◧ Let's Go writers travel on your budget.

"Guides that penetrate the veneer of the holiday brochures and mine the grit of real life."

—*The Economist*

"The writers seem to have experienced every rooster-packed bus and lunar-surfaced mattress about which they write."

—*The New York Times*

"All the dirt, dirt cheap."

—*People*

◧ Great for independent travelers.

"The guides are aimed not only at young budget travelers but at the independent traveler; a sort of streetwise cookbook for traveling alone."

—*The New York Times*

"A guide should tell you what to expect from a destination. Here *Let's Go* shines."

—*The Chicago Tribune*

"An indispensible resource, *Let's Go*'s practical information can be used by every traveler."

—*The Chattanooga Free Press*

◧ Let's Go is completely revised each year.

"A publishing phenomenon...the only major guidebook series updated annually. *Let's Go* is the big kahuna."

—*The Boston Globe*

"Unbeatable: good sight-seeing advice; up-to-date info on restaurants, hotels, and inns; a commitment to money-saving travel; and a wry style that brightens nearly every page."

—*The Washington Post*

◧ All the important information you need.

"*Let's Go* authors provide a comedic element while still providing concise information and thorough coverage of the country. Anything you need to know about budget traveling is detailed in this book."

—*The Chicago Sun-Times*

"*Let's Go* guidebooks take night life seriously."

—*The Chicago Tribune*

Let's Go Publications

Let's Go: Alaska & the Pacific Northwest 2002
Let's Go: Amsterdam 2002 **New Title!**
Let's Go: Australia 2002
Let's Go: Austria & Switzerland 2002
Let's Go: Barcelona 2002 **New Title!**
Let's Go: Boston 2002
Let's Go: Britain & Ireland 2002
Let's Go: California 2002
Let's Go: Central America 2002
Let's Go: China 2002
Let's Go: Eastern Europe 2002
Let's Go: Egypt 2002 **New Title!**
Let's Go: Europe 2002
Let's Go: France 2002
Let's Go: Germany 2002
Let's Go: Greece 2002
Let's Go: India & Nepal 2002
Let's Go: Ireland 2002
Let's Go: Israel 2002
Let's Go: Italy 2002
Let's Go: London 2002
Let's Go: Mexico 2002
Let's Go: Middle East 2002
Let's Go: New York City 2002
Let's Go: New Zealand 2002
Let's Go: Paris 2002
Let's Go: Peru, Ecuador & Bolivia 2002
Let's Go: Rome 2002
Let's Go: San Francisco 2002
Let's Go: South Africa with Southern Africa 2002
Let's Go: Southeast Asia 2002
Let's Go: Southwest USA 2002 **New Title!**
Let's Go: Spain & Portugal 2002
Let's Go: Turkey 2002
Let's Go: USA 2002
Let's Go: Washington, D.C. 2002
Let's Go: Western Europe 2002

Let's Go *Map Guides*

Amsterdam
Berlin
Boston
Chicago
Dublin
Florence
Hong Kong
London
Los Angeles
Madrid

New Orleans
New York City
Paris
Prague
Rome
San Francisco
Seattle
Sydney
Venice
Washington, D.C.

MIDDLE EAST
2002

Joey Shabot editor
Dave Newman associate editor
Elizabeth Ogburn associate editor

researcher-writers
Rim Abida
Deema Arafah
Christiaan Highsmith
Adam Kampff
Ebon Lee

Sharmi Surianarain managing editor

map editors
Noah Askin
Dan Barnes
Paul W. Guilianelli
Anna Malsberger

Macmillan

HELPING LET'S GO

If you want to share your discoveries, suggestions, or corrections, please drop us a line. We read every piece of correspondence, whether a postcard, a 10-page email, or a coconut. Please note that mail received after May 2002 may be too late for the 2003 book, but will be kept for future editions. **Address mail to:**

> **Let's Go: Middle East**
> **67 Mount Auburn Street**
> **Cambridge, MA 02138**
> **USA**

Visit Let's Go at **http://www.letsgo.com,** or send email to:

> **feedback@letsgo.com**
> **Subject: "Let's Go: Middle East"**

In addition to the invaluable travel advice our readers share with us, many are kind enough to offer their services as researchers or editors. Unfortunately, our charter enables us to employ only currently enrolled Harvard students.

Published in Great Britain 2002 by Macmillan, an imprint of Pan Macmillan Ltd.
20 New Wharf Road, London N1 9RR
Basingstoke and Oxford
Associated companies throughout the world
www.panmacmillan.com

Maps by David Lindroth copyright © 2002, 2001, 2000, 1999, 1998, 1997, 1996, 1995, 1994, 1993, 1992, 1991, 1990, 1989, 1988 by St. Martin's Press.

Published in the United States of America by St. Martin's Press.

ISBN: 0-333-90594-6
First edition
10 9 8 7 6 5 4 3 2 1

Let's Go: Middle East is written by Let's Go Publications, 67 Mount Auburn Street, Cambridge, MA 02138, USA.

CONTENTS

MAPS

✚ Hospital	🚌 Bus Station	▦ Baha'i Temple	Ⓐ Hotel/Hostel
✚ Police	TAXI Taxi Stand	✝ Church	Ⓐ Camping
✉ Post Office	✈ Airport	🕌 Mosque	Ⓐ Restaurant
ⓘ Tourist Office	🚂 Train Station	✡ Synagogue	☎ Telephone Office
$ Bank	M METRO STOP	🏛 Museum	Ⓐ Service
⚑ Embassy	⚓ Ferry Terminal	▲ Mountain	▲ Archaeological Site
▪ Site or Point of Interest	✂ Border Crossing	🌴 Oasis	👍 The Let's Go thumb always points NORTH.

RESEARCHER-WRITERS

▧ Rim Abida
Syria

Leaving belly-dancing Cambridge behind without a second thought, Rim forged through Syria like only a fun-loving Franco-Tunisian-Syrian polyglot could. Neither friend nor foe nor charming Syrian studmuffin impeded her superior researching, though we suspect that she may have subcontracted her grandmother as researching sidekick (how else could she have covered the breadth of Syria so seamlessly?). Ably researching new turf with humble competence, Rim was—though she had a hard time staying—cool.

▧ Deema Arafah
Lebanon

Cedar treehugger and poet extraordinaire, Deema broke our hearts with her inspired prose. Braving the mountains, valleys, ski slopes, forests, jazz clubs, post offices, and minefields of her beloved Lebanon, this native of Michigan (via Jerusalem) left nary a computer terminal unturned in her quest to reach out and touch her editors. Thanks to Deema, Lebanon is once again accessible to the budget traveler—and we will always remember to daaance, STRETCH, sing!

▧ Christiaan Highsmith
Alexandria, Nile Valley, Desert Oases

Determined to take our coverage to a new level, Cantabrigian Christiaan battled devilish heat, reluctant diving schools, and befuddling maps with the shrewdness of a true outdoorsman and experienced traveler. His unfaltering drive, wide-eyed appreciation for his surroundings, and ever-smiling dedication paid off in the end, as he finally learned how to spell Eygpt. He even remembered to let his mom know how he was doing—what a guy.

▧ Adam Kampff
Jordan

We couldn't have found a chiller dude to cover this laid-back kingdom. From the moment a skinhead hit him in the head with a *Let's Go* recycling bin, it was clear that Adam and this job were meant for each other. The budding astronomer and Albany native brought a relaxed attitude and fresh eye to every archaeological site and toilet stall he visited. Though his personal hygiene may have left something to be desired, his copy was impeccably clean. Whether cruising through the desert (Christina Aguilera blaring) with an Iraqi hitchhiker or sucking down 50 cups of tea out of respect for Hashemite hospitality, Adam was a pleasure to work with.

▧ Ebon Lee
Cairo, Nile Delta, Sinai

With nerves of steel, Ebon braved the 120°F heat, fleas, incapacitating sickness found only in 3rd-class train cars, Cairene bureaucrats who treated bus schedules like matters of national security, and detainment by tourist police—all without even batting an eyelash (or complaining to his editors). Instead, this Kansas native who had never before crossed the Atlantic consistently sent in reliable, opinionated copy from the vantage point of the ultimate budget traveler. Proof that good things come to those who wait: Ebon's luck finally turned around, as he watched the sunrise from the top of Mt. Sinai and landed a date with Jasmine, one of Egypt's top belly dancers.

Erzulie D. Coquillon	*Editor, Let's Go: Greece*
Ben Davis	*Editor, Let's Go: Turkey*
John Mazza	*Associate Editor, Let's Go: Greece*
Allison Melia	*Associate Editor, Let's Go: Turkey*
Alexandra D. Cooley	*Western Mediterranean*
Helen Dimos	*Southern Cyprus*
Kyle R. Freeny	*Aegean Coast*
Jeremy Greene	*Southeastern Anatolia*
Simon Lassman	*Ankara*
Cassim Shepard	*Istanbul*
Noah Carl Waxman	*Cappadocia, Eastern Mediterranean, Northern Cyprus*

ACKNOWLEDGMENTS

The Let's Go 2002 series is dedicated to the memory of Haley Surti

TEAM MID THANKS
Fourth floor crew, we love you. Thank you to all the girls we've loved before, including: Sharmilicious; Prodass Melissa and her cohorts; Noah, Anna and their mapland sidekicks; Batman; and you.

JOEY THANKS
Umm Kulthoum and Sharmi for hours of diversion and wonderful smoky voices; Eli, Rachel, Gautam, Ankur, Tal and Alex for a beautiful, lazy summer after all; Betsy for your smiling face; Dave for good humor and music; the Coöp, for alternativist thinking that makes it easier to say goodbye to this place; Lauren Grünsfeld and Paula for welcoming me back with open arms. Thank you Abba, Imma, Toby, Kathy, Ezra and Dina for your love and support.

DAVE THANKS
Mayo, Puja, Mike, Jen, DPM, MMI, KGS, VVG, and JML for distracting me from this job. Lauren, Mike, Chris, Phil, and Danielle for visiting. ABG and DMD for a great week off. PRC for being such a quiet roommate. Joey, Betsy, and Sharmi for your perpetual good spirits. Mom and Dad for your love and support.

BETSY THANKS
My family for raising me and for letting me come and go as I please, Mikey and Michelle for never-ending good times, and Tania for her over-the-top proofing skills. Also Salah al-Din for his antics, and my little sister Laura for being such an inspiring cream puff. And of course, the team: Dave, Sharmi, Joey.

Publishing Director
Sarah P. Rotman
Editor-in-Chief
Ankur N. Ghosh
Production Manager
Jen Taylor
Cartography Manager
Dan Barnes
Design & Photo Manager
Vanessa Bertozzi
Editorial Managers
Amélie Cherlin, Naz F. Firoz,
Matthew Gibson, Sharmi
Surianarain, Brian R. Walsh
Financial Manager
Rebecca L. Schoff
Marketing & Publicity Managers
Brady R. Dewar, Katharine
Douglas, Marly Ohlsson
New Media Manager
Kevin H. Yip
Online Manager
Alex Lloyd
Personnel Manager
Nathaniel Popper
Production Associates
Steven Aponte, Chris Clayton,
Caleb S. Epps, Eduardo Montoya,
Melissa Rudolph
Some Design
Melissa Rudolph
Office Coordinators
Efrat Kussell, Peter Richards

Director of Advertising Sales
Adam M. Grant
Senior Advertising Associates
Ariel Shwayder, Kennedy Thorwarth
Advertising Associate
Jennie Timoney
Advertising Artwork Editor
Peter Henderson

President
Cindy L. Rodriguez
General Manager
Robert B. Rombauer
Assistant General Manager
Anne E. Chisholm

Editor
Joey Shabot
Associate Editors
Dave Newman
Elizabeth Ogburn
Managing Editor
Sharmi Surianarain
Map Editors
Noah Askin
Dan Barnes
Paul W. Guilianelli
Anna Malsberger

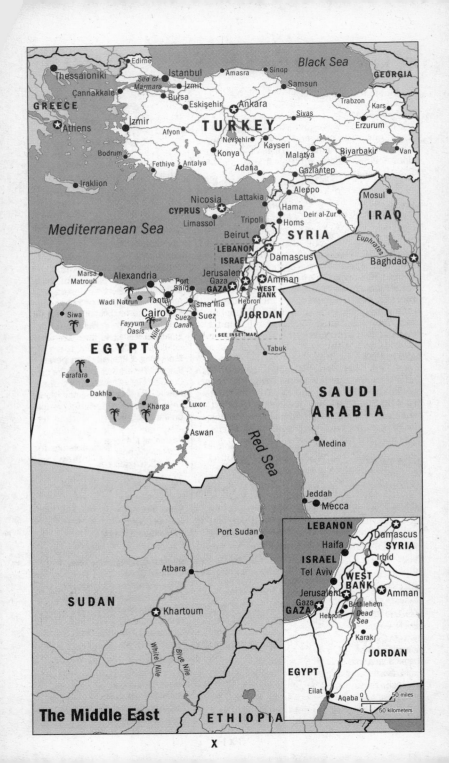

The Middle East

HOW TO USE THIS BOOK

Welcome to **Let's Go: Middle East 2002.** This book is a backpacker's guide to the Middle East, covering Egypt to Turkey overland and everything in between. If *Let's Go: Middle East* were an animal, it would be a camel. Like a camel, this book is rugged, intelligent, dependable, and a delightful shade of yellow. Unlike a camel, this book does not spit; please do not spit on it.

ORGANIZATION OF THIS BOOK

INTRODUCTORY MATERIAL. The first chapter, **Discover the Middle East,** provides you with an overview of travel in the region, including five **suggested itineraries** that give you an idea of what you want to see and how long it will take you to see it. The **Essentials** chapter outlines all the practical information you'll need to prepare for and execute your trip. The **Life and Times** chapter provides you with a general introduction to the history, religion, and culture of the Middle East.

COVERAGE. The chapters are organized by country, roughly south to north, beginning with **Egypt** and moving counterclockwise (and alphabetically) around the Mediterranean to **Turkey.** After Egypt comes **Israel**—including coverage of **Gaza,** the **West Bank,** and **Southern Cyprus** (an easy ferry ride from Haifa). The deserts and ruins of **Jordan** follow, then the diverse cultures and landscapes of **Lebanon**—including coverage of areas of South Lebanon recently opened to tourism—and then the ancient cities of **Syria.** Each country chapter begins with general information on the country, including historical and cultural background and practical information. Within each chapter, destinations are organized by city, town, or some other logical geographical subdivision. **Transportation** gets you from point A to point B (and how to get around B once you're there). **Orientation** untangles city streets, while **Practical Information** tips you off on how to get your laundry done, change your currency, and even check your email in the desert. **Accommodations, Food, Sights, Entertainment,** and **Nightlife** sections guide you to the Bedouin camps, shawarma stands, *sheesha* parlors, Crusader castles, camel markets, whirling dervish shows, and watering holes that will give you the most bang for your buck.

APPENDIX. The appendix contains a table of useful measurement **conversions** for the metrically-impaired, a **phrasebook** of handy phrases in Arabic, Hebrew, and Turkish, and a **glossary** of foreign words Middle Eastern foods.

A FEW NOTES ABOUT LET'S GO FORMAT

RANKING ESTABLISHMENTS. In each of the accommodations and food sections, we list establishments in order from best to worst. Our absolute favorites are denoted by the highest honor we give: the *Let's Go* thumbs-up (🖾).

PHONE CODES AND TELEPHONE NUMBERS. The **phone code** for each region, city, or town appears opposite the name of that region, city, or town, and is denoted by a ☎icon. **Phone numbers** are also preceded by the ☎icon.

GRAYBOXES AND IKONBOXES. Sometimes **grayboxes** provide cultural insight or historical background; at other times they are simply an excuse for crude humor. **Whiteboxes** provide important practical information, such as warnings (🛯), helpful hints and further resources (🛏), border crossing information (🛏), etc.

A NOTE TO OUR READERS The information for this book was gathered by *Let's Go* researchers from May through August of 2001. Each listing is based on one researcher's opinion, formed during his or her visit at a particular time. Those traveling at other times may have different experiences since prices, dates, hours, and conditions are always subject to change. You are urged to check the facts presented in this book beforehand to avoid inconvenience and surprises.

ABOUT LET'S GO

FORTY-TWO YEARS OF WISDOM

For over four decades, travelers crisscrossing the continents have relied on *Let's Go* for inside information on the hippest backstreet cafes, the most pristine secluded beaches, and the best routes from border to border. *Let's Go: Europe*, now in its 42nd edition and translated into seven languages, reigns as the world's bestselling international travel guide. In the last 20 years, our rugged researchers have stretched the frontiers of backpacking and expanded our coverage into the Americas, Australia, Asia, and Africa (including the new *Let's Go: Egypt* and the more comprehensive, multi-country jaunt through *Let's Go: South Africa & Southern Africa*). Our new-and-improved City Guide series continues to grow with new guides to perennial European favorites Amsterdam and Barcelona. This year we are also unveiling *Let's Go: Southwest USA*, the flagship of our new outdoor Adventure Guide series, which is complete with special roadtripping tips and itineraries, more coverage of adventure activities like hiking and mountain biking, and first-person accounts of life on the road.

It all started in 1960 when a handful of well-traveled students at Harvard University handed out a 20-page mimeographed pamphlet offering a collection of their tips on budget travel to passengers on student charter flights to Europe. The following year, in response to the instant popularity of the first volume, students traveling to Europe researched the first full-fledged edition of *Let's Go: Europe*. Throughout the 60s and 70s, our guides reflected the times—in 1969, for example, we taught you how to get from Paris to Prague on "no dollars a day" by singing in the street. In the 90s we focused in on the world's most exciting urban areas to produce in-depth, fold-out map guides, now with 20 titles (from Hong Kong to Chicago) and counting. Our new guides bring the total number of titles to 57, each infused with the spirit of adventure and voice of opinion that travelers around the world have to count on. But some things never change: our guides are still researched, written, and produced entirely by students who know first-hand how to see the world on the cheap.

HOW WE DO IT

Each guide is completely revised and thoroughly updated every year by a well-traveled set of nearly 300 students. Every spring, we recruit over 200 researchers and 90 editors to overhaul every book. After several months of training, researcher-writers hit the road for seven weeks of exploration, from Anchorage to Adelaide, Estonia to El Salvador, Iceland to Indonesia. Hired for their rare combination of budget travel sense, writing ability, stamina, and courage, these adventurous travelers know that train strikes, stolen luggage, food poisoning, and marriage proposals are all part of a day's work. Back at our offices, editors work from spring to fall, massaging copy written on Himalayan bus rides into witty, informative prose. A student staff of typesetters, cartographers, publicists, and managers keeps our lively team together. In September, the collected efforts of the summer are delivered to our printer, who turns them into books in record time, so that you have the most up-to-date information available for your vacation. Even as you read this, work on next year's editions is well underway.

WHY WE DO IT

We don't think of budget travel as the last recourse of the destitute; we believe that it's the only way to travel. Our books will ease your anxieties and answer your questions about the basics—so you can get off the beaten track and explore. Once you learn the ropes, we encourage you to put *Let's Go* down and strike out on your own. You know as well as we that the best discoveries are often those you make yourself. When you find something worth sharing, please drop us a line. We're Let's Go Publications, 67 Mount Auburn St., Cambridge, MA 02138, USA (feedback@letsgo.com). For more info, visit our website, www.letsgo.com.

DISCOVER THE MIDDLE EAST

Gertrude Bell, one of the most famous travelers to the Middle East (see **An English-woman in Arabia,** p. 479), said, "Few such moments of exhilaration can come as that which stands at the threshold of wild travel." The Middle East is, without a doubt, adventure country *par excellence.* Wide expanses of desert dotted with lush green oases, colorful underwater seascapes, and hidden cities carved in stone inspire exploration in the grand tradition of Lawrence of Arabia and Indiana Jones. The Middle East's long-standing and dynamic socio-political canvas is just as colorful as its landscape: ancient civilizations have left rich archaeological records of human struggle and achievement that are no less compelling than the contemporary drama of the Middle East peace process. Five of the seven wonders of the ancient world, numerous relics from three major faiths, and the first written alphabet are only pieces of the historical puzzle. The challenges of politics today range from the preservation of Bedouin traditional lifestyles in modern nation-states like Egypt to the attempts at peace between Israel and the Palestinians. Despite the vast diversity of political views, religious beliefs, and economic status in the region, all of its inhabitants adhere to one very strong belief: the profound importance of hospitality. As a traveler, you will encounter difficulties navigating shifty bus schedules, phantom trains, and stubborn camels. You will take in the Pyramids at Giza, gasp in awe at the lost city of Petra in Jordan, and admire Cappadocia's natural splendor in Turkey. And yet, at the end of the journey, your most striking memory is most likely to be sipping a cup of *ahwa* (coffee) while discussing the meaning of life with a spice vendor in a small corner of a *souq* (market).

FACTS AND FIGURES

PERCENTAGE OF WONDERS OF THE ANCIENT WORLD IN THE MIDDLE EAST: 71.4%

LARGEST BURIAL GROUND IN THE WORLD: Valley of the Mummies: 6 miles and of tombs holding 10,000 mummies

SINKING RATE OF THE DEAD SEA: 13 inches per year

QUALITY OF PRAYER DURING RAMADAN INSIDE THE DOME OF THE ROCK: 7,000 times more valuable than in any other mosque

---

WHEN TO GO

Take into account local holidays when arranging your itinerary (for a list of religious and national holidays, see **Holidays and Festivals,** p. 61). In Muslim countries, many businesses close on Fridays and during the afternoon on holidays, but are generally open in the morning. The most important event and the one most likely to complicate travel is **Ramadan,** the annual month-long fast during which Muslims abstain from food and drink from dawn to dusk (most restaurants close until sundown). Shops may be open for a few hours in the morning and a short time after *iftar*, the breaking of the fast; government services are either closed entirely or open only in the morning. It would be rude to smoke or eat in public at this time. In Israel, most businesses and public facilities close Friday afternoons for Shabbat, the Jewish sabbath, and reopen at sundown on Saturdays. They also close for Jewish holy days, which begin at sunset on the previous day.

DISCOVER

Also think about when everyone else in the region is vacationing. Egypt's high and low seasons depend partly on the region: Cairo is a year-round mob scene, while summertime is partytime in Alexandria and on the Mediterranean and Red Sea beaches. In the Sinai, Oases, and Upper Egypt, reasonable temperatures make winter the high season, but younger travelers revel in summertime bargains. North Americans and students favor summer for visiting Israel and the West Bank; Europeans prefer winter. Jordan's peak seasons are spring and autumn, while Syria and Lebanon receive more visitors in the summer. High tourist season runs between late June and early September in Turkey and Cyprus, bringing throngs of vacationers to Turkey's western coastal regions. If you can stand the climate, off-season travel means smaller crowds, lower prices, and greater local hospitality.

Average Temperature, Precipitation	January			April			July			October		
	°C	°F	mm	°C	°F	mm	°C	°F	mm	°C	°F	mm
Amman (Jordan)	8	46	63	16	60	17	25	77	0	20	68	6
Beirut (Lebanon)	14	56	195	19	65	48	27	81	1	24	75	35
Cairo (Egypt)	14	57	5	21	71	2	28	82	0	24	75	1
Damascus (Syria)	7	44	39	17	51	1	27	80	0	19	61	9
Jerusalem (Israel)	8	47	132	16	60	28	24	74	0	20	69	13
Istanbul (Turkey)	6	42	95	11	53	44	23	74	19	16	60	53
Limassol (Cyprus)	12	53	105	17	63	22	26	80	1	22	72	24

THINGS TO DO

While the Middle East's ancient ruins, religious traditions, and authentic *souqs* are delectable slices of the past on a backpacker's silver platter, the region contains more than just history. Beirut and Tel Aviv offer hopping, cosmopolitan club scenes, while the sandy shores of the Sinai Peninsula provide a backdrop to satisfy the most discriminating beach bunnies and hard-core hikers. For more specific regional attractions, see **Highlights of the Region,** at the beginning of each chapter.

SUN OF A BEACH

Much of the Middle East embraces the Mediterranean Sea, and cradling some amazing beaches in its arms. Bodacious **Bodrum** (p. 662) in Turkey is known the world over for its sizzling beaches (matched only by equally sizzling nightlife). For other perspectives on the Mediterranean party on down with sun-soaked hipsters at youthful **Tel Aviv** (p. 310) in Israel; kick back for a few days in **Jounieh** (p. 526) in Lebanon and **Herzliya** (p. 323) in Israel; and be sure to ferry over to the endless, sparkling beaches of **Cyprus** (p. 345), in the heart of the Mediterranean. Try banana boating, jet-skiing, or parasailing at the intersection of four countries in **Eilat** (p. 405), Israel. Savor the lazy daze of summer in Egypt at **Dahab** (p. 185), one of the many beachside treasures along the coasts of the **Sinai Peninsula** (p. 167), known the world over as a scuba paradise. Weary travelers can create their own resort by hiring a *felucca* to troll down the Nile (p. 208). Continuing northwest, they'll encounter countless stretches of undiscovered emerald coast: **Marsa Matrouh** (p. 158) in Egypt offers spectacular Mediterranean serenity without the Mediterranean crowds.

SHOP 'TIL YOU DROP

Bargaining is a fact of life in the Middle East, so it makes sense that the region is a shopper's paradise. Almost every city has a *souq*, an outdoor bazaar that sells everything from spices to stilettos. Grab silver and spice and everything nice at the

Grand Bazaar in **İstanbul** (p. 634), Turkey; head to **Beirut** (p. 510), Lebanon, for leather and gold; browse the intricately carved boxes and gold jewelry in **Damascus** (p. 575), Syria; **Cairo** (p. 80) is the place for tapestries and *sheeshas*. For less luxurious goods, head to **Petra** (p. 481), Jordan, for beautiful pottery or trek out to the camel markets in **Birqash** (p. 130) or **Daraw** (p. 232), Egypt. At the other extreme, high-end fashions can be found in the sparkling new malls and boutiques of Beirut, while **Israel** (p. 265) is also a haven for shoppers in search of modern luxuries: grab a pair of the world-famous *Naot* sandals anywhere in the country, and pamper yourself with **Dead Sea** (p. 386) mud baths and facial scrubs.

AIN'T NO MOUNTAIN HIGH ENOUGH...

Although the Middle East is better known for rising temperatures than rising peaks, there are many options for the alpine- and hiking-inclined. The **Negev Desert** (p. 394) and **Golan Heights** (p. 380) in Israel offer subtropical paths that cut through cliffside caves and breathtaking *wadis*. No trekking itinerary would be complete without a climb up holy **Mt. Sinai** (p. 175) in Egypt. For those of the skiing persuasion, Lebanon (known as "Little Switzerland" by those in the snow) boasts world-class skiing facilities at the twin resort towns of **Faraya** and **Faqra** (p. 529).

...AIN'T NO VALLEY LOW ENOUGH

What goes up must come down. Take a hike and check out the largest natural crater in the world, **Mitzpeh Ramon** (p. 403) in Israel. The depths of the **Dead Sea**, from either the **Israeli** (p. 386) or the **Jordanian** (p. 472) side, may seem like another great place to get down, but be content with floating peacefully on the water's surface.

▨ LET'S GO PICKS

BEST BODY-TO-TOMB RATIO: Nowadays, one body per tomb is standard, but the ancients of **Bab al-Dhira**, Jordan (p. 480), held a slightly different perspective. Their specialized shaft tombs contain 25 bodies a pop.

BEST PLACE TO LOOK, NOT TOUCH: Find your inner fish in the legions of brilliantly colored creatures as you flit through coral at the **Yemeniyyeh Reef** in Aqaba (p. 490) or the Red Sea in **Dahab** (p. 185), which rank among the world's best for scoping fish.

BEST WONDER OF THE WORLD: Five of the Seven Wonders of the Ancient World are in the Middle East, but if you only have time for one, head over to the **Pyramids at Giza** (p. 126)—which is the only one still standing anyway.

BEST CAFE FREQUENTED BY A NOBEL LAUREATE: Smoke *sheesha* and read *Palace Walk* amidst the bustle of Khan al-Khalili at **Fishawi's** (p. 124), the famous teahouse where Naguib Mahfouz spent endless *Arabian Nights and Days*.

BEST SEMITIC LANGUAGE: Tongue-tied? Head to Ma'alula (p. 586) in Syria, where **Aramaic**, the language in which Jesus preached, is still spoken.

BEST MAN-MADE LAKE: The imposing Aswan High Dam doubled Egypt's electrical output. It also created the 200m-deep **Lake Nasser** (p. 243), the world's largest artificial lake.

BEST REASON TO FINISH YOUR SPINACH: Dream your way into **al-'Abd** in Cairo (p. 101) for the creamiest whopping three scoops of ice cream you've ever had.

BEST TOILET SEAT VIEW: Speaking of buns, don't miss valuable sight-seeing minutes while on the can. The **Nabatean Museum** (p. 488) offers stunning, stall-side views of Petra, Jordan.

BEST MESSY FESTIVAL: Slide on over to the **Kırkpınar Grease Wrestling Festival** in Edirne, Turkey (p. 648), where competitors from all over Turkey don giant leather breeches, slather themselves in oil, and hit the mats.

BEST CRATER: When it slammed into Israel's desert many millennia ago, an asteroid created **Makhtesh Ramon** (p. 403). Measuring a mind-boggling 40km long, 9km wide, and 400m deep, it contains geological formations found nowhere else in the world.

DISCOVER

SUGGESTED ITINERARIES

1. BEST OF THE MIDDLE EAST (4-5 WEEKS)
If you want to sample everything the Middle East has to offer and more, this is for you. Start your journey in İstanbul (p. 634), where you can wander through old markets and bargain for gold, spices, and carpets amidst mosques and Ottoman palaces. Let Aya Sofia, the church transformed into a mosque and then finally into a museum, and the Blue Mosque take you from the past to the present. After a few heated days of sightseeing, cool off at a *hammam* (Turkish bath) before hopping a bus to **Damascus,** Syria (p. 575), the oldest continually inhabited city in the world. Shake it on over to fun 'n' funky **Beirut** (p. 510) in Lebanon. Party until dawn, then catch a breather at **Ba'albeck** (p. 545), the unforgettable home of some righteous ruins and host to an internationally known jazz festival where Ella and the Duke once swung it in 4/4 time. Next up is **Amman,** Jordan (p. 441), an excellent jumping off point to the rock-

hewn wonders of **Jerash** (p. 457) and the lost city of **Petra** (p. 481). Check in at Amman again on the way over to Israel, where your visit won't be complete without a stopover in **Jerusalem** (p. 277). Whether it's mosques, churches, or nightclubs, Jerusalem beats most other cities in the region. Plan to spend a few days here at least, if only to rest up before heading out to **Tel Aviv,** "The City That Never Takes a Break" (p. 310). Before you get down at the city's cutting edge hotspots, treat your homesick taste buds to a panoply of non-falafel foods in ethnic neighborhoods. Cross over to the **Sinai Peninsula** (p. 167) and tan your tired limbs in **Dahab** (p. 185) before diving into the azure depths of the Red Sea for some of the best snorkeling in the world. Finish your whirlwind tour of the region in tempestuous **Cairo** (p. 80), where beautiful, historic neighborhoods sprawl in the shadow of the **Pyramids at Giza** (p. 126).

2. ON YOUR MARK, JET-SET, GO! (3-4 WEEKS)
Jet-set like a pro while boning up on your ancient history with this supersonic tour of the Mediterranean. Dive into the sea of mosques and spice markets in İstanbul (p. 634), immerse yourself in one of the city's many famous

hammams, then make a splash at the many bars and "nomadic" discotheques. Head south to the massive classical ruins at **Ephesus** (p. 658), a notable ancient city which boasts a concentration of art and architecture surpassed only by Rome and Athens. Continue along the coast to the secluded coves and beaches of sunny **Bodrum** (p. 662). After partying until dawn in the city's many discotheques, shake it on over to **Antalya** (p. 675) and the **Turquoise Riviera,** Turkey's premiere tourist resort. Take a breather in the charming markets and tea gardens of **Antakya** (p. 679), then cross the border into Syria. Check out the birthplace of ancient and modern alphabets at **Ugarit** (p. 604) before daytripping to the spectacular Crusader castle at **Crac des Chevaliers** (p. 596). Ease your way back into modern life on the streets of leisurely **Tripoli** (p. 535), where you're sure to be taken in by the city's famed Lebanese sweets and even more famous hospitality. Take a breath of fresh air at **Bcharré** (p. 542), a tranquil mountain town 1400m above sea level. After stopping over at the ever-popular **Cedars of Lebanon** (p. 543) for world-class skiing and snowboarding in the winter, party on down at any one of the many hipster cafes, casinos, and discos in thrill-a-minute **Beirut** (p. 510) and her hip sister **Jounieh** (p. 526). Pass through the oldest continually inhabited city in the world, **Damascus,** Syria (p. 575), then muscle your way through the crowded traffic circles of **Amman,** Jordan (p. 441). Mudbathe and float your way along the **Dead Sea** (p. 472) en route to the calm seaside port of **Haifa** in Israel (p. 331). Ferry over to **Cyprus** (p. 345), where you can wander along unforgettable beaches and breezy mountains and trek through twisted streets in search of ancient ruins. Lay out on serene beaches with even more laid-back locals before heading to **Tel Aviv** (p. 310), a city that lives for the moment, grooving on beaches, in boutiques, and in booty-shaking dance halls. Finish your Mediterranean tour in the warm embrace of the vibrant seaside city of **Alexandria,** Egypt (p. 141), and be sure to travel a few hours west to the sleepy resorts and busy markets of the town of **Marsa Matrouh** (p. 158).

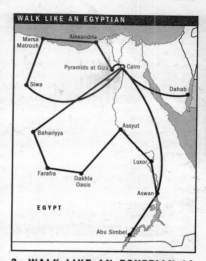

WALK LIKE AN EGYPTIAN

Marsa Matrouh
Alexandria
Pyramids at Giza · Cairo
Siwa
Dahab
Bahariyya
Assyut
Luxor
Farafra
Dakhla Oasis
Aswan
EGYPT
Abu Simbel

3. WALK LIKE AN EGYPTIAN (4 WEEKS) This is your chance to take part in a timeless adventure through the past and present. Hop on a train from Cairo to **Aswan** (p. 233), a city famous for its alabaster. You will love Aswan's unique Nubian flavor, which plays a large part in the surrounding villages and the comprehensive Nubian Museum, as well as its proximity to the ruins at Philae. Once you've had enough of Aswan, book a bus down to **Abu Simbel** (p. 245) to see some of the most awe-inspiring colossal remains in the world. Next on the ruins list is **Luxor** (p. 212), once the capital of ancient Egypt. It would take the rest of this page to list all that Luxor has to offer; make sure to see the Valley of the Kings and the tomb of Queen Nefertari. Though pricey, the latter attraction is Egypt's prized possession. Take a break from all the ruins by taking a leisurely *felucca* cruise up the Nile. Once you reach the town of Asyut, go west, pardner, and trek through the unforgettable desert oases, starting in the White Desert outside lush **Dakhla** (p. 254), then pause in **Farafra** (p. 253) before exploring the hot springs of **Bahariya** (p. 249). Emerge from the vast expanses of the western desert into bustling **Cairo** (p. 80), the largest city in the Middle East and Africa. The labyrinthine streets of the city are filled with beautiful mosques and churches, frenzied *souqs* where bargains abound, and a mile-a-minute nightlife unlike anything else in Egypt. The majestic **Pyramids at Giza** (p. 126) are also an easy daytrip from the city. The cosmopolitan calm of **Alexandria** (p. 141) may seem a shock after Cairo, but you'll fall easily enough into the beachside city's evening-strolling, *sheesha*-smoking pace. Head west from Alexandria and discover the dazzling Mediterranean gem that is **Marsa Matrouh** (p. 158), a resort town rarely visited by tourists except as a base to the verdant **Siwa Oasis** (p. 162). Return to Cairo and catch a bus to the **Sinai Peninsula** (p. 167), where you can find your inner fish by diving and snorkeling through world-famous coral reefs, and kick back with nomadic Bedouin near **Dahab** (p. 185).

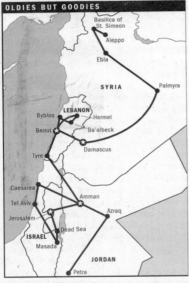

OLDIES BUT GOODIES

4. OLDIES BUT GOODIES (4 WEEKS) If you've always wanted to jump in a time machine, now you can: journey back in time to the ancient Levant. Begin in Syria, where the ancient trade center of **Aleppo** (p. 609) has wowed visitors since Ottoman times with its colossal Citadel and covered *souqs*. Springboard from Aleppo to the **Basilica of St. Simeon** (p. 614), a sacred stopover for Christian pilgrims since the 4th century, and **Ebla** (p. 615), the oldest of the old cities. The queen of **Palmyra** (p. 590), in central Syria, once rebelled against the Romans, and the stupendous

ruins of her city have also resisted the wear and tear of time. Spend a few days in **Damascus** (p. 575), the oldest continually inhabited city in the world—now a modern metropolis, but once the majestic capital of the Umayyad Empire—before jumping the border into Lebanon, where everything is but a day-hop from **Beirut** (p. 510). The Roman ruins and Crusader Castle in **Byblos** (p. 530) have toughed it out through centuries of bombardment; the town itself is so old that even the ancients considered it an ancient city. The Roman Temple of Bacchus in **Ba'albeck** (p. 545), east of Beirut, is one of the most celebrated in the world, and the Deir al-Maroun fortress in neighboring **Hermel** (p. 549) satisfies the independent explorer. Near the southern town of Sur, archaeologists have unearthed **Tyre** (p. 556), one of the great Phoenician city-states. Cut through **Amman,** Jordan (p. 441), and shimmy over to **Jerusalem** (p. 277), whose timeless wonders speak for themselves. Head for the **Dead Sea** region, the lowest point on earth (p. 472) and explore King Herod's palace in **Masada** (p. 390). Hungry for more Herod? His greatest achievement was the splendid city of **Caesarea** (p. 329), where Pontius Pilate ordered Christ's crucifixion in 33 CE. Back in Jordan, adventure like Lawrence of Arabia in 1500-year-old desert castles near **Azraq** (p. 469), then journey down the King's Highway to the Nabatean city of **Petra** (p. 481), whose rocky glory was lost for centuries.

THE BEST OF TURKEY

5. BEST OF TURKEY (3 WEEKS) Turkey is expansive, but here is what you absolutely need to see. Begin in **İstanbul** (p. 634), the traditional gateway to Turkey. You'll bargain for Turkish Delight at the Grand Bazaar (p. 645), marvel at luxurious Ottoman palaces, and stand awed in Aya

Sofia (p. 642). For post-sightseeing sweets, tea, and backgammon, head to one of İstanbul's chic waterfront cafes. Need a break from the city? The Bosphorus ferry will take you past stately waterfront mansions, stopping for fresh fish sandwiches and fried mussels along the way. **Edirne** (p. 648), the quietly proud former Ottoman capital, is now the capital of tea gardens and breathtaking architecture, including the finest mosque in all of Turkey. Then step off the beaten track and enjoy the serene beaches and small-town atmosphere of **Bozcaada** (p. 653), an Aegean island that has been producing wine since antiquity. Speaking of antiquity, the sparkling Aegean Coast houses the sun-bleached ruins of some of the ancient world's most powerful cities, including **Ber-**

gama (p. 654) and the eternally-popular **Ephesus** (p. 658). **Bodrum** (p. 662) lends new meaning to the phrase "Mediterranean party town." On the morning after, head to the secluded blue lagoon in **Ölüdeniz** (p. 671) to recover. Allow the waterfalls and butterflies of the nearby **Butterfly Valley** (p. 671) to enchant you before continuing along the Turkish Riviera. **Kaş** (p. 672) hosts the Mediterranean's only seal colony. Then on to **Demre** (p. 673) to explore the Basilica of St. Nicholas, a.k.a. Santa Claus. Scramble among the rock tombs of nearby **Myra** (p. 673). In **Göreme** (p. 689) and **Ürgüp** (p. 693) end your Turkish visit with the grand finale that is **Cappadocia:** a fantasy-world of underground cities, cave churches, and fairy chimneys.

ESSENTIALS

FACTS FOR THE TRAVELER

ENTRANCE REQUIREMENTS.
Passport (p. 8): Required for all travelers.
Visa (p. 9): Required for citizens of non-Arab countries.
Letter of Invitation: Not required.
Inoculations (p. 20): Polio, hepatitis A, immune globulin (IG), typhoid, cholera.
Work Permit (p. 9): Required for all countries.
Driving Permit (p. 38): Required for all countries.

EMBASSIES & CONSULATES

For information on Middle Eastern embassies and consulates abroad as well as foreign embassies and consulates in the Middle East, see the Essentials section of the individual country chapter (**Egypt,** p. 73, **Israel,** p. 273, **Jordan,** p. 436, **Lebanon,** p. 506, **Syria,** p. 570, **Turkey,** p. 629).

DOCUMENTS & FORMALITIES

PASSPORTS

REQUIREMENTS. Citizens of Australia, Canada, Ireland, New Zealand, South Africa, the UK, and the US need valid passports to enter Middle Eastern countries and to reenter their own countries. Some countries do not allow entrance if the holder's passport expires within six months; returning home with an expired passport is illegal, and may result in a fine.

PHOTOCOPIES. Be sure to photocopy the page of your passport with your photo, passport number, and other identifying information, as well as any visas, travel insurance policies, plane tickets, or traveler's check serial numbers. Carry one set of copies in a safe place, apart from the originals, and leave another set at home. Some consulates also recommend that you carry an expired passport or an official copy of your birth certificate separate from other documents.

LOST PASSPORTS. If you lose your passport, immediately notify the local police and the nearest embassy or consulate of your home government. To expedite its replacement, you will need to know all information previously recorded and show ID and proof of citizenship. In some cases, a replacement may take weeks to process, and it may be valid only for a limited time. Any visas stamped in your old passport will be irretrievably lost. In an emergency, ask for immediate temporary traveling papers that will permit you to reenter your home country. Your passport is a public document belonging to your nation's government. You may have to surrender it to a foreign government official, but if you don't get it back in a reasonable amount of time, inform the nearest mission of your home country.

NEW PASSPORTS. Citizens of Australia, Canada, Ireland, New Zealand, the United Kingdom, and the United States can apply for a passport at the nearest post office, passport office, or court of law. Citizens of South Africa can apply for a passport at the nearest office of Foreign Affairs. Any new passport or renewal applications must be filed well in advance of the departure date, although most passport offices offer rush services for a very steep fee. Citizens living abroad who need a passport or renewal services should contact the nearest consular service of their home country.

Australia: Info ☎131 232; www.dfat.gov.au/passports. Apply for a passport at a post office, passport office, or overseas diplomatic mission. Passports AUS$132 (32-page), valid for 10 years. Children AUS$66 (32-page), valid for 5 years.

Canada: Canadian Passport Office, Department of Foreign Affairs and International Trade, Ottawa, ON K1A 0G3 (☎613-994-3500 or 800-567-6868; www.dfait-maeci.gc.ca/passport). Applications available online, at post offices, passport offices, and Canadian missions. Passports CDN$60; valid for 5 years (non-renewable).

Ireland: Pick up an application at a Garda station or post office, or request one from a passport office. Apply by mail to the Department of Foreign Affairs, Passport Office, Molesworth St., Dublin 2 (☎(01) 671 1633; fax 671 1092; www.irlgov.ie/iveagh), or the Passport Office, 1A South Mall, Cork (☎(021) 272 525). Passports IR£45; valid for 10 years. Under 18 or over 65 IR£10; valid for 3 years.

New Zealand: Send applications to the Passport Office, Department of International Affairs, P.O. Box 10526, Wellington, New Zealand (☎(0800) 22 50 50 or (4) 474 81 00; fax (4) 474 80 10; www.passports.govt.nz). Standard processing time is 10 working days. Passports NZ$80; valid for 10 years. Children NZ$40; valid for five years.

South Africa: Department of Home Affairs. Passports are issued in Pretoria, but all applications must still be submitted or forwarded to the nearest South African consulate. Processing takes at least 3 months. Passports ZAR110; valid for 10 years. Under 16 ZAR85; valid for 5 years. For more information, http://home-affairs.pwv.gov.za.

United Kingdom: Info ☎0870 521 0410; www.open.gov.uk/ukpass/ukpass.htm. Request application from passport office, main post office, travel agent, or online. Apply by mail, in person at a passport office, or complete the online form. Passports UK£28; valid for 10 years. Children UK£14.80; valid for 5 years.

United States: Info ☎900-225-5674 (35 cents per min.); www.travel.state.gov/passport_services.html. Must apply in person at any federal or state courthouse, authorized post office, or Passport Agency (in major cities); see "US Government, State Department" in the telephone book for addresses. Processing takes 6 weeks. New passports US$60; valid for 10 years. Under 16 US$40; valid for 5 years. May be renewed by mail or in person for US$40. Add US$35 for 2-week expedited service.

VISAS AND WORK PERMITS

VISAS. As of August 2001, citizens of Australia, Canada, Ireland, New Zealand, South Africa, the UK, and the US need a visa—a stamp, sticker, or insert in your passport specifying the purpose of your travel and the permitted duration of your stay—in addition to a valid passport for entrance to Middle Eastern countries. Citizens of **South Africa** do not need visas in Egypt. Price, cost, and other visa details for each Middle Eastern country can be found in the country-specific essentials section. Note that Syria and Lebanon will not issue visas or allow entry if your passport indicates travel to Israel. US and UK citizens residing in the US can take advantage of the **Center for International Business and Travel** (**CIBT;** ☎800-925-2428), which secures visas to almost all countries for a variable service charge.

Be sure to double-check on entrance requirements at the nearest embassy or consulate for up-to-date information before departure. US citizens can also consult www.pueblo.gsa.gov/cic_text/travel/foreign/foreignentryreqs.html.

WORK PERMITS. Admission as a visitor does not include the right to work, which is authorized only by a business visa or work permit. Studying in Middle Eastern countries requires a permit. For more information, see **Alternatives to Tourism,** p. 43.

IDENTIFICATION

When you travel, carry two or more forms of identification on your person, including at least one photo ID; a passport combined with a driver's license or birth certificate is usually adequate. Many establishments, especially banks, may require several IDs in order to cash traveler's checks. Never carry all your forms of ID together; split them up in case of theft or loss. It is useful to bring extra passport-size photos to affix to the various IDs or passes you may acquire along the way.

For more information on the forms of identification listed below, contact the organization that provides the service, the **International Student Travel Confederation (ISTC)**, Herengracht 479, 1017 BS Amsterdam, Netherlands (☎ +31 20 421 28 00; fax 421 28 10; istcinfo@istc.org; www.istc.org).

TEACHER & STUDENT IDENTIFICATION. The **International Student Identity Card (ISIC)**, the most widely accepted form of student ID, provides discounts on sights, accommodations, food, and transport. The ISIC is preferable to an institution-specific card (such as a university ID) because it is more likely to be recognized (and honored) abroad. All cardholders have access to a 24hr. emergency helpline for medical, legal, and financial emergencies (in North America call 877-370-ISIC, elsewhere call US collect +1 715-345-0505, UK call collect +44 20 8762 8110, or France collect +33 15 633 144), and holders of US-issued cards are also eligible for insurance benefits (see **Insurance**, p. 24). Many student travel agencies issue ISICs, including STA Travel in Australia and New Zealand; Travel CUTS in Canada; usit in the Republic of Ireland and Northern Ireland; SASTS in South Africa; Campus Travel and STA Travel in the UK; Council Travel (www.counciltravel.com/idcards/default.asp) and STA Travel in the US (see p. 30).

The card is valid from September of one year to December of the following year and costs US$22. Applicants must be degree-seeking students of a secondary or post-secondary school and must be of at least 12 years of age. Because of the proliferation of fake ISICs, some services (particularly airlines) require additional proof of student identity, such as a school ID or a letter attesting to your student status, signed by your registrar and stamped with your school seal. The **International Teacher Identity Card (ITIC)** offers the same insurance coverage as well as similar but limited discounts. The fee is AUS$13, UK£5, or US$22.

YOUTH IDENTIFICATION. The International Student Travel Confederation issues a discount card to travelers who are 26 years old or under, but are not students. This one-year **International Youth Travel Card (IYTC;** formerly the **GO 25** Card) offers similar benefits to the ISIC. Look for the IYTC (US$22) where the ISIC is sold.

CUSTOMS

Upon entering the Middle East and when returning to your home country, you must declare valuable items purchased abroad and pay a duty on the value of those articles that exceeds the allowance established by the customs service. Keeping receipts for purchases made on your trip will help establish values when you return home. Make a list, including serial numbers, of carried valuables from home; if you register this list with customs before your departure and have an official stamp it, you will avoid import duty charges and ensure an easy passage upon your return. Goods and gifts purchased at **duty-free** shops abroad are not exempt from duty or sales tax at your point of return; you must declare these items as well. For more specific information on customs requirements, contact the customs information center in your home country.

MONEY

CURRENCY AND EXCHANGE

For currency conversion tables based on August 2001 exchange rates between Egyptian pounds (E£), Australian dollars (AUS$), Canadian dollars (CDN$), Irish pounds (IR£), New Zealand dollars (NZ$), South African Rand (ZAR), British pounds (UK£), US dollars (US$), European Union euros (EUR€), Jordanian dinars (JD), Lebanese pounds (L£), Syrian Pounds (S£), Israeli Shekels (NIS), and Turkish lira (TL), see the Essentials section of the individual country chapter (**Egypt**, p. 73, **Israel**, p. 273, **Jordan**, p. 429, **Lebanon**, p. 506, **Syria**, p. 564, **Turkey**, p. 629). For the latest exchange rates, check the currency converter on the Let's Go Homepage (www.letsgo.com/Thumb) or a large newspaper.

As a rule, it's cheaper to convert money at your destination than at home. You should bring enough foreign currency, however, to last for the first 48hr. of a trip to avoid being penniless should you arrive after bank hours or on a holiday. Travelers from the US can get foreign currency from the comfort of home: **International Currency Express** (☎ (888) 278-6628; www.foreignmoney.com) delivers most Middle Eastern currencies second-day (US$12) at competitive exchange rates.

When changing money abroad, try banks that have at most a 5% margin between their buy and sell prices. You lose money with every transaction, so convert large sums, but no more than you'll need.

If you use traveler's checks, carry some in small denominations (the equivalent of US$50 or less) for times when you are forced to exchange money at disadvantageous rates, but bring a range of denominations since charges may be levied per check cashed. Store your money in a variety of forms; ideally, you should carry some cash, traveler's checks, and an ATM and credit card. Travelers should consider carrying Western currency (i.e. US dollars; about US$50 worth). In the Middle East, foreign currency is often preferred to local, but throwing dollars around for preferential treatment may be offensive, and it can attract thieves. It also marks you as a stranger and can invite locals to jack up prices.

TRAVELER'S CHECKS

Traveler's checks (American Express and Visa are the most recognized) are among the safest and least troublesome means of carrying funds. Many agencies and banks sell them for a small commission. Each agency provides refunds if checks are lost or stolen, and many provide additional services, such as toll-free refund hotlines abroad, emergency message services, and stolen credit card assistance.

Buying traveler's checks in the currency of the country you are visiting is an exercise in futility in the Middle East. Lebanon and Syria accept only specific types of traveler's checks. **American Express** is the most widely recognized, and in some cities it is the only type accepted by businesses and banks. Other countries accept traveler's checks more widely. The most readily accepted checks are in US dollars or British pounds (the German mark will sometimes be taken as well); checks in other currencies won't get you very far—if a place will exchange it, you'll get a terrible rate.

While traveling, leave a list of check numbers with someone at home. Also, keep check receipts and records of which checks you've cashed separate from the checks themselves. Never countersign checks until you're ready to cash them, and always bring your passport with you to do so. If your checks are lost or stolen, immediately contact a refund center (of the company that issued your checks) to be reimbursed; they may require a police report verifying the loss or theft. Less-touristed countries may not have refund centers at all, in which case you might have to wait to be reimbursed. Ask about toll-free refund hotlines and the location of refund centers when purchasing checks, and always carry emergency cash.

American Express: Call 800 25 19 02 in Australia; in New Zealand 0800 441 068; in the UK 0800 521 313; in the US and Canada 800-221-7282. Elsewhere call US collect +1 801-964-6665; www.aexp.com. Traveler's checks are available at 1-4% commission at AmEx offices and banks, commission-free to Gold Card holders and AAA members.

Thomas Cook MasterCard: In the US and Canada call 800-223-7373; in the UK call 0800 62 21 01; elsewhere call UK collect +44 1733 31 89 50. Checks available in 13 currencies at 2% commission. Thomas Cook offices cash checks commission-free.

Visa: In the US call 800-227-6811; in the UK call 0800 89 50 78; elsewhere call UK collect +44 20 7937 8091. Call for the location of their nearest office.

CREDIT CARDS

Where they are accepted, credit cards often offer superior exchange rates—up to 5% better than the retail rate used by banks and other currency exchange establishments. Credit cards may also offer services such as insurance or emergency help, and are sometimes required to reserve hotel rooms or rental cars. **MasterCard** and **Visa** are the most welcome; **American Express** cards work at some ATMs and at AmEx offices and major airports. Budget travelers will find that few of the establishments they frequent accept credit cards; aside from the occasional splurge, you will probably reserve use of your credit card for financial emergencies.

Credit cards can be useful for **cash advances,** which allow you to withdraw currency from associated banks and ATMs throughout the Middle East instantly. Check the individual country listings for country-specific information on credit card acceptance. Hefty transaction fees and beefy interest rates for cash advances make credit cards a more costly way of withdrawing cash than ATMs or traveler's checks. In an emergency, however, the transaction fee may prove worth the cost. To be eligible for an advance, you'll need to get a **Personal Identification Number (PIN)** from your credit card company (see **Cash (ATM) Cards,** below). Be sure to check before you leave home about foreign transaction fees and interest rates.

CREDIT CARD COMPANIES. Visa (US ☎ 800-336-8472) and **MasterCard** (US ☎ 800-307-7309) are issued in cooperation with banks and other organizations. **American Express** (US ☎ 800-843-2273) has an annual fee of up to US$55. AmEx cardholders may cash personal checks at AmEx offices abroad, access an emergency medical and legal assistance hotline (24hr.; in North America call 800-554-2639, elsewhere call US collect +1 715-343-7977), and enjoy American Express Travel Service benefits (including plane, hotel, and car rental reservation changes; baggage loss and flight insurance; mailgram and international cable services; and held mail).

CASH (ATM) CARDS

Cash cards—popularly called ATM cards—are fairly widespread in the Middle East. Depending on the system that your home bank uses, you can most likely access your personal bank account from abroad. ATMs get the same wholesale exchange rate as credit cards, but there is often a limit on the amount of money you can withdraw per day (around US$500), and imperfect computer networks sometimes fail. There is typically also a surcharge of US$1-5 per withdrawal. Be sure to memorize your PIN code in numeric form since machines elsewhere often don't have letters on their keys. Also, if your PIN is longer than four digits, ask your bank whether you need a new number.

The two major international money networks are **Cirrus** (US ☎ 800-424-7787) and **PLUS** (US ☎ 800-843-7587). To locate ATMs around the world, call the above numbers, or consult www.visa.com/pd/atm or www.mastercard.com/atm.

Thomas Cook Road Cash (US ☎ 877-762-3227; www.roadcash.com) is a Visa travel money system allowing you to access money from any ATM with the Visa logo, common in major Middle Eastern cities outside of Syria. You deposit an amount before you travel (minimum US$300 plus a US$15 administration fee), and you can withdraw up to that sum. The cards, which give you a favorable exchange rate for withdrawals, are especially useful if you plan to travel to many countries.

GETTING MONEY FROM HOME

AMERICAN EXPRESS. Cardholders can withdraw cash from their checking accounts at any major AmEx office and many representative offices (up to US$1000 every 21 days; no service charge; no interest). AmEx "Express Cash" only works in Israel, where there are AmEx ATM's. Withdrawals from any AmEx ATM are automatically debited from the cardholder's checking account or line of credit. Green card holders may withdraw up to US$1000 in any seven-day period (2% transaction fee; minimum US$2.50; maximum US$20). To enroll in Express Cash, cardmembers may call 800-227-4669 in the US; elsewhere call the US collect +1 336-668-5041. AmEx national numbers are the AmEx office numbers in each country. Consult the country-specific sections for those listings.

WESTERN UNION. Travelers from the US, Canada, and the UK can wire money abroad through Western Union's international money transfer services. In the US, call 800-325-6000; in Canada, ☎800-235-0000; in the UK, ☎0800-833 833; in Egypt ☎202-355 50 23 to send and 202-594 07 41 to receive; in Israel ☎800 21 31 41; in Jordan ☎9626 462 72 95; in Lebanon ☎9611 39 10 00; in Turkey ☎90212 274 20 00; and in Cyprus ☎357 237 52 82. Western Union does not wire money to Syria. To wire money within the US using a credit card (D/MC/V), call 800-CALL-CASH (225-5227). The rates for sending cash are generally US$10-11 cheaper than with a credit card, and the money is usually available within 1hr. To locate the nearest Western Union office, consult www.westernunion.com.

FEDERAL EXPRESS. Some people choose to send money abroad in cash via FedEx to avoid transmission fees and taxes. While FedEx is reasonably reliable, note that this method is illegal. In the US and Canada, FedEx can be reached by calling 800-463-3339; in the UK, 0800 12 38 00; in Ireland, 800 535 800; in Australia, 13 26 10; in New Zealand, 0800 733 339; and in South Africa, 011 923 8000.

US STATE DEPARTMENT (US CITIZENS ONLY). In dire emergencies, the US State Department forwards money within hours to the nearest consular office, which will then disburse it according to instructions for a US$15 fee. Contact the Overseas Citizens Service, American Citizens Services, Consular Affairs, Room 4811, US Department of State, Washington, D.C. 20520 (☎202-647-5225; nights, Sundays, and holidays 647-4000; http://travel.state.gov).

COSTS

The cost of your trip will vary considerably, depending on where you go, how you travel, and where you stay. The single biggest cost of your trip will probably be the **airfare** to your Middle Eastern destination (see **Getting to the Middle East: By Plane,** p. 29). Before you go, spend some time calculating a reasonable per-day **budget.**

STAYING ON A BUDGET. Prices vary considerably between cities. To give you a general idea, a bare-bones day in Cairo (sleeping in a hostel, buying food at a market) would cost about US$8 (E£30), while a slightly more comfortable day (sleeping in the occasional budget hotel, eating one meal a day at a restaurant, going out at night) would run US$24 (E£95). Costs much higher in Israel and Lebanon, however, where it is difficult to get by with less than $US40 per day. Also, don't forget to factor in emergency reserve funds (at least US$200) when planning how much money you'll need.

TIPS FOR SAVING MONEY. Considering that saving just a few dollars a day over the course of your trip might pay for days or weeks of additional travel, the art of penny-pinching is well worth learning. Do your laundry in the sink (unless you're explicitly prohibited from doing so). You can split accommodations costs (in hotels and some hostels) with trustworthy fellow travelers; multi-bed rooms almost always work out cheaper per person than singles. The same principle will also work for cutting down on the cost of restaurant meals. You can also buy food in markets instead of eating out. With that said, don't go overboard with your budget obsession. Though staying within your budget is important, don't do so at the expense of your sanity or health.

Carry cash with you, and have small bills on hand while visiting sights or wandering the streets of a town. Most officials like *bakhsheesh* (see below) and most stores, *service* drivers, and the like cannot (or will refuse to) make change. No one to whom you are giving *bakhsheesh* will give you change. Keep small bills separate from larger bills, so that people cannot point to your stash and demand more.

TIPPING AND BARGAINING

Tipping and especially bargaining in the Middle East is a quite different and much more commonplace practice than you may be accustomed to; there are many unspoken rules to which tourists must adhere. Tipping (called *bakhsheesh* in Ara-

THE ART OF THE DEAL

Bargaining in Egypt is a given: no price is set in stone, while vendors and drivers will automatically quote you a price that is several times too high; it's up to you to get them down to a reasonable rate. Successful merchants enjoy the haggling (just remember that the shopkeepers do this for a living and have the benefit of experience). With the following tips and some finesse, you might be able to impress even the most hardened hawkers:

1. Bargaining needn't be a fierce struggle laced with barbs. Quite the opposite: good-natured wrangling with a cheerful smiling face may prove your biggest weapon.

2. Use your poker face. The less your face betrays your interest in the item the better. If you touch an item to inspect it, the vendor will be sure to "encourage" you to name a price or make a purchase. Coming back again and again to admire a trinket is a good way of ensuring that you pay a ridiculously high price. Never get too enthusiastic about the object in question; point out flaws in workmanship and design. Be cool.

3. Know when to bargain. In most cases, it's quite clear when it's appropriate to bargain. Most private transportation fares and things for sale in outdoor markets are all fair game. Don't bargain on prepared or pre-packaged foods on the street or in restaurants. In some stores, signs will indicate whether "fixed prices" prevail. When in doubt, ask tactfully, "Is that your lowest price?" or whether discounts are given.

4. Never underestimate the power of peer pressure. Bargaining with more than one person at a time always leads to higher prices. Alternately, try having a friend discourage you from your purchase—if you seem to be reluctant, the merchant will want to drop the price to interest you again.

5. Know when to turn away. Feel free to refuse any vendor who bargains rudely, and don't hesitate to move on to another vendor if one will not be reasonable about the final price he offers. However, to start bargaining without an intention to buy is a major *faux pas*. Agreeing on a price and declining it is also poor form. Turn away slowly with a smile and "thank you" upon hearing a ridiculous price—the price may plummet.

6. Start low. Never feel guilty offering what seems to be a ridiculously low price. Your starting price should be no more than one-third to one-half the asking price.

bic) will be encouraged (at times expected) everywhere you go in the Middle East. There are three kinds of *bakhsheesh*. The most common is similar to tipping—a small reward for a small service. *Bakhsheesh* becomes most useful when used to procure special favors. The second kind of *bakhsheesh* is the giving of alms. There are beggars everywhere in the Middle East who are willing to bestow rhetorical blessings in return for a little charity. There are also those who insist on opening a door before you can get to it or snatch your baggage from your hands and then demand *bakhsheesh*. Don't feel obligated to give money in this situation. The final form of *bakhsheesh* is simply a bribe—a bad idea. Don't bribe officials.

EGYPT. *Bakhsheesh* is your key to happiness in Egypt. The standard tip in a restaurant is usually included in the bill as a 10-15% service charge. Anything more on top of the bill is not expected. Taxi or *service* drivers do not expect tips. *Bakhsheesh* is also useful when sightseeing, as many places do not provide tour guides. The alternative is to find a local to show you around for some *bakhsheesh*. Egypt is a great place to bargain; use your skills in the bazaars.

ISRAEL. Tipping in Israel is increasingly moving toward American standards, but for the time being, a 10-15% tip will suffice in restaurants, bars and taxis. Check whether a service charge is already included in the bill: in restaurants, gratuity is frequently included for parties of six or more. Bargaining in Israel is the norm. There are very few places where you can't bargain: the "no's" are limited for the most part to department stores, drug stores, and supermarkets. Ask hostel owners if they offer any "discounts." Chances are they'll knock 5% or 10% of the price. However, insist that taxi rides be metered; if a driver quotes you a flat price do not accept it unless you are certain that it will not end up costing you more than the metered fare. Do not bargain in restaurants with fixed-price menus, or in stores where prices are barcoded as opposed to hand-labeled.

JORDAN. The appropriate tip in a restaurant is about 15%, and it is often included in the bill. For transportation, don't feel obligated to tip *service* drivers; taxi drivers do not usually expect tips but accept them. Like most Middle Eastern countries, bargaining is also crucial in Jordan for getting the best possible price.

LEBANON. In restaurants, gratuity is often included, but if not, 15-20% is expected. It is not the norm to tip *service* drivers in Lebanon.

SYRIA. Gratuity is never included in restaurant bills, and 10% is adequate for both restaurants and drivers. Be prepared to bargain your way around Syria.

TURKEY. Tips are usually not expected. Leaving a bit of small change, however, at your table after a meal or with a taxi driver is appreciated as a friendly gesture and a sign of gratitude. Bargaining occurs in outdoor food markets, bazaars, and some carpet and souvenir shops. Walk-in stores that stock conventional goods such as groceries, pharmaceuticals, and clothes have fixed prices.

TAXES

In general, figuring out exactly how taxes operate in the Middle East is tricky. Sometimes, the extra money is already included in the bill. Other times, taxes may be added on to a bill at the last minute. It is best to ask all hotels (and even restaurants) about the taxes they may charge in advance. In **Egypt**, there is no sales tax. In **Lebanon,** taxes are easily negotiable. They are the first part of a price to go, especially at hotels where taxes are the most hefty. **Israel** offers tourists tax-free shopping through a VAT (Value Added Tax) **refund** to visitors purchasing more than US$50 worth of goods at shops approved by the Ministry of Tourism. If you are a foreign passport holder who is not an Israeli citizen, and you pay for your purchase in foreign currency (cash or international credit cards), you may reclaim sales taxes at your point of departure. Approved stores will be marked: look for the Ministry of Tourism logo or a sign reading "V.A.T. Refund." In **Jordan,** a 13% tax (as well as a 10% service charge) is added to hotel and restaurant prices. Both are usually already added to the bill, though some hotels may add on the extra charges at the end. Taxes are nonexistent in **Syria.** Not all shops participate, but **Turkey** does have a 10-20% value-added tax (VAT) known as the *katma değer vergisi* or KDV. It is included in the prices of most goods and services (including meals, lodging, and car rentals). Before you buy, check if the KDV is included in the price to avoid paying it twice. Theoretically, it can be reclaimed at most points of departure, but this requires much persistence. An airport tax of US$15 is levied on international travelers, but it is usually included in the cost of the ticket.

SAFETY AND SECURITY

The number one concern for most travelers planning a trip to the Middle East is physical safety. There are regions in the Middle East in which travel remains unsafe. Of particular concern this year is travel to Israel and the Palestinian Territories, where hundreds have died in the most recent clashes since September 2001. Travelers in these areas are constantly under threat of terrorist and military acts; nevertheless, travel in Tel Aviv, northern, and southern Israel is considerably safer than movement around Jerusalem, the West Bank, and Gaza. The most important thing to do is keep updated on current events. Good sources for information are newspapers, television, and websites on travel safety run by your home country (www.state.gov for the US, www.dfait-maeci.gc.ca for Canada, www.fco.gov.uk for the UK, and www.dfat.gov.au for Australia). For country specifics, see individual chapters and **Terrorism** (p. 17).

PERSONAL SAFETY

Tourists are particularly vulnerable to crime because they often carry large amounts of cash and are not as street-savvy as locals. Keep your money on your person, preferably in a money belt concealed from sticky fingers. The key to avoiding unwanted attention is to **blend in** as much as possible. Respecting local customs by dressing more conservatively may placate would-be hecklers. The gawking camera-toter is a more obvious target than the low-profile traveler. This is particularly tricky in the Middle East because the dress code and attitudes often differ drastically from Western norms; read over the **Dress and Etiquette** and **Women Travelers** section at the start of each country chapter, as well as **Essentials: Women Travelers** (p. 39) before getting off the plane.

Familiarize yourself with your surroundings before setting out for the day; if you must check a map on the street, duck into a cafe or shop. Carry yourself with confidence; an obviously bewildered bodybuilder is more likely to be harassed than a stern and confident 98-pound weakling. If you are traveling alone, be sure that someone at home knows your itinerary and **never admit that you're traveling alone.**

FURTHER INFORMATION: SAFETY AND SECURITY.
Fielding's The World's Most Dangerous Places, edited by Kathy Knoles (US$22), gives detailed descriptions of dangerous destinations around the world. *Don't Go!: 51 Reasons Not to Travel Abroad, But If You Must...176 Tactics for Coping With Discomforts, Distress and Danger*, by Hannah Blank (US$11), provides great tips for taking care of oneself on the road. For the lighter side of coping, see *Worst Case Scenario Survival Handbook: Travel* by Joshua Piven (US$15). For specific safety and travel warnings, consult both the country's chapter in this book as well as your home country's department of State web page (see **Personal Safety,** above.)

PROTECTING YOURSELF (AND YOUR WALLET)

Find out about unsafe areas from tourist offices, the manager of your hotel or hostel, or a local whom you trust. You may want to carry a **whistle** to scare off attackers or attract attention; also memorize emergency numbers for the city or area. Whenever possible, *Let's Go* warns of unsafe neighborhoods and areas, but there are some good general tips to follow. When walking at night, stick to busy, well-lit streets and avoid dark alleyways. Do not attempt to cross through parks, parking lots or other large, deserted areas. The distribution of people can reveal a great deal about the relative safety of the area; look for children playing, women walking in the open, and other signs of an active community. Keep in mind that a district can change drastically from block to block. There are very few regions in the Middle East where violent crime against foreigners is a serious threat, and there are a few simple precautions travelers can take (see **Protecting Your Valuables,** p. 18). However, while many places have **pickpockets,** the most common thievery is simple scamming. Trust your instincts: if you feel you are getting something for nothing, be wary. On the other hand, if you feel that something is reasonably priced by Western standards, know that you may very well be paying too much for it. Labor and materials cost much less in most of the Middle East than they do in the Western world, and prices should reflect that.

TRANSPORTATION

If you are using a **car,** learn local driving signals and wear a seatbelt. Children under 40 pounds should ride only in a specially designed carseat, available for a small fee from most car rental agencies. Study route maps before you hit the road, and if you plan on spending a lot of time on the road, you may want to bring spare parts. If your car breaks down, wait for the police to assist you. For long drives in desolate areas, invest in a jerrycan for extra gas and a cellular phone. Be sure to park your vehicle in a garage or well traveled area, and use a steering wheel locking device in larger cities. **Sleeping in your car** is one of the most dangerous (and often illegal) ways to get your rest. For info on the perils of **hitchhiking,** see p. 38.

SELF DEFENSE. There is no sure-fire way to avoid all the threatening situations you might encounter when you travel, but a good self-defense course will give you concrete ways to react to unwanted advances. **Impact, Prepare, and Model Mugging**

can refer you to local self-defense courses in the US (☎ 800-345-5425). Visit the website at www.impactsafety.org/chapters for a list of nearby chapters. Workshops (2-3hr.) start at US$50; full courses run US$350-500.

TERRORISM

Although the Middle East has long been known for political and religious conflicts, travel in the region is relatively safe for a cautious traveler exercising common sense. Those planning to visit the region for longer periods of time should register with their home country's embassy in each destination country to obtain updated information on travel and security in specific areas.

EGYPT. Traveling in Egypt is safe except for **Middle Egypt** and the **Egyptian frontiers.** Since the summer of 1998, the US government has warned against traveling in Middle Egypt (especially near the governates of Minya, Asyut, Sohag, and just north of Qena), where terrorist attacks by extremist groups have occurred since the mid-1990s. Although there have been no attacks on foreign tourists since 1998, these areas should be considered risky (*Let's Go* has not sent researchers to these areas). Those wishing to visit areas near Egypt's frontiers should also be aware of the dangers of off-road travel and the possible threat of **landmines** (marked by barbed wire) from previous conflicts. The dangerous areas of Egypt's "frontier" include: the oases near the Libyan border (except for the relatively safe Siwa Oasis); off-road areas in the Sinai; and sights south of Aswan near the Sudanese border (an area known as the disputed "Ha'ib Triangle" area). Travel to the first two regions cannot be completed without permission from the Travel Permits Department of the Ministry of the Interior in Cairo.

ISRAEL AND THE PALESTINIAN TERRITORIES. Terrorists in **Israel** target crowded areas, such as outdoor markets, and public transportation. Terrorists set their sight to the busy shopping days of Thursday and Friday, when Jews are preparing for the Sabbath, for bombing outdoor markets, while most bus explosions in Israel occur in the early morning rush hour. If your plans are flexible, try to avoid shopping or bus travel at those times. As terrorism is sadly a part of life in the country, Israelis look at abandoned purses and backpacks in a different light. Leave nothing unattended, and alert authorities if you see an abandoned package.

Traveling in the **Palestinian territories** can be dangerous, especially in a car with the yellow, rather than blue, license plates that identify the vehicle as Israeli. Jewish travelers should avoid identifying themselves as such. Simply placing a baseball cap over a *kippah* can prevent stares and hostility. Especially since the most recent clashes during 2001, be aware of potential unrest in the West Bank by staying up to date with the news and contacting the consular division of the US Consulate General, at 27 Nablus Rd. in East Jerusalem.

JORDAN. Jordan is one of the safer places for travel in this region. Amman (via the King Hussein/Allenby Bridge) and Aqaba (by way of Eilat) are the only safe gateways into Israel from anywhere in the Levant. See **Jordan: Border Crossings** (p. 436) for detailed information on travel between Jordan and Israel.

LEBANON. Since August 28, 2000, the US Department of State has had a **travel warning** in place for Lebanon. In June 1998, the US Embassy in Beirut was the target of a rocket-propelled grenade attack, and the security situation in the city of **Sidon** has recently deteriorated, including the issuance from the Sidon area of an anti-American threat of undetermined credibility. Americans are cautioned to avoid travel into Sidon and adjacent Palestinian refugee camps until security stabilizes. As an added precaution, American air carriers are prohibited from the use of the **Beirut International Airport** due to continuing concern about passenger and aircraft security arrangements.

Despite the Israeli withdrawal in May 2000, South Lebanon (namely south of Beirut as far north as the Na'ameh Hills, sections of the Beqa'a Valley) is still a risky place to travel because of continuing political instability (for details, see **Lebanon: Modern History,** p. 501). **Ba'albeck** (home of Hezbollah headquarters, p. 545) is safe and comfortable for travel.

SYRIA. Syria is one of the safer places for travel in this region. The main problem travelers encounter involves traveling to Syria after visiting **Israel.** The Syrian government rigidly enforces restrictions on prior travel to Israel: authorities will refuse admission to travelers whose passports have Israeli stamps, Jordanian entry cachets or cachets from other countries that suggest prior travel to Israel, or whose passports do not bear any entry stamps from a country adjacent to Israel that the traveler has just visited. If you wish to visit Syria and Israel on the same trip, your best bet is to visit Israel first, ask border officials not to stamp your passport (they will give you a slip instead), and then cross via the West Bank and Jordan (see **Syria: Border Crossings,** p. 571). Although Syria is included on the US Department of State's list of state sponsors of **terrorism,** there is no record of terrorist attacks against foreigners or of a terrorist presence anywhere in Syria; the Syrian government has also repeatedly stated their commitment to protect foreigners.

TURKEY. The **PKK** (Workers' Party of Kurdistan) and the DHKP/C (formerly Dev Sol) commit most of the terrorist acts in Turkey, which have historically not targeted tourists. The PKK vowed to stop targeting civilians and declared a cease-fire in August 1999. Terrorist activities increased after the capture of PKK leader Abdullah Öcalan (see **Turkey: In The News,** p. 627). Since the autumn of 1999, however, tourism has been on the rise. *Let's Go* does not recommend that women travel alone in **Eastern Anatolia.** Incidents of terrorism are frequent in **southeastern Turkey,** which is under martial law because some provinces are in a state of civil war with Kurdish guerrillas fighting for freedom. Visitors to any part of southeastern Turkey are advised to travel only during daylight hours and on major highways. Although access to Mt. Ararat is officially prohibited, it is still possible to get near it. In most militarized cities, **roads close** during certain parts of the day. Photographs of military installations, bridges, and power stations are prohibited.

FINANCIAL SECURITY

PROTECTING YOUR VALUABLES. Street crime is not common in the Middle East, but there are a few steps you can take to minimize the financial risk associated with traveling. **Bring as little with you as possible.** Leave expensive watches, jewelry, cameras, and electronic equipment (like your Discman) at home; chances are you'd break them, lose them, or get sick of lugging them around anyway. Second, buy a few combination padlocks to secure your belongings either in your pack—which you should never leave unattended—or in a hostel or train station locker. Third, carry as little cash as possible; instead, use traveler's checks and credit cards, keeping them in a concealed money belt (not a "fanny pack") along with your passport and ID cards. Fourth, keep a small cash reserve separate from your primary stash. This should entail about US$50 (US dollars are best) sewn into or stored in the depths of your pack, along with your traveler's check numbers and important photocopies.

CON ARTISTS AND PICKPOCKETS. Among the more financially threatening aspects of large cities are **con artists.** Possessing an innumerable range of ruses, they often work in groups, and children are the most effective. Beware of certain classics: sob stories that require money, rolls of bills "found" on the street, mustard spilled (or saliva spit) onto your shoulder to distract you while they snatch your bag. Especially in Egypt, where thriving tourism has existed for years and it is often the only source of income, hustlers have fine-tuned the con into an art form (see **Scam Wars, Episode I,** p. 98).

Don't ever hand your passport to someone whose authority is questionable (ask to accompany them to a police station if they insist), and **don't ever let your passport out of your sight.** Similarly, don't let your bag out of sight; never trust a "station-porter" who offers to carry your bag or stow it in the baggage compartment or a "new friend" who wants to guard your bag while you buy a train ticket or use the restroom. Beware of **pickpockets** in crowds, especially on public transportation. Also, be alert in public telephone booths and around ATM machines. If you say your calling card number, do so very quietly; if you punch in a PIN, make sure no one can look over your shoulder.

ACCOMMODATIONS AND TRANSPORTATION. Never leave your belongings unattended; crime occurs in even the most demure-looking hostel or hotel. Bring your own **padlock** for hostel lockers, and don't ever store valuables in a locker.

Be particularly careful on **buses** and **trains;** horror stories abound about determined thieves who wait for travelers to fall asleep. Carry your backpack in front of you where you can see it. When traveling with others, sleep in alternate shifts. When alone, use good judgement in selecting a train compartment: never stay in an empty one and use a lock to secure your pack to the luggage rack. Try to sleep on top bunks with your luggage stored above you (if not in bed with you), and keep important documents and other valuables on your person.

If traveling by **car,** don't leave valuables (such as radios or luggage) in it while you are away. If your tape deck or radio is removable, hide it in the trunk or take it with you. If it isn't, at least conceal it. Similarly, hide baggage in the trunk, even though savvy thieves can tell if a car is heavily loaded by the way it sits on its tires.

DRUGS AND ALCOHOL

You are subject to the laws of the country in which you travel, not to those of your home country. **Illegal drugs** (including marijuana) are best avoided. Penalties for possession, use, or trafficking in illegal drugs are severe throughout the Middle East and include severe fines and jail time. Egypt and Syria may impose the **death penalty** on anyone convicted of smuggling or selling. Consulates can do no more than bring floral arrangements to prisoners, provide a list of attorneys, and inform family and friends. If you carry **prescription drugs** while you travel, it is vital to have a copy of the prescriptions themselves readily accessible at country borders.

Although there is an Islamic law forbidding **alcohol,** many people drink anyway. You may be asked to purchase alcohol for not-so-devout Muslims; unless they are underage, it is legal to do so if you are of age. The drinking age in **Egypt** is 21. It is strictly enforced in areas like Islamic Cairo, but may be quite lenient in other areas. In general, keep such practices to yourself and be careful. The drinking age in **Israel** is 18, and for the first time, bars are beginning to enforce it. Eilat in particular has begun to card stringently; a foreign driver's license usually serves as adequate identification. Many clubs in Israel have higher minimum drinking ages to target an older clientele. In **Jordan** and **Syria,** the drinking age is 18, but it doesn't seem to be enforced anywhere. The drinking age in **Lebanon** is also 18, but it is only strictly enforced in heavily Islamic areas, like Sur and Ba'albeck. Since Islam prohibits the consumption of alcohol, it is improper to drink in the more traditional towns of **Turkey,** and anywhere at all during the holy month of Ramadan (see **Holidays and Festivals,** p. 701, for dates). In all countries, **public drunkenness** can jeopardize your safety and earn the disdain of locals.

HEALTH

Common sense is the simplest prescription for good health while traveling. Travelers complain most often about their feet and their gut, so take precautionary measures: drink lots of fluids to prevent dehydration and constipation, wear sturdy, broken-in shoes and clean socks, and use talcum powder to keep your feet dry.

BEFORE YOU GO

Preparation can help minimize the likelihood of contracting a disease and maximize the chances of receiving effective health care in the event of an emergency. For tips on packing a basic **first-aid kit** and other health essentials, see p. 25.

In your **passport,** write the names of any people you wish to be contacted in case of a medical emergency, and also list any allergies or medical conditions of which you would want doctors to be aware. Matching a prescription to a foreign equivalent is not always easy, safe, or possible. Carry up-to-date, legible prescriptions or a statement from your doctor stating the medication's trade name, manufacturer, chemical name, and dosage. While traveling, be sure to keep all medication with you in your carry-on, not your checked, luggage.

IMMUNIZATIONS AND PRECAUTIONS

Take a look at your **immunization** records before you go; if you are coming from a tropical area with a risk of yellow fever or cholera, such as Sub-Saharan Africa, you may be required to show certificates of up-to-date vaccinations to enter some countries. For recommendations on immunizations and prophylaxis, consult the CDC (p. 20) in the US or the equivalent in your home country, and be sure to check with a doctor for guidance.

 REQUIRED IMMUNIZATIONS. Travelers over two years old should be sure that the following vaccines are up to date: Measles, Mumps, and Rubella (MMR); Diptheria, Tetanus, and Pertussis (DTP or DTap); Polio (OPV); Haemophilus Influenza B (HbCV); and Hepatitis B (HBV). A booster of Tetanus-diptheria (Td) is recommended once every 10 years, and adults should consider an additional dose of Polio vaccine if they have not already had one during their adult years. Hepatitis A vaccine and/or Immune Globulin (IG) is recommended for travelers to the Middle East as well. If you will be spending more than four weeks in Egypt, Jordan, Lebanon, or Syria you should consider the typhoid vaccine. Travelers to Syria and southern Turkey should also take malaria pills.

USEFUL ORGANIZATIONS AND PUBLICATIONS

The US **Centers for Disease Control and Prevention** (**CDC;** ☎877-FYI-TRIP; www.cdc.gov/travel) maintains an international fax information service and an international travelers hotline (☎404-332-4559). The CDC's comprehensive booklet *Health Information for International Travel,* an annual rundown of disease, immunization, and general health advice, is free online or US$25 via the Public Health Foundation (☎877-252-1200). Consult the appropriate government agency of your home country for consular information sheets on health, entry requirements, and other issues for various countries. For quick information on health and other travel warnings, call the **Overseas Citizens Services** (☎202-647-5225; after hours 202-647-4000), contact a passport agency or an embassy or consulate abroad. US citizens can send a self-addressed, stamped envelope to the Overseas Citizens Services, Bureau of Consular Affairs, #4811, US Department of State, Washington, D.C. 20520. For information on medical evacuation services and travel insurance firms, see the US government's website at http://travel.state.gov/medical.html or the **British Foreign and Commonwealth Office** (www.fco.gov.uk).

 FURTHER READING: USEFUL ORGANIZATIONS. For a detailed, country by-country overview of diseases, try the **International Travel Health Guide,** Stuart Rose, MD (Travel Medicine, $24.95). Information is also available at Travel Medicine's website (www.travmed.com). For general health information, contact the **American Red Cross,** which publishes *First-Aid and Safety Handbook* (US$5) available for purchase by calling or writing to the American Red Cross, 285 Columbus Ave., Boston, MA 02116-5114 (☎800-564-1234, M-F 8:30am-4:30pm). Useful **web pages** include CDC Travel Information's *Health Information for Travelers to the Middle East* (www.cdc.gov/travel/mideast.htm) and the United States State Department's *Tips for Travelers to the Middle East and North Africa* (travel.state.gov/tips_mid-east%26nafrica.html).

MEDICAL ASSISTANCE ON THE ROAD

Most Middle Eastern hospitals do not have the high quality of medical treatment found in North America, Europe, or Australia, and few doctors speak English. Jordan and Syria are a step above other Middle Eastern countries, but only in Israel are city hospitals on par with Western standards in training and technology. Many large hotels throughout the Middle East have English-speaking doctors on-call, who can either treat travelers or refer them to the nearest city hospital. Pharmacies are absolutely everywhere in the Middle East; many countries even have rotating 24hr. pharmacy duties.

If you are concerned about being able to access medical support while traveling, there are special support services you may employ. The *MedPass* from **GlobalCare, Inc.,** 2001 Westside Pkwy., #120, Alpharetta, GA 30004, USA (☎800-860-1111; fax 770-475-0058; www.globalems.com), provides 24hr. international medical assistance, support, and medical evacuation resources. The **International Association for Medical Assistance to Travelers** (**IAMAT;** US ☎716-754-4883, Canada ☎416-652-0137, New Zealand ☎03 352 20 53; www.sentex.net/~iamat) has free membership, lists English-speaking doctors worldwide, and offers detailed info on immunization requirements and sanitation. If your regular **insurance** policy does not cover travel abroad, you may wish to purchase additional coverage (see p. 24).

Those with medical conditions (diabetes, allergies to antibiotics, epilepsy, heart conditions) may want to obtain a stainless-steel **Medic Alert** ID tag (first year US$35, annually thereafter US$20), which identifies the condition and gives a 24hr. collect-call number. Contact the Medic Alert Foundation, 2323 Colorado Ave, Turlock, CA 95382, USA (☎888-633-4298; www.medicalert.org).

ONCE IN THE MIDDLE EAST

ENVIRONMENTAL HAZARDS

Heat exhaustion and dehydration: Heat exhaustion, characterized by dehydration and salt deficiency, can lead to fatigue, headaches, and wooziness. Avoid it by drinking plenty of fluids, eating salty foods, and avoiding dehydrating beverages (e.g. alcohol- and caffeine). Continuous heat stress can eventually lead to heatstroke, characterized by a rising temperature, severe headache, and cessation of sweating. Victims should be cooled off with wet towels and taken to a doctor.

Sunburn: If you're prone to sunburn, bring sunscreen with you (it's often more expensive and hard to find when traveling), and apply it liberally and often to avoid burns and risk of skin cancer. If you are planning on spending time near water, in the desert, or in the snow, you are at risk of getting burned, even through clouds. If you get sunburned, drink more fluids than usual and apply Calamine or an aloe-based lotion.

INSECT-BORNE DISEASES

Be aware of insects in wet or forested areas, while hiking, and especially while camping. Mosquitoes are most active from dusk to dawn. Use insect repellents, such as DEET. Wear long pants and long sleeves and buy a mosquito net. Wear shoes and socks, and tuck long pants into socks. Soak or spray your gear with permethrin, which is licensed in the US for use on clothing. Natural repellents can be useful supplements: taking vitamin B-12 pills regularly can eventually make you smelly to insects, as can garlic pills.

Malaria is transmitted by *Anopheles* mosquitoes that bite at night, malaria may be a risk to travelers in some parts of Turkey and Syria. The incubation period varies from 6-8 days to as long as months. Early symptoms include fever, chills, aches, and fatigue, followed by high fever and sweating, sometimes with vomiting and diarrhea. See a doctor for any flu-like sickness that occurs after travel in a risk area. Left untreated, malaria can cause anemia, kidney failure, coma, and death. It is an especially serious threat to pregnant women. To reduce the risk of contracting malaria, use mosquito repellent, particularly in the evenings and when visiting forested areas, and take oral prophylactics, like **mefloquine** (sold under the name Lariam) or **doxycycline** (ask your doctor for a prescription). Be aware that these drugs can have very serious side effects, including slowed heart rate and nightmares.

ESSENTIALS

ESSENTIALS

Dengue fever is an "urban viral infection" transmitted by *Aedes* mosquitoes, which bite during the day rather than at night. Risk to travelers in the Middle East is low. Dengue has flu-like symptoms and is often indicated by a rash 3-4 days after the onset of fever. Symptoms for the first 2-4 days include chills, high fever, headaches, swollen lymph nodes, muscle aches, and in some instances, a pink rash on the face. If you experience these symptoms, see a doctor, drink plenty of liquids, and take fever-reducing medication such as acetaminophen (Tylenol). *Never take aspirin to treat dengue fever.*

Leishmaniasis is a parasite transmitted by sand flies that can occur in the Middle East. Common symptoms are fever, weakness, and swelling of the spleen. There is a treatment, but no vaccine.

FOOD- AND WATER-BORNE DISEASES

Be sure that everything you eat is cooked properly and that the water you drink is clean. In the Middle East, where the risk of contracting traveler's diarrhea or forms of food poisoning is high, never drink unbottled water that you have not treated. To purify your own water, bring it to a rolling boil or treat it with iodine tablets, available at any camping goods store. In risk areas, don't rinse your toothbrush under the faucet, and keep your mouth closed in the shower. Salads and uncooked vegetables are also full of untreated water. Other culprits are raw shellfish, unpasteurized milk, and sauces containing raw eggs. Insist on having any lukewarm meats or meat-sauces reheated and anything slightly undercooked put back on the grill. Peel all fruits and vegetables yourself, and beware of watermelon, which is often injected with impure water. Watch out for food, fruit, or juices from markets or street vendors that may have been washed in dirty water or fried in rancid cooking oil. Always wash hands before eating and after using the restroom to minimize the risk of Hepatitis A; bring a quick-drying antibacterial hand cleaner. Your bowels will thank you.

◪ **Traveler's diarrhea** results from drinking untreated water or eating uncooked foods, and can last 3 to 7 days. Symptoms include nausea, bloating, urgency, and malaise. If the nasties hit you, eat quick-energy, non-sugary foods with protein and carbohydrates to keep your strength up. Over-the-counter remedies may counteract the problems, but they can complicate serious infections. **Avoid anti-diarrheals** if you suspect that you are at risk for other diseases. If possible, avoid taking such medication unless strictly necessary (i.e., before embarking on an overnight bus trip), as how long your stools remain loose is an important diagnostic clue that remains unclear for those using anti-diarrheals. The most dangerous side effect of diarrhea is **dehydration.** The simplest and most effective anti-dehydration formula is 8oz. of (clean) water with ½ tsp. of sugar or honey and a pinch of salt. Soft drinks without caffeine or salted crackers are also good. Down several of these remedies a day, rest, and wait for the disease to run its course. If you develop a fever or if your symptoms don't go away after 4 or 5 days, consult a doctor. If children develop traveler's diarrhea, see a doctor, as treatment is different.

Dysentery results from a serious intestinal infection caused by certain bacteria. The most common type is bacillary dysentery, also called *shigellosis*. Symptoms include bloody diarrhea or bloody stools mixed with mucus, fever, and abdominal pain and tenderness. Bacillary dysentery generally only lasts a week, but it is highly contagious. Amoebic dysentery develops more slowly, with no fever or vomiting. However, it is a more serious disease, and may cause long-term damage if left untreated. A stool test can determine which kind you have, so you should seek medical help immediately. If you are traveling in high-risk regions (especially rural areas) obtain a prescription before you leave home.

Hepatitis A (distinct from B and C, see below) is a **high risk** in the Middle East. Hep A is a viral infection of the liver acquired primarily through contaminated water, ice, shellfish, or unpeeled fruits and vegetables, and also from sexual contact. Symptoms include fatigue, fever, loss of appetite, nausea, dark urine, jaundice, vomiting, aches and pains, and light stools. Ask your doctor about the vaccine (Havrix or Vaqta), or ask to get an injection of immune globulin (IG).

Parasites such as microbes and tapeworms also often hide in unsafe water and food. **Giardiasis,** for example, is acquired by drinking untreated water from streams or lakes all over the world. Symptoms of parasitic infections include swollen glands or lymph nodes, fever, rashes or itchiness, digestive problems, eye problems, anal itching and anemia. Boil your water, wear shoes, avoid bugs, and eat only cooked food.

Schistosomiasis (also called **bilharzia**) is a parasitic disease caused by a flatworm. The larvae mature inside freshwater snails and escape back into the water, where they can infect humans by penetrating unbroken skin. Avoid swimming in fresh water areas, particularly in Egypt, where the disease is most prevalent. If your skin is exposed to untreated water, rub it immediately and vigorously with a towel and/or rubbing alcohol. You may notice an itchy localized rash; later symptoms include fever, painful urination, diarrhea, loss of appetite, night sweats, and a hive-like rash on the body. Schistosomiasis can be treated with prescription drugs.

Typhoid fever is common in villages and rural areas in the Middle East. While mostly transmitted through contaminated food and water, it may also be acquired by direct contact with another person. Symptoms include fever, headaches, fatigue, loss of appetite, constipation, and a rash on the abdomen or chest. Antibiotics can treat typhoid, but the CDC recommends vaccinations (70-90% effective) if you will be hiking, camping, or staying in small cities or rural areas.

OTHER INFECTIOUS DISEASES

Rabies is transmitted through the saliva of infected animals and is fatal if untreated. Avoid contact with animals, especially strays. If you are bitten, wash the wound thoroughly and seek immediate medical care. By the time symptoms appear (thirst and muscle spasms), the disease is in its terminal stage. A rabies vaccine, which consists of 3 shots given over a 21-day period, is available but is only semi-effective.

Hepatitis B is a viral infection of the liver transmitted through the transfer of bodily fluids, by sharing needles, or by having unprotected sex. Its incubation period varies, and symptoms may not show until many years after infection. The CDC recommends the Hep B vaccination for health-care workers, sexually active travelers, and anyone planning to seek medical treatment abroad. Vaccination consists of a three-shot series given over a period of time and should begin 6 months before traveling.

Hepatitis C is like Hep B, but transmission is different. Intravenous drug users, those with occupational exposure to blood, hemodialysis patients, and recipients of blood transfusions are at the highest risk, but the disease can also be spread through sex or sharing of items like razors and toothbrushes that may have traces of blood on them.

AIDS, HIV, STDS

Acquired Immune Deficiency Syndrome (AIDS) is a growing problem around the world. The World Health Organization estimates that at the end of 1999, there were more than 30 million people infected with the HIV virus, 27 million of whom were unaware of their HIV-positive status. The easiest mode of HIV transmission is through direct blood-to-blood contact with an HIV-positive person; never share intravenous drug, tattooing, or other needles. The most common mode of transmission is sexual intercourse. Health professionals recommend the use of latex condoms—take a supply with you before you depart for your trip. For detailed information on **Acquired Immune Deficiency Syndrome (AIDS)** in the Middle East, call the **US Centers for Disease Control** 24hr. hotline (☎ 800-342-2437), or contact the **Joint United Nations Programme on HIV/AIDS (UNAIDS),** 20, av. Appia, CH-1211 Geneva 27, Switzerland (☎ +41 22 791 36 66; fax 22 791 41 87). The Council on International Educational Exchange's pamphlet, Travel Safe: AIDS and International Travel, is posted on their website (www.ciee.org/Isp/safety/travelsafe.htm), along with links to other online and phone resources. Note that a number of countries, including those in the Middle East, screen incoming travelers for AIDS and may deny entrance to those who test HIV-positive. This is particularly true for travelers who plan to spend an extended period of time in the Middle East. Contact the nearest consulate for up-to-date information.

Sexually transmitted diseases (STDs) such as gonorrhea, chlamydia, genital warts, syphilis, and herpes are easier to catch than HIV, and some can be just as deadly. **Hepatitis B** and **C** are also serious sexually transmitted diseases (see **Other Infectious Diseases,** p. 23). Warning signs for STDs include: swelling, sores, bumps, or blisters on sex organs, rectum, or mouth; burning and pain during urination and bowel movements; itching around sex organs; swelling or redness in the throat; and flu-like symptoms with fever, chills, and aches. If these symptoms develop, see a doctor immediately. When having sex, condoms may protect you from certain STDs, but oral or even tactile contact can lead to transmission.

WOMEN'S HEALTH

Women traveling in unsanitary conditions are vulnerable to **urinary tract** and **bladder infections,** common and severely uncomfortable bacterial diseases that cause a burning sensation and painful and sometimes frequent urination. To try to avoid these infections, drink plenty of vitamin-C-rich juice and plenty of clean water, and urinate frequently, especially right after intercourse. See a doctor if symptoms persist: untreated, these infections can lead to kidney infections, sterility, and death.

Vaginal yeast infections are treatable but uncomfortable illnesses likely to flare up in hot and humid climates. Wearing loosely fitting trousers or a skirt and cotton underwear helps. Bring supplies from home if you are prone to infection, as they may be difficult to find on the road. In a pinch, some travelers use a natural alternative such as a plain yogurt and lemon juice douche.

Tampons, pads, and **reliable contraceptive devices** are sometimes hard to find when traveling, so take supplies along. Women on the pill should bring enough to allow for possible loss or extended stays. In case you need to get more, bring a prescription, since forms of the pill vary a good deal.

Women considering an **abortion** abroad should contact the **International Planned Parenthood Federation (IPPF),** Regent's College, Inner Circle, Regent's Park, London NW1 4NS (☎020 7487 7900; fax 7487 7950; www.ippf.org), for more information. Abortion is legal in Turkey. In Israel, Jordan, and Egypt it is only permitted on limited health grounds. In Lebanon and Syria it is illegal.

INSURANCE

Travel insurance generally covers four basic areas: medical/health problems, property loss, trip cancellation/interruption, and emergency evacuation. Although your regular insurance policies may well extend to travel-related accidents, you may consider purchasing travel insurance if the cost of potential trip cancellation/interruption or emergency medical evacuation is greater than you can absorb. Prices for travel insurance purchased separately generally run about US$50 per week for full coverage, while trip cancellation/interruption may be purchased separately at a rate of about US$5.50 per US$100 of coverage. **Medical insurance** (especially university policies) often covers costs incurred abroad; check with your provider. **US Medicare** does not cover foreign travel. **Canadians** are protected by their home province's health insurance plan for up to 90 days after leaving the country; check with the provincial Ministry of Health or Health Plan Headquarters for details. **Homeowners' insurance** (or your family's coverage) often covers theft during travel and loss of travel documents (passport, plane ticket, etc.) up to US$500. **ISIC** and **ITIC** provide basic insurance benefits, including US$100 per day of in-hospital sickness for a maximum of 60 days, US$3000 of accident-related medical reimbursement, and US$25,000 for emergency medical transport (see **Identification,** p. 9). Cardholders have access to a toll-free 24hr. helpline (run by the insurance provider TravelGuard) for medical, legal, and financial emergencies overseas (US and Canada ☎877-370-4742, elsewhere call US collect +1 715-345-0505). **American Express** (US ☎800-528-4800) grants most cardholders automatic car rental insurance (collision and theft, but not liability) and ground travel accident coverage of US$100,000 on flight purchases made with the card.

INSURANCE PROVIDERS. **Council** and **STA** (see p. 30) offer a range of plans that can supplement your basic coverage. Other private insurance providers in the **US and Canada** include: **Access America** (☎ 800-284-8300); **Berkely Group/Carefree Travel Insurance** (☎ 800-323-3149; www.berkely.com); **Globalcare Travel Insurance** (☎ 800-821-2488; www.globalcare-cocco.com); and **Travel Assistance International** (☎ 800-821-2828; www.worldwide-assistance.com). Providers in the **UK** include **Campus Travel** (☎ 01865 25 80 00) and **Columbus Travel Insurance** (☎ 020 7375 0011). In **Australia**, try **CIC Insurance** (☎ 9202 8000).

PACKING

Pack lightly: lay out only what you absolutely need, then take half the clothes and twice the money. The less you have, the less you have to lose (or store, or carry on your back). Any extra space will be useful for any items you pick up along the way.

LUGGAGE. If you plan to cover most of your itinerary by foot, a sturdy **frame backpack** is unbeatable. **Internal-frame packs** mold better to your back, keep a lower center of gravity, and can flex adequately on difficult hikes that require a lot of bending and maneuvering. **External-frame packs** are more comfortable for long hikes over even terrain (like city streets) since they keep the weight higher and distribute it more evenly. In addition to your main vessel, a small backpack, rucksack, or courier bag is useful as a **daypack** for sightseeing expeditions.

CLOTHING. Don't forget the obvious: it's always a good idea to bring a rain jacket (Gore-Tex is a miracle fabric that's both waterproof and breathable). Natural fibers are better than synthetics in the heat. Dark colors hide dirt, but light colors deflect sun. In many areas (especially holy sites), both men and women should cover their knees and upper arms to avoid offending local rules of modesty. Leave jeans at home: bring along khakis or light cotton trousers. Well-cushioned sneakers are good for walking. Lace-up leather shoes with firm grips provide better support and social acceptability than athletic shoes. A double pair of socks—light absorbent cotton inside and thick wool outside—will cushion feet, keep them dry, and help prevent blisters. If you only want to bring one pair, the best all-around footwear are sneakers-cum-hiking boots. Talcum powder in your shoes and on your feet can prevent sores, and moleskin is great for blisters. You should also bring a comfortable pair of waterproof sandals, as sneakers get very hot and uncomfortable when the temperature skyrockets.

FIRST-AID KIT. For a basic first-aid kit, pack bandages, pain reliever, antibiotic cream, a thermometer, a Swiss Army knife, tweezers, moleskin, decongestant, motion-sickness remedy, diarrhea or upset-stomach medication (Pepto Bismol or Imodium), an antihistamine, sunscreen, insect repellent, burn ointment, and a syringe for emergencies (get an explanatory letter from your doctor).

FILM. Film and developing in the Middle East are expensive, so consider bringing along enough film for your entire trip and developing it at home. Less serious photographers may want to bring a **disposable camera** or two rather than an expensive permanent one. Despite disclaimers, airport security X-rays *can* fog film; buy a lead-lined pouch at a camera store or ask security to hand-inspect it. Pack film in your carry-on luggage, since higher-intensity X-rays are used on checked luggage.

ELECTRIC CURRENT. In the Middle East, electricity is 220 volts AC, enough to fry any 110V North American appliance. Most outlets are made for round prongs, so even if your machine has a built-in converter, you'll also need an **adapter** to change the plug shape. **New Zealanders** and **South Africans** (who both use 220V at home) as well as **Australians** (who use 240/250V) won't need a converter, but will need a set of adapters to use anything electrical.

ESSENTIALS

OTHER USEFUL ITEMS. An umbrella, sealable plastic bags, alarm clock, water-proof matches, sun hat, needle and thread, safety pins, sunglasses, pocketknife, plastic water bottle, compass, string, towel, whistle, rubber bands, flashlight, cold-water soap, earplugs, electrical tape (for patching tears), tweezers, garbage bags, flip-flops for the shower, a money-belt and padlock for carrying valuables, deter-gent and a small rubber ball to stop up the sink (for doing laundry by hand), deodorant, razors, tampons, and condoms (see AIDS, HIV, and STDs, p. 23).

ACCOMMODATIONS

HOSTELS

Hostels are generally dorm-style accommodations in single-sex large rooms with bunk beds, although some hostels do offer private rooms for families and couples. The downside to traveling in the Middle East is that there aren't very many hostels. Those that do exist sometimes have kitchens and utensils for your use, bike or moped rentals, storage areas, and laundry services (but not facilities). A bed in a hostel will average around US$6-12. Some **colleges and universities** also open their residence halls to travelers when school is not in session, or even during term-time. These dorms are often close to student areas—good sources for information on things to do—and are usually very clean. Getting a room may take a couple of phone calls and require advanced planning, but rates tend to be low, and many offer free local calls. You can access university lodging worldwide by checking out *Campus Lodging Guide (19th Ed.)*, B&J Publications (US$15).

HOSTELLING INTERNATIONAL
Joining the youth hostel association in your own country (listed below) automati-cally grants you membership privileges in **Hostelling International (HI),** a federation of national hosteling associations. Only Egypt, Turkey, and Israel have HI hostels and only Israeli hostels accept reservations via the **International Booking Network**

(Australia ☎02 9261 1111; Canada ☎800-663-5777; England and Wales ☎1629 58 14 18; Northern Ireland ☎1232 32 47 33; Republic of Ireland ☎01 830 1766; NZ ☎03 379 9808; Scotland ☎8701 55 32 55; US ☎800-909-4776; www.hostelbooking.com). HI's umbrella organization's web page (www.iyhf.org), which lists the web addresses and phone numbers of all national associations, can be a great place to begin researching hostelling in a specific region.

CAMPING AND THE OUTDOORS

Camping is a viable option in many areas of the Middle East, particularly in Egypt, Jordan, Israel, Lebanon, and Turkey. It is generally free or close to free, but typically it will not be organized by a central camping agency, meaning that it is almost entirely unregulated. Always check with the local tourist agency, police, and other travelers before setting up camp to find out if there are certain places where camping is illegal. For information on hiking and camping, contact these companies for a free catalog: **Sierra Club Books,** 85 2nd St. 2nd fl., San Francisco, CA 94105-3441, USA (☎415-977-5500; www.sierraclub.org/books); **The Mountaineers Books,** 1001 SW Klickitat Way, #201, Seattle, WA 98134, USA (☎800-553-4453 or 206-223-6303; www.mountaineersbooks.org). .

DESERT SAFETY. Stay hydrated. The vast majority of life-threatening desert situations can be avoided by following this simple advice. Prepare yourself for an emergency, however, by always packing a first-aid kit, a reflector, a whistle, high energy food, and extra water for any hike. Dress in light, natural fibers. If spending the night in the desert, remember that temperatures drop dramatically at night. Spring and fall are the most temperate season for hikes. In summer, most of the day will be in the shade with the Bedouin until the sun calms down, and in winter you'll freeze. The nights are frigid year-round. You may be able to rent blankets from the Bedouin, but don't count on it; bring a sweater and a warm sleeping bag. **Check weather forecasts** and pay attention to the skies when hiking, since weather patterns can change suddenly. Whenever possible, let someone know when and where you are going hiking, either a friend, your hostel, a park ranger, or a local hiking organization. Do not attempt a hike beyond your ability—you may be endangering your life. See Health, p. 19, for information about outdoor ailments and basic medical concerns

KEEPING IN TOUCH
BY MAIL

SENDING MAIL TO THE MIDDLE EAST

Airmail letters under 1 oz. between North America and the Middle East or Turkey and Cyprus take four to seven days and typically cost US$0.80, or CDN$1.05 up to 20g. Allow at least five to seven business days from Australia (postage AUS$1.50 for up to 50 grams) and four to 10 days from the UK (₤0.65 for up to 20g). Envelopes should be marked "airmail" or "par avion." If regular airmail is too slow, **Federal Express** and **DHL** can move your mail quickly but will charge through the nose for their services. From New York, a half-pound letter costs US$32 plus tax to Cairo, Beirut, Tel Aviv or Istanbul, and is guaranteed to arrive in four business days. Rates from non-US locations are similarly expensive (London to Cairo costs US$48 and takes two days; Sydney to Cairo US$73.29, four days). Mail within the Middle East is not much cheaper: Dubai to Cairo runs US$25 and takes two days. Cheaper **Global Priority Service** is a slightly less expensive alternative, sending small and large flat-rate envelopes to the Middle East in 3-5 days, though it only services select countries (see http://ircalc.usps.gov for details).

RECEIVING MAIL IN THE MIDDLE EAST

There are several ways to arrange picking up letters sent from friends and relatives while you are abroad.

General Delivery: Mail can be sent to the Middle East through **Poste Restante** (the international phrase for General Delivery) to almost any city or town with a post office, though Poste Restante does not exist in Lebanon. Address letters in the following way: Paula SADOK, Poste Restante, City, COUNTRY. In Turkey, the address must either say *Markaz Postane* (Central Post Office), or specify which office should receive the mail. It is best to use the largest post office in the area, as mail may be sent there regardless of what is written on the envelope. When possible, it is safer and quicker to send mail express or registered. When picking up your mail, bring a photo ID, preferably a passport. There is generally no surcharge; if there is, it should not exceed the cost of domestic postage. If there is nothing for you, have them check under your first name.

American Express: AmEx's travel offices throughout the world will act as a mail service for cardholders. Under this free **Client Letter Service** they will hold mail for up to 30 days and forward upon request. Address the letter in the manner shown above. Some offices will offer these services to non-cardholders (especially those who have purchased AmEx traveler's checks); call ahead to make sure. Check the **Practical Information** section of the countries you plan to visit; *Let's Go* lists AmEx office locations for most large cities. A complete list is available free from AmEx (☎ 800-528-4800).

SENDING MAIL HOME

Aerogrammes, printed sheets that fold into envelopes and travel via airmail, are available at post offices. Mark them "airmail" or "par avion." Most post offices will charge exorbitant fees or simply refuse to send aerogrammes with enclosures. Delivery time averages four to 21 days. Costs for Europe, North America, and Australia are similar (about US$0.60); costs for Africa and Arab countries are lower. **Surface mail** is by far the cheapest and slowest way to send mail. It takes one to three months to cross the Atlantic and two to four to cross the Pacific—good for items you won't need to see for a while, such as souvenirs or other articles you've acquired along the way that are weighing down your pack.

BY TELEPHONE

CALLING THE MIDDLE EAST FROM HOME

To call the Middle East direct from home, dial:

1. The **international access code** of your home country. These include: Australia 0011; Ireland, New Zealand, or the UK 00; South Africa 09; Canada and the US 011.

2. The **country code** for the nation you are calling. Country and city codes are sometimes listed with a zero in front (e.g. 033), but after dialing the international access code, drop successive zeros (with an access code of 011 and country code of 033, dial 011 33). For individual country codes, see the **Phone Facts** box of each chapter.

3. The **city code** (see the city's **Practical Information** section) and local number.

CALLING HOME FROM THE MIDDLE EAST

A **calling card** is your best and cheapest bet. Calls are billed collect or to your account. **MCI WorldPhone** also provides access to MCI's Traveler's Assist, which gives legal and medical advice, exchange rate information, and translation services. Calling card use is limited in Jordan. **To obtain a calling card** from your national telecommunications service before you leave, contact the appropriate company. In **Australia,** call Telstra **Australia Direct** (☎ 13 22 00); in **Canada,** call **Canada Direct** (☎ 800-668-6878); in **Ireland,** call **Ireland Direct** (☎ 800 40 00 00); in **New Zealand,** call **Telecom New Zealand** (☎ 800 000 000); in **South Africa,** contact **Telkom South Africa** (☎ 10 219); in the **UK,** call British Telecom **BT Direct** (☎ 800 34 51 44). In the **US,** call **AT&T** (☎ 800-222-0300), **Sprint** (☎ 800-877-4646), or **MCI** (☎ 800-444-3333).

You can usually make **direct international calls** from pay phones. Look for pay phones in public areas, especially train stations, as private pay phones are often more expensive. In-room hotel calls invariably include an arbitrary and sky-high surcharge than can run as much as US$0.75 per minute, or a flat fee of around US$10. If you do dial direct, first insert the appropriate amount of money or a pre-paid phone card, then dial the international access code for the target country, and then dial the country code and number of your home. **Country codes** include: Australia 61; Ireland 353; New Zealand 64; South Africa 27; UK 44; US and Canada 1.

CALLING WITHIN THE MIDDLE EAST

In addition to coin-operated public phones, you can also buy **prepaid phone cards,** which carry a certain amount of phone time depending on the card's denomination. Phone rates tend to be highest in the morning, lower in the evening, and lowest on Sundays and late at night.

TIME DIFFERENCES

Greenwich Mean Time (GMT) is 5hr. ahead of New York time, 8hr. ahead of Vancouver and San Francisco time, 2hr. behind Johannesburg time, 10hr. behind Sydney time, and 12hr. behind Auckland time. All the countries in this book are 2hr. ahead of GMT.

BY EMAIL AND INTERNET

The **Cybercafe Search Engine** (www.cybercaptive.com) can help you find cybercafes in the Middle East, but although the site is updated daily, don't despair if it doesn't list cafes in your target town: they are cropping up so quickly that no index is current. In Egypt, Lebanon, Israel, and Turkey there should be no trouble finding Internet access. In Jordan and Syria, big cities have Internet access. One money-saving strategy is to befriend college students and ask if you can use their campus terminals. One hour usually costs between US$2 and US$5. For Internet cafe listings, refer to the **Practical Information** section of a given city.

GETTING TO THE MIDDLE EAST

BY PLANE

When it comes to airfare, a little effort can save you a bundle. If your plans are flexible enough to deal with the restrictions, courier fares are the cheapest. Tickets bought from consolidators and standby seating are also good deals, but last-minute specials, airfare wars, and charter flights often beat these fares. The key is to hunt around, to be flexible, and to ask persistently about discounts. Students, seniors, and those under 26 should never pay full price for a ticket.

AIRFARES

Airfares to the Middle East peak between mid-June and late September; holidays are also expensive. The cheapest times to travel are early November to mid-December and early January. Midweek (M-Th morning) round-trip flights run US$40-50 cheaper than weekend flights, but they are generally more crowded and less likely to permit frequent-flier upgrades. Traveling with an "open-return" ticket can be pricier than fixing a return date when buying the ticket. Round-trip flights are by far the cheapest; "open-jaw" (arriving in and departing from different cities, e.g. New York-Cairo and Tel Aviv-New York) tickets tend to be pricier. Patching one-way flights together is the most expensive way to travel. Flying from hub to hub (e.g. London to Cairo) will win a more competitive fare than flying to or from smaller cities. While some European airlines fly to Alexandria, it is not considered a hub and tends to be more expensive. The cheapest gateway cities in the Middle East are typically Cairo, Istanbul and Tel Aviv.

If the Middle East is only a stop on a more extensive globe-hop, consider a round-the-world (RTW) ticket. Tickets usually include at least 5 stops and are valid for about a year; prices range US$1200-5000. Try **Northwest Airlines/KLM** (US ☎800-447-4747; www.nwa.com) or **Star Alliance**, a consortium of 22 airlines including United Airlines (US ☎800-241-6522; www.star-alliance.com).

Fares will vary drastically from month to month. A round-trip student fare from the US or Canadian east coast to a Middle Eastern hub city will range US$700-1200; from the UK, UK£345-600; from Australia AUS$2600-3300; from South Africa ZAR7000-12,000.

Confirm international flights by phone within 72hr. of departure. Most airlines require that passengers arrive at the airport at least 2hr. before departure. One carry-on item and two checked bags is the norm for non-courier flights.

BUDGET AND STUDENT TRAVEL AGENCIES

While knowledgeable agents specializing in flights to the Middle East can make your life easy and help you save, they may not spend the time to find you the lowest possible fare—they get paid on commission. Students and under-27ers holding **ISIC and IYTC cards** (see p. 3), respectively, qualify for big discounts from student travel agencies. Most flights from budget agencies are on major airlines, but in peak season some may sell seats on less reliable chartered aircraft.

usit world (www.usitworld.com). Over 50 **usit campus** branches in the UK (www.usitcampus.co.uk), including 52 Grosvenor Gardens, **London** SW1W 0AG (☎0870 240 10 10); **Manchester** (☎0161 273 18 80); and **Edinburgh** (☎0131 668 33 03). Nearly 20 **usit NOW** offices in Ireland, including 19-21 Aston Quay, O'Connell Bridge, **Dublin** 2 (☎01 602 16 00; www.usitnow.ie), and **Belfast** (☎02890 32 71 11; www.usitnow.com). Offices also in Athens, Auckland, Brussels, Frankfurt, Johannesburg, Lisbon, Luxembourg, Madrid, Paris, Sofia, and Warsaw.

Council Travel (www.counciltravel.com). Countless US offices, including branches in Atlanta, Boston, Chicago, L.A., New York, San Francisco, Seattle, and Washington, D.C. Check the website or call 800-2-COUNCIL (226-8624) for the office nearest you.

CTS Travel, 44 Goodge St., **London** W1T 2AD (☎020 7636 0031; fax 020 7637 5328; ctsinfo@ctstravel.co.uk).

STA Travel, 7890 S. Hardy Dr., Ste. 110, Tempe AZ 85284 (24hr. reservations and info ☎800-777-0112; fax 480-592-0876; www.statravel.com). A student and youth travel organization with countless offices worldwide (check their website for a listing of all their offices), including US offices in Boston, Chicago, L.A., New York, San Francisco, Seattle, and Washington, D.C. Ticket booking, travel insurance, railpasses, and more. In the UK, walk-in office 11 Goodge St., **London** W1T 2PF (☎087 0160 6070). In New Zealand, 10 High St., **Auckland** (☎09 309 0458). In Australia, 366 Lygon St., **Melbourne** Vic 3053 (☎03 9349 4344).

StudentUniverse, 545 5th Ave., Suite 640, New York, NY 10017 (toll-free customer service ☎800-272-9676, outside the US 212-986-8420; help@studentuniverse.com; www.studentuniverse.com), is an online student travel service offering discount ticket booking, travel insurance, railpasses, destination guides, and much more. Customer service line open M-F 9am-8pm and Sa noon-5pm EST.

Travel CUTS (Canadian Universities Travel Services Limited), 187 College St., **Toronto,** ON M5T 1P7 (☎416-979-2406; fax 979-8167; www.travelcuts.com). 60 offices across Canada. Also in the UK, 295-A Regent St., **London** W1R 7YA (☎0207-255-1944).

COMMERCIAL AIRLINES

The commercial airlines' lowest regular offer is the **APEX** (Advance Purchase Excursion) fare, which provides confirmed reservations and allows "open-jaw" tickets. Generally, reservations must be made seven to 21 days ahead of departure, with seven- to 14-day minimum-stay and up to 90-day maximum-stay restrictions. These fares carry hefty cancellation and change penalties (fees rise in summer). Book peak-season APEX fares early; by May you will have a hard time getting your desired departure date. Use **Microsoft Expedia** (www.expedia.com) or **Travelocity** (www.travelocity.com) to get an idea of the lowest published fares, then use the

FLIGHT PLANNING ON THE INTERNET. The Web is a great place to look for travel bargains—it's fast, it's convenient, and you can spend as long as you like exploring options without driving your travel agent insane. Many airline sites offer special last-minute deals on the Web. Try **Cape to Cairo** (www.capecairo.com), **Cheap Tickets** (www.cheaptickets.com), **NOW Voyager** (www.nowvoyagertravel.com), **Travac** (www.travac.com), or **Travel Avenue** (www.travelavenue.com) for low fares to the Middle East. Other sites do the leg-work and compile the deals for you—try www.bestfares.com, www.one-travel.com, www.lowestfare.com, and www.travelzoo.com. **STA** (www.sta-travel.com), **Council** (www.counciltravel.com), and ■**StudentUniverse** (www.studentuniverse.com) provide quotes on student tickets, while **Expedia** (msn.expedia.com) and **Travelocity** (www.travelocity.com) offer full travel services. **Priceline** (www.priceline.com) allows you to specify a price, and obligates you to buy any ticket that meets or beats it; be prepared for antisocial hours and odd routes. **Skyauction** (www.skyauction.com) allows you to bid on both last-minute and advance-purchase tickets. To protect yourself, make sure that the site uses a secure server before handing over any credit card details.

resources outlined here to try and beat those fares. Low-season fares should be appreciably cheaper than the high-season (mid-June to Sept.) ones listed here. However, the fares listed here are also from "discount" airlines, which have fewer departure points and are less convenient than standard commercial centers like American and United, but probably offer better deals, unless you manage to grab a special promotion or airfare war ticket from one of the big boys.

TRAVELING FROM NORTH AMERICA

Lufthansa (☎800-399-5838; www.lufthansa-usa.com) has a wide variety of routes covering all major hubs of the Middle East via Frankfurt.

Air France (☎800-237-2747; www.airfrance.com) covers much of the Middle East mainly through Paris.

TWA (☎800-892-4141; www.twa.com) flies to some, but not all, Middle Eastern cities, like Cairo and Amman.

EgyptAir (☎800-334-6787; www.egyptair.com.eg) has the most routes within the country, and also serves major cities like New York and Los Angeles.

Royal Jordanian (☎800-755-6732; www.rja.com.jo) not only flies to all major Middle Eastern hubs, but also has extensive service to many smaller airports as well.

TRAVELING FROM THE UK AND IRELAND

British Airways (☎845 773 33 77; www.british-airways.com) has daily flights to nearly all major Middle Eastern cities, including Tel Aviv, Cairo, Istanbul, Beirut, and Amman. Virtually flights originate from London.

Austrian Airways (☎171 434 73 80; www.aua.com) connects to all major Middle Eastern cities via Vienna.

EgyptAir (☎171 734 94 90; www.egyptair.com.eg) serves the United Kingdom to the Middle East on a daily basis.

Royal Jordanian (☎207 878 63 00; www.rja.com.jo) provides connections between many cities in Europe and the Middle East through Amman.

TRAVELING FROM AUSTRALIA AND NEW ZEALAND

Qantas Air (☎13 13 13; www.qantas.com.au) flies from a variety of departure cities in Australia and New Zealand to London, from which connecting flights to the Middle East are easy to find.

Air New Zealand (☎02 92 23 46 66; www.airnz.com) has reasonable fares from Auckland to London, and often special sales at much lower prices. Again, it is necessary to find connecting flights to the Middle East.

EgyptAir (☎ 612 232 66 77; www.egyptair.com.eg) is one of the few airlines serving Cairo from Australia and New Zealand.

TRAVELING FROM SOUTH AFRICA

Basic round-trip fares to the Middle East range from roughly US$600-1600: to Cairo, US$800-1400; to Istanbul, US$600-1000; to Beirut, US$700-1200; to Tel Aviv, US$600-900; to Amman, US$1100-1600.

South African (☎ 11 978 10 00; www.saa.co.za) serves mostly Africa, but also connects to some cities in the Middle East.

Lufthansa (☎ 011 484 47 11; www.lufthansa.com) reliably offers direct flights to Cairo and Istanbul from South Africa, as well as provides connecting flights to the Middle East through Eastern Europe.

British Airways (☎ 011 441 86 00; www.british-airways.com/regional/sa) has flights from Johannesburg and Cape Town to places in Europe with easy connections to the Middle East.

KLM (☎ 11 881 96 96; www.klm.com) serves South Africa to the Middle East through Europe.

AIR COURIER FLIGHTS

Those who travel light should consider courier flights. Couriers help transport cargo on international flights by using their checked luggage space for freight. Generally, couriers must travel with carry-ons only and deal with complex flight restrictions. Most flights are round-trip only, with short fixed-length stays (usually one week) and a limit of a one ticket per issue. Most also operate only out of major gateway cities, mostly in North America. Round-trip courier fares from the US to the Middle East run about US$400-750 and are quite limited in destination; flights to Cairo or Tel Aviv may be all that you find. Most flights leave from New York, Los Angeles, San Francisco, or Miami in the US; and from Montreal, Toronto, or Vancouver in Canada. Generally, you must be over 21 (and in some cases 18). In summer, the most popular destinations usually require an advance reservation of about two weeks (you can usually book up to two months ahead). Super-discounted fares are common for "last-minute" flights (three to 14 days ahead).

Air Courier Association, 15,000 W. 6th Ave. #203, Golden, CO 80401 (☎ 800-282-1202; www.aircourier.org) provides their members with a list of opportunities and courier brokers worldwide for an annual fee.

International Association of Air Travel Couriers, 20 South Dixie Hwy., PO Box 1349, Lake Worth, FL 33460 (☎ 561-582-8320; courier@iaatc.com; www.courier.org) is another group that provides information on courier flights.

Now Voyager Travel, 74 Varick St., Suite 307, New York, NY 10013 (☎ 212-431-1616; www.nowvoyagertravel.com) offers both discount courier and non-courier fares.

TICKET CONSOLIDATORS

Ticket consolidators, or **"bucket shops,"** buy unsold tickets in bulk from commercial airlines and sell them at discounted rates. The best place to look is in the Sunday travel section of any major newspaper (such as *The New York Times*), where many bucket shops place tiny ads. Call quickly, as availability is typically extremely limited. Not all bucket shops are reliable, so insist on a receipt that gives full details of restrictions, refunds, and tickets, and pay by credit card (in spite of the 2-5% fee) so you can stop payment if you never receive your tickets. For more info, see www.travel-library.com/air-travel/consolidators.html or pick up Kelly Monaghan's *Air Travel's Bargain Basement* (Intrepid Traveler, US$8).

TRAVELING FROM THE US & CANADA

Travel Avenue (☎ 800-333-3335; www.travelavenue.com) searches for best available published fares and then uses several consolidators to attempt to beat that fare. Other consolidators worth trying are **Interworld** (☎ 305-443-4929; fax 305-443-0351), **Pennsylvania Travel** (☎ 800-331-0947), **Rebel** (☎ 800-227-3235; travel@rebeltours.com; www.rebeltours.com), **Cheap Tickets** (☎ 800-377-1000; www.cheaptickets.com), and **Travac** (☎ 800-872-8800; fax 212-714-9063; www.travac.com), **Internet Travel Network** (www.itn.com), **Travel Information Services** (www.tiss.com), **TravelHUB** (www.travelhub.com), and **The Travel Site** (www.thetravelsite.com). Keep in mind that these are just suggestions to get you started in your research; *Let's Go* does not endorse any of these agencies. As always, be cautious, and research companies before you hand over your credit card number.

TRAVELING FROM THE UK, AUSTRALIA, & NEW ZEALAND

In London, the **Air Travel Advisory Bureau** (☎ 020 7636 5000; www.atab.co.uk) can provide names of reliable consolidators and discount flight specialists. From Australia and New Zealand, look for consolidator ads in the travel section of the *Sydney Morning Herald* and other papers.

CHARTER FLIGHTS

Charters are flights that a tour operator contracts with an airline to fly extra loads of passengers during peak season. Charter flights fly less frequently than major airlines, make refunds particularly difficult, and are almost always fully booked. Schedules and itineraries may also change or be canceled at the last moment (as late as 48hr. before the trip, and without a full refund), and check-in, boarding, and baggage claim are often much slower. However, they can also be cheaper.

Discount clubs and **fare brokers** offer members savings on last-minute charter and tour deals. Study contracts closely; you don't want to end up with an unwanted overnight layover. **Travelers Advantage**, Trumbull, CT, USA (☎ 203-365-2000; www.travelersadvantage.com; US$60 annual fee includes discounts and cheap flight directories) serves most large Middle East cities, though not Beirut.

GETTING AROUND

BY PLANE

Egypt is served by **EgyptAir** (☎ 02 76 52 00); see **Cairo: Flights** (p. 82) for locations, prices, and destinations. EgyptAir's main office in the US is at 720 5th Ave., Suite 505, New York, NY 10019 (☎ 800-334-6787). **Air Sinai** (☎ (02) 76 09 48; 77 29 49), in the courtyard of the Nile Hilton in Cairo, serves the Sinai and Israel. **Royal Jordanian** (www.rja.com.jo) flies between all major Middle Eastern hubs, and has extensive service to many smaller airports. **El Al Israel Airlines** (www.elal.com) has flights between Tel Aviv and Cairo. **Middle East Airlines** (www.mea.com.lb) serves many Middle Eastern destinations from Beirut, and **Syrian Airlines** (www.syrianonline.com/syrair) from Damascus. **Turkish Airlines** (www.turkishairlines.com) serves numerous destinations throughout Turkey and the Middle East.

BY BUS

For specific information on stations, routes, and prices, consult the individual **Essentials** section in each country and **Transportation** section in each cities.

EGYPT. Though inexpensive, buses in Egypt can be slow, crowded, and hot. Companies include **Superjet, West Delta Bus Company**, and **East Delta Bus Company**. West Delta has a deluxe branch called **Golden Arrow** with vehicles sporting air-conditioning, refreshments, and bathrooms. Air-conditioned East Delta buses serve the Sinai.

AIRCRAFT SAFETY. The airlines of developing world nations do not always meet safety standards. The *Official Airline Guide* (www.oag.com) and many travel agencies can tell you the type and age of aircraft on a particular route. This can be especially useful in the Middle East, where less reliable equipment is often used for inter-city travel. The **International Airline Passengers Association** (US ☎800-821-4272, UK ☎(020 8681 6555) provides region-specific safety information. The **Federal Aviation Administration** (www.faa.gov) reviews the airline authorities for countries whose airlines enter the US. **US State Department** travel advisories (☎202-647-5225; travel.state.gov/travel_warnings.html) sometimes involve foreign carriers, especially when terrorist bombings may be a threat.

ISRAEL. Buses are the most popular and convenient means of travel in Israel. Except for the **Dan Company** and the Arab buses serving the West Bank, Galilee, and Gaza, the **Egged Bus Cooperative** has a monopoly on intercity and intracity buses. Students with ISIC receive a 10% discount on more expensive fares. Buses can get crowded, especially during rush hours and on Saturday after Shabbat.

JORDAN. The government owns a monopoly on intercity bus service, so the **Jordan Express Tourist Transport (JETT)** is your only option. Buses (infrequently) cover popular routes, including daily trips from Amman to Aqaba, Petra, Ma'an, the King Hussein/Allenby Bridge, Damascus, and Cairo. The air-conditioned JETT luxury coaches cost about 20% more than regular buses. Booking ahead is necessary.

LEBANON. Local buses in Beirut all cost L£500 and are surprisingly easy to use. There are two companies in Lebanon, both running nearly identical routes. **Government** buses are blue and white, while the red-and-white buses are those of the **Lebanese Commuting Company (LCC).** Over 20 different lines criss-cross the city, and are ideal for going to well-traveled destinations such as Cola Bridge, the National Museum, Dawra, or the Pigeon Rocks (Raouche). Stand on the proper side of busy streets and shout your destination as the bus slows down. Intracity buses finish their runs around 7 or 8pm; after that you're left with *service* or private taxis.

SYRIA. Karnak, the government-run bus company, has extensive routes and low fares on orange-and-white, air-conditioned buses. Buses occasionally depart on schedule, and reservations are required. **Pullman** buses are a step below Karnak. Over 50 private bus companies now operate in Syria; they have excellent coaches and competitive prices. Reservations are a good idea for these buses too. All tickets must be bought at the stations, as drivers do not handle money. **Microbuses** (MEEK-ro-bus) are easy, cheap, and relatively hassle-free. Fees in Damascus are set, but vary elsewhere depending on your destination; ask the person next to you (not the driver) how much to pay or wait to see what other people pay.

TURKEY. Frequent, modern, and cheap buses run between all sizeable cities. In large cities, the *otogar* (bus station) is often quite a distance from the city center, but many bus companies have branch offices downtown. Free shuttles called *service* take ticketed passengers to the otogar. Buy tickets in advance from local offices, or purchase them directly at the station. You will need to go from booth to booth to piece together a complete schedule; one company may not divulge competitors schedules. Many lines provide a 10% discount to ISIC-carrying students. Fares may increase during summer and religious holidays. Seats are assigned and passengers are expected to remain in their assigned seats for the duration of the trip. Road safety is a serious concern in Turkey, so *Let's Go* strongly recommends that you only travel on reputable bus lines, particularly for long trips. Although these are comparatively the most expensive tickets, they are still cheap. The extra money you pay allows the companies to take safety precautions such as giving the drivers rest breaks. Reputable companies include: Varan, Ulusoy, and Kamil Ko. Whenever possible, *Let's Go* quotes prices from these companies.

BY TRAIN

EGYPT. Egypt's railway system was the first established in both the Arab world and in Africa. Schedules and signs in the train stations are never in English, but can be obtained from the tourist office or from ticket windows. If lines are long and you're in a hurry, try boarding the train without a ticket—the conductor will usually sell one on board for an additional fee.

Trains offer student discounts (ISIC card required) of up to 50%, with an average discount of about 30%. Air-conditioned second-class cars are comfortably small, with reclining seats. Avoid the dangerous third class. Second-class sleeper cars might be more comfortable for trips of 10hr. or more but are overpriced. Reserve space in a sleeper at the wagon-lit offices in Cairo, Luxor, Aswan, and Alexandria. Seats for Cairo-Alexandria (especially in summer) and Cairo-Upper Egypt (especially in winter) trips should be reserved a day or two in advance. Reserve a week in advance during the last week of Ramadan and the following week, as well as before Eid al-Adha.

ISRAEL. Rail service in Israel is useful only for travel along the northern coast. Trains are slightly cheaper than buses, but they are slower and like most bus lines, stop running during Shabbat. Avoid traveling on Friday afternoons when the trains are most crowded. Students with an ISIC enjoy a 50% discount.

SYRIA. Strictly speaking, trains connect some cities in Syria. Frankly speaking, roller skates would serve you better. Trains are slow, crowded, and dirty, and in most places they drop you off about 30km out of town. Use the buses.

TURKEY. Trains run directly to Istanbul from Athens and Bucharest. Some lines may be suspended due to political crises in the Balkans. Eurail passes are not valid in Turkey, but InterRail passes are. The Under 26 InterRail Pass (from UK£159) allows either 15 days or one month of unlimited travel within one, two, three, or all of the seven zones into which InterRail divides Europe; the cost is determined by the number of zones the pass covers. The Over 26 InterRail Pass (also zone-based) offers unlimited second-class travel for 22 days for UK229. Overall, however, trains are slothfully slow and very expensive. Use the buses.

BY CAR

Driving is extremely dangerous in the Middle East. You should be prepared as a pedestrian, passenger, or driver for unorthodox and aggressive moves. Egypt has the highest rate of car accidents; Turkey has also achieved international notoriety for its unfortunate driving records. **Wear a seatbelt.** Child safety seats are usually not available: strap on children's seatbelts and don't let kids sit in the front seat, if possible. In many regions, road conditions necessitate driving more slowly and cautiously than you would at home. For long drives in desolate areas, invest in a cellular phone. **Sleeping in your car** is one of the most dangerous (and often illegal) ways to get your rest. If your car breaks down, wait for the police to assist you.

DRIVING PERMITS AND CAR INSURANCE

INTERNATIONAL DRIVING PERMIT (IDP). If you plan to drive while in the Middle East, you must be over 18. *Let's Go* also suggests purchasing an International Driving Permit (IDP): Egypt and Syria require one, while Israel, Jordan, Lebanon, and Turkey recommend one. The degree of enforcement of these rules varies from country to country. Even for the countries where an IDP is not required, it may be a good idea to get one anyway, in case you're in an accident or stranded and the police do not know English; information on the IDP is printed in ten languages, including Arabic.

Your IDP, valid for one year, must be issued in your own country before you depart. An application for an IDP usually needs to include one or two photos, a current local license, an additional form of identification, and a fee. To apply, contact the national or local branch of your home country's Automobile Association.

CAR INSURANCE. Most credit cards cover standard insurance. If you rent, lease, or borrow a car, you will need a **green card,** or **International Insurance Certificate,** to certify that you have liability insurance and that it applies abroad. Green cards can be obtained at car rental agencies, car dealers (for those leasing cars), some travel agents, and some border crossings. Rental agencies may require you to purchase theft insurance in countries that they consider to have a high risk of auto theft.

BY THUMB

Much of the Middle East is untraveled desert; never count on getting a ride— you'll die of **dehydration** first. *Let's Go* strongly urges you to consider the risks before you choose to hitchhike. We do not recommend hitchhiking as a safe means of transportation. Hitching is not common in urban parts of the Middle East, and not always in rural section, either. In recent years, the newspapers have been full of crimes perpetrated by hitchhikers along the roads between Cairo and Alexandria, making most drivers reluctant to pick you up anyway. Rides are reportedly easy to obtain in isolated areas (such as along the Great Desert Road in Egypt) or for short jaunts in remote parts, where public transportation is difficult to find. Many drivers who pick up hitchhikers expect money anyway, so public transportation should be used wherever it is available.

 Let's Go strongly urges you to consider the risks before you choose to hitchhike. We do not recommend hitchhiking as a safe means of transportation.

SPECIFIC CONCERNS

WOMEN TRAVELERS

Women exploring on their own inevitably face some additional safety concerns, but it's easy to be adventurous without taking undue risks. Foreign women traveling alone will be **harassed** by Arab men—and so will foreign men. The Middle East is not the place to visit if you want to be left alone, but harassment has more to do with socioeconomic exasperation and cultural misunderstanding than gender-based hostility. Harassment can take many forms, from overzealous salesmanship to touchy-feely *service* drivers, and from mildly sinister "hellos" to frightening and potentially harmful physical contact. The media has not helped the situation: movies and television tend to depict Western women as free and easy, and the racy nature of much Egyptian cinema has drastically altered expectations about how men and women should interact. If you are concerned, consider staying in hostels that offer single rooms that **lock** from the inside, or in religious organizations with rooms for **women only.** Communal showers in some hostels are safer than others; check them out before hopping in. Stick to centrally located accommodations and avoid solitary late-night treks or metro rides.

When traveling, always carry extra money for a phone call, bus, or taxi. **Hitchhiking** is never safe for lone women, or even for two women traveling together. Choose train compartments occupied by other women or couples; ask the conductor to put together a women-only compartment if he or she doesn't offer to do so first. Look as if you know where you're going (even when you don't) and approach older women or couples for directions if you're lost or feel uncomfortable.

Generally, the less you look like a tourist, the better off you'll be. Dress conservatively, especially in rural areas. Trying to fit in can be effective, but dressing to the style of an obviously different culture may cause you to be ill at ease and a conspicuous target. Wearing a conspicuous **wedding band** may help prevent unwanted overtures. Some travelers report that carrying pictures of a "husband" or "children" is extremely useful to help document marriage status. Even a mention of a husband waiting back at the hotel may be enough of an antidote in some places to your potentially vulnerable, unattached appearance. Women will find themselves approached much less frequently when escorted by a male over the age of 14, but should be wary of claiming to be "friends" with someone: the concept of friendship between men and women in the Arab world differs greatly from its counterpart in the West. Many Arabs see male-female relationships as euphemisms for something more ("friends with benefits," so to speak), and men often think that a woman's speaking to them implies sexual advance. Some hotels frown upon unmarried couples sharing a room and some have been known not to allow it, especially if one of the people is a native.

 DRESS LIKE AN EGYPTIAN. Foreign women in the Middle East are guaranteed to attract a great deal of attention. While it is not necessary for women to dress in traditional Arab clothing, they should cover their bodies as much as possible, especially their legs and upper arms. Stay away from the following items of clothing: short skirts, shorts, athletic gear such as biking shorts, midriff-baring halter tops, v-neck blouses that descend more than an inch or two from the neck, tank tops, visible bra straps, and tight shirts. Except in the heavily touristed parts, these restrictions hold true even at the beach. Generally, the less you look like a tourist, the better off you'll be. That said, in secular havens like Tel Aviv and Beirut local dress comes in many forms, from the long, draping dresses of Muslim conservatives to hip-hugging hotpants.

Your best answer to verbal harassment is no answer at all; feigning deafness, sitting motionless, and staring straight ahead at nothing in particular will do a world of good. The extremely persistent can sometimes be dissuaded by a firm, loud, and very public "Go away!" or "Shame on you!" in the appropriate language (for useful phrases to use, see **Kiss My As(wan)**, p. 238). Nothing reminds an Arab man of common manners better than public embarrassment. If this doesn't work, don't hesitate to seek out a police officer or a **passerby** if you are being harassed. Memorize the emergency numbers in places you visit and consider carrying a whistle or airhorn on your keychain. A self-defense course will not only prepare you for a potential attack, but will also raise your level of awareness of your surroundings as well as your confidence (see **Self Defense**, p. 17). Also be sure you are aware of the specific **health concerns** that women face when traveling (see p. 24).

FURTHER READING

A Journey of One's Own: Uncommon Advice for the Independent Woman Traveler, Thalia Zepatos. Eighth Mountain Press (US$17).

Active Women Vacation Guide, Evelyn Kaye. Blue Panda Publications (US$18).

Travelers' Tales: Gutsy Women, Travel Tips and Wisdom for the Road, Marybeth Bond. Traveler's Tales (US$13).

TRAVELING ALONE

There are many benefits to traveling alone, including independence and greater interaction with locals. On the other hand, any solo traveler is a more vulnerable target of harassment and street theft. Lone travelers need to be well-organized and look confident at all times. Try not to stand out as a tourist, and be especially careful in deserted or very crowded areas. If questioned, never admit that you are traveling alone. Maintain regular contact with someone at home who knows your itinerary. For more tips, pick up *Traveling Solo* by Eleanor Berman (Globe Pequot Press, US$17) or subscribe to **Connecting: Solo Travel Network,** 689 Park Rd., Unit 6, Gibsons, BC V0N 1V7 (☎604-886-9099; www.cstn.org; membership US$28).

Alternatively, several services link solo travelers with companions who have similar travel habits and interests; for a bi-monthly newsletter for single travelers seeking a travel partner (subscription US$48), contact the **Travel Companion Exchange,** P.O. Box 833, Amityville, NY 11701 (☎631-454-0880 or 800-392-1256; www.whytravelalone.com; US$48).

OLDER TRAVELERS

Discounts for senior citizens in the Middle East are few and far between, existing solely in Turkey, Israel, and Jordan. That being said, if you don't see a senior citizen price listed, ask, and you may be delightfully surprised.The books *No Problem! Worldwise Tips for Mature Adventurers*, by Janice Kenyon (Orca Book Publishers; US$16) and *Unbelievably Good Deals and Great Adventures That You Absolutely Can't Get Unless You're Over 50*, by Joan Rattner Heilman (NTC/Contemporary Publishing; US$13) are both excellent resources. For more information, contact one of the following organizations:

ElderTreks, 597 Markham St., Toronto, ON M6G 2L7 (☎800-741-7956; www.eldertreks.com). Adventure travel programs for the 50+ traveler in Turkey.

Elderhostel, 11 Ave. de Lafayette, Boston, MA 02111 (☎877-426-8056; www.elderhostel.org). Organizes 1- to 4-week "educational adventures" in the Middle East on varied subjects for those 55+.

BISEXUAL, GAY, & LESBIAN TRAVELERS

The Middle East is not a particularly rainbow-friendly locale—even though men hold hands in the street, this reflects a different cultural attitude about male physicality, not homosexuality (see **I Wanna Hold Your Hand,** p. 78). No one is out of the closet in any public fashion except in Beirut, Haifa, and Tel Aviv; although homosexuality is legal in Turkey, it is not prevalent. A few gay bars here and there do not mean that any same-sex public displays of affection will be socially acceptable—they may even be illegal in some areas.

Listed below are contact organizations, mail-order bookstores, and publishers that offer materials addressing some specific concerns. **Out and About** (www.planetout.com) offers a bi-weekly newsletter addressing travel concerns and a comprehensive site addressing gay travel concerns.

Gay's the Word, 66 Marchmont St., London WC1N 1AB (☎+44 20 7278 7654; www.gaystheword.co.uk). The largest gay and lesbian bookshop in the UK, with both fiction and non-fiction titles. Mail-order service available.

Giovanni's Room, 1145 Pine St., Philadelphia, PA 19107 (☎215-923-2960; www.queerbooks.com). An international lesbian/feminist and gay bookstore with mail-order service (carries many of the publications listed below).

International Gay and Lesbian Travel Association, 52 W. Oakland Park Blvd., #237 Wilton Manors, FL 33311, USA (☎800-448-8550; fax 776-3303; www.iglta.com). An organization of over 1200 companies serving gay and lesbian travelers worldwide.

International Lesbian and Gay Association (ILGA), 81 rue Marché-au-Charbon, B-1000 Brussels, Belgium (☎+32 2 502 2471; www.ilga.org). Provides political information, such as homosexuality laws of individual countries.

TRAVELERS WITH DISABILITIES

Unkempt roads, local ignorance, and lack of access ramps can make travel in the Middle East prohibitively difficult for travelers with disabilities. **Israel** has taken several steps toward making the businesses and sights in and around their modernized cities more accessible to disabled travelers.

FURTHER READING: BISEXUAL, GAY, & LESBIAN.
Spartacus International Gay Guide 2001-2002. Bruno Gmunder Verlag (US$33).
Damron's Accommodations, and *The Women's Traveler.* Damron Travel Guides (US$14-19). For more info, call 800-462-6654 or visit www.damron.com.
Ferrari Guides' Gay Travel A to Z, Ferrari Guides' Men's Travel in Your Pocket, and *Ferrari Guides' Inn Places.* Ferrari Publications (US$16-20). Purchase the guides online at www.ferrariguides.com.
The Gay Vacation Guide: The Best Trips and How to Plan Them, Mark Chesnut. Citadel Press (US$15).

Those with disabilities should inform airlines and hotels of their disabilities when making arrangements for travel; some time may be needed to prepare special accommodations. Call ahead to restaurants, hotels, parks, and other facilities to find out about the existence of ramps, the widths of doors, the dimensions of elevators, etc. **Guide dog owners** should inquire as to the specific quarantine policies of each destination country. At the very least, they will need to provide a certificate of immunization against rabies. The **Green Book** (http://members.nbci.com/thegreenbook/home.html) has a partial listing of accessible accommodations and sights in Egypt and Israel.

USEFUL ORGANIZATIONS

Mobility International USA (MIUSA), P.O. Box 10767, Eugene, OR 97440 (☎541–343-1284, voice and TDD; www.miusa.org). Sells *A World of Options: A Guide to International Educational Exchange, Community Service, and Travel for Persons with Disabilities* (US$35).

Moss Rehab Hospital Travel Information Service, www.mossresourcenet.org. An information resource center on travel-related concerns for those with disabilities.

Society for the Advancement of Travel for the Handicapped (SATH), 347 5th Ave., #610, New York, NY 10016 (☎212-447-7284; www.sath.org). An advocacy group that publishes free online travel information and the travel magazine *OPEN WORLD* (US$18, free for members). Annual membership US$45, students and seniors US$30.

Directions Unlimited, 123 Green Ln., Bedford Hills, NY 10507 (☎800-533-5343). Books individual and group vacations for the physically disabled; not an info service.

MINORITY TRAVELERS

People of all skin colors will encounter less active racism in the Middle East than they will ignorance about different ethnicities. **Ethnic Asians** may attract stares, especially in untouristed areas. In some regions of the Middle East, **black or dark-skinned travelers** may find that they encounter some negative attention. This response arises largely from the fact that Africans have traditionally been seen as interlopers. **Blondes** attract curiosity in the Middle East, since native blondes are nonexistent (as are, therefore, dumb blonde jokes——so you can stop desperately trying to think of comebacks).

All over the Middle East, the highly explosive ethnic and religious tensions mean that people will likely be curious about your origins. Natives you befriend will often ask where your father comes from and which religion you were raised to practice. In particular, travelers with Biblical names or German-sounding surnames may be asked if they are **Jewish.** While non-Israeli Jews aren't necessarily viewed with hostility in Arab countries, Jewish travelers should avoid revealing their religion, as it could result in tension or even confrontation.

TRAVELERS WITH CHILDREN

Family vacations often require that you slow your pace, and always require that you plan ahead. When deciding where to stay, remember the special needs of young children; if you pick a small hotel, call ahead and make sure it's child-

ESSENTIALS

friendly. If you rent a car, make sure the rental company provides a car seat for younger children. Be sure that your child carries some sort of ID in case of an emergency or in case he or she gets lost.

Children under two generally fly for 10% of the adult airfare on international flights (this does not necessarily include a seat). International fares are usually discounted 25% for children from two to 11. Finding a private place for **breast feeding** is often a problem while traveling, so plan accordingly. For more information, consult one of the following books:

Backpacking with Babies and Small Children, Goldie Silverman. Wilderness Press (US$10).

How to take Great Trips with Your Kids, Sanford and Jane Portnoy. Harvard Common Press (US$10).

Have Kid, Will Travel: 101 Survival Strategies for Vacationing With Babies and Young Children, Claire and Lucille Tristram. Andrews McMeel Publishing (US$9).

DIETARY CONCERNS

The Middle East is definitely a meat munching place, but there's always falafel and hummus, and eggs are sold scrambled or hard-boiled in all the local markets. You won't find tofu or soybeans anywhere but in Israel or in an expat-type store in Beirut. Many restaurants in Israel are vegetarian because of the kosher restriction on mixing milk and meat. To address dietary concerns at restaurants ("I am a vegetarian"), see the **Phrasebook,** p. 701.

The North American Vegetarian Society, P.O. Box 72, Dolgeville, NY 13329 (☎518-568-7970; www.navs-online.org), has information about vegetarian travel, including Transformative Adventures, a Guide to Vacations and Retreats (US$15).

Travelers who keep kosher should contact synagogues in larger cities for information on kosher restaurants. Your own synagogue or college Hillel should have access to lists of Jewish institutions across the nation. If you are strict in your observance, you may have to prepare your own food on the road. A good resource is the *Jewish Travel Guide,* by Michael Zaidner (Vallentine Mitchell; US$17).

For more information, visit your local bookstore, health food store, or library, and consult *The Vegetarian Traveler: Where to Stay if You're Vegetarian,* by Jed and Susan Civic (Larson Publications; US$16)

CUSTOMS AND ETIQUETTE

Keep your soles out of sight—in or out of you shoes. Bottoms of **feet** resting anywhere but on the ground is disrespectful. Before entering **mosques,** remove shoes and have socks ready to wear. Women must **cover** their heads and arms, and stand behind men. Outside of mosques, women usually congregate with other females, lining up with other women to buy tickets and sitting at the front of buses and trains. For men, except in the most secular areas like Israel or downtown Beirut, speaking to unknown women is a breach of etiquette and should be avoided.

It is customary for Arabs to refuse the first **invitation** of an offering; tourists should do the same, as a genuine invitation will be repeated at least twice. If ever invited to a home but unable to attend, the householder will often press for a promise from you to visit in the future, usually for a meal. If you make such a promise, keep it. Failing to arrive will humiliate your host. It is also offensive to offer *bakhsheesh* to professionals, businessmen, or others who would consider themselves your equals.

Middle Eastern countries outlaw drugs, and in many places, alcohol and pork. If you need to drink in the presence of others, ask first. Explicit sexual material, like magazines, photographs, tapes, or records is illegal and subject to confiscation.

ALTERNATIVES TO TOURISM

For an extensive listing of "off-the-beaten-track" and specialty travel opportunities, try the **Specialty Travel Index,** 305 San Anselmo Ave., #313, San Anselmo, CA 94960, USA (☎888-624-4030 or 415-455-1643; www.specialtytravel.com; US$6). **Transitions Abroad** (www.transabroad.com) publishes a bi-monthly on-line newsletter for work, study, and specialized travel abroad.

STUDYING ABROAD

Whether spending a summer, term, or semester abroad, the Middle East is a good place to learn a new language, boasting a rich culture and history to boot. Though most study programs for foreigners in the Middle East focus on intense language instruction, others offer classes in subjects like Middle Eastern studies and international affairs. Cairo, Tel Aviv, Amman, Beirut, Damascus, and Istanbul are home to universities and programs that welcome students from the West.

> **FURTHER READING & RESOURCES: STUDYING ABROAD.**
> StudyAbroad.Com Program Search (www.studyabroad.com)
> *Academic Year Abroad 2001-2002.* Institute of International Education Books (US$47).
> *Vacation Study Abroad 2000-2001.* Institute of International Education Books (US$43).
> *Peterson's Study Abroad 2001.* Peterson's (US$30).
> *Peterson's Summer Study Abroad 2001.* Peterson's (US$30).

Apply early for a student visa, as application processing can be stunningly slow. A visa is required for most Middle Eastern countries for both short and long stays; if you're unsure of visa requirements, consult an embassy or the university of your choice. An excellent place to find the Middle Eastern institution best suited to your study abroad needs is **Amideast Study Abroad,** 1730 M St. NW, #1100, Washington, D.C. 20036 (☎202-776-9600; inquiries@amideast.org; www.amideast.org).

UNIVERSITIES

Most American undergraduates enroll in programs sponsored by US universities. Those relatively fluent in Arabic or Hebrew may find it cheaper to enroll directly in a local university (though getting credit may be more difficult). Most universities in the Middle East offer language intensive courses. Some schools that offer study abroad programs to foreigners are listed below.

School for International Training, College Semester Abroad, Admissions, Kipling Rd., P.O. Box 676, Brattleboro, VT 05302, USA (☎800-336-1616 or 802-258-3267; www.sit.edu). Programs ranging from month-long homestays to year-long peace and conflict studies run US$4,100-13,700.

Council on International Educational Exchange (CIEE), 633 3rd Ave., New York, NY 10017 (☎800-40-STUDY; studyinfo@ciee.org; www.ciee.org/study) sponsors work, volunteer, academic, and internship programs in Jordan and Turkey.

International Association for the Exchange of Students for Technical Experience (IAESTE), 10400 Little Patuxent Pkwy. #250, Columbia, MD 21044-3510, USA (☎410-997-2200; www.aipt.org). 8- to 12-week programs across the Middle East for college students who have had 2 years of technical study. US$25 application fee.

American University of Beirut (AUB), P.O. Box 11-0236, Raid al-Solh, 11072020 **Beirut,** Lebanon (☎961-1-340460; fax 961-1-351706; www.aub.edu.lb), or 850 3rd Ave., 18th fl., **New York,** NY 10022-6297 (☎212-583-7600; fax 583-7650). Black-clad hipsters who haunt most of Beirut's hotspots hail exclusively from AUB, which offers programs in everything from philosophy to poultry science. Classes are conducted in English. Tuition is about US$7500 for the year, approximately US$325 per credit.

ESSENTIALS

LANGUAGE SCHOOLS

Language programs are run by foreign universities, independent international or local organizations, and divisions of a variety of Middle Eastern universities. They generally cost anywhere from US$400-$12,000 per semester (depending on the country) and may include room and board. Listed below are schools that offer study abroad programs to foreigners, organized by country.

EGYPT. Studying in Egypt means attending the **American University in Cairo** (AUC), 113 Sharia Qasr al-Aini (www.aucegypt.edu). AUC offers semester, year, and summer programs in intensive Arabic and undergraduate and graduate degree study conducted in English. Tuition (not including housing) is US$5,625 per semester; US$2,813 for the summer session. Contact the Office of Student Affairs, American University in Cairo, 420 5th Ave., 3rd fl., New York, NY 10018 (☎212- 730-8800; aucegypt@aucnyo.edu). **Center of Arabic Study Abroad (CASA)** is a private organization with a branch at AUC that offers a well-respected Arabic program to graduate students. Enrollment in classes is only by a series of examinations. Contact CASA, 428-B Candler Library, Emory University, Atlanta, GA 30322 (casa@emory.edu; www.sais-jhu.edu/languages/casa).

JORDAN. University of Jordan offers a 6-level intensive program in Arabic (Modern Standard) for non-native speakers. All levels are offered regularly and concurrently during the fall, spring, and summer semesters. Tuition fees for the fall and spring are JD340, for the summer JD205. For more information, contact University of Jordan, Amman 11942, Jordan (☎(06) 535 50 00; fax 535 55 22; www.ju.edu.jo).

ISRAEL. Before the study abroad semester begins, there is a 4-9 week *ulpan* to learn Hebrew, and university programs are preceded by *mekhina*, a year of intensive Hebrew at **Hebrew University of Jerusalem,** 11 E. 69th St., New York, NY 10021 (☎212-472-2288; fax 517-4548). For more information, contact British Friends of the Hebrew University, 126 Albert St., London NW1 7NE (☎020 7691 1478; fax 691 15 01; students@fhu.org.uk). More programs for foreign students are provided by **Tel Aviv University,** Office of Academic Affairs, 360 Lexington Ave., New York, NY 10017, or Ramat Aviv, Tel Aviv 69978 (☎03 640 83 17; fax 640 67 22) and University of Haifa, 220 5th Ave., Ste. 1301, New York, NY 10001 (☎888-562-8813 or 212-685-7880; fax 212-685-7883), or Haifa 31905 (☎972-4-824-0766; overseas@research.haifa.ac.il; www.haifa.ac.il).

SYRIA. Arabic Teaching Institute for Foreigners in Damascus offers beginning and intermediate classes in Modern Standard Arabic. Tuition is US$600 for either the 8-month winter course (Oct.-May) or the 3-month summer course (June-Sept.) and does not include housing, transportation, food, or living expenses. For more information, contact the Institute at Villat Sharqiyah (Eastern Villas), P.O. Box 9340, Damascus, Syria (☎11 22 15 38). The **National Council on US-Arab Relations** offers a six-week "Summer in Syria" program in Aleppo and Damascus for US$3400 that allows students to earn up to seven hours of college credit—four of which are for intensive Arabic (the remaining credits can be earned in anything from international policy to comparative literature). The cost includes roundtrip airfare, tuition, transportation, room and board. For more information, contact the Council at 1140 Connecticut Ave. NW, Ste. 1210, Washington, D.C. 20036 (☎202-293-0801; info@ncusar.org).

TURKEY. Summer Program at **Bogaziçi University,** Istanbul, offers two or three seven-week classes on the culture, language, and history of Turkey, Central Asia, and the Middle East. Contact the Study Abroad Office, 115 International Studies Building, 910 S. 5th St., Champaign, IL 61820 (☎217-333-6322; sao@uiuc.edu). **TÖMER,** 18/1 Ziya Gökalp Cad., Kizilay, Ankara (☎312 435 97 81; fax 433 81 90) is a university whose goal is to teach the Turkish language and culture. It has 13 branches across Turkey, including Istanbul, Antalya, Bursa, and Izmir. Contact Pitzer College in Turkey, Office of External Studies, Pitzer College, 1050 N. Mills Ave., Claremont, CA 91711 (☎909-621-8104; fax 621-0518; www.pitzer.edu) to learn more about their 4-month field study program.

WORKING AND VOLUNTEERING

A special type of visa and/or a working permit is required in order to work as a foreigner in the Middle East. For travel purposes other than tourism, Israel requires a work visa. In Jordan, Lebanon, and Turkey, working permits are required. Friends in the Middle East can often help expedite work permits or arrange work-for-accommodations swaps.

Few foreigners work in the Middle East because acquiring a work visa or permit is often a bureaucratic nightmare. Being an **English speaker** does wonders for your marketability (tutoring or teaching English is your best bet). Some travelers in the Sinai work for hotels or dive centers in **Na'ama Bay** (see p. 181). A note on **archaeological digs:** although they abound in this area, most sites offer hard work, menial labor, and no pay (the Archaeological Institute of America listed below is an excellent source for finding more rewarding digs). **Volunteer** jobs are readily available almost everywhere, particularly at Israeli **kibbutzim.**

COUNTRY-SPECIFIC RESOURCES

Egypt: You have to arrange for a working permit once you get to Egypt. Some people look for temporary jobs upon arrival in Na'ama Bay or Alexandria. **American Field Service (AFS)** runs the Egyptian Society for Intercultural Exchange, (ESIE), which sponsors summer-, semester-, and year-long homestay exchange programs in Egypt for current students and short-term service projects for adults. Programs for nearly every country of origin; financial aid available. Contact ESIE at 10 al-Thawra St., Apt. 5, Mohandiseen, Giza, Egypt (☎(02) 360 61 42; fax 337 60 01; info-egypt@afs.org; www.afs.org).

Israel: A special **work visa** is required, which your employer in Israel must apply for before you depart. Volunteers often work at one of Israel's 250 **kibbutzim,** communal settlements whose members divide work and profits equally. Volunteers work 6 8hr. days per week, with a few days off per month, and receive a small monthly allowance in addition to room and board; the work is generally in agriculture, industry, or service. To apply, contact the main **Kibbutz Aliya Office** at 633 3rd Ave., 21st fl., New York, NY 10017 (☎800-247-7852; fax 212-318-6134; kibbutzdsk@aol.com). Applicants must be ages 18-35 with no children. **Moshavim** are agricultural communities in which farms and homes are privately owned and operated. You will receive free lodging with a family or with other workers. In return, you work a 6-day week, at least 8hr. per day. Workers are paid about US$350 per month, and are expected to pay for their own food. Applicants must be ages 18-32 and physically fit, with no children. Contact **Volunteers Moshavim Movement,** 19 Leonardo da Vinci St., Tel Aviv (☎(03) 695 84 73).

Jordan: Get **work permits** from the Ministry of Labor. It's difficult for foreigners to find jobs in **Jordan;** a combination of perfect English and business or banking skills is optimal. Positions must be arranged before arrival in order to get a work visa. **Residence permits** are required for stays of more than 3 months.

Lebanon: People who seek to work in Lebanon must acquire a special **work visa.** Contact the nearest Lebanese embassy for details. **UNIPAL (Universities Trust for Educational Exchange with Palestinians)** sends volunteers to teach English to Palestinians and help with handicapped children in the West Bank, Gaza Strip, and Lebanon. Contact BCM Unipal, London, UK WC1N 3XX (☎(191) 386 7124).

Syria: Work for foreigners is scarce in Syria. A **residence permit** is required, as visitors on tourist visas are not allowed to work. The **American Language Center Damascus** employs 40 native speakers to teach English at their special learning facility in Damascus. Contact ALCD c/o USIS, P.O. Box 29, Damascus, Syria (☎(11) 332 72 36) or ALCD c/o USIS, Department of State, Washington, D.C. 20521-6110.

Turkey: Finding work in Turkey is difficult, as the government even restricts employment to citizens. Foreigners who wish to work in Turkey must obtain a **work permit,** issued by the Ministry of the Interior; contact a Turkish diplomatic mission for more information.

TEACHING ENGLISH

International Schools Services, Educational Staffing Program, P.O. Box 5910, Princeton, NJ 08543, USA (☎609-452-0990; www.iss.edu). Recruits teachers and administrators for American and English schools in the Middle East. US$150 program fee.

Office of Overseas Schools, US Department of State, Room H328, SA-1, Washington, D.C. 20522 (☎202-261-8200; fax 261-8224; www.state.gov/www/about_state/schools/). Keeps a comprehensive list of schools abroad and agencies that arrange placement for Americans to teach abroad.

ELS Language Centers/Middle East employs many English as a First Language (EFL) teachers in full- and part-time work in Egypt and Jordan. Contact them at their main office, P.O. Box 3079, Abu Dhabi, UAE (www.elsme.com; elsme@emirates.net.ae).

ARCHAEOLOGICAL DIGS

Archaeological Institute of America, 656 Beacon St., Boston, MA 02215, USA (☎617-353-9361; www.archaeological.org). The *Archaeological Fieldwork Opportunities Bulletin* (US$16 for non-members) lists field sites throughout the Middle East. Purchase the bulletin from Kendall/Hunt Publishing, 4050 Westmark Dr., Dubuque, IA 52004, USA (☎800-228-0810).

VOLUNTEERING

Volunteer jobs are readily available, and many provide room and board in exchange for labor. You can sometimes avoid high application fees by contacting the individual workcamps directly.

Earthwatch, 3 Clocktower Pl., P.O. Box 75, Maynard, MA 01754 (☎800-776-0188 or 978-461-0081; www.earthwatch.org). Arranges 1- to 3-week programs in Turkey, Jordan, and Israel to promote conservation of natural resources. Programs cost US$1600.

Habitat for Humanity International, 121 Habitat St., Americus, GA 31709, USA (☎800-422-4828; www.habitat.org). Offers international opportunities in Egypt to live with and build houses in a host community. Costs range US$1200-3500.

Service Civil International Voluntary Service (SCI-IVS), 814 NE 40th St., Seattle, WA 98105, USA (☎/fax 206-545-6585; www.sci-ivs.org). Arranges placement in workcamps in Palestine for those 18+. Registration fee US$65-150.

Volunteers for Peace, 1034 Tiffany Rd., Belmont, VT 05730, USA (☎802-259-2759; www.vfp.org). Arranges placement in workcamps in Israel and Turkey. Annual *International Workcamp Directory*, US$20. Registration fee US$200. Free newsletter.

OTHER RESOURCES

Let's Go covers all aspects of budget travel, but we can't put *everything* in our guides. Listed are resources that can serve as spring boards for your own research.

TRAVEL PUBLISHERS & BOOKSTORES

Hippocrene Books, Inc., 171 Madison Ave., New York, NY 10016 (☎212-685-4371; orders 718-454-2366; www.netcom.com/~hippocre). Free catalog. Publishes foreign language dictionaries and language learning guides.

Hunter Publishing, 130 Campus Dr., Edison, NJ 08818, USA (☎800-255-0343; www.hunterpublishing.com). Extensive catalog of travel guides and diving and adventure travel books.

Rand McNally, 150 S. Wacker Dr., Chicago, IL 60606, USA (☎800-234-0679 or 312-332-2009; www.randmcnally.com), publishes road atlases (each US$10).

Adventurous Traveler Bookstore, 245 S. Champlain St., Burlington, VT 05401, USA (☎800-282-3963 or 802-860-6776; www.adventuroustraveler.com).

Travel Books & Language Center, Inc., 4437 Wisconsin Ave. NW, Washington, D.C. 20016 (☎800-220-2665 or 202-237-1322; www.travelbks.com). Over 60,000 titles from around the world.

WORLD WIDE WEB

Almost every aspect of budget travel is accessible via the web. Within 10min. at the keyboard, you can make a reservation at a hostel, get advice on travel hotspots from other travelers who have just returned from the Middle East, or find out exactly how much a train from Luxor to Alexandria costs.

Listed here are some budget travel sites to start off your surfing; other relevant web sites are listed throughout the book. Because website turnover is high, use search engines (such as www.google.com) to strike out on your own.

THE ART OF BUDGET TRAVEL

How to See the World: www.artoftravel.com. A compendium of great travel tips, from cheap flights to self defense to interacting with local culture.

Rec. Travel Library: www.travel-library.com. A fantastic set of links for general information and personal travelogues.

Lycos: cityguide.lycos.com. General introductions to cities and regions throughout the Middle East, accompanied by links to applicable histories, news, and tourism sites.

INFORMATION ON THE MIDDLE EAST

Arabnet: www.arab.net. A one-stop guide to the Middle East (except Israel) with extensive country-specific resources on geographic, political, and historical elements. Though the page is not strongly political, it regularly features often inflammatory pro-Arab statements; Israel's absence further discredits Arabnet as a neutral news source.

CIA World Factbook: www.odci.gov/cia/publications/factbook/index.html. Tons of vital statistics on geography, government, economy, and people of the Middle East.

Foreign Language for Travelers: www.travlang.com. Provides free online translating dictionaries and lists of phrases in Arabic.

MyTravelGuide: www.mytravelguide.com. Country overviews, with everything from history to transportation to live web cam coverage of the Middle East.

Geographia: www.geographia.com. Highlights, culture, and people of the Middle East.

Atevo Travel: www.atevo.com/guides/destinations. Detailed introductions, travel tips, and suggested itineraries.

World Travel Guide: www.travel-guides.com/navigate/world.asp. Helpful practical info.

TravelPage: www.travelpage.com. Links to official tourist office sites in the Middle East.

PlanetRider: www.planetrider.com. A subjective list of links to the "best" websites covering the culture and tourist attractions of the Middle East.

AND OUR PERSONAL FAVORITE...

☒ **Let's Go:** www.letsgo.com. Our constantly expanding website features photos and streaming video, online ordering of all our titles, info about our books, a travel forum buzzing with stories and tips, and links that will help you find everything you ever wanted to know about the Middle East.

ESSENTIALS

LIFE AND TIMES

HISTORY

The Middle East gave birth to human civilization nearly 10,000 years ago in the **Fertile Crescent,** the lush valley between the **Tigris** and **Euphrates** rivers in what is now Iraq. Simple stone sickles used to harvest wild wheat have been found dating as far back as the 9th millennium BCE. In the 7th millennium BCE, someone in **Mesopotamia** (literally, "the land between the rivers") had the bright idea to invent farming. (Historians believe the innovation was probably made by women.) After millions of years of Earth being really boring, the **Agricultural Revolution** opened the floodgates of progress, ushering in a series of basic inventions in succeeding millennia—irrigation, pottery, writing, and the all-important and perennially reinvented **wheel.** At the same time, techniques of metal working were developed: first copper, then bronze, and finally iron. These technological advances led to the surpluses (of food, not federal budget) that leolmd to substantial population growth and the development of the earliest cities.

VERY ANCIENT EMPIRES

There is a rich archaeological record of early civilizations in the Middle East, including excavations of the ancient city of **Jericho** dating to 6500 BCE, with historical records going back to the 3rd millennium BCE, when writing was first introduced. The beginning of the historical period was marked by constant rivalry between the central Mesopotamian city-states of the **Akkadians,** who were **Semites** (people originally believed to be descended from Noah's son Shem, now grouped together linguistically) and those of the non-Semitic **Sumerians.** Sumerians dominated until the 24th century BCE, when **Sargon I,** an Akkadian king, established the world's first empire. Sargon's empire fell around 2250 BCE but was soon reestablished by the Sumerians under the famous **ziggurat**-building Third Dynasty of the **Kings of Ur.** After an invasion by Arabian nomads called **Amorites** and a period of anarchy, Amorite King **Hammurabi** laid the smack down in the 18th century BCE, creating the third Mesopotamian empire and developing the world's first comprehensive written legal system, best remembered for its "eye for an eye" system of punishment. Around the same time, Babylonian mathematicians discovered the famous **Pythagorean Theorem** (named after the Greek guy who rediscovered it 13 centuries later).

Across the Red Sea to the west, the Kingdoms of **Upper** and **Lower Egypt** were united early in the 3rd millennium under the first dynasty of the **Old Kingdom** of Egypt. The Old Kingdom split apart into independent kingdoms in 2250 BCE, only to be reunited (in a sequel called the **Middle Kingdom**) two centuries later. The Egyptians added their own innovations to Mesopotamian technologies. They used irrigation to harness the fertility of the Nile River and were the first to build with stone, starting with the pyramid of Zoser in the 27th century BCE.

In **Anatolia** (modern Turkey) and what is now Syria, another powerful kingdom was established by the **Hittites,** flourishing after 2000 BCE. The Egyptians, Hittites, and **Babylonians** vied for influence in the region of modern Israel and Lebanon, with the Egyptians generally in control. Armed conflict alternated with extensive periods of trade. In 1580 BCE, the princes of Thebes liberated Egypt once again, founding the **New Kingdom,** regaining Palestine, and moving into Syria. Around the same time, invaders from what is now Iran wrought havoc in Mesopotamia with a new military weapon, the horse-drawn chariot. The **Assyrians** built up a powerful kingdom with ties to the Hittites, and the Amorites were replaced by the **Aramaeans,** whose language eventually became widely used in Palestine and was spoken by such luminaries as **Jesus Christ.** The Aramaic alphabet is still used today in printed Hebrew.

Around 1375 BCE, wacky pharaoh **Akhenaton** introduced monotheism to Egypt, a brief religious revolution that ended with the victory of the traditional priesthood upon Akhenaton's death. Egypt expanded again into Syria after this disruption. In a critical battle, the Hittites defeated pharaoh **Ramses II** at Kadesh in 1280; the truce signed after this battle is the oldest surviving peace treaty. Ramses II is best known, though, in the shiny-headed guise of Yul Brenner; historians believe that the Exodus of the Hebrews from Egypt (recounted in the Old Testament and the Charlton Heston film *The Ten Commandments*) probably took place during Ramses's reign.

ANCIENT EMPIRES

About 1200 BCE, barbarians from Europe poured into Anatolia, wiped out the Hittite state, and invaded Syria. A few years later, more invaders poured down the coast of Palestine and were beaten back from Egypt with difficulty, settling finally along the coast of Palestine, ending Egyptian dominance there. Palestine takes its name from one of these peoples, the **Philistines.**

About 1000 BCE, as iron weapons became the new fad, the **Aramaeans** overran the whole Fertile Crescent, swept away the second Assyrian empire, and became the dominant force in Mesopotamia. The **Phoenicians** of Lebanon and the **Hebrews** of Palestine broke the power of the coastal Philistines, who were finally conquered under the leadership of **David** in 975. Under the warlike David and his more peaceful and wise son **Solomon** (famous for rebuilding the Holy Temple), the Hebrews dominated Palestine. But upon Solomon's death, the unified kingdom split—not to be reunited until 1948—and the Assyrian empire reestablished itself as the main power in the region.

Assyrian power peaked under Emperor **Tiglath-Pileser III** (745-728 BCE) and his successors. Their empire included all of the area of modern Israel and Syria, the bulk of Egypt, and a slice of Anatolia. However, invaders—again from modern-day Iran—soon teamed up with the **Babylonians,** who established a new empire, replacing the Assyrians at the top of the greasy pole.

The alliance with the eastern invaders came back to haunt the Babylonians. In 549 BCE, Emperor **Cyrus II** assumed control of **Persia**, which was already the most powerful kingdom in the region, and by 539, he had incorporated the whole of the Babylonian empire into his domains. Persian rule was good news for the Jews, who were allowed to return home from the exile that Babylonian Emperor **Nebuchadnezzar** had imposed in 586 BCE. With the conquest of Egypt by Cyrus' son, **Cambyses II,** the Persian empire covered all of the Middle East from Egypt to the borders of India. Egypt regained its independence around 400 BCE, but the rest of the empire held firm, as Persia remained the big cat in the region until the arrival of (drumroll, please) ■**Alexander the Great.**

FROM HELLENISM TO ISLAM

In 334 BCE, wonderboy general **Alexander of Macedon** invaded Anatolia; just nine years later, he controlled the Persian Empire. Not content with the entire Middle East, Alexander pushed on, extending his empire from Greece to the Khyber Pass in India. After Alexander's death (from jet lag) his empire broke up, and

6500 BCE	Stone Age town in present-day Jericho
3100-2183	Old Kingdom
2713-2494	Sphinx, Pyramids at Giza built
2370	Sargon I
2290-2250	Guti invasions
1991-1786	Middle Kingdom
1755	Code of Hammurabi
1720	Hyksos
1580	Egypt liberated from Hyksos domination
1573-1180	New Kingdom
1380	Hittite empire spans all of Anatolia and Jerusalem
1375	Monotheism introduced in Egypt
1280	Treaty of Kadesh
1200	Barbarian invaders wipe out Hittite state
1190	Philistines settle in Palestine
1000-962	David

MIDDLE EAST

962-931
Solomon

931
Judea splits into
two kingdoms

721-705
Sargon II

586
Nebuchadnezzar
deports Jews to
Babylon

539
Cyrus the Great
conquers Babylon

325
Alexander the
Great defeats Per-
sian Empire

301-121
Seleucids

121 BCE-224 CE
Parthians

224-651
Sassanians

622
Muhammad flees
Mecca to Medina

638
Jerusalem
becomes holy city
of Islam

661-750
Umayyad Dynasty

749-1258
Abbasid Dynasty

1099
First Crusade

1291
Rise of the Mamluks

1636
Libya breaks free
from Ottoman rule

1798
Napoleon con-
quers the Mamluks

1802
Wahhabbis capture
Mecca

Seleucus and his successors, the Seleucid kings, controlled most of Syria, Anatolia, Mesopotamia, and Persia from 301-121 BCE. These kings had no official policy of Hellenization, but Greek culture profoundly impacted the Middle East for many centuries.

The **Parthians** replaced the Seleucid kings, ruling from 121 BCE until 224 CE, when the **Sassanians**—stooges of the Roman Empire—took over. Relatively uneventful, the Sassanian Period did mark a gradual religious shift in the Middle East to monotheism. Many in the Roman Empire followed the lead of Emperor **Constantine I** after his 313 Edict of Milan legalized **Christianity** in the empire. Others adopted **Zoroastrianism,** a religion developed in the 6th century BCE in Persia; few adherents are left today (though modern Zoroastrians of note include former Queen lead singer **Freddie Mercury**).

In the early 7th century, an Arab merchant named **Muhammad** began preaching in the city of **Mecca**. In 622, Muhammad fled persecution in Mecca for **Medina,** where he preached until his death—after which his followers passed on his teachings. At first, **Islam** spread slowly because of well-organized Christian and Jewish communities, but soon Islam stretched throughout the entire Middle East.

Muhammad's flight from Mecca marked the dawn of the **Arabo-Islamic Period,** when Islam replaced Hellenism as the dominant cultural force, unifying Middle Eastern empires until the 13th century. Beginning in 630, **Muslims** (adherents of Islam) assumed control of the Middle East. The **Umayyads** ruled the region with Damascus as their capital and spread west toward North Africa. The **Abbasids** replaced the Umayyads farther east, while the **Zaydi** dynasty prevailed in southern Arabia.

In 1099, the armies of **Godfrey of Bouillon** invaded the Middle East, fulfilling Godfrey's (and God's?) will by incorporating parts of what are now Israel, Jordan, and Syria into the **Christian Kingdom of Jerusalem.** Over the next 200 years, three more Crusades left the land spotted with castles from which the Europeans staved off Muslim attacks. At the end of the 12th century, **Salah al-Din** led the **Mamluks** to reconquer what is now Syria. For the next three centuries, the Mamluks remained the dominant power in the Middle East.

TURKEY DAYS

At the same time as Salah al-Din's victory over the Crusaders, **Seljuk Turks** began migrating throughout the Middle East, gnawing away at the **Byzantine Empire.** In 1453, the Seljuks gained the ultimate prize when strategically vital **Constantinople** fell to **Mehmet the Conqueror** after a 54-day siege. Under **Selim I,** Ottoman armies conquered Palestine, Egypt, Arabia, and present-day Syria. Suddenly, the Ottoman Sultan was guardian of the three holy cities of Islam: Mecca, Medina, and Jerusalem.

Due to transportation and communication difficulties, the **Ottoman Empire** was relatively decentralized. The Ottoman governor's contact with satellite provinces was usually limited to issues of tax collection and military conscription. The huge empire thus remained heterogeneous, and by the 17th century, Ottoman power had been stretched too thin. Spurred by pirate loot, Libya began to assert greater autonomy. By 1744, Muslim factions also spurned Ottoman rule. **Muhammad ibn Saud,** a prominent sheikh, and **Muhammad ibn 'Abd al-Wahhab,** a preacher of a form of Islam called **Wahhabism,** united in the first **Saudi Empire.** By 1802, the Wahhabis captured Mecca, and the Saudi empire reached its peak, spanning most of modern-day Saudi Arabia and southern Iraq.

COLONIZATION AND INDEPENDENCE

With the dawn of the 19th century, European powers turned toward the Middle East, further hastening the Ottoman Empire's decline. In 1798, **Napoleon Bonaparte's** armies defeated the Mamluk forces at Imbaba. By 1802, Napoleon had been expelled by the British, who in turn were KO'd by **Muhammad 'Ali** three years later, but the European intrusion was significant. Napoleon's victory marked the first European conquest of a major Arab country in Islamic history and signaled the fall of the Middle East as a world political power.

Imperialist Britain and France began a string of colonizations extending to the early 20th century. Between the 1820s and 1870s, the British signed protection treaties with the Persian Gulf nations and established colonies in Somalia and the Sudan. But their biggest conquest came in 1882: spurred on by Egypt's newfound commercial significance (thanks to the construction of the **Suez Canal**), Great Britain pressured Egyptian ruler **Tawfiq Pasha** to relinquish control of his government. Not to be outdone, France invaded Algeria in 1830, beginning a 132-year occupation. The **Bardo Treaty** made Tunisia a French protectorate in 1881, and joint British and French intervention pressured the Ottomans into establishing a Christian settlement in 1860 in what would become Lebanon.

World War I marked the end of the decaying Ottoman Empire, which having allied itself with Germany and Austria-Hungary, collapsed when British forces occupied Baghdad in 1917. The power vacuum in the Middle East was filled by the **Mandate System,** in which the newly created **League of Nations** awarded the Western European powers control over the old Turkish turf with the stated purpose of preparing the Middle East for independence. Britain was given Palestine and Iraq, while France walked away with what are now Syria and Lebanon.

Throughout the interwar years, the British relinquished mandate control in the face of increasing Arab nationalism. In 1921, **King Abdullah** established the **Emirate of Transjordan** as a self-governing territory under British mandate. The British also ended their protectorates of Egypt, Yemen, and Morocco, though Egypt was a puppet kingdom until the 1936 **Anglo-Egyptian Treaty** recognized it as an independent nation under **King Farouk.**

World War II—in which many Middle Eastern leaders defied Britain and collaborated with the Nazis—provided the final impetus for a battered Britain to get the hell out of Dodge. In 1946, the British evacuated Syria and Jordan, creating modern-day states, and left the Suez Canal soon after. France was more stubborn, waging a brutally repressive war in Algeria to keep the colony—finally allowing a national referendum on independence in 1962. (Needless to say, the Algerians voted almost unanimously for independence.)

1805
Muhammad 'Ali defeats British forces

1820
Start of British and French colonization of the Middle East

1860
Ottomans establish Christian settlement in Lebanon

1881
Tunisia becomes French protectorate

1917
Balfour Declaration

1921
Emirate of Transjordan established

1922-1932
British end protectorates in Egypt, Yemen, and Morocco

1936
Anglo-Egyptian Treaty

1946
British evacuate Syria and Jordan

1947
British evacuate Suez Canal

1948
Israeli War of Independence

1949
Jerusalem divided under Israeli and Jordanian rule

1956
Suez Crisis

MIDDLE EAST

1958
Egypt and Syria
form United Arab
Republic

1960
OPEC formed

1962
French end 132-
year occupation of
Algeria

1963
Syrian Ba'ath Party
established

1967
Six Day War

1968-70
War of Attrition

1969
Arafat takes con-
trol of PLO

1970
Black September

1973
Yom Kippur War

1978
Camp David
Accords

1979
Islamic Revolution
in Iran

1980-88
Iran-Iraq War

1981
Sadat assassi-
nated

1987
Intifada begins

1991
Persian Gulf War

1993
Oslo Accords

1995
Rabin assassi-
nated

2000
Israel withdraws
from Lebanon;
Assad dies

NATIONALISM AND RELIGIOUS CONFLICT

RISE OF ISRAEL AND PAN-ARABISM

Britain's clean withdrawal from Syria and Jordan would not be repeated in Palestine. In the 1917 **Balfour Declaration** Britain had promised its support for both a Jewish and Palestinian state, and, in fact, the United Nations General Assembly voted in 1947 to split Palestine into two states. The Jewish leadership accepted the resolution reluctantly, while Palestinian Arab leaders and the governments of neighboring countries rejected it, vowing never to recognize a Jewish state in Palestine. As the British prepared to leave Palestine in accordance with the UN's **Partition Plan,** Jews and Arabs planned for full-scale war.

In 1948, the British mandate over Palestine ended, and **Zionist** leader **David Ben-Gurion** declared the independence of the state of **Israel.** The next day, a combined army of Syrian, Iraqi, Lebanese, Saudi, Egyptian, and Jordanian troops invaded. The ensuing **War of Independence** proved a disaster for the Palestinians. When the dust settled with armistices in early 1949, Israel had secured not only its UN-allotted territory, but also some land in the north and in the West Bank designated for Palestine. Thousands of Palestinian refugees crowded into camps in the West Bank, Gaza, and Jordan.

Egypt, weakened by struggles between nationalists and the monarchy, fell into shambles after its failed invasion of Israel. In 1952, a group of young army officers, led by charismatic heartthrob **Gamal 'Abd al-Nasser,** seized power from corrupt King Farouk. Advocating an ideology of **Pan-Arabism,** Nasser hoped to unify the Arab world into one state powerful enough to resist imperial encroachments and regain Palestine. In 1956, the US attempted to curtail Nasser's power by withdrawing its offer to finance the **Aswan High Dam.** Nasser thumbed his nose at the far less-handsome US President **Dwight Eisenhower,** nationalizing the Suez Canal and establishing—with Jordan and Syria—a joint military command directed against Israel. When Israel collaborated with Britain and France to retake the canal, world opinion forced the three countries to withdraw. After the Suez crisis and the merger of Egypt with Syria in 1958 to form the **United Arab Republic,** Nasser was heralded as the savior of the Arab world. But with the ascendancy of **Hafez al-Assad** and the nationalist (rather than pan-Arabist) **Syrian Ba'ath Party** in the 1960s and Nasser's death in 1970, the dream of a united Arab world was never to be realized.

THE PALESTINIAN DILEMMA

From bases sanctioned by the governments of Jordan, Syria, and Lebanon, the **Palestinian Liberation Organization (PLO)** raided Israel, attacks that came to a head with a Syrian-Israeli air battle in April 1967. Nasser successfully demanded the withdrawal of the UN buffer-zone troops stationed in the Sinai since 1956 and initiated a blockade on May 22, 1967. When Jordan, Iraq, and Syria deployed troops along Israel's borders, Israel launched a preemptive strike against air fields in the Sinai, obliterating the Egyptian air force before it got off the ground. The **Six Day War** that followed ended in another resounding

Israeli victory, as Israel annexed East Jerusalem, the Sinai Peninsula, Gaza Strip, West Bank, and Golan Heights.

Palestinian Arabs decided to take matters into their own hands. In 1969, **Yasser Arafat,** leader of the terrorist group **FATAH,** took over the PLO from its pro-Nasser leadership. The Arafat-led PLO sought liberation through propaganda and guerrilla warfare but was stymied by Jordan's **King Hussein.** Already aggravated by the 400,000 additional Palestinian refugees created by the Six Day War, Hussein was infuriated by the PLO hijacking of commercial airlines and declared war on the group. Fighting between Jordanian and PLO troops in September 1970 took over 3000 lives, causing the month to become remembered by Palestinians as **Black September.** After **Arab League** mediation and Nasser's personal intervention, an agreement was forged requiring the PLO to move its headquarters to Lebanon.

In October 1974, the Arab League declared that the PLO—not Jordan—was "the sole legitimate representative of the Palestinian people." This incensed King Hussein, but when the other 20 Arab nations assented to PLO representation in the League, he was forced to agree. In November, the UN General Assembly granted the PLO observer status in the UN.

(OILY) OCTOBER RAIN

After Nasser's sudden death, conservative-leaning Vice President **Anwar Sadat** assumed control of Egypt and its **War of Attrition** against Israel. Sadat sought to reopen the lucrative Suez Canal and reclaim the desperately needed Sinai oil fields. In October 1973 on **Yom Kippur** (the holiest day on the Jewish calendar), Egypt and Syria—armed with Soviet weapons—launched a surprise assault on Israel. After initial Arab gains, Israel launched a series of fierce missile attacks and ultimately broke through the Egyptian line, crossing the Suez Canal onto the mainland. After the **Geneva Peace Conference** and the subsequent **Sinai I** and **II** agreements, much of the Sinai was returned to Egypt, and the aura of invincibility Israel had earned over the years was gone.

The **October War** had serious repercussions outside the Middle East. The Organization of Petroleum Exporting Countries **(OPEC)**—a cartel of 11 mostly Middle Eastern nations, formed in 1960—responded to Western support for Israel by tightening the world oil supply. Prices skyrocketed and the international economy took a nosedive. Highly reliant on Middle Eastern oil and unable to manufacture fuel-efficient cars that didn't spontaneously explode (i.e. the **Ford Pinto**), the US battled stagflation throughout the 1970s.

By attacking Israel on Yom Kippur, Sadat shrewdly positioned Egypt to seek unilateral peace with Israel. In November 1977, Sadat was officially welcomed to Jerusalem. By September 1978, Israeli Prime Minister **Menaḥem Begin** and Sadat had forged an agreement (the **Camp David Accords**) with the help of US President **Jimmy Carter,** in which Israel relinquished the Sinai in exchange for peace and full diplomatic relations with Egypt. However, the Arab world viewed Egypt as a traitor, leaving the country isolated and forced to turn to the US for financial support. Right-wing Muslims, whom Sadat had courted in his battles against the Nasserist left, objected to this open alliance with the West. An extremist group assassinated Sadat in 1981.

Meanwhile, **Ayatollah Khomeini** and other fundamentalist Iranian leaders carried out an Islamic revolution in 1979, deposing the ruling shah and setting up an anti-Western theocracy. Iraq—a rising regional power under modernizing Iraqi President **Saddam Hussein**—renewed the area's age-old Persian-Arab conflict by attacking Iran in 1980, setting off the bloody **Iran-Iraq War** which lasted until 1988 and may have cost up to one million lives.

INFIGHTING AND INTIFADA

As the Soviet power dissipated in the 1980s and Egypt proved that coexistence with Israel was possible, Cold War tensions in the Middle East began to thaw a bit. The decade saw no major Arab invasion of Israel, though there was no end to violence in the region.

Though he stuck to the terms of the Camp David Accords, Sadat's successor **Hosni Mubarak** held Israel at arm's length, attempting to reintegrate Egypt into the Arab world it had once tried to unite. In 1984, Egypt restored relations with the USSR and was readmitted to the Islamic Conference. In 1988, the Arab League invited Egypt to rejoin, dropping demands that Egypt sever ties with Israel.

In 1982, Israel invaded civil war-plagued Lebanon in an attempt to create a protective buffer zone and wipe out PLO forces that had been attacking northern Israel. When the Israeli army, after surrounding the PLO in Beirut, began shelling the city at an enormous civilian cost, world public opinion turned against Israel. Under an agreement negotiated by the US, most fighting ended in 1983, and Israel withdrew in 1985, but maintained a strip of south Lebanon as a security zone.

In 1988, King Hussein dropped Jordan's claims to the West Bank and ceased assisting in the administration of the territories. Arafat seized the opportunity to secure a PLO role in negotiations, renouncing terrorism, recognizing Israel's right to exist, and proposing an independent Palestinian state. Israeli Prime Minister **Yitzhak Shamir** presented his own proposal but refused to negotiate with the PLO. With increasing Palestinian uprisings (known as the **intifada**) and no progress, the US and the PLO terminated their discussions in the summer of 1989.

LET'S MAKE A DEAL

Not deterred by a decade of war with Iran, Iraqi troops marched into oil-rich Kuwait in August 1990, marking the start of an international crisis. In six weeks of fighting during the winter of 1991, a coalition of the US, European countries, Egypt, Syria, Saudi Arabia, and the other Gulf states forced Iraq to withdraw. During the conflict, 39 Iraqi SCUD missiles fell on Tel Aviv and Haifa, cheered on by Arafat and the Palestinians. Israel, under pressure from the US, did not retaliate.

Paradoxically, the **Persian Gulf War** opened the door for peace in the region. Many hoped that parties such as Israel and Syria—for the first time on the same side of a regional conflict—could be brought to the bargaining table. As the USSR lay in shambles in October 1991, the **Madrid Peace Conference** was convened with Israel carrying on negotiations with Syria, Lebanon, Egypt, and a joint Jordanian-Palestinian delegation. Little progress was achieved. Then, almost a year later, Israel and the PLO shocked the world by announcing that representatives meeting secretly in Oslo had successfully negotiated a peace agreement. The Declaration of Principles on Interim Self-Government Arrangements (a.k.a. the **Oslo Accord**) was signed on the White House lawn on September 13, 1993. The DOP provided mutual recognition between Israel and the PLO, as well as a plan for the implementation of Palestinian autonomy in the Gaza Strip and the Jericho area. A five-year transitional period was to end with an agreement on final status of refugees, settlements, security arrangements, borders, foreign relations, and Jerusalem.

Oslo was followed by several other Israeli-Palestinian agreements, as well as a peace accord with Jordan in 1994. The **Gaza-Jericho Agreement** provided the details for Israeli withdrawal from these areas and the creation of a **Palestinian Authority (PA)** headed by Arafat. The two sides then signed the **Early Empowerment Agreement**, transferring some official responsibilities in the West Bank to the PA. Finally, the **Wye River Interim Agreement** promised that Israel would withdraw from parts of the West Bank and dismantle certain settlements.

IN THE NEWS

Since Oslo, obstacles continue to obstruct the peace process. In November 1995, a right-wing Jewish university student shot and killed aging Israeli hero and Prime Minister **Yitzhak Rabin.** The May 1996 election of polished, Clintonesque Likud leader **Benjamin Netanyahu** marked a turn away from Rabin's peace-oriented policies. The militant Islamic organization **Hamas** dealt another blow to the peace process with the suicide bombing of a crowded Jerusalem market on July 30, 1997.

In May 1999, Labor leader **Ehud** (rhymes with "Hey Jude") **Barak** was elected prime minister with a mandate to wrap up the peace talks. Barak appeared to be well on his way, negotiating simultaneously with Syria, Lebanon, and the PA. In May 2000, Israeli troops finally pulled out of southern Lebanon (though, due to heavy fire by **Hezbollah** guerrillas, it was a week earlier than Barak's deadline). And days later, hard-line Syrian President Assad died, leaving Syria to his Western-educated son, **Bashar al-Assad.**

But since Assad's death, the situation has largely deteriorated. In September 2000—against the wishes of Muslim authorities—hawkish Likud leader **Ariel Sharon** visited an area of Jerusalem containing Muslim and Jewish holy sites, in a move Palestinians found offensive and threatening. Riots escalated into months of full-fledged attacks on the Israeli military that led to hundreds of (mostly Palestinian) deaths. As violence showed no signs of letting up, Barak's popularity went into freefall, and Sharon trounced him in the February 2001 election. Some feared that Sharon would be as intransigent a prime minister as he was an opposition leader, but he has been reluctant to provoke Palestinians further. After Arab terrorists began a suicide bombing campaign in spring of 2001, Sharon and Arafat agreed to a ceasefire. Terrorist attacks continued throughout the summer, however. Prospects for a lasting peace in the Middle East seem as far away as ever, but both sides—and the ever-involved US—continue to work toward that goal.

RELIGION IN THE MIDDLE EAST

The Middle East is home to the three major monotheistic religions: **Judaism, Christianity,** and **Islam.** The **Druze, Baha'i, Karaites,** and **Samaritans** also call it home.

ISLAM

The Arabic word *islam* translates, in its general sense, as "submission," and the basic tenet of Islam is submission to the will of God **(Allah)**. Islam has its roots in revelations received from 610 to 622 CE by **Muhammad,** who was informed of his prophetic calling by the angel Gabriel. These revelations, the **Qur'an** (Arabic for "recitation"), form the core text of Islam. Muslims believe the Arabic text is perfect, immutable, and untranslatable—the words of God embodied in human language. Consequently, the Qur'an appears throughout the Muslim world (the majority of which is non-Arabic speaking) in Arabic. Muhammad is seen as the "seal of the prophets," the last and greatest in a chain of God's messengers that includes Jewish and Christian figures such as Abraham, Moses, and Jesus.

It is believed that the Prophet Muhammad received the Qur'an during the month of **Ramadan.** Fasting during this holy month is the fourth pillar of Islam. Between dawn and sunset, Muslims are not permitted to smoke, have sexual intercourse, or let any food or water pass their lips; exceptions are made for pregnant or menstruating women, the sick, and travelers—they must make up the fast at a later date. Fasting is meant for reflection; to teach Muslims to resist temptation and thereby control all their unchaste urges, better understand the plight of the poor, and be more thankful for the food with which God has provided them. As soon as the evening *adhan* is heard, Muslims break the fast and begin a night of feasting, visits to friends and relatives, and revelry. In busy metropolises like Cairo, the city stays up until just before dawn, but in quieter areas, a neighbor may circulate to houses, banging a drum and waking people for the *suhur*, a meal eaten just before the crack of dawn in an attempt to avoid extreme hunger upon waking.

HISTORY OF ISLAM

Muhammad rapidly gathered followers to his evolving faith. Staunchly monotheistic Islam met with ample opposition in polytheistic Arabia, leading to persecution in Muhammad's native city of **Mecca.** In 622, he and his followers fled to the nearby city of **Medina,** where he was asked to mediate a long-standing blood feud. This *hijra* (migration) marks the starting point of the Islamic calendar. In 630, Mecca surrendered to the Muslims, who had organized themselves into an army, thus making Muhammad the most powerful man in Arabia and leading numerous Meccans to convert to his new faith. This established the foundation for the concept of *jihad* ("struggle"), which refers first to the spiritual struggle against one's own desires, then to the struggle to make one's own Muslim community as righteous as possible, and lastly to the struggle against outsiders wishing to harm Islam.

Muhammad is not believed to be divine, but rather a human messenger of God's words. Several verses of the Qur'an demand obedience to the Prophet; his actions are sanctified because God chose him to be the recipient of revelation. The stories and traditions surrounding the Prophet's life and personal behavior have been passed on as *sunna* ("rules") and those who follow the *sunna* (from which the term "Sunni" is derived) in addition to the teachings of the Qur'an are considered especially devout. The primary source for *sunna* are the *hadith*, a collection of sayings and deeds attributed to Muhammad. *Hadith* narratives had to go through a rigorous verification process before they were accepted as true; the tale had to be confirmed, preferably by those who saw the action, and the greatest weight was given to testimony by Muhammad's closest followers and relatives.

SUNNIS, SHI'ITES, AND SUFIS

Muhammad's nephew and son-in-law 'Ali was the catalyst for the major split in the Muslim world. When 'Ali was murdered in 661, the *Shi'at 'Ali* ("Partisans of 'Ali" or **Shi'ites**) believed he was the only legitimate successor to Muhammad, thus separating themselves from **Sunni** Muslims, who accepted the leadership of a appointed Caliph. A minority sect within Islam, Shi'ism is a faith with a sharp focus on divinely chosen leaders (or *imams*) who are blood descendants of 'Ali and his wife, the Prophet's daughter Fatima. Today, Shi'ite Muslims are the majority in Iran, and a significant minority in Syria, Lebanon, and Iraq.

In the 10th century, Sunni Muslim scholars *(ulama)* proclaimed "the gates of *ijtihad* (individual judgment)" closed; new concepts and interpretations could no longer stand on their own but had to be legitimized by tradition. There have been numerous reform movements throughout the Islamic world, including the conservative Wahhabi movement on the Arabian Peninsula, which rejects any religious innovations that occured after the 3rd century of Islam. The movement of the thinker **Jamal al-Din al-Afghani** in the Middle East reacted to Western colonial activity in the Arab world and urged Muslims to reform themselves as the first step in rising to meet this challenge from an alien, more powerful culture. Another important figure in political Islam was **Muhammad Iqbal** in South Asia. An advocate of Pakistani independence, his poetry and philosophy stressed the rebirth of Islamic and spiritual redemption through self-development, moral integrity and individual freedom. There are four main schools of thought in the Islamic legal system, and the applicability of *sharia*, or Islamic law, is a subject of much strife in a number of Muslim countries, which have seen challenges to secular government institutions by movements carrying the banner of Islam.

Sufism is an ancient mystical movement within Islam, and Sufis stress the goal of unity with God. They are organized in hierarchical orders that prescribe different ways to reach God; some preach total asceticism, while others seem almost hedonistic in their pursuit of pleasure. Sufi *sheikhs* (masters) and saints are reputed to perform miracles, and their tombs are popular pilgrimage destinations. Jalal al-Din Rumi in the thirteenth century founded the famous order of the "whirling dervishes," who wear long skirts, dance and sing to produce a state of mind conducive to unity with God.

FIVE PILLARS OF ISLAM

Allahu akbar. Allahu akbar. Al-hadu an la ilaha illa Allah. Al-hadu anna Muhammadan rasul Allah. "God is greatest. God is greatest. I testify that there is no god but God. I testify that Muhammad is God's Messenger." These words are

TWIST AND SHOUT Known to Westerners as **whirling dervishes**, the **Sufi** sect of Islam began in Konya, Turkey, during the mid-13th century. The origin of the word Sufi is a mystery. Some think that it derives from the root *suf* (wool), used to describe the woolen garments worn by the first members of the sect. Another theory is that Sufi came from the Greek *sophos,* meaning wisdom. The Persian word *darwish* literally means the "sill of the door"—hence, *dervish* would refer to the Sufi who is at the doorstep of paradise or enlightenment. The dervishes hope to cast off mundane worries and reach a higher spiritual plane through their perpetually whirling dance. The ritual is an entrancing display of color and devotion, a dizzying spin during which the dervish throws off cloak after cloak of earthly possession, eventually left with the soaring white fabric of his inner robe. Their spiritual dance likely inspired the "spinners" made famous at **Grateful Dead** concerts.

the **testimony of faith,** or *shahadah,* which is the first of the **five pillars** of Islam. They are also the first lines of the Islamic call to prayer, which is broadcast five times a day from live or recorded *muezzins* perched atop the minarets of mosques. These words reflect the unity of God *(tawhid)* and the special place of Muhammad as God's ultimate messenger. Any person who wishes to convert to Islam may do so simply by repeating these lines three times. Enemies of Islam often memorized the lines before going into battle as an emergency survival tactic.

The second pillar is **prayer** *(salat),* performed five times each day while facing the holy city of Mecca. Each prayer is preceded by ablution (ritual cleansing), begins with a declaration of intent, and consists of a set cycle of recitation and prostration. The Arabic word for Friday *(yom al-jum'a)* means "the day of gathering," and communal prayer is performed on this day.

The third pillar is **alms** *(zakat).* Because all belongs to God, wealth is merely held in trust by human beings, and alms represent the bond between members of a community. Through required charity to those less fortunate, the contributor is purified from selfishness. *Zakat* has been historically administered as a tax, the level of giving is a percentage of the wealth and earnings of the individual.

The fourth pillar of Islam is **fasting** *(sawm),* required during the entire month of Ramadan, the most holy month of the Islamic calendar. Muslims believe that during this month the Qur'an was revealed to the Prophet Muhammad by the angel Gabriel. Muslims fast from sunrise until sunset every day of Ramadan. The holy month ends with Eid al-Fitr, a day of intense celebration and vigorous feasting.

The last pillar is **pilgrimage** *(hajj),* required once per lifetime for those who are financially and physically able to journey to the holy cities of Mecca and Medina (located in what is now Saudi Arabia) during the last month of the Muslim calendar. Worship is focused around the **Ka'aba,** which devout Muslims believe to be the first site of worship built by the first man, Adam, under instruction from God. The *Hajj* unites Muslims and stresses the equal status of all who submit to God. Every worshiper, from the Gulf oil prince to the Cairene street-sweeper, must dress in simple white cloth, remove all accessories, and perform the same rituals. If you travel during the month of *Hajj* (see **Holidays and Festivals, p. 61**), expect delays and pandemonium in airports.

JUDAISM

Neither theologians nor historians can pinpoint a date for the founding of Judaism, but the religion has been evolving for at least four millennia. According to the Bible, **Abraham** first established a covenant with God through his self-circumcision at the ripe old age of 99. This symbolic act is repeated with each generation of Jewish males, but now a ritual circumciser (the *mohel*) performs the honors on the eighth day of life. Abraham's grandson, Jacob, fathered 12 sons from whom the 12 tribes of the Nation of Israel descended. Abraham, his son Isaac, and his grandson Jacob are believed to be buried with their wives (Sarah, Rebecca, and Leah) in the Cave of Machpela in Hebron (see p. 428).

The descendants of Jacob moved to Egypt and settled there, and were eventually **enslaved** by the Egyptian Pharaoh. The Bible recounts that the Jewish nation was founded soon after the Exodus from Egypt, during the generation spent wandering with **Moses** in the Sinai desert en route to the Holy Land. This generation received the **Torah,** the central text of Judaism, from **Yahweh** (usually pronounced "Adonai") at Mt. Sinai. Once the Israelites arrived in the Promised Land, they conquered it from the idol-worshiping natives, most notably the Philistines and Canaanites. An Israelite Kingdom was formed, and worship was eventually centralized at the Temple in its capital, Jerusalem. (Remnants of the temple site can still be seen in the Old City of Jerusalem at the **Western Wall,** p. 297.)

Historians estimate the present form of the **Torah** to be 2500 years old. The Written Torah (a.k.a. the **Pentateuch,** or the Books of Moses), which consists of the first five books of the Bible, formed the foundation for the Oral Torah, a series of interpretations and teachings codified in 200 CE as the *Mishnah.* The *Mishnah,* along with the *Gemara,* is the basis of the Babylonian and Jerusalem Talmuds, edited over centuries and finalized during the 5th century CE. A legal document that forms the basis for *halacha,* or Jewish law, the Talmud was a springboard for interpretations and teachings that continue to build upon each other to this day.

In Judaism, faith in God is central, but the energy of Jewish life is concentrated on observing the commandments, or **mitzvot.** The Torah contains 613 *mitzvot,* including directives for ritual observances and instructions concerning moral behavior. Over the ages, rabbis have interpreted and expanded these commandments. This entire set of laws is called the *halakha* ("the way"). Much of modern Jewish life revolves around the **synagogue.** The *aron ha-kodesh* ("Holy Ark") houses the Torah scrolls and determines the orientation of the synagogue. Synagogues normally face Jerusalem; within Jerusalem, they face the Temple Mount. Above the *aron ha-kodesh* hangs a flickering *ner tamid* ("eternal flame"). Most orthodox synagogues contain a *meḥitza,* a divider between men's and women's sections, which have separate entrances. Men should cover their heads when entering; there is often a box of *kippot,* ritual skullcaps, by the entrance.

CHRISTIANITY

Christianity began in Judaea among the Jewish followers of **Jesus.** The most significant sources on the life of Jesus are the **Gospels.** Scholars agree that the "synoptic gospels" of Mark, Matthew, and Luke were written in that order some time after 70 CE, drawing on an oral tradition that recorded the words of Jesus. The Gospel of John was written about 100 CE but has roots as old as the others. These sources provide a history influenced by the experiences of the church fathers and the belief that Jesus was the **Messiah** ("anointed one").

Various historical events date the birth of Jesus between 7 and 4 BCE. The Bible says that Jesus was spontaneously conceived and brought forth by Mary, a virgin, making him a product of God's creative power and free from humanity's original sin. According to Matthew, **Bethlehem** was the birthplace of Jesus, and Mary and Joseph moved to **Nazareth** to protect him. Jesus was baptized in the Jordan River by **John the Baptist,** a popular evangelist later hailed as the reincarnation of the 9th-century BCE Israelite prophet Elijah, herald of the Messiah. Jesus later preached in the Galilee, speaking for the poor and the righteous, most notably in the Sermon on the Mount (Matthew 5-7). After about three years of preaching, Jesus went to Jerusalem, where the **Passion,** the events leading up to his death, took place. On Good Friday, he carried his cross down the **Via Dolorosa** until he reached the hill of Golgotha (or Calvary), now marked by the Church of the Holy Sepulchre, where he was crucified. According to the Gospels, three days after Jesus' crucifixion, on what is now celebrated as Easter, Mary and two other women went to Jesus' tomb to anoint his body and discovered the tomb empty. An angel announced that Jesus had been resurrected; Jesus subsequently appeared to the Apostles and performed miracles. The **Resurrection** is the point of departure for the Christian faith, the beginning of an age when the faithful await Christ's *parousia,* or second coming.

At first, Christianity was a sect of Judaism, accepting the Hebrew Bible. However, the sect's defining tenet—that Jesus was the Messiah—severed it from mainstream Judaism. **St. Paul** (originally Saul of Tarsus) successfully adapted the faith of Christianity to meet the spiritual needs of the largest body of converts: former pagans. The incorporation of ancient festivals, such as the winter solstice, helped draw the common people to the new religion, and the usage of Platonic doctrines converted many intellectuals. The Christian faith was officially legitimized by the Edict of Milan, issued by Emperor Licinius in 313 CE. In 325 CE, **Emperor Constantine** made Christianity the official religion of the struggling Roman Empire. Constantine also summoned the first of seven Ecumenical Councils, held in Nicaea, to elaborate and unify the content of the faith. The Council of Nicaea came up with an explicit creed, declaring that Jesus Christ was of the same essence as the Father and that there were three equal parts to God. This crucial doctrine of the **Trinity**, which is only implicitly supported in the Gospels, maintains that the Father, Son, and Holy Spirit are distinct persons, yet represent one God.

Despite these unifying dicta, the Christian community suffered many schisms through the centuries. The **Egyptian (Coptic) Church** broke off in the 3rd century (see below), when other eastern branches began to drift away from Western Christianity. In 1054, the **Great Schism** split Christendom into the Roman Catholic Church and the Eastern Orthodox Church. Whereas Rome upheld the universal jurisdiction and infallibility of the Pope, Orthodoxy stressed the infallibility of the church as a whole. In 1517, German monk **Martin Luther** sparked the **Reformation**, which split northern Europe from Roman Catholicism and led to the development of **Protestantism.** Protestantism is itself composed of many sects, which generally believe in salvation through faith rather than good works. Eastern Orthodoxy, too, is divided into multiple national traditions (Greek, Russian, Armenian).

THE COPTIC CHURCH

The term "Copt" is derived from the Greek word for Egyptian, *Ægyptos*, shortened in its Egyptian pronunciation to *qibt.* Copts in Egypt usually have tattoos of a domed cathedral or a tiny cross on their wrists. Of 58 million Egyptians, five to seven million are Copts, most of whom live in Cairo or Middle Egypt. Portions of the liturgy are still in Coptic, though most of the service is in Arabic.

St. Mark introduced Christianity to Egypt in 62 CE. Mass conversions transformed Alexandria into a Christian spiritual center, but Roman persecution also increased. The bloodiest days passed under **Diocletian,** who murdered so many Christians that the Copts date their Martyr's Calendar from 284 CE, the beginning of his reign. In 451 CE, the Alexandrian branch of the Church declared independence from Constantinople, forming the **Coptic Orthodox Church.**

Byzantine Emperor **Justinian** sought to restore unity by exiling Coptic clergy to isolated monasteries. Copts welcomed the Persians as liberators when they captured Egypt in 619. Since the 7th century, the community has lived as a religious minority in an Islamic state. Relations between the Copts and the Muslims have vacillated throughout history. Recently, the Copts felt besieged by Egypt's vocal Islamists, and acts of violence are often aimed at Coptic population centers.

Coptic Christianity served as a link between the Roman and Islamic eras, leaving its own mark on modern Egypt. Coptic art incorporates the influences of pharaonic and Hellenistic cultures. The Coptic cross borrows from the *ankh,* the hieroglyphic sign for "life" (vaguely resembling the human form), as well as from the crucifix on Golgotha. Embroidered tapestries and curtains displaying nymphs and centaurs descend from Greco-Roman mythology. Islamic art often borrows from the Coptic style. Many of Cairo's mosques were engineered by Coptic architects, and some are even converted Coptic churches.

Coptic churches usually have one of three shapes: cruciform, circular (to represent the globe, the spread of Christianity, and the eternal nature of the Word), or ark-shaped (the Ark of the Covenant and Noah's Ark are symbols of salvation). Above Coptic altars hang ostrich eggs, symbolizing Resurrection (life out of lifelessness) and thus God's eternal love and care.

MIDDLE EAST

OTHER FAITHS

THE DRUZE

The faith of the Druze, a staunchly independent sect of Shi'ite Muslims, centers around a hierarchy of individuals who are the sole custodians of a religious doctrine hidden from the rest of the world. Many Druze consider themselves a separate ethnicity as well as a religious group, while others consider themselves Arabs. The Druze believe that the word of God is revealed only to a divinely chosen few, and that these blessed few must be followed to the ends of the earth. Wherever the Druze settle, they generally remain politically loyal to their host country. Syria has a Druze population of about 500,000, Lebanon 300,000, and Israel 85,000.

The religion was founded in 1017 CE by an Egyptian chieftain, **al-Darazi,** who drew upon various beliefs in the Muslim world at the time, especially from Shi'ism. The Druze believe that God was incarnated in human forms, the final incarnation being the Fatimid Caliph al-Hakim. The Druze have suffered a history of persecution and repression for their beliefs, which may partially explain the group's refusal to discuss its religion. The late 1600s was a period of prosperity, however, and under **Emir Fakhr al-Din** the Druze kingdom extended from Lebanon to Gaza and the Golan Heights. In 1830, a Druze revolt against the Egyptian pasha was crushed, along with all but two of the 14 Druze villages in the Carmel. In the 1860s, Ottoman rulers encouraged the Druze to return to the Carmel.

Because the Druze will not discuss their religion, most of what Westerners know about them comes from British "explorers" who fought their way into villages and stole holy books. Some Druze believe in reincarnation. As far as outsiders know, Jethro, father-in-law of Moses, is their most revered prophet. The most important holiday falls in late April. In Israel, Druze gather in the holy village of Ḥittim, near Tiberias. Devout Druze are forbidden to smoke, drink alcohol, or eat pork, but many young Druze do not adhere strictly to these prohibitions.

THE BAHA'I

This movement began in Teheran in 1863 CE, when Mirza Hussein 'Ali renamed himself **Baha'ullah** ("Glory of God") and began preaching non-violence and the unity of all religions. Baha'ullah's arrival had been foretold in 1844 by the Persian **Sa'id 'Ali Muhammad** (or **al-Bab**, "the gateway"), the first prophet of the Baha'i religion. Baha'ullah was exiled to Palestine, where he continued to teach in Acre (Akko). Al-Bab is buried in **Haifa,** Israel (p. 331), which is now home to a large Baha'i population.

Baha'ullah's teachings, which incorporate elements of major Eastern and Western religions, fill over 100 volumes. Baha'i believe in a Supreme Being, accepting Jesus, Buddha, Muhammad, and Baha'ullah as divine prophets. The scripture includes the Bible, the Qur'an, and the Bhagavad Gita. A central doctrine of the faith regards their vision of the future: Baha'ullah prophesied a "flowering of humanity," an era of peace and enlightenment. Before this new age can arrive, however, the world must experience dreadful events to give civilization the impetus to reform itself. The Baha'i espouse trans-racial unity, sexual equality, global disarmament, and the creation of a world community. The faith currently boasts nearly six million adherents, with two million converts in the last decade alone.

THE KARAITES

The small sect of Jews known as the Karaites dwell principally in Ashdod, Be'er Sheva, and the Tel Aviv suburb of Ramla. The community, whose existence dates to the 9th century CE, numbers about 15,000 today. Formed out of the political and religious turmoil following the Muslim invasion, Karaites adhere strictly to the five books of the **written Torah** and reject all later Jewish traditions. They are generally cohesive and have their own synagogues and religious courts.

THE SAMARITANS

Today, the Samaritan community is a small one, with roughly 550 adherents divided between Nablus (on the West Bank) and Ashkelon (a suburb of Tel Aviv). Originally the residents of Samaria, Samaritans consider themselves the original Israelites, descended from the tribes of Joseph (Manasseh and Ephraim), from whom other Israelites learned monotheism. The religion is seen by non-members as an offshoot of Judaism marked by literal interpretation of the Samaritan version of the Old Testament and the exclusion of later Jewish interpretation (the *Mishnah*, the Talmud, and all books of the Hebrew Bible after Joshua). A gradual, centuries-long separation between the two religions culminated in the destruction of the Samaritan temple on Mt. Gerizim by the Hasmonean king **John Hyrcanus** in 128 BCE. The mountain is still the most holy site of the Samaritan religion. Centuries of persecution by the various rulers of Palestine and thousands of deaths in a 529 CE uprising against Byzantine rule shrank the community further. While the Rabbinate does not recognize Samaritans as Jews, the Israeli government applies the Law of Return, granting them settlement rights in Israel.

HOLIDAYS AND FESTIVALS

Islamic holidays are timed to local sightings of the moon, so dates are not set until the last minute and differ from country to country. **Jewish** holidays last from sundown one day until sundown the next day. For longer holidays, businesses are closed for the first and last day, but remain open the rest of the time. The **holy day** (when many business are closed) is Friday *(Juma'a)* in the Muslim world and Saturday *(shabbat)* in Israel. Businesses typically close on national holidays as well. **Christian** holidays listed are those of the Eastern Orthodox or Maronite Church, and are celebrated among Christians in Syria, Lebanon, and Cyprus.

DATE	FESTIVAL	TYPE
Nov. 1, 2001	All Saints' Day	Christian
Nov. 15	First Day of Ramadan (approximation)	Islamic
Nov. 22	Independence Day	Lebanese
Dec. 10-17	Ḥanukkah	Jewish
Dec. 12	Laylat al-Qadr	Islamic
Dec. 16	'Eid al-Fitr (end of Ramadan)	Islamic
Dec. 25	Christmas	Christian
Jan. 7, 2001	Epiphany	Christian
Jan. 30	King Abdullah's Birthday	Jordanian
Feb. 9	Mar Maroun (Feast of St. Maron)	Christian (Lebanon)
Feb. 23	'Eid al-Adha (Feast of the Sacrifice)	Islamic
Feb. 26	Purim	Jewish
Mar. 8	Revolution Day	Syrian
Mar. 16	Muharram (Islamic New Year)	Islamic
Mar. 21	Women's Day (Mother's Day)	Syrian
Mar. 22	Arab League Day	Syrian
Mar. 25	Ashoura	Islamic
Mar 28 - Apr. 3	Pesaḥ (Passover)	Jewish
Apr. 8	Yom Ha-Shoah	Israeli
Apr. 13	Good Friday	Christian
Apr. 15	Easter	Christian
Apr. 17	Yom Ha-Atzma'ut (Israel Independence Day)	Israeli
Apr. 17	Evacuation Day (Independence Day)	Syrian
Apr. 23	National Independence and Children's Day	Turkish
May 1	Labor Day	Cypriot, Jordanian
May 6	Martyr's Day	Lebanese, Syrian

MIDDLE EAST

DATE	FESTIVAL	TYPE
May 10	Yom Yerushalayim (Jerusalem Day)	Jewish
May 17	Shavuot	Jewish
May 19	Atatürk's Commemoration/Youth & Sports Day	Turkish
May 25	'Eid Mawlid al-Nabi (Birth of the Prophet)	Islamic
May 25	Independence Day	Jordanian
June 3	Pentecost	Christian
June 10	Army Day and Anniversary of the Great Revolt	Jordanian
June 18	Evacuation Day (Liberation Day)	Egyptian
July 23	Revolution Day	Egyptian
Aug. 15	Assumption of the Virgin Mary	Christian
Aug. 30	Victory Day	Turkish
Sept. 7 - 8	Rosh Ha-Shana (Jewish New Year)	Jewish
Sept. 16	Yom Kippur	Jewish
Sept. 21 - 22	Sukkot	Jewish
Oct. 4	Isra' and Miraj	Islamic
Oct. 6	National Day (Armed Forces Day)	Egyptian
Oct. 6	October War Day	Syrian
Oct. 24	Suez and National Liberation Day	Egyptian
Oct. 28 - 29	Simḥat Torah	Jewish
Oct. 29	Republic Day	Turkish
Nov. 1	All Saints' Day	Christian
Nov. 6	First Day of Ramadan	Islamic
Nov. 16	National Day	Syrian
Nov. 22	Independence Day	Lebanese
Nov. 20 - Dec. 7	Ḥanukkah	Jewish
Dec. 6	'Eid al-Fitr (end of Ramadan)	Islamic
Dec. 23	Victory Day	Egyptian
Dec. 25	Christmas	Christian

EGYPT مصر

EGYPTIAN POUND (E£)		
US$1 = E£4.00	E£1 = US$0.25	
CDN$1 = E£2.60	E£1 = CDN$0.40	
UK£1 = E£5.63	E£1 = UK£0.17	
IR£1 = E£4.40	E£1 = IR£0.22	
AUS$1 = E£2.00	E£1 = AUS$0.50	
NZ$1 = E£1.60	E£1 = NZ$0.60	
ZAR1 = E£0.50	E£1 = ZAR2.00	
EUR€1 = E£3.50	E£1 = EUR€0.30	
JD1 (JORDANIAN DINAR) = E£6.00	E£1 = JD0.17	
L£100 (LEBANESE POUNDS) = E£0.28	E£1 = L£358	
NIS1 (NEW ISRAELI SHEKEL)= E£1.00	E£1 = NIS1.00	
S£1 (SYRIAN POUND) = E£0.08	E£1 = S£12.6	
TL100,000 (TURKISH LIRA) = E£0.29	E£1 = TL347,000	

PHONE CODES   **Country Code: 20. International Dialing Prefix: 00.**

EGYPT

The Arab Republic of Egypt (*Gomhoriyyat Misr al-'Arabiyya*, or simply *Misr*) is home to natural and man-made wonders that are rivaled only by its 5000 years of rich recorded history. A quarter of the Arab world lives in Egypt, despite the fact that the driest desert in the world, the Western Desert, makes up almost all (97%) of the country's land mass. The Nile, the longest and most fertile river in the world, stretches its arms across this region full of ancient temple ruins and glittering desert oases, welcoming the Mediterranean with the open hands of its Delta. The Nile Delta cradles several jewels in its palm: the breathtaking Pyramids at Giza (and their predecessor at Saqqara, the oldest monument in the world); the dizzying streets and dazzling mosques of Cairo, the largest city in the Middle East and Africa; and cosmopolitan Alexandria, once home to the greatest library in the world. The mainland of Egypt is divided into Upper Egypt in the south (including Aswan, Luxor, and Nubia, the region where African and Egyptian culture merge), Middle Egypt, and Lower Egypt in the north. This orientation comes from the fact that the Nile flows upstream from the south toward the Mediterranean. The Sinai Peninsula is its own rugged wonderland: at its heart, hikers trudge through desert containing some of the oldest and most sacred religious sites in the world; along the coast, scuba divers plunge into the azure depths of the Red Sea, known as one of the planet's premiere underwater sightseeing spots.

Egypt is a budget traveler's paradise. The sights are stunning, the culture is fascinating, and bargains are a way of life. However, travel here requires plenty of time, stamina, and patience. Most travelers find that with a relaxed attitude, the difficulties of navigating the hassles are surpassed by the intensity and beauty of the experiences Egypt has to offer.

▨ HIGHLIGHTS OF EGYPT

MARVEL at the funerary monuments that are the **Pyramids at Giza** (p. 126).

PARLEZ-VOUS Siwi, language of the Berber community of the **Siwa Oasis** (p. 162)?

RELIVE the past with Mark Antony and Cleopatra at Lover's Beach, in **Marsa Matrouh** (**p. 161**), the jewel of the Mediterranean coast.

WALK like a pharaoh in the Temples of **Luxor** (p. 217) and **Karnak** (p. 218).

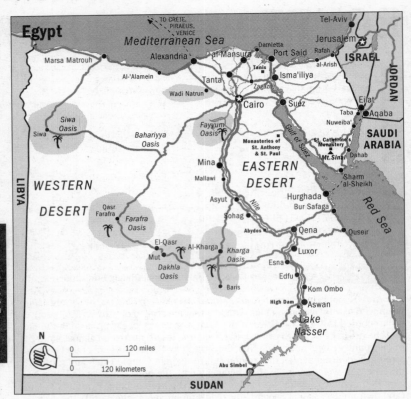

LIFE AND TIMES

Egypt is home to one of the principal civilizations of the ancient Middle East and one of the earliest urban and literate societies in the world. Its culture had an important influence on both ancient Israel and ancient Greece, which in turn helped to shape modern Western civilization.

Egypt has always been a transit hub—ships and caravans passed traveled westward along the coast of North Africa, northwest to Europe, northeast to the Levant, south along the Nile to Africa, and southeast to the Indian Ocean and the Far East. This natural advantage was enhanced in 1869 by the opening of the Suez Canal, connecting the Mediterranean Sea to the Red Sea. The concern of the European powers to safeguard the Suez Canal for strategic and commercial reasons has probably been the single most important influence on the history of Egypt since the 19th century.

HISTORY

ANCIENT HISTORY (2925 BCE–642 CE)

According to the famous **Narmer Palette** (an ancient mascara holder discovered along the Nile in 1898 CE), **King Menes** was the first true pharaoh of Egypt, uniting Upper (southern) and Lower (northern) Egypt in 2925 BCE. His kingdom, centered at Hierakonpolis, was one of the longest lasting and most powerful in all of history, enduring until Narmer was fatally mauled by a hippopotamus.

OLD KINGDOM. The pharaohs of the **Old Kingdom** (2575-2130 BCE) built a new capital at Memphis as Imhotep, history's first recorded architect, began constructing the step pyramids at Saqqara—the forerunners of the later pharoahs' self-indulgent mausolea at Giza. Most view this era as the pinnacle of ancient Egyptian civilization: at a time when even China had scarcely emerged from the Stone Age Egyptians had invented writing and papyrus, forged a national economy, recorded the history of eight dynasties of pharaohs, and built some of history's most impressive structures. Believed to be earthly manifestations of the falcon-god **Horus,** the all-powerful pharaohs feared only death; their most magnificent monuments represent attempts to defeat this ultimate enemy.

MIDDLE KINGDOM. The rise of **Mentuhotep II** ushered in the **Middle Kingdom** (1938-1600 BCE), an era of conservatism and order; nevertheless, internal political rivalries began to weaken the Egyptian dynasties in the 18th century BCE. Taking advantage of this vulnerable state, the chariot-riding **Hyksos** from the North penetrated the desert citadels at Thebes and ravished the Egyptian countryside.

NEW KINGDOM. Upon the expulsion of the Hyksos by the ever-plotting Theban princes almost a century later, Egypt was resurrected as the **New Kingdom** (1539-1075 BCE). Thebes became the center of a theocratic police state. The high priests of the sun (now embodied in the god **Amun**) wielded unimaginable power, often controlling the pharaoh himself. Egypt "modernized" its formerly primitive army by adapting the bronze weapons and horse-drawn chariots of the Hyksos and immediately proceeded to invade Africa, Palestine, and Syria. Now an empire ruled by warrior-kings, Egypt established control over most of the eastern Mediterranean. Trade in wood, olive oil, and slaves brought stability and prosperity, though the rivalry between the pharaoh and priests of Amun stirred things up a bit.

THE ROMANS. Despite the thriving economy and the achievements of aggressive pharaohs such as **Thutmose III** and the monumentally egotistical **Ramses II,** the New Kingdom slowly crumbled, and a slew of invaders had their way with it. First the Libyans, then the Palestinians, then the Assyrians, Kushites, and Persians took turns conquering and ruling Egypt. When **Alexander the Great** arrived in 332 BCE, he freed the Egyptians from Persian rule and was declared the son of Amun and the legitimate pharaoh of Egypt by the Oracle of Amun in the Siwa Oasis (oh yeah, he also founded a dinky little town and named it after himself: Alexandria). In 48 BCE, more than a century after Rome made its first overtures to the ever-feuding Ptolemies (descendants of Alexander's successor, Ptolemy), **Julius Caesar** came to Egypt and made similar advances to **Cleopatra VII,** Queen of Egypt. She accepted an alliance with Caesar that left her secure until his assassination four years later. Cleopatra also formed a politico-sexual alliance with **Marc Antony,** one of the three men vying to succeed Caesar. While Antony was otherwise occupied, third wheel **Octavian** grabbed the empire for himself in 30 BCE, ruthlessly crushing the affair and the Ptolemaic dynasty at the **Battle of Actium.** At the height of the battle, both Cleopatra and Antony withdrew. The two fled to Alexandria but could do little more than await the arrival of the victorious Octavian. Alexandria was captured and Antony and Cleopatra committed suicide—he by falling on his sword, she by the bite of an asp (or so the legend goes).

The Egypt of Imperial Rome and Byzantium was characterized by political stability and an increasingly entrenched bureaucracy (two traditions that modern Egypt has wholeheartedly embraced). During this period, Egypt was also the breadbasket of the Mediterranean, supplying most of the grain needed to support the empire's growing urban population. Christianity arrived in Egypt around 40 CE with **St. Mark** and helped maintain relative social tranquility. Some argument arose over the personage of Jesus Christ: the **Copts** worshiped him only as a divine figure, whereas the church at Constantinople believed he was both divine and human. This long-festering argument exploded in 451 CE when the Copts were excommunicated and forced to set up their own church in Alexandria. The modern-day Coptic minority in Egypt is descended from these original dissidents (see **Religion and Culture,** p. 69).

EGYPT

MEDIEVAL HISTORY (639-1798 CE)

Medieval Egyptian history opened and closed with outsiders' conquests: the Arab invasion led by **'Amir ibn al-'As** in 639 CE and the Napoleonic expedition of 1798 CE. In the interim, Egypt embraced a new language and religion.

DO THESE PANTS MAKE ME LOOK FATIMID? To facilitate the slow process of Arabization, the **Umayyad** and **Abbasid** caliphates adopted policies of tolerance toward Copts and other non-Muslims, as long as they paid their taxes. Ahmad ibn Tulun came to power and established the **Tulunid dynasty** in 868 CE. Though initially stable because of strong military and expansionist policies, the death of the dynasty in 905 created chaos, to be left unresolved by the **Ikhshidid dynasty.** In 969, the **Fatimids**—one of the most influential families in the history of Egypt—came to power. They enacted grand policies of Islamization, while also improving trade by means of low tariffs and good relations with merchants. The fall of Fatimid rule in 1171 came with the rise in power of **Salah al-Din,** a commander from Syria. He restored Egypt to Abbasid allegiance and founded the **Ayyubid** dynasty. The Ayyubids were generally well liked, but al-Din and his successors were too busy fighting the **Crusaders** to enjoy their popularity. The Ayyubids were also weakened by their nepotistic delegation of family members to provincial posts, a policy that led to unneccessary infighting.

MAMLUK WHO'S TALKING. The only real security for Ayyubid Egypt lay in its independent military strength. In order to maintain this advantage in the face of deteriorating control, one of the last sultans, **al-Malik al-Salih Ayyub** was forced to purchase Turkish slaves, **Mamluks,** to man his armies. After the death of al-Salih Ayyub in 1250 CE, the Mamluks were able to exploit a palace feud and elevate a member of their own ranks to the sultanate. Their rule lasted for two and a half centuries and brought Egypt to the peak of its evolution in the medieval period.

From 1250 to 1517, the Mamluks, a group of non-Arab, non-Muslims, established a regime that protected Muslims and preserved Muslim territory. Arabic became the national language, while the military established a haven for Muslims in Syria and Egypt. Under the Mamluks, mosques, colleges, hospitals, and monasteries were built and encyclopedias, chronicles, and dictionaries written. The **Ottomans** conquered the region in 1517, ending the Mamluks' 300-year reign and ushering in their own three-century-long rule.

MODERN HISTORY (1798-PRESENT)

FROM ZEUS TO SUEZ. The invasion of Napoleon Bonaparte's French expeditionary forces in 1798 CE was too short-lived and too universally loathed to have any major impact at the time, but as the first European conquest of an Arab country in the history of Islam, the invasion marks the beginning of a colonial trend that lasted into the 20th century.

Europe was still looking for a shortcut to the mysteries (and trade possibilities) of India, and all eyes turned to the Suez region. Europe and the Ottomans fought for control of the region, as Britain and France gradually emerged as the real rulers, as Egypt fell into deeper and deeper debt to the European powers. In 1859, the French Suez Canal Company began construction on the **Suez Canal,** which connected the Mediterranean Sea to the Red Sea upon its completion in 1869. The rigid Ottoman Empire grew flaccid in the later years of the 19th century, and in 1882 the Brits moved in, beginning their 74-year occupation of Egypt (though the Ottoman sultan maintained nominal control of the country until World War 1).

THE KINGDOM OF EGYPT. After World War I ended, the nationalist *Wafd* ("delegation") party rose to power and demanded complete autonomy from Britain, however the deportation in 1918 of *Wafd* leader, Sa'ad Zaghloul, showed that the British had other plans. Though they eventually recognized Egypt's independence in 1922, the British maintained control through puppet-king **Fouad I.** Not content to have his strings pulled by far-distant imperialists, Fouad struggled successfully for some power of his own; soon the British, Fouad, and the popularly supported *Wafd* party were all fighting for control of Egypt. The Anglo-Egyptian Treaty of 1936 ended the three-way tug-of-war for control by granting Egypt independence but allowing for continued British occupation of the Suez Canal Zone.

Egypt again came to center stage as an Allied base of operations during World War II. The decisive Allied victory at the **Battle of al-'Alamein** (just outside Alexandria, p. 157) allowed the Allies to sweep into North Africa and halt the advances of Nazi General Edwin Rommel's Afrika Korps once and for all. Resentment toward the British reached a fever pitch during and after World War II as Egyptians rioted against being forced to participate in a war they had nothing to do with. Continued rioting and striking led the British to finally leave Alexandria and the Suez in 1947.

The newborn Egyptian government didn't wait long before taking its first, hesitant steps. In 1948, Egypt and the entire Arab world was humiliated when a joint Arab army was easily defeated by the smaller army of the new state of Israel. Several young officers were so outraged at the incompetence of their elder leaders that they formed the **Free Officers** coalition and staged a bloodless coup of the government on July 26, 1952. The king, Farouk, was forced to abdicate, all political parties and Constitution were abolished, and General Muhammad Naguib was elected Prime Minister (although the government was really controlled by a nine-member Revolutionary Command Council led by Colonel **Gamal 'Abd al-Nasser**).

THE NASSER REVOLUTION(S). Nasser officially assumed presidency of the Egyptian Arab Republic in 1956. Equal parts brilliant strategist and power-obsessed dictator, he gained popularity because of his dedication to the plight of the *fellaheen* (peasant) majority in Egypt. One of Nasser's first major political moves was the controversial nationalization of the Suez Canal after a lack of Western financial support for the **Aswan High Dam.** During his presidency, Arabic nationalism was born, reached its peak, and died out; as a result, Nasser's name is synonymous with **pan-Arabism.** In 1958, Egypt and Syria united, forming the United Arab Republic; this ended during the **Six-Day War** (July 5–10) of 1967, when Israeli armies managed to gain control of the Sinai Peninsula (as well as other strategic locations). Three years later, the crumbling movement for pan-Arabism was dealt a fatal blow with the death of Nasser on September 28, 1970.

SADAT AND PEACE WITH ISRAEL. Following Nasser's death, Vice President **Anwar Sadat,** also a Free Soldier, took over the show. Sadat maintained the election-legitimated authoritarian regime (which it remains to this day) set up by Nasser, though he dismantled many of the most oppressive features of Nasser's nearly totalitarian rule. The conservative-leaning Sadat was more sympathetic to the West and free markets than the socialist Nasser, and he perceived peace with Israel and alliance with the United States as being in Egypt's long-term interests. But to pursue a course of reconciliation, Sadat decided first to go on the offensive.

On October 6, 1973 (Yom Kippur), Sadat attacked Israeli forces in the Sinai. Although this **October War** ended in a stalemate, the Arab world experienced an incredible morale boost. Having regained a stronger hand at the bargaining table, Sadat was able to work out the **Sinai I** and **II** agreements with Israel in 1974-75, returning parts of the peninsula to Egyptian control. On November 17, 1977, Sadat made a dramatic visit to Jerusalem to address the Israeli Parliament. In 1978, Sadat and Israeli Prime Minister **Menaḥem Begin** reached a comprehensive peace agreement, in which Egypt recognized Israel's right to exist and normalized relations with its neighbor in exchange for control of the Sinai. The West embraced Sadat, award him and Begin the 1978 **Nobel Peace Prize** for negotiating these **Camp David Accords.** But Sadat's domestic support was crumbling: never the debonair figurehead Nasser had been, many Arabs saw him as a sell-out and a yes-man to Western interests. Sadat was assassinated by Islamic fundamentalists at a military parade in October 1981.

EGYPT

IF IT AIN'T MUBARAK, DON'T FIX IT. Current President **Hosni Mubarak,** elected in 1981, continued his predecessor's policies with less derring-do and more domestic sensitivity. Mubarak was responsible for developing Egypt's growing tourism industry, resuming diplomatic and trade relations with moderate Arab countries, and bandaging the wounds made by the flamboyant swathe Sadat cut through Arab politics. Mubarak's support of Saudi Arabia and Kuwait in the **Gulf War** in 1990-91 was important in restoring Egypt's position at the center of Middle Eastern politics. The most significant political threat to President Mubarak's regime continues to be internal Arab dissidents, in the form of the Islamist parties. Sadat was assassinated by militants who wanted to overthrow the Egyptian government and establish an Islamic republic in its place. Mubarak has consistently appeased Islamic moderates (who are in the majority anyway) in order to isolate militants: alcohol was banned on EgyptAir flights, the American show *Dallas* was taken off television, and an Islamic newspaper, *al-Liwa' al-Islami,* was initiated. The past few years have seen a rise in Islamist-generated violence, with militants based in Middle Egypt striking at the status quo via attacks on government figures and assassinations of secularist intellectuals. The deadliest attack by Islamist militants killed 58 tourists at Luxor on November 17, 1997, leading the government to drastically tighten security throughout the country.

IN THE NEWS

Egypt's tourism industry, which was electrified by the shocking 1997 terrorist attack at Luxor, appeared to have made a brilliant recovery; but since the Israeli-Palestinian violence that broke out in September 2000, tourism in Egypt has gone back into a slump (though it remains safe to travel in the country). Relations with Israel, not surprisingly, have taken a similar turn. When Israeli troops bombarded the Gaza Strip in November 2000 in response to Palestinian terrorist attacks, Egyptians considered the reprisal to be an overreaction, and Mubarak recalled the Egyptian ambassador from Tel Aviv in protest. On the other hand, Egypt and Israel were able to reach a very different sort of agreement in January 2001, when the two nations inked a US$3 billion deal under which Egypt will supply its neighbor with natural gas until 2012. Despite regional conflict, it seems that business-as-usual is the order of the day in Egypt. In April 2001, US Secretary of Defense **Donald Rumsfeld** announced the Bush Administration's intention to remove American peacekeeping troops from the Sinai.

Meanwhile, Mubarak has come under increased fire for the persistent authoritarianism of his rule. Although reforms have been made, Egypt is still worlds away from being a legitimate democracy. No opposition candidates are permitted to stand in presidential "elections," which are really no more than referenda to rubber stamp Mubarak's continued rule. In the last four of these yea-or-nay propositions, Mubarak has won—on average—96 percent of the vote. In May 2001, Mubarak drew major heat when **Sa'ad Eddin Ibrahim**—a prominent Egyptian-American sociologist and advocate of civil rights and increased democracy in Egypt—was sent to prison for seven years. The trumped-up charges: accepting money from abroad without the government's permission, embezzling funds, and "defaming Egypt." Even after the conviction drew the outrage of human rights organizations, the United Nations, the European Union, and the Western media, Mubarak refused to override the verdict (which was reached by a panel of three Cairo judges even before the defense team had finished turning over its evidence). The trial has led many to question just how far Egypt has moved toward political liberalization—and whether the pressure of dealing with Egypt's substantial radical right (Muslim and otherwise) has gotten to the aging Mubarak. To make matters worse, 52 men were simultaneously charged in July 2001 with engaging in immoral acts—the largest **anti-gay** trial in Egyptian history—leading Egypt's increasingly vocal gay community to claim that the government has stepped up harrassment of gays in recent months.

RELIGION AND CULTURE

ISLAM

Islam is constitutionally established as the official religion of Egypt, with over 90% of the population belonging to the **Sunni Muslim** sect. Western mores do not apply, especially in matters of family and sex. The visibility and freedom of most Egyptian women is limited. Egypt is one of the most important centers of Islamic theological study in the world, with Cairo's **al-Azhar University** (p. 108) at its heart. Al-Azhar is the oldest continuously operating university in the world and has graduated Islamic scholars from every Muslim country on earth since it was first founded in 972 CE. For more on the history and theology of Islam, see p. 55.

COPTIC CHURCH

Orthodox Christians (who belong to the **Coptic Church**) make up Egypt's largest and most significant religious minority, with population estimates somewhere between three and seven million. The relationship between the Copts and the Muslim government has always been strained, but with the rise of Muslim fundamentalism, tensions between the Muslim majority and the Coptic minority have erupted, resulting in acts of vandalism. Another one million or so members of the Egyptian population are Roman Catholic, Greek or Armenian Orthodox Christian, Protestant, and Jewish. These groups thrived in colonial times but have dwindled in number due to emigration. For more on the Coptic Church, see p. 59.

LANGUAGE

ANCIENT EGYPTIAN LANGUAGE

One of the earliest forms of writing was Egyptian **hieroglyphs** (sacred carvings). Alongside this pictorial system developed the **hieratic,** an abbreviated cursive script that retained only the vital characteristics of the pictures. After the 22nd Dynasty, scribes began using the sacred hieratic writing in a secular context, leading to the rise of a form known as Enchorial or **Demotic.** Eventually, even the sacred *Book of the Dead* (a compilation of spells and cult rituals) was translated into this script. Modern scholars owe much of their knowledge of ancient Egyptian linguistics to the **Rosetta Stone,** a stone tablet dating from around 200 BCE that contains the same passage celebrating the crowning of King Ptolemy V recorded in hieroglyphic, Demotic, and Greek script. **Coptic,** today used only in liturgy, is a derivation of ancient Egyptian that uses the Greek alphabet plus six additional letters.

ARABIC

Egyptian is the most widely understood dialect because of Egypt's prolific film and television industry. It's also considered to be the best dialect in which to tell jokes. The main phonetic difference between the Egyptian and Levantine (includes the dialects of Jordan, Syria, Lebanon, the West Bank and Gaza) pronunciation is that in Egypt the Levantine *j* sound (as in Julia) becomes a hard *g* (as in gulf, so Egyptians would say "Gulia"). In Upper (south) Egypt, the Nubians, or Sa'idis, replace the Classical Arabic *q* with a hard *g*. For more on the Arabic language and a phrasebook of useful terms, see p. 701. For a glossary of Arabic terms and common Middle Easter foods, see p. 708.

THE ARTS

LITERATURE

Most of the writings of the ancient Egyptians, such as the *Book of the Dead*, deal with magic and religion. The ancients dabbled in poetic love songs as well. Modern literature in Egypt is synonymous with the name of Cairene novelist **Naguib Mahfouz.** In 1988, Mahfouz became the first Arab to win the Nobel Prize for literature.

MEET THE GODS

The ancient Egyptians didn't play that monotheism game. Here's a brief rundown on their many deities:

AMUN "The Hidden One." Amun is typically portrayed as a ram-horned man with blue-colored flesh. In the New Kingdom he became associated with the sun-god Ra, and "Amun-Ra" became the king of the gods and a father figure to the pharaohs.

ANUBIS The jackal-headed god of cemeteries and embalming, whose black skin represents either the silt of the Nile or mummy flesh treated with chemicals. He is usually depicted weighing the hearts of the dead (the heart was considered the center of intellect and emotions) against Maat, the feather of truth.

ATON The sun at noon, usually depicted as a disk from which rays extend ending in outstretched hands holding *ankhs* (a Coptic cross). The heretical 18th dynasty pharaoh Akhenaton worshiped Aton as the one and only god, with the pharaoh as his one and only priest.

GEB The earth god, usually depicted as a reclining man holding up his sister-wife Nut (the sky goddess). He divided Egypt in two, giving Lower Egypt to his son Osiris and Upper Egypt to his son Seth.

HAPY The symbol of the Nile's annual flooding. He is depicted as a seaweed-tressed man with breasts and a rounded abdomen (representing fertility).

HATHOR The daughter of Ra, the goddess of joy and love, and the protectoress of women and travelers. She usually hangs out on tomb walls sporting cow horns with a sun disk between them.

HORUS The hawk-headed sky god and son of Isis and Osiris. When Seth cut out his eyes (they were later glued back on with divine saliva), they came to represent perfection and were known as a guard against evil (the *wedjat* eye).

ISIS Another sister-wife (to Osiris), usually depicted with a throne on her head. She is the protectoress and healer of children.

KHNUM Ram-headed potter god who sculpted both gods and men out of clay. He is known for controlling the Nile's annual flood.

KHONSU As the moon god, this young man holds the posture of a mummy wearing a moon disk on his shoulders. He is the son of Mut and Amun, thus completing the Theban triad. Also revered as the god of time and known as a lover of games.

MAAT The personification of cosmic order, usually depicted as a woman wearing an ostrich feather on her head.

MUT Symbolic mother of the pharaoh and Thebes's principal goddess (wife of Amun), who often appears as a lion-headed woman wearing a vulture-shaped headdress.

NUT Cow-shaped goddess of the sky and yet another sister-wife (to Geb), usually depicted stretched across the ceiling of a tomb, swallowing the sun and making the night. She is the mother of Osiris, Isis, Seth, and Nephthys.

OSIRIS The mummified god of the underworld and fertility and brother of Isis. Seth was so bitter when Geb divided up Egypt that he dismembered his brother Osiris and buried his body parts across Egypt. Isis collected the pieces and bandaged them together, making the first mummy; as a thank-you gift, Osiris fathered Horus by Isis before he headed for Duat (the underworld) to rule as lord and judge of the dead.

RA Don't mess with Ra, the falcon-headed sun god with a sun disc upon his head who is so powerful that other gods often merge with him to enhance their own powers (Amun-Ra). He rides across the sky in his solar boat, rising from Duat (the underworld) in the east and reentering the land of the dead in the west.

SETH God of chaotic forces, synonymous with evil in much of Egyptian mythology. He performs his one good deed when he spears the evil snake Apophis as the boat of Ra begins its entry into the underworld every evening.

THOTH The ibis-headed scribe god, inventor of writing, and divine reckoner of time. Thoth sometimes took the form of a great white baboon with a giant penis.

Mahfouz's major work in the 1950s was *The Cairo Trilogy (Palace Walk, Palace of Desire*, and *Sugar Street)*, which seamlessly depicts the life of three generations in Cairo from World War I to the 1950s. His classic allegory *Children of Gebelawi* (1959), banned throughout the Arab world except in Lebanon, retells the stories of the Qur'an in a modern-day Cairo setting.

Notable among more contemporary authors is Alexandrene novelist and essayist **Edward al-Kharrat,** who is considered the father of modernism in Egyptian literature. His popular novels *City of Saffron* (1989) and *Girls of Alexandria* (1993) are both available in translation. Doctor, feminist, and novelist **Nawal al-Saadawi** stands out among women authors with her extensive writings (including the notable works *The Circling Song* and *The Naked Face of Arab Women*) on the psychological, sexual, and legal liberation of the Arab woman. Her works were once considered so controversial they were banned in her native country, and she herself has been imprisoned for a year and forbidden from practicing medicine in Egypt because of the perceived danger she poses to society.

Many non-Egyptians have written accounts of their travels and experiences within the country. In *The Innocents Abroad*, Mark Twain describes his misadventures in Egypt and other countries. For an engrossing—if oversexed—account of Alexandrene life, don't miss Lawrence Durrell's multi-narrator epic, *The Alexandria Quartet*. For an eye-opening account of early Western explorers roaming the Nile, read Alan Moorehead's *The White Nile* and its companion volume, *The Blue Nile*, which include hair-raising chapters on the French invasion of Egypt and the rise of Muhammad 'Ali. Michael Ondaatje's award-winning *The English Patient* contains sensual and incredibly accurate descriptions of early desert expeditions in the area.

MUSIC

Traditional Egyptian folk music incorporates nasal horns churning out repetitive melodies to the incessant beat of drums. **Nubian music** (called *musiqa nubiyya* in Aswan) is equally enthralling. In general, it eliminates the horns and focuses on slow drumbeats and chanting choruses. The music blaring from taxis, *ahwas*, and homes throughout Egypt is a slightly updated version of this traditional classical music. Egypt is the capital of the Arab music industry and the promised land for aspiring artists from all over the Arab world. Sayyid Darwish and the legendary **Muhammad 'Abd al-Wahhab** began as early as the 1910s and '20s to integrate Western instrumentation and techniques into Arabic song. Like Egyptian cinema, this type of music had its heyday in the '50s and '60s but shows no signs of waning in popularity today. In the '60s, the emphasis fell on strong, beautiful voices to unite Arabic music's disparate elements, and several "greats" of Egyptian music emerged. The greatest of these was the unmistakable and unforgettable **Umm Kulthum.** Her rags-to-riches story begins in the provinces, where her father dressed her up as a boy to sing with him at religious festivals; it ends in 1975 with a funeral that was bigger than President Nasser's five years earlier. In the interim, Umm Kulthum gave speeches, starred in musical films, and sang everything from post-revolutionary propaganda songs to love ballads. Travelers in Egypt cannot and should not escape without hearing Umm Kulthum's voice and seeing her sunglasses-clad face on a television screen or wall mural. Music in the '80s and '90s saw a wholesale incorporation of Western influences. Modern Egyptian pop is totally danceable, mostly pre-packaged, and rarely long-lived. Among these transitory teen dreams, **Amr Diab** has endured as the best-selling Arab recording artist of all time. His upbeat songs provide sing-along material at weddings, parties, and discos.

CINEMA

Egypt has had a near monopoly on the Arabic entertainment industry for most of the second half of the 20th century, ranking behind only Hollywood (United States) and Bollywood (India) in its prolific output. Egyptian films range from skillfully made modern dramas to comedies that pit down-and-out students against evil capitalists and bumbling police officers, with a smattering of southern Egyptians (portrayed as idiots) thrown in for comic relief.

The '50s and '60s were the golden age of Egyptian cinema, when Alexandrene **Omar Sharif** (*Doctor Zhivago*, *Funny Girl*) ruled as an international film superstar and his former wife Fatin Hamama presided as queen of Arab cinema. The musicals of that period are still very popular, and feature well-dressed hipsters knitting their brows in consternation over the cruelty of love, the generation gap, and the difficulty of college examinations. Controversial auteur **Yusef Chahine** (credited with discovering Omar Sharif in a Cairo cafe and catapulting him to fame with 1954's *Blazing Sun*) has gained international acclaim for his lushly filmed, genre-bending masterpieces that tackle everything from sexual discovery to the hypocrisy of Western society. *The Emigrant* (1994) was initially banned in Egypt for depicting images of the Prophet Muhammad (which is forbidden in the Muslim religion), but became a box office hit once the ban was lifted. His recent work includes *Destiny* (1997), which attacks modern Islamic fundamentalism by recounting the persecution of the Islamic philosopher Averroes.

The levying of heavy entertainment taxes in the '70s and the general atmosphere of profiteering in the '80s served to lower drastically the standards of modern Egyptian cinema to somewhere below chintzy tragicomedy. A new guard of young directors has begun to revitalize the industry by tackling such once-taboo topics as social conditions, terrorism, and the country's volatile relationship with Israel

FOOD AND DRINK

The Egyptian breakfast of choice is **fuul** ("fool")—cooked, mashed fava beans blended with garlic, lemon, olive oil, and salt that are eaten with bread and vegetables. What's known as falafel elsewhere—chick peas and/or fava beans mashed, shaped into balls, and fried—is called **ta'amiyya** in Egypt, and both *ta'amiyya* and *fuul* are sold at street stands everywhere. Street vendors also sell *kibdeh* (liver) sandwiches, which don't score high on the smell test but go down quite scrumptiously. **Shawarma** made its way from the Levant to Egypt only recently; it is supposed to be sinfully fatty lamb rolled into a pita with vegetables and *tahina*, but Egyptians will slap any sort of meat into bogus French bread and call it *shawarma*. Popular **kushari** is a cheap, filling meal of pasta, lentils, and dried onions in tomato sauce.

At times you might feel that all you will ever get to eat will be *kofta*, kebab, and chicken. These carnivore's wet-dreams are almost always served with salads, bread or rice, and *tahina*, a sesame-based sauce. *Kofta* is spiced ground beef grilled on skewers; kebab is chunks of lamb cooked the same way. Chicken is either fried (without batter), roasted on a rotisserie, or skewered, grilled, and called *shish tawouq*. Fried and stuffed pigeon *(hamam)* is a source of national pride, particularly in Alexandria, but most travelers are content to leave the dish, served whole, for the birds. *Biftek* (sometimes called *veal panné* on restaurant

PUFF THE MAGIC SHEESHA In Egypt, relaxation has become synonymous with gurgling and puffing noises accompanied by the smell of sugary honey, apple, or rose tobacco. The instrument of pleasure is a popular smoking apparatus known in Egypt as a *sheesha* (elsewhere as an *argileh* or *nargilah*), which can be plain or ornately colored and decorated with feathers. It consists of a snake-like tube and a small bowl filled with burning coals, tobacco, and spices. Water vapor carries the tobacco smoke through the one-meter tube and into the mouth, making each puff smooth and sweet. The *sheesha* is thought to have been introduced in Egypt by the Turks, and became fashionable among the elite during the late 17th century. For a long time *sheesha* smoking remained an upper-class pleasure, but as of late the apple and honey puffs of smoke have become a veritable national pastime.

menus) is a thinly sliced veal, breaded and fried. You can get feta cheese with a year-long shelf life in no-refrigeration-needed packs—great for long road trips or cheap breakfasts. The brand *La Vache Qui Rit* (The Laughing Cow) is so popular that it has been adopted as a disparaging nickname for President Hosni Mubarak.

Fatir are flaky, chewy, doughy delights, filled with anything and everything and eaten either as a meal or for dessert. Other desserts include *ba'laweh* and rice pudding flavored with rosewater *(roz bel laban)*. Egypt's ruby-red watermelons *(butteekh)*, though sometimes known to be color-enhanced with non-potable water, make a juicy, hydrating communal snack. Also try the unbelievable **figs** *(teen)* and, in late summer, the papaya-like *teen shoki* (cactus fruit).

A popular drink among travelers is **'asab,** sugar cane juice, said to increase sexual prowess. Egyptians themselves are coffee and tea fiends. Egyptian tea is taken without milk but with enough sugar to make it syrupy. Egyptians prefer **ahwa** (Arabic coffee). Especially when you are in Upper Egypt, try *karkadeh*, a red drink made by brewing hibiscus flowers that is served hot or cold. Egypt brews its own beer, **Stella,** which costs between E$5 and E$8 in restaurants and bars, as well as the surprisingly good **Sakara,** which usually costs a pound or two more.

HOLIDAYS AND FESTIVALS

Government offices and banks close for Islamic holidays, but most tourist facilities remain open. The month of Ramadan can be a wonderful (if occasionally inconvenient) time to visit, especially in festive Cairo and Alexandria. Along with the regular Islamic festivals, the two Sufi rituals of **Zikr** and **Zar** are not to be missed (both rituals are practiced on Fridays in populous areas). In the former, a group of dancers whirl themselves into a frenzy; in the latter, women dance in a group, primarily as an exorcism rite. The Coptic celebrations of Easter and Christmas are tranquil affairs marked by special church services. The festival known as **Sham al-Nissim** falls on the first Monday after Coptic Easter, but has developed into a secular celebration. Sham al-Nissim was originally an outdoor spring festival in which ancient Egyptians and enslaved Jews feasted on pungent *fisikh* (dried and salted fish) as equals; the highlight of the festival was the ritual casting of a young woman into the Nile. *Fisikh* is still eaten at modern celebrations, but the young women stay dry; even the ritual of throwing a doll into the Nile has all but disappeared from the present-day festivities. For a full list of holidays and festivals, see p. 61.

ESSENTIALS

DOCUMENTS AND FORMALITIES

CONSULAR SERVICES ABROAD

Egyptian embassies and consulates abroad include:

Australia: Embassy: 1 Darwin Ave., Yarralumla, Canberra, ACT 2600 (☎02 62 73 44 37; fax 62 73 42 79). **Consulates:** 124 Exhibition St., 9th fl., Melbourne, Victoria 3000 (☎03 96 54 86 34 or 96 54 88 69; fax 96 50 83 62). 112 Glen More Rd., Paddington, NSW 2021 (☎02 93 32 33 88; fax 93 32 32 88).

Canada: Embassy: 454 Laurier Ave. E., Ottawa, ON K1N 6R3 (☎613 234-4931; fax 234-6347). **Consulate:** 630 Rene-Levesque, Suite 2302, Montreal, PQ H3B 1S6 (☎514 861-6340; fax 861-6343).

Ireland: Embassy: 12 Clyde Rd., Dublin 4 (☎01 660 65 66 or 660 67 18; fax 668 37 45; embegypt@Indigo.ie).

UK: Embassy: 26 South St., London, W1Y 6DD (☎020 7499 3304; fax 7491 1542). **Consulate:** 2 Lowndes St., London, SW1 X9ET (☎020 7235 9777; fax 7235 5684).

US: **Embassy:** 3521 International Court NW, Washington, D.C. 20008 (☎202-895-5400; fax 244-4319). **Consulate:** 1110 2nd Ave., New York, NY 10022 (☎212-759-7120; fax 308-7643).

CONSULAR SERVICES IN EGYPT

Embassies and consulates of other countries in Egypt include:

Australian Embassy: World Trade Center, 11th Fl., Corniche al-Nil, Bulaq, Cairo (☎02 575 04 44; fax 578 16 38; cairo.austremb@dfat.gov.au).

Canadian Embassy: 5 al-Sarayah al-Cobrah Sq., Garden City, Cairo (☎02 794 31 10; fax 796 35 48).

Irish Embassy: 3 Abu al-Feda St., Zamalek, Cairo (☎02 340 82 64; fax 341 28 63).

South African Embassy: 21/23 Giza St., 18th fl., Giza, Cairo (☎02 571 72 34; fax 571 72 41; saembcai@gega.net).

UK Embassy: 7 Ahmed Ragheb St., Garden City, Cairo (☎02 794 0850, fax 794 08 59). **Consulate:** 1 Nile St., Luxor (☎95 382 838).

US Embassy: 5 Latin America St., Garden City, Cairo (☎02 795 73 71, fax 797 32 00; www.usis.egnet.net).

ENTRY REQUIREMENTS

PASSPORT. Citizens of Australia, Canada, Ireland, New Zealand, South Africa, the UK, and the US need valid **passports** to enter Egypt and to re-enter their home countries. Travelers with an Israeli stamp in their passports are allowed to enter the country.

VISA AND PERMIT INFO. As of August 2001, citizens of Australia, Canada, Ireland, New Zealand, the UK, and the US need a **visa** in addition to a valid passport for entrance to Egypt. Citizens of **South Africa** do not need a visa to enter Egypt. It is better to get your visa in advance; however, in case of emergency, visas can be obtained at the airport in Cairo or at the Port of Alexandria, with some restrictions. Visas cost US$15 and can be easily obtained by submitting an application to the nearest Egyptian embassy or consulate. Processing normally takes five business days, though sometimes may take significantly longer. These are good for one month, but renewable at police stations or at passport offices in major towns if you provide one photograph, E£12, and receipts showing that at least US$200 has been changed into Egyptian currency. There is a 13-day grace period after the 30-day visa expires; if you still fail to renew your visa during this time, you will face (at least) a E£100 penalty upon departure. If your visa has been expired for more than a couple weeks, you will be treated to an all-expenses paid trip to the interrogation rooms of the Egyptian immigration office in Cairo. Visits to the Sinai from Israel or Jordan can be made on a two-week **Sinai-only visa,** available at borders.

BORDER CROSSINGS

TO JORDAN. A **ferry** shuttles between the port at **Nuweiba** and **Aqaba.** Nobody really knows what time the ferries leave, but the latest schedule had them both leaving daily at 3pm. **Taxis** from Nuweiba or Tarabin to the port cost E£5. The ticket office for the ferries is in a small white building 100m south of the port, past a bakery. The slow ferry takes 3hr., barring technical difficulties, and costs US$33, payable in dollars or Egyptian pounds; a faster, less crowded, and more punctual **speedboat** takes 1hr. and costs US$43. Show up a few hours before the earliest possible departure time to deal with customs and ticketing. For general ferry information, call 52 00 52 or 52 03 60. Jordanian **visas** can be obtained on board (Australia JD16, Canada JD36, Ireland JD11, New Zealand JD16, South Africa free, UK JD23, US JD33). There is no departure tax from Egypt.

TO ISRAEL. The most convenient option is **Taba** to **Eilat** (border open 24hr.). *Service* drop you right at the border, but the East Delta bus stop leaves a 200m walk north to the Promised Land. See the **Transportation** sections of towns in the Sinai for information on transportation to Taba. On the Israeli side, **bus** #15 runs daily every 15 minutes from the border checkpoint to Eilat until about 11pm except on Fridays, when the last bus is at 5:30pm (NIS3.20). **Taxis** (US$6 to downtown) also go to Eilat. Rented **cars** are not allowed to cross in either direction.

At the border you will be issued a free visa, the length of which is entirely determined by the border guards' mood and your appearance (min. one week, max. three months). You will have to pay a E£2 exit tax if you have traveled beyond the Sinai. The walk through the stations shouldn't take more than 1hr. Keep your Israeli entrance card—you'll need it to leave the country. Israeli customs will often let you walk right through their station, but make sure to stop there because you can't pass the final checkpoint without the customs stamp on your gate pass.

POINTER FOR ENTERING ISRAEL. If you plan on traveling to Syria or Lebanon, have Israeli authorities stamp your visa on a separate piece of paper—you will not be allowed to enter these countries if there is an Israeli stamp in your passport. Israeli border authorities will often not let you leave Egypt without stamping your passport, so make trips to Syria or Lebanon beforehand.

GETTING AROUND

EGYPT

BY PLANE. Egypt is served by **EgyptAir** (☎02 76 52 00); see **Cairo: Flights** (p. 82) for locations, prices, and destinations. EgyptAir's main office in the US is at 720 5th Ave., Suite 505, New York, NY 10019 (☎800-334-6787). **Air Sinai** (☎(02) 76 09 48; 77 29 49), in the courtyard of the Nile Hilton in Cairo, serves the Sinai and Israel.

BY TRAIN. Trains in Egypt tend to take longer than buses. Schedules and signs in the train stations are rarely in English, but can be obtained from the tourist office or from ticket windows; fellow passengers can also help you. If lines are long and you're in a hurry, try boarding the train without a ticket—the conductor will usually sell one on board for an additional fee, even if the train is full.

Trains offer student discounts (ISIC card required) of up to 50%, with an average discount of about 30%. **Air-conditioned second-class** cars are comfortably small with reclining seats; shelling out more for first-class means only slightly larger seats and loud, braying Egyptian movies. Avoid the dangerous **third-class. Second-class sleeper cars,** available on some regular trains, might be more comfortable for trips of 10hr. or more, but are overpriced. Seats for Cairo-Alexandria and Cairo-Upper Egypt trips should be reserved a day or two in advance. Reserve a week in advance around the time of the two major Islamic holidays: 'Eid al-Fitr, occuring during the last week of Ramadan, and 'Eid al-Adha (Feast of the Sacrifice), which takes place about three months later.

BY BUS. Though inexpensive, buses in Egypt can be slow, crowded, and hot. Companies include **Superjet**, West Delta Bus Company, and East Delta Bus Company. **West Delta** has a deluxe branch called **Golden Arrow** with vehicles sporting air-conditioning, refreshments, and bathrooms; unfortunately, they often show Egyptian soap operas with women shrieking at unsustainable volumes. Air-conditioned **East Delta** buses serve locales throughout the Sinai.

BY TAXI. Flexibly-scheduled **service** (also known as *taxi bin-nafar* in Middle and Upper Egypt and *taxi ugra* in Lower Egypt) are a ubiquitous and surprisingly efficient method of getting around. *Service* are shared intercity taxis that run a specific route, and they depart when full or when passengers have agreed to split the price of a full carload. The local version of *service* is referred to as **minibus.**

Private taxis are inexpensive and convenient only in Cairo (black and white) and Alexandria (black and yellow or orange). Hail private taxis on the street instead of in front of a tourist trap, train station, or large hotel, and don't take a taxi if the driver approaches you. Discussing the price in advance only invites disagreement. *Never* ask the driver for the fare: open the door as you are paying with folded bills and leave the taxi without looking to the driver for approval. Have exact change and small bills ready, since change will never be made for you. "Special" means "rip-off:" if this word is mentioned in your presence, firmly repeat *La* ("No").

BY CAR. Renting a car is a useful option only for getting around the Sinai and the Western Desert Oases. Cheaper cars tend to be less reliable and harder to handle on difficult terrain. Less expensive 4WD vehicles in particular tend to be more top heavy, and are more dangerous when navigating particularly bumpy roads. You can generally make reservations before you leave by calling major international offices in your home country. Rentals in Egypt run about US$35 per day without a driver from the company, and US$50 with one. Expect to pay more for larger cars and for 4WD. Cars with **automatic transmission** can cost more than standard manuals (stick shift), and in some places, automatic is hard to find in the first place.

ROAD TRAVEL ADVISORY. Highway travel in Egypt is incredibly dangerous: Egypt has one of the highest road casualty rates in the world. **Intracity travel** is just as scary: at night, cars race by at 100kmph (60mph) without headlights. Avoid *service* after sundown. Check with local tourism authorities or the Ministry of the Interior before venturing in private transport off main roads, particularly in the following areas: the Western Desert (especially near the Libyan and Sudanese borders), along the Suez Canal and Red Sea Coast, and in the Sinai. If you need a permit, apply at the Ministry of the Interior in Cairo at 110 Qasr al-'Aini St. (☎354 83 00).

BY THUMB. Egypt is mostly untraveled desert; never count on getting a ride—you'll die of **dehydration** first. *Let's Go* does not recommend hitchhiking as a safe means of transportation. Hitching is not common in urban parts of Egypt. In recent years, the newspapers have been full of crimes perpetrated by hitchhikers along the roads between Cairo and Alexandria, making most drivers reluctant to pick you up anyway. Rides are reportedly easy to obtain in isolated areas (such as along the Great Desert Road) or for short jaunts in remote parts of the Nile Valley (where public transportation is difficult to find). Many drivers who pick up hitchhikers expect money anyway, so public transportation should be used wherever it is available.

TOURIST SERVICES AND MONEY

TOURIST OFFICES. Wherever you find yourself in Egypt, tourist offices will not be hard to find. More than 30 offices are spread throughout cities like Alexandria, Port Said, Fayyum, Luxor, Aswan, and in the Sinai. In general, English is spoken well and maps are available. For information on history, religions, and tourist attractions in Egypt, see the Egyptian Tourist Ministry's thorough website, **www.egypttourism.org.** The central offices in **Cairo** can provide information for most cities (see **Tourist and Financial Services,** p. 94).

CURRENCY AND EXCHANGE. The **Egyptian Pound** (E£), pronounced gin-EEH in Arabic, is divided into 100 **piasters** (pt), also called *irsh* (plural oo-ROOSH). Coins come in denominations of 5pt (٥), 10pt (١٠), and 20pt (٢٠); the last two look similar, so check the Arabic numbering. **Save exchange receipts** in case authorities ask for them when you are leaving the country. You are not allowed to carry more than E£1000 into or out of Egypt.

Bank hours are ordinarily Sunday to Thursday 8:30am-2pm (although some banks in big cities are open daily), with money exchange available daily 8:30am-noon and 4-8pm. Foreign banks keep longer hours, usually Sunday to Thursday 8am-3pm. **Trav-**

ARABIC FOR DUMMIES A brief lesson in Egyptian Arabic: After *min fadlak* (please) and *shukran* (thank you), the most important word to know is **khawaga** (kha-WA-ga), because you are one. *Khawaga* loosely means "tourist," and implies "clueless, idiotic, and rich." Aside from those in hotels and restaurants, most prices are not posted, which means that *khawaga*s may be charged more than Egyptians. Avoid souvenir shops and kiosks near tourist attractions at all costs. When shopping, the key concept is **bargain,** and the key words are *ana mish khawaga* ("I am not an idiot"). Another word to remember is **bakhsheesh,** the art of tipping: baggage handlers, guards, and bathroom and parking attendants expect to receive a tip of 50pt-E£1. For a detailed breakdown of the different types of *bakhsheesh* and the attitudes toward it in Egypt, see **Tipping and Bargaining** (p. 76).

eler's checks are not widely accepted in Egypt, except at ritzy hotels. They are, however, exchangeable for cash at many banks or at any American Express office. Credit cards can be useful for **cash advances,** which allow you to withdraw currency from associated banks and ATMs throughout Egypt instantly. Hefty transaction fees and beefy interest rates for cash advances make credit cards a more costly way of withdrawing cash than **ATMs,** which are fairly widespread in Egypt.

PRICES. Prices vary with competition and between high and low season. The high season in Alexandria is June to August, in the Nile Valley October to April. There is a hotel tax which varies by location, averaging around 20%. Unless otherwise noted, prices include tax but exclude breakfast. To give you a general idea, a bare-bones day in Cairo (sleeping in a hostel, buying food at a market) would cost about US$8 (E£30), while a slightly more comfortable day (sleeping in the occasional budget hotel, eating one meal a day at a restaurant, going out at night) would run US$24 (E£95). Don't forget to factor in emergency reserve funds (at least US$200) when planning how much money you'll need.

INFLATION SUCKS. Admission costs to major archaeological sights in Egypt are going up. Ticket prices for hotspots like the pyramids at Giza and the temples at Luxor, set by Egyptian authorities, are scheduled to gradually increase up to 50% by October 2002. Sight listings in this book were researched in August 2001, and reflect prices current at that time. In planning your budget, allow for variations of 25-50% for sight admissions.

TIPPING. The standard tip in a restaurant is usually included in the bill as a 10-15% service charge. Anything more on top of the bill is not expected. Taxi or *service* drivers do not expect tips. *Bakhsheesh* is also useful when sightseeing, as many places don't have tour guides. The alternative is to find a local to show you around for some cash. Egypt is *the* place to bargain; use your skills in the bazaars.

BUSINESS HOURS. On **Friday,** government offices, post offices and most banks are closed. Other establishments, such as restaurants, remain open seven days a week. Store hours are ordinarily Saturday to Thursday 9am-9pm, with many also open Friday. Government offices are open 9am-2pm. Archaeological sites and other points of interest typically open 8am-5pm, and close 1-2hr. earlier in winter.

HEALTH AND SAFETY

EMERGENCIES Police: ☎ 122. **Ambulance:** ☎ 123. **Fire:** ☎ 124.

MEDICAL EMERGENCIES. Most Egyptian hospitals do not have the high quality of medical treatment found in North America, Europe, or Australia, and few doctors speak English. Luxury hotels may have resident doctors, and other hotels can usually get someone dependable in an emergency. You can also ask your embassy for a list of recommended physicians and pharmacists. Even big-city **pharmacies**

EGYPT

do not carry Western brand-name drugs, but most Egyptian brands are equally effective and cheaper. Pharmacists in Egypt are authorized to write prescriptions (and are more lax about refills than most Western countries) and also able to give injections. There should be at least one pharmacy in each town, although finding a 24hr. store will prove difficult in small towns.

HEALTH. Called **Pharaoh's Revenge** in Egypt, an upset stomach can spoil any vacation. A change in water and diet can result in diarrhea and nausea. Stay away from raw fruit and vegetables (many are injected with unsafe water to improve their color), and drink plenty of liquids, especially bottled water, which is inexpensive and readily available. This will help you avoid **amebic dysentery**, ingested with unclean food or drink. Though malaria is not common to Egypt, **rabies** is endemic. Stay away from stray dogs around monuments. Rabies can be contracted not only from a bite, but also from saliva of the sick animal contacting an open wound. It is fatal if not treated in time. Medical treatment or help is available wherever you see a **red crescent,** the symbol of medical services in Egypt (equivalent to the red cross seen elsewhere); it designates hospitals, ambulances, and other medical services.

TERRORISM. Travel in Egypt is safe except in **Middle Egypt** and the **Egyptian frontiers.** Since the summer of 1998, the US government has warned against traveling in Middle Egypt (especially near the governates of Minya, Asyut, Sohag, and just north of Qena), where terrorist attacks by extremist groups have occurred since the mid-1990s. Although there have been no attacks on foreign tourists since 1998, these areas should be considered slightly risky.

WOMEN TRAVELERS. Women exploring on their own inevitably face some additional safety concerns, but it's easy to be adventurous without taking undue risks. Foreign women traveling alone will be **harassed** by Egyptian men—and so will foreign men. Egypt is not a place to visit if you want to be left alone, but harassment has more to do with socioeconomic exasperation and cultural misunderstanding than gender-based hostility. Harassment can take many forms, from overzealous salesmanship to touchy-feely *service* drivers, and from mildly sinister "hellos" to frightening and potentially harmful physical contact. The media has not helped the situation: movies and television tend to depict Western women as free and easy, and the racy nature of much Egyptian cinema has drastically altered expectations about how men and women should interact.

MINORITY TRAVELERS. People of all skin colors will encounter less active racism in Egypt than they will **ignorance** about different ethnicities. **Ethnic Asians** may attract stares, especially in untouristed areas, and will usually be assumed Japanese. In some regions of Egypt, **black** travelers may find that they encounter some negative attention. This response arises largely from the fact that Africans, especially Sudanese, have sometimes been seen as interlopers in Egyptian society. **Blondes** attract particular curiosity in Egypt, since native blondes are virtually nonexistent (as are, therefore, dumb blonde jokes—so you can stop desperately trying to think of comebacks).

BGLT TRAVELERS. Egypt is not a particularly rainbow-friendly locale—even though men hold hands in the street, this reflects a different cultural attitude about male physicality, not homosexuality (see **I Wanna Hold Your Hand,** below). As a country populated mainly by traditional Muslims, Egypt does not condone homosexual behavior. No one is openly gay in any public fashion, and homosexuality is technically **illegal** in Egypt. Be careful how you act in public—save displays of affection for somewhere safe.

I WANNA HOLD YOUR HAND Egyptian men may seem particularly affectionate to many travelers: they kiss each other on the cheeks, hold hands when strolling through bazaars, and even sit on each other's laps. Soldiers walk with a man on one arm and an AK-47 on the other. These amorous displays are merely manifestations of friendship and brotherhood in Egypt, as is evidenced by the very reserved manner in which Egyptian men treat their women. Women are considered very clean and chaste, and marriage is preceded by a strict courtship of two to three years.

ACCOMMODATIONS AND CAMPING

HOTELS. Some Egyptian "hotels" charge as little as US$2 for the privilege of sleeping on the roof. With a little searching, a comfortable, safe (indoor) bed could be yours for US$10. Egypt also proudly offers **five-star** hotels. If the sun gets too hot or the post offices too crowded, stop by these air-conditioned palaces, relax in their chandelieried lobbies and send some letters home, or even treat yourself to some nice clothes from their self-contained malls. A service charge of 12% applies to hotels as well as a 5-7% sales tax. An additional 1-4% tax is sometimes added to upper-end accommodations, so it is possible to find that a 23% tax has been added to the price of mid-range or top-end hotel rooms.

CAMPING. Camping in Egypt is generally free or nearly free, but typically it will not be organized by a central camping agency, meaning that it is almost entirely unregulated. Always check with the local tourist agency, police, and other travelers before setting up camp to find out if there are certain places where camping is illegal. For a free catalog on hiking and camping, contact these companies: **Sierra Club Books,** 85 2nd St. 2nd fl., San Francisco, CA 94105-3441, USA (☎415-977-5500; www.sierraclub.org/books); **The Mountaineers Books,** 1001 SW Klickitat Way, #201, Seattle, WA 98134, USA (☎800-553-4453; www.mountaineersbooks.org).

KEEPING IN TOUCH

MAIL. Standard **airmail** is the best way to send mail home from Egypt; be sure to write "**par avion**" in clear letters on the front. Airmailing postcards and letters weighing under 15g costs E$1.25 and normally takes 4-5 days to get to the UK and Ireland and 7-10 days to get to North America, Australia, or New Zealand, although delivery time can vary drastically for no apparent reason. If using post boxes, **blue** is for international airmail, while red and green boxes are for mail to other parts of Egypt. If your package is not time sensitive, **surface mail** is by far the cheapest alternative to send mail. It takes one to three months to cross the Atlantic and two to four to cross the Pacific—good for items you won't need to see for a while, such as souvenirs or books you've acquired along the way that are weighing down your pack. To speedily send packages by **Federal Express,** contact their office at 1079 Corniche al-Nil, Garden City, Cairo (☎02 357 13 00 or 355 10 63; fax 357 13 18). Mail can be sent via **Poste Restante** to almost any city or town in Egypt with a post office, and it is usually quite reliable.

TELEPHONE AND INTERNET ACCESS. A **calling card** is probably your cheapest bet. Calls are billed collect or to your account. You can frequently call collect without even possessing a company's calling card just by calling their access number and following the instructions. **To obtain a calling card** from your national telecommunications service before leaving home, contact the appropriate company listed below (using the numbers in the first column). To **call home with a calling card,** contact the operator for your service provider in Egypt by dialing the appropriate toll-free access number (listed below in the second column). You can usually make **direct international calls** from coin-operated pay phones in Egypt, but if you aren't using a calling card, you may need to drop your coins as quickly as your words. **Local calls** cost 10pt per 3min. from public phones, 50pt per 3min. from private phones in establishments.

In Egypt, there should be no trouble finding Internet access. **Internet cafes** and the occasional free Internet terminal at a public library or university are listed in the **Practical Information** sections of major cities. For lists of additional cyber cafes in Egypt, check out the **Cybercafe Search Engine** (www.cybercaptive.com). One hour usually costs between US$2 and US$5. Travelers with laptops can call an Internet service provider via a **modem.** Long-distance phone cards specifically intended for such calls can defray normally high phone charges; check with your long-distance phone provider to see if it offers this option.

CUSTOMS AND ETIQUETTE

Keep your soles out of sight—in or out of you shoes. Bottoms of **feet** resting anywhere but on the ground is disrespectful. Before entering **mosques,** remove shoes and have socks ready to wear. Women must **cover** their heads and arms, and stand behind men. Outside of mosques, women usually congregate with other females, lining up with other women to buy tickets and sitting at the front of buses and trains. For men, speaking to unknown Egyptian women is a breach of etiquette and should be avoided.

It is customary for Egyptians to refuse the first **invitation** of an offering; tourists should do the same, as a genuine invitation will be repeated at least twice. If ever invited to a home but unable to attend, the householder will often press for a promise from you to visit in the future, usually for a meal. If you make such a promise, keep it. Failing to arrive will humiliate your host. It is also offensive to offer *bakhsheesh* to professionals, businessmen, or others who would consider themselves your equals.

Egypt prohibits drugs, and in many places, alcohol and pork. If you need to drink in the presence of others, ask first. Explicit sexual material, like magazines, photographs, tapes, or records is illegal and subject to confiscation.

CAIRO القاهرة ☎ 02

I arrived at length at Cairo, mother of cities and seat of Pharaoh the tyrant, boundless in multitude of buildings, peerless in beauty and splendor, the meeting-place of comer and goer, the halting-place of feeble and mighty, whose throngs surge as waves of the sea.
——Ibn Battuta, 14th-century globetrotter

Cairo has been the jewel of the Middle East and Africa for nearly the past millennium. In 2600 BCE, the pharaohs of the Old Kingdom chose the sandy plateau just above the Nile Delta for their ancient capital of Memphis—one of the world's earliest urban settlements and Egypt's capital until the beginning of the first century CE, when St. Mark introduced Christianity to Egypt. For the next 600 years, the Coptic Church that grew out of St. Mark's teaching marked the wrists of its faithful with tattoos and left even more enduring marks in the architectural landscape of Old Cairo. The early decades of the 7th century CE found Cairo in the throes of a power struggle between the Persian and Byzantine empires. Memphis and Babylon (the glitzy settlement across the Nile) changed hands many times, while warfare near Babylon drove urban dwellers to the villages. The city thus lay bereft and deserted at the time of the Arab conquest in 641 CE. The leader of the Arab invaders, 'Amr ibn al-'As, set up camp at Fustat, the precursor of modern Cairo. The Arabs were responsible for giving the city its name: Fatimid leader Gawhar al-Sikelli dubbed it *al-Qahira*, or "the Conqueror."

The city swelled so much in size and grandeur under the Fatimids and their descendants that it soon became known simply as *Misr*, the Arabic name for all of Egypt. During the next three centuries—Cairo's Golden Age—it became the most advanced cultural center west of China. Although various conquerors throughout the Middle Ages managed to carry off pieces of Cairo's glory, it remained far more populous than any city in Europe. The Ottomans, however, reduced Cairo to the status of a provincial center in 1516. After a brief affair with Napoleon in the late 1700s, Cairo made a grand entrance onto the 19th-century scene after a face-lift by its modern political patron, Muhammad 'Ali. An Albanian emigré, 'Ali drove away Egypt's European conquerors and reinstalled Cairo at the forefront of the Arab world. His penchant for the extravagant resulted in the numerous Cairene streets dotted with lofty Turkish-style mosques and glittering European-style palaces.

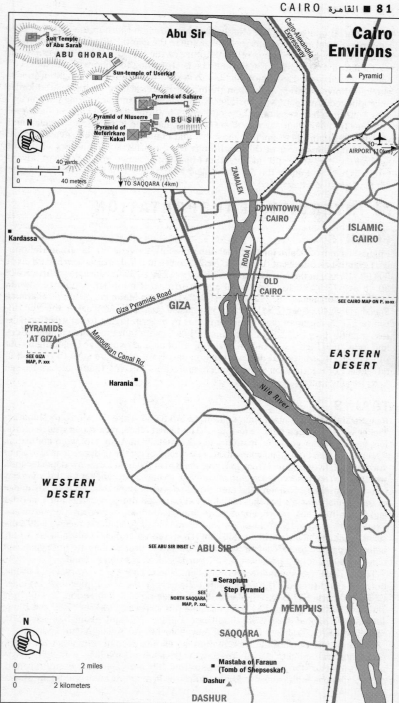

Cairo Environs

▲ Pyramid

Abu Sir

Sun Temple
of Abu Sarab

ABU GHORAB

Sun-temple of Userkaf

Pyramid of Sahure

Pyramid of Niuserre

ABU SIR

Pyramid of
Neferirkare
Kakai

N

0   40 yards

0   40 meters

↓ TO SAQQARA (4km)

Cairo-Alexandria Expressway

TO
AIRPORT (10km)

ZAMALEK

DOWNTOWN
CAIRO

ISLAMIC
CAIRO

RODA I.

OLD
CAIRO

SEE CAIRO MAP ON P. xx-xx

EGYPT

■ Kardassa

Giza Pyramids Road

GIZA

PYRAMIDS
AT GIZA

SEE GIZA
MAP, P. xxx

Marouityan Canal Rd.

Harania ■

EASTERN
DESERT

Nile River

WESTERN
DESERT

SEE ABU SIR INSET ABU SIR

SEE
NORTH SAQQARA
MAP, P. xxx

■ Serapium
▲ Step Pyramid

MEMPHIS

SAQQARA

N

0   2 miles

0   2 kilometers

■ Mastaba of Faraun
(Tomb of Shepseskaf)

Dashur ▲

DASHUR

The social upheaval of the Middle East has affected Cairo in the 20th century. Modern political and economic centralization in the capital is driving thousands of rural Egyptians into the arms of the "Mother of the World" (*Umm al-Dunya*, as the medieval Arabs called Cairo), and she is struggling to cope with the needs of her growing brood. Expansion has led to severely overcrowded neighborhoods, clogged thoroughfares, and urban pollution. Places where pharaohs and kings once lounged now teem with barking street merchants and silver-tongued con artists. Amid tangled webs of unlabeled streets and the dizzying calls of hawkers, Cairenes frequent their favorite *sheesha* halls, navigate labyrinthine bazaars, and worship in hundreds of ancient mosques and churches (and some synagogues). Cairo intimidates most of those who pay the city only a perfunctory visit. But beyond the Pyramids and the Egyptian Museum, patience and a sense of adventure will help you enjoy the apparent insanity of a city that seems always on the verge of some great event.

⊠ INTERCITY TRANSPORTATION

FLIGHTS

Flights leave from **Cairo International Airport** (☎291 42 55 or 291 42 66), in Heliopolis. **EgyptAir** has offices at 6 'Adly St. (☎392 7649), at 9 Tala'at Harb (☎393 28 36 or 393 03 81), and in the Nile Hilton (☎579 30 49 or 579 94 43 for the sales office, ☎579 30 46 or 575 97 03 for the travel agent office). Round-trip flights to: **Aswan** (US$368), **Hurghada** (US$240), **Luxor** (US$232), **Marsa Matrouh** (US$110), **Sharm al-Sheikh** (US$240), **Suez** (US$170), and **Wadi Gadid** (US$235). **Air Sinai,** in the Nile Hilton (☎577 29 49; open daily 9am-5pm), has round-trip flights to **Tel Aviv** (for trips less than 30 days US$238, longer trips US$320). Note that these are sample prices and individual flights will vary in cost. It is difficult and expensive to get flights out of Cairo to international destinations on short notice, so be sure to reserve in advance. For information on traveling to and from Cairo International Airport, see **Entry Requirements,** p. 74.

TRAINS

Ramses Station is the main train station. (☎575 35 55. Take the Metro to Mubarak. Ticket windows open daily 8am-10pm.) The **tourist office,** past the entrance on the left, can write out your destination and other details in Arabic to avoid confusion. (Open daily 8am-8pm.) The **information desk,** straight past the entrance, can also point you in the right direction. Which line you stand in at the ticket window depends upon whether you are reserving a seat in advance or trying to buy a ticket for the same day (often impossible). Women (and men traveling with women) should take advantage of the special **women's line** that may form at crowded times, which is much shorter and faster than the corresponding men's line. In addition, women are permitted and expected to push to the front of any line, head held high. Students receive a **30% discount** on almost all fares with an **ISIC card.** The trains enter their berths at least 30min. before departure time. None of the train numbers or destinations are in English, but other travelers, tourist police, or the information desk may lend a hand.

Trains leave for **Alexandria** every hr. 6am-10pm. There are two types of trains, both air-conditioned—the **French line** (3hr.; every 1½-2hr. 10 per day; 1st-class E£20, 2nd-class E£12) and the faster **Spanish line** (2hr.; 8, 9am, noon, 2, 3, 6, 7pm; 1st-class E£22, 2nd-class E£17). Trains also run to: **Aswan** (13-16hr.; 7:30 and 10am; 1st-class E£73, 2nd-class E£43) and **Luxor** (9-12hr.; 7:30 and 10am; 1st-class E£63, 2nd-class E£36). Trains to Luxor and Aswan via Minya, Sohag, Asyut, and Qena.

The area just outside the train station is chaotic, despite the numerous traffic police and traffic lights. Avoid crossing the treacherous roads by using the convenient tunnels of the Mubarak Metro station. But before heading underground, catch a glimpse of the massive **Statue of Ramses II,** standing calm amidst the storm.

Travel agents in the downtown area have been known to add airport taxes (there is no departure tax from Cairo) and other phantom fees to tickets. You should demand receipts for every pound you hand over and have them give you written estimates, including all taxes, for every flight you purchase. Once you have purchased a ticket, call the airline to make sure a seat is indeed reserved.

BUSES

The bus system in Egypt is a four-wheeled embodiment of the government bureaucracy—things are always changing, no one can explain what is going on, yet somehow it all works out. Taking a bus can be quite a fuss in Cairo (as in much of the Middle East), as schedules shift daily, prices fluctuate, and drop-off points change without warning. Check a day or two before you need to take a bus to make sure it's going where you want for a price you're willing to pay. The buses themselves are quite nice—they are frequently air-conditioned and always equipped with large, comfortable seats, and many even serve food. Make reservations in person a day or two in advance for popular destinations.

Cairo's intercity bus terminal has shifted locations frequently in the past years (even recent schedules can be out of date). Unless otherwise noted, buses leave from **Turgoman Station (Mahattat Turgoman)** near Ramses Sq. Buses go to:

Alexandria and the Mediterranean Coast: Superjet (☎579 81 81) goes to **Alexandria** (3hr., every 30min. 5:30am-11pm, E£55) and **Marsa Matrouh** (5hr., 8am, E£37). Connections to **Siwa** from both destinations.

The Canal Zone: The East Delta Bus Co. (☎576 22 93) travels to: **Isma'ilia** (2hr., every hr. 7:30am-6:30pm, E£6.50); **Port Said** (2hr., every hr. 7:30am-6:30pm, E£15); and **Suez** (2hr., every 30min. 7:30am-6:30pm, E£6).

Hurghada: Superjet (8:30am and 2:30pm, E£47; 11pm, E£52) and the **Upper Egypt Bus Co.** (9am, 12:30, 3, 9:40, 11:30pm, midnight; E£45.50).

The Sinai: The East Delta Bus Co. (☎576 22 93) runs buses to: **Dahab** (8hr.; 7:30am, 1, 4:30, 11:30pm; E£55); **Nuweiba** (8hr., 7:30am and 10pm, E£50-55); and **Taba** (9hr.; 7:30am, E£50; 10pm, E£70). **Superjet** (☎579 81 81) runs buses to **Sharm al-Sheikh** (7hr., 11pm, E£55).

Upper Egypt: The Upper Egypt Bus Co. sends buses to: **Aswan** (13hr., 5:30pm, E£55); **Bahariya** (4-5hr.; 7 and 8am, E£12.50; 6pm, E£15), **Farafra** (7½hr., 10am and noon, E£40); **Kharga** (12hr., 8am, E£40); **Luxor** (9hr., 9pm, E£50).

International Buses:

The Levant: The East Delta Bus Co. sends buses to **Jordan** and **Syria** (22hr., 8pm, E£114) and **Turkey** (50hr., 8pm, E£310.50). **Superjet** leaves from al-Maza Sq. to **Jordan** (M, Tu, Th, Sa 6am; E£231) and **Syria** (Sa 10pm, E£310.50).

Tel Aviv and Jerusalem: Buses leave daily from the **Cairo Sheraton** (10hr., about E£150). Make reservations the day before at the Sheraton or at **Misr Travel,** on the 1st block of Tala'at Harb St.

SERVICE

Service leaving from Ramses Station travel to: **Alexandria** (E£10-12), **al-Arish** (E£15), **Isma'ilia** (E£6), **Port Said** (E£9), and **Suez** (E£5-7). *Service* from Giza Sq. travel to: **Alexandria** (E£11), **Fayyum** (E£5), **Mansoura** (E£9), **Tanta** (E£6), **Wadi Natrun** (about E£10), and **Zagazig** (E£5). *Service* to the rest of the Delta leave from Ahmed Hilmi Sq. Station. Prices are approximate, so watch what other passengers are paying. Unlike taxis, relatively few foreigners use *service*, so those that do can "get away" with paying the same as everyone else.

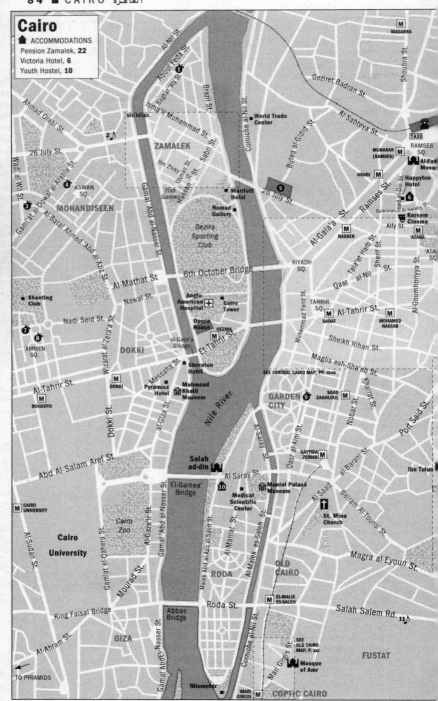

Cairo

🏠 **ACCOMMODATIONS**

Pension Zamalek, **22**
Victoria Hotel, **6**
Youth Hostel, **10**

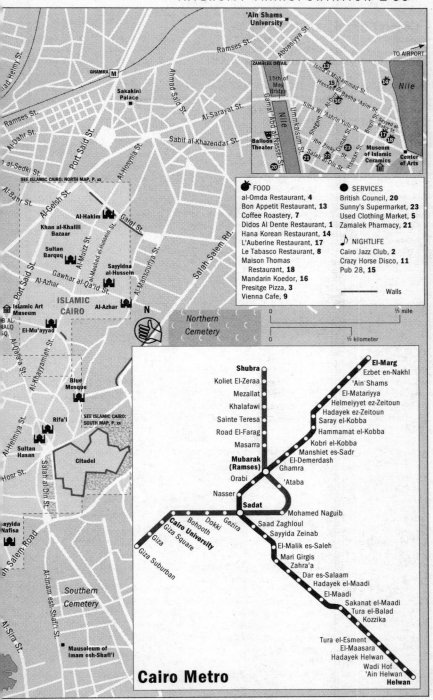

'Ain Shams University

ZAMALEK DETAIL

15th of May Bridge

Nile

Balloon Theater

Museum of Islamic Ceramics

Center of Arts

GHAMRA Ⓜ

Sakakini Palace

Ramses St.
Al-Sarayat St.
Sabil al-Khazendar St.
Port Said St.
Al-Hosnyia St.
Ahmad Said St.
Gamal Abd an-Nasser St.
Ummtaisum St.
Salah al-Din St.

SEE ISLAMIC CAIRO: NORTH MAP, P. xx

Al-Bahr St.
Al-Gelsh St.
Galal St.

Al-Hakim

Khan al-Khalili Bazaar

Sultan Barquq

Al-Muizz St.
Al-Masjad el-Hussein St.

Sayyidna al-Hussein

Gawhar al-Qa'id St.
Al-Azhar

Al-Mansouriya St.
Salah Salem Rd.

ISLAMIC CAIRO

Islamic Art Museum

El-Mu'ayyad

Al-Qala'a St.
Al-Khayyamien St.

Blue Mosque

Rifa'i

SEE ISLAMIC CAIRO: SOUTH MAP, P. xx

Sultan Hasan

Citadel

Al-Helmiya St.
Salah al-Din St.
Hosr St.

Sayyida Nafisa

Salah Salem Road

Southern Cemetery

Al-Imam esh-Shafi'i St.

Al-Sira St.

Mausoleum of Imam esh-Shafi'i

Northern Cemetery

FOOD
al-Omda Restaurant, 4
Bon Appetit Restaurant, 13
Coffee Roastery, 7
Didos Al Dente Restaurant, 1
Hana Korean Restaurant, 14
L'Auberine Restaurant, 17
Le Tabasco Restaurant, 8
Maison Thomas Restaurant, 18
Mandarin Koedor, 16
Presitge Pizza, 3
Vienna Cafe, 9

SERVICES
British Council, 20
Sunny's Supermarket, 23
Used Clothing Market, 5
Zamalek Pharmacy, 21

♪ **NIGHTLIFE**
Cairo Jazz Club, 2
Crazy Horse Disco, 11
Pub 28, 15

━━━━━ Walls

0   ½ mile
0   ½ kilometer

Cairo Metro

Shubra
Koliet El-Zeraa
Mezallat
Khalafawi
Sainte Teresa
Road El-Farag
Masarra
Mubarak (Ramses)
Orabi
Nasser
Sadat

El-Marg
Ezbet en-Nakhl
'Ain Shams
El-Matariyya
Helmeiyyet ez-Zeitoun
Hadayek ez-Zeitoun
Saray el-Kobba
Hammamat el-Kobba
Kobri el-Kobba
Manshiet es-Sadr
El-Demerdash
Ghamra
'Ataba

Dokki
Bohooth
Cairo University
Giza Square
Giza
Giza Suburban
Gezira

Mohamed Naguib
Saad Zaghloul
Sayyida Zeinab
El-Malik es-Saleh
Mari Girgis
Zahra'a
Dar es-Salaam
Hadayek el-Maadi
El-Maadi
Sakanat el-Maadi
Tura el-Balad
Kozzika
Tura el-Esment
El-Maasara
Hadayek Helwan
Wadi Hof
'Ain Helwan
Helwan

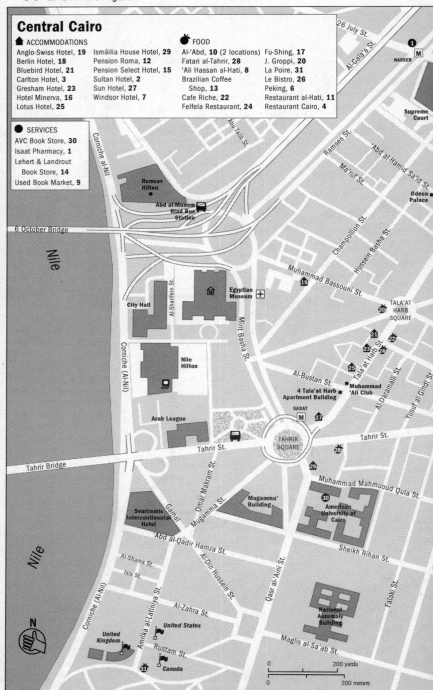

Central Cairo

🏠 ACCOMMODATIONS
Anglo-Swiss Hotel, **19**
Berlin Hotel, **18**
Bluebird Hotel, **21**
Carlton Hotel, **3**
Gresham Hotel, **23**
Hotel Minerva, **16**
Lotus Hotel, **25**
Ismáilia House Hotel, **29**
Pension Roma, **12**
Pension Select Hotel, **15**
Sultan Hotel, **2**
Sun Hotel, **27**
Windsor Hotel, **7**

🍎 FOOD
Al-'Abd, **10** (2 locations)
Fatari al-Tahrir, **28**
'Ali Hassan al-Hati, **8**
Brazilian Coffee
   Shop, **13**
Cafe Riche, **22**
Felfela Restaurant, **24**
Fu-Shing, **17**
J. Groppi, **20**
La Poire, **31**
Le Bistro, **26**
Peking, **6**
Restaurant al-Hati, **11**
Restaurant Cairo, **4**

⚫ SERVICES
AVC Book Store, **30**
Isaat Pharmacy, **1**
Lehert & Landrout
   Book Store, **14**
Used Book Market, **9**

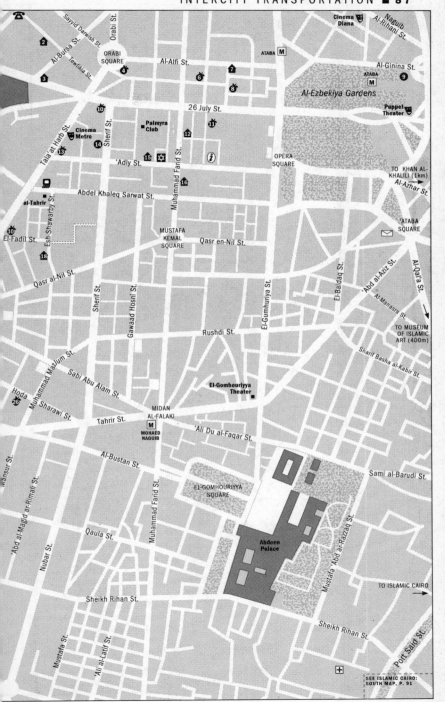

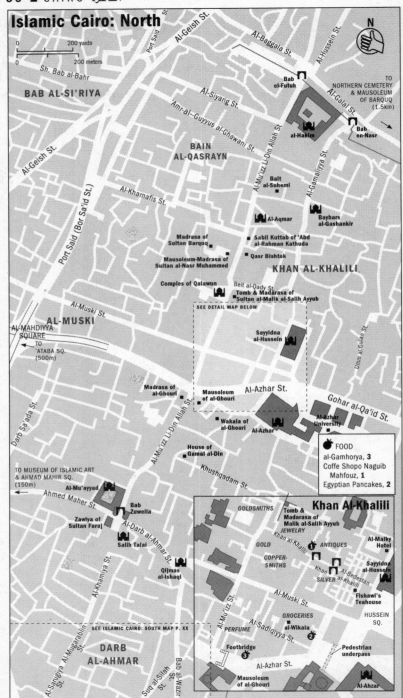

Islamic Cairo: North

0   200 yards
0   200 meters

Sh. Bab al-Bahr

BAB AL-SI'RIYA

Al-Geish St.
Port Said St.
Al-Geish St.
Al-Baggala St.
Al-Hussein St.
Al-Siyang St.
Amr-al-Guyyus al-Ghawani St.
Al-Mu'izz Li-Din Allah St.

Port Said (Bor Sa'id St.)

Al-Kharnafis St.

BAIN AL-QASRAYN

Bab el-Futuh

al-Hakim

TO
NORTHERN CEMETERY
& MAUSOLEUM
OF BARQUQ
(1.5km)

Al-Galai St.

Bab en-Nasr

Al-Gamaliyya St.

■ Bait al-Suhemi

■ Al-Aqmar

Baybars al-Gashankir

Madrasa of
Sultan Barquq

■ Sabil Kuttab of 'Abd
al-Rahman Kathuda

■ Qasr Bishtak

KHAN AL-KHALILI

Mausoleum-Madrasa of
Sultan al-Nasr Muhammed

Complex of Qalawun

Beit al-Qady St.

Tomb & Madrasa of
Sultan al-Malik al-Salih Ayyub

AL-MUSKI

Al-Muski St.

SEE DETAIL MAP BELOW

Sayyidna
al-Hussein

**AL-MAHDIYYA
SQUARE**

TO
'ATABA SQ.
(500m)

Umm al-Gulan St.

Al-Azhar St.

Madrasa of
al-Ghouri

Mausoleum
of al-Ghouri

Gohar al-Qa'id St.

Darb Sa'ada St.

TO MUSEUM OF ISLAMIC ART
& AHMAD MAHIR SQ.
(150m)

Al-Mu'izz Li-Din Allah St.

■ Wakala of
al-Ghouri

Al-Azhar

Al-Azhar
University

🍎 **FOOD**
al-Gamhorya, **3**
Coffe Shopo Naguib
Mahfouz, **1**
Egyptian Pancakes, **2**

House of
Gamal al-Din

Khushqadam St.

Al-Mu'ayyad

Ahmed Maher St.

Bab
Zuwella

Zawiya of
Sultan Faraj

Al-Darb al-Ahmar St.

Salih Talai

Al-Khamiya St.

Qijmas
al-Ishaqi

Al-Sarugiya al-Mugaribiin

Suq al-Silah St.

Bab al-Wazir St.

SEE ISLAMIC CAIRO: SOUTH MAP P. XX

**DARB
AL-AHMAR**

Khan Al-Khalili

GOLDSMITHS

Tomb &
Madrasa of
Malik al-Salih Ayyub

JEWELRY

Khan al-Khalili

GOLD

ANTIQUES

Al-Malky
Hotel

COPPER-
SMITHS

Khan al-Khalili

SILVER al-Bedestan

Sayyidna
al-Hussein

Fishawi's
Teahouse

Al-Muski St.

HUSSEIN
SQ.

Al-Mu'iz St.

GROCERIES

Al-Sadiqiyya St.

al-Wikala

PERFUME

Pedestrian
underpass

Footbridge

Al-Azhar St.

Mausoleum
of al-Ghouri

Al-Ahzar

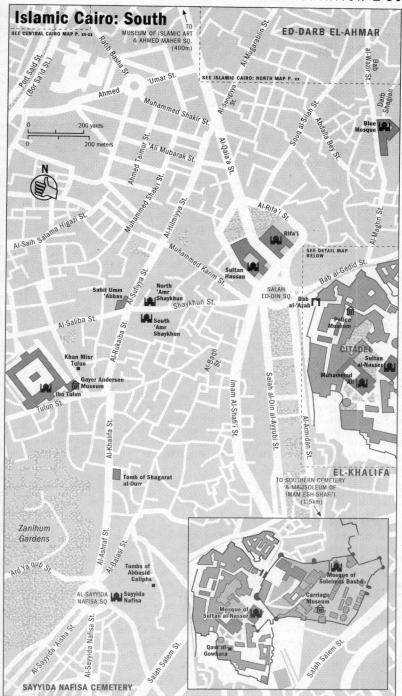

Islamic Cairo: South

SEE CENTRAL CAIRO MAP P. xx-xx

TO
MUSEUM OF ISLAMIC ART
& AHMED MAHER SQ.
(400m)

ED-DARB EL-AHMAR

Port Said St.
(Bor Sa'id St.)

Ratib Basha St.

'Umar St.

Ahmed

Muhammed Shakir St.

Al-Mugarablin St.

Bab al-Wazir St.

SEE ISLAMIC CAIRO: NORTH MAP P. xx

Al-Sangiya St.

Souq al-Silah St.

Abdalla Bey St.

Darb Shaglan

Blue
Mosque

Ahmed Taimur St.

'Ali Mubarak St.

Al-Qala'a St.

Al-Maghri St.

Muhammed Shakir St.

Al-Saih Salama Higazi St.

Al-Hilmiyya St.

Al-Rifa'i St.

Rifa'i

Muhammed Karim St.

Sultan
Hassan

SEE DETAIL MAP
BELOW

Bab al-Gedid St.

0   200 yards
0   200 meters

N

Al-Sufiyya St.

Sabil Umm
'Abbas

North
'Amr
Shaykhun

Shaykhun St.

SALAH
ED-DIN SQ.

Bab
al-'Azab

Police
Museum

Al-Saliba St.

Al-Rukalba St.

South
'Amr
Shaykhun

Al-Braqii St.

CITADEL

Sultan
al-Nasser

Khan Misr
Tulun

Gayer Anderson
Museum

Imam Al-Shafi'i St.

Salah al-Din al-Ayubbi St.

Muhammad
Ali

Ibn Tulun

Tulun St.

Al-Khalifa St.

Al-Amidan St.

EL-KHALIFA

Tomb of Shagarat
al-Durr

TO SOUTHERN CEMETERY
& MAUSOLEUM OF
IMAM ESH-SHAFI'I
(1.5km)

Zanihum
Gardens

Al-Ashraf St.

Al-Balasi St.

'Ard Ya'qub St.

Tombs of
Abbasid
Caliphs

AL-SAYYIDA
NAFISA SQ.

Sayyida
Nafisa

Al-Sayyida 'Aisha St.

Al-Sayyida Nafisa St.

Salah Salem St.

Mosque of
Suleimas Basha

Carriage
Museum

Mosque of
Sultan al-Nasser

Qasr al-
Gowhara

Salah Salem St.

SAYYIDA NAFISA CEMETERY

CAR RENTAL

If you're a daredevil or a maniac (or both), driving in Cairo is for you. **Avis** (☎794 74 00) has branches throughout the city. The branch at Cairo International Airport (☎265 24 29) is open 24hr. Join the millions of middle-class Egyptians driving Suzuki Swifts for US$50 per day, including insurance, taxes, and the first 100km. Most branches are open daily 8am-3:30pm. **Hertz** (☎347 41 72) has branches at Cairo International Airport (☎265 24 30), Ramses Hilton (☎574 44 00 or 575 80 00), Semiramis Intercontinental Hotel (☎354 32 39), and Meridien Hotel (☎383 03 83). They offer Toyota Corollas for US$60 per day with unlimited mileage and air-conditioning. All branches open daily 9am-5pm. Keep in mind that Cairene traffic barely manages to avoid catastrophe even with experienced drivers at the helm. Those who are not familiar with the conventions of driving in Cairo are a danger to themselves and other motorists.

UPON ARRIVAL. Upon arrival at the **Cairo International Airport,** there are several options for getting downtown. Taxis are the simplest, but the most expensive (at most E£25); only take those that leave from the official stand, as they are monitored 24hr. by tourist police. Taxis will most likely drop you off at Tahrir Sq. (center of Cairo), and you can get anywhere from there. **Minibus** #27 (٢٧) and **bus** #400 (٤٠٠) go to Tahrir Sq. from the Airport's old terminal for 50pt (piasters). Gem Travel also runs a 24hr. **shuttle bus** to downtown (US$4).

All **trains** into Cairo stop at Ramses Station. **Bus** #160 (١٦٠) runs from there to Tahrir Sq. Black and white **taxis** to Tahrir Sq. cost E£2. The **Metro,** opposite the station, runs to Tahrir Sq. for 50pt. To walk (30min.), climb the pedestrian overpass and walk south on Ramses St., away from the Ramses II statue.

Buses from Israel usually drop passengers off at 'Abbasiyya Station. To reach Tahrir Sq. from 'Abbasiyya Station, hop into a southbound black and white cab (E£4-5) or walk left down Ramses St. as you leave the station; go beyond the overpass, and to the first bus stop on the right. From here many buses travel to Tahrir Sq. Buses from Jordan usually drop you off at **'Abd al-Munem Riad Station.** To reach Tahrir Sq. from here, walk right onto Gala'a St. as you exit, until you come to the Corniche al-Nil. At the corniche take a left onto Tahrir St.

Some hotels, as well as a tour guide by the name of **Mr. Salah Muhammad** (☎/fax 298 06 50; samo@intouch.com), offer free 24hr. shuttle service (reserve ahead of time by email) from the airport to downtown Cairo for visitors who will stay at their establishments or take Muhammad's tour of the Pyramids at Giza, Memphis, Saqqara, and the carpet school at Harania (E£40, not including entrance fees to sights, E£5 *Let's Go* discount if you book with him). For more information on the package, see **Pyramids at Giza,** p. 126.

✵ ORIENTATION

DOWNTOWN

At the center of it all is **Tahrir Sq.** *(Midan Tahrir)*, one of the many central districts planned by British and French colonialists. Local buses depart here for every metropolitan destination. Facing the square to the north is the monumental sandstone **Egyptian Museum;** adjacent to it on the west side of the square is the **Nile Hilton.** Entrances to the Sadat Metro station ring the square. At the southern end of the square is the hulking, concave **Mugamm'a Building,** headquarters of the Egyptian bureaucracy. The placid gardens and excellent bookstore of the **American University in Cairo (AUC)** are directly to the east of the Mugamm'a Building across Qasr al-'Aini St. A few blocks east on Tahrir St. is the Bab al-Luq public bus depot.

The three most important streets coming out of Tahrir Sq. are Qasr al-'Aini St., Qasr al-Nil St., and Tala'at Harb St. **Qasr al-'Aini St.** runs south from Tahrir Sq. and ends at **Old Cairo** (also known as Coptic Cairo), the historic and spiritual

The area in the immediate vicinity of Tahrir Sq. has been the scene of some **pickpocketing** by youngsters who may barely reach waist-level. Be wary of large, playful groups of local kids in and around the Square, as it is easy to get distracted. Most of the rest of Cairo is theft-free at any time of day.

center of the Copts, Egypt's Eastern Orthodox Christians. The American University in Cairo (AUC), Parliament, and some of the city's most beautifully preserved 19th-century colonial mansions line Qasr al-'Aini St. Just south of Tahrir Sq., sandwiched between Qasr al-'Aini St. and the **Nile River,** foreign embassies and banks cluster along the streets of the serene **Garden City** residential area. Farther south, the exclusive district of **Ma'adi** serves as home for many of Cairo's American expatriates. **Qasr al-Nil St.** begins in front of the Nile Hilton, cuts through Tala'at Harb Sq., and continues on to **Mustafa Kamal Sq.** In between lie many of Cairo's Western-style stores, banks, travel agents, and the AmEx office. **Tala'at Harb St.** runs from the northeast side of Tahrir Sq. through **Tala'at Harb Sq.** toward Orabi Sq. and 26 July St. **Ramses Sq.** to the north (west of Orabi Sq.) and **'Ataba Sq.** (east of Orabi Sq., at the end of 26 July St.) form a rough triangle with Tala'at Harb Sq. enclosing the main business and shopping district, which is crammed with travel agents, banks, restaurants, clothing stores, and budget hotels. Due north of Tahrir Sq. lies **'Abd al-Munem Riad Sq.,** the starting point of **Ramses St.** and the city's main public bus depot. Heading northeast away from the Nile, Ramses St. runs up to **Ramses Sq.,** the Cairo train station (called **Ramses Station**), and the Mubarak Metro station. South of Ramses Sq. off Ramses St. is the Mahattat Turgoman (**Turgoman Bus Station**), where intercity buses come and go. Farther out on Ramses St. are **Cairo Stadium** and **Heliopolis,** a fashionable suburb where President Mubarak lives. Heading east from 'Ataba Sq., al-Azhar St. and al-Muski St. (a long shopping strip) both lead to the northern end of Islamic Cairo and the Northern Cemetery.

ISLAMIC CAIRO

Islamic Cairo was the heart of the city in the Middle Ages and continues to be the center of its religious life. It occupies the area southeast of downtown Cairo, marked by the **Citadel** and **Mosque of Ibn Tulun** in the south and **al-Azhar Mosque** and **University** in the north. Although this district has never benefited from a coherent urban plan, there are a few key streets and areas, the first of which is **Salah al-Din Sq.** (*Midan Salah al-Din*). Both the **Sultan Hassan Mosque** and **Rifa'i Mosque** border this square, as does the gargantuan Citadel. **Salah al-Din St.** runs south to the Southern Cemetery, while **al-Qala'a St.** is a main north-south thoroughfare. Branching off of al-Qala'a and heading toward **al-Azhar** and the market of **Khan al-Khalili** is **al-Mu'izz St.,** once the main avenue of the city. Finally, al-Azhar St. connects Islamic Cairo to 'Ataba Sq. and circumnavigates Khan al-Khalili and al-Azhar.

FRIEND OR FOE?

Downtown Cairo is the scene of Egypt's most aggressive street hustling. A walk from Tahrir Sq. to Orabi Sq. along Tala'at Harb is almost certain to gain you multiple "Egyptian friends," eager to help you get the best (for them) deals on perfume, papyrus, *felucca* rides, and hotel rooms. But you will also be approached by people who genuinely want to befriend you. Too often, jaded tourists treat everyone they meet with suspicion. There are a few ways to identify touts. First, be aware of your location. Anyone who approaches you downtown probably doesn't have your best interests in mind, while elsewhere the odds reverse. People who declare themselves your friend and ask you to go somewhere with them after 10 seconds are probably selling something (10min. is a different matter). One of the most certain giveaways is the phrase "Egyptian hospitality." Respectable Egyptians would never call attention to their own generosity.

EGYPT

A TRIP DOWN MEMORY LANE Many street names in Cairo have historical significance (for details, see **Modern History**, p. 66).

26 July Street: Commemorates the 1953 non-violent coup in which General Naguib and his Free Officers overthrew the king.

6 October Street: The date in 1973 when President Anwar Sadat staged a surprise attack on Israeli forces in the Sinai, earning him incredible popular support.

Sa'ad Zaghloul Street: Its namesake was the leader of the nationalist movement during World War I.

Salah al-Din Street: Salah al-Din al-Ayyubi (a.k.a. Saladin) assumed control of Egypt in 1171, fortified Cairo, and built its Citadel. His reign was a golden age for Egypt, and he is revered as one of the great heroes of Islamic history.

Tala'at Harb Street: Egypt's most famous economist, Muhammad Tala'at Harb, founded the country's first national bank (now the ubiquitous Banque Misr), which was the first bank in the world to conduct business in Arabic (as it still does).

OTHER NEIGHBORHOODS

The main bridge crossing the Nile from the downtown area is **Tahrir Bridge,** connecting Tahrir Sq. to the southern tip of Gezira Island. The northern half of the island (connected to downtown by the 26 July Bridge) is **Zamalek,** Cairo's ritziest residential area and home to European expats and expensive restaurants. South of Zamalek is **Roda Island,** site of the Nilometer. Past Tahrir Bridge on the western bank of the Nile, the Cairo Sheraton Hotel presides over the residential neighborhood of **Doqqi,** home to a handful of embassies. North of Doqqi lies **Mohandiseen** (Engineer's City), built in the late 1950s by Nasser as a neighborhood for engineers. South of Doqqi, past the Cairo Zoo and across the Giza Bridge, is **Giza Sq.** Southwest is **Pyramids Rd.,** where overpriced and disreputable bars run from the square all the way to the **Pyramids of Giza.**

The major streets in Cairo are sometimes labeled in both English and Arabic, but a good map is helpful (most find they need maps more detailed than the one given out by the Egyptian Tourist Authority). Maps cost E£10-30 and are available at most bookstores (p. 94). *The Complete Cairo Street-Finder: A-Z* is an authoritative map in book form. *Egypt Today* (E£10) publishes up-to-date street listings. Also, look for their *Dining Guide* and *Travel & Recreation Guide* (E£15 each).

▣ LOCAL TRANSPORTATION

METRO

The Cairo Metro is the fastest and cleanest ticket in town—worlds away from the rest of Cairo's bumpy and grumpy public transport. It was completed in 1987 as a joint project with France and Japan, and is the best (and only) subway system in all of Africa. Trains run along the main line, a 40km route linking the southern industrial district of Helwan to al-Marj in Heliopolis, with a number of stops downtown (look for the giant red "M" signs). An additional line connecting Giza was recently added; another line to Imbaba and al-Azhar via Zamalek is still under construction. Trains run about every six minutes (6am-midnight; 50pt-E£1.50). Save the ticket for exiting through the turnstiles or pay a fine of E£5. The stations downtown are **Mubarak** (Ramses Sq. and Railway Station), **Orabi** (Orabi St. and Ramses St.), **'Ataba** ('Ataba Sq.), **Nasser** (26 July St. and Ramses St.), **Sadat** (Tahrir Sq.), **Sa'ad Zaghloul** (Mansour St. and Isma'il Abaza St.), **Sayyida Zeinab** (Mansour St. and 'Ali Ibrahim St.), **al-Malik al-Saleh** (Salah Salem Rd.), and **Mari Girgis** (Old Cairo). Rush hour is before 9am and from 2-5pm. Although women can ride in any compartment, the first is always reserved for women; the second is, too, until 4pm.

MICROBUSES

Microbuses follow set routes to certain destinations, but tend to be flexible as long as all passengers are going to the same area. Stops are sometimes marked by a wooden shelter. If you don't have a basic command of Arabic, stick to the numbered, fixed routes. Microbuses go from **'Ataba Sq.** to Ramses Sq., Tahrir Sq., Northern Cemetery, Zamalek, Islamic Cairo, and Heliopolis. From **Tahrir Sq.**, microbuses leave for Heliopolis, Giza Sq., Doqqi, Mohandiseen, the Pyramids, and the airport terminals. Fares (25pt-E£1.50) depend on the length of the route.

MINIBUSES

Minibuses operate along many of the same routes as city buses. Although more expensive (50pt-E£1.50), minibuses are far more comfortable, and the orange-and-white buses operate on natural gas instead of unleaded. Minibus numbers appear in Arabic only. Beware: numbers with a strike through them travel completely different routes from their ordinary counterparts.

From the Nile Hilton:

#16 (١٦): al-Gala'a Bridge—Agouza

#27 (٢٧): Masr al-Gadida—Airport

#30 (٣٠): Nasser City—'Abbasiyya Sq.—Ramses Sq.—'Abd al-Munem Riad 2

#32 (٣٢): Hai al-Tamin—Mugamm'a—Ramses Sq.—'Abbasiyya

#35 (٢٥): 'Abbasiyya—'Abd al-Munem Riad 2—Roxy—al-Hijaz Sq.

#49 (٤٩): Falaki Sq.—Tahrir Sq.—Zamalek

#50 (٥٠): Ramses Sq.—'Ataba Sq.—Citadel

#52 (٥٢), **56** (٥٦): Bab al-Luq—Tahrir Sq.—Ma'adi—Old Cairo

#54 (٥٤): Bab al-Luq—Rifa'i Mosque—Ibn Tulun Mosque—Citadel—S. Cemetery

#55 (٥٥): Ma'adi—Bab al-Luq

#58 (٥٨): Ramses Sq.—Manial

#77 (٧٧): Bulaq al-Dakrur—Khan al-Khalili—al-Darasa

#84 (٨٤): 'Ataba/Tahrir Sq.—Doqqi—Giza

From Tahrir Square:

#77 (٧٧), **102** (١٠٢), **103** (١٠٣): Bulaq al-Dakrur—Khan al-Khalili—al-Darasa

#183 (١٨٣): Giza

From 'Ataba Square:

#26 (٢٦): Roxy—Tahrir Sq.—Doqqi—Giza

#48 (٤٨): Zamalek

#93 (٩٣): Mazalat—'Ataba Sq.—Basatin

BUSES

Few foreigners use the bus system, and with good reason: although very cheap (25-50pt), the buses are hot and cramped, and since they never come to a full stop, passengers must jump out the back to exit. Numbers and destinations are always in Arabic. Buses run 5:30am-12:30am (during Ramadan 6:30am-6:30pm and 7:30pm-2am), except for buses **#400** (٤٠٠) and **#400** (٤٠٠), which have 24hr. service to both **airport terminals** from Tahrir Sq. and Ramses Sq., respectively. Cairo's local bus depot is **'Abd al-Munem Riad Station,** north of the Egyptian Museum just below the towering, triangular Ramses Hilton. Several buses depart from the front of the old **Arab League Building,** to the west of the Mugamm'a along Tahrir St., adjacent to the bridge. Other bus stations are at **'Ataba Sq.** (to the Citadel, the Manial Palace, Giza, and Tahrir Sq.), and at **Giza Sq.** (to the Pyramids, airport, and Citadel).

TAXIS

Never let a taxi hail you. Major hotels, sights, and transportation centers are crowded with drivers who will offer you rides at several times the actual price. Stick to the **black-and-white taxis** that collect passengers along the way. Meters have been installed in all taxis, but drivers rarely use them due to outdated gas costs and the prohibitive price of getting them fixed. However, any driver that mentions money before you arrive at your destination is trying to rip you off. Passengers are

EGYPT

From 'Abd al-Munem Riad Station:

#8 (٨): Tahrir Sq.–Qasr al-'Aini–Manial–Giza–Mena House Hotel (Pyramids)

#63 (٦٣), **66** (٦٦): al-Azhar–Khan al-Khalili

#72 (٧٢): Sayyida Zeinab–Citadel–Imam al-Shafi'i Mausoleum

#82 (٨٢), **182** (١٨٢): Imam al-Shafi'i Mausoleum–S. Cemetery–Citadel

#99 (٩٩): Agouza–Sudan St.–Lebanon Sq. (Midan Lubnan)

#128 (١٢٨): 'Abbasiyya Sq.–'Ain Shams

#173 (١٧٣), **194** (١٩٤), **609** (٦٠٩): Tahrir Sq.–Citadel

#174 (١٧٤): Ramses–Sayyida Zeinab–Ibn Tulun–Sultan Hassan–Citadel

#400 (٤٠٠): Old Cairo Airport via Heliopolis (Roxy Sq.)

#403 (٤٠٣): Citadel–Sultan Hassan

#666 (٦٦٦): al-Gaili Museum

#900 (٩٠٠): Tahrir Sq.–Qasr al-'Aini–Manial (Youth Hostel)–Cairo University–Giza–Pyramids–Holiday Inn Hotel

#923 (٩٢٣): Basatin–Giza Sq.

#949 (٩٤٩): New Cairo Airport

From the Arab League Building:

#13 (١٣): Zamalek–Bab al-Luq

#19 (١٩), **203** (٢٠٣): Doqqi

#102 (١٠٢): Mazalat–Doqqi

#166 (١٦٦): 'Ataba Sq.–Doqqi

#815-173 (٨١٥-١٧٣): Medinat al-Talaba

From 'Ataba Square:

#214 (٢١٤): Qanatir

#404 (٤٠٤): Citadel–Tahrir Sq.–Medinat al-Talaba

#801 (٨٠١), **951** (٩٥١): Citadel–'Abd al-Munem Riad

#904 (٩٠٤): Mugamm'a–Pyramids

From Giza Square:

#3 (٣): Pyramids

#30 (٣٠): Ramses Station

#949 (٩٤٩): Airport (both terminals)

From Ramses Station:

#30 (٣٠): Pyramids

#160 (١٦٠): Citadel–Tahrir Sq.

expected to know the price, so have the fare in hand and pay with folded bills as you exit the vehicle, without discussion or glancing back for approval. Drivers who do not speak English tend to inflate prices less than their polyglot colleagues; so use landmarks and either say or show a written copy of your destination in Arabic. Showing a map to the driver never works. (For more information, see **Essentials: By Taxi,** p. 247). Rides in the downtown area (Ramses Sq., Tahrir Sq., Zamalek, and Islamic Cairo) should cost about **E£3-5.** Trips to the pyramids are about E£15; those to Ma'adi and Heliopolis run around E£8-10. A taxi to or from the airport should cost no more than E£20-25. These estimates are very generous, so be prepared to brush off taxi drivers who demand more.

🛂 PRACTICAL INFORMATION

TOURIST AND FINANCIAL SERVICES

Tourist Office: The **Egyptian Tourist Authority (ETA)** has offices scattered throughout the city. All provide free maps and info, and can make reservations or write out destinations in Arabic. The accuracy and utility of their information varies according to who is on duty. Some staff members tend to tell you what they think you should know rather than what you actually want to know. Locations include: **Cairo International Airport** (☎291 42 77; open 24hr.), at the entrance and next to the duty-free shops; **Giza** (☎385 02 59; open 24hr.), in front of Mena House Hotel; **Railway Station** (☎579 07 67; open daily 8am-8pm), on the left at the station's main entrance; **5 'Adly St.** (☎391 34 54; 8:30am-8pm), a 20min. walk from Tahrir Sq. If you want someone who speaks English well, your best bet is the 'Adly location. Follow Tala'at Harb St. and turn right on 'Adly St. The office is 3 blocks down on your left, just past the Tourist Police.

Student Cards: Medical Scientific Center, 103 Mathaf al-Manial St. (☎531 03 30), on Roda Island. South of the Manial Palace across the street from Kentucky Fried Chicken (look for the ISIC sign). Great source of information for travelers. Provides ISIC and

Go25 cards (E£25; bring a photo and proof of student status). Student volunteer staff speaks excellent English and will quote prices for sights and entertainment. The center gives out free maps and pamphlets and organizes excursions to see the Pyramids and whirling dervish dancing.

Passport Office, Mugamm'a Building, 2nd fl. (☎ 792 69 00). This gray edifice at the southern side of Tahrir Sq. was constructed during Nasser's flirtation with the USSR, and the spirit of the Cold War lives on in its Soviet-style inefficiency. To navigate the visa extension process, first stop at the information desk on the 2nd fl. Having what you want written down in Arabic beforehand helps. Registration open Sa-Th 8am-8pm, visa extensions 8am-1pm. For smaller crowds, check the 2nd fl. of the **Ministry of Economy and Foreign Trade Building,** 8 'Adly St. (☎ 390 43 63), next to the EgyptAir office. Bring a passport photo for visa extensions (2-6 months E£10, 1 year E£40). Open Sa-Th 8am-1:30pm.

Currency Exchange: Banks and exchange services litter the downtown area. **Banque Misr** (☎ 391 75 71) has branches at major hotels, with a main office downtown at 151 Muhammad Farid St. All open Sa-Th 8:30am-2pm and 6-9pm. **Cairo Barclay's International Bank,** 12 Sheikh Yusef Sq., Garden City (☎ 794 94 15 or 794 94 22), 3 blocks south of Tahrir Sq. along Qasr al-'Aini St., accepts traveler's checks and has worldwide money transfer services. Open Su-Th 8:30am-2pm; Ramadan 10am-1pm. Foreign banks closed F-Sa, but most Egyptian banks open Sa. Money wired to Egypt through **Citibank,** 4 Ahmed Basha St., Garden City (☎ 795 18 73 or 795 18 74; open Su-Th 8:30am-2pm) or **Western Union,** 1081 Corniche al-Nil, Garden City (☎ 797 13 00 or 797 13 74; open Su-Th 9am-8:30pm), in the FedEx office.

ATM: Egyptian British Banks have machines that accept Express Net, Global Access, PLUS, and V cards. Locations in Semiramis Intercontinental, Zamalek Marriott, Cairo Sheraton, and Ramses and Nile Hiltons.

Thomas Cook, 17 Mahmoud Bassouni St. (☎ 574 37 76, 574 39 55, or 574 39 67; fax 576 27 50). Half a block west of Tala'at Harb Sq. Other offices throughout the city. Travel agency, money transfers, currency exchange, and cash advances on MC and V. Cashes traveler's checks. Open daily 8am-5pm.

American Express, 15 Qasr al-Nil (☎ 574 79 91, 574 79 92, or 574 79 96). Off Tala'at Harb Sq., opposite EgyptAir toward Ramses St. Members can have money sent to the office and have mail held there. Cashes traveler's checks. Open Su-Th 9am-4pm; Ramadan 9am-3:30pm. Other locations at the Nile Hilton (☎ 578 50 02 or 578 50 03), Marriott Hotel (☎ 736 01 36), Pullman Ma'adi (☎ 790 78 51), and 4 Syria St. (☎ 570 79 08 or 570 79 14) in Mohandiseen.

EMBASSIES AND CONSULATES

Australia, World Trade Center 11-12th floors, 1191 Corniche al-Nil (☎ 575 04 44), in Bulaq. Past the 26 July Bridge. Passports generally replaced in 5 working days (32-page passports AUS$132, 64-page AUS$198, payable in E£ only). Immediate replacement in case of emergency. Open Su-W 8am-4:15pm, Th 8:30am-1:45pm.

Canada, 3rd fl. of Arab-African Bank Building, 5 Midan al-Saraya al-Kobr (☎ 794 31 10 or 794 31 19, emergencies ☎ 796 36 44), in Garden City. Passports replaced within one week for E£115. Open Su-Th 9am-2pm.

Israel, 6 Ibn al-Malik St. (☎ 761 03 80 or 761 04 58), in Doqqi. Cross over to Doqqi from Roda Island on University Bridge (al-Gam'a). The street to the right of and parallel to the bridge is Ibn al-Malik. Security guards by the entrance will ask to see your passport. Visas E£60. Open Su-Th 10am-12:30pm.

Jordan, 6 al-Goheina St. (☎ 748 55 66 or 749 99 12), in Doqqi. 2 blocks west of the Cairo Sheraton. Visas (photograph required) free for Australians, E£28 for New Zealanders, E£63 for Brits, E£231 for Americans, E£91 for Canadians. Same-day service. Open Sa-Th 9am-2pm; arrive early to avoid the crowd.

Lebanon, 22 al-Mansour Muhammad St. (☎ 738 28 23, 738 28 24, or 738 28 25), in Zamalek. Photograph required for passports. Visas E£123. Any evidence of having been to Israel prohibits obtaining a Lebanese visa. Consular services open M-Th and Sa 9:30am-12:30pm.

South Africa, 21 and 23 Giza St., 18th fl. of the Nile Tower (☎571 72 38 or 571 72 39), in Giza. File applications for new passports here; they're sent to South Africa for processing. Entire process takes 8 weeks. In the meantime, you are issued a one-page Emergency Passport good for 3 months (E£50). Open Su-Th 8am-5pm; consular services Su-Th 9am-noon.

Syria, 18 'Abd al-Rahim Sabri St. (☎337 70 20), in Doqqi. Bring 2 photographs for a visa. Visas free for Australians and New Zealanders, E£182 for Brits, E£195 for Canadians, and E£211 for Americans. Anywhere from 1 day to 1 week for processing, depending on nationality. You are advised to apply for visas in your home country. Americans are sometimes denied visas at Syrian embassies in other Arab countries. Evidence of travel to Israel prohibits obtaining a Syrian visa. Open Sa-Th 9am-2pm.

UK, 7 Ahmed Ragheb St. (☎794 08 50), in Garden City. Also handles **New Zealand** affairs. Will replace passports within 4 days and only accepts E£ (32-page passports E£270, 48-page E£330). Open Su-Th 9am-1pm.

US, 5 Latin America St. (☎794 82 11, emergencies ☎795 73 71), in Garden City. 2 blocks south of Tahrir Sq. For the consulate, enter on Lazoughli St. around the block. Lost or stolen passports replaced overnight for US$60 or E£ equivalent (US$40 for renewal). Open Su-Th 8am-noon.

LOCAL SERVICES

Luggage Storage: Avoid the unreliable Ramses Station lockers. Get bilingual written proof of having stored anything at a hotel. Make sure that "storage" in budget hotels is a safe at the front desk and not just a hallway.

English-Language Bookstores: Lehnert and Landrock, 44 Sherif St. (☎393 53 24), between 'Adly St. and 26 July St. "L&L" offers a superb, wide-ranging selection of guidebooks, maps, histories, and postcards. Open M-F 10am-2pm and 4-9pm, Sa 9am-11pm. MC/V. **Used Books,** left of the statue by the Cairo Puppet Theater near 'Ataba Sq. Metro: 'Ataba. Among tracts on dialectical materialism and US Boy Scout manuals are titles for as low as E£4. **AUC Bookstore,** 113 Qasr al-'Aini St. (☎797 53 77), in the Hill House at the American University in Cairo. University texts, classic novels, Arab literature in translation, maps, and guide books. ID needed to enter the campus. Open Su-Th 8:30am-5pm. MC/V.

Newspapers and Magazines: The *Egyptian Gazette, al-Ahram Weekly,* and *Middle East Times* are Egypt's English newspapers. *Egypt Today,* a monthly magazine (E£10), is handy for current restaurant and entertainment listings. All are sold at **The Reader's Corner,** 33 'Abd al-Khaleq Sarwat St., downtown. Open M-Sa 10am-7pm. Many hotels and street stands from Tahrir Sq. to Tala'at Harb Sq. sell foreign language publications.

American Cultural Center, 5 Latin America St., Garden City (☎794 96 01 or 576 27 04; library ☎795 05 32 or 797 34 12), inside the US Embassy, across from the British Embassy. Tourists in Egypt for at least 12 months are eligible to join no matter what their nationality (bring 2 photographs and a passport). Members can borrow books and watch videos. All American citizens have access to the A/C library's collection of popular magazines and books on America. Occasional free films and lectures. Call for a schedule. Open Su-F 10am-4pm; in winter M-F 10am-4pm.

Supermarkets: Seoudi Market, 25 Midan al-Missaha St., Doqqi (☎748 84 40 or 748 84 41); 20 Hijaz St., Mohandiseen (☎346 03 91); and 15 Ahmad Hishmat St., Zamalek (☎736 35 86 or 735 03 70). A fully stocked supermarket with low prices. All open daily 9am-2am. **Sunny Supermarket,** 11 al-'Aziz 'Osman St., Zamalek (☎342 11 21), up the road from the Pension Zamalek south of 26 July St. A more expensive option offering an impressive array of Egyptian and Western products. Sunny's also has a bulletin board where you can find information on anything from Arabic lessons to apartments for rent. Open daily 8am-10pm.

Laundromat: Circle Cleaning, 24 26 July St. (☎576 08 55), near the Supreme Court and the intersection with Tala'at Harb St. Open daily 9am-9pm. The place is a madhouse—be prepared to fight your way to a machine—so you're better off doing your laundry yourself or paying a maid in your hotel. 50pt per piece is reasonable.

Swimming Pools: Fontana Hotel (☎592 21 45 or 592 23 21), in Ramses Sq. has a teal-tiled pool on its 7th fl. patio (E£15 per day). Cairo's sporting clubs also sell day passes for E£20: the **Gezira Sporting Club** (☎735 60 00), in front of the Marriott Hotel in Zamalek; the **Ma'adi Sporting Club,** 8 al-Nadi Sq. (☎790 54 55); and the **Heliopolis Sporting Club,** 17 al-Merghany St. (☎291 00 65). Day passes at 5-star hotels up to E£30, though at some large, busy hotels, no one will notice if you jump in.

EMERGENCY AND COMMUNICATIONS

Emergency: Police: ☎122, 126, or 303 41 22. **Fire:** ☎125 or 391 01 15.

Tourist Police, 5 'Adly St. (☎390 19 44 or 390 60 28, emergencies ☎126). In the same building as the Tourist Office. Also at Cairo International Airport (☎637 25 84), the Manial Palace Hotel in Giza (☎385 02 59), and Ramses Station.

24-Hour Pharmacies: Victoria Pharmacy, 90 Qasr al-'Aini St. (☎794 86 04). **Isaaf Pharmacy** (☎574 33 69) on Ramses St. and 26 July St. **Seif Pharmacy,** 76 Qasr al-'Aini (☎794 26 78). **Zamalek Pharmacy,** 3 Shagarat al-Durr (☎735 24 06).

Hospitals: The best-equipped is **al-Salaam International Hospital** (☎524 02 50), Ma'adi, Corniche al-Nil. Other options: **Anglo-American Hospital** (☎735 61 62 or 735 61 65), Zamalek, on Botanical Garden St. below the Cairo Tower; and **Cairo Medical Center** (☎258 05 66, 258 02 17, or 258 10 03), in Heliopolis at Roxy Sq.

Fax Office: You can send and receive faxes at the business office of the **Ramses Hilton** (fax 575 71 52 or 578 22 21). Sending prices vary by destination; receiving costs E£4 per page. Most telephone offices can also send faxes.

Telephones: Main Telephone Office, on Ramses St., one block north of 26 July St. Other offices in Zamalek, Airport, Ma'adi, Tahrir Sq., 'Adly St., and Alfy St. (under the Windsor Hotel). All open 24hr. You can make **collect calls** and **credit card calls** with the USADirect, UKDirect, CanadaDirect, and JapanDirect phones in the lobbies of the Ramses Hilton, Marriott, and Semiramis Hotels (for access numbers, see **Keeping in Touch,** p. 79). Yellow Menatel and red NilePhones can make international calls. For a 25% surcharge, you can also place international calls at the business service offices in the Meridien, Sheraton, and Nile Hilton hotels. Open 24hr. **Directory Assistance:** ☎140.

Internet Access: Internet access has recently become cheaper and more widespread. A growing number of hotels offer access to their guests, usually for about E£10 per hr. The **Internet Egypt Cafe** (☎578 04 44) in the Nile Hilton Mall has fierce A/C and several banks of computers. 15min. minimum E£3; 30min. E£6; 1hr. E£12. Open daily 7am-midnight. The **Hany Internet Cafe,** 16 Sarwat St., 1 block north of the Berlin Hotel, offers a small but serviceable place to get online. 30min. E£3; 1hr. E£6.

Post Office, 55 Sarwat St. (☎391 26 14), in 'Ataba Sq. under the dome. Often crowded, but blissfully empty shortly before closing. Packages require export license, available from airport, hotels, and tourist shops. Open Sa-Th 8am-7pm; Ramadan 9am-3pm. Most post offices in Cairo sell stamps and have EMS. **24hr. EMS** on Bidek St. One convenient branch is at 13 Metitte Bash St. in Tahrir Sq. (☎575 43 13), opposite the Egyptian Museum. Open Sa-Th 9am-9pm. Stamps sold and letters mailed at major hotels.

Federal Express, 1081 Corniche al-Nil, 8th floor, Garden City (☎792 33 01), opposite the Meridien Hotel on the east bank of the Nile. Open daily 8am-8pm.

▗ ACCOMMODATIONS

Downtown Cairo, on and around **Tala'at Harb St.,** is littered with dozens of budget hotels and dorms occupying the upper floors of colonial buildings. All hotels listed below accept reservations, include breakfast in their prices, and have fans and

SCAM WARS, EPISODE I
Never underestimate the power of the con side. The most notorious con, the **hotel scam**, begins the moment you step off the plane. Have two or three hotels in mind and avoid taking a taxi or otherwise making verbal contact (besides a firm, polite "no") with anyone who offers you anything at the airport. Do not believe anyone who claims your chosen hotels are closed, whether they are taxi drivers, "tour guides," or even (underpaid) tourist police. Simply find another driver, get dropped off at a nearby landmark, or refuse payment. When in Cairo (or any other city) do not let yourself be a taken to a hotel by a taxi driver or "hotel manager." This only succeeds in inflating the price due to hefty commissions and in bringing you to a dishonest establishment that may have further designs on your wallet. The second con is the dreaded **tour con.** Even at reputable hotels, the management may push tours of high cost and low quality. Always check with the tourist office for a list of fair prices. Day excursions to the Pyramids and Saqqara may be an excuse to take you to perfume and papyrus shops along the way. Several hotels in Cairo offer *felucca* and Nile cruise trips between Aswan and Luxor: these are the most serious **rip-offs.** Skip the middleman and contact **Amigo Tours,** in the Isis Hotel in Aswan (☎097 31 68 43). Inclusive multi-day trips (excluding train fare) cost US$65 for a *felucca* and US$145 for a Nile cruise. As with any tour, seek to pay the balance directly to the tour company and only after you arrive at your destination—whether it be Alexandria or Alderon.

24hr. hot water in all rooms unless otherwise noted. "Hotels" and "hostels" are close cousins in Egypt. Many hotels have dorm beds available and many hostels have single or double rooms. Most maids will do your laundry (usually about 50pt per article). If you're in Cairo for a while or during low season, bargain for a reduced rate. Single-sex groups should have no problem renting a flat (E£500-2000 per month), but landlords often frown upon renting to coed groups. The billboards at the AUC entrance and the Sunny Market in Zamalek list available apartments.

BUDGET

Pension Roma, 169 Muhammad Farid St. (☎391 10 88 or 391 13 40), 1 block south of 26 July St. and two blocks east of Tala'at Harb St. Turn right on 'Adly St. and left after the synagogue, and look for the hotel's green sign above the Gattegno department store, between 'Ataba and Nasser Metro stations. Owner Madam Cressaty keeps her beautifully designed *pensione* immaculately clean and perfectly maintained. Well-furnished rooms may have a breezy balcony, but no fans. Towels, toilet paper, and soap provided. Fan rental E£2.50. Free storage. Singles E£29.50; doubles E£40, with shower E£55; triples E£73.50, with shower E£82. Reservations recommended.

Hotel Minerva, 39 Tala'at Harb St. (☎392 06 00, 392 06 01, or 392 06 02), one block toward Tala'at Harb Sq. from 26 July St. Entrance is on Mamar El Central St. between Tala'at Harb St. and Sherif St. Beautifully renovated bathrooms, vast balconies, and hardwood floors add a touch of elegance. Rooms come with sinks. Often full, so reservations are recommended. Singles E£23; doubles E£35; triples E£48. Fan rental E£2.

Sultan Hotel, Venice Hotel, and Safari Hotel, 4 Soug al-Tawfiqia St. (☎577 22 58, 574 32 69, and 575 07 52). These 3 hotels collectively occupy the 1st 5 floors of one address. All are extremely cheap, with friendly, honest management. **Venice** has Internet access for E£8 per hr. Japanese backpackers seem to find **Safari** particularly attractive. Breakfast not included, but a fruit market thrives just outside the entrance. Dorms E£6-8; the ones at **Sultan** are the most comfortable. Singles and doubles E£25.

Pension Select Hotel, 19 'Adly St., 8th fl. (☎393 37 07), next to a synagogue. High above the street noise, the Select offers rooms that are quiet and off the beaten path. Many rooms have access to a shared balcony with a sweeping view of the city. Singles E£25; doubles E£40; triples E£60.

Sun Hotel, 2 Tala'at Harb St., 9th fl. (☎578 17 86 or 773 00 87). Worshiped by budget travelers for its convenient location—less than a block from the Metro, on the left as you leave Tahrir Sq. Features satellite TV, a kitchen, and a lively lobby area with crammed couches. Comfortable beds in compact rooms. Bargain for longer stays. Dorm beds E£15; singles E£30; doubles E£40; triples E£51.

Youth Hostel (HI), 135 Malik 'Abd al-'Aziz al-Sa'ud St., Roda Island (☎364 07 29; fax 98 41 07). Metro: Sayyida Zeinab. Exit to the right and walk straight to the Nile. Cross the Sayala Bridge and continue straight across Roda Island to the Nile's main channel. Turn left just before the University (al-Gam'a) bridge (with Salah al-Din Mosque to your right); the hostel is 10m away on the left. The hostel is clean and quiet, a nice island retreat from downtown. A bit isolated from tourist sights (but not the Nilometer!). No lockout. Curfew 11pm. Call ahead for reservations. Single-sex 8- and 3-bed dorms E£15 and E£20; nonmembers E£1 extra.

Isma'ilia House Hotel, 1 Tahrir Sq., 8th fl. (☎796 31 22), by the exit of the Sadat Metro station in the direction of AUC. A warm, convenient hotel with diligent management. The rooms are fairly standard, but have stupendous views of Tahrir Sq. Singles E£20, with shower E£25; doubles E£40, with shower E£50; triples E£51, with shower E£60.

Bluebird Hotel, 42 Tala'at Harb St., 6th fl. (☎575 63 77), opposite 'Adly St. heading toward Ramses St. A fairly clean and well-maintained option, though some of the walls are rather thin. Separate baths for men and women, satellite TV, and common kitchen. Singles E£20; doubles E£40; triples E£60.

Anglo-Swiss Hotel, 14 Champollion St., 6th fl. (☎575 14 97), 2 blocks west of Tala'at Harb Sq. From Tahrir Sq., turn right on Champollion in the northwestern end of the square before the museum, by the parking lot. The hotel will be to your left at the intersection with Mahmoud Bassouni St. Play the piano in the sunny dining hall or watch some TV in a pleasant living room before retiring to quiet, if sometimes drab, rooms with shared baths, most with balcony. Friendly management, but not the most reputable around. Avoid the touts that hang around the hotel. French spoken. Singles E£20; doubles E£30. Student discount.

Gresham Hotel, 20 Tala'at Harb St. (☎576 20 94), just off Tala'at Harb Sq. Not all rooms come with fans. Travelers may find better deals on tours elsewhere. Singles E£25, with bath and A/C E£35; doubles E£40, with bath and A/C E£45; triples E£55, with bath and A/C E£65; quads E£70, with bath and A/C E£80.

A BIT SWANKIER

▨ **Berlin Hotel,** 2 al-Shawarby St. (☎/fax 395 75 02; berlinhotelcairo@hotmail.com). From Tala'at Harb Sq., walk up Qasr al-Nil toward Mustafa Kamal Sq. The entrance to this new hotel is on a pedestrian-only street. Friendly proprietor Hisham is generous with his wealth of information and advice and makes sure that all his customers are well cared for. Elegant rooms boast private showers, full-length velvet curtains, and quite possibly the most comfortable beds available for any price in Cairo. All rooms have A/C. Internet access E£10 per hr., MediaRing Internet phone calls to anywhere in the world available at E£2 per min. Hotel can arrange transportation from airport—a good idea, since Berlin's policy against paying commissions has earned some enemies among unscrupulous taxi drivers. Reservations recommended. Singles US$20; doubles US$25; triples US$30.

▨ **Victoria Hotel,** 66 Goumhoriyya St. (☎589 22 90 or 589 22 91; fax 591 30 08). From the 'Ataba Metro station, walk north along Goumhoriyya to reach this 3-star hotel. Professional service and amenities beyond the dreams of most budget travelers, including a bank, Internet cafe, and hairdresser. Restaurant and posh bar with satellite TV. Rooms with polished wood floors, A/C, bath, and TV. Full breakfast buffet included. Reservations recommended. Singles US$19; doubles US$25; triples US$30. AmEx/MC/V.

Windsor Hotel, 19 Alfy St. (☎591 58 10 or 591 52 77; fax 592 16 21; windsorcairo@link.com; www.windsorcairo.com). Clean facilities with excellent service in an atmosphere of old-time grandeur make this a character-ful place to spend a night in Cairo. The hotel's gem is the Barrel Bar (named for the barrel furniture), which once served as the British Officers' Club and retains nostalgic artifacts from the old days. Monty Python's Michael Palin hung out here while filming *Around the World in Eighty*

EGYPT

Days. Rooms have A/C, towels, crisp sheets, and comfy beds. Reservations recommended. Singles with shower US$29.50, with bath US$37- 46.50; doubles with shower US$38.50, with bath US$47-56.50. Prices include tax. 25% *Let's Go* discount, 15% during peak seasons. 5% credit card service charge may be added. AmEx/MC/V.

Happyton Hotel, 10 Aly al-Kassar St. (☎592 86 00). With your back to Tala'at Harb St., turn left on Emad al-Dein St. from Alfy St. at Cinema Diana. Turn right on Kassar St. to reach the entrance. This hotel offers the cheapest rooms with A/C and private bath in the city. Includes a small bar in the lobby, as well as a restaurant. Singles E£46; doubles E£66; triples E£84.

Lotus Hotel, 12 Tala'at Harb St. (☎575 627; fax 575 47 20; www.lotushotel.com). The sister hotel of the Windsor offers upscale accommodations close to Tahrir Sq. Restaurant and bar 2 floors up. Singles E£60, with shower and A/C E£90; doubles E£90, with shower and A/C E£120; triples with shower and A/C E£160. MC/V.

Carlton Hotel, 21 26 July St. (☎575 50 22; fax 575 53 23), beside the Cinema Rivoli and near the vegetable market and intersection of Tala'at Harb St. and 26 July St. Friendly management succeeds in maintaining the 1930s glory of this aging institution, though rooms often remain vacant. Each room comes with satellite TV, A/C, and furnished balconies. Dinner is served nightly on the rooftop garden, complete with stunning views. Breakfast not included. Singles E£65; doubles E£90.

Pension Zamalek, 6 Salah al-Din St. (☎735 93 18) in Zamalek. Turn south on Osman St. from 26 July St., then right on Salah al-Din. Pleasant rooms with a quiet residential atmosphere lead to furnished balconies. Breakfast served in a relaxing cafe. Reservations recommended. Singles E£50; doubles E£80; triples E£120.

🞂 FOOD

Sticking with the same old *fuul* and *ta'amiyya* will require only 50pt to amply fill your stomach. A good place for *kushari* (E£1.50-3) is **al-Tahrir,** on Tahrir St. near Bab al-Luq or on Abdel Khalek Sarwat St. near Tala'at Harb St. **Lux,** on 26 July St., is another tasty choice. Fresh **fruit juice,** on sale anywhere you see bags of fruit hanging around a storefront, is one of the highlights of the Egyptian culinary experience. As long as the place looks clean and has running water behind the counter, it is probably safe to drink, though you should know that glasses are merely rinsed between customers. At places without waiters, pay first and then exchange your receipt for food.

Sit-down meals are often relatively cheap by Western standards and are usually worth the small investment, as long as you choose wisely from the menu. Even at more expensive restaurants, you can create a handsome meal out of hummus, *baba ghanoush* (grilled eggplant dip), and salad for under E£10. *Fatir*—a filo dough-like bread stuffed and topped with vegetables, meats, or sweets—is far tastier than the imitations of Italian pizza in town, and usually cheaper (E£5-10). A 5% **sales tax** on food and a 10-12% **service charge** at sit-down restaurants are added to the bill. A **minimum charge** of about E£2 is common among more expensive restaurants. Additionally, a small **tip** (E£1) is usually in order.

Vegetarians have an advantage, as Cairo's veggie fare is cheaper and better-tasting than the poor-to-mediocre meat dishes found in most restaurants. Since cheap restaurants and street vendors often advertise vaguely labeled "meat" that could very well have been pulling a cart a few days before, even militant carnivores may discover a sudden empathy for animals.

While eating local food is an essential component of the Egyptian experience, you might also want to try the cleaner, faster, air-conditioned Western fast-food chains lined up across from AUC on Mahmoud St. **Pizza Hut** offers slices for E£2 each. (☎356 26 28. Open daily 9am-4am, delivery until 3am.) Next door, **Kentucky Fried Chicken** is a bit cheaper but serves buns in place of the biscuits so treasured by the Colonel and his cohorts. **McDonald's,** near AUC, offers combos for about E£9. (☎355 81 31. Open daily 10am-2am.) All have free delivery up to 2km away.

DOWNTOWN

RESTAURANTS

Al-Tabei, 31 Orabi St. (☎575 42 11), north of Orabi Sq., 100m south of Ramses St. The menu is primarily veg., though there are some meat dishes. A sprawling meal of *ta'amiyya*, *fuul*, oven-roasted eggplant, and a large plate of salads (choose 4 for E£3) will amount to only a few pounds. The interior is clean and bright, the service professional and blue-vested. Open daily 9am-1am.

Fatatri al-Tahrir, 166 Tahrir St., 1 block east of Tahrir Sq. If the decor is minimal, it's to keep your attention focused on the food, which includes the best *fatir* downtown. Get your filo topped with meat, vegetables, or sweets (E£6-10). A medium-sized *fatir* makes a large meal (E£8); small (E£6) and large (E£10) also available. Finish it off with a tall glass of fruit juice from the excellent stand next door. Open 24hr.

Felfela, 15 Hoda Sha'rawi St. (☎392 27 51 or 392 28 33), off Tala'at Harb St., one block south of Tala'at Harb Sq. The cool rainforest ambiance attracts a crowd of both tourists and locals, who sit at tables made of huge tree stumps, with vines hanging overhead. Full meal of *waraq 'einab* (stuffed grape leaves) E£12; stuffed pigeon E£17. Also delicious is *om 'ali*, a pastry baked with milk, honey, and raisins (E£6). Of more interest to the budget traveler is Felfela Take-Away, around the corner at 15 Tala'at Harb St. which excels at simple foods like *fuul* (50pt), *ta'amiyya* (50pt), and lentil soup (E£2). Both open daily 6am-midnight.

Restaurant al-Hati, 8A 26 July St. (☎391 88 29). The glitzier younger sibling of 'Ali Hassan al-Hati (see below), complete with marble tiles, mirrors, and far better food. Standard Egyptian entrees E£25-30. Take-out. Open daily noon-midnight. AmEx/MC/V.

Peking, 14 Saraya al-Azbakia St. (☎591 23 81), behind Cinema Diana between Alfy St. and 26 July St. Cairo's most popular Chinese restaurant. Pamper yourself with the complimentary steaming hand towels before a full meal with appetizer, 3 dishes, and dessert—don't miss the honey-walnut Tarte Lee (E£40-60). Alcohol served. Free delivery. Open daily noon-midnight. AmEx/MC/V. **Other branches:** Mohandiseen (☎349 98 60), New Ma'adi (☎516 42 18), and Heliopolis (☎270 56 78).

Le Bistro, 8 Hoda Sha'rawi St. (☎392 76 94), down the street from Felfela. Walk down the stairs, pick up a French newpaper, and sit down to a French menu that you can study as you listen to soft French music. By the time the bill comes *(en français, bien sûr)*, you will have enjoyed a decent imitation of Gallic cuisine. Entrees E£20-30. Open daily noon-midnight. AmEx.

Fu-Shing, 28 Tala'at Harb St. (☎576 61 84), in an alley running west from the street. Walk up the stairs past the Arabic and Chinese calligraphy. Exotic items (purple seaweed soup E£4) and diverse veg. options make this Chinese restaurant a delicious escape from ho-hum(mus) street vendor fare. Entrees E£15-25. Open daily noon-10pm.

Cafe Riche, 17 Tala'at Harb St. (☎392 97 93). This storied cafe-restaurant, once a favorite of radicals and revolutionaries, may intimidate budget travelers from the outside, but step inside for a diverse selection of foods ranging from traditional Middle Eastern to modern Western. Pasta E£10. Rib eye steak E£32. Stuffed quail E£30. Open daily 10am-midnight. AmEx/MC/V.

CAFES

■ **Al-'Abd,** 25 Tala'at Harb St. (☎392 44 07), opposite the Arab Bank building. This upscale bakery-cafe provides the perfect antidote to Cairo's heat: a whopping 3-scoop mango ice cream cone (E£1.50). Ask to sample any of the tempting pastries. Open daily 8:30am-12:30am. **Another branch:** 26 July St., 1 block east of Tala'at Harb St.

J. Groppi, on the west side of Tala'at Harb Sq. This confectionery opened its doors to Europeans and Europeanized Egyptians in 1891 and hasn't changed its decor since. Make your purchases in the bakery or linger in the A/C coffee shop. A great place for a date (chocolate-covered or not). The mango and apricot jams make for a tart retort to the excellent Turkish coffee. A snack will cost about E£5. Open daily 7am-midnight.

E G Y P T

La Poire, 18 Latin America St. (☎ 355 15 09), across the street from the British Embassy in Garden City. Come for the extensive selection of ice cream flavors (E£1.75 per scoop) but stay for the croissants, eclairs, and sticky-sweet *ba'laweh* (about E£1.50 per serving)—and don't leave until you're *poire*-shaped. Open daily 7am-midnight.

Brazilian Coffee Shop, 38 Tala'at Harb St., at the intersection with 'Adly St. This A/C restaurant upstairs from the Miami Cinema serves cappuccino and espresso (E£2.50 each). A great place to read the morning paper with your favorite middle management chums. Chicken sandwich E£6. Open daily 6am-midnight.

ZAMALEK

RESTAURANTS

■ **L'Aubergine,** 5 Sayyed al-Bakry St. (☎ 735 65 50). From 26 July St., turn right at Brazil St.; turn right again at the 1st opportunity and the restaurant is a few meters ahead. The atmosphere is Louis Armstrong covering Edith Piaf. Spinach lasagna (E£19), *l'aubergine moussaka* (E£18), and a refreshing gazpacho (E£8) typify the exclusively veg. selection. **Cafe Curnovsky,** the Eggplant's sister restaurant upstairs, serves meat (E£25-30). Both open daily noon-1am. Reservations accepted. V.

■ **Didos Al Dente,** 26 Bahgat Basha 'Ali St. (☎ 735 91 17). Walking north along the western corniche, take a right onto Muhammad Anis St.; Didos Al Dente is two blocks ahead on your left. Fashionable young Egyptians come for the wide selection of pastas with 18 different sauces (E£5-15), plus side dishes such as the excellent *insalata al-funghi* (E£11). Open daily noon-1am. Reservations a good idea for groups during the evening.

Maison Thomas, 157 26 July St. (☎ 735 70 57), on the right near the base of the bridge as you come into Zamalek from Cairo. Hip French/Italian bistro filled with hanging salamis and wheels of cheese that evoke the Mediterranean's other coast. A wide range of salads and baguette sandwiches at a wide range of prices, but it's the Italian-style pizza that brings the crowds (E£15-20). Gorge yourself like a pig on any of numerous pork options. Free delivery. Open 24hr.

Hana Korean Restaurant, 21 Ma'had al-Swissry St. (☎ 735 18 46), in al-Nil Zamalek Hotel. Take a right off 26 July St. onto Brazil St. and the restaurant is to the right after a bend in the road. This A/C haven, popular among tourists and expats, serves up shark-fin soup (E£9) and *bulgogi* (tender slices of beef you barbecue right at the table; E£23). Entrees come with a complimentary assortment of 7 side dishes, including two kinds of *kimchi* (cabbage or vegetables that have been spiced and fermented). Stella (E£7) is everyone's favorite gal. Open daily 11:30am-11pm.

Bon Appetit, 3 Isma'il Muhammad St. (☎ 735 43 82 or 735 91 08), one block from the Flamenco Hotel on the west side of Zamalek. The cleanest place in town to try tongue sandwiches (E£4.75). Main courses E£10-30. Open daily 9am-1am. AmEx/MC/V.

CAFES

■ **Simonds,** 112 26 July St. (☎ 735 94 36), just east of the intersection where Hassan Sabri St. becomes Brazil St. The New York chic feel lures an eclectic mix of locals and foreign emissaries who sip *café au lait* (E£2.75) and fresh-squeezed orange juice (E£2.50). A huge selection of savory desserts (E£1-2). Open daily 7am-9pm.

Mandarin Koedar, 17 Shagarat al-Durr St. (☎ 735 50 10). Take a right off 26 July St. at the Misr Gas Station onto Shagarat al-Durr St. and follow the crooked lane for 200m. Cool to the core: a wide selection of ice cream (E£1.50 per scoop) and pastries served up in an arctic A/C setting. Open daily 9am-11pm.

MOHANDISEEN

Le Tabasco, 8 'Ammen Sq. (☎ 336 55 83). From the Dokki Metro station, follow Tahrir St. west for 600m, then take a right at Babel St. and continue for another 600m. One of the best restaurants in Cairo, this perpetually trendy establishment stays en vogue by constantly shaking up the menu. Dim candlelight and soft jazz accompany the Mediterranean-centered cuisine. Appetizers E£10-24. Pasta E£10-20. Main dishes E£20-40. Open daily 1pm-midnight. Reservations required. AmEx/MC/V.

Al-Omda, 6 al-Gaza'ir St. (☎ 346 22 47), near the Atlas Hotel on Gam'at al-Duwal St. Full meals E£10-25. Dine-in (A/C) or delivery. Open daily noon-3am.

Prestige Pizza, 43 Geziret al-'Arab St. (☎ 347 03 83), just east of Wadi al-Nil St. Coming from Gam'at al-Duwal St., turn right before al-Ahli Bank. Inexpensive pizza served in a laid-back atmosphere. The "normal" size pizzas (E£12) are quite enough to satisfy most appetites. "Prestige" size E£17. Open daily noon-1am. AmEx/MC/V.

Coffee Roastery, 46 Nadi Seid St. (☎ 749 88 82). An Egyptian expat in San Francisco exported this cafe to Cairo. Sip a caffe latte (E£4) while reading through *Time* or your choice of Egyptian teenybopper magazines. Open daily 8am-midnight. AmEx/MC/V.

ISLAMIC CAIRO (KHAN AL-KHALILI)

Egyptian Pancakes, 7 al-Azhar Sq. (☎ 590 86 23), half a block from the intersection of al-Azhar St. and Gohar al-Qa'it St. Small (E£10), medium (E£12), or large (E£15) *fatir* topped with sweets (honey, coconut, or raisins) or meats. Open 24hr.

Coffee Shop Naguib Mahfouz, 5 al-Badistante Ln. (☎ 590 37 88), two blocks west of al-Hussein Mosque. Not on *Sugar St.*, as those familiar with Nobel laureate Mahfouz's work might hope. This pricey restaurant is a calm oasis of delectable food in the maddening bustle of Khan al-Khalili. Engage in *Small Talk on the Nile* as you sip on fresh fruit juices (said to be the favorites of Mahfouz, who was once a regular here). No doubt he also appreciated the clean restrooms and nightly live music. No *Autumn Quail,* but you can try a Lebanese kebab (E£39) or *tabbouleh* (E£6.50). Minimum charge E£10 per person, E£2 music charge. Open daily 10am-2am. AmEx/MC/V.

Al-Gamhorya, on al-Azhar St., one block east of the green pedestrian overpass at al-Ghouri Mosque and Mausoleum. A perfect *kushari* stop-off (E£1.50). Single women may feel out of place among the mostly male clientele. Open daily 9am-11pm.

◎ SIGHTS

Centuries of history come together in the streets of Egypt's capital, where the dusty ghosts of dynasties past fight to be remembered amid the emerging spirit of a metropolitan future. In **Islamic Cairo** (p. 103), the devout prostrate themselves before some of the Muslim world's most revered sites while small-time capitalists haggle in **Khan al-Khalili** (p. 108), the ancient bazaar nearby. In the **Cities of the Dead** (p. 111), mausolea and tombs coexist with a poor but vibrant community. Christian and Jewish minority communities are centered in the **Coptic** district of **Old Cairo** (p. 113), and the remains of **al-Fustat** (p. 115) house the earliest Egyptian mosque. **Modern Cairo** (p. 116) rushes to embrace the future, while the city's **museums** (p. 118) strain to weave together its four millennia of history. Note that **price hikes** of 25-50% on admission tickets to major sights are scheduled for the coming year; see **Inflation Sucks,** p. 77, for more information.

ISLAMIC CAIRO

The great 14th-century historian Ibn Khaldun once said, "He who has not seen Cairo cannot know the grandeur of Islam." The resplendent mosques and monuments of Cairo's medieval district rank among the world's finest examples of Islamic architecture. Unlike Damascus and Baghdad (the other capitals of the medieval Islamic world), Cairo was spared the devastation of Mongol invasions. Make sure to see the historical sights the area has to offer, but spare some time to wander through today's living Islamic Cairo and catch a glimpse at ancient way of life whose customs, like the domes and minarets above, have endured through the centuries.

GENERAL ADVICE

It takes at least two days to explore Islamic Cairo, and the area holds riches enough to fill many more. **William Lyster** and **SPARE (Society for the Preservation of Architectural Resources in Egypt)** publish a superb set of four 3-D maps of Islamic Cairo (E£10 per map). The *City Map of Cairo* (E£10) has an indexed map of Islamic Cairo. For in-depth descriptions and history, try *Islamic Monuments in Cairo: A Practical Guide,* by Caroline Williams (E£60). That book and most maps are available at the AUC Bookstore (p. 96).

EGYPT

Many of the important monuments charge entrance fees (E£6-12, half-price with ISIC). At free sights (mosques in particular), you will be expected to give *bakhsheesh* to the gatekeeper (E£1 should be adequate). At the biggest mosques, the man who "guards" your shoes while you are inside usually expects compensation of some kind. Students purchasing discounted tickets should pay 50pt-E£1 in *bakhsheesh*. Where permitted, climbing the minaret is included in the ticket price. Opening hours are estimates at best, so declare your interest to whomever is around and someone will let you in; a tour of Islamic Cairo confined to already-unlocked doors will miss many of the city's treasures.

Most "ornamental" mosques—those no longer used for regular prayer—are open daily from 8am to 5pm. Other mosques are open from dawn until dusk, but visitors are not welcome during prayer times. Wait a few minutes after the congregation has finished before entering. There are usually separate entrances for men and women. Night visitors are often not permitted, although some travelers rave about watching the sunset paint Cairo dusty pink from atop a minaret. Avoid visiting noon-2pm on Fridays, when the Muslim community gathers for afternoon prayer. Certain highly venerated mosques—namely, Sayyida Hussein, Sayyida Zeinab, and Sayyida Nafisa—are believed to contain the remains of descendants of Muhammad and are officially closed to non-Muslims.

Even more so than in the rest of Cairo, visitors must dress modestly in Islamic Cairo: revealing clothing will attract a great deal of unsolicited and unfriendly attention and will prevent admission to many mosques. Residents consider shorts, miniskirts, and exposed shoulders disrespectful. Women are encouraged to cover their hair with a hat or scarf in the mosques; when head coverings are required, they can usually be rented for a few piasters. In some mosques (such as Muhammad 'Ali) an entire *galabiyya* is provided for free. It is important to avoid sandals and wear clothes that you don't mind getting dirty: just as Islamic Cairo is full of charm, so are its streets full of trash and dust. Since you will often be asked to remove your shoes, socks are a good idea. Bring a plastic bag for your shoes to avoid the 50pt charged by custodians to watch them while you are touring. Never let the soles of your shoes touch a mosque floor.

> **SIGHTSEEING STRATEGY.** Although each of the following sights can be visited individually, *Let's Go* has divided Islamic Cairo into four easily navigable regions (each of which can be visited in a leisurely **half-day** walking tour): **Southern Islamic Cairo** and the **Mosque of Ibn Tulun** (p. 104), the **Citadel** (p. 106), **Central Islamic Cairo** (p. 107), and **North al-Mu'izz St. and the Walls** (p. 109). A stopover at al-Azhar University (p. 108) and the bazaar at Khan al-Khalili (p. 108), both centrally located, can easily be tacked on to any of these trips.

SOUTHERN ISLAMIC CAIRO

MOSQUE OF IBN TULUN. Built in 879 CE, the fortress-like Mosque of Ibn Tulun is the largest and third-oldest of Cairo's Islamic monuments. If you stand on Qadri St., the entrance is around the left side. Once inside the gate, the **Gayer-Anderson Museum** (p. 120) is to your left and the mosque's courtyard is straight ahead. The serene courtyard covers almost seven acres and has six *mihrabs* indicating the direction to Mecca. In the center of the courtyard, an ablution fountain (*mayda'a*), added in 1296 CE by a Mamluk sultan, is still used for washing before prayer time. The mosque, like many other early Islamic monuments, has pared-down decorative elements and an arcade-encompassed courtyard design modeled after the house of the Prophet Muhammad.

The mosque is named after Ahmed ibn Tulun, who served as the Abbasid governor of Egypt until he broke with the sultanate and established an independent city-state, Qatai'i, with its capital around this building. The minaret and its unusual external staircase (a harrowing climb culminating in a great view) were probably modeled after the Great Mosque of Samarra in Iraq. A less substantiated theory explains that after the mosque was built, it became clear that the *muezzin* could see impure things during his ascent to the top of the minaret. His glimpses of unveiled women relaxing in their homes led architects to build inner stairwells with hopes that the *muezzin* would stay more focused on prayer. *(Take minibus #54 (٥٤) or bus #72 (٧٢) from Tahrir Sq., or take the Metro to Sayyida Zeinab and then bus #501 (٥٠١) (35pt) to Qadri St., which leads to Ibn Tulun. Open daily 8am-6pm; Oct.-Mar. 8am-5pm; Ramadan 8am-4pm. E£6, students E£3.)*

TOMB OF SHAGARAT AL-DURR. Heading east on Tulun St., turn right onto al-Khalifa St. to find the small Tomb of Shagarat al-Durr on your left. Built in 1250 CE, the tomb is the burial place of a politically prominent Muslim woman (one of only a dozen women to have ruled in the Muslim world) and the last Ayyubid building constructed in Cairo. Shagarat al-Durr (Tree of Pearls) was a slave who rose to power after marrying al-Salih Ayyub, the final ruling member of Salah al-Din's Ayyubid Dynasty. After having her son murdered, Shagarat al-Durr declared herself queen and governed Egypt alone for 80 days before marrying the leader of the Mamluk forces and engineering the succession of the Mamluk Dynasty. The renegade couple managed to rule happily until the queen discovered that her new husband was considering a second marriage and had him murdered as well. Not to be outdone, the prospective second wife avenged the death of her lover by beating Shagarat al-Durr to death with a pair of wooden clogs and then hurling her body from the top of the nearby Citadel, leaving her corpse to the jackals and dogs. The remains were put together in this small, rather unremarkable tomb. Even so, the wall mosaics are worth the *bakhsheesh* (E£1).

If you continue on al-Ashraf Khalifa St. you will find the Mosque of Sayyida Nafisa (see p. 113). Retrace your steps to the left to return to the Mosque of Ibn Tulun. From the main entrance of Ibn Tulun, head left and take a right at the intersection with Khodairi St., which eventually turns into al-Saliba St.

SABIL UMM 'ABBAS. On the left side of Saliba St. is Sabil Umm 'Abbas, an Islamic endowment that became the home of the **Life and Culture Center** in 1990. Tucked away in Islamic Cairo, the artists rarely get visitors and are anxious to share their passions with interested travelers. The medieval exterior inscribed with Islamic calligraphy contrasts with the contemporary Egyptian art found inside, which includes paintings, textile designs, silk screens, and remarkable lamp shades. *(Open Sa-Th 9am-2pm. Free.)*

MOSQUE AND KHANQAH OF 'AMIR SHAYKHUN. Walk north on al-Saliba St. past the intersection with al-Siyuqiyya St. to find these two buildings facing each other on opposite sides of the street, complete with matching facades, doors, and minarets. The entrance to the mosque (the building on the right as you walk north on al-Saliba St.) is up an alley—pop in to check out the amazing stained glass windows installed to keep out evil *djinns*. General Shaykhun is buried in the *khanqah*, a Sufic monastery, parts of which are undergoing renovations. Slip up the stairway near the door to explore the long hallways of cells where Sufi mystics once lived.

SULTAN HASSAN COMPLEX. Compared with the mosque of Muhammad 'Ali which it faces, this masterpiece from the Mamluk era seems more genuine, striking for both its sheer bulk and intricate detail. Unlike the Pyramids at Giza, which convey the mighty power of the pharaohs with their own might and size, the majesty of Sultan Hassan's complex stands in complete contradiction of his weak rule. The only time Sultan Hassan ever slipped out from under the thumb of the Mamluk generals who controlled him was in 1356 CE, when he built this majestic *madrasa* and mausoleum; unfortunately, the tightwad generals murdered him when they got the bill. The spacious interior courtyard is surrounded by four vaulted arcades known as *irwans*, which once housed the four major schools of judicial thought in Sunni Islam. On either side of the easternmost *mihrab*, bronze doors open onto the beautifully decorated mausoleum—the inlaid marblework is the finest in Cairo. *(To reach Sultan Hassan and the Rifa'i Mosque (as well as the Citadel), continue down Saliba St. to Salah al-Din Sq. From Tahrir Sq., take bus #173 (١٧٣) or minibus #54 (٧٢). From the southern edge of 'Ataba Sq., take Muhammad 'Ali St., which becomes al-Qala'a (Citadel) St. To get back to Tahrir Sq., take bus #194 (١٩٤) or #609 (٦٠٩). Open Sa-Th 8am-6pm; F 9-11am and 2-5pm; Oct.-Mar. Sa-Th 8am-5pm, F 9-11am and 2-5pm; Ramadan Sa-Th 8am-4pm, F 9-11am and 2-4pm. E£12, students E£6.)*

RIFA'I MOSQUE. Next door to the Sultan Hassan complex stands the enormous Rifa'i Mosque, built by the mother of Khedive Isma'il, who is buried here with her son King Fouad and grandson King Farouk (Egypt's last monarch). In the room next to Farouk lies the tomb of Muhammad Reza Pahlavi, the last Shah of Iran, who was exiled in 1979 after the Islamic Revolution. Rifa'i's stupendous size and polished interior will make your neck sore. Near the ticket window is a pleasant lawn—a great place to catch your breath before moving on to other sights. *(Same directions, hours, and prices as Sultan Hassan Complex.)*

THE CITADEL (AL-QALA'A) القلعة

From Tahrir Sq., take bus #82 (٨٢), 83 (٨٣), or 609 (٦٠٩). From 'Ataba Sq., take bus #401 (٤٠١) or minibus #50 (٥٠) or 55 (٥٥). A taxi from downtown costs E£5. Enter from either the northern or southern gate. From Hassan and Rifa'i, head right (south) along the wall and circle the Citadel. The entrance is on Salah Salem St. Open daily 8am-6pm; Oct.-Mar. 8am-5pm; Ramadan 8am-4pm; closed Friday during prayer; entrance locked 1hr. before closing. E£20, students E£10, including all museums and mosques.

Crowned by the dome and tall minarets of the Muhammad 'Ali mosque, the enormous Citadel *(al-Qala'a)* watches over Islamic Cairo's tangled alleys. Salah al-Din began construction in 1176 CE, and the building has been continually expanded and modified since then (most notably by the Mamluks and Muhammad 'Ali). Almost all the rulers of Egypt from the 13th century until 1874 lived here. The complex contains three large mosques and four operating museums: as you walk around the curved road from the Citadel gate, the tin-helmeted **Mosque of Muhammad 'Ali** will be on your left and the **Mosque of Sultan al-Nasser** on your right; several courtyards away is the third mosque, the **Mosque of Suleiman Basha.** To the south of the Mosque of Muhammad 'Ali is **Qasr al-Gowhara** (Diamond Palace).

MOSQUE OF MUHAMMAD 'ALI. The mosque of Muhammad 'Ali is easy to spot from anywhere in the Citadel. Those flying into Cairo can see its metallic domes glistening in the sun. In 1830, 'Ali leveled the western surface of the Citadel, filled in the famous 13th-century Mamluk palace Qasr al-Ablaq, and built his mosque on the ruins as a reminder of Turkish domination. Modeled after the Aya Sophia in Istanbul, the mosque is a favorite of postcard-makers and tourists, but art historians disparage it as a third-rate copy of the great Ottoman mosques in Turkey. The edifice is also known as the Alabaster Mosque because it is covered inside and out with clear alabaster, hauled over from Beni Suef. Only one outer face remains bare: when sugar daddy Muhammad 'Ali died, so did the mosque's funding.

Visitors enter the mosque through a courtyard presided over by an ornate (and never-functional) gingerbread-house-like clock of French design. In 1845, when Muhammad 'Ali presented France with the obelisk from Luxor Temple (which now stands in Place de la Concorde in Paris), King Louis Philippe thanked the ruler by presenting him with this clock. Egyptians have always been somewhat ticked off about getting a dud of a clock in return for a first-rate obelisk—and perhaps have wondered why they didn't bring the obelisk next door to Switzerland—but this didn't stop Muhammad 'Ali from decorating the interior of his mosque in a 19th-century French-salon-inspired style, complete with lavish Parisian architectural details (visible mostly on the five main domes and 15 mini-domes), a chandelier, and 365 tiny lanterns. Any architectural shortcomings are redeemed by the view from the terrace by the exit, where you can see all of Cairo and the Pyramids.

At prayer time, you can hear a thousand simultaneous *muezzin* calls to prayer, a haunting chorus that seems projected from the belly of the city itself.

MOSQUE OF SULEIMAN BASHA. The Turkish-inspired Mosque of Suleiman Basha was the first Ottoman mosque in Cairo, built in 1527 by one of the Ottoman governors who headed the Janissary Army. The small-domed mosque, also known as **Sariat al-Gabal** (Mountain Palace), has a cozy prayer hall decorated with different calligraphic styles and a courtyard consisting of four *irwans*. Only punch-drunk Muhammad 'Ali fans should walk south to the **Carriage (Hantour) Museum,** which houses carriages used by the champ's family, and little else of interest.

MOSQUE OF SULTAN AL-NASSER. This is one of the few major buildings in the Citadel to escape the hand of architectural busybody Muhammad 'Ali (although the interior was stripped by Sultan Selin several hundred years before 'Ali arrived). The mosque is well known for the tile decoration on its minarets, constructed by Iranian craftsmen. Go through the gate with two flags on your left to enter another courtyard with superb views of Cairo and the mosques below.

QASR AL-GOWHARA (THE DIAMOND PALACE). This half-palace was built in 1811 by Muhammad 'Ali and named after one of his wives. In 1974, a burglary attempt resulted in a fire that destroyed half of the palace. The surviving half consists of a large gilded reception room, where 'Ali once received 500 of his closest Mamluk allies before having them murdered on their way out. Also on display are a few of the gold- and silver-adorned tapestries from the Ka'aba in Mecca; Mecca presented Cairo with one of these tapestries every year until 1961.

CENTRAL ISLAMIC CAIRO

From Salah al-Din Sq., walk north along the Citadel for 100m until Bab al-Wazir St.

BLUE MOSQUE (MOSQUE OF AQSUNQUR). This 14th-century edifice owes its name not to the words scrawled in blue marker on the main door, but to the colored Syrian tiles that line the interior, added in 1652 by a Turkish governor homesick for Istanbul's grand tiled mosques. The prayer hall to the right has one of the oldest marble *minbars* (pulpits) in the Islamic world. The top of the minaret is a great vantage point for viewing the Citadel to the south, Khan al-Khalili to the north, and the southern end of the City of the Dead to the east. *(On Bab al-Wazir St., several blocks down and on the right. Open daily 8am-6pm; in winter 8am-5pm; Ramadan 8am-4pm. E£6, students E£3.)*

MOSQUE OF QIJMAS AL-ISHAQI. This mosque, dedicated to the Chief of the Royal Stable and Chargé d'Affaires for the pilgrimage to Mecca, is on al-Darb al-Ahmar (Red Way), which commemorates Muhammad 'Ali's bloody massacre of the Mamluks. Its unremarkable exterior gives no inkling of the serene, colorfully lit interior of marble and wood inlaid with complicated ivory patterns. Under the prayer mats in the east *irwan* lies an ornate marble floor, an example of geometric Mamluk design. Tip the custodian to uncover it for you. *(Head 2 blocks north of Bab al-Wazir St. where it becomes al-Darb al-Ahmar. To get into the mosque, gesture to locals, and they will retrieve the custodian. Open daily 8am-4pm. Free, but bakhsheesh is appropriate.)*

BAB ZUWEILA. Bab Zuweila is the most imposing of the three remaining gates into Fatimid Cairo, named after the Berber tribe that once guarded it. Egyptians also call it *Bawwabat al-Metwali* (Gate of the Tax Collector) after the civil servant who used to wait for victims there. It is topped by two minarets from the Mosque of al-Mu'ayyad, an interesting juxtaposition of military might and Islamic culture. *(The gate is at the intersection of al-Darb al-Ahmar and al-Mu'izz St.)*

MOSQUE OF AL-MU'AYYAD. The Mamluk ruler al-Mu'ayyad was once imprisoned on the site of this mosque. Upon becoming sultan, he tore down the prison and built this house of worship over it between 1415 and 1420. The huge door may look familiar to you; it was taken from the Sultan Hassan Mosque. The arcaded building has a lovely garden and excellent inlaid marblework in the prayer hall. Give the guard *bakhsheesh* and he will let you climb the minaret for a spectacular view of Islamic Cairo. *(Go north through Bab Zuweila. The mosque is on the left. Open daily 8:30am-7pm. E£6, students E£3.)*

AL-AZHAR UNIVERSITY

Al-Azhar University is the oldest continuously operating university in the world and the foremost Islamic theological center. Established in 972 CE by the Fatimids (who belonged to the Shi'a Muslim sect), it rose to pre-eminence in the 15th century as a center for the study of Qur'anic law and doctrine. It is still considered to be the final arbiter on all doctrinal issues related to Sunni Islam, the sect to which the focus of study at al-Azhar was shifted once the Ayyubids came to power (and today the majority sect of Islam). Both the University and the Mosque of al-Azhar stand just a few steps from the midpoint of al-Mu'izz St. at the end of al-Azhar St., facing the square.

AL-AZHAR MOSQUE. To reach the central courtyard of this arcaded mosque, enter through the double-arched gate and pass under the **Minaret of Qaytbay** (built in 1469). Although the stucco decoration of the courtyard's facade is a reconstruction, the *mihrab* in the central aisle is original. The **library**, just left of the main entrance, holds over 80,000 manuscripts. For about E£1, the caretaker will allow you to climb one of the locked **minarets** for a fantastic view of Cairo and Khan al-Khalili below you. *(Open Sa-Th 7:30am-9pm, F 9am-noon and 2-7pm. E£12, students E£6. Women must cover their heads at the entrance.)*

UNIVERSITY. Around the corner from the mosque is where al-Azhar's 8000 students take classes from October to May. Students sit on the plush red carpets of the mosque's *riwaq* (the arcaded aisle around the central courtyard), cramming for exams. The theological curriculum has remained virtually unchanged since the Mamluk era, though more recent secular arrivals include physics and medicine. Women, though allowed in the mosque, may not study at al-Azhar; they attend a sister school near 'Abbasiyya Sq. The university uses the Socratic method of teaching, with a professor seated in the center of a circle of students, guiding the dialogue through questions. Give a small consideration to the caretaker and he'll show you the **tomb** of the university's founder.

SAYYIDNA AL-HUSSEIN MOSQUE. The Sayyidna al-Hussein Mosque was built in the Turkish style (note the pencil minarets) by Khedive Isma'il in the 1870s. It is highly revered throughout the Islamic world as the resting place of the skull of Hussein, grandson of the Prophet Muhammad. The head is rumored to have been transported to Cairo in a green silk bag in 1153, almost 500 years after its owner died in the Battle of Karbala in modern-day Iraq. On *'Eid Mawlid al-Nabi* (Birthday of the Prophet), the President of Egypt traditionally comes to pray at Sayyidna al-Hussein while boisterous festivities take place in the square. During Ramadan, this square is the best place to witness the breaking of the fast after evening prayers (at sundown). Restaurants display their fare 30min. before prayers begin, and famished patrons stampede to the tables afterward. After blood-sugar levels return to normal, the square erupts in celebration. *(Across al-Hussein Sq., 100m north of al-Azhar Mosque. Closed to non-Muslims.)*

KHAN AL-KHALILI AND ENVIRONS

KHAN AL-KHALILI BAZAAR. Khan al-Khalili, just west of al-Hussein Sq., is the largest and most notorious bazaar in Egypt. The Mamluk prince Gharkas al-Khalili established the market in the 1380s. Today it is still a requisite stop for countless tour buses, whose occupants pour forth to find that perfect little *tchotchke* for friends and family back home. As usual, however, the package tourists rarely stray far from the comfort of their air-conditioned buses and miss most of the good stuff. Revel in the free-market frenzy as you pass through the copperware, perfume, spice, gold, silver, and *sheesha* sections of this vast bazaar. Though the tacky souvenirs are often overpriced, the time-honored institution of bargaining still thrives. Be ferocious if you intend to strike a good deal (often one-fifth to one-third of the starting price, if not less); pretending to walk away usually elicits a discount. The farther you go from the heart of the market, the more authentic the wares become. A word of warning: Khan al-Khalili is a **thief's** paradise. Many a hard-won bargain has been rendered moot by a wallet disappearance. Also, be sure **not** to enter shops with any hustlers you meet in the street; the store will inflate the prices to include the hustler's commission. After a hard day of bargaining, Cairenes stay up late into the night at one of the Khan's many sidewalk cafes. The most renowned of these is **Fishawi's,** which offers respite from the market bustle with flavored *sheesha* and exotic juices (see **Ahwas,** p. 124). Although women traveling alone are safe, they should be prepared to deal with men who come close enough to whisper unsolicited "compliments."

AL-MUSKI ST. Considerably less tourist-ridden, but more crowded and dirtier than Khan's bazaar, this long avenue is where Egyptians come to shop for everyday items like cologne, shoes, cloth, furniture, pillowcases, and food. This is the place to come if you want to see Egyptians haggling over the price of underwear. Al-Muski stretches from al-Mu'izz St. all the way to Port Said St., running parallel to and one block north of al-Azhar St. It is also a convenient route between downtown and Islamic Cairo. For more places to shop in Cairo, see **Shopping,** p. 121.

AL-GHOURI COMPLEX. This al-Mu'izz St. complex consists of a *madrasa* and mosque (closed for renovations as of August 2001) across the street from a **mausoleum,** where whirling dervishes enchant visitors (W and Sa 9pm; see **Performing Arts,** p. 120). Al-Ghouri also hosts plays every once in a while; stop by and ask the guards about the calendar. From the *madrasa,* mausoleum, and mosque, head east on al-Azhar St., then right onto Sheikh Muhammad Abduh St. At No. 3 (on your right), you'll see the magnificently preserved *wikala* (inn for merchants; built in 1505), now transformed into a center for handicrafts and folk arts. *(Mausoleum and wikala open Sa-Th 9am-9pm. E£6, students E£3.)*

NORTHERN AL-MU'IZZ STREET AND THE WALLS

To minimize mileage in this area, walk from al-Azhar up al-Mu'izz St., through both Bab al-Futuh and Bab al-Nasser. Return by way of al-Gamaliyya St., which runs roughly parallel to al-Mu'izz St. from Bab al-Nasser past the Mosque of al-Hussein to the square in front of al-Azhar. Expect to shell out about E£15 at each of the sites below.

The section of al-Mu'izz St. between al-Azhar Mosque and Bab al-Futuh was once known as *Bayn al-Qasrayn* ("between the two palaces"—also the title of one of Naguib Mahfouz's novels) after the two Fatimid palaces that once stood here. Although those palaces were destroyed by the rulers of later dynasties, the area is still lined with many Fatimid and early Mamluk architectural attractions. A brisk walk through this part of al-Mu'izz St. is a wonderful way to see stunning Islamic architecture from the outside. This area is also home to a **bazaar** for restaurant supplies that is locally known as the best place to buy reasonably priced *sheesha* pipes. Forget that gaudy and overpriced tourist junk in the heart of Khan al-Khalili—and that second-rate bong you had your eye on back in your hometown's seedy record store—and shop here alongside Egyptian *ahwa* owners for the most authentic smoking equipment (E£15-45).

COMPLEX OF SULTAN AL-MALIK AL-SALIH AYYUB. The last ruler of Salah al-Din's Ayyubid Dynasty and the unfortunate husband of super-paranoid queen Shagarat al-Durr (see p. 105), Sultan Ayyub built this tomb, *madrasa*, and mosque in the 13th century. You'll recognize it by its square minaret pointing resolutely heavenward. The *madrasa* has ornate arched windows in the shape of boat keels. The custodian has keys to the adjacent domed mosque. *(Proceed north on al-Mu'izz St. from the intersection with Gohar al-Qa'id St. After passing 4 small side streets, you can see the tomb and madrasa on your right. The entrance is off a small alley on the right.)*

COMPLEX OF SULTAN QALAWUN. The Mamluk Sultan Qalawun sponsored the construction of this impressive mausoleum, *madrasa*, and hospital in 1284 (prior

EGYPT

to his death en route to attack a Crusader fortress in Palestine). Although the Mamluks and the Crusaders didn't get along very well, their architectural styles did—note the Romanesque windows borrowed from the Crusaders' Levantine castles. Only the three high *irwans* of the original *muristan* (mental hospital) remain. The ornate stucco work inside is original, though the undersides of the arches have been restored. The exquisite wood screen separating the tomb from the rectangular forecourt also remains untouched. Before the 14th century, Egypt was the world's center for glasswork, and the Qalawun mausoleum offers especially dazzling glass mosaic work. *(On al-Mu'izz St. Complex open daily 8am-6pm, though in practice hours vary. To gain access to the mausoleum, hunt down the guard, purchase a ticket, and have the guard unlock the door. E£6, students E£3. Video cameras not allowed without written permission from a tourist office; the nearest one is on al-Darb al-Asfar, next to Beit al-Suheimi.)*

COMPLEX OF SULTAN BARQUQ. Barquq, the first of the Circassian Mamluk sultans, led the wildly popular Circassian Invasion in the 14th century, rising to power through a series of assassinations. His **mosque** was erected in 1386. The inner courtyard has four *irwans*, the largest and most elaborate of which doubles as a prayer hall. Four porphyry columns (quarried in pharaonic times from mountains near the Red Sea) support the ceiling, while the floor is decorated with disks of marble that are actually slices of Greek and Roman columns. *Bakhsheesh* gets you into the Sultan's **tomb,** constructed of inlaid marble with an elegant green and gold vine motif decorating the drum of the dome. *(On al-Mu'izz St., next door to the complex of Sultan al-Nasser Muhammad. Open daily 10am-7pm. E£6, students E£3.)*

MOSQUE OF AL-AQMAAR. This Fatimid-era mosque was built in 1125 CE, the first Cairene mosque to have the stone-facade-and-shell motif (found within its keel-arched niche) that became popular during that era. Al-Aqmaar means "the moons," and refers to the way the stone facade sparkles in the moonlight. The northern corner is typical of later Cairene architecture; the height of the niche is just about equal to that of a loaded camel, and it was intended to make the turn onto the side street easier for the hump-backed creatures to negotiate. *(Bear left at the fork in al-Mu'izz St. and continue north along al-Mu'izz to the next right-hand side street. Mosque of al-Aqmar is on the corner.)*

BEIT AL-SUHEIMI AND ENVIRONS. The 16th-century Beit al-Suheimi was built by Suheimi, the *sheikh* of al-Azhar Mosque. Artisans have restored the finely carved wood ceilings and colorful stained-glass windows. The *khanqah* (Sufi monastery) known as **Baybars al-Gashankir** is nearby. Erected in 1310, it is the oldest surviving example of a *khanqah* in Cairo. *(Proceeding north from al-Aqmar Mosque, turn right onto al-Darb al-Asfar and follow the winding alley about 50m. The doorway on the left marked with a small, green plaque is the entrance to Beit al-Suheimi. Walk along al-Darb al-Asfar away from al-Mu'izz St. and you'll eventually come to al-Gamaliyya St. Across the street is Baybars al-Gashankir.)*

NORTHERN WALLS. Islamic Cairo is bordered on the north by the remains of the Fatimid walls. Built in 1087, these colossal fortifications are the best surviving example of pre-Crusader Islamic military architecture. Three of the rampart's original gates still stand: **Bab al-Nasser** ("Victory Gate"—at the top of al-Gamaliyya St.) and **Bab al-Futuh** ("Conquest Gate," literally "Opening Gate"—at the north end of al-Mu'izz St. in front of al-Hakim Mosque), and **Bab Zuweila.** Look for graffiti left behind by French soldiers during the Napoleonic invasion.

AL-HAKIM MOSQUE. The Fatimid-era al-Hakim Mosque was built between 990 and 1010 and remains the second-largest mosque in Cairo. Al-Hakim is often referred to as the "Mad Caliph" and was actually the inspiration for the crazy Ali-Hakim in Rodgers and Hammerstein's famous musical *Oklahoma!* Al-Hakim's unpredictable rages meant death to Christians, Jews, his enemies, his friends, and—on one occasion—all the dogs in Cairo. He ensured the confinement of women by forbidding cobblers to make shoes for them. He even banned the cooking of *mulukhiga* (a green vegetable eaten throughout Egypt), renaming it *mulukhiyya* (meaning "royal") and restricting its consumption to his family. He was assassinated soon after he announced that he was an incarnation of God. His chief theologian, al-Darazi, fled to Syria and founded the Druze sect there (see **The Druze,** p. 60). *(Just inside the walls between Bab al-Nasser and Bab al-Futuh. Entrance off al-Mu'izz St. Open daily 9am-6pm. E£6, students E£3. Climbing minaret permitted.)*

CITIES OF THE DEAD مدن الموت

The Cities of the Dead teem with life, serving as home to some of Cairo's finest Islamic architecture along with several hundred thousand living, breathing Cairenes. The areas to the northeast and south of the Citadel contain hundreds of spectacular tombs and mausolea; unlike their more pious predecessors, Mamluk sultans spared no expense in the construction of their final resting places, perhaps knowing their dynasties would not survive for long. During the late 1960s, a serious housing shortage for lower-income Egyptians, combined with the perennial issue of migration from the countryside to the city, sparked the trend of transforming burial chambers into homes. Unlike most graveyards, the Cities of the Dead have streets, house numbers (not even found in Cairo's city center), and even a regular bus system and postal service. The modern residents of the medieval necropoles dwell amid the funerary architecture, and many families have even incorporated the grave markers into their houses and yards. Tombs frequently serve as clotheslines and soccer goals. On Fridays, the gravesites swarm with visitors arriving to pay respects to the deceased. Many of the plots are enclosed by walls, encompassing an adjoining chamber and small house where families pray for their ancestors on holy days. The Egyptian custom of picnicking at the family tomb on feast days may be an ancient holdover from pharaonic times, when the corpse was believed to require nourishment for good health in the afterlife. Visitors are not permitted in the mosques on Fridays or during prayer times.

NORTHERN CEMETERY

Go east along al-Azhar St. from al-Azhar Mosque, hugging the wall on your left. When the road forks, turn left under the overpass; this leads to the southern section of the northern necropolis. Bus #176 (١٧٦) from 'Ataba Sq. stops in front of the Mausoleum of Barquq. Bus #77 (٧٧) or 904 (٩٠٤) from Tahrir Sq. stops in the cemetery.

The Northern Cemetery, northeast of al-Azhar, has broad avenues and courtyards containing the finest monuments in the Cities of the Dead. Posh modern mausolea sit alongside structures dating from the late (14th-16th century) Mamluk period.

TOMBS OF TULBAY AND TUGHAY. These tombs were erected to honor two wives of Sultan al-Nasser Muhammad. **Tughay** was renowned for her beauty and piety, and her grieving husband constructed an appropriately fine tomb for her. The base of the dome is decorated with tiles in the Iranian style, fashionable after a peace was reached with Iran two decades prior to the tombs' construction. Egypt's penchant for the cosmopolitan during that era is evidenced by the use of arabesques and Chinese peony designs on the central *mihrab*. Although the harems of the Mamluk sultans were frequently hotbeds of intrigue and jealousy (and even more frequently simply hot beds), Sultana **Tulbay** was quite close to Sultana Tughay and built her tomb next to that of her deceased co-wife and friend. *(From al-Azhar St., turn right at the 1st long street, and walk 1 block south. Facing the tombs with your back to the long street, Tughay's tomb is on the right; Tulbay's is on the left.)*

▧MAUSOLEUM AND MOSQUE OF QAYTBAY. Enter the complex through the marble northern doorway, passing through a rectangular sanctuary that affords the best views of the polychromatic striped brickwork of the complex, whose likeness graces the Egyptian one-pound note. Qaytbay was a Mamluk slave who rose through the ranks of the army to become leader of Egypt near the end of the 15th century, ruling for 28 years. Qaytbay was not without enemies, so he watched his back, designing his **mausoleum** with three secret doors for quick escapes. Apparently his efforts paid off—Qaytbay was the only Mamluk ruler who was not assassinated. Qaytbay designed the prayer niche such that it requires devotees to pray over the ruler's remains in order to face Mecca. The mausoleum also contains two black stones bearing footprints said to be those of the Prophet Muhammad. The **mosque** itself has a remarkable dome (with an unusual echo effect that the care-taker will demonstrate) that uses geometric and arabesque designs. Ask to climb the minaret to see the intricate workings on the outside of the dome. *(Upon leaving the alley, turn left and walk 2 blocks, then turn right at the 1st major street; there will be a small domed tomb on the left opposite the start of the street. Follow this street for 3 blocks; turn left up the lane with a stone arch, around 40m down the lane. This is the gate of Qaytbay's complex. Open daily 9am-9:30pm. E£6, students E£3. Bakhsheesh required to climb the minaret.)*

COMPLEX OF SULTAN ASHRAF BARSBAY. Originally intended as a *khanqah*, the 15th-century **mosque** of Sultan Ashraf Barsbay has meticulously fashioned mar-ble mosaic floors; lift the prayer mats to see the colorful tilework. Barsbay pulled out all the stops to construct his combined mosque, *khanqah*, and mausoleum complex in 1432. Adjoining the mosque to the north is Barsbay's **mausoleum** (a domed chamber containing his remains and those of his slaves), an elaborately decorated *mihrab*, and gleaming mother-of-pearl and marble mosaics. The dome decorations are complex geometric designs, which replace the chevrons used in earlier tombs (such as that of Barquq, below). The wooden *minbar* is one of the best in Cairo. *(3 blocks north of the Qaytbay complex and 50m south of the Mausoleum of Bar-quq, along the cemetery's main thoroughfare. Open daily 9am-7pm. Free.)*

MAUSOLEUM OF BARQUQ. Like the mausoleum of Sultan Barsbay, this mauso-leum (identified by its twin domes and minarets) was built in 1411 as a *khanqah*. There is limited decoration in the mausoleum, as excessive ornamentation was seen as a distraction from contemplating the full glory of Allah. This asceticism did not apply to Barquq's mausoleum in the northern corner, which has the largest stone domes in Cairo, though it is not as intricate as those of Barsbay and Qaytbay. Behind the mosque is a contemporary military cemetery. *(North of the Barsbay com-plex. Open daily 8am-6pm; Oct.-Apr. 8am-5pm. E£6, students E£3.)*

SOUTHERN CEMETERY

The Southern Cemetery is a sprawling expanse of tombs dating from the Fatimid period to the present. The silence in the cemetery is disturbed only by occasional noise from the squatters who inhabit the area (and make it unsafe for women to come here at night). The area is easily accessible by foot from the Mosque of Ibn Tulun, Sultan Hassan, or the Citadel. From Ibn Tulun or Sultan Hassan, proceed east to Salah al-Din Sq., just southeast of the Citadel, then head directly south fol-lowing the southern slope of the Citadel. When you reach the traffic circle, walk under the overpass and take the right-hand fork, al-Qadiriyya St., which becomes **Imam al-Shafi'i St.**, the main thoroughfare in the cemetery. You can also take bus #82 (٨٢) or minibus #54 (٥٤) from Tahrir Sq.

MAUSOLEUM OF IMAM AL-SHAFI'I. The Southern Cemetery's most impressive edifice is the celebrated Mausoleum of Imam al-Shafi'i. The largest Islamic mortu-ary chamber in Egypt, the mausoleum was erected in 1211 by Salah al-Din's brother and successor in honor of the great Imam al-Shafi'i, founder of one of the four schools of judicial thought of Sunni Islam. *Shafi'i* is still the dominant judi-cial system in Egypt and much of East Africa. In 1178, Salah al-Din first built a large monument over the grave of Imam al-Shafi'i, which is currently housed within the 13th-century mausoleum and often crowded with Muslims offering prayers. The teak memorial depicts the Imam himself, and is one of the finest sur-viving pieces of Ayyubid wood-carving. Two mosques adjoin the tomb chamber. The 1190 mosque is closed to non-Muslims. The 1763 mosque, open to all, remains a center of worship and has a distinctive boat that holds grain for birds on its dome. *(Bus #72 (٧٢) from 'Abd al-Munem Riad Station goes to the mausoleum. Open daily 6am-7pm. Free, but E£1 bakhsheesh appropriate.)*

TOMB OF THE FAMILY OF MUHAMMAD 'ALI. Just as Muhammad 'Ali spent plenty of time and money on his country, he put an equal amount of effort into pro-viding for his family and their remains. His favorite wife Tulun, her sons, and their families are all buried in these marble tombs, directly behind the tomb of the Imam

Shafi'i. Like 'Ali's mosque, which is criticized by art historians for cheesily imitating the mosques of Istanbul, the tombs fail stylistically, decorated in gaudy colors and outlandish designs. The headpieces on each tomb indicate the gender and rank of the deceased. *(Known to most public transportation drivers by its Arabic name, Haush al-Basha. Open daily 9am-9pm. E£6, students E£3.)*

MOSQUE OF SAYYIDA NAFISA. Those approaching the Southern Cemetery can't miss Sayyida Nafisa's tall, single minaret and ornate dome on the western edge. The mosque is Egypt's third-holiest Islamic shrine and one of Cairo's three congregational mosques. It honors the great-great-great-granddaughter of the Prophet, who died in 824 CE and began attracting droves of pilgrims to her tomb soon thereafter. So many mausolea were erected in the immediate vicinity of her tomb that historians suspect that it was this shrine that sparked the development of the Southern Cemetery. Although the mosque is closed to non-Muslims, the beautiful white dome, well-kept exterior, and nearby grassy lawns merit a visit.

OLD CAIRO قاهـرة القديمة

Old Cairo is a remarkable testament to the religious diversity of Egypt: mosques, Coptic churches, and a synagogue coexist here peacefully. The region known as Old Cairo consists of Christian **Coptic Cairo** (below) and Islamic **al-Fustat** (p. 115), also serving as the center of Jewish Cairo. Although most of the Jewish population left in 1949 and 1956, 42 families still inhabit this quarter and worship at the ancient **Ben-Ezra Synagogue** (p. 114). The easiest way to reach Old Cairo is to take the **Metro** from Tahrir Sq. toward Helwan to Mari Girgis station (50pt).

As you face the Church of St. George, a staircase to the left on Mari Girgis St. descends into an alley leading into the heart of Old Cairo. The churches here have their own quiet beauty, but the real charm of the neighborhood is in its twisting alleys. These narrow passages, barely marred by souvenir vendors, are cool and quiet. The sun bakes the ancient brick as the occasional Cairene ducks around the corner or underneath an arch to enjoy a smoke or visit a friend.

COPTIC CAIRO

Ancient Egypt inspires images of towering pyramids, hieroglyphs, and mummy cases dripping with jewels. Many mistakenly assume that this ancient pharaonic era shifted directly into the Islamic age of mosques and medieval fortifications. However, the interim period between Cleopatra and the caliphs was the time of the Roman conquest, which led to the spread of Christianity and the conversion of the Emperor Constantine in 324 CE. Indeed, Christianity was the dominant faith in Egypt for 300 years—from the fall of the pagan Romans until the arrival of Islam—and about 6 million Christian Copts currently live in Egypt, mostly in Old Cairo or Middle Egypt (see **Religion and Culture**, p. 69).

Most of Cairo's Coptic churches are tucked away from the street, and the older ones have simple entrances. Though the churches do not charge admission and do not usually require *bakhsheesh* (this neighborhood is pleasantly free of the hustlers that infest other sections of Cairo), all have donation boxes. A few congregations have programs in which their younger members take turns offering tours of their respective churches. No money is expected, and you'll see much more than you would on your own. Those seeking serenity should avoid churches on Sundays or on church saint's day, when hundreds of Coptic Cairenes and their children migrate from church to church, receiving blessings and pronouncing their faith. Ongoing renovations of the churches and other buildings in Coptic Cairo began in the summer of 2000; entrance to these buildings, however, is still allowed.

CHURCH OF MARI GIRGIS (CHURCH OF ST. GEORGE). This Greek Orthodox church, built in the 6th century over one of the towers of the Fortress of Babylon, is dedicated to the Roman soldier George, whose famed tussle with a dragon is shown in a large relief in the courtyard. The current building was renovated in 1909, and its steps spiraling into the air represent the infinity of God. Inside are some of the most vivid and best-preserved icons in Old Cairo. The church and the nunnery of St. George nearby (where a chain-wrapping ceremony commemorating the torture of St. George is sometimes performed) both claim to house the chains used to torture the famous saint. The small doorway to the right of the staircase leads to a room where you can try on the chains for yourself. *(From the Mari Girgis Metro station, take a left. The entrance is along the wall on the right. Open daily 8am-5pm. Free.)*

CHURCH OF THE VIRGIN (AL-MU'ALLAQA CHURCH). This beautiful Coptic church is referred to as *Mu'allaqa* ("Hanging One") because it was suspended 13m above the ground between two bastions of the fortress of Babylon; look for the trap door under the carpet alongside the wall to the right of the entrance to see the distance to the ground below. The building itself is ark-shaped, its roof held up by eight pillars on each side (one for every member of Noah's family). Pointed arches and colorful geometric patterns decorate the main nave; in the center, an elegant pulpit (used only on Palm Sunday) rests on 13 slender columns—one each for Christ and his disciples. The conspicuous black and gray marble columns symbolize Judas Iscariot (who famously betrayed Jesus for 30 pieces of silver) and Doubting Thomas (who didn't believe Jesus had been resurrected until actually having seen him). Though most of the icons have been removed for the duration of the renovation, some of the most famous remain, including one of the Holy Mother with an infant Jesus and John the Baptist.

This church holds a special place in the annals of Coptic history, thanks to its involvement in the miracle of **Mokattam Mountain.** A doubtful caliph issued an ultimatum to Pope Ibrahim ibn al-Zar'a and the Coptic population—prove that the faithful can move mountains, or die. The Copts in the area prayed for three days and three nights in the Church of the Virgin until, on the third night, their bowing and wailing of *Kyrie eleison* (Greek for "Lord, have mercy") supposedly shook the earth and moved Mokattam a few inches. *(On your left as you face the Mari Girgis Metro station. Coptic orthodox masses W 7-9am, F 8-11am, Su 6-8:30am and 9-11am.)*

COPTIC MUSEUM. Directly across from the Mari Girgis Metro station is the Coptic Museum, home to the world's largest and finest collection of Coptic art, texts, textiles, metalwork, and iconographic materials (see p. 119).

BEN-EZRA SYNAGOGUE. Named for the great Spanish poet and scholar Abraham ibn Ezra, this synagogue is the oldest in Egypt and a house of worship for the country's few remaining Jews. The synagogue was built in the 7th century BCE on a site Moses supposedly used for prayer before the Exodus. The Copts eventually took over the building (which explains why its design resembles that of the nearby churches), but in 1115 CE, the caliph returned it to the Jewish community. The temple is beautifully decorated, combining Islamic geometric patterns with the Star of David. The exquisite arabesque ceiling dates from the Coptic occupation of the site. Directly in front of the entrance is a cenotaph (empty tomb) commemorating Ben-Ezra. The staircase behind it is the pulpit where the rabbi stands. Jewish history buffs can check out the collection of Hebrew books in the adjacent library. *(With your back to the Church of St. Barbara, the synagogue is approximately 25m to the left. The library is directly behind the synagogue, at the end of the path to the right of the main entrance. ☎ 354 26 95. No photography.)*

CHURCHES OF ST. BARBARA, ST. CYRUS, AND ST. JOHN. St. Cyrus and St. John were torn apart by wild beasts during the notorious persecution of Christians by Roman Emperor Diocletian, but the only wild beast in the church now is an occasional wandering cat. Legend holds that when the caliph discovered that both churches were being restored, he ordered the architect to destroy one of them. Unable to choose, the architect paced back and forth between the two buildings until he died of exhaustion; the caliph was so moved he allowed both to stand.

The eponymous saint of the **Church of St. Barbara** was killed by her pagan father when she attempted to convert him. Her bones rest in the tiny chapel accessible through a door to the right as you enter her church. The bones of St. Catherine supposedly lie here as well (see **St. Catherine's,** p. 177). A 13th-century wooden iconostasis graces the church's ornate interior of carved wood and metalwork.

The Coptic Museum (p. 119) now holds most of the church's furniture. *(To the left, at the end of the alley that starts at the stairs next to Mari Girgis Church. Open Su-Th 11am-5pm)*

TRAJAN'S GATE AND BATTLEMENTS. Cairo's only substantial classical ruins are the **Iron Gate** of Roman Emperor Trajan's fortress (built during the first century CE) and parts of the battlements that accompanied it. The fort once covered 60 acres. The Muslims captured it when Coptic Patriarch Cyrus ordered the defenders to surrender. *(In front of the Coptic Museum, across from the Mari Girgis Metro station.)*

AL-FUSTAT الفسطات

*To reach al-Fustat, take the **Metro** to Mari Girgis (50pt). With your back to the station, head north along Mari Girgis St. until you see the minarets of the Mosque of Amir on your right. If you take a **taxi** from downtown (E£4), ask to go to Misr al-Qadima or Gami' Amir.*

Adjoining Coptic Cairo to the north are the partially excavated remains of al-Fustat, one of the oldest Islamic settlements and the seat of the Egyptian caliphate for 250 years. Al-Fustat was the name of a garrison town that some historians say comes from *fossatum*, Latin for "entrenchment." A different account of al-Fustat's founding holds that the conquering General 'Amir ibn al-'As sent word to the caliph in Medina that the magnificent Roman port of Alexandria would be the perfect place for the capital of Egypt. To 'Amir's dismay, the caliph preferred to establish his outposts along desert trade routes, which were invulnerable to the naval attacks of seafaring Christians. The disappointed general returned to the area (a Roman town called Babylon) to find that a white dove had nested in his tent during his absence. Interpreting this as a divine omen, 'Amir founded the new capital of Egypt there and dubbed it al-Fustat (City of the Tent). The military camp soon grew into a prosperous city with large houses, running water, and a sophisticated sewer system. Al-Fustat remained the capital of Egypt until the Fatimids established the neighboring city of al-Qahira ("the Conqueror") in 969 CE. In 1168, Crusader King Amalric of Jerusalem invaded al-Qahira, and the resident Fatimids burned al-Fustat to the ground to prevent it from falling into the hands of the Crusaders. The ruins were quickly scavenged for building materials, and al-Fustat's days of importance ended ignominiously as the city garbage dump.

As a result, the present-day architectural remains of al-Fustat are insubstantial, and a stroll through the site reveals little more than traces of cisterns, drains, cesspools, and rubbish. The main reasons to visit al-Fustat (aside from a few interesting churches) are the **Mosque of 'Amir**—Egypt's oldest mosque—and the pottery district. Al-Fustat sprawls over the large area behind the mosque. If you venture out to this district in the heat of summer, bring plenty of water. It is best to avoid the area at night, since it is isolated and lacks police protection.

MOSQUE OF 'AMIR. The present-day Mosque of 'Amir ibn al-'As, Egypt's first mosque, occupies the site of the original building of 642 CE, and is four times the size of its predecessor. The oldest portion of the current mosque is its crumbling southeast minaret, added during the Ottoman period. The mosque has been rebuilt countless times over the centuries, most recently in 1983. There is little of historical or architectural interest about the current building, especially in comparison with the nearby Coptic churches. Architectural fragments, thousands of pieces of Islamic pottery, and imported Chinese porcelain have all been discovered here, but most pieces are currently displayed at the Islamic Museum and in the new Islamic Ceramics Museum. Behind the Mosque of 'Amir is the **pottery district**, which provides the clay pots and pipes used to store water and transport sewage throughout Cairo. Watch modern-day artisans at work feeding smoke-belching kilns with leather scraps and garbage, but ask before you take their picture, or you may be slapped with a E£5 fee. *(Open daily 9am-5pm. E£6, students E£3.)*

OTHER SIGHTS. Walk straight down the street opposite the entrance to the Mosque of 'Amir to **Deir Abu Seiffein,** a complex of three 8th-century Coptic churches. The wooden entrance to the churches is about 500m ahead on the right. *(Odass, or liturgy, read in Coptic Su 6-10am, W 8am-noon, and F 7-11am. Open daily 8am-5pm.)* The oldest church with the finest icons in Deir Abu Seiffein is the **Church of St. Mercurius**

EGYPT

Felopatir (also called the Church of Abu Seiffein), dating from the 4th century but restored during the Middle Ages. Mercurius Felopatir, a Roman soldier, was beheaded because of his Christian beliefs, even after he helped fend off Berber attacks. The martyr is also called Abu Seiffein ("the dude with two swords") because an angel gave him a heavenly sword to go with his military saber.

The church's ebony, ivory, and cedar **iconostasis** separates the front vestibule from the nave. The elaborate, gabled roof is evidence of masterful Coptic carpentry, as pieces are fitted together without screws or nails. You can peer into the **Chamber of St. Barsoum,** where the saint supposedly lived with a cobra (not his wife) for 25 years. Upstairs are the ancient and miniscule churches of St. George of Rome, St. John the Baptist, and the 144,000 Martyrs, all of which were rediscovered when the plaster was accidentally chipped away from multiple layers of icons. As of August 2001, the chapels were closed for renovation.

Down the street is the 4th-century **Church of St. Shenouda,** dedicated to one of the most famous Coptic saints. This chapel contains seven altars and two fine iconostases of red cedar and ebony. The smallest of the three main churches at Deir Abu Seiffein is the early 8th-century **Church of the Holy Virgin,** a one-room chapel crammed with rare icons, paintings, and three altars. Across the Nile on Roda Island is a particularly interesting variation on the ubiquitous Cairene **Nilometer** (a glorified stairwell built to measure the depth of the Nile). The Abbasids built it around 850 CE and carved Qur'anic verses about water on its interior walls. The Ottomans added a dome in the 19th century. If both entrances to are locked, use *bakhsheesh.* Ask one of the many children playing nearby to pester the custodian.

MODERN CAIRO

The heart of Cairo beats in **Tahrir Sq.** (Liberation Sq.), with the **Egyptian Museum** on the north side, the **Mugamm'a** to the south, and cars speeding suicidally in between. However, the city's "downtown" also includes the many squares surrounding Tahrir Sq., particularly **Tala'at Harb Sq., Ramses Sq.,** and **'Ataba Sq.** You'll find yourself in an architectural wonderland whose cosmopolitan, French-influenced flavor may come as a welcome relief from the dusty ancient quarters and shantytowns of much of the rest of the city. To escape the hubbub, head to the quieter corners just outside downtown: posh **Zamalek** beckons from the middle of the Nile, and the small suburbs of **Heliopolis** and **Garden City** are only a few steps away.

TAHRIR SQ.

One block up from Tahrir Sq. at the intersection with Bustan St. are two particularly fine old buildings. On the south side of the intersection is the **4 Tala'at Harb St.** apartment building, elaborately decked out from its foundation to its richly decorated dome. Across the street, the more restrained and renovated **Muhammad 'Ali Club** glistens in the Cairo sun; look for the carved faces in the moldings.

TALA'AT HARB SQ.

Just north of Tahrir Sq. is Tala'at Harb Sq., named after the founder of the Egyptian National Bank and ringed with buildings in a variety of European styles. On the west side of the square is **J. Groppi's** (see p. 101), once *the* place to see and be seen (although the only things to see there now are the fabulous Italian mosaics at the entrance). Although the July Revolution brought that world to an abrupt end, Groppi's remains a stodgy reminder of Cairo's colonial heyday. Farther up Tala'at Harb St. is the **Cinema Metro,** a beautiful movie palace from the 1930s that often shows English-language films as well as Arabic flicks. Farther north, Tala'at Harb St. intersects with 26 July St. West of Tala'at Harb St. is the **Sha'ar Ha-Shamaim Synagogue.** The temple's name is Hebrew for "Gate to the Sky," and its 1920s architecture is indeed heavenly. (Open Sa. Free.) Three blocks east of the square on Qasr al-Nil St. is the beginning of al-Sherifein St., home to the Egyptian **stock exchange.** One block north of 'Adly St. on Tala'at Harb St. is the faux leaf-encrusted brick of the **Davins Bryan Building,** which once outfitted explorers. To the south is **St. Joseph's Church,** the center of the city's Catholic community.

'ATABA SQ.

To the west of downtown is 'Ataba Sq. and the **Ezbekiya Gardens.** A patch of thick trees remains in the south corner to hint at the gardens' old glory, first under the Mamluks and then during the colonial period (when it was redesigned by the landscape architects of the Bois de Boulogne in Paris). In the northeast corner of 'Ataba Sq., just past the skyscraper with an antenna, are the double brass domes of the **Sedanoui Department Store.** The building's interior is worth a stop, with a huge open center and two staggeringly large cut-glass chandeliers.

SAKAKINI SQ.

The merchant Sakakini struck it rich when he sent a caravan of camels to the rat-infested Suez Canal; to celebrate his luck, he built the **Sakakini Palace** in the middle of the square and festooned it with a bizarre assortment of statuary depicting ferocious beasts and frolicking maidens. The carving above the main entrance represents Sakakini himself. You can get a good view from the outside, but the caretaker will show you around the interior for a few pounds of *bakhsheesh* if you arrive midday. (Open daily 10am-2pm. Free.)

ZAMALEK

Zamalek was first settled in the colonial era, when the **Gezira Club** in the north (which still owns much of the island) was a second home to the British elite. A walking tour of the sights in and around Zamalek is a change of pace from the ancient sites and medieval architecture that characterize the rest of Cairo. Spend an afternoon browsing the exhibitions at the opera complex at the south end of the island (particularly those at the **Egyptian Modern Art Museum,** p. 120). When the sun sets, head for the restaurants for some of Cairo's best food (see p. 102).

CAIRO MARRIOTT. The building that now houses the Cairo Marriott, along the east bank of Zamalek, was built in 1869 for Empress Eugenie (wife of Napoleon III) during the grand opening of the Suez Canal. If the slings and arrows of budget travel have you down, the Marriott has good restaurants, cafes, shops, and a swimming pool. Across the river to the west are **houseboats** that housed cabarets and nightclubs during World War II. One was owned by a belly dancer, employed by the Germans, who used her charms to acquire secrets from British agents.

CAIRO TOWER. The tower dominates the city's skyline and has an excellent (if pricey) view of the city. Commissioned by Nasser and completed in 1961, it was built to commemorate the rise of industry in Egypt. At 187m (60 stories) high, the tower is 50m taller that the Great Pyramid. A rotating restaurant on the top floor sells expensive drinks and meals. *(Open daily 9am-midnight; lines form at sunset. E£30.)*

HELIOPOLIS

This suburb of Cairo was founded in 1906 by Belgian industrialist Edouard Empain as a community for foreigners. Its broad avenues and odd Euro-Islamic fusion architecture make it an interesting trip out of central Cairo. The highlight of Heliopolis is **Empain's Palace.** To get there, head south on Shahid Tayyar Nazih Khalifa. The estate is a strange riot of carved elephants and Cambodian motifs that you can explore on your own (with a little *bakhsheesh* to the caretaker). The huge building behind the high wall in Heliopolis is the **President's Palace.** Down Cleopatra St., across from Mubarak's pad, are the beautifully decorated offices of the **Heliopolis Company** (the suburb's planners). At night, Heliopolis comes alive, as residents flood the shops, malls, and cafes on Roxy St.

GARDEN CITY

Just southwest of Tahrir, historic Garden City has fine examples of British colonial architecture, housing a large part of Cairo's expat population. **Qasr al-'Aini Hos-**

pital, the first hospital in Cairo, lies in west Garden City on the north end of Roda Island. In northeast Garden City is **Maglis al-Sha'ab** (Parliament), close to the **Mugamm'a** building. Along the Nile are a plethora of **embassies,** including those of the US and UK, as well as five-star hotels like **Shephards** and the **Semiramis.**

MOHANDISEEN

Built in the 1960s to house Egypt's *mohandiseen* (engineers), this district is now home to many expats and well-to-do Egyptians and has some of the best bars and restaurants in Cairo. Its main boulevard, **Gam'at al-Duwal al-Arabiya,** is lined with palm trees, fast food joints, and duty-free shops. (Note that to purchase duty-free products you must bring your **passport.**)

🏛 MUSEUMS

EGYPTIAN MUSEUM متحف مصر

In Tahrir Sq. Open daily 9am-4:45pm. E£20, students E£10. Camera privileges E£10, video E£100. Mummy Room E£40, students E£20.

Of the world's great museums, this behemoth may very well have the single most amazing collection. More certainly, it's housed in one of the worst facilities. Priceless artifacts—any one of which would be the *pièce de resistance* at an ordinary museum—are stacked on top of each other and crammed into dusty corners. Though the museum is filled with mummies and pharaonic treasure, it manages to retain the atmosphere of a warehouse. The heavily touristed areas (such as the Tutankhamun and Akhenaton rooms) are very well-labeled, but many descriptions are unhelpfully banal ("Pot," "Clay"), and others are just plain wrong ("Woman," reads the desciption of a portrait of a bearded man). Other items have no explanation at all. The crowded rooms deserve their popularity, but some of the smaller, infrequently visited side rooms are equally fascinating and far away from the maddening tourist hordes. Unless you choose to buy the E£100 catalog, the first item to check out should be the wall map to the left of the entrance. Flash photography is not permitted, but most of the museum is fairly well-lit (though, amazingly, not air-conditioned), so bring a camera along.

⚅TUTANKHAMUN ROOM. Of all the collections in the museum, the treasures from **Tutankhamun's tomb** are the best-displayed and most popular. Originally squeezed into less than 100 cu. m, the booty now occupies a quarter of the second floor. The eastern corridor contains decorated furniture, golden statues, delicate alabaster lamps, weapons, amulets, fossilized undergarments, and other bare necessities for a King of the Underworld. **Room #4** displays King Tut's famous gold, glittering all over coffins and funeral masks, as well as an astounding collection of amulets, scarabs, and jewelry. The mask made to fit over the head of Tut's mummy contains more than 4kg of solid gold inlaid with quartz and lapis lazuli. In the hallway sit the king's internal organs, each in its own gilded coffin. The countless souvenir versions of these items, sold in tacky *souqs* and found on gaudy T-shirts and fake papyri, only make the originals look more amazing.

NARMER PALETTE. In the small glass case opposite the entrance (and surrounded by mobs of tourists with their guides) is the Narmer Palette, a stone slab commemorating the unification of Upper and Lower Egypt in about 3100 BCE by the mythical founder of pharaonic dynasties, King Narmer (a.k.a. Menes, see **Ancient History,** p. 64). From here, navigate the first floor in a clockwise direction around the central courtyard to get a sampling of pharaonic art from the Old Kingdom to the Greco-Roman period. Walking down the west corridor, you can visit the three rooms off to the right for a few minutes each. The first two rooms feature the best of the Old Kingdom, including a diarite statue of Chephren and a wooden statue named "Sheikh al-Balad" by workers who thought that it resembled their boss. The third room displays limestone artifacts from the Middle Kingdom.

AKHENATON ROOM. In the Akhenaton room (at the rear of the first floor) are statues of the heretical pharaoh who introduced Egypt to a monotheistic cult centered around the sun god Aton. Aton was represented as a disk with rays ending in hands that sometimes held *ankhs*, the Egyptian symbol for life. Artwork from this period is recognizable for its realistic portraits (versus the stiff and stylized portraits of other periods) and feminine body shapes. Read more about Akhenaton-era hijinks by sticking your head between the legs of the king's shapely statue to get a view of the informational plaque. Past the Akhenaton room are a collection of **statues** from the New Kingdom. In the room in the northeast corner, look for a painting of **Ramses II** clutching the cowering enemies of Egypt by their hair.

GREEK AND ROMAN ROOMS. Down the hall from the painting of Ramses II are the Greek and Roman rooms, where Classical art sits side-by-side with such oddities as a statue of a nude woman with the legs and tail of a chicken. Around the corner toward the entrance is a remarkable statue of **Alexander the Great.** His body is stiff and pharaonic, while his head is carved in the style of Greek naturalism.

FAYYUM PORTRAITS. Room #14, in the inner northwest corner of the second floor, exhibits the realistic portraits found on Ptolemaic-era mummies, mostly from the Fayyum region. The portraits depict their subjects as they looked just before death, in contrast to the statues and *stelae* of earlier Egyptians, who preferred a more timeless look. The result is haunting, with the long-dead expressively gazing back at their viewers.

MUMMY ROOM. The controversial mummy room is in the southeast corner of the second floor. Former President Anwar al-Sadat closed the famed room in 1981 because the display offended some Islamist groups who felt it was disrespectful toward the dead. (Unfortunately for Sadat, the gesture did little to appease the fundamentalists who assassinated him a few months later.) The reopening of the room was delayed by the mummies' continued decomposition, which left them offensive to just about everyone. Now restored and lodged in a dimly lit, air-conditioned room, the mummies require a separate ticket purchased outside the room (E£40, students E£20). Don't expect to learn how the mummification process worked, as there are no descriptions except identifications of each mummy. Nevertheless, the room does not lack in visceral impact: the well-preserved corpses (Seti I looks like he's sleeping) laid out in climate-controlled glass cases were once the most powerful people in the world. For more on mummies, see **Mummy Dearest,** p. 218.

OTHER ROOMS. The west corridor has layers of oblong **mummy cases,** and room #37 has square mummy cases used in the Middle Kingdom. The **papyri** in the middle of the second floor put those sold in the streets today to shame, while the fine gold jewelry collection in the room to the left of Tut's room #4 makes the necklaces of Khan al-Khalili look shoddy. At the opposite end of Level II from the gold of Tutankhamun is the modest **Tomb of Yuya and Thuyu,** more typical of the tombs in which most Egyptians rested for eternity. Animal-rights activists may cringe in nearby **room #53,** where mummified remains of cats, birds, monkeys, and a huge fish are slowly rotting to dust in their non-humidity-controlled surroundings.

OTHER MUSEUMS

Though one could spend an entire vacation with the mummies, Cairo has a number of other interesting museums housing everything from calligraphy to collage.

Islamic Art Museum (☎ 390 99 30), in Bab al-Khalaq Sq. at the intersection of Port Said, Muhammad 'Ali, and Ahmed Maher St. The hiding place of many of the artifacts missing from the mosques, mausolea, and *madrasas* of Cairo. Also contains Islamic art from the rest of the Middle East. Don't miss the miniature paintings and gold-leaf Qur'ans in the calligraphy room at the back, or the room that gleams with gilded swords and armor. Open Sa-Th 9am-4pm, F 9-11:30am and 1-4pm; in winter F 9-am12:30pm and 2-4pm. E£16, students E£8.

Coptic Museum (☎ 363 97 42), directly opposite the Mari Girgis Metro station. The world's finest collection of Coptic art. 14,000 textiles, paintings, icons, and other pieces. 2nd fl. icons include many superb paintings in a variety of styles; compare an icon of the Virgin Mary suckling baby Jesus with a carving of the Egyptian goddess Isis feeding her son Horus. The Nag Hammadi Library, next to the textiles, houses 12 Coptic Gnostic codices from the 4th century. Unlike most museums in Cairo, this collection is well labeled in French and English. Open daily 9am-5pm. E£16, students E£8. Camera privileges E£10, video E£100.

Egyptian Modern Art Museum (☎ 736 66 55), in the Opera Complex in Zamalek. Cross the bridge from Tahrir Sq. or take the Metro to the Opera. Work by Egyptian artists in a variety of media, exhibited in a modern, A/C gallery. A welcome reminder that Cairo's art is not confined to tombs and sarcophagi. Open Sa-Th 10am-1pm and 5-9pm. Free.

Gayer-Anderson Museum, 4 Ibn Tulun St. (☎ 364 78 22), in front of Ibn Tulun Mosque. Originally two separate buildings, these 16th- and 18th-century mansions were joined when Major Gayer-Anderson, an English art collector, arrived in the 1930s and proceeded to fill his home with eclectic artifacts and furniture. When he left Egypt in the '40s, he gave the mansion and its contents to the government. Ask the caretaker to show you the secret door behind a cabinet leading to a balcony overlooking the ballroom. To Egyptians, the museum is enigmatically known as "The House of the Cretan Woman." You may recognize some rooms from the James Bond flick *The Spy Who Loved Me.* Open daily 9am-4pm. E£16, students E£8. Camera privileges E£10, video E£100.

Mahmoud Khalil Museum, 1 Kafour St., Doqqi (☎ 336 23 76), 200m from the Cairo Sheraton. A fantastic collection, housed in an A/C mansion, consisting almost exclusively of paintings by such 19th-century European greats as Monet, Van Gogh, Degas, and Toulouse-Lautrec. Open Tu-Su 10am-6pm. E£25, students E£10.

♫ ENTERTAINMENT

CINEMA

A few cinemas run English-language films four to six months behind their release in the US; *al-Ahram Weekly* (75pt) has listings in English. All of these air-conditioned theaters are packed with Egyptian teenagers on Thursday nights. Films usually show at 10:30am, 1:30, 3:30, 6:30, and 9:30pm, with a midnight showing on Thursdays (E£10, in winter E£20). The cinema in the **Ramses Hilton Hotel Annex** has two screens, one of which always shows a film in English. (☎ 574 74 35). **Metro Cinema,** 35 Tala'at Harb St. (☎ 393 75 66), near Tala'at Harb Sq., and **Kareem Cinema,** 15 Imad al-Din St. (☎ 592 48 30), alternate English and Arabic movies.

DANCE

Mausoleum al-Ghouri (☎ 510 08 23), on al-Mu'izz St., just south of the pedestrian overpass near al-Azhar University in Islamic Cairo. Renovated 500-year-old palace hosts free Sufi music and whirling dervishes (spinning at over 100rpm) on W and Sa nights (9pm, in winter 8pm). Arrive early to the 1hr. show, as seats fill up fast.

Balloon Theater (☎ 347 17 18), on al-Nil St. at the Zamalek Bridge, Agouza. Regular performances of Rida's Troupe, one of the best Egyptian folk dance companies. Tickets E£10-30. Shows daily 9:30pm.

Falafel Restaurant (☎ 577 74 44), at the Ramses Hilton (behind the Egyptian Museum). Prix-fixe dinner (US$31) includes a fabulous folk dancing show by the Hassan Troupe. Dinner 8pm-10pm. Show 10:30pm. Open Sa-Th 9pm-midnight. Reservations required.

Coquillage (☎ 735 61 26), at the foot of Tahrir Bridge in Zamalek, connected to Qasr al-Nil Casino. Coffee shop by day, lavish hall of stained glass with Arabic dancing and singing by night. Fettuccine with chicken (E£35) dazzles the taste buds; variety show dazzles the eyes and ears 10pm-4am. Open 24hr. Reservations recommended. MC/V.

MUSIC AND THEATER

Cairo Opera Complex (☎ 737 06 01), outside the Opera Metro station in Gezira, south of Zamalek. Hosts the Cairo Symphony Orchestra, outdoor jazz performances, and visiting operas. Jacket and tie required for men attending main hall performances (travelers have been known to borrow snazzy clothing from kind hostel workers). Season runs Sept.-June; casual open-air performances held July-Aug. daily at 9pm. Main hall and small hall E£15-50, outdoors E£15-25. Student discount usually 30%. Check *al-Ahram Weekly* or *Egypt Today* for details. Box office open daily 10am-3pm and 4-9pm.

Al-Gomhoriyya Theater, 12 al-Gomhoriyya St. (☎390 77 07), at the intersection of al-Gomhoriyya with 'Abd al-'Aziz St. Performances by the Arabic Music Troupe and the Cairo Symphony Orchestra, usually F evenings.

Wallace Theater (☎797 63 73), in the AUC New Campus, on Muhammad Mahmoud St. near McDonald's. Features 2 plays in English per year. AUC also hosts a variety of concerts, from jazz to chamber music, and free movie festivals at the library. Open fall-spring. Call or check bulletin boards around the Old Campus (near the AUC bookstore).

Cairo Puppet Theater (☎591 09 54 or 591 83 67), outside the easternmost Metro entrance in Ezbekiya Gardens near 'Ataba Sq. World-famous shadow puppets perform in Arabic, but are universally comprehensible. W-M 7:30pm, F and Su 10:30am. E£5.

🎬 ACTIVITIES

FELUCCA RIDES. Consider hiring a swallow-winged **felucca** and lazing on the river during the day or night. Most *feluccas* can accommodate up to eight people comfortably. The more passengers, the cheaper; bargain for a good rate. *Feluccas* for hire dock just south of the Qasr al-Nil (Tahrir) Bridge on the east bank. Across the corniche (on the water) from the Meridian Hotel, shrewd negotiators can snag a boat for E£10 for a 1hr. ride. A nominal tip (E£1-2) is expected at the cruise's end. Travelers seeking multi-day cruises (especially popular in Upper Egypt, near Luxor and Aswan) should see **Tips on Traveling by Felucca,** p. 209. **Hantours** (horse carriages) are also enjoyable, especially on a breezy evening. Avoid the *hantours* in front of major hotels; catch one downtown, on the corniche under Tahrir Bridge. Don't pay more than E£10 for a 30min. ride.

GIZA ZOO. With wide walkways, picnicking families, and children playing soccer, the Giza Zoo doubles as a park. Nevertheless, for less than E£1 you can take pictures with the animals, feed them (20pt a pop), and get close enough to the lions to get goose bumps on the back of your neck. (*Right in front of you as you cross the University Bridge—al-Gama'a—west into Giza. Open daily 9am-4pm. 25pt. Camera privileges 20pt.*)

PHARAONIC VILLAGE (AL-QARIA AL-FARA'ONIYA). This Disney-fied village was founded by former Egyptian ambassador and self-proclaimed papyrus king Dr. Hassan Ragab. Visitors board motorboats and chug through canals past statues of the gods and historically reconstructed scenes of ancient papyrus-making, temple wall-painting, and mummification. All this is described in detail by a guide speaking the language of your choice. Disembark to view a temple, houses, and King Tut's tomb reconstructed to appear as it did when Howard Carter discovered it in 1922. The price is steep, but the village is high on information and low on hassle. It's definitely worth it if (and only if) you're not going to see the real thing in Luxor. (*5km south of downtown, on Jacob's Island in Giza. ☎571 86 76. Open daily 9am-9pm; in winter 9am-5pm. E£55, students E£40, groups of 10 or more E£30 per person. Lunch E£17.*)

🛍 SHOPPING

OUTDOOR MARKETS. Cairo's biggest and most famous market is **Khan al-Khalili** (see p. 108). Navigating the maze of alleyways that lie within the *khan* may seem like madness, but there is a method to it. Most gold, copper, and antique dealers lie along Khan al-Khalili St., which changes to al-Badestani St. as it heads east. Perfumes, spices, and cloth can be found a few blocks south, between al-Azhar and al-Muski St. In the market south of **Sayyida Zeinab,** each alley offers different wares.

VENI, VIDI, VENDI Buying and selling in the Egyptian capital transcends mundane business—it's an intricate give-and-take that has evolved over centuries. Think of it as a game to be relished, not a battle to be won. Bargaining is a given: no price is set in stone, and shopkeepers enjoy the haggling (just remember that they do it for a living and have the benefit of experience). If you play hardball, the vendors will not lower the price; chatting will bring you more success. Theatrics, rather than stubbornness, get results. Walk away in disbelief several times. Do a brief Mexican hat dance while you weigh the pros and cons of the purchase. Never get too enthusiastic about the object in question. Instead, point out flaws in workmanship and design. Have a friend discourage you from your purchase—if you seem reluctant, the merchant will want to drop the price to interest you again. Ideally, you should know the approximate worth of the item, then make an offer sufficiently below that to gain leverage. A good deal could be anywhere from one-tenth to three-quarters of the starting price. For more advice on driving a hard bargain, see **Tipping and Bargaining,** p. 14.

Take the Metro to Sayyida Zeinab, then walk 5min. toward the minarets of the Sayyida Mosque. Other major markets are northeast of **'Ataba Sq.** To get to 'Ataba Sq. from Tahrir Sq., go east along Tahrir St., then up 'Abd al-'Aziz St. **Souq al-Tawfiqia** runs between Ramses and Tala'at Harb St., one block north of 26 July St. Produce stalls stand beside kitchen-equipment booths, all laid out in brilliant displays.

DEPARTMENT STORES. If hard-core bargaining doesn't appeal to you, you can head to one of Cairo's upscale department stores. **Omar Effendi** has several branches downtown. More expensive shopping centers lure foreigners and wealthy Egyptians with higher-quality goods. The **World Trade Center** on the corniche, north of the Ramses Hilton, is the biggest. A bit less expensive is **al-Yamama Center,** at 3 Dr. Taha Hussein St. in Zamalek. For assuredly high-quality versions of wares found in the *khan* (copper, antiques, papyrus) and a minimum of bargaining, try Ma'adi's tree-lined **Road Nine** (Metro: Ma'adi).

CLOTHING AND TEXTILES. At the **Tent-Makers' Bazaar,** south of Bab Zuweila in Islamic Cairo, you can buy appliqué pillowcases (E£20) and bedcovers (E£300). The **Nomad Gallery,** 14 Saraya al-Gezira, Zamalek, near the Marriott, is known for its top-quality jewelry, textiles, and crafts. They're not big bargainers, but their prices are as low as they go at the Tent-Makers' Bazaar. (☎736 19 17. Open M-Sa 10am-3pm. AmEx/MC/V.) Across from the Ibn Tulun Mosque, **Khan Misr Tulun** sells quality handicrafts from all parts of Egypt and Africa. (☎365 22 27. Open M-F 9am-5pm.) The best places to shop for woven **rugs** are the stores along **Saqqara Rd.** near the Pyramids, where Harania artists weave up a storm (see p. 129). On Friday mornings there's a **junk market** at the Mausoleum of Imam al-Shafi'i.

 HOW TO GET RIPPED OFF. The touts in the street of Khan al-Khalili who try to get you into stores also get a commission. To make up for the commission, the store owner raises the price. You'll never get a good price at a store to which a hustler has brought you.

There's a colorful **used clothing market** daily at the east end of 26 July Bridge. The stands hawk modern and vintage Western clothing as well as some traditional Egyptian garb, much of it for less than E£10. Buy a *galabiyya* (E£15-30) at the **market** south of al-Ghouri Mosque and Khan al-Khalili on al-Mu'izz St. Casual clothing for several well-known Western brands is made in Egypt, and you may want to take advantage of the slightly lower (but fixed) prices. Most of these goods are available in boutiques on the main streets and in department stores. **Al-Wikala** (☎589 74 43), 73 Gawhar al-Qayid St., in the alley south of the Egyptian Pancake House, is considered one of the best places to buy bellydancing costumes.

BOOKS AND MUSIC. There's a huge **used book market** daily at the fringe of Ezbekiya Gardens, next to the puppet theater, with volumes in Arabic, English, French, and German. Most stalls also stock one- or two-year-old Western magazines bought as surplus from overseas vendors. Titles are not organized very well, so it's best to come for browsing. (For bookstores, see p. 96.) If you develop a taste for Arab pop music, the best place to pick up a few tapes is Shawarby St., a left turn off Abdel Khaleq Sarwat St. at the Misr gas station one block east of Tala'at Harb St. Look for **Intersound,** at the north end of the street. They have a wide selection of Arab classical and pop, and some Western music.

JEWELRY AND METALWARE. Cairo is a center of the jewel trade, and prices here tend to be markedly lower than in the West. Often, gold or silver jewelry can be made to order for barely more than the cost of the metal itself. Never ask for the price first. Look at a piece of jewelry carefully and then ask the shopkeeper to weigh it in front of you. Inquire about the grade of gold or silver; gold content under 18 karat is rare in Egypt. Always make sure you see the stamp indicating level of purity on both gold and silver items. One of the best shopping areas is in the **Khan al-Khalili Souq al-Fida** (silver market). Ceramic plates and trays are available throughout the *khan* for E£15-20, while an average-sized *sheesha* should cost about E£30-35. For the best *sheeshas* in Cairo, however, bypass the junk sold at the *khan* and head to the **restaurant supply bazaar** on al-Mu'izz St. (see p. 109).

PAPYRUS. The "papyrus" sold throughout Cairo is usually banana leaf, a cheap look-alike. Real papyrus can be scrunched up and will not retain any wrinkles, while banana leaf crackles and stays crunched. Handpainted papyrus is even rarer; if anything even vaguely looks like a print, it is. A smudged artist's signature is the usual tip-off. To see the real stuff at correspondingly higher prices, head to **Dr. Ragab's Papyrus Factory,** a right turn off al-Gala'a Bridge heading west from Tahrir Sq. Another authentic option is the **Sa'id Delta Papyrus Center,** 21 al-Ghouria St., 3rd fl. (☎512 07 47), by Darb al-Ahmar near the Umayyad Mosque. The bazaars are full of fake but colorful artwork for those who think a neon pink Osiris would look great next to a velvet Elvis portrait.

BACKGAMMON. *Tawila* boards cost E£60-120, depending on the quality and your bargaining skills. Make sure the board is absolutely flat when it's opened and laid on a table, as they are occasionally warped or wobbly. Pieces are often made (and sold) separately from the board. Check to see that they fit on the triangles, and that there are 15 of each color. You should pay less if the pieces are plastic. **Maka al-Mokarama,** 7 'Adly St. (☎393 89 80), next to the tourist office, has quality boards but lacks the hassle and fun of Khan al-Khalili, where scads of stores sell them.

SPICES AND PERFUME. Excellent Middle Eastern spices like *za'tar* are difficult or impossible to find in the West; here, they are sold by the kilo for a few pounds. The quality of perfumes ranges dramatically. Rub some on the back of your hand: if it's oily or shiny, oil has been added to the perfume to stretch the liquid weight. Vendors of perfume will often misquote the size of a container; they know most tourists (especially Americans) can't tell a milliliter from a millipede. A 60ml jar should be about the length of a middle finger. A gram costs 50pt-E£1. **Harraz Agricultural Seeds, Medicinal, and Medical Plants Co.,** east of Bab al-Khalq Sq. on Ahmed Mahir St., sells every imaginable spice and folk remedy at reasonable prices. (Open Sa-Th 9am-9pm.) If the "*sheikh* of spice" won't cut you a good deal, **Khodr,** next door, has similar wares, as do many vendors in Khan al-Khalili.

◪ NIGHTLIFE

As the sun sets on the Egyptian capital, *sheesha* smoke fills the air, strolling locals mill about the markets, and decked-out scenesters dance 'til (almost) dawn at the discotheques dotting the side streets of the city. The free publication *Croc*, available at most bars, is an up-to-date guide to the Cairene scene. During **Ramadan** (see

Holidays and Festivals, p. 61), Cairenes take to the streets around al-Azhar and Hussein Sq., along the corniche, and all over the bridges spanning the Nile. Starting around 10pm, there are street performances, magic shows, and general shenanigans and tomfoolery. Most cinemas also have midnight screenings during this month. The following listings are as easy to navigate as A-B-C-D—**Ahwas, Bars, Clubs, and** (belly) **Dancing**.

AHWAS (COFFEEHOUSES)

Cairenes love to relax, meet with friends, and contemplate the sweet mysteries of life. Much of this ruminating occurs in the *ahwas* (coffeehouses) that dot many street corners and alleys east of the Nile. A typical *ahwa* has gossipers in one corner, *tawila* (backgammon) players in another, and *sheesha* smoke and Turkish coffee steam winding throughout. *Sheesha* tobacco is smoother and more delicious than cigarette shag and comes plain or flavored (apple is ubiquitous). Foreigners and women are welcomed at all the *ahwas* listed below. Several others downtown welcome foreigners, but with the intention of cheating them. Tactics include trying to charge for bottled water whether customers ask for it or not, telling them that their *sheesha* is "finished" after 5min. and needs to be replaced (a good *sheesha* withstands at least 20min. of dedicated smoking). Specifically, **avoid** the *ahwa* on Tahrir St. just east of Tahrir Sq. Elsewhere, staff is usually honest, but women may feel uncomfortable in these houses of male bonding. Try to determine the mood of the place before you sit down. For further info on *sheesha*-smoking, see **Puff the Magic Sheesha**, p. 72.

■ **Fishawi's Khan al-Khalili** (☎590 67 55), 4 doors down from al-Hussein Hotel, just off al-Hussein Sq. The oldest of Cairo's teahouses, Fishawi's is also the least typical, with table after table of tourist families and nary a *galabiyya* in sight. The decor, however, is stunning. Nicknamed "Café des Miroirs," Fishawi's is furnished in a 19th-century Turkish style with panels of mirrors and woodwork, chandeliers, and brass tables. Customers spill out into the walkway, sipping their mint tea (E£2) and *karkadeh* (E£3) and smoking aromatic cappuccino, banana, apple, or cantaloupe *sheesha* (E£3). Open 24hr.

Vienna Cafe, on Qasr al-Aini St. south of Tahrir Sq., 70m past the Misr gas station. Frequented by middle-class Egyptians, this well-tended cafe in Garden City has great *sheesha* and friendly service. Tea E£1.50. *Sheesha* E£2.50. Open daily 7am-2am.

Maroush, 64 Lubnan St., Mohandiseen (☎346 68 91), a E£5 taxi ride from downtown. A ritzy *ahwa* for a ritzy neighborhood, but relaxed, even by coffeehouse standards. Outdoor patio makes for a great escape with a *sheesha* (E£5). Open daily 8am-2am.

BARS

Cairo isn't known for beer guzzling, but considering the strict Islamic prohibition against alcohol, it has a good number of bars. These fall into two categories: cheap places serving only Stella and catering to middle-aged Egyptian males, and livelier establishments filled with a combination of the young, the rich, and the expatriated. All of bars listed below fall into the latter category. Several examples of the first kind can be found around the north end of Tala'at Harb St., especially on Alfy St. Women should avoid those places.

■ **Barrel Bar**, at the Windsor Hotel, 19 Alfy St., 2nd fl. (☎591 58 10 or 591 52 77). No music or dancing, but the period atmosphere ensures a constant stream of AUC students and tourists, and the occasional movie star. The lounge resembles a museum documenting Cairo's days under British rule, but this museum serves Stella (E£8.50) and has a well-stocked bar. Open daily 10am-1am.

Cairo Jazz Club, 197 26 July St. (☎345 99 39). Groove nightly with a crowd of international scat cats who come here to grab some Ella and a Stella (E£12) or to jump, jive, and cocktail (E£20) around the clock. The best live music scene in Cairo. Restaurant serves up decent entrees (E£15-25). Shows start at 10:30pm. Open daily 8pm-2am.

EGYPT

El Gato Negro, 32 Jeddah St., Mohandiseen (☎361 68 88). Stylish hepcats scope the Mohandiscene from this classy lair while sipping on anything from water (E£3) to top-notch scotch and whiskey (E£18). The adjacent restaurant serves up a variety of delicious foods (pizza, pasta, Middle Eastern fare). Cover-less dance floor opens at 10pm. Open daily 1pm-2am. AmEx/MC/V.

Pub 28, 28 Shagarat al-Durr St., Zamalek (☎340 92 00), kitty-corner to the Mandarin Koedar ice cream store (p. 102). Take a right off 26 July St. at the Misr gas station; the pub's brick facade will be on your left. The closest you'll come to Dublin in Cairo, this dimly lit pub serves a wide selection of spirits (E£9+). Next thing you know, it'll be raining outside. Open daily noon-2am. AmEx/V.

CLUBS

The Cairene club scene is smaller, tamer, and less crowded than that of Beirut and Istanbul. The clubs on **Pyramids Road** in Giza overflow with Gulf Arabs, but are extremely expensive—a night out can cost over E£200. Elsewhere clubs are more affordable, but depending on the place, night, and mood of the bouncer, single men may have a hard time getting in. Always call to check on the latest rules, and wear something sleek, black, and non-denim to improve your chances. The summer of 2001 found Cairo in the middle of a salsa rage, and as of August 2001, most clubs featured a weekly salsa night. Otherwise, the playlist is a mixture of Arabic pop and American Top 40.

Jackie's Joint, Nile Hilton, Tahrir Sq. (☎578 04 44 or 578 06 66, ext. 285 or 214). One of Cairo's hotspots, with lines out the door most nights. Features themed nights 2 or 3 times a week—call to check what's on. Minimum charge E£35 (includes a drink). Happy hour Sa-Su 10pm-midnight. Open daily 9pm-4am.

Crazy House Disco, Cairoland Entertainment Center, 1 Salah Salem (☎366 10 82 or 366 10 83). Careen into dancing Cairenes at this local favorite, which features a hyperactive fog machine. E£25 cover includes 2 beers. Open daily 11pm-5am.

Hard Rock Cafe, in the Meridien Hotel. Brand new and hugely popular with pop-culture crazed Egyptian youth, this branch of the international chain looks and acts precisely like all the others around the world. Disco open daily midnight-4am.

BELLY DANCING

Authentic belly dancing is a popular evening diversion for those who can afford it. For a E£2-5 cover charge, you can watch a show at one of several inexpensive venues downtown. However, these are good only as a form of ironic entertainment and have more in common with a comedy club than anything else. A dancer will typically wander around the floor (sort of) in time with the blaring orchestra, and occasionally throw in one of the two or three moves in her repertoire. To divert attention from their ineptitude, dancers often drag spectators onto the floor, so sit away from the center if you'd rather watch the entertainment than become it. Avoid any appetizers placed at the table; these are not free and can add a zero to your bill if you're not careful. These joints have little in common with clubs operated by five-star hotels. A five-star dancer has complete creative control over her performance and employs her own orchestra. Women will have no problem attending shows alone, and the Gulf Arabs who form most of the audiences regularly bring their families. Such convenience has a price—up to E£200, including dinner. Keep in mind that the quality of the performance depends most on the skill of the dancer; call ahead to check who is scheduled for a particular night.

Palmyra Club, in an alley off 26 July St. west of Sherif St. The cleanest, largest, and most reputable of the downtown joints. Stella E£12. Shows run 1-4am. Cover E£5.

Nile Maxim Cruise (☎342 48 33), at the Marriott Hotel in Zamalek. Glitzy Nile cruiser with chandeliers, mirrors, enormous windows, and jacked-up A/C. Floating show features top-level dancer and whirling dervish for E£70, including salad and dessert. Add at least E£50 for dinner. Daily 8 and 11pm. Call for reservations. MC/V.

EGYPT

Other clubs: Respected venues include **Semiramis Intercontinental Hotel** (☎ 795 71 71), on the corniche, and **Pyramisa Hotel Cairo**, 60 Giza St. (☎ 336 70 00 or 336 80 00). Shows usually start at 1am, dinner at 10pm. Call for reservations.

▶ DAYTRIPS FROM CAIRO

PYRAMIDS AT GIZA (AL-AHRAM) الاهرام

For the best combination of speed and economy, take the Metro to Giza Square (60pt), then a microbus from the east side of the Metro station (left as you exit the station; 30pt). **Minibus #183** (١٨٣; *40pt) from Tahrir Sq. and* **#26** (٢٦) *from 'Ataba Sq. are slower. The last stop is often 1km from the Pyramids; cross the street and follow the main road to get there. A taxi from downtown should cost less than E£20, though drivers often ask more. The easiest and most comfortable way back is on a special tour bus that leaves outside the tourist office every 10-15min. (E£2.50). Hotel managers in Cairo can arrange* **tours**, *but be sure to compare prices.* **Mr. Salah Muhammad** (☎/fax 298 06 50; mobile 012 313 84 46; samo@intouch.com) *offers chauffeur-driven tours of Memphis, Saqqara, the carpet school at Harania, and the Pyramids at Giza for E£40 each (E£35 for Let's Go users who book directly), including a guide. Entrance fees not included (leave at 9am, return at 5pm). Book at least the night before. Although sunrise at the Pyramids is impressive, guards won't let you in until regular hours of operation. Site open daily 8:30am-5pm; Nov.-Apr. 9am-4pm. Pyramids and Sphinx complex E£20, students E£10. 2 smaller pyramids E£10, students E£5. Great Pyramid limited to the 1st 100 visitors who appear at 8:30am and 1pm. E£20, students E£10.*

A 12th-century Arab historian once said, "All things fear time, but time fears the Pyramids." Centuries later, these great stone monoliths inspire mixed reactions from their visitors. For some, the Pyramids are the highlight of a trip to Egypt; others come away disappointed. Since everyone wants to see these stirring testaments to human achievement, nowhere else is Egypt's ravenous tourism industry so persistent. For a solid mile leading up to the pyramids, souvenir shops, alabaster factories, and papyrus museums conspire to pawn off "ancient" artifacts that are manufactured while-u-wait. At the foot of the pyramids, an army of hustlers not unlike a biblical swarm of locusts hounds you: Bedouin imposters rent camels and Arabian "race" horses, children peddle tourist dreck at inflated prices, and self-appointed guides approach at every turn. A firm *"la, shukran"* ("no, thanks") can prove useful at the Pyramids, even with the man who claims to be the mayor of Giza (he isn't). That said, if you can blot out the racket below and forget your expectations, you will be able to see this wonder of the ancient world as generations of awe-struck travelers have before you.

The three main pyramids at Giza were built for three pharaohs from the 4th dynasty: **Cheops** (Khufu), **Chephren** (Khafre), and **Mycerinus** (Menkaure), a father-son-grandson trio that reigned during the 26th century BCE. The pyramids are lined up in order of size and age, from Cheops to Mycerinus. All three entrances face north, and the bases are aligned with the four cardinal directions. The smaller, surrounding pyramids belonged to the pharaohs' wives and children. Each of the pyramids was once attached to its own funerary complex, which included a riverside pavilion and a mortuary temple where the pharaoh's cult could continue for eternity. A long, narrow causeway linked the mortuary temple with the neighboring waters of the Nile. Attendants brought the mummy of the deceased ruler across the Nile by boat and up the causeway in a solemn procession, depositing it in its sacred resting place at the heart of the pyramid.

 SIGHTSEEING STRATEGY. The best time to visit the Pyramids is Friday, when some of the more pious hagglers take the day off, and most other attractions are closed anyway. Be wary of going before 9:30am from November to March, when fog shrouds the Pyramids in the morning, but crowds tend to pick up as the day progresses. Be warned that you can't get inside the Pyramids or boat museum after 5pm. Good shoes are key for those who plan on internal exploration. External climbing is not permitted.

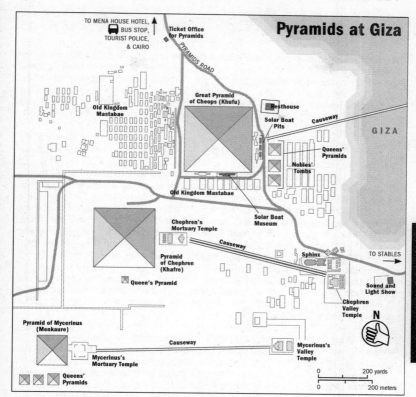

Pyramids at Giza

TO MENA HOUSE HOTEL,
BUS STOP,
TOURIST POLICE,
& CAIRO

Ticket Office
for Pyramids

PYRAMIDS ROAD

Great Pyramid
of Cheops (Khufu)

Resthouse

Solar Boat
Pits

Causeway

GIZA

Old Kingdom
Mastabae

Queens'
Pyramids

Nobles'
Tombs

Old Kingdom Mastabae

Solar Boat
Museum

Chephren's
Mortuary Temple

Causeway

Pyramid
of Chephren
(Khafre)

Sphinx

TO STABLES

Queen's Pyramid

Sound and
Light Show

Chephren
Valley
Temple

N

Pyramid of Mycerinus
(Menkaure)

Causeway

Mycerinus's
Valley
Temple

Mycerinus's
Mortuary Temple

Queens'
Pyramids

0   200 yards
0   200 meters

EGYPT

GREAT PYRAMID OF CHEOPS. Built around 2550 BCE, the Pyramid of Cheops is the first you'll encounter upon entering the site. It initially stood 146m high, but over the course of four and a half millennia its height has decreased by nine meters. While experts still debate the exact technology used in its construction, they generally agree that it took 10,000 workers about 11 years to build it. The total weight of Cheops is estimated at six million tons. One dubious story recounts that Cheops hired his daughter out as a courtesan and required each of her admirers to give her a stone for her dad's grave. (This seems unlikely. Considering that the pyramid contains 2.3 million blocks of stone and assuming that Cheops's daughter could secure one admirer per day, such a strategy would reach fruition sometime during the middle of the 38th century CE.) Stairs lead up the side to the entrance into the empty tomb, which is marked by graffiti left by 18th-century tourists.

PYRAMID OF CHEPHREN. The middle member of the Giza trio is three meters shorter than the Pyramid of Cheops, although it looks a bit taller because it's positioned on a higher plateau. Portions of the limestone casing that originally covered the monument still sheathe its apex, making it Egypt's most splendid pyramid. Also notice the granite on the summit; Chephren wanted to add a layer of granite atop the limestone, but died before he could start the addition.

PYRAMID OF MYCERINUS. What the Pyramid of Mycerinus lacks in size, it makes up for in the dysfunction of its occupant. Legend has it that instead of devoting his energy to his death chamber like any healthy, red-blooded pharaoh, Mycerinus lavished attention on his daughter, attempting to become her lover. After the grief-filled girl hanged herself, she was buried in a golden cow which was brought into the light of the sun once a year, in accordance with her (admittedly bizarre) dying wish. At the pyramid's northeast corner are the quarried remains of the **Mortuary Temple of Mycerinus.** Farther away, the ruins of the unexcavated Valley Temple of Mycerinus lie swathed in a blanket of sand.

THE SPHINX. Hewn almost entirely from a single rock, the Sphinx's poised figure is 80m long and 22m tall. His enigmatic smile—the Middle East's answer to Mona Lisa—once so unnerved visitors that Egyptians call him **Abu al-Hul** (Father of Terror). With civilization swirling around his paws, he now looks rather friendly. Many centuries have aged the Sphinx, and the Ottoman army didn't help things when it used him for target practice. A major renovation project has recently been completed, and the Sphinx now enters its 5th millennium in fine form.

Opinion is divided over the Sphinx's identity. Some believe that the face is a portrait of Chephren, whose pyramid lies directly behind it, while others maintain that the features represent the local deity Horan. Those who subscribe to the former theory believe that the Sphinx emerged from a sturdy knoll facing Chephren's complex. Failing to flatten it, architects transformed the knoll into the figure that lounges on the sand today. Another tale tells how Chephren, living a life of luxury, fell asleep by the sphinx's foot while hunting. The Sphinx spoke out and said, "I shall make thee Pharaoh if thou wilt dig me out of the sand." This theory does not sit well with archaeologists, who suggest that the body and head of the sphinx were carved at different times; they are not proportional to one another and have completely different erosion styles. (How would these archaeologists explain Michael Jackson?) Egyptian folklore asserts that Abu al-Hul is a half-human, half-tiger creature who protects the tombs from thieves, though he would seem to have performed rather poorly at his job. Whichever explanation you accept, the stunning visual majesty of the Sphinx remains indisputable.

EATING AT THE PYRAMIDS. The food situation in Giza is bleak, and it's best either to wait until you get back to the city or to bring a bag lunch (as many Egyptians do). There are several food stands near the sound and light show auditorium, as well as a Pizza Hut. **Pyramids Shishkebab Restaurant,** two blocks from the Sphinx Rest House along the main road, has a cheap *ta'amiyya* and shawarma stand outside and serves up traditional salads, *fuul,* and falafel inside. E£1-5 per item; meat dishes are more expensive. (☎385 10 78. Open daily 10am-2am.) **Khan al-Khalili Coffee Shop,** in the Mena House Oberoi Hotel at the end of Pyramid St., is a sleek spot to sip coffee or mint tea for E£3.50. (☎383 68 28. Open 24hr.)

At the foot of the Sphinx, just around the corner to the south, sits the I-shaped **Valley Temple of Chephren,** discovered in 1853. Sixteen great pillars, each 15m high, support the roof of this edifice, leading up to the ever-smiling pyramid guard.

SOLAR BOAT MUSEUM. This zucchini-shaped work of postmodern architecture rests against the south side of the Pyramid of Cheops. It holds the well-preserved Solar Boat of Cheops, the oldest boat in existence. It was used to transport Cheops' body and then buried so his soul could use it in the afterlife. Outside, his mortuary temple is little more than a few column segments and foundations. *(Open daily 9am-4:30pm. E£20, students E£10. Camera privileges E£10, video E£100.)*

CAMEL AND HORSEBACK RIDING. Innumerable animals are available for rent, and their owners *will* approach you incessantly. A 1hr. ride on a horse or camel should cost around E£15. For longer rides and more reliable beasts, walk beyond the Sphinx and turn right after the auditorium where the sound and light show takes place. You'll find a row of reputable establishments, including **AA Stables** (☎385 05 31; open daily 5am-8pm) and **SA Stables.** (☎385 06 26. Open 7am-11pm.) Both provide professional equipment (such as boots and hats) for a reasonable rate. The going price at these establishments is around E£20 for a guided trek on

MIDNIGHT MARAUDERS During the full moon, more adventurous travelers have been known to make nighttime excursions to the Pyramids by horseback. Both **SA** and **AA stables** stay open later around this time (call ahead to confirm) to accommodate those interested in seeing the Pyramids under the stars. The desert sands reflect much of the moon's light, making it rather easy to navigate. The dark outlines of the Pyramids themselves are an unforgettable sight against the purple backdrop of Cairo's sky. Rates are about the same as during the day (E£20 per hr.), but getting to the stables after dark is more difficult. Have a taxi drop you off near the stables (E£15) or take a series of microbuses from Doqqi. Go when the moon is full or very nearly so to ensure that there is enough light, and go only in a group. Women especially should not venture out to Giza alone after dark.

either a horse or a camel. E£10 is a fair price without a guide (in the unlikely occasion that the owner agrees), but only confident equestrians should inquire, as some mounts obey only hieroglyphs and may gallop swiftly off into the desert, ignoring their rider's hysterical yells and tugs.

SOUND AND LIGHT SHOW. As far as entertainment goes, it's the Pyramids or bust (unless you find fending off hustlers entertaining). The **sound and light show**, featuring lasers, runs two or three times each evening and can be entertaining if you are in the right sort of mood or under the right sort of influence (E£35, students E£17.50). Call ☎385 28 80 or check *Egypt Today* to find out when the Sphinx will reveal the answers to its riddles in the language of your choice. There is an English show every night. If you seek solitude, the people in the stables next to the Sphinx can arrange overnight expeditions through the dunes for E£30-50.

KARDASSA قردسة

On the road from Cairo to Giza, a turnoff to the right at the 2nd canal before the Pyramids leads to Kardassa. Taxis from Giza Sq. cost E£10-15; minibuses from Giza Sq. are 50pt.

The Western Desert and the camel road to Libya commence at the village of Kardassa. The village has become popular among tourists due to the variety of its local crafts, many of which appear in Cairo's tourist shops. The main products of the village are wool and cotton scarves, *galabiyyas* (E£10-30), rugs (1x1.5m rug E£50-60), and Bedouin weavings. The shops are in a sandlot across the canal from the village, usually in the back of a store or in the alleys off the main drag. Also for sale among the scarves and rugs are a disturbing number of professionally stuffed animals, including gazelles, jackals, and rabbits. Despite the efforts of the Egyptian Environmental Affairs Agency, this illegal but highly profitable trade continues. Tourism is beginning to rob Kardassa of its charm, though the prices are still lower and the quality of the merchandise higher than at Khan al-Khalili.

HARANIA هرنية

*The best way to visit is with **Salah Muhammad's tour** (see p. 90). To get there on your own, take a **minibus** or **bus** headed to the Pyramids along Pyramids Rd. and ask to be let off at Maroutiya Canal. A **taxi** may be willing to take you the rest of the way (E£4). Follow the road 3km along the west bank of the canal; the artists' school is 200m to the right, next to the Salome Campground. If you get lost, ask for Wissa Wisef, the school's founder. Open daily 9am-6pm. MC/V.*

More interesting is the artists' school at **Harania**, where young children and adolescents are encouraged to develop their creativity by weaving brilliantly colored carpets and making pottery. Since its inception in 1942, two generations of tapestry-weavers have studied at the school; many still practice as adults, countering the decline of the traditional craft industry. Some of the most notable works are showcased in the museum at Harania and in the book *Threads of Life—A Journey Through Creativity*, available at the center. The results of this creative process are stunning but expensive (E£300-2000).

EGYPT

BIRQASH CAMEL MARKET بـرقش

*Take a **taxi** from downtown Cairo (E£5) or **minibus** from Ramses Sq. to the site of the closed camel market in Imbaba (near Imbaba Airport). From Imbaba, **minibuses** (45min., E£2; ask for Souq al-Gamal) run to the Birqash Camel Market. The Sun Hotel (☎578 17 86) also offers an E£20 **tour** (not including admission) that leaves F at 6am and returns at noon; contact them W to reserve a spot. E£10. Camera privileges E£5, video E£20.*

If you came to Egypt expecting camels but feel like an ass because you've seen nothing but donkeys, the Birqash Camel Market is for you. The market is a bumpy half-day excursion from Cairo, convening every Friday from 6 to 11am in the small farming town of Birqash. Bypass the butcher shops with camel appendages on display (camel meat is low in cholesterol) and head to the market in the heart of town. Hundreds of camels stand around smiling enigmatically while Sudanese traders haggle over prices and smack the camels on the rear at the slightest hint of disobedience. If you think you know someone who could use a beating, you can buy one of the canes to take home (E£15). If you'd rather have a larger, more troublesome souvenir, prone to biting and spitting, camels run from E£1000-3000, with strong females being the most valuable. Give a boy some *bakhsheesh* to show you to the birthing pens to see the newborns. Traders are happy to answer any questions you might have about their wares.

SAQQARA AND ENVIRONS سقّارة

All sights officially open 8am-4pm; May-Sept. 8am-5pm. Some guards may lock up and go home a couple of hours early in low season and stay a bit longer in the winter. Some locked tombs may be accessed by paying an entrance fee (E£5-10) or bakhsheesh, depending on who is on duty. E£20, students E£10. Camera privileges E£5, video E£25. Ticket good for all Saqqara sites.

SIGHTSEEING STRATEGY The primary destination for most visitors is **North Saqqara** (p. 131), site of the funerary complex and the famous Step Pyramid of Zoser I. The three pyramids of **Abu Sir** (p. 134) are 6km north of North Saqqara, near the tiny village of the same name. The two pyramids and the funerary complex of **South Saqqara** (p. 134) are about 4km south of North Saqqara. The historically significant but scanty ruins of **Memphis** (p. 134) are even farther from Saqqara's necropolis, next to the Nile just south of the village of Mit-Rahine. The pyramids of **Dashur** (p. 135) form the southern tip of the row.

Named after Sokar, a Memphite god of death, Saqqara began as a royal necropolis in the early years of the Old Kingdom (3rd dynasty, around 2600 BCE), when nearby Memphis was the capital of Egypt. It was used as a burial site for the next 3000 years, acquiring a remarkable array of tombs and pyramids. Buses have begun depositing loads of tourists in North Saqqara, but only a handful of the most popular tombs catch most visitors' attention. At other sites, you stand a good chance of finding solitude as well as monuments. In contrast to those at Giza, the pyramids at Dashur and Abu Sir offer an opportunity to contemplate the wonders of antiquity in the stillness and stark beauty of the desert.

The two easiest ways to see Saqqara and its environs are to take **Salah Muhammad's tour** (see p. 90) or—for more flexibility—to hire a driver from the Berlin Hotel (see p. 99). If you choose to go on your own, you'll want to begin at the ruins of **North Saqqara**. Public transportation to and around the area is sparse, because a large swath of farms separates the ruins from Cairo. One option is to take a **taxi** from Cairo (E£20) and then try to find and share taxis at each site. However, some sites may have periods when taxis don't drive by for three or four hours. An easier and much more exciting option is to take a taxi to North Saqqara and then hire a **steed** to reach other areas. This is your chance to ride through the desert on a horse with no name, but it will cost you about E£15 per hr., more or less depending on demand—and you will probably also have to pay for a guide (and his ride).

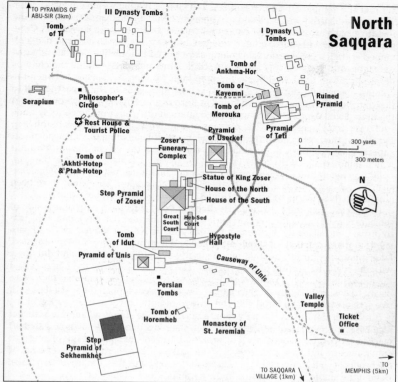

North Saqqara

TO PYRAMIDS OF ABU-SIR (3km)

III Dynasty Tombs

I Dynasty Tombs

Tomb of Ti

Tomb of Ankhma-Hor

Tomb of Kayemni

Ruined Pyramid

Serapium

Philosopher's Circle

Tomb of Merouka

Rest House & Tourist Police

Pyramid of Userkef

Pyramid of Teti

300 yards

300 meters

Tomb of Akhti-Hotep & Ptah-Hotep

Zoser's Funerary Complex

N

Statue of King Zoser

Step Pyramid of Zoser

House of the North

House of the South

Great South Court

Heb-Sed Court

Tomb of Idut

Hypostyle Hall

Pyramid of Unis

Causeway of Unis

Persian Tombs

EGYPT

Tomb of Horemheb

Valley Temple

Monastery of St. Jeremiah

Ticket Office

Step Pyramid of Sekhemkhet

TO SAQQARA VILLAGE (1km)

TO MEMPHIS (5km)

However you get there, wear **sneakers or boots** (not sandals) as the sand is quite hot. Bring lots of **water** and a hat, and try to get an early start, since the afternoon sun can be cruel. A **flashlight** also allows you to avoid paying the *bakhsheesh* the guards will request to illuminate some of the more poorly lit tombs. Tombs often close for preservational purposes in the summer, when there is less tourism.

NORTH SAQQARA

*A **taxi** to North Saqqara from Cairo costs about E£20. Another option is to take a **minibus** from Cairo, but this is only for those confident in their ability to untangle the complicated minibus schedule (with route information in Arabic). Begin by taking a minibus from Giza Sq. to the village of Abu Sir (50pt). From there, the killer 4km **walk** to the entrance takes between 30min. and 1hr., depending on your sand-speed. Walk south (to the left as you arrive) along the canal just before the village and follow the dirt road until you reach the paved road. Turn right and it's 200m to the site entrance. You can also hire a **pickup truck** at the canal in Abu Sir (E£1-2 per person) to take a group to the site.*

STEP PYRAMID OF ZOSER I. Saqqara's most famous site is the Step Pyramid of Zoser I (Zoser-Netcherikhe). Begun in 2630 BCE, it is the world's oldest funerary monument and the inspiration for the pyramids and other architectural wonders in Egypt. The brilliant architect **Imhotep** initially designed the monument as a stone *mastaba*, a low, rectangular building covering a burial shaft dug into the earth. Not satisfied with a simple rectangle, he modified the original structure, greatly expanding it and stacking several layers on top of the original base. Time and weather have taken their toll on history's first monument to postmortem egotism, but the pyramid has been renovated and the surrounding area excavated due largely to the efforts of French archaeologist Jean-Philippe Lauer.

Enter the complex from the southeastern side of the limestone enclosure wall. The paneled barrier was designed to resemble the mud-brick work that graced the fortifications surrounding the cities and palaces of the period. Two fixed stone panels, carved to resemble a huge wooden doorway, open onto a restored 40-columned entrance colonnade. The columns are ridged to look like bundles of papyrus stems and are probably the world's first stone columns—unlike the chumps before him who used mud brick, Imhotep built for eternity. Niches between the columns once held statues of Zoser. This corrridor leads to the **Hypostyle Hall** (a fledgling version of the hallways found at Karnak and Abydos), which opens onto the **Great South Court.** The two weathered altars in the center of the court symbolize Lower and Upper Egypt. The remains of a *mastaba* are at the base of the Step Pyramid at the north end of the site; scholars are still debating the purpose of this superfluous structure. Some think that the tomb is the original *mastaba* onto which Imhotep added the other layers of the pyramid. Others claim it is the symbolic representation of a second tomb. Earlier pharaohs had second tombs constructed (at Abydos) in addition to their tombs at Saqqara; Zoser may have been alluding to this custom by placing a small tomb at the south of his complex.

To the east, past the colonnade, the **Heb-Sed Court** runs the length of one side of the courtyard. During the Archaic Period (before the first dynasty), pharaohs had to prove themselves by performing various athletic feats at the annual Sed Festival. If a pharaoh failed, he would be killed and a stronger replacement crowned. Later pharaohs turned the Sed into a strictly symbolic ceremony and did away with the regicidal portion of the program. The Heb-Sed Court in the complex and the panels inside the pyramid that depict Zoser running a ceremonial race were meant to ensure his eternal rejuvenation. Twice, Zoser climbed the small dais with two sets of stairs, to be fitted with the crowns of both Lower and Upper Egypt.

Directly in front of the Step Pyramid's northern face stands a haunting **statue of King Zoser I.** The pharaoh stares out from a slanted stone hut (known as a **sardab**) pierced by two tiny apertures. The *sardab* allowed the spirit of the pharaoh to communicate with the outside world. The striking figure here is a plaster copy of the original (which now glares at visitors in the Egyptian Museum in Cairo; p. 118). Behind the statue is the entrance to the pyramid's locked interior.

OTHER PYRAMIDS. There are several other pyramids in the area, though the only one open to the public is the small **Pyramid of Teti.** Scramble down a ramp into the underground chambers to be greeted by protruding rocks—all that remains of a weak attempt to deter grave robbers. A massive black sarcophagus is inside, as well as a fine example of a **pyramid text** and a ceiling decorated with stars.

On the southwest corner of Zoser's complex, up the steps to the right of the pit and over the enclosure wall, looms the **Pyramid of Unis.** Unis was the last pharaoh of the 5th dynasty. Inside are wall carvings known as the **Pyramid Texts,** discovered by Thomas Cook (of traveler's check fame), also known for conducting the world's first package tours along the Nile in 1881. These writings are the earliest known example of decorative hieroglyphic writing on the walls of a tomb chamber. Sadly, the Pyramid of Unis has been closed permanently for preservation.

Extending east from the Pyramid of Unis is the **Causeway of Unis,** a beautifully restored sunken road lined by **solar boat pits** on its southern side. Over the low ridge of dunes lie the ruins of the **Monastery of St. Jeremiah,** barely jutting out from the desert. Founded in the 5th century, it was discovered in 1907. Many of the artifacts found inside are now in the Coptic Museum in Cairo (see p. 119).

TOMBS OF THE NOBLES. Noble families constructed tombs around the pyramids, mindful of their prestige even in death. All are relatively close together, and those open to the public have signs in English identifying their owners—who are always depicted in wall paintings as being bigger than their servants and companion animals. All tombs have several features in common. Most of them have narrow insets in the wall (called **spirit doors**) through which the ghosts of the deceased can pass, as well as paintings of food and entertainment for the dead to partake of in the afterlife.

Just east of the Pyramid of Teti, a ramp leads north to the entrance of the **Tomb of Mererouka.** This tomb has separate sections for Mererouka, his son, and his wife. There are fine carvings of desert hunts, jewelry making, and officials with big sticks collecting taxes. In addition, well-preserved, colored reliefs show the slaughtering and cutting up of cattle. A few meters to north of the Tomb of Mererouka is the **Tomb of Kayemni,** which contains reliefs depicting daily farming life along the Nile. In one hall, incredibly limber "acrobats" entertain Kayemni. Continue west to reach the often-closed **Tomb of Ankhma-Hor,** which contains several representations of medical operations (including toe surgery and circumcision).

The **House of the South** stands just east of the Step Pyramid. The inside walls are inscribed with ancient graffiti left by a visitor during the reign of Ramses II. The messages, expressing admiration for King Zoser, were hastily scrawled in a late cursive style of hieroglyphics known as hieratic. The lotus columns here represent Upper Egypt—hence the name House of the South. The **House of the North** is represented by the papyrus columns, the symbol of Lower Egypt. Some scholars believe that this emphasis on North and South throughout the site at Saqqara reflects the era's desire to unify Egypt geographically and spiritually.

To the south, a humble shack covers the shaft leading to three of Egypt's deepest burial chambers, the **Persian Tombs** of Psamtik, Zenhebu, and Peleese (of the 16th dynasty of Persian rulers). A dizzying spiral staircase drills 25m into the ground, ending in three vaulted burial chambers linked by narrow passageways. The colorful chambers make the walk worthwhile. According to the ancient inscriptions, Zenhebu was a famous admiral and Psamtik a high-ranking doctor of the pharaoh's court. Since the tombs are more isolated and usually locked, some asking around and *bakhsheesh* may be necessary to gain admittance—though even then you may not have any luck.

TOMB OF AKHTI-HOTEP AND PTAH-HOTEP. This unique tomb was built by two brothers; their fraternal affection is conveyed across the centuries. There are many superb reliefs here, including one of a cow giving birth. The color in some sections of the tomb shows that men, who were often in the sun, had much darker skin than women. *(Expected to be closed for renovations at least through the end of 2002.)*

TOMB OF TI. The Tomb of Ti, 300m northwest of the Serapium, was excavated in 1865 and has since been one of the primary sources of information about daily and ceremonial life during the 5th dynasty (25th century BCE). Serving under three pharaohs, Ti had many titles: Overseer of the Pyramids and Sun Temples at Abu Sir, Superintendent of Works, Scribe of the Court, Royal Counselor, Editrix, Royal Hairdresser, Royal Tea Brewer, and even Lord of Secrets. Some scholars also believe he was a practitioner of a martial arts discipline similar to that of the Japanese ninjas. He was such a high-ranking noble that he was allowed to marry Princess Neferhotep. Tomb paintings show his children wearing braided hairpieces, a sign that they were royal contenders for the throne.

SERAPIUM. The Serapium, discovered in 1854, is several hundred meters west of the Rest House, at the terminus of the main road. The complex is the legacy of a bull-worshiping cult that thrived during the New Kingdom. Believers traditionally associated the Apis bulls (the sacred oxen of Ptah) with the god Osiris and the afterlife. During the Roman occupation, the Apis bull cult combined with that of the Greek god Zeus, who often took the form of a bull, especially when he was fooling around with mortal women. The combined Zeus-Apis cult was especially strong around Alexandria. Work on the main portion of the underground complex was begun in the 7th century BCE by Psamtik and continued through the Ptolemaic era, though much older tombs adjoin this central set of chambers. In the oldest portion of the Serapium, two large, gold-plated sarcophagi and several canopic jars containing human heads were found, as well as the undisturbed footprints of the priests who had put the sacred animals to rest more than 3000 years earlier. Recessed tombs flank the main corridor on both sides, each containing a sarcophagus. It's difficult to imagine how these mammoth coffins were transported to the confines of the cave; their average weight is 65 tons. In the final tomb stands the largest sarcophagus, hewn from a single piece of black granite.

The mausoleum in the Serapium (a series of eerie underground tunnels with tiny lanterns) houses the **Tombs of the Apis Bulls,** where 25 sacred oxen representing Ptah's pets were embalmed and placed in enormous sarcophagi of solid granite. Only one of the bulls escaped theft; it now stands in Cairo's Agricultural Museum. At the end of the mausoleum tunnel metal steps ascend into one of the gigantic coffins. *(Go early to the Serapium early; it is a fair distance from other sites and often closes around 4pm. In summer, it may not be open at all.)*

OTHER SIGHTS. West of the Tomb of Akhti-Hotep and Ptah-Hotep is an expensive **rest house** with a bathroom and a small concession stand. Farther along the highway, where the road turns sharply to the west, are several decrepit and mostly decapitated Greek statues known as the **Philosophers' Circle.** These statues are said to represent (from left to right) Plato, Heraclitus, Thales, Protagoras, Homer, Hesiod, Demetrius of Phalerum, and Pindar.

ABU SIR أبوصير

*The pyramids of Abu Sir are 6km north of Saqqara and 2.5km from the village of Abu Sir. The site can be reached by **foot** or **hoof,** or a **taxi** can take you within 300m of the pyramids along a new asphalt road. Abu Sir is not technically open to the public, but E£5 **bakhsheesh** for the guard should get you in.*

PYRAMIDS OF ABU SIR. The most imposing of the three main pyramids at Abu Sir is the **Pyramid of Neferirkare,** which towers 68m above the desert and remains one of the best-preserved monuments in the Saqqara area. It once had a stone casing like its neighbors at Giza, but it has suffered a similar loss of face and currently bears a remarkable resemblance to a step pyramid. The **Pyramid of Niuserre** is the youngest, yet most dilapidated of the area's pyramids. The **Pyramid of Sahure** to the north completes the trio. The view from up the side of one of the pyramids allows you to see the entire width of the Nile Valley.

SUN TEMPLE OF ABU SARAB. If you are traveling by animal between Abu Sir and Giza, have your guide stop off along the way at the 5th-dynasty Sun Temple of Abu Sarab. On the fringe of cultivated fields, about 1.5km north of the Pyramid of Sahure, the temple was built by King Niuserre in honor of the sun god Ra. It features an altar constructed from five blocks of alabaster. *(A horse or camel ride from Zoser's Step Pyramid to the Sun Temple costs E£20; if business is slow, bargain to E£10.)*

SOUTH SAQQARA

*From North Saqqara, it is at least a 30min. **walk** to South Saqqara. **Taxis** from North Saqqara cost E£7.*

South Saqqara's most interesting funerary monument is the unusual **Tomb of Shepseskaf,** known as Mastabat Fara'un (Pharoah's Mastaba). The tomb is an enormous stone structure shaped like a sarcophagus and capped with a rounded lid. Although Shepseskaf reigned for only three years (he was the sixth king of the 4th dynasty and son of Mycerinus, whose pyramid stands at Giza), his stint on the throne was long enough to qualify him for a grand tomb—sort of. *Mastabat Fara'un* is neither a true *mastaba* nor a pyramid; scholars see it as a transitional experiment. A guard will admit you (E£1 *bakhsheesh* should suffice).

MEMPHIS ممفيس

*To get to Memphis on your own, take the **Metro** to Helwan (75pt) and then a **microbus** to the village of al-Badrasheen (25pt). After crossing the Nile in a **ferry** from the village, look for the **microbus** that occasionally passes by on its way to the ruins (25pt). Alternatively, take a **taxi** from Saqqara or Abu Sir.*

Memphis is not worth the detour today, though it might have been in 3000 BCE. The great pyramid-building pharaohs lived and ruled at Memphis, founded over five millennia ago by the legendary Menes and once populated by over half a million people. While the pyramids they built have endured, the pharaohs' city has faded away, leaving only palms, wandering goats, and the occasional ruin (usually closed to the public). There is a small **museum** that has a garden with well-worn statues and a large alabaster sphinx that probably stood at the south entrance of the Temple of Ptah. The only notable item in the collection is the 14m-tall **Colossus**

of Ramses II, displayed horizontally with cartouches engraved on its shoulders and waist. (E£14, students E£7. Camera privileges E£5, video E£25.)

DASHUR دشور

The four unique pyramids at Dashur—located south of Memphis—are definitely worth seeing. Closest to the road is the large **Pyramid of Senefru.** Senefru was the father of Khufu, whose pyramid at Giza beat his dad's by only 10m. You can scramble down a long ladder into the chambers of the pyramid. A quick drive or moderate walk away from the Pyramid of Senefru is the famous **Bent Pyramid.** This pyramid is unusual because it changes the angle of its sides halfway to the top, perhaps to keep it from collapsing under its untenable weight. Much of it is still cased in limestone, showing what pyramids looked like when they were first built. A few yards behind the Bent Pyramid is the small cone of a decaying pyramid. Though not too much to look at, it has a nice view of the desert at the top and flat stones that can be used as picnic tables. It's also a good place from which to view the fortress-like remains of the mud-brick **Black Pyramid.**

NEAR CAIRO

FAYYUM الفيوم ☎ 084

Fayyum, Egypt's largest oasis, is a vast agrarian settlement slightly over 100km from Cairo. Most of the 1.8 million residents of the oasis live in 157 small villages that dot the sandy landscape swathed with chrysanthemum and sunflower fields. Fayyum city, however, has no such charm. Enough tourists pass through to create an appetite for "money" (a term which has replaced *bakhsheesh* in local usage), but there are apparently not enough tourists to support a class of professional hustlers. It seems to the tourist, though, that the whole of the local citizenry has stepped in with glee, crudely and frantically demanding "money" whenever the fabled fat wallets of foreigners come within reach.

Fayyum was first developed through canal-building and irrigation by the rulers of ancient Egypt's 12th dynasty (20th-19th centuries BCE). The Ptolemies made the area into a rich province with its capital at Crocodopolis (near the site of modern Fayyum), the headquarters of a cult that worshiped Sebak and other reptilian deities. Roman conquerors used Crocodopolis as a vacation resort and as one of the primary granaries of the empire. An early center of Coptic Christianity, the oasis also sheltered a large population of exiled Jews in the 3rd century CE. Muslims believe the extensive canals to be the work of the biblical Joseph during his stay in Egypt; Bahr Yusef is named accordingly. Fayyum also boasts several out-of-the-way pharaonic ruins that are still under excavation and rarely touristed; discoveries await the independent traveler with a lot of patience.

▐▀ TRANSPORTATION

Buses and Service: Buses from Cairo to Fayyum city leave from Giza Sq. (2hr., about every 30min. 6am-6pm, E£4). Bus service from Turgoman Station is reportedly in the works; inquire at the tourist office for details. **Service** to Fayyum are available from the same area (E£5). Both arrive at Fayyum's **main bus and service station,** 1km from the city center, tucked surreptitiously under a bridge. To get to the station from the waterwheels, walk east on al-Gomhoriyya St. and take a left at the 1st bridge across the canal, about 300m later. Follow this road 200m and you will see a bridge; the station is under the bridge, across the train tracks. **Buses to Cairo** stop at Giza Sq. and Ramses Station (2hr., every 30min. 6am-6pm, E£4). In a fast-paced version of vehicular Russian roulette, *service* go to Giza Sq. or Ramses Station in Cairo until late at night (E£5). Another **bus and service station** serves **Beni Suef** and points south. Walk to the 3rd bridge over the canal west of the waterwheels, turn left, and walk 1km. Don't be misled by the local bus depot past the main crossroads—the station is 200m farther down on the right.

GETTING AROUND FAYYUM Two challenges confront Fayyum's foreign visitors: transportation and the determination of the tourist police to accompany any foreigners they see to all but the most commonly traveled areas. Hotels are required to report foreigners lodging in their rooms, so you'll wake up to a small entourage waiting in the lobby. (Do not be alarmed, as the tourist police are there for your own protection.) Both problems are best solved by renting a car in Cairo; all the sites listed below are accessible by well-maintained roads. It is possible to see Fayyum without your own car, but be aware that the police may require you to hire a private car to go any farther than Lake Qarun. For the adventurous, verdant scenery and a relative lack of pollution make Fayyum one of the best areas in Egypt for bicycling—a form of transport which combines freedom of movement with the chance to interact with locals. It is possible to rent a bicycle in Fayyum city for E£15 per day. Begin your inquiries at the sports center across the street from the Governate Club; someone there will point you in the right direction. As long as you stay within the oasis, getting lost isn't much of a danger; villages are spaced fairly close together and anyone can give you directions. Just get the police off your back by telling them you're going around the city, and be back by nightfall.

Local Transportation: Arabic-numbered **service** travel around town (25pt). *Service* to towns outside Fayyum city can be caught from these stations (50pt-E£1). You can also hire a **hantour** (horse carriage; E£1-5) or hop on a red **motorbike taxi** (E£1-3).

✦ 🛈 ORIENTATION AND PRACTICAL INFORMATION

Fayyum covers a roughly triangular area, stretching about 90km east to west. The eastern edge is bordered by the Nile. The saltwater **Lake Qarun** separates the northwest edge of Fayyum from the sandy plateau of the Western Desert. The city of Fayyum, almost in the center, serves as the area's transportation hub. Most hotels and offices sit around the four groaning **waterwheels** in the middle of town. The city runs along the **Bahr Yusef Canal**, which flows west from the Nile. At the waterwheels, **Bahr Tanhale** separates from Bahr Yusef and flows north toward the farmlands. About 200m to the west, **Bahr Sinnuris** branches off in the same direction. **Al-Gomhoriyya St.** and **al-Huriyya St.** run along the north and south banks of Bahr Yusef, respectively. The inverted pyramid dominating the east end of Bahr Yusef is Fayyum's **Culture Palace**, housing a theater, cinema, and public library.

Tourist Office: (☎34 23 13). With the waterwheels to your left and Bahr Yusef to your right, take the 1st left and walk 2km to the Governate Building on your right. Security guards at the entrance will direct you to the tourist office. Alternatively, take *service* #5 (ο) from in front of Banque Misr. Either way, it's not worth the journey, as the staff speaks little English and can offer only an outdated brochure and impossible-to-use map. Open daily 9am-4pm.

Currency Exchange: Banque Misr (☎35 01 62), on the same side of the canal as the Palace Hotel, on al-Gomhoriyya St. No traveler's check exchange. MC/V/Cirrus **ATM** outside. Open Su-Th 8:30am-2pm.

Tourist Police: (☎34 72 98). Usually on duty in the vicinity of the waterwheels, but they speak even less English and are even less helpful than the tourist office. Anyway, if you check into a hotel, you'll be seeing them soon enough.

Hospital: (☎34 22 49 or 33 35 96). From the waterwheels, turn left as if heading to the tourist office and continue for 1km; it's the large pink building to your right. Cash only.

Telephones: 100m south of the 1st bridge east of the tourist office, on the opposite side of the river. International calls available. Open 24hr.

Post Office: Same building as the post office. **EMS** and **Poste Restante** available. Open Sa-Th 8am-2pm.

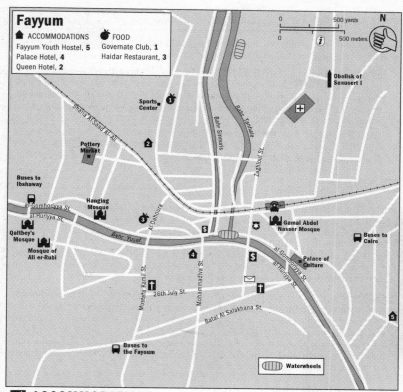

Fayyum

♠ ACCOMMODATIONS
Fayyum Youth Hostel, **5**
Palace Hotel, **4**
Queen Hotel, **2**

🍎 FOOD
Governate Club, **1**
Haidar Restaurant, **3**

Obelisk of
Senusert I

Sports
Center

Pottery
Market

Buses to
Ibshaway

Hanging
Mosque

Bahr Sinnuris

Bahr Tanhale

Zaghloul St.

al-Gomhoriyya St.
al-Huriyya St.

Qaltbey's
Mosque

Mosque of
Ali er-Rubi

Al-Dahoura

Bahr Yusef

Gamal Abdel
Nasser Mosque

Buses to
Cairo

al-Gomhoriyya St.

al-Huriyya St.

Palace of
Culture

Mustafa Kamil St.

26th July St.

Mohammadiya St.

Batat Al Salakhana St.

Buses to
the Fayoum

Waterwheels

EGYPT

⛺ ACCOMMODATIONS

Most visitors stay in Fayyum city only long enough to find the quickest way out, but if you have to sleep here, there are plenty of cheap beds available.

Palace Hotel (☎31 12 22), off al-Huriyya St., 1 block west of the waterwheels, on the other side of Bahr Yusef. Entrance behind a small watch store. Best bet for a clean room in the city center. Breezy rooms overlooking the canal with sheets, towels, and soap. Owner Ashraf Arafa speaks solid English and is much more helpful than the tourist office. Breakfast included. Lunch and dinner E£10 each. Singles E£20, with shower E£30, with A/C E£45; doubles E£35, with shower E£45, with A/C E£60.

Fayyum Youth Hostel, al-Hadaka, Block 7, Flat #7 (☎35 00 05). From the Cairo bus stop, take the bridge across the train tracks. Take the 1st left, pass a 4-way intersection after 1km, and take another left at the green FHYH sign 50m ahead. The hostel is the 2nd building on the right; continue around the corner to the right to find the entrance under a sign depicting a tree and a house. Ask for *beit al-shabab* if you get lost. A bit distant, but the best of the city's ultra-cheap accommodations. Slightly dingy rooms. Common kitchen. Inconvenient location and 46 beds ensure that there will always be vacancies. Breakfast included. Dorm beds E£8, members E£7.

Queen Hotel (☎33 78 28). Walk north along Bahr Sinnuris from the city center, turn left at the 2nd bridge, and continue for 250m until the road ends at Tawfikia St. The hotel is 1 block to your right, on the left side of the street. Probably the most appealing choice if you're staying in Fayyum for a while. Isolated from the worst aspects of the city, this hotel wraps around a peaceful courtyard. Deluxe doubles are the most luxurious and expensive rooms in town. Breakfast included. Singles E£20; doubles E£40, with A/C, TV, and bath E£60.

🕭 FOOD

Food options in Fayyum city are limited to small cafeterias serving grilled meats and the usual *fuul* and *ta'amiya*, plus a few restaurants.

Governorate Club, on Governorate St. Ask your *hantour* driver for *Nadi al-Muhafzah* or take *service #9* (٩) from the center of town. The restaurant is to your left as you enter the club grounds (E£3 entrance fee). Large, cheap meals. Kebab E£9. Chicken, lamb, or steak E£10. Spaghetti with vegetable salad and *tahina* (E£3) is the best veg. option around. Open daily until 1am.

Haidar Restaurant. From the Palace Hotel, turn left on al-Huriyya St., then turn right and cross the canal at the 2nd bridge. On the left side of the street after 200m, with an English sign. Stewed lamb E£9. Grilled chicken E£6.

👁 SIGHTS

MOSQUE OF QAYTBAY. Fayyum city doesn't have much to offer in terms of visual appeal, but visitors looking for sights should visit the Mosque of Qaytbay, along the canal about 1km west of the town center, at the very end of al-Huriyya St. The mosque is named for Mamluk Sultan al-Ashraf Seif al-Din Qaytbay, who ruled Egypt from 1468 to 1496. It was built beside a river that once flowed there, allowing worshipers to wash before prayers. The ivory on the *mihrab*, which marks the direction of Mecca, was imported from Somalia.

WATERWHEELS. For a quick introduction to the rural life of Fayyum, head north out of town along Bahr Sinnuris. It takes a while to escape the dreariness of the city into the green expanses of countryside, but after 2km, you'll reach the first of seven ancient waterwheels, still used in the irrigation system. Unlike Western versions, these great wooden devices are not used to power pumps but are themselves pumps, ingeniously using the flow of the stream to lift water from the canal to irrigation ditches leading to the fields.

🗺 DAYTRIPS FROM FAYYUM

KARANIS

*Catch a **service** or **bus** heading north from Fayyum and ask to be let out at Mathaf (MUT-haf) Kom Oshim. Museum open daily 8am-6pm; in winter 8am-5pm. E£16, students E£8.*

The mud-brick houses of the Greco-Roman settlement of Karanis, 30km north of Fayyum along the road to Cairo, have not fared well over time. The town was built by the Greeks in the 3rd century and occupied by the Romans for almost 800 years. Its two stone temples are in better shape, offering an interesting contrast of architectural styles (one temple was built by the Greeks, the other by the Romans).

The infrequently visited **Museum of Kom Oshim** holds a surprisingly wide collection of statues and *stelae* found both on-site at Karanis and around Saqqara and Giza. Comb through the exhibit of Greco-Roman terra cotta figurines, displaying a survey of ancient hairstyles. The second floor of the museum, devoted to Islamic and Coptic art, houses beautifully painted wood icons.

🏝 WADI AL-RAYAN

*If you have your own **car**, drive west along Lake Qarun. About 1km after you pass the distinctive domes and arches of Tunis village, turn left at the English sign. Other signs (in English) will direct you to the lake. Getting here without a car is tough, as no public transportation goes this way. You can take a **taxi** from Fayyum city (about E£100) or from Lake Qarun (E£40-60). **Hitchhiking** is common among the locals throughout the year, but is not recommended by Let's Go. Wadi entrance E£5, cars E£5 extra.*

Three freshwater lakes replete with wildlife adorn the Wadi al-Rayan area, 50km southeast of Lake Qarun, along what becomes a pure desert passage. Sand dunes and cool cobalt waters ripple side by side, separated by no more than a few meters of greenery. The **beach** around the three waterfalls is crowded with teenage boys on Fridays and holidays, but you can find an isolated spot elsewhere on the beach. Bring plenty of sunblock and insect repellent. Try to arrange for an overnight stay at the **Paradise Safari Camp**, owned by the exceptionally hospitable Muhammad Marzuk (E£20 per person). The camp, on the lake's shore but away from the some-times noisy beach, is surrounded by golden dunes ripe for exploration. Each large tent has two crisp-sheeted beds and a nightstand with a candle (electricity is used solely for the refrigerator in the kitchen). The camp's beautiful outdoor **restaurant** serves meals of chicken or fish (E£25). If you can get a group together, gather around a bonfire for Bedouin music and dancing.

WADI NATRUN وادى النطرون

If the chaos of Cairo has left you feeling slightly insane, Wadi Natrun's monaster-ies, flowering trees, cooing doves, and friendly monks are a wonderfully soothing antidote. For 1500 years, the 50 monasteries of Wadi Natrun were the backbone of the Coptic community in Egypt. The four that stand today (forming an ill-propor-tioned cross on the desert landscape) are more than relics; they are functional places of worship serving the spiritual needs of Egypt's Orthodox Christians, who flock here in tour buses all summer. The first Christian monastery in Egypt was established in the Eastern Desert by St. Anthony the Great (250-355 CE; see **St. Anthony's Monastery**, p. 199). In 330 CE, one of Anthony's disciples established the monastic lifestyle in Wadi Natrun. During the 1980s, interest in Coptic monasti-cism was so great that new rooms were added to accommodate the many novice ascetics arriving in the Natrun Valley. Wadi Natrun is also home to the last surviv-ing type of papyrus, which, due to the high salinity of the water (*wadi* = valley, *natrun* = salt), is a dwarf subspecies that never exceeds two meters (large papy-rus, found in the Delta, was last seen in the mid-19th century).

▐ TRANSPORTATION

A West Delta **bus** leaves from Cairo's **Turgoman station** (2hr., every 30min. 6am-6pm, E£4.50 at the ticket booth just to the right of the terminal's main entrance). Ride past the Wadi Natrun Rest House into Wadi Natrun town and get off at the bus stop near the gaudily painted statue of a soldier. Take a **pickup taxi** from here to the monastery Deir Anba Bishoi (10min., E£5). Coptic pilgrims are often willing to pick up travelers; hitching a ride with pilgrims is also the most convenient way to travel between monasteries, though *Let's Go* does not recommend hitchhiking. Start your journey early if you plan to return to Cairo or Alexandria in the evening. Note that there are no places to stay in Wadi Natrun town. To leave Wadi Natrun, wait at the Wadi Natrun Rest House for *service* or buses, which go to Alexandria (*service* leave about every hr., E£4.50) or Cairo (E£4 for frequent service; ask in Cairo or around Wadi Natrun for information about the less frequent buses).

NIGHT OF THE LIVING DEAD The monks who inhabit the four functional monasteries in Wadi Natrun live, eat, work, and pray in unison. Few are allowed to leave, unless for medical reasons or on monastery business. When a monk is ordained, his former self "dies" as he casts off the world of earthly desires, donning the black robe that symbolizes this metaphorical death. The black hood represents the biblical "helmet of salvation" (Ephesians 6:17), the cross embroidered on the back represents Jesus Christ, and the 12 crosses on the sides represent the apostles. A monk's day typically begins at 3:45am (even earlier on Sundays, when the monks of Deir Anba Bishoi rise at 12:45am for 6hr. of uninterrupted prayer), at which time the monks sing psalms and cantillate the Coptic liturgy amid clouds of incense, wide-eyed icons, and flickering candlelight. The service is punctuated by entrancing triangle and cymbal music. (Travelers must spend the night to attend.)

👁 SIGHTS

Deir Anba Bishoi is open every day of the year, while Deir al-Suryan, Deir Anba Baramus, and Deir Abu Maqar close for Lent. With the exception of those at Deir Abu Maqar, all monks happily receive foreign tourists and provide free tours of their monasteries. Some travelers try to arrange overnight stays, although this is primarily a privilege of religious pilgrims. For information on overnight stays, contact the Coptic Patriarch in Cairo at 22 Ramses St., Aboiyye (☎ 02 282 53 74), and see the specific monastery descriptions below for details. Non-pilgrims are often allowed to camp near the monasteries. As at most religious sites in the Middle East, you should wear modest attire (no shorts or sleeveless shirts) and remember to remove your shoes before entering the church. No flash photography.

DEIR ANBA BISHOI. With seven churches, the Monastery of St. Bishoi is the largest and most accessible of the four monasteries. Dating from 381 CE, Deir Anba Bishoi's original limestone and silt construction is now covered in plaster. It was rebuilt in 444 after being sacked by barbarians and now contains the remains of St. Bishoi, who is still believed to perform miracles for the faithful. Monks used to sleep in the desert, coming to the church only for services, but attacks by nomads in the 9th century prompted the construction of sleeping chambers, a protective wall, and a tower connected to the wall by a drawbridge. From atop the tower you can see a white swath in the distance—this is the salt that gives Wadi Natrun its name. The second floor's **Chapel of the Virgin Mary** exhibits 1500-year-old Gothic-style arches, an Egyptian innovation brought to Europe from Byzantium by the Crusaders. Don't leave without hearing the amplified echo in the old communal dining room, along with an amazingly well-preserved set of vestments from the Islamic conquests. (*15km from the Rest House. Ask for Father Sedrak or Teodoros, each of whom speaks excellent English and provides free tours. Open daily 8am-5pm.*)

DEIR AL-SURYAN. The "Monastery of the Syrians," named for the monks who once inhabited it, was established when a group of 4th-century monks left the Monastery of St. Bishoi following a theological dispute. With the resolution of the dispute in the 5th century, the Egyptian Copts no longer needed this alterna-monastery. In the beginning of the 8th century, a Syrian merchant purchased the monastery for use by monks from his homeland, the first of whom arrived at the beginning of the 9th century. The monastery was prominent throughout the 10th century, and by the 11th century it housed the largest community in Wadi Natrun. Today Deir al-Suryan is home to 130 resident monks and 15 monks-in-training.

The monastery is best known for frescoes the Syrians painted over the original Egyptian work. The monks here will be quick to tell you that they have what is widely considered the world's most beautiful fresco, depicting the Annunciation (when the angel Gabriel told Mary that she was pregnant), on the **altar room** ceiling to the right as you enter. To the left the ceiling is decorated with a Dormition fresco, in which Jesus, surrounded by the twelve apostles, receives the soul of his dead mother into his arms. Also in this room is an enormous set of ebony doors known as the **Door of Symbols,** whose leaves form the screen to the sanctuary in the Chapel of the Virgin Mary. The panels depict the seven epochs of the Christian era.

At the back of the church is a low, dark passageway leading to the private **cell of St. Bishoi.** The monks will show you an iron staple and chain dangling from the ceiling and explain how St. Bishoi would fasten it to his hair, thereby maintaining a standing position lest he fall asleep during his all-night prayer vigils. Set in the floor at the western end of the church is the **lakan** (marble basin), which is used for washing the monks' feet on holy days. Outside in the courtyard sits the **miracle tree,** which supposedly sprang from the staff of a Syrian saint in the 4th century. From the main entrance, go left past the courtyard garden and then take another left. The age-old Tamarind tree sits inside the building's corner. (*Facing away from the entrance to Deir Anba Bishoi, turn left and walk 5min. along the paved road. Open Su-F 9am-7pm, Sa 9am-7pm; in winter Su-F 9am-6pm, Sa 9am-3pm. Monks give free tours. No overnight stays.*)

DEIR ANBA BARAMUS. Founded in 342, this monky house is known as the Monastery of the Virgin Mary, though "Baramus" derives from the Coptic word "Romeos" (or Romans), in honor of Roman Emperor Valentinus's two sons, monks Maximus and Domitius. Tradition says that a crypt under the altar holds the remains of these two holy men who worshiped here. Relics of St. Moses and St. Isadore are kept to the left of the altar in the old church. The corpse of St. Moses once shook hands with passersby through a small aperture in his casket, but for the past 200 years, he has not been quite as cordial, and the opening has been sealed. *(4km northwest of Deir Anba Bishoi. Take a taxi from Wadi Natrun town or catch a ride from Deir Anba Bishoi. Open daily 10am-5pm. Find the resident English speaking monk for a free tour. Talk to the bishop about overnight stays, but they are usually reserved for pilgrims.).*

DEIR ABU MAQAR. The Monastery of St. Maccarius was founded by St. Maccarius the Great (300-390 CE) and is the oldest of the Wadi Natrun monasteries. St. Maccarius remained a religious hermit throughout his life and lived in a cell connected by a tunnel to a small cave. (Virtually none of that original building remains.) At the start of the 11th century, the monastery became the refuge of monks fleeing Muslim persecution. During the Middle Ages, the monastery was famous for its library, which remained intact until Europeans discovered the treasures in the 17th century and removed them. *(8km southeast of Deir Anba Bishoi. Visitors not permitted without prior approval. Fax the monastery at 048 60 10 57 or send a letter to P.O. Box 2780, Cairo. State the date and time of your visit, how long you wish to stay (no longer than 2hr.), and whether you would like to eat there. Overnight visits are granted to religious groups and students of theology or history. Hire a car at the Wadi Natrun Guest House for the 15min. drive.)*

ALEXANDRIA الأسكندرية ☎03

The population of Alexandria (al-Iskandariyya) swells to 12 million during the summer, as Gulf Arabs, Africans, and Egyptians flock to the city's gentle Mediterranean breezes. Outside the city center, apartment buildings dot the length of Alexandria's two harbors. Alexandria shares the dirt, crowds, and noise of Cairo, but a different spirit pervades Egypt's second-largest city. Only here can an evening meal combine Greek *souvlaki*, British ale, French pastries, and the serenade of a *muezzin*'s call to prayer. Western fashions are prevalent, alcohol flows freely, and French replaces English as the second language of choice.

Besides what can be found in an intriguing museum and a large catacomb complex, only bits and pieces of classical Alexandria remain to remind the visitor of its long and vibrant history as a Mediterranean seaport. It all started when a triumphant Alexander the Great stumbled upon this little fishing village (then called Rhakotis) en route to the Oracle of Amun at Siwa. The conquering hero became so enamored with the spot that he ordered a grand metropolis built upon it, then left for Siwa and never returned. Ptolemy was just as ptempted by the Mediterranean city as his predecessor and set about pampering Alexandria with the best ancient Greece had to offer. Alexandria's *Mouseion* (including the famous 500,000-volume library) soon became the greatest center of learning in the ancient world. Euclid invented his geometry there while Eratosthenes estimated the circumference of the earth; later, Ptolemy devised a tremendously popular faith in which Zeus and the pharaonic bull-god Apis were fused into the new deity Serapis.

Ptolemy's creatively named successor, Ptolemy II, fostered trade in the city, which soon became the richest commercial center of its day. To help the traffic along, Ptolemy II constructed the Lighthouse of Pharos Island, one of the seven wonders of the ancient world (now collapsed). After all the back-stabbing and booty-snatching involving Cleopatra, Mark Antony, Octavian, and others with tetrasyllabic names, the Romans took control of the city. With the return of political stability, Alexandria continued to grow in size and intellectual importance. Scholarly interests shifted to theology, and Alexandria was the site of the creation of the Septuagint (the first Greek translation of the Hebrew Bible) for the expatriate Jewish population after the destruction of the Temple in Jerusalem. Legend has it that

GIVING THEM THE FINGER When the Apostle St. Mark the Evangelist came to Alexandria to bring Christianity to Egypt in 64 CE, he quickly won many followers. Pagans and Gnostics, who made up the majority of the population, felt threatened by the new Bishopric of Alexandria. In 67 CE, they ambushed St. Mark while he was giving a Mass and dragged him behind some horses around the streets of the city until he was killed. Not content with his death, they tied the body to a stake and started a fire, but the corpse would not burn. Frustrated, they instead beheaded the dead saint and called it a day. His remains were gathered up by the local church, where they lay until the 9th century, when zealous visitors from Venice (a city notorious across the Eastern Orthodox world for its relic-snatching) stole the body to be reinterred at the Basilica di San Marco. Meanwhile, the head remained in Egypt after being transferred to the Church of St. George in Cairo, where it would be used, like other relics, during important religious celebrations. Fast forward to 1997, when at a summit of the Sees (the regional seats of church authority), Pope John Paul II returned one of St. Mark's fingers to the Coptic Pope Shenouda III. This gesture of papal reconciliation now rests at the Coptic Orthodox Patriarchate in Alexandria.

the translation was named for the 72 scholars who each labored in isolation but produced exactly the same text. Legend also teaches that St. Mark introduced Christianity to the city in 64 CE, founding what would become the Coptic Church. With Emperor Constantine's conversion in 314 CE, the influence of the Christians grew, and they turned on their pagan neighbors with vengeful glee, burning the *Mouseion* in the process (see **A Library Long Overdue,** p. 152). It was all downhill from there: the new capital in Cairo soon eclipsed Alexandria's glory, and a series of 13th-century earthquakes finally reduced the immense lighthouse to rubble.

A rejuvenated modern city burst forth when Muhammad 'Ali made Alexandria a port for his navy and redug the canal to the Nile. During the 19th century, breezy Alexandria became a favorite holiday spot for expatriate Europeans, wealthy Turks, and Egyptian nationals, as well as the setting for several major works of literature (like *The Alexandria Quartet*) In the 20th century, Alexandria continued to occupy a privileged position as the cooler of Egypt's two major cities, and the setting of choice for Egyptian filmmakers's famous melodramas.

In recent years, Alexandria's popular Governor al-Mahgoub has initiated a series of modernization projects to make the city even more accessible to visitors. Construction of the great Biblioteka is nearly complete and the coastal six-lane corniche is in the final stages of expansion. Known throughout Egypt for their shopping, the downtown streets are crowded with visitors in search of bargains. Late into the evening, sounds of street vendors hawking their wares mix with lively conversation from cafes. Twenty-somethings abound, hailing from the city's many universities, and Alexandrians of all ages are proud of their popular city and warmly welcome visitors into their midst.

✈ INTERCITY TRANSPORTATION

Alexandria lies at the junction of lush Delta farmlands, the barren Western Desert, and the Mediterranean coast. Cairo is a 3hr. drive to the southeast on either of two roads. The scenic Delta road (231km) crosses both branches of the Nile and passes through the industrial city of Tanta, while the desert road (225km) nudges Wadi Natrun and passes through Giza.

FLIGHTS

Al-Nozha is Alexandria's new **airport,** located several kilometers southeast of downtown. Local bus #203 (٢٠٣) and minibus #703 (٧٠٣) run between Orabi Sq. and the airport. **EgyptAir,** 19 Sa'ad Zaghloul Sq. (☎486 59 37 or 486 59 38), is just east of Ramleh Station Sq. Open daily 8am-8pm. **Lufthansa,** 6 Tala'at Harb St. (☎487 70 31), flies nonstop to Frankfurt on Sa, M, W, and Th at 7:35am; one-way E£2575. **Olympic**

Airlines (☎486 10 14 or 486 72 95; fax 482 89 01), in Sa'ad Zaghloul Sq. one block east of EgyptAir, flies to Athens Tu and F at 8:45am. One-way E£1035, youth E£730. Open M-F 8:30am-4:30pm, Sa 8:30am-12:30pm. **British Airways**, 15 Sa'ad Zaghloul Sq. (☎486 15 65 or 487 66 68.), flies to London Tu and F at 10:50am. One-way E£2800, student E£2300.

TRAINS

All trains leave from Misr Station, south of Sa'ad Zaghloul Sq., and arrive at Sidi Gabr Station, near May Sq., about seven minutes later. There are two options for trains to **Cairo:** the turbocharged **Turbini** trains (2hr.; 7, 8am, 2, 3pm, 7, 7:30; 1st-class E£30, 2nd-class E£22) or the slower **French** trains (3hr.; 6, 11am, 1, 3:30, 5, 8, 9:30pm; 1st-class E£23, 2nd-class E£14). The **third-class** trains run frequently (3:30am-11pm; E£6). A train also runs to Marsa Matrouh (5hr.; 6:45am; 2nd-class E£17, 3rd-class E£8.10). All trains offer student discounts.

BUSES

Find buses and tickets at the complex in 15 May Sq., behind Sidi Gabr Station. **Superjet** (☎429 85 66), offering air-conditioning, snacks, bathrooms, and ever-endearing Egyptian movies, runs to: Cairo with stops at Giza, Tahrir Sq., al-Maza, and Cairo airport (3hr., 4hr. to the airport; every 30min. 5am-1pm; downtown E£20, airport E£25); Hurghada (8hr., 8pm, E£80); Port Said (4½hr., 6:45am, E£22); and Sharm al-Sheikh (11½hr., 6:30pm, E£77). **West Delta** (☎428 90 92) runs daily to: Cairo via Giza Sq., Tahrir Sq., and usually the Cairo airport (3hr.; every 30min. 5am-1:30am; downtown E£20, airport E£25-28); Hurghada (11hr., 6:30pm, E£60); Marsa Matrouh (5hr.; 7, 7:30, 8, 8:30, 9, 10:30, 11am, noon, 1, 2:30, 3pm; E£15-23); Port Said (4½hr.; 6, 8am, 3:30, 4:30pm; E£17, with A/C E£22); Siwa (7½hr., 8:30, 11am, 2pm; E£27); Tanta (6:45am, noon, 1:15pm; E£6); and Zagazig (2hr.; 8, 10am, 2, 3, 4pm; E£13-15).

SERVICE

Service are cheap but packed (sometimes 20 people per minivan). Vans and station wagons depart from **Muharram Bey Station,** a 5min. drive out of town; *service* departing from Misr Station will take you there. Prices are approximate. *Service* go to: Abu Qir (30min., 80pt); Cairo (3hr. by the desert road, E£10); Marsa Matrouh (3hr., E£25); Port Said (4hr., E£10); Tanta (1½hr., E£4); and Zagazig (4hr., E£10).

CAR RENTAL

Avis, in the Cecil Hotel on Sa'ad Zaghloul Sq., rents Toyota Corollas to those over 25. (☎483 74 00; fax 483 64 01. US$50 per day, US$0.25 per km over 100km, plus tax and insurance. Open daily 8am-10pm.)

✈ ORIENTATION

Alexandria stretches from Abu Qir Bay to the western harbor. The entire 28km of coastline, lined by the main road referred to as the **corniche,** is crowded with glistening skyscrapers and deteriorating hotels jockeying for a spot near the Mediterranean. Alexandria's architect, Dinocrates, planned the city with broad boulevards rigidly arranged in a grid to harness sea breezes. The breezes still waft, but the order is long gone. Ancient Alexandria was built around **Pharos Island** (now a peninsula separating the eastern and western harbors), and the area still serves as the heart of the city. The downtown commercial district—called **al-Manshiyya,** or Midan Ramleh—is the hub of Alexandria's nightlife and tourist trade. Along the curve of the eastern harbor, northeast of downtown, is **al-Goumrouk,** a grandiose residential neighborhood that holds many old mosques. The **Karmouz** district, which encompasses Alexandria's main train depot **Misr Station,** borders the southern edge of al-Manshiyya. Its streets of overflow with students, workers, and the rest of the proletariat. Pompey's Pillar and the Catacombs of Kom al-Shoqafa are also here. **Al-Anfoushi,** home to Fort Qaytbay, occupies the tip of Pharos Island.

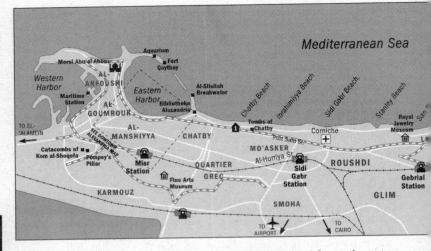

The best place to orient yourself downtown is **Sa'ad Zaghloul Sq.** on the water-front, which showcases a mamouth statue of the man himself. Bordering the southeast corner of Sa'ad Zaghloul Sq. is **Ramleh Sq.** (Midan Ramleh), the main depot for the intracity tramway and a hub for intercity buses. Many municipal buses and minibuses service the busy stop in front of the square on the corniche or on the south side across from Trianon Cafe.

Heading west on the south side of Ramleh Sq. is **Sa'ad Zaghloul St.** (which does *not* border Sa'ad Zaghloul Sq.), a main shopping artery that runs to **Orabi Sq.** The two squares serve as transportation hubs. All yellow trams out of Ramleh Station pass through here, as do a number of minibuses. The southern end is also called **Tahrir Sq.**, and the larger area **al-Manshiyya Sq.**

The corniche starts at the northern tip of al-Anfoushi and winds the length of the city's coastline to reach the **Sidi Bishr** district, **Montaza Palace**, and **Ma'mura Beach**, which demarcates the city's far eastern border. Note that the corniche is also called **26 July Ave.**

In addition to the corniche, two main arteries traverse the stretch from down-town to Ma'mura. **Alexander the Great (al-Iskandar al-Akbar) St.** lies several blocks inland. In Sidi Bishr, the street changes its name to Khalid ibn al-Walid St. to wel-come you to *(bienvenidos a)* Miami Beach, where it ends. The second major artery is **al-Huriyya St.**, which runs all the way to Montaza. East of its intersection with **Nabi Daniel**, al-Huriyya becomes **Sidi Metwalli**.

▐ LOCAL TRANSPORTATION

All of Alexandria's main squares, transportation centers, and the corniche lie within walking distance of each other. A brisk 30min. walk will take you from Old Pharos Island to the Shooting Club along the corniche. The rest of the city is acces-sible by municipal tram, bus, minibus, and private microbus or taxi. Riding the **tram** is by far the easiest way to get around the city. Look above the car's middle door for the train route in English. Minibuses are fast, frequent, and cheap, but they lack organization, and routes are at the whim of the driver.

BUSES

There are three terminals: in **Ramleh Station** (on the east side of Sa'ad Zaghloul Sq.), in **Misr Station.**, and in **Muharram Bey Station.** Buses run from approximately 5:30am to midnight or 1am (2am during Ramadan) and cost 25-35pt, or 50pt to out-side beaches like al-'Agami or Montaza. Buses are marked in Arabic numerals.

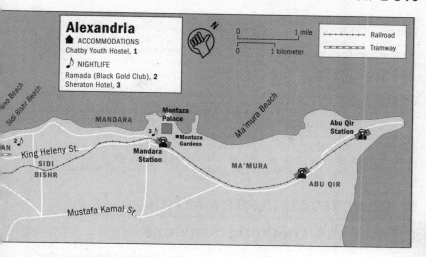

Alexandria

🏠 ACCOMMODATIONS
Chatby Youth Hostel, **1**

🎵 NIGHTLIFE
Ramada (Black Gold Club), **2**
Sheraton Hotel, **3**

E G Y P T

From Sa'ad Zaghloul Sq.:
#1 (١): Sidi Bishr & 15 May Station (A/C)
#2 (٢): al-'Agami (A/C)
#3 (٣): al-'Agami via Montaza (A/C)
#214 (٢١٤), **#215** (٢١٥): Maritime Station
#221 (٢٢١): Ma'mura
#403 (٤٠٣): Dakhla
#750 (٧٥٠), **#760** (٧٦٠): Hannoville

From Orabi Sq.:
#203 (٢٠٣): Airport
#220 (٢٢٠): Sidi Bishr
#231 (٢٣١): Citadel
#251 (٢٥١): Abu Qir via al-Huriyya St.
#260 (٢٦٠): Abu Qir via the corniche

MINIBUSES

A more appetizing alternative to the crowded city buses, minibuses run from 5:30am to 1am (2am and sometimes even later during Ramadan). They cost 50pt. Stand on the street and hold up the number of fingers equal to the number of passengers. Tell the driver or man in the passenger's seat where you are going, and he will motion for you to join them or stay put.

From Sa'ad Zaghloul Square:
#700 (٧٠٠), **#705** (٧٠٥): Muharram Bey
#703 (٧٠٣): Airport
#706 (٧٠٦): Citadel
#725 (٧٢٥): Citadel via the corniche
#735 (٧٣٥), **#736** (٧٣٦): Montaza
#750 (٧٥٠): Bitash
#760 (٧٦٠): Hannoville
#781 (٧٨١): International Gardens

From Orabi Square:
#703 (٧٠٣): Airport via Sa'ad Zaghloul
#704 (٧٠٤): Fishing club
#724 (٧٢٤): 15 May Station
#736 (٧٣٦): Ma'mura
#737 (٧٣٧): Abu Qir
#779 (٧٧٩): Mandara

From Misr Station:
#728 (٧٢٨): Montaza and Abu Qir
#729 (٧٢٩): Abu Qir
#755 (٧٥٥), **#765** (٧٦٥): al-'Agami
#770 (٧٧٠): Ma'mura

From Montaza:
#735 (٧٣٥): Sa'ad Zaghloul, Qaytbay

From Ras al-Tin:
#735 (٧٣٥): Montaza via the corniche

TRAMS

Trams all start from **Ramleh Station** and come in two colors. **Blue** trams (25pt) head east and pass by the Sporting Club before ending at al-Nasser Station. **Yellow** trams (20pt) head west and pass Orabi Sq. before turning north or south. They run every few minutes until midnight, occasionally until 1am, and until 2am during Ramadan. The middle car of every three-car tram is for **women only;** on two-car trams, one is marked "ladies" and the other "gentlemen." Hop on at any stop or flag one down, and pay on board. Look for the route number on the front of the train, not the longer car numbers painted on the sides. When in doubt, call out your stop to the driver or passengers, and maybe they'll stop to help.

TAXIS

A local taxi ride in Alexandria is marginally less death-defying than one in Cairo, and it is an inexpensive way to avoid the slow grind of the tram and the sardine-can squalor of the city buses. Hail one going in your direction and shout your destination into the window. The meters never run. No matter how big your group (three is the maximum), you can get away with E£5 to most places in the downtown area. Longer trips (Montaza or Abu Qir) are E£15-20, and past midnight you'll have to bargain harder. There is an E£1 minimum.

⑦ PRACTICAL INFORMATION

TOURIST AND FINANCIAL SERVICES

Tourist Office: Main office (☎484 33 80 or 485 15 56) on Nabi Daniel St., at the southwest corner of Sa'ad Zaghloul Sq. Fluent English speakers. Open daily 8:30am-6pm, Ramadan 9am-4pm, holidays 8am-2pm. Branch offices at **Misr Station** (☎392 59 85; same hours), **Maritime Station** (☎480 34 94; open 8am-5pm and additional hours for boat arrivals), and the **airport** (☎427 87 64 or 427 10 36). Free copies of *Alexandria by Night and Day* and *Alexandria and the Beaches.*

Passport Office: 22 Tala'at Harb St. (☎484 78 73). Walk west on Sa'ad Zaghloul Sq. from Ramleh Station Sq. and bear left on Falaky St. by the blue sign when Sa'ad Zaghloul curves toward the sea. Tala'at Harb St. is the 1st left. Open Sa-Th 8am-3pm, closed Fridays. Handle visa extensions in Cairo if at all possible.

Consulates: Israel, 15 Mena St., Loran (☎544 95 01). Open Su-Th 9:30am-3:30pm. **Lebanon,** 63 al-Huriyya St. (☎482 65 89). **UK,** 3 Mena St., Rushdi (☎546 70 01), off Kafr Abdou St. about 6km east of downtown, several blocks south of the corniche. Open Su-Th 8am-1pm. For **US,** contact the American Center (see **Cultural Centers,** below) or the US Embassy in Cairo (see p. 74).

Currency Exchange: Better rates than banks, but they only take cash. **National Bank of Egypt** in Cecil Hotel in Sa'ad Zaghloul Sq. is fast. Open daily 8:30am-noon and 5-8pm. **National Bank of Egypt** (☎484 09 53), a few blocks east of Sa'ad Zaghloul Sq. on al-Ghorfa al-Tigariayya St. on the corner of Nabi Daniel and Salah Salem, gives V and MC advances (no traveler's checks). Open Su-Th 8:30am-2pm, has ATM. **Banque Misr,** up the street and around the corner from the passport office on Tala'at Harb St., has ATMs.

American Express: 10 Patrice Lumumba St. (☎495 09 18; fax 495 09 17), near the Roman Amphitheater. Full service office, but doesn't hold mail. Open daily 9am-4pm.

Thomas Cook: 15 Sa'ad Zaghloul St. (☎484 78 30; fax 487 40 73; tcalex@att-mail.com), just east of Ramleh Station Sq. Here you can arrange plane tickets, holidays, and tours, cash traveler's checks, make hotel reservations, and pick up train schedules. Open daily 8am-5pm.

LOCAL SERVICES

English-Language Bookstore: The best is the **Alex Center for Multimedia & Libraries,** 181-183 Ahmed Shawky St. (☎545 37 14; alexcntr@ritsec2.com.eg; www.acml-egypt.com), which has an impressive collection of English titles, including a wide variety of classiscs, works of Egyptian history, numerous textbooks, maps, and even the *Guinness Book of World Records.* **Al-Ma'aref,** 44 Sa'ad Zaghloul St. (☎487 33 03); another entrance is on the south side of Sa'ad Zaghloul Sq. Strange selection of textbooks, translations of Arabic works, and trashy paperbacks. Open M-Sa 10am-9:30pm. **General Egyptian Book Organization,** 49 Sa'ad Zaghloul St. (☎486 29 25), just down the street from al-Ma'aref. Medium-sized selection ranges from *Sweet Valley High* to *The Art*

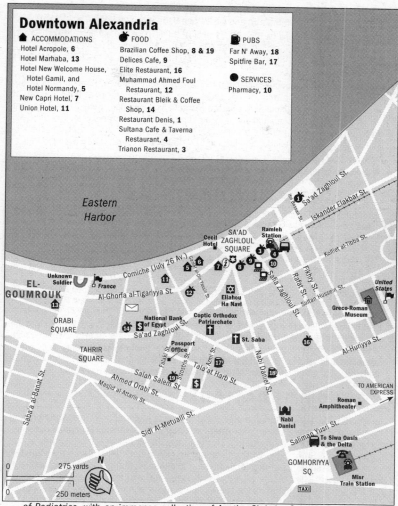

Downtown Alexandria

🏠 ACCOMMODATIONS
Hotel Acropole, **6**
Hotel Marhaba, **13**
Hotel New Welcome House,
  Hotel Gamil, and
  Hotel Normandy, **5**
New Capri Hotel, **7**
Union Hotel, **11**

🍎 FOOD
Brazilian Coffee Shop, **8 & 19**
Delices Cafe, **9**
Elite Restaurant, **16**
Muhammad Ahmed Foul
  Restaurant, **12**
Restaurant Bleik & Coffee
  Shop, **14**
Restaurant Denis, **1**
Sultana Cafe & Taverna
  Restaurant, **4**
Trianon Restaurant, **3**

🍺 PUBS
Far N' Away, **18**
Spitfire Bar, **17**

● SERVICES
Pharmacy, **10**

of Pediatrics, with an immense collection of Agatha Christie. Open M-Sa 10am-8pm.
The **Used Book Market,** at the southern end of Nabi Daniel St. near Misr Station, is an
entire block of obscure, inexpensive English titles.

Cultural Centers: British Council, 9 Ptolemies (Batalsa) St. (☎486 01 99). Open Su-Th
8:30am-8pm; library open Su-W 10am-8pm, Sa and Th 10am-3pm. **American Cultural
Center,** 3 Phara'ana St. (☎486 10 09). Turn left on al-Huriyya St. from Safia Zaghloul
St., walk 1 block past the 1st sign for the Greco-Roman Museum, turn left, then take the
1st right. Book and video library. Inquire about **teaching jobs** at the English Teaching
Program. Cultural events calendar posted outside. Open Su-Th 8:30am-6pm

EMERGENCY AND COMMUNICATIONS

Emergency: Ambulance: ☎123. **Police:** ☎122. **Tourist Police:** ☎483 33 78.

Tourist Police: Montaza Palace (☎547 33 95). Main office upstairs from tourist office in
Sa'ad Zaghloul Sq. (☎487 33 78). Both open 24hr. Other branches in **amphitheater**
(☎490 62 73), **Citadel** (☎480 91 44), and **Greco-Roman Museum** (☎482 89 12).

Pharmacy: Pharmacy Strand (☎ 486 51 36), opposite the tram at the intersection of Sa'ad Zaghloul St. and Safia Zaghloul St. Open 9am-1am.

Hospitals: Armed Forces (☎ 544 88 58 or 542 34 50), on the corniche in Sidi Gaber, take the blue tram to al-Shiekh Station. Open 24hr. **Al-Mowasah** (☎ 421 28 85 or 421 28 88), on al-Huriyya St. in al-Haddara is closer to the center of town but in shabbier condition. Open 24hr.

Telephones: Menatel phones scattered throughout downtown area. **Ramleh Station Sq.** office charges E£4 for 1min. to US. Open 24hr. Additional offices at **Misr Station,** at west end of Sa'ad Zaghloul St. on **Sultan Hussein St.** Open daily 8am-10pm. Lines are down for hours at a time, and you may be abruptly cut off. **Luxury hotels** (try the Cecil in Sa'ad Zaghloul Sq.) offer more reliable, but also more expensive, overseas connections. Rates to: US, Canada, and Europe E£4.85 per min., Australia E£6.25 per min.

Internet Access:

Al-Jaber CompuComm Services, 20 Mahmoud Azmi St. (☎ 483 27 95; aljaber@alexcomm.net), around the block from the Coptic Patriarchate heading south. Look for the sidewalk sign mentioning "Internet." Only has 1 terminal, but the owner serves tea while you're online. E£8 per 30min., E£15 per hr. Open daily 9am-11pm.

Zawia, 62 Safia Zagloul (☎ 484 80 14; zawia@iaa.com.eg; www.alex-cam.com). From Raml Station head south on Safia Zaghloul St. and take the 1st right onto Dr. Hassan Fadaly St.; Zawia is on the left. Look for the red and blue sign. Fast connection access the Internet on 8 computers, and there is a fax machine upstairs.

ICC Internet (☎ 487 44 59), on Safia Zaghloul St. just past Zawia. Look for a blue and red sign on the 2nd fl. Take a right into the alley before the pharmacy and follow the signs upstairs. Fast connections on 10 computers. A/C. E£5 per hr. Open daily 10am-1am, 24hr. in summer.

Global Net (☎ 495 89 81 or 491 28 89; Ghada-mehany@globalnet.com.eg), on Nabi Daniel St. across from the French Cultural Center, after al-Huriyya St. when heading toward Misr Station. No English sign; 6th fl. A/C room with fast connections. E£6 for 30min., E£10 per hr. Open 24hr.

Post Office: All open Sa-Th 8am-3pm, and most have **EMS** (until 2pm). A branch at the tram stop at **Ramleh Station Sq.** (☎ 486 07 46) and one on **al-Ghorfa al-Tigariyya St.** (☎ 480 53 29) 3 blocks west of Sa'ad Zaghloul Sq. **Poste Restante** until 1pm. Packages are held at the office of **Misr Station** (☎ 393 29 53 or 393 29 54), 10m south of al-Huriyya St. An office in front of the **Sidi Gabr Railroad Station** has EMS.

🛏 ACCOMMODATIONS

E.M. Forster liked Alexandria so much that he wrote a guidebook for it and named a character in *A Room with a View* after the Cecil Hotel. Nowadays, visitors are paying more for location than quality, though bargaining is always an option at the cheaper hotels. Steer clear of the ultra-cheap (E£10 per night) dives that line the streets running south from the corniche near Ramleh Station Sq. It's better to stay in one of the hotels listed below: all are clean, cheap, and within walking distance of the two main squares. None have fans, unless noted, as most Alexandrians depend on sea breezes for air-conditioning. In summer, look for corner rooms with cross ventilation.

Streets in **al-Manshiyya Sq.** teem with budget hotels. For a beachside retreat, head out to **Sidi Bishr** (14km) or **Montaza** (18km), where the posh amenities make up for the inconvenience of staying so far from the center of town. The only **camping** possibility is the beach at Abu Qir, but police generally only give permission to large groups. Interested travelers should inquire at the tourist office. Reservations are a good idea in summer, especially on weekends.

Hotel Union, 6 Muhammad Noaman St. (☎ 480 73 12; fax 480 73 50), off the corniche on the 2nd block behind the Cecil Hotel. This popular hotel has large, classy rooms with balconies and great views of the harbor. The comfortable lounge with the picture window and Mel Tormé tunes can't be beat. On the pricier side, but the comfortable beds, towels, and spotless bathrooms are well worth it. Breakfast E£6. Singles E£37; doubles E£63; triples E£67.

Chatby Youth Hostel (HI), 32 Port Said St. (☎ 592 54 59; fax 591 47 59), next to the tombs of Chatby. Clean, classy, comfortable, *and* inexpensive, this 175 bed hostel fills up quickly. Each spotless double and triple has a desk and occasionally a refrigerator. Restaurant serves 3 meals per day; breakfast included. 8-bed dorms E£12.60; doubles E£22.60 per person; triples E£17.60 per person.

New Hotel Welcome House, 8 Gamal al-Din Yassin St., 5th fl. (☎ 480 64 02), on the 1st block off the corniche behind the Cecil Hotel. Oddly named but well-maintained hotel with old but clean rooms, great prices, and views to match. Popular with the backpacking crowd. Rooms come with tiny baths. Singles E£16-22; doubles E£22; triples E£30.

New Capri Hotel, 23 al-Mina al-Sharkia, 8th fl. (☎ 490 93 10), same building as tourist office off Sa'ad Zaghloul Sq. A bit inland, but the rooms are spacious and the blue bathrooms immaculate. Corner rooms offer panoramic views of the square. Breakfast included. Singles E£37; doubles E£52; triples E£65.

Hotel Acropole, 27 Gamal al-Din Yassin St., 4th fl. (☎ 480 59 80), at end of the block behind the Cecil Hotel. Aging rooms include desk, dresser, and beds with thin mattresses. Prices vary with views, which range from panoramas to brick walls. Breakfast included. Singles E£15-35; doubles E£40-45; triples E£55-65.

Hotel Normandy, 8 Gamal al-Din Yassin St., 4th fl. (☎ 480 68 30). This dubious establishment was mentioned in Australian phenom Ted Simon's landmark travel narrative *Jupiter's Travels*. All rooms have three old (and crotchety) beds, high ceilings (with peeling paint), and shared baths (with stained tubs). Some have a nice view of the water. Bathrooms are adequate. Prices negotiable, especially if you begin to walk out. Singles E£15; doubles E£25; triples E£30; room with a view E£5-10 extra.

Hotel Marhaba, 10 Ahmed Orabi Sq. (☎ 480 09 57 or 480 95 10), on the northwest side of Orabi Sq. These posh digs were the former summer residence of the King of Libya, and it shows: wallpapered rooms come with towels, soap, sinks, and Egyptian TV. Louis XIV sitting rooms on each floor, and the rooftop sports breakfast buffet, a pool table, and a lonely bar. Singles E£35; doubles E£49, with shower E£57.50; triples E£68, with shower E£76.50.

🞉 FOOD

Meat, fruit, seafood, and vegetables can be found in the **souqs** of al-Mo'asker (take any blue tram six or seven stops east and walk south) and Bahary (take yellow tram #16 along the corniche, get off before the Mosque of Morsi Abu al-Abbas and walk inland two blocks). The fishmongers will cook purchases on the spot for E£3-5. **Supermarkets** dot the area around Sa'ad Zaghloul Sq. Gastronomic voyeurs should sneak a peek into **Muhammad Ahmed's Falafel Workshop,** which dishes out insight into the falafel-making process; green Industrial Revolution-era falafel churners spin chickpeas into a heavenly mash. Go up 'Abd al-Fattah al-Hadari St. from Muhammad Ahmed Fuul Restaurant, listed below, and turn right down the first alley to the brick building on the left.

RESTAURANTS

The restaurants of Alexandria are a delicious reminder of the city's cosmopolitan heritage. The cheap falafel and *fuul* found throughout Egypt are readily available, but Alexandria also boasts fine Italian and Greek restaurants downtown, where French pastries vie with *ba'laweh* and *kinafeh* for the affections of the strolling crowds. And of course, this "Queen of the Mediterranean" naturally features excellent seafood. Roam the streets of **al-Manshiyya** for a variety of tasty and reasonably-priced meals. Southeast of Sa'ad Zaghloul Sq., the streets teem with possibilities. If some of the smaller establishments have only Arabic menus, don't let that worry you. Communicate the old-fashioned way: follow your nose and point.

▧ Muhammad Ahmed Fuul, 17 'Abd al-Fattah al-Hadari St. (☎ 483 35 76). Walk away from Sa'ad Zaghloul Sq. on al-Ghorfa al-Tigariyya St. and take the 1st left, 10m up on the left. *Fuul*-lovers flock to this local family favorite. Scrumptious take-out for E£2 or less, a full sit-down meal nextdoor E£6. Open daily 6am-1am.

☒ **Elite,** 43 Safia Zaghloul St. (☎486 35 92), 1 block north of al-Huriyya St. Breezy, stylin' artists' cafe and restaurant since 1900, run by a friendly Greek matriarch. Wrap-around glass windows, high-beamed ceilings, and 2 decks of tables give a maritime feel. Steak E£18-33, chicken E£16-19, filling pasta E£3.50-10, Stella beer E£6.25. Open daily 8am-midnight.

Kadoura Restaurant (☎480 09 67), on the corniche about a block before the Tikka Grill sign, 2.5km west of Sa'ad Zaghloul Sq. toward Fort Qaytbay; look for the neon sign above the door. Locals rave about Kadoura's delicious seafood. Choose your prey downstairs from several varieties of fish, crab, and calamari (some still moving), then head up the slippery spiral stairs for a great view of the ocean and corniche crowd below. Waddle out after a massive meal of seafood, salad, bread, and drink (E£30). Fish prices seasonal. Open daily noon-midnight.

Restaurant Bleik, 18 Sa'ad Zaghloul St. (☎484 08 80). Walk west on Sa'ad Zaghloul until you're two blocks from Orabi Sq. A mixture of Lebanese and Egyptian cuisine. Enjoy such delicacies as quail and brain with rice (E£9) or sample from a range of Lebanese specials (E£4-14). Pastries E£2. Open daily 9am-10:30pm.

Restaurant Denis, 1 Ibn Bassam St. (☎486 17 09), located in the northeast corner of Sa'ad Zaghloul Sq. on a side street leading to the Corniche, adjacent to the corniche. Good seafood at fair prices. Waiter brings the day's catch to your table so you can sea food before eating it. Fish E£27-30 per kg. Calamari E£12. Shrimp E£40. Beer and wine served. Open daily 10am-midnight.

Taverna (☎487 85 91), on the southern side of Ramleh Station, across from the trams and next to KFC. A touristy crowd enjoys the "famous fish menu" (E£14-40), Italian specialties (E£4-14), and shawarma, pitched as "our nicest dish." Good prices and a convienent location. Branch at Montaza Gardens offers take-out only. Open daily 7:30am-3am (2am in winter).

Trianon (☎482 09 86), at the corner of Sa'ad Zaghloul and Ramleh Station Sq. A landmark from the city's *belle époque* and former hangout of illustrious literary types, this 80-year-old restaurant has both indoor and outdoor seating. Prices are reasonable (entrees E£13-26), with some great bargains: *mousaka* is E£13, and 3-course French breakfast with coffee is E£12. Open daily 7am-midnight; outdoor cafe open later.

CAFES

Sa'ad Zaghloul Sq. is packed with coffee and pastry shops while ice cream parlors cool off the Ramleh Station Sq. Along the corniche you'll find ritzy cafes and *sheesha* joints; cheaper, more traditional cafes (*ahwas*) await farther inland. **Ma'mura** offers a lively waterfront scene, where a youthful crowd buzzes until after midnight. Popular places to grab grub and *sheesha* include: the **Antazza Cafe,** serving food after 7pm (off of Sa'ad Zaghloul St. and across from the mosque, no English sign), **Minouche** (Italian food E£10-20), and **Cafino** (above Antazza, open late).

☒ **Brazilian Coffee Store,** in 2 locations: 20 Salah Salem St. and a stand-up joint at 44 Sa'ad Zaghloul St. (☎486 50 59). Cozy up to the bar at the Salah Salem location to examine green coffee plant tiles. The wonderfully rich coffee (E£1.50) draws a loyal local following. Croissants E£1.60. Both stores open daily 7am-11pm.

Delices (☎486 14 32 or 486 54 60), opposite the corniche in Sa'ad Zaghloul Sq. French and Middle Eastern desserts. More posh for your nosh: the sea-view terrace is a great place to enjoy savory pastries (E£2-5), ice cream (E£2.50-10), or coffee (E£4.25). Open daily 7am-1am.

Sofianopoulo Coffee Shop (☎487 15 17), on Sa'ad Zaghloul St., next to Restaurant Bleik. Classic coffee shop with outstanding prices: capuccino (E£2), tasty croissants (E£1.25). Aspiring astronauts can enjoy Tang on tap (E£1.25). Open daily 9am-11pm.

Sultana (☎486 27 69), on the south side of Ramleh Station Sq., across from the trams. Offers a luscious array of sundaes and ice cream (E£1.75 per scoop), waffle cones made while you wait. Turns into an animal house at night. Open daily 9am-1am, and (boy, do) they deliver.

Cafe Baudrot, 23 Sa'ad Zaghloul St. (☎486 56 87). With its expansive vine-trellised garden straight out of a *Town and Country* magazine, this cafe is a fine retreat from the busy streets. Perfect for musing over beer (E£9), coffee (E£4.50), cake (E£3), or even dinner (chicken or fish E£20). Tax and service not included. Open daily 7am-midnight.

◉ SIGHTS

The modern city of Alexandria was built atop the ruins of ancient Alexandria, leaving Classical remains eight meters underground. The scattered places where ancient foundations are visible offer fascinating glimpses of a city with a diverse cultural and religious history. That said, archaeological wonders are not the primary appeal of Alexandria as they are of other Egyptian destinations. This city's charm lies in its Mediterranean disposition—the people, the breezes, the beaches. Note that **price hikes** of 25-50% on admission tickets to major sights are scheduled for the coming year; see **Inflation Sucks,** p. 77, for more information. Also note that exorbitant camera privilege fees are not always enforced.

DOWNTOWN ALEXANDRIA

▨ROMAN AMPHITHEATER. This dazzling white marble structure is the only Roman amphitheater in all of Egypt. Stand on the round stone in the stage, whisper *Et tu, Brute?*, and your voice will be heard by conspirators all the way in the theater's back row. Archaeologists recently finished excavating a 100m-long Roman bath and villa behind the theater. The villa contains a stunning bird mosaic discovered in 1998. *(Just northwest of Misr Station and south of Cinema 'Amir. From Sa'ad Zaghloul Sq., walk up Nabi Daniel St. past al-Huriyya St. to the next big intersection. Turn left across from a gas station and go 200m; the entrance is on the left. ☎390 29 04. Open daily 9am-5pm; Ramadan 9am-3pm. E£6, students E£3. Camera privileges E£10; video E£150.)*

▨ GRECO-ROMAN MUSEUM. On display here are the most interesting and unusual relics of ancient Alexandria, including a mummified crocodile, exquisitely painted sarcophagi of Greco-Roman nobles (said to have provided inspiration for later Renaissance artists), and well-preserved statues of superstars like Caesar, Augustus, and Cleopatra. The pride of the museum is the beautiful mosaic of Alexandria as "Queen of the Ocean." *(5 al-Mathaf al-Roumani St. Walk south from the corniche along Safia Zaghloul St., turn left on al-Huriyya St., then left at the museum sign. ☎482 58 16. Open Sa-Th 9am-5pm, F 9am-noon and 2-5pm; Ramadan and holidays 9am-3pm. E£16, students E£8. Camera privileges without flash E£10, video E£150.)*

ELIYAHU HA-NAVI SYNAGOGUE. Guarded by a tall iron gate, this synagogue is still central for Alexandria's Jewish community and the greatest of the few Jewish sights still standing in the city. The gracious Joe Harari in the Communauté Israelite Grand Rabbinat office to the right as you enter the courtyard will show you around the building, let you look at old photographs, and tell you all about Alexandrian Jews. Although Alexandria once had more than 100,000 Jews and a synagogue in every neighborhood, this is the last one still in use for the 50 or so Jews who remain. The temple now holds an impressive collection of beautiful Torah scrolls from the closed synagogues. Built in 1885 by Baron Jacques L. de Menasce for the then-thriving community, the towering edifice sports five aisles, stained glass windows, pink Italian marble columns, dangling chandeliers, and wooden pews—check out the international assemblage of names on the brass seat markers. *(Walking away from Sa'ad Zaghloul Sq. on Nabi Daniel, take the 1st left after the intersection with Sa'ad Zagloul St. The iron gate is on the left. Open Su-F 10:30am-1pm.)*

COPTIC ORTHODOX PATRIARCHATE. The Patriarchate is in a beautiful church (founded in 67 CE and rebuilt in 1950) with mosaics, stained glass, hanging ostrich eggs, and a finely painted *iconostasis.* The first 47 patriarchs of the Alexandrian See (the regional seat of church authority), starting with St. Mark, some of whose remains are in a chapel to the left of the *iconostasis,* are buried within. Their names are listed in a niche on the right side of the church. *(Walking down Sa'ad Zaghloul St. from the square, take a left on Nabi Daniel continuing away from the square and then take the 1st right onto al-Akbat St. Open daily, services 6-8am and 8-10am.)*

E G Y P T

A LIBRARY LONG OVERDUE

The great **Biblioteka Alexandria** stood as an intellectual center of the ancient world for over 250 years. Alexander the Great's general Ptolemy I founded the library around 295 BCE, filling its shelves with scrolls from Athens. Unfortunately for academics, Julius Caesar caught up with Alexandria on his road to Rome in 48 BCE, allegedly destroying most of the ancient library and its collection of 500,000 scrolls. What remained was completely destroyed in 391 CE by crusading bibliophobe Bishop Theophilus, who led a pagan-hating mob to raze the building in the name of Christianity. Almost 2000 years later, Egypt has decided that it is time to try again. In 1987, UNESCO announced a project to resurrect the building that even Cleopatra could not save. A Norwegian firm designed the 45,000 sq. m behemoth in the shape of a circle. Built in the Royal Quarter where its predecessor is thought to have stood, the modern library's diameter stretches 160m, slanting down towards the ocean. Seven of the building's 11 floors have an ocean view, and the plan is for its shelves to hold an 8 million volume collection that will serve as the region's primary center study. Opening day keeps getting pushed back as Alexandrians continue to wait for their library. Not that waiting is anything new to a city in need of a library since the days of Julius Caesar. For information on the political obstacles facing the restoration team, see **In The News**, p. 68

MONASTERY OF ST. SABA. Sitting on the site of what was once a temple to Apollo, this 17th-century church in the Greek Orthodox Monastery of St. Saba is another testament to the historical importance of Christianity in Alexandria. Before 1965, there were 300,000 Greeks living in the city, though Nasser's assumption of power caused their numbers to dwindle, and the current population has settled around 1000. A giant bronze bell sits outside the church, while inside there are beautiful paintings, a spectacular collection of amulets, a giant bronze bell, and the marble table on which St. Catherine was beheaded. The church has recently been undergoing renovations; inquire at the tourist office about accessibility. (*Walk up Safia Zaghloul St. from Sa'ad Zaghloul Sq. to Sultan Hussein St. Turn right, then take the 2nd left. Open daily 7:30am-12:30pm and 3:30-6pm. Free.*)

WEST OF DOWNTOWN

MOSQUE OF MORSI ABU AL-'ABBAS. This is the city's largest mosque and Alexandria's most elaborate example of Islamic architecture. The holy Sidi Shehab al-Din Abu al-'Abbas ibn al-Khazragi came from Muslim Spain before the expulsion of the Moors to spread the teachings of the Qur'an in Egypt. His tomb rests underneath the mosque in the back, and legend has it that he rose from his tomb to catch bombs during World War II. Come nightfall, his coffin, like the exterior of the mosque, is bathed in a green neon glow. (*1km south of Fort Qaytbay along the corniche. Dress modestly. Women allowed in back room only. Open daily 5am-10pm, except during prayer times: 1, 4, 9:40pm, and sunset.*)

FORT QAYTBAY. The Islamic Fort Qaytbay was constructed on the ancient island of Pharos, on the foundations of the famous lighthouse. Fishermen and lovebirds alike congregate along the dramatic seaward walls, drawn by the waves and pleasant sunsets. Silt connected the island to the mainland, leaving the fort at the tip of a peninsula. Built in 1480 CE by Mamluk Sultan al-Ashraf Qaytbay, the Citadel houses the remains of the French fleet sunk by Admiral Nelson in the battle of Abu Qir (see **Abu Qir**, p. 155). There is a small mosque in the center of the tower, and the entire fortress is aligned so that the mosque's *mihrab* faces Mecca. Unfortunately, the main tower and mosque are under rennovation (call ahead for updates), but the ramparts offer a sweeping view of the city. On the road to the tramway is the **aquarium,** which has more visiting school groups than schools of Red Sea fish. (*Take yellow tram #15 west from Ramleh Station and get off at the sharp left turn, or take any bus going to Ras al-Tin. You'll find yourself in the middle of a fish market. At the point where the tram turns left, make a right on the road between the Kuwait Airlines sign and the mosque. The fort is at the end of this road. Minibus #707 (٧٠٧) or 719 (٧١٩) from Ramleh*)

Station Sq. takes you to the beginning of the street. ☎ 480 91 44. Fort open daily 9am-6pm summer; 9am-5pm winter. E£12, students E£6. Camera privileges E£10, video E£150. Aquarium open daily 8am-3pm. E£1. Camera privileges E£1, video E£5.)

ANFUSHI TOMBS. The Anfushi tombs were built for Greek occupants who had adopted Egyptian customs in the first half of the 3rd century BCE. Cut into the limestone of what was once Pharos Island, they are placed in two groups around a staircase leading into an open court and may well extend farther under the palace gardens. Many of the tombs were decorated with colorful geometric designs or painted to look like marble. On the wall facing the stairs of tomb #2 is an interesting painting depicting the purification of the dead. *(On Ras al-Tin St. Take the yellow tram from Ramleh Station and ask for Ras al-Tin St. Get off just before the palace. Open daily 9am-5pm. E£12, students E£6. Camera privileges E£5.)*

SOUTH OF DOWNTOWN

CATACOMBS OF KOM AL-SHOQAFA. This enormous, three-tiered complex of Roman tombs (descending some 35m below ground) is one of the best Classical sites in the city. The gate is decorated with winged serpents, Medusa heads, a pine cone (symbolizing Dionysus), and a *caduceus* (symbolizing Mercury, the *psychopompos* or leader of the dead to the Underworld). The main tombs are on the second level and are richly decorated with sculptures and reliefs of Egyptian gods with virile Roman bodies (a blend of pharaonic and Roman art). A statue of jackal-headed Anubis stands near the entrance to the innermost burial chamber. Scenes above the sarcophagi show the Egyptian gods and a mummification, along with the worship of the Apis bull. The sarcophagi are decorated in a Roman style, with garlands and bull skulls. Try to lift the lids—it's impossible, because the bodies were placed inside from passages behind. As you exit, notice two statues of Anubis, one in which he is dressed as a Roman legionnaire and one in which he has the body of a serpent. *(Facing the entrance to Pompey's Pillar, turn left and walk straight. Pass a mosque on the left and continue for another block. The tombs are on the left. Open daily 8am-4:30pm; Ramadan 18am-3pm. E£12, students E£6. Camera privileges E£10, video E£150.)*

POMPEY'S PILLAR. This 25m pillar of pink granite from Aswan is all that remains of the Serapium (Temple of Serapis, the bull-god), which was leveled once the Roman Empire adopted Christianity. The best finds from the ruins have been moved to the Greco-Roman Museum, but the pillar stands proud atop a small hill guarded by two granite sphinxes. Named in the Middle Ages by ignorant Crusaders with a flair for the alliterative, Pompey's Pillar actually dates from the time of Diocletian, a Roman who came to power several centuries after Pompey. One story holds that Diocletian was so incensed by an Alexandrian revolt that he swore he would massacre the rebellious people until blood stained the knees of his horse. As he entered the already defeated but mostly un-massacred town, his mount stumbled into a pool of blood, prematurely fulfilling his oath. The emperor spared the life of the city's inhabitants, and the lone pillar (once the tallest structure in Alexandria) remains as a symbol of the people's gratitude to him and his klutzy horse. Another story says that the pillar commemorates the time Diocletian gave the city free grain during a famine. *(Southwest of Misr Station. Take bus #309 (٣٠٩) or tram #16 from Ramleh Station Sq. and get off on Karmouz St. Enter on the southern side of the complex. Open daily 8am-5pm; Ramadan and other holidays 10am-3pm. E£6, students E£3. Video privileges E£150.)*

EAST OF DOWNTOWN

TOMBS OF CHATBY. Discovered in 1904, the Tombs of Chatby date from the 3rd century BCE and are believed to be the oldest surviving tombs in Alexandria. Before being carted off the Greco-Roman Museum postmortem trinkets filled the underground chambers. The ground above the small tomb is cluttered with random columns and Greco-Roman artifacts deemed unworthy for the museum. *(On Port Said St., across from St. Mark's College in the Chatby beach area. Open daily 8am-5pm. E£6, students E£3. Camera privileges E£5.)*

EGYPT

MUSTAFA KEMAL NECROPOLIS. This necropolis consists of four tombs from the 2nd century BCE decorated in a Hellenic style. Tomb #1 has an airy courtyard and a faded fresco depicting a libation scene over the middle doorway, complete with doric columns and sphinxes. *(Take tram #2 to the Rushdi tram station and walk towards the corniche on al-Mo'asker al-Romani St. Open daily 9am-4pm. E£12, students E£6. Camera privileges E£5.)*

ROYAL JEWELRY MUSEUM. Behind the governor's residence in Glim sits the architecturally intriguing Royal Jewelry Museum. Originally the Palace of Muhammad Ali's Granddaughter Fatima al-Zahra'a, the museum contains gleaming baubles of Egypt's last royal families. The gold figurines of a Persian chess set contain some 425 Flemish diamonds. But wait, if you think that's a lot, the E£10 million crown of King Fouad's first wife contains 2159 diamonds, among them a centerpiece 250 carat wonder. *(27 Ahmed Yahya St. Take tram #2 to Zezenia. Look for the Roman chariotieer painted on the side of the Faculty of Arts building. Facing away from the ocean, walk left until reaching Adly Yakan St., then turn left, go to the end of the block, and take another left. ☎ 586 83 48. Open Sa-Th 9am-4pm; F 9-11am and 1:30-4pm. E£20, students E£10. Camera privileges E£10, video E£150.)*

◪ BEACHES

Cairenes flood the Alexandrian waterfront during the summer months. For more peaceful surroundings, head to the **Sinai** (see p. 167) or the calm (but expensive) waters west of Alexandria (tram #1 or 2 from Ramleh Station Sq.). The 400 acres of flora at **Montaza Palace and Gardens** were once used as the summer retreat of King Farouk. Today, they are still the jewel of Alexandria's beaches. The palace and its museum have been closed to the public, but the beach is always busy despite its steep price (especially on weekends), and the gardens and groves are a favorite picnic spot for Alexandrians. Pizza Hut, Chicken Tikka, a supermarket, and juice and ice cream stands are all just outside the garden gates. (☎ 457 30 79. Beach E£10 via the Venesia Hotel; E£65 through the gates of the 5-star waterfront Helnan Palestine Hotel. Open daily 11am-1am. Gardens open 24hr.; E£4, holidays E£5.) Not far from Montaza, **Ma'mura** remains a favorite among vacationing Cairenes. (Beach access E£5; chair and table E£3; umbrella E£7; changing station E£1; paddle boats E£30.) Both beaches are reachable by bus #221 (٢٢١), #250 (٢٥٠), or #260 (٢٦٠), or by minibus #770 (٧٧٠). **San Stefano's Beach**, between Montaza and Sa'ad Zaghloul Sq., is much closer to the city center, as its weekday crowds and rubbish attest. (E£8 admission includes a chair and an umbrella. Closes at 9pm.) For more secluded beaches in the area, see **The Road to Marsa Matrouh**, p. 156.

♫ ENTERTAINMENT

BILLIARDS AND SPECTATOR SPORTS

Billiard tables charge by the hour throughout the city. A friendly owner runs the local favorite **Free Ball** in the southwest corner of Ramleh Station on the second floor (E£15 per hr.; snooker E£20 per hr.; coffee but no alcohol). The **Marhaba Hotel** in Orabi Sq. has a pool table (E£10 per hr.; alcohol served; open nightly 10pm-2am). If the sound of thundering hooves makes your pulse race, head to the **Antoniadis Palace and Gardens** in Smouha, on the wide road bordering the zoo. For over 50 years, Alexandria's working classes have gathered here on summer Sundays to watch working horses, with carriages of all kinds, race at breakneck speed. (Arrive by 6pm. 75pt.) Ask at the tourist office for info on the various **sporting events** at the Alexandria Municipal Stadium.

◪ NIGHTLIFE

CLUBS AND DISCOS

The cosmopolitan days of Alexandria's Hellenistic hedonism are long gone, replaced by the relaxed atmosphere of outdoor cafes. As the sun sets, *sheesha* cafes come alive with the sound of slapping dominos and the smell of fruity smoke. Evening strolls and waterfront cafes are some of the most attractive features of life in Alexandria. Arabic music eminates from the numerous storefronts in **al-Manshiyya**, as shoppers peruse the streets well past midnight. The action is concentrated downtown between Orabi Sq. and Sa'ad Zaghloul Sq., home to endless storefronts and the best bars, pastry shops, and coffee houses. Hopping between them is a great way to soak up liquor or wash down desserts.

Downtown, **Far 'N Away** is the best option for dancing on Thursday and Friday nights. A disco opens beside the bar, spinning a variety of American tunes. The **Lourantos** nightclub has drinks and Arabic dancing girls from 1am-6am (cover E£75). Dance the night away on Sidi Bishr's beachfront pavilions where weekends rock with late-night parties (cover E£5-10). **Nightclubs** can be found in most of the luxury hotels. There's no cover, but beware the stealthily levied **minimum charges.** Try the Ramada Renaissance on the corniche in Sidi Bishr, home to **Black Gold.** (Open daily 10pm-5am. Entrance on the corniche side. Min. E£30.) The ultrafab head to the **Sheraton** in Montaza to compare Rolexes. (Open daily Jul.-Sept., Th-Tu rest of the year; 10:30pm-4am. Minimum E£35.) Many discos don't allow single men or women, and some relegate lone males to the bar and forbid them from dancing. These rules are usually relaxed for foreigners, though, especially those willing to make a small donation.

BARS

Thursday and Friday are the big nights out in Alexandria, although "big" is relative in a town that places very little emphasis on drinking. During the week the bars are mostly empty. **Far 'N Away** the best pub in town is located at 14 al-Hurreyya past the intersection with Nabi Daniel St. Stylish American feel with a long wooden bar and hardwood floors (Stella E£15), also serves Tex-Mex and American fare. Just down al-Hurreyya, the upstairs bar at **L'Ossobuco** restaurant a welcomes foreigners with soothing jazz and Stellas for E£10. Another cool option is **Spitfire,** 7 Rue Bourse al-Hadema, at the west side of a small square where Sa'ad Zaghloul St. and Hassan al-Sheiko St. meet. Decals and posters cover every inch of this expat favorite, and mellow '80s music calms rattled nerves (Stella E£7.50). A unique find is **Sheik 'Ali,** around the corner to the south from the Sofianopoulo Coffeeshop when heading toward Sa'ad Zaghloul Sq. The long marble bar is a great place to enjoy appetizers or a Stella (E£7.50). The Athineos Hotel, between Ramleh Station and the corniche, also has a bar (Stella E£8.50) with an ocean view, comfortable chairs to lounge in, and *sheesha* (E£4). To fully relive World War II memories, head to **Monty's Bar,** on the second floor of the Cecil Hotel. Prints of classic paintings are barely visible in the dim lighting. General Montgomery's former headquarters now charges five-star prices for cocktails. (Open daily 4pm-2am. Stella E£8.50.) If Monty's high prices have got you down, head up to the roof garden for a fantastic view of the square and the water, but be careful where you sit—the sharp, green objects are actually cacti (Stella E£8).

⚡ DAYTRIPS FROM ALEXANDRIA

EAST OF ALEXANDRIA

ABU QIR   ابو قير

*From Alexandria's Misr Station, take local **bus** #251 (٢٥١) or #260 (٢٦٠), or **minibus** #728 (٧٢٨) to Abu Qir (20min., every 30min. 7am-10pm, 50pt). 3rd-class **trains** also leave from Misr or Sidi Gabr Station (45min., every 10min. 5am-1am, 45pt), local **taxis** from downtown (15min., E£15-20), or **service** from Misr Station (40min., E£1). Within Abu Qir, horse-drawn carriages (hantour) start trotting from al-Bahr al-Mayyit St. (E£2-3).*

On a small peninsula 5km east of Alexandria, Abu Qir has yet to be absorbed by the relentless expansion of the "Queen of the Mediterranean." It was here in 1798 that British Admiral Horatio Nelson took the French fleet by surprise without any navigational charts to guide him. Today, all hints of a military history are gone, and Abu Qir's **beach** is a peaceful and convenient place to enjoy the blue sea and its bounty of edible denizens.

EGYPT

IT'S ALL HIEROGLYPHS TO ME Hieroglyphic writing was used in instances of special religious significance, such as inscriptions on a temple wall or spells designed to speed a pharaoh to a happy afterlife. Since the inscriptions are in part decorative, they are often written in mirror-image pairs; in such cases, the writings are read from different directions. To tell which direction is the beginning, look for a human character; the direction the person or god is facing is usually the beginning. Before the discovery of the **Rosetta Stone,** the most popular theory was that each glyph represented an idea: elaborate, fanciful, and utterly incorrect translations were made from many papyri and inscriptions. The Rosetta Stone provided the revolutionary insight that each glyph stood for an individual sound, rather than a complex meaning. The stone became the key to the long-forgotten script because of its trilingual engraving—Greek, Demotic, and hieroglyphic. The hieroglyphic alphabet uses combinations of sounds to represent words, much like the English alphabet. To provide more exact syntax, the hieroglyphic alphabet also includes characters that clarify meaning and resolve the problem of homonyms.

There are no accommodations in Abu Qir, necessarily making it a daytrip from Alexandria. As always, produce and the ubiquitous *ta'amiyya*, shawarma, and *fuul* stands are found in the *souq* near the train station. Only sharks get seafood fresher than that served in Abu Qir's two major sit-down restaurants, both with great views of the beach. The Greek-owned, colorfully muraled ◪**Zephyrion,** 41 Khalid ibn al-Walid St. (☎560 13 19), is the oldest restaurant in town, founded in 1929. Blow on in for a full fish meal (E£25-35) and wash it down with a Stella (E£5.50). Nearby is the similarly priced and appropriately named **Bella Vista.** Nobel Prize-winning President Anwar Sadat was a cook here before he joined the army. Sit at his spot in the far left corner. (☎560 06 28. Open daily noon-midnight.)

One of the cleanest **public beaches** in the area is a short walk down any side street on the left as you face away from the train station. Most Alexandrians go on the weekends, so weekdays are best if you want the beach to yourself. As always, women should be wary of swimming uncovered, though a T-shirt and shorts are sufficiently modest for lounging around this beach.

RASHID (ROSETTA) رشيد

On the northern edge of the Nile Delta, about 1hr. east of Alexandria. A West Delta **bus** *runs from Muharram Bay Station in Alexandria (2:30pm, E£4).* **Microbuses** *leave from the Tikka Grill in Alexandria, 1 block inland from the corniche (E£3). 3rd-class* **trains** *run from Misr Station (every hr. 7am-8pm, E£2) via Ma'mura and return to Alexandria (9 per day 5:50am-8pm).* **Service** *are easy to catch at Muharram Bay in Alexandria, but the returning ones depart infrequently (E£3-5).*

Rashid (Rosetta) is the western meeting point of the Nile and the Mediterranean (Dumyat is the eastern meeting point). Not many visitors besides aspiring Egyptologists and those with plenty of time on their hands venture here. It owes its fame to the **Rosetta Stone,** the key to unlocking the hieroglyphs discovered here in 1799 by Napoleon's army. The port is dotted with provincial Ottoman mosques and houses from the 17th and 18th centuries. Unfortunately, trash-lined streets detract from Rashid's historic homes, many of which have been recently restored. A cast of the stone is on display in the museum here (the Rosetta Stone is in London's British Museum). It describes the coronation and numerous titles of Pharaoh Ptolemy V in three tongues: Demotic (the common language), ancient Greek (the royal language), and hieroglyphs (the holy language). Although hieroglyphs had previously been indecipherable, ancient Greek certainly was not; by comparing the three translations, scholars finally created a basic dictionary of hieroglyphs.

THE ROAD TO MARSA MATROUH

Microbuses *and* *service* *cruise the Alexandria-Marsa Matrouh road all day. Just flag one down (E£3.50 from Alexandria to the Atic Hotel, another E£5-8 to get to Marsa Matrouh).*

The coastline west of Alexandria stretches for several hundred kilometers along Egypt's Mediterranean coast, culminating in the beach resort **Marsa Matrouh.** The Mediterranean's natural beauty can do wonders for the tired body and soul. If you time your day right, you can bask and feast at the beach, stop to visit **al-'Alamein Memorials,** and make it to Marsa Matrouh by sunset. Though many coastline segments between Alexandria and Matrouh are depressingly devoid of budget hotels, opportunities for free and secluded **camping** are virtually unlimited (simply check in with the nearest police station or military office).

A number of resorts along the coast let passersby use their facilities for a fee. The plush **'Aida Beach Hotel** (☎410 28 02), 80km west of Alexandria, offers a low rate (E£30), which pays for pool use and a soft drink, or a high rate (E£100), which includes lunch and use of a beach cabin. Day use at the **Atic Hotel** includes a splendid shoreline, two pools, and a playground (a domed gatehouse 90km west of Alexandria with red letters above it. ☎410 63 93. E£20; with lunch E£45). The cheapest sandy spot is the **Marina Beach Club,** 95km west of Alexandria. It'll cost you E£20 (including umbrella and chair) to use the beautiful beach populated by wealthy Alexandrians zipping around on jet skis (E£200 per hr.).

AL-'AGAMI العجمى

Upper-middle-class Alexandrian sun worshipers flock to al-'Agami to escape the bustle of the city, instead embracing a world of concrete villas, chain restaurants, and private beaches. During the peak summer months, crowds compete elbow-to-elbow for beach space and women grow courageous in the quest to bare more than a knee here or a nape there. In winter, hours shorten, prices descend, hemlines drop, and the town quiets down.

To get to al-'Agami, take bus #2 (٢), 3 (٣) or 12 (١٢) from Sa'ad Zaghloul Sq. in Alexandria (E£1-2). Al-'Agami is actually two towns—Bitash and Hannoville. In **Bitash,** villas and expensive hotels mingle with restaurants and Western-style boutiques. In **Hannoville,** the quieter, more spinsterly sister city, a few budget hotels are crammed in between rows of apartments. When Egyptians say "al-'Agami," they're generally referring only to Bitash. Each town is oriented around a 2km-long main street (**Bitash St.** and **Hannoville St.,** respectively) that extends from the highway to the beach and is lined with stores and groceries.

There is no reason to stay in al-'Agami; Alexandria is 30min. away and the hotels here are pricey. Most beaches, such as the belly-and-bicep baring **Fardous (Paradise) Beach,** are private and hard to use. **Abu Qir** and **Montaza** are better bets. The greatest concentration of restaurants is in Bitash, where the main road forks into Bitash St. and al-Asal St. Along with various chain restaurants, **al-Omda** serves up copious quantities of meat, and **La Dolce Vita** scoops up sweet Italian-style gelato.

AL-'ALAMEIN العلمين

Al-'Alamein is a sober interruption in the giddy spree of villa construction that dominates the Mediterranean coast. Here, in November 1942, Allied forces led by British Field Marshal Sir Bernard Montgomery halted the advance of the German Afrika Korps, saving Alexandria, Egypt, and the Suez Canal and oil fields of the Middle East from Nazi takeover. The Allied victory here marked the beginning of the end for the Axis Powers in North Africa and crushed the mystique surrounding the "Desert Fox," German Field Marshal Erwin Rommel, whose force of Panzer tanks had previously seemed invincible. Nearly 10,000 soldiers lost their lives at al-'Alamein, and 70,000 were wounded.

Non-air-conditioned **West Delta buses** traveling between Marsa Matrouh and Alexandria or Cairo pass through al-'Alamein, though you can also go to a **service** depot and name your destination. Get off at the police checkpoint, right before the road to the British War Cemetery; the museum lies left of the main road connecting Alexandria to Marsa Matrouh. To leave town, flag down a *service* or **minibus** heading to Alexandria (1hr., E£5) or Marsa Matrouh (2hr., E£8-10) on the main road (the road leading to the museum and cemetery that merges with the main road Alexandria- Marsa Matrouh road. A hired **taxi** costs E£100, for either a round-trip from Alexandria or a cross-desert run.

WAR MUSEUM. The displays of weaponry and military garb are impressive but sterile. There are English descriptions of Rommel, Montgomery, and other participants in the battle. A map bedecked with hundreds of tiny red and green bulbs recreates the changing landscape of the North African campaign. *(On the west side of the village; near the bus stop and main square. Open daily 9am-5pm. E£5. Camera privileges E£5, video E£20.)*

BRITISH WAR CEMETERY. The British War Cemetery, about 250m east of the museum, is a more powerful testament to the cost of the battle. Here lie 7367 soldiers from all over the Commonwealth, 815 of whom have headstones bearing only the inscription "Known Unto God." Ringed by purple flowers and set against the seemingly interminable desert, the excruciatingly tidy rows maintained by the British War Graves Commission are made even more poignant by the personalized epitaphs. *(Open Sa-Th 7am-2:30pm. Free.)*

> **!** **WARNING:** Do not wander unguided through the desert. While the grounds themselves have been cleared of **landmines**, strips of land between cemeteries remain dangerous.

GERMAN AND ITALIAN CEMETERIES. The less frequently visited German and Italian cemeteries (8km and 12km west of town, respectively) perch on a small peninsula overlooking the sea. It is difficult to get directly to these monuments without a private car or hired taxi. Microbuses along the Alexandria-Matrouh road will let off passengers 2km from the monuments—lucky travelers may be able to convince *service* drivers to give them a door-to-tomb ride. Whichever way you travel, make sure you're armed with lots of water.

MARSA MATROUH مرسى مطروح ☎046

Fanning out from a bay of pure cobalt blue, this resort city—home to the best beaches on Egypt's north coast—makes a pleasant stopover for travelers in no rush to get to Siwa. In summer, Egyptian families pack the mold-and-pour concrete villas and bathe along the 5km crescent of white sands and gentle waves. At night, the streets fill with horn-happy drivers, gaggles of mothers looking for bargains, and shouting vendors selling useless junk. Marsa Matrouh's natural harbor has served travelers, merchants, and soldiers from Alexander the Great to Rommel the Desert Fox. Now the majority of sea vessels in Marsa are rented by the hour, and the police patrolling the Libyan border comprise the only major military presence in the area.

⌐ TRANSPORTATION

Flights: EgyptAir (☎493 43 98), on Gala'a St., 3 blocks west of Alexandria St. Flights to **Cairo** (1hr.; W, F, Su 10:30am; US$55). Office open June-Sept. Tu-Su 9am-2pm and 6-9pm. No flights in off season.

Trains: Station (☎493 39 36) is 1 block east of the south end of Alexandria St., and about 1km from the corniche. Runs trains to **Alexandria** (6hr., 3rd-class 7am and 3:30pm, E£3.50; 2nd-class and sleeper cars S, Tu, Th 11pm, E£26).

Buses: Station is 2km south of the corniche past the train tracks, to the left facing away from the ocean. Book ahead for Cairo buses, especially during summer. Arrive 30min. early to buy tickets and get a seat. Far fewer A/C buses Nov.-May. **Golden Arrow** (☎493 10 79) sends A/C buses to **Alexandria** (3hr.; 9, 11am, 2, 3, 4, 6pm, with additional buses in summer; E£20) and **Cairo** (5hr.; 8:30am, 10:30, noon, 2:30, 3:30, 4:30pm, with additional buses in summer; E£36). **Superjet** (☎493 48 98) offers A/C buses to **Alexandria** (3hr.; noon and 2:30pm; E£20) and **Cairo** (5hr.; 9, 11am, 1:30, 3, 4pm; E£37). Superjet buses do not always run in winter. **West Delta** (☎493 20 79) has non-A/C buses to: **Alexandria** (5hr.; 2 7, 11am, noon, 1, 5, 8pm, and additional buses in

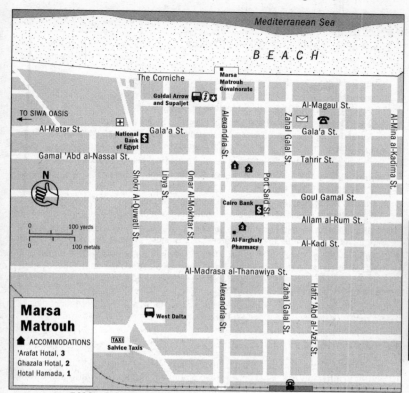

Marsa Matrouh

■ Marsa Matrouh Govalnorate

The Corniche

Goldai Arrow and Supaljet

TO SIWA OASIS

Al-Matar St.

National Bank of Egypt

Gala'a St.

Gamal 'Abd al-Nassal St.

Al-Magaul St.

Zahal Galai St.

Gala'a St.

Tahrir St.

Alexandria St.

Al-Mina al-Kadima St.

Shokri Al-Quwati St.

Libya St.

Omar Al-Mokhtar St.

Port Said St.

Goul Gamal St.

Allam al-Rum St.

Cairo Bank

Al-Kadi St.

Al-Farghaly Pharmacy

Al-Madrasa al-Thanawiya St.

Alexandria St.

Zahal Galal St.

Hafiz 'Abd al-'Aziz St.

N

0 — 100 yards
0 — 100 metals

Marsa Matrouh

▲ ACCOMMODATIONS

'Arafat Hotal, **3**
Ghazala Hotal, **2**
Hotal Hamada, **1**

West Delta

TAXI Salvice Taxis

E G Y P T

summer; E£20); **Cairo** (7hr.; 7:30am with additional buses in summer; E£28); and **Siwa Oasis** (5hr.; 7:30am, 1:30, 4, 7:30pm; E£12).

Minibuses: Leave for the surrounding beaches from where al-Matar splits into 2 streets behind the Omar Effendi store, 5 blocks west of Alexandria St.

Service: *Service* leave irregularly from the bus station to **Alexandria** (E£12); infrequently to **Siwa Oasis** (E£15) and nearby beaches.

Bike Rental: On Alexandria St., 2 blocks south of the corniche. E£2 per hr., E£10 per day; bargain for long-term rental.

■ ORIENTATION

Your feet will serve you well in Marsa Matrouh—a cross-town stroll should take no more than 15min. You only need to know two streets to find your way around town: the **corniche**, stretching the length of the bay, and **Alexandria St.**, running perpendicular to the corniche. Alexandria St. begins at the **Marsa Matrouh Governorate** and heads inland to the **train station** and hill 1km south of town. Most hotels and government offices cluster along the corniche and the streets running parallel to it. Heading inland from the corniche, the most important of these are **Gala'a St.**, **Tahrir St.** (also called Gamal 'Abd al-Nasser St.), **Goul Gamal St.**, and **Allam al-Rum St.** Parallel to Alexandria St. to the east are **Port Said St.** and **Zaher Galal St.**

While Marsa Matrouh is a resort town, it is also only 215km from Libya—hence the noticeable military presence in the surrounding areas. It is wise to carry your **passport** with you outside of town and at the more out-of-the-way beaches.

PRACTICAL INFORMATION

Tourist Office: Egyptian Tourist Authority (☎ 493 18 41), on the corniche 1 block west of Alexandria St., behind the Governorate building. Friendly English-speaking staff. Ask for the map booklet *Alexandria and Marsa Matrouh,* which lists some hotels and restaurants. Open daily 9am-8pm; in winter 9am-7pm.

Passport Office (☎ 493 38 10), 1 block north and ½ block east of the train station, just off Alexandria St. Open for **visa extensions** Sa-Th 8am-3pm.

Currency Exchange: The National Bank of Egypt, on Shokri al-Quwatli St., 4 blocks west of Alexandria St. Changes traveler's checks and has an **ATM.** Open daily 8:30am-5pm.

Police (☎ 93 33 76), 1 block south of the corniche, 2 blocks east of Alexandria St. Little English spoken. Contact the police in case of a **medical emergency.** Open 24hr.

Tourist Police (☎ 493 55 75), next door to the tourist office. Little English spoken; tourist office or Superjet staff can help you communicate when they're open. Open 24hr.

Pharmacy: Al-Farghaly Pharmacy (☎ 493 93 93), at the corner of Alexandria St. and Allam al-Rum St., 3 blocks south of the corniche. Open daily 8am-2am.

Hospital: Military Hospital (☎ 493 52 86 or 493 43 70), on Gala'a St., 3 blocks west of Alexandria St. It is better to seek treatment in Alexandria or Cairo if possible.

Telephone Office: Opposite the post office. Crowded and unreliable for international calls. Sells phone cards. Open 24hr. **Hotel Riviera Palace,** on the north end of Alexandria St., has pricier but more dependable phone and fax service. Open 24hr. There are **Menatel** phones along Alexandria St.

Post Office (☎ 493 23 67), 2 blocks east of Alexandria St. and 1 block south of the corniche. No *Poste Restante.* Open Sa-Th 8:30am-2pm.

ACCOMMODATIONS

High season in Marsa Matrouh runs from June to October, with the bulk of its tourist action in July and August. There is also a spurt of Egyptian vacationers during Ramadan. In the off season, upscale hotels along the corniche offer surprisingly low rates. No matter what time of year, you are sure to find a room at one of the budget hotels on and near Alexandria St. Because few foreigners frequent these places, many have neither English signs nor English speakers—sign language or Arabic experimentation (see **Phrasebook,** p. 701) may be in order.

Groups of two or more can rent one of the many available flats in town. From June to September, **Awam Beach Flats** (☎ 493 51 74), west of Alexandria St. off the corniche behind the Mosque of Awam, offers two-bedroom flats for up to six people with living room, bath, and kitchen for E£100 per night.

If they don't mind sharing the beach during the day, couples can relax at **Marine Fouad** (☎ 493 85 55) on Rommel's Peninsula, where wonderful rooms with baths and three meals a day for two people cost E£110. (Open June-Sept.). **Camping** is permitted on the beach in front of the Semiramis Hotel free of charge, but you must check in with the **tourist police** first.

■ **Hotel Lido** (☎ 493 22 48), on al-Gala'a St., east of Alexandria St. Impeccable rooms with new beds, fans, TVs, and balconies. Private baths have towels and soap. Breakfast E£4. Singles E£44; doubles E£53.

Hotel Hamada (☎ 493 33 00), on the corner of Tahrir and Alexandria St. Bare-bones, reasonably clean rooms with shared baths. Avoid the din from the streets below by getting a room away from the corner. Singles, doubles, and triples E£10 per bed.

'Arafat Hotel (☎ 493 36 06), east of Alexandria St. on Tahrir St., down a side street 1 block past the Hotel Hamada. Dusty rooms with clean baths. Singles E£20; doubles E£30; triples E£45.

Ghazala Hotel (☎ 493 35 19), on Allam al-Rum St., in a 3-story white building just east of Alexandria St., 6 blocks from the corniche. Around the corner from al-Farghaly Pharmacy. Dark but well-kept rooms with firm beds and great sofas. Dank baths don't always have hot water. Dorms E£10; singles E£15; doubles E£20.

🔥🎵 FOOD AND ENTERTAINMENT

Strolling along the corniche and chilling out in *ahwas* are the major after-hours recreational sports in Marsa, just as they are in most of the towns along Egypt's Mediterranean coast. The Beau Site Hotel, on the corniche 1.5km west of Alexandria St., serves pricey drinks in its comfortable **bar** (Stella E£11). They also run a **disco** beside the bar and a **bowling alley** across the street. A raised outdoor patio 100m west of the end of the corniche (across from the Armed Services hotel compound) hosts energetic **live music** in a breezy, friendly setting in July and August.

🍕 **Pizza Gaby** (☎ 493 07 91), just past the Negresco Hotel at the west end of the corniche. A/C haven on the sea is a perfect spot to admire the sunset. Tasty pizzas E£9-14. Grilled meats E£18-23. Middle Eastern salad buffet E£5. Open daily noon-1:30am.

Hammo al-Temsah Fish (☎ 494 33 83), on the corner of Port Said and Tahrir St. Choose your fish from the market next door and enjoy a hearty and inexpensive dinner (E£18) at one of the outdoor tables. Open daily 9am-midnight.

Abu Aly Pizza (☎ 494 23 04), on Alexandria St., 3 blocks south of the corniche. This 2-story restaurant offers a wide selection of soups, sandwiches, and desserts. Fresh pizza E£10.50-18.50. Shawarma E£2.50-6. Open daily 9am-3am; 9am-2am in winter.

Panayotis Greek Restaurant (☎ 493 24 74), on the west side of Alexandria St., 2 blocks south of the corniche. Simple menu includs a fresh fish dinner (E£30), calamari (E£25), pizza (E£8.50-16), and Stella (E£7.50). Open daily 8am-2am.

🏖 BEACHES

Marsa Matrouh's glorious beaches are its *raison d'être*. However, just as in Alexandria, some women swim fully clothed, and only the most liberal beaches allow bikinis or revealing one-pieces. No matter how tolerant a beach may be, women should arrive well-covered and gauge the mood of the crowd once there, as the level of acceptance can vary from day to day. Since most Egyptian visitors prefer to relax on the sand, even crowded areas have lots of open water for swimming.

To reach these beaches, catch a *service*, minibus, or pickup truck (E£2-4 per person to 'Agiba or Cleopatra beaches) from the eastern side of Anwar al-Sadat St., behind the Omar Effendi store. Drivers leave once there are enough passengers (usually every hr. 9am-4:30pm; summer only).

🏖 **'AGIBA BEACH.** Surely the most spectacular of the area's sights is 'Agiba ("miracle" in Arabic), about 25km from Marsa Matrouh. Golden limestone cliffs plunge down to meet azure waters, where waves crash over eroded rock formations and into sandy coves. Swimming is not always permitted, but a barefoot walk along the rocks is one of the best ways to spend a few hours around Marsa Matrouh. Bring **food**—there is only a soft-drink stand here. Archaeologists are currently excavating a tiny **Temple to Ramses II** 2km to the east, near Umm Araham village. The site is on the other side of the road, but as of August 2001, it was off-limits to visitors.

BEAU SITE HOTEL BEACH. At the far west end of the corniche, the Beau Site Hotel has one of the most beautiful beaches around. Though somewhat overrun by frolicking Egyptian children, the beach is cleaner and more liberal than most others. There is no charge for non-guests, but they ask that you rent an umbrella (E£12 per day) or a chair (E£3 per day). During off season, umbrellas are free. Security guards on the hotel's private beach ensure that bathers can wear bikinis without being harassed.

ROMMEL'S ISLE. The eastern part of the harbor is called Rommel's Isle, but it actually isn't an isle at all, and can be reached by donkey cart (E£3), bike (E£10 per day), boat (E£1), or pickup truck taxi (50pt). Nestled in the peninsula is the **Rommel Museum,** housed in the caves that Rommel used as his headquarters during Germany's North African campaign. On display are his overcoat (size 41L) and various German and Italian maps showing the order of battle, yet the small faux cave is hardly worth the price. The **beach** outside, however, is a favorite destination of Egyptian tourists and fills up quickly. *(Museum open daily in summer 9am-4pm. E£5.)*

THE LOVE BEACHES. West of the main beach, the **Beach of Love (Shati' al-Gharaam)** fondles the western horn of the bay and can be easily reached by foot or kayak. Inconsiderate visitors have begun to spoil the sand while enjoying the sun, and heaps of litter float out to sea every day. You'll encounter more wind, less trash, and the tantalizing **Cleopatra's Beach** 14km farther west, on the far right-hand side of a small cove called **Cleopatra's Bath.** Legend has it that the queen and Mark Antony would come here to bathe, and as the waves crashed into the cove, the water would shoot toward the heavens and cascade back down on the lovers' entangled bodies. The peaceful but shallow **Obayyid Beach,** 18km west of Marsa Matrouh, draws Egyptian families staying at their company's tents on the shore, making it pretty boring unless you're there with your friends from the office.

SIWA OASIS واحةسيوة ☎046

Emerging from 300km of barren sand, the palm trees and freshwater springs that comprise Siwa seem like a desert mirage. A walk among the people of this small town and its surrounding villages only deepens the sense of disbelief. Instead of Arabic, the Berber language of Siwi is spoken, and the few married women who venture outside cover themselves from head to toe in blue *tarfudit* veils. Electricity only came to Siwa about 10 years ago, and the thousands of TVs in this town of mud-brick homes are only the most recent in a long history of outside invaders.

The Temple of Amun, east of the central town, housed one of the most famous oracles of the ancient world. After taking Egypt from the Persians in 331 BCE, Alexander the Great set out across the desert to learn Amun's prophecy and conquer Siwa. With the centuries that followed came more conquerors: Muhammad 'Ali brought the territory under Ottoman control in 1820, the British occupied it in the early 20th century, and the Desert Fox trotted into town during World War II.

Even today, the people here are Siwans first, Egyptians second, and they look skeptically at the technological changes that are making their desert buffer just a short stretch of sand. In 1984, the Egyptian government completed the road connecting Siwa to Marsa Matrouh, turning a week-long camel trek into a quick 4hr. bus ride. Cairo has integrated the oasis into the national economy, and Arabic has replaced Siwi as the language of instruction in schools. Today, younger Siwan women don Egyptian fashions, and local folklore is losing ground to soap operas. These changes are not yet pervasive, and local tradition still regulates everyday life. Local festivals during fall and winter, especially the Feast of Siaha on the first full moon in October, are celebrated with relish and bring in droves of spectators. Older women still wear the traditional Siwan costume, with intricately braided hairdos and heavy silver jewelry. Residents request that visiting women cover their arms and legs. Alcohol and open displays of affection are forbidden.

▐ TRANSPORTATION

The most practical way to reach Siwa is by **bus** from Marsa Matrouh or Alexandria, but courageous groups with a **car** can travel the 420km stretch of rough road from the Bahar(iya Oasis. **Pickup trucks** can be hired to take you the other way for about E£700 per load. One-way overnight **tours** to Bahar(iya can also be arranged through the tourist office for E£900 for up to seven people.

Buses: To **Alexandria** (E£27) via **Marsa Matrouh** (8hr., 7am, 10, 5pm, and 10, E£10).

Local Transport: *Service* pickup trucks will bring visitors around the oasis. Pick them up in front of the tourist office, but first check inside for times.

SIWI MADE SIMPLE

Most Siwan children's first language is Siwi, an unwritten Berber dialect. It is incomprehensible to the rest of Egypt and sounds almost Scandinavian at times. As children grow up, parents and schools make sure they learn Arabic as well. The possible permutations of the following words should keep you occupied until the donkeys come home:

SIWI	ENGLISH	SIWI	ENGLISH
mashi	yes	oula	no
gaf lahk	go	shiek	you
oushi	give me	ehk sehk	I want
aksoom	meat	aman	water
azumur	olives	tene	dates
ihkseikh teswi aman	I want water	tanta elhal ineik	How are you?
tanta wook	What is this?	betin ismetinik	What's your name?

ORIENTATION AND PRACTICAL INFORMATION

Siwa Oasis is in a desert hollow about 300km southwest of Marsa Matrouh. Its western edge comes within 50km of the Libyan border. The valley spans 82km east to west and 30km north to south. Most visitors concern themselves only with Siwa town and nearby villages. **Buses** stop in the **market center** in the shadows of the ancient fortress of **Shali**. The **tourist office** and **police** are back up the road to Marsa Matrouh, while the **King Fouad Mosque,** the town's largest building, is nearby.

Tourist Office: (☎ 460 23 38), from the bus stop, walk towards the mosque and take a right, following the road to the white building opposite the post office. An oracle unto himself with regard to all things Siwan, **Mahdi Muhammad 'Ali Hweity**—sociologist, fluent English-speaker, and native Siwan—arranges sightseeing expeditions and obtains camping permits. Open Sa-Th 8am-2:30pm and 6-10pm; in winter Sa-Th 4-10pm.

English-Language Bookstore: Hassan's Handicrafts and English Bookshop, between the mosque and the tourist office. A few English books on Egyptian history and culture and some novels. Run by the fab Mr. Hweity of the tourist office. Open Sa-Th 8-11pm; in winter 3-10pm.

Police: (☎ 460 20 08), in the same building as the post office. Open 24hr.

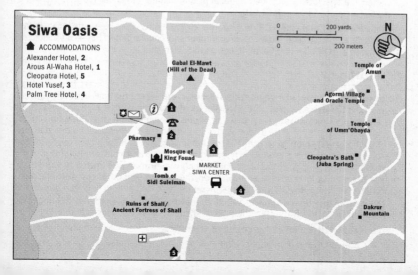

Siwa Oasis

🏠 ACCOMMODATIONS
Alexander Hotel, **2**
Arous Al-Waha Hotel, **1**
Cleopatra Hotel, **5**
Hotel Yusef, **3**
Palm Tree Hotel, **4**

Gabal El-Mawt
(Hill of the Dead)

Temple of Amun

Agormi Village and Oracle Temple

Temple of Umm 'Obayda

Pharmacy

Mosque of King Fouad

MARKET
SIWA CENTER

Cleopatra's Bath
(Juba Spring)

Tomb of Sidi Suleiman

Ruins of Shali/
Ancient Fortress of Shali

Dakrur Mountain

Pharmacy: Yusef's Pharmacy, on the road to the Cleopatra Hotel. Open daily 9am-2pm and 6pm-midnight; in winter 9am-noon.

Hospital (☎460 20 19). Go south 1km from the town square and take a right at the 1st 4-story building on the left. Open 24hr.

Telephone Office: Next to the Arous al-Waha Hotel.

Internet Access: Muhammad Ibrahem's Internet Service (☎460 20 49), next door to the Palm Trees Hotel. Siwa is, after all, the middle of the desert; connections are slow. Muhammad recommends composing on a word processor (E£8 per hr.) before going online (50pt per min.). Knock loudly if lights are out. Digital camera rental. Open 24hr.

Post Office: Across the street from Arous al-Waha Hotel. Open Sa-Th 8am-2pm.

▚ ACCOMMODATIONS

Most crash pads in Siwa cluster around the main square. Slow business in the summer means it is fairly easy to find a good room, but in winter Siwa has more tourists than donkeys, so make reservations or consider an outlying hotel. Unless otherwise noted, all rooms have fans. **Camping** is available free on **Dakrur Mountain,** 4km southeast of town, or for E£5 at ▨**Bir Wahad,** 12km south of town. (see **South of Siwa,** p. 167). Bring a warm sleeping bag and insect repellent. Check in with Mr. Hweity at the tourist office before pitching your tent.

▨ **Palm Trees Hotel** (☎460 23 04), 20m down a side road from the town square. Clean, comfortable rooms with fans and balconies, but the best part of this hotel is the idyllic grove filled with palm-leaf furniture out back. Laundry machine and bike rentals. Singles E£7.50-10; doubles E£15, with bath E£18; triples E£27.

▨ **Hotel Yusef** (☎460 21 62), in the center of town. The name is painted across the top floor. Cleanest rooms in town. Friendly owner Salameh is committed to guest satisfaction. Balconies overlook Siwa and beyond. Women can sunbathe on the roof terrace in peace. Bike rentals. Dorms, singles, and doubles E£6 per person.

Alexander Hotel (☎460 05 12; fax 460 00 06), opposite the post office. Clean but old, with dim rooms and private baths. Dorms E£7; singles E£10; doubles E£15. Prices 30% higher in winter.

Cleopatra Hotel (☎460 21 48), south of the town square on the main road, past the Shali fortress. A newer and slightly pricier establishment with stuffy rooms, but great balcony views and immaculate private bathrooms. Antony and Cleo would have preferred the spacious "bungalow" doubles in the building next door (E£34). Breakfast E£5. Singles E£14; doubles E£18.

Arous al-Waha Hotel (☎460 21 00; fax 460 20 28), across from the tourist office in the northwest part of town. Huge, spotless rooms and private baths. Breakfast included. Singles E£30.50; doubles E£49. Prices up to 50% higher in winter.

◖ FOOD

All Siwan restaurants are vegetarian-friendly, and many feature Indian-inspired meals. Local **stores** are well stocked with local produce (dates E£1.25 per kg). If you ask a local may offer you a taste of *lagbi*, a sweet palm-tree juice and local specialty served only before 10am—it ferments by noon. Because Siwans tend to be more reserved than most other Egyptians, only a few travelers receive **invitations** to eat or stay with a local family. Invitations are usually offered by children or adult men. At dinner, your hosts may try to sell you homemade crafts, or they may simply want to talk. Exercise caution before accepting hospitality—solo women should decline invitations from single Siwan men.

Restaurants line the two market squares and are generally open from 8 or 10am to midnight or 1am. In summer, the menus shrink. Siwan eateries are mainly indistinguishable from one another, but there are a few tried-and-true favorites.

'Abdou's Restaurant, on the street running along the north side of the square. Unusual quiche-style veg. pizza E£7-13. For breakfast, try the pancakes with banana, honey, and yogurt (E£3.50). Open daily 8am-midnight.

East-West, same street as 'Abdou's. Yummy grilled chicked E£10. Open daily 9am-1am.

Palm Trees Hotel, 20m down a side road from the town square, Marvelous garden restaurant with small but delicious portions. Breakfast E£1-4. Dinner E£2-10.

🐫 AROUND THE OASIS

Ringed by multicolored desert mesas and waves of sand dunes, all under a piercing blue sky, Siwa is Egypt's most beautiful oasis. Most of Siwa's sights are easily accessible by bike trips down smooth dirt roads lined with palm trees. The more distant surrounding villages can be reached by local bus or through one of many tours offered by hotels and restaurants. *Carettas* (donkey-drawn taxis) always stand ready, making for a slow and bumpy (but thoroughly Siwan) trip. Mr. Hweity of the tourist office has posted new blue signs around town to mark Siwa's important buildings and roads. A **half-day tour** is a bargain at E£15 per person.

SIWA TOWN

RUINS OF SHALI. From atop the ruins of the crumbling medieval fortress-town of Shali (which simply means "town" in Siwi), you can see the quiet streets of Siwa town wind through a cluster of mud houses and luxuriant palm gardens. The wall encircling Shali once protected Siwa from marauding Berbers and Bedouin. There was little room within the walls to build, so houses were cramped. Although the mud-brick structures were sturdy, torrential rains washed away most buildings about twice a century. After Muhammad 'Ali conquered Siwa in 1820, there was less need for fortification, so Siwans were quick to build more spacious homes outside the walls. Several days of fierce rain in 1985 severely damaged much of Shali, and what remains today is a surreal landscape of tangled walls and eroded mud-brick that may house a donkey here, a family there, or an abandoned gaggle of free-range chickens. The walls are quite secure, and it is safe to wander through the ruins. Every Thursday night after the last call to prayer (around 9pm, in winter 6pm), some local Muslims gather for religious ceremonies outside the mud-brick **Tomb of Sidi Suleiman,** who was the town's patron saint, beside the King Fouad Mosque. Visitors are invited to watch.

TRADITIONAL SIWAN HOUSE. The 1985 rains motivated a visiting Canadian ambassador to try to preserve Siwan culture, so he raised funds to construct the permanent Traditional Siwan House. The house serves as a museum of Siwan garb, silver jewelry, and children's toys. *(Down the road from the tourist office, opposite the King Fouad Mosque. Open Sa-Th 10am-noon; ask tourist office about other hours. E£1.50.)*

NORTHERN SIWA

GABAL AL-MAWT (HILL OF DEATH). The acropolis of Gabal al-Mawt rises 1km to the northeast of ancient Siwa. The hill is home to several Ptolemaic-era tombs that Romans robbed and reused. These tombs went undiscovered until World War II, when Siwan families crammed into caves to seek shelter from Italian bombs. The scattered human bones and mummy wrappings that litter the site belonged to the Romans, as did the niches that mar the ancient frescoes. The first sepulcher is the **Tomb of Si-Amun.** The intact decoration shows the bearded nobleman with Osiris, and the magnificent ceiling depicts the six stages of the sun's journey across the sky and a beautiful field of stars. The **Tomb of Mesu Isis,** 5m to the east, has damaged paintings of Osiris and Isis. The **Tomb of the Crocodile** features paintings of the scaly chomper once buried there, although his corpse has been removed. The **Tomb of Niperpathot,** the oldest in Siwa, housed the body of a nobleman of the 26th dynasty (around 662 BCE) and includes paintings of his Nubian and Greek wives and their multiracial sons. *(Tombs are to the left as you enter from the access road. A custodian unlocks tombs daily 9am-2:30pm. Free, but E£2-4 bakhsheesh is appropriate.)*

EASTERN SIWA

The Temple of Amun and the Temple of Umm 'Obayda lie 1km apart on the same road. A bike trip looping around the road might take in the two temples, followed by a dip at Cleopatra's Bath, then onto Dakrur Mountain, and from there back to town. Rent a bike from town or hail a *caretta* (E£10).

ORACLE OF AMUN. A 13th-century gate made of palm logs graces the entrance to the acropolis on which this oracle is perched. Some of the massive inner chambers (all that remains upright) are still adorned by extensive carvings. Follow the same path as Alexander the Great to reach the oracle: go through the stone temple's simple gateway into the outer court, then cross the inner court to reach the center. The Oracle of Amun is thought to date from the 26th dynasty (c. 660 BCE). It became widely celebrated in later dynasties and gained popularity even with the ancient Greeks, who constructed many shrines to Amun in their home city-states. Greek and Roman historians recorded the mystical rituals necessary to invoke an answer from the oracle: priests carried a sacred boat containing the image of Amun, while women sang and danced in procession. Alexander did all of this to seek the answer to the million-dollar question: Was he a god, the son of Amun? He also supposedly asked the oracle another question in private, but what he queried will never be known. The secret died with him, less than 10 years after his visit.

TEMPLE OF UMM 'OBAYDA. Down the curving road 1km south of the Oracle of Amun, are the remains of the Temple of Umm 'Obayda, also dedicated to Amun. Surviving the ravages of time and an 1877 earthquake, the temple was reasonably well-preserved until 1897, when a local official demolished the remains to collect stone for the construction of new public buildings. One wall remains upright, with inscriptions dedicated to the Egyptian gods.

CLEOPATRA'S BATH. A pleasant 1km bike ride through the quiet, green palm groves around Siwa leads to **Juba Springs,** renamed Cleopatra's Bath by the tourist authority. A tiled basin 15m in diameter now encircles a deep blue pool, which bubbles lightly from the large spring below. Although the pool is mostly frequented by men, fully clothed women should also feel comfortable swimming here (as comfortable as one can be swimming fully clothed), and may enter via the enclosure next to the spring. If you visit at sunrise or in the late evening, you may be the only person there.

HAMMAM RAMAL (SAND BATH). On **Dakrur Mountain,** 1km south of Cleopatra's Bath, nearly 1000 rheumatics congregate each summer for 10-day stints in the Hammam Ramal. The procedure may sound like a Siwan torture method, but it's actually painless: under supervision of a specialist, the "bather" is buried in sand from the neck down while his head is protected from the sun's heat. After a stint in the sand, the patient stays indoors for the rest of the day, then repeats the procedure. *(E£30, including room and board.)*

ABU SHROUF AND ENVIRONS. Abu Shrouf, 27km east of Siwa toward Bahariya, is a beautifully clear and deep spring, and cleaner than any of Siwa's pools. Local legend has it that Abu Shrouf is the only place in the oasis with female donkeys. If a male donkey escapes from Siwa, the first place his owner looks is Abu Shrouf. This myth has even influenced local slang: if a Siwan man has a pleasant night with his wife, he tells his friends, "Last night I went to Abu Shrouf!" You too can go there, either with the tour arranged by Mr. Hweity from the Siwa tourist office (4 people, E£15 each) or by private taxi (about E£80 for a half-day round-trip). A large spring called **Qurayshat,** 7km west of Abu Shrouf, was a major farming area during Roman times. Although the spring is not very interesting in itself, the drive past desert shepherds and wild scenery is worthwhile. A small **Bedouin village** lies 5km to the east. Though the government built them houses, the Bedouin preferred to live in tents and keep their livestock in the new homes. Unamused that its

> **GREASED LIGHTNING** Not long ago, Siwans ran a smuggling operation to carry goods on the sly from Libya into Egypt on donkeys. The nighttime treks would proceed perfectly until the beasts (unaware of the clandestine nature of the mission) would bray and alert the Border Patrol officials, thereby spoiling the whole operation. Siwans wracked their brains to figure out a way to pacify the carriers until someone somehow discovered that if the asses' asses were greased, the brutes would be unable to create the force needed to let air out of their mouths. A team of French scientists is currently researching this exciting discovery.

projects were being used as barns, the government destroyed many of the tents and forced the Bedouin to live in houses. The ruins of **al-Zaitoun** lie between the Bedouin tents and their small village. The settlement wallows in the hot desert, where a circular olive press still stands among the crumbling buildings.

WESTERN SIWA

■**FATNAS.** Plan to spend at least one sunset in idyllic Fatnas, or Fantasy Island, 4km west of town. Accessible by a small causeway, Fatnas Pool is not to be missed. The sun sets over the glistening salt lake as you sit by a palm grove sipping mint tea (E£1.50) and relaxing in a hammock or wicker chair. Ride a bike through palm tree fields and local settlements, passing the occasional donkey cart. From the far western corner of an adjoining garden, observe a limitless sea of sand.

BILAD AL-RUM (CITY OF THE ROMANS). An unidentified stone structure and several tombs in the hillside are known collectively as Bilad al-Rum. Up the road behind barbed wire are the remains of a **Doric temple.** Greek archaeologist Liana Souvaltzi caused a stir in 1995 when she announced that she had discovered the tomb of Alexander the Great within the temple walls. A team of 12 archaeologists quickly flew in from Greece and determined that the tomb's inscriptions were not Alexander's, but those of another important Greek official. Although Alexander wanted to be buried in Siwa, his general, Ptolemy, purloined the corpse and buried it in his capital, Alexandria, where it lies today (somewhere underneath the modern roads and high-rises). **Campers** can ask the tourist office for special permission to sleep here, then take the bus back to Siwa the next morning.

SOUTHERN SIWA

■**BIR WAHAD.** Bir Wahad ("Well #1"), lies 12km deep into the sand dunes south of Siwa. Riding a 4WD through the dunes is exhilarating, as your driver climbs high up and then races down the mountains of desert sand, until two small, lush oases rise from the nothingness. A cool pond sits on one side of a tall dune, while the other side boasts a hot spring with water clean enough for bathing. Nearby, a desert garden grows watermelon and cantaloupe. A number of Siwans offer **guided tours** for around E£60—inquire at the tourist office to find out who offers the best package. A **camp** is set up there where you can sleep under the stars (E£5; with dinner E£10). If you spend the night, bring insect repellent and a **blanket** from your hotel—it gets cold in the desert, even in July.

SINAI PENINSULA السيناء

The Sinai is a haven for turned-on, tuned-in, dropped-out beach bums. A handful of small towns and a major road occupy the sandy shelf where the mountains meet the sea, but only Bedouin brave the rest of the Sinai's dry, rough landscape. The greatest diversity of life in the area thrives below the sea: the Gulf of Aqaba's warm waters support a carnival of brilliantly colored coral reefs, tropical fish, and other subaquatic life. In sharp contrast to the earthy hues of the rest of the Middle East, the underwater environs explode with color—the reds and greens of coral broken by the flashes of yellow, blue, and orange fins, set against the sparkling turquoise backdrop of the so-called Red Sea.

For a desert wasteland, the Sinai has had a surprisingly long history of war. Since the pharaohs' troops first trampled the broad plains of the northern Sinai on their march to Syria and Canaan, the favor has been returned by marauding Egypt-bound Hyksos, Assyrians, Persians, Greeks, Arabs, and Turks. In 1903, the British drew the borders of the Sinai from Rafah to Eilat in an attempt to keep soon-to-be World War I collaborators Turkey and Germany at a safe distance from the Suez Canal. On the fourth day of the Six Day War of 1967, Israel seized control of the Sinai from Egypt and began to capitalize on the region's potential for tourism. The Israelis were first to establish the numerous Sinai hotels and dive centers, including those in Dahab and Sharm al-Sheikh. The new development altered the lives of many Bedouin, who began to work in the tourist industry, giving camel tours and staffing hotels, often abandoning their traditional nomadic lifestyle. In the 1973 Yom Kippur War, Egypt and Israel dueled over the Sinai. Israel retained the Sinai until it was returned to Egypt in two stages under the terms of the Camp David Accords—the first half in 1979 and the second in 1982.

The more recent Israeli-Palestinian violence, dating back to September 2000, has not threatened to spill over onto the peninsula, yet it has had a profound impact on the tourism industry. In many areas, especially those closest to Israel, camps that were once filled to capacity now lie virtually abandoned. On the bright side, the Sinai has become a haven for budget travelers. Some resorts, faced with near-zero occupancy, have reduced rates by half or more. With a little bargaining, it shouldn't be too difficult to score additional discounts. Should the peace process get back on track, it won't be long before tourism and prices increase. Until then, the few who come may enjoy the region's wonders cheaply, and in solitude.

TRANSPORTATION

BUSES. The noble machines of the **East Delta Bus Company,** battered cruelly by the rocks, ruts, and dust of Sinai roads, heroically tread the scorched highway, traversing the long distances between the Sinai's spread-out towns. Unfortunately, bus timetables are really no more than an administrator's *(sheesha)* pipe dream. At Sinai bus stations, patience is more necessity than virtue.

SERVICE. *Service* are a reasonably priced and convenient alternative to buses. Weathered old Peugeot 504s piloted by Bedouin cabbies are ubiquitous. Hop in with other passengers or negotiate with a driver and wait while he recruits more travelers to your destination. Women should avoid riding alone. *Service* are comparable in price to buses under ideal circumstances, but only with a full load of seven passengers. You'll get to where you're going a lot faster, but this speed has its perils: traffic laws do not apply, and the laws of physics are only grudgingly acknowledged. The law of supply and demand is in effect, though—*service* prices will drop just before the arrival of a bus, then skyrocket after the bus has departed.

ABOVE-WATER TIPS

Travel in the Sinai Peninsula is far easier than in the rest of Egypt. Women can comfortably wear shorts and sleeveless shirts in most places, and professional con artists are rare. However, a number of **regulations** govern travelers to the Sinai. Unguided travel is restricted to main roads and settlements, but you may visit parts of the desert interior with a Bedouin guide. Sleeping on the beach is prohibited in some areas (notably Na'ama Bay), and the police often harass dozing backpackers. Since these areas are not always marked, ask around before settling down for the night. **Nude sunbathing** is illegal, as is the oft-hawked **marijuana.** You cannot bring a rented car or any four-wheel-drive vehicle into the Sinai from Israel. **Prices** tend to be higher and currency exchange rates poorer than anywhere else in Egypt. If you're coming from the Nile Valley, change money before arriving. **Bug season** descends upon the Sinai in the spring and early summer. Dahab is peri-

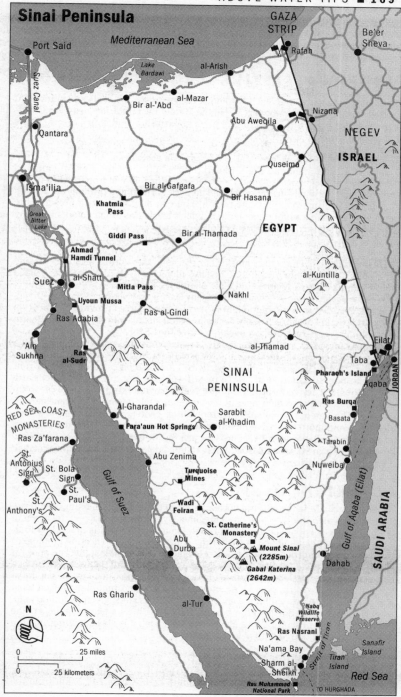

Sinai Peninsula

Mediterranean Sea

GAZA STRIP

Be'er Sheva

Port Said

Rafah

al-Arish

Lake Bardawi

al-Mazar

Suez Canal

Bir al-'Abd

Nizana

Abu Aweqila

NEGEV

Qantara

ISRAEL

Quseima

Isma'ilia

Bir al-Gafgafa

Bir Hasana

Khatmia Pass

EGYPT

Great Bitter Lake

Giddi Pass

Bir al-Thamada

Ahmad Hamdi Tunnel

al-Shatt

Mitla Pass

Suez

al-Kuntilla

Uyoun Mussa

Ras al-Gindi

Nakhl

Ras Adabia

'Ain Sukhna

Ras al-Sudr

al-Thamad

Eilat

Taba

Pharaoh's Island

Aqaba

JORDAN

SINAI PENINSULA

Al-Gharandal

Sarabit al-Khadim

Ras Burqa

RED SEA COAST MONASTERIES

Para'aun Hot Springs

Basata

Ras Za'farana

Tarabin

St. Antonius Sign

Abu Zenima

Nuweiba

St. Bola Sign

St. Paul's

Turquoise Mines

St. Anthony's

Wadi Feiran

Gulf of Suez

St. Catherine's Monastery

Abu Durba

Mount Sinai (2285m)

Dahab

Gabal Katerina (2642m)

Ras Gharib

Gulf of Aqaba (Eilat)

SAUDI ARABIA

al-Tur

Nabq Wildlife Preserve

Strait of Tiran

Ras Nasrani

Sanafir Island

N

Na'ama Bay

Sharm al-Sheikh

Tiran Island

0   25 miles

Red Sea

0   25 kilometers

Ras Muhammad National Park

TO HURGHADA

EGYPT

odically clouded by mosquitoes and flies with killer munchies. Some travelers rig mosquito nets; others advise sleeping near the beach. The Sinai is a laid-back place: in summer, no one wears or carries much, and it takes only a few days before travelers begin to reexamine conventions of hygiene and appearance.

UNDERWATER TIPS

Without question, the Red Sea has some of the greatest coral reefs and marine life in the world. Diving was not very big in the Middle East until Jacques-Yves Cousteau made his voyage through the Red Sea aboard the good ship *Calypso*, later chronicled in his famous book and movie *The Silent World*. Now that diving is a major part of many trips to the Sinai Peninsula, the regional administration has begun to face the serious problem of **irresponsible ecotourism.** All coral reefs from Dahab to Ras Muhammad are under the jurisdiction of the Ras Muhammad National Park. Regulations forbid the defacement or removal from the sea of any animal, plant, or shell—living or dead. The park is fighting a difficult battle with developers waiting to exploit the region. You can do your part to preserve the reefs by observing a simple rule: look, but **don't touch.** Ras Muhammad, like many James Bond movies, has underwater police that will chase you out of the water if they see you breaking this rule. Even accidentally bumping the coral can damage it (and you), so listen to Ice Cube and check yo' self before you wreck yo' self.

Diving, though cheaper than most other places in the world, can still be expensive—but you're paying for safety. The sites along the Gulf of Aqaba coast listed below emphasize safety above all else. **Snorkeling gear** can be rented anywhere, while **dive shops** are concentrated mainly in Dahab and Sharm al-Sheikh. Divers must be certified to rent equipment. Most five-day courses provide certification and cost around US$300. The only decompression chamber in the area is in Sharm al-Sheikh. If you're rusty, take a check-out dive for US$35.

Beginner divers should make sure their instructors speak their language flawlessly, as small misunderstandings can make a big difference underwater ("Tanks!" "You're welcome!"). The instructor must also be certified to teach your particular course, whether it's PADI or SSI—always ask to see his or her card. Some clubs are active in protecting the reefs, participating in annual clean-up dives, and making sure their operations have minimal impact on the marine ecosystems. The size of the club also matters: larger centers often have more scheduled dives and more extensive facilities, whereas smaller ones give you personal attention and will usually run a course for just one or two people rather than waiting for six to sign up. Quality of equipment and safety records are important; ask other divers for advice.

AL-'ARISH العريش ☎ 68

Al-'Arish is caught in the cultural vortex between the *sheesha*-smoking Mediterranean and the *who-knows-what*-smoking Sinai—yet manages to avoid the worst of both. Because it is only accessible through Isma'ilia, al-'Arish is much less touristed than the High Sinai and is free of the acres of concrete vacation complexes that line the Mediterranean coast near Alexandria. Al-'Arish is a favorite spot for vacationing Egyptian families, and Western tourists will find themselves a bit of a curiosity but less hassled here than in many parts of Egypt. Currently the capital of the North Sinai Governorate, al-'Arish was once an important stopover on what was perhaps the oldest military route in history. It has since given up military slogans and has settled down with a more mellow one: life's a beach. Some say the beach here is the best on Egypt's Mediterranean coast; it is clean, inviting, and the only one in Egypt dotted with palm trees.

TRANSPORTATION AND ORIENTATION. There are two roads to know in al-'Arish: **Fouad Zekry St.,** which runs along the beach, and **Tahrir St.,** perpendicular to Fouad Zekry. The **bus station** is at the south end of Tahrir St., 2km from the beach. Buses run daily to **Cairo** (5hr.; 8am and 5pm, E£25) and **Isma'ilia** (3hr., every 30min. 7am-5pm, E£10). **Service** (E£5) run to the **Israeli border** at Rafah. Getting around the downtown area is easy on foot, but it's a long walk to the beach—catch a *tut-tut* bus or one of the ancient Mercedes that serve as shared taxis (E£1). City **minibuses** run along the beach on Fouad Zekry St. (50pt). A private **taxi** within al-'Arish shouldn't cost more than E£5.

◗ PRACTICAL INFORMATION. The **tourist office** is just off the beach. Coming from the downtown/Tahrir St. area, bear left at the intersection with Fouad Zekry St.; the tourist office is on the right. The friendly staff speaks English but is short on hard information. (☎34 05 69. Open daily 9am-2pm and 4-8pm.) The **tourist police** (open 24hr.) is in the same building as the tourist office. There are banks along Tahrir St., including the **Bank of Cairo,** which exchanges traveler's checks or cash and gives cash advances on credit cards. (☎35 30 32. Open Su-Th 9am-2:30pm.) The **police station** is at the northern end of Tahrir Sq., but you're better off paying a visit to the tourist police. **Pharmacies** in the downtown area are generally open daily 8am-1am. The **government hospital** is on al-Geish St., just off Tahrir St. (☎34 00 11. Open 24hr.) The 24hr. **telephone office** is three blocks north and two blocks east of Tahrir Sq. Al-'Arish's **post office,** across the street from the telephone office, sends **faxes** for E£5.50 plus the cost of the call. (☎35 15 03; fax 35 15 01. Open Sa-Th 8:30am-2:30pm.)

◗◘ ACCOMMODATIONS AND FOOD. Most of al-'Arish's beachfront hotels are reasonably priced. In summer, reservations are strongly recommended. The **Moonlight Hotel** is on the beach, just west of the tourist office, off Fouad Zekry St. The shared baths could use a hosing down, but on the other hand, the hotel has a pleasant cafe on the beach. (☎34 13 62. Singles E£20; doubles E£35.) The **Green Land Beach Hotel** is east of the tourist office, just off Fouad Zekry St. Walk toward the beach on the road that angles behind William's Restaurant; the Green Land is on the beach side of the road. (☎34 06 01. Doubles and triples with fan, balcony, bath, breakfast, and the occasional TV E£30.) The airy **al-Salaam Hotel** is on Tahrir St., off the square and near the bus station. Ask for a room away from the street. (☎35 42 19. Private bath. Doubles E£20; triples E£25.)

Food is mostly standard Middle Eastern fare, with the exception of **William's** on Fouad Zekry St. near the Green Land Beach Hotel. Minimalist decor doesn't detract from the fish and meat entrees, complete with french fries and salad. (Entrees E£10-20. Open daily 8am-2am.) **'Aziz,** next to al-Salaam Hotel on Tahrir St., featuring a variety of grilled foods (E£5-15) and rice or noodle side dishes (E£1-3), wins the award for the best budget meal in town. (☎35 43 45. Open daily 9am-1am.) At the western end of al-'Arish, about 3km from the intersection of Fouad Zekry St. and Tahrir St., is the pleasant **Basata,** roofed and furnished with palm fronds and filled with palm frond furniture. (Full meals E£10-20. Open daily 11am-1am.) The part of the beach nearest town is lined with cafes and stands selling everything from *fuul* to pizza.

◖◗ SIGHTS AND ENTERTAINMENT. Life in al-'Arish revolves around the Mediterranean. The entire length of the **beach** is pristine and, except for brief sections in front of the Semiramis and Egoth Oberoi Hotels, there is no private shoreline. Women bathing in al-'Arish should still be fully clothed. There are a few **Bedouin craft stores** at the north end of Tahrir St. Every Thursday, **Tahrir Sq.** comes alive when local Bedouin sell silver, rugs, garments, and camel accessories at the weekly *souq.* A few kilometers east of town on the road to Rafah is the **Sinai Heritage Museum,** which details traditional Bedouin life on the Peninsula and has an excellent collection of clothes and jewelry. (Open Sa-Th 9:30am-2pm. E£2. Camera privileges E£5, video E£25.) In the evenings, many locals take to the *sheesha* parlors of Tahrir Sq., while the cafes along the promenade attract both locals and tourists. The expensive drinks (Stella E£12) sometimes outnumber the people at the **bars** of the Semiramis and Oberoi hotels.

EGYPT

Near al-'Arish is **Zaranik Protected Area**, a nature reserve where thousands of birds migrate in the fall. The park has a birdwatching area, nature trails, and campgrounds. (US$3; camping US$5 per person.) Get there via *service* running between Isma'ilia and al-'Arish.

'UYOUN MUSA عيون موسى

*Daily **buses** from Suez will drop you off, but it could take a couple hours to find a bus going back. Set off early in the day and bring a backpack full of food and water. A **taxi** from Suez costs E£40-50. Insist on seeing the wells—your driver may deny their existence.*

Moses buffs everywhere will be enthralled by this locale, 15km south of Suez, where the prophet devised an early water purification system with the help of a tree branch. 'Uyoun Musa continues Moses's work in several wells, some of which are open for swimming. When Napoleon visited in 1798, he discovered a canal linking the wells to the sea, used to resupply ships with fresh water.

RAS AL-GINDI راس القندى

*50km inland from Ras al-Sudr, where any **bus** running from Suez to the south Sinai will drop you off. You must then hire a **taxi** (at the petrol station after the turnoff for Ras al-Sudr) to Ras al-Gindi (E£80-100), so get a group together. To get back, flag down one of the **buses** which pass regularly on the south Sinai-Suez route. Bring water, a camera, and solid hiking shoes.*

Ras al-Gindi features the ruins of Salah al-Din's 800-year-old "Fortress of the Soldier," or **Qal'at al-Gindi**. The ruins stand atop a small mountain (a 1hr. climb). Be careful going up, as the path drops off considerably on either side; one misstep and you'll wind up next to your sleeping taxi driver below.

FARA'UN HOT SPRINGS نبوض الفرعون

Just off the main highway, 80km south of Suez. Hire a taxi from Suez for E£100.

Though the hot springs and beach at this southern spot are attractive, their remote location makes them more trouble than they're worth. The beach at 'Ain Sukhna is infinitely more convenient.

SARABIT AL-KHADIM سرابت الخديم

*Despite its location, Sarabit al-Khadim has become a popular destination from Sharm al-Sheikh and Na'ama Bay—the easiest but least exciting way to get here. Independent travelers have to rent or hire a 4WD vehicle for the 1½hr. drive and get permission from the military to venture into the desert. The best place to start is the Suez tourist office (see **Orientation and Practical Information**, p. 198). They can inform you of the latest regulations.*

This remote spot is the site of an ancient temple that extends over 200m of desert. During the 12th Dynasty (c. 1900 BCE), a small chapel was dedicated to the goddesses Sodpu and Hathor, "Mistress of Turquoise." In the 18th dynasty, the temple was elongated and expanded. Ramses VI, the last pharaoh to visit the temple, dropped by around 1100 BCE. The stones of the ruins are decorated with religious inscriptions and accounts of mining expeditions. Around the temple are ancient turquoise mines waiting to be explored.

ST. CATHERINE'S ☎069

St. Catherine's rich history of monasticism started in the 3rd century CE when Christian hermits, attracted by the tradition designating the valley below as the site of the Burning Bush in the Book of Exodus, migrated here in search of holiness and freedom from Roman persecution. Living in complete poverty and isolation (except on holy days, when they gathered at the Bush), these hermits often fell victim to harsh weather and raiding nomads. In 313 CE, Constantine the Great officially recognized Christianity, and soon afterward the monastery was founded by Constantine's mother, Empress Helena. The monastery thrived under the continual protection of rulers from the Prophet Muhammad to Napoleon Bonaparte over the next 1600 years. As a tribute to the monks' tradition of hospitality to Christians and Muslims alike, it has never been conquered. Modern pilgrims and curious tourists of all faiths visit St. Catherine's throughout the year. Though much of the interior of the monastery is closed to the public, its beautiful architecture and mountainous setting can be enjoyed just as well from the outside.

⬛ TRANSPORTATION

Buses: The bus station is at the main square; it's less a station and more a midtown parking lot where the bus is assumed to stop. Buses are notoriously scarce, but they do run to **Cairo** (9hr., 6am, E£35) via **Suez** (6hr., E£25) and **Dahab** (3hr., 1pm, E£25). Check the times with the bus driver who brings you and with someone at the Rest House—buses stop right in front of the establishment, and the staff seems to have a good grasp on the schedule. Should you need to leave in the afternoon, take a **taxi** to the crossroads between al-Tor and St. Catherine's 100km away (E£120 per carload; find an English speaker and say you want to go to the "crossroads" or "checkpoint"). East Delta **buses** stop (or at least slow down) at the military checkpoint on their way to Cairo and Suez about every hr. until 6pm, though not all have seats available. A rest house at the checkpoint sells water and snacks if you get stranded for any length of time.

Minibuses: Red minibuses leave daily to **Cairo** (E£50) via **Suez** (E£40) at 11am. Drivers meet most buses to advertise their service and will pick you up from your hotel.

Taxis: As a last resort, taxis are always available but very expensive; you will have to bargain hard. Popular destinations include: **Cairo** (E£500); **Dahab** (E£120-150 per car); **Nuweiba** (E£200); **Sharm al-Sheikh** (E£200).

✴ 🅿 ORIENTATION AND PRACTICAL INFORMATION

At an elevation of about 1600m, **St. Catherine's Monastery** is hidden away in the mountainous interior of the Sinai. Good roads run west to the Gulf of Suez and east to the Gulf of Aqaba, each about 100km away. Tiny **St. Catherine's town** lies about 3km east of the monastery. St. Catherine's town is home to the office of Sheikh Musa, the starting point for all tours and hikes in the area (see p. 177).

Bank: Banque Misr (☎ 47 04 63), in an arcade on 1 side of the main square. You can exchange money or traveler's checks and withdraw cash. Open daily 8:30am-1:30pm and 6:30-8:30pm. V.

Police: The **police station** (☎ 47 03 13) is up the hill near the mosque. The **tourist police** (☎ 47 00 46) are opposite the bus station in the main square. Open 24hr. Tourist police are also posted on the access road near the monastery.

Hospital: (☎ 47 03 68), opposite the bus station. Open 24hr.

Telephone Office: (☎ 47 00 10), opposite the mosque. International phone service. Open 24hr. The monastery also has 2 Menatel phones, one in the Auberge and another on the outside of the northern wall. **Supermarkets** in the village sell phone cards.

Post Office: (☎ 47 03 01), a few doors from the telephone office. Open daily 8am-3pm.

🛏 🍴 ACCOMMODATIONS AND FOOD

Apart from the free **camping** on Mt. Sinai, **Fox of the Desert Camp,** 1km from St. Catherine's town, provides the cheapest accommodations. Walk out of town toward the monastery, sticking to the main road at the fork. The signless camp is the last building to the right before the four-way intersection. Run by friendly Bedouin brothers Farag and Soliman, the camp offers tidy concrete huts. Prices include blankets, mosquito nets (upon request), and nightly tea around a campfire. (Camping E£5; single huts E£10; double huts E£20.) The closest place to the monastery and the mountain is the monastery's **St. Catherine's Auberge.** To get there, turn right at the fork just before the monastery. Clean rooms have private baths, and the location justifies the price. Delectable dinner and breakfast are included. Reservations are recommended if you intend to arrive after 11pm, or anytime in August or April. (☎47 03 53. Singles US$35; doubles US$60; triples US$75.) Bearing left at the fork outside the village and walking 5min. brings you to a row of hotels, including **al-Fairouz Hotel.** (☎47 03 33 or 47 03 23. Camping in the sand courtyard E£5; 10-bed dorms E£20; rooms with private baths E£35 per person.)

Gift shops, supermarkets, and **restaurants** surround the bus stop. Restaurants are virtually identical, all offering good, simple food (usually E£7-10 for a dish of spaghetti or rice and chicken) with a side order of flies. Some places will even cook food you've purchased from a supermarket. (Markets open daily 8am-11pm.) The most popular place is the **Rest House Restaurant,** right in front of the bus stop, where E£8.50 buys a hearty meal of chicken, rice, bread, and soup. (Open daily 6am-9pm.) Opposite the mosque is a brick-oven **bakery.**

ST. CATHERINE'S MONASTERY

*To get to the monastery from town, follow the road between the tourist police and the telephone office for 1km (going straight at the fork), then turn right at the 4-way intersection. Present your **passport** to the tourist police shortly before another fork in the road, where you bear left to reach the monastery's entrance. Spend the night on the mountain, watch the sunrise, and hike down at 7am and reach the monastery just as the doors open at 9am (to avoid the heaviest crowds). No shorts or bare shoulders allowed, though the monks keep sheets on hand for the benefit of the immodestly dressed. Open M-Th and Sa 9-11:45am; closed on Orthodox Christian holidays (Jan. 6; Feb. 26-28; Apr. 7, 12, 14, 16; May 24; June 4; Aug. 28; Sept. 27; Nov. 14; Dec. 8). Call in advance. Free. For more information, contact Father John (☎47 03 43) or the monastery's Cairo office, 18 Midan al-Dahr, 11271 Cairo (☎02 482 85 13; fax 485 28 06).*

St. Catherine's is believed to be the oldest example of unrestored Byzantine architecture in the world. The complex was named after the martyred Alexandrian evangelist, Catherine, whose body was found on top of Gabal Katerina to the south. About to be tortured on a wheel of knives for converting members of the Roman emperor's family, Catherine was miraculously saved by a malfunction in the wheel (they slit her throat anyway). Her body showed up centuries later atop the isolated mountain. Once home to hundreds of monks, the monastery now houses only a handful. These ascetics are members of one of the strictest orders; they never eat meat or drink wine, and they wake up each morning at 4am when the bell of the Church of the Transfiguration tolls 33 times.

Unfortunately, the most famed and accessible of Egypt's monasteries seems like little more than a photo opportunity from the inside. The occasional passing monk is immediately besieged by the religious and curious alike, while guards patrol the small part of the monastery open to visitors to control crowds. Those looking for a little solemnity should try the Red Sea monasteries (see **Monasteries of St. Anthony and St. Paul,** p. 199).

ICONS. The monastery houses many treasures, including over 2000 exquisite 5th-century icons. The icons with brushed gold halos have a holographic effect, an artistic style unique to the Sinai. In the 7th century, the Prophet Muhammad granted the monastery protection and exemption from taxes; a copy of this directive still hangs in the icon gallery, near a similar letter penned by Napoleon in 1798.

LIBRARY. The monastery's library, containing over 8000 books and manuscripts, is said to be second only to the Vatican library in the number and value of its religious texts. The collection is currently being copied onto microfiche in order to make it available to scholars everywhere.

BURNING BUSH. Upon entering the monastery, turn left to reach a thorny shrub, resting in a wire enclosure at about eye-level. This plant is alleged to have descended from the Burning Bush where God spoke to Moses. Tourists and pilgrims have the (bad) habit of snapping off tendrils within arms reach.

CHURCH OF THE TRANSFIGURATION. The first permanent structure in the monastery was erected in 330 CE, when the Empress Helena (Constantine's old lady) built a small church and tower (dedicated to St. Eleni) at the site of the Burning Bush. Around 530, Emperor Justinian ordered a splendid basilica within a walled fortress to be constructed on top of Mt. Sinai. When Justinian's trusted architect Stephanos found the mountain's peak too narrow, he built the Church of the Transformation next to St. Eleni's chapel instead. This structure became known as the Church of the Transfiguration, so named for its spectacular almond-shaped mosaic depicting this event in Jesus's life. The peeved emperor ordered Stephanos's execution, but the builder lived out his days in the safety of the monastery and eventually attained sainthood (his bones are in the **ossuary**). Both St. Helena and Justinian dedicated their churches to the Virgin Mary, since Christian tradition asserts that the Burning Bush foreshadowed the Annunciation, when the archangel Gabriel heralded the birth of Christ.

CHAPEL OF THE BURNING BUSH. Only the central nave of the Church of the Transfiguration is open to the public. On tiptoe you can see mosaics of a barefoot Moses in the Chapel of the Burning Bush, behind the altar. Should you manage to visit the icons back there, you'll have to remove your shoes, as the roots of the sacred shrub extend under the floor (a living descendant resides just outside). Such privileges are only accorded to true religious pilgrims, who are traditionally allowed to ask God for one favor. The monks themselves, with the help of the local Bedouin population (descended from Byzantine slaves), built a **mosque** within the fortress to convince advancing Ottoman armies that the complex was also Muslim.

MOSES'S WELL. Outside the main entrance of the Church of the Transfiguration is Moses's Well, where the prophet reportedly freshened up after his holy ascent. The **ossuary,** a separate building outside the walls, houses the remains of monks.

MT. SINAI جبل موسى

The holy peak of Mt. Sinai, or as locals call it, Mt. Moses (Gabal Musa), stands 2285m above sea level. The Bible describes a mountain engulfed in fire and smoke that Moses ascended to receive the Ten Commandments while the Israelites built a golden calf at its base. Mt. Sinai is one of only two places in the Old Testament where God revealed himself to the people, making the desolate peak sacred for both Christians and Muslims (Jews do not universally identify the modern Mt. Sinai as the peak made famous by the Bible). In the Book of Exodus, God warned the people, "Take heed that you do not go up into the mountain or touch the border of it; whoever touches the mountain shall be put to death" (Exodus 19:12). This prohibition seems to have been long forgotten—busloads of tourists climb the peak each day. God should have included an 11th commandment: "Thou shalt not trash holy places"—maybe then climbers would think twice before leaving litter on the trail. Despite the trash, the view from the summit is awe-inspiring.

🛈 PRACTICAL INFORMATION

You don't necessarily need a guide, but for safety neither men nor women should hike alone at night. Most people hook up with **organized groups** from the Gulf of Aqaba resorts and begin their climb (via the camel path) around 2am in order to catch sunrise at the top. Alternatively, you can take the bus to St. Catherine's and start the hike late in the afternoon. Sunset on the mountain is just as spectacular as sunrise, and there isn't a crowd. For a few hours after nightfall, the snack peddlers and blanket hawkers may turn off their lights and music and take a much-deserved nap, leaving you with a real chance to have the summit to yourself. No matter when you make the hike, bring a flashlight and wear walking shoes, or at least a sturdy pair of sandals. If you explore the small ravine between the peaks during daylight hours, you'll discover an ancient Byzantine **cistern** where water was stored during the summers.

EGYPT

HOLY MT. SERBAL? In some religious circles, the debate still rages over whether Mt. Sinai is actually the site where Moses received the Ten Commandments. Though most believe that Mt. Sinai is the real McCoy, some maintain that the actual mountain referred to in the Bible is Mt. Serbal, 20 miles to the west. According to most biblical scholars, however, the Mt. Serbalists are fighting a losing battle. The Bible mentions three characteristics of the mountain in question: it is surrounded by a vast plain, the summit is visible to all below, and it is accessible to all who surround it. All three describe Sinai, none Serbal. It is also doubtful that the Israelites would have chosen to camp for a year in the valley beneath Mt. Serbal—the site of fierce floods, little drinking water, and hordes of mosquitoes. Besides, who's going to tell 18 generations of pilgrims they've been climbing the wrong mountain?

Overnighters should bring ample **food,** and everyone should bring two or three bottles of **water** for the ascent. The cheapest places to buy these amenities are the supermarkets in St. Catherine's town (p. 172). The monastery **rest house** also sells snacks and water at reasonable prices. There are refreshment stands on the way up, along the camel path, but prices increase with altitude. A stand on the summit sells tea (E£3), water (E£5), and various snacks (E£5-6).

CAMPING

Secluded campsites protected by stone windbreaks are available on Mt. Sinai's secondary peak, just a few meters to the west. However, the National Parks administration that oversees the St. Catherine's Protectorate actually prefers that visitors not camp on this peak. Try Elijah's Hollow instead (see **Hiking Mt. Sinai,** p. 176), which is quieter and a little warmer, anyway.

If you plan to spend the night on the mountain, bring a **sleeping bag** and **warm clothes.** Even in summer, it's often only 8-10°C (46-50°F) at night, and the breeze makes it feel even cooler. Those without the necessary gear can rent blankets (E£5) and mattresses (E£10) at the top. There are also "toilets" west of the summit (holes in the ground with more flies than privacy). Hikers should bring a warm change of clothing—sweaty shirts will quickly turn to shirtsicles.

HIKING MT. SINAI

The hike to the top is not very challenging, but you should still leave all but the bare essentials behind. The monks of St. Catherine's (p. 174) will allow you to leave your bags in a room (E£5 per piece per day). There are two paths up the mountain: the **Steps of Repentance** and a **camel path.** To find either trail, walk up the hill to the monastery, bear left at the fork, and continue to the back of the monastery. From here, the camel path continues down the valley while the Steps start to the right, at a gap in a low external wall at the southeast corner of the monastery. The National Parks Administration publishes *Mount Sinai: A Walking Trail Guide,* a tract describing sights along the trails and on the summit, available at the monastery bookstore and the refreshment stand in Elijah's Hollow (E£10).

Most visitors experience only the small fraction of the mountain visible from the two paths and the peak. But for those without the time or money to make a full-blown desert trek, the mountain provides a unique opportunity to see the High Sinai. A Sinai-only or tourist visa grants access to the entire mountain. Hidden away around the mountain are enough hermitages, chapels, springs, and sights of natural beauty to occupy days of exploration. The sun beats down on wild herbs, releasing their scents into the air, while lizards and bees flit around flowers that somehow survive among the rocks. Start your hike at Elijah's Hollow; the owner of the snack stand there will point you in the direction of a couple of paths and let you store unnecessary baggage in a room. As always, bring tons of water.

EGYPT

STEPS OF REPENTANCE. Of the two paths up the mountain, this one is shorter and also more difficult, but you probably deserve it. It is said that the 3750 steps were built by a single monk in order to fulfill his pledge of penitence. The monk cut corners here and there, making many of the steps extra high. Though it requires more physical exertion, this route has fewer crowds and less trash than the camel path, and great views of the monastery below make it far more rewarding. The Steps take you past a number of interesting sights, which (in the order you see them when descending the mountain) include **Elijah's Hollow,** the 6th-century **Elijah's Gate,** the **Shrive Gate** (where pilgrims until the late 19th century had to confess their sins to a priest before continuing their ascent), and a small white **Byzantine chapel.** Stone walls, smoothed into graceful panels by eons of wind, hem in the Steps on either side. Do not chance the Steps at night—they are treacherous and difficult to follow even with a flashlight. *(Bedouin fly up and down the steps in a matter of minutes, but it will take the less sure-footed 1½- 2hr.)*

CAMEL PATH. The longer route, built in the 19th century, begins directly behind the monastery. **Camel rides** up the mountain usually cost E£35 during peak hours, but if you can stand the sun and the heat, you can get a ride up in the middle of the day for E£20. Unfortunately, the camels are not always available when you need them—you may arrive at the dispatch area at the beginning of the path and find only dung. The path forks a couple of times at the beginning; it doesn't matter which way you go, as the diverging paths always meet up later. There is one juncture that confuses hikers: near the top, the camel path intersects the Steps path after passing through a narrow, steep-walled stone corridor. Turn left to reach the summit; the camel path ends here. Riders will have to get off their high humps and huff up the rest of the way. *(At night about 2½hr. by toed foot, 1½hr. by cloven.)*

ELIJAH'S HOLLOW. After 3000 Steps of Repentence, you'll reach the plain known as Elijah's Hollow. To get there via the camel path on the way up, turn right at the intersection with the path leading to the Steps. The hollow, marked by a 500-year-old cypress tree and a half-dozen of its younger peers, is visible from the north side of the summit. This is where the prophet Elijah is said to have heard the voice of God and the sound of silence after fleeing Jezebel (I Kings 19:8-18). The small **Chapel of Elijah** occupies the site. Another chapel inside is dedicated to Elijah's successor, Elisha. Neither is open to visitors. The **cave** by the chapel supposedly concealed Elijah during his flight.

CENTRAL SINAI DESERT

The natural wonders of the Sinai Peninsula will win you over if nothing else will. *Wadis* shrouded in misty heat lead in every direction, snaking their way around mountain ranges, lush oases, and Bedouin homesteads. The region is fairly untouristed, meaning you'll have all the time and space you want to explore.

ⓩ PRACTICAL INFORMATION

WHEN TO GO

Spring and fall are the most temperate seasons for hikes. In summer you'll spend most of the day resting in the shade until the sun calms down, and in winter you'll freeze. The nights are frigid year-round. You may be able to rent blankets from Bedouin, but don't count on it—bring a warm sleeping bag.

PLANNING YOUR TRIP

To venture into any of the mountains other than Mt. Sinai, you must be accompanied by a **Bedouin guide** and have a regular **Egyptian tourist visa**—the Sinai-only visa won't do. **Organized tours** can be arranged in Israel through **SPNI** (see **Tourist and Financial Services,** p. 276). The Israeli travel outfitter **Neot Ha-Kikar** (see **Tourist and**

Financial Services) specializes in Sinai tours, with trips beginning in Eilat and Cairo. (Offices in Tel Aviv, Jerusalem, and Eilat. 6-day circuit US$360). No matter where in Israel you book your tour, however, you'll eventually end up at Sheikh Musa's office; you'll save a lot of money by starting there, too.

Sheikh Musa, head of Mountain Tours, has a monopoly on all the hikes in the mountains, and trips must be arranged through him. (☎ 06 947 04 57. Reservations accepted.) You are required by law to leave your passport with Musa—he will notify the army of your whereabouts. To get to his office in St. Catherine's town, walk from the town square past the petrol station. Take the second right; Mr. Musa's office is straight ahead up the hill.

Sheikh Musa will procure both a guide and permit for you. His price, which includes guide, food, camels, and equipment, is US$20-30 per person per day, depending on the size of your party and where you go. The minimum total charge is US$90 per day, making individual travel very expensive. If you're willing to wait a few days, you may be able to join a group. Surplus gear can be stored in Musa's house. You'll leave for your hike within 2hr. of arriving at his office (15min. if you've made a reservation). You and your guide will camp with the Bedouin, so be prepared for long nights by the fire smoking "Bedouin tobacco," drinking tea, and learning a great deal about a little-known culture. Tell Sheikh Musa what you want to see and how quickly, and he'll tailor an itinerary.

HIKING THE SINAI DESERT

Routes include the following possibilities. For most of these trips, you need bring nothing more than a sleeping bag and warm clothes; some may require a rope.

Al-Galt al-Azraq: The most popular trek, a spring-fed pool shaded by a willow tree (2 days).

Gabal Banat: A mountain north of St. Catherine's overlooking a vast desert (2 days).

Gabal Bab: From this peak you can see west all the way to the Gulf of Suez (2 days).

Gabal Katerina: The highest mountain in Egypt (2642m), south of Mt. Sinai. The path to the top is difficult, secluded, and beautiful. A chapel at the summit (11hr. round-trip).

Gabal 'Abbas Pasha: A rock with palace ruins and excellent views (2 days).

Gulat al-Agrod: A deep, crystal-clear mountain pool where you can swim in the shade of overhanging trees and dive off the surrounding rocks (3 days).

Wadi Talla: There are two *wadis,* one large and one small. Swim in the big one (3 days).

Wadi Nogra: A rocky valley with a natural dam (Nogra Dam). The water trickles off moss-covered boulders to form a natural shower (3 days).

Sheikh Owat: A picturesque oasis with palm trees, a well, and a lot of goats (3 days).

Farsh Romana: A campground with showers on the way to Gabal Banat (2 days).

Wadi Feiran: An amazingly lush oasis 50km west of St. Catherine's Monastery. Islamic tradition holds that Hagar fled there when banished from Abraham and Sarah's camp in al-Tantawi. Today there is a convent there. The best way to get there is by taxi from St. Catherine's (E£100 round-trip); hiking overland is prohibited by the military. Buses to and from Cairo pass by but the schedules are unpredictable; you might get stranded.

SHARM AL-SHEIKH شرم الشيخ ☎ 069

In the words of a wise Dahab dive master, "Sharm sucks." The people who stay in Sharm al-Sheikh are not merely package tourists; they are package tourists gullible enough to pay large sums of money to spend their vacation at a resort that appears to have been built on the site of a nuclear blast. The hotels are a fairly wretched bunch, gathered around a bay polluted by constant boat traffic. Still, a couple of factors partially redeem the city. Accommodations, however wretched, are cheaper here than in Na'ama Bay, and the area around the old market is crowded with cheap coffee shops, fruit stands, and butcher shops displaying hanging sides of meat—tails still attached. The diving, also, is pretty amazing.

⊏ TRANSPORTATION

Flights: The **Egypt Air** office (☎66 10 58) is along the road leading to Na'ama Bay, not far from the bay. It's easily identified and makes a good landmark. Open Sa-Th 9am-2pm and 6-9pm. Another **branch** at the airport (☎60 06 40).

Buses: From the East Delta station behind the Mobil station between Na'ama and Sharm al-Sheikh, buses leave daily to: **Cairo** (7-10hr., 10 per day 7:30am-midnight, E£50-65); **Dahab** (1½hr., 8 per day 6:30am-11:30pm, E£10); **Nuweiba** (2½hr.; 9am, 2:30, 5pm; E£15); **Suez** (7hr., 9am and 2pm, E£26-35); **Taba** (3hr., 8 and 9am, E£25). To get to **St. Catherine's,** take the earliest bus to Dahab, from where a bus leaves for the monastery at 9:30am. Some buses to Cairo and Suez also leave from a smaller station, down the street from EgyptAir.

Ferries: The ferry to **Hurghada** (☎66 01 66) leaves three times per week from the port just west of Sharm al-Sheikh bay (6hr.; M, W, Th 9am; E£125). From the Sharm Marina, keep walking around the harbor and over the hill at the southern end. Book tickets a day ahead, either through a hotel or at **Thomas Cook** (☎60 18 08), 50m south of the Pigeon House Hotel in Na'ama.

Local Transportation: Take a green and white **minibus** to any destination up to and including Na'ama Bay (50pt). You can catch a minibus going up or down the hill. Other destinations include the Old Market and the marina west of the bay. **Taxis** (☎66 03 57) are much more expensive, charging E£10-15 to go to the main East Delta bus station.

✴ 🛈 ORIENTATION AND PRACTICAL INFORMATION

Sharm al-Sheikh is divisible into two parts: up-the-hill and down-the-hill. If you are arriving by minibus from the bus station, get off when the bus makes a right off the main road near EgyptAir. You are now down the hill. The hill in question is marked at the top by the sign of the Aida Hotel. A road leads up the hill—continue straight and signs will direct you to the bank area.

Banks: Bank of Alexandria (☎66 03 55). Allows cash withdrawal with MC/V. Open 8:30am-2pm and 6-9pm. **National Bank of Egypt** and **Banque du Caire** have **ATMs** that accept MC/V.

Supermarket: Sharm Express Supermarket (☎60 09 24). From the hill, turn right at Safetyland and left just past EgyptAir to reach the Old Market entrances. Take the 2nd entrance on the right. Open daily 9am-2am. To get to **Supermarket al-Sheik Abdallah,** follow signs less than 100m past the International Hospital. Those serious about cooking for themselves will find the low prices and wide selection of this western-style market well worth the minibus trip. Open 7:30am-3am.

Police: (☎66 04 15), 300m from the banks. **Tourist police** (☎60 03 11 or 60 05 54) are open 24hr.

Pharmacy: Pharmacy Sharm al-Sheikh (☎66 03 88), next to the Bank of Alexandria. Open daily 9am-1am. **Pharmacy Nada'a** is near the Sharm Express Supermarket.

Ambulance: ☎60 05 54.

Hospital: (☎66 04 25), down the hill, just north of EgyptAir. Open 24hr. **Sharm al-Sheikh International Hospital** (☎66 08 93; fax 66 09 81), halfway between Sharm al-Sheikh and Na'ama Bay. Better-equipped than the hospital in town. Open 24hr.

Telephone Office: (☎66 04 00), just before the banks. Open 24hr.

Post Office: (☎66 05 18), in the same complex as Pharmacy Sharm al-Sheikh. **Poste Restante** and **EMS.** Open Sa-Th 8am-3pm.

⌂ ACCOMMODATIONS

Youth Hostel (☎66 03 17), at the top of the hill and to the left. The cheapest place to stay in the region. Old dorms are more cramped and running water is unreliable, but breakfast is included. New section sparkles, but breakfast costs E£8. Both sections have A/C. Old section E£19; new section E£40. Non-members add E£1.

Al-Kheima Camp (☎/fax 66 01 66), 1.5km past Safetyland along the road that rings the bay. The "camp" has spacious rooms with A/C and bath, as well as a bit of greenery in the almost-pleasant courtyard. Bungalow singles E£40; bungalow doubles with portable fans E£60; single rooms E£80; double rooms E£120.

Safetyland (☎ 66 34 63), at the bottom of the hill at the intersection of the road leading to Na'ama Bay and the road running along the bay. The only hotel on the beach and a last resort. Stuffy concrete bungalows are situated in what looks like a construction site. Breakfast included. Open tent sites E£20 per person; singles E£40; doubles E£80.

🍴 FOOD

Restaurants are concentrated in the Old Market. Turn left off the Sharm-Na'ama highway at EgyptAir to find Sharm's finest asset: a small, unmarked **liquor store** that sells beer (Stella E£5, Sakara E£5.50) and the usual assortment of dodgy wine and spirits. You'll be hard-pressed to find beer for less than twice those prices elsewhere. (Open daily 11am-3am.)

La Trattoria Restaurant (☎ 66 22 40), opposite the liquor store. Standard Italian fare. Pizza E£10-18. Pasta E£7-10. Ostrich E£40. Open daily 10am-1am.

Sinai Star Restaurant. Take the 2nd entrance into the Old Market, then the 1st right. Fish, calamari E£15. Meals include rice, salad, and *tahina*. Open daily 11am-midnight.

🐚 SCUBA DIVING

The Sharm al-Sheikh and Na'ama Bay area is undoubtedly the mecca of Red Sea diving and the epicenter of the Sinai's tourism. Despite the large number of wealthy Germans and Italians in five-star hotels, Sharm al-Sheikh still has several unexplored gems in and around the Straits of Tiran, Ras Muhammad National Park, and the wreck of the *Thistlegorm*.

DIVE CENTERS

■ **Camel Dive Center,** P.O. Box 10, Na'ama Bay, Sharm al-Sheikh, South Sinai, Egypt (☎ 60 07 00; fax 60 06 01; reservations@cameldive.com; www.cameldive.com), in the Camel Dive Hotel. One of the oldest dive centers in the area, and probably the friendliest. Offers an average of 6 boats, state-of-the-art equipment, and highly trained multilingual guides, as well as inexpensive accommodations by Na'ama's standards (dorm rooms US$30). 2 guided dives US$60; full equipment US$25; O/W course US$350. Reserve ahead for a 10% discount on all services. MC/V.

Sinai Divers (☎ 60 06 97; fax 60 01 58; info@sinaidivers.com; www.sinaidivers.com), next to the Ghazala Hotel on the promenade. Offers a huge variety of courses, liveaboards, excursions, and an ironclad reputation. English, Arabic, French, Italian, and German spoken. PADI or SSI O/W course US$330; 3 days with 6 dives US$160. Accepts traveler's checks, MC/V.

Oonas Dive Club (☎ 60 05 81; fax 60 05 82), at the northern end of the bay. Slightly cheaper rates and much better after-hours camaraderie than the other centers. 5-day PADI course US$295; certification US$30. Intro dives US$50-65 including equipment. Full gear rental US$24. Full day at Ras Muhammad with 2 dives US$60.

DIVE SITES

■ **RAS MUHAMMAD NATIONAL PARK.** Jutting out into the Red Sea at the tip of the Sinai peninsula, Ras Muhammad National Park is the most famous dive site in Egypt and one of the most spectacular in the world. The tiny neck of land is bordered on the west by the Gulf of Suez and on the east by the Gulf of Aqaba. The waters of Ras Muhammad contain over 1000 species of fish, many of which are unique to the Red Sea. The aquatic wonders found here outweigh the time and expense of the trip, making it by far the best daytrip from Sharm al-Sheikh or Na'ama Bay. The most famous sites are the **Shark** and **Yolanda Reefs.** The latter includes the wreckage of the freighter *Yolanda* (the actual ship has slipped off the continental shelf and lies 220m below the surface). This surreal sight is possibly the only place in the world where you can swim with sharks among broken toilets.

In the early 1980s, it became clear that tourist and fishing traffic was destroying Ras Muhammad's underwater treasures, so the Egyptian government declared the area a national park. Most of the fragile underwater habitat is now closed to the public, and it is against Egyptian law to remove any material, living or dead, from the park. Diving, snorkeling, and swimming are only permitted in specified areas, mostly around the very tip of the peninsula. On rough days, snorkeling at Ras Muhammad can be difficult. (For underwater advice and warnings, see **Scu-better Watch Out,** p. 184.) Camping is permitted in designated sites; check with the park's Visitors Center for details. Call the Sharm al-Sheikh info office (☎66 06 68 or 66 05 59) for further information about the park. *(The park is accessible by boat and taxi for E£100. Since it is beyond the jurisdiction of a Sinai-only visa, you must have your passport and a full Egyptian tourist visa. Park open daily 8am-5pm. US$5 per person, additional US$5 per car.)*

▓THISTLEGORM. The World War II cargo ship *Thistlegorm* was sunk in 1941 by long-range German bombers off the southern coast of the Sinai. Discovered years later by Jacques-Yves Cousteau (who kept the location secret until it was rediscovered in the early '90s), the *Thistlegorm* has become legendary among divers and is widely considered the best wreck dive in the world. Quite far offshore, the *Thistlegorm* requires at least one day and two dives to explore. The cargo bays are crammed full of tires, rifles, motorcycles, aircraft wings, tanks, trucks, and railway carriages. The commander's deck and outer shell are downright eerie. Although a more expensive dive (US$120-150), it is simply unforgettable.

JACKSON'S REEF. Of the four reefs extending down the center of the spectacular **Straits of Tiran,** this is the best and northernmost dive. The strong current is particularly challenging to negotiate, but it also encourages the growth of some of the most beautiful and abundant coral in the entire Sinai, bringing nutrients to feed the coral and schools of fish that congregate on the reef, as well as a variety of sharks and turtles. Schools of hammerheads are seen during July and August.

RAS GHOZLANI. In the area just north of the famous Ras Muhammad National Park lie many peaceful and often overlooked local dive sites. Many of the sites are incredibly beautiful and tranquil; Ras Ghozlani is the best. Divers here are less likely to see the big predators found prowling the deep at other sites, but this location is rarely crowded, uniquely preserved, and full of colorful fish.

NA'AMA BAY خليج نعمة ☎69

This five-star hotel nexus is the center of Egypt's anti-backpacker sentiment—the budget traveler is about as welcome in Na'ama as a narcotics agent in Dahab. However, if you look clean-cut (and act like you own the place), you can freely roam the waterfront shops and hotels. As soon as you don your hip new tie-dye from Dahab, however, you invite stares along the promenade and may be barred from certain areas. Many budget travelers do flock here each year, drawn by the world-class diving and snorkeling as well as the most active nightlife in the Sinai. Travelers have been known to get jobs at hotels or dive centers (see **Working & Volunteering,** p. 45). If you work for a hotel, you usually get free accommodations; if you work at a dive club, you get free diving lessons or courses. Knowledge of Arabic is not necessary, but French and Italian are helpful.

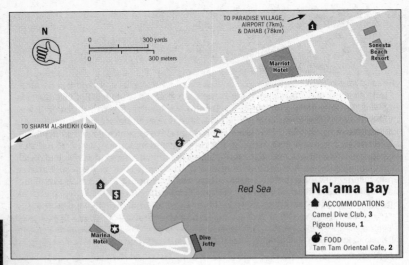

TO PARADISE VILLAGE,
AIRPORT (7km),
& DAHAB (78km)

Sonesta
Beach
Resort

N

0   300 yards

0   300 meters

Marriot
Hotel

TO SHARM AL-SHEIKH (6km)

Red Sea

Marina
Hotel

Dive
Jetty

Na'ama Bay

▲ ACCOMMODATIONS
Camel Dive Club, **3**
Pigeon House, **1**

♠ FOOD
Tam Tam Oriental Cafe, **2**

EGYPT

▌ TRANSPORTATION

By far the best way to go from Sharm al-Sheikh to Na'ama (and anywhere in between) is to hail one of the green and white **service minibuses** (50pt) along the main highway. They run constantly in both directions and will stop anywhere. Any taxi driver who tells you otherwise is lying, and will charge no less than E£10-15 for the same journey. **Intercity buses** leave from behind the Mobil station halfway down the road to Sharm and from the Sharm bus station.

✦ ▐ ORIENTATION AND PRACTICAL INFORMATION

Na'ama Bay is one long strip of resorts on both sides of the highway, which is the town's main street. Most of the beach is owned by five-star resorts. Between the beach and hotels is a **promenade,** where restaurants, bars, and diving clubs cluster.

Banks: National Bank of Egypt, in the Marina Sharm, Ghazala, and Mövenpick Hotels. Exchanges money. Open Sa-Th 9am-1pm and 6-9pm, F 9-11am and 6-9pm. **Banque Misr** (☎60 16 67), at the Marriott Hotel. Cash advances on MC/V. Open Sa-Th 9am-2pm and 7-10pm, F 10am-12:30pm and 7-10pm. **Commercial International Bank** has 2 locations—next to the Camel Dive Center and across from the Mövenpick Hotel. Both open daily 9am-2pm and 6-9pm.

ATMs: In the Mövenpick Hotel lobby and along the promenade in front of the Ghazala Hotel. MC/V.

Ambulance: ☎123.

Tourist police: (☎64 03 01), just north of the Helnan Marina Hotel.

Pharmacy: Towa Pharmacy (☎60 07 79), in the bazaar south of the Mövenpick. Open daily 10am-1am.

Hospital: The closest hospital is the Sharm al-Sheikh International Hospital between Na'ama and Sharm (see Sharm al-Sheikh **Practical Information,** p. 179).

Telephones: Menatel card phones stand between the promenade and the highway.

Internet Access: Neama Internet, on the 2nd fl. of a building next to McDonald's. E£20 per hr. Open 10am-3am.

Post Office: In Sharm al-Sheikh, but most hotels will drop off mail.

ACCOMMODATIONS

If you have the money, opt for accommodations in Na'ama rather than in Sharm. Hotels are nicer, restaurants and clubs are nearby, and you won't have to take a minibus to and from the beach.

Pigeon House (☎ 60 09 96; fax 60 09 95), on the highway in the north end of town, past Thomas Cook. The only relatively cheap place to roost in Na'ama. Happening court-yard is *the* place for a Stella or *sheesha*. Comfortable rooms. Breakfast included. Singles E£65, with A/C E£105; doubles E£85/E£120; extra bed E£20.

Camel Dive Club (☎ 60 07 00), in the center of the small bazaar near the cliffs that over-look the southern end of the bay, a block in from the promenade. This slightly pricey option is worth it for the location as well as the A/C rooms, private baths, and views of a flowery courtyard with pool. The hotel is wheelchair-accessible and features 5 rooms designed for disabled guests. Breakfast included. Dorm rooms US$30; singles US$91; doubles US$108. Reserve ahead for a 10% discount. MC/V.

Shark's Bay Camp (☎ 60 09 43; fax 60 09 44), 4km north of town. A ship-shape Bedouin camp that overlooks a quiet bay. Features a breathtaking view of Tiran Island, an excellent restaurant, and a dive club, but the cost of a taxi (E£20) to Na'ama makes these clean bungalows an expensive choice. Bedouin tent on the beach E£125. Singles E£50-60; doubles E£65-75; triples E£90-100.

FOOD

Food in Na'ama Bay is high in quality, a fact underscored by correspondingly high prices. Only a few places offer low-cost meals, but a little extravagance pays off with a first-rate dining experience.

Seahorse Restaurant (☎ 60 01 51), also part of the Ghazala Hotel complex, next to Sinai Divers. If you're going to blow the budget, you may as well do it at this excellent Swiss restaurant. The steaks (E£40-42) are considered the best in the Sinai by those who keep track of such things. They also serve veg. entrees (E£22-25), while the daily-changing lunch special could even be considered a borderline budget meal (E£20). Open daily noon-1am. Reservations strongly recommended for dinner. MC/V.

Tam Tam Oriental Corner (☎ 60 01 51), attached to the Ghazala Hotel. The best Egyptian restaurant in town. Enormous bowl of *kushari* E£8. *Fuul* and falafel E£3-5. Salads E£3.50. Open daily noon-midnight.

Viva Restaurant (☎ 60 09 64), next to the Red Sea Diving College. The cheapest meal on the promenade. Tasty pizzas E£10. Open daily 10am-midnight. AmEx/MC/V.

Pigeon House Restaurant, in the hotel of the same name. Excellent pork, meat, and fish. Pasta E£10.50-16.75. Kebab E£19.75-22.75. Open daily until 11pm.

Tandoori (☎ 60 07 00 ext. 329), at Camel Dive Club. Serves good Indian cuisine in a relaxing outdoor courtyard. Lamb and chicken dishes, as well as a number of veg. entrees (E£28-32). Open daily 6:30pm-11:30pm. Reservations encouraged. MC/V.

WATERSPORTS

Na'ama Bay itself has no spectacular coral reefs, but a veritable colossus of coral lies just outside the bay to the north and south. Dive centers have maps of the reef-scape; pick one up and put on your flippers. The closest free site is **Near Gardens** at the northern tip of Na'ama Bay, a moderate walk down the beach. The nearby **Tower** and **Sodfa** are a decent walk south of Na'ama Bay, but both require a E£10 fee, payable at the Tower Hotel. Ask at a dive center which sites are accessible by land; some are tricky to reach. For snorkeling, many swear that boat-based is the best. For US$15-25, spend a day on a boat and explore spectacular waters. Arrange trips through the dive clubs. The legendary reefs of the **Straits of Tiran** are distant

SCU-BETTER WATCH OUT... Scu-better not die! Hidden

among the crevices in the coral reefs around the Sinai Peninsula are creatures capable of inflicting serious injury and even death. If you see something that looks like an aquatic pin cushion, it's probably a **sea urchin** or a **blowfish,** both of which should be touched only in sushi form. Avoid the feathery **lionfish** as well—its harmless-looking spines can deliver a paralyzing sting. The well-named **fire coral** can bloat a leg to mammoth proportions, leaving welts the size of croquet balls. The **stonefish** is camouflaged flawlessly to resemble a mossy lump of coral or rock. If you step on one, you'll puff up and may die within hours. Reach into a hole and a 2m-long **moray eel** may lock its jaws onto your hand. The list goes on. Before plunging in, ask at any dive shop for a look at one of the picture cards that identifies these underwater uglies.

When snorkeling, try to enter the water in a sandy area to avoid damaging underwater plants and animals. If you have no choice but to enter where sea creatures and coral may dwell, wear foot protection. **Sharks** are attracted by blood, so never enter the water with an open wound or if menstruating. Panicking and thrashing tends to excite sharks. If you see one, calmly climb out of the water and casually share the news. Most sharks, however, are not aggressive and wouldn't give you the time of day even if they could; most marine animals become aggressive only if *you* have done something threatening or irritating. If you see an animal getting defensive, simply back away slowly. *Let's Go* does not recommend messing with sharks.

and accessible by boat only. **Ras Nasrani** and **Ras Umm Sidd** are good sites a little closer to town. Water activities are not restricted to diving. **Sun-n-Fun** booths (☎ 60 01 37 ext. 170; open 9am-7pm) at the Hilton and Aquamarine beaches rent equipment for **windsurfing** (E£50 per hr.; lessons E£65 per hr.), **water skiing** (E£40 per 15min.), and **sailing** (E£50 per hr.; lessons E£55). Try a **glass bottom boat** (every hr. 10am-4pm; E£25 per person) or the big **Discovery** (every 2hr. 11am-5pm; E£55, children E£30). Frolic for free at the tiny **public beach** just south of Gafy Land Hotel.

⚔ OUTDOOR ACTIVITIES

Landlubbers can throw on some plaid pants and tee off in a game of **miniature golf** at the Hilton. (E£10 per game, E£55 deposit on clubs.) **Horseback riding** (E£60 per hr.) is available across from the Novotel Hotel. **Safari Tours,** next to the Pigeon House, offers **ATV** trips (US$35 per hr.) out in the desert. Most leave before sunset.

WADI KID. Here's looking at you: this *wadi*, 40km north of Na'ama Bay, is a deep, fertile canyon where you can hike among rock formations and fruit trees. Most hotels are affiliated with a tour company that goes once a week. (*Mövenpick Hotel organizes half-day trips to Nabq and Wadi Kid for US$30 per person, with a 4-person minimum.*)

NABQ WILDLIFE RESERVE. On the coast 20km north of Na'ama Bay, Nabq's most notable site is a strip of coastline where the largest **mangrove forest** in the Sinai flourishes, attracting herons, ospreys, foxes, and hard-to-spot gazelles. The mangroves sprout in a few feet of warm, clear water with a sandy bottom, ideal for swimming and relaxation. The problem of maintaining traditional Bedouin lifestyles in the modern world is being actively addressed in Nabq: a Bedouin "reservation" attempts to preserve the culture and openly welcomes visitors. (*Most hotels organize daytrips to Nabq. Wandering off the path in the park is extremely dangerous, as there are still a number of* **landmines** *in the area.*)

DESERT EXCURSIONS. Na'ama, first popular with divers and snorklers, then with European sunbathers, is now taking aim at the adventure market—teeming with companies promising "a genuine Bedouin experience." A jeep will take you to St. Catherine's or the Colored Canyon for US$50, while a couple of hours on a camel usually costs about US$20. The people who take these overpriced trips are gener-

EGYPT

ally package tourists, so unless you relish being stranded in the desert with insipid whiners ("Do we *have* to eat this?"), start your journey in Dahab or Nuweiba.

🎵 LIBATIONS 'N' GYRATIONS

Na'ama nights are usually spent tossing back Stellas and swapping diving stories.

Pirate's Bar (☎ 60 01 36, ext. 850), in the Hilton. With cutlasses and rigging hanging from the wall, the bar attracts an appropriately ridiculous mix of swashbucklingly tan diving instructors and suave Europeans. Stella E£10. Imported draught beer E£18-20. Free bar munchies. Open daily 11am-1:30am.

Camel Dive Club, upstairs from the dive center of the same name. Local dive masters congregate here. The 1st fl. is packed and often features live music; the low-key rooftop patio overlooks the main street. Stella E£12, E£9 for divers.

Hard Rock Cafe (☎ 60 26 65 or 60 26 66), around the corner from the Camel Dive Club. Transforms into an extremely popular disco at midnight, with a line snaking out the door most nights. Open until 4am.

Casino Royale (☎ 60 17 31), opposite the Mövenpick Hotel. Give the roulette wheel a spin at this Las Vegas-style joint. 18+. No shorts. Open daily 8pm-4am.

DAHAB دهب   ☎069

Like Kathmandu or Amsterdam, Dahab is one of those places that has grown larger than life in the minds of travelers. For most, it conjures up images of glossy-eyed, tie-dyed hippies lounging on the shore, blissfully asphyxiating themselves in blue clouds of marijuana smoke. Now, Tommy Hilfiger is more popular than tie-dye and cell phones more prominent than joints. Dahab is now a resort for back-packers and budget travelers, a kind of Club Med on US$10 a day. More than any other factor, the diving industry has driven the changes in Dahab. The most common story around is that of the backpacker who means to stay a few days and wakes up a dive instructor six months later (so think hard before you take that introductory dive). Regardless of how long you plan to stay in Dahab, "Bedouin" camps are the cheapest, most social places to crash, though travelers seeking more comfort can choose from a number of more expensive, middle-range hotels with air-conditioning and a family atmosphere.

▐ TRANSPORTATION

Buses: East Delta Buses leave daily from the station in Dahab city to: **Cairo** (8hr.; 8:30am, 12:30, 10:30pm; E£55-70); **Nuweiba** (1½hr., 10am and 6:30pm, E£10); **Sharm al-Sheikh** (1hr.; 8:30, 10am, 12:30, 3:30, 5:30, 10:30pm; E£10); **St. Catherine's** (3hr., 9:30am, E£15); **Taba** (3hr., 10:30am, E£20). An **Upper Egypt** bus leaves daily at 4pm from the same place, stopping by **Sharm al-Sheikh** (E£15), **Suez** (E£40), **Hurghada** (E£76), **Luxor** (E£90) along the way. Most camps post current bus schedules. Prices fluctuate depending on departure time—the last bus of the day usually costs about one-third more than earlier buses.

Service: If you get a group together, you can convince a driver to go to almost any destination. *Service* end up being more expensive, but the rides are much faster.

Taxis: Pickups are the cheapest and most common way to get from the bus station to the village. The ride can cost as little as 50pt per person if there are multiple pickups in attendance, or the driver may ask for as much as E£5 if he is alone. You can always bargain him down to E£1-2 by threatening to walk or wait for another ride. **Taxis** charge E£5 for the same trip. Many drivers of both taxis and pickups are paid commissions by some of the less desirable camps to deliver customers, so don't believe anyone who claims the camp of your choice is closed, inferior, or expensive.

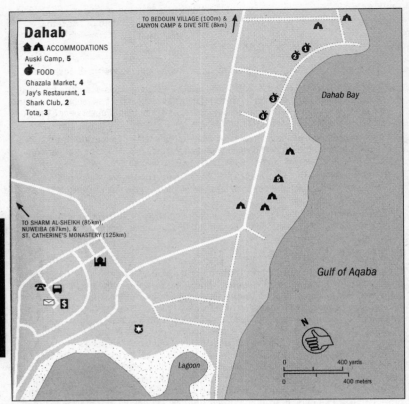

Dahab

🏠 🏚 ACCOMMODATIONS
Auski Camp, **5**

🍎 FOOD
Ghazala Market, **4**
Jay's Restaurant, **1**
Shark Club, **2**
Tota, **3**

TO BEDOUIN VILLAGE (100m) &
CANYON CAMP & DIVE SITE (8km)

Dahab Bay

TO SHARM AL-SHEIKH (85km),
NUWEIBA (87km), &
ST. CATHERINE'S MONASTERY (125km)

Gulf of Aqaba

Lagoon

0   400 yards

0   400 meters

EGYPT

✦ 🛈 ORIENTATION AND PRACTICAL INFORMATION

Dahab city is of almost no significance to the budget traveler, who only glimpses it between climbing off the bus and getting into a pickup headed for the village. A quick glance around should provide enough in the way of orientation. The more relevant part of town lies 3km to the northeast, along the coast. The village is sickle-shaped; the curved part that rings the bay is called Masbat, and the handle to the south is Mashraba. Even farther north (and rarely frequented by tourists) lies the current Bedouin settlement of 'Aslah, home to acrobatic goats, tethered camels, and the occasional dive instructor.

Banks: National Bank of Egypt (☎ 64 02 42), down the road from the bus station to the left. **ATM** accepts MC/V. Open daily 8:30am-2pm and 6-9pm. **Banque du Caire** (☎ 64 04 44), on the bay. Withdraw money with MC/V or change **traveler's checks** with an outrageous commission. Open Sa-Th 9am-2pm and 6-9pm. **Western Union** (☎ 64 04 66), a few doors north of Tota (see **Food**, p. 188). Open daily 10am-midnight.

Supermarket: Near the National Bank of Egypt. Open daily 6am-2am.

Tourist Police: (☎ 64 01 88), opposite the Novotel Resort near the beach. Open 24hr.

Medical Assistance: Dr. Adel Shafey (☎ 012 33 07 97) and Dr. Ahmed Sadek (☎ 012 348 62 09) both have **clinics** in Mashraba.

Telephones: The **telephone office** is across the street from the supermarket. Open 24hr. Another office next to the Muhammad 'Ali Camp provides international **phone** and **fax** service. E£7 per min. for calls to the US.

Internet Access: The bay boasts more than a dozen Internet cafes, most of which charge in the neighborhood of E£10 per hr.

Post Office: (☎64 02 23), opposite the supermarket. **Poste Restante.** Open Sa-Th 8am-3pm. Down the road from Western Union, a shop next to Neptune Restaurant has an airmail dropbox and sells stamps.

▓ CAMPING

Several dozen **camps** crowd all parts of the village. Dahab camps are an unfortunate bastardization of the thatched beach hut—someone came up with the brilliant idea of casting the huts in concrete, connecting them in rows around a central courtyard, and creating bare cells with minimal ventilation. Fortunately, the huts mostly serve as storage space for your belongings while you lounge outside in one of the restaurants. Rooms with only a mattress are cheapest (E£5-10); those with private bath are a bit pricier (E£15-30). Thatched huts, rare nowadays, provide the best ventilation but also the least resistance to mosquitoes. Camps on the beach south of the bay are the quietest and most relaxed places to stay. Make sure huts have wire screens on the windows; otherwise, you may have to choose between stifling heat and mosquitoes.

Bedouin Moon Hotel (☎64 06 95; bedouinmoon@menanet.net), about 3km north of the village, just past the Bedouin settlement. Owned and operated by 2 Bedouin brothers, the Bedouin Moon is a beautiful hotel situated at the foot of the mountains with a sandy beach and the dive center Reef 2000 (see **Scuba Diving**, p. 189). Rooms have private bath and attractive brick dome ceilings. 3-bed dorm rooms US$14; singles US$20-30; doubles US$35-45 (depending on whether you want a fan or A/C, mountain view or sea view). 10% *Let's Go* discount.

Auski Camp (☎64 04 74), on the beach south of the bay, near the Sphinx Hotel. Friendly owner keeps rooms fresh-smelling and spic-and-span. Doubles E£15.

Venus Camp (☎64 08 38), 50m south of the bay. Clean and laid-back, this camp features an outdoor lounge on the beach—perfect for reading that novel you've been carrying around. Huts E£7; single thatched bungalows E£20; double bungalows E£25.

Cleopatra's (cleopatra140@hotmail.com). A camp in Mashraba whose thatched huts are hot commodities in the Dahab market. Rooms with shower and toilet E£25-30; 2-person huts E£15; 4-person huts E£25.

Oasis Fighting Kangaroo (☎64 00 11; bedouinn@yahoo.com), down a small alleyway across from Napoleon's Restaurant in the middle of the village (don't confuse it with the Fighting Kangaroo Camp). The OFK has some of the best huts in Dahab (E£5) and a Bedouin-style TV room (with hammocks) outside. Singles E£5; doubles E£10. Nicer rooms cost up to E£60.

▓▓ FOOD AND DRINK

If you find yourself with the munchies, fear not: Dahab is home to some of the best cheap food in Egypt, but quality varies in the extreme. The beach is lined with inexpensive restaurants which—when they're not harassing passers-by in an attempt to drum up business—serve good, simple dishes like pancakes with chocolate and fruit. However, many travelers report becoming ill after consuming fish at some of these places. Be wary of ordering anything slightly undercooked, especially meat. If you're feeling ambitious, try one of the restaurants listed below. If you want complete control over food preparation, try **Ghazala Market** at the southern end of town.

Jay's Restaurant (☎335 33 77; julie_jays@yahoo.com), just north of the middle of the bay. You have to step out of the Dahab daze and think ahead if you want to eat at this excellent restaurant. Stop by before 6pm to order dinner for that night (the menu changes daily, and always includes veg. options), and Jay's will have the food ready when you come back. The food is not only some of the best in Dahab, it is also among the cheapest. A main dish, side, and beverage usually amounts to less than E£10. Open for dinner 6-10:30pm. Open for reservations at 10am.

Tota (☎64 92 71), near the southern end of the bay. A *Let's Go* favorite for 17 years. Despite the tugboat architecture and the waiters' sailor costumes, Tota specializes in pasta (E£7.50-9.50), not seafood, but you can drink like a fish—the restaurant has a liquor license. Cocktails E£7.50-8.50. Stella E£6. Open 8am-12:30am.

Tarabouche's (☎012 235 63 38), on the pathway past the Banque du Caire and the Sunrise Camp, across the small parking lot. 3-course, home-cooked Egyptian meals (E£25-50) include salad, choice of fish or meat, and dessert. Food is known to be hygienically prepared. Reservations necessary.

Shark Club, on the beach south of Jay's; look for the shark emblem on the restaurant's kitchen across the beach. Featuring shakes that will leave you speechless, this restaurant wins the Dahab dessert title. The owner speaks perfect English, and the gigantic portions may cause feeding frenzies among patrons. Small pasta E£3-6, large E£5-10. Shakes E£3-5. Open for dinner only 6pm-"when the last customer leaves."

♫ SHAKE 'N' BAKE

SHAKE. The social event of the week in the village is the Friday night dance party at the Nesima Resort's **Roof Bar,** where the crowd forms around 11pm and persists until closing time at 2am. The Helnan Hotel in Dahab city is the site of the **Zanzibar Disco,** which can draw quite a crowd on weekends. On Wednesday nights, rock out to a live local band at the **Hilton Hotel** (also in the city) until dawn. Free hors d'œuvres ease the pain of pricey Stellas (E£10).

BAKE. Alcohol is widely available in Dahab and, like most other things, relatively inexpensive. There are six main sources of booze: the restaurant at the Nesima Dive Club, the Sphinx Hotel, Green Valley, the Crazy House Pub, Tota, and Neptune Billiards, where pool sharks can also rack up a game. (E£10 per hr. Open 10am-2am.) Though the **dope scene** is less noticeable nowadays, marijuana is known to be available. People generally do not actively advertise what type of smoke is coming out of their *sheesha*. The possession of drugs is illegal in Egypt, and Egyptian jails rate low on the Michelin system. Dealers may win an all-expenses-paid trip to the hereafter via firing squad. *Let's Go* just says no.

⚑ OUTDOOR ACTIVITIES

OVERLAND DAYTRIPS. Daytrips to nearby natural wonders, offered by most camps, are great ways to escape the haze of Dahab. Four-wheel-drive trips to the **Colored Canyon** cost E£50 per person for a group of six. You can travel by camel or truck to the brackish oasis of **Wadi Gnay** (E£30 per person). A one-day camel trip to Nabq (see p. 184) is also an option (E£35-50). Hamed the Lobster Man runs **Crazy Camel Camp** (☎64 02 73) and organizes jeep and camel safaris. He also takes people on night **lobster hunting** trips that culminate in lobster feasts on the beach. **Blue Hole Travel** (☎64 02 36; blueholetravel@n2mail.com), across the street from the Sphinx Hotel, runs camel safaris, trips to St. Catherine's, and daily snorkeling excursions to the company's namesake. If you want to go anywhere nearby, ask around the Bedouin community; the Bedouin know these hills better than anyone and will often be happy to organize a trip.

SNORKELING. The snorkeling in Dahab is excellent; enter at either end of the bay where the waves break on the reefs (just be sure to wear shoes or flippers, because if the sea urchins don't get you, the coral will). Trips to the **Blue Hole** and the **Canyon** are arranged every morning by most camps, and you can rent snorkel gear at camps or on the beach (E£5-10). Before paying, make sure the flippers fit, the mask is air-tight, and the snorkel is unobstructed. **Paddleboats** are available for rental near the northern part of the village (E£15 per hr.); use them to explore some of the more secluded spots.

SCUBA DIVING

DIVE CENTERS

The Dahab diving scene has unfortunately turned into a cutthroat operation in which inexperienced and ill-equipped dive centers cut corners on services and prices. There are very few dive centers in Dahab, aside from those listed here, that offer safe and first-rate services at relatively inexpensive rates. Some others charge substantially less, but you're paying for the peace of mind of knowing that air will keep flowing. Keep in mind that a change in management—which happens regularly in Dahab—can turn a reputable establishment in the wrong direction. **Certifications,** by the way, mean next to nothing, though the Egyptian tourist board has plans to institute a more rigorous inspection process sometime in the next year. When choosing a club, there's no substitute for local expert advice. You'll find the entire Dahab diving community—instructors, masters, owners, and managers—congregated on the Nesima's beach on Friday evenings after 6pm for their weekly volleyball tournament. Ask around, and try to get a feel for the consensus as to which clubs are currently the best.

Reef 2000 (☎64 00 87; reef2000@intouch.com, www.reef2000.com), at the Bedouin Moon Hotel in its own bay, just north of the Bedouin village. Run by a British couple who offer low prices and a safe atmosphere where even the most inexperienced will feel comfortable (especially since most of the guides and instructors are English-speaking expats). One guided dive with full equipment US$45; PADI O/W courses US$315. **Camel safaris** to Ras Abu Galum include full equipment, lunch, water, and two dives (US$100). 15% *Let's Go* discount. MC/V.

Nesima Dive Club (☎64 03 20; nesima@menanet.com; www.nesima-resort.com), in the Nesima Resort south of the bay. One of the best reputations in the village. Equipment is well cared for and regularly replaced. PADI O/W course US$315. MC/V.

Fantasea (☎64 04 83; ☎/fax 64 00 43; fdc@intouch.com), at the northern end. Offers everything from open-water dives to assistant instructor courses. PADI O/W courses US$295. Three days of guided dives US$120. AmEx/MC/V.

DIVE SITES

Dahab offers some of the best dives reachable by land. The dive sites, on the Red Sea, are all accessible by car (usually 4WD vehicles) and cover the areas both north and south of the main lighthouse region.

ISLANDS. The most plentiful and beautiful supply of coral and aquatic life in Dahab is here. The labyrinth of pathways, valleys, and coral peaks can make it a difficult but rewarding site to visit, as divers often navigate new and different routes while weaving through delicate cities of coral. Many guides believe that this is the best-preserved coral in the entire Sinai area.

CANYON. Most of the coral have now died due to over-tourism, but the long, narrow canyon ranging in depth from 18-50m still thrills divers looking for deep adventure. At the end of the canyon, divers move through a man-sized crack into the "fish bowl," an enclosure almost completely filled with schools of glass fish.

BLUE HOLE. The most famous site in Dahab is well known for all the wrong reasons. The site should be recognized for the incredibly blue dive, starting at the Bells and continuing along the cliff of coral to the Blue Hole. Every year, though, some of Dahab's best (or just most reckless) divers try to swim through the arched passage (52m below sea level) or even touch the bottom (160m) of the Hole. Some are successful; others lose their lives. *Let's Go* does not recommend being stupid.

NUWEIBA نويبع ☎ 069

One of the Sinai's natural oases, Nuweiba lies at the mouth of an enormous *wadi* that is filled with drifting sand for 10 months of the year. About the only excitement in town occurs in winter, when sudden, rampaging walls of water 3m high charge down the *wadi*. Nuweiba resembles a younger version of Dahab: a town with no inherent appeal or style that happens to be blessed with a cheap, carefree Bedouin camp and a great beach (complete with its own friendly dolphin; see **A Tale of Two Dolphins,** p. 191). Nuweiba's importance rests primarily on its role in interstate travel: a ferry shuttles tourists and workers to **Aqaba, Jordan** (see p. 490). Its proximity to Israel and former popularity with Israeli tourists means that Nuweiba has suffered a more severe decline in trade from recent regional unrest than any other Gulf of Aqaba resort city. Aside from Dolphin Beach, you are not likely to encounter many other travelers in the area.

E TRANSPORTATION. Nuweiba, named after the Bedouin tribe whose territory reaches Taba, is divided into a **port** and a **city.** The city lies 10km to the north of the port; a taxi between the two costs E£10. **Ferries** to Aqaba, Jordan leave from the port. The **bus stop** is in the port, in front of the post office. **Buses** are supposed to leave daily to: Cairo (6hr., 10am and 3pm, E£50); Sharm al-Sheikh (2½hr., 6:30am and 3:30pm, E£15) via Dahab (1½hr., E£10); St. Catherine's (6:30am, E£15); Suez (7hr., 7am, E£25); and Taba (1hr., 6am and noon, E£10). Reality is more complicated, and since there is rarely anyone on duty at the station, you'll have to arrive early and ask around.

▓▐ ORIENTATION AND PRACTICAL INFORMATION. For credit card cash advances, use the **Banque du Caire** in the Hilton Hotel. (Open Su-Th 9:30am-noon and 6-9pm.) Across the street from the bus station in the port is **Banque Misr,** with a MC/V **ATM.** Most stores are in either the **new** or the **old commercial center**—both of which are in the city, neither one larger than a few blocks. The new center is near the Helnan International Hotel; the old is north, closer to Tarabin. Both have **supermarkets,** but the old center keeps longer hours. A **newsstand** next to Dr. Shishkebab in the old center has English-language newspapers, international telephone service, and mostly accurate bus schedule information available. Next to the Helnan stands the **tourist police** (☎50 02 31). The old center also houses the **Nuweiba Pharmacy.** (☎50 06 05. Open 24hr.) Across the street from the old center and clustered around the communications antenna are a handful of other services: The **hospital** is inferior to Israeli health care just over the border, but it's there if you need it. (☎50 03 02. Open 24hr.) The **telephone office** is open 24hr. The **post office** has **Poste Restante** and **EMS.** (☎50 02 44. Open daily 8am-3pm.)

▐▐ ACCOMMODATIONS AND FOOD. Budget travelers are better off staying in nearby Tarabin. The camps are cheaper and more plentiful, the restaurants closer to the beach, and the landscape unmarred by socialist buildings. The only budget accommodation in Nuweiba city is **al-Waha Village,** 500m south of the Helnan, which sports garden shed-style bungalows. (☎50 04 21; fax 50 04 20. Breakfast E£10. Singles E£25; doubles E£35; triples E£45; camping E£8 per person.) The **Helnan International Hotel,** near the old commercial center, offers relatively cheap rooms with access to a private beach. (☎50 04 01. Breakfast included. Single huts E£46; double huts E£62; triple huts E£78. Pitch your own tent for E£15.)

Dr. Shishkebab, in the old commercial center, has the best budget meals in the city. (☎50 02 73. Sandwiches E£3-4. Meat entrees E£15-25. Veg. dishes E£3-5. Open daily 10am-1am.) **'Ali Baba,** around the corner from Dr. Shishkebab, serves up meat dishes for E£12-15. (Open daily 9am-midnight.) Also around the corner, the bakery **Sugar** has pastries for E£1-2.

A TALE OF TWO DOLPHINS Uleen is one of 12 dolphins in the world that have chosen to live and play with humans. The competing versions of this fish tale are like fatuous episodes of *Flipper*. One story is that in 1994, Awda, a Bedouin fisherman, noticed that Uleen's mother was beached on the shore. Attempting to save her, Awda pulled the dolphin back into the water; but she didn't survive the transition. The next day, Uleen followed Awda and his deaf-mute brother, Abdullah (who could only make one sound: "Uleen"), on their daily fishing trip. Abdullah jumped into the water to swim with her, forging a bond that neither would soon forget. Another version has it that Uleen's male companion was caught in a net and shot by soldiers who mistook him for a shark. Grief-stricken, the lovelorn female lay crying in the water while Abdullah stroked her silvery skin to calm her—again, forging that special interspecies bond. Scientists assign more, well, scientific reasons to her behavior: she was ejected from her pod (perhaps due to some illness or weakness) and sought social interaction, which she eventually found with humans. Whatever the explanation, Uleen has not left the vicinity of the beach, where visitors swim with her every day.

◪ SIGHTS AND SAFARIS. Nuweiba's most rewarding sight is **Dolphin Beach,** named for the friendly dolphin who lives there (see **A Tale of Two Dolphins,** p. 191). Dolphin Beach is a 20min. walk south of Nuweiba Port or a E£5 taxi ride. Tell your driver "Dolphin." Bedouin will charge you E£10 to swim, and another E£10 for mask, snorkel, and fins. The beach is open until 6pm.

Nuweiba is an excellent starting point for **camel** or **jeep safaris** through the desert terrain. All camps in Tarabin either offer their own trips or can refer you to someone else's. It generally costs E£40-50 to go to the Colored Canyon. Camel tours of the interior are in the range of E£80-100 per day; 4WD tours are about E£20 per day less. You may save E£10-15 per day by dealing directly with a guide—look for one at Tarabin if none approach you. Guides here are generally trustworthy. Desert trips require a **permit,** achieved by some mysterious passport fermentation process at your friendly neighborhood police station (your guide will take care of it for you). Tour prices always include food but not necessarily **water.** The price of water rises dramatically during the safari, so start with a large supply.

◪ SCUBA DIVING. Like all towns on the Sinai coast, Nuweiba is surrounded by beautiful coral reefs, but unlike Dahab, Na'ama Bay, and Sharm al-Sheikh, there are only three dive clubs on Nuweiba's shores. **Emperor Divers,** in the Hilton Hotel, opened in 2000. (☎52 03 20 or 52 03 21, ext. 900. Two suited dives with full equipment and transport US$70. PADI O/W training and certification around US$325. Open daily 8am-6pm.) **Diving Camp Nuweiba** is in the Helnan Hotel. (☎50 04 02. 2 dives with vehicular transport US$60, with boat US$65; introductory dives US$45. O/W training US$325. Open 10am-6pm.) Divers can arrange trips to Ras Abu Galum through either center. **Sinai Dolphin Divers** is in the Nakim Inn. (☎50 08 79; sinaidolphin@yahoo.com. Dives with full equipment and transport US$40.)

NEAR NUWEIBA: THE ROAD TO TABA

The 70km stretch between Nuweiba and Taba—the main point by which you can cross into Israel (see **Border Crossings,** p. 74)—is one of the most magnificent parts of the Sinai: mountains tumble to the sea, reefs and sand turn the water a magnificent shade of turquoise, and the peaks of Saudi Arabia tower in the distance. Unfortunately, the view will soon be ruined by the five-star resorts that are popping up like weeds along this beautiful stretch. The coastline is dotted with **Bedouin camps,** which are accessible by bus or *service* from Taba or Nuweiba. East Delta buses leave Taba for Nuweiba at 9am and 3pm (1hr., E£10). Drivers may not know the names of some camps, so keep your eyes peeled for signs. The camps follow a standard layout: a couple of huts, a central lounge, and a restaurant. Some huts do not have electricity (and those that are electrified rely on sputtering generators), so bring a flashlight. It's quiet out here: people spend the days reading and swimming, while night brings on backgammon, stargazing, shagging like rabbits, and all that good stuff.

TARABIN طربين

*Taxi drivers try to extort a completely unjustified E£10 from Nuweiba to Tarabin and E£20 from the port. If you bargain, they may accept as little as ¼ of the asking price. To **walk** from Tarabin to Nuweiba, simply follow the road south. When you see Dr. Shishkebab on your left, you're in the old center.*

Within spitting distance of Nuweiba, Tarabin is a miniature Dahab in spirit. Unlike Dahab, however, Tarabin actually has a beach, and the water is warm and clean. There is only one road, and camps, restaurants, and bazaars line the shore. At present, very few people stay here, and Bedouin children far outnumber foreigners at the beach. Except for the drug-smuggling 4WDs that occasionally speed by at night, there is little to detract from the stunning natural scenery. The quality of the huts varies little from camp to camp. Most charge E£10-15 and have their own Bedouin-style restaurant. Muhammad, who runs **Carmina Camp** at the southern end of town, will make you feel right at home. The cafe here is one of the better restaurants in Tarabin. (☎50 04 77. Two-person huts E£20 for one night, E£15 per night for two nights or more.) **Blue Bus Camp** is the only place with a remnant of a social scene, likely due to the free camping on the beach. It also has a popular restaurant. (Single huts E£10; double huts E£20.) **Soft Beach,** at the southern end of the village, is a quiet place right on the beach. (Single huts E£10; double huts E£15.) A few of the camps have **supermarkets** attached. A cheaper supermarket option, north of the main cluster of camps, is **Safari,** which has a limited selection but boasts a computer with **Internet access.** (E£20 per hr. Open daily 8am-10pm.)

BEACH CAMPS

Some of the most beautiful camps lie 10-15km north of Nuweiba. All camps should cost E£10-20 per person per night. Prices go down the longer you stay, the larger your party, and the fewer the people already staying there. Always **bargain;** camps will probably take less than the prices quoted here. All accommodations are fairly basic, with few amenities to distract you from the neighboring natural splendors. **Magana Beach,** a Bedouin camp near colorful rock formations 10km north of Nuweiba, has reefs and a restaurant. **Devil's Head** *(Ras Shaytan)*, named for a rock formation 3km north of Magana, contains four camps. The southernmost, **Moon Island,** is the most simple and secluded. (Bamboo hut singles E£20; doubles E£40; triples E£50.) Moving north, the second and fourth camps have more huts. Farther north, and close to the Basata camp, the ritzy **Bawaki** has a few budget-priced, non-air-conditioned sheds for US$20 (including use of the pool).

BASATA بسطة

Basata means "simplicity" in Arabic, and this environmentally conscious camp midway between Nuweiba and Taba is unlike anything you will encounter on the Sinai coast—a gorgeous place you can enjoy without pangs of ecological guilt. Glass, metal, and plastic are all recycled, water is desalinated, organic trash is used as livestock feed, and there are plans to have electricity generated by solar panels. Owner Sharif Ghamrawi cultivates a family-oriented atmosphere with communal dinners, a comfy common area, and lots of **rules:** no nudity, no drugs or alcohol, no sleeping in the common area, and no dirty dishes. A vegetarian (E£20) or fish (E£25) **meal** is prepared every evening, though you can save money by cooking for yourself. The kitchen runs on trust: take what you want and write down what you take. All prices are subject to a 10% tax. Sharif also organizes **tours** by camel (E£75 per day) and jeep (E£60). At the moment, huts are almost always available, but make reservations just in case. (☎ 069 50 04 81. Camping E£18; bamboo hut singles E£40; doubles E£56.)

Between Basata and Taba is a remote and beautiful spot called the **Fjord,** where a small inlet cuts into the steep hills. The **Salima Restaurant and Camp** is right off the highway on a small ledge overlooking the sleepy bay. There are a few rooms crammed between the restaurant and the rock slope behind it. (☎ 069 53 01 30. E£25 per person). **Camping** is also available on the beach.

PHARAOH'S ISLAND

Ferry to the island E£15, JD25 from Aqaba. Castle admission E£20, students E£10. Taxis from the ferry terminal to Taba cost E£20.

The rocky outcrop of Pharaoh's Island (called Gezirat Fara'un by Egyptians, Coral Island by Israelis), 8km south of the Taba border crossing, holds the ruins of a Crusader castle built around 1115 CE. Salah al-Din took the fortress in 1171 but abandoned it in 1183 after European counterattacks. The ruins have towers and passageways as well as a large water cistern. En route to the island, the view of Sinai from the castle is ruined by the five-star Salah al-Din Hotel (the best view is from the mainland). The coral reef formations off the northeastern tip of the island draw divers and snorkelers, but neither the reefs nor the wildlife compares to that of the lower Sinai. Meals on the island are overpriced and often unavailable when few other tourists are around.

SUES السويس

One of the most ambitious feats of engineering ever attempted, the Suez Canal was once just a glimmer in the eye of Napoleon Bonaparte, who considered digging a canal between the Mediterranean and the Red Sea but feared that the waters of the latter were too high. Years later, another Frenchman, Ferdinand de Lesseps, persuaded Sa'id Pasha (the *khedive* of Egypt) to give the idea a shot. Excavation started on April 25, 1859, and took 10 years to complete. On August 18, 1869, the canal was opened in a grand ceremony attended by over 6000 dignitaries.

Spanning 195km and reaching a maximum depth of 15m, the canal connects Port Said on the Mediterranean to Suez on the Red Sea. The average transit time for ships through the canal is 15hr. Because it allowed for rapid travel from Europe to the Indian Ocean, the canal became a crucial element in the infrastructure of the British Empire. Nasser nationalized the canal in 1956, precipitating a British-French-Israeli invasion (to read more about the **Suez Crisis** and the rise of **Pan-Arabism,** see p. 67). During the 1967 Six Day War with Israel, Nasser blocked the canal with sunken ships. It remained closed through the 1973 Yom Kippur War and was finally cleared and reopened in 1975.

PORT SAID بور سعيد ☎ 048

Founded in 1860 upon the start of the Suez Canal's construction, Port Said *(Bor Sa'id)* became Africa's gateway to the Mediterranean once the canal was finished. Since the city was declared a tax-free zone in 1976, Port Said has developed into a shopping resort for Egyptians cashing in on duty-free deals. The main streets are saturated with clothing stores fronting styles (mercifully) unseen in the West since the '70s, while the scene near the waterfront faintly reflects the days when even the most hedonistic of sailors could get more than his fill of hashish and prostitutes. Port Said doesn't really come alive until nighttime, when everyone takes to the streets to window shop and enjoy the cool breeze and twinkling lights of the canal. The men of Port Said are well-known for their politeness, and women here (at least, those who are not prostitutes) will experience noticeably less harassment than in other parts of Egypt

📧 TRANSPORTATION

Trains: The **station** is on Mustafa Kamal St., 500m from the southwest end of al-Gomhoriyya St. Trains run to **Cairo** (4½hr.; 6, 8am, 7:30pm; 2nd-class E£14) and **Suez** via **Isma'ilia** (1¾hr., 2nd-class E£6).

Buses: The **East Delta** bus depot is on Salah al-Din St., on the northern side of Ferial Gardens, 2 blocks west of al-Gomhoriyya St. Daily buses to: **Alexandria** (4hr.; 7, 9am, 2:30, 4:30pm; E£15-20); **Cairo** (2hr., every hr. 6am-7pm, E£12-15); **Suez** (6, 10am, 1, 4pm; E£7.50). The **Superjet** depot is next to the train station on Mustafa Kamal St., also with daily buses to **Alexandria** (8:30pm, E£22) and **Cairo** (10 per day 7am-7pm, E£15). A 3rd station is on al-Nasr St. (ask for "Mubarak"), with buses to **Isma'ilia** (1½hr., every hr. 6am-7pm, E£4).

Service: Near the train station and the Superjet depot. Ask for *"taxi ugra."*

Bike Rental: Bikes are a great way to get around the city. Rent them on the south side of Hafiz Ibrahim St., between Palestine and al-Gomhoriyya St. E£5 per hr.

🔆🛈 ORIENTATION AND PRACTICAL INFORMATION

Port Said is 343km east of Alexandria and 220km northeast of Cairo. The town is surrounded by water on three sides: the Mediterranean to the north, the Suez Canal to the east, and **Lake Manzala** to the south. The point at which the canal meets the Mediterranean is Port Said's northeastern corner. **Atef al-Sadat St.** runs along the sea, and **Palestine St.** follows the edge of the canal. **Memphis St.** and **al-Gomhoriyya St.**, one and two blocks inland, respectively, run parallel to Palestine St. Another important thoroughfare, three blocks inland, is **23 July St.**, which runs parallel to Atef al-Sadat St.

Tourist Office: 5 Palestine St. (☎23 52 89), 2 blocks from the south end of the street. Gives out a good map, and information about restaurants, hotels, and sights in the area. Open Sa-Th 9am-2pm. Another branch at the **train station** keeps similar hours.

Currency Exchange: Small offices abound. The most convenient is **Thomas Cook,** 43 al-Gomhoriyya St. (☎33 62 60; fax 23 61 11). Open daily 8am-5pm. **ATM** at Banque Misr, 30 al-Gomhoriyya St.

American Express: 83 al-Gomhoriyya St. (☎23 98 31), across from al-Salaam Mosque. Cash advances and traveler's check exchange. Open daily 10am-4pm.

Emergency: Ambulance: ☎123. **Police:** ☎122.

Tourist Police: (☎22 85 70). Stationed on the 5th fl. of the abandoned post office building on al-Gomhoriyya St.

Pharmacy: Hussein (☎33 98 88; fax 33 97 77), on al-Gomhoriyya St., a block south of Muhammad Mahmoud St. Open daily 9am-midnight. Many other pharmacies also line al-Gomhoriyya St.

Hospital: Delivrand (☎22 36 63 or 22 56 95), on al-Shaid al-Gaya St.

Telephones: (☎22 01 66; fax 32 57 05), 2 blocks north of the tourist office on Palestine St. Phone cards available for E£15, E£20, and E£30. Direct international dialing (E£10.50 per 3min. to the US). Open 24hr.

Internet Access: Internet and Information Club, on al-Gomhoriyya St. Entrance next door to Popeye Restaurant, 3rd fl. US$3 or E£ equivalent for 1hr.

Post Office: In the southeast corner of the Ferial Gardens, at the intersection of Muhammad Mahmoud St. and al-Geish St. For **Poste Restante,** take the 1st left south of the post office and walk 30m. Both open Sa-Th 8am-5pm.

🏠 ACCOMMODATIONS

Most accommodations in town are either on or near **al-Gomhoriyya St.** There are many mid-range and luxury hotels, but super-cheap hotels are hard to come by, especially near the beach.

EGYPT

Port Said

▲ ACCOMMODATIONS
Akri Palace Hotel, 8
Hotel Delaposte, 5
Youth Hostel, 2

★ FOOD
El-Borg Restaurant, 1
Gionala Restaurant, 7
Lord's Pastry, 3
Popeye Restaurant, 6

● SERVICES
Delirand Hospital, 4
Service Station, 9

TO ALEXANDRIA (343km)

Port Said Stadium

Muhammad al-Sayed Sirhan St.

Nabeh St.
Beni Swef St.
El Minia St.
Aswan St.
El Giza St.
El Dakhlia St.
El Gory St.
El Roda St.
Hamed El Alfy St.
Abu El Hassan St.
Nabil Mansor St.
Shohada St.

Sabah St.
Nasr St.
Ismail St.
Salam St.

Buses to Isma'ilia

23 July St.

Sa'ad Zaghloul Garden

Fahmy El Nokrashy St.
Sa'ad Zaghloul St.
Ahmed Maher St.
Mohamed Farid St.
Safia Zaghloul St.

Al-Nasr St.

Military Museum

Atef al-Sadat St.

Mediterranean Sea

TO CAIRO (220km)

Superjet

Al-Nahda St.

Oraby St.

Memorial Monument

Salah Salem St.
Salah al-Din St.
Ramses St.
El-Geish St.

Mustafa Kamel St.

Muhammad Mahmoud St.

Tourist Police
West Delta Bus Company

Ferial Gardens

Al-Gomhoriyya St.
Memphis St.
Palestine St.

Hafiz Ibrahim St.

Sedke St.

American Express

Thomas Cook
Port Said National Museum

Palace Gardens

Al-Salaam

TO PORT FOUAD

PORT FOUAD

Suez Canal

N

0   300 yards
0   400 meters

Youth Hostel (HI) (☎ 22 87 02), on Muhammad al-Sayyid Sirhan St. opposite the stadium. Your only budget option if you want to roll out of bed and onto the beach every morning. Modern and sterile. Large bathrooms. Fans. 20min. walk or E£2 taxi ride from the town center. Breakfast included. 6-bed dorm E£17.50; nonmembers E£1 extra.

Akri Palace Hotel, 24 al-Gomhoriyya St. (☎ 22 10 13). 2 blocks from the south end of the street. Owned by the friendly Greek Nicolandis brothers. A 19th-century elevator transports you to charming but run-down rooms, with high ceilings, wood floors, sinks, and desks. Ask to see what you're getting before bedding down. Balcony doors provide a nice breeze. Singles E£13; doubles E£26; triples E£31; add E£10 for private bath.

Hotel Delaposte, 42 al-Gomhoriyya St. (☎ 22 96 55 or 22 40 48). Look for the English "Hotel" sign, next door to a pastry shop. Deserves its 2 stars for rooms with private baths, TV, and fridge. Singles E£38; doubles E£47; triples E£53; with A/C add E£14.

🍴 FOOD

🖼 **Lord's Pastry** (☎ 23 52 02), just south of the intersection of al-Gomhoriyya and 23 July St. You'll thank your sweet Lord for the sweets. Friendly staff. Pastries E£1.25.

Popeye Restaurant (☎ 23 94 94), on the corner of al-Gomhoriyya and Safia Zaghloul St. Your deck may be pooped after a long day shopping or swimming, but you'll be strong to the finish after a meal here. Zesty chicken kebab E£17. Banana splits E£5.70. No spinach. Open daily 8am-midnight. MC/V.

Gionala Restaurant, 15 al-Gomhoriyya St. (☎ 24 00 01). Across Safia Zaghloul St. from Popeye. Clean, sophisticated setting. Pasta E£11-15. Fish and meat dishes E£20-35. Generous sandwiches E£4-14. Open daily 8am-2am.

Al-Borg (☎ 32 34 42), on the beachside corniche. A local favorite for fresh seafood. Full meals around E£30. Open 24hr.

👁 SIGHTS

PORT SAID NATIONAL MUSEUM. This museum houses a fine collection of items from all periods of Egyptian history, ranging from exquisite mummy cases to Coptic icons and Qur'anic calligraphy. See the carriage from which Khedive Isma'il presided over the 1869 opening of the canal. With labels alongside each of the artifacts, not to mention air-conditioning, this museum is a must-see. (*At the northern end of Palestine St.* ☎ *23 74 19. Open Sa-Th 9am-5pm, F 9am-noon and 2-5pm; Ramadan 8:30am-1pm. E£12, students E£6. Camera privileges E£10, video E£20.*)

OTHER SIGHTS AND EXCURSIONS. Free **ferries** to Port Fouad leave every few minutes from the southern tip of Palestine St. The shell-covered **beach,** cleaner and quieter than Port Said's, lies along the Mediterranean shore to the north. Beach umbrellas can be rented for E£3 per day, and showers are every 100m. If the words "duty-free" make your wallet tremble, **shopping arcades** stretch three blocks inland from Palestine St. For more affordable goods, hop on a minibus (25pt) and ask to be taken to **al-Souq al-Togary** farther inland. Here you'll find street after street of local merchants with cheap clothing, fabric, shoes, and other goods.

SUEZ CITY السويس ☎ 062

Suez (al-Suweis) sits at the junction of the Red Sea and the Suez Canal. Besides counting the unnatural number of dead cats by the roadside, there's not much to see or do here. The young men of Suez are prolific marijuana smokers, and they don't seem to care who knows it. There are, nevertheless, some ways to kill a few hours between buses. **Port Tawfiq** provides an excellent perch from which to watch the canal at work, and it's probably the only place you can dangle your toes in the canal waters. A promenade running parallel to the Suez-Port Tawfiq road provides a great view of the Suez bay and is a good place to meet the exceptionally friendly locals, many of whom will offer you a joint as a sign of their goodwill. (*Let's Go* does not recommend going to jail.)

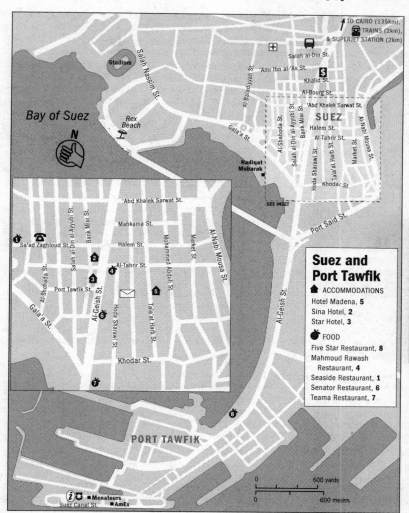

Suez and Port Tawfik

▲ ACCOMMODATIONS
Hotel Madena, **5**
Sina Hotel, **2**
Star Hotel, **3**

🍊 FOOD
Five Star Restaurant, **8**
Mahmoud Rawash
  Restaurant, **4**
Seaside Restaurant, **1**
Senator Restaurant, **6**
Teama Restaurant, **7**

EGYPT

Most travelers pass through Suez en route from Cairo to the Sinai by way of the **Ahmed Hamdi Tunnel** (which runs under the canal 17km north of town), or on their way south along the Red Sea coast. Others stay a few days looking for passage on a boat at the Yacht Club. Nearby **'Ain Sukhna** is downright spectacular; its proximity to Cairo provides a convenient sun-swim-snorkel option.

▢ TRANSPORTATION

Buses: There are two bus stations around al-Geish St. in the north part of town. Both stations are easily accessible by **minibus.**

East Delta Bus Station: On Salah al-Din St., 1 block west of al-Geish St. Buses leave to: **'Ain Sukhna** (1hr.; 6:30, 7:30, 8:30, 10, 11am, noon, 1, 2pm; E£2); **Alexandria** (5hr., 7am and 2:30pm, E£23); **Cairo** (2hr., every 30min. 6am-8pm, E£7); **Isma'ilia** (1¼hr., every 30min. 6am-4pm, E£4); **Port Said** (3hr.; 7, 9, 10:30am, 3:30pm; E£9). Reserve tickets to Alexandria a few days in advance. Suez is also the main launching ground for forays into the Sinai. Buses leave for: **Dahab** (7hr., 11am, E£30); **Nuweiba** (11am, 1, 5pm; E£29); **Sharm al-Sheikh** (6hr.; 8,

11am, 1:30, 3, 5, 6pm; E£20); **St. Catherine's** (2pm, E£20); **Taba** (3pm, E£25); **'Uyoun Musa** (8, 11am, 1:30, 2, 3, 5, 6pm; E£6).

Superjet Bus Station: 2km north, near the train station. Buses go to **Hurghada** (6hr., 8 per day until 10pm, E£22) and **Upper Egypt.** Reserve tickets to Hurghada a few days in advance.

Service: *Service* travel to most of the destinations reached by bus (except Alexandria) at similar prices: **Cairo** (E£7); **Hurghada** (E£22); **Isma'ilia** (E£4); **Port Said** (E£7). *Service* don't go to the Sinai, and **private taxis** are generally prohibitively expensive.

Minibus: For transport within the city, flag down a blue **minibus** and see if it's headed your way. Common destinations include: Port Tawfiq, the East Delta bus station, the Superjet bus station, and the train station. A flat fare of 25pt gets you anywhere. A few drivers may try to claim that you're destination is "special" and overcharge, but most are very honest and will help you find another minibus if theirs is going somewhere else.

✴🛈 ORIENTATION AND PRACTICAL INFORMATION

Al-Geish St. runs roughly north-south through the center of Suez, from the **bus stations** all the way down to **Port Tawfiq,** where the **tourist office** stands at the westernmost end of town. The tourist office is one of the most knowledgeable and helpful in Egypt and provides a map of Suez and Port Tawfiq, plus a useful listing of local restaurants, sights, and services. (☎33 11 41 or 33 11 42. Open daily 8am-8pm.) **Banque Misr,** at the intersection of 'Amr ibn al-'As and al-Geish, has an **ATM** that accepts MC and V. (☎22 05 71. Open Su-Th 9am-3pm.) **American Express** services are available for all travelers at Menatours (☎22 88 21), next to the tourist office in Port Tawfiq. The **tourist police** (☎33 11 40) share a building with the tourist office. Suez's main house of medicine is the **General Suez Hospital** (☎33 11 89), just west of the East Delta bus station. The **telephone office** is about three blocks west of al-Geish St., on the corner of Shohada'a St. and Sa'ad Zaghloul St. (Open 24hr.) The **post office,** on Hoda Sharawi St., one block east of al-Geish St., offers **Poste Restante.** (☎22 39 17. Open Sa-Th 8am-3pm.)

🛏 ACCOMMODATIONS

Even if you're not planning to continue to the monasteries of St. Anthony and St. Paul, the budget hotels of Suez will give you a taste of the monks' ascetic lifestyle. The city's importance as a transportation hub means that even the grottiest hotel often has no vacancies. Single rooms in particular seem to be in short supply, so call ahead (all hotels listed here accept reservations).

Sina Hotel, 21 Banque Misr St. (☎33 41 81). A mirrored and gilded lobby and friendly management welcome travelers. Unsullied rooms sport fans and may have a balcony and 1-channel TV. Shared bathrooms have hot water. Many rooms are defective in some way (the fan doesn't work, the balcony door locks automatically behind you, etc.), so ask to see the room before signing off on it. Singles E£15; doubles E£26.

Star Hotel, 17 Banque Misr St. (☎22 87 37), 1 block south of the Sina. Large, clean rooms with turbo fans. Stellar showers and balconies. Singles or doubles E£20, with bath E£25; triples E£30, with bath E£35.

Hotel Madena (☎22 40 56). Walk 3 blocks east on Tahrir St., take a right, and proceed to the next street; the hotel is on the left. Rooms are bare and tiny, but functional and decently priced. Singles E£13, with bath E£18; doubles E£26, with bath E£30.

🍴 FOOD

Eating cheaply is no problem in Suez. There's a good **fruit market** near the East Delta bus station. Near the intersection of al-Geish and Tahrir St., there are sandwich stands, small bakeries, and vendors selling kebab and roast chicken. Some recent additions have bolstered the city's formerly meager middle-range options.

Senator Restaurant (☎ 34 87 35), on al-Geish St., 2 blocks south of Tahrir St. The best of the new joints. Slick exterior. The food is high quality and reasonably priced. Thick-crust pizza E£7-14. Pasta E£7-10. Seafood E£15-25.

Mahmoud Rawash Restaurant, on Tahrir St. just off al-Geish St. Sandwiches 25pt.

Seaside Restaurant (☎ 22 32 54), 1 block west of the telephone office on Sa'ad Zaghloul St. Seating in an A/C interior (with satellite TV) and on a rooftop terrace. Sandwiches E£2. Grilled fish and shrimp E£25.

Teama Restaurant (☎ 34 14 90), next to the Renaissance Cinema toward Port Tawfiq on al-Geish St. Outdoor cafe with basic Egyptian food. Kebab E£18. Salads E£3-5.

Five Star Restaurant, on al-Geish St. in Port Tawfiq. Neither 5 stars nor a restaurant, but they do have desserts (E£1.50) to snack on while watching the ships roll in.

👁 🎵 SIGHTS AND ENTERTAINMENT

If you get stuck here for any length of time, there are few sites to keep you entertained. **Hadiqat Mubarak,** on the corniche, displays American-made Israeli tanks captured in 1973 and other military vehicles. The dirty water from the many ships at **Rex Beach,** in town near the stadium, isn't very regal, but the beach at **'Ain Sukhna** (Hot Spring), 60km south along the Red Sea, rivals those of the Sinai. **Buses** go there early in the day (1hr.; 6:30, 7:30, 8:30, 10, 11am, noon, 1, 2pm; E£2) and return about 1½ hours later. The hot spring (35°C), originating in the Ataka Mountains, empties out onto a gorgeous sandy beach. Get off the bus when you see the large green-and-white sign for the **'Ain Sukhna Hotel** (☎ 32 84 88). Daytrippers can pay the hotel a E£15 fee for chairs and umbrellas if they only plan to visually enjoy the crystal-clear water, though the mouth of the hot spring is also available for prolonged soaks. The hotel offers an expensive but incredible fish, salad, and hummus meal (E£30). It's not just the best choice, it's the only choice—bring your own food if you'd rather not put your money where your mouth is.

MONASTERIES OF ST. ANTHONY & PAUL

These centers of faith, dating from the early Christian monastic tradition, are inhabited by monks whose austere lifestyle has changed remarkably little over the past 16 centuries. They warmly welcome visitors, and some speak excellent English. While a few hours suffice to see the monasteries, spending the night can be transcendent (although you'll need a letter of recommendation). Men and women of any religious persuasion can stay in the dorms at both St. Anthony's and St. Paul's. The monasteries are not tourist attractions; rather, they are functioning centers of worship where most guests take religion seriously, so be prepared to field questions about your own beliefs. The monks provide water and generous portions of food (simple fare from their own gardens and orchards). There is no charge, but donations are welcome (even the most ascetic life requires some financing) though not actively solicited.

▇ TRANSPORTATION

Reaching the monasteries is a serious endeavor without a car, since no organized tours go there. Plenty of patience and water are required, as travelers are completely dependent upon **pilgrims** for transportation. Of the two possible options for getting to the monasteries, the safer and more hassle-free is to contact the **monasteries' administration offices** in Cairo and ask when local Coptic churches are planning pilgrimages to the monasteries so you can tag along. A group may be leaving as soon as tomorrow or as late as a month from next Sunday. (St. Paul's ☎ 02 590 02 18; St. Anthony's 02 590 60 25. Call daily 10am-noon or 8:30-9:30pm.)

The less desirable option is to take public transportation as far as you can. The closest stop to St. Paul's (12km from the monastery) from a Hurghada-bound bus from Suez is by the **St. Bola sign,** near a road running directly to the monastery. Pilgrimage groups have been known to pick up travelers along the way and take them to the monasteries and back. Although pilgrims tend to be friendly, catching a ride can be difficult. Hitchhiking, especially in the desert, is an inherently risky proposition, and *Let's Go* does not recommend it.

⚡🛈 ORIENTATION AND PRACTICAL INFORMATION

The isolated monasteries of St. Anthony and St. Paul lie 30km apart (84km by road), near the Red Sea. You must have a **letter of recommendation** from the administration office in Cairo (see below) to stay overnight at either of the two monasteries, though the monks certainly won't make you spend the night in the desert if you straggle in late in the day without a way back to where you came from. Both monasteries are open daily 9am-5pm.

👁 MONASTERIES

ST. ANTHONY'S MONASTERY

St. Anthony was raised in the Nile Valley in the 4th century CE and became the first famous ascetic of the Christian Church when he scorned worldly concerns and retreated into the Eastern Desert. Anthony's dramatic move reflected the restlessness that overtook some Christians after Constantine made Christianity the official religion of the Roman Empire—a disturbing development for those who felt that the church had gained worldly security and wealth at the expense of its spiritual focus. In Egypt, some of these Christians (mostly educated upper-class men) sought to escape the secular world by retreating into the desert where they could pray in solitude and render their lives unto God rather than Caesar.

St. Anthony was victimized by his own success: his desert hermitages became popular pilgrimage sites, and crowds of the pious and the curious deprived the recluse of precious penitent isolation. Frustrated in his quest for solitude, St. Anthony came up with the solution of organizing his most persistent followers into a loose-knit group that prayed and ate together once a week, creating the model followed by many Orthodox monasteries to this day. Soon after the saint's death, his disciple St. Athanasius told the story of St. Anthony's choice of poverty and hardship, his wild battles with demons, and his wise counsel to monks and laymen. Athanasius's *Life of Anthony* became the prototype for much of later Christian hagiography (biographies of saints). Around the same time, Anthony's followers settled at the present site and established the first Christian monastery. The Monastery of St. Anthony served as a refuge for some of the monks of Wadi Natrun when their own sanctuaries were attacked by the Bedouin in the 6th century. During the 7th and 8th centuries, the monastery was occupied by Melkite monks, and in the 11th century it was pillaged by the army of Nasser al-Dawla. About 100 years after the sacking, it was restored and transferred to Coptic hands.

The **Church of St. Anthony** and the monastery's southern walls are the only remains predating the 16th-century construction of the present monastery. With ancient frescoes embellishing each of their sections, Anthony's church and its small chapel are the most impressive parts of the monastery. The monks are still awaiting permission from Orthodox Pope Shenouda III before the church can be consecrated and opened to visitors. Inquire at the Cairo office if this fortuitous event has occurred. East of the Church of St. Anthony is the **Church of the Apostles.** Like other early Coptic churches, it is divided into three sections, the closest to the altar reserved for the baptized who can receive communion, the farthest for transgressors, and the middle for those falling somewhere in between. Morbid visitors will appreciate the glass-encased remains of an early 19th-century bishop to the right of the altar. The monks claim his body lies perfectly preserved, though a cloak precludes verification. During Lent, the monks cantillate the liturgy in the 18th-century **Church of St. Mark.** The **Chapel of St. Michael** is on the top floor of the keep. The extensive **library** contains more than 1700 manuscripts.

The major religious attraction in the vicinity of the church is the **Cave of St. Anthony,** where the ascetic himself is said to have lived. The vista from the cave, 276m above sea level, rewards the requisite 45min. of hoofing and huffing. Before entering the fissure, remove your shoes or risk offending nearby Copts. Inside, a small nook at the end of the cave is stuffed with written supplications for divine assistance. The best time to start the climb is when the sun is low (before 7am or after 4pm). Try to return before dark and bring a bottle of water. The **spring** at which St. Anthony drank resurfaces within the monastery and still delivers a healthy 100 cu. m of water daily. A monk will unlock the gate built around it and allow you to taste the water—it's safe to drink. St. Anthony's also has several **shops**—a snack shop selling soda and cookies, a bookstore, and a gift shop.

ST. PAUL'S MONASTERY

St. Paul (not the Apostle) was born into an affluent Alexandrian family in the 3rd century CE. When his father died, he left his estate to young Paul and his brother. Naturally, this caused squabbling between the two, and when the family had heard enough, the brothers were sent off to consult with a judge. In the end, the two young men took separate routes. Paul happened to pass the funeral service of a wealthy man and was, for some reason, profoundly affected (why he wasn't so moved at his own father's funeral no one knows). Like St. Anthony, St. Paul cast off all worldly concerns and—guided by an angel—headed for the hills. He lived in a cave near Mt. Nemra and made his garments from palm leaves and branches. Legend has it that his strict diet of half a loaf of bread per day was dropped to him by a crow, and water came from a secret source high in the mountains. These divine provisions enabled St. Paul to live alone for over 80 years.

The original monastery was built on the cave site not long after St. Paul's death—probably before 400 CE. St. Paul's has been attacked by Bedouin throughout its history, most notably in 1484, when the churches were burned, the library destroyed, and all the monks killed. When the Bedouin left 80 years later, Coptic Patriarch Gabriel VII sent new monks to rebuild the churches, but the buildings were destroyed again. Finally, at the end of the 16th century, Patriarch Ioannis ordered St. Anthony's monks to reconstruct and inhabit St. Paul's. These monks built a five-story tower with a drawbridge leading to the fourth story. The first two floors of the tower were for food and water storage and allowed the monks to endure sieges of up to three months. The monastery was renovated in 1974 with few changes, aside from the addition of electrical generators and a guesthouse.

St. Paul's gets fewer visitors than its neighbor, and the monks are even friendlier to guests. The highlight of the monastery is the **Church of St. Paul,** built in the cave where the famed hermit dwelt. Many of the church's 4th- and 7th-century **frescoes** have somehow survived. Ostrich eggs symbolizing the Resurrection hang from the roof. Past the gardens, you can fill your Baraka bottles with holy water coming from the same secret source St. Paul depended on. If you're spending the night, you may be allowed to attend evening prayer, which is most interesting when a large group of pilgrims is in attendance. Amid thick clouds of incense, believers grasp and kiss icons paraded around the chapel by monks, as ancient chants are punctuated by the occasional ululating woman overtaken by religious fervor.

WHEN TONY MET PAULIE According to Christian lore, St. Anthony and St. Paul met in one dramatic encounter at the end of Paul's life. Wanting to reveal the holiness of St. Paul, God led St. Anthony to his cave. As the two conversed, Paul's crow dropped a whole loaf of bread for them (double what the bird usually brought). Paul, realizing that he was talking to another holy man, told Anthony that he was nearing death and made one final request: to wear the robe of Pope Athanasius. Anthony immediately departed to fetch the garment. On his return, he had a vision of angels carrying St. Paul's soul to heaven, and arrived at the cave to find Paul dead. While Anthony pondered what to do with the body, two lions descended from the mountain, mourned for their lifelong companion, and dug a grave. Anthony wrapped Paul in the papal robe and buried him. He then carried St. Paul's palm leaf garment back to Athanasius, who wore it every Christmas, Epiphany, and Easter.

HURGHADA الغردقة ☎ 065

The Red Sea near Hurghada ("al-Ghardaqa") is dotted with small islands and chains of coral reefs where schools of tropical fish swim through the sun-dappled, tranquil cobalt waters. Since the early 1980s, when peace with Israel opened Egypt to foreign investors and tourists, scores of resorts have sprung from the sands of Hurghada. The town continues to expand along the coast at a rapid pace that shows no signs of slowing down. The underwater splendors find their skewed counterparts on land in a profusion of tourist bazaars selling gaudy souvenir dreck to the foreign visitors who flock here for the superb diving and snorkeling.

▐ TRANSPORTATION

Flights: Hurghada Airport (☎ 44 28 31 or 44 37 94), 3km south of town and about 1.5km inland, is served by **EgyptAir**, with flights to **Cairo** (2 per day 8:50am and every evening at varying times, E£480) and **Sharm al-Sheikh** (M and F 10:40am, E£320). Tickets should be booked in advance through **Karnak Travel** (☎ 54 78 93), opposite the mosque on al-Nasser Rd. Open daily 8am-8pm.

Buses: Upper Egypt Bus Co. launches from al-Nasser Rd., 300m from the southern end of town. Buses to: **Alexandria** (10hr., 7pm, E£60); **Aswan** (7hr.; 10am, 3:30, 10:30pm, midnight; E£25-30); **Cairo** (6hr., 14 per day 8am-2am, E£35-50); **Luxor** (4hr.; 12:30, 1, 2:30, 9am, 1, 3:30, 7, 10:30pm; E£15-20); **Sharm al-Sheikh** (10hr., 9pm, E£65); **Suez** (5hr., 12 per day 10am-1:30am, E£21). Schedules vary with the seasons; consult the station for the most up-to-date timetable.

Ferries: To **Sharm al-Sheikh** from the "New" Harbor (1½hr.; M, Tu, Th, Sa 8am, returning at 6pm; US$40). Reserve at least one day in advance through a hotel manager, at the ferry office, or with **Sherif Travel** (☎ 54 51 47) near the Sand Beach Hotel.

Service: From Dahar, through Saqala, south to the resorts, and back (50pt-E£1). Al-Nasser Rd. and the corniche are the best places to catch one. **Intercity service taxis** congregate off al-Nasser Rd., beside the rotary just south of the telephone office, and go to: **Cairo** (5hr., E£30); **Qena** (2½hr., E£10); **Suez** (5hr., E£20).

Taxis: Local destinations E£5-15 depending on distance. Intercity private taxis can be found at the *service* taxi station. Prices are per car; it's best to form a group and bargain. Taxis travel to: **Cairo** (5hr., E£300); **Luxor** (4hr., E£200); **Suez** (4hr., E£200).

◪ ⁊ ORIENTATION AND PRACTICAL INFORMATION

Paved highways link Hurghada with other cities, but the town itself is remote. Suez lies 410km north at the end of the Gulf of Suez, and Cairo is another 130km west. Hurghada extends along the coast in a narrow strip. Downtown Hurghada (known as **Dahar**) lies 2km north of **Saqala**, the original fishing town out of which Hurghada grew. Buses and *service* arrive in Dahar, where budget hotels and restaurants await. Saqala has a more authentic Egyptian flavor with plenty of dive shops, cafes, and bars—but few budget hotels. South of Saqala, the five-star resorts preside over private beaches.

Al-Nasser Rd. begins inland from the coastal road and connects the town and harbor. Almost everything, from the passport office in the north to the bus station in the south, lies along a 2km stretch of this street. Smaller streets to the east of al-Nasser Rd. contain budget hotels, restaurants, tourist bazaars, and the **souq**, all separated from the sea by a sandy mound posing as al-Arish "mountain."

Tourist Office: (☎ 44 44 21; fax 44 44 20), just south of the airport on the corniche. From Dahar, get on a microbus headed towards Saqala and ask for Marine Kalab. The poshest tourist office in Egypt is on the right. Open Sa-Th 8am-8pm.

Passport Office: (☎ 54 67 27), on al-Nasser Rd. at the north edge of town, 2km from the bus station. Behind the Red Sea Security Dept. building. Provides visa extensions. Open daily Sa-Th 8am-2pm.

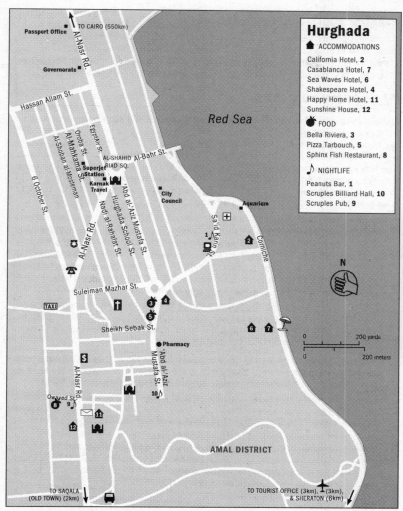

Hurghada

🏠 ACCOMMODATIONS

California Hotel, **2**
Casablanca Hotel, **7**
Sea Waves Hotel, **6**
Shakespeare Hotel, **4**
Happy Home Hotel, **11**
Sunshine House, **12**

🍅 FOOD

Bella Riviera, **3**
Pizza Tarbouch, **5**
Sphinx Fish Restaurant, **8**

♪ NIGHTLIFE

Peanuts Bar, **1**
Scruples Billiard Hall, **10**
Scruples Pub, **9**

E G Y P T

Currency Exchange: National Bank of Egypt, on al-Nasser Rd., 500m north of the bus station, changes traveler's checks and has an **ATM**. Open Su-Th 8:30am-2pm and 6-9pm. Next door, **Banque Misr** also changes money and has an **ATM** (MC/V, Cirrus, PLUS links). Open daily 8:30am-2pm and 3-9pm. **Thomas Cook** (☎54 18 71) is just past the bus station on al-Nasser St. Open 10am-2pm and 6-10pm.

Police: (☎54 67 23), on al-Nasser Rd., at a bend 900m north of the bus station. The **tourist police** (☎44 77 74) is past the telephone building on the left.

Pharmacy: Talat Pharmacy (☎54 43 14), on 'Abd al-'Aziz St. just past the Sherry Hand Restaurant. Open daily 10am-1am.

Hospital: General Hospital of Hurghada (☎54 67 40), on Sa'id Karin St., around the corner from Three Corners Empire Hotel. **Ambulance:** ☎54 64 90 or 54 67 40.

Telephones: Office on al-Nasser Rd., on the left after the road turns at the police station. Calls to US, Europe, and Australia: E£7 per min. Open 24hr. Send **faxes** from a hut across from the phone office (☎/fax 54 88 45). E£14-20 per page to the US or Europe. Open Sa-Th 8am-2pm and 8-10pm.

Internet Access: Prince Cafe (☎ 54 43 50), 1 block before the Three Corners Empire Hotel as you head towards the ocean on Sa'id Karin St. 2 computers in the back. E£8 per hr. Open daily 9am-11pm. **Malibu,** inside the tourist bazaar next to Peanuts Bar on Sa'id Karin St., has 4 computers. E£10 per hr. Open daily 10am-12:30am.

Post Office: On al-Nasser Rd., 300m north of the bus station, on the right. **Poste Restante, EMS,** and orange international **phones.** Open Sa-Th 8am-2pm.

📍 ACCOMMODATIONS

Hurghada is a piaster-pincher's paradise, but watch out for spontaneous price inflation, especially during peak season. Many of the cheaper hotels work with diving centers and get hefty commissions for the customers they bring. This either means that you'll be strongly encouraged to dive or snorkel or that you cannot stay in a hotel unless you book a trip through them. It is far more convenient to book through your own hotel than through another establishment, so look at hotels' trip prices before checking in. All hotels listed below have ceiling fans. In the summer it's a good idea to reserve a room in advance.

California Hotel (☎ 54 91 01). Friendly owner 'Abdul is justifiably proud of his hotel amd its cozy muraled rooms. Breakfast E£2.50. Singles E£10; doubles E£20, with bath and breakfast E£25; triples with breakfast E£30. California dreamin' on the roof E£5.

Sea Waves (☎ 54 50 71), across from the public beach. Take a right by the Golden Dolphin Dive Center. Clean rooms, shiny floors, and a cute cafe-style dining room. Breakfast E£2. Singles E£10; doubles E£20; triples E£30. Add E£5 for private bath.

Casablanca (☎ 54 82 92), on the corniche opposite the public beach. Enter through the side door of the Cowboy Restaurant and it'll be lookin' at you, kid. Some rooms have beautiful ocean-view balconies, but the private bathrooms have been known to smell. Guests get 20% discount at Cowboy, but some rooms hear the hee-hawing all night long. Singles E£10; doubles E£20; triples E£30.

Happy Home Hotel (☎ 54 96 11), on Mosque St. behind the post office. Amiable manager makes sure that his hotel, though not in the center of town, is where the heart is. Discounts at the building's diving center. Singles E£15; doubles E£30; triples E£45.

Sunshine Hotel (☎ 54 51 13), 2 blocks north of the bus station. Small hotel with a homey feel and well-maintained single-sex bathrooms in the hall. Friendly and knowledgeable Hassan arranges snorkeling (E£40-45) and dive (US$35-45) trips. Breakfast E£2.50. Singles E£10; doubles E£15; triples E£25.

Shakespeare Hotel (☎ 44 62 56), at the corner of 'Abd al-'Aziz Mustafa and Sa'id Karin-General Hospital St. Tangled in a copse of weather'd trees/This taintless inn entices families/Its fragrant garden sweetens as it blooms/As do the pink and private bathing rooms. Some rooms have A/C. Singles E£25; doubles E£35; triples E£45.

🍴 FOOD

In terms of grub, Hurghada is a veritable Little Italy. Other than the usual street fare, it appears that the only foods that have made their way to the coasts of the Red Sea migrated here from a boot-shaped peninsula in the Mediterranean.

▨ **Bella Riviera** (☎ 54 89 85), south of the Shakespeare Hotel on 'Abd al-'Aziz Mustafa St. One of Hurghada's best deals, with A/C to boot. Watch the waiters scamper in and out of the secret door in the wall. Cheap drinks, lasagna (E£4), salads (E£2-3), meat dishes (E£8-12), fish (E£10-40), and pizzas (E£12-25). Open daily 9am-1am.

▨ **Pizzeria Tarbosh** (☎ 54 84 56), on 'Abd al-'Aziz Mustafa St. past the Shakespeare Hotel. No relation to the fez-like hat. Owner 'Amir cooked pizza in Italy, and it shows in some of the best crusts in Egypt. Over 20 types of pizza served in generous personal pies (E£9-20). Special student menu: salads E£2.75; meat dishes E£8.

Sphinx Fish Restaurant, under Scruples bar on the corner of al-Nasser and Owayed St. (no English sign). This tiny eatery serves up great fish dinners complete with 2 whole fish, rice, and salad (E£10). Calamari dinners E£15.

Felfela (☎ 44 24 11), south of Saqala on Sheraton Rd., 10min. from Dahar by minibus. This installment of the national chain has the best ocean view in town from its clifftop terraces. Vegetarian-friendly *fuul* (E£2-4) and salads (E£2.25), as well as meats (E£15-35). Open daily 9am-12:30am.

🍺 DRUNKEN NIGHTS

Just like the reefs, Hurghada's active nightlife attracts creatures of all shapes and sizes. The area's best bars are in Saqala, a quick 10-15min. minibus ride south of Dahar. Conveniently, minibuses operate well past midnight, so you can party it up and then ride back to Dahar. Dutch-run **Papa's Bar**, past the McDonalds in Saqala, is the most happening place in town (Stella E£11). Two blocks south is the beach-front **Chill**. Relax with a Stella (E£10) in one of their hammocks, or groove to the guest European DJs on the dance floor. **Peanut's Bar**, next to Three Corners Empire Hotel on Sa'id Karin-General Hospital St. in Dahar, fills its patio every night. The Stellas (E£10) come with complimentary all-you-can-eat shelled peanuts. **Scruples** pub and steakhouse, on al-Nasser Rd. near the center of town, buzzes and pops with neon lights and beer bottlecaps. Scruples also has a classy **billiard hall** near the southern end of 'Abd al-'Aziz Mustafa St. with several pool tables and a full bar. (Pool E£10 per hr. Stella E£8.50. Cocktails E£11.50.) Bars in town are supplemented by the resorts, which have their own pubs, bars, or nightclubs. **Kalaboush Disco** (☎ 54 50 87), at the Arabella Hotel on the corniche, is a popular club with a different theme every night (E£10 minimum).

👁 SUNKEN SIGHTS

DRY AND MIGHTY. Landlubbers rejoice! Hurghada's underwater splendor can now be enjoyed without even getting your feet wet. Aspiring Captain Nemos can go a couple of leagues under in the **Sinbad Submarine** (☎ 44 46 88). US$50 buys a seat aboard a real 44-person sub for a 1hr. undersea voyage. Sign up at any luxury hotel and leave from the Sinbad Resort. Many of the larger hotels run **glass-bottom boat tours** for E£15-20 per hr. Make reservations at any luxury hotel or over the phone. Get an inkling of the subaquatic splendors at the **Hurghada Aquarium**, which features a variety of fish accompanied by remarkably informative descriptions. (Open daily 9am-10pm. E£5.)

ON YOUR MARK, GET WET, GO! There are a variety of beaches to choose from around Hurghada. **Public beaches** next to the Geisum Hotel and just past the Beirut Hotel on the way to Saqala are the smelliest and most packed. Local rumor has it that sand is buried beneath all the dirt. Women will feel uncomfortable baring anything more than toes. Head to the hotels for more liberal bathing fashions. Just north of the public beach downtown, the **Shedwan, Three Corners**, and **Sand Beach Hotels** all open their beaches and pools to non-guests for E£15; **Geisum Hotel** charges E£10. **Shellghada Beach,** between Safir and Le Meridien hotels, charges E£10 for a day on their soft sand and use of their showers. These beaches can be reached by minibus (E£1 from Saqala) or taxi (E£5-10).

🤿 DIVING DELIGHTS

Hurghada's real attractions are silent and submerged. Red Sea creatures will astound you with their array of colors, shapes, and sizes. Buck-toothed triggerfish, iridescent parrotfish, rays with blue polka dots, sea cucumbers, giant clams, and a million others star in this briny show. The shimmering, variegated blues of Hurghada's waters have been spared the horrors of oil exploration (see **Sinai: Underwater Tips,** p. 170, for information on snorkeling and scuba diving).

GEFTUN ISLAND. There are a few reefs you can reach without a boat, including one near the Sheraton, but to reach Hurghada's most brilliant aquatic scenery you must take a barge. Hotels offer an all-day trip to Geftun Island, usually including two 1hr. snorkeling stops near the island and a fish meal prepared on board. Most hotels advertise the trip at E£40, but bargaining often works wonders. Some Geftun-bound boats are as crammed as cattle cars and stop only once for snorkeling. There is a US$1 environmental tax here, so many snorkeling boats are heading to different destinations.

EGYPT

SNORKELING. Snorkeling from a dive-boat might give you access to better underwater sights, but is a bit more expensive (US$10-15). The best reefs are north of Hurghada. The northern waters aren't shielded by islands like the southern ones, so calm weather is a must in order to go. To save money, a group can make independent arrangements with a boat owner—perhaps a fisherman in Saqala—or with one of the sea-trip offices around town. Excursions to other locales can be less crowded and cheaper. For information, talk to: Sayad of **Sunshine Dive Center** (☎54 51 13), on al-Nasser Rd., between the post office and bus station; Bart or Sylvie of **Blue Paradise Diving Center** (☎54 43 54), a block past the Casablanca Hotel on the corniche; or **Son Bijou Diving Center** (☎54 46 80), behind the Casablanca Hotel. Rent your own gear (E£10-15 per day for mask, snorkel, and fins) at any office in town. ISIC or IYTC (GO 25) discounts are available.

SCUBA DIVING. While Hurghada may have some of the best scuba diving in Egypt, it also has some of the worst dive shops. Many of the shops that have sprung up to profit on rising tourism don't have very much experience, so choose your shop carefully. Inspect the equipment to make sure it has been maintained properly, then ask to see the workshop (a reputable dive center should have a workshop where they repair equipment). Ask about the number of guests per dive boat; any boat with more than one guest per meter is overcrowded. Also check into the diver-to-guide ratio, and be wary of any shop that requires advance payment. Be sure to check your instructor or guide's certification and experience, as well as the ship's gear, and especially its emergency equipment. Dive shops that are members of HEPCA, a marine protection organization, are often more environmentally conscious underwater. **Subex** (☎54 86 51), on the corner next to the California Hotel; **Blue Paradise Diving Center** (☎54 43 54); and **Sea Ray Diving Center** (☎54 33 90), one block past Subex, are all reputable and experienced establishments with full-day diving excursions including two dives, transportation to and from your hotel, equipment, buffet lunch, dive boat, and guide for US$40-50.

Hurghada is also a great place to earn open-water dive certification (for more tips on choosing a dive center, see p. 170). Belgian-run **Blue Paradise Diving Center** offers a reliable 4- to 5-day PADI course for US$280 (PADI book is US$40 extra). Manager Bart brings years of diving experience and an easygoing teaching style to to his small classes. **Subex** is a well-established professional dive center offering open-water certification for US$460. Their high price is worth it, as the instruction is top-notch, all dives are in the ocean, and everything is included in the price.

NILE VALLEY وادى النيل

How doth the little crocodile
Improve his shining tail
And pour the waters of the Nile
On every Golden Scale.
—Lewis Carroll

Originating at the equatorial high water marks of Lake Victoria and Lake Taru, the Nile winds north through Uganda, Ethiopia, and the Sudan, pouring into Lake Nasser and Egypt, where its banks are home to 95% of the country's population.

Before the construction of the Aswan High Dam in 1971, the Nile overflowed its banks every year, depositing the rich silt that made the valley the most fertile region in the world. This yearly inundation was the most important time of the year for ancient Egyptians and the reason for ancient religions to focus on the river's cycles. No major temple along the length of the Nile Valley was without a **nilometer,** a graded pit used to measure and predict the river's depth. For millions of ancient Egyptians, no oracle was more influential.

The region between Cairo and Luxor is known as **Middle Egypt,** home to the majority of the country's Coptic Christian population. Akhenaton built his capital at Tel al-Amarna; farther south stand the temples at Abydos and Dendera. Luxor marks the northern boundary of **Upper Egypt,** stretching upstream (south) to Lake Nasser and the Sudanese border. Tourists flock here to see the underground maze of ancient architecture on Luxor's west bank and the imposing temples at Edfu and Abu Simbel.

Lower Nile Valley

MEDITERRANEAN SEA

Abu Qir
Rosetta (Rashid)
TO DAMIETTA
Alexandria
Damanhur
Tanta
Mansura
Zagazig
Deir Anba Baramus
Deir al-Suryan
Benha
Bubastis
WADI NATRUN
Qanatir
Deir Anba Bishoi
Deir Abu Maqar
Giza
Cairo
Pyramids of Giza
Helwan
Abu Sir
Memphis
Saqqara
Dashur
Lake Qara'un
Qara'un
Fayyum
Hawara
al-Lahun
Beni Suef
WADI AL-RUWAYAN
al-Fashn
Magagha
Beni Mazar
Nile River
Deir Gabal al-Teir
Tehna (Acoris)
Mina
Tuna al-Gabal
Beni Hassan
Ashminein (Hermopolis)
Mallawi
Tel al-Amarna
Dairut
Manfalut
Abnub
EASTERN DESERT
TO KHARGA
Asyut
Al-Badari
Tima
WESTERN DESERT
Akhmim
Deir Anba Shenouda (Deir al-Abayyad)
Sohag
al-Mansha
al-Balyana
Abydos
TO UPPER NILE VALLEY
Qena
Dendera

Upper Nile Valley

Hurghada

0   75 miles
0   75 kilometers

TO LOWER NILE VALLEY
N
al-Balyana
Qena
Dendera
Qus
Naqada
Valley of the Kings
Deir al-Medina
Karnak
Armant
Luxor
EASTERN DESERT
TO KHARGA
Esna
Al-Kab
Edfu
Nile River
Gabal al-Silsilah
Kom Ombo
Daraw
Aswan
Elephantine Island
Philae
Kalabsha
Beit al-Wali
Aswan High Dam
WESTERN DESERT
Lake Nasser
al-Sibu
Abu Simbel
EGYPT
SUDAN
Lake Nubia

EGYPT

In summer, temperatures average over 45°C (113°F), frequently breaking 50°C (122°F). This is *a bit* warm, but the complete lack of humidity makes it possible to continue most essential biological processes, even as the sand slowly drips into beads of glass. Hotel managers, guides, and others of their ilk are desperate for business in the summer, so bargain hard. To avoid the heat, plan most of your touring for between 6 and 11am; to avoid the crowds, shoot for late afternoon. In November through May, temperatures drop and prices rise.

GETTING AROUND THE VALLEY

BY SERVICE, BUSES, AND TRAINS

Traveling by **service** is the cheapest and most convenient option for shuttling between the river towns at almost any time of day. Unfortunately, security throughout Upper and Middle Egypt prohibits *service* trips between more distant cities. "Special" (i.e. "ripoff") **taxis** are a possibility, but prices are high. Another option is to travel with the police escorted **convoy** (check with the local tourist office for schedule). As regulations regarding tourist travel in Egypt are constantly changing, inquire at a tourist office or *service* stop to determine the best way to go. Don't let yourself get too frustrated trying to find a ride; you'll need your nerves in top form to cope with drivers' recklessness. **Buses** are often slightly cheaper than *service*, and run more frequently, but they can be horribly slow, hot, and unreliable. Most stop running at 6pm. Buses are best for transport out of Luxor or Aswan, where you can reserve air-conditioned buses by going to the station a day or two in advance. In the smaller towns between, you may not find an empty seat, and schedule reliability plummets. **Trains** can be a hassle for short trips, but first- or second-class air-conditioned compartments are a great value for the long Luxor-Aswan haul or for more distant sights north of Luxor. Third-class travel is possible, but authorities discourage tourists from taking third-class trains and obtaining schedules may be difficult. See listings in **Luxor** (p. 212) and **Aswan** (p. 233) for more specific information.

BY NILE CRUISER

Tough times for tourism in Egypt have opened up an option for budget travelers on a binge: the **Nile Cruiser.** Book a cabin on a triple-decker, pool-topped cruise ship and slip from Luxor to Aswan or vice versa (one-way is 2 nights), hobnobbing with French tourists the whole way. Travel agents can book for you at a mark-up (US$45-80 per person per night) or you can go to the dock yourself and chat with the boat receptionist about open cabins (as low as US$35 per person per night). The air-conditioned two-room suites come with TVs and showers. All meals are included, but drinks are extra pricey. A *kalish* will cart you to the temple and back at each stop. Several travel agents (including Eastmar and Misr Travel) dot the corniche south of the Winter Palace in Luxor. In Aswan, agencies can be found around the southern end of the corniche. If you find a bargain, you'll enjoy two days of pure bliss: sunning by the pool and watching the palms float by, interrupted only for daily feedings.

BY FELUCCA

For those who want to get up close and personal with the Nile while still sticking to a tight budget, a **felucca** (sounds like "bazooka") cruise is a slow-paced way to absorb the Egyptian countryside and regain sanity after days in overcrowded *service. Feluccas* (Nubian for "boats") have been sailing the Nile for thousands of years—and *felucca* scams have been going on for at least that long. The more careful you are in navigating the crowded docks, the more carefree you can be while your captain navigates down the river.

The typical Nile-cruising *felucca* sleeps up to eight people (though some can hold more), has a single tall mast with a characteristically angled boom, and is piloted by an English-speaking Arab or Nubian Egyptian. When traveling alone, gather a group of like-minded tourists (aim for six) in hotel lobbies, the many restaurants along the Nile, or on a tour to Abu Simbel. You can also ask at the tourist office. As a last resort, join a group already assembled by a captain. Be sure to meet these people beforehand, or you may find yourself stuck in a horrifying Middle Eastern version of MTV's *Road Rules*. Your bargaining position is strongest when a full group is assembled, so rounding up a posse may be worth the effort.

Members of a six-to-eight-person group leaving Aswan pay E£35-40 each to Kom Ombo (1 day, 1 night), E£50-90 to Edfu (3 days, 2 nights). These prices include a E£5 registration fee and all meals on board. For registration in Aswan, the captain will ask for your passport, and in some cases, a deposit or the E£5 registration fee. Have an assembled group ready, or the captain may try to hold your passports hostage until he can corral other passengers. Prices don't vary much from captain to captain, so the most important variable is the vibe you get. During the summer, prices may dip a bit due to the shortage of tourists, but it's harder to find a full group. Conversely, prices rise in winter, but finding a full group is easier. As of August 2001, *feluccas* are not allowed in Luxor—all stop in Edfu. The quick trip to Kom Ombo cuts the adventure short, but most find the voyage to Edfu just right.

ROLLIN' ON THE RIVER Top *felucca* captains to avoid:

10. *Captain Hook.* Good at fencing, not so good at dodging crocodiles.

9. *Captain Ahab.* Dude has to take his mind off that stupid white whale and watch where he's steering the boat.

8. *Captain Kangaroo.* Beloved TV personality has trouble navigating without the help of Mr. Green Jeans, Mr. Moose, and Grandfather Clock.

7. *Captain Morgan.* Rum pitchman unlikely to pass sobriety checkpoints on the Nile.

6. *O Captain! My Captain!* Famous Walt Whitman poem. Unfortunately, the skipper isn't much help after having "fallen cold and dead."

5. *Soy capitán.* Yo no soy marinero, soy capitan, soy capitan, soy capitan. If he crashed Ritchie Valens's plane, you shouldn't get on a boat with him.

4. *Cap'n Crunch.* Sugary breakfast cereal will rot your teeth.

3. *Captain Kirk.* Rule #17: Never trust a *felucca* captain with a bad toupee.

2. *Captain Marvel.* Nega-Bands give this superhero the power to fly faster than the speed of light, to breathe in space, and to shoot energy blasts. But he can't swim.

1. *George Clooney.* Star of *The Perfect Storm* drowned Marky Mark, lost all the fish, and wasted millions of moviegoers' money. Stay out of his *felucca* at all costs.

TIPS ON TRAVELING BY FELUCCA

CHOOSE THE CAPTAIN ON YOUR OWN. From the moment you step off the train in Aswan, you will be constantly approached by *felucca* captains or—more often—middlemen sent out to round up suckers. Every hotel manager and every man in the local *ahwa* has his favorite *felucca* captain (from whom he receives a commission), so the word on the street is almost useless. Commission-charging hotels, even if they don't add to the price of the trip, will take money away from your captain who may then be inclined to cut corners on the trip to make up for his losses. From the northern local ferry terminus on Elephantine Island (p. 238) in Aswan, Captain Jamaica runs a polished, though somewhat pricey, *felucca* operation. The charismatic captain owns seven feluccas and runs by far the most popular trips. If you're in a pinch for time or are having a hard time rounding up fellow travelers, pay Jamaica a visit, as he is likely to have one of the seven *feluccas* sailing soon. Keep in mind that Captain Jamaica sells the trips but his relatives actually captain the boats, so make sure to meet your captain before sailing.

LOOK FOR EXPERIENCED CAPTAINS. Go down to the river yourself, meet and talk with several captains, inspect several boats, and take a list of potential candidates to the tourist office to make sure they aren't pirates or perverts. Ask to see comment books and talk to fellow travelers. Check for lifejackets. Be skeptical of any cute aliases the captain uses (the Most Inappropriate Boat Captain Nickname Award goes to Captain Titanic)—an honest captain will tell you his real name if asked. Also be wary of captains who speak little English: these typically younger captains often lack the experience necessary to handle sailing emergencies (several capsizings in recent years have been caused by high winds and inept sailors). You're better off with a gnarled, salty old man who speaks English well (if a bit colorfully) than with some wet-behind-the-ears pollywog who is just learning the ropes. If you decide to back out of a trip or switch captains, you should receive a full refund, minus E£10-15 if your captain has already bought food.

PRE-ARRANGE THE FINAL DESTINATION. Make sure that the captain clearly understands the final stop. For example, many *felucca* trips to Edfu actually stop at a way-station 40km from a town where pre-arranged microbuses take passengers the rest of the way. Captains are tempted to stay close to home to save themselves a time-consuming return against the current. Unscrupulous boatsmen have been known to drop their passengers off without mentioning such arrangements, claiming that it was "close enough."

CHECK YOUR PROVISIONS. Choose a captain who takes care of the cooking. An extra-special captain who cooks Nubian dishes in the *felucca* or stops at his village for a home-cooked meal is a godsend. A captain should also bring at least two cartons of bottled **water;** make sure it is aboard before you depart and check that the tabs are sealed, as they may be filled with tap water. In addition, bring at least three bottles of water per person per day for drinking, cooking, and brewing tea. You can also ask for a big jerry can of tap water to be brought along to be used instead of the Nile for washing dishes and faces. For those looking for more exciting libations, beer can be procured at the liquor store on the corniche.

QENA قنة ☎096

Sixty-five kilometers north of Luxor, Qena rests quietly by the Nile, oblivious to the hordes of tourists descending on her southerly neighbor. Tour buses pass through town in droves on their way to the spectacular Temple of Hathor, but few visitors stay beyond their temple tour. Those who do will be rewarded with Egypt's cleanest streets and the opportunity to be the sole traveler in town. The new governor has made modernization and cleanliness his priorities: apartment buildings have fresh coats of white paint, and a corps of orange-clad street cleaners keep the roads spotless (in marked contrast to the rest of Egypt). Agriculture dominates the the life and economy of Qena, but in the evenings, the streets come alive with strolling people and the sound of slapping dominoes.

⬛ TRANSPORTATION

The train station lies at the center of town, 2km east of the Nile. **Trains** go to Luxor (45min.; 5:30, 8am, 2:30, 4, 5:30, 9pm; E£5) and Cairo (8½hr., 10 per day 4am-12:15am, E£36-46). The bus station is 1.5km west of the train station and 500m from the Nile on al-Manshiya St. (take a taxi for E£3-4). **Buses** go to: Luxor (1hr., 6 per day 7am-7pm, E£3-5); Cairo (10½hr., 5 per day 6:30am-10:30pm, E£50); Hurghada (3hr., every hr. 6am-10pm, E£15).

⬛ ORIENTATION AND PRACTICAL INFORMATION

Qena has only a few main streets. Shops and cafes are concentrated in front of the train station along **Sidi 'Abd Rahima St.** Perpendicular to the main entrance of the train station is **al-Gamil St.,** which winds 2km to the Nile. A large **clock** marks the traffic circle 500m down al-Gamil St. from the train station. Take a right two blocks before the clock to reach the **police station** (emergency ☎122). Next to the police is the **post office** (open Su-Th 8am-2pm) and the **National Bank of Egypt** (exchange open Su-Th 8:30am-2pm). Another post office, with **EMS,** is 150m down the street on the left after the clock. The Telecom Egypt **phone office** is on a street to the right after you pass the clock. Qena's **hospital** (☎33 43 94) is by the Nile on the road to Dendera, past the bus station. Dr. Kamal Mahmoud Mustafa's **pharmacy** is to the right of the train station on Sidi 'Abd Rahima St. (open 24hr.).

⬛ ACCOMMODATIONS AND FOOD

There is little incentive to remain in Qena beyond a temple visit, as the cleanest hotels are overpriced and often full. To get to **New Palace Hotel,** walk away from

THE LAST OF THE ANCIENT EGYPTIANS

The sacred symbols of the ancient Egyptian religion are the stuff of souvenir shops these days, but for one woman, they were much more. After falling down the stairs of her home in England in 1907, three-year-old Dorothy Eady was declared dead. When the town doctor returned an hour later to the room where he had laid the young girl's body, he was shocked to find her contentedly playing on her bed. Alive and well, the normal (if slightly rambunctious) British lass began insisting she was an ancient Egyptian and started begging to be taken "home." She was, she later said, a former priestess-in-training at the Temple of Seti in the holy city of Abydos. After a chance meeting on the temple grounds, she fell deeply in love with the Pharaoh Seti I and found herself in a rapturous affair that contravened all the rules of the priesthood. When the temple's high priest demanded a confession, ancient Egyptian Eady-as-priestess eventually took her own life rather than betray the name of her lover.

The real-life Eady devoted her life to "returning home," fulfilling her destiny at the temple, and taking her place at Seti's side in the afterlife. In 1956, after 20 years as a distinguished employee of the Egyptian Department of Antiquities (where she worked with and won the respect of some of the most distinguished Egyptologists there), Eady transferred to the ancient site of Abydos. There, known in the village as *Omm Seti* (mother of Seti), she helped to guide work at the temple, exhibiting an uncanny familiarity with the grounds. Eady treated the temple as the sacred sanctuary it once was, praying and making offerings to the gods until her actual death in 1981. She was buried in the desert to the northwest, at last ready to take her place at Seti's side.

the train station on **al-Gamil St.;** the hotel is in an alley on the left. New Palace offers the best combination of cleanliness and economy, with clean sheets, balconies, and air-conditioning. The quality of rooms varies, so ask to look around. (☎32 25 09. Singles E£25; doubles E£50.) One block past the pharmacy on Sidi 'Abd Rahima St. is the substantially cheaper and much dirtier **al-Bait Hota Hotel**. Small rooms come with fans. (☎33 37 55. Singles E£10; doubles E£15.) The **souq,** past the pharmacy to the left, provides fruits, vegetables, *fuul,* and falafel.

🢒 DAYTRIP FROM QENA: DENDERA

Take a taxi from Qena to the temple (E£7). Temple open 7am-5pm. E£12, students E£6. In summer, bats inhabit the temple, so bring a flashlight.

The Temple of Hathor at Dendera is one of the few sights in Middle Egypt that remained accessible throughout the fundamentalist uprising. While it is a bit out of the way, those who make the trip will find a structure unique in the options it offers the exploring tourist. Built of Nubian sandstone, the temple dates from the first century BCE. It is one of the most complete ancient temples in all of Egypt, second only to the temple at Edfu. The late Ptolemies and the Romans found it politically expedient to associate themselves with the benevolent goddess, and her temple thus escaped destruction. Hathor is depicted with a cow's head or ears, or wearing a crown of two horns cradling the sun disk. Because her specialty was love, Hathor was identified by the Greeks as Aphrodite. During an annual festival, a statue of Hathor was carried in a sacred procession down the Nile to meet Horus of Edfu (see p. 230).

Eighteen columns are topped by cow heads in the **Great Hypostyle Hall.** In the temple's inner sanctum, paintings depict the embalmer's art, while the ceiling is decorated with pictures of the goddess Nut. The second hypostyle hall, also called the **Hall of Appearances,** gives way to the **Hall of Offerings,** where daily rites were performed. In the artsy kiosk in the southwest corner of the roof, priests performed the ceremony of "touching the disk," in which the soul of the sun god Ra appeared in the form of light. To the right is a gently sloping staircase leading up to the roof. Turn your flashlight off for a moment as you make your way up the stairs. The lights are dim, the smell is strange, and it is hard not to feel that you are a part of the sacred religious procession chiseled on the wall to your right.

The **Hall of the Ennead** immediately precedes the inner sanctuary. The chamber on the left is the wardrobe; opposite it, a doorway leads through a small treasury into the **Court of the New Year,** where sacrifices were performed during the New Year festival. On the ceiling of the colorful portico, Nut gives birth to the sun, whose rays shine upon the head of Hathor. The so-called **Mysterious Corridor** surrounds the **Sanctuary** on three sides, and 11 chapels—each with a distinct religious function—open off it. A small chamber known as the **Throne of Ra** sits behind the northernmost of the three doorways behind the sanctuary. A miniscule opening in its floor leads to the crypt, a subterranean hallway embellished with reliefs. some of inlaid alabaster. Many rooms on the upper floors have ceiling paintings of Mut swallowing the sun at sundown and giving birth to it at dawn. On the roof of there is graffiti left by French soldiers in 1799.

LUXOR الاقصر ☎ 095

This ancient capital of Upper and Lower Egypt still humbles visitors three millennia after the height of its power. Luxor is built on the site of Ta Ipet (known by its Greek name, Thebes), which flexed its muscles during the rule of the New Kingdom (18th-20th dynasties, 1539-1075 BCE). Egypt's ancient history is more tangible here than anywhere else in the Nile Valley, and droves of tourists come to marvel at Luxor's sandstone temples and mysterious tombs. Unfortunately, the tourism industry has spawned a society of ruthless hoteliers, greedy guides, and cunning cab drivers: be wary of anyone who uses the word "free" in Luxor. With proper bargaining, however, a few pounds a day can net refreshing accommodations, satisfying cuisine, and access to unforgettable sights.

▣ INTERCITY TRANSPORTATION

Flights: The airport, 8km northeast of town (no bus; taxi E£20), is served by **EgyptAir** (☎ 38 05 80), next to the Old Winter Palace Hotel. Flights to: **Aswan** (3 per day, E£203); **Cairo** (1hr., 4 per day, E£456); **Sharm al-Sheikh** (3 per week, E£401). While it is possible to purchase EgyptAir tickets at the airport (☎ 38 05 86 or 38 05 89), it is not recommended. Tickets to international destinations must be purchased in Luxor.

Trains: The train station (☎ 37 20 18) is at the head of al-Mahatta St., 750m inland from Luxor Temple. Lockers E£1.25 per day. Trains to **Aswan** are less comfortable than *service* or *feluccas* (3hr.; 7:30am and 5:30pm; 1st-class E£23-27, A/C 2nd-class E£14-18; students 1st-class E£16-20, 2nd-class E£11-15). Tourists are restricted to 2 crowded trains to **Cairo** (8-10hr.; 8:20am and 8:50pm; 1st-class E£56-70, A/C 2nd-class E£36-46; students 1st-class E£31-35, 2nd-class E£23-24). Reserve sleeper cars 1 day in advance. Walk on for a fee; reserve a seat to be safe.

Buses: The bus station is near the exit of Karnak Temple. Buses to: **Aswan** (4½hr., 6 per day 7:15am-8pm, E£8) via **Esna** (1hr., E£3), **Edfu** (1½hr., E£8), and **Kom Ombo** (3hr., E£10); **Cairo** (11½hr., 7pm, A/C E£50); **Dahab** (18 hrs, 5pm, E£95) via **Sharm al-Sheikh** (E£85); **Hurghada** (8 per day, 6:15am-8pm, E£15-20) via **Qena** (1hr., E£3-5) and **Suez** (E£31-40); **Port Said** (11½hr., 8pm, E£50). Hours and rates change often.

Service: Off al-Karnak St., 1 block inland from the Luxor Museum. Early morning and late afternoon *service* leave when full, usually about every 15min. Out-of-town trips must be made with police convoys. Daily convoys by expensive "special" taxi leave from a side street near the Antiquities Museum and go to **Aswan** (7, 11am, 3pm); **Abydos** and **Dendera** (8am and 2pm, full-day taxi E£250; 2pm departure is for Dendera only). Check with the tourist office for updates and changes.

✺ ORIENTATION

Luxor is easily negotiated on foot. The city lies on the east bank of the Nile, 670km upstream from Cairo and 220km downstream from Aswan. Surrounded by a heavily cultivated floodplain, the city is at the heart of an agricultural area, with a farmers' *souq* on Tuesdays. The metropolis can be divided into three sectors: the **city of Luxor** proper on the east bank, the village of **Karnak** a few kilometers north, and **Thebes** on the west bank. Finding your way around is easy as long as you know the main thoroughfares. **Al-Mahatta St.** (Station St.) runs perpendicular to the Nile. The **train station** is on this street, 750m inland, on the eastern edge of Luxor. Exit the train station at a 45-degree angle to the left and you will eventually reach **Television St.**, where signs advertising the many budget hotels and pensions in town appear. **Al-Nil St.** (**the corniche**) runs south along the river, turning into Khalid ibn al-Walid St. past the Novotel. **Al-Karnak St.** begins just north of the temple and runs parallel to the corniche. **Luxor Temple** is on the corniche at the center of town, and **Karnak Temple** is 3km farther. The **bus station** is at the exit of Luxor Temple.

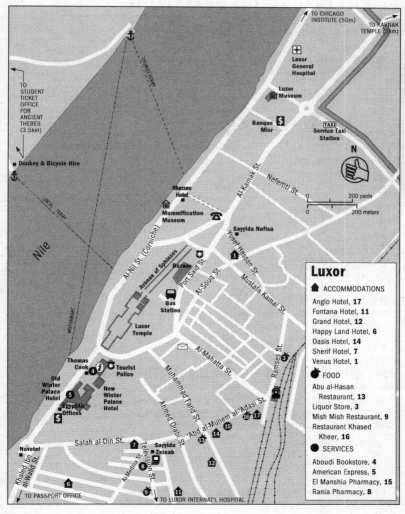

EGYPT

Luxor

🏠 ACCOMMODATIONS

Anglo Hotel, **17**
Fontana Hotel, **11**
Grand Hotel, **12**
Happy Land Hotel, **6**
Oasis Hotel, **14**
Sherif Hotel, **7**
Venus Hotel, **1**

🍎 FOOD

Abu al-Hasan
Restaurant, **13**
Liquor Store, **3**
Mish Mish Restaurant, **9**
Restaurant Khased
Kheer, **16**

● SERVICES

Aboudi Bookstore, **4**
American Express, **5**
El Manshia Pharmacy, **15**
Rania Pharmacy, **8**

◪ LOCAL TRANSPORTATION

Minibuses: The cheapest and quickest transportation in the city is (25pt). The most common route goes from al-Karnak St. to al-Mahatta St. to Television St.

Kalish: Riding to Karnak Temple on a **kalish** (carriage) can be pleasant (E£5). Kalishes are also good for baggage transport.

Bike Rental: You can rent a bike (E£5-7 per day) on al-Mahatta and Television St., or ask at a hotel. **Motorbikes** available at the Sherif Hotel and a small shop off Television St. Turn left after the Takia Cafe. (E£50-60 per day; no helmets). To visit the west bank sites on motorbike, catch a ferry in front of Luxor Temple.

Flying Pigs: On the corner of Television and Radio St. (50pt).

◪ PRACTICAL INFORMATION

TOURIST AND FINANCIAL SERVICES

Tourist Office: (☎37 22 15 or 37 32 94), left of the New Winter Palace Hotel. Open daily 8am-8pm. Additional branches at the **train station** (☎37 02 59; open daily 8am-8pm) and **airport** (☎37 23 06). Low on free and useful literature, but the one in the bazaar has bus and train schedules with price listings.

Passport Office: (☎38 08 85), on the left of Khalid ibn al-Walid St., 1km south of the Novotel, on the left before the tan CIB Bank. Visas extended. Open Sa-Th 8:30am-2pm; Ramadan 9am-2pm.

Currency Exchange: Available in most hotels and numerous banks on the corniche. **National Bank of Egypt,** on the corniche 50m south of the Old Winter Palace Hotel, accept traveler's checks and offers cash advances on MC/V. Open daily 8:30am-10pm, in winter 8:30am-9pm.

ATM: Outside the two branches of **Banque Misr,** one at the north end of Television St. and another a block inland from the corniche, north of the Mercure Hotel. Also at **National Bank of Egypt.** All accept AmEx, MC, V, PLUS, and Cirrus.

American Express: (☎37 83 33; ☎/fax 37 28 62), on al-Nil St. in front of the Old Winter Palace Hotel, south of Luxor Temple. Holds mail, sells traveler's checks, wires and exchanges money and checks. Open Su-Th 8am-7pm, F-Sa 9am-3pm.

Thomas Cook: (☎37 24 02), on al-Nil St. in front of the Old Winter Palace Hotel. Cashes traveler's checks and organizes tours of Thebes (half-day E£135).

LOCAL SERVICES

English-Language Bookstore: 'Aboudi Bookshop has 3 locations in the tourist bazaar complex on al-Nil St. Good but costly Egyptology books, countless sappy romances, and a few paperbacks in English, French, and German. Open daily 8am-10pm. Kiosks in front of tourist bazaar and in the train station sell foreign periodicals.

EMERGENCY AND COMMUNICATIONS

Emergency: ☎ 123.

Police: ☎ 122. The police station is off al-Karnak St., 200m north of Luxor Temple. **Tourist Police** (☎37 66 20), in the tourist bazaar on al-Nil St. Also in the train station (☎37 38 45). Both open 24hr.

Late-Night Pharmacy: 24hr. duty rotates—inquire at any hotel. **Rania Pharmacy** (☎37 12 86), at the north end of Television St., is well stocked with Egyptian drugs and basic toiletries. Open daily 8am-midnight. **Al-Manshia** (whose sign reads "nshia"), on 'Abd al-Munem al-Adasi St., carries mostly medicine. Open daily 7:30am-noon.

Hospitals: Luxor International Hospital (☎38 71 92), on the south end of Television St. New, modern facility. Accepts cash, credit cards, and medical insurance. **Luxor Public Hospital** (☎37 20 25 or 37 28 09), on al-Nil St. north of the museum, is a definite step down. Cash only.

Telephones: Central Telephone Office, west off al-Karnak St., just north of Luxor Temple. Open 24hr. Other less crowded offices are on **al-Nil St.** in front of the Old Winter Palace Hotel (the cheapest **fax** services in the city are here) and in the **train station.** Both offices open 8am-8pm. Hotels may charge twice as much as telephone offices.

Internet Access: 'Aboudi Internet Cafe (☎37 23 90; aboudishop@yahoo.com), on the 2nd fl. of the 'Aboudi Bookshop on al-Nil St. just south of the Luxor Temple. E£12 per hr. Refreshments E£2. Open daily 9am-10:30pm. **Abu Khaled Internet** (☎37 00 67), 50m from the intersection with Salah al-Din St. E£8 per hour. Open daily 10am-2am.

Post Office: On al-Mahatta St., 100m east of Luxor Temple. Offers **Poste Restante** (passport required for pickup) and **EMS.** Open Su-Th 8am-2pm; EMS 8am-noon. Other branches near the tourist office and in the train station. Open daily 8am-2pm.

⊓ ACCOMMODATIONS

If you come to Luxor by train, you will disembark into a writhing mass of arms waving hotel cards. Decide where you want to go and stick to your guns. Many hawkers will quote incorrect prices or tell you the hotel you have in mind is full or shut down. *Kalish* drivers may take you to a different hotel from the one you request, assuming you don't know any better or are too tired to complain. Demand to be taken to your hotel or withhold payment. Women traveling alone should be prepared for sexual overtures from employees in some of the small hotels. If a firm refusal doesn't do the trick, complain to the manager or the tourist police.

For the most part, though, staying in Luxor is a treat. Air-conditioning comes quite cheap and there are ample opportunities for hard-core bargaining. Shop around and enjoy the wildly exaggerated accounts of just how much a breakfast costs the owner. Travelers with patience or those with groups of three or four will be rewarded: air-conditioned rooms can be had for as low as E£4-6 if you play your cards right, and roof or terrace mattresses for E£3-4. The majority of the budget hotels are clustered around Television St. and Yusuf Hassan St. Most hotels have laundry service (50pt-E£1 per piece) and bike rentals (E£5-7).

Hotel managers make their money from overpriced tours of the west bank, so count on being encouraged to take one. Happy Land offers guided air-conditioned bus tours for E£45 and donkey tours for E£35. Never accept prices higher than these.

🏨 **Happy Land Hotel** (☎37 18 28; fax 37 11 40; happylandluxor@hotmail.com), 150m off al-Medina St., a few blocks past Television St. (look for the huge sign). The owner will go to great lengths to demonstrate his establishment's nearly obsessive cleanliness. Towels and toilet paper in each room. Comfortable rooftop restaurant with satellite TV serves hearty breakfast. Internet E£10 per hr. Trips to west bank (E£45) and Dahab (E£85). A/C dorms E£7.50. Singles with fan E£15; doubles E£18; add E£5-7 each for bath and A/C. Triples E£12.50 and quads E£9.50 per person; bath and A/C included.

🏨 **Fontana Hotel** (☎38 06 63), off Television St. Super-clean rooms (try to get one with a balcony) and incredible shared baths. Breakfast included. Ask the owner to use the laundry machines yourself for no fee. Fans in every room. Singles E£8, with A/C E£10; doubles E£10, with A/C E£15, A/C and bath E£20; small triples with bath and A/C E£25-30; prices a few pounds higher in winter.

Venus Hotel (☎37 26 25), on Yusef Hassan St. Convenient (if hectic) location, with fairly clean tiled rooms and large windows. As always, insist on the correct price for rooms and tours if at first you are quoted something that seems too high. Breakfast included. Singles E£10, with A/C and bath E£15; doubles E£20/E£25; triples E£22.50/E£30; quads E£30/E£40; prices E£5-10 higher in winter. **Mars Bar** on the 2nd fl. features pool table, foosball, satellite TV, and cheap drinks (Stella E£6).

Anglo Hotel (☎/fax 38 16 79), in the alley to the left of the train station. Some of the clean rooms have balconies. Pricey tours. Breakfast included. Singles E£15, with A/C E£20; doubles E£25-30/E£35; triples E£30/E£45.

Oasis Hotel (☎36 59 00), on Muhammad Farid St. Clean, spacious rooms, but the bathrooms could stand to be renovated. Prime location, with restaurants and fruit stands nearby. Can be pushy about tours. Breakfast included. Dorms have fans; all other rooms have bath and A/C. Dorm beds E£6; singles E£10; doubles E£15; triples E£18. Bargain with the manager for lower prices.

Sherif Hotel (☎37 07 57; khaeli@hotmail.com), on Badr St., the 1st right off Television St. Bob Marley's image, music, and habits thrive in this friendly establishment. Breakfast E£3. Rooms with fan E£7 per person; for A/C add E£5 per room.

Grand Hotel (☎38 29 05), on Muhammad Farid St. Less frequented by travelers, tucked into a quiet corner just past the Oasis on the right. The small, covered rooftop patio is pleasant. Sizeable rooms have seen better days. Beware the markups on the tours lest ye be ripped off. Breakfast E£3.50. Singles with fan E£6, with A/C E£7.50; doubles E£12, with A/C E£15; triples E£15, with A/C E£18.

🍴 FOOD

Luxor may be an archaeologist's paradise, but it's purgatory for the frugal gourmet. Two *kushari* houses stand out from the pack: **Sayyida Zeinab,** on Television St., and **Sayyida Nafisa,** on Yusef Hassan St. The **coffee shop** in the New Winter Palace Hotel has a paltry but cheap all-you-can-eat dessert buffet (E£16). A **liquor store** on Ramses St. is on al-Mahatta St. to your right as you leave the train station. (Open daily 8am-2pm and 5-11pm.) Hotel managers can also procure beer for you.

The west bank in particular lacks decent budget restaurants. **Tutankhamun,** next to the ferry landing, offers the usual chicken and kebab dinners (E£15-20). Most hotels have restaurants, but they're often closed and the quality is inconsistent, especially in the summer when business is slow.

Mish Mish (☎38 17 56), on Television St., across from al-Houda. A big hit with travelers. Good prices, tasty food. Pasta E£3-5. Pizza E£4-12. Meat E£8-12. Free delivery and 9% student discount. Open daily 10am-midnight.

Amoun Restaurant (☎37 05 47), just north of the Luxor Temple and the bus station in the tourist bazaar. A tourist favorite, Amoun serves a variety of Western dishes in A/C comfort. Try the refreshing lime juice and delectable banana milkshakes. Pizza starts at E£7, entrees average E£10. 10% student discount wipes out service charge and tax. Open daily 7am-midnight.

Restaurant Khased Khear (☎38 45 80), on 'Abd al-Munem al-Adasi St. (al-Manshia St.), 1 block from the train station. Cozy and cool interior has a nautical feel, but Khased's specialty is kebab (E£6-10). Take-out available. Open daily 11am-1am.

Abu al-Hasan al-Shazly (☎37 12 14), on the corner of 'Abd al-Munem al-Adasi St. and Muhammad Farid St., near the Oasis Hotel. Locals and tourists alike enjoy the Ottoman decor of this 2-story behemoth of a restaurant. Big portions of budget fare. Pizza E£8-12. Meat dishes E£8-20. Pasta E£3.50. 2-egg omelets (E£3.50) get the job done when hotel breakfasts fall short. Open daily 8:30am-3am.

Classic Restaurant (☎38 17 07), on Khalid ibn al-Walid St. in the St. Joseph Hotel; look for the yellow sign before the passport office. Classy establishment with excellent food. Perfect for a well-deserved meal after conquering Thebes (especially if mild heat stroke has loosened the grip on your wallet). 4-course meal E£24. Stella E£7. On Fridays when they have sufficient numbers the Classic offers a belly dancing buffet (9pm; in winter 7pm. E£50). Add 19% tax. Open daily 6-10:30pm. AmEx/MC/V.

👁 SIGHTS

EAST BANK الضفة الشرقية

Luxor has two major temples and two museums. **Luxor Temple** (p. 217) stands in the heart of the city, adjacent to the Nile. The temple's lighting and late hours make it perfect for a first date. Going north on al-Nil St., the **Mummification Museum** (p. 221) and the small but excellent **Luxor Museum of Ancient Egyptian Art** (p. 221) house sculptures and artifacts unearthed at Karnak and elsewhere. **Karnak Temple** (p. 218), the Leviathan of pharaonic architecture, sprawls just a few kilometers north. The entire 3km route between the temples of Luxor and Karnak was once connected by the sacred **Avenue of the Sphinxes,** built by Queen Hatshepsut (Hat-*Cheap*-Suit). The ever-modest Ramses II took the liberty of adding a small statuette of himself to each sphinx. The final stretch of the avenue remains complete, with two rows of sphinxes near the **Temple of Khonsu,** to the right of the main entry to Karnak Temple. Karnak Temple is best seen early in the morning, while the museums are perfect for an afternoon cool-off, and Luxor Temple is best at night. Note that **price hikes** of 25-50% on admission tickets to major sights are scheduled for the coming year; see **Inflation Sucks,** p. 77, for more information.

LUXOR TEMPLE هيكل الاقصر

Enter on al-Nil St. side, 400m north of the New Winter Palace. Evening is the best time to visit, as temperatures are comfortable and the temple looks cool in the dimmed light. Open daily 6am-10pm, in winter 6am-9pm. E£20, students E£10.

Although Karnak gets all the glory, Luxor Temple is grand in its own right and much more comprehensible to the visitor than its big brother. Most of the temple was built around 1380 BCE by Amenhotep III. Significant portions were also erected by famous pharaohs from Ramses II to Tutankhamun, each striving to make his mark. Luxor Temple was meant to serve as a **love nest for the gods.** Once a year, during the Opet festival, the statues of Amun and his consort Mut would be taken from Karnak Temple and loaded onto a sacred boat. Amidst much rejoicing and beer guzzling, priests carried the statues on their shoulders to Luxor Temple, where the happy couple spent 24 days and nights together in the sanctuary. During one of their retreats the moon god Khonsu was conceived, completing the Theban triad (see **Meet the Gods,** p. 70). Romans used the temple as a military camp in the 4th century CE. The Mosque of Abu al-Haggag, added by the Fatimids in 1077 CE and still in use today, prevents work on the gallery on the left, so only the end portions of the Avenue of the Sphinxes (the 3km road connecting the Luxor and Karnak Temples) have been unearthed and restored.

Ramses II built the enormous **First Pylon,** nearly 24m tall and 65m wide. The pylon is inscribed with images of Ramses II smiting the Hittites. In front of the pylon stand three of the six original **Colossi of Ramses II,** two seated and one standing. A red granite obelisk flanks the doorway; its twin was given to France in 1831 in exchange for a fake clock (see **Mosque of Muhammad 'Ali,** p. 106) and now graces the Place de la Concorde in Paris. The granite statues of the **Court of Ramses II,** past the pylon, originally portrayed Amenhotep, but were altered when ancient Egypt's favorite egomaniac assumed the throne. Seventy-four enormous columns and the **Mosque of Abu al-Haggag** occupy the temple's largest chamber. The right wall of this court shows the sons of Ramses II leading a funerary procession. On the right after entering through the first pylon is a small shrine built by Hatshepsut and Thutmose III, 100 years before Amenophis III began construction on the larger temple.

Continue through the court's papyrus columns to the **Colonnade of Amenhotep III,** where the 14 columns have open lotus crowns. Tutankhamun had the walls of the colonnade inscribed with scenes from the festival of Opet. From here, proceed into the **Court of Amenhotep III.** Beyond this court rises the hypostyle hall antechamber with its 22 columns. The back wall depicts Amenhotep III being coronated by the gods. The Egyptian government is spending E£9 million to restore these columns, whose foundations crumbled when the construction of the Aswan High Dam raised the water level in the area (see **Moving a Mountain,** p. 245).

Roman legionaries converted the next room into a chapel by covering the ancient inscriptions with plaster. A side room contains Latin inscriptions to Julius Caesar. The second antechamber, with pictures of the pharaoh making sacrifices to Amun, escaped the Romans' wrath. To the left is the **Birth Room,** displaying the divine birth of Amenhotep III. His mother Mutemuia delivers under the watchful eyes of Isis and Khnum (who sits at his potter's wheel molding the great pharaoh's soul). Alexander himself had the bas-reliefs (in which he appears in pharaonic attire before Amun and other deities) added when he built the **Sanctuary of Alexander the Great,** in the third antechamber. Fertility god Min receives disproportionate attention in this sanctuary, complete with a shrine for the sacred barque of Amun. Storage rooms on either side are engraved with inventory lists.

MUMMY DEAREST The ancient Egyptians wanted to live forever, so they had to be certain their bodies were fit for the long haul of the afterlife. In predynastic times, people were buried in simple pits in the sand. The heat and arid conditions dried the bodies out and prevented decay. As civilization advanced, efforts were made to provide for a more comfortable afterlife. Elaborate tombs served to speed decay, separating corpses from the drying sands; the process of mummification was perfected during the New Kingdom era. Before a body was wrapped in white linen bandages, it was preserved in a number of different ways. The least effective and least expensive was a simple washing and cleansing of the corpse. The next level involved filling the body's orifices with a caustic, corrosive fluid, then plugging up the holes. Several days later, the plugs were removed and the putrid fluid drained. The super-deluxe preservation package required that an incision be made in the abdomen. All of the viscera, save the heart and kidneys, were removed (including the brain, either through the base of the skull or through a nostril) and preserved in canopic jars. These jars were amphora-shaped alabaster containers with engravings on the sides and lid. The body was then packed with *natrun,* a natural salt found in Wadi Natrun. After 40 days, the salt was removed and ointments, spices, and oils such as frankincense were applied in combination with intricate wrappings. The essences reacted over time, forming a pitch-like substance that gives mummies their names (*moumiya* is Arabic for pitch).

MUMMIFICATION MUSEUM

100m north of Luxor Temple on the bank of the Nile. ☎38 15 02. *Open daily 9am-1pm and 5-10pm; in winter 9am-2pm and 4-9pm. E£20, students E£10. Free monthly lectures are offered in English during the winter; call ahead for schedules.*

This new riverside museum gives an insightful view into the meticulous and often misunderstood process of mummification (see **Mummy Dearest,** p. 218). English descriptions take the visitor through the entire process from purification of the body to the fields of the afterlife. A well-preserved mummy and elaborate wooden sarcophagi highlight the collection. Also on display are sophisticated surgical instruments and a mummified menagerie consisting of a monkey, goose, and crocodile—and a cat in a Pez dispenser-shaped coffin.

LUXOR MUSEUM OF ANCIENT EGYPTIAN ART

A 15min. walk north of Luxor Temple on al-Nil St. Open daily 9am-1pm and 5-10pm; in winter 9am-1pm and 4-9pm. E£30, students E£15. Wheelchair accessible.

The Luxor Museum contains a wonderfully edifying collection of antiquities—proof that less is sometimes more. Unlike the heaps of objects squeezed into Cairo's Egyptian Museum (see p. 118), the treasures here have multilingual descriptions, and the exhibits have been thoughtfully arranged with the help of the Brooklyn Museum of Art in New York. The recreated **mural** of 283 sandstone blocks on the second floor, found within Karnak Temple, depicts Akhenaton and Nefertiti in adoration of the sun god Aton, along with numerous artisans and peasants at work. The first floor contains several small statues, including one of Thutmose III that is considered one of the best ancient Egyptian statues in existence. The gallery also includes smaller artifacts such as drinking vessels, precious jewelry, bronze statuettes, and Alexandrian coins from the 2nd century CE. The **Cachette Hall** holds 16 marble and granite statues found in the 1980s beneath Luxor Temple. The coolest is the red granite likeness of Amenhotep III (1405-1367 BCE).

KARNAK TEMPLE هيكل كرنك

*Local **minibuses** run between Karnak Temple and the train station (25pt). Make sure the driver is going as far as the temple, and don't let him hike up the price at the end of the ride. You can also reach the temple by **bike, foot,** or **kalish** (E£3-5). The Karnak complex covers over 5 acres of land and is difficult to cover thoroughly, so bring water and come early in the day. Open daily 6am-6:30pm; in winter 6am-5:30pm. E£20, students E£10; use of a tripod*

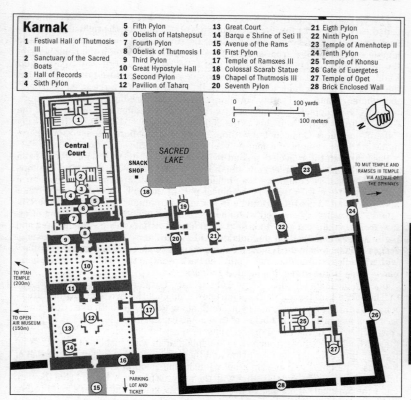

Karnak

1 Festival Hall of Thutmosis III	**5** Fifth Pylon	**13** Great Court	**21** Eigth Pylon
2 Sanctuary of the Sacred Boats	**6** Obelisk of Hatshepsut	**14** Barqu e Shrine of Seti II	**22** Ninth Pylon
3 Hall of Records	**7** Fourth Pylon	**15** Avenue of the Rams	**23** Temple of Amenhotep II
4 Sixth Pylon	**8** Obelisk of Thutmosis I	**16** First Pylon	**24** Tenth Pylon
	9 Third Pylon	**17** Temple of Ramsxes III	**25** Temple of Khonsu
	10 Great Hypostyle Hall	**18** Colossal Scarab Statue	**26** Gate of Euergetes
	11 Second Pylon	**19** Chapel of Thutmosis III	**27** Temple of Opet
	12 Pavilion of Taharq	**20** Seventh Pylon	**28** Brick Enclosed Wall

E£20. *If you seek more than a general impression of the place, a* **guided tour** *is useful, and latching onto one is easy. The* **sound and light show** *is a fascinating way to explore the temple for a 1st-time visit and pique your curiosity for a more in-depth visit the following morning. English shows M and Th 8pm, Tu-W and F-Su 9:15pm; in winter M 6pm, Tu 9pm, W-Su 7:30pm. Times may change, so check at your hotel or at the tourist office. E£33.*

Karnak Temple is overwhelming in its intricacy and proportions. Every major period in Egypt's ancient history since the collapse of the Middle Kingdom is represented in the additions to this complex of shrines dedicated to the sun god Amun and his family. Karnak Temple is the product of centuries of one-upmanship, as pharaoh after pharaoh added his mark to the temple in an effort to demonstrate the greatness of Amun (and himself). It was also the center of power for Amun's high priest, whose powers often exceeded even those of the pharaoh.

The temple is a hodgepodge of additions and alterations spanning millennia, but because of long-lasting pharaonic architectural traditions, the different pieces comprise a harmonious whole. As you push your way inside, think of each section as a layer of history built onto the original shrine at the core. The deeper you proceed into the building, the farther back in time you go. The temple is oriented along two axes: a primary east-west axis following the path of the sun god Amun and a secondary axis proceeding north-south to Luxor Temple.

Enter the temple from the west, with the Nile behind you, and pass through the **Avenue of the Rams,** another double-rowed boulevard of creatures (this time, lions' bodies with rams' heads) dedicated to Ramses II. The curly-horned ram was one of Amun's sacred animals.

The first and largest pylon was never completed and probably dates from the 25th dynasty. Look for the ancient mud-brick scaffolding, on the right as you enter, used to erect the massive wall. The **Great Court,** the single largest element of the temple complex, dates from around the same time. Seti II built the chambers on the left to house the sacred barques of the Theban triad of Amun, Mut, and Khonsu. The largest room housed the barque of Amun, pictured on the wall. On the right is a temple built under Ramses III, consisting of a large open court and three inner chambers. Twenty 7m statues of the warrior-king line the open court, while its walls depict his conquests. An open papyrus column in the center of the Great Court is all that remains of the 25th-dynasty (689-664 BCE) Ethiopian King Taharq's pavilion. Constructed without a roof, the pavilion was used for a ceremony in which a statue of Amun-Ra was recharged by the sun's rays.

Pass through the recycled second pylon (Ramses II made it with blocks from one of Akhenaton's temples) into the **Great Hypostyle Hall.** With 12 central columns and 122 subsidiary columns, it's a pinnacle of pharaonic architecture. The central colonnade (from 1375 BCE) is the oldest part of the hall; Ramses II made other additions, and his royal cartouche is featured prominently on many of the columns. The walls are covered with images of Amun, who is often receiving offerings from the kings. A side door on the left allows visitors to view the hunting and battle scenes inscribed on the outside wall. A path here leads north to the small **Temple of Ptah.** Inside the temple a columned path leads to a small inner sanctuary with a headless statue of seated Ptah. The dark room on the right contains an eerie black stone statue of the lion-headed goddess Sekhmet.

Back in the main temple, emerge from the forest of sandstone to find the obelisk of Thutmose I on the right. This courtyard connects the two sections of Karnak temple; a turn to the right takes you south along the north-south axis. Continuing east, the 30m-high granite **Obelisk of Queen Hatshepsut,** the tallest obelisk in Egypt, towers in front of the fourth pylon. Hatshepsut, who considered herself a female king, brought the stones from Aswan and inlaid them with bushels of gold. Passing through the rubble of the fifth pylon and the granite sixth pylon, enter the **Hall of Records,** containing two elegant granite pillars, one decorated with carvings of the lotus of Upper Egypt and the other with the papyrus of Lower Egypt From the hall, enter the **Sanctuary of the Sacred Boats,** built by Alexander the Great's half-brother Philip around 300 BCE. A room to the north of the sanctuary contains colorful images of the gods, placed there by Hatshepsut. Her images were erased by her ungrateful son and successor Thutmose III, who had the wall completely covered, unknowingly preserving it until the present day.

Straight ahead across the open courtyard, the **Festival Hall of Thutmose III** dominates the eastern edge of the Karnak complex. Built to commemorate the pharaoh's victories in the mysterious north, it contains carvings of strange plants and animals brought back from his campaigns. The star-studded ceiling survives intact, supported by 52 tapered pillars. Some of the bases were actually whittled down to make room for large processions. In the 6th century CE, the hall was converted into a church; frescoes of haloed saints still adorn the interior walls and column shafts. Beyond a low wall to the east, the **Gate of Nectanebo** marks an early entrance to the complex. South of the Festival Hall, the limpid waters of the **Sacred Lake** sizzle in the heat. Priests purified themselves every morning in the holy waters of this rectangular pool before performing ceremonies in the temple. Note the large **scarab beetle** at the northwest corner of the lake. It is said that if a woman runs clockwise around the scarab three times, she will soon be pregnant.

Circle back to the junction of the two temple axes to explore the secondary north-south axis. The **Cache Court** in front of the seventh pylon is named for the thousands of statues uncovered during excavations, some of which can be seen in front of the pylon. The south face of the pylon is covered with images of Thutmose III battling enemies. Also in front of this face sit the bottom half of two large statues. The eighth pylon also depicts victorious Egyptian kings in the heat of battle while several statues guard its south face. As of August 2001, the gate in front of the eighth pylon was closed for renovations.

KARNAK OPEN-AIR MUSEUM. The museum is north of the great court; look for a small sign and go back toward the entrance. The museum is comprised of three excavated chapels and a motley crew of well-labeled wall fragments. The **Red Chapel** of Queen Hatshepsut is displayed in rows of blocks, along with the Middle Kingdom **Alabaster Chapel.** The latter has flowing white walls streaked with brown, a welcome relief from the acres of sandstone. *(E£10, students E£5.)*

WEST BANK الضفة الغربية

*The cheapest way to get to the west bank is on the local tourist **ferry,** which docks directly in front of Luxor Temple (E£1; bicycles 25pt extra). Ferries run from 6am to 4pm. **Private motorboats** take passengers across for E£5 per boat. From the local ferry landing, it is a 1km walk north to the ticket kiosk, then 3km to the Colossi of Memnon. See **Sightseeing Strategy,** p. 222, for information on getting around once you are on the west bank.*

When they weren't preoccupied with empire-building and invader-expelling, the rulers of Thebes busied themselves preparing for eternity. As followers of the sun god Amun, the elite of the New Kingdom aspired to tombs on the west bank, where the sun sets and the afterlife supposedly begins. Pharaonic obsession with the afterlife made the necropolis of Thebes into the world's fanciest graveyard. Over millennia, robbers and archaeologists have nabbed much of the treasure, but the site still features an unparalleled collection of Egyptian funerary art.

New Kingdom rulers took no chances with the security of the afterlife. Earlier pharaohs had been too convinced of the mortality of their sacred tombs. Thieves had mastered the delicate art of pyramid pilfering at Memphis, making off with afterlife amenities of a grandeur that can now only be imagined. A radical change in burial practices was in order. The pharaohs of Thebes would not have their treasure rest anywhere but beside their mummified remains.

To conceal the location, contents, and design of the tombs, the work was done in secrecy by a team of laborers who dwelt within the necropolis. Perfecting techniques of tomb construction, decoration, and mummification, these 300 artisans devoted themselves to the City of the Dead over the course of generations, passing expertise down through familial lines. The remains of **Deir al-Medina** (Valley of the Artisans, see p. 227) have been thoroughly excavated and are among the most complete town remains in Egypt. Tomb design reflected the new emphasis on secrecy. Instead of one ostentatious pyramid, there were pairs of funerary monuments: an underground grave, lavishly outfitted with the articles demanded by the hectic afterlife and sequestered in an obscure recess of the desert; and a grandiose mortuary temple where the monarch could be worshiped for eternity. Architects incorporated dead-end passages, fake sarcophagi, hidden doorways, and deep shafts to foil the most cunning robbers. Once a pharaoh was safely stowed, workers immediately began to construct the tomb destined for his successor.

One region in particular seemed ideal for entombment: a narrow, winding valley walled on three sides by jagged limestone cliffs and approachable by a single rocky footpath. This isolated canyon, known as the **Valley of the Kings** (p. 223), became the burial place of New Kingdom pharaohs. Although it looked promising on papyrus, it failed to deter hoodlums, and few of the tombs escaped pillage. Queens, favored consorts, and select offspring were accorded ceremonial burial with full honors and security precautions in a separate corner of the west bank, the **Valley of the Queens** (p. 228). Esteemed members of the Theban aristocracy also practiced elaborate burial customs, and several of the resulting **Tombs of the Nobles** (p. 228) rival royal burial chambers in craft and design. Last but not least, the **Valley of the Artisans** has two very impressive tombs of pharaonic artists. Over 400 tombs continue to decay in the necropolis, but only a handful are accessible. The most imposing of the west bank's massive **mortuary temples** (p. 226) are the **Colossi of Memnon,** the **Temple of Hatshepsut** (Deir al-Bahri), and the Temple of Ramses III (better known as **Medinat Habu**) near the Valley of the Queens. The ruins of the **Ramesseum** (the Temple of Ramses II), though shattered, also merit a visit.

EGYPT

EGYPT

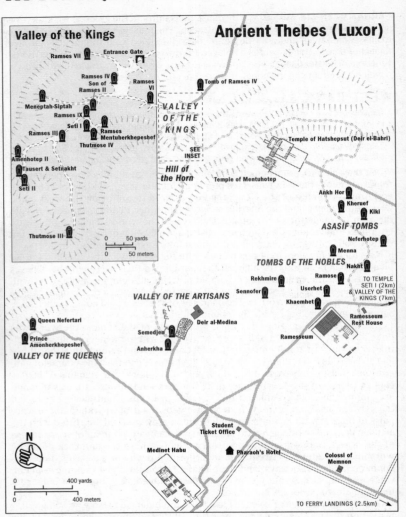

Valley of the Kings

Ancient Thebes (Luxor)

Ramses VII

Entrance Gate

Ramses IV
Son of
Ramses II

Ramses
VI

Tomb of Ramses IV

Meneptah-Siptah

Ramses IX

Seti I

Ramses
Mentuherkhepeshef

VALLEY
OF THE
KINGS

Temple of Hatshepsut (Deir el-Bahri)

Ramses III

Thutmose IV

SEE
INSET

Amenhotep II

Tausert & Setnakht

Hill of
the Horn

Temple of Mentuhotep

Seti II

0   50 yards

0   50 meters

Ankh Hor

Kheruef

Kiki

ASASIF TOMBS

Thutmose III

Neferhotep

Menna

TOMBS OF THE NOBLES

Nakht

Rekhmire

Ramose

Sennofer

Userhet

TO TEMPLE
SETI I (2km)
& VALLEY OF
THE KINGS
(7km)

Khaemhet

VALLEY OF THE ARTISANS

Ramesseum
Rest House

Queen Nefertari

Semedjen

Deir al-Medina

Ramesseum

Prince
Amonherkhepeshef

Anherkha

VALLEY OF THE QUEENS

N

Student
Ticket Office

Medinet Habu

Pharaoh's Hotel

Colossi of
Memnon

0   400 yards

0   400 meters

TO FERRY LANDINGS (2.5km)

🄖 **SIGHTSEEING STRATEGY: NILE WEST BANK.** In **summer**, explore the necropolis in the early morning; in **winter**, afternoons are sometimes less crowded. Guards at the less-visited sites tend to lock up and head home a little early, especially in the summer. All sites open at 6am and officially close at 5pm (4pm in winter); stragglers won't be kicked out as long as they get in before closing. Bring plenty of **water** and a **flashlight.** Tomb guards have been known to turn off the lights to force you to rely on them for guidance. Here are some transportation options once you're at the west bank:

On foot: If you have time and stamina, walking is the best and probably safest way to see the sights on the west bank. All of the sights (except for the Valley of the Kings) are within 3km of the Colossi of Memnon. Once on the main road (1km from the ticket office), catch a covered pickup truck to the Colossi of Memnon (25pt). Special taxis travel directly from the ticket office to the Colossi of Memnon for E£5 (more in summer). The Valley of the Kings is 8km by paved road, but the walk is worth it for the chance to follow the donkey trail up and over **Gabal al-Qurn** (Hill of the Horn). The peak was once sacred to the goddess of silence, Mirtseger, and with good reason—the serene quiet at the top of the hill is matched only by the view of the ruins. A simple geographic division is **North** (Valley of the Kings, Seti Temple, Hatshepsut, Ramesseum, the Tombs of the Nobles) and **South** (Valley of the Queens, Medinat Habu, the Valley of the Artisans); this division makes for a two-day exploration.

Guided tour: Tours in air-conditioned coaches with English-speaking guides are most popular. All budget hotels book tours, but many charge a hefty commission. Do not under any circumstances book tours for Luxor in Cairo, as travel agents are likely to slap a hefty commission onto an already inflated price. There's no need to pay more than E£45 for a tour; simply negotiate with your hotel manager or join the Happy Land tour. Some tours include up to 40 people, so check in advance with your hotel about numbers. A better option (with a better price) is to book a tour directly with noted guide and Egyptologist **Mahmoud 'Abd Allah** (☎37 28 21, or 01 22 15 71 45). Better known as Sunshine, he speaks English and has been giving good, cheap tours for 24 years.

By donkey: Mark Twain wrote that riding a donkey in Egypt "was a fresh, new, exhilarating sensation worth a hundred worn and threadbare pleasures." The novelty of donkey travel (which wears thin as quickly as the seat of your pants) and the fantastic views afforded by the trail as it climbs its way up to the Valley of the Kings have led to a burgeoning burro-borrow market. Arrange an excursion through your hotel that includes donkey and ferry ride (E£35) or hire your own animal in the village of Gezira (just inland from the ferry) or at the local dock. One suggested donkey route starts at the Valley of the Kings, circles to the Temple of Hatshepsut and the Ramesseum, then returns home.

By bike: A few serious hills are challenging, especially during the summer. Rent bikes in Luxor or by the local ferry landing (E£5). Many hotels, including the Sherif, rent motorbikes (E£50-60 per day).

By taxi: Taxis lack air-conditioning and are more expensive (E£25-35 per hr. is reasonable), but they allow you to cover the most ground. Hordes of drivers wait at both ferry landings. You can hire a taxi in Luxor, but a trip by the new bridge can drive up prices. When bargaining, ignore nonsense about government rates and per person charges.

VALLEY OF THE KINGS وادى الملوك

5km from the Nile, but there's no direct path. Two possible routes to the beginning of the Valley road exist. You can go past the Colossi of Memnon, continuing straight toward the Valley of the Artisans; at the end of the road, hike 3km over the Hill of the Horn. Alternately, turn right at the ticket office (follow the signs), pass the Ramesseum, then turn left at the military checkpoint (after 2km) where the road gently winds for 5km through desolate mountain valleys. Tombs open daily 6am-5pm; in winter 6am-4pm. A single ticket provides access to 3 tombs. E£20, students E£10. The rest house near the entrance has overpriced water, warm juice, and public toilets.

The Valley of the Kings, no more than 400m long and 200m wide, can easily be toured on foot using the clearly marked, well-groomed gravel paths. Over 64 known tombs honeycomb the valley, numbered in the order they were discovered. Most are closed to the public, but the best-known tombs are almost always accessible. Every few months the open tombs are rotated to minimize wear and tear and to add a little variety—which, after all, is the spice of afterlife. Ask at the tourist office to find which are currently open.

TOMB OF RAMSES IV (#2). The second tomb on the right is the tomb of Ramses IV. The tomb was once used as a Byzantine church, and Coptic graffiti adorns the wall to the right of the entrance. Damaged decorations in the corridor give way to a bath of color and well-preserved adornments closer to the burial chamber. The tomb contains wall paintings excerpted from the *Book of the Dead* and the *Book of Gates* (look for the beautiful solar boat in the burial chamber). The 365 small statues in the tomb portray the pharaoh's guardian spirit and were believed to facilitate his resurrection each night of the year, when Amun-Ra crossed to the west bank. The figures on the left wall, facing the sun god, will be resurrected, while the upside down figures on the right wall represent doomed non-believers. A vividly colored ceiling and huge, cartouche-shaped sarcophagus make this one of the best tombs in the valley. Royal cartouches were thought to preserve the king's name forever inside their oval shape; Ramses figured that a cartouche-shaped sarcophagus ought to preserve his body forever.

TOMB OF RAMSES IX (#6). The intricately detailed ceiling of the 12th-century BCE tomb of Ramses IX (on your left when you enter the valley) features gold figures displaying their *joie de mort* against a deep blue background. To the right of the entrance, the pharaoh is shown offering a gazelle to Amun-Ra. Farther on the right, the reliefs show Ramses making offerings to the god of justice, who holds a balance, and to Osiris, god of resurrection, and making 136 negative confessions (I never lied, I never spent time in a Turkish prison, etc.). Directly opposite these reliefs, Ramses is playing the same game with Horus to gain safe passage through the two lakes of fire. A long corridor descends to an anteroom covered with protective demons, serpents, and wild beasts. A pit beyond the long corridor in the burial chamber holds Ramses IX's sarcophagus. The ceiling of the chamber was not smoothed and the text appears in shorthand because Ramses IX died before his tomb was ready. Most of the painting had to be completed during the 70 days needed for mummufucation.

TOMB OF RAMSES VI (#9). The third-largest tomb in the valley after those of Ramses II and Seti I, this crypt is known for its ceiling of winged cobras, decapitated enemies, and a spectacular 18m-long depiction of the sky god, Mut. The various red disks along Mut's body depict the daily path of the sun—she would give birth to it every morning and then swallow it in the evening. The vast sarcophagus in the burial chamber was split by tomb robbers who heated it and doused it in water, causing the stone to expand and crack—you can see the charred marks.

TOMB OF RAMSES III (#11). Nicknamed the "Tomb of the Harp Players" after the two plucky musicians depicted on one of its interior antechambers. The size and artistic skill of the decorations reflect Ramses III's successful 31-year reign. Left of the entrance, the pharaoh prays to Ra-Hurakhti (looking suspiciously like Horus in his hawk form). Colorful side rooms are decorated with paintings of their former contents. The penultimate chamber boasts a vivid portrayal of ancient chariot races on its left wall. Past the first chamber, the sacred barque of Ra is piled high with gods as it travels through the secret gates towards the afterlife. The pillared chamber is filled with pictures of the peoples of the world. On the right wall, non-believers are tied to plants. Luckless Ramses III was killed in a palace plot, burgled post-mortem, and—as a final insult—stolen and shipped in his magnificent sarcophagus to the Louvre in Paris.

GET DOWN AND DIG IT An archaeologist's work is never done, especially in Luxor. Although it would appear that most of the treasures of the old tombs and temples have been whisked away, archaeologists are still concerned with what they can learn through excavation (and finding a little new treasure never hurt anyone, either). The Department of Antiquities oversees and conducts many ongoing projects, from the restoration of the Ramesseum to current digs at the Karnak Temple and Valley of the Kings. A recent promising find is the discovery of the largest tomb ever found in Egypt, a vast 107-room (and counting) complex being excavated by a team led by the American archaeologist Kent Weeks. The name of Ramses II has been identified four times, giving rise to speculation that this could be the final resting place of the great pharaoh's many sons. Entry into the tomb, designated **KV5,** has been hampered by falling rocks, and it is completely off-limits to the public. Other avenues of research include remote sensing, which detects irregularities beneath the surface without costly digging, and excavation within the city of Luxor itself.

TOMB OF RAMSES I (#16). The steep entrance next to the tomb of Seti I (#17, see **Other Tombs** below) descends into the tomb of Ramses I, a single burial chamber dominated by Ramses's pink granite sarcophagus. The tomb walls are some of the best in the valley. The first corridor is also the shortest in the valley, perhaps a reflection of Ramses's brief rule (1320-18 BCE).

TOMB OF TUTANKHAMUN (#62). The west bank's most renowned tourist attraction, the tomb of Tutankhamun, stands directly in front of the rest house in the middle of the valley and requires a special ticket (E£40, students E£20). The real treasures are at the Egyptian Museum in Cairo (see p. 118), and the interior of this small tomb may not be worth the extra cash. If you plan to see it, visit it first or you'll probably be disappointed after seeing the others.

The only pharaonic tomb to evade grave robbers, Tut's treasure box was discovered in 1922 by archaeologist Howard Carter and has toured the world several times before returning to its permanent home in the Egyptian Museum. Tutankhamun's mummy was encased in the innermost of four snugly nested, superbly decorated cases, three of which can be seen in Cairo. Fortunately, the raiding Egyptologists left behind the outermost case (a gilded wood extravagance covered in rich jewels) and Tut's exquisitely carved sarcophagus. The perfectly preserved interior walls of the burial chamber depict colorful scenes from the *Book of the Dead*, which were transcribed from the pyramid writings at Saqqara (see p. 130). Egyptologists had expected that the tomb would contain little of interest because Tut reigned only two years, but Carter ignored professional censure and toiled for six years in the Valley of the Kings. After more than 200,000 tons of rubble had been moved, Carter's patron reluctantly decided to abort the project. Before admitting failure, Carter explored one more possibility: a site in front of the tomb of Ramses VI, in an area covered with workers' huts. Confounding the critics, he chanced upon an ancient doorway beneath the shanties. The tomb had been opened by robbers, but the thieves had apparently been caught in the act by necropolis guards, because the treasures had been hastily stacked and the entrance resealed. Three mummies, including that of Tut, were found in the tomb.

TOMB OF MERENPTAH (#8). Across from the rest house and down a short path, Merenptah's tomb descends past several pillared halls. On the left as you enter, a colorful painting depicts the pharaoh addressing Ra-Hurakhti. Farther down in the first pillared hall, pictures of Nubians and Syrians from the *Book of Gates* adorn the walls to the left. A detailed scene of Merenptah making offerings to Osiris and an unfinished statue also decorate the room. A huge granite sarcophagus rests in the middle of the burial chamber with the pharoah's visage carved into the top. The top walls contain the only remaining images of what once must have been an intricately decorated burial room.

TOMB OF THUTMOSE III (#34). The most dramatically situated burial site in the necropolis is the cliffside Tomb of Thutmose III, reached by a long, steep staircase that ascends a precipitous ravine squeezed between towering limestone cliffs. To get to the tomb, follow the dirt road that begins next to the Tomb of Ramses III (#11) leading southeast up the hill. The tomb's location provides the ultimate example of the 18th-dynasty pharaohs' attempt to hide their tombs. Thutmose III's is built in a fault, where it became naturally concealed by debris left by flash floods, but the ingenious design did not deter grave robbers. Queen Hatshepsut appointed her freakishly short stepson Thutmose III as a military leader; he became her rival and eventually took the throne from her. His conquests reached as far as the fourth cataract of the Nile to the south, Crete and Cyprus to the north, and the Euphrates to the east. His grave is decorated with unusual hieratic text (shorthand hieroglyphics, see **Ancient Egyptian Language,** p. 69) and strangely beautiful stick-figures of Khnum and other gods. The first pillared hall holds 741 figures from the *Book of the Dead*. The cartouche-shaped burial chamber still contains his red granite sarcophagus (don't tip the guard for showing you that it's empty).

EGYPT

MORTUARY TEMPLES

MEDINAT HABU (TEMPLE OF RAMSES III). This complex of well-preserved edifices stands to the left at the end of the road after the Colossi. Relatively few tourists visit this site; a tranquil hour is enough to take it in. The best part of the complex is the Mortuary Temple of Ramses III, decorated with reliefs of the pharaoh's many successful military campaigns, including his victories over the mysterious "Sea People" (who dangle by their hair from his fist). Enter the temple through its large fortified gate. Climbing the stairs on the gate's opposite side leads to a small open chamber where Ramses III is believed to have stayed while visiting the temple. (It was likely also the site of his assassination.) The temple is warrior-themed throughout: the main pylon, also known as the Royal Pavilion, resembles a military fortress rather than a temple. One relief explains the importance of securing houses of worship so that peace and order could then spread elsewhere, and several reliefs show prisoners being put to death. On the back of the main pylon are savory piles of conquered hands and tongues. Beyond the gate are two relief-rich courts. On the left side of the second court a window opening is supported by statues of human heads. Behind the second pylon are the remains of large statues of Osiris standing in front of eight papyrus-shaped columns. This "window of appearances," used for royal speeches, was meant to show the king standing on the heads of his vanquished enemies. *(Public bathrooms and a refreshment stand outside the gates.)*

RAMESSEUM (TEMPLE OF RAMSES II). Farther north, beyond the student ticket office, is the Mortuary Temple of Ramses II. A tour of the Ramesseum may not be worth a long side-trip and shouldn't exceed 30min. In most of the ravaged temples, visitors attempt to gather from the ruins an idea of the spectacle that once was, but at the Ramesseum, the ruins themselves are the grandest statement of all. The same pharaoh who had Abu Simbel tailor-made to his specifications built the Ramesseum to house another mammoth exercise in narcissism. The shattered remains of the 1000 ton, 17m **Colossus of Ramses II** (his fingers are over 1m long) were the inspiration for Percy Bysshe Shelley's famous poem: "My name is Ozymandias, king of kings: / Look on my works, ye Mighty, and despair!" Their broken enormity leads many to similar sentiments. The colossus, which was transported in one piece from the pharaoh's granite quarries in Aswan to Thebes, originally overlooked the passageway leading into the second court. Even shattered, the remnants (including head, upper arms, and one foot) are imposing.

MUMMIES IN THE NIGHT In the late 1870s, members of the Antiquities Service noticed many New Kingdom funerary objects appearing on the European black market. **Charles Wilbur,** a wealthy American antiquer, was enlisted to go undercover and identify the source of the treasures. After making clear that he would pay high prices for authentic pieces, Wilbur was eventually led to Luxor. Across the river in the town of Qurna, he was shown an item that had come from a recently opened royal burial. Wilbur secretly telegraphed Gaston Maspero, the Director General of the Antiquities Service, who rushed to Luxor and began intense questioning of all involved. Several weeks later, **Muhammad 'Abd al-Rasul,** the head of the most prominent antiquities-dealing family in Luxor, confessed that his family had found a tomb near the Mortuary Temple of Hatshepsut. Archaeologists were quickly summoned and found the deep shaft burial containing the mummies of the New Kingdom's greatest kings: Thutmose III, Ahmose (founder of the New Kingdom), and Ramses II, among many others. The 'Abd al-Rasul family had kept the shaft a secret for 10 years, quietly selling their stash. The Antiquities Service, aware of the security risk that a public disclosure would cause, employed hundreds of men to load the mummies onto ships. The bodies were hurried down the Nile and now reside in the Egyptian Museum in Cairo.

DEIR AL-BAHRI (TEMPLE OF HATSHEPSUT). Just north of the Ramesseum, a paved road leaves the main north-south thoroughfare and heads northwest, winding around to the Temple of Hatshepsut. If on foot, you can save some time by cutting through the village on the left side of the road (before it splits). In the center of the necropolis, the temple is 500m north of the Tombs of the Nobles. The temple's ancient Egyptian name, *Djeser Djesern*, means "most splendid of all," and with good reason: Hatshepsut's masterpiece rises in three broad, columned terraces from the desert floor against a dramatic backdrop of sheer limestone cliffs.

After the death of her husband Thutmose II, Hatshepsut became the ruler of the kingdom, the only woman ever to assume the title of pharaoh (see **Ancient History,** p. 64). Her temple was excavated by French and Egyptian archaeologists and is currently being restored by a joint Polish-Egyptian team with support from the US and France. No images of Hatshepsut remain intact. After her death, her stepson Thutmose III—who had to wait 20 years before coming into his own as pharaoh because she refused to marry him—defaced virtually all of them, and placed his name on the statues of a bearded Hatshepsut that line the third level. Men: can't live with 'em, can't be reincarnated with 'em.

If you walk from the lower court up a wide ramp to the central court, you'll come upon a colonnaded back wall that contains, from left to right, the Shrine of Hathor, the Colonnade of the Expedition of Punt, the Birth Colonnade, and the Shrine to Anubis. Inside the shrine of Hathor lies the only remaining image of Queen Hatshepsut as she stands between Hathor and Amun-Ra. If you look hard enough it is possible to spot her through the bars at the end of the chapel. The Punt reliefs show Egyptian expeditions to modern-day Somalia, and the exchange of goods with the locals. The Birth Colonnade details Hatshepsut's birth and childhood. Another huge ramp leads to the upper court with a rock-cut sanctuary. This court is closed to the public because it was badly ruined and sadly defaced by 7th-century Copts who used the temple as a monastery.

TEMPLE OF SETI I. You'll have a fair amount of trouble getting to this place, and there's not that much to see once there. Go north on the main road and follow it to the military checkpoint. Turn right to visit what remains of the Mortuary Temple of Seti I, father of Ramses II, a warrior who enlarged the Egyptian empire to include the island of Cyprus and parts of Mesopotamia. Seti was also one of the first men to wear earrings—a fact archaeologists gleaned from his well-preserved mummy-lobes. Although the booty from his successful campaigns has been stolen, the relief work, ranked among the finest executed in ancient Egypt, still remains.

VALLEY OF THE ARTISANS

One ticket includes the Workers' Walled City, the Temple of Deir al-Medina, and the two tombs. E£12, students E£6.

TOMBS OF THE ARTISANS. The accessible artisans' tombs are in such excellent condition that it is hard to believe they were painted so many centuries ago. Unlike the formal decorations on the walls of royal tombs, these tombs contain very creative drawings of the afterlife. Some artisans spent almost 30 years building their tombs, as they could only work on their own tombs on the single rest day of the ancient 10-day week. Two amazing tombs are open to the public: the **Tomb of Sennedjen,** artist for Ramses III, and the **Tomb of Anherkha,** "Deputy Master of the Two Egypts in Truth Square"—i.e. head artist for Ramses IV.

WORKERS' WALLED CITY. To reach the plentiful though visually uninspiring remains of the Workers' Walled City, go past the Colossi of Memnon and follow the small road west, past the ticket office. The Workers' Walled City was the only area of the west bank inhabited during the New Kingdom, and it is the best window archaeologists have found into the nature of urban life in ancient Egypt. Since the workers and artists knew the whereabouts of the tombs they were digging, their movements were strictly controlled, and they lived in isolation (the entire walled city was roofed over). To prevent any leaks, the priests had many of the workers' tongues cut off when construction was over. A typical house consisted of a kitchen, living room, and bedroom. Some had stairways for access to the roof-tops, a welcome relief from the heat and smell below.

TOMBS OF THE NOBLES قبور النبلاء

A few hundred meters southeast of the Temple of Hatshepsut is the west bank's sardine-packed burial site for nobility, with more than 400 tombs. Tickets (E£12, students E£6) are usually good for two tombs. The 1st pair listed provides the most punch for your pound. Many villagers will volunteer their services, but a guide is unnecessary. Maps are available in bookstores on the east bank.

TOMBS OF REKHMIRE (#100) AND SENNOFER (#96). The westernmost tomb belongs to Rekhmire, a governor of Thebes who advised Thutmose III and prided himself on his administrative genius. A historian's delight and perhaps the most absorbing of the tombs in the Theban necropolis, the **Tomb of Rekhmire** contains biographical narratives depicting the range of activities Rekhmire oversaw.

In the first chamber, tax evaders are tried by Rekhmire, who sits with a set of rolled papyrus texts strewn at the foot of his judgment throne; the presence of the papyrus suggests that written law existed as early as 1500 BCE. On the inner, left-hand wall, processions of tribute-payers arrive from Crete (top), Syria (middle), and the African kingdoms of Punt (modern-day Somalia) and Nubia (bottom). Other scenes show Egyptians drinking themselves silly during what was known as the Festival of the Valley. The niche at the top of the rear wall was intended to contain a statue of Rekhmire himself.

Trek 50m up the hill west of Rekhmire's tomb to reach the **Tomb of Sennofer,** known as the "Tomb of the Vines." A delightful lattice of purple and green filigreed grapevine crawling all over the ceiling simulates a shady arbor for Sennofer, over-seer of the royal gardens of Amun under Amenhotep II. The plan of the tomb is as unusual as its decor: a curving wall leads into the first room, which in turn leads straight back into the pillared burial chamber. The big, wet eyes of **the love-cow Hathor** follow you around the tomb from the tops of the columns. The superb condition and expressiveness of the paintings make this small tomb worth the detour.

VALLEY OF THE QUEENS وادى الملكات

During the later years of the New Kingdom, a special burial area was chosen for the wives and children of the pharaohs. Traditionally, the pharaoh's closest relatives were buried beside the monarch, but this arrangement changed during the reign of Ramses I (14th century BCE), when princes, consorts, and wives were buried in the Valley of the Queens. Directly west of the Colossi of Memnon at the end of the main road, the Valley of the Queens contains fewer than 30 royal tombs. Check at the ticket kiosks to find out which are currently open.

TOMB OF TITI (#52). As the favorite wife of Ramses III, Titi's tomb is richly decorated—but small. Reliefs show Titi praying and presenting musical instruments to Ra. In Roman times her tomb was used as a house, so the decorations lack the well-preserved freshness of some of the other area tombs.

TOMB OF AMONHERKHEPESHEF (#55). The tomb of Amonherkhepeshef, the son of Ramses III, is richly adorned with bas-relief carvings. In one, Ramses III introduces his nine-year-old son (wearing the groomed topknot of a pharaonic prince) to each of the major deities. Colored scenes of deities and farmers fill entire walls—a rare sight in Theban tombs. The sarcophagus that held the prince's mummy stands in the rear burial chamber. A dessicated fetus lies curled in a small glass display next to the remains of a still-born younger brother of the prince. The lively paintings make this tomb a cheaper, welcome alternative to the much more famous tomb of Queen Nefertari.

TOMB OF QUEEN NEFERTARI (#66). Touted as Egypt's finest tomb, the pricey tomb of Queen Nefertari is open to the first 150 people who can afford a ticket (E£100, students E£50). Stay alert: the moisture on your breath damages the tomb's colors, so you'll only have 10min. to absorb what you can. The vivid tones of the tomb walls are breathtaking, and it's a good thing they are: it took seven winters, US$6 million, and the expertise of the Getty Institute to preserve and restore this masterpiece dedicated to the favorite wife of Ramses II. The reliefs in the first chamber include the cow-goddess Hathor leading Nefertari by the hand, thousands of hieroglyphs, and a scarab-faced goddess. A sea-green and starry ceiling canopies the stairs down to the queen's burial chamber. Columns in the burial chamber portray green-skinned Osiris and Hathor.

🎭 ♟ ENTERTAINMENT AND ACTIVITIES

FELUCCAS. For a truly Luxorious diversion, while away the hours aboard a *felucca* on the Nile. **Banana Island,** a small, palm and fruit tree-studded peninsula 2mi. upriver, is a popular destination (2hr.; E£35-40; E£5 entrance fee paid to the family living on the island). Overpriced souvenir stands detract from an otherwise rustic experience. Banana Island can also be reached by bicycle: follow the Nile 5km south past the Novotel and turn left onto a tiny dirt road before the turnoff for **Crocodile Island.** Tourists have replaced the thousands of crocs of yore on Crocodile Island. *Feluccas* are prohibited from sailing after sunset.

SWIMMING. For E£10 you can beat the heat by the pool at **Emilio Hotel** (down the street from the Venus Hotel), **St. Joseph Hotel** (on Khalid ibn al-Walid St.), **Shady Hotel** (on Television St.), or **Luxor Wena Hotel** (on the corniche, fee includes unlimited rounds of billiards and backgammon).

CAFES. The many **ahwas** on the streets of Luxor are filled with Egyptians smoking *sheesha*, drinking coffee, and playing dominoes and backgammon. Foreigners are usually welcome, but solo women may attract unwanted comments. **Tikia,** on Television St., is more comfortable and friendlier than the other shops. Locals enjoy meeting foreigners, so don't be surprised if you are invited to a **wedding party** while in Luxor (or at least asked to buy liquor from duty-free store "for my sister's wedding tomorrow"). Think twice before disrupting a wedding party—"guests" are often expected to pay admission.

🎷 NIGHTLIFE

The King's Head on Ibn Walik St. is a popular pub in the British tradition, with pizza (E£13) and a wide drink selection (Stella E£10; cocktails E£12). Play pool for E£20 per hr. **Mars Bar** in the Venus Hotel (Stella E£6) has a foosball table, billiards, and satellite TV. Most discos in Luxor are not hip, not cheap, and not worth it. Dance floors are about the size of a large table, and most DJs play songs you don't like and terrible remixes of the songs you do. If you're set on going anyway, try the popular disco at **Mercure Hotel** (also called the ETAP), on al-Nil St. At 12:30am, the music changes from Top 40 dance remixes to Arabic music, and the belly dancing starts. An older crowd joins the youngsters for the nightly display of undulating flesh. (E£30 minimum. Stella E£12. Open daily 10pm-2am.) Most popular among local swingers is the Disco on **Le Lotus** at the Novotel (at the intersection of Salah al-Din and al-Nil St.), on a boat docked beside the hotel. (No minimum. Stella E£14, cocktails E£19. Usually open W-Sa 10pm-3am, but schedule changes seasonally—inquire at the front desk.)

🏛 DAYTRIP FROM LUXOR

ABYDOS ابيد وس

*Although Abydos is officially open to the public, security concerns in Middle Egypt mean that visitors to the temple will probably be transported by **police convoy.** The site is accessible from the town of al-Balyana, a 45min. **microbus** ride from Sohag (E£1.50-2). You can also get to al-Balyana from Luxor: take north-bound **train** #981 (٩٨١) to al-Balyana from Luxor (2hr., 8am, E£9-11). If you aren't able to catch a tourist bus back, you will be stranded at the train station until 1:15 or 2:30pm. From al-Balyana, you and a mandatory party of your clos-*

est armed friends will continue to the temple (E£7). Bring food and water; the nearby restau-
rant has inflated prices and may not have any food if business is slow. Open 6am-6pm. All
sites E£12, students E£6.

The ancient city of Abydos was the site of a necropolis and temple dedicated to
the god Khenti-Amentiu. Pharaohs from the first dynasty onward chose to be buried at the site, which attracted corpses from all over Egypt **Osiris,** god of the dead,
subtly co-opted Abydos and the worshipers of Khenti-Amentiu during the 3rd
dynasty. Legend has it that the body of Osiris himself lies buried on these grounds.
After his famed dismemberment at the hands of his brother, Seth (see **Meet the
Gods,** p. 70), Osiris's head was said to have landed here. The cult of Osiris centered
here ritually reenacted the battle between Osiris and Seth as a sacred annual custom. The city that was Abydos has all but vanished, but after a look at the magnificent white limestone **Temple of Seti I,** dedicated to a 19th-dynasty pharaoh, it is not
hard to imagine the wonder that drew pilgrims from all over the Kingdom.

The Temple of Seti has been partially reconstructed. Three of the original seven
doors remain on the **Portico of Twelve Pillars,** which guarded the entrance into the
temple proper. The central doorway leads to the **First Hypostyle Hall,** lined with 24
colossal columns in the shape of papyrus plants. This grandiose entrance gives
way to the **Second Hypostyle Hall,** which contains some of the finest bas-reliefs ever
carved in Egypt At the far left corner of the Second Hypostyle Hall, a long narrow
corridor known as the **Gallery of the Kings** leads southeast. This simple passage
houses one of Egypt's most treasured finds, the **Kings' List,** which mentions the
names of 76 Egyptian rulers from Menes of Memphis to Seti I, the temple's royal
patron. Adding this list to previous knowledge, historians were able to map the
sequence of Egyptian dynasties.

In the south wing of the temple, beside the entrance to the Gallery of the Kings,
a doorway leads to a chamber with a tiny chapel to its right. The chapel contains a
kinky relief showing the mummy of Osiris, in the form of a falcon, impregnating
Isis. At the temple's rear is the elaborate **Inner Sanctuary of Osiris,** painted with
scenes of Osiris's life. The sanctuary is flanked by three small shrines bedecked
with the temple's best-preserved reliefs. Immediately behind the temple is the **Osir-
ion,** a now partially submerged tomb that Seti built for himself in the style of the
Old Kingdom. Ask a tomb guard to take you to the much less well-preserved **Temple of Ramses III** through a desert of broken ceramic to the north. The temple contains some interesting hieroglyphs and a mix of Coptic and pharaonic styles. Only
the bottom of the temple remains, but the colors in the small antechambers are
vivid. In one, Ramses II drinks the milk of cow goddess Hathor; in another, impri-
sioned Syrians are tied together by their necks.

BETWEEN LUXOR AND ASWAN

EDFU ادفو   ☎ 097

Only 50km south of Esna, Edfu is more than worth the short trip. Even the most
templed-out traveler won't be able to resist Edfu's intricately detailed **Temple of
Horus.** The vast, stunningly preserved temple is one of Upper Egypt's most spectacular sights, rivaling the serenity of Kalabsha and even the awesome scale of
Abu Simbel. Mysteriously, the temple hasn't made such a big impression on locals.
When archaeologists began excavating the temple in the mid-19th century, they
had more than sand and rubble to clear; the people of Edfu had also built a number
of homes on the half-buried temple's roof.

◪ **TRANSPORTATION.** The **train station** is remotely positioned on the east bank,
away from town. The **service station** sits just right of the small square where the
bridge reaches the west bank. Trains run north to Luxor (9:30, 11:30am, 1:30pm;
E£1.50) and south to Aswan (9:30, 11:30am, 5:30pm; E£1.50) These times change

often, so make sure to check within the train station for up to date information. **Kalishes** (E£2-3) or **private taxis** (E£3-5) can take you from either station to the temple. When facing the mosque in Temple Sq., follow the street on the mosque's right side to the **bus station,** 50m up the street. Buses run to Luxor (6pm, E£8) and Aswan (6, 7, 8am; E£2.50). Another set of buses bound for Luxor (7:30, 8, 9, 10, 11am, 1:30, 2:30, 3, 5, 7pm; E£8) and Aswan (9, 10, 11am, noon, 2, 3, 5, 6, 9:30pm; E£5-7) stop across the river in front of the train station. Schedules change often, so ask around for the latest developments.

■✈️🚹 **ORIENTATION AND PRACTICAL INFORMATION.** Edfu lies on the west bank of the Nile, roughly halfway between Luxor and Aswan. The center of town, **Temple Sq.,** lies about 1km inland, while a bridge crosses the Nile at the northern edge of town. The **Bank of Cairo** is on the west bank, 200m east (towards the river) of Temple Sq. on the right. (☎71 36 97. Open Su-Th 8:30am-2pm and 3-9pm.) Across the street from the bank is **Ezzat Pharmacy.** (☎71 38 60. Open M-Sa 7:30am-11:30pm.) About 100m from Temple Sq. is a tourist bazaar, the **temple,** and the **tourist police.** (☎70 01 34. Open 7am-7pm, in winter 7am-4pm.) The **post office** is on Tahrir St., 50m south of Temple Sq. (Open Sa-Th 8am-2pm.) From the bridge, the riverfront road runs 100m south to the **central telephone office** (☎71 17 77; open 24hr.) and another 200m to **al-Maglis St.,** which links the Nile with Temple Sq. The **telegraph office,** on the south side of Temple Sq., can help with **calling cards.** Several **telephone offices** line the riverfront where the cruise ships dock.

🚹🏠 **ACCOMMODATIONS AND FOOD.** The cleanest budget hotel in town—though that's not saying much—is the musty **al-Madina Hotel,** just off Temple Sq. The included breakfast, however, is impressive. (☎71 13 26. Singles E£20, less without bath; doubles E£30, with bath E£40; triples with bath E£45.) The cheap but run-down **Semiramis Hotel** is near the bank; at E£6 per bed it's not hard on the pocketbook, but you get what you pay for. A handful of restaurants lie in the square by the bridge. The **New Nesma Tourist Restaurant** serves up large portions of chicken and kebab (E£6-10) with heaps of potato chips (Stella E£6). Edfu's produce **souq** encompasses the streets off Temple Sq.

◙ **SIGHTS.** The spectacular ▨**Temple of Horus** took almost 200 years to construct and wasn't completed until 57 BCE, making it one of the last great Egyptian monuments. The Ptolemies designed this temple and the temple to Hathor at Dendera (see p. 246) as a matching set. Several important religious festivals dealing with the life of Horus were celebrated at Edfu. During the annual Union with the Solar Disk, Horus's earthly form was brought to the roof of the temple to be rejuvenated by the sun's rays. In another important ritual, the Festival of the Happy Reunion, the god's icon (once held in the polished black granite shrine in the temple's inner sanctuary) was removed from the temple in a ceremonial boat, then taken to Dendera to escort gal-pal Hathor back to his humble abode for some play. In a chamber behind the sanctuary there is a modern reconstruction of the ceremonial boat used to carry the statue during festivals; the original is in the Egyptian Museum in Cairo. (*Open daily 7am-6pm, in winter 7am-4pm. E£20, students E£10. Bring a flashlight.*)

The path from the ticket office takes you to the temple's shapely rear end. Wind your way around the complex to the front, decorated with inscriptions galore and a large depiction of Horus on either side of the entrance. Enter through the 12 gargantuan columns of the **Great Hypostyle Hall** and look to the right for the small **library,** where papyrus was found indicating the dates of the temple's festivals. A symmetric doorway on the left served as a **purification chamber** for the pharaoh. On the left-hand wall, inscriptions show Ptolemy building the temple—first digging the foundation and then opening his grand edifice. Proceed to the second hypostyle hall, outfitted with a similar arrangement of smaller pillars. Doorways on either side lead to the **ambulatory,** a narrow exterior passageway running between the temple and its protective wall. Charred ceilings mark the period when Christians used the temple to store and burn their garbage. The doorway on the right side of the second hall leads to a side **chapel** ceiling depicting the sky goddess Nut, reaching around the Zodiac (see **Meet the Gods,** p. 70). Sadly, monotheists of later eras chiseled away most of the faces, but the rest of the temple's reliefs remain untouched.

Outside the temple, in front of the main entrance, is a well-preserved Roman **mammisis** (birthhouse), where the birth of Horus was reenacted annually with appropriate hoopla. How many breast-feeding scenes can you count? Coptic Christians defaced images on the columns. Note the pictures of **pot-bellied pygmies,** brought to court for the royalty's entertainment, atop the exterior side columns.

KOM OMBO كوم امبو

Where the temples at Philae, Kalabsha, and Abu Simbel once stood, only water now remains (see **Moving a Mountain,** p. 245). But Kom Ombo still stands in its original spot, 45km north of Aswan, cutting the same striking figure today as it did during Ptolemaic times. The beautiful temple ruins make Kom Ombo worth the visit, but finding a parking spot may be difficult: Nile cruisers carrying an assortment of European tourists and their translators barge in on every available inch of the coastline. One look at the adjacent town will make most travelers want to make like a temple and relocate.

A series of temples has occupied this spot since the Middle Kingdom, and parts of the older versions of the **Temple of Kom Ombo** now rest at the Louvre in Paris and the Egyptian Museum in Cairo (see p. 118). The current edifice dates only to 150 BCE and was built by Ptolemy VI. Later, Ptolemy XIII added the outer and inner hypostyle halls. In 30 BCE, Caesar Augustus left his own mark—though his additions lie in ruins today, as the rising waters of the Nile buried the lower part of the temple in silt. In later years, the above-ground portion was used as a quarry for new construction projects; as a result, the side walls have vanished.

Nevertheless, the temple that remains (open daily 7am-9pm, in winter 7am-7pm; E£10, students E£5) provides more deity for your dollar than you will get anywhere else. **Sobek,** patron of the many crocs that lurked in the waters nearby in ancient times, came to **Horus** the elder, avenger of Osiris and the source of the pharaohs' divine power, asking for food. Horus apparently complied, and the two gods subsequently agreed to share this temple. Kom Ombo is therefore rigorously symmetrical throughout: double halls and double colonnades lead to double doorways which open onto double chambers and double sanctuaries. The right side of the temple honors Sobek, and the left Horus. (Sobek's crocodiles have since relocated to Lake Nasser.) On the ceiling of the left vestibule, bright blue images of Horus still hover protectively over the chamber. A tunnel in the floor of the inner sanctuary allowed clergy to climb in so they could overhear entreaties to the gods. Ask the guard to show you the reliefs of **Cleopatra II and VII,** and take it upon yourself to decipher the risqué hieroglyphs: can you spot the two dripping phalluses and the dismembered bodies?

Predating the Catholic tradition of confessionals by several centuries, a window in the west wall opening into the sanctuary, decorated with ears and eyes, is where the plebeians came to confess their sins to the gods and ask for forgiveness. This section of the temple also houses reliefs honoring yet another deity: Aesculapius, the Greek god of medicine.

West of the temple are remains of a Roman *mammisis*, and adjoining the northern edge of the temple are now-putrid Roman water supply tanks, once crawling with crocodiles. The **Chapel of Hathor,** to your right as you enter the compound, has crocodile mummies which were unearthed near the road leading to the site. Cleopatra's bubble bath is also rumored to be nearby.

▶ DAYTRIP FROM KOM OMBO: DARAW CAMEL MARKET

Service careen to Daraw from Kom Ombo (8km, 10min.) and Aswan (37km, 1hr.), but check with local authorities to make sure they take non-Egyptians. **Trains** and **buses** running between Luxor and Aswan may also stop in Daraw. The taxi stand, bus station, and train sta-

*tion lie along the main highway. To reach the camel market from the stations, walk 300m north, cross the tracks, and head down the road for 15min. Take a right after you pass the open fields. You've arrived when you see 200-odd people smacking the rear ends of bound, groaning camels to display their vigor. If you're gliding by on a **felucca**, have the captain stop at the Daraw ferry landing and a pickup truck will take you to the market. Market open Sa-Tu 7am-2pm; slows down after 11am. Ask around for most up-to-date market days.*

Sudanese merchants, Bishari tribespeople, and Egyptian *fellaheen* gather Saturday to Tuesday mornings in Daraw for the unforgettable **camel market.** Waking up very early in Aswan, you can visit the market and move on to the temple at Kom Ombo. Saturdays and Sundays are the best days to scope out camels. On Tuesdays, various other livestock are sold as well.

The Bishari (Saharan nomads with their own language and culture) purchase camels for the equivalent of E£1000 in the Sudan, where camels are as plentiful as sand, and take them by caravan through the desert from the Sudan to Abu Simbel on the Forty Days Road. From Abu Simbel, trucks take the camels to the vet in Daraw before the Saturday market. Look for the occasional businessman in full traditional dress: flowing pants, a sword and dagger, and a cloak draped over the shoulders. Typically, a Sudanese camel owner will pay a Sudanese or Bishari shepherd to drive his camels north to Egypt The owner then flies up to oversee the sales, coming away with big profits. Camels are used for work, tourism, racing, and meat (the meat is said to be quite tender). Prices range E£2000-4000, savings of E£1000 over Cairo prices. A camel's hump size determines its health and value.

ASWAN اسوان ☎ 097

Aswan, one of the southernmost cities in Egypt, lies at the junction of the Middle East and Africa, evinced by the city's ethnic and cultural pluralism. In 1971, the completion of the Soviet-designed High Dam created nearby Lake Nasser (the world's largest reservoir) and boosted Egypt's agricultural and energy potential. The dam flooded most of Nubia, forcing large-scale migrations to Egypt and Sudan. Darker-skinned Nubian immigrants now thrive in Aswan, giving the city its African flavor. The city's name comes from the Nubian phrase *assy wangibu*, meaning "too much water," although the high daytime temperatures will often make you wonder if there could ever be enough water. This far south, the fertile strip nourished by the Nile is not very wide, and often there are only a few trees separating the desert from the river. Though summer temperatures average over 40°C (104°F), the thermometer dips to a chilly 35°C (95°F) in winter. During this time, the city becomes an all-out resort.

Aswanis' gentle charm makes up for the stuffy weather. Somehow tourists are coaxed into extending their stay, whether by the pesky street vendor stopping passersby mid-stride to hawk his wares, or by the friendly old lady giving directions in broken English. The cool breezes along the corniche in the evenings are a welcome surprise for those foolish enough to go out during the day. Women, however, should experience Aswan's pleasures with company; women traveling alone will get loads of catcalls, suggestive glances, and more-than-friendly hellos.

Aswan is a convenient base for exploring southern Egypt and deserves a spot on any itinerary. Plan on four days if you want to see the sights and stay sane. You can take *felucca* trips to Kom Ombo, Edfu, and Luxor (see **The Nile Valley: Getting Around,** p. 208). Summer, when temperatures are high and captains are desperate to capture the few tourists, is the best time for a *felucca* trip. Not only may prices be lower, but drifting on the Nile provides escape from the sun-soaked sands.

▐▌ TRANSPORTATION

Flights: The airport (☎ 48 03 20) is 23km south of town, near the High Dam. E£20 oneway by taxi, less if you haggle. Served by **EgyptAir** (☎ 31 50 00; fax 31 50 05), on the southern end of the corniche near Ferial Gardens. Office open daily 8am-8pm. Another EgyptAir office at the airport (☎ 48 05 68), but tickets are not sold there. 4 flights daily to Cairo, 8 during the winter (E£577 one-way). Daily flights to **Abu Simbel** leave at least twice a day Apr.-Sept; more frequently Oct.-Mar. (E£275 round-trip). MC/V. **Airport Police: ☎48 05 09.**

Trains: Station (☎31 47 54) at the northern end of al-Souq St. 1st- and 2nd-class A/C trains depart for **Cairo** (14hr.; 1st-class E£73, student E£49; 2nd-class E£42, student E£33) and **Luxor** (3½hr.; 1st-class E£27, student E£20; 2nd-class E£17, student E£15). Frequent trains run to the **High Dam** (30min.; 8, 9:30, 11:30am, 1:45, 3, 4:45pm; 70pt) and back (11:30am, 2, 2:30, 4pm). Prices and schedules subject to the whim of the Egyptian Transportation Department. Morning trains tend to be about E£5 less. The tourist office can provide current fares.

Buses: station (☎30 32 25) on Abtal al-Tahrir St. behind Abu Simbel Hotel. To: **Abu Simbel** (4hr.; 8, 11:30am, 5pm, returns to Aswan 7am, 2, 5pm; only four non-Egyptians allowed per bus; E£40 round-trip); **Asyut** (9hr., 7am, E£20); **Cairo** (12hr., 3:30pm, E£55); **Edfu** (2hr., E£5); **Hurghada** (7hr.; 6, 8am, 3:30, 5pm; E£35); **Kom Ombo** (1hr., E£1.50); **Luxor** (3½hr., E£6.50); **Qena** (4hr.; 6, 7, 8, 9, 11am, 12:30, 1:30, 3:30, 5pm; E£13) via **Daraw** (45min., E£1.50); **Suez** (13hr.; 6, 8am, 5pm; E£50).

Ferries: Range from large *feluccas* to small motor boats. Local ferries depart for **Elephantine Island** from al-Shatii Restaurant on the southern end of the corniche, or even farther south across from the EgyptAir office (every 15-20min. 6am-8pm, E£1). Hotel Oberoi's cheap ferry floats to the northern part of Elephantine Island from a ramp on the south side of the corniche gardens (E£1; see **Sights**, p. 238). The **Seti** ferry (not Seti Tours) departs from the north end of the corniche across from the park to the northern part of the western bank (every 20min., 6am-8pm, 25pt). Ignore captains who tell you the ferry is not running.

Service: As of Aug. 2001, buses and *service* were unavailable to tourists due to road closures and safety concerns, but they may be available later in the year. *Service* leave from the covered station 1km south of the train station (every 15-30min. 4am-6pm, depending on demand). To get there, take the overpass just left of the train station, make a left at the end of the road, then take another right. To: **Daraw** or **Kom Ombo** (40min., E£1); **Edfu** (1¼hr., E£7); **Esna** (2-3hr., E£8); **Khazan/Old Dam** (25pt); **Luxor** (3hr., E£10); and **Qena** (4hr., E£9). *Service* also occasionally depart from the corniche and Abtal al-Tahrir St. across from the bus station.

Taxis: Pick up a taxi anywhere along the corniche. Not more than E£5 within the city.

Bike Rental: Abtal al-Tahrir St., past the Arab Land Bazaar next to Poste Restante office. Open daily 10am-10pm. E£18 per day, E£3 per hr. Haggle if prices are not posted.

Kalish: After haggling, a horse-drawn *kalish* should cost E£5 for a short ride, E£10 for a 30min. tour.

✦ ORIENTATION

In Aswan, you're rarely more than two blocks from the Nile. The northern half of the city lies along three long avenues that run parallel to the Nile. The riverfront **Corniche al-Nil** ("the corniche") is the most picturesque, featuring several hotels, shops, banks, floating restaurants, and docks. Two blocks inland, the market-lined **Sa'ad Zaghloul St.** showcases everything from watermelons to water pipes. Also called **al-Souq St.,** it begins at the train station at the northeast corner of town and runs south 2km to **'Abbas Farid St.** For the block-long stretch behind al-Salaam and Hathor Hotels, this path of many names curves to the right, narrows, and changes its name to **Ahmed Maher St.** At this point, a crowded shopping street called **al-Sayyida Nafisa** runs perpendicular to al-Souq St. In the southern half of town, the corniche continues for another 1km and ends at the **Ferial Gardens.** South of the *souq*, inland streets form a labyrinth of alleys. Sandwiched between the corniche and al-Souq St., **Abtal al-Tahrir St.** begins at the youth hostel in the north and culminates in a small cluster of tourist bazaars, resuming as a narrow lane farther south. Unless you're an expert at reading signs in faded Arabic, don't plan on being able to identify streets. Asking for directions or using a map is your best bet.

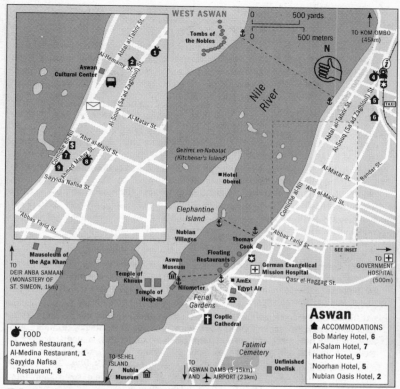

WEST ASWAN

Tombs of the Nobles

TO KOM OMBO (45km)

N

Aswan Cultural Center

Nile River

Geziret en-Nabatat (Kitchener's Island)

Hotel Oberoi

Elephantine Island

Nubian Villages

Thomas Cook

Floating Restaurants

German Evangelical Mission Hospital

Qasr el-Haggag St.

Mausoleum of the Aga Khan

TO DEIR ANBA SAMAAN (MONASTERY OF ST. SIMEON, 1km)

Temple of Khnum

Aswan Museum

Nilometer

Temple of Heqa-ib

Ferial Gardens

AmEx

Egypt Air

Coptic Cathedral

SEE INSET

TO GOVERNMENT HOSPITAL (500m)

TAXI

Al-Matar St.

Corniche al-Nil

Abd al-Majid St.

Bandar St.

Abbas Farid St.

Sayyida Nafisa St.

Abbas Farid St.

Al-Souq (Sa'ad Zaghloul) St.

Abtal al-Tahrir St.

Al-Hemamy St.

Ahmed Maher St.

Abd al-Majid St.

Al-Matar St.

Fatimid Cemetery

Unfinished Obelisk

TO SEHEL ISLAND

Nubia Museum

TO ASWAN DAMS (5-15km) AND AIRPORT (23km)

0   500 yards
0   500 meters

FOOD
Darwesh Restaurant, **4**
Al-Medina Restaurant, **1**
Sayyida Nafisa
   Restaurant, **8**

Aswan
▲ ACCOMMODATIONS
Bob Marley Hotel, **6**
Al-Salam Hotel, **7**
Hathor Hotel, **9**
Noorhan Hotel, **5**
Nubian Oasis Hotel, **2**

ⓘ PRACTICAL INFORMATION

TOURIST AND FINANCIAL SERVICES

Tourist Office: (☎31 28 11). Domed structure on the right as you exit the train station, at the northern end of al-Souq St. Few brochures, but knowledgeable and multilingual staff can help you. Open daily 9am-3pm and 7-9pm; in winter 9am-3pm and 6-8pm.

Tourist Police: (☎30 31 63). On the south side of the train station. Open 24hr.

Passport Office: (☎31 22 38). On Corniche al-Nil, on the 3rd fl. of the police building. Registers passports and extends visas. Open Su-Th 8am-2pm.

Currency Exchange: Banque Misr, 103 Corniche al-Nil (☎31 66 92 or 31 66 93; fax 31 66 94). MC and V advances. Open Su-Th 8:30am-2pm and 6-9pm. **ATM** on the corniche next to Banque Misr takes MC/V, PLUS, and Cirrus cards. Next to Memnon Hotel, the **National Bank of Egypt** also has an ATM that takes PLUS and Cirrus.

American Express: (☎/fax 30 29 09) At the south end of the corniche, on the 2nd fl. of the New Cataract Hotel. Arranges itineraries, cashes traveler's checks, and holds mail for cardholders. Open daily 8am-5pm.

Thomas Cook: 59 Corniche al-Nil (☎30 40 11; fax 30 62 09), just north of the police building. Travel and financial services. Discounts on tours and hotels if you book through Cook. Open daily 8am-2pm and 4-8pm; in winter 8am-8pm.

LOCAL SERVICES

Bookstore: Large hotels usually have small bookstores carrying European newspapers. Books in Arabic, English, French, and other languages can be found in shops along al-Souq St. and Corniche al-Nil.

Laundromat: Most hotels do laundry for E£1-2 per garment. Laundry and dry-cleaning service under the Nubian Oasis Hotel (see p. 236). Open daily 8am-2pm.

Swimming Pools: The Oberoi Hotel pool is a swanky but expensive option (E£21). Other 4- and 5-star hotels may allow use of their pools during the slow summer season for E£20-30. The rooftop pool at the Hathor Hotel is cheaper (E£5; free if you stay at the hotel) but it is only about 4ft. deep.

EMERGENCY AND COMMUNICATIONS

Emergency: Few places have English speakers, so call the **tourist police** (☎31 43 36 or 31 40 15) or **tourist office** (☎31 28 11) first. **Medical Emergency:** ☎123.

Pharmacy: Aswan Pharmacy (☎30 31 65), on the north end of Abtal al-Tahrir St., between the bus and train stations. Open daily 9:30am-1am. Numerous other pharmacies line the corniche and *souq*.

Hospitals: In decreasing order of English proficiency: **Mubarak Military Hospital** (☎31 79 85), in the flamingo-pink building behind the Nubian Museum. Clean new facility offers everything from family planning to emergency gynecological care. Travelers pay in cash. **German Evangelical Mission Hospital** (☎30 21 76 or 31 21 76), 100m south of the police station down an alley on the left. Look for steel doors with flower symbols. Recommended by the tourist office. The **Government Hospital** (☎30 28 55 or 24 19), on Qasr al-Hagga St., should be a last resort. Every hotel reception can provide the name of a **doctor**.

Internet Access: Enter **Oriental Cafe Garden** at the youth hostel sign and head to the outdoor garden cafe. In the back right corner is a pleasant A/C room with 3 computers. E£15 per hr., E£5 minimum. Open daily 9:30am-2am. **Rohab Internet Cafe,** inside the Aswan Rowing Club, charges E£5 for 15 min. Open daily 9am-midnight.

Post Office: On the corniche, toward the north end of town, right before the park. Offers **EMS** and **telegraph** services. Open Sa-Th 8am-2pm. For **Poste Restante,** walk south from the main post office and turn left down Salah al-Din St., then immediately right. In the yellow building with black columns. Open Su-Th 8am-2pm.

Telephones: Telephone office (☎31 06 10), two doors down from EgyptAir on the south end of the corniche near Ferial Gardens. Calls to US E£20 for 3min. Open 24hr. **Telegraph service** and **fax** available 8am-9pm. **Information:** ☎16.

■ ACCOMMODATIONS

Prices are higher in winter and lower in summer; rates listed are approximate. If you have the energy when you arrive, you may be able to play hotel hawkers off one another to land a better price. All listed hotels have laundry service and breakfast unless otherwise stated, but none dance the credit card tango. Spend the extra money in the summer and get air-conditioning, unless you want to wake up in the morning to find half your body mass evaporated. Be sure to ask for student and group discounts, but be careful of discounted group tours and *felucca* trips, which are often rip-offs. Do not agree to anything until you have checked out the competition on your own.

Nubian Oasis Hotel, 234 Sa'ad Zaghloul St. (☎31 21 23; fax 31 21 24; nubianoasis@infinity.com.eg). From the train station, turn left on Sa'ad Zaghloul and then right 2 streets after Cleopatra Hotel. Simple and clean, with great views from the rooftop sitting area. The restaurant serves inexpensive meals and the management organizes reliable tours at good prices. TV lounge with cable and pool. Internet access E£15 per hr. Rooms come with fans, soap, and toilet paper. Check-out noon. Singles E£10; doubles E£15; private bath and A/C E£5 each.

Noorhan Hotel (☎31 60 69), on Sa'ad Zaghloul St. From the train station, turn left onto Sa'ad Zaghloul, then take the 2nd left, at the Noorhan sign. At sundown, sip a Stella (E£6) on the terrace. Check-out noon. Rooms without A/C come with fans. Singles E£12, with A/C and private bath E£20; doubles E£12/E£25; triples E£18/E£30.

Hathor Hotel (☎31 45 80; fax 30 34 62), in the middle of Corniche al-Nil, next to al-Salaam Hotel. It's all about the rooftop pool (guests free, visitors E£5). All rooms have clean, fully tiled baths and A/C. Lunch E£12. Dinner E£15. Check-out noon. Singles E£30; doubles E£45; triples E£60. In winter add E£10 to room rates.

Queen N. Hotel (☎32 60 69). From the train station, walk to your right and towards the Nile. In a pink building 100m down the road. Brand new and super clean, this small, homey hotel offers rooms with comfortable mattresses, refrigerators, private baths, and A/C. The lobby offers welcoming chairs, TV, and a cafe. Plans for a small rooftop swimming pool by winter 2001-02. Laundry service available. Singles with huge double bed E£25, doubles E£35. Add E£5 for in-room TV with limited channels.

Al-Salaam Hotel, 101 Corniche al-Nil (☎30 36 49; fax 30 26 51). Carpeted hallways, an elevator, and clean rooms (some with balconies over the Nile). All rooms have pristine bathrooms and A/C. Check-out noon. Singles E£35; doubles E£50; triples E£65.

Bob Marley Hotel (☎30 18 39). From the train station, turn left onto al-Souq St., and take a left at the sign for the hotel. Low on cash? Don't mind lumpy beds? Bob's is your place, mon. No private baths or A/C. Check-out noon. Breakfast E£1. Singles E£5.

FOOD

Aswan's **souq** sells fruit, vegetables, bread, and pigeon (a local specialty)—not to mention *ta'amiyya*, liver sandwiches, *fuul*, falafel, and *kushari*. Vegetarians may find their choices limited to a few rice dishes. For legendary legumes, **vegetable souqs** are tucked away across the tracks from the train station and on the east end of 'Abd al-Majid St. Come in the morning for a full range of options. Small restaurants hide in the corners of al-Souq St. and Abtal al-Tahrir St. At the other end of the price spectrum are the huge buffets of luxury hotels. The Oberoi offers an elegant E£44 **breakfast buffet** (6-10:30am) in its cupola-covered ballroom restaurant. Don't leave Aswan without trying *karkadeh*, a sweet purple drink made of hibiscus. Local legend says downing a glass before bedtime mellows you out.

Sayyida Nafisa (31 71 52). Turn left on al-Souq St. from the train station and continue onto Ahmed Maher St. As you approach the restaurant, the ground in the *souq* turns rosy red from colored wood shavings. Named after a relative of Muhammad, this restaurant has both indoor and outdoor seating. Chicken and beef dishes E£6-11, refreshing juices E£2. Add 10% for service. 10% student discount. Open daily 7am-2am.

Al-Medina (30 56 96). On al-Souq St., across from the Cleopatra Hotel. Street vendors and tourists lunch here in A/C comfort. Beef, chicken, and veg. dishes served with rice, veggies, and salad (E£7-18) fill you up, and the speedy service won't slow you down. Add 15% for service and tax. Open daily noon-midnight.

Darwesh Restaurant, on Sa'ad Zaghloul St., opposite the south end of the train station. All meals (E£6-10) come with vegetables, soup, rice, and salad. Add 13% for service and tax. Open daily noon-midnight.

FLOATING AND RIVERSIDE RESTAURANTS
Popular with locals and tourists alike, these pseudo-aquatic eateries offer decent meals and the perfect setting to watch the sun go down over the desert hills of the west bank. All serve basically the same array of meat dishes, salads, tahini, drinks, and desserts. They are all relatively close together along the corniche, starting across the street from Thomas Cook and running down to about 100m north of the EgyptAir office. Expect an additional 15% added to all bills for tax and service.

Aswan Moon Restaurant (☎31 61 08). Popular with locals and tour groups alike, the atmosphere at this floating restaurant can't be beat. Oriental red drapes provide shade and a relaxing setting. Main dishes E£8-18.

Panorama (☎30 61 69). "The best food money can buy" is the motto of this riverside restaurant, set amidst luscious fruit trees. Delicious food and garden seating are worth the walk down the corniche. Try the Bedouin coffee served on coals, filtered with dried grass, and flavored with cardamom, cinnamon, and cloves (E£4). Main dishes E£7-9. Open daily noon-9pm.

Monalisa, with pleasant outdoor and indoor seating and a comfortably covered garden patio. The overbearing heat outdoors might wipe the enigmatic smile off your face, but turn that frown upside down with a Monalisa fruit cocktail (E£2). Well-prepared meat and fish entrees E£7-12. Breakfast E£3.50. Open daily 6am-3am.

👁 SIGHTS

Most of Aswan's attractions can be found on the isles in the middle of the Nile. Although some of Aswan's ancient Egyptian ruins are only second-rate compared to those of Giza and Luxor, its Nubian artifacts can't be found anywhere else. Just a short train ride away, the Aswan High Dam and Lake Nasser demonstrate the continuing Egyptian penchant for grandeur.

To reach the sights on the west bank of the Nile, it's easiest to hire a *felucca*. The official rate for *felucca* transport in the vicinity of Aswan is E£15 per hr. regardless of the number of passengers, but getting this price may take some negotiation. A complete tour of Elephantine Island, Kitchener's Island, the Aga Khan's Mausoleum, St. Simeon's Monastery, and the northern tombs goes for E£18 per hr. per group and takes 3-4hr. A cheap alternative is to break the west bank and Elepaphantine Island into two trips and trek between the sights on foot. Take the local ferry to the west bank (25pt) and back to Aswan and then take the other ferry over to Elephantine Island. From the west side you can hire a small rowboat (E£2-3) to take you to Kitchener and back. Then hop back on the local ferry to Aswan (E£1). Just make sure you don't get stranded late in the day, or you will be at the boatmen's mercy.

MAUSOLEUM OF THE AGA KHAN. The most placid attraction on the Nile's west bank is the Mausoleum of the Aga Khan, a short climb from the *felucca* dock. Aga Khans, the hereditary titles of Isma'ili Muslim *imams*, are believed to be direct descendants of Muhammad and the inheritors of his spiritual responsibilities of guidance. Aswan became the favorite winter retreat of **Sultan Muhammad Shah al-Husseini**, Aga Khan III (1877-1957). Upon his death, the Aga Khan's wife Begum oversaw the construction of the mausoleum, where the feisty nonagenarian still spends part of her year. Unfortunately, the mausoleum has been closed by the Egyptian government since June 1, 1997, due to a dispute with Begum over entrance fees. It sports an imposing fortress-like exterior, while the interior has a quiet simplicity modeled after Cairo's Fatimid tombs. Opposite the entrance stands a beautiful marble sarcophagus inscribed with passages from the Qur'an. *(Once the mausoleum re-opens, hours will be Tu-Su 9am-4pm. Call the tourist office for updates. Dress conservatively and remove shoes.)*

KISS MY AS(WAN)

The top ten ways to get rid of *felucca* captains and other undesirables:

10. *"La, shukran."* (No thank you.)
9. *"Ultilak la."* (I said no.)
8. *"Bas."* (Enough.)
7. *"Imshee."* (Go away.)
6. *"Haraam 'alayk."* (Shame on you.)
5. *"Kib nafsik."* (Scram.)
4. *"Iza arabit minni, badribak."* (If you get any closer, I'll hit you.)
3. *"La hawla wa la quwata illa billah...la!"* (By all the force and power of Allah...no!)
2. *"Ya haywan."* (You animal.)
1. *"Ibn kalb."* (You son of a dog.)

Let's Go does not recommend using phrases 1 or 2.

MONASTERY OF ST. SIMEON. The isolated and majestic **Deir Anba Samaan** (Monastery of St. Simeon) is a 1km walk up the stone path from the ferry landing. Built in the 6th and 7th centuries, the monastery is on a terrace carved into the steep hills. With its 6m-high turreted walls, it looks more like a fort than a religious sanctuary. The original walls stood 10m high but were not strong enough to keep the 300 resident monks from being driven out by 14th century Arab conquerors. Upstairs, the monks' cells and stone beds (with Bible and *galabiyya* wall slots) are currently occupied by bats. Simeon's chamber is open to visitors, complete with remnants of the baptismal font and drain pipe, well-preserved paintings of Mary and Joseph, Communion wine-making facilities, and a slot in the roof for a rope he tied around his beard to keep him on his feet during all-night prayer vigils. The dining room and kitchen are outside, to the west of the main hall. The monastery had a church and enough accommodations for several hundred pilgrims and their camels (the domed stables are outside to the south of the main hall).

To get to the monastery, follow the paved path that starts in front of the Mausoleum of the Aga Khan or, if you don't mind a chafed rear, hire a camel near the *felucca* stop (E£20 per camel for a 20min. ride for 2 people). Despite what the camel driver says, women do not need to cling tightly to him for safety, nor should he need to grab his passengers' legs to ensure stability. If you feel at all uncomfortable, forget the drivers' beastly manners and leave their camels behind. *(From the Tombs of the Nobles, head down the stairway towards the Nile and turn right. Walk 1.5km through the sand to the camels by the ferry landing. Hitch a camel or continue on up the hill. Open Tu-Su 7am-4pm. Tickets occasionally required.)*

TOMBS OF THE NOBLES. The Tombs of the Nobles lie farther north along the west bank of the Nile, carved into the face of desert cliffs. These tombs of governors and dignitaries date from the 23rd to the 18th century BCE and are significantly better preserved than those on Elephantine Island. Climb up the 100-odd stairs to ogle the bright color and detail of the reliefs in the **Tomb of Sarenput II**, a garrison commander during the 12th dynasty. Note the sacrificial stone slab with a blood drainage spout. The mummy was taken to Cairo, but there are plenty of other things to see. If you ask nicely, the guard will move the grating and let you peer into the enclave where baskets of yummy camel bones are stored; or, you can take a moment to examine the altar where meals were offered to the gods. The interconnected 6th-dynasty **Tombs of Mekhu and Sabni,** father and son, have images of the ancients getting high on lotus blossoms. The cheapest way to visit the tombs is to take the ferry (E£1) from the corniche, across the small park from the tourist office. Once across, walk uphill and to the left to the shack-like office on the left. *(Open daily 7am-5pm, 7am-4pm in winter. E£12, students E£6. Camera privileges E£10.)*

NUBIAN MUSEUM. Nubian culture is more alive and prominent in Aswan than anywhere else in Egypt Ten years in the making, Aswan's Nubian Museum is a magnificent sandstone building south of the Old Cataract Hotel. It features a vast collection of Nubian artifacts from all over Egypt, described in detailed Arabic and English (a rarity in Aswan). Also check out the wonderful models of Abu Simbel and Philae, as well as the interesting exhibit on the High Dam and the numerous temple relocation efforts associated with its construction. If you have to choose, the Nubian Museum is a better deal than the Aswan Museum on Elephantine Island. *(Open daily 9am-1pm and 6-10pm. E£20, students E£10.)*

NUBIAN VILLAGES. For a more authentic and enjoyable taste of Nubian life, the central section of Elephantine Island has several Nubian villages, where you'll find friendly residents, adoring youngsters, and brightly painted homes. The ferry to the west bank tombs (E£1) can take you to **Gharb Aswan,** a series of Nubian villages less touristed than Elephantine Island's. From the ferry dock walk 500m or take a pickup truck (about E£1) north to the villages.

The large Nubian houses, made of Nile mud, consist of six rooms around a courtyard; each cluster of rooms has its own dome or cylindrical roof. When the

High Dam threatened to destroy this traditional style, architect Hassan Fathy whipped up these reconstructed and relocated villages. Just as many Arab Muslims take pride in having made the *hajj* (pilgrimage to Mecca) by adding the prefix "hajj" to their last name, Nubian families celebrate this accomplishment by painting their huts in bright colors.

You may even be invited to join the celebrations and ululations of a wedding ceremony; Nubians consider it a mark of honor to have guests from far-flung villages attend their nuptial festivities. Nubian weddings traditionally involved 15 days of partying, but the demands of modern life have trimmed the celebration down to a mere three or four. Nubians feel slighted if you reject their offers of hospitality, so be diplomatic if you must decline. At all times, be modest in your dress and behavior. Women traveling alone will feel more comfortable amongst polite and hospitable Nubians than with the harassing men on the east shore.

🎵 ENTERTAINMENT

Nightclubs in Aswan feature a group of drummers and tambourine players, with a loud organ player and a male singer/emcee, plus the hip-notizing gyrations of a sequin-clad belly dancer enticing men into tossing bills. The action starts around 1am and lasts almost until sunrise. Check out the scene at **Salah al-Din Restaurant** or **Isis Hotel.** There is often a cover charge or minimum for discos and nightclubs, but prices change frequently (usually E£13-25 cover or two-drink minimum). The **Oberoi Hotel** has a piano bar where even you can sit down and play (drinks E£18), and a mini-disco during the winter with a pounding dance mix. The bastard love child of Eastern and Western dance scenes can be found at the dank pub and disco at the **New Cataract.** (Open daily 7pm-2am, E£15 cover for disco. Pool table E£20 per hr. Stella E£12.40.) The Pullman Bar in the **Old Cataract** is a more legitimate alternative with no cover. Try the pool and snooker tables at the **Basma Hotel** on the corniche, just behind the Cataract Hotels (no charge to play if you buy drinks).

🛍 SHOPPING

If you want more authentic souvenirs than hieroglyph-emblazoned t-shirts—or even if you do want hieroglyph-emblazoned t-shirts—take a stroll down **al-Sayyida Nafisa St.,** where tailors measure and cut with lightning speed. (Pants E£10-25, shorts and shirts E£10-15, shirts with collars and buttons E£25-40.) For traditional Egyptian clothing, there are numerous *galabiyya* (the Egyptian name for the ubiquitous Arab gown) and *qaftan* merchants in the *souq.* A tailor will make one out of his cloth for E£30-50. If you have the time, buy high-quality government cloth (at posted government prices) from one of the government shops on the corniche, then have garments made to order by the tailors on Sa'ad Zaghloul St. To tell if the tailor is experienced or not, look at his right hand. If the fingers are callused, he's authentic; if they're soft, he's probably just a salesman. For authentic papyrus, head down the stairs by the waterfront to **Dr. Rayab's Papyrus Museum,** across from the Horus Hotel. (Open daily 8am-midnight.) Papyrus ranges from E£20 to E£1200, depending on whether you want a sketch of a hieroglyph or an elaborate picture of an ancient Egyptian ritual. From October to May, the **Aswan Palace of Cultures** on Corniche al-Nil, north of the post office and across from the Rowing Club, features Nubian dancing and crafts. (Open Sa-Th 9-11pm. E£10.)

🔆 DAYTRIPS FROM ASWAN

An excellent road follows the Nile from Aswan to Khazan (a village near the Old Dam), providing access to both the dam and the motorboat launch to the Temple of Isis at Philae. The route to Khazan is serviced by **service** (50pt-E£1, depart from *service* stand) and by public **bus** (50pt-E£1). Both run until about 9:30pm.

TOURS. The tourist office and most hotels in Aswan arrange minibus trips to the ruins there. The trips generally cost E£40-55. Options usually include a short trip to Abu Simbel (E£40, with A/C E£45) or a long trip that also includes Philae temple, the High Dam, and unfinished Obelisk (E£50, with A/C E£55). Entrance fees are not included in tour prices. If your hotel charges more than the price listed here, shop around, as hotels pool their guests into the same tour, regardless of the price you are paying. Arranged tours generally leave at 4am and return to Aswan by 2pm; overzealous authorities insist that tourist groups travel in a police convoy. You'll be miserable if your minibus doesn't have air-conditioning, since blowing sands may preclude opening the windows for much of the trip. A roundtrip flight to Abu Simbel booked through EgyptAir costs E£275.

ELEPHANTINE AND KITCHENER'S ISLANDS

The local ferry drops you just north of the museum on Elephantine Island. From the landing, walk left towards the green metal gate. To continue to Kitchener's Island, find a rowboat from the west side of Elephantine Island: make your way through the gardens and fields to the water's edge, where you should be able to spot a rowboat along the shore. **Elephantine Island** *open daily 8:00am-6pm, in winter 8am-5pm. E£10, students E£5; includes the museum, the adjacent ruins, and the Nilometer. Camera privileges E£15.* **Kitchener's Island** *open daily 8am-5pm. E£5.*

While historically very significant, Elephantine Island is not as exciting as the west bank. The island got its name from the black, elephant-shaped stones at its southern tip. The remains of the ancient settlement on the southeast corner of the island, behind the museum, have been excavated. The local ferry from the corniche provides the cheapest transport to Elephantine Island (E£1, see p. 234).

The **Aswan Archaeological Museum** houses a rather small collection of ancient artifacts, either hand-labeled or completely unmarked. Even the "Head of a Man Mummy," resting on a cloth sack in the museum's sarcophagus room, looks bored. An annex augments the collection with a wide array of items recently excavated from the nearby ruins. Outside the museum, past the gardens, the **Nilometer** near the waterfront is nothing more than a staircase with a few engravings on the banister. The most interesting sections of the island are the temples behind the museum. The **Temple of Khnum** lies mostly in ruins, but you can see the remains of the temple door covered with pictures of the ram-headed god Khnum and his wife Seti. Several different **Temples of Satet** also sit amongst the ruins. The temples were built over the course of several dynasties. One displays a picture of 11th dynasty ruler Monthuh II. The **Temple of Heqa-Ib** houses several interesting statues in its courtyard, and a Ptolemaic temple among the ruins is dedicated to Alexander II. Make sure to bring a ball of string to trail behind you; some of the chambers are labyrinth-like, complete with dead ends and false doors.

Behind Elephantine Island and not visible from central Aswan, Kitchener's Island (*Geziret al-Nabatat*, or "Island of the Plants") is a lovely botanical garden planted by British General Kitchener, best known for crushing the Sudanese rebellion of 1898. Flamboyant birds congregate among the tropical plants that flourish here. To reach the island, hire a *felucca* to combine an island visit with stops along the west bank and Elephantine Island (a full afternoon rental runs E£15-18 per hr.). It is also possible to hire a rowboat from the west side of Elephantine Island (about E£3 for 1-2 passengers only). Make sure boats will wait for you or come back to pick you up by withholding payment until the end of the trip. If you're a real cheapskate, you can still get a gorgeous bird's eye view of this miniature paradise from the south face of the Tomb of the Nobles on the west bank.

PHILAE فيلة

Visited most easily by **minibus** *as part of a tour organized through your hotel. A* **taxi** *will take you to Philae for E£20 or as part of an itinerary including other sights.* **Bus** *service for foreigners is prohibited. After paying admission, you must hire a* **motorboat** *to reach the* *island at the official round-trip rate of E£20 per boat or E£2.50 per person when the boat is full. Prices may drop in the off-season. Find a few travelers to share the expense of a boat. The captain will try to con you into paying more, but be firm. If there are serious problems, complain at the tourist office in town. The boat captain is obligated to wait for you as you tour the site, so there is no need to rush.*

Called "the pearl of Egypt" by one of Napoleon's soldiers, the beautiful Temple of Isis at Philae has attracted the pious and the curious since classical times. The completion of the Old Dam in 1902 partially submerged the buildings only a few years after their resurrection as a popular tourist destination. Victorian vandals then gathered around the pillars and chipped their names into the protruding columns; the graffiti now mark the earlier water level. Archaeologists feared the waters would eventually undermine the foundations of the temples and hasten their collapse, and the construction of the High Dam would indeed have utterly destroyed Philae were it not for the efforts of UNESCO and the Egyptian Antiquities Department. Between 1972 and 1980, the entire complex of temples was transferred from Philae Island to higher ground on nearby Agilkia Island. In 1980, the new site of the temples re-opened to tourism (see **Moving a Mountain,** p. 245). Philae offers a sound and light show. (English performances M, F, Sa 6:30pm, and Tu, W at 7:45pm in winter; M, F, Sa at 8pm and Tu, W at 9:15pm in summer.)

TEMPLE OF ISIS. The Temple of Isis, dominating the island's northern edge, is the last bastion of ancient Egyptian religion. Isis was a goddess in the truest sense: mother of nature, protector of humans, goddess of purity *and* sexuality, and sister-wife of the legendary hero Osiris (see **Meet the Gods,** p. 70). It was on Philae that she supposedly found her husband's heart after he was dismembered, making the island the most sacred of Isis's homes. Her cult following continued long after the establishment of Christianity, fizzling out only in the 6th century during the reign of Justinian, who successfully replaced her with the Virgin Mary. Nearly all the structures on Philae date from the Ptolemaic and Roman eras, when Egyptian art was in decline—hence the inferior quality of the decorative relief work. *(Open daily 7am-5pm. E£20, students E£10.)*

PORTICO OF NECTANEBO. From the landing at the southern tip of the island, climb the short slope up to the temple complex past Philae's oldest structure, the **Portico of Nectanebo,** with several pillars and numerous inscriptions that once formed the vestibule of a temple. A great colonnade with pillars on either side runs from the portico to the massive main walls of the Temple of Isis. The outermost courtyard in Philae was for commoners, while each successive inner courtyard was reserved for increasingly important people—the innermost for High Priests. The larger edifice has been washed away, but the eastern side of the colonnade remains. Ptolemy, Isis, and Horus are depicted on the **first pylon,** which rises 18m on either side of the temple's main entrance. Note the channels cut into the face of the pylon on either side of the doorway, where brightly painted square-cut cedar flagpoles once stood. The space on the left side of the threshold was for hinges that once supported an enormous door.

Through this entrance is the **central court,** with a Roman *mammisis* (birth-house) devoted to Horus, its columns emblazoned with the head of his consort, the cow-goddess Hathor. The walls depict the falcon god in the marshes of his birth. On the temple wall opposite the *mammisis* (to the right as you enter the central court), Horus is transported in a boat on the shoulders of servants en route to visit another member of the divine family.

To the north is the slightly off-center **second pylon,** marking the way to the temple's inner sanctum. The *pronaos* (vestibule) was converted into a church by early Christians, who inscribed Byzantine crosses on the chamber walls and added a small altar. Farther north is the *naos*, the temple's innermost sanctuary. With a little *bakhsheesh* it may be possible to climb to the roof of the temple or enter a trap door on the interior right side leading to an inscribed crypt

OTHER SIGHTS. Behind the temple to the left is a **Nilometer** with a stairwell and the grooves used to measure the depths of the water during the river's yearly floods. The stairwell is across from a French inscription from Napoleon's expedition. Because Egyptian gods supposedly liked to make house calls, to the right of the temple is **Trajan's Kiosk,** a beautifully columned, open-air garage/divine carport (mistaken as a pharaoh's bed by the Victorians), which housed the barque of whichever god-icon came to visit Isis.

ASWAN HIGH DAM السد العالى

*Until tourists can once again use the buses and service, the best way to get to dam is the frequent **train** or a taxi which can take you by the dams and Kalabsha (E£30). Train stops are not labeled, so make sure to ask veteran-looking passengers for help identifying stations. Neither vehicles nor pedestrians are allowed to cross the dam after 6pm.*

The best-known attraction in the area is modern Egypt's greatest monument, the High Dam (al-Sidd al-'Ali), completed in 1971. The dam is interesting intellectually as well as incredibly impressive visually. It lacks the aesthetic magnificence of ancient Egypt's colossi, but it could teach them a thing or two about size: 1km thick at the base, 3.6km long, and 100m high, the dam contains more than 17 times the material used in the Great Pyramid of Cheops. The construction of the dam created **Lake Nasser,** the world's largest artificial lake, and covered all of Lower Nubia in waters as deep as 200m. Because of it, thousands of Sudanese and Nubians were forced to relocate, and ancient Nubia's archaeological treasures were threatened. The Egyptian government sent out an international plea for help—many countries responded, both individually and under an ambitious UNESCO plan. A rise in the Sahara's water table has been noticed as far away as Algeria, and archaeologists suspect that this effect has damaged the necropolis at Luxor and the base of Giza's Sphinx. Another danger of the dam is the possibility of sabotage. Should the dam be destroyed, the flood that would follow would wipe out 98% of Egypt's population. Nearby hills have radar installations and anti-aircraft missiles to guard against such a disaster. On the brighter side, the dam's 12 turbines doubled Egypt's electrical output, agricultural productivity has been enhanced, and the acreage of Egypt's arable soil has increased by 30%. The dam enabled Egypt to enjoy a healthy water supply during the drought of the past decade, and in August 1988 it saved Egypt from the floods suffered by Sudan when the Nile overflowed after heavy rains. For a few extra pounds or a little sweet talk, have a taxi go behind the gates to the **power plant** where itsy-bitsy workers crawl around the base of the dam like industrious ants.

SOVIET-EGYPTIAN FRIENDSHIP MONUMENT. Crossing the dam to get to this monument is a bit of a pain. The soldiers at the eastern end won't let you walk across, but they will stop passing vehicles and make them give you a ride—but you have to pay E£5. On the other side is the towering Soviet-Egyptian Friendship Monument, arguably premature given the alacrity with which the Egyptians spurned their Soviet benefactors once the dam was complete. A stylized lotus blossom sitting in its own pond, the monument would fit perfectly into a museum of modern art. Amid Egypt's ancient wonders, however, it looks a little out of place. Due to the rise in terrorist activity, tourists should secure police permission to go to the top, either in Aswan or in the large yellow gift shop and cafeteria west of the monument, although some have been known to *bakhsheesh* (E£5) their way to the top if the dam authorities are closed. *(Open daily 6am-6pm, in winter 5am-5pm.)*

NEAR THE HIGH DAM. Built by the Brits between 1898 and 1902, the **Old Dam** supplied most of Egypt's power for years. Cab-oglers can fully appreciate the impressive sheer granite wall; there are no tourist facilities here. The fertile area known as the **First Cataract** is one of the most idyllic spots in the Aswan area. Viewing what is left of the rapid waters, churning around rocky outcrops north of the Old Dam, gives some idea of the perils of early Nile expeditions (when ships were hauled past this dangerous spot with ropes). In the village of **Khazan** on the south side of the Old Dam, 90-year-old British villas (now Brit-less) sit peacefully within walled gardens.

EGYPT

KALABSHA كلبشة

The well-preserved temple at Kalabsha is considered by many Egyptologists to be second only to the temple at Abu Simbel, but the building—situated dramatically above the placid waters of Lake Nasser—is more impressive on the outside than on the inside. Dedicated to the Nubian god Mandulis, renowned for his hundreds of wives and legions of children, the temple was built by Amenhotep II, augmented during the reign of Augustus, and used as a church during the Christian era. In 1962-63, the West German government paid to have the entire temple dismantled and transported in 13,000 pieces from its Nasser-flooded home to the present site, 50km north of the original (see **Moving a Mountain,** p. 245).

The temple is somewhat difficult to reach and poorly publicized, but it offers a relatively peaceful and quiet (if dimly lit) temple experience for those intrepid travelers wary of the pesky crowds at Abu Simbel. The cheapest way to reach Kalabsha is to take the **train** to the east end of the dam, ride to the west end (you'll have to pay the dam E£5 fee), then walk to the boat landing for the temple. To get to the landing from the western checkpoint, continue straight ahead for 100m, then veer left through the shipyard, following the curve of the water for about 1km. A **taxi** from Aswan to the boat landing is less of a hassle but more expensive; try bargaining down to E£25-30 (even less for large groups). Adding this stop to your taxi tour of the High Dam, Philae, and the Unfinished Obelisk should cost around E£5. At the dock, a **motorboat** (E£20 for a load of 10 or so) takes you to the temple's island. Remember to bring lots of water, cover your head, and watch your step on the dock. (High Dam open until 6pm.)

TEMPLE CAUSEWAY. An immense causeway of dressed stone leads from the water to the temple's main entrance. The first pylon is off-center from both the causeway and the inner gateways of the temple itself. The grand forecourt between the pylon and the vestibule is surrounded by 14 columns, each with a unique capital. On the wall to the left of the doorway in front of you, baby-god Horus is nursed by his mother Isis. A small picture of St. George slaying the dragon is carved into the bottom left side of the right-hand wall.

HOLY OF HOLIES. Because the temple faces east, light flows into the Holy of Holies (innermost chamber) only in the early morning. Bring a flashlight at other times and be prepared for bats. A passageway leads north through the vestibule to an inner encircling wall; around the wall to the south is a **Nilometer.** Extraordinary carvings of Mandulis, Isis, Horus, and Osiris cover the outside walls.

NUBIAN SHRINE. Outside the huge fortress-like wall, the remains of a small shrine are visible to the southeast; the present structure is largely a reconstructed facade. Nubian reliefs, including pre-dynastic elephants, a large giraffe, and gazelles, grace large boulders on the southern side of the temple. The double-image technique, characteristic of Nubian art, is used to portray motion in some of the drawings. Carcasses of enormous desiccated fish are surrealistically scattered on the sand, as are disembodied stone heads.

TEMPLE OF KERTASSI. Slightly southwest of the Temple of Kalabsha are the ruins of the Temple of Kertassi. Two Hathor columns remain, as well as four columns with elaborate floral capitals and a lone monolithic architrave. A stone pathway leads up the hill behind and to the right of the Temple of Kertassi to the **Rock Temple** (*Beit al-Wali* or "House of the Holy Man"), rescued from the encroaching waters of Lake Nasser with the aid of the US government. Ask the guard to let you in. One of many Nubian temples constructed by Ramses II, it features typically humble scenes of Ramses conquering foreigners, Ramses receiving prisoners, and a particularly understated scene of Ramses storming a castle half his size. Like a miniature Abu Simbel, this cave-temple was hewn from solid rock. Examine the bas-relief scenes closely: political and social history are portrayed in everything from chariot battles to squabbles over whose turn it is to walk the camel.

MOVING A MOUNTAIN

As the water level of Lake Nasser rose in the mid-'60s, Egypt realized that flooding would claim a large piece of the country's heritage if quick action was not taken. The United Nations and individual governments responded by funding a US$36 million relocation effort. The international concern was not entirely selfless: any country that assisted could claim half of the antiquities it helped to rescue and receive concessions for future archaeological research. As a result, the Temple of Dendera is now enclosed in New York's Metropolitan Museum of Art, Debed Temple can be found in Madrid, and al-Lessiya was claimed by Turin. The initial plan was to raise each temple, remove the surrounding mountain, and encase the structures in protective concrete boxes. The boxes would be slowly jacked up, and a thick concrete base would be built beneath them. Another possibility was to build a second small dam around the temples to keep the water at bay. Both of these schemes were deemed too expensive. To the chagrin of Egyptologists, the cheapest method was chosen—cutting the temples into pieces. The mountain had to be cut away, a job that endangered the sandstone statues below. Bulldozers covered the facade of Abu Simbel with sand, forming a mound that was penetrated with a steel tunnel so that workers could set up supportive steel bars inside. It took months to saw the temple apart and move the 3000 pieces to higher ground. When it was reassembled, hollow concrete domes were engineered to support the new artificial mountain.

ABU SIMBEL أبوسمبل

*Abu Simbel is 50km from the Sudanese border and a treacherous 297km south of Aswan. Due to political tensions, the Sudanese border is not passable and should not be approached by tourists for any reason. The government shut down ground transportation to Abu Simbel in 1997 due to terrorist threats, but it has been reopened and is considered quite safe. The easiest and most popular way to travel to Abu Simbel is by **microbus** arranged through hotels in Aswan. Prices may vary but the service is the same (hotels pool their guests together), so shop around. There are two options: Abu Simbel on its own (4am-1pm; E£40, with A/C E£45), or Abu Simbel plus stops at the **High Dam, Philae,** and the **Unfinished Obelisk** (4am-3:30pm; E£50, with A/C E£55). Two local **buses** travel between Aswan and Abu Simbel (11:30am and 5pm; returning to Aswan 7am, 2, 5pm; E£40). The morning bus gives you 2½hr. to explore the temple. Public buses are only permitted to carry four non-Egyptians per trip, so buy your ticket at the Aswan bus station a day ahead of time. **Planes** fly to Abu Simbel daily (E£275 roundtrip). Book a flight through EgyptAir (see Getting Around, p. 75) at least 2 days in advance. Airline buses meet you at Abu Simbel Airport and shuttle you to and from the sight free of charge. Another option is to take a **ferry** from Aswan to Abu Simbel (4 days/3 nights or 5 days/4 nights; US$100-120 per person per night). Site open 6am-5pm. E£36, students E£19.50; includes admission to Temple of Hathor. Flash photographers will be escorted out.*

Swiss explorer John Lewis Burkhardt happened upon the Great Temple of Abu Simbel in 1813. Until then, its mighty statues had been buried by the desert sands that had built up over the centuries.

BIG HEADS (COLOSSI). The grandeur of the pharaonic monuments reaches its peak at Egypt's southernmost tip. Four 22m tall statues of **Ramses II**, carved from a single slab of rock, greet the sunrise over Lake Nasser and guard the entrance to the Great Temple of Abu Simbel. Each statue wears Old and New Kingdom versions of the crowns of Upper and Lower Egypt An earthquake in 27 BCE crumbled the upper portion of one of the colossi. Modern engineers were unable to reconstruct the figure (and there were debates about whether they should—if it's been broken for 2000 years, don't fix it), so they left it in its faceless state. There are (much) smaller statues of wife Nefertari and some of the kids at the feet of Ramses. A row of **praying baboons** stand above the statues, framing the top of the temple entrance nearly 30m above the desert floor. Ancient Egyptians admired the baboons' habit of warming themselves in the sun's rays, thinking the beasts quite pious to pray to the sun god every dawn.

GREAT TEMPLE OF ABU SIMBEL. This is Ramses II's masterpiece. The temple is supposedly dedicated to the god Ra-Hurakhti, but as in all of Ramses' monuments, the focus is clearly on the great pharaoh himself. Ramses II couldn't seem to get enough self-celebrating statues, and the large first hall is lined with two rows of statues of the king. The walls vividly depict battle scenes of Ramses's Nubian victories. Proceeding through the temple, Ramses undergoes the characteristic god-king metamorphosis: near the entrance he is depicted as a great king, then as a servant of the gods, next as a companion of the gods, and finally, in the inner sanctuary, as a card-carrying deity.

Off the main temple chambers are **antechambers** that once stored implements of worship. Inscriptions on the walls show Ramses making sacrifices to the gods. At the rear of the temple, in the inner sanctum, four seated statues facing the entrance depict Ramses and the gods Ra-Hurakhti, Amun, and Ptah. Originally encased in gold, the statues now wait with divine patience for February 22 and October 22, when the first rays of the sun reach 100m into the temple to bathe all except Ptah (the god of darkness) in light. February 21 was Ramses' birthday and October 21 the date of his coronation, but when the temple was moved, the timing of these illuminations shifted by one day (they just don't build temples like they used to). A door to the right of the temple's facade leads into the dome that supports the new and improved mountain.

TEMPLE OF HATHOR. Next door to Ramses's temple was a temple dedicated to his favorite wife Nefertari and to Hathor, the young fertility/sky goddess. Six 10m statues of Ramses and Nefertari (as Hathor) adorn the façade. Along with the temple of Hatshepsut in west Thebes (see **Deir al-Bahri,** p. 227), this is one of the only temples in Egypt dedicated to a woman. Vivid pictures depicting the voluptuous queen and offerings to the gods adorn the walls of the main chamber. Still, images of Ramses abound—scenes on the walls depict his coronation, with the god Horus placing the crowns of Egypt on his head. The temple was constructed in the typical three-room style: the first chamber was open to the public, the second to nobles and priests, and the inner sanctuary only to the pharaoh and the high priest.

WESTERN DESERT OASES

"The call of the desert, for thinkers of the city, has always been irresistible. I do not think they find God there, but that they hear more distinctly in the solitude, the living verb they carry within themselves."
—T.E. Lawrence

The Western Desert (known as the Libyan Desert until World War II) is the largest and driest in the world, covering two-thirds of Egypt's area but supporting only 1% of its population. It boasts some of the highest temperatures on record, despite the fact that its oases—**Bahariya, Farafra, Dakhla,** and **Kharga**—mark the trail of a prehistoric branch of the cool, wet Nile. Each oasis sits in a depression surrounded by an escarpment, the top of which marks the usual level of the desert floor. Subterranean water seeps through these depressions, which lie at or near sea level. The water flow begins as the rains of equatorial Africa replenish the wells and springs annually, and it takes thousands of years to journey north through underground fissures. The Romans were the first to irrigate the area by tapping deeper reserves with their waterwheels and aqueducts, known as **'Ain Romani.** The Egyptian government is finally following suit by spending vast sums on its **New Valley Project** to use underground water to promote agriculture and the relocation of landless peasants from the Delta to the New Valley.

The desert oases are still somewhat off the beaten tourist path. Though the popularity of the oases is rising and the number of visitors steadily increasing, sights remain uncrowded and prices low, especially during the summer. The best time for all but extreme penny-pinchers to visit the oases is between October and April,

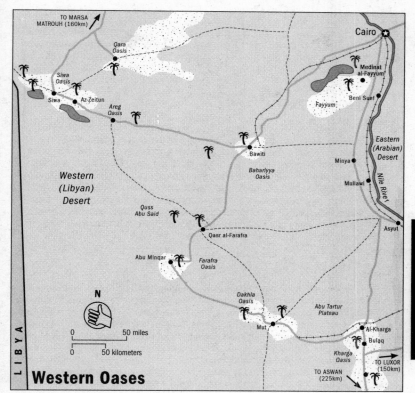

To Marsa Matrouh (160km)
Qara Oasis
Siwa Oasis
Siwa
Az-Zeitun
Areg Oasis
Cairo
Medinat al-Fayyum
Beni Suef
Fayyum
Eastern (Arabian) Desert
Minya
Mullawi
Nile River
Asyut
Western (Libyan) Desert
Bawiti
Bahariyya Oasis
Quss Abu Said
Qasr al-Farafra
Abu Minqar
Farafra Oasis
Dakhla Oasis
Abu Tartur Plateau
N
0   50 miles
0   50 kilometers
Mut
Al-Kharga
Bulaq
Kharga Oasis
To Luxor (150km)
To Aswan (225km)
LIBYA
Western Oases

EGYPT

as it is not unusual for summer temperatures, especially at Dakhla or Kharga, to reach 52°C (126°F). Even at night, summer temperatures persist into the upper 20s (over 80°F). Air-conditioning is making its way across the desert, but at present, only Dakhla and Kharga offer it. Similarly, traveler's checks can only be cashed in Dakhla and Kharga, so have plenty of money on hand before venturing westward. For important **desert safety** information, see **Essentials**, p. 27.

TRANSPORTATION

BY BUS

Inexpensive buses run from Asyut to Kharga and Dakhla. Bus travel between the oases requires even more flexibility and patience than in the rest of Egypt Published schedules are no more than rough guesses, so you should get to the station at least 30min. before the scheduled departure time. When there is no published material available, ask as many people as possible, follow the consensus, and arrive early. The most accurate information will come from local tourist offices and bus officials.

BY TAXI OR SERVICE

Special taxis travel from Cairo to all of the oases, from Asyut to Kharga, and from Kharga to Luxor. They sometimes offer a faster and more comfortable journey—check out what the vehicle looks like and ask how many people will be crammed in. *Service* between all oases are affordable, and often quicker than buses.

BY CAR

Car rental is convenient and comfortable—albeit expensive—for desert travel. A giant loop along the Great Desert Road and the Lower Nile Valley in either direction beginning in Cairo is about 1700km. Any car must be in top condition and fully outfitted for intense desert travel in order to survive the long, hot, poorly maintained roads. **Four-wheel-drive** is highly recommended. Another option is a **trailer** (caravan); renting one can solve a lot of problems, including those of transporting food, water, and extra gas, and finding a comfortable place to sleep.

CAR CAVEATS. First and foremost, it is always a long way between gas stations. While every oasis has at least one fuel pump, it is essential to buy jerry cans and fill them with enough gas to cover the vast distances between towns. A trailer guzzles huge quantities of fuel, so bring extra to fill an entire tank. Additionally, several containers of potable water are vital in case you get stranded. Try to drive in the cool morning or late afternoon, but never drive at night—the chances of getting lost on unlit roads increase dramatically, and hidden potholes are especially lethal. Note that foreigners are prohibited from leaving the main road. Don't pull an *English Patient*: never drive in a sandstorm. If you do get caught in one, stop, turn the car's rear to the wind, and wait.

ACCOMMODATIONS

The best alternative to staying in hotels is **camping**. Several budget campsites are run by hotels near Bahariya and Dakhla. Otherwise, most fertile land belongs to farmers who will usually permit you to pitch your tent. The ideal spot is just outside the main town of an oasis, where there is usually a small pool of water (ask the locals for the '*ain*, or spring) and nothing to keep you company but the sound of silence. Or trek out into the desert where cool temperatures and breezes carry away the mosquitoes, and the sand makes a soft mattress. Sleeping on the dunes has its own set of dangers—you might be sharing the desert expanse with ticks, wasps, scorpions, cheetahs, foxes, rats, amorous strangers, and tiny hedgehogs that roll into spiky balls when frightened. You might roll up yourself if you encounter one of the seven kinds of **poisonous snakes** in Egypt, among which is a family of lethal vipers. They rest under rocks and sand, coming out to drink at night. If you see snake tracks going in one direction, calmly go in the other. Common sense, a first aid kit, and a snake bite kit are recommended, even though snakes are rare and snake attacks rarer still. If you prefer mosquito bites to the threat of reptile venom, each of the oases has at least one cheap, clean hotel or rest house.

FOOD

Oasis groundwater tastes much better than that of the other Egyptian municipalities; however, while safer than water near the cities, it can still ruin a trip. The main towns of all the oases have restaurants and markets where you can fill up on food, but don't expect variety or refinement. The best meals are at locals' homes—with a winning smile and a little luck, you can taste for yourself.

SAFETY AND SECURITY

WOMEN TRAVELERS

Women should follow certain guidelines when swimming in springs. They are unlikely to be bothered in isolated springs not frequented by locals. The same goes for pools cordoned off and connected to tourist rest houses. Women should not, however, enter pools where men are already bathing. Sometimes women can bathe in a separate pool (local women bathe separately in the evening), provided they wear a *galabiyya* (loose-fitting robe). Women traveling without men should not embark on overnight desert excursions unless pre-arranged by a tourist official. Even then, care and common sense are key. Solo women heading for the oases should be prepared to deal with harassment. For more on what women can expect traveling in Egypt, see **Women Travelers**, p. 78.

TAXES, TOURISM, AND TRUST

Despite what out-of-date sources may tell you, you need only flash a **passport** at the numerous military checkpoints, and sometimes not even that. In Dakhla, Kharga, or Farafra, you will be asked to pay a one-time **tourism development tax** (E£5) by a tourist officer or by an employee of your hotel. Keep the receipt as proof or you may have to pay again.

The Western Desert has been attracting an increasing number of visitors with its traditional village lifestyle, stunning landscapes, and low prices. Bahariya, in particular, is seeing an exponential increase in tourism thanks to the recently discovered Roman ruins and "Valley of the Mummies," as well as overnight tours to the Black and White Deserts (see p. 252). With this sudden bumper crop of tourists comes the creeping influence of the smell of tourist money. Each oasis has people whose English is good, knowledge of the area fair, and sense of capitalism extraordinary. They are often friendly and helpful, but their assistance has a bloated price tag attached. For the best information, head for the New Valley's **tourist officials:** Muhammad 'Abd al-Qader in Bahariya, Umar Ahmed in Dakhla, and Ibrahim M. Hassan in Kharga. They will answer your questions in excellent English for free and can arrange for fairly priced **guides and transportation.** Without them, you are at the mercy of the wolves.

BAHARIYA OASIS واحة البحرية ☎018

The land turns a deep shade of red as you approach Bahariya, thanks to the vast deposits of iron that are quarried in an immense mine just off the highway, 40km away from Bawiti. This small oasis, 330km south of Cairo, has been a stopover for caravans traveling between the Nile Valley and the rest of North Africa since pharaonic times, when merchants used to load their donkeys with wine from al-Qasr (the present-day town of Bawiti). In later centuries, Bahariya enthusiastically welcomed Mecca-bound pilgrims, who would often join the traders on their transdesert trek. Today, the only "pilgrims" in Bahariya are the caravans of rip-roaring European adventurers gallivanting through the oasis in Land Rovers—because of its relatively close proximity to Cairo, Bahariya attracts visitors who crave a few days in the desert. Factor in the opening of several Roman-era sights in 1999, in addition to growing interest in the recently unearthed "Valley of the Mummies," and it's easy to see why Bahariya has become far more commercial and cutthroat than the other oases. Unfortunately, Bahariya's ancient ruins are spread over several kilometers, so hire a car for the day or truck it on a bicycle. The nearby gardens, springs, and desert offer relief, but not enough to make anyone stay longer than necessary. Food stores, coffee shops, and gas stations make this oasis an unavoidable stop en route to Farafra.

▐▀ TRANSPORTATION

The Bahariya Oasis is linked to Cairo by a decently paved road that heads past the Pyramids of Giza, then turns southwest across the desert to the town of **Bawiti.**

Buses: Touts congregate by the bus ticket and reservation office in a blue shed across from the Paradise Hotel (open daily 7am-noon and 8-11pm). A 3pm bus also leave. Get there early for a seat. Daily buses to **Cairo** (5hr.; 7am, noon, 3pm, midnight; E£12.50).

Minibuses: Minibuses run daily between Bahariya and **Cairo's** Sayyidna Zeinab bus station (5hr., E£11). Infrequent service to **Farafra** (E£11). Look for groups gathering by pickup trucks and minibuses in Bawiti on the main street. Minibuses leave when full.

EGYPT

▌ ORIENTATION AND PRACTICAL INFORMATION

Tourist Office: (☎ 80 30 39 or 80 30 35; 80 26 00 in the evening), 1st fl. of the government compound, which is just before the post office. It is the largest building in town, surrounded by a metal fence, and counts among its staff city council member Muhammad 'Abd al-Qader, who is the best source of information in Bahariya (after 2pm, find him in the lobby of the Paradise Hotel). Open daily 8am-2pm.

Currency Exchange: The **National Bank for Development** is next to the post office. Exchanges cash only. Open Su-Th 8am-2pm.

Gas Stations: 2 on the main road, about 1km out of town towards Cairo.

Pharmacy: (☎ 80 36 55), on the left 50m past Bayoumi's Popular Restaurant as you head towards Cairo on the main road. Open daily 8am-1am.

Hospital: (☎ 80 23 90), on the road toward Cairo. Take the 1st left and walk to the end of the dirt road. The hospital is on the left. Open 24hr.

Telephone Office: Opposite the Paradise Hotel. No international service, but you may be able to get through using MCI, AT&T, or an Egyptian calling card, all of which use local access numbers to connect you with the rest of the world. Open daily 8am-10pm.

Post Office: 2 doors down from the government compound as you head toward Farafra. Limited services. Open Sa-Th 8:30am-2pm.

▌ ACCOMMODATIONS

Ahmed's Safari Camp (☎ 80 33 99; ☎/fax 80 20 90; ahmed_safari@hotmail.com), 4km south of Bawiti. The massive grapevine-covered veranda, good food, free rides to and from town, and occasional live Bedouin music sweeten the bitter taste of isolation. Ahmed's friendly drivers meet each bus as it arrives in front of the Paradise Hotel. Numerous improvements and additions are in the works for winter 2001-02. Bare huts E£5 per person, breakfast an additional E£2.50. Concrete cabanas with breakfast included E£10-25 per person. Deluxe domed gazebos with shower and breakfast E£50.

Pyramid Mountain Safari Camp (African Camp) (☎ 80 21 84), 17km west of Bawiti. Turn off the main road near the northern end of town. Most visitors come through Hotel Alpenblick, but you can arrange your own transportation out to this clean, tranquil camp run by friendly Sudanese (E£30-35 round-trip per car). The nearby hot spring Bir Ghaba is the highlight of this camp. Breakfast E£15. Basic dinner E£5. Huts E£10 per person.

New Oasis Hotel (☎/fax 80 30 30), 300m down the road leading past Bayoumi's Restaurant and 'Ain Bishmu spring, behind al-Bishmu Hotel. Resembling something out of a honeymoon package deal, clean and classy rooms sport new beds and baths, wall-to-wall carpeting, and colorful decor. Call ahead to reserve a room, especially during the winter, as large tour groups often claim rooms well in advance. Breakfast included. E£25 per person.

Hotel Alpenblick (☎ 80 21 84), a white-domed building 250m past the "cheapest shop in town" sign as you walk with your back to the city council building and the tourist office. Lodgings here are a bit nicer than other options in Bawiti, but they're not quite worth the added expense. Rooms have carpets, fans, and mediocre bathrooms. Mahmoud, the general manager, organizes trips to the hot springs. Restaurant serves dinner. Breakfast included. Singles E£20; budget doubles E£20; regular doubles E£40, with bath E£56; triples E£60, with bath E£84.

▌ FOOD

Pickings are slim for restaurants in Bawiti. Most hotels serve three meals a day. **Bayoumi's Popular Restaurant,** across from the police station, sits next to the government compound just off the main road to Cairo. Ask in advance about prices. (Full meal around E£10. Stella E£7. Breakfast E£5. Open 5am-midnight.) **Restaurant Rashed,** about 200m out of town on the right side of the Cairo road heading east, serves breakfast (E£4), meat and rice (E£8), macaroni (E£4 with meat, E£2 without). Open 8am-midnight. **Al-Gahsh,** in the main square, also serves up morning *fuul* and falafel. Don't miss the **falafel stands** down the main road toward Farafra.

🅖 SIGHTS

Hotel managers run group tours of all the area's springs and sights, (E£60 per car accommodates 6 people or more). You can hire a taxi through the tourist office or on your own for E£30 for a 2-3hr. trip; E£80 for a full day.

HOT SPRINGS. Bahariya's hot springs give you the chance to get in touch with your inner lobster and are quite clean despite the faint scent of sulfur. **'Ain Bishmu,** down the road from Bayoumi's Popular Restaurant following the signs for al-Bishmu Hotel, holds steady at a lukewarm 30°C. The cold (25°C) and hot (44°C) springs at **Bir al-Mattar,** eight kilometers southeast of Bawiti, pour out of a viaduct into a small cement pool (taxi E£15-20 round-trip). Men bathe here by day, women by night. The bumpy "road" to Bir al-Mattar (really just a desert track—drivers beware) continues southeast through the desert to ⛰**Bir al-Ghaba,** 17km from Bawiti. This site has both a hot and cold spring in another sumptuous oasis landscape. Both men and women can swim here (taxi E£30-40 round-trip). Less appealing is **Bir al-Ghilis** (also known as Bir al-Dahkema), a steamy, pump-activated spring only a 10-minute walk out of town on the same road as 'Ain Bishmu; head to Bayoumi's Popular Restaurant and ask for directions (taxi E£5 round-trip).

MUSEUMS. The **Antiquities Museum** (or **Mummy Hall**) is where some of the finds from the surrounding ruins, including pottery shards and five mummies, are kept. Ask the Inspector of Antiquities to dig up the key to the painted subterranean tomb dating from the pharaonic era. Nature is Bahariya's real attraction, but the **Oasis Heritage Museum** in Bawiti is also worth a visit. Talented local artist Mahmoud Eed creates life-like clay figurines to populate dioramas depicting traditional oasis life. *(Antiquities is 500m out of town, on a dirt road that turns right off the road toward Cairo. Ask at the tourist office to arrange a visit. Open Sa-Th 8am-1:30pm. Free. Oasis Heritage is 900m out of town, on the left, heading toward Cairo. Drop E£5 in the box at the back.)*

AL-QASR. Explore the narrow streets and ancient squares of Bahariya's oldest town and ancient capital. A Zawian (as Libyan exiles under Italian rule were called) mosque, Bahariya's oldest town square—Midan Abusti—and traditional oasis homes on old, narrow streets are highlights of a trip through Bawiti's western sibling and the capital of Bahariya in pharaonic times. *(Head down the road past al-Bishmu Hotel and take a left at the square. Take the 1st left to reach Midan Abusti.)*

TOMBS AND TEMPLES

Head 500m out of Bawiti on the main road towards Cairo and turn right onto the 1st dirt road. Past the foodstands, take the 1st left to reach the grey stone ticket office. All sights open daily 9am-5pm. E£30, students E£15. Camera privileges E£25, video E£100.

In spring 2001, five newly excavated ancient ruins were opened to tourists. A single ticket gives admission to the Antiquities Museum plus the five sights listed below and can be purchased in a small grey hut across from the museum. The sights are spread over several kilometers in and around Bawiti. Rent a bicycle or arrange a taxi through the tourist office to see each sight.

🅣TOMB OF BANNENTOIU. Descend a small staircase and duck through the door to enter the main chamber of this 26th-dynasty tomb. Strikingly vivid and colorful pictures grace the walls. On the right-hand side, Bannentoiu stands between Anubis and his priest, who is introducing the golden-haired wonder to an erect Amun-Ra. The great god is pictured missing an arm and a leg—his punishment for impregnating all the women of Bannentoiu's town. The back right wall of the main chamber was damaged by a Cairene thief who removed the plaster and paintings (he was later caught and the paintings recovered, but they have not been returned to Bahariya). In the second chamber, the right wall shows gods Tehuti and Maat weighing Bannentoiu's life for admission into the afterlife. (*Cross the Cairo road and walk straight down a dirt path. Buildings give way to a barbed wire fence after 100m. Enter through the opening in the fence on the left.*)

TOMB OF ZED-AMUN EF ANKH. Banneltoiu's father is buried next door in a similarly styled 26th-dynasty tomb. In two different frescoes Zed-Amun Ef Ankh makes sacrifices to his gods. At the back of the chamber you can see the work of Romans who unsuccessfully dug away at a false door. Silly Romans, tombs are for kids!

TEMPLE OF 'AIN AL-MUFTELLA. The temple of the "mother of the spring on the sand dune" is composed of two separate buildings with faint inscriptions on the inside of the stone walls. At the back of larger building, behind a locked door, are the clearest inscriptions of this 18th-dynasty temple. Look for a troupe of 7 dancing girls performing in front of the god of happiness and love. The god's small body, large head, and lion's tail indicate that he may have been a foreign god from the East. (*4km outside of Bawiti in al-Qasr. Facing Ahmed's Safari Camp, travel towards Bawiti and turn left onto the well-paved asphalt road. Where the road branches, go straight onto the dirt road leading to the temple.*)

TOMB OF AMENHOTEP HUY. Most of the inscribed drawings on this late 18th-dynasty tomb have faded away, but some images can still be seen. On the wall to your right as you enter is a drawing of Amenhotep Huy's servants storing wine while he and his wife sit on mats. In the right corner of the far wall is a large image of Amenhotep seated with his wife, facing the goddess Hathor, who is pictured as a cow. This is one of the less impressive tombs around. (*1½km from Bawiti on the road toward Farafra. Take a right onto the dirt road 150m past the military compound.*)

TEMPLE OF ALEXANDER THE GREAT. There isn't much to see at the ruin of Alexander's only Egyptian temple. Discovered in 1938, the back wall of the temple shows a faint image of Alexander with Amun and other Egyptian gods. His official stamp was found there, but it has been removed and taken to Cairo. Behind the temple lie the ruins of the priests' housing. (*4km outside Bawiti. Take the dirt road behind Ahmed's Safari Camp and continue left behind the sheet metal building. Continue down the dirt road 50m until you reach the caretaker's hut.*)

◪ DAYTRIP FROM BAHARIYA OASIS: DESERT TOUR

The best way to ensure a reasonable price for a **tour** from Baharia is to arrange one through Muhammad 'Abd al-Qader at the tourist office. Organizing overnight desert tours from Farafra may be cheaper; call ahead to al-Badawiya Hotel. You can also see the area from a public **bus** (sit on the driver's side). Every site except al-Wadi Oasis can be reached by a regular car, but a 4WD is more fun. Overnight tours including food, transportation, and sleeping arrangements for a desert camping experience should run E£350 per car (5 people can fit), E£450 for a 4WD, and E£750-800 for a 3-day, 2-night extended tour. Summer is the cheapest time to go but the hardest time to find riding partners. Drivers will begin by demanding E£800 for trips to Farafra, so bargain hard.

The 183km road from Bawiti to the Farafra Oasis runs through spectacular canyons, wind-blown mesas, and rugged desert landscapes from which precious gemstones were exported during the reign of Ramses II. The eastern and western escarpments of the Baharia depression meet at a point about 60km south of Bawiti; the road winds through this pass and onto a brief plateau before plummeting into the Farafra Oasis.

Leaving Bawiti, you'll first pass through the **Black Desert,** known for its dark mesas and crumbly flats peppered with sun-blasted rock and tufts of dry desert grass. Tours usually drop groups at the base of **Black Mountain,** where a short but steep 300m climb yields a striking view of the surrounding desert. The idyllic oasis village of **al-Hayiz** (E£60 per truckload as a daytrip from Bawiti) lies 5km off the main road to Farafra, 40km from Bawiti. Gardens and a spring make this simple village a nice spot to camp overnight and enjoy fresh watermelon or apricots for breakfast. **Crystal Mountain** (nothing more exciting than a roadside hill with quartz deposits) rises about 100km from Bawiti. Farther along is **al-Agabat,** which means "strange," "beautiful," or "difficult" in Arabic. Camel caravans that struggled to cross this desolate land of rugged plateaus rising sharply from the sandy desert floor gave the area its name. The palm trees and the small, desolate **Magic Spring** of the empty **al-Wadi Oasis** (the only location that requires a 4WD) are about 140km from Bawiti and usually included in 3-day trips. The oasis is striking amidst the towering dunes and grazing gazelles. About 40km outside Farafra, the black buttes suddenly give way to the **White Desert,** known for its breathtaking views and stunning chalk formations. For more on the White Desert, see p. 254.

FARAFRA OASIS واحة الفرافرة ☎ 010

Farafra claims a whopping 16% of Egypt's entire territory and borders both Libya and Sudan. Five years ago the area was home to a mere 5000 people, but immigration since then has brought that figure to over 14,000. Nonetheless, the oasis's main town, Qasr al-Farafra, still the smallest of the oasis capitals, attracts fewer tourists than its counterparts. The main road through this dusty, sleepy town hosts all three supermarkets, a handful of restaurants, and three small cafes. Farafra makes a good starting point for overnight desert tours, but not much else. However, recent increases in tourism have led to a bit of development, and province president Muhammad Ra'afat Amin has done much to redefine the region's image: hotels have been privatized, over 60,000 acres of land have been reclaimed through a large-scale irrigation effort, and an airport is in the works.

▐ TRANSPORTATION. Buses and **service** arrive and depart from Tamawy Cafe, under the bus station sign on the Bahariya-Dakhla road; ask around for the latest bus schedule quirks. Reception staff in al-Badawiya Hotel and Aiman in Hossin's Restaurant speak English and are helpful with bus information. **Buses** run daily to Dakhla (5hr., 2pm and 2am, E£12) and Bahariya (2½hr., 10am and 10pm, E£12), continuing on to Cairo (8hr., E£25). **Minibuses** and *service* are also a good way to get to Dakhla. Around 6am and 6pm are the best times to travel; ask around the night before to secure a seat (4hr., E£12-15). A **gas station and repair shop** is on the main road, 500m down from the bus stop. *Let's Go* never recommends **hitchhiking.**

▓ PRACTICAL INFORMATION. All services are on or just off the Bahariya-Dakhla road. As you head toward Bahariya, you'll pass the **police station** and **post office** (open Su-Th 8am-2pm) on your left, followed by the **telephone center,** which offers unreliable international service (open daily 8am-midnight). Next to the post office is the **city hall,** where government officials may be of assistance planning desert excursions, but don't count on it. (Open Sa-Th 8am-2pm.) For better, honest assistance talk to chef Aiman at Hossin's Restaurant. The **hospital** sits 1.5km out of town on the main road toward Bahariya. (☎ 51 00 47. Open 24hr.)

▐▐ ACCOMMODATIONS AND FOOD. Al-Badawiya Hotel (☎ 51 00 60, fax 51 04 00, badawya@link.net), 750m from the bus stop in the direction of Bahariya, has beautifully decorated, painstakingly cleaned rooms and toilets, and stunning bedouin architecture. Don't miss the rooftop terrace. Breakfast E£2-15; lunch and dinner E£5-20. Laundry service E£1-2. (Dorms E£15; rooms E£20 per person, with bath E£40 per person.) **Camping** in the nearby desert or at **Bir Sitta** (6km from town) might make for a more organic experience, but bring plenty of insect repellent. Also check your shoes and pants before getting dressed—scorpions and huge biting ants thrive in these parts. Don't let them thrive in yours. The huts of several budding gourmands are clustered around the bus station. **Hossin's Restaurant,** opposite Tamawy Cafe and 30m toward Dakhla, offers traditional desert fare, outdoor seating, and a friendly English-speaking chef named Aiman who serves up tasty meals and good advice for E£6.

EGYPT

☉ SIGHTS. The **art museum,** conveniently situated across from the oxymoronic Military Intelligence Office, displays sculptures and paintings made of local materials (sand, mud, and sticks) by the talented local artist, Badr, depicting life in Farafra. (Open daily 9am-1pm and 4pm-sunset. Free.) The hot spring **Bir Sitta** (Well #6), 6km west of town, is an idyllic spot to swim and camp (transportation E£15-20 per carload). If you're fed up with the flatulent scent of the sulfur wells, head to **Birkat Abu Noss,** 15km outside of town, to cool off. This lake is 2km off the road to Bahariya; turn left just before the checkpoint (round-trip transportation E£30).

NEAR FARAFRA OASIS

WHITE DESERT · صحراء بيضاء

*An average overnight trip in a **4WD** from Farafra should cost about E£250-500 per carload, depending on the type and length of trip. An average desert safari should cost about E£350 per carload. More establishments in Bahariya and Dakhla are beginning to offer reasonable White Desert tours (see **Dakhla: Accommodations and Food,** p. 256); inquire ahead to compare prices. The incorrigible Mr. Saat, manager of al-Badawiya Hotel often insists on outlandish prices. If you don't mind being stranded in the desert for several hours on the way back, take a **bus** to Bahariya (10am, E£12) and ask to be let out at the White Desert (make sure the driver will do this before you leave Farafra) and then catch the next bus back to Farafra, which may be after 6pm.*

The White Desert (about 40km from Farafra) has overnight camping and breathtaking views. Spooky fungoid chalk formations stand stark white in daytime, glow shades of bashful fuchsia by dusk, and turn orange by dawn. A typical tour of the desert from Farafra (the best starting point for a trip to the White Desert) passes through both verdant **Wadi Henis** and the village of **Karaween,** which has marvelous springs and gazelles. Visiting during or near a full moon can be a particularly otherworldly experience. As you leave the White Desert, you'll pass a **cold spring.**

DAKHLA OASIS واحات الداخلة   ☎ 088

If traveling through some of the other desert oases seems like a challenge, Dakhla (also known as the "pink oasis" for the surrounding pink cliffs) is the reward. Affordable food, appealing lodgings, and picture-book Islamic sights and natural backdrops all come together in and around **Mut,** the oasis capital, unlike anywhere else in the Western Desert. The work of 75,000 Dakhlans has resulted in a widening wave of greenery, including peanuts, rice, and other crops. Yet this posterchild for the New Valley Project has not allowed itself to be urbanized in the manner of Kharga; a mix of Nubians, Sudanese, Libyans, and Berbers peacefully inhabit this laid-back oasis without abandoning their traditional way of life.

▚ TRANSPORTATION

Flights: The **airport,** 10km south of Mut, is served by **EgyptAir** (☎82 28 53 or 82 28 54), which has an office in the courtyard opposite the police station in town. Flights to **Cairo** (W 8:50am; E£615, US$160). Open Sa-Th 8:30am-2:30pm.

Buses and Service: Buses and *service* depart from **Mut Station** (☎82 15 38), in New Mosque Sq. Arrive early and don't expect to leave on time. Buses to **Cairo** (7pm and 9pm, E£35-40) via **Kharga** (2½hr., E£8) and **Cairo** (12hr., 6am and 6pm, E£30) via **Farafra** (5hr.). Local buses run to **Asyut** (6am, 8:30, 1pm, 5pm, 10pm; E£16) via **Kharga** (E£8) and **Balat** and **Bashendi** (E£1), leaving Tahrir Sq. across from the police station and stopping frequently along the way. Bus schedules change frequently so ask the tourist office for updates. *Service* are more reliable, especially early in the morning. *Service* and minibuses to: **Farafra** (5hr., 6am or when full, E£15), **Kharga** (3hr., 6am or when full, E£8), and **Asyut** (6hr., 6am or when full, E£16).

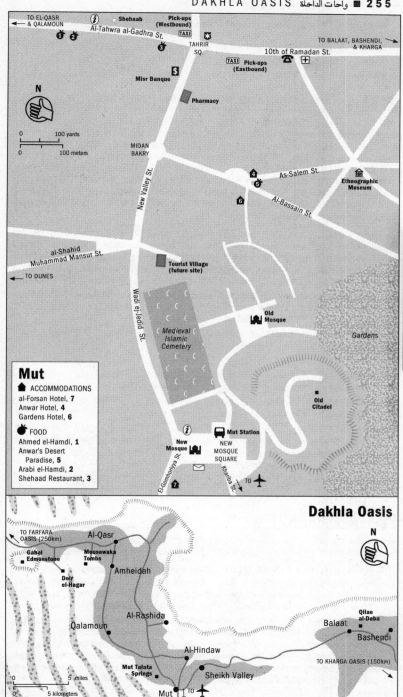

TO EL-QASR
& QALAMOUN

Shehaab

Pick-ups
(Westbound)

Al-Tahwra al-Gadhra St.

TAXI

TAHRIR
SQ.

TO BALAAT, BASHENDI,
& KHARGA

10th of Ramadan St.

TAXI Pick-ups
(Eastbound)

Misr Banque

Pharmacy

N

0   100 yards

0   100 meters

MIDAN
BAKRY

New Valley St.

As-Salem St.

Al-Bassain St.

Ethnographic
Museum

al-Shahid
Muhammad Mansur St.

Tourist Village
(future site)

TO DUNES

Wadi ej-Jedid St.

Medieval
Islamic
Cemetery

Old
Mosque

Gardens

Old
Citadel

Mut

ACCOMMODATIONS
al-Forsan Hotel, 7
Anwar Hotel, 4
Gardens Hotel, 6

FOOD
Ahmed el-Hamdi, 1
Anwar's Desert
  Paradise, 5
Arabi el-Hamdi, 2
Shehaad Restaurant, 3

Mut Station

New
Mosque

NEW
MOSQUE
SQUARE

El-Gomhoriyya St.

Kharba St.

TO

EGYPT

Dakhla Oasis

TO FARFARA
OASIS (250km)

Al-Qasr

N

Gabal
Edmonstone

Mousawaka
Tombs

Deir
el-Hagar

Amheidah

Al-Rashida

Qilae
al-Daba

Qalamoun

Balaat

Bashendi

Al-Hindaw

TO KHARGA OASIS (150km)

Mut Talata
Springs

Sheikh Valley

0   5 miles

0   5 kilometers

Mut   TO

Taxis: Taxis offer sightseeing tours (one day E£50-60, shorter one-sight-only trips E£10-20); ask in New Mosque Sq. or at the tourist office. Covered pickup trucks shuttle frequently between Tahrir Sq. and Balaat, Bashendi, and al-Qasr (E£0.50-1). The early bird catches the truck: around 6am and early afternoon are the best times to try.

Bike Rental: In Abu Muhammad Restaurant on al-Thrawa al-Khadra St. E£10 per day.

⊞ 🛈 ORIENTATION AND PRACTICAL INFORMATION

The Dakhla Oasis, 320km from Farafra and 190km from Kharga, is bounded by **West Mawhub** (80km west of Mut) on one side and the fertile **Tineida** (40km east of Mut) on the other. Cultivated regions also dot the well-paved main highway. The most appealing of these are **al-Qasr** (30km west of Mut), **Balaat** (30km east of Mut), and **Bashendi** (35km east of Mut). The capital of the Dakhla Oasis is **Mut** (pronounced "moot"), named for the Egyptian mother goddess and wife of Amun (see **Meet the Gods**, p. 70). Mut has two focal points: **Tahrir Sq.**, at the intersection of New Valley St. and the southeast-northwest Kharga-Farafra Hwy., and **New Mosque Sq.**, one kilometer south on New Valley St.

Tourist Office: The **new office** (☎82 16 86 or 82 16 85) is 400m away from Tahrir Sq. on the road to Farafra, across the street from Abu Muhammad Restaurant. The **old office** (☎82 04 07) is across from the mosque in New Mosque Sq., in the same building as the Tourist Rest House. The knowledgeable Omar Ahmed (☎94 07 82) speaks English and helps arrange transportation. Both open Su-Th 8am-2pm and 8-10pm.

Currency Exchange: Banque Misr (☎82 00 63), in Tahrir Sq., on the road towards New Mosque Sq. Changes traveler's checks and cash. Open Su-Th 8:30am-2pm and 6-9pm, and sporadically Sa 8am-2pm for changing money.

Gas Station: On the outskirts of eastern Mut, on left side of the road to Kharga. Another station west of Mut, 1km from Tahrir Sq. Open 24hr.

Police: (☎82 15 00), in Tahrir Sq.

Pharmacy: There are 7 pharmacies in Mut. One is directly across the street from the new mosque in New Mosque Sq. Open daily 8am-2pm and 4-10pm.

Hospital: The **main hospital** (☎82 15 55 or 82 13 32) is 1km from Tahrir Sq., toward Kharga. Smaller hospitals are in each village. Open 24hr.

Telephones: From New Mosque Sq., walk east along 23 July St. to Anwar Restaurant, then veer left toward the red-and-white tower about 30m ahead on the left. Open 24hr. For **international service,** try the 2 private telephone offices by the Tourist Office on the road to al-Qasr or the office by New Mosque Sq.

Post Office: One in New Mosque Sq., another on al-Ganeim St., around the corner from the telephone office. Both open Su-Th 8am-2pm.

🏕 ACCOMMODATIONS

If you don't want to sleep in the dunes, Dakhla has the choicest lodgings of the oases, making it the place to go for a couple of days' respite from the sand.

Al-Forsan Hotel (☎82 13 43; fax 82 13 47; elforsan@usa.net), close to New Mosque Sq. on the main road running to Tahrir Sq. wins the location and cleanliness awards. Pool table and a satellite TV on the covered patio. Spacious rooms are ideal for larger groups. Breakfast E£5. E£10 per person, E£15 with bath; E£25 with A/C and bath.

Gardens Hotel (☎82 15 77), 20m down a dirt road from Anwar's Desert Paradise Restaurant and Hotel, has a leafy garden and very polite management. Stick to the breezy rooms with fans unless you don't mind stuffy rooftop dorms. Breakfast included with rooms over E£20. A curious washing machine churns out clean clothes in small batches; E£1 per load. Dorm beds E£8; singles E£12, with bath E£15; doubles E£16, with bath E£20; triples E£18, with bath E£24.

Anwar Hotel (☎ 82 00 70, ☎/fax 82 15 66), at the intersection of al-Salem and al-Bassain St., boasts breezy rooms and balconies. Rooms and common baths are very clean and neat. Breakfast included with private rooms. Throw a mattress on the roof for E£7. Dorms E£15, some have A/C; singles E£10, with A/C E£20; doubles E£20, with A/C E£35; triples E£30, with A/C E£55.

Bedouin Camp (☎ 85 08 05; ☎/fax 85 04 80), 7km northwest of Mut on the road to al-Qasr. If you came to the oasis for a break from the same old hotel scene, ditch Mut and head to this hilltop camp. Clean, wooden huts with concrete floors and well-kept shared baths. Breakfast included. Dinner E£10-15. Large common area used for impromptu bongo performances. Inquire about desert jeep and camel tours. E£15 per person.

FOOD

The desert oases are not known for their filling cuisine, but Dakhla's is the best around. Three brothers have restaurants on the road between Tahrir Sq. and al-Qasr. **Hamdy,** just before the Mebarez Hotel, serves large multi-course chicken and meat meals (E£10), **Arabi** offers the same fare as well as fresh duck, rabbit, and pigeon specialty meals from his farm out back (E£20). Both open 8am-11pm. Around the corner from the Garden Hotel is **Anwar's Desert Paradise Restaurant,** so named, perhaps, for the aging air-conditioning (full meal E£9). **Shehaab,** whose English sign reads "restaurant," is the first restaurant outside of Tahrir Sq. on the road to al-Qasr. This local favorite with sawdust under the tables offers traditional fare (full meal E£4). **Al-Forsan Hotel** has a classy outdoor restaurant offering meals at plebeian prices (kebab meal E£12-15).

AROUND THE OASIS

There's little of interest in **Mut,** but the oasis capital is a great starting point for **Western Dakhla,** which includes the village of al-Qasr and surrounding archaeological digs, and **Eastern Dakhla,** which includes the villages of Balaat and Bashendi (see **Dakhla: Practical Information,** p. 256, for more information). In the cooler months, biking to some spots is feasible, although you'll still need to bring plenty of water—and then some.

WESTERN DAKHLA

Hire a pickup for a day (E£50-70) or hop on the pickup truck taxis that circle the sites. Ask the Dakhla tourist office for help on tours, itineraries, and prices.

QALAMOUN. The distinctly medieval hilltop village of Qalamoun was the capital of Dakhla in Mamluk times. In the Islamic era, Qalamoun functioned as an administrative center. Its inhabitants today claim Turkish and Mamluk ancestry. The town's name has two possible translations: "Amun's pens" (*qalam* means pen), for the scribes who lived here, or "Amun's citadel" (*qala'a* means fortress), as Qalamoun's panoramic perch offers military defense. Near the center of town is an Ayyubid **mosque,** uphill through the maze of narrow passages and traditional mud-brick houses. *(5km west of Mut is the Bedouin village of al-Douhous, where the road splits for 25km before joining up again; the left fork takes you to Qalamoun.)*

AL-GEDIDA. Al-Gedida ("New Town," so named because it's only 300 years old) is known for its **arabesque factory.** In cooperation with 'Ain Shams University and the German Embassy, locals make decorated woodwork with palm tree branches. For more delicious handiwork, sample the town's sweet harvests: apricots in May, mangos in late July, and dates in October. *(5km past Qalamoun, on the road to al-Qasr. Factory open Sa-Th 8am-2pm. Free.)*

MOUSAWAKA TOMBS. These tombs are closed for renovations as of August 2001, though a worker may be present to show you around the jagged rock headstones dating from the first and 2nd centuries CE and the slightly newer domed tombs.

Outside, small caves dug into the hill house skeletons and mummies; nowhere in Egypt can you get more up close and personal with a mummy than here. *(3km west of al-Gedida, on the left or 5km south of al-Qasr, take a right at the white Arabic sign leading to a dirt road.)*

DEIR AL-HAGAR. Half the fun of this Roman temple is the road leading up to it, which twists and turns around a small village and passes three Roman remains before leading up to a ridge which affords a striking view of Deir al-Hagar rising out of the desert dunes. Dedicated to the immortal Theban trio of Mut (a.k.a Nut), Amun-Ra, and Khonsu, the temple was built during the reign of Nero and added to by his immediate successors. Roman emperors ruling in Egypt had no problem playing the role of pharaoh, and this temple combines Egyptian gods with the hieroglyphic names of Roman emperors. A long colonnade lines the path to a small temple and its vivid inscriptions. Ask to see the small exhibit by the entrance. *(8km from al-Qasr. Across the street from the Mawhoub building, follow the road to the village, where a dirt road takes you 1½km to the desert temple. Open daily 8am-5pm. E£20, students E£10.)*

AL-QASR القصر

The most edifying daytrip from Dakhla is al-Qasr, a twisty 32km from Mut on the northern fork. This charming contemporary town was built in and around the substantial remains of Dakhla's medieval Islamic capital. The older buildings, adorned with lively accounts of pilgrimages to Mecca, are a model of comfortable architecture, as their mud buildings remain cool in summer and warm in winter. The **old village** of al-Qasr lies 400m to the north of the main road through the new village. On the main road at the western edge of town, there is a large **map** of the village. Within the old village, arrows direct you to the sights. Still, sights are hard to find without a guide (E£5 tip expected). The number of old village residents is dwindling, replaced by children selling handicrafts. **Al-Qasr Rest House,** on the main road at the turnoff to the old village, serves up traditional desert fare as well as ice cream and cold drinks. (☎87 60 16. Breakfast E£2, lunch E£5, dinner E£7.) The hotel upstairs offers basic rooms (E£10 per person) and rooftop mattresses (E£2). There is also a market, 30m from the hotel on the same side of the road. A **medical clinic** is 50m toward Mut.

OLD VILLAGE SIGHTS. The **Minaret of Nasser al-Din** is the only extant part of an 11th-century Ayyubid mosque; a 19th-century mosque surrounds the old tower. Down the gnarled alleys north of the minaret stands **Qasr Madrasa,** an intact two-story mud-brick building thought to have been either an Ayyubid schoolhouse or the entertainment hall of an Ottoman palace. Villagers later used the building as a courtroom and the nook on the left as you enter was a small prison. Also inside the maze of buildings are a grain mill and olive press. Many of the doorways of the old village are adorned with ornate wooden lintels that reveal the name of the owner, builder, and carpenter as well as the date of construction. Bits of a pharaonic arch and a Roman doorway hint at al-Qasr's pre-Islamic past. On the southern fringes of the old town you can see a waterwheel and a functioning **pottery works,** where villagers churn out everything from ashtrays to chamberpots.

EASTERN DAKHLA

BALAAT. In the crowded old section of Islamic Balaat (pop. 5000), long, dark passageways burst into a courtyard with palm fronds and grapevines. These pathways were built with ceilings as a defense tactic—during invasions, the enemies' camels and horses could not fit through the alleys. Ask to see the **mayor's house,** with its assembly courtyard, speech balcony, and Ottoman wrought iron lamps and bedframes. Outside the old village are several markets selling snacks and drinks.

QILAE AL-DABA. Dakhla's pharaonic governors were buried in these red-brick tombs during the 6th dynasty. A team of French archaeologists has uncovered three unusual inverted step pyramids as well as a mummified governor. *(Behind Bal-*

aat; walk past the bus stop toward Bashendi on the main road for 500m and then take a left before a row of trees onto the dirt road marked by twin sign poles. Follow the electric wires into the desert. One pyramid can be seen from the road. Follow the dirt road 1km into the desert and head for the brown tomb rising from the desert sand. Ask locals for al-Maqabr al-Fara'oniya. Open daily 8am-5pm. E£20, with ISIC E£10—but there is often nobody there to collect the toll.)

BASHENDI. Though less picturesque than its younger brother Balaat, Bashendi sits atop a recently discovered temple and various Roman-era tombs that make a visit worthwhile. This isolated village has tiny, twisting streets and is more of a working town than the other old Islamic villages of Dakhla. The large stone **Tomb of Ketenus** contains six rooms, including one decorated with scenes of a 2nd-century Roman mingling with the gods Min and Seth. Before you can mingle with the ghosts of Romans past, you'll need to get the key from the tombkeeper. Next door to the Tomb of Ketenus is the prominent **Tomb of Bashendi,** which consists of a distinctly Bedouin domed roof atop a Roman foundation. The tomb commemorates the village's beloved namesake; you might join locals who decorate the inside of the holy man's tomb with henna. If the guard isn't around to open the tombs, another villager will do the honors. There are also a number of hot and cold springs to which residents can direct you, though local touts would rather lead you to the Bashendi **carpet works,** where youths weave beautiful rugs for E£100 and up. *(5km east of Qilae al-Daba, 40km from Mut. Ask locals for al-Maqabr al-Romaniya. Tomb of Ketenus E£16, students E£8.)*

KHARGA OASIS الواحة الخارجة

☎ **092**

Kharga is the capital of the New Valley Province *(al-Wadi al-Gideed)* and Egypt's most effective attempt at a desert boomtown. Little is known about Kharga's early pharaonic history, although it must have been agriculturally productive—its hieroglyphic name is *hibis,* or "plow." Kharga became prosperous during Roman times due to its proximity to trade routes, including the Darb al-Arba'een (Forty Days Road), between Egypt and Sudan. Beginning in the 4th century, Kharga was a large Christian settlement and center for monasticism, to which sundry Christian figures (including Bishop Nestorius, founder of the heretical Nestorian sect) were exiled by religious and political rivals. The oasis's role as Egypt's Siberia continued into the 20th century, when Nasser banished Mustafa Amin, founder of *al-Akhbar* (Egypt's largest circulating daily), to Kharga after the 1952 revolution.

When the New Valley Project began in earnest in the early 1980s, the town again prospered. The

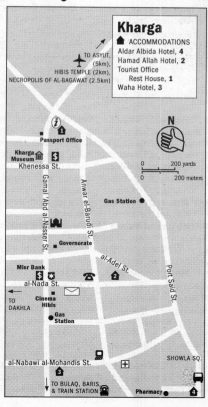

EGYPT

Kharga

ACCOMMODATIONS
Aldar Albida Hotel, **4**
Hamad Allah Hotel, **2**
Tourist Office
Rest House, **1**
Waha Hotel, **3**

TO ASYUT
(5km),
HIBIS TEMPLE (2km),
NECROPOLIS OF AL-BAGAWAT (2.5km)

Passport Office

Kharga
Museum
Khenessa St.
Gamal 'Abd al-Nasser St.
Anwar el-Baudi St.

Gas Station

Governorate

al-Adel St.

Misr Bank
al-Nada St.

Port Said St.

TO DAKHLA
Cinema
Hibis
Gas
Station

al-Nabawi al-Mohandis St.
SHOWLA SQ.

TO BULAQ, BARIS
& TRAIN STATION
Pharmacy

N

0   200 yards
0   200 meters

streets of Kharga, filled with new cookie-cutter apartments, are largely lifeless and boring by Egyptian standards, but the ruins on its periphery astound. Welcome relief from Kharga's New Town can be found in the narrow alleyways of the Old Town, where locally made ceramics and carpets are available in the *souq*. The recent rise of tourism may be causing Kharga to rapidly modernize, but a side trip from one of the area temples to small oasis towns provides a glimpse of the friendly agricultural life that thrives there. Be aware of local customs; women are asked not to wear shorts or sleeveless tops. While Kharga is safe, visitors may encounter the local tourist police who trail tourists as they move throughout the oasis. Ditch them if you can, or use them to your advantage as a (free) personal taxi service.

Kharga is the closest oasis to the Nile Valley, a mere 240km from Asyut. A newly paved road heads south from the city, skirting dunes and small oases on the way to **Bulaq** (15km south), **Baris** (90km south), and **Luxor** (270km west).

TRANSPORTATION

Flights: EgyptAir (☎92 16 95), in the Governorate, 2 blocks north of the Banque Misr intersection on Nasser St. Open Sa-Th 8am-2pm. **Airport** turnoff is 3km north of town on Asyut Rd., then another 2km southeast. Flights to **Cairo** (25 min., Su 7:50am, US$40) via **Asyut** (US$54) or via **Dakhla** (W 7:50am, E£450). Minibus or taxi to airport from Showla Sq. E£5.

Trains: 5km south of the intersection of al-Nabawi al-Mohandis and Nasser St. Take a taxi from town for E£5. Check with the tourist office for schedule updates; trains do not run every day. Trains go to **Luxor** and **Baris,** leaving Kharga at 6am and leaving Baris for Kharga at 2pm.

Buses: Intercity buses arrive and depart from Showla Sq. to: **Asyut** (3hr.; 6, 7, 8, 11am, noon, 2, 7:30, 10pm; E£7); **Cairo** (11hr.; 6am E£23, 9 and 11pm E£30); **Dakhla** (2½hr.; 1, 8, 11am, 2, 10pm; E£7). **Local buses** to **Baris** (3hr.; 1, 3, 7am, noon, 2:30pm; E£1.60) and **Dush** (1½hr., 6 and 11am, E£2). Schedules change, so see tourist office for updates.

Service and Minibuses: Catch *service* and minibuses in Showla Sq. 6-10am and 5-10pm are the best times to find *service,* as locals stay out of the midday sun. *Service* to **Asyut** (2½hr., E£8), **Dakhla** (2hr.; E£8, "special" unshared E£100), and occasionally **Baris** (E£3). With a group, a special taxi to Luxor may be feasible (4hr., E£300-350 per car). Hiring a *service* or minibus to Baris for the day costs E£50-75. For sights north of town, a roundtrip "special" pickup **taxi** should cost around E£10. Within town, **covered truck taxis** scurry along al-Nabawi St. from Showla Sq., turn up Nasser St., and head for the tourist office at the northern end (10pt).

ORIENTATION AND PRACTICAL INFORMATION

Gamal 'Abd al-Nasser St. runs north-south and is bisected by **al-Nada St.,** which heads west to Dakhla. At this intersection you'll find Cinema Hibis, **Banque Misr** (traveler's check exchange, V cash advances; open Su-Th 8:30am-2pm), and the **police station** (☎122). The main branch of the **post office** is just off al-Nasser St., behind Cinema Hibis. (**EMS** service. Open Sa-Th 8am-2pm. Smaller branch in Showla Sq.) At the northernmost end of al-Nasser St., just before it heads off to the ruins and Asyut, stand the rest house and **tourist office,** where the resourceful Ibrahim Hassan, regional director of oasis tourism, will make your stay in the oases as pleasant as possible by smoothing over any bumps with his excellent English. (☎92 12 06; ☎/fax 92 12 05. Open daily 8:30am-8pm and occasionally until midnight. Mr. Hassan is in Kharga Su-Tu and in Dakhla Th-Sa.) The **passport office** (open Sa-Th 8am-2pm) faces the tourist office, and the **tourist police** is next door. (☎92 13 67. Open 24hr.) Grab a **pickup taxi** (10pt) to get to this part of town.

The southern end of al-Nasser St. intersects **al-Nabawi al-Mohandis St.,** which runs east-west. This street curves slightly northeast to **Showla Sq.,** where you'll find the intercity bus, *service*, and minibus stations. The main **hospital** is off al-Mohandis St. toward Showla Sq. (☎ 122 or 92 07 77. Open 24hr.) **Aleman Pharmacy** sits between Aldar Albiadaa Hotel and Showla Sq. (Open daily 9am-midnight.) Get online at **Computer Technology Center,** on al-Nabawi St. (Open Sa-Th 9am-midnight. E£10 per hr.) One block south of Showla Sq., on the left as you walk past Aldar Albiadaa Hotel, is a small blue Internet office without an English sign. (Open 24hr. E£30 per hr.) **Al-Dawati Telephone Central,** in Showla Sq., has the most reliable international service. (Open Sa-Th 8am-midnight.)

ACCOMMODATIONS

Rooms with fans are essential in the summer, and they don't hurt in the winter.

Waha Hotel (☎ 92 03 93), on al-Nabawi al-Mohandis St., close to the corner of Gamal 'Abd al-Nasser St. A 30min. walk from Showla Sq., near grocery stores and restaurants. Simple, tidy rooms with balconies and crisp linen. The common bathrooms are strictly cold water affairs. Dorm beds E£5-8; singles E£7, with hot water, bath, and fan E£16; doubles E£16, with bath E£22.

Aldar Albiadaa Hotel, only steps away from the bus station, is a favorite among travelers. The rooms and baths are well-cleaned but noisy due to the bustle below. Singles E£15, with bath E£20; doubles E£20, with bath E£28; triples E£24, with bath E£30.

Hamad Allah Hotel (☎ 92 50 17) on al-'Adel St., one block from the Telecom tower. Shady trees circle the building, which features posh and peaceful doubles with wall-to-wall carpeting, refrigerator, A/C, TV, bath, and towels. Breakfast included. Lunch E£15, dinner E£17. Singles E£38, with A/C E£63; doubles E£54, with A/C E£90.

Tourist Office Rest House, (☎ 92 12 05) directly behind the tourist office on Gamal 'Abd al-Nasser St. Villas come with living rooms, TV, fully equipped kitchens, and A/C. Ideal for groups of four or more. E£22 per person.

FOOD

Cuisine in Kharga is adequate on a good day, and a decent rotisserie chicken seems to be the specialty (half of a bird with rice, vegetables, salad, and bread E£5-8). Clusters of budget eateries and coffee shops can be found on al-Nabawi al-Mohandis St. between Gamal 'Abd al-Nasser St. and Showla Sq. The greatest concentration of restaurants is around al-Basatin Sq. Vegetarians have to make do with beans and rice. A restaurant at the entrance to the *souq* street offers *fuul* and falafel (50pt) for breakfast.

SIGHTS

MUSEUM AL-WADI AL-GADID (NEW VALLEY MUSEUM). This is the *pièce de resistance* of the New Valley's tourism drive, housing an extensive collection of artifacts from ruins throughout the New Valley oases, and a few pieces from the Egyptian Museum in Cairo. Displays include prehistoric stone tools, wooden sarcophagi, sandstone sphinxes, mascara jars, and Roman coins. *(Open Sa-Th 9am-5pm, F 9am-noon and 3-5pm. E£20, with ISIC E£10. Camera privileges E£10.)*

TEMPLES OF HIBIS AND NADURA. The **Temple of Hibis** was begun in 588 BCE (during the 26th dynasty) by Apnias and completed in 522 BCE by Darius I, making it one of only two Persian-built Egyptian temples. Although dedicated to the Theban trio of Amun, Mut, and Khonsu, the temple is distinguished by its depictions of Persians and of Seth, god of the Oases, with a blue body and a falcon head. First-century Roman inscriptions on display discuss legal issues, including women's rights. Crowning a knoll across the road from the Temple of Hibis is the **Temple of Nadura,** built in the 2nd century BCE during the reign of Roman Emperor Antonius. Little of it stands today, but the site offers an excellent view of the oasis and some

EGYPT

faint hieroglyphic inscriptions. *(At the northern end of town, 2km north of Hotel al-Kharga and close to the road on the left. A shared covered taxi will take you to the tourist office (and possibly farther) for E£1. From there, walk or try to hop on an intertown taxi (E£2). The scaffold-covered Hibis will be closed for several years for renovation but you can walk around the outside. Nadura, closer to town on the right, is open to the public. Free.)*

NECROPOLIS OF AL-BAGAWAT. The 263 above-ground tombs (also called chapels) of the Christian Necropolis of al-Bagawat stand eerily at the desert's edge. From the 3rd through 8th centuries, a sizeable Christian community (including many hermits and some of the religion's first monks) inhabited Kharga. The necropolis is visible from the road, and an asphalt lane leads to the ticket booth. If you go up the hill along the marked path, you'll come to the **Chapel of Exodus,** with ceiling murals depicting the pharaoh's army chasing Jews as they flee from Egypt From the doorway, you can see Moses on the left, to the right of a tree. Adam and Eve stand below him next to a doorway with ankh-like crosses. On the other side of the tree, slightly underneath it, is Daniel. In front of the Chapel of Exodus are the interconnected frescoed chapels #23-35, the resting places of members of a wealthy local family. The interior frescoes of biblical scenes in the **Chapel of Peace (#80)** exemplifies Coptic painting in the early Alexandrian style. Greek inscriptions identify Adam and Eve, Noah's Ark, and the Virgin Mary. Atop the cemetery's central hill stands a ruined 4th-century mud-brick basilica. *(500m past the Temple of Hibis on the road to Asyut. Open daily 8am-6pm, in winter 8am-5pm. E£20, students E£10.)*

NEAR KHARGA

For a full day of exploration, hire a pickup **taxi** for the day from Kharga (E£50-75). Plenty of shared taxis go from Kharga as far as **Bulaq** (50pt). Catch them at north end of Showla Sq. Each day, **buses** go to **Baris** (2hr., 7am and 2pm, E£1.50) and back (11am). *Service* run infrequently between Kharga and Baris (E£3). Morning is the best time to travel. **Hitchhiking** is difficult and dangerous in the extreme heat.

DARB AL-ARBA'EEN (FORTY DAYS ROAD)

If you've come all the way to Kharga, don't miss the road along the old camel trail that leads south to the town of Baris, known as Darb al-Arba'een (the Forty Days Road). The road follows the floor of the valley east of Kharga. The temples of Ghwita, Nadura, and Dush were lighthouses of the desert, notifying weary traders that shelter, food, and rest were near. From any of those hilltop temples, look eastward for a view of this legendary caravan route. Extending from the western Sudan to the Egyptian Nile Valley, Darb al-Arba'een trafficked more slaves than any other land route in history.

GHWITA TEMPLE. Vast sandscapes are all that thrive between Kharga and Ghwita Temple, 17km to the south. The 10m-high walls of the temple-fortress dominate a hill 2km east of the road. The mud-brick exterior gives way to a multi-chambered stone temple dedicated to Amun, Mut, and Khonsu. Built by Darius I, the temple served as the center of a thriving, grape-producing community in pharaonic times. *(Take a pickup taxi from Showla Sq. (50pt) and get off after the big orange gas tanks. From the main road, the temple is 1km to the left. Open daily 8am-5pm; in winter 8am-6pm. E£16, students E£8.)*

ZAYAN TEMPLE AND WELLS. At the 25km mark you'll come across the village of **Nasser** and its shaded, dirty Nasser Wells. **Zayan Temple,** dedicated to Amun, sits 5km east of Nasser Wells, near the village of Araf, on a road that loops around from north of Ghwita Temple to a point north of Bulaq. Originally built in the Ptolemaic era, the Romans restored the site and built a fortress, of which there are still remnants. A colonnade leads to the small interior temple, where hieroglyphs decorate the doorways. *(To get to Zayan Temple, hop on a pickup or public bus headed for Baris and have the driver drop you off at Araf. A round-trip taxi should cost no more than E£20 for both Ghwita and Zayan. Zayan is 5km outside Ghwita Temple on the asphalt road. To return to Kharga or continue on to Baris, walk 1km to Bulaq and catch a pickup taxi, bring lots of water and* *wait by the road. Let's Go does not recommend hitchhiking. Open daily 8am-5pm, in winter 8am-6pm. E£16, students E£8.)*

BARIS بارس

The secluded desert outpost of Baris (the sign at the edge of the town ironically reads "Paris") est 90km au sud de Kharga et comme l'enfer en été (over 50°C), mais il fait beau en avril. Until 10 years ago, merchants made a 40-day camel trek from here to the border of Chad to purchase an ingredient used in local soap, each expedition reputedly bringing the merchant E£20,000. More recently, difficulties with the Sudan have closed the border, making the profitable journey impossible. Today Baris is quiet and dusty, but it offers beautiful views of the surrounding desert and a window into the typical agricultural oasis lifestyle, free from the tourist influences that have infiltrated Kharga. Since there is no place to spend the night, start your trip to Baris early. The nearby temple is worth a visit, and the friendly locals make this town a nice rest stop before heading back to Kharga.

Mr. Farkhat from the Kharga **tourist office** is available in Baris (Th-Sa). If you walk down the central street, perpendicular to the main road, old Baris will be on your right and the gardens straight ahead. The blue building resembling a doghouse sells kebab, *fuul*, and falafel every day except Friday. Numerous cafes line the street and a few markets offer snacks.

An abandoned **public housing complex** designed by Egyptian architect Hassan Fathy stands 300m northwest of the **rest house.** Construction was halted when war broke out in 1967 and never resumed, as the government correctly assumed that the villagers wouldn't want to live in buildings resembling tombs.

DUSH TEMPLE هيكل دوش

A paved road leads 23km southeast from Baris to the Dush Temple. Baris pickup taxi drivers will make a special round-trip to Dush for E£20, wait included, but are hard to find. Open daily 8:30am-5pm. E£20, students E£10.

The temple has an overabundance of heat and a shortage of visitors during the summer, but there's more to the deceptively large temple than meets the eye. Particularly thrilling are the decorated, seemingly endless inner chambers that lead you deeper and deeper into the heart of the temple. Originally built for the worship of Serapis and Isis, the building dates back to the rule of Roman emperors Trajan and Hadrian. The sand around the temple is slowly parting to reveal a church, pottery shards, and a well with clay pipes. These pipes tunnel down to an underground city, leading archaeologists to believe that Dush was a prosperous settlement that was abandoned when the wells ran dry.

EGYPT

Mooooore Room.

Real American Airlines deals
for students and faculty,
online at StudentUniverse.
Earn AAdvantage miles and
enjoy *more room throughout
Coach only on American*.

 StudentUniverse.com

featuring
AmericanAirlines

ISRAEL ישראל

NEW ISRAELI SHEKEL (NIS)

US$1 = NIS4.23	NIS1 = US$0.24
CDN$1 = NIS2.74	NIS1 = CDN$0.37
UK£1 = NIS6.12	NIS1 = UK£.16
IR£1 = NIS4.89	NIS1 = IR£0.20
AUS$1 = NIS2.25	NIS1 = AUS$0.44
NZ$1 = NIS1.86	NIS1 = NZ$0.54
ZAR1 = NIS0.51	NIS1 = ZAR1.98
EUR€1 = NIS3.87	NIS1 = EUR€0.26
E£1 (EGYPTIAN POUND) = NIS1.00	NIS1 = E£1.00
JD1 (JORDANIAN DINAR) = NIS5.99	NIS1 = JD0.17
L£100 (LEBANESE POUNDS) = NIS0.28	NIS1 = L£357
S£1 (SYRIAN POUND) = NIS0.079	NIS1 = S£12.6
TL100,000 (TURKISH LIRA) = NIS0.32	NIS1 = TL309,000

PHONE CODES   Country Code: ☎972. Police: ☎100. Emergency: ☎101.

A NOTE TO OUR READERS This book was last updated based on information gathered from May to August of 2000, as political instability in the region in and around Israel and the Palestinian Territories during the summer of 2001 prevented *Let's Go* researchers from gathering information at that time.

Halfway through its first century, Israel has yet to resolve a psychological struggle between secularism and reverence. An inevitable sense of religion and history permeates its modern cities, where pensive philosophers and microchip millionaires sit on park benches with patriotic Zionists and day-seizing disco-goers. The sacred and the profane jockey side by side on Friday evenings, when Tel Aviv clubs and Eilat pubs explode with revelry that can almost be heard in the reverent streets of Tzfat and Jerusalem's Jewish Quarter. Israel has always been controversial. As a result of persecution culminating in the Holocaust, Jews of all cultures came together to fashion a new kind of state and to remake themselves, sometimes at the expense of Palestinian Arabs. With the country's identity and culture in constant flux, all Israelis have their own visions of what Israel could or should be. Amos Oz, the nation's leading novelist, sees in Israel "a warm-hearted, hot-tempered Mediterranean people that is gradually learning, through great suffering and a tumult of sound and fury, to find release both from the bloodcurdling nightmares of the past and from delusions of grandeur, both ancient and modern." Ask Israelis about their bewildering national situation, and they will tell you at length how *they* see their country—there is no lack of impassioned political or apolitical opinions. But a fundamental optimism shines through; talk with them long enough, and they will eventually smile or shrug and say, *"Yihiyeh tov"* (It will be okay). For the full coverage of the sights and sounds of Israel, try *Let's Go: Israel 2002*.

⚑ HIGHLIGHTS OF ISRAEL

SHAKE IT to *salsa and* disco in the **Russian Compound** club scene (p. 309)

HAGGLE your head off at the **Shuk Ha-Pishpeshim** (p. 322) in old Jaffa.

CHAT with the architect-inhabitant of the Surrealist **Hermit's House** (p. 324) before strolling down to Herzliya's beautiful shoreline for a quiet afternoon of sun.

HIKE Nahal David (p. 387) at Ein Gedi and glimpse some of the world's rarest wildlife.

ISRAEL

LIFE AND TIMES

HISTORY

ANCIENT HISTORY

BIBLICAL ISRAEL. Want to "know" Israel in the biblical sense? The Bible begins the recorded history of the area with the story of Abraham (Avraham in Hebrew, Ibrahim in Arabic), the first of the Patriarchs. Local leaders united the Israelite tribes in the region under a single deity, **Yahweh,** and established an 11th-century BCE kingdom under **Saul** that reached its peak during the reign of Saul's successors **David** and **Solomon** (who built the Holy Temple in Jerusalem). After Solomon's death in 922 BCE, the empire split into the northern Kingdom of Israel and the southern Kingdom of Judah.

The Assyrians conquered Phoenicia and Israel in the late 8th century BCE, forever removing the 10 tribes of northern Israel from their homeland. King **Nebuchadnezzar** wreaked widespread havoc and again deported the Jews to Babylon in 587 BCE, a period known as the Babylonian Captivity. The Israelites prospered intellectually and economically under the **Persians** (who ousted the Babylonians and allowed the Jews to build the Second Temple in Jerusalem). **Alexander the Great** ushered in a period of Hellenism that swept through the region from his invasion in 332 and lasted until 198 BCE, after which the Syrian-based **Seleucids** took over under King Antiochus IV and forbade all Jewish practices. The Jewish lower classes successfully revolted under **Judah Maccabee** (an event commemorated by the holiday Chanukah) and founded the Hasmonean dynasty.

In 44 CE, **Pompey** conquered the territory and declared it a Roman province (Judaea), leading to Jerusalem's rebellion in 65-66 CE. In 70 CE, the Roman general **Titus,** faced with the choice of sparing Jerusalem's Second Temple at great military cost or burning the city, chose the latter. The destruction of the Second Temple led to dramatic upheaval and despair among the Jewish people. Three years later, the Romans captured the last Jewish stronghold at **Masada** (see p. 390). The Romans then exiled the majority of Jerusalem's population, dispersing them throughout the empire. Perhaps to obliterate the land's historical connection with the Jews, they gave the territory the name **Palestine,** after the Philistines.

EMPIRES AND SUFFIXES. With the division of the empire into Latin West and Byzantine East in 330 CE, Palestine came under the supervision of **Constantinople.** Although little changed administratively, the adoption of Christianity by the Emperor Constantine in 331 CE created increased interest in what to many was the "Holy Land." In the 10th century, Muslim Fatimids captured most of Palestine (including Jerusalem) and destroyed many Christian holy sites, such as the **Church of the Holy Sepulcher.** Enraged **Crusaders** recaptured the Holy Land in 1099, beginning the short-lived era of the Crusader states before falling to the Kurd **Salah al-Din** and his own short-lived Ayyubid Dynasty. The age of "-uks" (Mamluks, Seljuks, etc.) nipped at the heels of the age of "-ids" (Fatimids, Ayyubids, etc.), which was followed by the lavish **Ottoman Empire.** By the end of the 17th century, however, the Ottoman ports in Palestine, Syria, and Egypt (which had once provided the sole access to the East) were rendered insignificant as Portuguese sailors steered their way around the Horn of Africa. The once-formidable Ottoman Empire became "the sick man of Europe."

MODERN HISTORY

ZIONISM AND THE BRITISH MANDATE. Although small Jewish communities were present in Palestine over the 18 centuries following the Roman exile, the vast majority were in **Diaspora** communities in Europe, the Middle East, North Africa, and the Americas. These Jews hoped to someday return to and rebuild their

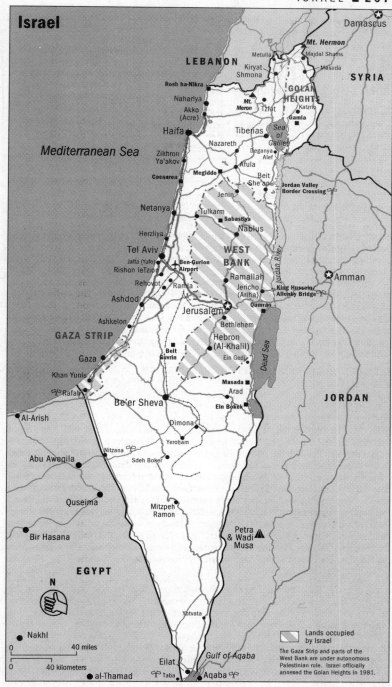

Israel

DAMASCUS

LEBANON

SYRIA

Mt. Hermon

Metulla
Majdal Shams
Kiryat
Shmona   Masada

Rosh ha-Nikra

GOLAN
HEIGHTS

Nahariya
Akko
(Acre)   Mt.   Tzfat   Katzrin
               Meron
                                       Gamla
Haifa   Tiberias

Mediterranean Sea   Nazareth   Sea
                                     of
               Zikhron   Deganya   Galilee
               Ya'akov   Alef
            Megiddo   Afula
Caesarea   Beit
                         She'an   Jordan Valley
                                    Border Crossing
                         Jenin

Netanya   Tulkarm
                      Sabastiya
Herzliya   Nablus

Tel Aviv   WEST
Jaffa (Yafo)   Ben-Gurion   BANK
Rishon leTzion Airport
Rehovot   Ramallah
            Ramla   Jericho
Ashdod   (Ariha)   King Hussein/
                                   Allenby Bridge   Amman
Ashkelon   Jerusalem   Qumran

GAZA STRIP   Bethlehem
                       Hebron
Gaza   Beit   (Al-Khalil)
              Guvrin   Ein Gedi
Khan Yunis
Rafah   Masada   Dead Sea
                       Arad
Al-Arish   Be'er Sheva   Ein Bokek   JORDAN

              Dimona

Nitzana   Yeroham
Abu Awegila   Sdeh Boker

Quseima

Bir Hasana   Mitzpeh
              Ramon
                       Petra
                       & Wadi
                       Musa

EGYPT

N

Yotvata

Nakhl   Lands occupied
                               by Israel
0   40 miles
                               The Gaza Strip and parts of the
0   40 kilometers   West Bank are under autonomous
                               Palestinian rule. Israel officially
al-Thamad   Eilat   Gulf of Aqaba   annexed the Golan Heights in 1981.
       Taba   Aqaba

I
S
R
A
E
L

ancient homeland. This hope became the focus of the movement of **Zionism** in the late 19th and early 20th centuries, when various writers promoted a return to Israel as a solution to the problems of the Jews; **Theodor Herzl** was the first to encourage political means to achieve Zionist ends. The first **aliyah** ("going up," the term for Jewish immigration to Israel) occurred in 1882; the second, in 1904-1914, witnessed the development of **kibbutzim,** cooperative agricultural settlements.

During World War I, the British government, at war with the German-allied Ottomans, made muddled promises of sovereignty to the Arabs, Jews, and French, including the November 1917 **Balfour Declaration,** a document that declared that the British would support a Jewish homeland in Palestine if it would not affect Palestine's non-Jewish communities. After the war, however, the League of Nations handed Palestine wholesale to Great Britain. British indecisiveness continued during their interwar control of the region, as the rise of Nazism drove tens of thousands of European Jews into Palestine. After World War II, the UN partitioned Palestine into separate Jewish and Arab states. The leaders of the former reluctantly accepted the resolution, while the leaders of the latter (and the governments of neighboring Arab states) rejected it outright, denying the UN's authority to divide and distribute territories they considered Arab patrimony.

INDEPENDENCE. On May 14, 1948, the British mandate over Palestine ended and **David Ben-Gurion** declared the independence of the State of Israel. The next day, a combined army of Syrian, Iraqi, Lebanese, Saudi, Egyptian, and Jordanian troops marched in from the north, west, and south. Few gave the new state much chance for survival, but the war's results became clear with the signing of armistices in early 1949. Israel had secured not only its UN-allotted territory, but also land designated for Palestine in the north and in the West Bank. The Gaza Strip, which had also been designated for Palestine, was secured by Egypt, and the West Bank and half of Jerusalem by Jordan. Thousands of Palestinian refugees crowded into camps in the West Bank, Gaza, and bordering Arab states. The dispossessed Palestinians came to bitterly remember the 1948 war as **al-Naqba,** the Catastrophe.

THE SUEZ CRISIS AND THE RISE OF PAN-ARABISM. After Colonel **Gamal 'Abd al-Nasser** took control of Egypt in 1952, he promoted a highly emotional brand of pan-Arabism, hoping to unify the Arabic-speaking masses into one state powerful enough to resist imperial encroachments and take control of Palestine. The US and other foreign powers, who had begun to develop the oil fields of Arabia, feared their arrangements with local monarchs would collapse if Nasserism spread. In 1956, the US clumsily attempted to curtail Nasser's power by withdrawing its offer to finance the Aswan High Dam. Rather than yield to the snub, Nasser nationalized the Suez Canal to use its revenues for the dam. On October 24, 1956, Jordan, Syria, and Egypt established a joint military command directed against Israel. Israel, Britain, and France devised a scheme to take the canal. Israel would attack Egypt, and a Franco-British "peace-keeping" force would follow. Initially, the conspiracy worked: Israel took the **Sinai Peninsula,** opened its port of Eilat to international shipping, and dealt Nasser's military a major blow. The military victors, however, had not considered world reaction to their adventure. When Israel, Britain, and France withdrew their troops to placate the furious US, Nasser was heralded as the savior of the Arab world without having won a battle.

SIX DAY WAR. From bases sanctioned by the governments of Jordan, Syria, and Lebanon, the **Palestinian Liberation Organization (PLO)** raided Israel during the 1960s; in return, Israel hit Palestinian refugee camps. The cycle of raids and reprisals created tension on Israel's northern border, and a Syrian-Israeli air battle took place in April 1967. When Syria's hard-line government turned up the rhetoric, Nasser stepped in and initiated a blockade of the Gulf of Aqaba on May 22, 1967, sparking what is known as the 1967 War or **Six Day War.** Israeli leaders had made it clear that such a blockade would be considered a declaration of war, and on June 5, Israel launched a preemptive strike on Egyptian airfields; less than a week later, all parties had accepted the cease-fire. To Israel went the spoils: they annexed

East Jerusalem and got the Sinai and the Gaza Strip from Egypt, the Golan Heights from Syria, and the West Bank from Jordan. The defeated Palestinians decided to take things into their own hands; the extremist group FATAH, led by **Yasser Arafat,** took over the PLO in 1969, encouraging propaganda and guerrilla warfare.

The stakes of the game were now higher than anyone could have imagined: with the United States behind Israel and the Soviet Union behind Nasser, any local conflict affected the world's major superpowers. **UN Resolution 242** stipulated "withdrawal of Israeli armed forces from territories occupied in the recent conflict." The intentional ambiguity of the document caused bickering immediately, while the situation along the Suez Canal degenerated into the **War of Attrition.**

The 1967 War created 400,000 more Palestinian refugees, most of whom went to Jordan, throwing the Jordanian government and the PLO into a tense relationship: Hussein wanted to hold secret peace negotiations with the Israelis, while the PLO hoped to use Jordan as a base for attacks on Israeli-held territory. In September 1970 (known to Palestinians as **Black September,** see p. 432), Hussein's frustrations and conflicts with Arafat's PLO, already at boiling point, overflowed; a brutal war was declared and martial law imposed. It was only after 3000 lives were sacrificed that the PLO reluctantly agreed to move its headquarters to Lebanon.

YOM KIPPUR WAR AND CAMP DAVID. Egyptian and Syrian forces launched a surprise assault on Israel on October 6, 1973, when most Israelis were in synagogues for Yom Kippur (the holiest day of the Jewish year); the bloody fighting of the **Yom Kippur War** and the subsequent Arab oil embargo ended only when the Arabs decided to settle matters under the supervision of the US and the Soviet Union in the Geneva Peace Conference of December 1973. After much manuevering by US Secretary of State **Henry Kissinger,** all parties agreed to disengage forces over the next five months (one month after Israeli Prime Minister **Golda Meir** resigned amidst public uproar against the country's unpreparedness for the war). Soon after, the PLO was granted "observer" status in the UN.

Throughout the 1970s, an increasing number of Israelis began to settle in the occupied territories, an act discouraged by Prime Minister Yitzhak Rabin but encouraged by his successor, **Menahem Begin.** In 1979, Begin, Egypt's Anwar Sadat, and the US's Jimmy Carter met at Camp David in Maryland to sign the **Camp David Accords,** which returned the Sinai to Egypt but left the question of West Bank and Gaza control more muddled than before. Things cooled off in the 1980s under Sadat's successor, current Egyptian President Hosni Mubarak, but on June 6, 1982, Israel invaded **Lebanon** under "Operation Peace for Galilee," an attack aimed at wiping out guerrilla forces that had been shelling northern Israel. Tensions led to bloodshed, ending only when the US intervened and the Israelis withdrew in 1985, leaving a buffer zone in southern Lebanon.

THE PLO AND JORDAN. Mourning at a funeral for several Palestinians killed in an Arab-Israeli car crash in Gaza erupted into a Palestinian **intifada** (uprising, literally "throwing or shaking off") that spread to the West Bank. Palestinians in the territories began establishing networks to coordinate their hitherto sporadic acts of civil disobedience, and it soon became apparent that the *intifada* was not abating. In the summer of 1988, Jordan suddenly removed itself from the situation, and the PLO seized the opportunity to secure a role in negotiations with the rest of the world by renouncing terrorism, recognizing Israel's right to exist, and proposing an independent Palestinian state. Israeli Prime Minister Yitzhak Shamir retaliated with a proposal whose underlying tenet was that Jerusalem, whole and undivided, was Israel's eternal capital, but the PLO and Egypt refused to accept this and turned on Arafat, whom they blamed for the weakening of the strong position Palestinians had gained from the *intifada*.

THE GULF CRISIS AND OSLO ACCORD. The Gulf Crisis began when Iraqi President Saddam Hussein ordered his troops to march into Kuwait on August 2, 1990; he then slyly suggested "linkage" as a way of solving the Gulf Crisis: he would withdraw from Kuwait when Israel withdrew from the West Bank, Gaza, and

ISRAEL

Golan, and when Syria withdrew from Lebanon. SCUD missile rockets rained down on Israel (supported by Arafat) as tensions skyrocketed, but hopes were high at the 1991 Madrid peace conference because Syria entered negotiations on the side of Israel (the first time in years such a thing had happened). The year 1992 saw both the election of Palestinian autonomy-promising Prime Minister Yitzḥak Rabin and increased terrorist attacks by **Hamas,** an Islamist Palestinian faction. In 1993, Israel and the PLO surprised the world by announcing a successfully negoti-ated, peaceful framework for solving the Israeli-Palestinian conflict. It was known as the Declaration of Principles on Interim Self-Government Arrangements (the DOP or **Oslo Accord**), which was signed on the White House lawn on September 13, 1993 with US President Bill Clinton presiding. The DOP provided mutual recogni-tion between Israel and the PLO and the implementation of Palestinian autonomy (expanding over five years) in the Gaza Strip and Jericho area, leading to an even-tual finalizing of the entire messy situation. Other agreements created the **Palestin-ian Authority (PA),** a 24-member council headed by Yasser Arafat that would have some governmental control in the West Bank.

RECENT HISTORY AND THE PEACE PROCESS. On November 4, 1995, 25-year-old **Yigal Amir,** a right-wing Jewish university student, shot and killed Israeli Prime Min-ister Yitzḥak Rabin. Over one million mourners (50 of them world leaders) filed by the slain leader's coffin in the days following the murder. **Benjamin Netanyahu** barely scraped through elections in May 1996, in which he promised to continue Rabin's peace-oriented politics, but tensions (ignited by Hamas) over his conser-vative policies lead to widespread violence. Hamas suicide-bombers twice tar-geted Jerusalem's crowded thoroughfares in 1997, killing 20 and injuring over 10 times as many. In response, Israel cordoned off the West Bank and the Gaza Strip and arrested Palestinians.

On May 30, 1998, Israel celebrated its **50th anniversary** with widespread partying in Jerusalem. The anniversary turned grim as Palestinians mourned the 50 years since **al-Naqba** ("the Catastrophe"). Violent rioting broke out in Hebron and East Jerusalem, and Israeli soldiers fired on crowds, leaving five Palestinians dead. The PA and the US set a deadline that same month for Israel to withdraw from 13% of the West Bank, but Netanyahu ignored their decision, insisting that anything over a 9% withdrawal would pose an unacceptable security risk.

IN THE NEWS

The summer of 1999 marked a tit-for-tat bombing struggle between the Israeli Army occupying South Lebanon and **Hezbollah** guerrillas. In September 1999, Labor leader and Prime Minister **Ehud Barak** (who defeated Netanyahu with a sweeping mandate to secure a comprehensive Arab-Israeli peace) announced plans for a historic Israeli pullout scheduled for July 2000. Barak hoped that the gesture of Israeli goodwill would encourage peace talks with Syria. Escalating skirmishes through the winter, however, prompted Barak to advance the pullout first to June 1, 2000, and then to May 24, when Israel's 20-year occupation of South Lebanon finally came to a close. In July 2000, Arafat and Barak met for the Camp David II summit under the auspices of the US government. These talks marked the first time that Israel was willing to consider discussing the status of Jerusalem; Arafat and the Palestinian Authority have repeatedly pressed for a Palestinian cap-ital in heavily Arab East Jerusalem. No progress was made, however, and at press time no date had been set for future talks.

However, In September 2000—against the wishes of Muslim authorities—hawk-ish Likud leader **Ariel Sharon** visited an area of Jerusalem containing Muslim and Jewish holy sites, in a move Palestinians found offensive and threatening. Riots escalated into months of full-fledged attacks on the Israeli military that led to hun-dreds of (mostly Palestinian) deaths. As violence showed no signs of letting up, Barak's popularity went into free-fall, and elections were called in February 2001—before the end of his term. Sharon defeated Barak in a landslide. The Israeli political system in turmoil, Sharon attempted to draw Barak and Labor into a national unity government. Barak, however, opted to step down as Labor leader and has removed himself from the political scene (though from the sidelines he has begun to call for the removal of Arafat, whom he now labels a "thug"). Sharon, a strong critic of the peace process as an opposition leader, has surprised many with his moderate policies. After terrorists began a suicide bombing campaign in spring and summer of 2001, Sharon and Arafat agreed to a cease-fire, though the agreement did little to stop the carnage. Palestinian terrorist attacks have continued, and the Sharon government's response of assassinating suspected terrorist masterminds has been roundly condemned by Arafat and other Arab leaders.

RELIGION AND ETHNICITY

Freedom of religion is safeguarded by the state under the 1948 Declaration of the Establishment of the State of Israel. Israel's population of 5.8 million is 80% Jewish and 15% Muslim; the remaining 5% includes Christians and Druze. Each community operates its own religious courts, funded by the Ministry of Religion, and controls its own holy sites. Every religion's days of rest are guaranteed by law.

About half of Israeli **Jews** are secular, while 30% identify themselves as Orthodox and 18% as Ultra-Orthodox. The religious-secular divide is something of a fault line in society. The religious establishment is quite powerful—rabbinical courts even have a state monopoly on matrimonial issues among Jews. Many Israeli Jews are either first- or second-generation immigrants, and are often divided along ethnic lines: **Sephardi** Jews come from Arab or other Mediterranean countries, while **Ashkenazi** Jews have northern or eastern European origins. The deep rift in Israeli society goes back to the 1950s, when Sephardi Jews from Morocco and Iraq were brought to an already established, Ashkenazi-dominated state. Although Sephardim comprise roughly half of the Jewish population in Israel, Ashkenazim still fill most of the positions of power in the government, military, and academia, and Sephardim are generally poorer. The last decade has brought massive immigrations from the former USSR and Ethiopia, clouded by questions concerning the religious status of immigrants claiming to be Jewish.

Among other religious and ethnic groups in Israel are the **Muslims,** who have flourished in Israel since the 7th century. After Mecca and Medina, the most important Muslim holy site—**al-Aqsa Mosque** (see p. 296)—is in Jerusalem. A Muslim *hadith* tells of Muhammad's journey from Mecca to al-Aqsa ("The Farthest") and up through the Seven Heavens to meet God. Many **Christian** sects are also represented in Israel, including the Armenian Orthodox, Abyssinian, Anglican, Baha'i, Coptic, Greek Orthodox, Roman Catholic, and Syrian Orthodox churches. Most are Arab by language and origin. Israel's **Druze** population is divided between those living in the Galilee and in the Golan Heights. Those in the Galilee remain loyal to Israel and often serve in the army, while those in the Golan support their return to Syria. Druze generally live in separate villages and have their own communal institutions.

LANGUAGE

Hebrew and **Arabic** are the official languages of Israel. Most Israelis speak some English; many speak English with near fluency, particularly in bigger cities like Jerusalem and Tel Aviv and popular tourist destinations such as Eilat. Signs are usually written in English (sometimes Russian) as well as Hebrew and Arabic. For more information on the Hebrew language, see the **Appendix,** p. 703.

THE ARTS

LITERATURE. The compilation of the biblical narrative was followed by the age of the **Mishnah** (200 BCE-700 CE), when *halakha* (laws derived from the Bible) and *agada* (elaboration on the Bible) were compiled. The revival of Hebrew as a secular language in the 18th century brought a drastic shift in Hebrew literature. Josef Perl and Isaac Erter parodied Ḥasidic works in their writings. **Joseph Brenner** was popular at the turn of the century, thanks to his hallmark character—the tragic, uprooted settler. In the 1920s and '30s, Nobel Laureate **Shmuel Yosef (Shai) Agnon** confronted the breakdown of cultural cohesion among modern Jews in *A Guest for the Night*, *The Bridal Canopy*, and *Twenty-One Stories*. In the late 1950s, writers such as **Amos Oz** began to experiment with psychological realism, allegory, and symbolism, paving the way for the skepticism of the '60s (such as *The Palace of Shattered Vessels* by David Shaḥar, considered the Proust of Israeli literature). *Past Continuous* by **Ya'akov Shabtai,** about Tel Aviv in the 1970s, is perhaps the best Israeli novel of the decade. The poetry of **Yehuda Amichai** will ensure that you never look at Jerusalem stone in the same way again.

Israeli literature today increasingly focuses on the Israeli-Palestinian conflict. Oz's *In the Land of Israel* is a series of interviews that documents the wide range of political sentiment. For Palestinian accounts, check out *The West Bank Story* by Rafik Halabi, an Israeli Druze television reporter, and Fawaz Turki's autobiographical *The Disinherited*. A cadre of young writers such as Etgar Keret and Gafi Amir highlight the disaffected and cynical outlook characteristic of what has been called the **post-Zionist** era. Israel's tumultuous history has inspired a number of over-idealized, highly entertaining histories, including Ḥayim Potok's *Wanderings*, James Michener's *The Source*, and Leon Uris's *Exodus*.

MUSIC. After World War I, Jews in Palestine assembled chamber groups, a symphony orchestra, an opera company, and a choral society. With the rise of Nazism in Europe, Jewish musicians fled to Israel, and this influx also spurred the formation of several music groups. Today seasonal music activities from October to July are held in such varied settings as the historic Crusader Castle at Akko (see p. 358) and the modern, 3000-seat Mann Auditorium in Tel Aviv. Israeli **popular music** emerged from its folk-chant origins (often echoing Russian folk melodies) in the late 1960s. Since the 1970s, Israel has been catching up with international music fashions; local bands experiment with punk, reggae, heavy metal, grunge, and even rap. **MTV** now keeps Israeli youth abreast of the goings-on in London and New York, and they expect nothing less of their own local acts. Tel Aviv is the unequivocal hub of the cutting-edge music scene in Israel. The most popular artists perform music that's somewhere between hard rock and acoustic pop. Some native classics still on the performance circuit are Shlomo Artzi, Yehudit Ravitz, Rami Klinestein, and Gidi Gov. Achinoam Nini blends American rock with Middle Eastern sounds, while David Broza also throws in Latin American influences. Zahava Ben, a Sephardic Jew, is one of the more popular Israeli singers. She frequently tours in the Palestine Authority and has achieved a great deal of success in Egypt singing the songs of the legendary Umm Kulthum. Drag queen Dana International brought Israeli pop international fame in 1998 when she won the Eurovision Song Contest. In many places, Middle Eastern-style music (*muzika mizrahit*, or "oriental music") blasts from car stereos and boomboxes and is very popular with Sephardim (Avihu Medina is the big name in *mizrahi* music).

FILM. Israel has a thriving film industry with numerous festivals and award ceremonies, including an Israeli version of the Academy Awards. In the award-winning *Wedding in Galilee* (1987) by Palestinian director Michel Khleifi, a Palestinian is granted permission to waive curfew in order to hold his son's wedding, on the condition that Israeli officers be allowed to attend. Other successful films include *Clara Ha-Kedosha* (St. Clara) and *Etz Ha-Domim Tafus* (Under the Domim Tree, 1994) which deals with teenage survivors of the Holocaust in the 1950s.

FOOD AND DRINK

Some Israelis' diets are affected by **kashrut** (literally translated as "proper"), the Jewish dietary laws. Observant Jews will not eat or shop in a place that carries non-kosher goods; to keep kosher clientele coming, the big supermarket chains in

Israel carry only kosher products, and many restaurants (and most hotels) serve only kosher food. Observance of *kashrut* is not necessarily the norm in Israel, and many restaurants (particularly in Haifa and Tel Aviv) are avidly non-kosher.

The typical Israeli eats a large breakfast, a big midday meal, and a light, late supper. Because of the poor quality and high cost of beef and lamb, Israelis rely largely on chicken, dairy, and vegetable products. Popular items in the Israeli diet include ever-present **hummus** (mashed chick-peas, garlic, lemon, and *tahina,* a sesame concoction); "salad," finely chopped tomatoes and cucumbers garnished with oil and vinegar; *gvina levana,* soft white cheese; *schnitzel,* breaded and fried chicken breast; chips (french fries); and a variety of sweet dairy snacks.

You can prepare your own meals from food purchased at the *shuk* (outdoor market, like the *souqs* elsewhere in the Middle East), the *makolet* (small market), or a supermarket. *Burekas* (cheese-, potato-, spinach-, or meat-filled filo dough) are available at patisseries and some fast-food shops. Aside from the standard falafel and shawarma, street vendors also sell what look like hand grenades—these are only **sabras,** prickly cactus fruits with edible innards (the seeds cause indigestion). *Sabra* is also a term for a native Israeli; both the fruit and the people are said to be thorny on the outside, sweet on the inside.

Two Israeli **beers** are the decent, deep-amber Goldstar (a draft beer) and the lesser Maccabee lager. The not-strictly-enforced minimum drinking age is 18. Strong, sweet **Arabic coffee,** or *ahwa,* is sometimes referred to as *turki* (Turkish); for less potent brews, ask for *hafukh* (mixed with milk) or *filter. Shahor* (black) or *botz* (mud) coffee is Turkish coffee brewed in a cup.

FESTIVALS AND HOLIDAYS

In Israel, most businesses and public facilities close Friday afternoons for **Shabbat,** the Jewish sabbath, and reopen at sundown on Saturday. They also close for Jewish holidays, which begin at sundown on the previous day. **Pesah,** or Passover (Mar. 21 - Apr. 3 2002), celebrates the exodus of the Jews from Egypt. Observant Jews refrain from eating bread and pastries; products made leavening agents may be hard to come by. **Rosh Ha-Shana** (the Jewish New Year; Sept. 18-19) is only slightly less holy than **Yom Kippur** (Sept. 27), the holiest day of the Jewish calendar; observant Jews fast in atonement for their sins, and Israel shuts down entirely. In Muslim areas, many businesses close on Friday for prayer. On holidays, they may close during the afternoon, but are generally open in the morning. For a list of religious and national holidays, see the **holidays and festivals,** p. 61.

ESSENTIALS

DOCUMENTS AND FORMALITIES

EMBASSIES AND CONSULATES

Most foreign embassies and consulates in Israel are in **Tel Aviv** (see **Practical Information,** p. 314), though a few countries also have consulates in Jerusalem, Haifa, and Eilat. Israeli embassies and consulates abroad include:

Australia: Embassy: 6 Turrana St., Yarralumla, Canberra ACT 2600 (☎02 6273 1309; fax 6273 4273). **Consulate:** 37 York St., 6th fl., **Sydney** NSW 2000 (☎02 9264 7933; fax 9290 2259).

Canada: Embassy: 50 O'Connor St., #1005, Ottawa, Ont. K1P 6L2 (☎613-567-6450, 567-6453, or 567-6455; fax 237-8865; embisrott@cyberus.ca; www.israelca.org). **Consulates:** 180 Bloor St. W., #700, **Toronto,** Ont. M5S 2V6 (☎416-640-8500; fax 640-8555; hasbara@idirect.com); 1155 Boulevard Réné-Lévesque Ouest, #2620, **Montréal,** Québec, H3B 4S5 (☎514-940-8500; fax 940-8555; cgisrmtl@videotron.net).

Ireland: Embassy: Carrisbrook House, 122 Pembrook House, Dublin 4 (☎01 668 03 03; fax 668 04 18).

New Zealand: Embassy: 13th Floor, Equinox House, 111 The Terrace, P.O. Box 2171, Wellington (☎04 472 23 68 or 472 23 62; fax 499 06 32; israel-ask@israel.org.nz; www.webnz.com/israel).

South Africa: Embassy: 339 Hilda St., Pretoria 001, P.O. Box 3726 (☎12 342 26 93 or 342 26 97; fax 342 14 42; cgijhb@global.co.za).

UK: Embassy: 2 Palace Green, London W8 4QB (☎020 7957 9500; fax 7957 9555; info@israel-embassy.org.uk; www.israel-embassy.org.uk/london).

US: Embassy: 3514 International Drive NW, Washington, D.C. 20008 (☎202-364-5500; fax 364-5423; ask@israelemb.org). **Consulates:** 800 2nd Ave., **New York,** NY 10017 (☎212-499-5410; fax 499-5425; nycon@interport.net); 6380 Wilshire Blvd., #1700, **Los Angeles,** CA 90048 (☎323-852-5500; fax 852-5555; israinfo@primenet.com). Israeli consulates are also in **San Francisco, Miami, Atlanta, Chicago, Boston, Philadelphia,** and **Houston.**

ENTRY REQUIREMENTS

Visas are not required for citizens of Australia, Canada, Ireland, New Zealand, South Africa, the UK, and the US. Flights arrive at **Ben-Gurion International Airport.** Buses leave from the airport to Tel Aviv (NIS10), Jerusalem (NIS21), and other major cities. **Studying** or **working** in Israel requires a special visa and permit.

BORDER CROSSINGS

TO JORDAN. There are three border crossings into Jordan: from Jericho in the West Bank, from **Beit She'an** in northern Israel, and from **Eilat** (by far the simpler and more popular option). Crossing from Eilat to **Aqaba** (info ☎07 633 68 12) should take less than 1hr.—just pay the NIS57 exit tax and walk the 1km no-man's land between the two countries (there's no public transport). Get Jordanian visas valid for one month at the border (citizens of Australia JD16, Canada JD36, Ireland JD11, New Zealand JD16, South Africa free, UK JD23, US JD33). Taxis from Eilat to the border cost NIS15-20; from the border to Aqaba JD4. (Border open Su-Th 6:30am-10pm, F-Sa 8am-8pm; closed Yom Kippur and 'Eid al-Adha.) For more info, see **Border Crossings: To Israel,** p. 437.

TO EGYPT. The border crossing from **Eilat** to **Taba** is somewhat arduous. Passports must be valid for at least three months; Israeli visas must be valid for the day of travel. For travel outside Sinai, get a visa at the Egyptian consulate. The border (info ☎637 31 10) is open 24hr., but is closed on Yom Kippur and 'Eid al-Adha. Allow at least 1hr. to cross. Take the #15 bus from Eilat and keep your passport handy. There are 11 exciting steps: (1) Bus drop-off. (2) Little Taba snack bar ("last beer before Sinai"). (3) Passport pre-check. (4) Passport control booth (pay NIS57 exit tax). (5) Israeli last passport check; they automatically stamp your passport at this point unless you ask them not to. (6) Stroll through no-man's land. (7) Egyptian passport control—fill out entry form, get stamp. (8) Egyptian security (X-ray machine). (9) Post-border passport check. (10) Passport check and E£17/US$6 Egyptian border tax. The Taba Hilton is the best place to **change money** (open 24hr., no commission for foreign currency converted to Egyptian pounds). (11) Welcome to Egypt! The bus station is a 10min. walk from the border. From Taba, there are buses to: **Cairo** (7hr., E£70); **Nuweiba** (1½hr., E£12); **Dahab** (2½hr., 3pm, E£15-17); and **Sharm al-Sheikh** (3-4hr., E£25).

TO LEBANON AND SYRIA. Israel's borders with Lebanon and Syria are closed. The most common route into Syria is via Jordan. Travelers with Israeli stamps in their passports will not be granted Lebanese or Syrian visas. Ask that your passport not be stamped if you eventually plan on traveling to Lebanon or Syria.

GETTING AROUND

BUSES. Buses are the most popular and convenient means of travel in Israel. Except for the **Dan Company** (☎ 03 639 44 44) in Tel Aviv and the **Arab buses** serving the West Bank, Galilee, and Gaza, the **Egged Bus Cooperative** (www.egged.co.il) has a monopoly on intercity and most intracity buses. The modern, air-conditioned buses are direct *(yashir)*, express, or local *(me'asef)*, with an occasional 10% ISIC discount. Most bus stations have printed schedules, often in English. Egged has intercity **information lines** in the major cities (Tel Aviv ☎ 03 694 88 88, Haifa ☎ 04 854 95 49, Jerusalem ☎ 02 530 47 04). A *kartisia*, available from any bus driver, gives you 11 local rides for the price of 10 (NIS47); a one-month pass that includes unlimited local rides in Haifa, Jerusalem, and Tel Aviv costs NIS188. Most local bus rides cost NIS5. Buses between cities usually leave from the central bus station *(tahanah merkazit)*. Round-trip tickets may be 10% cheaper.

TAXIS AND SHERUT. Regular private taxi rides are called **special** (pronounced "spatial"). City taxis operating as *special* must use a meter *(moneh)*; insist that the driver turn it on. Refuse offers of unspecified "discount" rates (translation: no meter and an exorbitant fare). Otherwise, set a price before you enter the taxi. **Sherut** (the equivalent of the Arab *service*) taxis hold up to seven people. Certain companies operate *sherut* seven days a week from offices in each city. Intercity *sherut* operate on loose schedules, departing when full; on Saturdays, they often whiz along the streets in search of passengers. Intracity *sherut* don't follow schedules. Most routes have set fares comparable to bus prices; ask for quotes at tourist offices or from the nearest Israeli. Always settle on a price before you depart.

TRAINS. Rail service in Israel (10% ISIC discount on tickets over NIS20.50) is useful only for travel along the northern coast. Trains are slightly cheaper than buses, but they don't run on Shabbat. Avoid traveling on Friday afternoons when trains are most crowded. See www.isarail.com for more information.

CAR RENTAL. More Israelis have been killed in car accidents than in all of the country's wars combined. Drunk driving is prevalent and the windy, hilly roads don't help. Widespread public transportation makes cars generally unnecessary, but some places (especially the Golan and Negev) are most easily reached by car. Some roads, particularly in the Negev and the Golan, have poor (or nonexistent) shoulders or few gas stations. "Scenic routes" are barely wide enough for one car, and buses often blast by in the opposite direction. The legal driving age is 17, but most agencies will only rent to credit-card holders 21 years or older (a few rent to 18-year-olds). Rentals cost about US$55-70. Deals arranged beforehand from overseas are often much cheaper. Roads are well marked and maps are available at all tourist offices. Israelis drive on the right side of the road. Car phones and cellular phones (Israelis call them "pelephones") are everywhere; most rental cars have them built in, so decide at rental time if you want the more expensive with-phone plan. Cell phones are responsible for many accidents, so laws regarding them are stringently enforced. **Sleeping in your car** is one of the most dangerous (and often illegal) ways to get your rest. If your car breaks down, wait for the police to assist you. See **Practical Information** in each city for agency addresses.

HITCHHIKING. Sexual harassment and assault related to *tremping* (as it is called in Israel) have increased in recent years. License plates carry meaning; yellow are Israeli, black with a צ are army, red are police, blue or gray are occupied territory, and white are diplomatic. Hitchers in the Negev or Golan (where sometimes the only option is a military vehicle) risk being stranded by a ride that doesn't go all the way to their destination. Hitchers flag cars by pointing to the far side of the road with the index finger. *Let's Go* does not recommend hitchhiking.

ISRAEL

MONEY MATTERS

CURRENCY AND EXCHANGE. The primary unit of currency is the **New Israeli Shekel (NIS)**. There are 100 **agurot** in a shekel. Notes come in denominations of NIS200, 100, 50, and 20; coins come in NIS10, 5, and 1, as well as 50, 10, and 5 agurot. It is cheaper to buy shekels in Israel than in your home country. **ATMs** in Israel are open 24hr. and accept most major American credit cards. **Post offices** usually have the best rates and charge no commission. Since you lose money with each transaction, **convert in large sums** (unless the currency is depreciating rapidly). Banks are generally open Su, Tu, and Th 8:30am-12:30pm and 4-5:30pm; M and W 8:30am-12:30pm; F and holidays 8:30am-noon. An ATM card or credit card garners the best possible rates. Traveler's checks are not accepted in some places.

TAXES. Israel offers a **VAT** (Value Added Tax) refund to tourists who purchase over US$50 worth of goods at a shop approved by the Ministry of Tourism. To collect the 17% refund, you must be a non-Israeli citizen, pay in foreign currency (cash or international credit card), and present a VAT invoice/receipt at your point of departure from Israel (if leaving from Ben-Gurion International Airport, go to the 24hr. Bank Leumi Counter). Eilat is a free trade zone, so there is no VAT.

TIPPING AND BARGAINING. Tipping in Israel is increasingly moving toward expensive American standards, but for the time being, a 10% tip will suffice in restaurants, bars, and hotels. Taxis are mostly metered with standardized prices; drivers do not expect tips but accept them. Bargaining in Israel is the norm, the only exceptions being department stores, drug stores, and supermarkets.

TOURIST AND TRAVEL SERVICES

MEDICAL EMERGENCIES AND HEALTH. Medical care in Israel is equivalent in quality to that in the West. For minor illnesses, go to a pharmacy (at least one pharmacy in a neighborhood is open or on-call 24hr.). Pharmacists offer medical advice and medication; most speak English. Doctors can help with more serious illnesses; almost all Israeli doctors speak fluent English. Because Israel's system of socialized medicine has only recently begun to privatize, private practices are very expensive and medical insurance is a must.

BUSINESS HOURS. Most businesses are open 8:30am-7pm, but many stay open until 10pm, particularly in shopping malls. Most have longer hours on Thursdays. **Shabbat** (the Jewish day of rest) lasts from sundown on Friday to sundown on Saturday; most businesses close by 2pm on Friday and stay closed on Saturday.

USEFUL ADDRESSES. Society for the Protection of Nature in Israel (SPNI) runs expertly guided tours throughout Israel and Sinai. Tours range from half-day explorations of Jerusalem to 15-day Israel odysseys. Their main office is at 13 Heleni Ha-Malka St. in Jerusalem (☎02 625 23 57).

KEEPING IN TOUCH

MAIL. Post offices are usually open Su-Tu and Th 8am-12:30pm and 3:30-6pm, W 8am-2pm, F 8am-1pm, and are closed Sa and holidays. On the street, yellow mailboxes are for mail sent within the same city; red mailboxes are for all other mail. Most post offices offer international **Express Mail Service (EMS),** which supposedly takes three days. Mail can be sent through **Poste Restante** to almost every town in Israel. **American Express** offices will hold mail for up to 30 days and forward upon request, but only for cardholders. **Aerogrammes** are available at post offices for NIS1.40. Airmail from Israel averages five to nine days, although times are unpredictable from smaller towns.

TELEPHONE AND INTERNET ACCESS. To call Israel direct from home, leave off the 0 from the city code. Within Israel, major calling cards that can be used include: **AT&T** (☎ 800 949 49 49); **Sprint** (☎ 800 938 70 70); **MCI WorldPhone Direct** (☎ 800 940 27 27); **Canada Direct** (☎ 800 949 41 05); **BT Direct** (☎ 177 440 27 27); **Telecom New Zealand Direct** (☎ 177 640 27 27); and **Telkom South Africa Direct** (☎ 177 270 27 27). **Public telephones** are everywhere. Avoid older telephones—they devour coins even for local calls (50 agurot). Far more common are the beige-colored public phones (marked with yellow signs) that operate with **Telecards** (20 units NIS10.50, 50 units NIS23, 120 units NIS52; buy them at post offices). Telecards are good for long distance calls (NIS5.90 per min. to the US). International rates drop up to 50% late at night and on Saturdays and Sundays. **Bezek,** Israel's phone company, has offices with metered phones for international calls in Tel Aviv and Jerusalem. It may be more economical to call overseas from a phone office, because they charge for the exact time spent on the phone, not in calling units as telecards do. Dial ☎ 144 for the **operator** or **information.**

Israel is a highly networked country, with computer technology as one of its major industries. There are **cybercafes** in all major cities and most hostels offer inexpensive use of Internet and email.

SPECIAL CONCERNS

WOMEN TRAVELERS. Women travelers in Israel do not attract undue attention, but it's always best to take basic safety rules into account. Western women can blend in easily in Israel, as women generally dress in Western styles, but it is advisable to dress modestly (nothing sleeveless or tight, with skirts and pants well below the knees) in Orthodox Jewish and Arab sections of the country. Fashions in Tel Aviv, however, are about as liberal as they get. Persistent harassers may be dissuaded by a loud, public "*lech!*" ("Go away!"), or even an English scolding.

BGLT TRAVELERS. Tel Aviv is one of the few cities in the Middle East with a thriving gay and lesbian community. The main organization for gay and lesbian concerns in Israel is the **Society for the Protection of Personal Rights,** P.O. Box 37604, Tel Aviv 61375 (☎ 03 629 36 81; fax 525 23 41), or P.O. Box 3592, Haifa (☎ 04 867 26 65). A community center, library, and coffee shop are at 28 Naḥmani St., Tel Aviv. The **White Line** (*Ha-Kav Ha-Lavan;* ☎ 03 732 55 60, operating Su-Th 7:30-11:30pm) is the society's gay and lesbian hotline.

JERUSALEM ירושלים القدس ☎ 02

Your name will scorch my lips forever,
Like a seraph's kiss, untold,
If I forget thee, golden city,
Jerusalem of Gold.
　　—Naomi Shemer

When the sun sets over the Judean hills, Jerusalem's white stone turns gold and peace seems to be within the city's grasp. The domes, spires, and minarets of three major faiths' places of worship rise over crenelated walls in quiet harmony. But Jerusalem is not always as serene as its evening breeze and rooftop view. The white stone, a requirement for all of Jerusalem's buildings, is indelibly, if invisibly, stained with the blood of centuries. During Jerusalem's 5000 years, 18 conquerors have presided over the city. David established Jerusalem as the capital of the Israelite kingdom, and his son Solomon extended it northward to the present-day Temple Mount (where the Ark of the Covenant was kept and the First Temple stood). The split of the Israelite kingdom led Judah's citizens to develop the Jewish identity in the city until 596 BCE, when King Nebuchadnezzar besieged the city and exiled the Jews to Babylon.

Jerusalem Overview

JERUSALEM FOREST

MOTZA ILIT

Sderot Ben Gurion

Kanfei Nesharim

HAR NOF

BEIT ZAYIT

JERUSALEM FOREST

SEE WEST JERUSALEM MAP, PP. xxx-xxx

Sderot Herzl

Wolfsohn

Bank of Israel $

Hebrew University (Giv'at Ram Campus)

Giv'at Ram

Yad Vashem

Mt. Herzl

Herzl's Grave

Herzl Museum

Jerusalem Forest Recreation Centre

Sderot Herzl

Shmuel Beyth

Ein Kerem

Hantke

Church of St. John

EIN KEREM

Hantke

Bezalel Barak

Church of the Visitation

Russian Convent

KIRYAT HA-YOVEL

Ha-Rav Uzlel

TO HADASSAH MEDICAL CENTER

Ha-Ma'ayan

Szold

KIRYAT MENAHEM

Golomb

Ha-Rav Herzog

ORA

Golomb

N

0 _____ 1000 yards

0 _____ 1 kilometer

Kenyon Yerushalayim (Shopping Mall)

Teddy Stadium

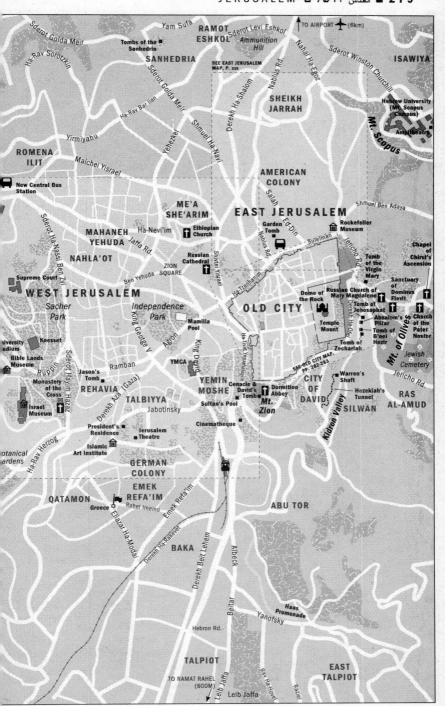

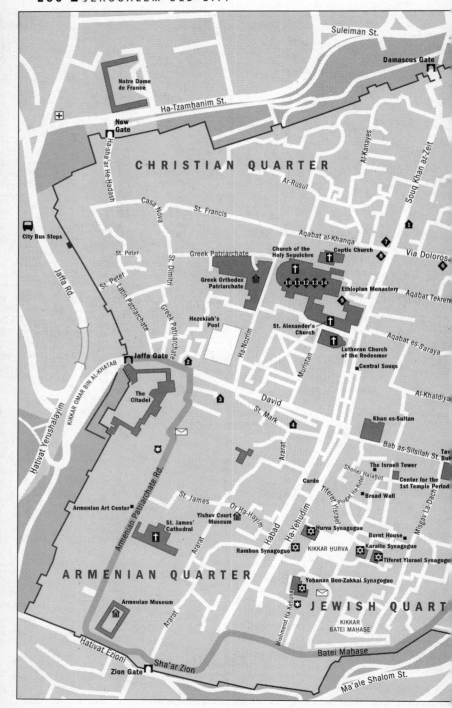

Suleiman St.

Damascus Gate

Notre Dame
de France

Ha-Tzamhanim St.

New
Gate

Al-Kanayes

Souq Khan az-Zeit

CHRISTIAN QUARTER

Ar-Rusul

City Bus Stops

Casa Nova

St. Francis

Aqabat al-Khanqa

1

Jaffa Rd.

St. Peter

Greek Patriarchate

Church of the
Holy Sepulchre

Coptic Church

7

8

Via Doloros

6

St. Peter

Latin Patriarchate

St. Dimitri

Greek Orthodox
Patriarchate

10 11 12 13 14

Ethiopian Monastery

Aqabat Tekreh

Ha-Nozrim

9

Greek Patriarchate

Hezekiah's
Pool

St. Alexander's
Church

Aqabat es-Saraya

Jaffa Gate

2

Lutheran Church
of the Redeemer

Central Souqs

KIKKAR OMAR BIN AL-KHATAB

The
Citadel

Muristan

Al-Khaldiya

3

David

Hativat Yerushalayim

St. Mark

Khan es-Sultan

4

Bab as-Silsilah St.

Tas
Bul

Armenian Patriarchate Rd.

Ararat

Shonei Halahot

The Israeli Tower

Center for the
1st Temple Period

Cardo

Tiferet Yisrael

Plugat Ha-Kotel

Broad Wall

Misgav La-Dach

Armenian Art Center

St. James

Or Ha-Hayim

Habad

Ha-Yehudim

St. James'
Cathedral

Yishuv Court
Museum

Hurva Synagogue

Burnt House

Ararat

Ramban Synagogue

KIKKAR HURVA

Karaite Synagogue

Tiferet Yisrael Synagogu

ARMENIAN QUARTER

Yohanan Ben-Zakkai Synagogue

Mishmerot Ha-Kehuna

JEWISH QUART

Armenian Museum

KIKKAR
BATEI MAHASE

Hativat Ezioni

Batei Mahase

Zion Gate

Sha'ar Zion

Ma'ale Shalom St.

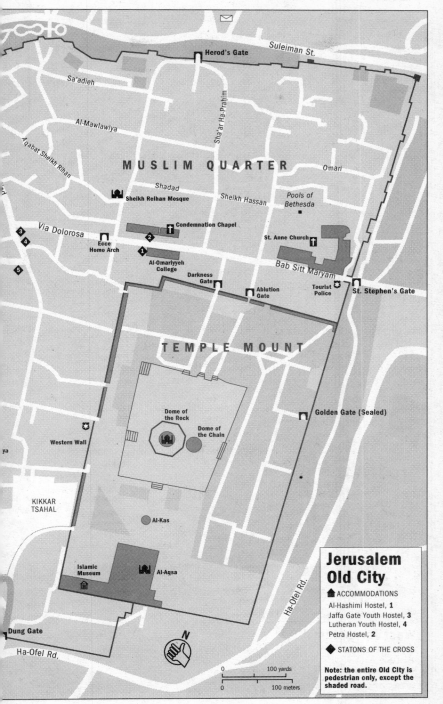

Jerusalem Old City

⌂ ACCOMMODATIONS

Al-Hashimi Hostel, **1**
Jaffa Gate Youth Hostel, **3**
Lutheran Youth Hostel, **4**
Petra Hostel, **2**

◆ STATONS OF THE CROSS

Note: the entire Old City is pedestrian only, except the shaded road.

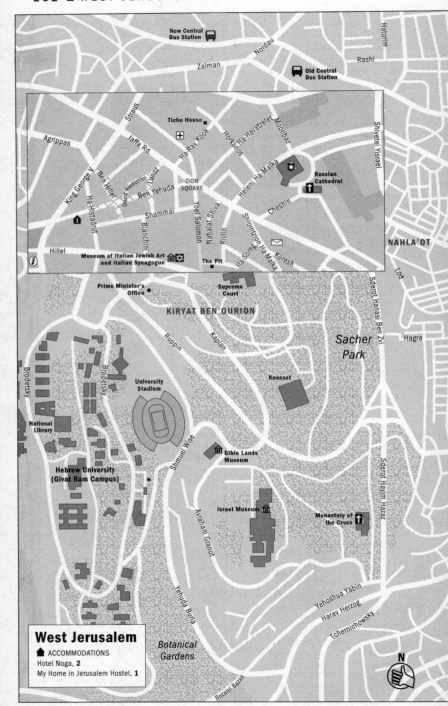

New Central Bus Station

Old Central Bus Station

Nordau

Zalman

Rashi

Haturim

Straus

Ticho House

Ha-Havatzelet

Moonbaz

Shivetei Yisrael

Agrippas

Jaffa Rd

Ha-Rav Kook

Horkanos

Heleni Ha-Malka

Russian Cathedral

King George V

Ben Hillel

Dorot Rishonim

Ben Yehuda

Lunz

ZION SQUARE

Cheshin

Ha-Histadrut

Shammai

Bianchini

Natalat Shiva

Yoel Salomon

Rivlin

Shlomtzion Ha-Malka

Ha-Soreg Ha-Malka

Koresh

NAHLA'OT

Lod

Hillel

Museum of Italian Jewish Art and Italian Synagogue

The Pit

Prime Minister's Office

Supreme Court

KIRYAT BEN GURION

Sderot Hanasi Ben Zvi

Hagra

Ruppin

Kaplan

Sacher Park

Brodetsky

Brodetsky

University Stadium

Knesset

National Library

Hebrew University (Givat Ram Campus)

Shmuel Wise

Bible Lands Museum

Sderot Hayim Hazaz

Avraham Granot

Israel Museum

Monastery of the Cross

Yehoshua Yabin

Harav Herzog

Tchernichowsky

Yehuda Burla

West Jerusalem

⌂ ACCOMMODATIONS
Hotel Noga, **2**
My Home in Jerusalem Hostel, **1**

Botanical Gardens

Bezalel Bazak

N

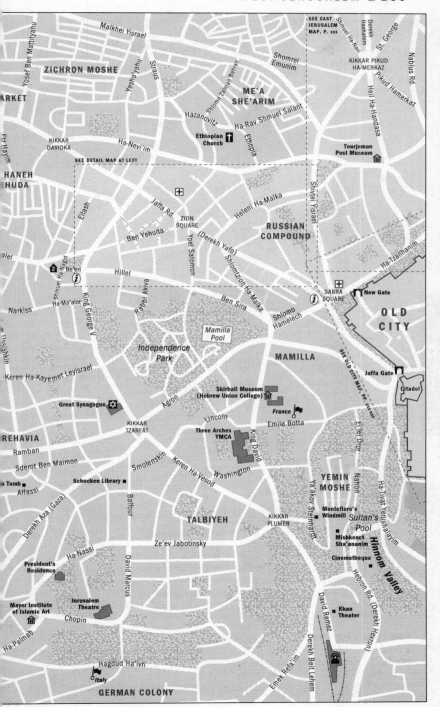

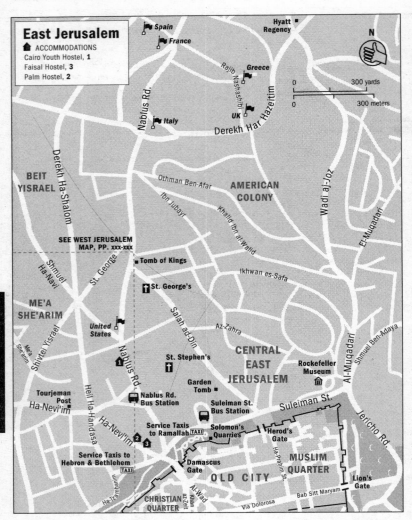

East Jerusalem

ACCOMMODATIONS
Cairo Youth Hostel, **1**
Faisal Hostel, **3**
Palm Hostel, **2**

Jerusalem enjoyed more than a century of revival under the Persians, until Alexander the Great rode in on a tide of Hellenism that swept through the city in 332 BCE. The renaissance ended in 198 BCE, when Seleucid King Antiochus IV forbade all Jewish practices. Led by Judah Maccabee, the Jews successfully revolted and founded the Hasmonean dynasty that lasted until the Romans set up the province of Judaea. Six centuries of Roman rule began with Herod the Great, child of a Jewish father and Samaritan mother. The Jews revolted but failed, then tried once more (the 123 CE Bar Kokhba Revolt) and failed; when Hadrian razed the city after this third revolt, he divided his new *Aelia Capitolina* into quarters (that remain today) using two major roads (the Cardo and Decumanus). When Roman Emperor Constantine adopted and legalized Christianity in 331 CE, his mother Eleni visited the Holy Land in order to identify and consecrate Christian sites.

Muslim caliph Omar conquered *Aelia* in 638, beginning an era of tolerant rule; his successors built the Dome of the Rock soon after. The Fatimids and Seljuk

Turks who followed were not so kind to the city and its synagogues and churches. Fired up by the rumored closing of pilgrimage routes, the Crusaders stormed and captured Jerusalem in 1099, and they subsequently began massacring Muslims and Jews mercilessly. The year 1187 saw the city do its time (as all cities in the Middle East did) under Salah al-Din, who allowed both Muslims and Jews to resettle the city—so tolerantly that the city became a thriving center for Muslim scholarship in the Mamluk era. Ottoman rule saw restructuring and expansion until 1917, when the city fell without resistance to the British army. Both Jews and Arabs came to resent the increasing influence of the British, who promised autonomy to both during World War I but ended up keeping Palestine for themselves, heightening tension between the two sides that almost turned into a civil war in 1936 and 1939.

The next World War ignited violence that divided Palestine into separate Jewish and Arab states, but left Jerusalem an international city. In the post-evacuation war of 1948, West Jerusalem and the Jewish Quarter were besieged by Arabs. Jordanian control of the city saw the synagogues and ancient quarters dynamited, and the city was divided into Jordanian and Israeli sectors for nearly two decades. In the Six Day War of 1967, Israel captured East Jerusalem, the Old City, and the West Bank from the Jordanians. On June 29 of that year, Israel declared the newly unified Jerusalem its "eternal capital." The walls separating the Israeli and Arab sectors were torn down, and life under Israeli rule began for Jerusalem's Arabs.

The 1987 *intifada* (uprising) of Palestinians protesting Israeli occupation saw violent clashes that turned East Jerusalem and the Old City into alien territory for Jewish Israelis. Bus explosions, suicide bombings, and street fighting have fueled the fires of Jerusalem's recent history, and the future of Jerusalem is perhaps the most sensitive issue in the current Israeli-Palestinian negotiations. Israel adamantly refuses to discuss withdrawing from its capital, while Palestinians fervently oppose the idea of abandoning claims to their most important city.

✈ INTERCITY TRANSPORTATION

FLIGHTS

Ben-Gurion Airport (info for all airlines ☎ 03 972 33 44. El Al English info ☎ 03 972 33 88. Automated flight reconfirmation ☎ 03 972 23 33.) is only 1hr. from Jerusalem and easily accessible; you do not need to go to Tel Aviv first, no matter how early your flight, thanks to the 24hr. *sherut* service offered by Nesher (see **Taxis,** below). For a hassle-free airport experience, bags for El Al flights can be checked in and inspected in advance at 7 Kanfei Nesharim St., 1st fl. (☎ 651 57 05; fax 651 57 03), on the corner of Jaffa Rd. near the central bus station. Open Su-Th 2-10pm for next-day flights, 2-7pm for same-night flights.

BUSES

Egged Central Bus Station (☎ 530 47 04; www.egged.co.il), on Jaffa Rd. (see **Getting Around,** below). 10% ISIC discount on long-distance trips. Drivers often inspect ISIC cards upon boarding. Times, frequencies, and prices listed here are based on the summer 2000 schedule; call for current info (or go to the station). Info desk open Su-Th 6am-8:30pm, F 6am-3pm. To: **Arlozorov terminal** (#480; every 15-20min. Su-Th 6am-10:30pm, F 6am-4:30pm, and Sa 8:20-11pm); **Be'er Sheva** Direct (#470; 1½hr.; every 45min.-2hr. Su 6:20am-6:15pm, M-Th 6:45am-6:15pm, F 10:20am-sundown, Sa 8:20pm; NIS27) or via **Kiryat Gat** (#446; 1¾hr.; every 15min.-1hr. Su-Th 6am-9pm, F 6am-sundown, Sa sundown-10:35pm); **Ben-Gurion Airport** (#423, 428, 945, or 947; 1hr.; every 15-40min. Su-Th 6am-8:35pm, F 6am-sundown, Sa sundown-10pm; NIS21); **Eilat** (#444; 4½hr.; Su-Th 7, 10am, 2, 5pm; F 7, 10am, 2pm; no buses on Sa; less frequent in winter; NIS61); **Haifa** Direct (#940; 2hr.; every 15-45min. Su 6am-7:30pm, M-W 6:30am-7:30pm, Th 6:30am-8:30pm, F 6:45am-sundown, Sa sundown-10pm; NIS40) or via **Netanya** (#947; 2hr.; every 20-40min. Su-Th 6am-8:30pm,

F 6am-sundown, Sa sundown-10pm); **Tiberias** (#961, 963, or 964; 3hr.; every hr. Su-Th 7am-7:30pm, F 7am-3pm, Sa 8:15-9:15pm); **Tel Aviv Central Station** (#405; 1hr.; every 10-25min. Su-Th 5:40am-midnight, F 6am-sundown, Sa sundown-midnight; NIS18). Egged buses don't go into any Palestinian towns in the West Bank; they stop only at Jewish settlements or sites. 2 bus stations serve the West Bank. Suleiman Street Station, in East Jerusalem between Herod's and Damascus Gates, serves routes south while Nablus Road Station serves points north. See **West Bank: Entry,** p. 416, for information on travel to the West Bank from Israel.

TAXIS

Jerusalem is served by 2 main **intercity sherut taxi** companies. **Ha Bira** (☎ 625 45 45), at the corner of Ha-Rav Kook St. and Jaffa Rd. (near Zion Sq.) goes to **Tel Aviv** (every 20min. 6am-2am; NIS18, after 11:30pm NIS19, Shabbat NIS20.) Office open Su-Th 5:30am-11pm and F 5:30am-5:30pm. **Nesher,** 21 King George St. (☎ 625 72 27 or 623 12 31), provides 24hr. door-to-door service to the airport from anywhere in Jerusalem (NIS40, reserve at least 4hr. ahead). *Sherut* taxis to other locations leave from the central bus station. Split among a group they can be as cheap as buses. To West Bank towns, *service* (the Arab equivalent of the *sherut*) leave from outside of Damascus Gate (see **West Bank: Transportation,** p. 417).

CAR RENTAL

Many companies have offices on or near King David St., not far from the Hilton and King David Hotel. Prices include full insurance. Many increase their prices during July-Sept., sometimes by as much as US$15 per day. **Budget,** 23 King David St. (☎ 624 89 91; fax 625 89 86; www.budget.co.il), has cars starting at US$45 per day, US$40 per day for 3-day rentals with unlimited mileage; 23+. **Eldan,** 24 King David St. (☎ 625 21 51; www.eldan.co.il), has one-day rentals beginning at US$38 (100km included), US$38 per day for one week minimum with unlimited mileage.

✦ ORIENTATION

Known as **Yerushalayim** in Hebrew and **al-Quds** (the holy) in Arabic, Jerusalem is a sprawling city, most of which was only developed in the last 50 years of the capital's three-millennia history. Most distances in Jerusalem make for reasonable, pleasant walks for those who don't mind the heat and the hills.

WEST JERUSALEM. This section includes Jewish parts of Jerusalem, from French Hill in the northeast and East Talpiyot in the southeast, to Kiryat Menaḥem in the southwest and Ramot in the northwest. The main street is **Jaffa Rd.** (Derekh Yafo), running west-to-east from the central bus station to the Old City's **Jaffa Gate.** Roughly midway between the two, **Zion Sq.** (Kikkar Tzion) sits at the corner of Jerusalem's triangular *midraḥov* bounded by Jaffa Rd., **Ben-Yehuda St.,** and **King George St.** Upscale eateries line **Yoel Salomon St.** and **Rivlin St.,** off Zion Sq.

North of the city center, the **Russian Compound's** hip bar scene hugs the old-world **Mea She'arim** like spandex on a *yenta*. Northwest on Jaffa Rd. are the teeming outdoor markets of **Maḥaneh Yehuda** and, farther down, the central bus station. Southwest of the triangle are the Knesset building and the hilltop Israel Museum complex. The beautiful **Independence Park** lies south of the city center, ringed by luxury hotels; farther south are the cafes of **Emek Refa'im** and the discotheques of **Talpiyot.** The artists' district of **Yemin Moshe** huddles southeast of Zion Sq.

OLD CITY. Jerusalem's most important historical and religious sites are concentrated within the walls of the Old City, which is still divided into the four quadrants laid out by the Romans in 135 CE. To get from West Jerusalem's center to the Old City, take Jaffa Rd. past the post office to Jaffa Gate. Here you can follow the promenade along the ancient walls to most of the seven other gates. The two main roads in the Old City are the roof-covered **David St.,** an extension of which,

Bab al-Silsilah St. (Gate of the Chain), runs up to the Temple Mount, and **Souq Khan al-Zeit,** from Damascus Gate, which enters directly into the **Muslim Quarter** and turns into the **Cardo** as it crosses David St. and enters the **Jewish Quarter.** The Jewish Quarter is also directly accessible through **Dung Gate.** The **Armenian Quarter** is to the right as you enter through Jaffa Gate and is directly accessible via **Zion Gate.** Left of Jaffa Gate is the **Christian Quarter,** which can also be reached directly from the **New Gate.**

EAST JERUSALEM. The old, invisible **Green Line** separating Jordan from pre-1967 Israel runs along **Derekh Ha-Shalom** (Peace Rd.) and is still a good general demarcation between Palestinian and Jewish areas of Jerusalem. East Jerusalem is the name normally given to the Palestinian parts of Jerusalem just outside the Old City to the north and east; it sometimes includes the Old City. **Suleiman St.,** in front of Damascus Gate, and **Salah al-Din St.,** which runs out from Herod's Gate, are the main roads in central East Jerusalem. **Ha-Nevi'im St.** (Musrada in Arabic), which runs in from Jaffa Rd. in West Jerusalem, converges with **Nablus Rd.** at Damascus Gate; the small, busy area has falafel and shawarma stands, fruit vendors, dry goods stores, and hostels, all cheaper than practically anywhere else in Jerusalem. Central East Jerusalem is the financial and cultural hub of the Arab community.

▐ LOCAL TRANSPORTATION

BUSES

All sections of the city are accessible by bus from the **central bus station** (info ☎ 530 47 04) on Jaffa Rd., west of city center just past the Maḥaneh Yehuda district (NIS5 per ride within Jerusalem; NIS47 *kartisia* buys 11 rides, 20 for those under 18). The current central bus station is temporary; the old one, farther west on Jaffa Rd., across from the Binyanei Ha-Umma Convention Center, is being rebuilt and will supposedly be finished sometime in 2001. A dazzling (and dizzying) **city bus map** is available at the information desk. Arab buses run irregularly every day; Egged service stops at about 4:30pm on Friday and resumes after sunset on Saturday. Taxis are widely available. Try **Reḥavia Taxi** (☎ 625 44 44 or 622 24 44) for 24hr. service.

COMMON BUS ROUTES:

BUS #1: To Mea She'arim and Dung Gate/Western Wall.

BUS #3: To Jaffa Gate, Shivtei Yisrael, Ha-Nevi'im, and Maḥaneh Yehuda.

BUS #4 AND 4A: To Emek Refa'im, Keren Ha-Yesod, King George, Ramat Eshkol, and Mt. Scopus.

BUS #6, 8, 13, 18, AND 20: To Zion Sq.; get off at the intersection of Jaffa Rd. and King George St. Buses #6 and 20 continue to Jaffa Gate; #6 goes on to the Kenyon mall.

BUS #9 AND 27: To the Knesset, the Israel Museum, the Hebrew University at Givat Ram, West Jerusalem center, and Mt. Scopus.

BUS #17: To Reḥavia, Mt. Herzl, and Ein Kerem.

BUS #21: To Talpiyot, Hebron Rd., King David St., and Mt. Herzl.

BUS #23: To Damascus Gate, Suleiman St. bus station, East Jerusalem, and Herod's Gate.

BUS #99 (THE JERUSALINE): From Jaffa Gate or central bus station, passes 34 major tourist sights on a 2hr. loop. Su-Th at 10am, noon, 2, and 4pm; F 10am and noon. Runs less frequently in winter. One loop NIS28.

◪ PRACTICAL INFORMATION

OLD CITY

TOURIST AND FINANCIAL SERVICES

Tourist Office: The tourist information office in Safra Sq. in West Jerusalem is superior to those in the Old City and worth the 10min. walk from Jaffa Gate (see p. 288).

Special Interest Tourist Offices: Christian Information Center (☎627 26 92; fax 628 64 17; cicts@netmedia.net.il; www.cits.org), inside Jaffa Gate, opposite the Tower of David. Offers information on Jerusalem's pilgrimage sights and Christian accommodations. Open M-Sa 8:30am-1pm. **The Jewish Student Information Center,** 5 Beit El St. (☎628 26 34; fax 628 83 38; jseidel@netmedia.net.il; www.geocities.com/athens/7613), in Ḥurva Sq. in the Jewish Quarter. Run by the friendly and enthusiastic Jeff Seidel, who leads tours of the Western Wall tunnels. Shabbat home hospitality available with Orthodox Jewish families.

Tours: The highly recommended **Zion Walking Tours** (☎628 78 66; mobile ☎050 305 552; www.zionwt.co.il) offers 8 inexpensive guided routes in and around the Old City. Their most popular tour is of the four quarters of the Old City (3hr.; daily 9, 11am, 2pm; US$10, students US$9, entry fees included). Their office is right inside Jaffa Gate, opposite the Tower of David. **Israel Archaeological Seminars,** 34 Habad St. (☎627 35 15; fax 627 26 60; office@archesem.com; www.archesem.com), in the Jewish Quarter, offers walking tours in addition to day-long archaeology excursions all over Israel. A guided tour of the politically sensitive **Western Wall tunnels** requires reserving a ticket **in advance** for a 1hr. tour (NIS30-40). Individuals cannot enter the tunnels or excavations without a guide (☎627 13 33; fax 626 48 28; www.hakotel.org). Most hostels organize daily sunrise tours of the Dead Sea area (3am-3pm), run by **Alternative Palestine Tours** (NIS90 for transportation and guide).

Bank: Bank Mizrahi, 26 Tiferet Yisrael St. (☎627 31 31; fax 628 84 29), in the Jewish Quarter. Look for the blue sign in Ḥurva Sq. Hefty commission for foreign exchange. Open Su-Th 9am-2pm and 5-7pm; M, W, F 9am-noon. Has the only **ATM** and automated **currency exchange machine** in the entire Old City.

EMERGENCY AND COMMUNICATIONS

Police: (☎622 62 22). Inside Jaffa Gate to the right, next to the Tower of David. 24hr.

Pharmacies: Jaffa Gate Pharmacy (☎628 38 98), the 1st left from Jaffa Gate, immediately on the right. Open daily 9am-8pm. **Habash Pharmacy,** 104 al-Wad St. (☎627 24 27; fax 628 81 57), in the Muslim Quarter. Open daily 8:30am-8pm.

Medical Assistance: Austrian-Arab Community Clinic, Qanatar Khadeir Rd. (☎627 32 46), off al-Wad St., in the Muslim Quarter, and across from the Austrian Hospice. Open Sa-W 8am-7pm and Th 8am-4pm. **Kupat Holim** (☎627 16 08), in the Jewish Quarter above the Cardo and across from Ḥurva Sq. Hours are erratic.

Internet Access: The cheapest connections are found mostly in the Muslim Quarter. **Mike's Center,** 172 Khan al-Zeit St. (☎628 24 86), at the turnoff for the 9th Station of the Cross, boasts "the fastest line in Israel." NIS12 per hr.

Post Office: (☎629 06 86), inside Jaffa Gate, across from the Tower of David, marked by a red sign. Open Su-Th 7:30am-2:30pm and F 8am-noon.

WEST JERUSALEM

TOURIST AND FINANCIAL SERVICES

Tourist Office: MTIO, 3 Safra Sq. (☎625 88 44), in the City Hall complex off Jaffa Rd. From behind the large water fountain in the municipal plaza, the entrance is on the right. Excellent computerized information. Offers pamphlets and maps, but doesn't have Carta's Map (NIS36), the best map available at Steimatzky's (see **English-Language Bookstores,** p. 289). MTIO open Su-Th 8:30am-4pm and F 8:45am-1pm.

Tours: The municipality sponsors a free Shabbat **walking tour** in English (☎625 88 44) from 32 Jaffa Rd. near Zion Sq. (2½hr., Sa 10am, rotates among several routes). *This Week in Jerusalem* lists guided tours (also posted at the MTIO office). Sunrise tours to Masada and the Dead Sea (NIS90) and day tours to the Galilee (NIS120) are available through most hostels in the area, or by contacting **Alternative Tours** (☎/fax 628 32 82; raed@jrshotel.com; www.jrshotel.com). The **Society for the Protection of Nature in Israel (SPNI),** 13 Heleni Ha-Malka St. (☎625 23 57), runs guided tours throughout Israel and Sinai. Tours range from half-day explorations of Jerusalem to 15-day Israel odysseys. Office open Su-Th 9am-6:45pm and F 9am-12:30pm.

Budget Travel: Neot Ha-Kikar, 5 Shlomtzion Ha-Malka St. (☎623 62 62; fax 623 61 61; www.neot-hakikar.com). Specializes in 1- to 6-day Sinai tours from Eilat (US$59-US$290). Open Su-Th 9am-5pm and F 9am-12:30pm. **ISSTA,** 31 Ha-Nevi'im St. (☎621 36 00). ISIC NIS40; bring photograph and proof of student status. Student discounts on airfare, car rentals, and **Eurail** passes. Open Su-Tu and Th 9am-7pm; W and F 9am-1pm. Additional offices in La-metayel camping store (☎624 31 78) and Hebrew University campuses on Mt. Scopus (☎582 61 16) and Givat Ram (☎651 87 80).

Consulates: UK, 19 Nashashibi St. (☎541 41 00), in East Jerusalem near Sheikh Jarrah. Open M-F 9am-noon. **US,** 27 Nablus Rd. (☎622 72 00, after-hours emergency ☎622 72 50; www.uscongen-jerusalem.org/consular), in East Jerusalem. Open for passport renewals and other services M-F 8:30-11:30am, notary service Tu 1-3pm. Closed for Israeli and US holidays and last F of each month. Administrative offices at 18 Agron St. in West Jerusalem (☎622 72 30). Other consulates in Tel Aviv (see p. 289).

Currency Exchange: City Change, 30 Jaffa Rd. (☎625 87 58). Open Su-Th 9am-6pm, F 9am-1pm. **Money Net,** 8 Ben-Hillel St. (☎622 23 18; fax 623 27 88), on the *midraḥov.* Open Su-Th 9am-6pm, F 9am-1pm. Both give better rates than banks and charge no commission. The **post office** (see **Central Post Office,** p. 290) offers the same rates, also commission-free. **Bank Ha-Poalim** (emergency ☎03 567 49 99), in Zion Sq. Open Su and Tu-W 8:30am-1pm; M and Th 8:30am-1pm and 4-7pm; F 8:30am-12:30pm. **ATM** accepts Cirrus, Plus, and major credit cards.

American Express: 19 Hillel St. (☎624 69 33; fax 624 09 50), near McDonald's. Full service office with commission-free traveler's check cashing, purchasing, and replacement for cardholders. Holds mail, but not packages. For traveler's check emergencies, call 24hr. ☎800 943 86 94. Open Su-Th 9am-4:30pm and F 9am-noon.

LOCAL SERVICES

English-Language Bookstores: Steimatzky, 39 Jaffa St. (☎625 01 55); other locations at 7 Ben-Yehuda St. and 9 King George St. Great for maps, magazines, and travel books. Open Su-Th 8:30am-7pm (Ben-Yehuda location until 8pm) and F 8:30am-2pm. Open Su-Th 8:30am-7:30pm and F 8:30am-2pm. **SPNI Bookstore,** 13 Heleni Ha-Malka St. (☎625 23 57), often has the lowest prices on guidebooks and maps.

Cultural Centers: American Cultural Center, 19 Keren Ha-Yesod St. (☎625 57 55; fax 624 25 60; acc-jer@usis-israel.org.il), near the Agron-King George intersection, right after King George St. turns into Keren Ha-Yesod St. Free and open to anyone. Open Su-Th 10am-4pm and F 9am-noon. Closed on all Israeli and US holidays. **Alliance Française,** 8 Agron St. (☎625 12 04), across from Supersol. French culture club for francophones of any nationality. Nominal charge for events.

Gay and Lesbian Services: Jerusalem Open House (JOH), 7 Ben-Yehuda St., 3rd fl. (☎625 31 91; gayj@hotmail.com; www.poboxes.com/gayj), on the *midraḥov.* Call or visit for a schedule of events. Office open Su, Th 4-8pm; Tu 10am-3pm; F 10am-2pm. Open house every Su and Th 8-10pm. **KLAF** (☎625 12 71; www.aquanet.co.il/vip/klaf), is an organization for lesbian feminists, with activities all over the country. On the line every W 8-10pm. **The Other 10%** (**Ha-Asiron Ha-Aḥer;** ☎653 54 54; www.poboxes.com/asiron), is Hebrew University's organization for gay, lesbian, bisexual, and transgender students. Hosts activities during the school year (Oct.-June).

ISRAEL

Ticket Agencies: Bimot, 8 Shammai St. (☎625 09 05), and **Kla'im,** 12 Shammai St. (☎625 68 69), have discount tickets for students and tourists for concerts, shows, and sporting events around Jerusalem. Both open Su-Th 9am-7pm and F 9am-1pm.

Laundromat: Laundry Place, 12 Shammai St. (☎625 77 14), near the *midraḥov.* Self-service NIS19 per load, includes dryer and detergent. Membership for long-term stays. Open Su-Th 8:30am-midnight, F 8:30am-sunset, and Sa sunset-midnight.

Camping Supplies: La-metayel, 5 Yoel Salomon St. (☎623 33 38; fax 623 33 52; www.lametayel.com) has the most extensive (and expensive) stock of camping gear (and an impressive array of travel books). Open Su-Th 10am-9pm and F 10am-2:30pm. **Orcha Camping,** 12 Yoel Salomon (☎624 06 55), near Cafe Kapulsky, is affiliated with SPNI (members get discounts on merchandise). Open Su-Th 8am-7pm and F 8am-3pm.

EMERGENCY AND COMMUNICATIONS

Medical Emergency: ☎101. **Magen David Adom First Aid,** 7 Ha-Memgimel St. (☎652 31 33). Turn right at the end of Jaffa Rd. (past the bus station) and take the next left. Their **Terem Clinic** (☎652 17 48) is open 24hr. and will see anyone on a walk-in basis for both emergencies and non-emergencies; most insurance plans are accepted, as is direct payment by credit card. Newspapers list hospitals on duty for emergencies.

Police: In the Russian Compound (☎539 11 11), off Jaffa Rd. in West Jerusalem. **Tourist desk** (☎675 48 11), on Cheshin St., just off Jaffa Rd., near the post office.

Help Lines: M'Lev Center for Crisis Counseling (☎654 11 11 or (800) 654 111) has a general help line and referrals for English speakers. The **Rape Crisis Center** (☎1202 from anywhere in Israel) is staffed 24hr. **Eran Emotional Health Hotline** (☎1201) assists tourists daily 8am-11pm. **Alcoholics Anonymous,** 24 Ha-Palmaḥ St. (☎563 05 24 or 583 00 92). **AIDS Hotline** (☎03 528 77 81), staffed M and Th 7:30-10pm. The weekly "In Jerusalem" insert in *The Jerusalem Post* lists many other support groups.

Services for the Disabled: Yad Sarah Organization, 124 Herzl Blvd. (☎644 44 25; fax 644 44 23; info@yadsarah.org.il; www.yadsarah.org.il). Free loans of medical equipment. Offers wheelchair van for airport pick-ups (NIS150, order 2 weeks in advance) and rides anywhere within Jerusalem for fares comparable to those of taxis. Open Su-Th 9am-7pm and F 9am-12:30pm.

Pharmacies: Superpharm, 3 Ha-Histadrut (☎624 62 44; fax 624 75 75), between Ben-Yehuda and King George St. Open Su-Th 8:30am-11pm, F 8:30am-3pm, and Sa sundown-11pm. **Alba Pharmacy,** 42 Jaffa St. (☎625 37 03). Open Su-Th 7am-7pm and F 7am-2pm. Two pharmacies rotate night duty and on Shabbat; check newspaper listings.

Telephones: Solan Communications, 2 Luntz St. (☎625 89 08; fax 625 88 79), on the *midraḥov,* off Ben-Yehuda St. Telegram and international fax services (NIS13 1st page, NIS8 each additional page), private booths for local and international calls (NIS3 per min. to most countries). Open Su-Th 8am-11pm, F 8am-5pm, Sa 5pm-midnight. An additional branch is inside Jaffa Gate. **Global GSM,** 22 King David St. (☎625 25 85 or (800) 252 585), rents cellular phones at a reasonable rate (US$1 per day, plus US$0.49 per min. for outgoing calls within Israel; free incoming calls). Open Su-Th 9am-7pm and F 9am-1pm. **Bezeq 24hr. Information:** ☎144.

Internet Access: Cheaper in the Old City (see p. 288). **Netcafe,** 9 Heleni Ha-Malka St. (☎624 63 27), uphill from Jaffa Rd. NIS7 for 15min.; NIS25 per hr. Open Su-Tu 11am-10pm, W-Th 11am-late, F 10am-3pm, and Sa 9pm-late. **Strudel Internet Cafe and Wine Bar,** 11 Moonbaz St. (☎623 21 01; fax 622 14 45), in the Russian Compound. It doubles as a bar at night. NIS6 for 15min. Happy hour 7-9pm and midnight-12:30am (15min. computer time and a beer NIS13). Open M-F 10am-late and Sa 3pm-late.

Post Office: 23 Jaffa Rd. (☎629 06 47) is the main office. **Poste Restante** for no fee. **Money exchange, Western Union, telegram,** and **fax** services available. Also sells phone cards. Open Su-Th 7am-7pm, F 7am-noon. For telegrams, dial ☎171 (24hr.). Branch post offices in most neighborhoods; look for a bright red awning.

♪ ACCOMMODATIONS

OLD CITY

Most of Jerusalem's cheapest hostels are in the Old City, but these vary tremendously in quality and safety (neither price nor location are good barometers). Solo women should be especially discriminating about where to stay and should dress modestly: t-shirts are okay, but exposing anything more than forearms will attract undue attention in the conservative Old City. Accommodations here fall into two categories: quieter, cleaner establishments with curfews; and less clean or safe places (but sometimes more fun) with bars or lax alcohol policies. Both kinds have priceless rooftop views of the surrounding sights. Bargain for discounts on multiple-night stays or if business seems slow.

Al-Hashimi Hostel and Hotel, 73 Souq Khan al-Zeit St. (☎628 44 10; fax 628 46 67). Take the right fork from Damascus Gate. Single-sex dorms are available. Fans in dorms; A/C and bathrooms in private rooms. Heat in winter. TV lounge. Internet access. Reception 6am-3am. Check-out 10:30am. Curfew 3am. Dorm beds NIS20; singles US$25-35; doubles US$30-45; triples US$50-70. 15% discount for stays longer than two nights (not applicable to dorm prices). Credit cards and traveler's checks accepted.

Lutheran Youth Hostel (☎628 21 20; fax 628 51 07), on St. Mark's Rd., the 1st alley off David St., on the right when coming from Jaffa Gate. Half hostel and half guest house. The large fountained garden and overhanging dining hall are reserved for private guests, but the hostel part has its own calm garden and enormous kitchen with free tea and coffee. Breakfast included for private rooms. Reception 6am-10:45pm. Check-in noon. Check-out 10am. Lockout for hostel guests 9am-noon. Curfew 10:30pm, flexible until midnight. Guests must be under 35 (also flexible, especially when business is slow). Large single-sex dorms NIS33; singles US$40-48; doubles US$72-80; prices fluctuate according to the value of the Deutschmark. No reservations for dorms. Credit cards accepted for guest house only.

Petra Hostel, 1 David St. (☎628 66 18), just inside Jaffa Gate, on the left before the entrance to the market. Built more than 175 years ago, this is the oldest accommodation in the Old City. Mark Twain and Herman Melville stayed here. Has fantastic rooftop views (some say the best in the city) and a vast, sunny lounge. Pool table, bar, Internet, laundry, and kitchen. Full breakfast NIS14. Luggage storage NIS1 per hr., NIS5 per day. Check-out 10am. Roof mattresses NIS20, with sheets and blanket NIS25; roof-top tents (in winter only) NIS25; dorms NIS32, weekly rate (paid in advance) NIS28 per night; private rooms US$35-50. Reservations accepted only for morning arrivals.

Heritage House. Office: 90 Ḥabad St. (☎627 19 16). Men's hostel: 2 Or Ha-Ḥayim St. (☎627 22 24). Women's hostel: 7 Ha-Malakh St. (☎628 18 20). Free nightly classes (optional) at the men's hostel. Kosher dairy kitchen for guests. Lock-out 9am-5pm. Curfew midnight, 1am in the summer and on Shabbat. Dorm accommodations only; free except on Shabbat (NIS20).

Al-Arab Hostel (☎628 35 37; alarab@netvision.net.il), on Khan al-Zeit St. Take the right fork from Damascus Gate, before al-Hashimi. A crowded party hostel with some of the cheapest beds in town and all the amenities: kitchen/cafe, *argileh*, free tea and coffee, Internet service, laundry, satellite TV, luggage storage, and 24hr. reception. Roof-beds NIS14; dorms NIS18; singles and doubles NIS60; triples NIS70.

Jaffa Gate Youth Hostel (☎627 64 02), in the Jaffa Gate area across from the Tower of David; a black and pink sign points down a short alley to the reception. TV lounge, patio, tiny common kitchen, and priceless rooftop view. Check-in until midnight. Check-out 10am. Curfew midnight. No smoking or alcohol. Small dorms NIS40; singles NIS60, with A/C and bath NIS80; doubles NIS100, with bath NIS160. Ask for a discount.

WEST JERUSALEM

Accommodations in West Jerusalem are generally roomier, cleaner, and safer than their Old City counterparts (and correspondingly more expensive). Hostels here are better for club-hoppers; most establishments have no curfew, and some are directly above the action. Avoid the 17% VAT by paying in non-Israeli currency.

■ **Zion Square Hostel,** 42 Jaffa Rd. (☎624 41 14; fax 623 62 45; jrpool@inter.net.il; www.zionsquarehostel.homestead.com/opening.html), in a fantastic location. A/C, laundry service, Internet (with a web camera), cable TV, 24hr. reception and security, lockers, and luggage storage. Some rooms have balconies overlooking Zion Sq. Breakfast included. Check-out 10am. Dorms NIS60; doubles NIS190.

Hotel Noga, 4 Bezalel St. (☎625 45 90, after 2pm ☎/fax 566 18 88; ask for Mr. or Mrs. Kristal). From the city center, walk down King George, turn right onto Be'eri, left onto Shmuel Ha-Nagid, and right onto Bezalel. Comfortable walk to Maḥane Yehuda or to the area of the Knesset and Israel Museum. Feels like having a private apartment; each floor has one full bath and kitchen. Managers leave after 2pm. For longer stays, ask about the apartment down the block. Singles US$32; doubles US$40; triples US$50; small roof-top bungalow US$25 for 1 person, US$35 for 2. 2-night min. stay. Reservations highly recommended.

Beit Gesher, 10 King David St. (☎624 10 15; fax 625 52 26), across from the Hilton Hotel. Clean and airy 39-room hostel in a beautiful, old building, frequented by youth groups in the summer but quieter the rest of the year. All rooms with private bath and A/C. No double beds. Breakfast US$7. Reception 24hr. Check-in after noon. Check-out 11am. Singles US$38; doubles US$54; add US$14 per person for 3rd and 4th people. Reservations highly recommended.

My Home in Jerusalem Hostel, 15 King George St. and 2 Ha-Histadrut St. (☎623 22 35; fax 623 22 36; myhome@netvision.co.il; www.myhome.co.il), on the left, 1 block from Jaffa Rd.; a newer building with more rooms is around the corner. Take bus #8, 9, 31, or 32 from the central station. Decently clean rooms, cable TV lounge, and prime location. Shared bathrooms. The 2nd building has more stairs, but nicer, carpeted rooms. Breakfast included. Reception and check-in 24hr. Check-out 10:30am. Dorms US$16 (more if you pay in NIS); doubles US$60. Prices vary by season.

Diana's House, 10 Hulda Ha-Neviah St. (☎628 31 31; fax 628 44 11; dradiv@zahav.net.il). From Safra Sq., take Shivtei Yisrael past the municipality, turn right through the small park, and continue down Natan Ha-Navi; Hulda is the next left. Israel's 1st gay B&B ("straight-friendly"). The architect proprietor named the house for his now-departed dog. Cable TV, VCR, whirlpool with view of the Dome of the Rock, laundry, and Internet. Breakfast included. Singles US$45; doubles US$75. Studio apartments also available. Call ahead.

EAST JERUSALEM

SAFETY WARNING. Tensions sometimes make East Jerusalem and parts of the Old City unfriendly to Israelis and Jewish foreigners. Jewish travelers should make their tourist status as pronounced as possible. Wearing a *kippah* is a bad idea in the Arab parts of town.

■ **Cairo Youth Hostel,** 21 Nablus Rd. (☎627 72 16), on the left when coming from Damascus Gate; from the central bus station take bus #27. Perhaps not the most aesthetically pleasing hostel, but it wears its age well; the friendly, laid-back atmosphere will quickly overshadow the drabness of the walls. Comfortable TV sitting area, a view-lover's roof, and an immaculate kitchen. Heat in winter. Reception 24hr. Check-out 10am. Curfew 1am (flexible). Roof mattress NIS15; coed and single-sex dorm beds NIS20; private room for 1-4 people NIS90.

Faisal Hostel, 4 Ha-Nevi'im St. (☎628 75 02; faisalsam@hotmail.com), in the parking lot opposite Damascus Gate, on the right. Crowded bunks, satellite TV lounge, cramped kitchen, and a computer with Internet access (NIS10 per hr.; a 5min. email check is free). Large but cozy bar on patio overlooking Ha-Nevi'im St., where *service* drivers can be heard yelling at almost all hours (don't expect to sleep in if your room is on that side). Reception 24hr. Check-out 11am. Curfew 1am. Coed and single-sex dorm beds NIS20; private doubles and triples NIS80.

Palm Hostel, 6 Ha-Nevi'im St. (☎627 31 89), opposite Damascus Gate, just past the Faisal Hostel. Small but comfortable; has the same noise problem as Faisal. Upper common room for eating, smoking, and watching videos. Heat in winter. Reception 24hr. Check-out 10am. Curfew midnight. Dorms NIS25, students NIS20; private rooms NIS100-120, students NIS80-100. Ask for discounts for longer stays.

▣ FOOD

OLD CITY

Cheap restaurants crowd the narrow alleys of the Old City. The chicken restaurants on **Souq Khan al-Zeit Rd.,** inside Damascus Gate, are popular with locals. Interchangeable sit-down restaurants line al-Wad Rd. and Bab al-Silsilah St. Street vendors sell fresh, soft sesame *ka'ak* with *za'tar* in the *souq* (NIS2-3). The market also drips with honey-drenched Arab pastries for NIS12-24 per kilo. ▣**Ja'far Sweets,** 42 Souq Khan al-Zeit St., offers the hottest, gookiest, most authentic pastries in the market, bar none. Take out or eat in with the locals. (☎628 35 82. Open daily 8am-8pm.) Small **supermarkets** can be found throughout the Old City, particularly in and near the Jewish Quarter.

▣ **Abu Shanab Pizza and Bar,** 35 Latin Patriarchate Rd. (☎626 07 52), the 1st left from Jaffa Gate. An old favorite of natives and tourists alike. Candlelight gleams off the stone walls and intimate tables. Mini individual pizzas NIS13-18; Oriental salads NIS7-10; assortment of cocktails NIS20. Happy hour every night 6-7pm, all drinks 2-for-1. Live jazz occasionally. Open M-Sa 10am-11pm.

▣ **Michael's Bar,** 3 St. Mark's St. (☎052 94 95 60), off David St., uphill from the Lutheran Hostel. Possibly the best falafel in Jerusalem, but the real reason to come is for Michael, one of the Old City's most charming residents. Falafel NIS8; shish kebab or shawarma NIS12. Open daily 10am-10pm.

Green Door Pizza Bakery (☎627 62 71), off al-Wad St. Coming in Damascus Gate, make a sharp left when the road forks. Abu Ali has been serving his renowned Arabic-style pizza for over 2 decades. Filling, personal pizzas (NIS6) are topped with cheese, egg, meat, and as many vegetables as he has. He'll also do individual orders, including veg. Eat in and you get free tea and coffee. Open daily 6am-11pm.

WEST JERUSALEM

Restaurants here serve everything from shawarma to sushi (with a corresponding array of prices), reflecting the international make-up of its population. Choose your own meal adventure from among the many "business lunch" specials at the city center restaurants. To choose your own ingredients, head for the raucous open-air **Maḥaneh Yehuda** market between Jaffa Rd. and Agrippas St. (best time Sa-Th 7-8pm, F 1-2hr. before sundown). *Me'orav,* a mix of inner parts grilled with onions and packed in pita pockets, is a specialty of the stands on Agrippas St., behind Maḥaneh Yehuda. The stands along Etz Ha-Ḥayim St. sell the best *ḥalva* (a sesame marzipan) at NIS14 per kg. **Ma'adei Mickey** (Mickey's Deli), halfway between Jaffa and Agrippas on Etz Ha-Ḥayim St., sells excellent hummus and salads for NIS18 per kg. **Marzipan Bakery,** 44 Agrippas St. (☎623 26 18), at one end of the Maḥaneh Yehuda market, sells *ruggelah* to die for—eat a kilo (NIS18.40) and you just might.

RESTAURANTS

▣ **Spaghettim,** 8 Rabbi Akiva St. (☎623 55 47), off Hillel St. Bear left at the sign, through the gates of an Italian-style villa. Snappy and elegant restaurant serves spaghetti prepared in over 75 different methods, from "gorgonzola spinachi" (NIS38) to "vanilla and brandy" (NIS25). Interior and refreshing outdoor seating. Open daily noon-midnight.

◪ **Alumah,** 19 Agrippas St. (☎ 625 50 14), just between King George St. and Maḥaneh Yehuda. The one-time restaurant has turned into a factory, but still maintains a storefront and tables for the discriminating eater. The ultimate in health food: completely natural *pareve* (non-dairy) meals made using whole grains milled on location, homemade *tempeh*, purified water, rice milk, and olive oil. No margarine, sugar, yeast, aluminum, or microwaves used. Meals are served with rice, chunky veggies, and two slices of crusty, thick sourdough bread. Open Su-Th 7am-7pm and F 7am-2pm.

Nevatim, 10 Ben-Yehuda St. (☎ 625 20 07), under a large but subtle wooden sign. Unquestionably the crunchiest place on the *midraḥov;* also one of the most affordable. Impressive assortment of soups (from *miso* to *borscht;* small bowl NIS15), plus veggie burgers (NIS17), grilled tofu (NIS17), and delicious, unlimited homemade bread. Open Su-Th 10am-10pm and F 10am-before sundown.

The Yemenite Step, 10 Yoel Salomon St. (☎ 624 04 77). Grand stone building with high ceilings and outdoor seating. Try the heavenly *malaweh,* their specialty, which resembles a large, flat, flaky croissant (with honey NIS18; with meat or veggie fillings NIS38 and up). Open Su-Th noon-12:30am, F noon-4pm, and Sa after sundown-1am.

Misadonet, 12 Yoel Salomon St. (☎ 624 83 96), when coming from Zion Sq., turn right into the marked alleyway and right past Orcha Camping. Authentic Kurdish kitchen; serene atmosphere with traditional decor. Traditional specialties include *kubeh* (made from semolina and stuffed with minced meat or vegetables) and *mujadara* (rice and lentils doesn't begin to describe it). Many veg. options. Soups NIS18-22; entrees NIS24-58. Open Su-Th noon-11pm, F noon-sundown, and Sa sundown-11:30pm.

Taco Taco, 35 Jaffa Rd. (☎ 625 50 70), marked by a bright green sign between Yoel Salomon St. and Naḥalat Shiva. Affordable Mexican bar with fast service and fresh ingredients made to order 'round the clock. Beef or chicken taco with cheese NIS12. Quesadilla NIS18. Happy hour daily 7-8pm. Open Su-W 11:30am-2am and Th-Sa 24hr.

QUICKIES

◪ **Babbette's Party,** 16 Shammai St. (☎ 814 11 82), near the corner of Yoel Salomon. A happy addition to the sweet-tooth scene. Israelis flock just to get a whiff of Babbette's 14 amazing Belgian waffle varieties (butter and cream NIS14; Grand Marnier NIS17). Also hands-down the best hot chocolate in Israel, some would say in the world (NIS8). Open Su-Th 4pm-2:30am, F 11am-sunset, and Sa after sundown-2:30am.

◪ **Melekh Ha-Falafel V'ha-Shawarma** (King of Falafel and Shawarma; ☎ 636 53 72), on the corner of King George and Agrippas St. Acclaimed parlor dominates the midtown scene; the tiny store is always packed, no matter what hour. Savory falafel NIS8; shawarma NIS12. Open Su-Th 8:30am-11pm and F 8:30am-3pm.

CAFES

◪ **Tmol Shilshom,** 5 Yoel Salomon St. (☎ 623 27 58; www.tmol-shilshom.co.il). Enter from Naḥalat Shiva St. This bookstore-cafe, named after a Shai Agnon book, is frequented by writers and poets such as Yehuda Amiḥai; he and other local greats give occasional readings here (sometimes in English; call in advance or check the web site for dates), while aspiring writers scrawl over coffee and tea (NIS8-14). Renowned all-you-can-eat breakfast buffet every Friday morning (NIS39.50). Internet NIS7 for 15min. Gay-friendly. Open Su-Th 8am-2am, F 8am-before sunset, and Sa after sundown-2am.

EAST JERUSALEM

◪ **Kan Zaman** (☎ 628 32 82; www.jrshotel.com), on the patio of the Jerusalem Hotel, just behind the bus station on Nablus Rd. Glass-enclosed garden restaurant with tables shaded by vines. Sandwiches NIS30-35; meat and fish meals NIS40-60. Famed Lebanese buffet (NIS70) with live Arabic music Sa after 8pm. Open daily 11am-11pm.

Omayyah Restaurant, 21 Suleiman St. (☎ 628 61 02), across the street and to the right from Damascus Gate. Authentic Palestinian kitchen dishes up standard shawarma and *shishkebab*, but also some less commercial specialties like the "upside down" rice patty (a.k.a. *maqlubeh;* NIS22). Soft drinks NIS3. Open daily 9am-midnight.

◉ SIGHTS

OLD CITY

WALLS AND GATES

RAMPARTS PROMENADE. For an amazing overview of the Old City, walk along this promenade, which tops the walls built by Suleiman the Magnificent in 1542. Begin at **Jaffa Gate** (one of the two gates from which you can access the ramparts) by climbing the hidden steps immediately on the left (just before the jewelry store). The most picturesque part of the walk stretches from here to **Damascus Gate** (20min.), where you can either descend into the market or continue on to **St. Stephen's Gate** (Lion's Gate), the beginning of the **Via Dolorosa**. To ascend the ramparts from Damascus Gate, face the gate from the plaza outside and go down the steps on the right, passing under the bridge and entering through the carriageway to the left of the plaza. (*Promenade open daily 9am-5pm. NIS14, students NIS7; combined ticket to ramparts, Temple Mount excavations (Ophel), Roman Plaza, Zedekiah's Cave, and Hezekiah's tunnel NIS35. Tickets good for 5 days.*)

JAFFA GATE. Jaffa Gate is the traditional entrance for pilgrims and the entrance in the western Old City wall (and thus the most convenient from West Jerusalem). A gate has stood here since 135 CE.

DAMASCUS GATE. Damascus Gate is built over the Roman entrance to the Cardo, facing East Jerusalem and providing direct access to the Muslim Quarter. Scholars recently discovered a plaza at the gate's entrance with a statue of Hadrian mounted on a huge column, explaining the Arabic name for Damascus Gate: *Bab al-Amud* ("Gate of the Column"). Also near Damascus Gate is the biblical **Zedekiah's Cave,** where stones for the Jewish Temple were hewn.

OTHER GATES. New Gate, just a few steps from Jaffa Gate, was opened in 1889 to facilitate access to the Christian Quarter. **Herod's Gate** is to the east of Damascus Gate and reaches the deeper sections of the Muslim Quarter. **St. Stephen's Gate,** also known as **Lion's Gate,** is along the eastern wall. It faces the Mount of Olives and marks the beginning of the Via Dolorosa. **Golden Gate** is blocked by Muslim graves and has been sealed since the 1600s. It is thought to lie over the Closed Gate of the First Temple, the entrance through which the Messiah will purportedly pass (Ezekiel 44:1-3). **Dung Gate,** on the southern wall, opens onto the Western Wall plaza. It was given its name in medieval times because dumping feces here was considered an especially worthy act. **Zion Gate,** on the opposite end of the Cardo from Damascus Gate, connects the Armenian Quarter with Mt. Zion.

TOWER OF DAVID (THE CITADEL)

To the right inside Jaffa Gate. 24hr. info ☎ 626 53 33. Museum open Apr.-Oct. Sa-Th 9am-5pm and F 9am-2pm; Nov.-Mar. Sa-Th 10am-4pm and F 10am-2pm. NIS35, students and seniors NIS25, children 5-12 NIS15; includes tour in English Su-F 11am. Nighttime programs several nights per week. Occasional international jazz shows Oct.-June; call for dates.

The Citadel complex gives an outstanding historical introduction to the Old City. The Citadel, also called the Tower of David (*Migdal David* in Hebrew), resembles a Lego caricature of overlapping Hasmonean, Herodian, Roman, Byzantine, Muslim, Mamluk, and Ottoman ruins, but nothing from David's era (during his reign, this area was outside the city and unsettled). The tower provides a superb vantage point for surveying the Holy City. As you wind through the rooms of the fortress, listen to the high-tech museum tell the story of the city in Hebrew, Arabic, or English. Begin with the excellent 14min. introductory movie.

ISRAEL

TEMPLE MOUNT

The entrance to the Mount is up the ramp, just right of the Western Wall. It is also accessible from the end of Bab al-Silsilah St. Visitors may enter the Temple Mount area Sa-Th 7:30-11am and 1:30-2:30pm, though the Mount is sometimes closed to visitors without notice. Hours subject to change during Ramadan and other Islamic holidays, but it is usually open 7:30-10:30am. Tickets sold until 3pm at a booth between al-Aqsa Mosque and the museum (to the right when entering from the ramp). NIS38, students NIS25.

 SECURITY. Remember that the area is highly sensitive—incidents in the past have resulted in violence. Any conspicuous action, no matter how innocent, may result in ejection. **Modest dress** is required and wrap-around gowns are provided for those who need them. Be aware that many sections considered **off-limits** by the police are not marked as such, including the walls around al-Aqsa, the area through the door to the south between al-Aqsa and the museum, the garden walkway along the eastern wall, and the Muslim cemetery. Bags and packs are not permitted inside al-Aqsa or the Dome of the Rock and must be left outside along with your shoes; theft is not usually a problem, but you should refrain from bringing valuables when you visit. **Photography** is permitted on the Temple Mount, but not inside al-Aqsa or the Dome of the Rock.

Known as *al-Haram al-Sharif* in Arabic and *Har Ha-Bayit* in Hebrew, this 35-acre area in the southeastern corner of the Old City is one of the most venerated religious sites in the world. The **Temple Mount** is central to both Judaism and Islam and a holy site for at least 10 ancient religions. God asked Abraham to sacrifice his son Isaac here (Genesis 22:2), and King Solomon built the **First Temple** here in the middle of the 10th century BCE (2 Chronicles 3:1) before it was destroyed in 587 BCE, when the Jews were led into captivity (I Kings 5-8; II Kings 24-25). The **Second Temple** was built in 516 BCE, after the Jews' return from exile (Ezra 3-7). In 20 BCE, King Herod rebuilt the temple and enlarged the Mount, reinforcing it with four retaining walls (parts of which still stand). The Second Temple is remembered by Christians as the backdrop of Christ's Passion. Like the First Temple, the Second Temple lasted only a few hundred years until it was sacked by Roman legions in 70 CE. Hadrian built a temple to Jupiter over the site, but the Byzantines destroyed it and used its platform as a sewage facility. After Caliph Omar arrived in 638, he ascended the Mount and began cleaning up, personally removing an armful of brown gook. According to Muslim legend, the arches on the Temple Mount will be used to hang scales for weighing people's good and bad deeds. The **Islamic Museum** is filled with fantastic relics, including elaborately decorated Qur'ans and a collection of crescent-topped spires that once crowned older domes. The museum is accesible from the ramp entrance beside the Western Wall.

DOME OF THE ROCK AND AL-AQSA MOSQUE. The Umayyad Caliphs built the two Arab shrines that still dominate the Temple Mount: the silver-domed **al-Aqsa Mosque** (first built in 715 CE), and the magnificent **Dome of the Rock** (691 CE). A stunning display of mosaics and metallic domes, the complex is the third-holiest Muslim site (after the Ka'aba in Mecca and the Mosque of the Prophet in Medina). This is where Allah took Muhammad on his mystical Night Journey *(miraj)* from the Holy Mosque at Mecca to the outer Mosque *(al-aqsa* means "the farthest") and then on to heaven. The Dome of the Rock surrounds what Muslims believe to be the makeshift altar where Abraham almost sacrificed Ishmael, his son by Sarah's maid Hagar (not Isaac, as Christians and Jews believe).

The dome, once of solid gold, was eventually melted down to pay the caliphs' debts. The domes of the mosques and shrines were plated with lead until the structures received aluminum caps during the restoration work of 1958-64. Renovations in 1993 re-coated the domes with new metal plates and a thin layer of 24-karat gold. Many of the tiles covering the walls of the Dome of the Rock were affixed during the reign of Süleyman the Magnificent, and are easily distinguishable from the ceramic tiles added with the private funds of the late King Hussein of Jordan.

Next to the Dome of the Rock is the smaller **Dome of the Chain,** the exact center of al-Haram al-Sharif, where Muslims believe a chain once hung from heaven that could be grasped only by the righteous. Between al-Aqsa and the Dome of the Rock is **al-Kas,** a fountain where Muslims perform ablutions before prayer. Built in 709 CE, it is connected to cisterns capable of holding 10 million gallons.

WESTERN WALL. Religious scholars believe the **Holy of Holies** (the most sacred spot in the temple, where the High Priest was allowed to enter only once a year) was closest to what is now the Western Wall, making this wall the holiest approachable site in Judaism. Some Jews won't ascend the Mount in the off-chance that they will walk on the Holy of Holies, which is off limits until the Messiah arrives. Most of the Western Wall stands in the Jewish Quarter (see below).

JEWISH QUARTER

Known as *Ha-Rovah* by Israelis, the picturesque Jewish Quarter is in the southeast quadrant of the Old City, on the site of the posh Upper City of the Second Temple era. After being exiled when the Second Temple was destroyed, Jews resettled here in the 15th century. Much of the Quarter was damaged in the 1948 War, and lay in ruins after two decades of Jordanian rule. The Israelis annexed the Old City after the 1967 War and began extensive restoration of the neighborhood, unearthing archaeological wonders with every lift of the shovel. They have managed to integrate the ancient remains into the new neighborhood quite gracefully. Today the Quarter is an upper-middle-class neighborhood of about 650 families (many American) who are almost exclusively Orthodox Jews.

The Jewish Quarter extends from Ha-Shalshelet St. to the southern wall, and from Ararat St. to the Western Wall. From Jaffa Gate, go down David St. and turn right at the first intersection just before it becomes Bab al-Silsilah St., or turn right past the Tower of David onto Armenian Orthodox Patriarch Rd. (in the direction of traffic) and make the first left onto St. James Rd. The high arch over the Ḥurva Synagogue marks Ḥurva Sq., a convenient reference for Jewish Quarter sights. The Quarter is home to the **One Last Day Museum** and **Wohl Archaeological Museum.**

WESTERN WALL. The 18m-tall wall (*Ha-Kotel Ha-Ma'aravi*, or just "The Kotel") is part of the retaining wall of the Temple Mount. Built around 20 BCE, the Wall was the largest section of the Temple area that remained standing after its destruction in 70 CE. Nearly 20m of Herodian wall (identifiable by its carved frames) still lie underground. Byzantines, Arabs, and Turks added the smaller stones above. The **Wailing Wall,** a dated moniker, refers to the Jewish worshipers who visited the wall in centuries past to mourn the destruction of the Temple. Today's visitors, Jewish or otherwise, often see the Wall as a direct connection with God and tuck written prayers into its crannies. Don't expect your scribble to wait there for the Messiah: all notes are periodically removed and buried in accordance with Jewish law. Pre-1948 photographs show Orthodox Jews praying at the wall in a crowded alley; after the 1967 War, the present plaza was built. Israeli paratroopers are now sworn in here to recall the Wall's capture. The prayer areas for men and women are separated by a screen, with the Torah scrolls kept on the men's side, along with recently excavated sections of the Wall. On Fridays, Yeshivat Ha-Kotel organizes dancing to usher in Shabbat. The festivities start before sundown and continue until late. Bar Mitzvahs (ceremonies marking a Jewish boy's coming of age) are held at the Wall on Monday and Thursday mornings. Photography is appropriate at these occasions, but not on Shabbat or holidays. On other nights, the Wall is brightly lit, the air cool, and the atmosphere reflective and quiet. *(The Wall can be reached by foot from Dung Gate, the Jewish Quarter, Bab al-Silsilah St., or al-Wad Rd.)*

WILSON'S ARCH. Wilson's Arch is inside a large, arched room to the left of the Wall. It was once part of a bridge that allowed Jewish priests to cross from their Upper City homes to the Temple. A peek down the illuminated shafts in the floor of this room gives a sense of the Wall's original height (women may not enter). The Wall continues from here through closed tunnels for over 500m. Women and

ISRAEL

groups can enter the passageways through an archway to the south, near the telephones. Underneath the Wall is an underground passage where Jewish radicals hid explosives in the early 1980s in a plot to destroy the Dome of the Rock. For tours of the passage, contact the MTIO, Archaeological Seminars, or the Jewish Students Information Center (see **Tours**, p. 288).

CARDO. The staircase down Or Ḥayim St. past Ḥabad St. descends to the remains of Jerusalem's main Roman and Byzantine thoroughfare, which has also been heavily excavated alongside Jewish Quarter Rd. The enormous remaining pillars suggest its original monumental proportions: it was built over a Byzantine extension of Emperor Hadrian's Cardo Maximus, which ran from Damascus Gate to David St. Archaeologists suspect that Justinian constructed an addition so the Cardo would extend as far as the Nea Church (beneath Yeshivat Ha-Kotel). Sheltered by the Cardo's vaulted roof are the best (and thus most expensive) **Judaica shops** in Jerusalem. Near the entrance to the Cardo is an enlarged mosaic reproduction of the **Map of the Holy Land,** the 6th-century plan of Jerusalem discovered in Jordan (see p. 476). *(Make a left at the bottom of the stairs on Jewish Quarter Rd. Cardo open and illuminated Su-Th until 11pm.)*

BURNT HOUSE. The Burnt House is the remains of a priest's dwelling from the Second Temple era. In 70 CE, the fourth year of the Jewish Revolt, the Romans destroyed the Second Temple and broke into Jerusalem's Upper City, burning its buildings and killing its inhabitants. Near a stairwell, the grisly bones of a severed arm reach for a carbonized spear. Sound and light shows inside the Burnt House recreate the events of its destruction. *(On Tiferet Yisrael St. From Ḥurva Sq., turn right at the Mizrahi Bank. ☎ 628 72 11. Open Su-Th 9am-4:30pm, F 9am-12:30pm. NIS9, students NIS7. English presentations every hour on the half hour.)*

OPHEL ARCHAEOLOGICAL GARDEN. The excavations at the southern wall of the Temple Mount are known as "Ophel," though the name technically refers to the hill just outside the southern wall, at the City of David. Scholars have uncovered 22 layers from 12 periods of the city's history. A tunnel leads out to the steps of the Temple Mount. *(From the Western Wall, head out past the security point toward Dung Gate; the entrance to the ruins is on the left just before the gate. ☎ 625 44 03. Open daily 7am-5pm. NIS14, students NIS7. Combination tickets for Ophel, Burnt House, Herodian Quarter, and Last Ditch Battle Museum NIS26, students NIS24.)*

FOUR SEPHARDIC SYNAGOGUES. Mediterranean Jews in the 16th century built the Synagogue of Rabbi Yoḥanan Ben-Zakkai, Prophet Elijah Synagogue, Middle Synagogue, and Istanbuli Synagogue in accordance with a local law that prohibited the construction of synagogues taller than the surrounding houses. To attain a semblance of loftiness, the synagogues were built in underground chambers. The renovated structures date from 1835 and remain the spiritual center of Jerusalem's Sephardic community. *(Down Mishmerot Ha-Kehuna St., near the Jewish Quarter parking lot. ☎ 628 05 92. Open Su-Th 9am-4pm, F 9am-noon. NIS7, students NIS4.)*

ḤURVA SYNAGOGUE. A single stone arch soars above the ruins of the synagogue in the square named for it, forming the center of the Jewish Quarter. Built in 1700 by followers of Rabbi Yehuda the Ḥasid, the synagogue was destroyed by Muslims, thereby earning its ominous title (*ḥurva* means "ruin"). In 1856 the building was restored as the National Ashkenazic Synagogue, only to be destroyed again during the 1948 War. In 1967, renovators opted to rebuild only the single arch as a reminder of the destruction. *(On Ha-Yehudim Rd. around the corner from Ḥurva Sq.)*

ARMENIAN QUARTER

Jerusalem's Armenian Christian population of about 1000 is cloistered in the southwestern corner of the Old City. The Quarter lives in the shadow of tragedy: the Turkish massacre of up to one-and-a-half million Armenians in 1915 (see **Turkey: Modern History,** p. 626) remains one of the century's little-noticed genocides, and persecution of those fleeing to Palestine has caused their numbers to dwindle even farther. Posters mapping out the genocide line the streets. The residential Armenian Compound is not open to the public, but the few available glimpses of Armenian culture are mesmerizing.

ST. JAMES CATHEDRAL. The massive spiritual center of the Armenian Quarter was originally constructed during the 5th century CE, Armenia's golden age, to honor two St. Jameses. St. James the Greater was beheaded in 44 CE by Herod, and his head (supposedly delivered to Mary on the wings of angels) rests under the gilded altar. St. James the Lesser, entombed in a northern chapel, was the first bishop of Jerusalem, but was run out of town by Jews who disliked his version of Judaism. Persians destroyed the cathedral in the 7th century, but Armenians rebuilt it in the 11th century, and Crusaders enlarged it in the 12th. *(The massive cathedral is on Armenian Orthodox Patriarchate Rd., the main paved road leading right from Jaffa Gate. The entrance is on the left past the tunnel, under an arch reading "Couvent Arménien St. Jacques."* ☎ *628 23 31; www.armenian-patriarchate.org. Open daily 6-7:30am during the morning service and 3-3:30pm during the Vespers service. Modest dress required.)*

SYRIAN ORTHODOX CONVENT. Aramaic, the ancient language of the Levant, is spoken here during services and in casual conversation. Also known as St. Mark's Church, the Syrian Church believes the room in the basement to be the site of St. Mark's house and the Last Supper (most other Christians recognize the Cenacle on Mt. Zion as that hallowed place). Decorated with beautiful gilded woodwork, the chapel contains a 150-year-old bible in Old Aramaic and a painting of the Virgin Mary supposedly painted by St. Mark himself. *(Turn left from Armenian Patriarchate Rd. onto St. James Rd. and left onto Ararat St. The convent, marked by a vivid mosaic, is on the right after a sharp turn in the road. Open daily 8am-4pm. Ring the bell if the door is closed.)*

CHRISTIAN QUARTER

The Christian Quarter, in the northwest corner of the Old City, is centered around the **Church of the Holy Sepulcher,** the site traditionally believed to be the place of Jesus' crucifixion, burial, and resurrection. The alleyways of the Quarter pass small churches and chapels of various denominations, and the streets bustle with pilgrims, nuns, monks, and merchants peddling rosaries and holy water.

CHURCH OF ST. ANNE. Commemorating the birthplace of Jesus' mother Mary, the church is one of the best preserved pieces of Crusader architecture in Israel. It survived the Islamic period because Salah al-Din used it as a Muslim theological school (hence the Arabic inscription on the tympanum above the doors). Extensive excavations behind the church clearly show the layers of history; the ruins of a 5th-century basilica cover those of a 2nd- or 3rd-century chapel. The church itself has fantastic acoustics. *Let's Go* used to suggest that visitors try singing quietly in the front rows, but there's now a sign informing people that "This is a holy place for prayer and religious hymns only"—oops. The cool, beautiful crypt has a beaten-copper cross and inlaid stone floors.

Within the grounds of the church is the **Pool of Bethesda,** straight ahead and down the stairs. Crowds of the infirm used to wait beside the pool for an angel to disturb the waters since the first person in after the angel would supposedly be cured. Jesus also healed a sick man here (John 5:2-9). *(Near St. Stephen's Gate, through the large wooden doors on the right. Church and grounds open M-Sa 8am-12:45pm and 2-6pm; in winter M-Sa 8am-12:45pm and 2-5pm. NIS6, students NIS4.)*

VIA DOLOROSA (STATIONS OF THE CROSS)

The Via Dolorosa (Path of Sorrow) is the route that the cross-bearing Jesus followed from the site of his condemnation (the Praetorium) to the site of his crucifixion and grave. Each event on his walk has a chapel commemorating it; together these chapels comprise the 14 **Stations of the Cross.** The present route was mapped out during the Crusader period and passes through the Muslim and Christian Quarters, although modern New Testament scholars have suggested alternate routes based on recent archaeological and historical reconstructions. The Via Dolorosa begins at St. Stephen's Gate; most Stations are marked, but many are hard to find. On Fridays (3pm, July-Aug. 4pm), you can join the Franciscan monks who lead pilgrims along the Via Dolorosa beginning at al-Omariyyeh St.

ISRAEL

STATION I. Just past an archway 200m from St. Stephen's Gate, a ramp with a blue railing leads back to the courtyard of **al-Omariyyeh College,** the site identified as the First Station, the **Praetorium** where Jesus was condemned. One bone of contention between sects involves the starting point of Jesus' final walk as a mortal. It is generally agreed that Jesus was brought before Pontius Pilate for judgment. Normally, Roman governors fulfilled their duties in the palace of Herod the Great, south of Jaffa Gate and the Citadel area. But on feast days such as Passover, the day of Jesus' condemnation, the governor and his soldiers presumably based themselves at the Antonia Fortress to be closer to the Temple Mount. Reflecting this holiday relocation, the **Tower of Antonia,** in the courtyard of **al-Omariyyeh College,** is considered to be the **First Station,** where Jesus was condemned. The station is not marked. For one of the best views of the Dome of the Rock plaza, walk into the courtyard of the school, turn left, and ascend the steps on the right.

STATION II. Across the Via Dolorosa from the ramp is a Franciscan monastery; inside on the left is the **Condemnation Chapel,** complete with a relief above the altar. This is the Second Station, where Jesus was sentenced to crucifixion. On the right is the **Chapel of Flagellation,** where he was first flogged by Roman soldiers. A crown of thorns adorns the dome. The Via Dolorosa passes beneath the **Ecce Homo Arch** (site of Pontius Pilate's mansion), named for Pilate's exclamation as he looked down upon Jesus (*Ecce Homo* means "Behold the Man"). The arch is actually part of the triumphal arch that commemorated Emperor Hadrian's suppression of the Bar Kokhba Revolt in the 2nd century CE. The nearby **Convent of the Sisters of Zion** sits atop a large chamber thought by some to be a judgment hall, making it yet another First Station contender. The convent is closed to the public, but the excavations are not. *(Chapels open daily Apr.-Sept. 8-11:45am and 4-6pm; Oct.-Mar. 8-11:45am and 1-5pm. Excavations: walk down the Via Dolorosa from the 2nd Station to the brown door on Aqabat al-Rahbat St., on the right off the Via Dolorosa. Knock to enter. Open M-Sa 8:30am-5pm. NIS6, students NIS4.)*

STATIONS III-VII. Immediately after the Via Dolorosa turns left onto al-Wad Rd., look to the left for the door to the Armenian Catholic Patriarchate. To the left of the door is the **Third Station,** where Jesus fell to his knees for the first time. A small Polish chapel inside a blue gate marks the spot; a relief above the entrance (marked "III Statio") depicts Jesus kneeling beneath the cross. At the **Fourth Station,** on the left just beyond the Armenian Orthodox Patriarchate, a small chapel commemorates the spot where Jesus saw his mother. Look for a carving above light blue iron doors, to the left of an arched alleyway. Turn right on the Via Dolorosa to reach the **Fifth Station,** where Simon the Cyrene volunteered to carry Jesus' cross (look for the brown door on the left, with the inscription "V St."). Fifty meters ahead, the remains of a small column designate the **Sixth Station** (marked with a "VI"), where Veronica wiped Jesus' face with her handkerchief. The mark of his face was left on the cloth, now on display at the Greek Orthodox Patriarchate on the street of the same name. Look for a pair of doors on the left, one green and one dark brown; the column is set into the wall between the doors. The **Seventh Station,** straight ahead at the intersection with Khan al-Zeit Rd., marks Jesus's second fall, precipitated by the sudden steepness of the road. Tradition holds that notices of Jesus's condemnation were posted on a gate at this spot.

STATIONS VIII AND IX. Crossing Khan al-Zeit Rd., ascend Aqabat al-Khanqah and look left past the Greek Orthodox Convent for the stone Latin cross that marks the **Eighth Station.** Here Jesus turned to the women who mourned him, saying "Daughters of Jerusalem, do not weep for me, weep rather for yourselves and for your children" (Luke 23:28). The small stone is part of the wall and difficult to spot; a large red-and-white sign was recently installed to mark it, but may not last long on such a narrow road. Backtrack to Khan al-Zeit Rd., take a right, walk for about 50m through the market, ascend the wide stone stairway on the right, and continue through a winding passageway to the Coptic Church. The remains of a column in its door mark the **Ninth Station,** where Jesus fell a third time.

ST. ALEXANDER'S CHURCH. Built over the Judgment Gate, the church marks the end of the Roman Cardo, through which Jesus exited the city on his way to Calvary. First-century stones line the floor, and two pillars from the original Cardo are visible. Next to the gate is a small hole in the ancient wall—this is the famed **Eye of the Needle,** through which latecomers would sneak into the city when the gates were closed. *(On the right just after turning off al-Wad St. toward the Holy Sepulcher.* ☎ *627 49 52. Open M-Sa 9am-1pm and 3-5pm. Ring bell. Prayers for Czar Alexander III Th 7am. NIS5.)*

CHURCH OF THE HOLY SEPULCHER. Retrace your steps to the main street and continue to the next right, which leads from the marketplace to the entrance of the Church of the Holy Sepulcher, one of the most revered structures on earth. The placement of the last five stations (X-XIV) inside the church contradicts an alternative hypothesis that Jesus was crucified at the skull-shaped Garden Tomb in East Jerusalem (see p. 301). The Church of the Holy Sepulcher marks **Golgotha,** also called **Calvary,** the site of the Crucifixion. The location was first determined by Eleni, mother of Emperor Constantine and Jerusalem's first archaeologist, during her pilgrimage in 326 CE. Eleni thought Hadrian had erected a temple to Venus and Jupiter on the site in order to divert Christians from their faith. Constantine built a small church over the site in 335, and part of the original church's foundations buttress the present Crusader structure (from 1149). The Crusader architects united all the oratories, chapels, and other sanctuaries that had cropped up around the site under one cruciform shape. By 1852, tremendous religious conflicts had developed within the Holy Sepulcher. The Ottoman rulers divided the church among the Franciscan order, the Greek Orthodox, Armenian Orthodox, Coptic, Syrian, and Ethiopian churches; the first three are the major shareholders, entitled to hold masses and processions and burn incense in the shrines and chapels.

The church is in somewhat bad shape. Restoration work in any part of the basilica implies ownership, making each sect hesitant to assist and eager to hinder the others. In 1935, the church was in such a precarious state that colonialists propped it up with girders. Since 1960, partial cooperation has allowed the supportive scaffolding to be gradually removed. To this day, the question of who gets to change a given light bulb can rage into a month-long controversy. The portions of the church not directly related to the Stations of the Cross are a dark labyrinth of small chapels through which priests, pilgrims, and chatty tourists wander. Because a denomination's ability to hang objects on the church's walls also indicates ownership, the building houses only religious paintings and spindly oil lamps. Steps lead down to two cavernous chapels commemorating the discovery of the true cross. In a small chapel on the ground floor just below Calvary, a fissure runs through the rock, supposedly caused by the earthquake following Jesus's death. According to legend, Adam (of "and Eve" fame) was buried beneath Calvary, allowing Jesus's blood to drip through this cleft and anoint him. *(Church open daily 5am-8pm; in winter 4am-7pm. Men and women must cover their knees.)*

ETHIOPIAN MONASTERY. Over part of the Church of the Holy Sepulcher is the Ethiopian Monastery; since the Ethiopians possess no part of the church itself, they have become squatters on the roof. The modest compound houses a small but spiritual church; enter through the roof and descend, exiting next to the Holy Sepulcher. Watch your head. *(Next to the Ninth Station, the 1st left from Khan al-Zeit Rd. when backtracking from the Holy Sepulcher. Open all day.)*

STATIONS X-XIII. The church's entrance faces the slab on which Jesus was supposedly anointed before he was buried. To continue along the Stations, go up the stairs to the right just after the entrance. The chapel at the top is divided into two naves: the right one belongs to the Franciscans, the left to the Greek Orthodox. At the entrance to the Franciscan Chapel is the **Tenth Station,** where Jesus was stripped of his clothes, and at the far end is the **Eleventh Station,** where he was nailed to the cross. The **Twelfth Station,** to the left in the Greek chapel, is a clearly marked Crucifixion site: a life-size Jesus in a metal loincloth hangs among oil lamps, flowers, and candles. Between the Eleventh and Twelfth Stations is the **Thirteenth Station,** where Mary received Jesus's body. The station is marked by an odd statue of Mary adorned with jewels, a silver dagger stuck into her breast.

STATION XIV. Jesus' tomb on the ground floor is the **Fourteenth Station.** The Holy Sepulcher, in the center of the rotunda, is a large marble structure flanked by huge candles. The first chamber in the tomb, the **Chapel of the Angel,** is dedicated to the angel who announced Jesus's resurrection to Mary Magdalene. A tiny entrance leads from the chapel into the sepulcher itself, a small chamber lit by scores of candles and guarded by priests. The walls of the tomb have been covered, but the priest in charge may be willing to reveal a small section of the original wall hidden behind a picture of the Virgin Mary. The raised marble slab in the sepulcher covers the rock on which Jesus's body was laid. Nudging the back of the Holy Sepulcher is the tiny **Coptic Chapel.** To the right of the sepulcher, the **Chapel of Mary Magdalene** marks the spot where Jesus appeared to her after his resurrection.

MUSLIM QUARTER

This sprawl of Ayyubid and Mamluk-era architecture is the largest, most heavily populated quarter in the Old City, as well as one of the most exciting. It is also the most conservative; women should dress modestly, and everyone should be particularly careful: although the Quarter is busy during the day, it becomes dark, isolated, and potentially dangerous at night.

Damascus Gate, the main entrance to the Quarter, is one of the finest examples of Islamic architecture in Jerusalem. The main thoroughfare and western border of the quarter is **Khan al-Zeit Rd.,** leading from Damascus Gate to David St., with an infinite array of booths selling spices, candy, clothing, sandals, and souvenirs in between. **Al-Wad Rd.** connects the Western Wall area to Damascus Gate. A right off al-Wad Rd. onto the Via Dolorosa leads to an array of small ceramics shops.

MUSLIM QUARTER SOUQ. The *souq* is crammed at all hours (watch for wagons and tiny tractors that charge gleefully at the crowds of shoppers) and a great place to buy Palestinian crafts such as Hebron-style wine glasses, mother-of-pearl inlaid boxes, ceramic tiles, and spherical Jerusalem candles. The *souq* is a Mamluk masterpiece of stone set within stone. Paintings of the Dome of the Rock and the Ka'aba adorn doorways; a painting of the latter signifies that a member of the family has been on the *Hajj*, the Islamic pilgrimage to Mecca and Medina.

BAB AL-SILSILAH STREET. The stretch of Bab al-Silsilah St. (Gate of the Chain St.) extending from the end of David St. to the Temple Mount is partially founded on the ancient Mamluk causeway that crossed the Tyropoeon Valley, linking the upper city to the temple platform. At the end of the first alley to the left stands the **Khan al-Sultan** (a.k.a. *al-Wakala*), a well-preserved Crusader-era *caravanserai* (an inn that provided lodging for merchants and their donkeys). Farther down Bab al-Silsilah St. on the right, just past Misgav Ladakh St., is the **Tashtamuriyya Building,** housing the tomb of its namesake (d. 1384). The multitude of Mamluk institutions in the area can be attributed to a system of succession that prevented parents from passing wealth on to their children; constructing public institutions was the best way to preserve a family's legacy. Continuing down Bab al-Silsilah St. to its intersection with Western Wall (Ha-Kotel) St. leads to the **Qilaniyya Mausoleum** and its Mamluk stalactite half-dome; the **Turba Turkan Khatun** (Tomb of Lady Turkan) is at #149. At the end of Bab al-Silsilah St., on the right and often surrounded by tour guides in training, is the **Tankiziyya Building,** built by a Mamluk slave who worked his way up to become governor of Damascus in 1312. This venerated structure, on the site of the original seat of the Sanhedrin, is currently controlled by the Israelis due to its proximity to the Western Wall and the Temple Mount.

NEAR THE OLD CITY

KIDRON VALLEY AND THE MOUNT OF OLIVES

The historic Kidron Valley, which runs between the Old City and the Mount of Olives, is revered by Christians as the path of the Last Walk of Jesus. To get there, turn left from Dung Gate and walk up the narrow Ha-Ophel Rd. A newly paved sidewalk leads to an observation point for the valley, the Mount of Olives in front of it, and the four tombs directly below; a map on the floor explains the vista. Running north-to-south are the **Tomb of Jehosaphat** and **Absalom's Pillar**, allegedly the tomb of David's favored but feisty son (II Samuel 15-18). A dirt path on the left leads to the impressive rock-hewn **Tomb of B'nei Hezir** and the **Tomb of Zechariah**. The tombs are accessible from the base of the Mount of Olives or via a new staircase near the observation point just past Ma'alot Ir David St. on Ha-Ophel Rd. Women travelers are advised not to visit the Mount of Olives alone.

MOUNT OF OLIVES. The bone-dry slopes of the Mount of Olives (*Har Ha-Zeitim* in Hebrew) to the east of the Old City are dotted with churches marking the sites of Jesus' triumphant entry into Jerusalem, his teaching, his agony and betrayal in Gethsemane, and his ascension to heaven. Jews believe that the Messiah will arrive in Jerusalem from the Mount of Olives. Tradition holds that the thousands of people buried here will be the first to be resurrected upon his arrival. Ogle a monumental view of the Old City from the observation promenade outside the Seven Arches Hotel. The bell tower of the **Augusta Victoria Hospital** on Mt. Scopus to the north marks the highest point in Jerusalem (903m above sea level).

CHAPEL OF CHRIST'S ASCENSION. Built in 392, this was the first church to commemorate the event for which it is named. It is the geographical (if not aesthetic) apex of the noteworthy sites in the area. In the 11th century, Crusaders adorned the chapel with columns and arches, and in the 12th century Salah al-Din constructed a domed roof. The interior contains a candle-lighting stand and sacred footprint, unidentifiable after wear and tear from generations of relic-happy pilgrims. *(Open daily 8am-5pm; ask a guard in the mosque courtyard if closed. NIS3.)*

CHURCH OF THE PATER NOSTER. St. Eleni founded this church in the 4th century as the Church of the Disciples; it is also referred to as the Church of the Eleona ("olive grove" in Greek). This was the site of the grotto where Jesus revealed the "inscrutable mysteries" to his disciples, foretelling the destruction of Jerusalem and his Second Coming. The church commemorates the first recitation of the Lord's Prayer (hence the current moniker, *Pater Noster*, Latin for "Our Father"). Polyglots can read the prayer in 78 languages (including Old Frisian) on the tiled walls. In the midst of the translations is the tomb of the Princesse de la Tour d'Auvergne, who worked here for 17 years (1857-74) and financed the excavations and renovations: she was determined to uncover the long-lost grotto where her favorite prayer was originally taught. *(Below the Chapel of Christ's ascension, under an orange sign reading "Carmelite Convent." Open M-Sa 8:30-11:45am and 3-4:45pm.)*

TOMBS OF THE PROPHETS. This site is the supposed resting-place of the prophets Malachi and Ḥaggai. Archaeological evidence, however, suggests that the graves are far too recent—probably dating from the 4th century CE. The glass-enclosed home on the premises is the residence of the caretaker, who will show visitors around downstairs with a kerosene lamp if asked. To the left of the tombs is an easy-to-miss orange sign with rubbed-off black lettering marking "This Common Grave" of those who died defending the Jewish Quarter in 1948. Next to the Common Grave lies the **National Cemetery,** and farther down the path sprawls the immense **Jewish Graveyard,** the largest Jewish cemetery in the world. Take the stone staircase on the left for another small observation point and access to the Jewish graves. *(With your back to the Seven Arches, turn right and go down the gray cement path to the left. Several meters down, a large green gate on the left leads to 2 cavernous tunnels. Open Su-F 8am-3pm.)*

SANCTUARY OF DOMINUS FLEVIT. This sanctuary was erected in 1955 to mark the spot where Jesus wept for Jerusalem (Luke 19:41), hence its Latin name ("The Lord Wept"). The chapel has a Byzantine mosaic and altar in an apse with a beautiful view of the Dome of the Rock. The glass shards of bottles cemented to the top of the walls protect the property of competing sects from trespassers. *(Downhill from the Tombs of the Prophets, on the right. Open Mar.-May 8am-5pm; June-Oct. 8am-6pm.)*

ISRAEL

RUSSIAN CHURCH OF MARY MAGDALENE. Czar Alexander III built this church in 1885. Constructed in the lavish 17th-century Muscovite style, it is adorned with seven golden onion domes. The crypt houses the body of a Russian grand duchess, smuggled to Jerusalem via Beijing after her death in the Russian Revolution. Now a convent, the church claims a part of the Garden of Gethsemane. *(Past the Sanctuary of Dominus Flevit. ☎ 628 43 71. Ordinarily open Tu and Th 10am-noon.)*

CHURCH OF ALL NATIONS AND THE GARDEN OF GETHSEMANE. Built with contributions from many European countries, the Church of All Nations faces west toward the Old City. Among its highlights is a magnificent gold and red facade portraying Jesus bringing peace to all nations. Inside, mosaics and sculptures depict Jesus' last days, including the proverbial kiss of death, but the real highlight is the **Rock of the Agony,** where Jesus was so impassioned that he sweat blood (Luke 22:44). Although the site has been venerated since the 4th century, the present building, designed by Barluzzi, was built after World War I. The garden outside is where Jesus spent his last night in prayer and was betrayed by Judas (Mark 14:32-43). *(The church is on the left near the bottom of the main path; the entrance is on the side. Open daily Apr.-Oct. 8am-noon and 2:30-6pm; Nov.-Mar. 8am-noon and 2:30-5pm.)*

TOMB OF THE VIRGIN MARY AND GROTTO OF GETHSEMANE. The steep stairs down to Mary's tomb were built to prevent pagans from riding horses into the sacred space. To the right, the natural grotto is another candidate for the site of Jesus' betrayal and arrest. *(At the bottom of the main path, on the right. Open daily 8am-noon and 2:30-5:30pm. At the exit onto the main road are telephone booths and taxis. Damascus and St. Stephen's Gates are within walking distance. A taxi to the city center should cost NIS15.)*

WEST JERUSALEM

NEAR ZION SQUARE

Zion Sq. (Kikkar Tzion) is the center of West Jerusalem and the epicenter of the pedestrian malls of Ben-Yehuda, Yoel Solomon, Naḥalat Shiva, and Rivlin St. Downhill on Ben-Yehuda St. and to the left is King George St., a bustling extension of the city center. Three blocks farther downhill, the enormous and ornate Great Synagogue of Jerusalem, 58 King George St., is an inspiring architectural compromise between modernity and religion. (☎ 624 71 12. Open Su-Th 9am-1pm and F 9am-noon.) Services here on holidays and the first day of Jewish months feature an excellent men's choir meant to recall the Levites' choir in the ancient Temple. Across from Zion Sq. on the other side of Jaffa Rd., Ha-Rav Kook St. eventually crosses Ha-Nevi'im St. and turns into the quiet, stone-wall-lined Ethiopia St. At the end of Ethiopia St. on the right is the handsome Ethiopian Church, built between 1874 and 1901. Inscriptions in Ge'ez adorn the gate and doors; black-robed monks and nuns live in the surrounding compound and care for the distinctive, blue-domed church. (☎ 628 28 40. Open daily 9am-1pm and 2-6pm. Remove your shoes before entering.) Directly across from the entrance to the church, at #11, is the one-time home of the founder of the modern Hebrew language, Eliezer Ben-Yehuda. **Ticho House,** 9 Ha-Rav Kook St. (☎ 624 50 68 or 624 41 86), about 2 blocks up the hill from Zion Sq., displays watercolors and drawings by artist Anna Ticho, who lived here with her prominent oculist husband Dr. Avraham Albert Ticho. His collection of *menorahs* is also on display. The elegant building and well-groomed gardens are a relaxing city respite; the attached restaurant serves a classy all-you-can-eat wine, cheese and salad buffet on Tuesday nights for NIS65. Open Su-Th 10am-5pm, Tu 10am-10pm and F 10am-2pm. Free.

MEA SHE'ARIM

Mea She'arim ("Hundredfold," an invocation of plenty), lies just north of Ethiopia St., on the other side of Ha-Nevi'im St. To get there from Zion Sq., take Jaffa Rd. and turn right onto Nathan Strauss St. (the continuation of King George St.); continue until it intersects with Ha-Nevi'im St. (Bank Ha-Poalim is on the corner). This intersection is known as Kikkar Shabbat (walk through on a Friday night around 11pm to find out why), the unofficial beginning of Mea She'arim.

WARNING! Signs in the area caution, "Do not enter our neighborhood unless your dress and conduct conform to the standards described below," and then proceed to request that women wear at least knee-length skirts (not pants), elbow-length sleeves, and nothing tight-fitting. Men should wear below-the-knee pants. Visitors are also advised not to enter in groups. Be warned that extremists have been known to stone tourists whom they deem improperly dressed. Whether you're Jewish or not, take these warnings seriously to avoid offending local Ḥasidim and being asked to leave the area.

The neighborhood, one of Jerusalem's oldest, is among the few remaining Jewish *shtetl* communities like those that used to flourish in pre-Holocaust Eastern Europe. Several thousand Ultra-Orthodox Jews live here and in the neighboring **Geula** (Hebrew for "redemption"), preserving traditional habits, dress, customs, and beliefs with pains-taking diligence. If your newfound grasp of Hebrew lets you down, it may be because you're hearing Yiddish, spoken by residents who consider Hebrew too holy for daily use. The neighborhood, just like the Orthodox suburbs to the north and northwest of the city, is largely conservative, but Mea She'arim's relatively few extremists receive a good deal of publicity for opinions and actions that do not necessarily reflect those of the entire community. The Neturei Karta ("City Keepers"), the most extreme sect of the Satmar Ḥasidim, oppose the Israeli state, arguing that Jewish law prohibits the legitimate existence of a Jewish country until the coming of the Messiah. While other Ultra-Orthodox Jews hold similar views, the Neturei Karta once went so far as to ask Yasser Arafat to accept them as a minority in the future Palestinian state.

Mea She'arim St. is probably the cheapest place in the world for Jewish books and religious items. Although the quality is not as high as in the Jewish Quarter of the Old City, the stores along Mea She'arim St. have affordable selections. The neighborhood also has some of the city's best **bakeries,** most of which are open all night on Thursdays, baking *ḥallah* and cake for Shabbat.

GIVAT RAM

ISRAELI SUPREME COURT. This building, completed in late 1992 by designers Karmi & Associates, combines Modern flair with themes from ancient Jerusalem's building traditions. This architectural masterpiece is also worth visiting for a glimpse of the justice system. Anyone may sit in on a trial—it's like Court TV, only live and in Hebrew. (☎675 96 12; fax 652 71 18; marcia@supreme.court.gov.il. Open Su-Th 8:30am-2:30pm. English tour Su-Th noon; call for summer schedule. With advance notice, tours can accommodate most special needs, including touch tours for the blind.)

KNESSET. Discover why Israeli schoolteachers compare excessively rowdy pupils to members of the Knesset, Israel's Parliament. Passports are required for entrance as part of a detailed search. (On Eliezer Kaplan St. directly across from the Israel Museum. From the central bus station or Jaffa Rd. take bus #9 or 24 and ask the driver where to get off. ☎675 33 33. Su and Th tours last 30min.; call to find out when the English tours begin and arrive at least 15min. early. Open sessions M and Tu 4pm, W 11am; call to make sure that the Knesset is in session.)

OTHER SIGHTS. The **Wohl Rose Garden,** which forms a walking path between the Supreme Court and the Knesset, is a sublime picnic spot with beautifully mani-cured lawns and flowers. Take the path on the right when exiting the Supreme Court building, or climb up to it from anywhere on the main street. The **Ardon Window** in the **National Library,** one of the largest stained-glass windows in the world, depicts Jewish mystical symbols in rich, dark colors. (Take bus #9, 24, or 28 from the city center. ☎658 50 27. Open in summer Su-Th 9am-7pm, F 9am-1pm. Free.)

TALBIYYA AND QATAMUN

Farther south are the neighborhoods of **Talbiyya** (Komemiyut) and **Qatamun** (Gonen), still known by their pre-1948 Arabic names. The ornate villas, one of which was the home of renowned cultural theorist Edward Said, have become favorites of Hebrew University faculty and, more recently, well-to-do profession-als. The official residence of the **Israeli President** is on Ha-Nassi (President) St., and the plush **Jerusalem Theater** is on the other side of the block, on the corner of Chopin St. and Marcus Rd.

On the other end of Jabotinsky St. from the President's House is **King David St.**, running north to the base of Shlomtzion Ha-Malka St. and Shlomo Ha-Melekh St. Just south of the intersection with Jabotinsky St. is the sprawling, green **Liberty Bell Park** (Gan Ha-Pa'amon). An amphitheater, basketball courts, climbable sculptures, and a Liberty Bell replica grace the lawns. On Saturday nights, the park hops with folk dancing festivities (take bus #14, 18, or 21 from the city center). Three hundred meters up King David St. toward the city center, the **Three Arches YMCA,** built in 1933, has an imposing bell tower with fine views of the whole city. (☎569 26 92. NIS5.) Directly across the street, the historic **King David Hotel** retains an aura of old-world luxury, making it a favorite accommodation for international celebrities. The King David served as the British headquarters during the 1948 War of Independence and was bombed by Jewish underground forces.

YEMIN MOSHE

In the valley between King David St. and the Old City is the restored neighborhood of Yemin Moshe. It was here that Sir Moses Montefiore, a British Jew, first managed to convince a handful of residents from the Old City's overcrowded Jewish Quarter to spend occasional nights outside the city walls, thus founding West Jerusalem. To strengthen the settlers' confidence, Montefiore built **Mishkenot Sha'ananim** ("Tranquil Habitations"), a picturesque small compound with crenelated walls resembling those of the Old City. The original buildings now house an exclusive municipal guest house and a pricey French restaurant, and are at the bottom of the hill. Montefiore also erected his famous stone windmill, which now contains a tiny free **museum.** (Open Su-Th 9am-4pm and F 9am-1pm.) Yemin Moshe is crammed with artists' studios and galleries; a plaza with a fountain beneath the exclusive King David Apartments makes this a lovely spot to wander. The stepped street of Ḥutzot Ha-Yotzer leads up to Ḥativat Yerushalayim St.; at #16 is the studio of Motke Blum, whose subtle cityscapes brilliantly evoke Jerusalem in oil. The now-dry **Sultan's Pool** sits in the valley below. Named after Suleiman the Magnificent, the renovator of this Second Temple reservoir in the 16th century, the pool figures prominently in Palestinian novelist Jabra Ibrahim Jabra's *The Ship.* Today, the Sultan's Pool is most famous for its open-air concerts and annual **art fair** in July or early August (info ☎625 44 03).

GERMAN COLONY AND HAAS PROMENADE

The **German Colony,** a leafy neighborhood of somber European houses and spacious Arab villas, surrounds Emek Refa'im St., an upscale avenue with a lively cafe scene. Buses #4, 14, and 18 run here from the city center. To the southeast, the **Haas Promenade** is a hillside park that commands unbelievable views of the Old City and the Dead Sea. The dusk experience alone is worth the trip. On foot, walk south on Derekh Hevron, bear left onto Albeck St., and turn left onto Yanofsky St. Bus #8 runs from King George St. to the corner of Albeck St. and Yanofsky St.

NORTHERN OUTSKIRTS

AMMUNITION HILL. Before the Six Day War, this was Jordan's most fortified position in the city, from which it commanded much of northern Jerusalem. Taken by Israeli troops in a bloody battle, the hill now serves as a memorial to the Israeli soldiers who died in the Six Day War. The architecturally striking museum, which details the 1967 battle, is housed in a reconstructed bunker. *(Buses #4, 9, 25, and 26 stop at the foot of the hill, in Ramat Eshkol, north of the Old City. ☎582 84 42. Open Su-Th 8am-6pm and F 8am-2pm; closes 1hr. earlier in winter. NIS10, students NIS8.)*

HEBREW UNIVERSITY OF JERUSALEM. After 1948, the Hebrew University of Jerusalem had to relocate from Mt. Scopus (Har Ha-Tzofim), where it was founded in 1925, to this new campus in Givat Ram. From 1948 to 1967, Mt. Scopus was a garrisoned Israeli enclave in Jordanian territory. Every week for 19 years, UN supplies were flown in to relieve the community; every week seven Israeli soldiers were let in, and seven were let out. After 1967, all but the natural and physical sciences departments moved back to the original campus. Massive reconstruction was funded largely by international donors, whose names emblazon the libraries, promenades, and pebbles that comprise modern Mt. Scopus. Pick up a map from the Reception Center for an unguided stroll around Israel's top university and browse through the bookstore, library, computer labs, and botanical gardens. For a fabulous view of Jerusalem, head to the overlook point, outside the university gates along the south side of the campus. The **Hecht Synagogue** in the Humanities building overlooks the Old City and is reputed to be have the best view of Jerusalem in the entire city. Enter the synagogue via the Sherman Building. The university's gorgeous **amphitheater** faces the Palestinian Territories. *(Take bus #4a or 9 from the city center. Tours Su-Th 11am.)*

WESTERN OUTSKIRTS

CHAGALL WINDOWS. The synagogue at the Hadassah Medical Center (not to be confused with Hadassah Hospital on Mt. Scopus) houses the magnificent Chagall Windows, Marc Chagall's stained-glass depictions of scenes from Genesis 49 and Deuteronomy 33. Chagall donated the windows to the hospital in 1962 and was sent an urgent cable when four of the windows were damaged in the 1967 War. Chagall replied, "You worry about the war, I'll worry about my windows." Two years later he installed replacements; three of the windows still contain bullet holes. *(From Jaffa Rd., take bus #27 or 19 to the end, about 45min. ☎ 677 62 71. Synagogue open Su-Th 8am-1:15pm and 2-3:45pm, F 8am-1pm. NIS10, students and seniors with ID NIS5. Free tours in English Su-Th every hr. 8:30am-12:30pm and 2:30pm, F every hr. 9:30-11:30am.)*

JERUSALEM FOREST AND EIN KEREM. The scenic Jerusalem Forest and the pastoral village of Ein Kerem, just west of Mt. Herzl, are perfect for picnics and short hikes. Formerly an Arab village, tiny Ein Kerem (Fountain of Vines) is the traditionally recognized birthplace of **John the Baptist.** The tranquil streets of this thriving artists' colony are now lined with charming studios and craftshops. *(To get to the village, take city bus #17, west from the central bus station or Zion Sq. Every 20-30min.)*

The **Church of St. John,** with its soaring clocktower, marks the spot where John was born. The church displays several paintings, including the *Decapitation of St. John*. In the church's **Grotto of the Nativity** there is a lovely Byzantine mosaic of pheasants—the symbol of the Eucharist. Ask the guardian for a key. *(☎ 641 36 39. Open Apr.-Sept. Su-F 8am-6pm; Oct.-Mar. Su-F 8am-5pm. Free.)*

Across the valley, down Ma'ayan St. from St. John's gate, the **Church of the Visitation** recalls Mary's visit to Elizabeth and contains a rock behind which the infant St. John hid when the Romans came to kill babies. *(☎ 641 72 91. Open May-Sept. Su-F 8am-6pm; Oct.-Apr. Su-F 8am-5pm. Free.)* The newer Upper Chapel depicts the glorification of Mary. The pink tower belongs to the **Russian Monastery.** *(☎ 625 25 65 or 641 28 87; only Russian spoken. Visit by appointment only.)*

🏛 MUSEUMS

ISRAEL MUSEUM

The Israel Museum is the largest and most comprehensive museum in and about Israel. With extensive collections of antiquities, books, sculptures, ancient and modern art, the legendary Dead Sea Scrolls, and even a children's exhibit, the museum has nearly as many facets as the country itself. *(Take bus #9 or 17 from King George St. On foot, walk up King George St., turn onto Ramban St., cross Hazaz St., and walk up Ruppin St. ☎ 670 88 11; fax 563 18 33; www.imj.org.il. Open Su-M and W-Th 10am-5pm, Tu 4-10pm, F 10am-2pm, Sa 10am-4pm; English tours Su-M and W-F 11am, Tu 4:30pm. The Shrine of the Book is also open Tu 10am-10pm; English tours Su-M and W-Th 1:30pm, Tu 3pm, F 12:45pm. Museum and Shrine NIS37, students NIS30, children 3-17 NIS20, family NIS108.)*

SHRINE OF THE BOOK. The display of the Dead Sea Scrolls is by far the museum's biggest attraction. Hidden for 2000 years in the Caves of **Qumran** near the Dead Sea, the scrolls date from the 2nd century BCE to 70 CE and were written by the Essenes, an apocalyptic, monastic Jewish sect. The scrolls contain fragments of every biblical text except the Book of Esther, and are nearly identical to the modern texts, supporting claims for the dating of the Hebrew Bible. The building's white dome and black walls symbolize the struggle between the Sons of Light and Dark, an important theme to the Qumran sect, and were designed to resemble the covers of the pots in which the scrolls were hidden.

ARCHAEOLOGY AND ETHNOLOGY EXHIBITS. Rock and rust enthusiasts should go straight to the archaeology section, which has an extensive collection of tools and weapons recording 30,000 years of human habitation in the Fertile Crescent. Straight ahead from the bottom of the steps is the **ethnography** exhibit, tracing the important events of the Jewish life cycle. *(Archaeology tours in English M and Th 3pm; guided tours of the Judaica and ethnography galleries S and W 3pm.)*

ART COLLECTIONS. The museum boasts a fabulous collection of art, including the largest display of Israeli art in the world. There is a sizeable Impressionist and Post-Impressionist collection, and even a few period rooms (including a spectacular French Rococo *salon* donated by the Rothschilds). The **Weisbord Pavilion,** across from the ticket building, houses a few Rodin sculptures, early modern paintings, and rotating contemporary exhibitions. **Billy Rose Sculpture Garden** displays some incredible masterworks by Henry Moore, Auguste Rodin, and Pablo Picasso. Pick up a schedule of evening outdoor concerts at the museum, and try to visit on a Tuesday night, when the garden is illuminated.

YAD VA-SHEM

Don't plan to do too much right after a visit; the museum's several buildings deserve some time and take an emotional toll. To get to Yad Va-Shem, take bus #13, 16-18, 20-21, 23-24, 26-27, or 39 and get off at the huge, red arch just past Mt. Herzl. Turn around and take a left on Ein Kerem St., then follow the signs down Ha-Zikaron St. for about 10min. Info ☎ 644 35 65 or 644 35 62; www.yad-vashem.org.il. Open Su-Th 9am-5pm, F 9am-2pm. Free. Guided tours in English available by appointment.

Meaning "A Memorial and a Name," Yad Va-Shem is the largest of Israel's Holocaust museums. An event as broad-sweeping and traumatic as the Holocaust cannot be memorialized by any single medium; the juxtaposition of Nazi records, victim testimony, and documentation of resistance creates a powerful and disturbing experience. It's best to start at the **Historical Museum,** which traces the origins of the Holocaust through photographs, documents, and relics. The exhibit ends with a simple, powerful memorial: symbolic tombs showing the number of Jews who were killed in each country, and a tiny shoe that belonged to one of the Holocaust's younger victims. The nearby **art museum** displays drawings and paintings created by Jews in the ghettos and concentration camps. By far the most haunting part of Yad Va-Shem is the stirring **Children's Memorial.** Mirrors are positioned to create the illusion of an infinite sea of candles while a recorded voice recites the names and ages of young victims.

♫ ENTERTAINMENT AND NIGHTLIFE

Tel Aviv hipsters hate to admit it, but Jerusalem's nightlife is no longer joke-worthy. Once the city's conservative majority is tucked into bed, the bar and club scene comes to life; from Thursday to Saturday nights, the city's energy is so high it would make a rabbi's hair curl. The best weekly info in English is the "In Jerusalem" insert in Friday's *Jerusalem Post.* The tourist office in Safra Sq. (see p. 288) also has detailed monthly calendars in English.

BARS

In the shadow of the stately Orthodox churches of the **Russian Compound** (Migrash Ha-Russim), two blocks down Heleni Ha-Malka St., neon beer signs lure liquor lovers like moths. After midnight, stylish bars in old stone buildings fill to capacity with a young, hip crowd jivin' to jazz, krooning along to karaoke, and doing everything in between. The **midraḥov,** just 5min. away, offers less rowdy but equally popular escapes.

RUSSIAN COMPOUND

Mike's Place, 7 Heleni Ha-Malka (☎052 67 09 65), on the corner of Horkanos. Tightly packed (in a cozy way). English-speaking crowd puts away Guinness, smokes *argileh* (NIS15), and digs great live music every night starting around 10:30pm. Happy hour daily 5-8pm (drinks half-price) and midnight-12:30am (cocktails and shots half- price). Light pub food. Pizza NIS10. Cheese fries NIS20. No cover. Open daily 5pm-3am.

Kanabis, 11 Moonbaz St. (☎623 29 29), upstairs from Tarabin. Large bar-restaurant-dance floor with outdoor terrace overlooking the Moonbaz scene. Karaoke M-Tu nights beginning at 10pm. Beautiful circular bar with 3-page cocktail menu. Individual pizzas and salads NIS30-35. Cover Th-Sa NIS30; M-Tu NIS25 works as a food and drink voucher; W free. Open M-Sa 8:30pm-4am.

Sergey, 15 Heleni Ha-Malka St. (☎625 85 11), at the corner of Moonbaz St. No-frills bar serving a 20-something crowd of Bezalel Art Institute students so hip that they don't even wear black. Pizza NIS30. Crepes NIS28. Salads NIS30-36. Beer NIS16-25. Mixed drinks NIS30+. Weekend min. charge NIS20. Open daily 7pm-late.

ON OR NEAR THE MIDRAḤOV

Syndrome, 18 Hillel St. (☎054 805 210), on the corner of Rabbi Akiva, underneath Cafe Aroma, at the end of the row of stores. Friendly and casual atmosphere. No food, no coffee, just alcohol, chips, *argileh* (NIS15), and music. Happy hour nightly 8-9pm (half-price draft beer). Live music performances (mostly blues and rock) on small stage almost every night 10pm-1am. Cover NIS10-30 (depending on who's playing), including a beer. Open daily 8pm-2am or later.

The Tavern Pub, 16 Rivlin St. (☎624 45 41). Supposedly Jerusalem's oldest pub—putting it at the ripe old age of 30. A magnet for all types, from European tourists and American college students to Israeli locals hoping to meet tourists and students. Eight kinds of draft beer (1 pint NIS16-20) and innumerable international beers. Cocktails NIS22 and up. Live music every other Th in winter. Open daily 3pm-5am.

CLUBS

Most clubs are clustered in the city center or on Ha-Umman St. in **Talpiot,** a southern industrial neighborhood down Hebron Rd. (taxis from the city center NIS15-20). They also open, close, and move more frequently than the city-center clubs; go to Ha-Oman 17 first and ask where to find other local hot spots.

Ha-Oman 17, 17 Ha-Oman St. (☎678 16 58; www.haoman.com), in Talpiyot. The city's largest and best dance club. Still relatively unknown among tourists (which is either good or bad, depending on who you ask). Huge after-parties on major holidays. Two huge indoor dance floors with large bar, populated mostly by scantily-clad Israeli university students. Mostly techno and pop. Th 23+ and F 19+. Cover NIS70. Open Th-F midnight-dawn (or later). Closed July-Aug.

The Underground, 1 Yoel Salomon St. (☎625 19 18), is the dance club everyone hates but goes to anyway, with a bar and batcave-like disco below. Sweaty, grinding dancers shed layers of clothing as the hours go by. Drinks NIS15 and up; buy one get one free during happy hour (daily 8-9pm). 18+. Cover Su-W after 10:30pm NIS20 and Th-Sa NIS30; includes one drink. Open nightly 7:30pm-4am.

Glasnost, 15 Heleni Ha-Malka St. (☎625 69 54), past Moonbaz when coming from Jaffa Rd. In the heart of the bar scene in the Russian Compound. Large outer courtyard overflows with toe-stepping Israelis. Live salsa every M 9pm-3am (NIS25), crash course 8-9pm (NIS35 includes both); Tu Reggae; Th house party; F-Su pub only with tables and chairs crowding out the dance floor (no cover). 21+.

TEL AVIV-JAFFA תל אביב-יפו ☎03

Proudly secular and downright sexy, Tel Aviv pulses with cutting-edge energy. Not surprisingly, given its never-ending quest to stay current, Tel Aviv is a very political city. Despite the effort to make Jerusalem the recognized capital, most countries keep their foreign embassies here. For a brief period during the Gulf Crisis in the winter of 1991, Tel Aviv became a target for Saddam Hussein's SCUD missiles. As modern and international as the city is, CNN videos of gas masks being distributed to children demonstrated the unique tension that exists here. It was also here in November 1995 that Yigal Amir, a Jewish student, fired the bullet that killed Prime Minister Yitzḥak Rabin (see **Assassination of Rabin,** p. 270). The Middle East peace process has taken its toll since then; in the last few years, Hamas bombings have claimed a number of lives in the city. However, political developments in the peace process leave residents hopeful that the recent calm will remain the norm.

Tel Aviv sprouted from Jaffa (*Yafo,* or "beautiful," in Hebrew; *Yafa* in Arabic), its neighboring city, at the end of the 19th century. Jewish settlers, unhappy with the crowded and dilapidated condition of Jaffa and its high Arab population, founded the first two exclusively Jewish neighborhoods in 1887 and 1891. In 1909, the Jewish population of Jaffa parcelled out another northern area, naming it Atuzat Bayit (Housing Property). One year later, the suburb was renamed Tel Aviv (Spring Hill) after the town Theodore Herzl had envisioned in his turn-of-the-century utopian novel, **Altneuland** (Old-New-Land; see **Zionism,** p. 266). Appealing to bourgeois Jewish immigrants from Eastern Europe, the new town quickly developed in the 1920s and '30s and soon became the largest Jewish town in Palestine.

■ INTERCITY TRANSPORTATION

FLIGHTS
Ben-Gurion Airport (English recorded info ☎ 972 33 44), 22km southeast of Tel Aviv in Lod. Egged bus #475 to the airport leaves from the 6th floor of the New Central Bus Station (every 30min. Su-Th 5:20am-11:40pm, F 5:20am-4:50pm, Sa 8:30-11:30pm; NIS10). Shuttle bus #222 makes a round-trip between the airport and Tel Aviv, passing most of the major hostels (every hr. Su-Th 4am-midnight, F 4am-7pm, Sa noon-midnight; NIS16; last shuttle departs from airport Sa-Th 11pm). Taxis from the airport to Tel Aviv run at a fixed tariff (about NIS70 during the day, NIS88 at night or on Shabbat; each piece of luggage NIS2).

TRAINS
Central Train Station (☎ 577 40 00), on Arlozorov St., opposite Namir Rd. Take bus #10 or 18 from the city center or bus #27 from New Central Bus Station. (Open Su-F 6am-11pm.) Air-conditioned trains leave every 30min. to: **Acre** (NS29); **Ashdod** (every 2hr., NIS13) via **Be'er Sheva** (NIS23.50); **Hadera** (NIS16); **Haifa** (NIS21); **Nahariya** (NIS39.50) via **Netanya** (NIS11). 10% ISIC discount on fares NIS20.50+. **Lockers** NIS5-10.

BUSES
Operated by **Egged** (☎ 694 88 88). 10% discount with ISIC on fares NIS20.50+.

NEW CENTRAL BUS STATION. New Central has departures on the 6th floor to: **Be'er Sheva** (#370; every 20min. Su-Th 6am-11pm, F 6am-4:40pm, Sa 8:30-11pm; NIS20.50); **Hadera** (#852 or 872; 1hr.; every 30min. Su-Th 7am-11:30pm, F 8am-4:30pm, Sa 8:30pm-midnight; NIS17); **Haifa** #900 direct (1¼hr.; every 25min. Su-Th 7:30am-8:40pm, F 7:30am-4:35pm, Sa 8:30-10pm; NIS20.50) or late-night #901 express (1¼hr.; every 20min. Su-Th 9:15-11pm; NIS20.50); **Jerusalem** (#405; 1hr.; every 15min. Su-Th 5:40am-midnight, F 6am-5:30pm, Sa 8:30pm-midnight; NIS18); **Netanya** (#605; 45 min.; every 25min. Su-Th 8am-9:15pm, F 8am-4:30pm, Sa 8:30am-10pm; NIS13); **Zikhron Ya'akov** (#872; 2hr.; every 30min. Su-Th 7am-11:30pm, F 8am-4:30pm, Sa 8:30pm-midnight; NIS22.50).

Tel Aviv

🏠 **ACCOMMODATIONS**

Dizengoff Square Hostel, **4**
Gordon Hostel, **3**
Gordon Inn Guest House, **2**
Ha-Yarkon 48 Hostel, **5**
Tel Aviv Youth Hostel (HI), **1**

Levi Eshkol

Namir (Haifa) Rd.

Einstein

Klausner

Tel-Aviv University
(Beit Hatfusot)

TO
HERZLIYA,
HAIFA

**RAMAT
AVIV**

Reading

Broderzky

Levanon (University)

Ayalon Hwy.

Sderot Rokakh

Ha-Yarkon
Park

Eretz Yisrael
Museum 🏛

Sderot Rokakh

Bnei Dan

**SHIKUN
BAVLI**

Yirmiyahu

Yehuda Ha-Macabi

Ha-Halakha

Derekh Aba Hillel

Bialik

**RAMAT-
GAN**

*Sheraton
Beach*

Nordau

Pinkas

Weizmann

Namir

Jordan 🚩

*Hilton
Beach*

Basel

Remez

KIKKAR
HA-MEDINA

Central
Train
Station 🚌

Jabotinsky Rd.

Egypt ℹ 🚩

Jabotinsky

Ibn Gvirol

Ben Yehuda

Dizengoff

Arlozorov

Arlozorov

Weizmann

Petah Tikva Rd.

Arvey Nahal

Ayalon Hwy.

**KIKKAR
ATARIM**

Ha-Yarkon

Ben-Gurion

Shlomo Ha-Melekh

City
Hall

Bloch

David
Ha-Malekh

🏥

Australia 🚩

**GIV'
ATAYIM**

2

Gordon

KIKKAR
YITZHAK
RABIN

Tel Aviv
Museum 🏛
of Art

3

Frischmann

Ibn Gvirol

Sha'ul Ha-Melekh

Ha-Shalom
Station

Herbert Samuel Promenade

4

KIKKAR
DIZENGOFF

Azrieli
Center

Ha-Shalom

TO
ZOOLOGICAL
CENTER
(1.5km)

Ben Yehuda

Bograshov

Dizengoff

Kaplan

Moshe Dayan

ℹ GTIO

Trumpeldor

Dizengoff
Center

Ben Zion

Ha-aashmona'im

Carlebach Rd.

Ha-Masger

*Opera
Tower*

5

Allenby

King George

Sderot Rothschild

Ha-Levi

He-Halutz

Ayalon River

**YAD
ELIYAHU**

**KEREM
HA-TEMANIM**

KIKKAR
MAGEN
DAVID

Sheinkin

Allenby

Ahad Ha-Am

Petah Tikva

Canada ⛵

**SHUK
HA-CARMEL**

Ha-Karmel

Nahlat Binyamin

Levi

Yad Eliyahu
Stadium

LaGuardia

Shalom
Tower ■

Mikye Yisrael

Old Central
Bus Station 🚌

**NEVE
TZEDEK**

Ha-Mered

Kaufman

Shomron

KIKKAR
HA-MOSHAVOT

**HA-TIKVA
MARKET**

Herzl

Levinsky

*Suzanne
Delal
Center* ■

Abarbanel

Ha-Aliyah

New Central
Bus Station 🚌 ℹ

Salameh Rd.

Ha-Hagana

HA-TIKVA

Eilat Rd.

FLORENTIN

Ha-Tikva St.

Lehi

Salameh Rd.

Kibbutz Galuyot Rd.

Mifratz Shlomo St.

Yefet

Jaffa
Clock-
tower

Sderot Yerushalayim

TO
BEN-GURION
AIRPORT,
JERUSALEM ✈

Yehuda Ha-Yamit

N

0   400 yards

0   400 meters

ARLOZOROV TERMINAL. On Arlozorov St., across from Namir Rd. To: **Be'er Sheva** (#380; 1¾hr.; every 15min. Su-Th 6am-8:30pm, F 6am-4:30pm, Sa 8:30-10:30pm; NIS20.50); **Haifa** (#910; 1¼hr.; every 15min. Su-Th 7:45am-8:45pm, F 7:45am-4:30pm, Sa 8:30-10pm; NIS20.50); **Jerusalem** (#480; 50min.; every 15min. Su-Th 6am-10pm, F 6am-4:30pm, Sa 8:30pm-midnight; NIS18).

FERRIES

Caspi, 1 Ben-Yehuda St. (☎517 57 49), in the Migdalor Building. 20% discount for passengers under 24 and students under 30. Port tax NIS100/US$22. Fares drop for round-trip tickets. To: **Piraeus** (3 nights; Su and Th 8pm, NIS424/US$106; in winter Th 7pm, NIS384/US$96) via **Cyprus** (1 night; NIS232/US$58; in winter NIS192/US$48) and **Rhodes** (2 nights; NIS404/US$101; in winter NIS364/US$91).

SHERUT

Across from New Central Bus Station exit (platform 410), to your left (with your back to the station). *Sherut* leave whenever mostly full. To: **Haifa** (1hr., NIS22); **Jerusalem** (45min., NIS18); **Nazareth** (1hr., NIS25); **Netanya** (20min., NIS10).

CAR RENTAL

Gindy Ltd. Rent-a-Car, 132 Ha-Yarkon St. (☎527 83 44). Manual NIS200/US$50 per day; automatic NIS240/$60 per day. 200km per day limit but weekly rental discounts with unlimited mileage available. 21+; drivers under 24 must have $1000 deductible in case of accident. **Avis,** 113 Ha-Yarkon St. (☎527 17 52). Manual NIS184/US$46 per day; automatic starts at NIS200/US$50 per day. 23+, 26+ for larger automatics. 250km per day limit.

◼ ORIENTATION

In the center of Israel's Mediterranean coastline, Tel Aviv is 63km northwest of Jerusalem and 95km south of Haifa. The two main points of entry into Tel Aviv are **Ben-Gurion Airport** and the **New Central Bus Station.** Frequent bus and *sherut* (minibus) service from the airport is supplemented by the vans that warring hostels send to lure potential customers.

Tel Aviv is rather easy to navigate once you learn the few main roads that run parallel to the coastline and a few big intersections. The **tayelet** (promenade) extends from Jaffa up to Gordon beach (about two-thirds of the way to the port). Parallel and one block inland is **Ha-Yarkon St. Ben-Yehuda St.** is another block inland. All three streets are lined with hotels, cafes, and restaurants—prices generally go down as you go farther from the shore. **Dizengoff St.,** home to some of Tel Aviv's trendy cafes and bars, runs parallel to Ben-Yehuda before swerving away from the coast toward **Kikkar Dizengoff,** an elevated plaza surrounded by shops and a cineplex. Dizengoff St. then continues to intersect the next big coastal-parallel street, **Ibn Gvirol St.,** with its arcades and cafes. On Ibn Gvirol, a few blocks above this intersection is **Kikkar Yitzhak Rabin,** in front of City Hall.

The third main square is **Kikkar Bath November,** where Ben-Yehuda intersects **Allenby St.** Most hostels are on or near Ben-Yehuda or Allenby. Farther down, Allenby intersects **King George St.** and **Sheinkin St.** at **Kikkar Magen David.** This is also the starting point of **Shuk Ha-Carmel** and the **midrahov** (pedestrian mall) of **Nahalat Binyamin.** Between the *shuk* and the shore are the winding alleyways of **Kerem Ha-Temanim** (the Yemenite Quarter). Below the *shuk* lies the neighborhood of **Neve Tzedek,** which has profited from a recent infusion of yuppies. Allenby continues most of the way to the bus station. Below the bus station, framed by **Herzl St., Ha-Aliya St., and Salame St.,** is the bohemian **Florentin** neighborhood.

Still another parallel street, much farther from the coast, is **Namir Rd.,** a major thoroughfare that leads to Tel Aviv's north exit; the **train station,** which has service to all major cities, is at the intersection of Namir Rd. and **Arlozorov St. Jaffa** and its waterfront lie farther south, outside the downtown area. The entrance to **Old Jaffa,** marked by a famous **clocktower,** lies at the intersection of **Eilat St.** and **Goldman St.**

▣ LOCAL TRANSPORTATION

Tel Aviv is mostly manageable on foot. On a hot August afternoon, though, a NIS4.70 bus ride may seem like the deal of the century. Buses in Tel Aviv are frequent, air-conditioned, and comfortable; definitely take them to sights north of the Yarkon, in Ha-Tikva area, in the Tel Aviv University area, or in Jaffa, which are all beyond easy walking distance from the city center.

BUSES

The **New Central Bus Station,** 108 Levinsky St. (☎638 40 40) can be scary and painful the first time you experience it, but the basics are easy enough. Most local buses (Dan) and local and intercity *sherut* leave from the fourth floor; exit at platform #416 for local buses and platform #410 for *sherut*. A few local buses with destinations outside Tel Aviv (Ramat Gan, Ramat Aviv) leave from the first floor. Intercity buses (Egged) leave from the sixth floor; the fourth and sixth floors have information kiosks. **Baggage check** rooms are on the sixth floor, down a small flight of stairs near the information kiosk. (NIS10 per item per day. Open Su-Th 7am-7pm, F and holiday eves 7am-3pm.)

Buses within Tel Aviv are operated by **Dan,** 39 Sha'ul Ha-Melekh. (☎639 33 33 or 639 44 44. Buses run Su-Th 5:30am-midnight, F 5am-5pm, Sa 8:15pm-12:30am; do not run on Shabbat and some stop earlier. NIS4.70.) For extended stays, consider buying Dan's **monthly bus pass** (NIS176). Unlike intercity buses, local buses travel both ways, so you must be conscious of the direction. Fortunately, bus stops have English signs with a green marker pointing to the current stop. Decide whether you need to follow the blue or red directional path and stand on the side of the street where the appropriately colored arrow matches the flow of traffic.

SEVEN MOST FREQUENTED ROUTES

4: From the New Central Bus Station (4th fl.), runs parallel to the coastline up Allenby and Ben-Yehuda St. and back. Every 5min.

5: From the New Central Bus Station (4th fl.), runs up Rothschild Blvd. and Dizengoff St. to Dizengoff Ctr., then turns right to run down the lengths of Nordau and Yehuda Ha-Maccabee before turning around. Every 5min.

10: Runs from train station along Arlozorov St., turns left to go down the coast along Ben-Yehuda St., Herbert Samuel St., and Kaufman St. to Jaffa. Weaves back up through the Florentin area along Herzl St. to Rothschild Blvd. before turning back. Every 15min.

18: Runs from the train station along Sha'ul Ha-Melekh through Dizengoff Sq. to Ben-Yehuda and then Allenby before heading down to Florentin along Ha-Aliya and Salame Rds. and turns around after reaching Bat Gam. Every 5-10min

25: Runs from Tel Aviv University down Namir Rd. then Yehuda Ha-Maccabee to Ibn Gvirol. After turning right and going for a few blocks on Arlozorov, turns left to follow Shlomo Ha-Melekh and King George down to Shuk Ha-Carmel. Until 9:30pm, continues to Bat Yam along the coast, but otherwise turns around at the *shuk.* Every 15 min.

27: From the New Central Bus Station (1st fl.), runs along Petaḥ Tikva Rd. and to Haifa Rd.; Central Train Station, then along Levanon St. to Tel Aviv University, the kenyon (shopping mall) in Ramat Gan, and back. Every 10-15min.

46: From the New Central Bus Station (1st fl.) to Jaffa and back along Yefet St. Every 8-10min., every 15min. at night.

Sherut taxis run along the routes of buses #4 and 5, and are numbered accordingly. At NIS4.50, they're cheaper than the bus and will stop anywhere along the route. Call a taxi anytime (☎524 90 90 or 527 19 99). **Rent-A-Scooter,** 136 Ha-Yarkon St. (☎681 57 78), provides an alternative to public transportation (NIS100/US$25 per day; 10% discounts for a week, 20% for two weeks; 18+).

⁊ PRACTICAL INFORMATION

TOURIST AND FINANCIAL SERVICES

Tourist Office: (☎639 56 60; fax 639 56 59), in the New Central Bus Station, 6th fl., near platform 630. From the city center, take bus #4 or 5. Provides hotel and tour reservations and maps of Tel Aviv and other Israeli cities. Open Su-Th 9am-5pm, F 9am-1pm. A kiosk in the City Hall Lobby (☎521 85 00) gives out maps and information about Tel Aviv only. Open Su-Th 9am-2pm.

Tours: SPNI, 19 Ha-Sharon St. (☎638 86 74), near the intersection with Petaḥ Tikva Rd. Their English-speaking guides lead the best 1-12 day tours, year-round. Day tours NIS200/US$50 to NIS300/US$75. Open Su-Th 8am-4:30pm, F 8-11am. **United Tours,** 113 Ha-Yarkon St. (☎522 20 08), offers tours around the country in English, Hebrew, French, and German. Day tours NIS232-296/US$58-74; 10% student discount with ISIC if booked directly from their office.

Budget Travel: ISSTA, 128 Ben-Yehuda St. (☎521 05 55), at Ben-Gurion St. For ISICs, bring a photograph, current student ID, and NIS40; Youth Hostel cards NIS35. Open Su-Th 9am-noon and 3-7pm and F 9am-noon. **Mona Tours,** 25 Bogorochov St. (☎621 14 33), specializes in student and charter rates. Must be under 28 to book flights; proof of age required. Open Su-Th 9am-6pm, F 9am-1pm. Both take credit cards.

Embassies and Consulates: Australia, 37 Sha'ul Ha-Melekh Blvd., Europe House, 4th fl. (☎695 04 51). Open M-Th 8am-noon. **Canada,** 3 Nirim St. (☎636 33 00), next to basketball stadium in Yad Eliyahu. Open for visas M-Th 8am-4:30pm, F 8-1:30pm. **South Africa,** Top Tower, Dizengoff Ctr., 16th fl. (☎525 25 66). Enter through gate #3. Open M-F 9-11am, W 9-11am and 2-3pm. **UK** (also serves travelers from **New Zealand**), 1 Ben-Yehuda St., Migdalor Building, 6th fl. (☎510 01 66 for passports and visas). Open M-Th 1:30-3:30pm, F noon-1pm. **US,** 71 Ha-Yarkon St. (☎519 75 75), just a few blocks north of Allenby St., on the left side. Open for passports M and W 8:30-11am and 2-3:30pm, Tu and Th 8:30-11am, F 8:30am-12:30pm; for visas M-F 7:30am-2:30pm. **Egypt,** 54 Basel St. (☎546 51 51 or 546 51 52), just off Ibn Gvirol. For a visa, bring a passport, photograph, and NIS75 (US citizens NIS50). Be sure to specify planned visits beyond the Sinai, or they'll automatically issue a "Sinai Only" visa. Open Sa-Th 9-11am. **Jordan,** 14 Aba Hillel (☎751 77 22), in Ramat Gan. Pre-arranged visas (NIS30) are required for crossing to Jordan via King Hussein/Allenby Bridge (see p. 417). Open Su-Th 9:30am-12:30pm.

Currency Exchange: Any post office will change money without commission. **Change Point,** 106 Ha-Yarkon St. (☎524 55 05; open Su-Th 9am-6pm, F 8:30am-1pm), and **Change Spot,** 140 Dizengoff St. (☎524 33 93; open Su-Th 9am-7pm, F 9am-2pm), also offer no-commission exchange. Banks usually exchange currency M-Th 8:30am-2pm, F 8:30am-noon; US$6 or 5% commission.

Banks: Most banks are open Su, Tu, Th 8:30am-12:30pm and 4-5:30pm; M, W, F, and holiday eves 8:30am-noon. Main bank offices: **Bank Ha-Poalim,** 104 Ha-Yarkon St. (☎520 06 12); **Israel Discount,** 16 Mapu St. (☎520 32 12); and **Bank Leumi,** 130 Ben-Yehuda St. (☎520 37 37). Branches throughout the city and suburbs.

LOCAL SERVICES

Shopping Hours: In general, 8:30am-7pm, but many stores stay open until 10pm, especially in malls. Most are open late on Th night and almost all close F by 2pm.

Camping Supplies: LaMetayel (☎528 68 94), Dizengoff Center, on the 3rd fl., near the Lev Cinema. Full range of equipment and information. Open Su-Th 10am-8:30pm, F 10am-2pm. **Steve's Packs** (☎525 99 20), next door, has a narrower selection, but may be more affordable. Open Su-Th 9:30am-8:45pm, F 9:30am-3pm, Sa 7-10:45pm.

Ticket Agencies: Rococo, 93 Dizengoff St. (☎527 66 77). Open Su-Th 9am-7pm, F 9am-2pm. **Hadran,** 90 Ibn Gvirol St. (☎527 97 97), north of Kikkar Yitzḥak Rabin. **Castel,** 153 Ibn Gvirol St. (☎604 76 78). **Le'an,** 101 Dizengoff St. (☎524 73 73). All sell tickets for concerts, plays, sporting events, and other performances. Discount student tickets sometimes available. MC/V. No checks.

EMERGENCY AND COMMUNICATIONS

Help Lines: Rape Crisis (☎517 61 76 for women, 517 91 79 for men). **Alcoholics Anonymous** (☎578 66 63). **Drug Counseling** (☎688 64 64). All speak English. All 24hr.

Pharmacy: Superpharm (☎620 37 98 or 620 09 75), on the bottom floor of Dizengoff Center. Open Su-Th 9:30am-10pm, F 9am-3:30pm, and Sa 6:30-11pm. Another location, in the London Minister building, at the intersection of Ibn Gvirol and Sha'ul Ha-Melekh St. Open 24hr. **Nayanpharm**, 75 Ben-Yehuda St. (☎522 91 21) next to the Supersol. Open Su-Th 9am-11pm, F 9am-3pm, Sa 7:30-10:30pm.

Hospitals: Ichilov Hospital, 6 Weizmann St. (☎697 44 44). **Assuta,** 58-60 Jabotinsky St. (☎520 15 15).

Telephones: Solan Communications, 13 Frischmann St. (☎522 94 24; fax 522 94 49). Private booths for international calls (NIS7 per min). Telecards, international calling cards, fax services. Open Su-Th 10am-9pm, F 8am-3pm. **RSM Communications,** 80 Ha-Yarkon St. (☎516 83 66; fax 516 81 26; fones@rentafone.co.il) Cellular phone rentals with voice mail NIS4/US$1 per day; local calls NIS2 per min.; international calls NIS5 per min. Open Su-Th 9am-5:30pm, F 9am-2pm.

Internet Access: Private Link, 78 Ben-Yehuda St. (☎529 98 89). Time purchased can be used over the course of one month: NIS18 per hr., NIS85 for 5hr. Open 24hr. MasloolTravelers' Equipment and Information Center, 47 Bogroshov St. (☎620 35 08). NIS8 for 30min. Open Su-Th 9am-10pm, F 9am-4pm, Sa 7:30pm-10:30pm.

Post Office: 7 Mikveh Yisrael St. (☎564 36 51), 2 blocks east of the south end of Allenby St. **Poste Restante, fax, telegram, and telex.** Open Su-Th 8am-6pm, F 8am-noon. Other branches throughout the city.

ACCOMMODATIONS

Most hostels cluster on Ben-Yehuda and Ha-Yarkon St., with some just off Allenby Rd. or Dizengoff St. Bus #222 makes a round trip between the airport and Tel Aviv and passes most hostels. When choosing, keep in mind that drunken revelry and honking horns downtown may continue through the wee hours. Also, consider the hostels in Jaffa (see p. 321). Hostels fill up quickly in the summer, especially the private rooms, so make reservations if possible. Almost all have 24hr. reception, kitchen, safe and storage, and Internet access. A huge influx of long-term travelers and day-laborers gives a lived-in feel to some places; daily work can often be found through the hostel managers. Sleeping on the beach is illegal; theft and sexual assault are not uncommon, and the zamboni-like machines that sweep the beaches every night for bombs could crush a traveler or at least give a rude awakening.

Ha-Yarkon 48 Hostel, 48 Ha-Yarkon St. (☎516 89 89; fax 510 31 13; info@hayarkon48.com; www.hayarkon48.com). Take bus #4 or 16 from the central bus station. The bright rooms and showers win popularity contests, but everyone spends their time in the TV lounge playing pool for free, drinking beer in reception, or on the rooftop bar. Small breakfast included. Key deposit NIS20. Check-out 10:30am. 6-bed dorms NIS42/US$10.50, NIS120/US$30 for 3 nights, NIS142/US$38 for 4 nights, NIS252/US$63 for 7 nights. Private rooms NIS176/US$44, with fan and bath NIS208/US$52, with A/C and bath NIS228/US$57. Rooftop mattress NIS35/US$8.75 in summer if all beds are taken.

Gordon Hostel, 2 Gordon St. (☎522 98 70; fax 523 74 19; sleepin@inter.net.il), on the corner of Ha-Yarkon St. Take bus #4 or 5 from the central bus station, and get off at Gordon St. Though the hostel is as close to the beach as you can get without getting sand in your sheets, most of the clientele sunsoaks on the rooftop lounge. Wash and dry NIS14. Check-out 10:30am. Lockout 11am-2pm. Dorms (coed or female-only) NIS36/US$9, NIS224/US$57 per week. Rooftop mattress NIS27/US$6.75. Students and repeat visitors receive 10% discount.

Gordon Inn Guest House, 17 Gordon St. (☎523 82 39; fax 523 74 19; sleepin@inter.net.il, www.psl.co.il/gordon-inn), just off Ben-Yehuda St. From the central bus station take bus #4 to Ben-Yehuda and Gordon St. More polished and proper than

ISRAEL

most in the price range, the Guest House resides conveniently between Dizengoff Center and the beach. Breakfast included. Max. stay 2 weeks, negotiable. Check-in 2pm. Check-out 11am. All rooms have A/C, some have balconies. Rooms in back are quieter. 7-8 bed dorms (coed) NIS64/US$16; singles NIS184/US$46, with bath NIS228/US$57; doubles NIS236/US$59, with bath NIS284/US$71; triples NIS288/US$72, with bath NIS340/US$85; quads NIS340/US$85, with bath NIS396/US$99. Prices 10-15% lower Nov.-June, except holidays.

Dizengoff Square Hostel, 13 Ben-Ami St. (☎522 51 84; fax 522 51 81; dizengoff@trendline.co.il; www.dizengoff-hostel.co.il), off Dizengoff Sq., across from the Chen cinema. Take bus #5 from the central bus station to Dizengoff Sq. Colorful paint, plaster sculptures in the TV/pool table room, and a breezy rooftop terrace keep the oldest hostel in Tel Aviv fresh and funky. Small breakfast included. Laundry NIS6. Checkout 10:30am. Lockout 10:30am-2:30pm. 4-8 bed dorms (coed and single sex) NIS38/US$9.50, with A/C NIS46/US$11.50. Private rooms NIS188/US$47, with A/C, bath, TV, and fridge NIS216/US$54. Dorms NIS232/US$58 per week.

Tel Aviv Youth Hostel/Guest House (HI), 36 B'nei Dan St. (☎544 17 48; fax 544 10 30, telaviv@iyha.org.il), near Ibn Gvirol St. Take bus #5, 24, or 25 to the Weizmann St. and Yehuda Ha-Macabbe intersection and walk up one block to B'nei Dan. This spotless and shiny hostel has a large breakfast included. Check-out 10am. All rooms have A/C and private rooms have bath. 4-bed dorm NIS70/US$17.50, with bath NIS88/US$22; singles NIS148/US$38; doubles NIS224/US$56; triples NIS288/US$72. NIS6 surcharge for nonmembers. Discounts for longer stays.

Home Hostel, 20 al-Sheikh St. (☎517 67 36). Take bus #4 from the central bus station along Allenby St. until Bialik St.; go behind Allenby 56 and turn right. As cheap as it gets, and, in terms of rooms and facilities, you get what you pay for. But, the family-like atmosphere, meals on Saturday, and a bed on your birthday are all free. Saintly owner can get discounts at local bars and clubs and find jobs for clientele. Breakfast included. Kitchen available. Dorms (coed and female-only) NIS30/US$8, students NIS27/US$7.

◨ FOOD

Come mealtime, Tel Aviv rises above and beyond the call of duty. Restaurants range from Tex-Mex to Southeast Asian, from falafel and hummus to French *haute-cuisine*, but after a brain-melting day at the beach, fast food and frozen yogurt may sound just as good. For quick, cheap belly-fillers, head for the self-service eateries on Ben-Yehuda St. (sandwich with chips or stuff-your-own falafel under NIS12). The eateries near Shuk Ha-Carmel and along Bezalel St. off Allenby and King George St. stay open the latest (1:30am or later).

Kerem Ha-Temanim (the Yemenite Quarter), south of Allenby St. between Ge'ula and Shuk Ha-Carmel, boasts cheap, spicy fried-dough, often stuffed with meat (NIS12-25). Israelis down kebab and *la'afa* in the **Shechunat Ha-Tikva** area in the southeasternmost quarter, renowned for its cheap beer and lamb, chicken, or beef skewers. Pastry stands, falafel joints, and ice cream shops line **Dizengoff Sq.** and the stretch of **Dizengoff St.** just north, where crowds of tourists and throngs of hungry young Israelis test the limits of spandex technology. **Yermiyahu St.** has a better, pricier selection (NIS20-35).

◪ **Itzik Ve' Ruthie,** 53 Sheinkin St. (☎685 27 53), serves the most scrumptious sandwiches (NIS5-15) in the city. The homemade soda (NIS2) alone is worth squeezing past all the locals crammed into this tiny shop. Open Su-Th 5am-4pm, F 5am-2pm.

◪ **Falafel 101,** 99 Dizengoff St., near the corner of Frischmann St., should be the model for all other falafel stands. For NIS10, get piping-hot falafel, a large selection of salads, and a drink. Open Su-Th 8am-midnight, F 8am-4pm.

Big Mama, 13 Najara St. (☎517 50 65). Look for the blue and red neon sign on the back right corner of the walkway behind Allenby 58. Gobble down the best pizza this side of Italy (NIS25-34), or try one of the indulgently creamy pasta dishes (NIS28-34). Open Su noon-2am, M-W and F noon-3am, Th noon-4am.

A Taste of Life, 60 Ben-Yehuda St. (☎ 620 31 51). A vegan paradise run by members of the Black Hebrew community, a group whose dietary laws prohibit both milk and meat (see **Dimona,** p. 399). Entrees like wheatfurters, veggie shawarma, and soy barbecue twists served à la carte (NIS15) or with 2 sides and a salad (NIS42). Cleanse your palate on the excellent soymilk ice cream (NIS6.50) and other non-dairy, no-egg desserts. Open Su-Th 9am-11pm, F 9am-3pm, Sa after sundown-midnight.

Hungarian Blintzes, 35 Yermiyahu St. (☎ 544 16 97 or 605 06 74), near the port. Turn right off Dizengoff St. and continue one block. Locals jonesing for Hungarian goulash blintzes (NIS32) flock to this intimate bistro. Sweeter jam (NIS25) and poppy seed cream (NIS30) also available. Open Su-Th 1pm-1am, Sa sundown-1am.

Yotvata B'Ir, 78 Herbert Samuel St. (☎ 510 79 84). There's a green and orange neon sign off the tayelet. Kibbutz Yotvata, renowned producers of dairy goods, ventures into the city with this well-lit oasis of fresh veggies, cheeses, and fruits. Menu highlights include salads large enough to feed a small army (NIS45-47) and pancakes masquerading as sundaes (NIS27-39). Open daily 7am-3am.

Dallas Restaurant, 68 Ezel St. (☎ 687 43 49), in Ha-Tikva neighborhood, a few blocks past the shuk. Bus #15 and 16 go past the restaurant. Outstanding Yemenite restaurant serves every cow part, including heart (NIS13), testicles (NIS10), and udder (NIS10). Open Su-Th noon-2am, F 11am-1hr. before sundown, Sa 8:30pm-2am.

New York Bagel, 215 Ben-Yehuda St. (☎ 605 35 72), above Jabotinsky St. Something from the Diaspora makes a welcome return to Israel, namely bagels (NIS3), with cream cheese (NIS13) and nova lox (NIS22). Open Su-Th 7:30am-11pm, F 7am-3pm.

■ CAFES

Crowd-gazing is an art in Tel Aviv; chairs on the sidewalk and café-au-lait can be found just about anywhere in the city. **Sheinken St.,** one of the hippest promenades in town, has a long tradition of artsy liberalism. Along the parallel **Ben-Yehuda, Dizengoff,** and **Ibn Gvirol St.,** a number of cafes serve local neighborhood folk and weary shoppers alike. **Basel St.** (near its intersection with Ibn Gvirol St., a block above Jabotinsky St.) recently sprouted its own crop of chichi cafes for hipper-than-thou Sheinken expats.

Tamar Cafe, 57 Sheinken St. (☎ 685 23 76), provides a quintessential Sheinken experience. Immortalized in a song by the Israeli pop trio Mango ("Living on Sheinken/drinking coffee at the Tamar Cafe/my dream is to make a short film"), the Tamar is crammed with locals arguing about who's more liberal. Open Su-Th 7am-8pm, F 7am-5pm.

Babblefish, 13 Rabbi Akiva (☎ 516 45 85), near the corner of Najara St., to the right of the shuk from Allenby. Adorable, cherry-pink hole-in-the-wall cafe. Sangria NIS12. Salads NIS15-20. Live percussion and funk DJ on F nights. Open Su-F noon-2am.

Ilan's Coffee Shop, 90 Ibn Gvirol St. (☎ 523 53 34). Tables are a prized commodity in Tel Aviv's 1st espresso bar. Renowned for their fantastic home brew "Angela Mia" (NIS6-16), they also just crossed the fence into the whole-leaf tea business (NIS6-14). Another location at 20 Carlebach St. Open Su-Th 6:30am-10pm, F 6:30am-3pm.

◎ SIGHTS

ROOFTOP OBSERVATORY. When haggling, shoving, and sunning take their toll, rise above it all. Look down on the chaos of the market and the city from the observatory in **Migdal Shalom.** The tower rises 34 stories skyward and the penthouse affords a breathtaking view, although the gating does give it a somewhat caged-in feel. The mosaic walls were made by artists Naḥum Gutan and David Sharir. (1 Herzl St. and Aḥad Ha-Am St. Enter through the Eastern Wing beneath the underpass. ☎ 517 73 04. Open Su-Th 10am-6:30pm, F 10am-2pm. NIS15, students and seniors NIS10.)

KIKKAR YITZHAK RABIN. Formerly Kikkar Malkhei Yisrael (Kings of Israel Sq.), the square was renamed in 1995 in memory of Prime Minister Yitzhak Rabin. On November 4, 1995, Rabin was assassinated by Yigal Amir, a Jewish student, during a crowded peace rally. The square has since drawn mourners who have painted large portraits of Rabin and left candles, flowers, and poetry. The official memorial, surrounded by five years' worth of candlewax, is next to the City Hall. *(Just off Ibn Gvirol St., between Arlozorov St. and Ben-Gurion St.)*

GREAT SYNAGOGUE. Completed in 1926 and renovated in 1970, this huge domed building showcases arches and stained-glass windows that are replicas of those from European synagogues destroyed during the Holocaust. *(110 Allenby St., near the corner with Rothschild Blvd. ☎560 49 05 or 560 40 66. Open Su-F 10am-5pm and Sa 7:30-11:30am. Sa prayer open to the public; head coverings and modest dress required.)*

Near the synagogue is **Independence Hall,** where the founding of the State of Israel was proclaimed in 1948. *(16 Rothschild Blvd. ☎517 39 42. Open Su-Th 9am-2pm.)*

ZOOLOGICAL CENTER. This combination drive-through safari park, circus, and zoo features 250 acres of African game in a natural habitat. Stare over a *wadi* at impossibly cute gorillas and Syrian bears, or let an ostrich poke its head into your car for a bite of candy. People without picnics can have lunch at the moderately priced restaurant, and those without a car can ride the park's own vehicles through the habitat. Pedestrian tours are offered as well. *(In Ramat Gan. Take bus #30, 35, or 43 from Tel Aviv or bus #67 within Ramat Gan. From the bus stop, go ½km down Ha-Tzvi Blvd. with the park on your right; the zoo entrance is on the right. ☎631 21 81 or 674 49 81. Open Su-Th July-Aug. 9am-5pm, Mar.-June and Sept.-Oct. 9am-4pm, and Nov.-Feb. 9am-2:30pm; open year-round F 9am-1pm and Sa 9am-3pm. Visitors may remain on the grounds 2hr. after entrance gate closes. NIS42, students and children NIS32; with circus NIS49, students and children NIS42; extra NIS5 charge to ride on park's bus.)* The beast-watching madness continues outside the Zoological Center in the massive **Ramat Gan National Park,** which rents boats. *(Open 24hr. Free.)*

🏛 MUSEUMS

ERETZ YISRAEL MUSEUM

2 Levanon St., in Ramat Aviv, the northernmost part of the city. Buses #7, 24, 25, or 74 from the New Central Bus Station stop at the museum. ☎641 52 44. Open Su-Tu and Th 9am-3pm, W 9am-5pm, F-Sa 10am-2pm. NIS28, students NIS22, children NIS20; includes access to all 8 pavilions and the Eretz Yisrael Library. Planetarium NIS20, in Hebrew.

A veritable eight-ring circus, the Eretz Yisrael museum consists of eight pavilions covering vastly different topics spread over an archaeological site that is still being excavated. The most famous attraction in the complex is the **Glass Pavilion,** with one of the finest collections of glassware in the world. The **Nehushtan Pavilion,** with its cave-like entryway, holds the discoveries of the excavations at the ancient copper mines of Timna, better known as King Solomon's Mines, just north of Eilat. Across the patio, the **Kadman Numismatic Museum** traces the history of the region through ancient coins. The **Ceramics Pavilion** contains ancient Canaanite pottery, exhibits explaining its production, and artist Moshe Shek's ceramic sculptures. Across the entrance area, past the grassy amphitheater, is the **Man and His Work Center,** an exhibition of Middle Eastern folk crafts and techniques. Follow the road to the right and go upstairs to reach the **Tel Qasile Excavations,** which have revealed a 12th-century BCE Philistine port city and ruins dating from around 1000 BCE. The area at the top of the hill contains the remains of three separate Philistine temples built on top of each other. Down the hill to the south are scattered remnants of the residential and industrial quarter of the city. Past the Philistine town is the **Folklore Pavilion,** with Jewish religious art, ceremonial objects, and ethnic clothing. The Eretz Yisrael complex also houses a library of over 30,000 books and periodicals (some in English) and the **Lasky Planetarium.**

TEL AVIV MUSEUM OF ART

27 Sha'ul Ha-Melekh Blvd. Buses #7 and 18. ☎696 12 97 or 695 73 61; www.tamu-seum.co.il. Open M and W 10am-4pm, Tu and Th 10am-10pm, F 10am-2pm, Sa 10am-4pm. Tours in English W 11:30am. NIS30, students NIS24, seniors and children NIS15.

The museum holds a sizeable collection of Israeli and international art. The handsome lobby boasts a Lichtenstein, and the museum itself runs the gamut from Impressionism (Renoir, Monet, Corot, and Pissaro) to Surrealism (including de Chirico and Magritte) to cutting-edge multimedia installations by more recent artists. Rotating thematic exhibits are exceptionally well-curated and range from "Music in Art" to "Stage Design." An English program listing special exhibits and events is available in the ticket booth or the "This Week in Tel Aviv" insert in Friday's *Jerusalem Post.*

◪ BEACHES AND PROMENADES

BEACHES. The beaches within the city are sandy, clean, and free, and all have showers, toilets, and changing rooms with varying degrees of cleanliness. All of Tel Aviv's beaches are rife with theft; lock up valuables before hitting the sand. The southern coastline, with fewer amenities and no luxury hotels, tends to be quieter during the day, but that is gradually changing now that the *tayelet* (promenade) has been extended all the way to Jaffa. **Gordon Beach** overflows with foreign tourists and Israelis trying to pick them up, while the **Hilton Beach** (behind the hotel) swarms with native surfers and tourists trying to pick them up. The **Sheraton Beach** is quite peaceful. From north to south, the beaches are: Sheraton, Hilton, Gordon, Frischmann, Trumpeldor, and the Jerusalem beach at the end of Allenby Rd.; the last four are almost one continuous beach. The Hebrew word for beach is *hof*, but it's more important to learn the **flag language** of the beach: black means swimming is forbidden, red means swimming is dangerous, white means swim on. Most beaches have lifeguards on duty 7am-5pm.

PROMENADES. If the beach doesn't sate your bare-flesh needs, perfect the Mediterranean art of nonchalant people-watching from Tel Aviv's streets and cafes (see **Cafes**, p. 317). Work that cover-girl look along the wide, high-fashion boutique-lined sidewalks of **Dizengoff St.**, no longer at the peak of their glory but still among the more crowded catwalks in town. **Dizengoff Sq.** hosts an ever-changing scene, from retirees feeding flocks of pigeons in the midday sun to late-night punks who flock to the overpass stairs.

▧ NIGHTLIFE

PUBS

After an exhausting day of tanning at the beach, many travelers just want an evening of good company and icy Carlsbergs. Rowdy but generic bars abound around hostel-heavy **Ha-Yarkon St.** and **Allenby Rd.** Israelis—often charged cover when tourists are not because of their tendency toward smaller bar bills—head inland to bars with a little more character. Several great options are hidden away on the Ibn Gvirol sidestreets and in Florentin. As with clubs, the general closing time is "when the last customer leaves," which can be as early as midnight or 1am on weekdays, but as late as 6am on weekends.

1942, 27 Rosh Pina St. (☎688 96 92 or 052 448 516), a few blocks from the central bus station. For all your nightlife needs, this gorgeous place has a mod checkerboard dance floor, a pub with the city's cheapest (and best decorated) cocktails (NIS20-28), and an Arabian-style loft for *argileh* (NIS20). Cover NIS40 (includes one drink), NIS60 for all you can eat and drink. Prove it's your birthday and everything is free. Open daily at 9pm, but only a dance bar Th-Sa. Also hosts an after-party Sa 6:30am.

Shweball at Rival 27, 27 Rival St. (☎ 687 43 64), off Ha-Massger St. Look for the graffiti mural reading "Rival 27." Relive your childhood, this time with alcohol. Join the friendly, young Israeli crowd for beer (NIS14-20), cocktails (NIS28, 35 for flaming versions), and games like pick-up sticks, Connect Four, and *taki*, the Israeli version of Uno. Open M-Th and Sa at 9pm, F at 10pm. Fills up at about 11pm.

End of the Night, 16 Ibn Gvirol St. (☎ 695 00 91), just above Dizengoff. Look for a big orange sign that reads "Mongol". Twenty-something locals pile on top of each other to jam to the well-chosen hip-hop and funk. 21+. Open Th-Sa at 11:30pm.

Florentine 5, at that address (☎ 682 66 34), just off Herzl St. If the candlelight, Israeli classics, and sophisticated crowd don't mellow you out, the *argileh* (NIS15) just might do the trick. Open daily at 9pm.

He-She, 8 Ha-Shomeret St. (☎ 510 09 14), off Shefer St. Tel Aviv's most popular gay bar, thanks to a devoted crowd of locals and tourists. Beer NIS20. Open M-Sa at 8pm.

The Out, 45 Naḥalat Binyamin (☎ 560 2391), a few blocks after the pedestrian mall, on the corner of Montefiore. Two-floor cozy gay bar with red lights and wood floors that lend a mellow ambiance, especially on romantic-themed Tuesdays. Israeli rock on Mondays, but the house goes house on weekends. Beer NIS12-18. Happy hour prices until 11pm. Open Sa-W at 9pm, Th-F at 10pm.

DISCOS

Tel Aviv's dance scene is always on the move; the *only* club one year may be empty the next and a hardware store after that. To really enjoy Tel Aviv's nightlife, you may have to reset your internal clock. The music sometimes starts early, but no one arrives before midnight and places tend to peak around 3am. Friday is the hottest. Those who really want to earn their nocturnal merit badges should keep an eye out for after-party signs; different clubs take turns hosting these 6:30am (Saturday morning) bashes that tunnel on until noon.

The Octopus (☎ 620 01 31), at the port. Turn right at the end of Yermiyahu St., near the Superpharm, and continue 300m to the cluster of clubs. After Th and F of hard-core trance, the crowd chills out at the Sa sundown party (5:30pm) then grooves up for '70s night fever (midnight). Cover Th NIS80, F-Sa NIS60.

The Scene, 56 Allenby Rd. (☎ 510 85 23). A catwalk of a club, the Scene serves as the prime stomping grounds for Tel Aviv's starlets in sequins. Club goes loco for salsa on Thursday. Monday is gay night. 23+. Cover NIS50. Open M-Sa 10pm-4am.

The Second Floor, 67 Allenby Rd. Head under the blue wooden sign around back and up the stairs. Wild crowd spills out onto the balcony of this '70s-style apartment or retreats to the many chill-out rooms to enjoy pool, *argileh*, or rooftop jazz. 20+. Cover NIS30. Open Th-F at 10pm. Occasional jazz soirées on F afternoons.

Dynamo Dvash, 59 Abarbanel St. (☎ 683 51 59), a small street off Salame St., on your left when coming from Herzl St. DJs from all over the world craft "brain dance" electronica high above the warehouse floor. 21+. Cover NIS40-70. Open Th-F at midnight.

LIVE MUSIC

Young Israeli rock bands have appointed Tel Aviv their headquarters and play the clubs nightly. In addition, two amphitheaters at Ha-Yarkon Park hold concerts. *Ha-Ir (The City)*, a weekly Hebrew magazine, has a section called "Akhbar Ha-Ir," with comprehensive listings. For listings in English, check the brochure *This Week in Tel Aviv*, produced by *The Jerusalem Post*.

Barbie, 40 Salame Rd. (☎ 681 67 57), halfway between Herzl St. and Marzuk Veezar. Only accessible by taxi. Look for a gray striped awning or a big crowd. Garage-like place is frequented by some of the best rock bands in Israel. Cover NIS10-50 depending on the band's fame. Shows Su-F 10pm and midnight.

Heineken Habima (☎ 528 21 74), on the left side of Kikkar Habima, at the top of Rothschild Blvd. Locals groove to local bands by the neon and candlelight. Beer NIS15-20. Cover NIS25, weekends NIS30. Open M-Sa at 10:30pm.

DON'T ASK, DON'T TEL AVIV Today, Tel Aviv is home to Israel's most thriving gay community. From the soaring attendance at the annual gay pride day party (now held in Ha-Yarkon Park) to the large number of gay clubs, pubs, and establishments with "gay nights," the community is present, active, and powerful. The best ways to find out what's going on are by catching leaflets on Sheinken St. and reading *Ha-Zman Ha-Varod*.

Camelot, 16 Shalom Aleichem St. (☎ 528 52 33). The basement echoes with live blues and R&B, while the upstairs pub stays mellow, with DJs on W, F, and Sa. Cover NIS35-80 for downstairs. Open daily 9pm-4am. Reserve at least a day before for good bands.

JAFFA (YAFO) יפו יאפا

An Israeli folk song describes Jaffa (*Yafo*, or "beautiful," in Hebrew; *Yafa* in Arabic) as possessing a "mysterious and unknown" element that allows its atmosphere "to seep like wine into the blood." Jaffa's stone houses and winding streets are truly intoxicating. An integral part of Tel Aviv, Jaffa has one of the oldest functioning harbors in the world, nearly 6000 years old. According to the Bible, the recalcitrant prophet Jonah shirked his divine calling and fled to Jaffa to catch a boat to Tarshish, and subsequently had his fateful encounter with the whale. The earliest archaeological finds in Jaffa date from the 18th century BCE, from which point on the city played host to a series of conquerors. In 1468 BCE, the Egyptians captured Jaffa by hiding soldiers in human-sized clay jars that were brought into the city market. King David took the city around 1000 BCE, and under Solomon it became the main port of Judea. During the 12th century CE, Jaffa was captured by the First Crusaders, Salah al-Din, Richard the Lionheart, the Muslims, and Louis IX, who built magnificent walls and towers which partly remain today. The Mamluks overpowered the city in 1267; apart from a brief stay by Napoleon around 1800 (during which much of the Jewish community vanished), Jaffa remained an important Arab stronghold until 1948. In the 1960s, the Tel Aviv municipality began a massive renovation project here, resulting in today's abundance of small museums and a thriving artists' colony amid green parks and Crusader walls.

◼ ORIENTATION

The **Jaffa Clocktower,** completed in 1906, stands by the entrance to Jaffa from Tel Aviv and is a useful landmark. A free 2hr. **tour** of Old Jaffa by the Tourism Association begins here Wednesday at 9:30am, though many people line up at 9am. Bus #46 from the New Central Bus Station lets off in front of the clocktower, and bus #10 from Ben-Yehuda St. or Allenby St., near the Opera Tower, stops just a couple minutes before it. A couple blocks past the clocktower, head right and the road becomes the **Mifratz Shlomo Promenade,** which leads to the **Old City** and provides stunning views of Tel Aviv's action-packed coast and skyline. Alternatively, a left turn onto **Beit Eshel St.** will you bring you to the *shuk*.

◼ ACCOMMODATIONS

If all the beds in Tel Aviv are full, or if you just want something that feels a little less like a college dorm, the two hostels in Jaffa provide fabulous alternatives.

▨ **Old Yafo Hostel,** 8 Olei Tzion St. (☎ 682 23 70; fax 682 23 16; ojhostel@shani.net). Walk one block past the clocktower on Yefet St. and turn left onto Olei Tzion St. It's rare that a hostel feels enchantingly antique without an accompanying layer of grime, but the Old Yafo manages superbly. Fully stocked bookshelves and a large rooftop garden make for delightful finishing touches. Kitchen available. Storage for non-guests NIS1. Laundry NIS10. Internet NIS10 per 15min. Reception 8am-11pm. Check-out noon. No curfew, but lights off at 11pm. Payment in any major foreign currency avoids 17% VAT. 6-bed dorms (coed or female-only)

NIS40/US$8.50. Singles NIS147/US$30; with TV, bath, A/C, and kitchen NIS226/US$46. Doubles NIS168/US$34; with TV, bath, A/C, and kitchen NIS246/US$50.

Beit Immanuel Hostel, 8 Auerbach St. (☎682 14 59; fax 682 98 17; beitimm@netvision.net.il; www.inisrael.com/beitimmanuel). From the clocktower, head toward Tel Aviv on Raziel St. for 5min. until it turns into Eilat St. Turn right after 12 Eilat St. onto Auerbach St. On bus #46, get off on Eilat St. near the gas stations. This family-oriented Christian hospice has a garden and playground. Breakfast included. Dinner NIS40. Shabbat NIS60. Laundry NIS10. Reception 7am-11pm. Check-in 3pm. Check-out 1pm. Lockout 10am-noon. Curfew 11pm. All rooms have A/C. Dorms NIS48/US$12; singles with bath NIS180/US$45; doubles with bath NIS280/US$70.

🍴 FOOD

The maze of narrow streets surrounding the Jaffa Clocktower is peppered with cheap falafel stands (NIS7-10), *al-ha'esh* (barbecue) meat establishments, and sweets vendors, some of which are open 24hr. The cafes and restaurants in the Old City tend to be generic, but the surrounding gardens and views of the Mediterranean make them some of the loveliest tourist traps imaginable. For a touch of romance and a big hit to the wallet, head to Jaffa Port, off Pasteur St. on the far side of the artists' colony, where picturesque waterfront restaurants offer seafood so fresh the gills are almost moving (daily catch entrees NIS42 and up). Jaffa is also one of the best places to get a great meal on Shabbat.

- 🍽 **Said Abou Elafia and Sons,** 7 Yefet St. (☎681 23 40), 1 block behind the Jaffa clock-tower. Popularly known as "Aboulafia," this bakery is so famous that its name is used by Israelis to denote all stuffed-pita foods. Try the *za'tar*-spiced toasts, flaky Iraqi pita with cheese, or honey-drenched baklava (NIS3-8). Take-out only. Open 24hr. Cash only.

- 🍽 **Parabin Yafo,** 20 Ogan St. (☎518 09 62), in the port, about 400m past the fancy fish restaurants. Feel like a *sheikh*, or at least incredibly chic, while lounging on pillows and puffing *argileh* (NIS17) in this lantern-lit hideaway. From 10pm, there's a line of large groups. Huge salads NIS25-27. Creamy hummus plates NIS12-18. Orgasmic chocolate cake NIS24. Open Sa-Th 8:15pm-3am, F 10:45pm-6am. Credit cards accepted.

- **Shipudei Itzik Hagadol/Big Itzik's Skewers,** 3 Raziel St. (☎518 18 02), a couple blocks before the clocktower. Green neon Hebrew sign. Hungry locals meet, greet, and eat skewered meat at this clean, friendly establishment. Herbivores and carnivores can achieve peaceful coexistence over a sampler platter of 18 salads (NIS14 per person), sizzling kebabs (NIS15 each), and huge, warm pita. Open Sa-Th 11am-1am.

- **Dr. Shakshuka,** 3 Beit Eshel (☎682 28 42), corner of Yefet St. Libyan food in the heart of Old Jaffa. Eponymous dish is the *shakshuka*—a mouth watering tomato and egg concoction (NIS18). Open Su-Th 9am-1am, F 9am-sundown, Sa sundown-midnight.

👁 SIGHTS

SHUK HA-PISHPESHIM. Jaffa's large Shuk Ha-Pishpeshim is one of the livelier markets in Israel, with roofed rows of overflowing stalls offering dust-covered knick-knacks, modern hand-dyed clothing, Persian carpets, leather goods, and brassware. A vast selection of enormous *argilehs* is also available. (*To reach the flea market, go 1 block past the clocktower along Yefet St., and turn left.*)

CLOCKTOWER AND ENVIRONS. Built in 1906 to celebrate the 25th anniversary of Sultan 'Abd al-Hamid II's ascension to power, the clocktower marks the entrance to Jaffa from Tel Aviv. Originally, the clocktower's four faces were split between Israeli and European time for the convenience of European sailors. On the right of the clocktower is **al-Mahmudiyya Mosque,** an enormous structure erected in 1812 that only Muslims may enter. Head to the right and up the hill along the Mifratz Shlomo Promenade to the **Museum of Antiquities of Tel Aviv-Jaffa,** which contains artifacts from Neolithic to Roman times and a collection of coins found in the area. (☎682 53 75. Open Su-Th 9am-1pm. NIS10, students and seniors NIS5.)

KIKKAR KEDUMIM. The old city's tourist center is Kikkar Kedumim. Following signs to the visitors center, head down to the underground plaza to the excavations from 2300-year-old Tel Yafo, get a short history lesson, and pick up free maps. (*Continue along Mifratz Shlomo past the Napoleonic Cannons, pass the Church of St. Peter and go up a large staircase. Open Su-Th 9am-10pm, F 9am-2pm, Sa 10am-10pm. Free. Church open daily 8-11:45am and 3-5pm; public masses in English Sa 8pm and Su 9am.*)

To the right of the Kikkar, just before the cafes and shops, a small alleyway leads to the colorful **Greek Orthodox Church of St. Michael,** which is worth a brief tour. (*Open daily 8-11:45am and 3-5pm.*)

The wooden footbridge from Kikkar Kedumim leads to **Ha-Pigsa Gardens,** used by both Arab and Jewish couples to take wedding pictures. The point offers Jaffa's best view of the coast, Tel Aviv, and **Andromeda's Rock.**

JAFFA PORT. The port, past the bottom of the artists' colony to the right along Pasteur St. was the perfect depth for King Solomon when he imported rafts of cedars from Lebanon to build his temple. It was too shallow, however, for larger ships. The infamous port caused Dutch sailors to term the impossible as "entering Jaffa." Today, the port is more accessible and is an active fishermen's wharf.

NEAR TEL AVIV

HERZLIYA הרצליה ☎ 03

Named after Theodore Herzl by the seven Zionist pioneers who settled the area (see **Zionism,** p. 266), Herzliya is more colloquially known as "the Bank of Israel" because of the affluent tourists and Israeli vacationers who flock to its beautiful shores. In the never-ending battle for the "best beach in Israel" title, Herzliya is a prime contender. Only 15km outside of Tel Aviv, Herzliya makes a great daytrip from the city; there are no budget accommodations.

TRANSPORTATION. Herzliya's **bus station** is at the corner of **Ben-Gurion St.** and **Ha-Atzma'ut Rd.** Buses #501 (35min., every 20min. 5:30am-11:30pm, NIS7) and 502 (30min., every 15min. 9am-7pm, NIS7) run between Herzliya and Tel Aviv. They stop running at around 5:30pm on Friday and start again at 8:20pm on Saturday.

ORIENTATION AND PRACTICAL INFORMATION. The town's cultural hub, the **Yad Labanim Memorial Center,** is at the corner of Ben-Gurion and **Ha-Banim St.;** from the bus station, go two blocks left on Ben-Gurion St. The main shopping area in Herzliya can be found by turning right from the central bus station, and making a left on **Sokolov St.** after a few blocks. City bus #29 goes to the beaches in Herzliya's suburb, Herzliya Pituah. (10-30min. depending on traffic, NIS5).

FOOD. It's a good idea to eat in town before hitting the beach. There are refreshment stands right off the ocean, but they have high prices and little variety. Ben-Gurion has a number of cheap eats, including the falafel stand at 10 Ben-Gurion St., diagonally across from the central bus station. Tuvya, an Egyptian expat who charms his patrons in English, French, Arabic, and Hebrew, serves deliciously fresh falafel (NIS7) and a variety of salads. There is also a **supermarket** in the shopping center on the left side of Ben-Gurion St., one block before Sokolov St. (Open Su-Th 9am-7pm, F 9am-1pm.)

BEACHES. The beaches in Herzliya Pituah range from the large, soft-sanded variety to the small and rocky type. The **Dabesh Beach** and **Arcadia Beach,** near the marina at the end of the bus line, belong to the former category and accordingly, charge admission (NIS12, children NIS8). While the size and sand of the **Sidna Ali** beach pales in comparison, admission is free, and it is the only beach without wall-to-wall umbrella lounge-chairs. People walking 1km from Sidna Ali to the pay-beaches (left as you face the sea) or those claiming to stay at one of the hotels (for example, Hotel Arcadia or Hotel Ha-Sharon) are often not required to pay. From the bus stop in Sidna Ali, the beach is up the hill and through the gate.

The Sidna Ali beach has other reasons to visit as well. The **Sidna Ali Mosque** allows modestly dressed visitors to visit when it is not prayer time. Women must cover their heads and shorts are forbidden. After the Mamluks destroyed the area during the Third Crusade, the mosque was named after one of Salah al-Din's soldiers who died in a battle on the hill on which the mosque stands.

HERMIT'S HOUSE. Herzliya's most worthwhile attraction is an inhabited sand castle known as the Hermit's House. This fantastical residence built into the side of a cliff by "hermit" **Nissim Kakhalon** is a must-see for anyone to whom "arts and crafts" is not incompatible with Surrealism. Kakhalon claims, "I make it from my love. I make it good." In other words, he spent 29 years turning other people's garbage (tires, toys, tiles, etc.) into this hallucinogenic maze of winding tunnels, flower-strewn antechambers, and plush gardens. Even more impressive, everything in the artful interior is absolutely functional, from the bathroom ceiling made entirely of Maccabee Beer bottles to the loveseat with a mirrored mosaic on one side and a huge sculpted stone face on the other. Nothing goes to waste here: Kakhalon even uses the manure from his family of goats to grow fragrant basil. Kakhalon's tours depend on the extent to which his guests are appreciative. This hermit is quite friendly, after all, and more showman than recluse. During the week, Kakhalon runs a cafe serving hummus (NIS15) and smoked fish (NIS50). (9am-sundown; hours erratic; closed for Shabbat.)

BEIT RISHONIM. Zionist history buffs may enjoy the Beit Rishonim (Founders' Museum), 8-10 Ha-Nadiv St. From Sokolov St. turn right on Ha-Nadiv St. and continue two blocks. The museum narrates the history of Herzliya, beginning with its days as a colony in 1924, using computerized presentations as well as items from the early settlement period. (☎950 42 70. Open M 8:30am-12:30pm and 4-6:30pm, Tu-Th 8:30am-12:30pm. NIS8, students and children NIS4, seniors free.)

OTHER SITES. The **Yad Labanim Memorial Center** houses the diminutive and avant-garde **Herzliya Museum of Art.** The contemporary exhibits are well worth the short trip from the bus station. (☎09 955 10 11 or 950 23 01; www.adgo.co.il/herzliya_museum. Open Su, Tu, and Th 4-8pm; M, W, F, and Sa 10am-2pm. Free.) An outdoor amphitheater is attached to the building and overlooks the museum's modern **Sculpture Garden,** which is the setting for concerts by the **Herzliya Chamber Orchestra** (☎09 950 07 61), as well as an annual theatrical festival in May.

ASHKELON אשקלון ☎07

Ashkelon's strategic position along major naval and land routes made it desirable property for almost every ancient empire, from the Greeks to the Muslims. First rising to prominence as one of the Philistines' five great cities (although settlements here date back to the 3rd millennium BCE), Ashkelon reached its zenith as an independent city-state in the Roman period. Today, its main attractions are its sandy beaches, seaside national park, and well-known archaeological sites.

⊏ TRANSPORTATION. The **Central Bus Station** (☎677 82 22) on Ben-Gurion Blvd., a 30min. walk from the beach, runs **buses** to: **Be'er Sheva** (#363 and 364; 1½hr.; every 45min.-1hr. 5:45am-8:05pm; NIS23.50); **Jerusalem** (#437; 1½hr.; every 45min.-1hr. 5:50am-7:15pm; NIS22.50); and **Tel Aviv** (#300, 301, and 311; 1¼hr.; every 15-30min. 5:20am-9pm; NIS18.20-21.50). **Local bus** #5 goes to Zephania Sq. in the heart of the Afridar neighborhood and to the *midrahov* in the Migdal area, stopping at the central bus station. Catch it on the Ben-Gurion (front) side of the station for Migdal, or on the right side of the station for Afridar (every 12-20min., NIS4). **Bus** #6 (bus #13 July-Aug.) goes to the National Park and shoreline (NIS4). **Sherut** go to **Tel Aviv** (NIS16) and **Be'er Sheva** (NIS20).

◪ PRACTICAL INFORMATION. The **Tourist Office** (☎ 673 24 12) is in City Hall, behind the bus station. Walk down the alley between the bus station and the Giron Mall to Ha-Gvurah St., turn left, and continue halfway down to the shopping center on the right. A Hebrew sign and flags fly in front, but the entrance is on the right. Ask about tours to local sights and activities. (Open Su-Th 8am-1pm and 4-6pm.) Change money at **Bank Ha-Poalim** (☎ 567 33 33), one block past the City Hall. **ATMs** accept NYCE, Cirrus, and major credit cards. (Open Su, Tu, and W 8:30am-1:15pm, M and Th 8:30am-1pm and 4-6:30pm, and F and holiday eves 8:15am-12:30pm.) The **post office** in Migdal on the *midraḥov* has good rates with no commission. For **first aid** call ☎ 672 33 33. The **police** (☎ 677 14 44) are at the corner of Ha-Nassi and Eli Cohen St. From the tourist office continue on Ha-Gvurah, and bear right. The **post office** (☎ 672 36 06) is behind the building with the town hall, near the *kenyon* Giron. (Open Su-Th 8am-2:30pm, F 8am-noon.)

▟◖ ACCOMMODATIONS AND FOOD. Cheap accommodations are lacking in Ashkelon. Free **camping** is normally available at the **Park Leumi Ashkelon** (Ashkelon National Park; ☎ 673 64 44). Call before your visit to see if any are available to tourists. There is no guard on duty from 8pm until 7am. Entrance to the park is free by foot, NIS15 by car. The snack bar and beach-side restaurants in the park are convenient and relatively inexpensive (steak, *shishlik*, or hamburger in a pita NIS15-25). Camping on the beach adjacent to the city is **dangerous** and not recommended.

The Herzl St. *midraḥov* in Migdal has the highest concentration of affordable eateries. Near the *midraḥov* is a lively *shuk*. From the *midraḥov*, take Ha-Kerem St. toward David Remez St.; the *shuk* is on the right. (Open M, W-Th 7am-7pm.) There are a number of outdoor, locally frequented, inexpensive restaurants on the corner of Ha-Nasi and Zephania St. at the Afridar Center, with *schnitzel*, hamburger, steak, and pizza for about NIS20. **Delilah Beach boardwalk,** a stone plaza up toward the street from the beach, showcases the city's collection of fish restaurants (meals NIS35-80). From the station, take bus #5 toward Afridar, get off at Zephania Sq., and backtrack a street to the highly visible front of the **Chinese Restaurant Furama,** 24 Ort St. Chow down on sweet and sour pork for NIS40 or wonton soup for NIS10. (☎ 673 84 97. Open daily noon-3pm and 7pm-midnight. Credit cards accepted.) In the middle of the *midraḥov* is **Titanic,** one of the more popular falafel joints. Get a falafel (NIS10) or satisfy your iceberg-sized hunger with a shawarma sandwich on delicious *lafah* bread. (NIS18. Open daily 8am-9pm.)

◙ SIGHTS. The Ashkelon National Park was built on the site of 4000-year-old Canaanite remains, buried beneath ruins of Philistine, Greek, Roman, Byzantine, Crusader, and Muslim cities. Traces of the once-thriving Philistine city surround the picnic tables and snack bars. The **Bouleuterion,** a series of Hellenistic and Roman columns and capitals, graces the park's center. It served as the Council House Sq. when Ashkelon was an autonomous city-state under Severius in the 3rd century CE. The courtyard-like area next to the Bouleuterion is actually the inside of a Herodian assembly hall; it contains two **statues** of Nike, the winged goddess of victory, and an Italian marble statue of the goddess Isis with her god-child Horus, sculpted between 200 BCE and 100 CE. Behind the Bouleuterion lies a preserved **amphitheater.** Along the southern edge of the park are segments of a wall from the 12th-century **Crusader city.** A short hike past the amphitheater affords a close-up view of the walls and a glimpse of Ashkelon's Rothenberg Power Station. Most peculiar is the assembly of Roman columns jutting out of the ancient Byzantine sea wall on the beach. These massive marble columns were used to support the walls, which were destroyed in 1191 by Salah al-Din. Richard Lionheart partly restored them in 1192, as did Cornwall in 1240, only to have them demolished by the Sultan Baybars in 1270. *(30min. walk from the bus station. From the station, turn right onto Ben-Gurion Blvd. and follow it to the T junction at the coast, before the soldiers' recreation facility (note the striking sculpture of Samson). Turn left onto the road to the park; a small orange sign points the way. Bus #6 to the park is infrequent. ☎ 673 64 44. Open daily 7am-7pm; in winter closed Sa. Free, NIS15 with car. Maps at the main entrance.)*

ISRAEL

◖◖ ⎚ **BEACHES AND ENTERTAINMENT.** Ashkelon's coast has four beaches where swimming is permitted; **Delilah Beach** is the most popular. White flags signal safe bathing and black flags signal dangerously rough water. At Delilah Beach, breakwaters lessen the chance of black-flagging, and shady canopies and snack bars provide relief to sun-scorched bathers.

▶ DAYTRIP FROM ASHKELON: BEIT GUVRIN

*To reach Beit Guvrin, first travel to Kiryat Gat, which is easily accessible by bus from Tel Aviv (#369, 1¼hr., every 30min., NIS18); Jerusalem (#446, 1¼hr., every hr., NIS23.50) and Ashkelon (#025, 35min., every 30min, NIS11.50.) Bus #011 from Kiryat Gat goes directly to Kibbutz Beit Guvrin (25min.; Su-Th 8:05am and 5:10pm, F 8:05am and 2pm; return Su-Th 8:30am and 5:30pm, F 8:30am and 2:30pm; NIS8.50). If you miss the bus from Kiryat Gat, **Kiryat Gat Taxis** (☎ 393 60 09), in the back of the gas station to the left, takes you to Beit Guvrin (NIS60, but try haggling). Call for a taxi from Beit Guvrin back to Kiryat Gat. The park is just off Rte. 35, near Kibbutz Beit Guvrin, across from the gas station. Bring a hat or white scarf, sunglasses, sunscreen, and at least 1.5L of water.*

Beit Guvrin was a flourishing Jewish metropolis in the 4th and 3rd centuries BCE and in the years between the destruction of the Second Temple and the Bar Kokhba Revolt (132-135 CE). The Arab village of Beit Jibrin stood nearby until the 1948 War, when its inhabitants were evacuated; since 1949, the modern kibbutz of Beit Guvrin has rested on its ruins. Once known as the biblical city of **Maresha,** one of the cities of Judah fortified by Rehoboam (Joshua 16:44), the area was settled by Edomites after the destruction of the First Temple, Sidonians during the 4th century BCE, and eventually Greeks, who converted it into a bustling economic center. The complicated caves and magnificent views of **Beit Guvrin National Park,** encompassing the ruins of Maresha and Beit Guvrin, are some of Israel's buried treasures. The park also contains some of the 800 glaringly white and chalky **bell-shaped caves** that characterize the Beit Guvrin region, hidden among the cacti and fig trees. Most of the caves were carved by Greeks, Byzantines, and others as they quarried for limestone. Once dug, the caves were used for storage, penning animals, and water collection, and later became sanctuaries for hermits and monks. St. John and others came here seeking solitude, and they often carved crosses and altars into the walls. The walls of the **Columbarium Cave** contain hundreds of small holes once used for storing pigeons for food, fertilizer, and cult rituals. The ruins in the lower city, near the *tel*, are worth the hot and hefty walk. Most impressive are the Hellenistic houses with their maze-like series of underground cisterns.

BETWEEN TEL AVIV AND HAIFA

The stretch of coastline north of Tel Aviv is home to much of Israel's population and most of its agricultural output. Zionists and refugees poured onto the beaches in the beginning of the 20th century and drained the swamps of the coastal plain, clearing the path for a modern, industrial state.

NETANYA נתניה ☎ 09

Netanya celebrates laziness in all its glorious forms—baking on the beach, strolling aimlessly along the Promenade, and sipping coffee and people watching in Ha-Atzma'ut Sq. In the 1920s, the town was established itself with a citrus farm and a few diamond factories, but the tantalizing call of idyllic beaches and the prime location between Tel Aviv and Haifa soon made Netanya one of the most popular hotspots in Israel. In both location and ethos, Netanya leans closer to Tel Aviv; there are even rumors among the locals of mafia infiltration, but crime is far from a glaring problem in this resort town. A significant minority of the tourists hail from land-locked parts of Israel, but there is a decidedly European, especially French, presence in Netanya. Because of the large Russian immigrant population, signs and menus are more often in French and Russian than in English. While the crowd is mostly affluent retirees and families (increasingly more of the latter), students and lone travelers are heartily welcomed into the chilled-out subculture of the young locals.

ISRAEL

TRANSPORTATION

Buses: Central bus station, 3 Binyamin Blvd. (☎860 62 02 or 860 62 22), on the corner of Binyamin Blvd. and Ha-Halutzim St. To: **Haifa** (#947, 45min., every 30min., NIS21.50); **Jerusalem** (#947, 1½hr., every 30min., NIS38); **Tel Aviv** (#601 and 605; 1hr.; every 15min. 5:40am-10:30pm; NIS13).

Sherut: Across from the station on Binyamin Blvd. To Tel Aviv NIS11.

Taxis: Main services include **Ha-Shahar** (☎861 44 44), **Ha-Sharon** (☎882 23 23), **Hen** (☎833 33 33), and **Netanya** (☎834 44 43).

Car Rental: Hertz (☎882 88 90), **Avis** (☎833 16 19), and **Eldan** (☎861 69 82) have offices at Ha-Atzma'ut Sq.

ORIENTATION AND PRACTICAL INFORMATION

To get to the center of town from the **central bus station** (☎860 62 02), cross the intersection to **Sha'ar Ha-Gai St.** and follow the falafel stands one block to **Herzl St.**, the town's central artery and main shopping area. Turn left and after a few blocks, just past **Dizengoff St.**, Herzl St. empties into the **midraḥov** (pedestrian zone), lined with expensive outdoor cafes and shawarma stands. At the end of the *midraḥov* is **Ha-Atzma'ut Sq.** (Independence Sq.), marked by a central fountain, benches and palm trees. Most Netanyans spend their days and nights milling around this area. Stairs to the beach are at the back of the square. Also at the back of the square, on your right as you face the sea, is the entrance to the **Promenade,** a walkway along the cliffs overlooking the sea with an **outdoor amphitheater** and a few playgrounds.

Tourist Office: (☎882 72 86), at the very back corner of Ha-Atzma'ut Sq., next to the Diamond Center in a tiny brick building with an oddly angled roof. City maps, bus schedules, and event schedules. Many languages spoken. Don't be fooled by the large Foreign Resident and Tourist Center at 15 Herzl St.; it's an investment center. Open Su-Th 8am-6pm, F 9am-noon; in winter Su-Th 8am-4pm and F 9am-noon.

Currency Exchange: Global Change (☎872 47 56; fax 872 47 59), on the left of Ha-Atzma'ut Sq., changes money with no commission. Open Su-Th 8am-7pm and F 8am-1pm. **Bank Ha-Poalim,** on the right as the *midraḥov* empties into Ha-Atzma'ut Sq. Open Su-Tu and Th 8:30am-3pm, W 8:30am-1:30pm, and F 8:30am-12:30pm. **Bank Leumi** (☎860 73 33; fax 860 73 29), on the corner of Herzl and Weizmann St. Open Su and Tu-W 8:30am-1pm, M and Th 8:30am-1pm and 4:30-7pm, F 8:30am-noon. No exchange Su. Commission NIS25.

English-Language Bookstores: Steimatzky Booksellers, 4 Herzl St. (☎861 71 54), on the left of the *midraḥov*. Sells books and magazines in Hebrew, English, and a variety of other languages. Open Su-Th 8am-8pm, F 8am-2pm.

Emergency: Magen David Adom First Aid: ☎862 33 33 or 862 33 35. **Police:** ☎860 44 44. **Fire:** ☎862 22 22.

Hospital: Laniado Hospital (☎860 46 66) is the main hospital. From the central bus station, walk down Binyamin Blvd. past Herzl (street will become Sderot Weizmann). Turn left on Rabbi Akiva and right on Divrei Ha-Yamim; the hospital is on the right.

Telephones: Solan, 8 Ha-Atzma'ut Sq. (☎862 21 31). Private booths for international calls. Fax, telegrams, and cellular phone rental. Open daily 8am-11pm.

Internet Access: Solan (☎862 21 31) has private A/C booths with dial-up connections. NIS12/US$3 per 15min., NIS20 per 30min., NIS28 per hr. Open daily 8am-11pm. **Pinati Internet Cafe,** 15 Remez St. on the corner of Remez and Smilansky (☎862 46 04). In a small cafe selling ice cream (NIS6) and light meals (NIS19-35). NIS8 per 15min., NIS15 per 30min., NIS500 per 5hr. Open Su-Th 9am-9pm, F 9am-1pm.

Post Office: The central branch, 57 Herzl St. (☎862 15 77), offers **Poste Restante.** Another **branch** at 2 Herzl St. (☎862 77 97). Open Su-Tu and Th 8am-12:30pm and 3:30-6pm, W 8am-1:30pm, F 8am-noon.

ISRAEL

ACCOMMODATIONS

A cheap sleep can be hard to find in Netanya. The hotels, most of which line the beach along **Gad Machnes St.** and **David Ha-Melekh St.,** are fairly expensive (singles NIS240/US$60; doubles NIS300/US$75; add NIS110 for each additional adult). American cash can be used as a bargaining tool, hence prices in dollars don't often jive with standard conversion rates. Reservations are necessary to secure one of the few pleasant and affordable options; call at least two weeks ahead in the summer and a month in August. The most popular areas for **beach-sleeping** are near the cafes and on benches that line the promenade. Since camping on the beach is unsafe, especially for solo women, *Let's Go* does not recommend it.

■ **Orit Hotel,** 21 Ḥen Blvd. (☎/fax 861 68 18; orith@bezenqint.net), off Dizengoff several blocks to the left of Ha-Atzma'ut Sq. This hotel provides a peaceful atmosphere and many perks, including beach towels and a library of Scandinavian and English books. The amiable Swedish management will even pick up guests from the airport (NIS140/US$35). Scrupulously clean rooms, private baths, fans, and balconies. No smoking. Breakfast included. Reception 7am-11pm, but guests can borrow keys to return after it closes. Check-out 10am. Singles NIS170/US$35; doubles NIS240/US$50; each additional bed NIS95/US$20.

Atzma'ut Hostel, 2 Usishkin St. (☎862 13 15; fax 882 25 62), at the corner of Ha-Atzma'ut Sq. and Usishkin St., on the left as you walk through the square from the *midraḥov*. Within stumbling distance of both the square and the beach. The warm and accommodating owners allow early check-ins if a room is ready and luggage storage if it is not (NIS10). To avoid late night noise, ask for a room that does not overlook the square, preferably one with a view of the sea. A/C, fridges, and private baths in all rooms. Reception 24hr. Check-out 11am. 6 and 10-bed (coed) dorms NIS50/US$10; singles NIS100/US$20; doubles NIS150/US$30.

FOOD

Cheap food *is* available in Netanya. During the day, the **Shuk Ha-Ir** (the City Market) one block north of Herzl St. overflows with cheap produce and fresh pastries; Pita and hummus for NIS15 on the beach but prices go down and quality goes up closer to the central bus station. **Sha'ar Ha-Gai St.** is lined with self-service falafel stands where one can stuff just about anything into a pita. Just about any place in the square offers a Sabra breakfast—with two eggs, salad, roll and jam, coffee and juice—for NIS20. The blue-and-white **Telad Cafe,** on the right side of the square, serves particularly magnanimous portions. Stock up at the **Nitza Supermarket,** 8 Nitza Blvd. (☎862 82 16), off David Ha-Melech St.

Mini Golf Restaurant and Pub, 21 Nitza Blvd. (☎861 77 35), perches on the edge of a cliff overlooking the sea. Ideal for a lazy lunch or snack, the restaurant serves up inner peace, a great view, and scrumptious stuffed vegetables (NIS18, with pita), but no putt-putt. Closed on Shabbat.

Bat Ikar, 14 Sha'ar Ha-Gai St., across from the bus station, fills the tummies of weary travelers and locals alike. Open 24hr., except for Shabbat. The house specialty, *sambusa* (delicate bread folded around your choice of stuffings, such as cheese and sauce or potatoes), is substantial enough for a light meal (NIS9-10). Pastries go for NIS1-4, any one of their 102 types of bread NIS1-3.

Kinamon, 13 Remez St. (☎832 25 44), on the corner of Dizengoff St. This candlelit restaurant serves more than *schnitzel*. The munchies platter, a heaping basket of stuffed pastries and vegetables, serves 2-3 (NIS33, add pesto for NIS2). Open Su-Th 8:30am-12:30am, F 8:30am-4:30pm and 7:30pm-12:30am, Sa 6pm-12:30am.

Le Moulin, 13 Ha-Atzma'ut Sq. (☎862 77 13), on the right side at the end of the *midraḥov*. This creperie adds a little French flair to the standard fare of the square. People-watch from the outside or chill inside with the A/C while noshing on entree crepes of egg, cheese or meat (NIS17-28) or dessert crepes oozing at the seams with chocolate, fruit, or ice-cream (NIS12-25). Open daily 8am-1am; closed for Shabbat.

👁 🎵 SIGHTS AND ENTERTAINMENT

ABECASSIS STUDIO. The art scene in Netanya is limited, but this small studio displays the work of Raphael Abecassis, an internationally acclaimed artist who uses brilliant colors and modern design to portray ancient Sephardic themes. (*4 Razi'el St. next to the post office; from the* midraḥov, *walk 1km along Herzl St. and turn left on Razi'el St.* ☎ *862 35 28. Open Su-Th 10am-1pm and 4-8pm and F 10am-1pm).*

BEACHES. Netanya's **beaches** are certainly its *raison d'être*. The stunning Mediterranean coast in Netanya is clean, free, and stretches on for 11km. **Herzl Beach,** the most crowded one, just below Ha-Atzma'ut Sq., has waterslides, playing courts, and surfboards for rent. **Sironit Beach,** just to the left of Herzl as you face the sea, is the only one open year-round; the others are open from May to October. **Kiryat Sanz Beach,** farther north, caters to the religious sunsoakers with separate bathing hours for men and women. (*Men: Su, Tu, Th mornings and M, W, F afternoons. Women: M, W, F mornings and Su, Tu, Th afternoons).*

FREE ENTERTAINMENT. The Netanya municipality organizes various forms of free entertainment almost every night during the summer and often during the winter. Stop by the tourist office for a complete listing of concerts, movies, and other activities. During the summer, you can watch the sun set over the Mediterranean while listening to classical music in the **Amphitheater** on the Promenade (check the tourist office for times). On Saturdays in summer, folk dance performers in Ha-Atzma'ut Sq. passionately incite the crowd to come join their revelry. Every Monday at noon, talented Russian musicians give classical concerts at 11 Ha-Atzama'ut Sq. (*☎ 884 05 34. NIS18, includes food at pre-concert reception.)*

🎭 NIGHTLIFE

Uranus Pub, 13 Ha-Atzma'ut Sq. (☎ 882 99 19), on the right as you enter Ha-Atzma'ut Sq. from the *midraḥov.* Fashioned after traditional English pubs, Uranus skips the froufrou and gets back to basics with a wide selection of beer (NIS13-17), straight-up liquor (starting at NIS26), and a laid-back twenty-something crowd. Open daily 8pm-5am.

Ropongi Pub, 9 Herzl St. (☎ 882 92 99), about halfway between the *midraḥov* and Binyamin Blvd. Packed with locals and an international crowd tossing back whatever beer and eating whatever sandwich happens to be Ropongi's special (each NIS14-19).

The Place (☎ 844 32 11), down a flight of stairs from 11 Ha-Atzma'ut Sq. Attempts to stem the exodus to Tel Aviv dance clubs with a barrage of bouncers, a strictly enforced dress code (no jeans, but spandex and cleavage almost mandatory), and plenty of neon and blacklight. Russian locals groove to international pop music. Those who opt against the steep cover (NIS50) can still hang out in the adjacent bar. Beer NIS14-20, cocktails NIS33-38. Open Th-Sa 10:30pm-6am.

CAESAREA קיסריה ☎ 06

At the end of the first century BCE, **Herod the Great,** vassal king of Judaea, established *Caesarea Maritima* (Caesarea of the Sea; Kay-SAHR-ya in Hebrew), a resplendent city of innovative architecture and huge entertainment complexes. The multi-layered ruins—astonishingly resilient despite riots and rebellions, pillage and plunder, and a partial sinking of the coastline—now constitute one of Israel's finest archaeological sites and most popular tourist attractions. The city rapidly became a great commercial center and was soon the headquarters of the Roman government in Palestine; the procurator of Caesarea from 26 to 36 CE was Pontius Pilate, who ordered Jesus' crucifixion in 33 CE.

Not only Romans, but also Samaritans and Jews flocked to the town, and ethnic conflict expanded with the population. This clash between Jews and pagans ignited the six-year **Jewish Rebellion** (the Great Revolt), which resulted in the destruction of Jerusalem's Second Temple in 70 CE (see **Ancient History,** p. 266). The Romans celebrated Jerusalem's fall by slaughtering thousands of Jews in Caesarea's amphitheater and crowning the commanding general Vespatian as Caesar. Despite the widespread eradication of the Jews, Caesarea's Jewish community remained cohesive and staged a revolution 62 years later, led by **Simon Bar Kokhba.** Legend has it that **Rabbi Akiva,** one of the greatest Jewish sages, supported Bar Kokhba and was jailed in Caesarea by the Romans. They tore him apart with iron combs, and to this day some Jews of the region wear their hair unkempt to memorialize him. Jews returned to the city en masse when Judah the Prince lifted the ban on living there a few centuries later; previously, the city had been deemed impure. In the 3rd century, a school for rabbinical studies was founded, and the city's rabbis are mentioned frequently in the Talmud.

▐ TRANSPORTATION

Getting to Caesarea can be difficult. The only practical way is via **Ḥadera,** the nearest town. Buses to Ḥadera are plentiful: from **Tel Aviv** (#852 or 872; 1hr.; NIS17.20); **Netanya** (#706, 35min., every 30min., NIS8.30; #921, 1hr., every 40min., NIS17.2); **Haifa** (#945, 40min., every 1½hr., NIS17); and **Jerusalem** (#945, 2hr., a few times per day, NIS33). From Ḥadera, however, only bus #76 goes to the ruins (30min., NIS8.30) and travels only a handful of times per day. The bus stops at the three entrances to the archaeological park: next to the Roman theater, near the eastern gate of the Crusader wall, and just south of the Crusader city wall (this stop upon request only). While it is possible to get a taxi from the station in Ḥadera (NIS30), finding one for the ride back from the ruins requires advance arrangements and costs about NIS10 more.

▐ ACCOMMODATIONS

Friendly **Kibbutz Sdot Yam** (☎636 44 70 or 44; fax 636 22 11; kef-yam@sdot-yam.org.il; www.kef-yam.co.il) feels like a ritzy summer camp. To get to the reception office, get off bus #76 at the Roman theater. The kibbutz's main gate is on the left of the theatre, next to the snack bar. Walk about 100 yards behind the tile factory, turn right at the fork in the road just after the tile factory, and follow the signposts to the "Kef Yam" office building at the end of the road. Fifteen private apartments (all with air-conditioning, private bath, refrigerators, TV, and telephones) are ideal for families or for three- to four-person groups, while 6-bed dorms come with bath, TV, linens, and air-conditioning. (Reception open daily 7am-5pm; in winter 7am-4pm. Check-out 10am. Safe available in office. Call at least one week in advance. 6-bed dorms Apr.-June NIS120/US$30 per person; NIS80/US$20 each additional adult; NIS72/US$18 each additional child. Prices up NIS10-20 July-Oct. and down NIS10-20 Nov.-Mar. Extra 15% weekends and holidays.) Many visitors unroll their sleeping bags on the beach, but **camping** in some places, such as Hof Shonit Beach, is forbidden. **Sleeping on the beach** is unsafe; *Let's Go* does not recommend it.

▐ FOOD

Restaurant prices in Caesarea are as high as the Crusader walls. Establishments within the ruins (right at the harbor), such as **Herod's Kosher Restaurant** (☎636 11 03) and **Charley's Restaurant** (☎636 30 50), offer great views but mostly standard fare at outrageous prices (*schnitzel* NIS40-55). The **Sdot Yam Cafeteria,** in the kibbutz, offers a taste of kibbutz life and kibbutz food like *ktsitsot*, salads, and mashed potatoes. (☎636 45 14. All-you-can-eat breakfast buffet 7-10am, NIS23; lunch noon-3pm, NIS38; dinner 6:30-8:30pm, NIS23.) Stock up on picnic supplies like fresh produce and other staples at Sdot Yam's mini-market **Markol** in the lower level of the dining hall building. (☎636 43 58. Open Su, Tu, and Th 11am-1pm and 4-6pm; M and W 11am-1pm. Non-kibbutzniks pay 20% more. Cash only.)

☉ SIGHTS

Caesarea's main sights are the Roman city, ancient port, and large Crusader fortress. A map (NIS10) sold at the three entrances to the **Caesarea National Park** provides a good history of Caesarea, and a well-illustrated booklet (NIS17, includes map) explains each well-labeled site. *(Park open Su-Th 8am-5pm, F 8am-4pm; in winter Su-Th 8am-4pm, F 8am-3pm. NIS18, students NIS15. Hold onto your ticket stub!)*

OTHER SIGHTS. A stroll through the peaceful **Kibbutz Sdot Yam** (see p. 330) provides a good antidote to the feel of the ruins. Shaded paths wind lazily through the well-manicured landscape, past kibbutzniks' cottages and a **playground** constructed from an airplane donated by the Air Force in gratitude for seven kibbutzniks who served about 25 years ago. The two museums in the kibbutz (follow the signs) are small but staffed by knowledgeable and amiable curators.

Most of the relics unearthed at Caesarea are on display at the **Sdot Yam Museum of Caesarea Antiquities** (☎636 43 67). The new archaeological garden and the museum's three rooms contain Jewish, Christian, Samaritan, and Muslim artifacts, Canaanite pottery, 3500-year-old Egyptian urns, and Roman coins and statues. Shield the eyes of any small children from the erotic oil lamps. Next to the museum is the **Hannah Senesh Memorial Center** (☎636 43 66), built in honor of a Sdot Yam parachutist who died while trying to save Jews from the Nazis during World War II. Admission includes a short film about Senesh's life offered in six different languages. *(Both open Su-Th and Sa 10am-4pm, F and holidays 10am-2pm. Museum and center NIS10, students and seniors NIS9.)*

☎♫ BEACHES AND ENTERTAINMENT

While the intensely blue water is cool and inviting, swimming within the walls of the city is not very economical (NIS25, NIS19 children). Tickets can be bought at Charley's Restaurant (see p. 330) or at the office inside the Crusader fortress walls. Unless you wish to snorkel in the ancient harbor, the free public beach behind the aqueduct is a better place to swim. Diving in the harbor is an expensive but rewarding experience. The Caesarea Diving Center provides full scuba equipment, beginner lessons, and snorkeling gear. Those who plan to dive without a guide must bring their license, insurance, and log. (☎/fax 626 58 98. Full equipment NIS170 per day; snorkeling gear NIS58 per day. Half-day lessons NIS190/US$50; full-day lessons including trip to sunken port NIS380/$US100. Open daily 9am-4pm.) The Kef Yam Office in the kibbutz offers glass-bottomed boat tours of the harbor (NIS32), wild tornado-boat rides off the beach (NIS45), and jeep tours to the Carmel Mountains. (☎636 44 44. Reservations required. NIS520/US$130 per 2hr. trip with up to 4 people.)

HAIFA חיפה حيفا ☎04

Since the prophet Elijah fled the wrath of King Ahab to the caves of Mt. Carmel (I Kings 18-19), Haifa has harbored religious minorities. Crusaders built the first of several monasteries above Elijah's Cave, which eventually gave shelter to the wandering Carmelite Order of Monks. German Templars established Haifa's German colony, and the Baha'i built their world headquarters here. In the 1930s, waves of European Jews seeking refuge from Nazism poured onto Haifa's beaches.

As a result, Haifa developed the philosophy, "live and let live." When the British decided to construct a port in the city, Arabs and Jews flocked to the economic opportunities and worked side-by-side in factories. Though they went home to separate neighborhoods, the municipality as a whole employed and was supported by members of both communities. Of course, the War of 1948 affected Haifa like all other areas, with thousands of Arabs abandoning the city; but today, Haifa's population of a quarter million includes a sizeable Arab minority and a small Orthodox Jewish community, who live together with little tension. Haifa University has the largest Arab population of any university in Israel and a joint community center promotes relations at the local level, especially among children. Not surprisingly, supporters of the Israeli-Palestinian peace accords often cite Haifa as the paradigm for peaceful Jewish-Arab co-existence.

✈ INTERCITY TRANSPORTATION

Trains: Central station in Bat Galim (☎856 44 44), is connected by tunnels to the central bus station. Trains to: **Akko** (30min., NIS11); **Hadera** (50min., NIS16); **Nahariya** (40min., NIS13); **Netanya** (NIS19.50) via **Binyamina** (45min., NIS16); **Tel Aviv** (1hr., NIS21). The trip to Jerusalem requires a station change and will take longer than the bus. Trains are generally the best choice when traveling north. 10% discount with student ID. The tourist office has schedules. Credit cards accepted.

Buses: The **central bus station** (intercity info ☎851 22 08), is at Jaffa Rd. and Rothschild Blvd. Intercity buses generally run Su-Th 5:15am-11:30pm, F 5:15am-5pm, Sa 5pm-midnight. Buses to: **Ben-Gurion Airport** (#945 and 947, 2hr., every 30min., NIS28); **Jerusalem** (#940 (direct) 2hr., #945 and 947 (via Ben-Gurion) 3hr.; NIS40); **Nahariya** (#251, 271, and 272; 1¼hr.; every 15-20min.; NIS13.80) via **Akko** (50min., NIS11.50); **Nazareth** (#331 and 431, 1½hr., every 40min., NIS18.20); **Tel Aviv** (#900 (direct) and 901 (express), 1½hr., every 20min., NIS20.50); **Tiberias** (#430 (direct) and 431, 1½hr., every hr. 5:30am-8pm, NIS23.50).

Ferries: Terminal (☎851 82 45) next to Merkaz train station, off Ha-Atzma'ut St. Ferries to Cyprus and mainland Greece (Th 8pm, F 7pm, and sometimes Su 8pm). Security checks are often several hours prior to departure. Check ahead. South Africans need visas to enter both countries. Tickets at **Caspi Travel,** 76 Ha-Atzma'ut St. (☎867 44 44. Open Su-Th 9am-5pm, F 9am-1pm.) Ferry tickets also available through ISSTA.

Taxis: Most taxis leave from Eliyahu St. in Paris Sq., near the Carmelit stop or from Ha-Ḥalutz St. and Herzl St., near bus stops in Hadar. For *special* (home pick-up) taxis, call **Kavei Ha-Galil** (☎866 44 44 or 22). To: **Akko** (NIS80), **Nahariya** (NIS120), or **Lod** (NIS280). **Amal's Sherut Service** (☎866 23 24) will take you from 6 Ha-Ḥalutz St. in Hadar to **Tel Aviv** (NIS22) and **Ben-Gurion Airport** (NIS45). Other taxi services include **Carmel Ahuza** (☎838 27 27) and **Merkaz Mitzpeh** (☎866 25 25 or 866 83 83). For 24hr. direct service to Ben-Gurion Airport, try Kavei Ha-Galil or Amal.

Car Rental: Avis, 7 Ben-Gurion Blvd. (☎851 30 50); **Budget,** 46 Ha-Histadrut Blvd. (☎842 40 04); **Hertz,** Ha-Histadrut Blvd. (☎840 21 27); **Reliable,** 140 Yafo Rd. (☎850 79 07); **Eldan,** 95 Ha-Nassi Blvd. (☎837 53 03). All open Su-Th 8am-6pm, F 8am-2pm. Most rent to 24+; Eldan will rent to 21+ with double insurance payments.

⚏ ORIENTATION

Situated on a small peninsula, Haifa rises from the Mediterranean coast up the steep, northern slopes of Mt. Carmel. It calls itself the "gateway of the North" for good reason; the cliffs of Rosh Ha-Nikra (and the Lebanon border) are less than 50km to the north. The Sea of Galilee is 70km to the east, and the ruins of Caesarea 40km to the south. The city itself is divided into three terraces and in this vertically oriented town, social stratification is more than just a metaphor; the rich really do live on the top, the poor at the bottom.

The **Ir Ha-Tachtit area** (downtown) fans outward from the port and **Ha-Atzma'ut Rd.** The **Old City** is one block back around **Yafo Rd.,** and it extends to the right (if facing the port) toward **Kikkar Paris,** the lowest stop of the Carmelit subway. Slightly higher up and to the left, the traditional Middle Eastern neighborhood **Wadi Nisnas** lies on and around **Khuri St.** Farther to left, **Ben-Gurion St.** runs uphill and intersects Yafo Rd. at the bottom, **Ha-Meginim Ave.** near the German Colony, **Allenby Rd.** near the **tourist office,** and **Ha-Geffen St.** at the first of the Baha'i gardens. Much farther left on the lower terrace, the **central bus station** adjoins the **train station** at the inter-

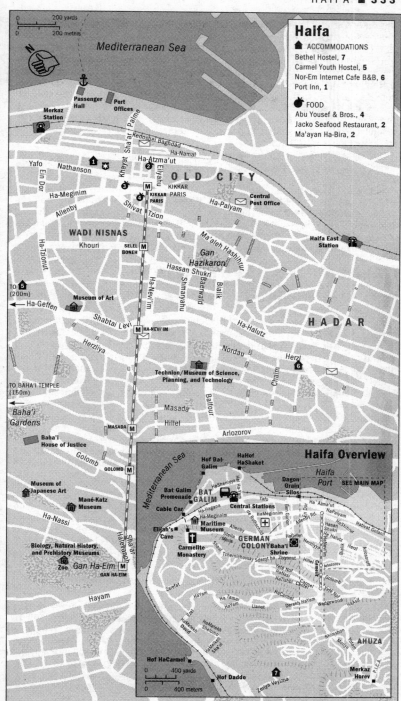

Haifa

⌂ **ACCOMMODATIONS**
Bethel Hostel, **7**
Carmel Youth Hostel, **5**
Nor-Em Internet Cafe B&B, **6**
Port Inn, **1**

🍎 **FOOD**
Abu Yousef & Bros., **4**
Jacko Seafood Restaurant, **2**
Ma'ayan Ha-Bira, **2**

Mediterranean Sea

Passenger Hall
Port Offices

Merkaz Station

Yafo
Nathanson
En Dor
Ha-Meginim
Allenby
Ha-Tzionut
Khayat Sha'ar Palme
Kedoshei Baghdad
Ha-Atzma'ut
Ha-Namal
Eliyahu
KIKKAR PARIS
KIKKAR PARIS
Shivat Tzion
Central Post Office
Ha-Palyam

OLD CITY

WADI NISNAS
Khouri
SELEL BONEH

Ma'aleh Hashihrur
Gan Hazikaron
Hassan Shukri
Simayahu
Baerwald
Bialik

Haifa East Station

TO (200m)
Ha-Geffen
Museum of Art
Shabtai Levi
Ha-Nevi'im
HA-NEVI'IM

HADAR
Ha-Halutz

Herzliya
Nordau
Chaim
Herzl

Technion/Museum of Science, Planning, and Technology

TO BAHA'I TEMPLE (150m)
Baha'i Gardens

Masada
Hillel
Balfour
Arlozorov

MASADA

Baha'i House of Justice
Golomb
GOLOMB

Museum of Japanese Art
Mané-Katz Museum
Ha-Nassi

Biology, Natural History, and Prehistory Museums
Zoo
Gan Ha-Eim
GAN HA-EIM

Sha'ar Halevanon

Hayam

Haifa Overview

Mediterranean Sea

Hof Bat-Galim
HaHof HaShaket

Bat Galim Promenade
BAT GALIM
Cable Car

Central Stations
HaMeginim
Ha-Hagana
Ha-Meginim
Maritime Museum

Elijah's Cave

Carmelite Monastery
GERMAN COLONY
Baha'i Shrine

Dagon Grain Silos

Haifa Port

SEE MAIN MAP

Yafo
Ben Gurion
Ha-Azma'ut
HaPalyam
Hassan Shukri
Hativat Golani
Ma'aleh Hashihrur
Ha-Halutz
Herzl

Stella Maris
HaGefen
Herzliya
Allenby Rd.
Allenby

Tchernichovsky Sderot ha-Ziyyonut

Yefe Nof
HaNasi
HaTishbi
Zarefat
HaYam
Llanot
Center
HaCarmel
Derekh HaYam

Yefe Nof
Hillel
Arlozorov
Golomb
Yefe Nof
Wedgewood
HaSfek

Ein
HaMelekh David
NaMelekh Shelomo
HaMelen Shaul

AHUZA
Shimshon
Moriah
Yasmin
P.I.C.A.

Merkaz Horev

Hof HaCarmel
Hof Daddo
Zeiya Veyizha

0   400 yards
0   400 meters

0   200 yards
0   200 meters

ISRAEL

section of Yafo Rd. and **Rothschild Boulevard,** in the **Bat Galim** neighborhood. Yafo then becomes **Ha-Haganna Ave.,** which curves around the peninsula to the beaches.

The middle terrace, the **Hadar** district, teeters precariously on the trendy-trashy border and is home to many clothing stores, cheap hotels, bakeries, and bazaar stands. The two main streets are **Herzl St.** and **Ha-Halutz St.** Ha-Halutz runs parallel to Herzl but one block down. Buses from Herzl go up the mountain, while buses from Ha-Halutz go to the central bus station. The street parallel to and above Herzl is the quiet **Nordau midrahov** (pedestrian zone). **Balfour St.,** perpendicular to these three and bordering Nordau on the left as you face the port, leads up to **Masada St. and Hillel St.** Hadar's Carmelit stop is at the intersection of Herzl St. and **Ha-Nevi'im St.,** a few blocks past Balfour.

The highest area, known as **Carmel Center,** glitters with posh homes, five-star hotels, restaurants, and bars. This district is traversed by **Ha-Nassi Boulevard** and **Yefeh Nof St.** Both pass the Dan Panorama Hotel, next to the **Louis Promenade,** which offers a view of the lower city and the port area. One block up Ha-Nassi is **Gan Ha-Eim,** a peaceful park, near the last Carmelit stop. **Hayam Road** branches to the right off Ha-Nassi and **Wedgewood Ave.** to the left as you walk from the Carmelit stop. The **Cultural Center** and several cafes and bars are farther up Ha-Nassi as it curves right. From Carmel Center, it's a long walk on Moriya St. or a quick ride on bus #24 or 37 to Ahuza—a yuppie district with cafes, restaurants, and Merkaz Horev, a large shopping center.

▤ LOCAL TRANSPORTATION

BUSES. The **central bus station** (city line info ☎854 91 31), like the city itself, has three tiers. Intercity buses leave from the first floor, city buses depart from the second, and all buses arrive on the third. Intercity buses stop at the bus station and in Hadar along Herzl after 8pm. All urban rides cost NIS5; a 15-ride pass is NIS47.

On weekdays, buses run from about 5:30am to 11pm. On Fridays, they stop at around 4:30pm, depending on when Shabbat starts. **Saturday buses** usually begin running at 9:30am, run less frequently than on weekends, and do *not* run from the central bus station; instead they run from the Hadar area (many from Daniel St.) until about 6pm, when they switch back. **Sherut** taper off a couple hours later than buses; many go to Hadar only (NIS4.50), while others follow specific bus routes.

Haifa's bus routes are extremely circuitous and a 20min. walk (though uphill) may be a 30min. bus ride. To get **Downtown (Ha-Ir)** from the central bus station, take bus #17 or 41; from other parts of town, take any bus in the 70s. Almost every bus numbered 1-40 eventually stops in Hadar, but from the central bus station, #15 and 18 run most frequently. Those in the 20s go to **Carmel** and **Ahuza,** and #24 and 37 continue on to the **University of Haifa.**

SUBWAY. The best way to travel within Haifa is the Carmelit subway system, a train slanted just enough to make the ascent or descent seem flat. Though this subway has only one line, its six stops conquer steep hills and put most neighborhoods within walking distance. Starting from the bottom, the subway stops at Kikkar Paris, Solel Boneh, Ha-Nevi'im, Masada, Golomb, and Gan Ha-Eim. Yellow pavilions indicate entrances. (☎837 68 61. Every 6-7min.; Su-Th 6am-10pm, F 6am-3pm and 8pm-midnight, Sa in winter 7pm-midnight. NIS4.70 per ride for adults and children, NIS3 for seniors; 10-ride pass NIS42, NIS32.50 for seniors and those under 18. Credit cards accepted.)

CABLE CARS. A more scenic, but also more expensive alternative for getting from bottom to top and back again is to take the **Rakbal cable cars** (☎833 59 70). Colloquially known as "the Carmel's Eggs" for their ellipsoidal shape, the cable cars run down the Carmel's northwestern slope, shuttling between the orange-and-turquoise **Yotvata B'Ir** dairy restaurant on the Bat Galim Promenade and the **Stella Maris monastery** area at the mountain's peak. To Bat Galim, take bus #41 or 42; to Stella Maris take #25 or 26. (Open daily 9am-midnight; in winter 9am-7pm. NIS16, round-trip NIS22.)

7 PRACTICAL INFORMATION

TOURIST AND FINANCIAL SERVICES

Tourist Office: 48 Ben-Gurion St. (☎853 56 06; fax 853 56 10; haifa5@netvision.net.il). Take bus #22 to the corner of Ben-Gurion and Ha-Gefen St. or walk several blocks to the left of Kikkar Paris Carmelit along Ha-Meginim Ave. and turn left on Ben-Gurion. Distributes free maps (more detailed ones NIS3), and the bimonthly *Events in Haifa* booklet. Free short film on Haifa's highlights. Open Su-Th 8:30am-6pm, F 8:30am-2pm.

Tours: Society for the Protection of Nature in Israel (SPNI), 18 Hillel St. (☎866 41 35), on the 4th fl. Information and maps (NIS62, in Hebrew) on hiking trips into the Carmel Mountains. Tours arranged with the Tel Aviv office. Open Su-Th 9am-2pm, F 8am-1pm.

Budget Travel: ISSTA, 20 Herzl St. (☎868 22 22). ISIC NIS40; HI membership NIS30. Student rates on plane and ferry tickets. Open Su-Tu and Th 9am-7pm; in winter 9am-6pm. Also at: **Technion** (☎832 67 39; fax 832 67 41), in the Student Building. Open Su-Th 9am-5pm; in summer F 9-11:30am. **Haifa University** (☎825 39 51; fax 834 53 06), next to the #37 bus stop.

US Consulate: 26 Ben-Gurion St. (☎853 14 70; fax 853 14 76; consage@netvision.net.il), in Hadar. Open Su-Th 9am-1pm (call first). In an emergency, call 03 519 73 70.

Currency Exchange: Any post office will exchange money without charging a commmission. Also, no-commission services cluster around Palmer Sq., by the port, and by the Gan Ha-Eim Carmelit stop. Banks generally charge a commission: min. US$6, max. 15%. **Bank Ha-Poalim,** 1 Ha-Palyam Blvd. (☎868 14 11). Currency exchange open M-Th 8:30am-2:30pm, F 8:30-11:30am.

American Express: Meditrad Ltd., 6 Ha-Yam St. (☎836 26 96). **Client Letter Service** available. Open Su-Th 8:30am-5pm, F 8:30am-12:30pm.

LOCAL SERVICES

Shopping Hours: Most shops open Su-Th 8:30am-1:30pm and 4-7pm, F 8:30am-1pm; some open Sa 8-11pm. Larger stores and malls usually open 8:30am-7pm.

English-Language Bookstore: Steimatzky, 16 Herzl St. (☎866 50 42), has paperbacks, magazines, and travel books. Open Su-Th 8:30am-7pm, F 8:30am-2pm.

Camping Supplies: Ha Metayel, 2 Balfour St. (☎864 42 44), next to ISSTA. Open Su-M and Th 9am-7pm, Tu 9am-6pm, W 9am-2pm, F 9am-1pm. Also on the 2nd fl. of the central bus station.

Ticket Offices: Haifa Municipal Theatre, (☎860 05 00) puts on everything from classic Neil Simon to edgy new Israeli playwrights. There are also general ticket offices for an array of plays, musicals, and concerts. **Haifa,** 11 Baerwald St. (☎866 22 44). Open Su-W 9am-1pm and 4-7pm, Th-F 9am-1pm.

Laundromat: Wash and Dry, 5 Ha-Yam Rd. (☎810 78 50), in Carmel Center. NIS12 for up to 7kg; NIS1 per min. to dry. Open Su-M 8:30am-5:30pm, Tu 8:30am-3pm, W-Th 8:30am-5:30pm, F 8:30am-2pm.

Swimming Pools: Maccabee Pool, 19 Bikurim St. (☎838 83 41), in Central Carmel. Heated and covered in winter. Open Su, Tu, and Th 6am-2pm and 4-10pm; M and W 6am-2pm and 6:30-10pm; F 6am-2pm and 4-6pm. NIS40. The **Dan Panorama Hotel,** 107 Ha-Nassi Blvd. (☎835 22 22), has a pool open to the public Su-F 7am-5pm, Sa 7am-2pm and 4-5pm. NIS40.

EMERGENCY AND COMMUNICATIONS

Emergency: First Aid: 6 Yitzḥak Sadeh St. **Police:** 28 Jaffa St. **Emotional First Aid** (☎867 22 22). English spoken. Open 24hr.

Pharmacies: Ha-Ḥalutz, 12 Ha-Ḥalutz St. (☎862 06 29), in Hadar. Open Su-Th 8:30am-1pm and 4-7pm and F 8:30am-1pm. **Merkaz,** 130 Ha-Nassi Blvd. (☎838 19 79), in Carmel Center. Open Su-Th 8am-7pm, F 8am-2pm.

ISRAEL

Hospitals: Rambam (☎854 31 11), in Bat Galim; **Benei Zion (Rothschild),** 47 Golomb St. (☎835 93 59); **Carmel,** 7 Michal St. (☎825 02 11); **Herzliya Medical Center** (HMC), 15 Ḥoret St. (☎830 52 22).

Internet Access: Nor-Em Internet Cafe. See accommodations below.

Post Office: Main branch at 19 Ha-Palyam Blvd. (☎830 41 82), offers **Poste Restante.** Other branches at Shabtai Levi and Ha-Nevi'im St. (☎864 09 17); 152 Jaffa Rd., on the corner of Sha'ar Palmer; 63 Herzl St. in Hadar; and 7 Wedgewood Blvd. next to #37 bus stop at Haifa University. Most open Su-Th 8am-5pm, F 8am-noon, except for the Shabtai Levi St. branch, which is open until 6pm on Su-Th.

⚑ ACCOMMODATIONS

Options are slim, but growing in Haifa. The two *Let's Go* thumbpicks listed here have made enormously welcome contributions to the budget scene. Also, the Haifa Tourist Board (☎853 56 06) now arranges **B&B stays in private homes** (NIS25-60). Religious hostels offer immaculate premises, but strict curfews thwart night-life revelry. Beyond these options, buyer beware and take a good look around before committing.

▧ **Nor-Em Internet Cafe Bed & Breakfast,** 27-29 Nordau St. (☎866 56 56; info@norem.israel.net; www.norem.israel.net), off Haim St., between Herzl St. and the Nordau *midraḥov.* Brand spanking new, this B&B offers spacious rooms, all with A/C and immaculate bathrooms. Laid-back, backpacker-friendly staff serves up drinks, sandwiches, and advice on the city 24hr. a day in the posh cafe. Check-out noon. 6-bed dorms (coed) NIS80/US$20; singles NIS160/US$40; doubles NIS220/US$55. 10% discount for stays longer than 3 days; 20% discount for stays longer than a week.

▧ **Port Inn,** 34 Yafo St. (☎852 44 01; fax 852 10 03; port_inn@yahoo.com), downtown. From the central bus station, take bus #3 or 5 to the intersection of Ha-Atzma'ut St. and Ben-Gurion. The Port Inn yearns to be your home away from home with a den-like social room, free use of the kitchen and coffee supplies, and a warm and advice-laden manager, who will even do your laundry (NIS30). Internet NIS0.50 per min. A/C in all rooms. Reception 7:30am-midnight; ring the bell anytime. Check-out 11am. 6-bed dorms (single-sex and coed) NIS45/US$11.25, with breakfast NIS55/US$13.75; singles and doubles NIS170/US$42.50, with bath NIS200/US$50.

Carmel Youth Hostel (HI) (☎853 19 44; fax 853 25 16), 4km south of the city at Ḥof Ha-Carmel (Carmel beach). Bus #43 from the central bus station and 44 *alef* from Hadar go directly past the hostel. Though extremely far from the center of town and a schlep from the beach, this simple hostel offers large rooms, cool breezes, and shaded woods. All rooms with A/C and bath. Breakfast included. Lockers NIS6. Check-in 2pm-8pm. Check-out 10am. 6-bed dorms (single-sex) NIS80/US$20; singles NIS128/US$38; doubles NIS224/US$56; triples NIS288/US$72; quads NIS352/US$88; quints NIS416/US$104. HI-card carriers get NIS5 discount.

Bethel Hostel, 40 Ha-Geffen St. (☎852 11 10). Take bus #22 from central bus station to Ben-Gurion St., walk up to Ha-Geffen, and turn right. The hostel is on the right after a couple blocks. A buzz-killer during party time, but in a quiet neighborhood close to the center of town. Christian volunteers keep the rooms sparkling. All rooms have fans. Shared bath in hall. Free dinner on Shabbat and sometimes M and Th. No smoking. Under 18 must be with an adult. Check-in Sa-Th 5-10pm and F 4-9pm. New arrivals may leave bags in locked storage and return after 5pm to register. Lockout 9am-5pm; strict 11pm curfew; wake-up 7am. 8- to 12-bed single-sex rooms NIS56/US$14.

◗ FOOD

Downtown overflows with shawarma and falafel shops, the best option for meals on Shabbat. There's more falafel (there's always more falafel) to be found in Hadar along Herzl and Ha-Ḥalutz St., and slightly more expensive cafes dot the **Nordau midraḥov** (pedestrian section). The lower, even-numbered end of Herzl St.—where the heady fragrance of fresh burekas and croissants wafts from a strip of bakeries—indulges a sweet tooth, but only until early evening. The area around the Gan Ha-Eim Carmelit stop serves a late night crowd with a mix of chain restaurants, ice cream stands, and several popular cafes and bars along Natanson St.

There is an inexpensive **fruit and vegetable market** just west of the Kikkar Paris station. Another **shuk** lies one block down from Ha-Ḥalutz St., around Yehiel St., where Haifans purchase cheap clothes, groceries, and wine. Finally, Khuri St. in Wadi Nisnas can satisfy any *shuk*-cravings on Shabbat. Be stubborn and bargain.

Iraqi Shishkebab, 59 Ben-Gurion St. (☎852 75 76). The owner will put anything in a pita to make the mother of all meals. Divine kebab skewers (NIS3 for 2) set a new standard for the culinary arts. Open Su-Th 12:30-10:30pm.

Ma'ayan Ha-Bira, 4 Natanson St. (☎862 31 93), in the midst of the *shuk,* look for Carlsburg signs on your left if coming from the Kikkar Paris Carmelit station. This diner's claim to fame is its home-smoked meats (NIS20-38). Eastern European delicacies like *ikra* (fish salad, NIS15) and *kisonim* (meat dumplings, NIS15) also served. Open Su-F 8am-6pm. Credit cards accepted.

Jacko Seafood Restaurant, 12 Kehilat Saloniki St. (☎866 88 13), near the Kikkar Paris Carmelit station and parallel to, but 1 block past, the *shuk.* Owner is a former fisherman who still gets fresh seafood daily (entrees NIS30-60). Enjoy cheap Turkish desserts like *malaby* or semolina with coconut (NIS10). Open Su-F noon-11pm, Sa noon-6pm. Credit cards accepted.

Abu Yousef and Brothers (☎866 37 23), in Kikkar Paris across (away from the port) from the Carmelit. This spacious restaurant in the heart of downtown serves up Middle Eastern delights including kebab, *shishlik,* and *sinaya* with pine nuts (NIS30-40). All dishes come with fries, coffee, and pita on the side. A shot of licorice-flavored *'araq* (NIS7) makes a good *digestif.* Open Sa-Th 8am-midnight, F 8am-6pm.

👁 SIGHTS

BAHA'I SHRINE. The golden-domed Baha'i Shrine that dominates the Haifa skyline commemorates the Persian Sayyid Ali Muhammad (the Bab), the first Baha'i prophet. In 1890, Baha'ullah, the founder of the Baha'i faith (see **The Baha'i,** p. 60), selected this spot on Mt. Carmel, near where he pitched his tent following his exile from Persia to Akko, and instructed his son 'Abd al-Baha to bury the Bab here and build a great temple in his honor. Though the Bab was executed in 1850 for his religious teachings, devotees transferred his remains numerous times for almost 60 years to prevent them from falling into enemy hands. Finally, in 1909, the Bab was laid to rest as Baha'ullah had wished, inside the shrine, beneath the red carpet. 'Abd al-Baha built the preliminary structure and Shoghi Effendi, Guardian of the Baha'i religion from 1921 to 1957, embellished and expanded the structure. Modest dress is required and visitors must remove their shoes before entering the shrine. For a stunning view of the entire grounds, look up from Ben-Gurion St. or down from Yefeh Nof St., just past the Louis Promenade. *(Take bus #22 from the central bus station or downtown or bus #23, 25, 26, or 32 from Ha-Nevi'im and Herzl St. to Ha-Tzionut Ave., just above the shrine. Once the project is completed, visitors can ascend the stairs from Ben-Gurion at the bottom, or weave down through magnificent gardens from Yefeh Nof St. ☎835 83 58. Open daily 9am-noon; gardens open daily 9am-5pm. Free.)*

MONASTERY OF THE CARMELITE ORDER. A Latin monk named Berthold founded the Carmelite order in 1156, but the Sultan Baybars destroyed the monastery in 1291. Originally built because the monks were not allowed to live in Elijah's Cave, the beautiful monastery, which stands on a promontory over Haifa bay, seems a more than reasonable replacement. The monks currently live in a relatively new church and monastery complex called Stella Maris (Star of the Sea), built in 1836 on the ruins of an ancient Byzantine chapel and a medieval Greek church. The monastery's small museum contains finds from the Byzantine and Crusader settlements on Mt. Carmel, including toes from a large statue of Jupiter that once stood on an altar on the mount. Because of the Carmelites' affinity for Elijah (St. Elias), the Feast of St. Elias (July 20) is a great time to visit. In the days preceding the Feast, Christian Arabs set up booths with food and games, and a carnival atmosphere takes over the complex. Knees and shoulders must be covered. *(Buses #25, 26, 30 and 31 climb Mt. Carmel to the monastery; get off at to the Seminar Gordon stop. A more expensive and scenic way to get to the monastery is via the Rakbal cable car from Bat Galim; see p. 334. ☎833 77 58. Open daily 6am-1:30pm and 3-6pm.)*

ELIJAH'S CAVE. Judaism, Christianity, and Islam all revere these grounds as sacred and even magical. According to the Bible, the caves at the base of Mt. Carmel sheltered Elijah from the wrath of the evil King Ahab and Queen Jezebel. They were more than a bit peeved at the prophet's drastic attempt to win the hearts of northern Israelites from Ba'al in the 9th century BCE when he brought down a heavenly fire to consume his sacrifices and then slaughtered the 450 priests of Ba'al (I Kings 18). Muslims revere Elijah as al-Khadar, the "green prophet" of the same-colored mountains, Jews believe he will return as the harbinger of the Messiah, and Christians hold that the caves safeguarded the Holy Family upon their return from Egypt. Adherents of each religion now pray quietly in the dim light. Modest dress is required, and there is no eating or drinking inside the cave. The religious (and not so religious) worshipers offering their blessings for you expect pocket change in return. *(230 Allenby Rd. The stairs leading to the cave's entrance are just across from the National Maritime museum, but construction may force you to go around to the left as you face the cave. Just across from the monastery entrance, an inconspicuous trail leads 1km down the Stella Maris ridge to the shrine at Elijah's Cave; do not attempt in sandals. ☎852 74 30. Cave open Su-Th 8am-5pm, F 8:30am-12:45pm. Free.)*

TECHNION. Real nerds can check out the Technion, Israel's internationally acclaimed institute of technology. The Coler Visitors Center has English-language newsletters and computerized displays describing the institution's history and achievements from its inception in 1913 to the present. *(Take bus #17 or 19 from downtown, Hadar, or central bus stations; or, #31 from Carmel Center to Kiryat Ha-Technion. ☎832 06 68 or 832 06 64. Open Su-Th 8am-2pm. Free.)*

🏛 MUSEUMS

HAIFA MUSEUM

The museum consists of three separately located buildings, each on a different level of the city. All are open M, W, and Th 10am-5pm; Tu 10am-2pm and 5-8pm; F 10am-1pm; Sa 10am-2pm. A ticket admits the bearer to all 3 museums for 3 days in a row. NIS22, children under 18 and students NIS16, seniors NIS11.

MUSEUM OF ART. This avant-garde collection ranges from simplistic blank canvases to downright wacky shoebox architecture. The museum has a small permanent collection but prides itself on its ever-changing, multi-national exhibits. *(26 Shabtai Levi St. in the Hadar district. Take bus #10, 12, 21, or 28. ☎852 32 55.)*

TIKOTIN MUSEUM OF JAPANESE ART. The Japanese tradition of displaying beautiful objects in harmony with the season has been embraced by this branch of the Haifa Museum. *(89 Ha-Nassi Blvd, in Carmel Center, between the Nof Hotel and the Dan Carmel Hotel. Take bus #3, 5, 21-23, 28, or Gan Ha-Eim Carmelit. ☎838 35 54.)*

NATIONAL MARITIME MUSEUM. The lowest branch of the Haifa Museum (in altitude, not quality). Chronicles 5000 years of maritime history. The intricately detailed ship models, the marine mythology collection, and the Department of Marine Ethnology have the most appeal for the average landlubber. *(198 Allenby Rd., opposite Elijah's Cave. Take bus #3, 5, 44, or 45. ☎853 66 22.)*

OTHER MUSEUMS

REUBEN AND EDITH HECHT MUSEUM. This museum houses a permanent exhibit called *The People of Israel in the Land of Israel*, a magnificent collection of archaeological finds from excavations across the country, as well as changing exhibits in its new wings. The small art wing contains Hecht's personal collection of Impressionist paintings and a few others from the Jewish School of Paris. *(On the 1st fl. in the main building of Haifa University. ☎825 77 73 or 824 05 77. Open Su-M and W-Th 10am-4pm, Tu 10am-7pm, F 10am-1pm, Sa 10am-2pm. Call for tour info. Free.)*

MA'AGAN MIKHEAL SHIP PROJECT. The main exhibit for the next several years is the reconstruction of an amazingly preserved Phoenician ship from 500 BCE. It was found off the coast of Caesarea, which didn't even have a port in 500 BCE. *(Within the Hecht museum, but affiliated with Haifa University. Hours and information number the same as the Hecht museum.)*

CLANDESTINE IMMIGRATION AND NAVAL MUSEUM. Devoted to *Ha-Apala*, the story of European Jewish immigrants smuggled into Palestine during the British mandate (see p. 266). The museum showcases impressive displays on Jewish underground movements and a recreation of a Cyprus deportation camp. Perched atop the museum is the *Af-Al-Pi-Khen* (In Spite Of Everything), a ship that once ran the British blockade in the 1940s. *(204 Allenby Rd., next to the National Maritime Museum and opposite the lower cable car station. Take bus #3, 5, 43 or 44. ☎853 62 49. Open Su-Th 9am-4pm. NIS10, children and students NIS5, free for soldiers from any country.)*

MANÉ KATZ ART MUSEUM. While the museum usually displays sculptures and canvases by Mané Katz, a member of the Paris group of Jewish Expressionists that included Modigliani, Chagall, and Cremegne, it packs everything up in storage a few times a year for special exhibits of contemporary Israeli artists. *(89 Yefe Nof St., just behind Panorama Center. ☎838 34 82. Take bus #21, 22, 23, or 28, or Gan Ha-Eim Carmelit. Open Su-M and W-Th 10am-4pm, Tu 2-6pm, F 10am-1pm, Sa 10am-2pm. Free, except during special exhibits when the price ranges between NIS10-25.)*

◨ ◪ BEACHES AND ENTERTAINMENT

The beaches surrounding Haifa may not be as large as Tel Aviv's or as beautiful as Netanya's, but they're still a great place to sun-worship or take a see-and-be-seen stroll. Although free beaches sprawl all along the northern coast, the best lie just outside of the city in **Dor** (see p. 342) and **Atlit**, both accessible by bus #921. Within Haifa, **Ḥof Ha-Carmel** and **Ḥof Dado** are most pleasant (bus #43, 44 or 45; 15min.). Hordes of Israelis pour down to these beaches on Friday and Saturday afternoons to play *matkot* (paddleball) and people-watch on the promenade; in summer, the bikini-clad and the men who love them hang out long after sunset. Near the central bus station **Ḥof Bat Galim** (bus #41, 42) has a more sedate promenade. On Tuesday evenings in summer, folk dancers kick it up at both promenades. **Ḥof Ha-Shaket** (Quiet Beach), is a true-to-name, separate-sex beach. (Women Su, Tu, and Th; men M, W, and F; co-ed Sa.) Lifeguards work from 8am-6pm at each of the beaches.

In the beginning of July, the nearby town of Carmiel fills with people coming to see the **Israeli Music and Dance Festival.** Carmiel is normally accessible from Haifa by buses #261 262, 361 and 501 (every 20-45min., NIS18), and Egged provides extra transportation during the festival. The artsy **Cinematheque,** 142 Ha-Nassi Blvd. (☎835 35 30), is next to the Cultural Center, a few blocks up from the Carmelit station, just after Ha-Nassi curves right. This theater shows cult classics, new Israeli films, film noir, and the latest US fare. (Su-Th shows 7, 9:30pm, and occasionally 5pm; F shows 2 and 10pm; Sa shows 5, 7, and 9:30pm. NIS27.)

🎵 NIGHTLIFE

PUBS

The Bear, 135 Ha-Nassi Blvd. (☎838 17 03), on the corner of Ha-Nassi and Wedgewood Ave., a few blocks up from the Carmel Center Carmelit stop. Everything seems sexier (even before the 4th beer) in this mellow, candlelit bar. Pleases the upper twenty-some thing crowd with indoor and outdoor seating and a monstrously large drink menu. Beer NIS15-22. Cocktails NIS27. Open daily 6pm-3am.

Little Haifa, 4 Sha'ar Ha-Levanon St. (☎838 16 58), between Ha-Nassi and Yefe Nof St., a block down from Gan Ha-Eim park. The oldest pub in the area, with a raucous decibel level matching its age. Drunk American sailors sing about home. Beer NIS10-12. Open M-Sa from 8:30pm until the ship leaves port.

Camel Cafe, down the coast at Hof Ha-Carmel. Almost every customer has a delicious fruit shake (NIS18, with alcohol NIS27) and a navel ring. Skinny dipping is rumored to occur. Beer NIS15-21. Open daily 8am-sunrise.

CLUBS

Hurva (☎862 12 65), on Qedoshe Baghdad St. off Ha-Atzma'ut St. Probably best to take a cab. A veritable carnival of a club, Hurva offers 1 dance floor with alternative and Euro-techno downstairs and another on the roof with MTV standards. Henna tattoos (NIS18). Beer NIS10-13; cocktails NIS18. Th 21+ and F 18+. No dress code. Cover NIS30, students with ID NIS25. Open Th-F from 12:15am.

City Hall (☎862 88 02), on Shabtai Levi St., which Herzl turns into after crossing Ha-Nevi'im St. Recently relocated from downtown to Hadar, this Haifan institution opened its doors in the '80s, and its DJ has yet to leave the decade. Beer NIS12-15, free on Th. F men 23+ and women 21+. No dress code. Beer NIS12-15. Cover Th-F NIS40 and Sa NIS35. Open Th-Sa until the dancers collapse.

🎵 DAYTRIPS FROM HAIFA

ISFIYA AND DALIYAT AL-KARMEL ☎04

Bus #22 (40min., departs infrequently 1-4:30pm, NIS5) leaves from the central bus station, stops in Isfiya, and then continues along the main road to Daliyat. The best option is to take a sherut; they leave from Kikkar Paris off Ha-Atzma'ut St. (to Isfiya NIS11, to Daliyat NIS12) and return from the Egged bus stops in Isfiya (across from the Stella Hospice) and Daliyat (at the top of the shuk). It is also possible to catch a bus or sherut to or from the University of Haifa. The last bus leaves Daliyat at 2:10pm, but sherut run until 5pm, when stores close.

Isfiya and Daliyat al-Karmel are all that remain of 14 Druze villages that once prospered on the Carmel. In 1830, the Egyptian *pasha* crushed a rebellion and then destroyed the area's villages. Thirty years later, the Turks welcomed Druze back to Isfiya and Daliyat, hoping that the towns would serve as buffers against Bedouin marauders and Christian missionaries. Today, some 17,000 Druze make their homes here. Religious Druze elders sport thick mustaches, baggy pants, and flowing white headdresses. Observant Druze women wear dark robes and long white shawls (for more information, see **The Druze,** p. 60). A large portion of the population, however, is secular. Unlike those residing in the Golan Heights, the Druze of the Carmel acknowledge their Israeli citizenship, and young men enlist in the army. Although Daliyat is by far the more touristed and interesting of the Druze villages, a visit to Isfiya provides more authenticity.

The scenic mountain road to the Druze villages inspires even the most agoraphobic travelers to explore the outdoors. The ridges and forests of the Carmel Mountains spread dramatically into the Yizre'el valley to the southeast and the Mediterranean to the west. SPNI has detailed trail maps, but ideal picnic spots are often just a few steps from the main road (see Haifa: Practical Information, p. 331). Down the road from the hospice, Wadi Chiq has well-marked forest trails.

Tourists come to Daliyat al-Karmel to shop in the small *shuk* on the main road. The bazaar is busiest on Saturdays, but weekdays make for low prices and better conversation with locals. In a back room of the bazaar's **Mifqash Ha-Akhim Restaurant** is the **Druze Heritage House** (☎839 31 69), full of artifacts, photographs, and explanations of all things Druze. Ask the restaurant owner, Sheikh Fadel Nasser al-Din, to let you take a peek. The house also hosts groups of 30 or more for lectures about the Druze people followed by tea and baklava (NIS12). Call ahead to ask about joining in.

The Zionist and Christian mystic **Sir Lawrence Oliphant** was one of few outsiders close to the Druze sect. In the late 19th century, he and his wife lived in Daliyat for five years, helping the Druze build their homes. **Beit Oliphant** now serves as a memorial to the scores of Druze soldiers killed in Israel's wars. A simple but eloquent memorial on the second floor displays the photographs of all the Druze slain in Israeli wars. Sir Lawrence sheltered Arab and Jewish insurgents against the British in a cave between the sculpture garden in the rear and the main house. Oliphant's secretary, the Hebrew poet **Naftali Hertz Imber,** wrote the words to "Ha-Tikva" (The Hope), Israel's national anthem, on the premises. At the far side of the football field, **Kir Ha-shalom** (Hebrew for "the wall of peace"), commemorates the Oslo Peace Accords. Turn right at the same end of the bazaar street as Mifqash Ha-Akhim restaurant and continue for 10min. Beit Oliphant is the stone building across from the domed marble sculpture, shortly after the road veers to the right.

Four kilometers from Daliyat al-Karmel is the site where Elijah massacred 450 priests of Ba'al (I Kings 18:40), a weather-god who had been enjoying popularity because of a harsh drought. **Muhraqa,** the site's Arabic name, refers to the burnt sacrifice that the prophet offered to God on an altar here. Pleased with the Israelites' renewed faith, God sent life-giving rain clouds. The Carmelites later interpreted the clouds as symbols of the Virgin Mary, to whom their order is devoted. In 1886 they built a small **monastery** here. A short flight of stairs leads to rooftop views; on clear days Mt. Ḥermon is visible on the horizon. *(There are no buses to the monastery. A taxi ride costs NIS20-25. If walking from Daliyat—though Let's Go does not recommend this—bear left at the only fork along the way. Monastery open M-Sa 8am-1:30pm and 2:30-5pm, Su 8am-1:30pm. NIS1.)*

EIN HOD עין הוד ☎04

To get to Ein Hod, take bus #921 from Haifa, which heads south along the old Haifa-Ḥadera road (20min., every 30min., NIS10). From the junction where the bus stops, the town is a 2km walk uphill, but the magnificent view compensates. To get to the center of town, turn right at the colorful sign and then right again at the fork.

Though perched on the western slopes of Mt. Carmel, 14km south of Haifa, Ein Hod ("Spring of Grandeur") seems to reside in its own surrealist universe. Tin soldiers stand guard along winding, nameless streets, funky mobiles swing between trees, and bronze nudes recline lazily against fences in this small artists' colony. Established in 1953 by Marcel Janco (one of the founders of Dadaism), Ein Hod functions as a cooperative with about 90 members whose talents range from glassblowing to needlework.

The **Main Artists' Gallery,** one of the largest galleries in Israel, displays the work of resident artists. The fantastic exhibits change every four or five months. (☎984 25 48. Open Sa-Th 9:30am-5pm and F 9:30am-4pm. Free.) The **Janco-Dada Museum** (☎984 23 50) features paintings and *objets d'art* by contemporary Israeli Dadaist artists, a permanent display of Janco's work, a constantly changing exhibit introducing a new artist in the village, and a hilarious and informative film entitled "Excuse Me, What is Dada?" that outlines the origins of the Dada movement. (Open Sa-Th 9:30am-5pm, F 9:30am-2pm. NIS10, students NIS5.) In addition to the main gallery and the museum, residents have their own studios and shops throughout the village which are fun to browse around for window-shopping or chatting with the artist.

ISRAEL

Workshops in glass-blowing, pottery, and other crafts are offered on Saturdays at which time no buses run and only residents can park their cars in the village (visitors park in the lot up the hill). The numerous "Pottery" signs lead to **Naomi and Zeev's Pottery Studio,** which offers 45min. workshops in wheel-throwing for adults and hand-building for children. They also sell a wide variety of ceramics, including a large selection of clay whistles for NIS15-150. (☎984 11 07. Workshops offered Sa 10am until dark. NIS30, children NIS15. 50% off for *Let's Go* readers. Open 24hr. Just ring the bell outside for service anytime.)

DOR דור

Take bus #921 from either Haifa (30min., every 30min., NIS12) or Tel Aviv (2hr., every 30min., NIS22.50), or bus #202 from Zikhron Ya'akov (20min., every 1½hr., NIS8.50). After getting off at the Kibbutz Dor intersection, it's a 4km walk on a well-trafficked road past banana fields to the beach. Many people hitch rides from kibbutzniks going down this road. ☎639 09 22. Open Sa-Th 7am-5pm, F 7am-4pm. NIS15, children NIS10.

The pristine **beach** at Dor is protected by four small, rocky islands. Each has a bird sanctuary, and all can be explored at low tide. The Tel Dor archaeological site is on the hill to the right as you face the sea, just past the Kibbutz Naḥsholim beach; footwear is recommended. The site includes temples dedicated to Zeus and Astarte, as well as the ruins of a Byzantine church. Facing the sea, you can see Atlit on the right, Caesarea (or at least its power-generating towers) to the left, and Zikhron Ya'akov and the Arab village of Faradis on the hills behind you.

Next to the beach, within the boundaries of **Kibbutz Naḥsholim,** the **Center of Nautical and Regional Archaeology** (a.k.a. Hamizgaga Museum), displays objects found at Tel Dor and underwater archaeological treasures retrieved by the center's diving team. See 4000-year-old anchors and seashell-encrusted muskets thrown overboard by Napoleon's troops as they retreated from Acre. (☎639 09 50. Open daily 10:30am-3pm. Admission and English film NIS10, students and seniors NIS7.)

A few kilometers north, next to **Kibbutz Ein Karmel,** is the **Naḥal Me'arot Nature Reserve,** with prehistoric caves inhabited some 200,000 years ago. These caves are the only evidence in the world of Neanderthals and Cro-Magnons living simultaneously. Experienced guides explain the significance of the caves and can recommend or lead longer hikes in the surrounding area. English tours and film available. (☎984 17 50. Bus #921 goes to the site from Haifa (20min., every 30min., NIS10) and from Tel Aviv (2hr., every 30min., NIS23). Get off at Ein Carmel Junction and walk a few minutes south along the road until you see a sign indicating the Nature Reserve. A few hundred meters east of the main road is the entrance to the caves. Open Su-Th 8:30am-4pm, F 8:30am-3pm. NIS18, under 18 NIS9.)

ROSH HA-NIKRA ראש הנקרה

*You must go **via Nahariya,** accessible by train, bus, or sherut from Haifa. **Bus #20 and 32** depart from Nahariya to the site a few times per day (NIS8). **Sherut** to Shlomi will stop at the Misrafot Junction (NIS6); the site is a 3km uphill walk on the main road from there. ☎985 71 09. Cable car down to grottoes runs Apr.-June and Sept. Sa-Th 8:30am-6pm and F 8:30am-4pm; July-Aug. Sa-Th 8:30am-11pm and F 8:30am-4pm; Oct.-Mar. daily 8:30am-4pm. NIS34, students and seniors NIS29, children NIS27; discount ticket includes Akko sites.*

The spectacular white chalk cliffs and grottoes of Rosh Ha-Nikra occupy the northernmost point on Israel's coastline. Rosh Ha-Nikra's caves, sculpted by millennia of lashing waves, nearly make one forget the mountain of barbed wire and the Uzi-toting soldiers who guard the tense Lebanese border only a few steps from the parking lot. The British enlarged the natural chalk grottoes when they bore a tunnel through the cliffs during World War II in order to complete a railway line linking Turkey with Egypt. The nearby kibbutz, smelling the chance for a new tourist trap, blasted additional tunnels through the rock to improve access to the sea caves, topped the cliffs with an observation point and cafeteria, and connected the highway to the caves with a cable car. Don't expect arduous spelunking here, a pleasant walk through the slippery grottoes is a half-hour affair. Arrive early or be caught in the afternoon throngs of youth and tour groups.

MONTFORT AND NAḤAL KEZIV

*You must go via Nahariya, accessible by train, bus, or sherut from Haifa. Frequent **buses** leave Nahariya from platform #6 for the Christian Arab village of Mi'ilya (#40, 41, 43, 44, and 45; 20min.; every 30min.; NIS10). From the stop, turn left and climb up the steep road toward Mi'ilya for about 30min. At the wooden sign for Montfort, the road veers right to Hilla. Continue straight and follow the red-and-white markers down the rocky path to the castle (another 30min.). The set of stone steps on the right is an alternate path to the ruins. The original trail turns to the right shortly, then travels across a small bridge and up the rocks to the castle. The site is currently under renovation and officially **closed,** but visitors have been known to prowl around. Bus #25 (8:15pm only) goes from the park to Shlomi, where there are **sherut** to Nahariya (NIS7). Bus #28 from Kibbutz Eilon goes back to Nahariya (8:10am, noon, 3:15, 5:15, 7:45pm; NIS10).*

The Crusader **castle** of Montfort splendidly rewards a challenging hike; the wind-swept ruins overlook the western Galilee's steep Keziv Valley. The Knights Templar built the main structure early in the 12th century; Salah al-Din partially destroyed it in 1187. The Hospitaller Knights enlarged the fortress in 1230 and called it Starkenburg or Montfort ("strong mountain" in German or French). The complex's impressive 18m tower and 20m main hall stand among its remains.

Those who enjoy more strenuous pleasures can visit by way of a longer hike. The 4hr. hiking loop has spectacular views and begins at the lookout point on the road to Hilla (coming from Mi'ilya, turn right at the wooden sign). It descends into the **Naḥal Keziv Valley** and then circles back up to Montfort. Follow black- or blue-and-white markers down into the valley, green-and-white while along the river, and red-and-white up to the castle and back to Mi'ilya. Several other trails branch off the loop. Following the river away from Montfort, green-and-white markers lead to the **Ein Tamir** and **Ein Ziv** springs. Ascending the slope opposite Montfort leads to **Goren Park** (follow red-and-white markers), a perfect vantage point for the castle (amazing at sunset).

Just north of Montfort is the **Naḥal Betzet Nature Reserve,** another fabulous stomping ground for hikers. Take a bus from Nahariya (#24; 30min.; departs 8:25am, 1, 3:30pm; NIS12) and ask the driver to stop at the path to Me'arat Keshet, or **Bow Cave.** Ascend the red-and-white marked trail for 20min. to reach the enormous cave, a natural arch affording dramatic views of the forested Galilean hills and cliffside caves. Descending into the cave requires ropes, and spelunkers should consult beforehand with SPNI (see **From Sea to Shining Sea,** p. 344).

PEKI'IN (BKE'AH) פקיעין بقيعة

*You must go via Nahariya, accessible by train, bus, or sherut from Haifa. **Bus #44** (50min., 7 per day, NIS14) makes the round-trip to Peki'in from Nahariya and will stop just above the cave upon request. Be sure to get off at Peki'in Ha-Atika (Old Peki'in), not Peki'in Ha-Ḥadasha (New Peki'in). At the blue-and-white sign, turn right and descend the stairs. At the large bush with houses behind it, turn right and walk between the two large rocks; the cave is a tiny hole about 3m away. Donation requested.*

Rabbi Shimon Bar-Yoḥai and his son Eliezer fled to Peki'in (Bke'ah in Arabic) when a Roman decree during the Bar Kokhba revolt banned the study of Torah. For 12 years, this erudite duo hid in a small hillside cave and, sustained by a nearby spring and generous carob tree, delved into their illicit book of learning. It is during this period that Bar-Yoḥai is said to have composed the *Zohar*, the central text of Kabbalah (Jewish mysticism), though most evidence suggests it was composed about a millennium later. According to popular legend, Bar-Yoḥai's gaze started **angry fires** in the fields of those less worthy. When God saw this, he sent Bar-Yoḥai back into the cave to chill out for another year. In its present state, the cave does not live up to the legend surrounding it.

Peki'in is the only city in Israel claiming continuous Jewish occupation since the Second Temple period. Though now predominantly Druze, it has a Jewish presence, which endures in one remaining Jewish family and an 18th-century synagogue with Temple-era stones built into the wall. To visit the synagogue, continue down the staircase near the cave to Kikkar Ha-Ma'ayan with its oddly shaped pool. Follow the street at the far right of the square, turn left at the first intersection, and take the curving road down to the synagogue's white gate on the right. If the gate is closed, knock on the door with a blue star, around the corner and upstairs.

AKHZIV אכזיב

*You must go via Nahariya, accessible by train, bus, or sherut from Haifa. **Buses** from platform #5 in Nahariya (#22-25 and 28) stop at the national park (10min., every hr., NIS7).* **Sherut** *NIS6.*

The first historical records of Akhziv are 15th-century BCE Egyptian letters found in Tel Amarna, which describe it as a fortified Canaanite port city. The city switched hands during every major conquest, and eventually the Crusaders built the large **L'Ambert Castle** to defend the coastal road. Akhziv's war days are over now, and its current claim to fame is its sunny shoreline.

Built on the site of an 8th-century BCE Phoenician port town, the sprawling lawns and sheltered beach of **Akhziv National Park** are perfect for a relaxing day. Facilities include showers, changing rooms, and a playground. (☎04 982 32 63. Open daily Apr.-June and Sept.-Oct. 8am-5pm; July-Aug. 8am-7pm. NIS20, students NIS10.) Two roads lead to the **Akhziv Beach:** one along the coast, currently closed off by the military, and a noncoastal road where buses stop. Every July a **Reggae Festival** stirs it up on the beach; call for details. (Begins 4km north of Nahariya and to the left of Akhziv National Park as you face the sea. ☎04 982 82 01. NIS18, children NIS9. Open Apr.-June and Sept.-Oct. 8am-5pm; July-Aug. 8am-7pm.)

The state of **Akhzibland** was founded in 1952 by the eccentric **Eli Avivi.** As the story goes, Eli was walking along the beach and saw the remnants of a village that the Israeli government had destroyed. Hopelessly in love, he claimed the land. **Eli's Museum,** housed in a deteriorated but striking Arab mansion, exhibits the benevolent dictator's extensive collection of mostly Phoenician implements and statue fragments. (☎04 982 32 50. Open 24hr.) Beds in one of Eli's breezy **guest rooms** above the museum or cabins next door cost NIS100, and sleeping in the rugged **camping area** costs NIS80 per person; the beach costs NIS20 for non-guests. These prices are entirely negotiable and may be waived for those who get on Eli's good side or help him with menial chores (such as landscaping, cleaning, or passing legislation) for 3hr.; 4hr for lodging and food.

FROM SEA TO SHINING SEA
One of Israel's most popular and challenging hikes is the three-to-four-day Yam L'Yam trek from the Mediterranean to the Sea of Galilee (or vice versa). The best place to start is at the Keziv Bridge in Akhziv, about 1km south of the SPNI Field School (☎982 37 62; also rents rooms). Contact SPNI for information and maps before attempting this hike. Cross the bridge and follow the green markers upstream along Nahal Keziv for the first day. On the second day, the green path leads to the Druze village of Hurfish, a good place to restock on food. From Hurfish, follow the green or red markers up to the Hurbat parking lot, the next sleeping station. Black markers line the way from Hurbat to the peak of Har Meron (1½hr.). It's all downhill from here: follow the black marker down Nahal Meron, which leads to Nahal Amud, named for the large pillar carved out by the river. Israelis who haven't been to the Grand Canyon call it the eighth wonder of the world. The black markers on upper and lower Nahal Amud lead to Kibbutz Hokkuk, next to the Sea of Galilee. From the kibbutz, buses #459 and 963 go to Tiberias. Plan ahead, bring a compass, and do as much walking as possible in the early morning. With proper planning, this trek can be the experience of a lifetime.

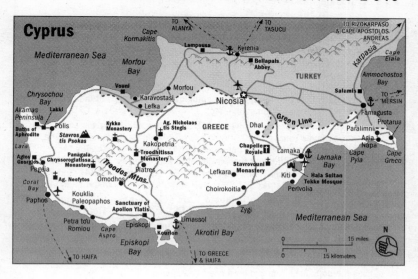

NEAR HAIFA: SOUTHERN CYPRUS

The ancient playwright Euripides once wrote that Cyprus is "where the Loves who soothe mortal hearts dwell." The lovely port cities of Limassol and Paphos—easy ferry trips from Haifa—will surely soothe you with their sunny beaches, breezy ruins, and friendly locals, who have grown accustomed to the growing number of tourists that pass through their hometowns. Inland, the fascinating city of Lefkosia remains the last divided city in the world. For further coverage of the sights and sounds of Southern Cyprus, check out *Let's Go: Greece 2002*.

 ENTERING SOUTHERN CYPRUS: Ferries from Haifa leave frequently for Limassol and Paphos. Residents of Australia, Canada, New Zealand, the UK, and the US need only present a valid **passport** for entry into Cyprus (good for 90 days). Residents of South Africa will need a **visa** to enter (NIS32), available from the South African consulate in **Tel Aviv** (see p. 314). Southern Cyprus is **not** accessible from northern Cyprus (nor is northern Cyprus accessible from southern Cyprus). If you have a Turkish stamp in your passport, you can *never* enter the south. Ask the Turkish authorities not to stamp your passport: a **Taşucu** stamp reveals that you've been to North Cyprus.

☎ **PHONE FACTS** | **Country Code:** 357. **Police and Emergency:** ☎ 199.

LIMASSOL Λεμεσος ☎ 05

Equal parts fast-paced industrial hub and laid-back resort town, Limassol is a cordial, if unrepresentative, introduction to Cyprus. An array of cultural festivities entertains visitors and natives year-round, while the city's elegant restaurants and architecture add an air of sophistication lacking in other Cypriot cities.

█ TRANSPORTATION

Intercity Buses: Check times at the CTO. **Intercity Buses** (☎ 06 643 492) and **Nea Amoroza Bus Service** both go to **Lefkosia** from the Old Port. (M-F 6 per day 6am-6pm, Sa 4 per day 7am-2:30pm; C£1.50.) **Intercity** also goes to **Larnaka** (M-F 4 per day 8am-4pm, Sa 3 per day; C£1.70) and **Paphos** (M-Sa 9:15am and 1:30pm, C£1.70.) The **Episkopi Village** and **Kourion** archaeological site **bus** stops at the **Limassol Castle** (every hr. 9am-1pm; returns June-Sept. 11:50am, 2:50, 4:50pm; C£0.70).

Ferries: Poseidon Lines (☎575 666; fax 575 577). Open M-F 8am-1pm and 3-7pm, Sa 9am-1pm. **Salamis Tours** (☎860 000; fax 367 374) run to: **Haifa,** Israel (11hr., 2 per week, C£70); **Rhodes** (18hr., 2 per week, C£64); **Piraeus** via **Rhodes** (45hr., 2 per week, C£74). Ask for student discounts on ferry tickets. **Cruises: Salamis Tours** (☎860 000; fax 367 374), **Louis Tourist Agency** (☎363 161; fax 363 174), and **Paradise Island Tours** (☎357 604; fax 357 884) stop at Haifa, Israel, and Port Said, Egypt.

Service: Run 6am-6:30pm to **Lefkosia** (C£3.45), **Larnaka** (C£3), and **Paphos** (C£2.50). Contact **Travel and Express** (☎362 061 or 365 550.) Free port pickup.

Local Buses: Most city buses run up and down the main sea-side road and come every 10min. **Bus #1** runs to the port from the station near the Anexartisias market, and **bus #30** runs from the **new port** to downtown Limassol (every 10 min., Sa every 30min., C£0.35). After ships arrive, buses wait near the customs building; otherwise, the stop is outside the port gates. A taxi to town costs C£2.50.

Bike and Moped Rentals: Agencies cluster on the shore road, near the luxury hotels. Try **MikeMar** (☎327 611) on Ag. Georgiou A, next to Pizza Hut. C£10 for a 50cc scooter, C£3 for a mountain bike. Open M-F 8:30am-7pm, Sa 8:30am-1pm.

█ PRACTICAL INFORMATION

Tourist Office: CTO, Spiro Araouzos 115a (☎362 756; fax 746 596), on the waterfront 1 block east of the old port along the main beach road. Open M-Tu and Th-F 8:15am-2:30pm and 4-6:30pm, W 8:15am-2:30pm, Sa 8:15am-1:15pm. Office at the **New Port** (☎571 868) opens immediately following arrivals.

Police: (☎805 050), on Gladstone and Leondios next to the hospital. Open 24hr.

Hospital: Government General Hospital (☎305 777), outside Limassol near the village Polemidia; take bus #15, which stops near the Municipal Market.

Telephones: CYTA on the corner of Markos Botsaris and Athinon.

Internet Access: C&P Computer Center 286C and 288A Agiou Andreou beyond the footpath (☎746 210). A bit expensive, but worth the convenience. High speed modems and the closest Internet to the center of town: C£3 per hr., minimum charge C£2. Printing available. Open M-Sa 8am-3pm.

Post Office: The main office (☎802 259) is next to the central police station on Gladstone. Open May-Sept. M-Tu and Th-F 7:30am-1:30pm and 4-6pm, W 7:30am-1:30pm, Sa 9-11am; Oct.-June Su-T and Th-Sa 3-5pm.

Postal Code: 3900.

█ █ ACCOMMODATIONS AND FOOD

Quirky yet friendly guest houses around the town center are Limassol's budget best. ◼**Luxor Guest House,** Ag. Andreou 101, one block in from the CTO and to the left on the footpath has a convenient location and an understated, simple elegance. (☎362 265. Some private baths, most shared. Singles C£6; doubles C£10; triples C£18.) Tapestries, fish tanks, animal skins, lawn ornaments, and chandeliers make for a kitschy combo at **Guest House Ikaros,** Eleftherias 61. Take Eirinis off the main road and take the fourth left. (☎354 348. Cheap, big rooms with shared bath. Call ahead for reservations. Singles C£5; doubles C£10.)

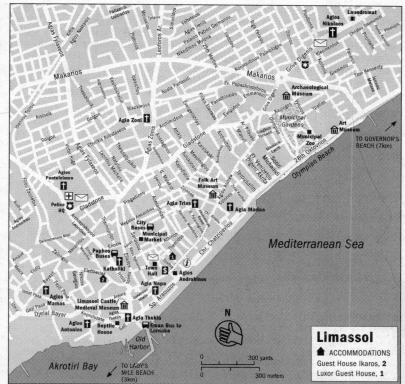

Limassol

Limassol

⌂ ACCOMMODATIONS
Guest House Ikaros, **2**
Luxor Guest House, **1**

ISRAEL

There are tavernas, small kebab houses, and cafes throughout the city. The best option for the health and wealth-conscious traveler is the **Municipal Market**, in a huge warehouse on the corner of Saripolou and Kanari. (Open M-F 6am-1pm.) **Sidon**, Saripolou 71-73, is a Lebanese restaurant in a beautiful setting—softly lit, open air rooms with flowering vines. Walk along the footpath of Ag. Andreou with the Luxor guest house on the right, go down two blocks and Saripolou will be on the right. (☎ 871 614. Main dishes C$5.50-12, wine C$6. Open daily 7-11pm.) At **Cuckoo's Nest**, Ag. Andreou 228, past the footpath with the Luxor glasshouse on the left, cheap village wine (C$3 per bottle) and local gossip flow freely under the fishing nets strewn across the ceiling. (☎ 362 768. Main dishes C$1.25-3. Open 10am-late.) The zebra hides at **Ta Kokkalakia**, Ag. Andreou 239, aren't likely to win points with animal rights activists, but the exotic garden and bar will please even the toughest critic. Eclectic African menu including ostrich steak and South African sausage, and an impressive South African wine selection. (☎ 340 015. Main dishes C$5-11. Open M-Sa 7pm-2am.)

👁 🎵 SIGHTS AND ENTERTAINMENT

KOURION. First settled during the Neolithic period, Kourion was colonized during the 14th and 13th centuries BCE by Achaeans from Argos; it would become famous for its **Sanctuary of Apollo Hylates** (8th century BCE, 3km west from main road), and its **Stadium** (2nd century CE, 1km west of the main settlement and the basilica). The **Temple of Apollo** and other parts of the Sanctuary of Apollo are largely reconstructed. The majestic 2nd century Roman **amphitheater** was used for dramas during Greek and Roman times, but by 300 CE, the stage had fallen to animal fights and professional wrestling. Adjacent to the amphitheater lie the **Baths and Annex of Eustoios,** built in 360 CE with exquisite 5th-century mosaic floors. Across the road from the basilica lies a group of ruins under excavation. In the northwest corner are the remains of the **House of Gladiators** and the **House of Achilles;** both have beautiful mosaic floors. *(Buses leave Limassol Castle for Kourion every hour on the hour. 10am-1pm; returning at 11:50am, 2:50, and 4:50pm; C£0.80. Drivers to Kourion usually go via Episkopi village. Open year-round 8am-7:15pm. C£1. Handicapped accessible.)*

LIMASSOL CASTLE. The **Limassol Castle,** where Richard King of England married Queen Berengaria in 1191 (crowned the Queen of England), served as a prison for much of its existence: the Knights of St. John turned the chapel into a series of prison cells, and when the Ottomans claimed the castle in 1570, the West Hall was used as a prison under the British regime until 1940. Today, it is the **Cyprus Medieval Museum,** home to a scattered collection of medieval armor and religious objects. (☎ 305 419. Open M-F 9am-5pm, Sa-Su 10am-1pm. C£1.)

SPECIAL EVENTS. At summer's end, Limassol's gardens flow with wine in the grand style of Dionysus for the Limassol **wine festival.** Participants fill bottles with as much local wine as they can guzzle. The general intoxication is enlivened by music, dance, and theater. (Admission C£1.50.) From May to August, people flock from around the world for **Shakespeare Nights** at the theater of ancient Kourion. **Carnival,** 50 days before Orthodox Easter (usually in February), is celebrated with more vim and vigor in Limassol than anywhere else in Cyprus. Limassol hosts a plethora of events throughout the year; pamphlets are available at the CTO.

◖ BEACHES

The city's long stone beach might be a little too rocky and too near the busy port for the discerning beach bums, but a new breakwater past the town center has made the area more pleasant for swimming. **Dassoudi Beach,** 3km east of Limassol, is a slightly better option. *(Take bus #6 from the Kanaris market. Every 15min., C£0.50.)* Farther east, about 7km beyond Dassoudi beach, surprisingly uncrowded **Governor's Beach** is perhaps the best bet near Limasso, offering sand, clean waters, and quiet. *(A bus leaves the Old Port at 9:50am each morning for the beach. C£2 round-trip; children under 10 free).* **Ladies Mile Beach,** just west of the new port, is popular with locals and tourists alike. *(Take bus #1.)* When making the excursion to Kourion, be sure to spend some time at happily undiscovered **Kourion beach.**

◖ NIGHTLIFE

Local bars and cafes are sparse near the center of Limassol, but a few can be found on Ag. Andreou and near the castle. Dance clubs, discos, and bars are at the edge of town in the tourist district. **The Hippodrome** disco dance club, on Georgiou, is the place to get down as the neighboring bars die down after 1am. **The Basement Club,** a few bars down from the Hippodrome on Georgiou, hosts a diverse crew of merrymakers and is one of the last clubs to close down. The 200-year-old building that houses **The Green Movement,** Ag. Andreou 259, is a testament to Limassol's fine architectural past with white columns and a marble patio. It serves as a bar, a stage for spontaneous jam sessions, and a meeting room for political and environmental discussions. (☎ 369 595. Open M-Sa 6pm-2am.)

PAPHOS Πάφος ☎ 06

Paphos, reputably the favorite city of Aphrodite, was the capital of Cyprus under the Ptolemies of Egypt. A 4th-century BCE earthquake ended its supremacy; it has since reemerged as hotspot of crystal beaches and historical treasures.

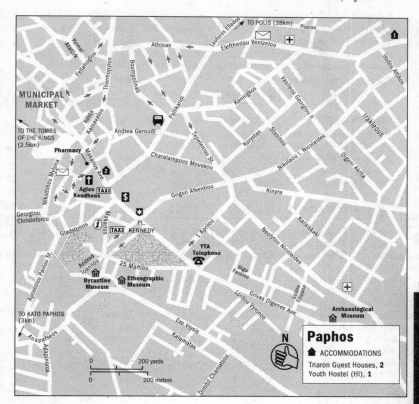

Paphos

ACCOMMODATIONS
Triaron Guest Houses, **2**
Youth Hostel (HI), **1**

TRANSPORTATION

Buses: Nea Amoroza Co., Pallikaridi 79 (☎236 822 or 236 740), in Pl. Kennedy goes to **Limassol** (M-Tu and Th-F 2:30pm, W and Sa 10:30am and 1pm; C£2). The **municipal bus #11** runs between Ktima Paphos and Kato Paphos (every 15min., C£0.50). Catch one in Ktima Paphos, up the road from the post office, or in Kato Paphos at any of the yellow benches on the road to town. **Bus #10** goes to **Coral Bay** (20 per day, C£0.50). **Bus #2** starts at Geroskipou Beach with stops along the coastal road (every 15-20min. 6am-7pm). Check the schedules available in the tourist office.

Service: To **Limassol** (every 30min. M-Sa 6am-6pm, Su 7am-5am; C£2.75). Contact **Travel & Express** on Eagorou (☎933 181).

Moped Rental: There are several shops in Kato and Ktima Paphos and along Apostolos Pavlou, the coastal road. C£3-8 per day. **4U Car & Bike rentals** (☎944 085 or 09 466 026) is on Tomb of the Kings Ave. Mountain bikes C£3, scooters C£7 per day.

ORIENTATION AND PRACTICAL INFORMATION

Paphos is divided into two sections. The upper section, **Ktima Paphos** (or just "Paphos"), is centered around **Pl. Kennedy,** with its shops, budget hotels, and services. The lower section, **Kato Paphos,** is roughly 1km south, with luxury hotels and the city's nightlife. **Apostolou Pavlou St.,** connecting Ktima and Kato Paphos, is lined with monuments to the Roman, early Christian, Byzantine, and Venetian periods of Cypriot history. Unless noted, everything below is in Ktima Paphos.

ISRAEL

Tourist Office: CTO, Gladstone 3 (☎932 841; fax 932 841), just outside of Pl. Kennedy. Open in winter M-Tu, Th-F 8:15am-2:30pm and 3-6:15pm, W and Sa 8:15am-1:30pm. In summer afternoon hours are 2:45-7pm.

Police: (☎806 060) on Grivas Digenes, in Pl. Kennedy, opposite the Coop Bank. English spoken; provide helpful tourist information. Open 24hr.

Hospital: Paphos General (☎803 100), a long walk on Neophytos Nicolaides. Free first aid. English spoken. **St. George's Private Hospital,** El. Venizelou 29 (☎947 000), on the way to the youth hostel, has ambulance services. English spoken. Open 24hr.

Telephones: CYTA (☎930 228), on Grivas Digenes. Open 7:30am-1:30pm.

Internet Access: Scattered throughout the city. **Maroushia Fashion Cafe,** 6 Pl. Kennedy (☎947 240; maroushia@cylink.com.cy). C£2 per hr.

Post Office: Main branch (☎940 223), on El. Venizelou. Open M-F 7:30am-1pm and (except W) 3-6pm, Sa 8-10am. **Kato Paphos** (☎940 226), branch Ag. Antoniou. **Postal Code:** Ktima Paphos 8900; Kato Paphos 8903.

ACCOMMODATIONS AND FOOD

Finding affordable accommodations in Paphos is a chore. Solo travelers should stick to the youth hostel or the guest house. Prices are higher in Kato Paphos. Ideally located ◼**Triaron Hotel Guest House,** Makarios 99, is a brilliant choice. (☎932 193; fax 936 227. Shared bath. Singles C£5; doubles C£8-12.) **Youth Hostel (HI),** El. Venizelou 45, is a 15min. walk from the plateia on Pallikaridi to Venizelou, then turn right. (☎932 588. C£5 per bed for the 1st night, C£4 per night thereafter.)

Restaurants in Kato Paphos are geared to money-laden foreigners. ◼**Vasano Kebab House,** Agapinoros 25 in Kato Paphos, has only the basics, but every morsel is prepared to perfection, and the locals know it—no evening passes without a full house. On the road from Ktima to Kato Paphos take a left onto Pinelopis and then a right onto Agapinoros. (☎242 635. Main dishes C£1-2.) **Athens,** Pallikaridi 47, bakes fresh pastries, and *pites* every morning. (☎32 613. Pastries C£0.40 and less.)

SIGHTS

MOSAICS OF KATO PAPHOS. The mosaic floors of the House of Dionysus, the House of Theseus, and the House of Aion in Kato Paphos are the city's most dazzling ancient relics. Discovered accidentally in 1962 by a farmer plowing his fields, they were excavated by a Polish expedition that found mosaics covering 14 rooms of the **House of Dionysus.** Using the stones' natural varying hues, the floors depict vibrant scenes from mythology and daily life. The decadent **House of Theseus** (dating from the 2nd to 6th centuries CE), with marble statues, columns, and mosaic floors, is towards the water. (☎940 217. Open daily 8am-7:30pm. C£1.50.)

TOMBS OF THE KINGS. About 2km before Kato Paphos, a sign directs you to Paleokastra's **Tombs of the Kings.** Although those interred in the stone tombs were local aristocracy, not kings, the 2nd-century remnants bear a strong resemblance to Egyptian peristyle court tombs. The most impressive are tombs #3, #4, #5, and #8, which have extensive underground passages to wander through. (☎940 295. Open 7:30am-7:30pm. C£0.75.)

MUSEUMS OF KTIMA PAPHOS. The **Archaeological Museum,** on Grivas Digenes, 1km from Pl. Kennedy, has an array of Bronze Age pottery, tools, sculpture, statues, and artifacts from the houses of Dionysus and Theseus. (☎940 215. Open M-F 9am-2:30pm and 3-5pm, Sa 10am-1pm. C£0.75.) Across the way, the **Byzantine Museum,** Andreou Ioannou 5, has icons and religious relics from local monasteries and churches, including frescoes, vestments, and manuscripts. The main attraction is the oldest icon in Cyprus, of Agia Marina, dating to the 7th or 8th century. (☎931 393. Open M-F 9am-4pm, Sa 9:10am-1pm. C£1, guidebook C£3.)

CATACOMBS OF AGIA SOLOMONI. Descend into these dark catacombs that include a chapel with deteriorating Byzantine frescoes. Dedicated to Ag. Solomoni (Hannah), the chapel sits on the site of an old synagogue. A marked tree, said to cure the illnesses of those who tie a cloth to it, denotes the entrance to the catacombs. St. Paul was whipped for preaching Christianity at nearby **St. Paul's Pillar,** where a Catholic church stands today. *(Tombs on Ag. Pavlou. Open 24hr. Free.)*

◢ BEACHES

The two most popular beaches stretch along **Geroskipou** to the east and **Coral Bay** to the north (big, sandy, and touristy—luxury hotels line the way). For Geroskipou, take bus #2 from Ktima Paphos (5 per day, 6:25am-7pm, C$0.50); to reach Coral Bay, take bus #10 from the Market in Pano Paphos (every 20min., C$0.50). **Cape Lara** is host to lovely, empty beaches, and is a nesting site for Green and Loggerhead Turtles from June until September. The ◼**Lara Sea Turtle Project** was conceived in 1971 to protect the turtles by ensuring that nesting continues. Turtle nests can be viewed in the Project's hatchery enclosure. Alas, there's no public transportation to Cape Lara; your best bet is a jeep excursion or motorbike. **Sundy Beach,** 2km down the road to Cape Lara, parades umbrellas for rent. Farther along a nearly deserted, unnamed beach stretches for about 1km.

◣ NIGHTLIFE

Virtually all of the area's nightlife centers on Ag. Napas and Ag. Antoniou, a couple of blocks inland from the waterfront in Kato Paphos. **Club 12,** on Ag. Andreou, draws all the crowds after 1am with heavy bass and the latest techno tunes—be prepared for wild dancing on the bars and tables. (☎0191 230 4848. Cover C$5.) **Summer Cinema** (☎247 747 or 09 632 229), on the waterfront, is a trendy open-air club just far enough from package hotels for the locals to call it their own. **Bubbles,** on Ag. Antoniou, hops from 10pm til 3-4am. Every Thursday, "Carwash Night Back in Time" turns back the clock with '70s and '80s hits. A more laid-back atmosphere is found at gay-friendly **Different** (☎934 668), farther down on Ag. Antoniou. Panos, the owner, enthralls all with stories and jokes.

◪ DAYTRIP FROM PAPHOS: KOUKLIA

*The sites are best seen from excursion **buses**. Renting a **moped** is not advisable—the road is hazardous; **service** are a much safer bet. ☎432 180. Open M-F 8am-7pm, Sa-Su 9am-5pm. Admission to ruins, city, and museum C£0.75.*

Adjacent to the modern village of Kouklia are the ruins of the great **Temple of Aphrodite** and **Paleopaphos** (Old Paphos), once the capital of a kingdom encompassing nearly half of Cyprus. The temple was the kingdom's religious center and a destination for pilgrims from all over the Roman empire. Built in the 12th century BCE, it thrived until the 4th century CE, when the edicts of Emperor Theodosius and a series of earthquakes reduced it to rubble. The scant remains make little sense without a guide. *A Brief History and Description of Old Paphos,* published by the Department of Antiquities, is available in the adjoining **Paleopaphos Museum.**

LEFKOSIA (SOUTH NICOSIA) ☎02

Landlocked Lefkosia, sliced in half by the barbed-wire Green Line, has the dubious distinction of being the last divided city in the world. The modern New City is separated from the Old by Venetian walls, built on top of the ancient Roman town of Ledra in a failed attempt to fend off Ottoman cannons. The British governed Cyprus until it gained independence in 1960, when Lefkosia became the capital of the island. In the aftermath of 1974, Lefkosia split into Turkish Nicosia to the North and Greek Lefkosia to the South, and remains under the watchful eye of the UN. You can cross the Green Line from the Ledra checkpoint on the southern side.

ISRAEL

The Old City of Lefkosia appeals to history buffs and politically inclined tourists. At the moment, the city is restoring the old Laiki Yitonia (the pedestrian area of the Old City) and constructing new museums and monuments, catering to tourists as it preserves its history. The New City is geared toward bureaucrats rather than backpackers. Lefkosia offers a poignant, intimate view of the political strife that has shaped modern Cyprus.

⧉ TRANSPORTATION

Buses: Intercity Buses (☎ 665 814), in Pl. Solomos, run to **Larnaka** (7 per day M-F 9am-6:30pm, Sa 11am, 1pm; C£1.50). **Intercity Buses** and **ALEPA** (☎ 09 625 027) both depart from Pl. Solomos for **Limassol** (9 per day M-F 6am-5:45pm, Sa 10am, 12:45, 2pm; C£1.50). **Nea Amorza** (☎ 236 822) and **ALEPA** (☎ 664 636), near Pl. Solomos, run to **Paphos** (M-F) via **Limassol** (2 per day 6:30am and 3:45pm, plus W and Sa 12:45pm; C£3). Get free maps of all the urban **Lefkosia bus** routes at the CTO.

Service: Travel & Express (☎ 07 774 74 or 757 616) runs (M-Sa every 30min. 6am-6pm, Su 7am-5pm) to: **Limassol** (C£3.45); **Larnaka** (C£2.40); **Paphos** (C£6). Call ahead. **Solis** (☎ 666 388), on Tripolis Bastion, runs *service* (M and W-Sa noon, C£5) and a minibus (M-Tu and Th-Sa noon, C£4) to **Polis** via **Limassol** and **Paphos.**

Private Taxis: Are easily summoned from sidewalks and corners. Taxi stations are in Pl. Eleftherias, or call **Travel & Express** (☎ 757 616) for private service as well. Open 24hr. Private taxis are expensive, running about C£0.65 initial charge and C£0.22 per km daytime, or C£0.88 initial charge at night and same amount per km.

✴ 🛈 ORIENTATION AND PRACTICAL INFORMATION

The easiest way to orient yourself in Lefkosia is to use the Venetian walls. The Green Line, running east to west at the north end of the city, divides the **Old City** into Greek and Turkish sectors. Within the walls, travelers can find most budget lodgings, museums, tavernas, and sights. From **Pl. Eleftherias,** Evagoras heads southwest into the New City, while **Lidras St.,** the primary pedestrian and tourist throughway, runs to the north, where it intersects the **Green Line.** Intersecting Evagoras are **Makarios Ave., Diagoras,** and **Th. Dervis,** which leads to the youth hostel. **Laiki Yitonia,** southeast of Lidras street, is the prominent pedestrian and tourist district. The New City is more spread out, making navigation on foot difficult. Sheet metal barriers or white and blue dividers confront you when you walk down the streets of the Old City. **Do not ignore the signs forbidding photography.**

Tourist Office: CTO, Aristokypros 11 (☎ 674 264; fax 660 778), in Laiki Yitonia. Entering Pl. Eleftherias from the New City, turn right and follow signs from the post office. Free maps, a list of buses, and a guide to city events. Open M-F 8:30am-4pm, Sa 8:30am-2pm. Free English-language walking tour through the old village of Kaimakli offered M, more general walking tour of Lefkosia Th; both leave from the CTO at 10am and last 2hr.

Banks: Bank of Cyprus: main branch, Phaneromeni 86 (☎ 674 064), offers **ATM** and **currency exchange.** Open M-F 8:15am-12:30pm. A convenient branch (☎ 436 161) in Laiki Yitonia on Drakos with 24hr. **ATM.** Open M-F 8:30am-12:30pm. Additional ATMs throughout the city, most 24hr.

American Express: A.L. Mantovani and Sons, Agapinoras 2D (☎ 763 777), 1km south of Pl. Solomos down Makarios. Open M-F 8am-12:45pm and 2:30-5:30pm, Sa 9am-noon. Currency exchange, and traveler's check exchange.

Public Toilets: In the parking lots along the Venetian walls (follow the W/C signs). Surprisingly sanitary and toilet paper is blessedly abundant.

Police and Fire Station: (☎ 802 200). The 2 buildings are next door to one another, 150m east of Paphos Gate on Digenis, inside the wall. Additional police station in the New City at the corner of Santaroza and Makarious (☎ 304 967). Both open 24hr.

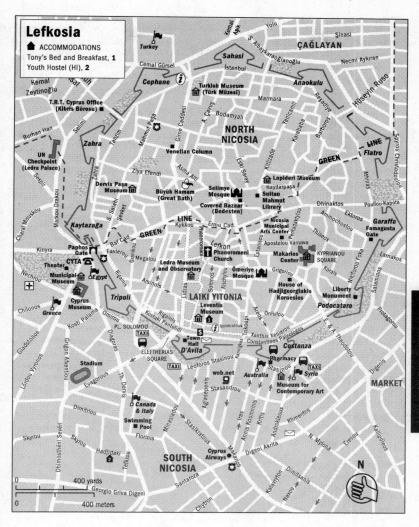

Lefkosia

⌂ ACCOMMODATIONS
Tony's Bed and Breakfast, **1**
Youth Hostel (HI), **2**

Hospital: (☎ 801 400), at Omirou and Nechrou St. Open 24hr.

Telephone: CYTA, Egypt 14 (☎ 702 276). Customer service open M-F 7:15am-1:30pm; cashier open M-F 7:15am-6pm, Sa 7:15am-1pm. 24hr. telecard machine outside.

Internet Access: Web.net Cafe at Stasandrou 10C (☎ 753 345; fax 753 184), at the border of the New City. New computers and efficient service. C£2.20 per hr. Student discount. Drinks C£0.60-1.30. Open M-Sa 10:30am-midnight, Su 5:30pm-midnight.

Post Office: Main office (☎ 303 219 and 303 123) on Constantinos Paleologos, east of Pl. Eleftherias. Open M-F 7:30am-2pm and 3-6pm; W no afternoon hours; Sa 8:30-10:30am. Offices on Digenis, Palace, Loukis Akitas (☎ 302 531).

Postal Code: 1903.

ACCOMMODATIONS

◼**Tony's Bed and Breakfast** is on the corner of Solon and Hippokratous, in the Laiki Yitonia. Traditional decorations and a Victorian staircase lead to sparklingly clean rooms, all with radio, phone, hot water pots, fridge, air-conditioning, and TV. Guests can eat breakfast on a spacious rooftop patio. (☎666 752 or 667 794; fax 662 225. Singles C$20; doubles C$25-28; triples C$30; quads C$35. 20% discount with student ID.) An old home with a sprawling, enclosed garden, the **Youth Hostel (HI),** Hadjidaki 1 in the New City off Diagoras Dervis, feels like grandma's house. The 11pm quiet hour keeps the peace and attracts older travelers. (☎674 808 or 09 438 360. 2 rooms for women, 2 rooms for men, 2 for families/couples, and 1 attic room as a single. Full kitchen, shared bath. Sheets C$1. Dorms C$4; attic room C$6.)

FOOD

Options in Lefkosia include tavernas with live music, pubs, pizzerias, and full restaurants. Touristy joints around Laiki Yitonia serve Cypriot *mezedes;* smaller restaurants cater to locals in the backroads of the Old City. For a cheap option, head to the **municipal market** on the corner of Digenis Akritas and Kallipolis, a huge warehouse filled with food stands. Hanging pigs will either stir your hunger or turn you vegetarian. (Open 6am-1pm and 4-6pm.) A colorful streetside **produce market** near Pl. Eleftherias along Constantinos Paleologos beckons veggie lovers. (Open W 9am-1pm and 4-6pm.)

◼**Zanettos Taverna,** Trikoupi 65 (☎765 501), near Omeriyeh Mosque in the Old City. Open since 1938, this oasis in the center of Cyprus's capital manages to provide its guests with a taste of *kypriatiko paradosiako faghito* (traditional Cypriot cuisine). The *Halloumi* specials (C£2) make for splendid starters and the meat *meze* for 2 (C£14) will satisfy all your carnivorous cravings. Open daily 12:30-4pm and 7:30pm-midnight.

Savvas, Solon 65 (☎668 444), in the Laiki Yitonia. Serves up exactly what a Cypriot mother would put on the table for her children. Join the locals on lunch break for traditional homemade dishes; for a true native experience try the *bambies* (baked okra stewed in a tomato, onion, and garlic sauce). All main dishes C£1-2, with a glass of local wine (C£0.50). Open 10am-5:30pm.

Berlin #2 Cafe (☎474 935), on the corner of Lefkon and Phaneromni. This popular takeout joint serves up *kebab*, salad, and pita (C£2) in the shadow of a UN guard station. Open M-Sa 7am-midnight.

SIGHTS

◼**STATE GALLERY.** Formerly known as the Lefkosia Municipal Gallery of Contemporary Art, this gallery is housed in a graceful converted hotel building constructed in 1925. Small rooms off spacious hallways showcase the paintings and sculpture of renowned contemporary Greek artists, such as Andreas Charalambides and Georghios P. Georghiou. Be sure to check out the installations on the third floor as well. (Crete 1. ☎304 992. On the edge of the New City across from the Bayraktar Mosque. Open M-F 10am-5pm, Sa 10am-1pm. Free.)

FAMAGUSTA GATE. Along the Venetian Walls at the end of Theseus St. is the recently restored Famagusta Gate, the largest, best preserved, and most famous of all the gates that surround old Nicosia. The main entrance to old Lefkosia, built in 1567, it now hosts plays, concerts, exhibitions, and lectures; check the schedule at the CTO or pick one up at the Town Hall. (Open M-F 10am-1pm, 4-7pm in winter and 5-8pm in summer. Free.) Not far down Korais street, walking away from Famagusta gate toward the Laiki Yitonia, is a marble monument, the **Freedom Statue** (Agalma Eleftherias), depicting 14 Cypriots, each representing a period of the island's history, being released from the iron bars that have restrained them.

LEVENTIS MUNICIPAL MUSEUM. This museum, which won the European Museum of the Year award in 1991, chronicles the history and social development of Lefkosia from 3000 BCE to recent years. Peer through the glass at your feet as you walk over an excavated portion of a Medieval House from the Nicosia area. The second floor consists mainly of traditional costumes, household items, and weaponry. Don't overlook the photographic chronology or the courtyard garden with its authentic Turkish baths. *(Hippocratis 17 in the Laiki Yitonia, off Solon. ☎ 671 997 or 661 475. Open Tu-Su 10am-4:30pm. Free. Handicapped accessible.)*

PHANEROMENI CHURCH. A point of nationalist pride to Greek Cypriots, the Phaneromeni Church survived a Turkish attempt to transform it into a mosque. Dating to the 14th century, the ornate *iconostasis* is engraved with Old Testament images. *(In the center of the Old City off Ledgras St. Open daily 6:15am-1pm and 3:45-7pm. Free, but donations are welcome.)*

PLATEIA ARCHBISHOPRIC KYPRIANOS. The Plateia consists of four main buildings of historical and touristic interest: the first is the **Makarios Cultural Center,** the largest of the buildings, in the middle of the plateia. The Center contains four galleries, the most impressive of which is the **Byzantine Museum** on the first floor. The museum contains over 150 icons from the 8th to 18th centuries, most of which were collected by the first Bishop of Cyprus, Makarios III. On the second floor is an **Art Gallery** containing an impressive collection of European oil paintings mostly from the 17th century. The **1821 War of Independence Gallery,** on the third floor, hosts a varied selection of war-related paintings from the 17th century to the modern day. On the second and third floors the **Cypriot Contemporary Painting Gallery** displays a collection of constantly shifting exhibits by contemporary Cypriot painters. *(☎ 430 008. Byzantine Museum open M-F 9am-4:30pm, Sa 9am-1pm. All other galleries share the same hours, but close from 1-2pm. C£1.)* The second building of interest is **Saint John's Cathedral,** in the courtyard of the Makarios Center, built in 1662 by Archbishop Nikiforos with a single nave and five pointed arches. The tablets adorning the entrance were transferred from Venetian and Frankish buildings. *(Open M-F 9am–noon and 2-4pm, Sa 9am-noon. Free.)* The third building is the **Ethnographic Museum of Cyprus,** previously called the Folk Art Museum, to the left of the Makarios Center. The Museum is housed in a magnificent 15th-century monastery, and contains Cypriot woodcarving, embroidery, pottery, basketry, and metalwork from the 18th to 20th centuries. *(☎ 432 578. Open M-F 9am-4pm, Sa 10am-1pm. C£1.)*

HOUSE OF HADJIGEORGIAKIS KORNESIOS. Near Pl. Kyprianos is the luxurious, 18th-century home of the famous *dragoman,* or Ottoman tax-collector and interpreter. Kornesios was actually a Greek Cypriot who, through clever strategy and knowledge of many languages, rose to the prestigious and lucrative position of tax-collector in Cyprus for the Ottoman Emperor. In 1804 the Cypriots raided his house, but the *dragoman* and his family escaped through a hidden passage. With an enchanting courtyard and a floor plan in the shape of the letter π, the monument is a significant example of the urban architecture of the last century of Ottoman rule. *(Patriach Gregory 18. ☎ 305 316. Open M-F 8am-2pm, Sa 9am-1pm. C£0.75.)*

CYPRUS MUSEUM. Here you'll find the most extensive collection of ancient art and artifacts on the island, from pre-Hellenic periods through the Byzantine era. Amateur archaeologists can compare local jewelry across eras, while everyone will feel dwarfed by ancient, larger-than-life terracotta figures. *(Mouseiou 1, near the Paphos Gate. ☎ 303 112. Open M-Sa 9am-5pm, Su 10am-1pm. C£1.50.)*

■ NIGHTLIFE

For late night entertainment, scattered coffeeshops, pubs, and dance clubs keep Lefkosia jumping. Most of Lefkosia's **bars** and **pubs** can be found in the Old City near or around Pl. Eleftherias. A word of caution: many cabaret clubs surround Pl. Eleftherias, but women should not walk alone through this neighborhood after 2am, when the bars have closed and the younger crowd at surrounding cafes has dispersed. **Dance clubs** are on the outskirts of the New City, while Makariou is filled with **cafes** for the younger crowds. For popular tunes, the neighborhood of Engomi, around Leoforou Goudia, has some of the most popular **clubs,** including **Martini.** (☎781 059. Open Su-Th 8pm-2am, F-Sa 8pm-4am.) Expect **Sfinakia,** Santaroza 2, to be packed every night of the week. (☎766 661. Open daily 9pm-3am.)

Mike & Alexander's Pub and Restaurant, on Pantelidi St. in Pl. Eleftherias, Laiki Yitonia, caters to a varied clientele, with a cafe for relaxation and a pub for revelry. (☎451 17. Beer C$1.50-2.60. Open daily 8am-2am.) **Ta Kala Kathoumena,** Nikokleous 21, tucked into an alley behind Phaneromni Church, is where Lefkosia's young collegiate intellectuals gather at night for debate, backgammon, and drinks. (☎664 654. Drinks C$0.40-C$1.20. Open M-Sa 11am-midnight, Su 6pm-midnight.)

NORTH OF HAIFA

AKKO (ACRE) עכו عكا ☎04

Dominated by the emerald-domed 18th-century **Mosque of al-Jazzar,** the Old City of Akko (*Akka* in Arabic, historically written "Acre" in English) is surrounded on three sides by the Mediterranean Sea. It gazes across the bay at Haifa's crowded skyline, but the city's stone fortresses and underground Crusader City lend it a character far removed from that of its modern coastal neighbor. Visitors can stroll through the colorful maze of the *souq* or escape to the city's South Promenade and toss back a Tuborg while the waves crash against the city's white walls.

The Canaanite city-state of Akko is first mentioned in the *Book of Curses,* which records the curses of pharaohs on their enemies in the 19th century BCE. After this happy entry onto the international stage, Akko was conquered by the usual suspects: Egyptians, Persians, Greeks, Hasmoneans, Romans, and Umayyads. Crusaders came to the city in 1104 on their campaign to recapture the Holy Land for Christianity. In 1187, with the battle of the Horns of Hattim, Salah al-Din defeated the Crusader forces in Akko; three years later, Richard the Lionheart arrived from England and recaptured the city. During the next century, Crusader kings transformed Akko into the greatest port of their empire and a world-class showpiece of culture and architecture. The Mamluks ended Crusader rule in 1291, and Akko remained impoverished until the Druze prince Fakhr al-Din rebuilt it almost 500 years later. The Muslims built their city directly over the Crusader network of tunnels and basements and left the subterranean labyrinth for wide-eyed tourists. After his unsuccessful siege of the city in 1799, Napoleon claimed that had Akko fallen, "the world would have been mine." After a stint under the Egyptian Ibrahim Pasha, Akko returned to Ottoman control. When the British captured the port in 1918, it held a predominantly Arab population of about 8000.

Akkan locals are eager to share thoughts on their home and their lives while offering much-needed guidance around the dizzying network of Old City streets. However, women traveling alone are strongly advised to be cautious with many of these would-be guides, and all solo travelers are advised to avoid the alleys of Old Akko after dark; stick to the well-lit promenade by the port for a safer stroll.

▐ TRANSPORTATION

Trains: The **train station** (☎856 44 44) is on David Remez St., 1 street behind the central bus station. Trains are often the best way to get to and from Haifa, especially during rush hour. To: **Haifa** (40min., NIS11); **Nahariya** (10min., NIS6.50); **Tel Aviv** (1¾hr., NIS29). Trains run every hr. Su-Th 5:30am-8:30pm, F 5:30am-3:30pm.

Buses: The **central bus station** (☎854 95 55) is on Ha-Arba'a St. in the new city. Buses go to **Haifa** (#271, 272, and 361; 45min.; every 20min.; NIS11.50; #251 makes local stops) and **Nahariya** (#271 and 272; 15min.; every 20min.; NIS7.20). Buses from platform #16 go to the **old city** until 6:30pm (NIS4).

Taxis: Sherut: off Ha-Arba'a St., across from the bus station. To: **Haifa** (NIS9); **Nahariya** (NIS7); **Tel Aviv** (NIS25). **Special Taxis: Akko Ba'am** (☎981 66 66).

✴☀ 🛈 ORIENTATION AND PRACTICAL INFORMATION

In **New Akko**, the central bus station is on **Ha-Arba'a St.** and the train station is one block behind it on **Remez St.** To get to the old city, turn left on Ha-Arba'a St. (with your back to the bus station), and after one block make a right on **Ben-Ami St.** Continue for a few blocks (past the bustling *midraḥov*) and turn left on **Weizmann St. Ha-Atzma'ut St.,** the new city's major thoroughfare and home to the main post office and city hall, and **Herzl St.** also run between Ha-Arba'a St. and Weizmann St. Once in **Old Akko**, visitors will likely be dismayed by the lack of street signs—locals and monuments are the best (and only) navigational tools. **Al-Jazzar St.** and **Salah al-Din St.** extend in opposite directions from slightly different points near the main entrance on Weizmann St. Most museums are on al-Jazzar St., and the **souq** begins from a plaza off the right side of Salah al-Din St. when coming from Weizmann St. **Ha-Hagana St.** runs from the far side of the peninsula to the coast of the **Pisan Harbor,** which is lined with touristy restaurants, a pleasant promenade, and sitting areas with great bay views.

Tourist Office: Municipal Tourist Information Office Booth (☎/fax 991 17 64), on al-Jazzar St. and across from the mosque, inside the same building as the post office. Open Su-Th 8:30am-6pm, F 8:30am-2:45pm, Sa 9am-5:45pm; in winter Su-Th 8:30am-5pm, F 8:30am-2:30pm, Sa 9am-5pm.

Currency Exchange: Mercantile Discount Bank (☎955 46 67), corner of al-Jazzar St. and Weizmann St. Open Su, Tu-W 8:30am-1pm; M and Th 8:30am-noon and 4:30-7pm; F 8:30am-1pm. **Bank Leumi** (☎995 63 33), on Ben-Ami St. near Weizmann St. Open Su, Tu, W 8:30am-1pm; M, Th 8:30am-1pm and 4:30-7pm; F 8:30am-noon. **ATMs** at both banks. **Change Spot** (☎991 68 99), at the end of al-Jazzar St., across from the post office, changes currency with no commission. Open Su-F 8am-5pm.

Emergency: Magen David Adom (☎991 23 33).

Police: 16 Ha-Hagana St. (☎987 68 68).

Pharmacy: Merkaz (☎991 47 02), at the corner of Ben-Ami and Weizmann St. Open Su-Th 8am-1pm and 4-9pm, F 8am-1pm. Pharmacies rotate 24hr. duty; schedules are posted in the windows.

Hospital: Mizra Hospital (☎955 95 95), north of new Akko.

Post Office: Central branch at 11 Ha-Atzma'ut St. (☎306 66 66) offers **Poste Restante.** Open M, Tu, and Th 8am-12:30pm and 3:30-6pm; W 8am-1:30pm; F 8am-noon. Other **branches** at 53 Ben-Ami St. and on al-Jazzar St.

▐ ACCOMMODATIONS

Dorm rooms are some of the cheapest in the area, yet remain rather empty. Quality varies greatly for even small price changes, so consider carefully before committing. All of the following will pick you up from the bus or train station; just call when you arrive. There are unofficial and unregulated rooms for rent in the old city; signs tend to cluster near the bus station, on the *midraḥov* in the new city, or around the entrance to the old city. Get an opinion from the tourist office before making a decision. **Beach camping** is forbidden and dangerous.

Lighthouse Hostel, 175 Ha-Hagana St. (☎991 19 82; fax 981 55 3), at the end of Ha-Hagana St., a few minutes before the lighthouse. This gorgeous Turkish mansion is the place to stay in Akko. The huge dorms may be plain, but they are clean. The large, airy lounge with marble pillars can make even the grimiest backpacker feel like a sultan. Bike rental NIS35 per day. Kitchen available. Breakfast NIS15. Reception 24hr. Checkout 10am. Single-sex and coed dorms NIS25/US$6.25; singles NIS105/US$26.25; doubles NIS120/US$30. Cash only.

Walied's Akko Gate Hostel (☎ 991 04 10; fax 981 55 30), near the eastern Nikanor Gate on Salah al-Din St., a mere stumble from the beach. Sports a rooftop bar and a pool table (NIS25 per hr.). Kitchen available. Breakfast NIS25. Check-out 10am. Single-sex and coed dorms NIS25/US$6.25; rooms NIS120/US$30, with A/C and bath NIS200/US$50. Credit cards accepted.

Paul's Hostel and Souvenir Shop (☎ 991 28 57 or 981 76 86). Souvenir shop doubling as reception is just across from the lighthouse at the southern end of Ha-Hagana St. under a large yellow awning. For a down-and-dirty backpacker experience, this hostel has one large room stuffed with bunkbeds and a single bathroom. Climate control, summer and winter, consists of a few ceiling fans. Reception 24hr. Check-out noon. Coed 20-bed dorms NIS20/US$5; private room with bath NIS100/US$25.

◖ FOOD

The *souq*, a tumultuous avenue of butchers, bakers, candlestick-makers, and copper, brass, and leather vendors, bustles from 6am-5pm, though supplies start to run out after noon on busier days. Food stands along the *souq* offer kebab, falafel, and sandwiches (NIS5-10) as well as cheap, fresh produce and exotic spices. There are also food stands and supermarkets on Ben-Ami St. and Yehoshafat St. in the new city. More expensive options can be found in the Pisan harbor, where standard Middle Eastern meat and fish entrees go for NIS35-65.

Hummus Said's (☎ 991 39 45), in the midst of the *souq*, on your right when coming from the plaza off Salah al-Din St. Kick, shove, bribe: do whatever it takes to get through the hordes of locals. NIS12 buys 3 piping hot pitas, a plate of vegetables, and a deep dish of creamy hummus. If there are no tables open (and there won't be), try the take-out version, a pita stuffed with hummus, hot chickpeas, and vegetables (NIS3.50). Open M-Sa 6am until the food runs out, usually around 2pm.

Oriental Sweets, right next to Said's. Every possible combination of filo dough, nuts, and honey goes for NIS1-3. Even cheaper in large quantities. Open daily 8am-5pm.

Ptolmais Restaurant (☎ 991 61 12), on the left side of the marina, when facing the sea. One of the cheaper options on the marina, Ptolmais serves up lamb *shishlik* (NIS45) and various kebabs (NIS33), but herbivores just there for the great view might opt for hummus or tahini and pita (NIS13). Open daily 11am-midnight.

◉ SIGHTS

The moats and dungeons of **Old Akko** speak clearly of the city's war-filled history. Guides—a.k.a. juice bar workers, waiters, and shopkeepers in their spare time—offer tours of varying quality and for varying prices. Ballpark figures are NIS15 for a sight and NIS120 for all of Akko, but make sure to verify beforehand. Women, especially, should ascertain what is expected in return for these tours.

CRUSADER CITY. Archaeologists first thought that the rooms in the Crusader City were built underground; they have since determined that al-Jazzar simply built his city on top of once above-land buildings. Much of the Crusader City still remains buried, but excavations expose more treasures each year. Most visible structures are part of the "Hospitaller's Quarter." Decorations on the columns with images of flowers or human forms are Crusader work, while abstract embellishments and Arabic calligraphy come from Ottoman artisans. The 12th-century halls were probably part of a medical complex where the Hospitaller Order treated pilgrims. From the courtyard beyond the entrance hall, fortifications built by Fakhr al-Din and Tahir al-Omar are visible. Halfway down the stairs on the left and along the wooden path are the giant rooms of the Hospitaller Castle, called the **Knights' Halls**, built on top of 3rd-century BCE Hellenistic foundations. (*Across from the mosque on al-Jazzar St., in the same building as the tourist office. ☎ 991 17 64. Open Su-Th 8:30am-7pm, F 8:30am-3pm; in winter Su-Th 8:30am-4:45pm, F 8:30am-2pm. NIS25, children and students NIS22. For groups over 20: NIS21, children and students NIS18. Ticket includes access to all sights in the Crusader City and the Okashi Museum and comes with a hand-held audio tour in English, Hebrew, or German. Combination ticket available with Rosh Ha-Nikra.*)

MOSQUE OF AL-JAZZAR. The third-largest mosque in Israel, it dominates the city with its green dome and towering minaret. Ahmed al-Jazzar ordered its construction in 1781 on what is believed to have been the site of San Croce, the original Christian cathedral of Akko. Inside is an attractive courtyard with Roman columns taken from Caesarea. Legend has it that al-Jazzar buried a large treasure underneath the mosque to ensure that there would be plenty of money to rebuild the place if it were ever destroyed. The tower was destroyed by an earthquake in 1927, but was promptly restored; the rest of the complex is in magnificent condition. Inside, in the green cage on the right side of the balcony, is a shrine containing a hair from the beard of the prophet Muhammad. Prayers are conducted five times a day, and visitors who arrive during a prayer session may be asked to wait.

To the right of the mosque is a small building containing the **sarcophagi** of al-Jazzar and son; peek through the barred windows at the marble boxes, now covered with soil and green plants. Al-Jazzar turned the buried Crusader cathedral into an underground water reservoir that received rainwater from the nearby Pasha gardens. The reservoir is accessible through a door and underground stairway at the left end of the mosque. Look for the small green sign and red arrows. *(The mosque entrance is a short walk on al-Jazzar St., across from the post office. Open daily 8am-7pm; in winter 8am-5pm. Closed periodically for 20min. during prayer time. NIS5, NIS3 after 4pm. Modest dress required; scarves available for those not already covered.)*

CITADEL. This stronghold, used by the British as their central prison, now houses the **Museum of Heroism,** a monument to Zionist fighters imprisoned by the British during the Mandate. The Citadel, built in the late 1700s on 13th-century Crusader foundations, was used as an **Ottoman prison.** The most famous inmate during the Ottoman rule was Baha'ullah, founder of the Baha'i faith, who was imprisoned on the second floor in 1868. During the British Mandate, the prison housed about 560 inmates under the guard of about half as many British soldiers. Members of the Etzel, Ha-Ganah, and Leḥi, including Ze'ev Jabotinsky, were incarcerated here for violent anti-British activities. Nine members of the resistance were sentenced to death by hanging between 1938 and 1947. The **Gallows Room** displays the noose, along with photographs of the nine fighters. On May 4, 1947, Etzel members staged a prison break that freed 41 of their peers and enabled the escape of 214 Arab prisoners (later depicted in the movie *Exodus*, shot on location). Across from the museum looms **Burj al-Kuraim** (Fortress of the Vineyards), often referred to as the British Fortress despite its Crusader and Ottoman construction. *(The Citadel adjoins the Crusader City on Ha-Hagana St., opposite the sea wall. To reach the museum from the Old City, exit on Weizmann St. and take an immediate left on the path. At the entrance, follow the stone stairs down to the lower garden, then the metal stairs up and around the side of the prison. ☎ 991 82 64. Open Sa-Th 9am-6pm, F 9am-1pm. NIS8, students NIS4.)*

CITY WALLS. A stroll along the Old City's cannon-spotted perimeter yields an interesting look at Akko's seaside defenses. Akko's security in recent centuries has relied upon **al-Jazzar Wall,** running along the northern and eastern sides of the city and surrounded by a sea water moat. The best place from which to view the wall, which originally ran the length of the harbor, is **Burj al-Kommander** (Commander's Fortress), an enormous Crusader bastion at the northeastern corner. To enter the watchtower, climb the steps beginning where Weizmann St. meets the wall. Follow the green signs, which describe Napoleon's siege in reference to the walls, despite the fact that they were built after Napoleon's retreat; the deception works because the new walls are in form, if not appearance and dimensions, the same as the old. England blew up the original walls in the siege of 1840 (almost half a century after Napoleon), when the Egyptians were using them as an ammunition dump. The **Tower of the Flies,** the site of the original lighthouse, solemnly broods in the middle of the bay. Its fortifications were toppled by a devastating earthquake in 1837. At the eastern corner near the shoreline is **Land Gate** (also known as Nikanor Gate), once the only entrance to the city. Next to the marina, locals like to leap into the water from windows in the walls.

⚡ DAYTRIP FROM AKKO: LOHAMEI HA-GETA'OT

*Lohamei Ha-Geta'ot lies between Akko and Nahariya. To reach the kibbutz, take **bus** #271 from Akko or Nahariya (10min., every 20min., NIS7) or a **sherut** (NIS6.50).*

Lohamei Ha-Geta'ot ("Fighters of the Ghettos") is a kibbutz founded in 1949 by survivors of concentration camps and the Warsaw Ghetto uprising. It now houses an entire building dedicated to the stories of children, and is one of Israel's most powerful Holocaust museums. The **Ghetto Fighter's House** examines Jewish life in Eastern Europe during the years leading up to World War II and during the Holocaust. The exhibits on Jewish Youth resistance movements during the war and ghetto uprisings are particularly intriguing. An entire floor chronicles the Nazi invasion of Europe and more specific exhibits relate the stories of Jews in Holland and Greece. (☎995 80 80; fax 995 80 07; mgans@gfh.org.il. Open Su-Th 9am-4pm; May-Sept., Su-Th 9am-6pm and F 9am-1pm. Free, but donation requested.) The recently constructed **Yad La-Yeled** in a nearby building is a memorial to the 1½ million children who perished in the Holocaust.

GALILEE הגליל الجليل

When the ancient Israelites described their country as flowing with milk and honey, they must have been talking about the Galilee. This lush and fertile region, bordering the West Bank to the south, the Golan to the east, Lebanon to the north, and the Mediterranean coast to the west, is laced by cool, refreshing rivers and carpeted with rolling, green hills. The Galilee was originally a province of the ancient Israelite kingdom, called *Ha-Galil* (the district) in Hebrew, whose inhabitants prospered by fishing and farming. As communities in the Galilee grew, religious leaders flocked to the area. Jesus grew up in Nazareth, performed many of his first miracles near the Sea of Galilee, and gave his famous sermon atop the Mount of Beatitudes. His apostles lived and taught in nearby Capernaum. Fifty years later, when Romans destroyed the second Temple in Jerusalem, the Sanhedrin relocated to the Galilee and resided there for the next 250 years. Dozens of armies swept through the region during the following millennium.

Despite a history of almost continuous war, today Galilee is one of the most peaceful areas in Israel. Since Israel captured the strategic Golan Heights in 1967 (see p. 268), putting the Galilee out of range of Syrian rockets, the region has blossomed into a tourist mecca. Busloads of pilgrims descend a massive metal staircase into the Jordan River at the site where John is believed to have baptized Jesus, banana boats and booze cruises skim over the Sea's blue waters to deposit passengers upon the bustling Tiberias promenade, and hikers crowd the trails of the Upper Galilee where Crusader fortresses keep watch over forested valleys. Meanwhile, the ancient synagogues of Tzfat and the churches of Nazareth continue to attract the faithful.

NAZARETH נצרת الناصرة ☎06

A vibrant center of Arab life in the Galilee, Nazareth (al-Nassra in Arabic, Natzrat in Hebrew) is a far cry from Christmas-card pictures of pastoral churches, quiet convents, and grazing sheep. Nazareth is indeed dear to Christian pilgrims as the setting of Jesus' younger years and the traditional home of Mary and Joseph, but it is also a gritty town. While devotees throng to a handful of neo-Gothic churches, drivers charge through dusty construction sites on the main road and crowds drift through the winding alleys of the hillside market.

Nazareth's population is roughly one-third Christian and two-thirds Muslim, with a small Jewish population. Unlike nationalist Palestinians in the West Bank, Nazarean Arabs are content as Israeli citizens. Life here, however, is worlds away from the beaches of Haifa and Tel Aviv. Visitors—especially women—should dress modestly to avoid harassment on the streets and difficulty entering churches. Parts of the city may be unsafe after dark.

▐ TRANSPORTATION

Buses: The **"bus station"** consists of several stops on Paul VI St., near Casa Nova St. When taking a bus to Nazareth, make sure it goes to Natzeret Ha-Atika, not Natzrat Illit. The upper city is a 20min. local bus ride from the old city. Buses leaving town head west on Paul VI St. The **Egged** info booth is on Paul VI St., just east of the intersection with Casa Nova. Open Su-F 7am-3pm. To: **Afula** (#355, 356, 357, 823, 824, and 953; 20min.; every 40min.-1½hr. Su-Th 5:25am-7:55pm, F 6am-3:30pm, Sa 4:15-9pm; NIS8); **Akko** (#343; 1½hr.; every 1-2hr. Su-Th 6:45am-5pm, F 6:45am-4:15pm; NIS21.50, students NIS19.50); **Haifa** (#331 and 431; 1hr.; every 1-2hr. Su-Th 5:40am-8:10pm, F 5:40am-5:10pm; NIS18); **Jerusalem** (#953, 3½hr., 6:30am, NIS40); **Tel Aviv** (#823 and 824 go from Natzrat Illit by way of Nazareth; 2½hr.; every 30min.-1hr. Su-Th 5:10am-7:40pm, F 5:45am-3:15pm, Sa 4-8:45pm; NIS32) via **Tel Megiddo** (45min., NIS13); **Tiberias** (#431; 1hr.; every 1-2hr. Su-Th 6:50am-9:30pm, F 7am-5:30pm, Sa 7-10pm; NIS18).

Taxis: Ma'ayan (☎655 51 05), Abu al-Assal (☎655 47 45), Galil (☎655 55 36), and Saiegh (☎646 35 11). Taxis can be found all along Paul VI St.

Service: *Service* gather on a small side street just off of Paul VI St. and across from the central bus stop. To: **Haifa** (NIS15); **Jenin** (NIS12); **Tel Aviv** (NIS25); and **Tiberias** (NIS18). *Service* run every day.

Car Rental: Europcar (☎655 41 29), at casa Nova St., next to the tourist office. 24+. Cars start at US$40 per day, automatics US$60 per day; min. 3-day rental. Open M-F 8:30am-6pm and Sa 8:30am-2pm. Credit card required.

✳▐ ORIENTATION AND PRACTICAL INFORMATION

Nazareth is 40km southeast of Haifa and 30km southwest of Tiberias, on a hill north of the Jezreel Valley. All the Christian sights are in the Arab **Old Nazareth** (Natzeret Ha-Atika). Upper Nazareth (Natzrat Illit), the newer, Jewish section of town, is residential and of little interest to tourists. The Arab town's main road, **Paul VI St.**, lies to the east of the sights. Its intersection with **Casa Nova St.,** just

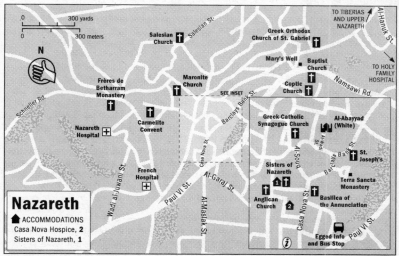

Nazareth
▲ ACCOMMODATIONS
Casa Nova Hospice, **2**
Sisters of Nazareth, **1**

below the Basilica, is the busiest part of town. Uphill from Casa Nova St., among churches, is the market area. Higher quality accommodations and panoramic views are farther up the hill toward **Salesian St.** and Mary's Well. Obtain a **map** of the city from the GTIO (see **Tourist Office,** below), as few of the streets have signs. Nazareth's Christian community shuts down on Sundays, but most establishments are open on Shabbat. Although Arabic is the major language, everybody speaks Hebrew and the proprietors of most tourist sites also speak English.

Tourist Office: Government Tourist Information Office (GTIO) (☎ 657 30 03; fax 657 30 78), on Casa Nova St., near the intersection with Paul VI St., next door to Israel Discount Bank. Staff distributes brochures and colorful new maps. Computerized information available. Open M-F 8:30am-5pm, Sa 8:30am-2pm.

Currency Exchange: Money Net (☎ 655 25 40), on the south side of Paul VI St., just west of Casa Nova St. Exchanges cash and traveler's checks with no commission. Open M-Tu and Th-F 8:30am-7pm, W and Sa 8:30am-3pm. The **post office** also exchanges cash and traveler's checks with no commission.

Banks: Israel Discount Bank (☎ 602 73 33), on Casa Nova St. by tourist office, has an **ATM.** Open Su, W, and F 8:30am-1pm; M-Tu and Th 8:30am-12:30pm and 3:30-6pm. **Bank Leumi** and **Arab Israeli Bank,** on Paul VI St. opposite the station, have **ATMs.**

Police (☎ 602 84 44), next to the post office by Mary's Well.

Pharmacy: Farah Pharmacy (☎ 655 40 18), next to Egged info, on Paul VI St. across from Bank Ha-Poalim. Open M and F 9am-7pm, Tu and Th 9am-1:30pm and 4-7pm, W and Sa 9am-2pm.

Hospitals: Nazareth Hospital (☎ 657 15 01 or 657 15 02), **Holy Family Hospital** (☎ 650 89 00), and **French Hospital** (☎ 650 90 00).

Post Office: Central branch (☎ 655 51 88), 2 blocks uphill from Paul VI St. from Mary's Well. Exchanges cash and traveler's checks; offers **Western Union** and **Poste Restante.** Open M-Tu and Th-F 8am-12:30pm and 3:30-6pm, W 8am-1:30pm, Sa 8am-noon.

ACCOMMODATIONS

During Christian holidays, it takes divine intervention to find a room here. At other times, hospices are crowded with tour groups but often have a bed to spare. There are very few budget accommodations in Nazareth, so call ahead if possible.

Sisters of Nazareth, P.O. Box 274 (☎ 655 43 04; fax 646 07 41). From Paul VI St., walk uphill on Casa Nova St. and turn left at the Basilica's entrance. This 150 year-old Catholic convent still looks brand new. The courtyard was built over ruins from the first century, which the sisters claim contain the grave of St. Joseph. They offer tours of the excavations M-Sa 8:30am. Breakfast NIS16; lunch and dinner NIS36 each. Reception 6am-9pm. Check-in 4pm. Check-out 10am (flexible). Strict 9pm curfew. Private rooms have bathrooms and great views. Single-sex dorms NIS32/US$8; singles NIS100/US$24; doubles NIS160/US$38; triples NIS240/US$57. Reservations recommended.

Galilee Hotel (☎ 657 13 11; fax 655 66 27), on Paul VI St., two blocks west of Casa Nova St. This modern hotel offers clean, spacious rooms with A/C, telephones, and bathrooms with tubs. Reception 24hr. Check-in 2pm. Check-out noon. Singles NIS210/US$50; doubles NIS330/US$80; triples NIS420/US$100. Credit cards accepted.

Casa Nova Hospice (☎ 645 66 60; fax 657 96 30), on Casa Nova St. opposite the Basilica of the Annunciation. Comfortable and clean rooms with A/C, private bath, and phones, usually full of tour groups. Breakfast included. Lunch and dinner US$8 each. Check-out 8:30am. Curfew 11pm. Singles NIS160/US$40; doubles NIS200/US$48; triples NIS290/US$72. 5% service charge. Traveler's checks accepted.

FOOD

Nazareth's cuisine is not known for diversity. Dozens of falafel stands and identical "Oriental" restaurants line the downtown streets. Restaurant hours are generally 7am-9pm, and many places are closed on Sunday. Several **food kiosks** can be found along the streets, but the biggest one is directly opposite the bakery. Besides that, the only options for late-night snacks are the shawarma stands along Paul VI St. near Casa Nova St. These usually stay open until midnight.

La Fontana di Maria (☎ 646 04 35), on Paul VI St., to the right of Mary's Well. Inside a Turkish *khan* with high vaulted ceilings, this is Nazareth's only classy sit-down restaurant. House specialties include steak (NIS50), kebab (NIS40), and cornish hen (NIS50). Soups (NIS15) and salads (NIS10-25) are a bit cheaper. Open daily 11am-11pm. Credit cards accepted.

Abu Hani's Falafel and Shawarma, on Paul VI St., just west of the intersection with Casa Nova St. Look for the large sign in front advertising falafel and shawarma deals. This tiny place has some of the best and cheapest falafel (NIS7) and shawarma (NIS10) in town. Soda NIS2 extra. Open M-Sa 9am-9pm.

Fahoum Restaurant (☎ 655 33 32), on Casa Nova St., on the left, just up from Paul VI St. This modern-looking restaurant actually dates back to before the creation of the state of Israel. Delicious chicken *shishlik* NIS35; St. Peter's Fish NIS50; kebab with chips NIS40; hummus plate NIS15. Open daily 8am-9pm. Credit cards accepted.

Mahroum Sweets (☎ 656 02 14), on Paul VI St., at the intersection with Casa Nova St. Gooey, sweet pastries in a shiny, mirrored interior. *Baklava* NIS30 per kg. Cookies NIS20 per kg. Coffee and tea NIS5. Open daily 8:30am-11pm.

🔆 SIGHTS

Nazareth received a much-needed US$60 million face-lift for the millennium that included repaving many of the old city streets, constructing new promenades with scenic vistas, and putting up prominent signs to help pilgrims find their way to the numerous religious sights in town. The majority of sights are clustered around Paul VI St. and the *souq*, but the new Nazareth Village hopes to draw tourists up the hill to experience life as it was in ancient times. Nazareth's churches are all free to visitors, but they happily accept donations.

BASILICA OF THE ANNUNCIATION. Nazareth is synonymous with churches and none is more prominent than the huge basilica that dominates downtown with its faceted lantern dome. Completed in 1969, the basilica is built on the site believed to be Mary's home, where the archangel Gabriel heralded the birth of Jesus. Inside the huge, bronze doors depicting the life of Jesus is the **Grotto of the Annunciation,** the site of Mary's home. A gallery overlooking the grotto is lined with a series of artistic interpretations of the Annunciation. Outside, Madonna and Child mosaics from nearly every country in the world grace the courtyard walls. Churches have marked this spot since 356 CE; excavations of churches and ancient Nazareth lie in a garden underneath the plaza, accessible from the upper floor of the basilica. *(Walk up Casa Nova St. from Paul VI St.; the entrance is on the right.* ☎ 657 25 01. *Open Apr.-Sept. M-Sa 8am-5:30pm; Oct.-Mar. M-Sa 8am-4:30pm. Shorts not allowed.)*

ST. JOSEPH'S CHURCH. This church was built in 1914, on top of the cave thought to have been Joseph's house. The present structure incorporates remnants of a Byzantine church. Inside, stairs descend to caves that once stored grain and oil, as well as an early baptismal bath. Although this is usually referred to as Joseph's workshop, evidence suggests that these caves have been used since the late Stone Age. *(Next to the Basilica of the Annunciation, in the same plaza on Casa Nova St.)*

GREEK-CATHOLIC SYNAGOGUE CHURCH. Recently restored by a group of Italian archeology students, the church is built on the site of the synagogue where young Jesus is believed to have preached. Next door is the beautiful 18th-century Greek-Catholic Church of the Annunciation. Two hundred meters up from the church on street 6126, on the left in a small chapel, is the **Mensa Christi** stone where Jesus supposedly ate with his disciples after his resurrection. *(In the center of the Arab market. Enter the souq from Casa Nova St., turn left after the music shop, and follow the street to the right. Open M-Sa 8am-6pm. If closed ring the bell on the door to the left.)*

ISRAEL

SOUQ. Nazareth's outdoor market is the best place in the city to buy olive wood camels and Bart Simpson underwear. It has been gutted and repaved in the last two years; today its white stones sparkle. Although perfectly safe in daylight, the market area is best avoided at night, when dope fiends lurk in its dark alleyways. *(Best reached via Casa Nova St. Open M-Sa 9am-5pm.)*

MARY'S WELL. Many believe that the well's water miraculously heals; recently it has begun to heal its once-ugly surroundings. Over the past few years, a new plaza, a few restaurants, and souvenir shops have sprouted nearby. The recently-built scenic promenades begin near here. From the well, continue right along Paul VI St. to the Namsawi Promenade and then up the hill to the promenades and the Salesian Church. *(The well is northeast of the bus station on Paul VI St.)*

GREEK ORTHODOX CHURCH OF ST. GABRIEL. The Church of St. Gabriel stands over the town's ancient water source. The original church was erected in 356 CE over the spring where Mary drew water and where the Greek Orthodox believe Gabriel appeared. The present structure, built in 1750, has elaborate Byzantine-style paintings and an ornate gold chandelier in the center. *(Left and uphill from Mary's Well, just off Paul VI St. Open M-Sa 7am-9pm, Su 7am-1pm and 2-9pm.)*

TIBERIAS טבריה طبرية ☎06

To accommodate its diverse group of visitors—vacationing Israeli families, party-seeking youths, weary backpackers, and Christian pilgrims from Hong Kong, Alabama, and everywhere in between—Tiberias has become a bizarre mix of flash and trash. Stores hawking Virgin Mary night lights and baby Jesus key-chains shut down just when the disco ball starts to twirl in the bar next door, and cafe waiters, hostels owners, and shopkeepers stand ready to pounce on any passerby. Despite proposals to clean up the city, Tiberias remains a whiff of Israel at its rawest.

Though its central location and cheap beds make it an ideal touring base for the Galilee and the Golan, its position 200m below sea level guarantees a hot, humid, and mosquito-ridden July and August. Of course, the action in Tiberias is also hottest during those months, with increased transportation, the best parties, street fairs, and everybody's favorite—price gouging.

▮ TRANSPORTATION

Buses: Bus station (☎672 92 22) at the corner of Ha-Yarden St. and Ha-Shiloah St. To: **Haifa** (#430 (express) and 431; 1¾hr.; every hr. Su-Th 6am-6:30pm, F 6am-4:30pm, Sa 4:45-7pm; NIS23.50, students NIS21); **Jerusalem** (#961, 963, or 964; 3hr.; every 30-60min. Su-Th 5:50am-7pm, F 7:30am-3pm, Sa 4:30-9:45pm; NIS42, students NIS38); **Tel Aviv** (#830, 835, 836, 840, or 841 (local); 2½-3hr.; every 30min. Su-Th 5:30am-9pm, F 6am-5pm, Sa 4-10pm; NIS35.50, students NIS32).

Taxis: *Sherut* and private cabs wait in the parking lot below the bus station and on Bibas St. To **Haifa** (NIS20) and **Tel Aviv** (NIS32). **Taxi Haemek** (☎672 01 31), at the corner of Ha-Shiloah St. and Ha-Yarden St.

Car Rental: Avis (☎672 27 66), in the parking lot below the bus station. All of the following are on Ha-Banim St. **Arad** (☎672 49 99). 21+, under 23 NIS90 extra. **Eldan** (☎679 18 22). 24+, 10% student discount. **Hertz** (☎672 39 39). 21+, under 23 NIS60 extra. **Budget** (☎672 08 64 or 672 34 96). 23+. All open Su-Th 8am-5pm, F 8am-2pm. Min. 2 years driving experience required.

▰▰ ORIENTATION AND PRACTICAL INFORMATION

Tiberias has three tiers: the **old city** by the water, **Kiryat Shmuel,** the new city up the hill, and **T'verya Illit** (Upper Tiberias) at the top of the hill (bus #7-10, every 10min., NIS4.10). The upper sections are residential; all boozing, boating, and beaching takes place in the old city. **Ha-Galil St.** and **Ha-Banim St.** run parallel to the water; **Ha-Yarden St.** runs perpendicular to them to the north. **Ha-Yarkon St.** and **Ha-Kishon St.**

intersect Ha-Galil St. and Ha-Banim St. to the south. The central **midraḥov** (pedestrian mall) runs from Ha-Banim St. to the waterfront **promenade.**

Tourist Office: Government Tourist Information Office (☎672 56 66), on Ha-Banim St., in the archaeological park next to the Jordan River Hotel. Free city maps and brochures. Open Su-Th 8am-1pm and 2-5pm (until 7pm in Aug.), F 8am-noon.

Tours: Matan Tours (☎672 45 74 or 054 61 61 48), offers a one-day tour from Tiberias of both Tzfat and Nazareth (NIS150).

Currency Exchange: Discount package paid in US dollars are the way of business here. The post office on Ha-Yarden St. gives top rates with no commission. **Money Net** (☎672 40 48), next to Bank Leumi on the corner of Ha-Banim St. and Ha-Yarden St., also charges no commission. Open Su-M and W-Th 8:30am-1pm and 4-7pm, Tu 8am-1:30pm, F 8:30am-1pm. **Bank Ha-Poalim** (☎679 84 11), on Ha-Banim St. between Ha-Yarden St. and Ha-Yarkon St., has a 24hr. **ATM.**

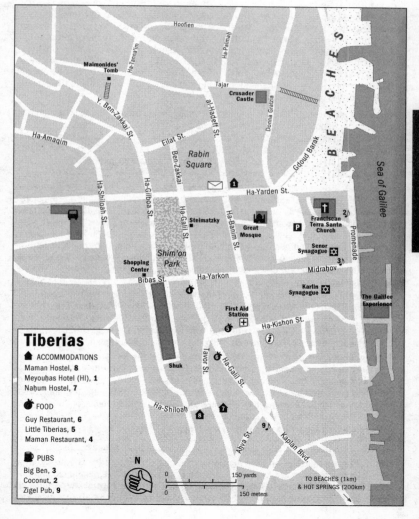

ISRAEL

Tiberias

🔺 ACCOMMODATIONS

Maman Hostel, **8**
Meyouḥas Hotel (HI), **1**
Naḥum Hostel, **7**

🍴 FOOD

Guy Restaurant, **6**
Little Tiberias, **5**
Maman Restaurant, **4**

🍺 PUBS

Big Ben, **3**
Coconut, **2**
Zigel Pub, **9**

Camping Supplies: Terminal La-Metayel, 38 Ha-Yarden St. (☎672 39 72), between the bus station and Ha-Galil St. Open Su-M and W-Th 9am-1:30pm and 4-7:30pm, Tu and F 9am-1:30pm.

Emergency: First Aid (☎679 01 11), corner of Ha-Banim St. and Ha-Kishon St. Open 24hr. **Police** ☎679 24 44. **Fire** ☎679 12 22.

Internet Access: Big Ben, at the end of the *midrahov* on the left. NIS20 per 30min. Open daily 8:30am-late. **Immanuel Internet Cafe** (☎672 36 20), in the Galilee Experience gift shop. NIS10 per 15min. Open Su-Th 8am-10pm, F 8am-5pm, Sa 5-10pm.

Post Office: Central office, 1 Kikkar Rabin (☎672 22 66), in parking lot off Ha-Yarden St., between Ha-Atzma'ut St. and al-Hadef St. **Poste Restante, EMS,** and **Western Union.** Open Su-Tu and Th 8am-12:30pm and 3:30-6pm, W 8am-1:30pm, F 8am-noon.

▮ ACCOMMODATIONS

Competition is fierce in Tiberias; at peak times, hostel "runners" swoop on visitors as they get off the bus. Don't be afraid to ask to switch to a different room if there's something wrong with the first one; Tiberias is not the place to value politeness over sanity. Speaking of sanity, all rooms (dorms included) have air-conditioning.

Prices rise between July and September and reservations for private rooms are recommended. The Jewish holidays of Pesah, Rosh Ha-Shana, and Sukkot are mob scenes. There are many "Room For Rent" signs throughout the city, but be aware that private homes are unlicensed and therefore not subject to inspection. Lone travelers should avoid sleeping in private houses.

Maman Hostel (☎679 29 86), on Atzmon St. From central bus station, walk right on Ha-Shiloah St. Bubbly international crowd keeps cool in the pool or on a stool at the tropical bar. If the atmosphere doesn't compensate for the thin dorm mattresses, at least private rooms are tasteful. Kitchen available. Free safe and storage. Check-out 10am. Dorms NIS25/US$6, July-Aug. NIS30/US$7.50; singles with bath NIS100/US$25, July-Aug. NIS120/US$30; doubles NIS100/US$25, July-Aug. NIS150/US$37.50.

Hostel Aviv, 66 Ha-Galil St. (☎672 00 07 or 672 35 10), one block past the intersection with Ha-Banim St. Stomping grounds for the rough-and-rugged but oh-so-friendly backpacker crowd, Aviv has some of the cheapest (and smallest) rooms in the city. Management offers copious discounts and freebies. Kitchen available; free coffee supplies. Free safe; lockers NIS10. Internet NIS20 per 30min. Reception 24hr. Check-out 10am. Single-sex and coed dorms with bath NIS25/US$6, July-Aug. NIS30/US$7.50; singles with bath, TV, and fridge NIS60-80/US$15-20; doubles with bath, TV, and fridge NIS100-120/US$25-30. Credit cards accepted.

Meyouhas Hostel (HI) (☎672 17 75 or 679 03 50; fax 672 03 72), at corner of Donna Gratzia St. and Ha-Yarden St., in a local black basalt rock building. Breakfast included. Free safe; lockers NIS6. Reception 24hr. Check-in 2pm. Check-out 10am. Coed dorms NIS52/US$13, July-Aug. NIS78/US$19.50; singles with bath NIS128/US$38, July-Aug. NIS172/US$43; doubles with bath NIS224/US$56, July-Aug. NIS252/US$63. NIS8 student discount; NIS7 member discount. Credit cards accepted.

Nahum Hostel (☎672 15 05; fax 671 74 37). Head right (as you face the sea) on either Ha-Shiloah or Ha-Galil and turn onto Tavor St. Backpackers relax with a Goldstar in the rooftop bar before heading back to their huge dorms with kitchenettes, bathrooms, and thin foam mattresses. Coed and single-sex dorms NIS25/US$7; private rooms with bath NIS100/US$25. Prices rise 20% in high season. 10% discount for stays longer than three days. Credit cards accepted.

▮ FOOD

Tiberias can easily meet all your beach and hiking picnic needs. The *shuk*, in a square block starting at Ha-Yarkon St. across from Shimron Park, sells cheap produce and baked goods every day except Shabbat. There is a **Supersol** supermarket on Ha-Banim St. (open Su-Th 8am-8:30pm, F 8am-4pm, and Sa after sundown-

10pm) and a **Hafer** supermarket on the corner of Ha-Banim and Ha-Yarden St. (Open Su-Th 8am-9pm, F 8am-3pm, and Sa 9-11pm.)

The restaurant scene, plagued by too many tourists, is not nearly so ideal. Grilleries on Ha-Banim St. near the *midraḥov* serve *shishlik* with salad and pita (NIS20). Waterfront seafood restaurants offer idyllic settings complete with jet skiers and plastic bottle flotillas. A dinner of **St. Peter's fish**, a Sea of Galilee specialty, costs about NIS35-50. Ha-Galil St., Ha-Banim St., and the squares in between burgeon with culinary possibilities, but beware of menus that don't list prices.

Guy Restaurant (☎ 672 30 36), on Ha-Galil St., past Ha-Kishon St. when coming from the center of town. No frills and no big bills found at this fabulous Moroccan place. Stuffed veggies with rice NIS7-15, with meat NIS12-15. Spicy meatballs NIS15. Meanest coffee around NIS4. Open Su-Th noon-11pm, F noon-5pm.

Decks (☎ 672 15 38), at Lido Beach. Turn left at the end of the promenade and continue 200m down Gdoud Barak St. Cleanse your palate on the lemon and mint slushes (NIS20) and finish off with the heavenly apple crepes, drenched in sorbet and wine-soaked cherries (NIS25). Open Su-Th 6pm-midnight, Sa sundown-midnight.

Maman Restaurant (☎ 672 11 26), 21 Ha-Galil St. Packed with Israeli regulars. Excellent hummus with pita and olives NIS12. St. Peter's fish at the lowest price around (NIS30). Open Su-Th 11am-11pm, F 11am-4pm, Sa sundown-11pm.

Little Tiberias (☎ 679 21 48 or 679 28 06), on Ha-Kishon St. *midraḥov*. Families flock to this homey retreat from *midraḥov* mayhem. Huge salads (Greek and Caesar) NIS28; grilled meat NIS40-60; and indulgently creamy veg. dishes NIS34. Open daily noon-midnight. AmEx/MC/V.

🜚 SIGHTS

As the seat of Talmudic study in the 2nd and 3rd centuries CE, Tiberias hosted a number of influential scholars. Buried in the hills around Tiberias are several of the giants in Jewish thought, history, and Torah commentary. Modest dress is required for visiting the tombs; head coverings are provided for men. All that's left of the **Old City**, shaken by earthquakes and conquerors, is a few black basalt wall fragments scattered throughout the modern town. A **free tour** leaves from the Sheraton Moriah-Plaza hotel every Saturday at 10am.

TOMB OF MAIMONIDES. The best-known of the scholars laid to rest in Tiberias is Moses Maimonides, the hugely influential 12th-century physician and philosopher whose works synthesized neo-Aristotelian-Arab philosophy with Judaism. According to legend, an unguided camel carried his coffin to Tiberias. The white half-cylinder is the actual tomb; the Hebrew inscription is a Jewish saying: "From Moses [the original] until Moses [Maimonides] there was no one like Moses [Maimonides]." Ask for the tomb of "Rambam," the Hebrew acronym for his full name (Rabbi Moshe Ben-Maimon). *(Walk out Ben-Zakkai St. from Ha-Yarden St.; the tomb is two blocks up on the right, up a wide stairway. Look for the red metal sculpture above the tomb.)*

BEN-ZAKKAI'S TOMB. Rabbi Yoḥanan Ben-Zakkai snuck out of besieged Jerusalem in a coffin, popped out of the casket in front of the Roman General Vespasian, and prophetically addressed him as "Caesar." When news of the old Caesar's death arrived, Vespasian graciously granted Rabbi Yoḥanan one wish. The rabbi chose to found a house of study with his students. *(Next to Maimonides' tomb on Ben-Zakkai St.)*

RABBI AKIVA'S TOMB. Rabbi Akiva, a woodcutter who began to study only after age 40, is one of the more frequently quoted rabbis in the Talmud and was one of the students who helped carry Rabbi Yoḥanan out of Jerusalem. Believers gather to have their illnesses cured at the hillside tomb of Akiva's student, **Rabbi Meir Ba'al Ha-Nes**, above the hot springs. *(On the hillside directly above the city. See the GTIO city map for walking directions, or take bus #4, 4-aleph, 6, or 6-aleph and ask for directions.)*

FRANCISCAN TERRA SANCTA CHURCH. Also known as St. Peter's, the Terra Sancta Church was built in the 12th century to commemorate St. Peter's role in the growth of Christianity. The church is set back next to the Papaya Bar; look for the five crosses on the brown door (the symbol and color of the Franciscan church). The apse behind the altar is arched like the bow of a boat in honor of Jesus' fishing career. In the courtyard is a statue of the Virgin Mary created by Polish troops who lived in the church from 1942 to 1945. *(On the promenade in front of the Caesar Hotel. ☎672 05 16. Open daily 8:30am-6pm. Modest dress required.)*

CRUSADER CASTLE. The crumbling remains of a 12th-century **Crusader castle** overlook the Sea of Galilee. Admission includes coffee, a short historical tour, a sentinel's view of the water, and entrance to the art galleries now housed in the castle. *(A block past the Meyohaus Youth Hostel on Donna Gratzia St. ☎672 13 75. Gallery open Su-Th 9am-1pm and 3-6pm, F 9am-1pm. NIS10.)*

◪ BEACHES

For many **beaches** on the Galilee, you'll have to bring your own sand—otherwise, bring sandals for walking over the sizzling rocks. Most beaches are owned by hotels that charge hefty fees in exchange for changing rooms, showers, boat rentals, and food. The beaches just north of town are along Gdoud Barak Rd., off Ha-Yarden St.; those to the south lie off the main coastal road (Rte. 90, with which Ha-Galil merges). **Lido Kinneret,** just off Ha-Yarden St., charges NIS20 for 45min. boat rides on the lake, but they are often only available for groups. Waterskiing is NIS200/US$50 for 15min. (☎672 15 38. Open daily 8am-5:30pm.) Just north of Lido, **Quiet Beach** (Ḥof Ha-Sheket), with a pool, an energetic DJ, and hordes of school kids, is anything but quiet. (☎670 08 00. Open daily 9am-6pm. NIS25, children NIS20.) Next in line to the north, **Blue Beach** boasts the largest swimming area and best view on the lake. (☎672 01 05. Open daily 9am-5pm. NIS25, children NIS20; NIS5 more on Shabbat.) A 15min. walk from the city center or a short ride on bus #5-aleph south of Tiberias leads to **Ganim Beach.** (☎672 07 09. Open daily 9am-6pm. NIS20.) Next to it is **Holiday Inn Beach.** Look for the bridge connecting hotel and lakefront. Banana boats cost NIS30 for 15min. (☎672 85 36. Open daily 9am-6pm. NIS25, students NIS20.) To avoid the hefty admission prices of most beaches, circle the old city walls at the southern end of the promenade and walk 200m along the dirt path to a small **free beach.**

Those seeking a hotter and slimier time are in luck: Tiberias is home to the world's earliest-known hot mineral spring, **Ḥamei T'verya.** One legend maintains that the springs were formed in the Great Flood when the earth's insides boiled. Another holds that demons heat the water under standing orders from King Solomon. Cleanse body and wallet (NIS53, Sa NIS58; 20% student discount). The older building, **Tiberias Hot Springs,** has single-sex baths. (☎672 85 00. Open Su-F 7am-4pm.) The newer, coed building, **Tiberias Hot Springs Spa,** contains a fitness room and whirlpools. A massage is NIS133 and a private mineral bath NIS99. (☎672 85 00. New spa open Su-M, W, and F-Sa 8am-8pm; Tu and Th until 11pm.) The springs are 2km south of town on the coastal road; bus #5-aleph runs from the central bus station and Ha-Galil St. (every 30min.).

◪ NIGHTLIFE

Nightlife in Tiberias centers on the *midraḥov* and promenade area. In summer, street musicians, popcorn vendors, and occasional palm-readers set up shop. Get out the white polyester duds and thigh-highs for Lido Kinneret Beach and Kinneret Sailing's **disco cruises,** one of Tiberias' trademarks. (Daily 8-11pm. NIS15-25.) The **Sea of Galilee Festival** brings international folk troupes to Tiberias during the second week of July. Check the GTIO for info on this and other area festivals, including Ein Gev's **Passover Music Festival** and Tzemaḥ's **Tu b'Av Love Fest** (mid-Aug.), where happy young Israelis gather for some love, sweat, and rock 'n' roll.

Kibbutz Kinneret Discotheque (☎675 96 89 or 05 195 30 36), at the Kibbutz. Volunteers from neighboring kibbutzim and Tiberias expats guzzle cheap beer (NIS10) or groove inside at what is widely considered the best discotheque in the area. Cover NIS25 not always applicable for tourists. Open W at 9:30pm and F at midnight.

Coconut (☎05 328 85 25). Turn left at the end of the *midrahov* and walk to the end of the promenade. This Gilligan's Island-esque hut has a nice view of the lake and a flashy little dance floor. Hot dancing F, bad music (karaoke) Sa, and quiet candlelight Su. Beer NIS16-20. Tequila drinks NIS25. Open daily 8pm-late.

Zigel Pub (☎05 285 35 82), where Ha-Galil St. and Ha-Banim St. merge. Israeli youth headquarters. If the disco trance and strobe light in the downstairs dance bar give you a headache, head upstairs to the comfy couches and cheap *argileh* (NIS10). F-Sa Dancebar, Tu, Th karaoke. Beer NIS16; cocktails NIS28. Open daily 10pm-late.

Big Ben, on the left near the end of the *midrahov*. This tourist bar gets rowdy late at night with young, drunken Brits (and a healthy dose of Americans and Israelis) giving each other the time of day. Beer NIS14-17; tropical cocktails like a 'Big Ben Kiss' NIS29. Fried snacks NIS19. Open daily 8:30am-late.

DAYTRIPS FROM TIBERIAS

BEIT SHE'AN בית שאן

From Tiberias, take bus #928, 961, 963, or 964 (50min., NIS19) to the Beit She'an bus stop. Walk to the main road through the mall, turn left, and make a right at the Bank Leumi, following signs to the site. ☎658 71 89. Open Sa-Th 8am-5pm, F 8am-4pm; in winter Sa-Th 8am-4pm, F 8am-3pm. NIS18, students NIS15, children NIS9.

One of the finest archaeological sites in the country, Beit She'an is a Sephardi (Jews of Middle Eastern descent) development town containing a vast complex of mostly Roman and Byzantine ruins. Excavations on and around **Tel al-Husn,** the oldest archaeological mound, have revealed 20 layers of settlements dating back as far as the 5th millennium BCE (Neolithic period). Of particular interest is the **Roman theater,** one of the largest extant Roman constructions in Israel. Long before it became a Philistine, Jewish, Greek, Roman, and eventually Turkish city, the region was occupied by the Egyptians; the 14th-century BCE ruins of the **Ashtaroth Temple,** built on the *tel* by Ramses III for his Canaanite allies, is a remainder of that period. North of the *tel* is the **Monastery of the Noble Lady Maria,** founded in 567 CE and abandoned after the Persian invasion of 614. The best time to visit the site is in the early morning, before the sun makes climbing the *tel* unbearable.

PEACE BRIDGE BORDER CROSSING. This is one of Israel's busiest border crossings into Jordan; allow at least 1hr. to cross, especially Thursday through Saturday. From Beit She'an, take bus #16 (NIS8) or a taxi (☎658 84 55 or 658 64 80; NIS35) to the border. Once there, you'll pay a NIS64 **exit fee,** go through passport and customs control (where you can reclaim your VAT), and take a shuttle bus (NIS4) from in front of the Duty Free shop to the Jordanian side. A visa to enter Jordan (US$44) can be purchased on the spot. From the Jordanian border, a taxi to Amman is JD25. Coming from the Jordanian side, the exit fee is JD4; there is no entrance fee for Israel, but travelers who need a visa (see p. 274) must purchase one at the Israeli embassy in Amman. (☎658 64 44, 658 64 22, or 658 64 48; Jordanian terminal ☎02 655 05 23. Open Su-Th 6:30am-10pm, F-Sa 8am-8pm. For info on crossing into Jordan, see p. 274.)

THE ROAD TO AFULA

Buses traveling between Beit She'an and Afula stop at any site upon request (#411, 412, 415, 417, 829, or 953; 45min.; every 30min. 6am-8pm, breaking for Shabbat.)

Along the beautiful valley road from Beit She'an to Afula are several sights of natural and historical interest. **Gan Ha-Shlosha,** also known as **Sahne,** is about 8km west of Beit She'an and worth an afternoon excursion. Its waterfalls and swimming holes are refreshing in both summer and winter (at a constant 28°C). The springs have been popular since Roman times; the covered pool and waterslides haven't. Watch out for theft on overcrowded weekends. (☎ 06 658 62 19; fax 658 78 22. Open Sa-Th 8am-5pm, F 8am-4pm; in winter Sa-Th 8am-4pm, F 8am-3pm. NIS27, children NIS16.) A 10min. walk along the road behind the park leads to the **Museum of Regional and Mediterranean Archaeology,** a collection of Hellenistic and Islamic art and pottery gathered from a local Canaanite temple, an Israelite community, and a Roman colony. (☎ 658 63 52. Open Su-Th 9am-2pm, Sa and holidays 10am-2pm. Park admission required for museum.)

Within **Kibbutz Hefziba,** another 3km down the road toward Afula, is the beautiful 6th-century CE **Beit Alpha Synagogue,** whose highlight is a magnificently preserved mosaic of a zodiac wheel surrounding the sun god Helios, identified with the prophet Elijah. (☎ 06 653 20 04. Open Sa-Th 8am-5pm, F 8am-4pm; in winter Sa-Th 8am-4pm, F 8am-3pm. NIS9, students NIS8, children NIS4.) Buses from Afula and Beit She'an stop at the entrance to the kibbutz. Don't be misled by the sign for Kibbutz Beit Alpha (1km closer to Beit She'an).

SEA OF GALILEE (LAKE KINNERET)   ☎06

Pleasant beaches, scenic trails, and historically and religiously significant sites grace the area that surrounds the Sea of Galilee. Campgrounds are available at several of the beaches around the Kinneret (contact the GTIO), or take advantage of cheap accommodations in Tiberias.

▐ TRANSPORTATION

All the sights on the Sea of Galilee are in some way accessible by bus from Tiberias, but renting a mountain bike is the more convenient and scenic way to go (see **Tiberias: Practical Information,** p. 364). A complete circuit of the lake (55km) takes 4-5hr. Leave as early as possible and bike clockwise around the lake to get the hilly part between Tiberias and Capernaum finished while your energy is high and the sun is low. Spring is the best time for biking; in July and August, the hills reach unbearable temperatures, but the ferries run more frequently and it's easier to catch one half-way around the lake. Bring a lot of **water.**

The **Lido Kinneret Sailing Co.** operates a ferry from Lido Beach to Capernaum, Ginnosar Beach, Mount of Beatitudes, and Tiberias. Individuals with bicycles are welcome, but schedules are at the mercy of tour groups. (☎ 672 15 38. 30-45min., 8am-6pm. NIS30.) The **Kinneret Sailing Company** runs cruises from Tiberias to Ein Gev on the east coast of the Sea of Galilee. Boats leave Tiberias daily (10:30am, 12:30, 3pm; return from Ein Gev 11:30am, 2:15, 5:45pm) during the second half of July and all of August. (☎ 665 80 08 or 665 80 09; fax 665 80 07. NIS20, children NIS15, with bicycle NIS30; round-trip NIS30, children NIS20.)

▐ ACCOMMODATIONS

The best accommodation option in the area is **Karei Deshei,** with beautiful gardens, a serene, private beach, and wonderful views of the Sea of Galilee. (Breakfast included. Reception 7am-10pm. Check-in 3pm. Check-out 10am; noon on Shabbat. Reservations recommended. A/C 4-6 bed dorms with bath NIS90; July-Aug., F, and holidays NIS112. Credit cards accepted.)

Camping is a good way to escape the city heat. Check out the MTIO/SPNI information office at Tzemaḥ on the southern tip of the lake, in the shopping strip across from Jordan Valley College. Their map (NIS22) shows the 25 lakeside campgrounds interspersed among the private beaches. (Take bus #26 or 28. ☎ 675 20 56. NIS60 per car; free without car. Open daily 8am-4pm.) Be wary of **theft.** Women should never camp alone.

◤ SIGHTS ON THE SHORE

YIGAL ALLON CENTER. The low water level of the Galilee in 1985-86 had one serendipitous effect—the discovery of an **ancient boat** under a segment of a newly exposed lake bed off the beach of Kibbutz Ginnosar. Authorities encased its wooden frame in a fiberglass brace and hauled it to shore. The boat, dating from between 100 BCE and 100 CE, has been restored to near-pristine condition. *(Take bus #840, 841, 963, or 964. NIS6.60. ☎ 672 14 95. Open Su-Th 8am-5pm, F-Sa 8m-4pm. NIS16, children and students NIS14.)*

HAMMAT GADER. These hot baths, known as *al-Himmeh* in Arabic, lie in former Syrian territory. In Roman times, the town, combined with its other (Jordanian) half on the western side of the Yarmouk River, formed part of the Decapolis. At the southwest corner of the complex sits the hottest spring in the area—so hot (51°C) that the Jews call it *Ma'ayan Ha-Gehinom* (Hell's Pool) and the Arabs call it *'Ain Maqla* (Frying Pool). Hammat Gader also boasts an **alligator park,** where hundreds of large, sleepy gators sun themselves and slog through murky water. *(30min. southeast of Tiberias. Bus #24; 9 and 10:30am, returns 1 and 3pm; F 8:45 and 10:30am, returns noon and 1:15pm; NIS7.20. ☎ 665 99 99. Open M-Sa 7am-noon, Su 7am-4pm. Weekdays NIS50, after 5pm NIS43; F-Sa NIS55.)*

DEGANYA ALEF. Founded by Russian immigrants in 1909, Deganya Alef is Israel's first kibbutz and the birthplace of General Moshe Dayan. Today, the kibbutz manufactures diamond tools. A 1948 Syrian tank marks the entrance. *(Near the spot where the Jordan River flows out of the Sea of Galilee, about 8km south of Tiberias and west of Hammat Gader. From Tiberias take bus #22 for NIS7.)*

MT. ARBEL. Among the best hikes in the area, the Mt. Arbel trail is to the northwest of the Sea of Galilee. The red trail leads from Moshav Arbel to the Arab village of Wadi Hamam. To start the hike, turn right and walk 1km. After another right turn on the next main road, walk 1km to Migdal Junction and take a bus back to Tiberias. The entire hike should only take 3-4hr. *(To get to Mt. Arbel, take bus #42 (7am, NIS7) to Moshav Arbel. Ask at the moshav for directions to Matzok Arbel. To get back to Tiberias, bus #459, 841, or 963; NIS7.)*

NAHAL AMUD. The Nahal Amud stream flows from Mt. Meron all the way to Hukkok Beach on the lake. Along the banks are beautiful flowers and a natural pillar of rock. Serious backpackers use the trail as either the first or last leg of a multi-day **Yam Le-Yam hike** (see **From Sea to Shining Sea**, p. 344).

◉ NEW TESTAMENT SIGHTS

According to the New Testament, Jesus walked on the waters of the Sea of Galilee, and four of the most significant stories in Christian history are set in the steep hills of its northern coast. Modest dress is required for entrance to New Testament sights—no shorts above the knees or bare shoulders.

TABGHE

Take bus #459, 841, or 963 (20min., every hr., NIS11.50) to the Capernaum Junction (Tzomet Kfar Nahum). Walk toward the sea, following the brown signs to Tabghe and Capernaum. Tabghe (Arabic), Heptapegon (Greek), or Seven Springs (English) houses 2 sites and lies about 1km down the road.

CHURCH OF THE BREAD AND FISH. This is the site where Jesus is said to have fed 5000 pilgrims with five loaves and two small fish (Matthew 14:13-21). The church is built around the rock upon which Jesus placed the bread, and a section of the mosaic has been removed to reveal part of the rock and the original 4th-century foundations. *(Open M-Sa 8am-6pm, Su 10am-5pm. Free.)* Around the right side of the church, past the "private" sign and down the stairs, is a small hospice for Christian pilgrims; inquire at the office inside the church for information. *(☎ 672 10 61. Singles with A/C and bath NIS140/US$35; doubles with A/C US$30/NIS120.)*

CHURCH OF THE PRIMACY OF ST. PETER. This church commemorates the miracle of the loaves and fishes and the spot where Jesus made Peter "Shepherd of his People." A Persian invasion in 614 CE destroyed the 4th-century church at this spot. Franciscans rebuilt it with black basalt in 1933. On the seaward side of the church are the steps where Jesus called out his instructions; on the shoreline are the "thrones of the Apostles," a series of six double column bases. *(50m past the parking lot of the Church of the Bread and Fishes. ☎ 672 47 67. Open daily 8am-4:30pm. Free.)*

MOUNT OF BEATITUDES. Jesus is supposed to have delivered his Sermon on the Mount (Matthew 5) and chosen his disciples at this site. A church funded by Benito Mussolini stands on the Mount; its octagonal shape recalls the eight beatitudes. Symbols surrounding the altar inside the church represent the seven virtues (justice, charity, prudence, faith, fortitude, hope, and remembrance). The gardens around the site offer a spectacular view of the Sea of Galilee, Tiberias, and the Golan Heights. *(The small path to the Mount is next to the stop for bus #16, across from the entrance to St. Peter's Church. It's a 20min. walk uphill to the church. From the Mount, follow the road back 1km to catch bus #459, 841, or 963 back to Tiberias (NIS11.50). ☎ 672 67 12. Open daily 8am-noon and 2:30-5pm.)*

OTHER SIGHTS

CAPERNAUM. It was in Capernaum (Kfar Naḥum in Hebrew, Tel Num in Arabic), Peter's birthplace, that Jesus healed Simon's mother-in-law and the Roman Centurion's servant (Luke 4:31-37 and 7:1-10). A modern church arches over the ruins of a 5th-century octagonal church, marking the site believed to have held Peter's house. The ruins of a nearby **synagogue,** discernible by the black, basalt foundation, is built on top of an older, first-century CE synagogue in which Jesus may have preached. Since Capernaum did not participate in the first- and 2nd-century Jewish revolts against the Romans, it survived unscathed. *(Buses #459, 841, or 963 from Tiberias pass the Capernaum junction about once per hr. on the way north to Kiryat Shmona and Tzfat. Get off near the Capernaum ferry port and walk 1km to your left. From Tabghe, Capernaum is 2km farther east on the coastal road. Synagogue open daily 8:30am-4pm. NIS2.)*

MIGDAL. The birthplace of Mary Magdalene lies north of Tiberias. An agricultural community founded in 1910 now accompanies the white-domed shrine and largely unexcavated ruins. *(Buses #50, 51, or 52 go to Migdal from Tiberias (10min., infrequent). Buses #459, 841, or 963 run to the Migdal Junction, "Tzomet Migdal," a short walk away.)*

KURSI. The ruins of this Christian settlement, also known as Gergessa or Gerasa, date from early Byzantine times (5th-6th centuries CE). According to the New Testament, it was at Kursi that Jesus exorcised several demons from a man's body and caused the demons to possess a herd of pigs; the pigs raced into the sea and drowned. The site harbors impressive remains of a large, Byzantine **monastery** and a small chapel, both reconstructed and with mosaic floors. *(On eastern side of the lake, 7km north of Ein Gev. Ruins 50m from the bus stop. Buses #15, 17, 18, 19, 20, or 22 run from Tiberias to Tzomet Kursi (30min., every 30min. noon-7pm, NIS14). ☎ 673 19 83. Open Sa-Th 8am-5pm, F 8am-4pm; in winter Sa-Th 8am-4pm, F 8am-3pm. NIS9, students NIS8.)*

KORAZIM. These ruins are on the site of the unrepentant towns chastised by Jesus (Matthew 11:21). The **synagogue** here dates from the Talmudic period, or the 3rd-4th centuries CE. *(Take bus #459, 841, or 963 (NIS11.50) and get off at Tzomet Korazim Junction. Walk east 2km on the main road, past Vered Ha-Galil and Moshav Korazim to a parking lot on the right. Signs there lead to the town. ☎ 693 49 82. Open Sa-Th 8am-5pm, F 8am-4pm; in winter Sa-Th 8am-4pm, F 8am-3pm. NIS14, students NIS10.50.)*

YARDENIT. The Gospels say that John baptized Jesus in the Jordan River. Today, dozens of pilgrims and tourists come to the Yardenit Baptismal Area on the banks of the Jordan. *(Right off the coastal road. Take bus #17, 19, 21, 22, 23, or 26 to Kibbutz Kinneret. ☎ 675 94 86. Open Su-Th 9am-6pm, F-Sa 8am-5pm.)*

TZFAT (SAFED) צפת صفد ☎06

Situated on Mt. Kenaan, the third-highest peak in Israel, Tzfat is a city of mesmerizing tranquility. Streets wind through this city on a hill, raising aimless wandering
to an artform. Stone buildings, spotted with turquoise-colored doorways, fall over
each other. Tzfat's beauty reflects not only its physical setting, overlooking the
cool, lush greenery of the Galilean hills, but also a mystical way of life. In 1777, a
rabbi who had trekked to Tzfat all the way from Europe ultimately packed up and
left for Tiberias, complaining that the angels had kept him up at night.

Tzfat hasn't always been a bastion of spirituality. Its Crusader-built castle was
captured by Salah al-Din in 1188, reconquered by the Knights Templar in 1240, and
then lost again in 1266 to the Mamluk Sultan Baybars. It wasn't until the Middle
Ages that many Jews arrived in Tzfat, seeking refuge in the relatively tolerant Ottoman Empire. After the Expulsion from Spain in 1492, Jewish exiles flocked to
Tzfat, bringing with them the seeds of a mystical tradition. New settlements began
in the second half of the 19th century and triggered violent Arab protest. By 1948,
12,000 Arabs lived in uneasy coexistence with 1700 Jews. In May 1948, Israeli
Palmaḥ troops defeated the Iraqi and Syrian forces entrenched in the fortress at
the top of Mt. Kenaan, and the Arab population fled with their armies.

▐ TRANSPORTATION

Buses: Central bus station (☎692 11 22). Info booth open Su-Th 6:30-8:30am and
9am-1:30pm and 2-3pm; F 6:30-8:30am and 9am-1:30pm. To: **Haifa** via **Akko** (#361
and 362; every 30min. Su-Th 6:15am-7pm, F 6:10am-3:15pm, Sa after sundown; 2hr.;
NIS30); **Jerusalem** (#964, daily 7:15am, NIS47); **Kiryat Shmona** (#501 and 511;
1hr.; every hr. Su-Th 5:50am-7:30pm, F 5:50am-4pm; NIS18); **Tel Aviv** (#846, 3hr.,
5:35 and 8:15am, NIS44); **Tiberias** (#459, 1hr., every hr. 6:50am-7pm, NIS17).

Taxis: Kenaan Taxis (☎697 07 07), next to the bus station. *Sherut* to **Tiberias** and **Rosh
Pina.** Look for white minivans.

✴❼ ORIENTATION AND PRACTICAL INFORMATION

The city can be divided into three districts: the **park area,** at the top of the mountain (ringed by Jerusalem St.), the **artists' quarter,** southwest and down the hill, and
the **synagogue quarter** (Old City), immediately to the north of the artists' quarter on
the other side of Ma'alot Olei Ha-Gardom St. Tzfat is arranged in curved terraces
descending on the west from the castle ruins atop **Gan Ha-Metzuda** (Citadel Park).
Jerusalem (Yerushalayim) St., behind the central bus station, follows the lines of
what was once the castle's moat and makes a complete circle around Citadel Park.
Heading left from the major intersection beside the bus station, on the western
side of the park, Jerusalem St. becomes the *midraḥov.* The **midraḥov** (pedestrian
mall) is the strip of Jerusalem St. running southwest of the park area, up the hill
from the artists' and synagogue quarters. **Ha-Palmaḥ St.** begins off Jerusalem St.
near the central bus station and crosses the main street over a stone bridge. **Ha-Ari
St.** also begins off Jerusalem St. near the bus station and circles around the western edge of the city, descending down to the cemetery grounds. Tzfat is a compact
walking city, and getting around in the old city with a car is nearly impossible.

Tourist Office: Visitors Center (☎692 74 84 or 692 74 85), Kikkar Ha-Atzma'ut. At the
intersection of Aliya Bet and Ha-Palmaḥ, inside the Wolfson Community Center, through
the main entrance on the right. Has a small exhibit on the history of Tzfat, updated
maps (NIS5), and free brochures about sights. Open Su-Th 10am-3pm.

Currency Exchange: There are several banks on Jerusalem St. on and near the *midraḥov.*
Bank Ha-Poalim (☎699 48 00), on the *midraḥov,* near Ha-Palmaḥ bridge. Hefty com-
mission for changing cash and traveler's checks (NIS24). **ATM** outside. Open Su and Tu-
W 8:30am-1:15pm, M and Th 8:30am-1pm and 4-6:30pm, F 8:15am-12:30pm.

Police: (☎697 84 44), outside of the main city, up the hill on the road to Rosh Pina.

First Aid: Magen David Adom, next to the central bus station, downhill on the side away from the main intersection.

Post Office: (☎692 04 05), on Kikkar Ha-Atzma'ut. At the intersection of Ha-Palmaḥ St. and Aliya Bet, through the parking lot on the other side of the Yigal Allon Theater and Cultural Center. **Poste Restante.** Open Su-Tu and Th 8am-12:30pm and 3:30-6pm, W 8am-1:30pm, F 8am-noon. A more convenient **branch** at 37 Jerusalem St., past the British Police Station at the end of the *midraḥov*, has the same hours.

ACCOMMODATIONS

Rooms are plentiful, though finding quality at the right price can take a bit of planning, particularly during summer weekends (call ahead for stays over Shabbat). In high season, inexpensive **guest rooms** and flats are often available from town residents. The best way to find a rental is to walk around Jerusalem St. and the old city looking for signs. Always inspect potential quarters before paying (blankets are a plus for Tzfat's chilly nights, even in summer), and feel free to bargain.

Shalom Inn, 3 Korchak St. (☎697 04 45 or 691 18 61), at the beginning of the artists' quarter. From the bus station, take a left on Jerusalem St. and a left on Aliya Bet St.; just past the cultural center take the unmarked street on the right with a small wooden sign that says "Artists' Quarter." The inn is on the left, just after the paved road curves left. Fresh and modern rooms recently redone. Views of the mountain and the artists' quarter. Private bathrooms, cable TV, A/C, and kitchen. Singles NIS75-110; doubles NIS150-200. Aug. singles NIS110-120; doubles 200-240. Credit cards accepted.

Beit Binyamin (HI), 1 Loḥamei Ha-Geta'ot St. (☎692 10 86; fax 697 35 14), near the Amal Trade School in South Tzfat. Take bus #6 or 7. From the bus station, take a left on Jerusalem St. and another left on Aliya Bet St. Pass the community and cultural centers and continue on to Ha-Nassi St., which curves down to the right. Stay on this street, through its curves, and look for the hostel sign on the left. Exceptionally clean, recently renovated rooms have private baths and refrigerators. Breakfast included. Check-out 9am. Wheelchair accessible. 4- to 6-bed dorms NIS78 per person; singles NIS162; doubles NIS224. Credit cards accepted.

Hotel Hadar (☎692 00 68), on Ridbaz St., in an alley off Jerusalem St. Take a right onto Jerusalem St. when coming from the bus station and look for the sign on the right that points down the alley. Comfortable, homey atmosphere. Rooms have bath and A/C or fans. Rooftop lounge has a great view of the city. Check-out 11am. Ring after the midnight curfew. Singles NIS100/US$25; doubles NIS200/US$50. Aug. and on Jewish holidays NIS10 more per person; in winter NIS10 less per person.

FOOD

Mountain View, 70 Jerusalem St. (☎102 04 04), in the middle of the *midraḥov*. Trendy cafe specializes in veg. dishes. Terrific view down the mountain is best at sunset. Huge salads NIS34-38. Stir-fry dishes NIS34. Pasta NIS32-36. Sandwiches NIS20. Smoothies NIS14-20. Open Su-Th 8am-midnight. Credit cards accepted.

Pita Ha-Mama, Jerusalem St., at the top of the Ma'alot Olei Ha-Gardom stairs. This popular bakery is a great place for a quick snack. Baked pitas stuffed with potato or spinach and onions (NIS5) are perfect for munching while strolling through the old city. Try the *lafah* bread with *za'tar* (NIS8). Open Su-Th 7am-8pm, F 7am-2pm.

Pinati (☎692 03 30), on the *midraḥov*, near Ha-Palmaḥ bridge. Elvis plays the role of the Messiah here, and all await his coming. The walls are plastered with memorabilia from the tumultuous life of the swivel-hipped dreamboat. No peanut butter and banana sandwiches, but the fun keeps going. Kebabs and spaghetti NIS30-40. Open Su-Th 9am-midnight, F 9am-4pm, Sa after sundown-midnight.

Ha-Mifgash Restaurant, 75 Jerusalem St. (☎692 05 10), at the lower end of the *midraḥov*. The restaurant is inside a 150-year-old stone-vaulted room that used to be part of a large underground well. Chicken soup connoisseurs must try the velvety brew (NIS12). Veggie options include stuffed pepper (NIS14) and eggplant (NIS16). Open Su-Th 8am-midnight, F 8am-4pm, Sa sundown-midnight. Credit cards accepted.

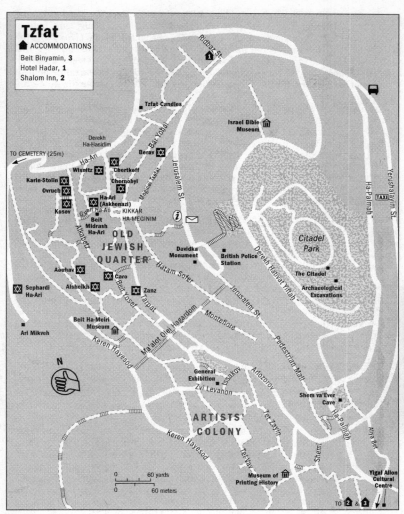

Tzfat

🏠 ACCOMMODATIONS

Beit Binyamin, **3**
Hotel Hadar, **1**
Shalom Inn, **2**

👁 SIGHTS

The best—and inevitably, the only—way to see Tzfat is to get lost in its circuitous sidestreets. Fortunately, there are a few **tour guides** on hand to inject some order into the chaos of navigating the city. **Aviva Minoff** gives entertaining tours starting from the Rimonim Hotel. (☎ 692 09 01, mobile ☎ 050 40 91 87. 2hr. tour NIS40/US$10; M-F 10:30am; min. 5 people; reserve in advance.) **Yosi Reis** gives good but expensive tours with advance notice. (☎ 692 28 03, mobile ☎ 051 60 36 06. 2hr. tour NIS200/US$50.) Otherwise, try Yisrael Shalem's *Six Self-Guided Tours to Tzfat* (NIS25), available at the candle shop and at Ascent (see **Accommodations,** above).

SYNAGOGUE QUARTER

ASHKENAZI HA-ARI SYNAGOGUE. Across from the post office on Jerusalem St. is a small cobblestone terrace; head down the steps and turn right to reach **Ha-Meginim Sq.** ("Sq. of the Defenders"), which was the Jewish city center until the earthquake of 1837. Through the square, under the stone archway, and down the stairs by the "Synagogue Ha-Ari" sign is the Ashkenazi Ha-Ari Synagogue, built in 1580, three years after the death of its namesake, **Rabbi Isaac Luria** (*Ha-Ari* is the acronym of the Hebrew for "our master Rabbi Isaac" and also means "lion"). It was to this site that the famous mystic and founder led congregants to welcome Shabbat. He is most famous for penning the *Kabbalat Shabbat*, an arrangement of prayers in preparation for the Sabbath; Alkabetz, his student, wrote the now standard hymn, *Lekha Dodi*.

The altarpiece was modified by locals, who were concerned that it was idolatrous. They smeared the paintings, replacing the lion's head with a human face. The synagogue features two notable curiosities. One is the fertility chair, more formally used as a ceremonial circumcision chair. It is rumored to bless women who sit in it with miraculous pregnancies. The other is a small hole in the central pulpit, where visitors place notes for wishes and good luck. The hole was made during the War of Independence, when a grenade flew into the synagogue and exploded while worshipers were bowed in prayer, allowing the shrapnel to sail over their heads and leave a mark only in the pulpit's side.

ABUHAV SYNAGOGUE. Exiting Ha-Ari synagogue, take a left down the stairs, a left at the bottom, a right on Simtat Abuhav St., and then a quick left after going down more stairs; the Abuhav Synagogue will be on the left. Rabbi Isaac Abuhav was a 15th-century Spanish mystic who never actually made it to Tzfat. His 550-year-old Torah scroll, however, is contained in the first ark to the right, inside the entrance. The second ark contains Rabbi Luria's four-century-old Torah scroll. The scroll inside the blue ark is rumored to have been the only object left intact in Tzfat following the 1837 earthquake that leveled the town. Hanging below the mural in the middle of the synagogue is a chandelier brought over from Europe as a reminder of those who suffered in the Holocaust. The chair at the back of the synagogue has been used to circumcise 8-day-old Jewish boys for 213 years, making it perhaps the single most unpleasant piece of furniture in the world.

AL-SHEIKH SYNAGOGUE. Exiting this synagogue, continue straight down the same alleyway. On the left will be al-Sheikh Synagogue, named for a student of Rabbi Yosef said to have been escorted to his grave by 12 doves that attended his Saturday afternoon lectures.

CARO SYNAGOGUE. Up the stairs on the left and through the door in the purple walls is the back entrance to the Caro Synagogue, one of the most famous in Tzfat. It was here that Yosef Caro, chief rabbi of Tzfat and author of the vast *Shulḥan Arukh* ("The Set Table," a standard guide to daily life according to Jewish law), studied and taught in the 16th century. Caro was well-known as a philanthropist who served simultaneously as rabbi, counselor, shelter provider, and soup kitchen coordinator. Notice the glass cabinet in the sanctuary full of Jewish books dating back to the 17th century. Caro Synagogue is also accessible by taking Ma'alot Oleh Ha-Gardom St. off Jerusalem St. and turning right at Beit Yosef St.

CHERNOBYL AND CHERTKOFF SYNAGOGUES. Back at Ha-Meginim Sq., down the narrow Bar-Yochai St., is the Chernobyl Synagogue, marked by a blue box, window grates, and a small English sign on the door. The modest Bar-Yochai St. is believed to be the alley down which the Messiah will make his way on his journey from the nearby mountains to Jerusalem. Off of Ha-Meginim Sq., on Ha-Ḥasadim St., one street above Najara St. and Ha-Ari Synagogue, is the Chertkoff Synagogue. The chief rabbi here predicted in 1840 that the messianic redemption would begin when 600,000 Jews inhabited the Land of Israel. Both of these synagogues are closed to the public.

CEMETERIES. Three adjoining cemeteries sprawl on the western outskirts of the old city, off Ha-Ari St. at the bottom of the hill. Follow the steps all the way down, past the new stone buildings on the left. The small building on the left when the path turns into the cemetery is Ha-Ari *mikveh*, or ritual bath. This natural spring

TOUCH NO EVIL Above doorways all over the old city of Tzfat, as well as on keychains, in windows, and behind picture frames throughout Israel, is the likeness of a hand. The hand has special significance in Jewish mysticism because of the Kabbalistic meaning of the numbers: a hand (generally) has five fingers, and people have two hands for a total of ten, a number that represents God in mystic texts. Some noteworthy variations on the hand symbol are the hand with an eye in its palm, which represents the evil eye, and the six-fingered hand above the doorway on the right after exiting left from Abuhav Synagogue. One of the builders had six rather than five fingers on one hand and left his mark after finishing the construction project.

was the bathing place of Ha-Ari himself, and its vibes have attracted the interest of mystics the world over, including the Dalai Lama. The local rabbinical court has ruled that women may not enter the *mikveh*'s icy waters, but renegade females have been known to take a dip late at night while a male friend guards the door.

The oldest cemetery contains the 16th-century graves of the most famous Tzfat Kabbalists. Most prominent is Ha-Ari's blue tomb, where religious Jews come at all hours to pray, light candles, and seek inspiration. Also notice the domed tomb built by the Karaites of Damascus to mark the grave of the prophet Hosea. Legend has it that hidden under this same hill are Hannah and her seven sons, whose martyrdom at the hands of the Syrians is recorded in the Book of Maccabees. This cemetery is the domain of eighth-generation Tzfat resident Mordekhai Shebabo, who left his position as a pedicurist to single-handedly restore the graves. Every visible grave is the result of his efforts.

ARTISTS' QUARTER AND GENERAL EXHIBITION. These alleys and galleries display a wide range of art inspired by the local colors. The quality varies, but a keen eye might discern a few real jewels. Gallery highlights include **microcalligraphy** (creating pictures out of verses from traditional Jewish texts) and Ruth Shany's silk artwork. A number of artists, including Avraham Loewenthal and David Friedman, create mystical art inspired by the Kabbalah. Not to be missed is Mike Leaf's studio, full of satirical paper mache sculptures. The General Exhibition is a collection of works by local artists. The art is displayed in the town's former mosque, which has been empty of worshipers since the 1948 War. *(The artists' quarter is below the Jerusalem-Arlozorov intersection. Most shops open 10am-1pm and 4-7pm. The General exhibition, well-marked by English signs, is on Arlozorov St., at the bottom of the hill south of Ma'alot Oleh Ha-Gardom St.* ☎ *692 00 87. Open Su-Th 9am-6pm, F 9am-2pm, Sa 10am-2pm.)*

SHEM VA'EVER CAVE. This site is said to be the burial grounds of Noah's son Shem and grandson Ever. Muslims call it the "Cave of Mourning" because they believe that it was here that Jacob learned of the death of his son Joseph. *(The cave is near the top of Ha-Palmah bridge, at the intersection of Jerusalem and Arlozorov St. If the shrine around the cave is locked, knock at the small, domed synagogue nearby.)*

🏛 MUSEUMS

BEIT HA-MEIRI MUSEUM. The 150-year-old stone building is as interesting as the exhibits on display. Its restored three floors tell Tzfat's history through colorful biographies of its elders—including the town matchmaker and the resident man-with-the-evil-eye—and exhibits on how they worked and lived. *(From the midrahov on Jerusalem St. take the Ma'alot Olei Ha-Gardom stairs all the way down to the bottom and make a right.* ☎ *697 13 07. Open Su-Th 9am-2pm, F 9am-1pm. NIS10, students NIS7.)*

MEMORIAL MUSEUM OF HUNGARIAN-SPEAKING JEWRY. This small museum is dedicated to preserving the heritage of Jewish life in Hungary. Personal items on display (including prayer books, diaries, clothing, and paintings) illustrate the vibrancy of a culture that was virtually destroyed by the Holocaust. *(From Jerusalem St. walk down Aliyah Bet St. and turn left at the Wolfson center; the museum is through the parking lot on the left.* ☎ *692 58 81; www.hungjewmus.org.il. Open M-F 9am-1pm. NIS10.)*

ISRAEL

CRAFTS

One of the must-see sights in the old city is the **Tzfat Candle Factory.** From Ha-Meginim Sq., head down to Najara St. and take a right past Ha-Ari Synagogue; the factory is on the right. All of the imaginatively colored and shaped candles on display are produced by the workers at the back of the shop, busily bent over blocks and sheets of beeswax. Make your own for NIS10-40. (☎682 20 68. Open Apr.-Sept. Su-Th 9am-6pm, F 9am-1pm; Oct.-Mar. Su-Th 9am-6pm, F 9am-1pm. Candles start at NIS12.) In Ha-Meginim Sq. is **Torah scribe** Zalmon Bear Halevy Tornek, who can be observed hand-copying Jewish religious texts. (☎692 42 77. Open Su-Tu and Th noon-6pm, F 11am-2pm.)

♫ ENTERTAINMENT

Having a wild night in Tzfat takes some creative thinking. The most prominent bar is **Adios,** 73 Jerusalem St. on the *midraḥov,* in a hip, two-story seating area, which serves beer (NIS10-15) and cocktails (NIS15) to that unbelievably bluesy beat of classic American rock. (☎682 12 62. Open Su-Th 8am-1am, F 8am-4pm, and Sa 9pm-2am.) Movies, often in English with Hebrew subtitles, are screened at the **Yigal Allon Theater and Cultural Center** a couple nights a week. Call ahead or stop by around 8pm to see if one is showing. The cultural center is next to the main post office, near the traffic circle where Ha-Palmaḥ St. and Aliyah Bet St. meet. (☎697 19 90. NIS20. Movies begin around 8:30pm.)

Travelers planning a visit to Tzfat well in advance should consider arriving in time for the annual **Klezmer Festival** in late July or early August, a three-night extravaganza during which the city sways to the strains of everything from old-world Yiddish tunes to modern Ḥasidic rock. Outdoor concerts are plentiful and free, as is the spontaneous dancing that seems to erupt in front of each stage.

🏛 DAYTRIPS FROM TZFAT

MERON AND MT. MERON הר מירון

Buses go to Kibbutz Sasa (#43 or 367; 25min.; 6:45, 9, 11:40am, 12:30, 5:30pm; NIS11.50). In summer, catch the early bus to avoid the midday heat. From the kibbutz, continue 1km along the main highway to the turnoff on the left marked with a green sign that indicates "Meron Field School." After 1km, there is a brown sign for the SPNI Field School, which is up the small hill to the right. To get to the tomb from the bus stop, walk to the intersection with a sign for Meron and follow the road up for about 5min.

For two days every spring, the tranquil hillside surrounding Rabbi Shimon Bar-Yoḥai's tomb at Meron transforms into the scene of a frenzied religious carnival. Some believe that the 2nd-century Talmudic scholar **Bar-Yoḥai** authored the *Zohar,* the central work of the Kabbalah. Thousands of Jews converge upon the town to commemorate the date of his death (the holiday of **Lag Ba'Omer,** in the first week of May 2002). Tzfat's Visitors Center (☎692 74 85) has more details on the festival.

Near the tomb stand the ruins of a historically noteworthy synagogue dating from the 3rd century CE, when Meron was important in the booming olive oil trade. From Bar-Yoḥai's grave, go past the *yeshiva* and follow the uphill path on the left. The **lintel,** an engraved stone slab that once decorated the entrance to the synagogue, is virtually all that remains of the edifice. Legend holds that this lintel's fall will herald the coming of the Messiah. To reach Meron from Jerusalem, take any one of hundreds of buses running all night from Malaḥi St. in Geulah.

Just west of the village is **Har Meron** (Mt. Meron), the highest mountain in the Galilee (1208m). A good trail affords tremendous vistas of Tzfat and the surrounding countryside—on clear days Lebanon and Syria to the north, the Mediterranean to the west, and the Sea of Galilee to the southeast are all visible. The **information office** offers limited hiking advice. (☎698 00 23. Trail map NIS62. Open Sa-Th 8am-7pm, F 8am-2pm.) To reach the trail, continue past the field school turnoff, past the army base on the right, and a small parking lot on the left. The **trail** begins at the back of the lot and follows striped black-and-white, as well as orange, blue, and white trail markers. A 1hr. walk uphill through sweet-smelling, wonderfully wooded surroundings leads to an observation area with striking views of the area. Continue along the red-and-white marked trail skirting the summit and follow the trail to the left when it reaches a rocky area near the army radio towers. Twenty minutes farther along the path leads to a picnic site and a traffic circle; make a quick left back into the forest to where the trail begins again. An easy 1hr. descent, again marked with black-and-white, ends at a paved road just above the village of Meron. A 15min. walk to the right leads to the tomb of Shimon Bar-Yohai. To get to the village, turn left onto the road, follow it into the town, and take a left at the grocery store on the right. After reaching the main gate, turn right down the highway and go left and across the highway at the major intersection to reach the bus stop (#361, every 20min. 6am-8pm, NIS8).

A gorgeous 3½hr. **hike** starts from Nahal Amud at the bottom of the Tzfat cemeteries. Interested travelers should get directions from SPNI or the tourist office or consult the rough map on file at Ascent (see **Accommodations,** p. 374).

ALMA CAVE מערת עלמה

*A **bus** leaves Tzfat for Rehania (#45; 20min.; Su-Th 8:45am and 1:30pm, F 8:45am, noon, and 3:30pm; NIS11.50). Bus #45 also makes the return trip from Rehania to Tzfat (Su-Th 9:15am and 2pm; F 9:15am, 12:30, and 4pm). By **car,** drive north along the Tzfat-Meron highway and continue past the Zeition Junction to Rehania. Across from the entrance to Rehania village is the dirt path to Alma cave. The path is marked by red and white stripes painted on the light pole beside the main highway; from there, red-and-white trail markers are infrequent. Stay on this path for about 30min., steering close to Alma (left), and away from the hilly, tree-lined area to the right (don't make any sharp turns). The walk goes past farmers' fenced-off fields, to the hill covered with tree clusters and stones toward the left. The marked trail leads to the cave entrance.*

Legend has it that the maze-like tunnels of Alma Cave form an underground bridge between the holy cities of Tzfat and Jerusalem and contain the corpses of 900,000 "righteous men." The entrance to the cave is hidden in a gorge, behind clusters of large trees; from the green nature reserve sign on the hillside of gray stones, go right and uphill toward the metal poles—the gorge and cave entrance are just beyond this. Notice the black ropes hooked into the stone to aid in climbing down into the gorge and toward the cave entrance. Climb (or slide) down the hole, keeping to the right. At a depth of approximately 60m (one-half to three-quarters of the way down), there are two phallic rocks near the right-hand wall. Behind those lies a small hole leading to the "inner chambers" of the cave. There are markers indicating the correct path: white for the way in, red for the way out. Once inside the large room with a ridge and a steep slope, veer to the far right along the ridge instead of continuing down the slope.

 CAVE SAFETY. Bring water and one reliable flashlight per person as well as candles and matches for backup, and prepare to get muddy. Alma Cave should be tried only by those who feel they can remain up to 108m beneath the earth for several hours. Keep in mind that it is slippery in and around the cave, and large packs will not fit through the tighter spots. It is safest to go during daylight hours with a group of people and to let someone know where you're headed.

TEL HAZOR תל חזור

***Buses** from Tzfat (#501 or 511; 35min.; NIS13) and all buses that run between Rosh Pina and Kiryat Shmona stop near the site. Don't get off at Hazor Ha-Gelilit; continue north to Kibbutz Ayelet Ha-Shahor. The kibbutz houses a small museum (☎ 693 48 55) displaying Canaanite and Israelite artifacts and explaining some of the tel's layers. From there, the site's entrance (☎ 693 72 90) is 250m up the main road. Museum and site open Sa-Th 8am-5pm and F and holidays 8am-4pm. NIS14, students NIS12, children NIS6.*

Hazor was once a fortified city on the main trading route that linked Egypt to Syria and Mesopotamia. Hazor served as a major commercial center in the Fertile Crescent, and the Bible calls it "the head of all those [northern Canaanite] kingdoms"

ISRAEL

(Joshua 11:10). At the *tel's* northern foot lies a vast, lower city built in the 9th century BCE. The most impressive of the *tel's* ruins is the 38m-deep tunnel, engineered during Ahab's reign to bring water into the city in case of a siege. Today, archaeologists are still searching for the city's archives.

BAR'AM בר עם

A bus from Tzfat goes to Bar'am (#43; 6:45am, 12:30, 5pm; return 7:45am, 1:45, 5:45pm; NIS13). Ask the driver for the synagogue ruins, marked by a small brown sign that says Bar'am and points right, not the Bar'am Kibbutz a few kilometers down the road. Open Sa-Th 8am-5pm, F 8am-4pm. NIS9, students NIS8, children NIS4.

These 3rd-century ruins constitute one of the best-preserved synagogues in Israel. Archaeological evidence shows that Bar'am was home to a prosperous Jewish community in the middle centuries of the first millennium. The ruins of two synagogues have been uncovered here. Bar'am was a Maronite Christian village until the 1948 War of Independence. A few steps up the hill on the left beyond the old synagogue ruins is a beautiful stone Maronite Church that is still used by the Maronites on holidays and special occasions. In front of the church is an observation point with a view of Mt. Meron to the south.

ROSH PINA ראש פינה

Buses go to Tzfat (#401, 459, 461, 501, or 511; every 30min.; NIS10), and buses go to Kiryat Shmona (#480, 500, 842, 845, or 909; every 30min.; NIS13).

Because many buses heading north pass through, the town serves as a gateway to the Upper Galilee and Golan. There's not much to do in quaint and quiet Rosh Pina except visit the **Rothschild Garden,** on Ha-Ḥalutzim St., a beautifully maintained park with shady poplars and dozens of varieties of roses lining its terraces or **Drora's Herb Farm,** 25 Ha-Ḥalutzim St., up the hill on the way to the hostel, one block past the post office, a sweet-smelling shop that sells everything organic. (☎693 43 49. Herb teas NIS5-20. Open Su-Th 10am-7pm, F 10am-6pm, and Sa 7-10pm.) The **Nature Friends Youth Hostel** has two tidy rooms with fridge, air-conditioning, and shared bath, as well as a small camping area. (☎693 17 64, mobile 051 57 21 41. Dorms NIS5; singles NIS15, shower and bath available. Guests must pay at the Beit Binyamin Hostel in Tzfat; call ahead.) The rest of the hostel's rooms are occupied by **SPNI field offices** (☎693 70 86; fax 693 43 12). To reach the hostel, walk straight up the hill from the main bus stop and look for a sign on the left.

GOLAN HEIGHTS רמת הגולן

This formerly volcanic plateau overlooking the Ḥula Valley has a sparse population of 35,000 equally divided between recent Jewish settlers and longtime Druze inhabitants, many of which strongly identify with Syria and have relatives across the border. To Israelis, the region is a major source of water as well as the home of ski slopes, apple orchards, wineries, and cattle pastures. The region's natural borders include the Jordan River and Sea of Galilee to the west, Mt. Ḥermon and the Lebanese mountains to the north, and the Syrian plains to the east.

Recent history has cast the Golan Heights into the jaws of political controversy. Throughout the 1950s and '60s, Israeli towns in Galilee were assailed by artillery fire from Syrian gunposts atop the mountains. Israel captured the Golan in the 1967 Six Day War but was pushed back by Syria's surprise attack in the 1973 war. Israeli forces quickly recovered and launched a counter-attack, capturing even more territory. As part of the 1974 disengagement accord, Israel returned both the newly conquered territory and part of the land captured in 1967. Israel officially annexed the remaining 768 sq. km territory in 1981, arousing international protest. Today, Jewish settlements are scattered among Israeli army bases, Druze villages, live minefields, and destroyed bunkers.

The political necessity of compromise became apparent with the election of Ehud Barak in May 1999, when it was revealed that even Benyamin Netanyahu had been close to making an agreement with the Syrians. The recent death of Hafez al-Assad has added an additional twist to the story. The international community awaits to see how Assad's son, now in power, will handle negotiations with Israel. Israel's goal is to reach an agreement with Syria that will not leave Israel dependent on the US for its security, as it was during the withdrawal from Sinai. Since the most recent outbreak of violence between Palestinians and Israelis in September 2000, no progress has been made on Israel's relationship with Syria. For current news on Israel, see **In the News,** p. 270.

NATURE RESERVES

The Golan offers some of the most beautiful hikes in all of Israel. Although the region gets very hot from late spring to early fall, most hikes go through streams, pools, and waterfalls, offering natural refreshment from the summer sun. Bus service to the trails, where it exists, is very irregular; call Egged and plan carefully. Be aware that many trails do not loop back to where they started and may leave you far away from your car. Start hiking early in the morning to avoid the busloads of Israeli children and remember that it is not safe to drink water from Golan streams.

▐ TRANSPORTATION

Egged buses reach some sights in the Golan, but infrequent service along remote roads necessitates careful planning. Double-check schedules, and anticipate some walking. Buses to sights near the Sea of Galilee generally leave from Tiberias. The Upper Galilee, Ḥula Valley, and northern Golan are served by buses from Kiryat Shmona and Hatzor Ha-Galilit. It is nearly impossible to get to Gamla and many hiking trails by bus. Few cars traverse the Golan, and hitchhiking is not recommended. If you decide to set out alone, take a good map (see Golan Hikes, p. 382.)

There is a rarely-open **tourist information office** for the Golan Heights at the Maḥanayim Junction between Rosh Pina and Kiryat Shmona, where Rte. 91 branches off of Rte. 90 (look for the gas station on the right and turn right; the information office is in the strip of shops on the left). The office sells maps and has brochures, mostly in Hebrew, on activities, restaurants, and accommodations in the region. (☎ 693 69 45. Open F 8:30am-3:30pm, Sa 9am-2pm.) There is a **24hr. grocery** next door to the tourist office; bring several bottles of water and at least a day's worth of food on any hike.

Organized **tours** are faster, more convenient, and sometimes less expensive than other forms of transportation; they also go at a quicker pace than many would like. **Matan Tours,** in Tiberias, attracts a young backpacker crowd with one-day professionally guided tours of the Golan and Upper Galilee that include sightseeing and light hiking. (☎ 06 672 4574 or 05 461 61 48. NIS160/US$38 per person.) **Egged** also offers professionally guided full-day tours of the region from Tel Aviv every Thursday. (☎ 03 527 12 12. NIS290/US$68; 10% ISIC discount.) **Moshe Cohen** makes military-history-oriented rounds in a van. (☎ 672 16 08. NIS140 per person; min. 4 people.) **SPNI** offers a three-day hiking tour of the Golan and Upper Galilee that includes kayaking on the Jordan River. (☎ 03 638 86 88. US$298. Leaves from the SPNI office in Tel Aviv.) For those who'd rather skip all the touristy kitsch and just get outside and hike, **Devorah Leah Rice** leads hikes in the Upper Galilee and Golan. (☎ 06 682 00 83. Half day NIS80, whole day NIS200.)

Jeep Plus in Moshav Ramot, on the eastern bank of the Sea of Galilee, runs guided jeep trips. (☎ 673 23 17. 2hr. trip for 7-8 people NIS540/US$145.) **Tractoron B'Rama,** also in Ramot, rents one-person ATVs to tourists with driver's licenses. (☎ 05 053 17 84. NIS120 per hr.) **Jimmy Jeep,** at Givat Yoav, southeast of Kursi on Rte. 789, runs 2hr. jeep trips for NIS550. (☎ 676 34 05. Jeep seats 8 people.)

▐ PRACTICAL INFORMATION

When wandering the Golan in summer, bring a hat, sunscreen, and water bottles. The cool pools of water often found on hikes reward weary walkers ready to take a dip, but don't drink the water. Try to avoid the cold, damp, foggy, and often snowy winter. The best time to visit the Golan is spring, when the temperature is mild, the hills are green, and the streams and waterfalls are satiated with icy-cold water from the melting snow on Mt. Ḥermon. The best way to see the Golan is to **rent a car** in Tiberias or Kiryat Shmona. Those who don't plan to hike can hit the major sights in two days. Don't be afraid to lean on your horn (passing other cars in the Golan is as common as passing breathtaking views), but take care when navigating the narrow, curving roads.

 ## HIKING

Those who wish to hike in the Golan should purchase the 1:50,000 trail map available at SPNI offices and in Steimatzky's (NIS62). SPNI offices also have useful booklets with descriptions and directions for hiking routes in the area, such as the *Israeli Landscapes Vol. 1: Guide to the Golan Heights* (NIS55) and a more general map of the upper Galilee and Golan Heights, with roads and popular sights marked (NIS20). For more detailed directions and alternative trail options in the Golan, check out a copy of Joel Roskin's *A Guide to Hiking in Israel*, on sale at Steimatzky bookstores (NIS39). Consult the SPNI field schools in Katzrin or Ḥermon for up-to-date advice and information; the information desk at **Yehudiyya Reserve** (☎696 28 17) also offers helpful hiking advice.

> **! DANGER! MINES!** The Golan Heights still contain active landmine fields. They are marked off by barbed-wire fences with square yellow signs that have red triangles and say, "Danger! Mines!" in English, as well as in Hebrew and Arabic. In some areas, the fences are marked only with red triangles. Be sure to stay on paved roads and clearly marked hiking trails. As a rule, avoid fenced-off areas whether or not you see the yellow-and-red warning signs.

YA'AR YEHUDIYYA NATURE RESERVE

By car from Tiberias, drive north along the lake, head east toward Katzrin, pass the Yehudiyya Junction, and continue along Rte. 87 until you reach the orange sign. By car from Kiryat Shmona, head toward Katzrin and the junction with Rte. 87, take a right, and look for the sign and parking lot on the right. Open Sa-Th 7am-5pm, F and holidays 7am-4pm; leave no later than 1hr. after closing time. NIS10, students NIS8, children NIS7. Most trails begin in Ḥenion Yehudiyya (☎696 28 17), a parking lot with an SPNI information booth, snack stand (1½L water NIS9, sandwiches NIS12), toilets, phones, and camping facilities accessible by bus from Katzrin. At the Ḥenion, bags can be stored for NIS12 per locker. Camping next to the Ḥenion parking lot costs NIS10 per person; facilities include showers and bathrooms. Before beginning a hike, check in with the information desk and get a map.

The most exciting and challenging hiking in the Golan is in the Ya'ar Yehudiyya Nature Reserve, southeast of Katzrin. The highlight of the reserve, and one of the best hikes in Israel, is the action-packed **Naḥal Yehudiyya** trail, which consists of an upper and a lower section. From the Ḥenion parking lot follow the red-and-white markers across the street, past the 1800-year-old Jewish and Byzantine town ruins, and into the valley. Upon completion of the **upper trail,** ascend the green-and-white trail to return to Ḥenion (3hr. round-trip) or continue along the red-and-white marked lower trail for a longer hike (5-6hr. round-trip). The lower trail ends with an extremely difficult climb up a boulder-strewn hill (be careful: the rocks are hot during summer), a peaceful stroll through a beautiful yellow field, and a 1½km walk to the right along the highway back to the Ḥenion. Both trails feature enticing waterfalls and pools, some of which you must swim across to complete your hike (bring a bathing suit and plastic bags to protect food and valuables). Rocks are slippery when climbing from dry parts of the trail into the water, so look for the strategically placed metal foot- and hand-holds in the cliffs. Jumping off the 9m cliff at the second waterfall is dangerous—people have died doing this. A much safer option is to climb down the slippery ladder into the water to enjoy the swim.

SPIES LIKE US In the early 1960s, Israeli spy **Eli Cohen,** posing as an Arab businessman, infiltrated the Syrian government. Rising through the ranks, he virtually became the president's right-hand man. One of Cohen's suggestions was that the Syrian army plant tall eucalyptus trees to camouflage their Golan Heights bunkers; he then tipped off the IDF, and the air force began targeting the eucalyptus clusters. The Syrian government eventually caught and hanged the Israeli spy, but the destroyed Syrian bunkers sprinkled over the Golan stand as a testimony to his espionage.

The reserve also harbors the slightly drier but equally beautiful **Naḥal Zavitan;** most of its trail options also start at the Ḥenion Yehudiyya parking lot. Start on the green-and-white marked Lower Zavitan trail. A left turn on the red-and-white trail leads to the **Ein Netef** spring, which purportedly contains the only drinkable water in the reserve. From the spring, backtrack along the red-and-white trail and turn left on the black-and-white trail to reach a pleasant pool and waterfall. This trek eventually crosses the red-and-white one and returns to Ḥenion Yehudiyya (3hr.). Alternatively, turn left and continue on the red-and-white trail for 45min. to reach the spectacular **Brekhat Ha-Meshushim** (Hexagon Pool), where hundreds of hexagonal rock columns skirt the water's edge in a wonderful geological phenomenon. From here, backtrack to Ḥenion (total 6hr.). The **Upper Zavitan** (black-and-white trail) tends to be good for all seasons. It begins near the field school in Katzrin and leads to less impressive hexagonal pools; after becoming a purple-and-white trail, it ends in Ḥenion Yehudiyya (3hr.). The more difficult **Lower Zavitan** should be avoided in the winter due to occasional flash floods. The dangerous **Black Canyon,** is near the Lower Zavitan trail, and can only be negotiated by rapelling. Many hikers have died here. Do not attempt to hike the Black Canyon without an experienced guide.

NAḤAL EL-AL. This beautiful hike lies southeast of the Zavitan and Yehudiyya Rivers. In winter and spring, enough water flows through to allow swimming beneath the falls. The red-and-white trail begins at the northeast end of the kibbutz. Follow the markers to **Mapal Ha-Lavan** (white waterfall) and continue on to **Mapal Ha-Shaḥor** (black waterfall). The trail ends at Kibbutz Avnei-Eitan. From there, take a right on Rte. 98 and walk 2km to return to Kibbutz Eli-Al. *(By car from Tiberias, head south on Rte. 90. At Zemaḥ Junction, turn onto Rte. 98 and follow it to Kibbutz Eli-Al. The site is fairly close to Yehudiyya: turn left out of Ḥenion Yehudiyya, take Rte. 87 to Rte. 808 on the right, turn right onto Rte. 98, and look for the kibbutz sign. Without a car, this hike is impossible to do in a day, as the 1st bus arrives at 12:30pm and the last one leaves at 1pm.)*

NAḤAL DEVORAH AND NAḤAL GILABON. From the main parking lot, red-and-white markings lead to the left around a building and down into the canyon. Join the hundreds who have left their mark by sticking a masticated glob of gum onto the **Even Ha-Mastik** ("The Gum Rock"). The first waterfall on the trail is the Devorah Waterfall. Continuing on the red-and-white path another hour leads to the 21m Gilabon Waterfall; wonderful views of the lush Ḥula Valley await at its top. The trail continues another 2hr. to the Jordan River and Rte. 918, but getting back to the parking lot may be difficult if you don't have a car waiting. Otherwise just retrace your steps to return to the parking lot. *(From Tiberias, take Rte. 90 north and the turnoff for Rte. 91 east. Continue 30min. on Rte. 91; watch for a brown sign and red-and-white trail marker 3-4km after the turnoff for Road 9088. Turn left onto the dirt road and make a right farther up to reach a parking lot surrounded by destroyed Syrian bunkers.)*

NAḤAL ZAKI. Naḥal Zaki makes for a refreshing hike. In August or September, ripe grapes hang overhead and the sweltering heat makes the cool stream a godsend. Wear a bathing suit and bring plastic bags to protect valuables—half the hike is spent wading in knee-deep water. In winter, the current is strong and this trail could be dangerous. Hike in the stream following the green-and-white trail for 3km; at the pipe that stretches across the river, get out of the water on the left side and return by way of a dirt path. *(Off of Rte. 92, just south of the Yehudiyya Junction on the left. Drive along the green trail to a lot, then park and begin the hike.)*

GAMLA. In 67 CE, the Romans laid siege to this hilltop fortress, then a haven for 9000 Jewish refugees. As the siege wore on, Roman commanders became impatient and decided to storm down the corridor of land leading to the town from nearby hills. As the legion penetrated Gamla's walls, hordes of Jews fled to the upper part of the city, where slopes were so steep that one house's rooftop touched the floor of the house above it. The Romans followed, but so many soldiers crowded on the rooftops that the houses collapsed; the Jews quickly turned and killed their pursuers. Some weeks later, three Roman soldiers sneaked into Gamla in the middle of the night and pulled out foundation stones from the watchtower, causing it to collapse. In the ensuing confusion, the Roman army burst into the city and began to slaughter the inhabitants, many of whom hurled themselves into the deep ravine next to the Citadel rather than die by enemy hands. Two women survived to tell the tale (some archaeologists take issue with Josephus's proclivity for over-dramatization and claim that Gamla's inhabitants were pushed over the cliff in the mayhem of battle). Inside the city lie remnants of what some archaeologists call the oldest synagogue ever found in Israel, dating from around the 2nd century BCE.

There are three **light hiking** trails at Gamla. The 2hr. trail through the ancient city is marked in black and begins at the upper left corner of the parking lot (when facing away from the ticket booth). The climb back up from the ruins to the parking lot can be brutal on a hot summer day; there is a shuttle bus that runs every hour down to the ancient city and returns to the parking lot on the half hour (NIS15). The **Mapal Gamla,** or Gamla waterfall, is the highest in the Golan (51m). The trail to the waterfall leads past another fall, usually dry in summer, as well as ancient **Dolmens,** table-like stone graves built 4000 years ago during the middle Bronze Age. The trail is marked in red, takes about 1hr., and begins out of the upper right corner of the parking lot, near the water spigots and bathrooms. The **Daliyot trail** (2hr.), marked red and white, starts out of the left corner of the parking lot nearest the ticket booth and runs through fields and along a river canyon. While hot and less interesting during the summer, it boasts a seasonal waterfall. (Take a right out of modern Katzrin, a left onto Rte. 87 at the junction, and a right onto Rte. 808. The road to Gamla is on the right, labeled with a sign. Gamla is **not accessible by public transportation;** those without cars often ask for rides from Katzrin and walk the 1km to the ridge overlooking the ruins. The descent to the ruins along the Roman route takes about 20min. Allot 1-2hr. to see the site. ☎ 676 20 46. Open Su-Th 8am-5pm, F 8am-4pm; closes 1hr. earlier in winter. NIS18, students NIS15.)

BANYAS בניס

Buses leave Kiryat Shmona once a day on their way through the Golan and stop by Banyas (#55 or 58; 1:30 and 4:40pm; NIS11.50). By car, Banyas lies just off Rte. 99, which runs between Kiryat Shmona and the north-south Rte. 98. ☎ 695 02 72. Park open Sa-Th 8am-5pm, F 8am-4pm. NIS18, students NIS15, children NIS9.

The most popular site in the Upper Galilee-Golan area, Banyas lies only a few minutes down the road from Dan and Ḥorshat Tal at the foot of Mt. Ḥermon. The Banyas springs in the Naḥal Ḥermon Nature Reserve have witnessed an odd religious mix: Jesus gave the keys to heaven and earth to St. Peter here, Muslims built a shrine over the Prophet Elijah's (Nebi Khadar) supposed grave in the adjacent hill, and an ancient sanctuary dedicated to the Greek God Pan remains carved into the cliffside. King Herod built a temple in honor of Caesar Augustus and called the place Caesarea Philippi, after his son Philippus. Because of its ancient association with Pan, however, the area became known as *Paneas* (Pan's Place).

The first brown sign on the road that points to Banyas leads to a parking lot and the entrance closest to the 10m **Banyas waterfall,** the largest falls in the region. From the waterfall, a 1hr. trail winds through woods toward the springs, which contain small pools of rare fish. Swimming is forbidden in the pool's icy-cold water, but some visitors wade in to refresh themselves anyway. From here, head toward the parking lot where the ruins of **Pan's temple** are up and to the left. Those short on time can drive from the waterfall to Pan's Temple by making a right on the main road and following the signs.

NIMROD'S FORTRESS קלעת נמרוד

*The **trail** to the fortress begins just off bus route #55 between Kiryat Shmona and Katzrin. The road to the castle sits across from the bus stop (NIS16.50). The 1hr., uphill approach leads to a view into the Druze village of Ein Qinya. The castle is accessible by a **footpath** from Banyas beginning directly above the springs and Pan's temple. This shadeless walk takes about 45min. each way. By **car,** continue on Rte. 99 past Banyas to Rte. 989; the fortress is up a curvy road on the left. Open daily 8am-5pm. NIS14, students NIS12, under 18 NIS6.*

Nimrod's Fortress (Qal'at Nemrud) stands 1.5km northeast of Banyas on an isolated hill. According to the biblical list of Noah's descendants, Nimrod claims the title, "the first on earth to be a mighty man" (Genesis 10:8). Legend holds that besides building the Tower of Babel, he erected this gigantic fortress high enough to shoot arrows up to God. The extensive fortress has two main sections; the one farther away from the entrance was built earlier. A look around the grounds reveals a secret passageway and game boards carved into the stone sidewalks by bored guards. The 815m-high view from the top of the fortress to the region below remains unrivaled anywhere in the Upper Galilee or Golan.

Up the road about 1km past Nimrod's Fortress is a Muslim tomb and hiking route at **Nebi Hazuri.** The location is marked on the left by a brown sign in Hebrew. A white gravel road begins in the parking lot and winds around picnic areas, trees, and monuments. The hiking route, marked in blue and white, heads right and downhill from beside the large wooden sign in the parking area (rocks are marked a bit farther down). After 2hr., the trail ends outside the entrance to the road leading up to Nimrod's Fortress; take a left and head up the main highway to return to the Nebi Hazuri parking area.

MAS'ADA AND MAJDAL SHAMS مسعدة و مجدل شمس

The Druze of these two villages at the foot of Mt. Ḥermon differ from the Galilee's Druze in one major respect: most have remained loyal to Syria and many refuse to accept Israeli citizenship. Many of them have close relatives on the other side of the Syrian border and do not want to fight against them in the event of a war. In 1982, they staged a protest against Israeli rule, and the Israeli Defense Forces were sent in to restore control. Since then, the villages have been quiet.

Mas'ada is at the foot of Mt. Ḥermon, at the intersection of Rte. 99 (leading west to Kiryat Shmona) and Rte. 98 (leading south to Katzrin). Mas'ada's farmers cultivate the valley and terrace the low-lying ridges around the mountain. Two kilometers north on Rte. 98 rests the locally famous lake **Breiḥat Ram** (Hebrew for "High Lake"). The perfectly round body of water fills the crater of a volcano that has not erupted in over 1000 years. The lake is on the right, past large green gates with a big white sign in Hebrew.

Majdal Shams (Arabic for "Tower of the Sun"), the largest town in the Golan (pop. 8000), is 5km north of Mas'ada through a pleasant valley. The town abuts the border with Syria; an Israeli lookout tower that looms above the village sees eye-to-eye with its Syrian counterpart on the opposite peak, while a white UN base spans the neutral valley in between. Because the electric-fence border is closed and pocked with land mines, the lookout area on the outskirts of town provides the setting for a sad, but fascinating, daily ritual. Majdal's Druze line up on the hillside (aptly dubbed *Givat Ha-Tza'akot* or "Shouting Mountain"). Armed with bullhorns, they make small-talk with their relatives on the Syrian side; the best time to communicate seems to be Friday and Saturday afternoons.

MT. ḤERMON

The 2800m high peaks of the majestic Ḥermon mountain range tower over the rest of the Golan. In the wintertime there is skiing, which can be challenging; it has no trees, and steep dips in the wide expanses are easy to miss. Beginners should not fret, however—gentle runs descend from the top of each lift. On clear days, skiers can see Galilee stretch out beneath them. In summer the same chairlift brings tourists up to a panoramic lookout atop Mt. Ḥermon. The mountain is particularly striking in late spring and early summer when it is covered in brightly colored wildflowers. (Info ☎ 06 698 13 37 or 03 565 60 40.)

ISRAEL

Ten kilometers south of Mt. Ḥermon lies **Moshav Neveh Ativ** (☎ 698 13 33), founded after Israel captured the Golan. The moshav has developed an expensive resort village to take advantage of the ski slopes. Bus #55 goes from Kiryat Shmona to the moshav twice a day (1:30 and 4:40pm, NIS13). A *sherut* from Mas'ada to Kiryat Shmona in the late afternoon is usually the same price. The road from Mas'ada to Kiryat Shmona runs west along a gorge and past the hilltop village of Ein Qinya and Nimrod's Fortress. For information on outdoor activities in the area or in the Golan in general, try the **Ḥermon SPNI field school,** near Kibbutz Senir, to the right off Rte. 99 on the way from Kiryat Shmona to Banyas and just beyond Tel Dan. The field school is down a turnoff marked by a wooden sign on the right, then through the gates. In addition to patient and friendly advice, the field school has air-conditioned double rooms with private bathrooms. (☎ 694 10 91. NIS245/US\$60; additional person NIS70; July-Aug. and holidays NIS25 extra per person. Breakfast included. Office open daily 8am-8pm.)

DEAD SEA ים המלח لبحر الميت

How low can you go? At 412m below sea level, this is it—the Dead Sea is the lowest point on Earth. If that factoid doesn't sound impressive, wait until you're driving on the highway, pass a "Sea Level" signpost, and then round a bend to see entire mountains whose *peaks* lie below you.

The Dead Sea is actually a large lake—65km long, 18km wide, and 412m deep. Its coasts are shared by Israel and Jordan, with the peaceful border drawn smack down the sea's middle. The sea's formation is the result of a geological phenomenon called the "Syrian-African Rift," essentially a mega-valley between shifting tectonic plates extending from southern Africa to Turkey. The resulting image of hollowness has led some to nickname the Dead Sea area "the navel of the world."

Water flows into the sea from the Jordan River and underground water sources from the surrounding desert. But with no outlet for the lake's water, the intense sun evaporates it faster than you can say "Ra." Inadequate rainfall, coupled with Israeli, Jordanian, and Syrian reliance on the sea's freshwater sources for drinking and irrigation, has begun to take its toll. The sun now evaporates more water than flows in; the sea is shrinking so severely that the southern tip has been cut off by a sand bar, and the northern part now recedes at the frightening rate of 80cm a year. Emergency measures to save the Dead Sea, driven by both ecological and economic incentives, are in the planning stages.

The **tourist information** hub for the entire area is in the central Dead Sea region is near Ein Gedi. Check in at the kibbutz reception center for information on local sights and events (☎ 07 658 44 44; fax 07 658 43 67; eg@mishkei.org.il; www.ein-gedi.co.il). It is possible to join the crowds on the popular one-day **tour** from Jerusalem that shuttles lemmings—er, tourists to Masada (in time for sunrise), Ein Gedi (Naḥal David and the Dead Sea beach), Qumran (jump out of the bus, take a picture, jump back in), Jericho (in time for a late lunch), and photograph stops at the Mount of Temptation, St. George Monastery, and the Mount of Olives. Tours cost NIS90 (entrance fees not included) and can be booked through most of the hostels in the Old City.

TRANSPORTATION

The Egged buses that serve the rest of the country well do poorly in this region. Fares are outrageous (up to NIS10 for a 10min. ride), and the routes don't cover every destination. These difficulties, in conjunction with the nasty heat and the great distance between the main roads and sights, make renting a car an excellent idea. Most companies offer a daily rental rate of US\$40-50 for single-day rentals, US\$35-45 per day for longer-term rentals. Driving in the Dead Sea region provides spectacular vistas, but be careful—steep, windy roads mean nothing to speed-demon Israeli drivers. The best place to rent is Jerusalem, since cut-throat competition drives prices down (see **Car rental,** p. 286). In the Dead Sea region, try **Hertz** (☎ 658 44 33 or 658 45 30) in Ein Bokek.

The few Egged lines that travel along the Dead Sea coast have erratic schedules with pauses often lasting 45-90min., so check times (Central Bus Station in Jerusalem ☎ 02 530 47 04) and plan ahead. Buses #421, 444, and 486 between Jerusalem and Eilat stop at Qumran, Ein Feshkha, Ein Gedi, and Masada. Bus #487, also from Jerusalem, runs only to Qumran, Ein Feshkha, and Ein Gedi. Buses #384 and 385 combined make about four trips per day (Su-F) between Be'er Sheva and Ein Gedi via Arad, Ein Bokek, and Masada. Buses will stop at many stations only upon request, so **confirm destinations** with the driver. Several sites listed, including Metzokei Dragot and Neot Ha-Kikkar, are **not accessible by public transportation.** On Saturdays, none of the buses head to or from the Dead Sea until the evening; to get there earlier, find a *service* across from Damascus Gate (NIS30-45 depending how far south you want to go). Locals claim hitchhiking is relatively safe in this part of the country; *Let's Go* does not recommend hitchhiking.

DESERT SAFETY

The Dead Sea region does not have an ordinary desert climate—instead of being hot and dry, it's hot and humid. The sticky air, the very high temperatures, and 330 days a year of cloudless, steady sun are barely tolerable. While the air does have a 10% higher oxygen concentration, exertion is recommended only in the early morning. The steamroom-like weather has been known to dehydrate people simply waiting at a shaded bus stop. Keep your head covered, take a **water** bottle wherever you go, and chug liberally at the rate of about 1L per hr. (more if you're hiking). Bring a large bottle with you and keep refilling at faucets to avoid getting ripped off by the 8-Shekel-a-pop street vendors once you're there. While the tap water is drinkable in most places in Israel, don't assume that shower and faucet water is safe to drink—check for "Drinking Water" signs or ask someone.

There is **no money changing office or ATM** anywhere in the Dead Sea region, so come prepared. The nearest facilities are in Arad and Be'er Sheva.

ADDING INSALT TO INJURY. Dead Sea water is powerful stuff. When it's good, it may cure arthritis, but when it's bad, it's like applying acid as aftershave. If Dead Sea water gets into your eyes, you're in for several minutes of painful blindness. Rinse your eyes immediately in the fresh-water showers, found on all beaches. Don't shave the morning before you go swimming; the water will sear minor scrapes. And, of course, resist the urge to taste it.

EIN GEDI עין גדי

After a hot morning hike or a muggy bus ride, the only thing better than drinking cold water is sitting in it. The Ein Gedi oasis, the epicenter of the Dead Sea region, has a long history of providing shelter and romantic getaways. The cascading waterfalls of the Ein Gedi oasis thrive just a few minutes' hike from the lifeless shores of the Dead Sea. Rare desert wildlife, including ibex, fox, and hyrax, and rare species of birds and flowers inhabit this verdant nature reserve. In 1994, the land in and around the Ein Gedi kibbutz was officially recognized as an International Botanical Garden, boasting over 800 species of trees, shrubs, and flowers from all over the world, as well as about 1000 species of cacti and desert plants. Tired hikers can relax in the afternoons at the free beach.

⊏ TRANSPORTATION

From Ein Gedi, **buses** go to: **Be'er Sheva** (#384 and 385; 2½hr.; Su-Th 4 per day 8am-6pm, F 8am-3:30pm, Sa 3:30pm; NIS35) via **Masada** (20min.), **Ein Bokek** (30min., NIS18), and **Arad** (1½hr.); **Eilat** (#444; 3hr.; Su-Th 4 per day 7:50am-5:50pm, F 7:50am-2:50pm; NIS50); **Ein Bokek** (#486; Su-Th 4 per day 10am-2:05pm, F 9:50am and 2:05pm); and **Jerusalem** (#421, 444, 486, and 487; 1¼hr.; Su-Th 11 per day

5:45am-6pm, F 5:45am-5pm, Sa 6:25pm-10:30pm; NIS32). Students with ISICs can receive discounted fares on all bus routes. Departure times are erratic; get a schedule from the bus station in Jerusalem or check with your hostel.

✴ ⁊ ORIENTATION AND PRACTICAL INFORMATION

Ein Gedi's 6750-acre nature reserve is the heart of this desert attraction. Around it, a kibbutz, several accommodations, a field school, a public bathing area, and a luxury spa have all been built. There are four **bus stops** in the area. The first one serves the **nature reserve** and the two youth **hostels.** Farther south is the beach stop, which is convenient for the public beach, food, a gas station, a **first-aid** station, and the yellow-roofed **tourist information** booth, which covers the entire Dead Sea region. (☎658 44 44; fax 658 43 67; eg@kibbutz.co.il; www.ein-gedi.co.il. Open daily 9am-4pm.) The third stop, by advance request only, serves the kibbutz and its guest house. At the fourth stop are the thermal baths and spa. The hostels and public beach are a 10-15min. walk apart, but the spas are 6km south of the beach. Food kiosks crowd the entrances to and exits from all attractions, beaches, and hikes.

⌂ ⍾ ACCOMMODATIONS AND FOOD

The **Beit Sara Youth Hostel (HI),** uphill at the turnoff for Naḥal David, has clean and uncrowded rooms with air-conditioning and private baths. Ask about discount tickets (15%) for the nature reserve, Ein Gedi Spa, and Atraktzia water park. (☎658 41 65; fax 658 44 44. Breakfast included; dinner US$8.50, child US$7.50. Packed lunch on request NIS22. Office open 7am-9pm; 24hr. phone reception. Check-in 3-7pm. Check-out Su-F 9am, Sa 10am. Dorms NIS72/US$17.50; doubles US$56. HI members receive US$1.50 discount on dorms. Credit cards accepted.) The **Ein Gedi Field School,** in a less touristed, more scenic spot, is a steep 10min. climb up the road behind the more accessible youth hostel. Run by the Society for the Protection of Nature in Israel (SPNI), the field school offers free sound and light shows on the Judean Desert every night. This peak is the only place on Earth to get a glimpse of a rare species of bird called *Leilit Ha-Midbar* (Hume's Tawny Owl). A few feet from the TV room is a special bird-shrine and lookout point. Each spartan room is equipped with a coffee station and towels for the shared showers. (☎658 43 50; fax 658 42 57. Common kitchen and TV room. Office open Su-F 8am-7pm. Check-in 3pm. Check-out 10am. Call ahead. Dorms NIS75. Students and SPNI members 20% discount; membership available at check-in for NIS82, family NIS108. Credit cards accepted.)

Quick snacks are available at kiosks throughout Ein Gedi, including near the entrance to the nature reserve at **Kiosk Naḥal David.** (Beer NIS10. Open 8am-5pm.) A few sandwiches and some juice can provide a relatively cheap alternative to expensive tourist joints, although prices are still higher than in the cities. The cafeteria-style **Pundak Ein Gedi,** in the parking lot of the beach bus stop, serves hungry beach-goers. (☎659 47 61. Chicken with two side dishes NIS30. Open daily 10am-6pm.) The kiosk next door is open later. (Sandwiches NIS12. Open daily 7:30am-8pm.) Another dining possibility in the central Dead Sea region is **Gofrit Restaurant** at the Ein Gedi Spa. (Main course NIS20, with side dishes NIS35. ☎659 48 13. Open daily 11am-4pm.) Hostels in the area will provide an inexpensive **packed lunch** if ordered the previous night.

⚑ HIKING

Of the two entrances to the huge **Ein Gedi Nature Reserve,** only the **Naḥal David** entrance (☎658 42 85), below the youth hostels, is accessible by bus. (Open daily 8am-4pm. Several hikes end after 1:30pm. NIS18.) **Naḥal Arugot** (☎652 0224), 3km past the Naḥal David entrance, is accessible only by car.

Some sections of the Ein Gedi trails are steep, but well-placed railings and steps have been built into the rock. Once noon rolls around, high temperatures can make even inhaling strenuous, so get going by **8am.** Always bring at least 1L of water per hour of hiking (there are faucets just outside the gate), and don't forget your **swimsuit** for dipping in the occasional freshwater pool or waterfall. The names of the different pools and springs repeat frequently and are almost interchangeable (David this, Ein Gedi that), so get a free map at the entrance and pay attention to the fine print to prevent confusion. Possible hikes vary from easygoing to double diamond difficult. Some suggested trails follow:

HIKING TRAILS

1. For a short hike of 45min. each way, enter from the Naḥal David entrance and follow the path straight until **Shulamit Falls**, a delicious, slender pillar of water dropping into a shallow pool. Turning left at the falls leads to a trail that climbs up the cliffside to **Shulamit Spring** (an additional 30min. each way).

2. For a longer hike, continue from Shulamit spring along the cliff and down a ladder to **Dudaim Cave** (Lover's Cave), a mossy niche at the top of the fall (30min. from the spring). Proceed left, passing the 3000-year-old remains of a **Chalcolithic Temple** once dedicated to worship of the moon, on the way to **Ein Gedi Spring** (20min. from the Temple), whose cool water is perfect for a refreshing dip. Resist the urge to dive from the high niches into the pool—it's not deep enough in some places. Next to the spring is a sugar or flour mill from the Islamic period which was powered by water from the spring.

3. The 2nd entrance to the reserve is at **Naḥal Arugot** (no bus; parking lot 3km inland from Rte. 90, between the beach and Naḥal David entrance). A somewhat challenging hour's hike along the river leads to a hidden waterfall and a beautiful, deep blue pool.

4. One long but highly recommended trail connects the David and Arugot entrances, with the Ein Gedi Spring smack in the middle. The trail passes the newly restored ancient **synagogue** and leads directly to the beachfront in time for an afternoon of sunbathing. The trail begins at the **SPNI Field School** and follows the "Zafit Trail" until Ein David. At Ein David, turn left and follow the main marked trail to Shulamit Falls. For a shorter hike, bear left and follow the main trail out; for the full hike, bear right and continue toward Shulamit Spring and the Chalcolithic temple. **Ein Gedi Spring** is a few hundred meters farther. Continue straight, due south, until **Tel Goren**. Turn left toward the sea, passing the ancient **synagogue** after a few hundred meters. The light blue building toward the end is the Ein Gedi mineral water bottling plant, a refreshing stop.

◤ BEACHES

For good ol' Dead Sea floating and mud, Ein Gedi has its own crowded **beach.** Use of the beach and umbrellas is free, but bathrooms and lockers cost NIS1 and NIS5, respectively. **Lot's Wife,** a boat touring around the Dead Sea area, departs from the small dock to the left (when facing the water) of the Ein Gedi beach. (mobile ☎ 054 91 50 04. Regular trips Tu and Sa at 2:30pm, but private tours arranged for groups. Call ahead. NIS40, children NIS30.) About 5km south of the beach is the **Ein Gedi Spa,** with indoor sulfur pools, therapeutic mud, and a restaurant. (NIS50, Sa NIS55; children NIS44. ☎ 659 48 13. Spa open Sa-Th 7am-6pm, F 7am-5:30pm.) Local hostels provide tickets for a 15% discount.

◗ DAYTRIPS FROM EIN GEDIT

KALYA BEACHES

This area in the northern Dead Sea region is only 25min. from Jerusalem (Rte. 90), and its shores are the least touristed by foreigners. Take bus #480 or 487 from Jerusalem. From Ein Bokek, take bus #421 or 966 (originating from Tel Aviv and Haifa, respectively). Remember to confirm your destination with the bus driver, and make sure you tell him you're going to the beach or else you'll end up at the Kalya kibbutz by Qumran. All of the Kalya beaches are accessible from the same turnoff and bus stop, but you'll still have to walk 1km in the sun.

Farther down the road, two private beaches offer luxuries that might appeal more to the adults. **Siesta Beach** (☎ 994 41 11) follow a salty float with a Thai massage to calm your sunstroked bod (NIS85 for 10min.). A Jordanian/Palestinian restaurant on the beach serves "authentic" cuisine at unauthentic prices. (Falafel plate and salad NIS25. Open daily 8:30am-7:30pm; in winter 8:30am-6:30pm.) Next door, **Neve Midbar** (☎ 994 27 81) complements black mud with Desert's Magic holistic treatments, which include water therapy using the Dead Sea's healing properties (NIS80 for a 30min. "half-treatment"). An outdoor restaurant features pricey drinks and meals. (*Schnitzel* NIS40. Open daily 8:30am-7:30pm.)

METZOKEI DRAGOT (WADI DARJA) מצוקי דרגות

This **nature reserve,** with soaring cliffs, is for serious hikers only. About 20km south of Qumran and Ein Feshkha, a steep, winding road branches off on the right. Buses go no farther than the turnoff; the only ways to reach the reserve and the hostel are by car or a 5km hike. The ascent culminates in a view of soaring cliffs and ravines on one side, the Dead Sea and not-so-distant hills of Jordan on the other. Heed the warnings on the green welcome-board—be sure to carry a trail map and a 20m security rope, both of which are usually available at the office. Climbers and rappellers with their own equipment may wish to take advantage of the excellent conditions in the reserve; unfortunately, there are no longer any organized trips or equipment rental. **You may not begin hiking in the wadi after 9am,** so it is a good idea to stay at the hostel the night before, and be on your feet at the crack of dawn. There is no place to refill water bottles; carry enough for the hike.

Owned and managed by the Mitzpeh Shalem Kibbutz a few kilometers away, the **youth hostel,** a great alternative to often-booked Ein Gedi accommodations, lies at the top of the winding road. (Check-in after 2pm; check-out Su-F 10am, Sa noon. Dinner NIS45 with advanced notice. A/C 6-8 bed dorms NIS32; singles NIS149; bed and breakfast doubles NIS230.)

MASADA מצדה

"Masada shall not fall again," swear members of the **Israel Defense Forces** each year at this site. Jewish Zealots' tenacious defense of Masada in the first century CE has been fashioned into a heroic symbol of the defense of modern Israel. Political significance aside, legions of tourists from around the world continue to storm this mountain fortress to catch the spectacular view of the Dead Sea, visit the extensive ruins, and envision the martyrdom of Masada's rebels.

At the outset of the Jewish rebellion against Rome in 66 CE, a small band of Zealot rebels, members of a small Jewish sect, captured the prize fortress from its unsuspecting garrison. As the Romans gradually crushed the revolt, taking Jerusalem in 70 CE and destroying the Second Temple, Masada became a refuge for surviving Zealots, and eventually the last Jewish holdout in all of Israel. With years' worth of food, water, and military supplies, the 967 men, women, and children held off 15,000 Roman legionnaires through a five-month siege. The Romans called in their best engineers to construct a wall and camps in a ring around the mount. Capitalizing on their superior strength, they built an enormous stone and gravel ramp up the side of the cliff, using Jewish slaves as laborers in order to prevent the Zealots from shooting them down as the ramp was built.

When the defenders realized that the Romans would break through their walls the next morning, the community leaders decided that it would be better to die, as their leader Eliezer Ben-Yair said, "unenslaved by enemies, and leave this world as free men in company with wives and children." Because Jewish law forbids suicide, ten men were chosen to slay the others, and one chosen to kill the other nine before falling on his own sword. Before burning the fortress and all their possessions, the Jews placed stores of wheat and water in the Citadel's courtyard to prove to the Romans that they did not perish from hunger. The following morning, when the triumphant Romans burst in, they encountered only smoking ruins and deathly silence. The only survivors, two women and five children, told the story of the Zealots' last days to Josephus Flavius, a Jewish-Roman general and chronicler. Flavius, always eager to embellish a good tale, never actually visited Masada. He based his dramatic history on the survivors' accounts, later describing the two to be "of exceptional intelligence for women." Although strong corroborating evidence for the story has been found at the site, such as the murder-lottery slips Josephus describes, archaeologists have yet to unearth the Zealots' actual remains. Where the bones of almost 1000 people have gone is still a mystery.

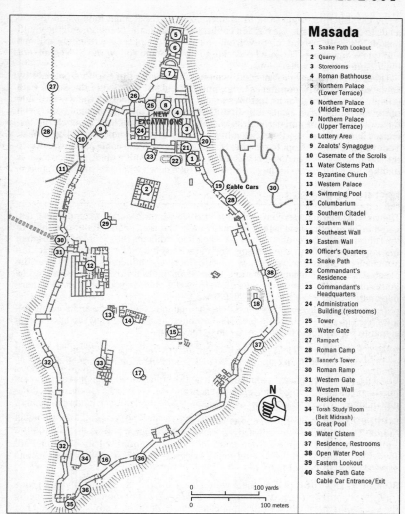

Masada

1 Snake Path Lookout
2 Quarry
3 Storerooms
4 Roman Bathhouse
5 Northern Palace (Lower Terrace)
6 Northern Palace (Middle Terrace)
7 Northern Palace (Upper Terrace)
8 Lottery Area
9 Zealots' Synagogue
10 Casemate of the Scrolls
11 Water Cisterns Path
12 Byzantine Church
13 Western Palace
14 Swimming Pool
15 Columbarium
16 Southern Citadel
17 Southern Wall
18 Southeast Wall
19 Eastern Wall
20 Officer's Quarters
21 Snake Path
22 Commandant's Residence
23 Commandant's Headquarters
24 Administration Building (restrooms)
25 Tower
26 Water Gate
27 Rampart
28 Roman Camp
29 Tanner's Tower
30 Roman Ramp
31 Western Gate
32 Western Wall
33 Residence
34 Torah Study Room (Beit Midrash)
35 Great Pool
36 Water Cistern
37 Residence, Restrooms
38 Open Water Pool
39 Eastern Lookout
40 Snake Path Gate Cable Car Entrance/Exit

0   100 yards
0   100 meters

ISRAEL

▐ TRANSPORTATION

Masada lies 20km south of Ein Gedi, a few kilometers inland from the Jerusalem-Eilat road (Rte. 90). Buses leaving Masada generally start around 8:30am; only a few leave after 4pm. Check at the Taylor Youth hostel for a current schedule, and make sure you are heading in the right direction. Buses go to: **Be'er Sheva** (#384 and 385; Su-Th 4 per day 8:15am-6:15pm, F 4 per day 8:15am-3:15pm, Sa 3:45pm; NIS35.50, students NIS31) via **Ein Bokek** (NIS11.50); **Eilat** (#444; Su-Th 4 per day 8am-6pm, F 3 per day 8am-3pm; NIS50, students NIS45); **Jerusalem** (#444 and 486; Su-Th 8 per day 8:35-7:20pm, F 5 per day 8:35am-3:20pm, Sa 6:50 and 9:20pm; NIS37.50, students NIS34) via **Ein Gedi** (NIS14); and **Tel Aviv** (#421; Su-F 2:25pm; NIS47, students NIS42). Buses #384 and 385 also go to Ein Gedi.

By car, Rte. 3199 runs from Arad to the base of the Roman Ramp, and Rte. 90 leads to the Snake Path, the eastern cable car entrance, the bus stop, and the youth hostel. The walk around the base from one path to the other is extremely arduous and time-consuming. Those who decide to do it should follow the SPNI trail, not the incline with the water pipe.

There are three ways to ascend the mountain: by either of two foot paths or by cable car. The more popular, scenic, and difficult of the two is the **Snake Path** (45min. hike), named for its tortuous bends. The **Roman Ramp,** on the western side of the mountain, is an easier hike than the Snake Path and the original path. Even the most grumpy of non-early birds will appreciate a dawn hike to catch the legendary sunrise over the Dead Sea and avoid tour group insanity and blazing heat. Today many warriors opt to take the Snake Path up and the cable car down; due to the steepness, the hike down is just as strenuous as the hike up. Another option is to take the cable car up in the afternoon and hike down when the sun is less fierce.

◉ THE FORTRESS

The ruins at Masada were unearthed from 1963-64; thousands of volunteers excavated in 11 months what would normally have taken 26 years. About one-third of the ruins is actually reconstructed—a black line indicates the extent of the original findings. The re-excavation of the Northern Palace by a group of expert Italian archaeologists has unearthed new mosaic floors and hundreds of coins near the bathhouses. The **Masada Sound and Light Show** lights up the fortress like a Las Vegas marquee. The show is not visible from the Masada youth hostel. For more information, call 995 93 33 or 995 89 93.

The following suggested route covers the highlights of Masada and roughly follows the sign-posted walking tour. The numbers listed following the sites correspond to the numbers labeled on the map on p. 391.

SNAKE PATH LOOKOUT (1). This lookout offers views of the Snake Path, the earthen wall, the Roman camps, the Dead Sea, and the Mountains of Moab.

QUARRY (2). This quarry supplied much of the stone for the extensive construction throughout Masada. Between the quarry and the Western Wall, there is a large pile of large round rocks, too perfectly shaped to be anything but catapults' ammo.

STOREROOMS (3). Food, weapons, and other supplies were stored within these rooms. Though the Zealots destroyed most of their valuable possessions and the fortress, they left the storeroom containing mass amounts of food untouched. Josephus explains that the Zealots wanted to prove that their suicide was a means of escaping slavery, not famine.

ROMAN BATHHOUSE (4). Bathers would leave their clothes in the *apodyterium* (dressing room) before proceeding to the *caldarium* (hot room), recognizable by the small pillars, which used to support a secondary floor. A stove channeled hot air between these two floors. Bathers then cooled off in the *tepidarium* (lukewarm room) before a quick dip in the *frigidarium* (cold pool). Built by Herod, the bathhouse served no purpose for the austere Zealots.

NORTHERN PALACE (5-7). Go down the nearby stairwell to Herod's thrice-terraced private pad. The frescoes and fluted columns, still intact on the lower terrace, attest to the splendor Herod enjoyed even on a remote desert butte. In the bathhouse of the lowest section, the skeletons of a man, woman, and child were found, along with a *tallit* (prayer shawl), *ostraca* (lots), and arrowheads.

LOTTERY AREA (8). Climb back up from the Palace to the Lottery Area, to the left of the bathhouses as you face the Palace. The Zealots used this area as a ritual bath for cleansing and purification, but it is most notable for the dramatic discovery of 11 *ostraca*. The uniform shards of pottery inscribed with names (including one with the name Ben-Yair, Zealot commander of Masada) most likely served as lots that decided who would kill the others.

ZEALOTS' SYNAGOGUE (9). Following the western edge of the mountain leads to the Zealots' synagogue, the oldest synagogue in the world. Scrolls were found here containing texts from several books of the Torah; most are now on display at the Israel Museum in Jerusalem (see p. 307). The scrolls and other discoveries, such as a *mikveh* (ritual bath), indicate that the community followed Jewish strictures despite mountainous isolation and the siege.

CASEMATE OF THE SCROLLS (10). A number of important archaeological relics were found within the casemate, including scrolls, papyrus, silver *shekels*, a *tallit* (prayer shawl), a wooden shield, arrows, sandals, keys, and baskets.

WATER CISTERNS PATH (11). The huge cisterns can still be seen dotting the mountaintop from the western wall; they are lined with a nearly perfect water-repellent plaster that still won't absorb a single drop. Rainfall used to drain from the surrounding mountains into Masada's reservoirs, filling the entire cistern within a few hours on the one annual day of rain. The Zealots were able to store up to eight years' worth of precious water in these cavernous structures.

BYZANTINE CHURCH (12). Remote Masada, with caves and buildings for shelter, made an ideal hideout for Christian hermits in the 5th and 6th centuries. The chapel with preserved mosaic floors is the most impressive of their remains.

WESTERN PALACE (13). Farther along the edge stands the site of Herod's throne room and offices of state. A system of water cisterns underlies the western wing; the northern wing surrounds a large central courtyard; the southern wing was the royal wing, and it includes a waiting room, courtyard, dining hall, kitchen, and a throne room. Though just as sumptuous as the Northern Palace, this was Herod's "working palace." He went to his northern "country residence" to relax.

SWIMMING POOL (14). Although water was a rare commodity in the fortress, Herod insisted on maintaining a swimming pool in the backyard of the Western Palace. The Zealots used this as a ritual bath.

COLUMBARIUM (15). The small niches in the walls of this round building, farther back and slightly to the left, sparked an archaeological debate. One team contended that it was a *columbarium*, where the ashes of the non-Jewish members of Herod's garrison were placed, while others thought the niches housed pigeons. After highly scientific tests the former opinion emerged victorious; small pigeons could not fit inside the niches.

SOUTHERN CITADEL (16). At the southern tip of the mountain, the Southern Citadel looks out at the Masada *Wadi*, the Dead Sea, and Roman encampments.

SOUTHERN WALL (17). Along the southern wall lie a tower with a Zealot installation (the building might have been a bakery), a ritual bath, a dressing room (the narrow niches held clothes), and a courtyard. The path is no longer in use.

SOUTHEAST WALL (18). There is a memorial inscription for "Lucius" (possibly a soldier in the Roman Garrison) engraved in the wall of the tower. On the plaster of the southern wall, there are four impressions of the name "Justus" in Latin and Greek. There is also a lookout from which the outer wall is visible.

EASTERN WALL (19). The outer and inner walls are joined by partitions, forming casemates. The higher and thicker sections of the inner wall are the sole remains of a series of towers that lined the wall. A channel under the floor of the Zealot additions is older than the wall itself. A small grove of fir trees toward the Snake Path Gate was the site of a 1988 interpretive reenactment of the battle.

EIN BOKEK עין בוקק ☎07

About 15km south of Masada, Ein Bokek, hemmed in by hordes of luxury hotels, international tour-groups, and racks upon racks of postcards, is the gaudy cubic zirconia in the tiara of Dead Sea beaches. For all the glitzy tourist-wooing of this most crowded of Dead Sea beaches, it is still a good spot for some old fashioned fun: floating and coating. Use of the beach and outdoor showers is **free** (8am-5pm); a package of mineral-rich mud from beachside vendors costs NIS10.

Farther to the right is a small **mall**, featuring a **grocery store,** Hertz office, and several restaurants, including the 24hr. **Peace and Love BBQ.** (☎658 43 71. Fruit shake NIS15. Hamburger NIS12. Fries NIS12.) To the left of the beach, **Me'al Hahof** (☎652 04 04), a bar on the beach, features a great view, French pop music, and a variety of beer (NIS10-16) and baguettes (NIS17). **Hertz** car rental is inside the Amiel Tours office in the mall.

Ein Bokek is 30min. east of Arad and 10min. south of Masada. **Buses** on the Masada/Dead Sea route pass through Ein Bokek and stop at each hotel along the strip. For the public beach, get off at **Ḥof Ein Bokek.** Minivans operating as *sherut* go to Arad (NIS10). **Hassan Taxi** (☎05 276 62 46) goes to Masada for NIS60 and Ein Gedi for NIS100. (☎658 45 30. 21+. About NIS350/US$55 per day. Open Su-Th 8:30am-4pm, F 8:30am-1:30pm.)

MOSHAV NEOT HA-KIKKAR מושב נאות הככר ☎07

About 20km south of rowdy Ein Bokek, Moshav Neot Ha-Kikkar is a desert of serenity and desolation. Take Rte. 90 toward Sodom to the Arava junction, passing the Dead Sea Works plant on the left and the southern edge of the sea. The Eilat-bound bus from Jerusalem or Tel Aviv will stop at the junction upon request. Make a left and follow the road for about 10km to the entrance to the moshav.

Taking the road to the end of the moshav leads to ▧**Fata Morgana,** an amazing oasis featuring large, clean and comfortable Bedouin-style guest-tents, a coffee-bar, and a restaurant. Fata Morgana arranges hiking tours of the region (including the famous Sodom flour caves), meeting individual requests whenever possible. It also offers **Shiatsu** massages and lessons in a special shrine tent every Friday and pick-your-own cherry-tomatoes or flowers. Work 4hr. in the field and sleep free. (☎655 79 92, mobile 050 69 15 85; ask for Koreen or Ya'akov. Beer NIS9. Hot fish meals NIS60. Veg. meals NIS40. Free use of spotless bathrooms and showers, fridge, and BBQ grill. Tents NIS40; own tent NIS30. *Let's Go* discount.)

NEGEV הנגב

The Negev covers roughly half of Israel's territory, but for many years the region received only a small fraction of Israel's tourists. In recent years, tourism has skyrocketed, but these 12,000 sq. km of desert have become no more accommodating. Temperatures soar at midday—those caught without a hat and water will see vultures circling overhead in a matter of minutes. Desert outfitters recommend that hikers drink 1L of water for every hour in the sun.

It's possible to tour the desert on Egged seats; air-conditioned lines run through all major towns and past several important sites. However, buses may be infrequent and late, and some sites and trailheads are only accessible by car. Renting a car or taking a guided tour are excellent options for those who can afford it. A more exciting way to see the Negev is on a **camel** or **jeep** tour.

BE'ER SHEVA באר שבע ☎07

Be'er Sheva has a long-standing tradition of serving as a point of replenishment and departure for people traversing the Negev. In recent years, however, increasing numbers of immigrants have decided to settle down in the city rather than just pass through, and the pre-fabricated apartments are as unavoidable and constricting as the spandex in Eilat discotheques. Despite the din of constant traffic and the overpowering presence of a glassed-in monster mall in the center of town, Be'er Sheva still has a few pockets of romance left, including the old city and the famous Thursday morning Bedouin market. The old city, museums in the surrounding area, and Be'er Sheva's hopping nightlife make it both a convenient base for short forays into the Negev and a destination in and of itself.

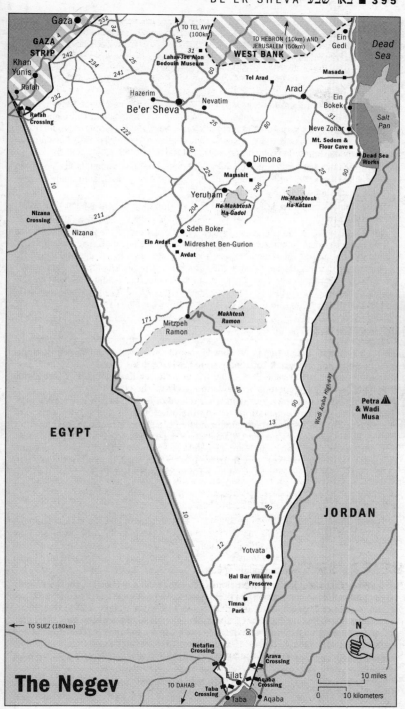

ISRAEL

The Negev

⌐ TRANSPORTATION

Intercity Buses: Egged (☎ 629 43 11) to: **Dimona** (#48, 56, or 375; 45min.; every 20min. 6:30am-11pm; NIS14); **Eilat** (#392, 393, or 394; 3½hr.; every 1½hr. 7:30am-11:45pm; NIS52); **Jerusalem** (#470 (direct) or 446; 2hr.; every 40min. 6am-8pm; NIS33); **Tel Aviv** (#369 or 370; 1½hr.; every 20min. 5:45am-9:45pm; NIS20.50).

Local Buses: Central bus station (☎ 627 73 81), on Eilat St., next to the *kenyon*. Buses #2, 3, 7, 8, 9, 11, 12, 18, 21, and 22 all go to the *shuk* and old city (5:20am-11pm), and bus #13 follows Ha-Atzma'ut St. to the Negev Museum and Beit Yatziv Youth Hostel (every 20min. 5:20am-11pm). Buses #7 and 8 go north on Yitzhak Rager Blvd., passing the hospital and Ben-Gurion University. All local rides NIS3.10.

Sherut: Moniot Ayil (☎ 623 53 33), in back of the central bus station, in the kiosk with the blue awning. *Sherut* to **Dimona** (NIS10) and **Tel Aviv** (NIS20) are slightly cheaper than buses, but don't leave until they fill up.

Taxis: Moniot Gan Zvi (☎ 623 93 32 or 623 93 33), next to the bus station, or **Moniyot Ha-Halutz** (☎ 627 33 33 or 627 07 07), across from Bank Ha-Poalim.

Car Rental: Avis, 8 Henrietta Szold (☎ 627 17 77), just before the Paradise Hotel. The #5 bus passes by. From the *kenyon* walk 2 blocks up Yitzhak Rager Blvd. and turn right through the parking lot behind the New York Cafe. Red Avis sign in the shopping strip across the street. 23+. Cars start at NIS195/US$42 per day. Open Su-Th 8am-6pm, F 8am-2pm. **Traffic Rent-a-Car,** 5 Ben-Zvi St. (☎ 627 38 78), behind the bus station, in the shopping strip on Ben-Zvi. Rents to people ages 21-23 for an additional US$12. Rates increase in July and Aug. Open Su-Th 8am-7pm, F 8am-2pm.

✳ ORIENTATION

The city's **central bus station** is on **Eilat St.,** across the road from **Kenyon Ha-Negev** (Negev shopping mall; ask for the *kenyon*), whose glass facade faces the three-way intersection of **Tuviyahu Blvd.,** Eilat St., and **Yitzhak Rager Blvd.** The **Ben-Gurion University** Be'er Sheva campus is a few minutes from the city center.

The old **Muslim Cemetery,** sitting in a wasteland of fenced-in sand, is across Eilat St. behind the central bus station. Just on the other side of it lies the neat grid of the **old city.** This pedestrian haven holds most of the city's attractions. In the center of the Old City is **Keren Kayemet L'Yisrael St.** (**Kakal** or **KKL** for short), a pedestrian-only street between **Herzl** and **Mordei Ha-Geta'ot St.** lined with shops, kiosks, and restaurants. To reach the old city from the bus station, walk in front of the *kenyon* to Eli Cohen Sq., cross Eilat St., and take Herzl St. or Ha-Halutz St.

❷ PRACTICAL INFORMATION

Tourist Office: 1 Derekh Hevron (☎ 623 46 13), at Abraham's Well. From Herzl St. in the old city, walk down from the top to the end of the pedestrian KKL. The office is on the left-side corner across from the intersection. Helpful staff sells an excellent English map (NIS5). Office arranges bus tours of the city's historical sights. Call ahead for English screening of the brief movie on Be'er Sheva. Open Su-Th 8:30am-4pm.

Currency Exchange: The main **post office** exchanges cash and traveler's checks at excellent rates without commission. **Bank Ha-Poalim,** 40 Ha-Atzma'ut St. (☎ 629 26 62), is on the corner of Ha-Halutz St. Open Su and Tu-W 8:30am-1:15pm; M and Th 8:30am-1pm and 4-6:30pm; F 8:15am-12:30pm. Min. charge $6. **Bank Leumi** (☎ 623 92 22), is just past the post office on Ha-Nesi'im Blvd. Open Su and Tu-W 8:30am-1pm; M and Th 8:30am-1pm and 4:30-7pm; F 8:30am-noon. **ATM** accepts V and DC.

Emergency: First Aid: Magen David Adom, 40 Bialik St. (☎ 627 83 33). **Police:** 30 Herzl St. (☎ 646 27 44), at the corner of KKL St. **Fire:** (☎ 627 96 91).

Hospital: Soroka Medical Center (☎ 640 01 11), on Yitzhak Rager Blvd., with a green walkway and a blue and green sign in Hebrew. Bus #7 or 8. Open daily 5:20am-11pm.

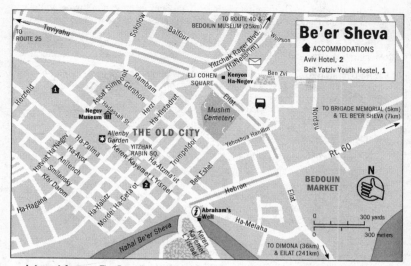

Internet Access: The Paradise Hotel on Henrietta Szold St. has Internet access at a computer on the mezzanine level for US$0.50 per min. Credit cards only.

Post Office: (☎629 58 32), at the corner of Yitzhak Rager Blvd., just across from the back entrance of the mall and Ben-Zvi St. This main branch has **Poste Restante, Western Union, EMS** services, international calling, fax, phone cards, and commission-free cash and traveler's check exchange. Smaller branches on Hadassa St. and in the City Hall building. All branches open Su-Tu and Th 8am-12:30pm and 4-6:30pm, W 8am-1pm, F 8am-12:30pm.

ACCOMMODATIONS

Be'er Sheva has several options for budget accommodations, including one youth hostel and a few reasonably-priced hotels. Conveniently, the following accommodations are all within a 5-10min. walk from the *midrahov* in the old city.

Beit Yatziv Youth Hostel (HI), 79 Ha-Atzma'ut St. (☎627 74 44), in the old city. Three blocks up from Herzl St., on the left behind the HI sign (walk or take bus #13). Clean rooms with bath, closet, A/C, and table. Pool in back. Full breakfast. Check-out 9am. Reception 24hr. 4-bed dorms US$22; 3-bed dorms US$24. The **Guest House** next-door is run by the same reception desk. Singles US$38-42.50; doubles US$56-59. HI members NIS5/US$1.50 discount. Credit cards accepted.

Aviv Hotel, 48 Mordei Ha-Geta'ot St. (☎627 80 59 or 627 82 58). Walk down Herzl St. and turn right on KKL St. Run by a sweet Bulgarian woman. All rooms have private baths and high-powered A/C; some have balconies. Breakfast NIS20. Laundry available. Reception 24hr. Check-out 11am. Singles NIS160/US$35; doubles NIS215/US$47. 15% student discount. Cash only.

Arava Hotel, 37 Ha-Histadrut St. (☎627 87 92). Turn right off KKL from Herzl St. Close to the popular cafes at the top of KKL. Rooms are fairly comfortable, with small bathrooms and A/C. Reception 24hr. Check-in 1pm. Check-out noon. Singles NIS80/US$25; doubles NIS100/US$35. Cash only.

🍴 FOOD

Lined with falafel, shawarma, pizza, and sandwich store fronts, the **Keren Kayemet LeYisrael St. (KKL)** *midrahov* is the best place for affordable eats. For a fast food fix, head to the food court on the lower floor of the *kenyon* across from the bus station. (Most

in the *kenyon* open Su-Th 10am-midnight, F 10am-3pm, Sa after sundown-midnight.)
A **Hypershuk supermarket** exists in the supermall. There is a small grocery store in the
old city on Mordei Ha-Geta'ot, just off KKL toward Ha-Palmaḥ St. (Open daily 7am-
7pm.) The cheapest place to buy fresh produce, meat, and fish is the **shuk,** just south of
the Muslim burial ground on Beit Eshel St. The listings below are all in the **old city** area.

▨ **Sof Ha-Derekh** (☎ 627 91 55), at the corner of Ha-Palmah and Ha-Tivat Ha-Negev. Feast
on one of 22 spicy salads with homemade *lafah* bread (NIS7), or order meat from the
grill. Chicken NIS15; steaks NIS55-70. Complimentary dessert of *baklava*, fresh fruit,
and mint tea. Open Su-Th 11:30am-1am, F 11:30am-1hr. before sundown, and Sa
after sundown-1am. Credit cards accepted.

Cafeteria Panorama (☎ 623 52 49), at the corner of Ha-Histadrut and KKL St., on the
2nd fl. Entrance near Rabin Sq. Francophone owner serves veg. blintzes, pizza, and
pasta (NIS11-22) in spartan simplicity. Juice stand downstairs NIS12. Open Su-Th
10am-3pm and 6pm-1am, Sa after sundown-2am.

Beit Ha-Ful, 15 Ha-Histadrut St., at the corner of Smilansky St. Walk past the park; the
restaurant's outdoor seating will be on the left. Popular with locals. *Fuul* (Egyptian
beans in pita with salads) NIS11, in bowl with garnish NIS25. Eat *al fresco* or in A/C
dining room. Open Su-Th 8am-midnight, F 8am-3pm, Sa after sunset-midnight.

👁 SIGHTS

BEDOUIN MARKET. Established in 1905, the famous Thursday market is a nirvana
for bargain hunters. Amid the clamor of screaming vendors are cheap Bedouin
food and excellent garments. Years ago, the Bedouin hawked camels, sheep, and
other wares at the end of agricultural seasons and during winter—now year-round
they've added snow globes and t-shirts to the much-ballyhooed wares. Farther
south, the quantity of rusty cans, scraps of paper, and dust increases, along with
the smell of dung from the live animals for sale. The southern part of the market,
however, houses the real gems: beaten copperware, Bedouin robes, fabrics, rugs,
and ceramic items. Get there early to see the trading at its peak and to get more of
a selection of genuine Bedouin goods. Many Bedouin here speak English, and
some may compliment your beautiful eyes while charging six times the going rate
for olive wood camels. *(The market is on the south side of the city, off Eilat St., south of the
intersection with Derekh Hevron. Most local buses will stop at the market upon request. By foot,
walk to Eilat St. from the central bus station and cross over to the market. Open Th.)*

ABRAHAM'S WELL. The well dates back to at least the 12th century CE, and many
believe it to be the original well dug by Abraham. A free, 5min. tour of the site illu-
minates Be'er Sheva's biblical history, the well's archaeological significance, and
its camel-powered hydrotechnology. From June to September, the well also serves
as a nighttime entertainment venue with live music and dancing. *(On the corner of
Derekh Hevron and Keren Kayemet LeYisrael St. ☎ 623 46 13. Call ahead.)*

JOE ALON BEDOUIN MUSEUM. At a time when approximately half of the
Negev's Bedouin live in urban "settlements," this museum showcases all facets of
the nomads' traditional lives, including tools, embroidery, medicine, and customary desert garb. An audio-visual presentation describes Bedouin culture and their
famous hospitality. Outside the indoor exhibit are two Bedouin tents. In one, a
Bedouin woman serves traditional pita and tea; in the other, Bedouin men con-
verse with guests and serve bitter coffee. The museum also has an observation
tower with a 360-degree view of the northern Negev. *(Several kilometers north of the tel,
on the outskirts of Kibbutz Lahav. Drive 15km north on Rte. 40 to Lahav junction or take bus
#369 (20min., every 30min., NIS12) and ask to be let off there. An orange sign behind the bus
stop points down the road in the direction of the kibbutz and museum, 8km away. Numbered
vehicles from the kibbutz drive by often and may offer a lift. After arriving, walk along the asphalt
road and follow it to where it curves to the right, up to the gate of the museum. Taxi NIS75. ☎ 991
33 22 or 991 85 97. Open Sa-Th 9am-5pm, F 9am-2pm. NIS15, students NIS13.)*

PARK YOUR OWN ASS. When approaching a Bedouin tent, it is customary to cough to let your host know that he has a visitor. If you have arrived on a horse or a camel, your host will graciously take your animal and tie it to his tent. However, if you rode in on a donkey, he will refuse his tie-down services, and you must tether it yourself.

ISRAELI AIR FORCE MUSEUM. This museum displays over 100 airplanes from several generations of Israeli aerial combat, including airplanes captured from and shot down by neighboring countries. Free guided tours by Israeli soldiers relate the history behind each of the displays. *(At the Haterim air force base 8km west of town on the Be'er Sheva-Haterim Rd. City bus #31 stops directly in front of the entrance. Walk up Ha-Atzma'ut St. from the youth hostel and cross over the Derekh Joe Alon Highway at the major intersection to reach the bus stop headed away from town. ☎990 68 55. Open Su-Th 8am-5pm, F 8am-1pm. NIS23, ages 3-13 NIS15, senior citizens NIS18. Call ahead for free tours.)*

TEL BE'ER SHEVA. Five kilometers northeast of the city are the ruins of a 3000-year old planned city, recently upgraded to a national park. One pile of unearthed rubble is a 2nd-century Roman fortress, another an 8th-century BCE house, and a third a 12th-century BCE well. The view from the top of the tower in the back right corner of the site is fantastic. Fashionable Israelis flock to conduct their marriages in trendy Bedouin style at nearby marriage hall **Ohalei Kidar.** *(By car, take Rte. 60 out of the city, and turn right at the set of lights after the gas stations. Taxi NIS28 each way. Buses to Arad and Omer run by the road that leads to the site: #388, every 35min. 6:45am-10:30pm, NIS6.20. The walk from the turnoff takes about 30min. There is a rotary approximately halfway down the road; keep straight to get to the ruins, which are through a parking lot on the right; an orange sign leads the way. Park open Su-Th and Sa 8am-5pm, F 8am-4pm; entrance closes 1hr. earlier. NIS9, students NIS8, children NIS4.50.)*

📷 NIGHTLIFE

Forum, 232 Kiryat Yehudit, in the old industrial area of town, a short drive out of Be'er Sheva's old city (taxi NIS15). Includes multiple dance floors, the largest bar in Israel, and a swimming pool. Open on Friday nights from mid-June through Aug. Call ahead to find out about theme nights like karaoke and techno. Beer NIS15-20. Cover NIS30-70. Open Tu and Th-Sa 10:15pm-5am; F after-party until noon on Sa.

Baraka, 16 Hadassah St., on the corner of B'nei Ein Harod St. This historic stone building once served as an Ottoman hospital and now serves beer (NIS15-22) outside in a desert-motif courtyard and inside to the beat of pop music. Line forms outside on weekends. No cover. Open nightly 10pm-early morning.

Punchline, 4 Smilansky St., below the Trumpeldor St. intersection. Beer NIS20. Salsa dancing on W and F. Cover charge for salsa nights and special performances NIS19, students NIS15. Open M-Sa 10:30pm-late.

NEAR BE'ER SHEVA

DIMONA דימונה

Since immigrating in 1969, the **Hebrew Israelite Community,** referred to as the **Black Hebrews** by non-members, has been working to combine the ideals of religious and communal living. A unique sect of English-speaking immigrants, the Hebrew Israelites trace their roots to ancient Israel. The community, which bases its religion on the revelations of spiritual leader Ben Ami Ben-Israel (formerly Ben Carter), believes that the ancestors of black slaves in antebellum America lived in Israel until they were forced to migrate to Western Africa after the Roman onslaught in 70 CE. Ben-Israel's vision included a return to the Holy Land; the group's vanguard left Chicago in 1967 and spent 2½ years in Liberia before coming to Israel. Another group from Chicago followed in 1970, and a third exodus took place from Detroit in 1973. The Israeli government at first refused to grant them citizenship unless they converted to Judaism, but the

ISRAEL

Hebrew Israelites insisted they were already Jews. In 1990, the government and the sect came to an agreement on a process for normalizing the community's legal status.

Every summer, the Hebrew Israelites host the two-day **Naisik Ha-Shalom Music Festival,** which highlights community entertainment, Hebrew Israelite singers, and Israeli bands. (Call Elisheva Eli-El ☎ 05 199 63 17 for information.) Singing groups from Dimona tour the country when they're not performing at home. Their music is a unique rendition of traditional Jewish and other religious texts in gospel and hip-hop style. Though the village welcomes solo wanderers, a tour can be much more informative. Call ahead to schedule a free tour. (☎ 07 655 54 00, 657 32 86, or 657 32 87. Donations accepted.)

Buses to Dimona leave from: **Be'er Sheva** (#48, 56, and 375; 45min.; every 20min. 6:30am-11pm; NIS13); **Eilat** (#393 and 394; 3hr.; every 1½hr. 5am-5pm; NIS43, students NIS39); and **Tel Aviv** (#375, 393, and 394; NIS30, students NIS27). To reach the village from the bus station, turn left on Herzl St., pass the tall red monument on the right, and continue for 10min. The village is on the left, past a school.

MAMSHIT ממשית

The sunbleached sandstone ruins of ancient Mamshit, the only city in the Negev that was walled in on all sides, lie 15km east of Dimona. Built in the first century CE, Mamshit reached its height as a garrison town in the Roman and Byzantine periods. From Mamshit, one of the six Nabatean cities in Israel, the Nabateans ruled the Petra-Gaza spice route stretching from India to Rome. On one side is a vast desert plain; on the other, the precipitous canyon of **Naḥal Mamshit** (Mamshit River). Following attacks by desert nomads in the 6th century CE, the city was destroyed and abandoned. Particularly impressive among the ruins are the Eastern Church, with its altar remains at the top of the market area, the 2nd-century CE tower which once guarded the dams of the river below, and the mansion, or "House of the Affluent." Also be sure to take a look down into the canyon from the observation point. (Open Su-Th 8am-5pm, F 8am-4pm. NIS9, student NIS8, youth NIS4; brochure of the site including small map and descriptions free.)

To view the canyon from a camel's back and with a Bedouin guide, contact the **Mamshit Camel Ranch,** 1km east of the ruins. (☎ 665 10 54; 2hr. tour NIS100.) Bedouin coffee and overnight stays available for groups of 20 or more.

Buses running between Be'er Sheva and the Dead Sea will stop 1km outside Mamshit, along the main highway, as will bus #394 to Eilat (1¼hr., every 1½hr., NIS19). Call **Mayam Taxi** (☎ 07 655 66 88) to get here from Dimona (10min., NIS33). Be sure to tell the bus or cab driver to stop at Atar Mamshit, the Nabatean ruins, not the new cinderblock city several kilometers to the west.

SDEH BOKER שדה בוקר ☎ 07

When experts advised that developing the Negev was a waste of time and money, first prime minister and Zionist visionary David Ben-Gurion insisted on searching for unconventional methods of "making the desert bloom," asking, "If the Nabateans could do it, why can't we?" When he visited the fledgling Sdeh Boker at the age of 67, he was so moved by the young pioneers that he decided to resign from office and settle on the kibbutz. Soon after, he founded the *Midresha* (institute) of Sdeh Boker, which houses laboratories and a field school devoted to the management of desert resources. Established in 1952, the kibbutz raises olives, kiwis, and other fruit, as well as wheat, corn, and livestock (though few cows).

Steeped in Ben-Gurion tributes, sights, and memorabilia, Sdeh Boker now serves as a base for desert exploration in the nearby **Ein Avdat National Park** and **Zin Valley.** There are a tremendous number of truly astounding hikes in this area, traversing jagged desert cliffs, natural springs, canyons, and monk's caves.

▉ TRANSPORTATION

The only public transportation to or from Sdeh Boker is Egged **bus** #60, which runs between Be'er Sheva and Mitzpeh Ramon (35min.; 6:35am-9:30pm; NIS19, students

NIS17.50). The bus stops at three different points a few kilometers apart: the gate of Kibbutz Sdeh Boker, the turnoff to Ben-Gurion's Hut (at the edge of the kibbutz), and the traffic circle outside the gate of the Ben-Gurion Institute.

ORIENTATION AND PRACTICAL INFORMATION

To reach the SPNI Field School, accommodations, Ein Avdat National Park, Ben-Gurion's grave, and the Ben-Gurion Heritage Institute, get off outside the gate. From the roundabout, the road on the right with the orange sign leads to the grave, Heritage Institute, and down the canyon to Ein Avdat. The road straight ahead leads to the SPNI office and accommodations. The institute buildings are arranged around a central square, inside of which are the restaurant, supermarket, and **post office.** (☎653 27 19. Open Su-M and W-Th 8:30am-noon and 1-2pm, Tu 8:30-11am, F 8:30-10:30am.) To reach the **SPNI Field School,** turn right at the end of the road inside the main gate and then left at the large parking lot. The helpful staff answers questions about hiking routes and desert flora, sells maps of nearby trails (NIS62), and stores bags during day hikes. (☎653 20 16; fax 653 27 21; www.boker.org.il/bet-sadeh. Open Su-Th 8am-4:30pm, F 8am-1pm and 5-7pm.)

ACCOMMODATIONS AND FOOD

The **SPNI Hostel** (☎653 20 16 or 05 393 04 59; fax 653 2721; orders@boker.org.il), on the edge of the canyon, has modern rooms with air-conditioning and private baths. The six-bed dorm rooms, Sdeh Boker's only budget lodgings, are reserved for students. (Breakfast included. Dorms NIS60; singles NIS195; doubles NIS245. Call ahead.) The field school also runs the **Hamburg Guest House** next door; the reception is in the SPNI field school's office. The rooms include air-conditioning, TV, refrigerator, and bathroom. (Singles NIS225; doubles NIS295. Prices increase during Passover, Sukkot, and Chanukah. Credit cards accepted.) Both accommodations include discounted use of the community swimming pool (NIS10). Guests are entitled to **Internet** access in the field school office. Camping is free at designated locations within the Zin Valley; contact the **SPNI Field School** for information about facilities and transportation.

Food options are slim. The **Super Zin** supermarket in the institute's center is the place to stock up on food before hitting the trail. (Open Su-Th 8am-7pm and F 8am-2pm.) The **Zin Restaurant,** on the other side of the post office, serves tasty breakfasts. (NIS10-32. Open Su-Th 8am-11pm, F 8am-2pm, Sa 10am-6pm. Credit cards accepted.) The **Sdeh Boker Inn,** next-door to Ben-Gurion's Hut, serves cafeteria-style meals, including excellent baked zucchini and goulash. (☎656 03 79. Open daily 8am-3pm. Credit cards accepted.) For Shabbat stays in Sdeh Boker, stock up before stores close on Friday night.

HIKING IN SDEH BOKER AND ENVIRONS

Although many tourists come to Sdeh Boker to see its Ben-Gurion memorials, Ben-Gurion was attracted to the kibbutz because of its majestic setting. The best way to appreciate the natural beauty of the region is to try some of its spectacular hikes. These, however, require careful preparation. Trails may be poorly marked, distances deceptive, and the Negev sun unforgiving. Detailed maps and explanations for all of these hikes are available at the SPNI field office, which you should visit before attempting any hike. With advance notice, SPNI offers guided hikes across the Avdat Plateau or Zin Valley; call ahead for more information. Wear a hat, get an early start, and drink 1L of water every hour.

EIN AVDAT NATIONAL PARK. This easily accessibly park is in the Zin Canyon. From the institute gate, the steep road to the park's lower, the main entrance snakes down the canyon (1hr. on foot, 15min. by car). From the entrance, the hike to **Ein Avdat** (Avdat Spring; the lower pools) is 15min. Allot about 1hr. for the full hike to the upper gate. Getting to the upper gate requires climbing one-way ladders; unless there's a car waiting at the end of the hike, you'll either need to make a U-turn at the base of the ladders and miss the view or extend your hike a few hours by walking along the rim of the canyon after reaching the top.

Gleaming white walls tower over the green, puddled path that runs through the canyon to the lower pools of the Avdat Spring. The eerie echoes of wildlife resound through the high caves carved in the sides of the canyon, which once served as homes to **Byzantine monks.** A small dam pools water that flows down the rocks from the Avdat Spring; just before the dam an easy-to-miss small set of stairs in the rock leads up to the rest of the hike and the one-way ladders. The foliage becomes denser along the upper part of the trail, where a grove of **Mesopotamian poplar trees** sits below a series of ladders that lead to a dazzling view at the top of the canyon. From the end of the trail on the canyon's rim, a trek along the riverbed to the nearby Nabatean ruins in Avdat takes about 2hr. (see **Avdat,** p. 402); the trail markings are difficult to follow so consult SPNI for details before going. To either return to Sdeh Boker or head on to Avdat on wheels, exit the park through the parking lot near the upper pools and walk down the road to the highway where there are stops for bus #60 headed in both directions. (☎655 56 84. Park open May-Sept. daily 8am-5pm; Oct.-Apr. 8am-4pm. Entry permitted until 1hr. before closing. NIS14, seniors and students NIS12, children NIS6. Free brochure).

KARAKASH WADI. This magnificent 3hr. hike passes an inviting pond and water-fall (water flows 1-2 times per winter). The Karakash Wadi eventually runs into the Ḥavarim Wadi. A 1hr. hike along the Ḥavarim Wadi passes a Nabatean cistern and slopes of smooth, white rock that are striking (and slippery) in moonlight. The cis-tern is below ground, down a flight of stairs from the beginning of the Ḥavarim Wadi hike. Part of the spice traders' efforts to squeeze water out of the desert, the cistern was used to catch and hold water from rain storms. A 1hr. hike along the trail leads to the bottom of the road and park entrance. The brush and rocky hills are popular spots for idling ibex. Turn right on the road to reach Ein Avdat or left to make the uphill haul back to Sdeh Boker. (To begin the hike, turn left on the Be'er Sheva-Eilat highway from the end of the entrance road to the midresha and walk approximately 1km; the trailhead is to the left. For the entrance to the Havarim cistern and Wadi hike, continue along the highway past the Karakash trailhead to an orange sign on the left, a 20min. walk from the institute. The sign points into the parking lot, where a blue-and-white marked trail descends on the left. Free.)

EIN AKEV. This 5½hr. hike offers magnificent views from above the Zin Canyon and leads to an oasis where chilly spring water provides a refreshing respite from the desert sun. From the SPNI field school walk down the winding road toward Ein Avdat. From the bottom of the canyon, walk for 20min. and look on the left for a trail with green and white markers that ascends the canyon. This trail goes southeast across a desert plateau for several kilometers and reaches a green pool surrounded by lush green vegetation. After a swim in the pool head north along a trail with blue markers. Turn left at the junction and return to Sdeh Boker on the trail marked by orange, blue, and white, which leads from Lebanon to Eilat. (This hike winds along the edge of cliffs at times. Be very careful and walk slowly in these areas. The return from Ein Akev is along the floor of the canyon and gets very hot during the middle of the day. It's best to start hiking as soon after sunrise as possible.)

🔋 DAYTRIP FROM SDEH BOKER: AVDAT עבדת

Bus #60 (40min.; 6:35am-10pm; NIS20, students NIS18) runs from Be'er Sheva to Mitz-peh Ramon, stopping in Avdat. Tell the driver you're going to the Nabatean archaeological site and not Ein Avdat (the oasis). You can also hike from Sdeh Boker via Ein Avdat (3-4hr.); consult the SPNI guides in Sdeh Boker for info. Bus #60 runs to Avdat from Sdeh Boker (NIS11) and from the highway near the end of the Ein Avdat trail (NIS5). ☎658 63 91; fax 655 09 54. Drinking water and bathrooms across from the ticket booth; bring water for the 20min. uphill hike to the entrance. Open Su-Th 8am-5pm, F 8am-4pm; in win-ter Su-Th 8am-4pm, F 8am-3pm. NIS18, students NIS15, children NIS9.

The magnificently preserved ruins of a 4th-century BCE **Nabatean city** are perched upon a hill 11km south of Sdeh Boker. Avdat once thrived as a pit stop for caravans along the spice route from the Far East to Gaza (via Petra) that continued on to Europe. Nabateans used their strategic perch at Avdat to spy on caravans as far away as present-day Mitzpeh Ramon or Sdeh Boker. After the Romans captured the city in 106 CE, it continued to flourish, reaching its economic peak during the Byzantine period. Most of the ruins date from this time. The most important Nabatean remains are a handsome esplanade on top of the hill, a winding staircase that led to a Nabatean temple, and a potter's workshop, all dating from the first century CE. When the Nabateans converted to Christianity around 300 CE, the temple became a church. The best of the 6th-century Byzantine remains include a 7m surrounding wall, a monastery, two churches, and a baptistry. In this century, the site was resurrected on film as the setting for the movie *Jesus Christ Superstar*. The small grove of crops just below the ruins is irrigated through ancient Nabatean techniques.

MITZPEH RAMON מצפה רמון ☎ 07

Mitzpeh Ramon sits on the rim of **Makhtesh Ramon** (Ramon Crater), the largest natural crater in the world. At 40km long, 9km wide, and 400m deep, its sheer size is mind-boggling. Since some of the geological formations are found nowhere else in the world, hikes pass through what seem to be landscapes of desolate, far-away planets. Uphill treks wind toward phenomenal views of the desert expanse, a rainbow of multi-colored sand. Today, the crater is a 250,000-acre national park with well-marked trails through mazes of geological stunners. From campsites in the crater, the lack of artificial light offers a spectacular view of the starry sky.

▛ TRANSPORTATION

From the main stop at the Delek gas station, **buses** #60 and 392 run to Be'er Sheva (1hr.; Su-Th 5:30am-9:30pm and F 5:30am-2:15pm; NIS22.50, students NIS20). Bus #392 uses Mitzpeh Ramon as a waystation between Be'er Sheva and Eilat; it stops for 15min. at the gas station and will pick people up if there are empty seats. Drivers are instructed to take 10min. breaks if they feel drowsy on long desert treks; don't panic if the bus is 10-40min. late.

✳❷ ORIENTATION AND PRACTICAL INFORMATION

From the gas station, the tan, flat-roofed **visitors center** is visible on the left edge of the crater. Clustered around it are the **youth hostel, Bio-Ramon,** and the crater-rim **promenade.** Cross the street, turn left at the gas station, and then take a right to get to the visitors center.

A commercial center containing a **Bank Ha-Poalim** branch is a bit downhill to the right from the gas station, across **Ben-Gurion Blvd.** (Open Su and Tu-W 8:30am-12:45pm, M and Th 8:30am-12:30pm and 4-6:30pm, F 8:30am-12:30pm.) The **post office** is upstairs behind the bank and across the parking lot. It houses Western Union and offers fax services, EMS, and Poste Restante. (Emergency ☎630 73 30. Open Su-Tu and Th 8am-12:30pm and 4-6:30pm; W 8am-1pm; F 8am-12:30pm.) **Police** (☎100), **first aid** (☎101 or 658 83 33), and **fire** (☎102) offices are up the walkway through the park across from the commercial center on Ben-Gurion Blvd.

▛ ACCOMMODATIONS

Staking out a **campsite** in the middle of the *makhtesh* is **forbidden** and environmentally destructive. Those who camp there run the risk of being awakened by an angry ranger or an even angrier **Asiatic wild ass.** There are inexpensive accommodations both in the town and in the crater, as well as interesting alternatives to hosteling and camping. There are campgrounds in town at the municipal park next

ISRAEL

to the gas station and at the SPNI field school. The **SPNI Field School** is directly on the crater's rim and has a trail leading down it. From Camel Observation Point, turn right at the Har Gamal dirt road at the crater's rim and walk along the black-marked cliffside trail toward the tall antennae. To get to the Observation Point, take bus #60 through town or turn left from the visitors center and follow the crater-rim promenade about 15min. (☎658 86 15 or 658 86 16; fax 658 83 85. A/C and private bath. No showers. Reception Su-Th 8am-6pm, F 8am-noon; Sa call ahead. Check-in 3pm. Check-out 8:30am. 6-bed student dorm NIS83; doubles NIS275/US$58; each additional person NIS110; children NIS65. Sleep outside under the bedouin tent, or pitch your own. NIS20. MC/V.) The **Mitzpeh Ramon Youth Hostel (HI)**, on the canyon's rim, is across from the visitors center and next to the promenade. (☎658 84 43; fax 658 80 74; mitzpe@iyha.org.il. Breakfast included. Reception 24hr. Check-in 3pm. Store bags for early arrivals. Check-out 10am. 6-bed dorms NIS89/US$19.50; singles NIS190/US$43.50; doubles NIS260/$US63. HI discount US$1.50. Credit cards accepted.)

▧ HIKING MITZPEH RAMON AND ENVIRONS

Far-flung trailheads are best reached by car or four-wheel-drive vehicle. For trailheads off of the main highway, bus #392 to Eilat travels through the crater and can stop at the turnoff for the Be'erot Camping Site. Locals say hitchhiking on the highway is safe, though the highway is not heavily trafficked. The **Park Ramon Visitors**

> ❗ Makhtesh Ramon is a spectacular park, but it should not be hiked casually. Always consult with Nature Reserve or SPNI personnel before setting out. Wear a hat, hike as early as possible in the morning, and carry food and 1L of water per person per hr. Heatstroke and dehydration can be deadly in the Negev.

Center, one of two hiking resources in Mitzpeh Ramon, is housed in the round building with the flat top overlooking the crater. Nature Reserve Authority staffers help plan hikes and provide an excellent map of the crater. If only Hebrew maps are available, ask the guides to write English names. (☎658 86 91 or 658 86 98; fax 658 86 20. Open Su-Th and Sa 8am-5pm, F 8am-4pm. NIS18, child NIS9; combo ticket with Bio-Ramon NIS21, children NIS11.) The **SPNI Field School,** near the edge of the crater, 500m southwest of Camel Observation Point, occasionally offers organized tours (call ahead to schedule). Although the trails are well marked, picking up maps at the visitors center is a good idea for an unguided expedition. Leave your route description and estimated trip duration at the field school before hiking—they have an on-site rescue team and are in direct communication with army units in the area. While hiking, keep a fix on the main highway or Be'erot Campsite. (☎658 86 15 or 658 86 16; fax 658 83 85. Open Su-Th 8am-6pm, F 8am-noon.)

HAR ARDON. Har Ardon (Mt. Ardon) is a full-day hike, combining challenging terrain with unbeatable views. To climb Har Ardon, turn left out of the Be'erot campsite and follow the black markers north for 3km to the sign marked Mt. Ardon. From here, follow the blue path on the right to a parking area, where the mountain ascent begins. The steep climb up follows a narrow trail that changes about halfway up into a smoother and wider trail. The descent from the mountain can be quite a physical feat; take it slow since the narrow, white-rock-and-sand trail is steep and slippery. Down the mountain and along the trail in the crater are the remarkable sand and hills of the **Red Valley,** which range in color from yellow to crimson. After passing the black hill of Givat Harut, turn right on the black trail and follow the signs back to the campsite to complete the hike.

WADI ARDON. South of Mt. Ardon, this hike leads past unique geological formations and Nabatean ruins. From the campsite, walk along the black-marked trail for 500m, and turn right on a dirt road marked in red. After about 1km, take the dirt road on the left marked in black. From the parking lot, continue south through

Wadi Ardon. Along the colorful borders of Wadi Ardon are a pair of vertical magma intrusions, one big and one small, known as the Father and Son Dikes. To continue on, take the blue path. It points toward **Parsat Nekarot** (the Horseshoe of Crevices), which includes **Sha'ar Ramon** (the Ramon Gate), where water exits the crater. The Parsat Nekarot river bed is flanked by soaring cliffs and cave-like enclaves that make welcome shady stops.

From Parsat Nekarot, follow the blue markings to **Ein Saharonim.** The vegetation lasts all year, but the water evaporates to mere puddles in summer. The remains of a **Nabatean caravanserai** stand at the end of the spring on the right. This is also the spot where animals are most likely to be seen wandering around in search of water sources. To return to the campsite from here, take the orange trail away from Parsat Nekarot. To start hiking from Ein Saharonim, go left from the campsite, and follow the orange trail next to a sign on the right.

SHORT HIKES FROM MITZPEH RAMON. Along the southern edge of the crater rises **Har Saharonim** (literally, Mountain of the Crescent-Shaped Ornaments). Start the climb from the western side, closest to the main road. Take a right from the campsite and turn left onto the "Oil Pipeline Route" black trail. After about 40min., follow the steep incline past the green trail to Ein Saharonim and the Naḥal Gevanim turnoff. Turn left at the green markers at the top, which lead to "Mt. Saharonim." The green-trail descent from Har Saharonim goes to **Ein Saharonim.** From there, follow the blue path through Parsat Nekarot in reverse.

Trailheads for the most interesting hikes are outside of town; two beautiful trails that pass by significant points of geological interest originate in Mitzpeh Ramon. An excellent 3hr. hike begins at the end of the western promenade, near the mini-amphitheater, and leads to **Ha-Minsarah** (Carpentry), where piles of prism-like rocks, configured and baked by volcanic heat, resemble carpenters' supplies. Follow the promenade from the visitors center. Past two iron ball sculptures, a green-marked trail makes a rocky descent from the cliff. At the bottom of the crater, follow the green trail left to Ha-Minsarah. A dirt road leads east toward the highway. A turnoff point marked in red along the green Carpentry trail leads south to a 5hr. hike along **Ramon's Tooth,** a rock formation of cooled magma that was exposed during the crater's creation. The hike also goes past the **Ammonite Wall,** a collection of crustacean fossils embedded in rock. From the red Ammonite Wall path, a black path eventually leads off to the left and to the highway. Bus #392 from Eilat usually passes on its way to Mitzpeh Ramon (Su-Th around 3 and 5pm).

EILAT אילת ☎07

Eilat has two goals—to get you tan and to make you poor. The city is soaked with the sweat of rowdy Israelis, international backpackers, and European tourists; the air is abuzz with jet skis and cell phones. Some swear by Eilat's sun, coral, and nightlife, while others see the city as a huge tourist trap attached to a nice beach. In between the cocktails and Coppertone, stick your head in the ocean and you may notice some of the most spectacular underwater life the world's seas have to offer. Above the waves, the wildlife is bikini-clad and muscle-bound.

The busiest times of the year are Passover, Sukkot, and Israel's summer vacation (July and Aug.), when nearly 100,000 Israelis descend upon the city. Don't fool yourself into thinking that this is a good time to visit. True, there are more parties and crowded pubs, but hostels and restaurants charge double their normal rates, petty theft runs rampant, and every inch of beach crawls with human flesh.

▐ TRANSPORTATION

Flights: The **airport** (☎636 38 38) is on the corner of Ha-Tmarim Blvd. and Ha-Arava Rd. **Arkia Airlines** (☎638 48 88) flies to: **Haifa** (2 per day, NIS370); **Jerusalem** (2 per day, NIS370); **Tel Aviv** (every hr., NIS370). **Israir Airlines** (☎634 06 66) flies to Tel Aviv (every hr., NIS268-298).

Intercity Buses: Central bus station (☎636 51 20) on Ha-Tmarim Blvd. Reserve tickets at least one day in advance, 3 days during high season. Buses to: **Haifa** (#991; 6hr.; Su and Th 8:30am, 2:30, 11:30pm; M-W 2:30 and 11:30pm; F 8:30am; Sa 5 and 11:30pm; NIS68); **Jerusalem** (#444; 4½hr.; Su-Th 7, 10am, 2, 5pm; F 7, 10am, 1pm; Sa 4:30 and 7pm; NIS58); **Tel Aviv** (#394; 5hr.; Su-Th 10 per day, F 7 per day, Sa 8 per day; NIS58). If these are full, it is possible to take a bus to **Be'er Sheva** and transfer. ISIC discounts. Bus schedules change frequently.

Local Buses: Bus #15 runs down Ha-Tmarim Blvd. and Ha-Arava Rd., through the hotel area, and past the HI hostel and Coral Beach to **Egypt** (every 20-30min. Su-Th 4:45am-8:30pm, F 4:45am-5pm, Sa 8:30am-8:30pm; NIS2.10-3.20). Buses #1 and 2 run from downtown to the hotel area (every 30min. Su-Th 7am-8pm, F 7am-2:15pm, Sa every 2hr. 10am-6pm; NIS3).

Taxis: King Solomon (☎633 33 38). City rides NIS10; to observatory NIS20; to Egyptian border NIS25-30; to Jordanian border NIS20. Taxi sharing is common. In winter, *sherut* run along the #1, 2, and 15 bus routes.

Car Rental: Hertz (☎637 50 50 or 637 66 82), in Red Canyon Center. 23+. **Budget** (☎637 41 25), in Shalom Center. **Avis** (☎637 31 64), next to the tourist office. All offer similar plans: NIS45/US$11 plus NIS1 per km. or unlimited mileage NIS160-200/US$40-50 per day. Insurance starts at NIS50/US$12 per day; NIS50/US$12 extra per day in high season. Rentals can't go into Egypt or Jordan. Open 8am-6pm.

Bike Rental: Red Sea Sports (☎633 08 66) in the marina. NIS90 per day. Open Su-Th 8am-9pm and F-Sa 8am-6pm. Rental recommended for winter only.

✦ ORIENTATION

Eilat is a 5km strip of coastline on the Negev's sandy bottom, the precarious intersection of Israel, Jordan, Egypt, and Saudi Arabia; at night the lights of all four are visible on the horizon. The city is divided into three sections: the town on the hills, the hotel area and Lagoon Beach to the east, and the port to the south.

The main entrance to the central bus station is on **Ha-Tmarim Blvd.,** which crosses the center of the city from the southeast (downhill) to the northwest (uphill). Across from the bus station is the **Commercial Center.** Uphill and to the right are most hostels and cheap restaurants. Walking downhill along the bus station side of Ha-Tmarim Blvd. leads to the **Red Canyon Center,** which resembles a futuristic Bedouin tent and houses the **post office,** supermarket, and cinema. Farther downhill is the **Shalom Center** mall. Ha-Tmarim Blvd. ends here, perpendicular to **Ha-Arava Rd.** If you turn right onto Ha-Arava Rd., you will soon find the main entrance to the Eilat airport on your left. A block past the airport, to the right of the intersection with **Yotam Rd.,** a three-level conglomeration of cheap restaurants and shops calls itself the **New Tourist Center.** On the other side of Yotam Rd. is the tourist office. Ha-Arava Rd. leads to Dolphin Reef, the Coral Beach reserve, the Underwater Observatory, and finally Taba Beach and the Egyptian Border. Bus #15 runs this route (every 15-20min., NIS2-3). Turning left at the intersection of Ha-Arava Rd. and Yotam St. leads to the **promenade** and the **public beach.**

🛈 PRACTICAL INFORMATION

Tourist Office: (☎637 21 11; fax 632 58 67), at the corner of Yotam Rd. and Ha-Arava Rd. Maps and brochures. Will help find accommodations for no commission. Open Su-Th 8am-6pm and F 8am-2pm. **SPNI,** the Society for the Protection of Nature in Israel (☎637 20 21), opposite Coral Beach, has maps and info about local hiking. Open Su-Th 8am-8pm.

Consulates: Egypt, 68 Ha-Efroni St. (☎637 68 82). From the bus station, turn right on Ha-Tmarim Blvd. and left onto Ḥativat Ha-Negev. Continue 900m until Sderot Argaman St., and turn right. Ha-Efroni St. is the 1st street on the right; look for the flag. Submit a visa application in the morning; pick it up at noon. Visas must be paid for in NIS (US nationals NIS50; South Africans free; all others NIS70). Bring a passport photograph. Free, Sinai-only visas are available at the border. Open Su-Th 9-11am. **UK** (☎637 23 44), above the New Tourist Center (next to the Adi Hotel). By appointment only.

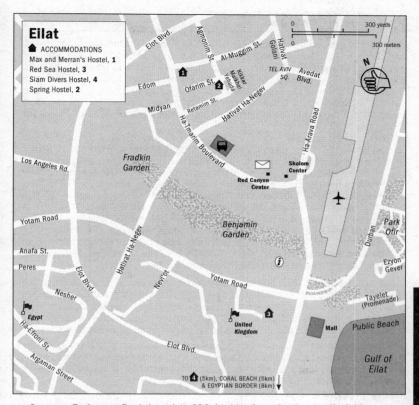

Eilat

🏠 ACCOMMODATIONS
Max and Merran's Hostel, **1**
Red Sea Hostel, **3**
Siam Divers Hostel, **4**
Spring Hostel, **2**

Currency Exchange: Bank Leumi (☎636 41 11). Open Su, Tu, and Th 8:30am-noon and 5-6:30pm; M, W, F 8:30am-noon. **Bank Ha-Poalim** (☎637 61 57). Open Su, Tu, and Th 8:30am-noon and 4:30-6pm; M, W, and F 8:30am-noon. Both banks are opposite the central bus station. Post office changes traveler's checks with no commission.

ATM: 24hr. machines (MC/V, Plus, Cirrus) outside Bank Ha-Poalim, next to the post office, and in the marina.

Camping Equipment: Azimut, The National Center for Hiking Equipment (☎634 11 12), on the bottom floor of the mall at the corner of Yotam Rd. and Ha-Arava Rd. Good selection of pricey gear. Open Su-Th 9:30am-midnight, F 9am-4pm.

Emergency: First Aid (☎637 23 33). **Magen David Adom** first-aid stations are on some beaches. **Police** (☎633 24 44), on Avdat Blvd. at the eastern end of Ḥativat Ha-Negev. "Lost and found" for packs stolen from the beach.

Hospital: Yoseftal Hospital (☎635 80 11), on Yotam Rd. **Maccabee Healthcare Services** (☎676 49 00; emergency ☎633 31 01), on the corner of Eilat St. and Ha-Tmarim Blvd. Modern facility that offers services for dental emergencies.

Internet Access: Internet access in Eilat is easy to find and prices are standard. **BJ's Books** (☎634 09 05; bjsbooks@eilatcity.co.il), in the New Tourist Center. NIS30 per hr. Open Su-Th 9:30am-10pm and F 9am-6pm. **Unplugged Internet Bar** (☎632 62 99), next to the Unplugged Bar, in the New Tourist Center. Fast but oddly old-fashioned coin-operated machines accept NIS5 coins for 15min. per coin. Open 24hr.

Post Office: (☎637 44 40), in the Red Canyon Center. Traveler's check cashing, Western Union, **Poste Restante.** Open Su-Tu and Th 8am-12:30pm and 4-6:30pm, W 8am-1pm, F and holidays 8am-12:30pm.

ACCOMMODATIONS

Finding a cheap room in Eilat is easy. Finding a safe, comfortable, convenient, and cheap room is another story. New arrivals to the bus station are attacked by a gaggle of apartment hawkers. Most hostels are less than three blocks from the bus station—walk up the hill on Ha-Tmarim Blvd. and take a right on Retamim St. Some of the bigger hostels are unfriendly and have been known to put out backpackers in favor of large groups or have patrons switch rooms in the middle of the night. The tourist office can assist if hostels are full. Prices for rooms rise in the summer.

There are two camping options in Eilat: expensive and legal or free and illegal. For the latest info on the former, stop by the **SPNI Field School** (☎ 637 20 21), across from Coral Beach. SPNI's campsite (NIS20 per person) offers showers and toilets; huts on the campground cost NIS300, but you have to call the Tel Aviv office (☎ 03 638 86 88) to reserve ahead. Most hostels allow camping on their roof or in their backyard for NIS15-20. In July and August, hundreds of people ignore the "No Camping" signs on the public beach or in the park; many are victims of theft. If sleeping on the ground and taking communal showers sounds appealing, take bus #15 to **Coral Beach Campground,** the municipal campground opposite the beach of the same name. The site's small huts have only their prime location to the reefs to recommend them. (☎ 637 19 11 or 637 50 63. Breakfast included. Refrigerator NIS10 per day. Pitch-your-own-tent NIS30; huts NIS300.)

Red Sea Hostel (☎ 637 60 60), in the New Tourist Center directly above the Unplugged and Underground Bars. Location, location, location! These small, crowded rooms are just a beer bottle's throw from the rest of Eilat's hot spots on the promenade. A/C; free safe. Mattress on the roof NIS15; dorms NIS25-30; singles NIS100; doubles NIS120; triples NIS150. Prices double during high season, but bargain for multiple night stays.

Siam Divers Hostel (☎ 637 05 81), right on Coral Beach. Priority goes to divers, but the location and atmosphere make this a great pick for any traveler. Oddly shaped rooms are simple, with common bath. Only 10min. by bus from Eilat. Dorms NIS60; doubles NIS150; triples NIS180.

Villa Kibel, P.O. Box 8304 (☎/fax 637 69 11, mobile 050 34 53 66; russell@eliat.ardom.co.il). Fully furnished, upscale apartment-style rooms with TV, mini-fridge, fresh linen, and cooking facilities. Within 1km of the beach; some rooms have ocean view. Two are wheelchair accessible. Call for bus station pick-up. Doubles NIS150-220. Larger rooms also available. Prices negotiable, especially for longer stays.

Spring Hostel, P.O. Box 1278 (☎/fax 637 46 60), halfway down Retamim St., around the corner. Immaculate but basic rooms. Billiards, pub, a pool, and very tight security. Dorms NIS30-60; singles NIS100-160; doubles NIS120-200.

Max & Merran's Hostel, P.O. Box 83 (☎ 637 13 33; fax 637 35 13), off Almogim St. Under new ownership and in a new location next to the Home Hostel (they share a courtyard), this hostel has lost none of its friendly atmosphere. Clean and newly built rooms with kitchen and common bathrooms. Dorms NIS25.

🍴 FOOD

- 🍴 **Pedro's Steak House,** 14 Ye'elim St. (☎ 637 95 04). Moderately expensive, but unbelievable food. A local favorite. Steak NIS63. Ostrich NIS75. Veg. options NIS38. Don't miss the freshly baked bread (NIS2) or divine crème brûlée. Open daily 5-11:30pm.

- 🍴 **Tandoori** (☎ 633 38 79), in the Lagoon Hotel on the King's Wharf. Excellent Indian food. Friendly waitstaff will help arrange a menu to meet a lower budget. Filling 3-course lunch special NIS49. Curry NIS30-50. *Naan* NIS5-16. Open daily noon-3:30pm and 7pm-1am.

- **The Spring Onion** (☎ 637 74 34), at the marina. This popular veg. and dairy restaurant serves fresh salads and pasta (NIS30-40) and offers a wide selection of tea and coffee. Large breakfast NIS32; fish NIS50. Open daily 8am-3am. AmEx/MC/V.

Malibu Restaurant (☎ 634 19 90), adjacent to Siam Divers, near the end of Coral Beach. A great place to get a sandwich (NIS16) on the beach or dinner on the dock. Dinner specials NIS60; pizzas NIS28-35. Open daily 10am-midnight.

Mai Thai (☎ 637 25 17), on Yotam Rd. just uphill from the New Tourist Center, overlooking the city. A bit expensive, but a treat. Try the egg rolls (NIS15) or get a set menu for two (NIS78). Main course NIS40-47. Open daily 1-3:30pm and 6:30-11pm.

👁 SIGHTS

Some say that the best of Eilat's wildlife is in the air. Avid birdwatchers flock to the salt ponds north of the lagoon mid-February through May and mid-September through November, when 30 species fly overhead on their way to or from Africa. The **International Birdwatching Center (IBC)**, P.O. Box 774, Eilat 88106, near the northern end of the airport on Eilat St., runs walking tours (US$5) and jeep tours (US$50). There's a bird watching festival in March. Contact the IBC for more information. (☎ 633 53 39. Open Su-Th 9am-1pm and 5-7pm, F 9am-1pm.)

Visitors pretend to be birds at the skydiving simulator **Airodium** (☎ 637 27 45), behind the Riviera Hotel. An air-vent contraption makes for an expensive but fun 10min. (NIS120). For stimulation beyond simulation, jump with **Skydive Red Sea,** P.O. Box 4139, Eilat 88150 (☎ 633 23 86).

🎵 ENTERTAINMENT

Eilat's entertainment is not exclusively limited to bars and clubs. The tourist office has information on events at the **Phillip Murray Cultural Center.** Kids of all ages like **Luna Park,** in front of the Queen of Sheba Hotel. Bumper cars and pirate ships cost NIS10; kiddie thrills are NIS5. (☎ 05 031 50 49. Open M-Sa 6pm-midnight.) The end-of-August international **Red Sea Jazz Festival,** with ten daily performances, is Eilat's most popular annual event. Ask the tourist office for information.

▨ **Unplugged** (☎ 632 62 99), in the New Tourist Center. Loud music and big TVs. Free Sony Play Station, Sa karaoke, and foosball attract the masses. Internet NIS5 for 15min. Happy hour 4-9pm. Heineken NIS12. Local beer NIS7-15. Open 24hr.

▨ **Green Beach** (☎ 637 70 32), on the promenade close to the shopping mall. A sprawling beach bar frequented by beautiful people at all hours. During the day, scantily clad waiters shoot water guns to cool the crowd, and at night they keep the liquor and coffee coming—whatever you need to stay until the sun rises over the Red Sea. Half-liter drafts NIS11 and up. Cocktails NIS26 and up. Coffee NIS8. Open 24hr.

Nisha (☎ 631 55 55), in the basement of the Neptune Hotel. This dance bar is Eilat's trendiest and craziest night spot. Reserved for the chic and beautiful. Travelers are advised to pull out their best duds for this place. Beer NIS12 and up; cocktails NIS26 and up. Cover NIS20-40. Open daily 11:30pm-4:30am.

Dolphin Reef (☎ 637 18 46), just before Coral Beach. The place to be on Th once the dolphins have gone to sleep. Beach parties are known as the kinkiest in Eilat. Th cover NIS50-80. Open daily until sunset and Th 11:30pm-4:30am.

Dolphin Bar (☎ 637 04 19), on Almogim St., across from Hard Luck Cafe, close to most hostels. Escape Eilat's exorbitant prices in this hole-in-the-wall pub. Serves the cheapest beer in town. Half-liter bottles of Tuborg NIS2.50. Billiards and Internet. Open 24hr.

🌀 SCUBA DIVING

Several underwater observatories exist to help those who want to experience underwater Eilat without getting wet. The **Coral World Underwater Observatory and Aquarium** features shark and turtle tanks and an underwater observation room. Though interesting, it is best for those who won't be snorkeling. (☎ 637 66 66. Open Sa-Th 8:30am-5pm, F and holiday eves 8:30am-3pm. NIS63, children NIS145.) Live a life of ease beneath the sea of green in the observatory's **Yellow Submarine,** which goes 60m below the surface. (☎637 66 66. Observatory and submarine NIS255, children NIS145.) The **Galaxy** is one of the city's many glass-bottomed boats. (☎631 63 60. 1½hr. NIS60.) The **Jules Verne Explorer** may not venture 20,000 leagues down, but glass walls make it a true underwater observatory. (☎633 36 66. 2hr. cruise to Japanese Gardens NIS80.) Both the Galaxy and the Explorer are at the marina. For an up-to-date list of dive sites and activities, try www.eilat.net.

DIVE CENTERS

■ **Siam Divers,** P.O. Box 1020, Eilat 88000 (☎637 05 81; fax 637 10 33; siamdive@netvision.net.il; www.siam.co.il), at the end of Coral Beach next to the Nature Reserve. While many may initially be attracted to the glossy finish of the larger clubs, this is Eilat's friendliest, safest, and most experienced dive center. Introductory dives (no certificate necessary) NIS160; 2 guided dives with full equipment NIS170; 5-day O/W course NIS790/US$190. Convenient dorms NIS60, with course NIS40. Amazing 3- to 5-day dive safaris to Sinai start at NIS1600/US$340. 10% student discount. For more info, email or write.

Red Sea Sports Club (☎637 65 69 or 637 00 68; fax 637 06 55; manta1@netvision.net.il), in the Ambassador Hotel; also has an office at the King Solomon Hotel. PADI O/W courses NIS1164/US$291; dives with dolphins NIS265/US$56. Office on North Beach near the lagoon offers windsurfing (NIS68 per hr.), waterskiing (NIS120 per 15min.), and parasailing (NIS150 per 10min.). Arranges horseback riding lessons at **Texas Ranch** (☎632 65 02. 1hr. NIS150; 2hr. NIS170; 4hr. NIS235).

Aquasport, P.O. Box 300 (☎633 44 04; fax 633 37 71; info@aqua-sport.com; www.aqua-sport.com), on Coral Beach next to Siam Divers. This large and active beachfront houses a PADI-certified diving center (O/W beginner course NIS1100/US$275) and windsurfing rentals (NIS75 per hr.).

DIVE SITES

JAPANESE GARDENS. Arguably the finest in Eilat, this dive site gets its name from the placid, "manicured" look of the coral, which almost completely covers the sandy bottom. Sushi and sashimi lovers will be glad to know that the Japanese Gardens are home to the most plentiful fish life in Eilat. *(Take bus #15; 10min. from the central bus station. Entrance is on the right by the underwater observatory. Diving available only through established dive clubs (see p. 410); snorkeling is free and open to the public.)*

CORAL BEACH NATURE RESERVE. This national reserve (which includes Moses' and Joshua's Rocks) offers a wealth of coral species and fish life, making the entry fee well worthwhile. Five water trails marked by buoys go through the reef, and two bridges into the water protect coral from human feet and vice versa. *(Take bus #15 from the central bus station toward the sea. ☎637 68 29. Open Sa-Th 9am-6pm, F 9am-5pm. NIS18, children NIS9. Lockers NIS6.)*

DOLPHIN REEF. The commercially operated scuba and snorkeling center at Dolphin Reef allows divers to observe semi-wild dolphins in a somewhat natural environment. Although the project has raised some ethical eyebrows, the dolphins are free to swim away at any time (although it would be difficult for any mammal to refuse a free feeding, as most budget travelers will agree). The dolphins perform a variety of tricks daily at the four "interaction" sessions, but observing them underwater is a more rewarding experience. The four original dolphins brought from the Black Sea have added seven new babies to the group. *(Beyond the port on bus #15. ☎637 18 46. Open daily 9am-5pm. NIS29, children NIS22. Interaction sessions every 2hr. 10am-4pm. Snorkeling NIS202, children NIS193. Beach open and free after 5pm.)*

◥ HIKING

The beauty of the red granite mountains towering over Eilat matches that of the coral reefs thriving beneath it. The **SPNI Field School,** across from Coral Beach (bus #15), is an essential stop for independent hikers. It sells extensive trail maps and provides good advice on hikes. (☎637 20 21. Open Su-Th 8am-4pm.) Many of the sites are accessible by northbound bus #393, 394, or 397. Buses fill up fast during high season and on Sundays and Fridays—make reservations at the central bus station two days in advance.

RED CANYON. The most exciting and accessible terrain north of Eilat includes **Ein Netafim, Mt. Shlomo,** and **Ha-Kanyon Ha-Adom** (Red Canyon). Buses will stop nearby upon request. From Red Canyon, hike to the lookout above **Moon Valley,** a pocked canyon in Egypt, and to the unusual **Amram's Pillars.** These hikes are not advisable in summer; October through April is the best season. Before attempting any of these hikes, consult SPNI (see **Tourist Offices,** p. 406). SPNI also runs guided hikes to Moon Valley; call its Tel Aviv office for details (☎ 03 638 86 75).

TIMNA NATIONAL PARK. Timna National Park is another hiking destination. The 6000-year-old Timna copper mines remain a fascinating destination. Some people believe the Israelites passed through here on their way out of Egypt. The park houses remains of workers' camps and cisterns dating from the 11th century BCE. The sandstone **King Solomon's Pillars** dominate the desert at a height of 50m near the 14th-century BCE Egyptian Temple of Hathor. The park's lake offers **camping** facilities (including showers) and a restaurant on its artificially created shores. *(Most buses that go to Tel Aviv or Jerusalem will stop at the sign for Alipaz. Don't get off at the Timna Mines signpost; the entrance is 2km away, which is too far to walk in summer.* ☎ *635 62 15; fax 637 25 42. Open daily 7:30am-6pm. NIS27, ages 5-18 NIS21.)*

GAZA

| ☎ PHONE CODE | The telephone code for Gaza is 07. |

The distance separating Israel from the Gaza Strip is covered in a 1min. car ride from one side of the border checkpoint to the other. Once in Gaza City, however, it becomes apparent that the short distance from Israel's booming industrial centers to Gaza City's Palestine Square sets the two regions worlds apart. A 46km long and 6-10km wide sliver along the Mediterranean coast, the Gaza Strip contains some of the most densely populated areas of the world. Population has increased dramatically in recent years, swelling to more than 1 million people with an influx of over 570,000 Palestinian refugees since 1951.

SAFETY WARNING. Since 1994, the Gaza Strip has been governed by the autonomous Palestine Authority (PA). While Israeli citizens cannot travel into Gaza without special permission, foreign tourists can generally visit without problems. Tourists should register with their respective consulates in Israel before going and should keep abreast of current events in the region so as to avoid visiting during times of unrest or tension. **Do not** speak any Hebrew during your stay; counter any taunting *"shalom"* with an Arabic *"marhaba."* Many people, especially children, are eager to practice their English on a native speaker. For some basic Arabic words and phrases, see the **Arabic Phrasebook,** p. 701. Women must **dress modestly**—long sleeves and a long skirt—and men should not wear shorts. Have your **passport** on hand at all times.

Gaza's history stretches back to 3000 BCE, when it was inhabited by Arab Canaanites. It grew as a stopping point for traders traveling from Africa and the Sinai to the southwest and from parts of the Middle East and Asia to the east. The Prophet Muhammad's grandfather, Hashem ibn 'Abd Manaf, is said to have been one such trader. He died when passing through Gaza City and is purportedly buried in one of the city's mosques (see p. 416). Gaza is perhaps most well-known for its history of occupation and uprising under Israel. The region was administered by Egypt from 1948 until the 1967 Six Day War. Refugees flooded the area after the

The West Bank and Gaza Strip

Israeli occupation of that year, and of the 770,000 refugees living in Gaza today, over 420,000 continue to live in the overcrowded UN-sponsored camps. The *intifada* (see p. 269) began in 1987 in Gaza in the Jabalya camp near Gaza City. The peace process intensified with the onset of the *intifada*, and the Oslo and Cairo agreements of 1994 placed the Palestine Authority in control of the Gaza Strip.

Gaza now seeks to reinvigorate its long history as an intercontinental crossroads, as evidenced by widespread construction and the growing numbers of international trade and investment signs that line Gaza City's streets. Renewed attempts are being made to rehabilitate refugee camps with the help of the UN, the European Union, and other international resources. Tourist officials hope that the sea and beaches will entice crowds of visitors. However, it is the disorderly everyday life of Gaza's present—the mosques, churches, and unearthed archaeological finds that blend haphazardly into side-streets and vending stalls—that makes for the most fascinating and affordable random wandering for travelers. Gaza throbs with the activity of its capital's outdoor markets, chokes in the dust and cramped quarters of the refugee camps, and embraces its visitors with hospitality and an eagerness to communicate the experience of life in the strip.

✈🚌 BORDER CROSSINGS AND TRANSPORTATION

As of press time, **Erez** was the only border checkpoint open for crossing from Israel into Gaza. Passing through the checkpoint is relatively easy for foreign tourists. From **Jerusalem,** *service* meet across from Damascus Gate and go directly to the checkpoint (1hr.; infrequent, depart when full; NIS30). Though it is not possible to enter Gaza by car, it is helpful to understand the system of colored **license plates** that differentiates vehicles (see **West Bank: Transportation,** p. 417, for an explanation of the various plates).

Crossing the checkpoint takes three steps. First, Israeli soldiers will inspect your passport and record the reason for and proposed length of your stay in Gaza. They will then give you a slip of paper for presentation when entering Gaza. Taxis cross the border for NIS10, but the walk is very short. After crossing into Gaza, your information will once again be entered into a ledger. On the Gaza side of the checkpoint, taxis heading into Gaza City abound. A *service* should cost NIS5 to Palestine Square on the main street, **Omar al-Mukhtar.** A *special* taxi can cost anywhere from NIS20-50.

Rafah, the Gaza Strip's third-largest town, is its border crossing point with Egypt. To get there from Gaza City, take a bus (1½hr., NIS2.50) or *service* (45min., NIS5). From Khan Yunis, backtrack along the main street from the *khan* toward the fruit and vegetable market, until reaching the corner with two-way traffic. Then, take a taxi from the *khan* (NIS2).

The bus system in Gaza Strip tends to be erratic, slow, and uncomfortably warm. Taxis are far more convenient and almost as cheap. Within Gaza City, where there is no intracity bus service, seemingly half of all cars serve as taxis. *Special* taxis are more expensive than *service.* Rides anywhere along Omar al-Mukhtar St., which runs from the Palestine Sq. market to the hotel strip along the beach, cost NIS1. Destinations off the main road will cost more; pay NIS1 and negotiate an additional fare upon entering the taxi. Buses and taxis to destinations in the Gaza Strip outside of Gaza City, such as Khan Yunis and Rafah, leave from a parking lot in Palestine Square, just beyond the Gaza City municipality building. Long yellow *service* depart whenever they fill with passengers.

Flights: Gaza Airport (☎ 213 5696 or 213 4228), near Rafah. **EgyptAir** (☎ 282 51 80) is on Jala'a St. at the corner with al-Wihda St. Flights to **Cairo** (NIS240/US$80 one-way, NIS668/US$167 round-trip). Cash only. **Royal Jordanian** (☎ 282 54 03) flies to Amman (US$120 one-way, US$190 round-trip). **Palestinian Airlines** (☎ 282 28 00) also flies to Cairo (US$142 one-way) and other destinations.

Buses: In Palestine Sq., in front of where the taxis leave. **Gaza Bus Company** (☎ 282 26 16) sends non-A/C buses to **Rafah** (1½hr., NIS2.50).

Taxis: *Service* (NIS1 for trips along Omar al-Mukhtar St.) depart when full to **Rafah** (45min., NIS4.50). **Imad** (☎ 286 40 00) will pick up passengers.

Car Rental: Yafa Rent-a-Car (☎ 282 51 27), on Omar al-Mukhtar St. 1 block toward Palestine Sq. from Ahmed Orabi St. Look for the blue sign on the left side of the street. 1-day car rentals NIS120-200/US$30-50. Min. age 24. Open Sa-Th 8am-10pm.

✴ 🛈 ORIENTATION AND PRACTICAL INFORMATION

Taxis from the Erez checkpoint let off in **Palestine Sq.** *(Midan Filisteen)*, the site of the main market, the Gaza City municipality building, taxis and buses to other destinations in the Gaza Strip, and many of the historical sights of the city. The main street, **Omar al-Mukhtar St.,** runs from Palestine Sq. to the coast. Almost all hotels are in the **Remal** (beach) district of the city, lined up along the coastal road **Ahmed Orabi,** which forms a T-junction at the end of Omar al-Mukhtar St. Another commercial center is built around the **Unknown Soldier Garden,** a grassy walkway median that divides the lanes of Omar al-Mukhtar St. Only major streets have both English and Arabic street signs and establishments are rarely numbered.

Tourist Office: Gaza City's **Public Relations and Information Office** (☎ 282 47 00), beginning of Palestine Sq., near the Arab Bank and under an English sign. Enter from Omar al-Mukhtar St. through the gate for the Municipality Building and walk through the parking lot and under the overhang to the door on the left. Open Su-Th 8am-2:30pm.

Human Rights Organizations: UNRWA (☎ 677 74 88), on Gamal 'Abd al-Nasser St. Take a taxi to the "UN." Once there, go to the public information office. Offers tours to

Jabalya refugee camp, a 15min. ride from the city. Call in advance to arrange a tour—the office has limited finances. Donations requested. Open Su-Th 7:30am-3pm.

Currency Exchange: Private agencies on Omar al-Mukhtar St. and near Palestine Sq. change money for no commission: look for dollar signs. Open Sa-Th 9am-9pm. **Western Union** (☎282 10 77), on Omar al-Mukhtar St., 20m past the Bank of Palestine toward Palestine Sq. Open Sa-W 8:30am-12:30pm and 2-4pm, Th 8:30am-12:30pm.

Pharmacy: Masoud (☎286 18 79), at the corner of Charles de Gaulle St. and Omar al-Mukhtar St. Open daily 7:30am-midnight. Call 24hr. for emergency.

Hospitals: Ahli Arab Hospital (☎282 03 25), on the 1st street to the right just beyond the bus and taxi stand in Palestine Sq. **Shifa Hospital** (☎286 55 20), on Ez al-Din al-Qassam St. From the beach, turn left on Omar al-Mukhtar St. just before the Rashad Shawwa Cultural Center.

Telephones: Al-Baz (☎286 01 20), on Omar al-Mukhtar St. just after Canal St., on the left, coming from the beach. International calls NIS4 per min. Open Sa-Th 9am-10pm. The blue public phones in Gaza operate on phone cards that can be purchased in small shops and groceries throughout the city (NIS15-60). Phone calls from hotels are pricier.

Post Office: 183 Omar al-Mukhtar St., next to the Municipal garden, halfway between the Unknown Soldiers' Park and Palestine Sq. Palestinian (not Israeli) stamps are issued here. Open Su-Th 8am-2:30pm.

ACCOMMODATIONS

Gaza City has the only accommodations in the Gaza Strip, along the coastal al-Rashid road in the Remal district, a short walk from the end of Omar al-Mukhtar St. Proprietors generally speak

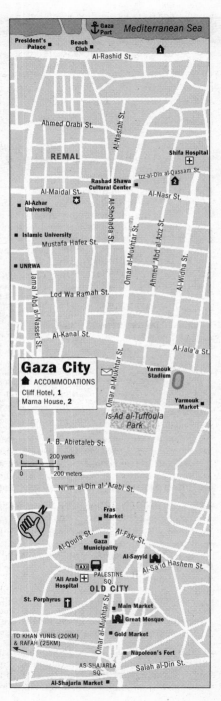

English and are eager to offer suggestions of sights and places to eat. ◪**Marna House,** on Ahmed 'Abd al-'Aziz St., is a good bet. From Palestine Sq., walk along Omar al-Mukhtar St. and turn right on Ez al-Din al-Qassam St., just past the Rashad Shawwa Cultural Center. Ahmed 'Abd is on the right and the hotel is on the left. The lounge downstairs has English books on Gaza, maps of Gaza City, and the infamous talking bird. Rooms are tastefully decorated, with bath, satellite TV, and air-conditioning. (☎282 26 24 or 282 33 22. Singles NIS200/US$50; doubles NIS240/US$60. Traveler's checks accepted.) **Adam Hotel,** on Ahmed Orabi St., 120m past Cliff Hotel, has small rooms with red decor, abundant mirrors, private bath, TV, and air-conditioning. (☎286 69 76. Reception 24hr. Singles NIS160/US$40; doubles NIS220/US$55. NIS20/US$5 student discount. Cash only.) At **Palestine Hotel,** on Ahmed Orabi St., 100m past the Cliff Hotel, all rooms behind the glitzy facade have balconies with a seaside view, as well as satellite TV, fridge, bath, and air-conditioning. Beds are especially large. (☎282 33 55; fax 282 68 13. Check-out noon. Singles NIS220/US$55; doubles NIS260/US$65. Additional person NIS60/US$15. 15% student discount. MC/V and traveler's checks accepted.)

🍴 FOOD

Seafood is Gaza City's speciality, served up in restaurants along the coastal road that offer the most after-dark activity in the city. Drinking water is of inconsistent quality: for bottled water, as well as other basics, try the **Yazji Supermarket** on Omar al-Mukhtar St. When coming from the beach, look for the red awning on the right side of the street, one block past Charles de Gaulle St. (Open daily 8am-11pm. MC.) Keep in mind that the Islamic prohibition of alcohol makes asking for or consuming alcohol in Gaza a bad idea.

◪ **Palestine Restaurant** (☎284 85 83), on Omar al-Mukhtar St.; the building overlooks Palestine Sq. Offers affordable food high above the city. Hamburgers NIS10. Kebab NIS20. Pizza NIS20-45. *Sheesha* NIS5-6. Open Sa-Th 8am-1am, F noon-midnight.

Al-Samak Restaurant (☎286 43 85), on Ahmed Orabi St., on the corner of Omar al-Mukhtar St. Inviting seafood restaurant with a beautiful ocean view. Fish or shrimp NIS40-60. Large salads NIS30. Soup NIS10. Open daily 9am-midnight. Cash only.

👁 SIGHTS

Despite an initial assault on the senses by the bustle, noise, sights, and smells of the city, visitors soon settle into the remarkably laid-back rhythm of urban life. Roaming around the centers of activity brings a glimpse of present-day life but also offers encounters with the city's architectural and cultural treasures.

GREEK ORTHODOX CHURCH OF ST. PORPHYRUS. Gaza's major historical church abuts the minaret of a small mosque to the right. The church was first built on the site in the beginning of the 5th century and was named after Saint Porphyrus of northern Greece, who was charged with spreading Christendom in Gaza. When he predicted the birth of the empress's child, St. Porphyrus won a mandate for the city's temples to be torn down and for a Christian church to be built. March 10, the day of the saint's death, is still celebrated by Gazan Christians. The church has a remarkable, sky-blue arched ceiling dotted with white stars. There also is an impressive collection of dark Orthodox icons along the walls of the church. *(Across Palestine Sq., on the 2nd street that curves down to the right beyond the bus station. To see the inside of the chapel go to the 2nd fl. of the modern church building to the left and ask to see the church. ☎282 68 06. Open daily 9am-1:30pm).*

AL-REDWAN CASTLE. This 17th-century fortress was built from the remains of a 13th-century Mamluk Palace. Napoleon spent three nights here in 1799 while waging a war against Egypt and Syria. During Ottoman rule, the building served as the governor's residence, and during the British mandate, it was a prison.

Today, the dilapidated fort is hidden behind an overgrown garden on the grounds of a girls' school. *(Streets branching off to the left from the souq and the gold market lead to al-Wihda St. and the fort. Look for an opening in the gate. Caretakers usually let visitors see the fort 7am-7pm.)*

AL-SAYYID HASHEM MOSQUE. The great-grandfather of the Prophet Muhammad, a merchant who died while traveling through Gaza City, is said to be buried under one of the four porticos of the courtyard, built in 1850 by an Ottoman Sultan. *(From Palestine Sq., take the side street on the right when facing the Palestine Restaurant. At the intersection bear left, and the minaret and mosque walls will come into view.)*

WEST BANK الضفةالغربية

PHONE CODES	Country Code: 972. Police and Emergency: ☎ 100.

For the first time ever, the Palestinian flag flies over much of the West Bank, but the long and arduous process of establishing self-rule is far from over, and its outcome unpredictable. Daily fluctuations in Israeli-Palestinian relations and extremist actions on both sides frequently disrupt daily life, but well-informed and cautious travelers should have little problem visiting the area's major sites. Tourists may be invited into Palestinian homes, where hot spiced tea and muddily delicious coffee are accompanied by discussions of the *intifada* and occupation. Modest dress will make both men and women's experiences more enjoyable. For now, the best way to visit towns in the West Bank is as separate daytrips from Jerusalem, using transportation from the Suleiman St. Station in East Jerusalem.

SAFETY WARNING. In the last year, the West Bank has seen deadly conflict between Palestinian residents, Israeli settlers, and security forces. Carry your **passport** at all times. Be aware of the situation in each town before visiting. **Avoid visiting** on the anniversaries of uprisings or terrorist attacks. **Do not travel** if Israel has just announced a new building program or territorial acquisition. Visibly Jewish travelers are in danger and should cover *kippot* with a baseball cap. Tourists may be invited into Palestinian homes, where hot spiced tea and coffee are accompanied by discussions of the *intifada* and occupation. **Refrain** from expressing political opinions. **Jewish travelers should not** reveal their religion. Visitors should make their tourist (i.e. non-Israeli) status apparent.

ENTRY

Travelers in Israel do not need any additional visas or permits to visit the West Bank; be sure to bring your passport, though. The West Bank is accessible by car, but the numerous Israeli checkpoints preclude a smooth ride. East Jerusalem is the transportation hub for the West Bank, but travel restrictions have made it impossible for Palestinians who do not live there to use Jerusalem as a transit terminal. As a result, most bus lines have been re-routed to Ramallah, in the northern West Bank; Ramallah's Manara Circle is a hub for East Jerusalem-northern West Bank connections. When possible, travel from Jerusalem into the West Bank rather than from one West Bank city to another. Direct roads from Jerusalem can often cut travel time by more than half. Check with the Israeli tourist office before going. They'll probably issue a standard governmental warning worthy of serious consideration; some may find the warning heavy-handed and decide to go anyway.

Be sure to pick up the monthly *This Week in Palestine*, available in hotel lobbies and restaurants in the West Bank and East Jerusalem, for extensive listings of events and resources throughout the Palestinian Territories.

BORDER CROSSING: JORDAN

Tourists crossing through Jericho's **King Hussein/Allenby Bridge** must obtain visas in advance; get them either in Tel Aviv, at the Eilat-Aqaba crossing, or from a Jordanian embassy or consulate. Allow at least 1½hr. to cross. At the bridge, your passport and belongings will be inspected (you may reclaim your VAT here). Everything remains unpredictable; get thorough, up-to-date information from your embassy or consulate before trying to cross. (NIS126. Border open Su-Th 8am-midnight, F-Sa 8am-3pm.)

CALLING HOME. Blue Telecard-operated phones are conveniently located in most post offices, where cards can also be purchased, but these phones do not accept Israeli Bezeq cards.

TRANSPORTATION

SERVICE. Although **service** are slightly more expensive than buses, they are faster and more reliable, and they depart more frequently (whenever they fill up). **Private taxis** (called *"special,"* pronounced SPAY-shal) are much more expensive and not usually equipped with a meter; be sure to bargain for a price before getting in. Private taxis are often the only way to reach remote sites. Drivers will take you to the site and (for a few extra shekels) wait around to make the return trip. Some West Bank cities, including Nablus and Ramallah, have color coded taxis: yellow cabs are private and orange cabs are *service*. As always, insist that the driver turn on the meter if there is one and have an idea of an appropriate price beforehand. Even for the most remote sites, do not pay more than NIS50 per hr. Most local rides average around NIS10; none should cost any more than NIS15.

BUSES. Both **Arab** and **Egged** buses serve the West Bank. Arab buses leave from two bus stations in East Jerusalem: the Suleiman St. Station, between Herod's Gate and Damascus Gate, for the south and the Nablus Rd. Station (a few steps away) for the north. Catch Egged buses at the West Jerusalem central bus station on Jaffa Rd. Egged buses cost more and often stop only at the outskirts of Palestinian towns, but they are convenient for traveling to the Jewish settlements. Arab bus schedules to the West Bank are unpredictable; the intervals listed in this book are approximate. Transportation to Nablus and Jericho is erratic. For the former, take a *service* to Ramallah and continue to Nablus from there. For Jericho, connect from Abu Dis or al-Izariyyeh (Bethany). Buses run from Jerusalem to: **Bethlehem** (every 15min., NIS2); **al-Izariyyeh** (every hr., NIS2); **Abu Dis** (every hr., NIS2); **Ramallah** (every 30min., NIS3); and **Nablus** (Tamini Bus Co., every hr., NIS6).

CARS. A system of colored license plates differentiates vehicles. Those registered in Israel, Jerusalem, and Jewish settlements have yellow plates. White plates with green numbers belong to vehicles registered with the Palestinian Authority. Blue plates are a remnant from the days when the Palestinian territories were the Occupied Territories; they signify Arab cars not registered with Israel. Others are black-on-white (UN or diplomatic), red (police), and black (army). It's probably safer to travel with white or blue plates, but many Arab-owned cars that are registered in Israel (with yellow plates) travel hassle-free in the West Bank.

TOURS. An easy way to see the West Bank is to hire a Palestinian guide for the day. **Alternative Tourism Group** (see **Bethlehem Tours**, p. 420) is a reliable company with excellent guides. Alternatively, look for a taxi driver who speaks decent English (there are many) and ask whether he can drive by the major sights. Specify how many hours you wish to spend and agree on a price in advance; something in the range of NIS45 per hr. is reasonable for transportation and waiting time.

HISTORY AND LITERATURE

The West Bank represents the most complex facet of the Arab-Israeli conflict, due to its relevance to three major groups: Palestinian Arabs, Israelis, and Jordanians. Palestinian Arabs form the region's largest indigenous group and have resided throughout Israel and the West Bank for hundreds of years. Jews lived in the West Bank long before the 1967 and even the 1948 wars. For the most part, Jews were drawn to the holy city of Hebron, but in 1929 they fled after an Arab massacre claimed 80 Jewish lives. Over 70% of Jordanians are of Palestinian origin.

The political region now called the West Bank was created in the 1948 Arab-Israeli War, when Jordan conquered the "west bank" of the Jordan River (see p. 268). The Jordanian government subsequently did little to develop the West Bank and discriminated against its Palestinian residents. Overall, Palestinians in the West Bank fared slightly better than those in the Egyptian-occupied Gaza Strip, since the fertile West Bank was economically vital to Jordan. In the 1967 Six Day War (see p. 268), Israel captured the West Bank, placing the area under temporary military administration (except for East Jerusalem, which was annexed). Arab mayors and police kept their offices, Jordanian school curricula continued to be taught, public welfare programs were established, National Social Security payments made, and Israeli medical treatment instituted. Israeli occupation was not all benevolent, however. Because the area was administered under martial law, basic rights granted to Jews and Israeli Arabs were denied the Palestinians, who suffered curfews and mass arrests. Houses were destroyed in retaliation for the terrorist actions of one family member. There was no freedom of assembly—Palestinians could not have weddings without permits from Israeli authorities. Flying the Palestinian flag was illegal, and the infrastructure, schools, and public works of the West Bank were neglected in comparison with those of Israel proper. Palestinian attempts at establishing economic independence were thwarted. **Birzeit University** was denied a building permit for years and shut down frequently. Israeli settlements in the West Bank were, and continue to be, a source of constant controversy. Some 160,000 Israeli Jews have settled in the West Bank since 1967. Launched by Labor governments eager to establish an Israeli presence in areas of strategic importance such as the Jordan Valley, the settlement project has been an ideological cornerstone of right-wing Likud governments since 1977. The settlements are motivated primarily by strategic considerations, but also by the desire to maintain the historical boundaries of *Eretz Yisrael* (the biblical land of Israel), an area including Israel, the West Bank, the Gaza Strip, and a bit beyond. Often strategically situated on hilltops overlooking Palestinian towns, some settlements resemble military installations more than housing developments.

In December 1987, a traffic accident in the Gaza Strip sparked the Palestinians of the occupied territories to begin the **intifada;** two decades of occupation, economic stagnation, and increasing Israeli settlement erupted into stone-throwing, demonstrations, the unfurling of the Palestinian flag, and other expressions of nationalism. The *intifada* (see p. 269) led to major changes in the nature of the Palestinian-Israeli conflict. The populist nature of the uprising and the televised suppression by the Israeli army managed to draw more international attention than decades of PLO terrorism. The *intifada* had stopped making headlines by the time of the 1991 **Gulf War,** when the PLO and most Palestinians supported Iraq, rather than supporting the US-led movement, like most Arab governments.

In the aftermath of the Gulf War, Middle Eastern governments became convinced that it was high time for a regional peace conference. Since the historic Madrid conference in October 1991, negotiations have gone on intermittently. Most recently, Israel's 20-year occupation of southern Lebanon came to a close. Former prime minister Ehud Barak hoped the pullout would isolate Israeli good will and encourage peace-talks with Syria (see **Recent History,** p. 270).

Much recent Palestinian literature concerns the agony of foreign occupation and exile, touching also on the themes of reconciliation with the Israelis. **Ghassan Kanafani,** perhaps the greatest contemporary Palestinian fiction writer, recreates the desperation and aimlessness of the refugee in his short stories *All That Remains: Palestine's Children* and *Men in the Sun and Other Palestinian Stories*. His *Return to Haifa* is an electrifying account of a face-to-face encounter between an exiled Palestinian family and an elderly Jewish couple who are Holocaust survivors. The poetry of **Mahmoud Darwish** depicts Palestinians' attachment to the land. The poems of **Fouzi al-Asmar,** collected in *The Wind-Driven Reed and Other Poems*, share the longing for a homeland. **Jabra Ibrahim Jabra's** novel *The Ship* is engrossing, as is his autobiography *The First Well*, an idyllic account of his Christian upbringing in Bethlehem. In *Wild Thorns*, **Sahar Khalifeh** describes an expatriate's return to Palestine and his conversion from an intellectual to an ideologically committed terrorist. Israeli Arab **Anton Shammas's** *Arabesques* documents Palestinian identity crises; Fawaz Turki's autobiographical tomes discuss life in exile. The works of **Liyana Badr, Raymonda Tawil,** and **Samih al-Qassem** all deserve note; most of these authors and others are translated in **Salma Khadra Jayyusi's** behemoth *Modern Palestinian Literature*.

BETHLEHEM بيت لحم בית לחם ☎ 02

Bethlehem and its environs were the backdrop for some of history's quieter religious moments: Rachel's death, the love between Ruth and Boaz, the discovery of the shepherd-poet-king David, and of course, the pastoral birth of Jesus. Bethlehem, which is almost entirely Christian, and the surrounding villages of Beit Sahour and Beit Jala are home to most of the Palestinian Christian minority. The glow-in-the-dark Virgin Marys and plastic crowns of thorns may take crass commercialism to a new level, but some visitors still manage to see past the blinding flashbulbs to a site of true religious significance.

Besides being home to one of Christianity's most important sites, Bethlehem is a prime example of what independence can achieve. In 1995, Bethlehem celebrated Christmas for the first time under Palestinian rule. The changing of the guard has breathed new life into this town; grants from other countries have been pouring in. The most crowded and interesting time to visit Bethlehem is during a Christian holiday, especially Easter 2002, for which you should make hotel reservations well in advance (i.e. it might already be too late). Other times allow more personal space to explore and a more accurate portrait of life in Bethlehem.

▐▘ TRANSPORTATION

Buses: Buses make the 8km trip from the Suleiman St. Station in East Jerusalem, right outside Damascus Gate to **Bab al-Zaqaq** (30min., daily every 15-30min. until 5pm, NIS2.50). Buses stop running after dark.

Taxis: Taxis are the only local transportation; you can find them on Beit Sahour Rd. behind the Peace Center. To get back to Jerusalem, take a taxi to Bab al-Zaqaq or Rachel's Tomb (NIS1.50) and flag down a Jerusalem-bound *service*. A private taxi from the checkpoint to Jerusalem is NIS25-30; set a price before you leave.

▰✶▱ ORIENTATION AND PRACTICAL INFORMATION

The three Wise Men followed a star to a peaceful manger; today's pilgrims can follow **Star St.** to bustling **Manger Sq.**, where most of the Christian sights are clustered. **Rachel's Tomb,** on the northern outskirts of Bethlehem, is a 30min. walk (or NIS2 *service*) from there. Manger St. forks into Star St.; **Paul VI Rd.** branches off this, and a right turn leads into Manger Sq. Alternatively, take a *service* from Rachel's Tomb to **Bab al-Zaqaq,** the transportation hub for the region, at **Hebron Rd.** and Paul VI Rd. The walk from Bab al-Zaqaq to Manger Sq. takes 15min. Star St. and **Najajreh St.** are home to the town's shopping district and open-air market.

Tourist Office: PA Ministry of Tourism (☎276 66 77; fax 274 10 57), in the Peace Center in Manger Sq. Distributes a free PA **town map** with a glossy pamphlet of major sights, details about special events during Christmas and Easter, and transportation information. Open M-Sa 8am-6pm.

Tours: Alternative Tourism Group (ATG; ☎277 21 51; fax 277 22 11; atg@p-ol.com; www.patg.org), in Beit Sahour, runs inexpensive tours of Palestinian cities and refugee camps throughout the West Bank. Prices are in the vicinity of $16 per day.

Currency Exchange: Mercantile Discount Bank (☎274 25 95), in Manger Sq. Open M-Th and Sa 8:30am-12:30pm, F 8:30am-noon. There are **no ATMs** for foreign bank cards in Bethlehem. Most services accept US dollars and many take credit cards as well.

Police: (☎274 49 35). **Tourist Police:** (☎277 07 50 or 277 07 51), in Manger Sq. beneath the Andalus Hotel; another branch in the new bus station.

Hospital: Beit Jala Government Hospital (☎274 11 61), on Main St. (the continuation of Paul VI Rd.), on the Beit Jala side of Hebron Rd.

Internet Access: ICC Internet Center (☎276 58 48), on Manger St. just past the new bus station, has the fastest connection in the Manger Sq. area. NIS7 per 30min. Open M-Sa 9am-10:30pm, Su 10am-1pm. Farther up Manger St., **Speed Net** (☎276 48 47), in the Middle East Building opposite Moradeh St., complements speedy computers with an espresso and cappucino maker. Open daily 10am-10pm.

Post Office: (☎274 27 92), in Manger Sq., beneath the Municipality Building. Open Sa-Th 8am-2:30pm. Send and receive mail via Israel and buy PA telecards and stamps.

▌ ACCOMMODATIONS

There's no problem finding a place to stay during the off-season, but at Christmas there's no room unless you reserve a year in advance. One attractive addition to Bethlehem's options is a **bed and breakfast** program intended to give individuals a taste of Palestinian family life at a reasonable cost.

Franciscan Convent Pension (Franciscaines de Marie; ☎274 24 41), on Milk Grotto St., on the left past the Grotto. Look for a set-back gray gate with small "White Sisters" plaque. Welcoming French nuns rent 3 sparkling flower- and Bible-bedecked rooms. Breakfast NIS20. Check-out 9am. Curfew 9pm; in winter 8:30pm. Reservations recommended. "Dorms" (for 2-3 people) NIS50; singles NIS100. No credit cards.

Casa Nova (☎274 39 80; fax 274 35 40), off Manger Sq., in a corner to the left of the basilica entrance. Modern rooms and plenty of hot water. Heated in winter. Reception 24hr. Check-out 8am. Flexible midnight curfew. Faxed reservations recommended. Bed and breakfast US$22 per person; half-board US$27; full board US$33; single supplement US$15. 5% service charge.

Al-Andalus Guest House (☎274 35 19; fax 276 56 74; andalus@p-ol.com), in Manger Sq. across from the Peace Center. Basic rooms with fans, private baths, and views of Jerusalem or Manger Sq. Guests can use the kitchen. Bed and breakfast rooms US$25 per person, US$30 during peak times.

Alternative Tourism Group (ATG; ☎277 21 51; fax 277 22 11; www.patg.com). This B&B program overseen by ATG has 27 double rooms in private homes, all with clean private baths and some with telephones. NIS95 per person with breakfast. Lunch or dinner NIS25. Contact George Rishmawi at ATG in Beit Sahour.

◆ FOOD

Cheap falafel and shawarma stands in Manger Sq. and on Manger St. provide *fuul* for church-hopping excursions. Bethlehem's one-and-only nightspot, **Balloons,** on Hebron Rd. near Rachel's Tomb, dishes up renowned pizza. They only serve soft drinks, but don't let that burst your balloon—the alcohol pours at **Memories,** the pub upstairs. (☎274 10 36. Open Sa-Th 1pm-1am.) **St. George,** in Manger Sq. next door to the post office, gets most of the tourist traffic from the basilica with its impressive bar and extensive menu. (☎274 37 80. Salads NIS18. Omelets NIS20. Meat plates NIS35-50. Open daily 8am-6pm.) One of Bethlehem's nicer lunch options is **Sababa,** on Manger St., near the junction of Star St. Their set daily menu includes a salad, traditional main dishes, coffee, and dessert for

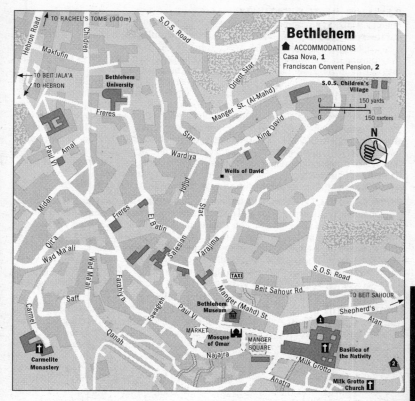

Bethlehem

⌂ ACCOMMODATIONS
Casa Nova, **1**
Franciscan Convent Pension, **2**

NIS55. (☎274 40 06. Open daily 11am-4pm.) At **al-Andalus Restaurant,** just off Manger Sq., around the corner from the affiliated guest house, affordable meals are disguised as "snacks." Hot dogs and hamburgers (NIS12-20) come with salad and fries. They offer a large variety of Middle Eastern foods for NIS28-45. Ask for a free, excellent map of Bethlehem, edited by the owner. (☎274 35 19; fax 276 56 74. Open daily 8am-midnight.) **Al-Atlal (The Ruins) Restaurant,** one block from Manger Sq. on Milk Grotto St., provides needed respite from the hordes. (☎274 11 04. Lamb *me'orav* (mixed grill) NIS35; cheese toast NIS16. Open daily noon-4pm and 8pm-midnight.)

◉ SIGHTS

There are two ways to "do" Bethlehem. Traditionally, tourists arrive from Israel, hop from one Christian holy place to another in several hours, and return to Jerusalem before dinner. A less common, but arguably more interesting, alternative is to stay the night or to use Bethlehem as a base for forays into the rest of the West Bank. Because no reliable public transportation is available, the best way to see the sights is to hire a guide with a vehicle for an afternoon. Guides gather in Manger Sq.; be sure to choose someone wearing a PA-issued ID tag. Tours should cost no more than US$10-12 per hr., including transportation. Guides will ask for double that, so be sure to bargain. To explore the villages and other West Bank cities from Bethlehem, contact ATG (see **Tours,** p. 420).

BASILICA OF THE NATIVITY

Manger Sq. is dominated by the Basilica of the Nativity, a massive basilica honoring the spot generally considered to be Jesus' birthplace and the oldest continuously used church in the world. Erected in 326 CE by Queen Helena, mother of Constantine, it was spared the Persian invasion (when virtually every other Christian shrine in the Holy Land was demolished) because of its mosaic of the three (Persian) wise men. The church lapsed into disrepair after the Crusader kingdom fell, but its importance as a holy shrine never waned; during the ensuing centuries, struggle for its control repeatedly led to bloodshed. In the 1840s, the church was restored to its former dignity, but squabbles between the various sects continue. An elaborate system of worship schedules, established in 1751, has worked through competing claims, but the confusion resulting from the Greek Orthodox Church's rejection of summer daylight savings time demonstrates the teetering balance of this arrangement. (As of summer 2000, Catholic mass was held M-Sa at 6am, Armenian at 1:30pm, and Greek Orthodox at 4pm; Su has a schedule of its own. Check at the entrance to St. Catherine's Church for the exact times.)

DOOR OF HUMILITY. Despite its impressive history, the Basilica of the Nativity is not particularly attractive from the outside. The main entrance and windows were blocked up as a safety precaution during medieval times. To enter, assume a kneeling position and step through the narrow Door of Humility—a remnant of Christian attempts to prevent Muslims from entering on horseback. Fragments of beautiful mosaic floors are all that remain of Queen Helena's original church. View them beneath the huge wooden trap doors in the center of the marble Crusader floor. England's King Edward IV offered the oak ceiling as a gift. The Russian royal family bequeathed the handsome icons adorning the altar in 1764.

GROTTO OF THE NATIVITY. The sanctuary beneath the church is the Grotto of the Nativity. Crosses are etched into the columns on both sides of the cramped doorway—religious graffiti from centuries of pilgrims. The focus of the hubbub is a silver star bearing the Latin inscription: *Hic De Virgine Maria Jesus Christus Natus Est* (Here, of the Virgin Mary, Jesus Christ was born). The 14 points represent the 14 stations of the Via Dolorosa (see p. 299). The star, added by Catholics in 1717, was removed by Greeks in 1847 and restored by the Turkish government in 1853. Quarrels over the star are said to have contributed to the outbreak of the Crimean War. *(In Manger Sq.,Tour guides often roam the square and nave; a reasonable fee is NIS15 for a 1hr. tour with a licensed guide. Basilica complex open daily 5:30am-7pm; in winter 5am-5pm. Free, though donations are encouraged. Modest dress required.)*

OTHER SIGHTS

ST. CATHERINE'S CHURCH. Built by the Franciscans in 1881, this simple and airy church is a welcome contrast to the grim interior of the adjacent basilica. Superbly detailed wood carvings of the 14 stations of the cross line the walls. The first of the downstairs crypt rooms, the **Chapel of St. Joseph,** commemorates the carpenter's vision of an angel who advised him to flee with his family to Egypt. The burial cave of children slaughtered by King Herod (Matthew 2:6) lies below the altar and through the grille in the **Chapel of the Innocents.** Beyond the altar, a narrow hallway leads to the Grotto of the Nativity, although it is blocked by a thick wood door pierced by a peephole. During times of greater hostility between Christian sects, this glimpse was as close as Catholics could get to the Greek Orthodox shrine. To the right of the altar, a series of rooms contains celebrity sepulchers including the **Tomb of St. Jerome,** as well as those of St. Paula and her daughter Eustochia. These lead to the spartan cell where St. Jerome produced the **Vulgate,** the 4th-century translation of the Hebrew Bible into Latin. The Franciscan fathers conduct a solemn procession to the basilica and underground chapels every day. To join in the 20min. of Gregorian cantillation and Latin prayer, arrive at St. Catherine's by noon. St. Catherine's also broadcasts a **midnight mass** to a worldwide audience every Christmas Eve. *(Adjoins the basilica. Use the separate entrance to the left of the basilica entrance, or face the altar in the basilica and pass through one of the doorways in the wall on the left. Open daily 6:30am-8pm.)*

MILK GROTTO CHURCH. The cellar of this church is thought to be the cave in which the Holy Family hid when fleeing from Herod into Egypt. The cave and church take their names from the original milky white color of the rocks, most of which have now either been blackened by candle smoke or painted blue. According to legend, some of Mary's milk fell while she was nursing the infant Jesus, whitewashing the rocks. Today, women with fertility problems can request small packets of white dust as a charm. Male visitors may be slightly uncomfortable amid the women who come here to pray for fertility and the photo-diorama of suckling babies born to those whose prayers were rewarded. *(A 5min. walk down Milk Grotto St. from the Basilica of the Nativity. Facing the line of stores in Manger Sq., turn left and take the narrow alleyway to the Franciscan flag; the grotto is on the right. ☎274 38 67. Open daily 8am-6pm; in winter 8am-5pm. If the door is locked, ring the bell.)*

MUSEUMS. The two adjacent stores that comprise the **Palestinian Heritage Center** display and sell traditional crafts. The small but interesting exhibit features a "traditional Palestinian sitting room" complete with handwoven carpets and teapots. The stores sell inexpensive needlework and other crafts, most of which are made by women from the Bethlehem area and nearby refugee camps. The **Bethlehem Museum** showcases Palestinian crafts, traditional costumes, and a 19th-century Palestinian home. *(Heritage Museum: on Manger St. near the intersection with Hebron Rd. ☎274 23 81. Open M-Sa 9am-7pm. Bethlehem Museum: off Star St., between the market and Manger Sq. ☎274 25 89. Open M-W and F-Sa 8am-5pm, Th 8am-noon. NIS8.)*

JERICHO أريحا יריחו ☎02

The first city to fly the Palestinian flag and the headquarters of the Palestinian Authority, Jericho vibrates with ground-breaking activity. Streets strewn with banners, flags, and portraits of Yasser Arafat convey Palestinian pride and optimism, which shines through in the hospitality and openness of the city's residents. Settled 10,000 years ago, Jericho is believed to be the world's oldest city. At 250m below sea level, it's also the world's lowest. Its location in the middle of the Judean Desert leaves Jericho brutally hot in the summer and pleasantly hot in the winter, making it a winter resort for vacationers as far back as the 8th century, when Syrian King Hisham built a magnificent winter palace here. Excavations at several sites around Jericho have been extensive, but besides several beautiful mosaic floors, the ruins themselves aren't that spectacular—after all, the city walls are famous for having tumbled down.

After Joshua destroyed the city with a blast of his trumpet (Joshua 6:20), Jericho remained in shambles for centuries. The oasis town was partially rebuilt in the days of King Ahab in the early 9th century BCE (I Kings 16:34), embellished by King Herod during the Hasmonean Dynasty, and further strengthened under Roman, Crusader, and Mamluk rule. The population skyrocketed after 1967, when thousands of Palestinian refugees fled here from Israel. Free from Jordanian control, the refugee camps were replaced by apartment buildings, and the standard of living drastically improved. Today, Jericho is the site of several noteworthy million-dollar investment projects, including a new luxury resort popular with wealthy Palestinians, a cable car-hotel complex at the foot of the Mount of Temptation, and the Oasis Casino, the region's very own mini-yet-majestic sin city. Jericho is under the custodianship of the Palestinian Authority and can be visited without difficulty. All travelers should dress modestly, and women travelers may feel safer with a male companion.

▆ TRANSPORTATION

Forty kilometers east of Jerusalem, Jericho is on the road to Amman, at the junction of the highway to Galilee (for information on crossing to **Jordan**, see p. 417). The quickest and most reliable way to get to Jericho is by **service**. Direct transportation from Jerusalem (across the street from Damascus Gate) is possible, but expensive (NIS15) and infrequent. Take a *service* to Abu Dis instead (NIS2.50; coming out of Damascus Gate turn right and head toward the end of the line of taxis), get out at the gas station, and switch to a Jericho-bound *service* (NIS6), which will stop in the central square or at the Oasis Casino. There is no schedule—*service* leave when full, and they fill most quickly during morning and afternoon rush hours. Repeat this process backwards to return to Jerusalem; from the casino, however, you might be better off going into Jericho first because *service* usually only depart for Abu Dis or Jerusalem when full.

There is no public transportation within the city, but there are a multitude of yellow taxis. Hiring a taxi for several hours is the recommended way of seeing the sights, since the blistering heat most of the year makes even walkable distances unbearable. Pay no more than NIS30-40 per hr. A great way to see the sights on cooler days is by bike. **Zaki Sale and Rent Bicycle,** in the main square by the corner of al-Kastal, rents 21-speed mountain bikes with locks. Bring water and watch out for cars. (☎ 232 40 70. Open daily 8am-10pm. NIS3 per hr. or NIS12 per day.)

■✿🛈 ORIENTATION AND PRACTICAL INFORMATION

There's no official tourist office, but you can get free maps and information at the municipality building in the main square or at the **Elisha's Spring complex** (☎232 24 17; info@jericho-city.org), across the parking lot from the old city. Exchange currency at the **Cairo Amman Bank,** in the main square (☎232 36 27. Open Sa-Th 8:30am-12:30pm.) The **police** are in the main square, next to the bank. (☎232 21 00 or 232 14 26. Open 24hr.) The **tourist police** are across from Elisha's Spring. (☎232 40 11. Open daily 8am-6pm.) **Arabi Pharmacy,** 74 Ein al-Sultan St., by Hisham's Palace Hotel, has the latest bedtime in town. (☎ 232 23 25. Open Sa-Th 8am-11pm.) If it turns out to be more serious, go to the **Palestinian National Authority Ministry of Health Clinic,** 51 Jerusalem Rd. just off the square. (☎232 24 06. Open Sa-Th 8am-2:30pm.) The **New Jericho Hospital** (☎232 19 66), farther down Jerusalem Rd., is open 24hr. Head down Amman St. from the police station to get to the **post office.** (☎232 25 74; fax 232 36 09. Open Sa-Th 8am-2pm.)

■🏠 ACCOMMODATIONS AND FOOD

With only a few sights to see and a relatively easy commute to Jerusalem, there isn't much reason to sleep here. **Jerusalem Hotel** (also known as al-Quds Hotel), is down Amman St., about 1.5km east of the city center, on the right. Its "dorms" (no more than 4 beds per room) are airy (fan, no A/C) and have shared baths. Upstairs, medium-sized rooms have air-conditioning, satellite TV, and phone; most have balconies. (☎232 24 44; fax 232 13 29. Breakfast included. Check-out noon. Dorms US$25 per person. Singles US$60; doubles US$80; triples US$100.) **Jericho Resort Village,** off Qasr Hisham St. near Hisham's Palace, is a full-fledged resort complex with swimming pools, restaurants, cafes, bars, and luxurious lounge areas—a magnet for wealthy Palestinian families. (☎232 12 55; fax 232 21 89; reservation@jericho-resort.com; www.jericho-resort.com. Breakfast included. Check-out noon. Singles US$100-120; doubles US$120-140. 4-person bungalows including kitchenette and sitting room US$140-150.) **Hisham's Palace Hotel,** on Ein al-Sultan St., close to the city center, isn't quite palace-like anymore. Rooms, hallways, and bathrooms are time-ravaged to the extreme and only borderline clean. Rooms have either air-conditioning or fans; some have balconies and private baths. (☎ 052 48 38 08. Flexible check-in and check-out. NIS30-80 per person, depending on season, type of room, and bargaining skills. No credit cards.)

Many cheap and tasty restaurants cluster around the city center. Falafel should be about NIS3, shawarma NIS6. Cheap fruit and vegetable bins are crowded in the southeastern corner of the square (near al-Kastal St.). The city's best restaurant, catering to native tastes and pockets, is **Abu Nabil,** under the red awning in the main square. A full lunch or dinner includes grilled meat, salad, pita, and hummus for NIS25. (☎232 21 60. Open daily 6am-midnight.) **Green Valley,** on Ein al-Sultan St., on the way to Hisham's Palace, has excellent local specialties in a well-touristed and spacious indoor-outdoor restaurant. (☎232 23 49. Live music on F and Sa nights in winter. Open daily 8am-midnight.)

👁 SIGHTS

Hire a taxi for several hours from the city center and beat the heat (NIS30-40 per hour; set a price in advance). Visit Hisham's Palace first, as a cluster of restaurants and a cooling spring near the ancient city provide a pleasant post-tour rest stop.

HISHAM'S PALACE. Begun in 724 CE and completed in 743, Hisham's Palace was ravaged only four years later by an earthquake. Known as Khirbet al-Mafjar in Arabic, the palace was designed for the Umayyad Caliph Hisham as a winter retreat from Damascus—although there is no evidence that the caliph ever actually spent any time here. The most renowned feature is a courtyard window in the shape of the six-pointed Umayyad star. In the "guesthouse," a beautifully preserved mosaic depicts a sinister tableau in which a lion devours a gazelle as its naive playmates frolic beneath the Tree of Life. Get a guide from the entrance to show you around (tip NIS5-10). *(To reach the palace from the square, head 3km north from Qasr Hisham St., following the signs to the turnoff at a guard post. Coming from ancient Jericho, head east on Jiftlik Rd., past the synagogue and the Ein al-Sultan refugee camp. After 1.5km, turn right on the road back to Jericho; the turnoff to Hisham's Palace appears on the left. ☎ 232 25 22. Open daily 8am-6pm. NIS10, students NIS7, children NIS5.)*

ANCIENT JERICHO. Thought to be the oldest city in the world (as opposed to Damascus, the oldest continually inhabited city), ancient Jericho is now a heap of ruined walls. Called **Tel al-Sultan,** the mound contains layer upon layer of garbage from ancient (and modern) cities. Some of the finds date from the early Neolithic period, leading archaeologists to suspect that Jericho was inhabited as early as the 8th millennium BCE. The oldest fortifications are 7000 years old. A limited amount of excavation has exposed many levels of ancient walls, some of them 3½m thick and 5½m high. Imagination will have to substitute for visible splendor at this site, which is distinctly unimpressive. *(To get to ancient Jericho from the city center, follow Ein al-Sultan St. to its end. The entrance is through a parking lot around the corner, opposite the Elisha's Spring complex. From Hisham's Palace, 2km away, turn right onto the road that runs past the Palace (away from the city center), cross a narrow bridge, then take a left at the next junction, following the "Tel Jericho" signs. ☎ 232 29 35. Open daily 8am-6pm; in winter 8am-5pm. NIS10, students with ISIC NIS7, children NIS5.)*

MOSQUE OF NABI MUSA. About 8km from Jericho on the road to Jerusalem, the huge Mosque of Nabi Musa stands in a sea of sand on a hill a short distance from the road, topped with a complex of white domes. The mosque was built in 1269 CE on a spot revered throughout the Muslim world as the grave of the prophet Moses. Islamic tradition holds that Salah al-Din had a dream about the location of the place where God carried the bones of Moses. The tomb is said to have special powers—run your hands over the velvet cloth of Moses' Tomb while making a wish and see for yourself. Across from the tomb, stairs lead upward into a minaret with incredible views of the surrounding Judean desert. Ask the souvenir vendors to unlock the gate if it is wired shut. *(The only way to visit is by car or taxi (NIS40 from Jericho). To get to the mosque, head toward Jerusalem about 5km, then turn left at the sign, and follow the road for another 5km. Open daily 8am-sunset. Free but donations welcome.)*

MONASTERY. An imposing Greek Orthodox monastery stands on the edge of a cliff among the mountains west of Jericho; the peak is believed to be the New Testament's **Mount of Temptation,** where the Devil tried to tempt Jesus. The complex of buildings stands before a grotto, said to be the spot where Jesus fasted for 40 days and 40 nights at the end of his ministry (Matthew 4:1-11). Three Greek monks now live in the monastery, built in 1895. The summit of the mountain, named **Qarantal** after the Latin word for "forty," is also a pedestal for the Maccabean **Castle of Dok,** beside which lie the remains of a 4th-century Christian chapel. *(The monastery can be reached by climbing up the mountain from the base, not far from the ancient city; the hike takes under 1hr., but bring plenty of water. A much easier way up is to take the téléphérique (see below), which still requires a short hike to reach the monastery. Open M-F 9am-1pm and 2-5pm, Sa 9am-2pm, Su 10am-2pm. Modest dress required.)*

WEST BANK

ENTERTAINMENT

The beautiful public **Spanish Garden,** on Amman St., near the center of town, was built recently through the contributions of the Spanish government. Reminiscent of a medieval Andalusian *hadeeqa*, the garden livens up after 6pm, when families, small children, and teenagers show up to enjoy Arabic music, coffee, and *argileh*. A small cafe serves inexpensive snacks next to an game-room. (☎ 232 39 31, mobile 050 51 55 18. Open daily sunset-1am; in winter sunset-9pm. NIS2, children NIS1.) Few visitors to this city of temptation can resist the **Oasis Casino Hotel,** several kilometers before the city center. This state-of-the art casino, with the full array of slot machines, blackjack, poker, and other tables, would hold its head high even in Las Vegas. All gambling is in US dollars, which can be exchanged from any currency at the door. (☎ 231 11 11. Min. bids at most tables US$10-25, though some are US$5. No T-shirts. Passports required. Open 24hr.)

RAMALLAH رام الله ☎ 02

Perched 900m above sea level, Ramallah, along with its smaller sister city al-Bireh, is famous for its cool, pleasant mountain air. Before 1967, the then-prosperous town was a summer haven for Arabs from Jordan, Lebanon, and the Gulf region. With vacationers long gone by the time of the *intifada*, Ramallah and the energetic young intellectuals at nearby Birzeit University joined Nablus as leaders of West Bank resistance. Now under PA control, the city has become a transportation hub and will replace Gaza as the administrative hub of the PA when Palestinian self-rule expands. It already houses several important Palestinian Authority offices, including the Ministries of Transportation and Education.

Ramallah is known for its religiously relaxed atmosphere (alcohol flows freely and movie theaters are well attended) and the cafes along its main streets. It is, without question, the cultural capital of the West Bank, with a highly educated and fashionable population. It is also the hub of Palestinian feminist activity; the city's women frequently attend university rather than marry early, and several women-run cafes are used to fund local feminist organizations.

▐ TRANSPORTATION

Due to its location 16km north of Jerusalem and the frequent closures of East Jerusalem roads, Ramallah has become a transportation hub. It is possible to get from Ramallah to most northern West Bank towns by direct **service.** From **Jerusalem,** take a *service* from outside Damascus Gate (20min., NIS3.50) or an Arab bus from the station on Nablus Rd. (40min., NIS2). Buses and *service* to Jerusalem leave from the second floor of the bus station on al-Nahda St., just off **Manara Circle** ("al-Manara"), the town's epicenter. The last bus leaves at about 5pm.

▐ PRACTICAL INFORMATION

Tours: Palestinian Association for Cultural Exchange (PACE; ☎ 295 88 25; fax 298 68 54; pace@palnet.edu), on Nablus Rd. in al-Bireh, organizes full- and half-day tours throughout the West Bank and Gaza Strip. Full day in Ramallah and vicinity NIS120. Also serves as an unofficial tourist office.

Currency Exchange: Money changers and banks can be found on all major streets and at Manara Circle. The only bank that accepts foreign ATM cards is **HSBC,** at the corner of Jaffa St. and al-Rashid St., downhill from al-Bardouni's Restaurant.

Police: (☎ 295 70 20), on al-Nahda St., past al-Wehdeh Hotel from Manara Circle.

Hospital: Ramallah General Hospital (☎ 995 65 61 or 995 65 62) is more accessible than Ramallah's **pharmacies,** which close at 8pm or earlier.

Internet Access: Carma Cyber Club (☎ 298 48 54), on the 6th fl. of the Lo'lo'at al-Manara building, near Manara Circle on Main St. NIS4 per hr. Open Sa-Th 8am-1am, F

3pm-1am. **Leader Net** (☎ 296 52 31), on the 6th fl. of Burj al-Sa'a building in Mughtarbin Sq. NIS5 per hr. Open Sa-Th 9am-midnight, F noon-midnight.

Post Office: (☎ 295 66 04), on Park St., off Main St., downhill from Rukab's Ice Cream, sells beautiful Palestinian stamps and serves the rest of the world with Israeli stamps. Open Sa-Th 8am-2:30pm.

ACCOMMODATIONS

Although a night in Ramallah is very worthwhile, accommodations are expensive compared with nearby Jerusalem. There are no true hostels in Ramallah.

Panorama Inn (☎/fax 295 68 08), on Jaffa St., downhill from Al-Bardouni Restaurant near the Faisal St. intersection. Not too far from the center of town, but surprisingly quiet with a sunny patio. Rooms with private bath, TV, and phone. Some with balcony and/or small fridge; large balcony in the hall on both floors. Knowledgeable and helpful staff. Breakfast included. Check-out noon. Singles NIS120; doubles NIS150.

Al-Wehdeh Hotel (☎ 298 04 12; fax 295 48 72), on al-Nahdah St. 1 block from Manara Circle. Ramallah's cheapest accommodation and also the most central, if you don't mind the noise from the street (it does quiet down eventually). Recently renovated. Rooms with TV, fans, and private bath; some with balconies. Breakfast included. Check-out flexible. Singles NIS100; doubles NIS150; long-term discounts available.

Royal Court Suite Hotel (☎ 296 40 40; fax 296 40 47; rcshotel@rcshotel.com; www.rcshotel.com), on the corner of Jaffa St. and Faisal St., next to the Panorama Inn. Snazzy new luxury hotel. All rooms have kitchenettes, balconies, A/C, cable TV, phones, Internet access lines (you supply the laptop), minibars, safe boxes, and even hair dryers. Breakfast included. 24hr. reception. Singles US$69; doubles US$99.

FOOD

Ramallah's streets are lined with falafel and shawarma stands. Good, inexpensive restaurants look down on the city from the tops of the buildings all around Manara Circle, especially along Main St. Most restaurants serve international dishes as well as traditional Palestinian cuisine. Ramallah's hip cafes attract Arabs from all over the West Bank and even Israelis from across the green line.

Rukab's Ice Cream (☎ 295 64 67), at the corner of Main St. and al-Exhibition St., one block from Manara Circle. Possibly the best ice cream in the hemisphere; their gum-thickened, gooey goodness comes in a rainbow of blissful flavors. Try the popular pistachio. Tiny cones NIS3; large, multi-flavored cones NIS9. Open daily 8am-1am.

Angelo's (☎ 295 64 08), a left turn off Main St. 1 block after Rukab's; the restaurant is on the corner. Flings pizza (small cheese NIS20; large "Angelo's Supreme" NIS55) into the air and onto the plates of plucky budget travelers. The garlic bread (NIS8 per basket) is a local favorite. Open daily 11am-midnight.

Al-Bardouni (☎ 295 14 10), on Jaffa St., several blocks from Manara Circle. A stone's throw from the city center, but in a quiet part of town. Especially beautiful (and packed) on sunny afternoons. Salads NIS8-12. BBQ dishes NIS38-50. *Musakhan* (traditional dish with half a chicken) NIS35. Open daily 11am-midnight.

Tal al-Qamar (☎ 298 79 05), on the 5th fl. of the Nasser Building on Main St., on the right, 1 block past Rukab's. Beautiful view. Sandwiches NIS15. Grilled meats NIS25-50. Su-W live *oud* after 9pm. Th nights live Arabic music. Open daily noon-1am.

SIGHTS AND ENTERTAINMENT

The main attraction is the city itself; on Saturdays, Manara Circle is a crammed jungle. For a more historical view, the **Palestinian Folklore Museum,** in the town of al-Bireh a few blocks away, exhibits traditional costumes, handicrafts, and rooms of a Palestinian house. (☎ 240 28 76. Open Sa-Th 9am-2:30pm.) **Al-Siraj Theater** (☎ 995 70 37) near Clock Circle, the **Ashtar Theater** (☎ 82 72 18) on Radio St., and the

Popular Arts Cinema (☎995 38 91) on al-Bireh St. produce performing arts and dance: call or ask around town for details. **Al-Walid Cinema,** on al-Nahda St., screens three films daily and caters to a predominantly male clientele. There's a **swimming pool** at Ramallah First Sarriyeh. It is in lower Ramallah; walk about 25min. along Main St. or take a taxi. (☎995 20 91. Tu women only. NIS15.)

█ NIGHTLIFE

On weekends, many restaurants offer live music (in particular the *oud*, a bass-like Middle Eastern stringed instrument). As comparatively liberal as Ramallah may be, local single women rarely congregate in the evenings unchaperoned; neverthe-less, it is perfectly acceptable for foreign women to go out.

Mocha Rena (☎298 14 60), on Mafad St., off Main St., to the right before Rukab's. The funky, modern atmosphere in this French-Italian cafe attracts a suave, young crowd. One of the few places in Ramallah where you can get a breakfast that doesn't involve salad (pancakes NIS10-18; omelets NIS18). Lunches and dinners run about NIS15-35; a slice of delicious NY-style cheesecake is NIS15. Open daily 9am-midnight.

Cafe Ole (☎298 41 35), on the 2nd fl. of a building on al-Anbyara St., off Main St., a block from Manara Circle. However, there is no food. One of Ramallah's most popular bars, with Thursday night disco parties (cover NIS25, includes 1 beer) and drunken rev-elry all other nights (no cover). Open daily 4pm-midnight, Th until 2am or later.

HEBRON الخليل חברון

Today, Hebron is the most important industrial center in the West Bank. The enclave of about 500 Israelis who live here engenders strong resentment from the Palestinian population; visitors should make their tourist status obvious.

The primary tourist site in Hebron, the half-synagogue, half-mosque **Tomb of the Patriarchs** is thought to lie directly above the underground tombs of Abraham, Isaac, Rebecca, Jacob, and Leah. The tomb of Abraham is visible through bars from both sides; the tombs of Isaac and Rebecca, however, are entirely within the mosque. The cave itself may not be visited but can be seen through an opening in the floor of the mosque, in front of Abraham's tomb. While in the same room, note the huge, oak lectern from which the *imam* delivers the Friday sermon. Added by Salah al-Din in the 12th century, it is one of the few in the world carved from a sin-gle block of wood. In the same room, the longest Herodian cut stone ever discov-ered forms part of the walls. More than 4m in length, it lies in the southeast corner of the room. Lift the carpet to get a glimpse or ask someone to point it out.

Service to Hebron leave frequently from the parking lot across the street from Damascus Gate in Jerusalem (45min., NIS7). From Bethlehem, *service* leave from Bab al-Zaqaq, at the corner of Hebron Rd. and Paul VI Rd. (30min., NIS6). To find a *service* back to Jerusalem or Bethlehem, take the right fork uphill from the center of town. Security has been very tight since the shootings several years ago by a Jewish extremist. All Jews are officially barred from entering the mosque portion of the building, and all entrants are required to present a passport (without a Jew-ish-sounding last name) and pass through several metal detectors. Due to recently rising tensions, tourists are **strongly advised** against visiting Hebron. (Modest dress required. Mosque closed F. Synagogue open M-F; Jews only Sa.)

JORDAN الأردن

JORDANIAN DINAR (JD)

US$1 = JD0.71 (JORDANIAN DINAR)	JD1 = US$1.41
CDN$1 = JD0.46	JD1 = CDN$2.18
UK£1 = JD1.02	JD1 = UK£0.98
IR£1 = JD0.82	JD1 = IR£1.22
AUS$1 = JD0.38	JD1 = AUS$2.66
NZ$1 = JD0.31	JD1 = NZ$3.21
ZAR1 = JD0.085	JD1 = ZAR11.8
EUR€1 = JD0.65	JD1 = EUR€1.55
E£1 (EGYPTIAN POUND) = JD0.17	JD1 = E£5.99
L£100 (LEBANESE POUNDS)= JD0.047	JD1 = L£2130
NIS1 (NEW ISRAELI SHEKEL) = JD0.17	JD1 = NIS5.97
S£100 (SYRIAN POUNDS) = JD1.33	JD1 = S£75.2
TL100,000 (TURKISH LIRA) = JD0.054	JD1 = TL1,850,000

PHONE FACTS | **Country Code: 962. International dialing prefix: 00.**

Take it from the late King Hussein, the world's longest-ruling head of state: "Jordan is a beautiful country: wild, with limitless deserts where the Bedouin roam....The mountains of the north are clothed in green forests, and where the Jordan River flows it is fertile and warm in winter. Jordan has a strange, haunting beauty and a sense of timelessness. Dotted with the ruins of empires once great, it is the last resort of yesterday in the world of tomorrow."

In ancient times, what is now the Hashemite Kingdom of Jordan was where John the Baptist baptized Jesus, desert trade routes flourished during the Roman Empire, and the mysterious Nabatean people carved an entire city into red rock at Petra—all in the course of a few decades. Modern Jordan *(al-Urdun)* now sits in the middle of a rough neighborhood, sandwiched between some of the roughest players: Saudi Arabia, Israel, Syria, and Iraq. The memory of Black September, 1970 (a brutal repression of Palestinian political activity by Jordanian authorities), has not disappeared, nor has the trauma of the Gulf War, in which Jordan supported Saddam Hussein. However, Jordan's former King Hussein (and his wife, US-born and educated Queen Noor) did much to raise morale within the country's borders and raise support outside them. A growing tourism industry has been the key to drawing Jordan into the hearts (and pockets) of outsiders, but despite this growth, most of the country and its sites of interest are largely untouched by the sticky fingers of commercialism. Close your eyes as you wander through Jordan's many natural and man-made wonders—you could be in any century.

▐ HIGHLIGHTS OF JORDAN

HIT the spectacular **Azraq and the Desert Castles** (p. 469) en route to the once-lost Nabatean city of **Petra** (p. 481).

RELAX, the only thing better than the desert beauty of **Wadi Rum** (p. 497) is the hospitality of its Bedouin community. No wonder Lawrence of Arabia stayed so long.

MARVEL at the impressive Roman ruins at **Jerash** (p. 457), also home to the **Jerash Festival,** a summertime musical and cultural extravaganza.

LIFE AND TIMES

Though not quite as chock-full of sights as its neighbors, Lebanon and Syria, two things make Jordan worth the trip: Petra, and the unparalleled hospitality of the Jordanian people.

HISTORY

ANCIENT HISTORY

THE HYKSOS. Sometime in the Middle Bronze Age (around the 18th century BCE), a mysterious martial people known as the **Hyksos** (a Greek bastardization of the Egyptian *hkaw haswt*, "rulers of foreign lands") descended on Egypt and Arabia from the north. Their newfangled horse-drawn chariots and bronze weapons helped them easily conquer the area and permanently change military practices in the region. The identity of these strangers is still up for debate, but most archaeologists agree that they came from the region that is modern-day Jordan.

EGYPTIAN AND GREEK RULE. For all their inventiveness, the Hyksos' rule was short-lived; the Egyptian pharaohs eventually took over, ruling Jordan (along with Palestine and Syria) as one empire called **Canaan.** During the Iron Age, small city-states that developed along trade routes rose into three major kingdoms in Jordan. These kingdoms bickered constantly, both with their Israelite neighbors and among themselves. The arrival of Macedonian superstar **Alexander the Great** in 332 BCE ushered in an age of social and artistic development heavily influenced by Greek culture. The Greeks founded new cities (such as **Gadara,** see p. 465) and renamed others: **Jerash** (p. 457) became Antioch, and **Amman** (p. 441) became Philadelphia. Hellenistic influence lasted through the reign of Alexander's successor **Ptolemy,** invasion by the **Seleucids,** and conquest of the area by the Romans under **Pompey** in 63 BCE.

THE NABATEANS. Before Alexander's conquest, a thriving new civilization had emerged when a nomadic tribe from Arabia known as the **Nabateans** settled in southern Jordan during the 6th century BCE. Their capital was at **Petra** (translation: rock), where they carved buildings, temples, and tombs out of—you guessed it—solid rock. As desert dwellers, the Nabateans were also skilled water engineers who irrigated their land using an extensive system of dams, canals, and reservoirs. Petra became a center of trade routes between Assyria, China, India, Egypt, Syria, Greece, and Rome, and the dialect of Arabic spoken by its inhabitants (rather than the Aramaic that most tribes in the area spoke) helped spread that language around the region. Sometime during the 4th century CE, the Nabateans left their capital at Petra without explanation. Everything from localized famine to alien invasion has been cited as the cause for their exodus.

ROMAN AND BYZANTINE POWER. The departure of the Nabateans inaugurated a period of Roman control that would last until 324 CE. In northern Jordan, the Greek cities of Philadelphia (Amman), Antioch (Jerash), Gadara (**Umm Qeis,** p. 465), **Pella,** and **Irbid** (p. 462) joined with cities in Palestine and southern Syria to form the **Decapolis League,** a confederation of cities linked by economic and cultural bonds. Jerash became the most splendid city in the flourishing League, and one of the greatest cities in all of the Roman provinces, while Pella was a center for Christian refugees fleeing Roman persecution. Under Byzantine control, beginning in the 4th century CE, rural Jordan provided crops and livestock to caravans travelling between the Far East and the Mediterranean. Jordan's cities were noted for their impressive Byzantine mosaics, the most beautiful of which can be found at **Madaba**—including the intricately detailed 6th-century **Map of the Holy Land.** At the same time the Map was crafted, however, Jordan underwent severe depopulation: the plague of 542 CE took the lives of many inhabitants, while many more died as a result of the **Sassanian** invasion of 614 CE.

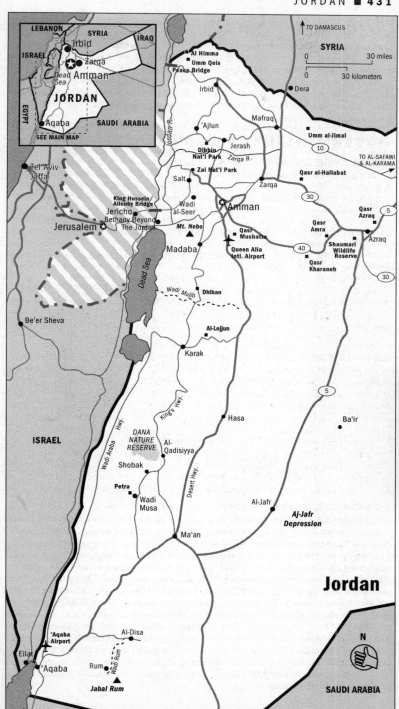

TO DAMASCUS

SYRIA

0   30 miles
0   30 kilometers

LEBANON   SYRIA
                    IRAQ
Irbid
ISRAEL Zarqa
Dead Amman
Sea
JORDAN
           SAUDI ARABIA
Aqaba
SEE MAIN MAP

Al Himma
Umm Qeis
Peace Bridge

Irbid

Dera

'Ajlun
Mafraq

Umm al-Jimal

Jerash

Dibbin
Nat'l Park   Zarqa R.

TO AL-SAFAWI
& AL-KARAMA

10

Qasr al-Hallabat

Jordan R.

Zai Nat'l Park

Salt

Zarqa

30

Qasr
Azraq

Tel Aviv-
Jaffa

King Hussein/
Allenby Bridge

Wadi
al-Seer   Amman

Qasr
Amra

5

Jericho
Bethany Beyond
The Jordan

Qasr Mushatta

Azraq

Jerusalem

Mt. Nebo

Queen Alia
Intl. Airport

Shaumari
Wildlife
Reserve

40

Madaba

Qasr
Kharaneh

30

Dead Sea

Wadi Mujib   Dhiban

Be'er Sheva

Al-Lejjun

Karak

5

ISRAEL

Hasa

Ba'ir

DANA
NATURE
RESERVE

Al-
Qadisiyya

King's Hwy.

Aj-Jafr
Depression

Shobak

Al-Jafr

Petra
Wadi
Musa

Desert Hwy.

Jordan

Ma'an

Wadi Araba Hwy.

'Aqaba
Airport

Al-Disa

N

Eilat
'Aqaba

Rum   Wadi Rum

Jabal Rum

SAUDI ARABIA

THE RISE OF ISLAM. The invading Sassanians paved the way for two centuries of Muslim rule by the **Umayyad** and **Abbasid** dynasties, based in Baghdad and Damascus. European Crusaders hoping to turn back the Islamic tide arrived in Jerusalem in 1099 and built two castles in Jordan—at **Shobak** and **Karak**—to fortify their position. Finally, **Salah al-Din** defeated the Crusaders at Karak in 1187, expelling the Christians from the region and beginning 300 years of **Mamluk** control of Jordan. The Mamluks' rule was followed by the invasion of the **Seljuk Turks** and Jordan's incorporation into the **Ottoman Empire,** which ruled the area until the outbreak of World War I.

MODERN HISTORY (1916-PRESENT)

JORDANIAN INDEPENDENCE. Once the Ottoman Empire had heaved its last breath at the end of World War I (in part because of Arab revolts led by **Lawrence of Arabia**), the League of Nations gave Britain control of Iraq and Palestine (which included modern-day Israel, the West Bank, the Gaza Strip, and Jordan) with the understanding that the Brits would prepare the territories for independence. In 1921, Britain established the area east of the Jordan River as the **Emirate of Transjordan.** A 40th-generation direct descendant of the Prophet Muhammad, **Abdullah,** was set up as emir, and the British-controlled emirate spent most of the period until the end of World War II keeping the peace between local Arabs and immigrant Jews fleeing to Palestine from Europe. After World War II, Great Britain handed the Palestine problem over to the newly formed United Nations, which granted the Hashemite Kingdom of Jordan independence under King Abdullah. After Israel became a state in May 1948 and expelled the invading armies of Jordan and other Arab neighbors, Jordan offered Palestinian refugees full citizenship (the only Arab country to do so)—to the chagrin of most Arab leaders. Jordan formally assumed control of the West Bank, home of many refugees, in 1950.

KING HUSSEIN. Efforts to unite with the Palestinians were cut short in 1951, when Abdullah was assassinated by a Palestinian youth while praying at **al-Aqsa Mosque** in Jerusalem. Abdullah's eldest son, **Talal,** ruled for six months before resigning, and Talal's son **Hussein** (who had also been shot but survived thanks to a well-placed medal) took over the throne just before his 18th birthday. King Hussein ruled until his death 48 years later, making him the longest serving executive head of state in the world. Hussein's moderate political stance (a result of his British education) and two (of four) Western wives (including his widow, **Queen Noor**) made him a favorite of Western leaders. Even domestically he was known as *al-Malik al-Insani* ("The Humane King"), particularly for his reception of Palestinian and (more recently) Kuwaiti refugees. Hussein opened his powerful cabinet to Palestinians and Bedouin, who form the bedrock of the monarchy's support.

JORDAN AND THE PALESTINIANS. The greatest black mark on Hussein's record came in the aftermath of the 1967 war with Israel. Over 400,000 additional Palestinian refugees fled to Jordan, throwing the Jordanian government and the newly-militant Palestinian Liberation Organization (PLO) into a tense relationship: King Hussein wanted to hold peace negotiations with the Israelis, while the Yasser Arafat-led PLO hoped to use Jordan as a base for attacks on Israeli-held territory. After the PLO hijacked several commercial airlines to protest its exclusion from negotiations between Egypt, Jordan, and Israel, Hussein put his foot down. In September 1970 (known to Palestinians as Black September), King Hussein declared war on the PLO, imposing martial law. Clashes between Jordanian and PLO troops took over 3,000 lives. After mediation by the Arab League and the intervention of Egyptian President Gamal 'Abd al-Nasser (shortly before his death), an agreement was forged requiring the PLO to move its headquarters to Lebanon. The break between Jordan and the PLO was completed in 1974, when the PLO was declared the true representative of the Palestinian people by the Arab League and won observer status in the UN.

THE GULF WAR. The crisis in the Persian Gulf that began with Saddam Hussein's August 1990 invasion of Kuwait and ended with the **Gulf War** of 1991 was also bad news for Jordan, as a tide of **pan-Arabism** and resentment of Western power led many Jordanians to support Saddam Hussein. Jordan's refusal to join the US-led anti-Iraq coalition devastated both the nation's economy and its geopolitical clout after the war. Most foreign aid was suspended, and the annual per capita income fell from US$2000 in 1990 to US$1400, where it stands today. Unlike its neighbors, Jordan has neither oil reserves nor abundant natural resources, and is dependent upon Arab and American financial aid to augment its income, which consists largely of the export of phosphates and vegetables grown in the Jordan Valley. The country's main source of income had been money sent home by Jordanians working in the Gulf States, but after the war they were largely replaced by Egyptian workers, who were considered more acceptable by the anti-Iraq coalition.

PEACE WITH ISRAEL. Hussein improved international relations in August 1994, when he and Israeli Prime Minister **Yitzhak Rabin** signed the **Washington Declaration,** ending the state of war between the two countries and opening the border between **Aqaba** (p. 490) and Eilat. The financial lifeline from the West was reestablished, and the US and Great Britain relieved millions of dollars of Jordan's foreign debt. An increase in tourism, heartily encouraged by Hussein and his successor, has given the country a much-needed economic boost.

KING ABDULLAH II. On February 7, 1999, **King Hussein** died of cancer-related health complications. The King's brother, former **Crown Prince Hassan,** was to inherit the throne from Hussein, but shortly before Hussein's death, he relieved Hassan of his duties and promoted his eldest son, 37-year-old **Abdullah,** to the position of Crown Prince. Hussein had criticized Hassan for exercising too much power when Hussein went abroad; Hassan had dismissed Hussein's loyalists in the army and altered some of Jordan's domestic policies. However, many have speculated that Hussein acted out of fear that if Hassan became king, it would be his sons and not Hussein's who would ascend to the throne in later years. Many have also questioned whether the young and relatively inexperienced Abdullah is capable of being king, but his lack of political baggage has been perceived by some as an asset. The Palestinian heritage of his wife, **Queen Rania,** has also made the couple popular with the dueling sectors of Jordan's population.

IN THE NEWS

Since his ascension to the throne, King Abdullah II has visited Syria a number of times to discuss the peace process. Relations between the two countries have improved dramatically since the late Syrian President **Hafez al-Assad** made a surprise attendance at King Hussein's funeral. (Abdullah then showed up at Assad's funeral in 2000, proving the old Yogi Berra saying that you should always go to other people's funerals so that they will go to yours.) Abdullah has also made overtures to Iranian President **Muhammad Khatami,** meeting for the first time in New York in September 2000. Jordan's ties with Iran, severed after the Islamic Revolution there in 1979, were renewed in 1991.

In October 2000, Jordan and the US signed a free trade agreement that was lauded by labor and environmental groups for its protection of workers and of the environment (though US President **George W. Bush** has since backpedaled from some of these provisions). But as Jordan won this economic victory, Israeli-Palestinian violence flared up again, leading many Jordanians to protest US support for Israel and call for end of relations with Israel. In June 2001, Jordan temporarily tightened immigration laws restricting Palestinian immigration from the West Bank. In recent months, Abdullah has come under fire from all sides—some Jordanian traditionalists are upset by his push for globalization, while liberals are disappointed at his focus on the economy at the expense of political reform efforts.

RELIGION AND ETHNICITY

The vast majority of Jordanians are **Sunni Muslims,** though there are communities of Shi'ite Muslims as well. Centuries of Byzantine rule and Crusader occupation have left their mark; Jordan has a sizable **Christian** community (roughly 8% of the population). Most Jordanians are ethnic Arabs (including many Palestinian expatriates), but about 2% of the population are Armenian, Circassian, or Druze.

LANGUAGE

The official language of Jordan is **Arabic,** but the spoken dialect differs from classical Arabic and the variations spoken in Egypt, the Gulf States, and North Africa. Due to decades of British colonial rule, **English** is Jordan's second language, taught at both public and private schools. Most signs are written in both Arabic and English, and Jordan Television's second channel broadcasts subtitled British and American programs as well as some French programs after 8:30pm.

THE ARTS

LITERATURE. The Jordanian region itself has a long tradition of prose: the oldest example of a Semitic script, the 9th century BCE relic known as the **Mesha Stele,** was found in Karak. Jordanian literature does not exist as its own genre as Egyptian or Lebanese literature does, although there are many prolific Jordanian writers. **Diana Abu-Jaber** recently achieved prominence for her first novel, *Arabian Jazz,* which was a finalist for the national PEN/Hemingway award. Many exiled Palestinian authors have written from Jordan, the most famous of whom is **Mahmoud Darwish.** Of Western non-natives writing in and about Jordan, the most famous is the British rabble-rouser T.E. Lawrence, also known as **Lawrence of Arabia.** His *Seven Pillars of Wisdom* contains vivid descriptions of the battles fought and the territory explored during the Arab Revolt of 1916. Even if you don't reach Lawrence's old haunts at **Wadi Rum,** don't miss *Lawrence of Arabia,* the film that won the 1962 Oscar for Best Picture. **Gertrude Bell,** one of the first female Western travelers in the region, writes of her journeys through Jordan and Syria in *The Desert and the Sown* (for more info on Bell's life, see **An Englishwoman in Arabia,** p. 479). The last word in desert mystery is **Agatha Christie's** *Argument with Death,* which introduces readers to the mesmerizing power of Petra (see p. 409).

VISUAL AND PERFORMING ARTS. Both the Jordanian government and private groups have taken measures to promote the **visual arts,** and Jordan's architecture, painting, and sculpture have all developed substantially in the past century. Skillful **weavers** use techniques developed over hundreds of years to make traditional rugs and tapestries out of wool and goat hair. Leather handicrafts, pottery, ceramics, and coral curios are also very common, but **wood-carving** is the Jordanian specialty. Jordanian art often expresses Arab and Muslim identity; recurring themes include traditional Bedouin life and a desire to return to the Palestinian homeland. **Dabke** is a traditional line dance performed to the rhythmic beat of feet pounding on the floor. Two decades ago, Queen Noor founded the annual **Jerash Festival.** The summer festival features diverse international offerings, from Romanian choirs to Indian dance troupes to traditional Arab and Bedouin art. For more information on the Jerash Festival, see p. 457. Jordan's film industry has been at a standstill since the '60s and '70s, when it produced mostly documentaries dealing with the Palestinian-Israeli conflict. Today, Jordan mainly produces television sitcoms. In 1999, the World Bank announced it would help fund a film on Jordan's Hijaz railway, the first feature film made in Jordan since the '70s. Jordanians have a strong oral tradition of storytelling and ballad singing. For a taste of traditional folk music, eavesdrop on a wedding—and listen for the women's shouts and ululations (*ha-WEEE-ha!*), known as **zaghroutah.**

SUGAR AND SPICE Jordan has long been a safe haven and cultural breeding ground for Syrian and Palestinian refugees. Nevertheless, immigrant kitchens guarded their native dessert recipes like the secret formula for Coke—that is, until the **Jabri** and **Habiba** pastry chains came onto the scene around 1950. Jabri introduced Damascene **ba'laweh**, while Habiba hooked the country on **kinafeh** from the Palestinian villages of Nablus. Half a century later, the Jordanian sweet tooth can only be satisfied by the honey-coated, nut-filled pockets of filo-dough joy that have become an inseparable part of the country's more established traditions.

FOOD AND DRINK

Jordanian cuisine has evolved through centuries of Bedouin and Palestinian cooking. The national dish is **mensaf**, and its main ingredients appear in most other Jordanian dishes. *Mensaf* consists of rice on a large tray of flat bread, topped with pine nuts, an entire lamb or goat, and a tangy yogurt-based sauce known as *jamid*. It is eaten from a communal dish while standing: the right hand is used to ball the rice while the left hand holds the flat bread which is used to pull off chunks of meat and dip them into the warm sauce. The Bedouin serve the head of the lamb on top, reserving the prize delicacies (tongue and eyes) for speechless guests.

A combination of hummus, cheese, honey, jam, bread, and sometimes *fuul* (beans) form a standard breakfast. Traditional dinners are served around 2 or 3pm; popular dishes include *musakhan* (chicken baked with olive oil, onions, and spices, served on bread) and *mahshi* (a tray of vine leaves, squash, or eggplant stuffed with mincemeat, rice, and onions). Supper is usually smaller and lighter. A staple at any time of the day is *za'tar*, a sauce of thyme mixed with sesame seeds and spices, eaten either by dipping the bread into olive oil and then into the mix, or pizza-style (*mana'eesh*).

Drink bottled water (300fils, more at restaurants and tourist haunts) or use iodine tablets. Coffee and tea are expressions of Jordanian hospitality, and tourists are likely to be offered refreshment many times a day. If a hot drink doesn't tickle your fancy, ask for *barid* (Arabic for "cold"). Jordanians drink tremendous amounts of tea *(shay)*, almost always made with mint *(na'na')*. According to stereotypes, *fellaheen* (peasants) drink their tea syrupy sweet; restaurants will assume you do too unless you prove your gentility by asking for *sukkar aleel* (just a little sugar). A cup of the thick, black, bittersweet Arabic coffee (*ahwa*) is stronger than espresso. Islam prohibits drinking **alcohol,** so imbibing in Jordan is subject to some restrictions and social conventions. Anyone who looks older than 16 may buy at a liquor store (usually owned by Christians). Locally brewed Amstel is the most popular alcoholic drink (600fils); imports are also available. 'Araq is a popular aniseed hard alcohol (similar to the Greek *ouzo* and Turkish *raki*) that is mixed with water until it turns cloudy and white.

FACTS AND FIGURES

OFFICIAL NAME: Hashemite Kingdom of Jordan

GOVERNMENT: Constitutional monarchy

CAPITAL: Amman

LAND AREA: 91,860 sq. km.

GEOGRAPHY: Arid plateau; the Great Rift Valley (Jordan Valley and Dead Sea) runs to the West

MAJOR CITIES: Amman, Jerash, Aqaba, Karak

CLIMATE: Dry, hot summers with occasional dust storms; wet, cool winters; hottest in Aug., coolest in Jan.

POPULATION: 4.5 million; 0-14 yrs 43%

LANGUAGE: Arabic

RELIGIONS: Muslim (92%), Christian (8%)

GNP PER CAPITA: US$1650

MAJOR EXPORTS: Phosphates, fertilizers, potash, agricultural products

ESSENTIALS

DOCUMENTS AND FORMALITIES

CONSULAR SERVICES ABROAD

Jordanian embassies and consulates abroad include:

Australia Embassy: 20 Roebuck St., Red Hill ACT 2603, Canberra (☎02 295 99 51, 2950 5663; fax 239 7236).

Canada Embassy: 100 Bronson Ave. #701, Ottawa, ON K1R 6G8 (☎613-238-8090; fax 232-3341).

South Africa Embassy: 209 Festival St., Hatfield, P.O. Box 14730, Hatfield, 0028, Pretoria (☎12 342 80 26 or 342 80 27; fax 12 342 78 47; embjord@embjord.co.za; www.embjord.co.za).

UK Embassy: 6 Upper Philimore Gardens, London W8 7HB (☎020 7937 3685; fax 937 8795).

US Embassy: 3504 International Dr. NW, Washington, D.C. 20008 (☎202-966-2664; fax 966-3110; www.jordanembassyus.org). **Consulate:** 866 2nd Ave., 4th fl., New York, NY 10017 (☎212-832-0119; fax 832-5346).

CONSULAR SERVICES IN JORDAN

Embassies and consulates of other countries in Jordan include:

Australian Embassy: (☎962 673 246; fax 673 260; ausemb@nets.com.jo), on Zahran St. between 4th and 5th Circles, Amman.

Canadian Embassy: (☎06 666 124; fax 689 227; www.cns.com.jo/directory/embassy/canada/index.htm), P.O. Box 815213, Shmeisani, Amman.

New Zealand Consulate: 4th fl., Khalaf Building, 99 al-Malek al-Hussein St. (☎06 462 51 49), Amman.

UK Embassy: (☎06 592 3100; fax 592 3759; www.britain.org.jo), P.O. Box 87, Abdoun, Amman.

US Embassy: (☎06 592 0101; fax 592 0121; rjaradat@usembassy-amman.org.jo; www.usembassy-amman.org.jo), P.O. Box 354, Abdoun, Amman.

ENTRY REQUIREMENTS

Visas can be obtained at Amman's Queen Alia International Airport and are valid for one month but renewable at any police station (US$44). Visas may also be obtained in person or by mail from any Jordanian embassy or consulate (takes up to five days). Requirements include a passport (valid for at least six months), a completed application form with one photo, and a self-addressed, stamped envelope. A group visa can be issued for tours of five or more.

BORDER CROSSINGS

Getting a visa to enter Jordan is a breeze, as the government issues visas at all international border crossings (except King Hussein/Allenby Bridge). There are three separate **departure taxes:** JD4 for departure by land (except for travel to the West Bank), JD6 by sea (from Aqaba), and JD10 by air (does not apply to transit travelers in Jordan less than 72hr.).

TO EGYPT. A ferry shuttles between Aqaba and Nuweiba. There is a slow ferry (3½hr. or more, noon, JD6), and a faster, less crowded, and more punctual **speedboat** (1hr., noon, JD20 plus JD4 departure tax). Tickets can be purchased at any travel agency in Aqaba; be sure to show up a few hours before departure. You can get a free **Sinai-only visa** if you only plan to visit the Sinai; otherwise, you'll need an

Egyptian visa (two-week or one-month), which can be obtained in one day at the Egyptian Consulate in Aqaba for JD12 (see p. 490). Visas can also be obtained on board the ferry for an extra charge, or you can risk it and wait to obtain a tourist visa upon arrival in Nuweiba.

TO IRAQ. There are two JETT buses from Amman to Baghdad (14hr., 8:30am and 2pm, JD12). Citizens of Western countries are unlikely to be granted Iraqi visas.

TO ISRAEL. There are three border crossing points between Israel and Jordan. There is no entrance fee into Israel and **free visas** are given at the border, though most Western citizens do not need visas (see **Israel: Entry,** p. 416). However, a **departure tax** is required if crossing in either direction. The simple crossing between **Aqaba** and **Eilat** should take less than 1hr.; take a taxi from Aqaba to the border (JD4), then walk the 1km no-man's land between the two countries (there's no transport). Once over the border, Israeli authorities will call you a taxi into Eilat (NIS15-20). There is no bus service on either side of the border. Though it is more of a hassle, travelers coming from Amman can cross the **King Hussein Bridge** (*Jisr Sheikh Hussein;* called Allenby Bridge on the Israeli side) to just outside of Jericho, from which buses and *service* frequently run for Jerusalem. There is a third border crossing in northern Jordan, at the **Peace Bridge,** which goes to the Israeli town of Beit She'an in Galilee. (Bridge open Su-Th 8am-7pm, F 8am-noon.)

TO SAUDI ARABIA. The crossing points between Jordan and Saudi Arabia are on the coast of the Gulf of Aqaba at al-Durra and farther east at al-Mudawwara. JETT and SAPTCO buses (JD31) run from Amman to: **Jeddah** (10am), **Dammam** (11am), and **Riyadh** (11:30am). The hardest part about traveling to Saudi Arabia is getting a **visa;** tourists can only register for transit visas, which sometimes let you travel along the Trans-Arabia Pipeline but usually only allow for one day in Riyadh.

TO SYRIA. The official road to Syria runs through the town of **Dera.** Daily buses and *service* run from Amman to **Damascus** and **Aleppo.** Although *service* are faster (and more expensive) than the buses (2-3hr., JD5), they are usually detained longer at the border, meaning *service* travelers may end up spending more money for a trip that takes just as long as the cheaper bus route. The painfully slow **Hijazi** railway chugs between Amman's Abdali Bus Station and Damascus (9hr.; to Damascus M 8am, to Amman Su 7:30am; US$3.50).

TO THE WEST BANK. The **King Hussein/Allenby Bridge** between Amman and the West Bank is a very popular (and crowded) option. (Border open Su-Th 8am-10:30pm, F-Sa 8am-1pm.) Visas are not issued at this border, but most Western citizens do not need a visa to enter the West Bank. Take a JETT bus (45min., 6:30am, JD6) from either station in Amman or a minibus or *service* (45min., JD1.5) from Abdali Bus Station.

GETTING AROUND

BY PLANE. There are three airports in Jordan: Queen Alia International Airport and Amman-Marka International Airport in Amman, and Aqaba International Airport. Flights between Amman and Aqaba take 50min. and cost approximately US$84 round-trip.

BY LOCAL TRANSPORTATION. Camel caravan trips can be arranged in Wadi Rum. Horse and camel rides through Petra are also available.

BY TAXI. Private taxis are yellow and have "taxi" written on them. They are most useful (and crowded) in Amman. Insist that drivers use the meter; the starting fare is 150fils. Women should always sit in the back seat, whether or not there are other passengers; men should always sit in the front when alone. It's rude to give exact change; drivers expect you to round up from the meter fare. Public taxis or **service** (ser-VEES) are usually white or gray Mercedes with a white sign written in

JORDAN

Arabic on the roof (سقف). The front doors display the fixed route and number (in Arabic numerals only). *Service* travel set routes in Amman and between the central terminals of larger cities. Schedules are unpredictable—*service* leave when full but can be hailed en route.

BY MINIBUS. Although minibus schedules are somewhat disorganized and inconsistent, minibuses are such a popular form of transportation that there is almost always one going your way. They are not as fast as taxis, but they may be more comfortable than the often crowded and claustrophobic *service*, and they are cheaper. Minibus travel is also a great way to meet friendly Jordanians; just be sure to know the name of your destination in Arabic and have small denominations of money to pay the fare, as drivers won't be able (or won't want) to make change for a bill more than 10 times the fare. Hail a bus en route by extending your right hand, palm down. Western men should not sit next to Jordanian women when other seats are available.

BY BUS. The government owns a monopoly on intercity bus service, so the **Jordan Express Tourist Transport (JETT)** is the only option. However infrequently, these buses cover the most popular routes, including daily trips from Amman to Aqaba, Petra, Ma'an, the King Hussein/Allenby Bridge, Damascus, and Cairo via Aqaba. Bus fares are slightly lower than *service* rates, but buses are slower and their routes sometimes confusing. The air-conditioned JETT luxury coaches cost 20% more than regular buses; those from Amman to Aqaba come with hosts, professional wrestling videos, and screeching Egyptian movies. Booking ahead is often necessary. In Amman, most buses follow the pattern of *service*, with traffic to the north leaving from Abdali Station and buses to the south from Wahdat Station.

BY CAR. For groups of four to six, renting a car (in Amman or Aqaba only) can be an affordable and efficient way to reach less accessible sights. The beautiful King's Highway route, barely served by other modes of transportation, can be toured by private car in a full day. Desert heat and police regulations require fire extinguishers in cars. **Four-wheel-drives** (4WDs) are only needed to reach Wadi Rum. The law requires **seatbelts** (JD5 fine for those flying unfettered). Unless you are a lunatic, do not try to drive within the city of Amman.

BY THUMB. Hitchhiking is very difficult during the major holidays. At other times, it is possible, though groups of females will never pick up male hitchhikers. You should offer a small amount of money to the driver, but less than the cost of bus fare. Hitchhiking is dangerous, however, and *Let's Go* does not recommend it.

TOURIST SERVICES AND MONEY

TOURIST OFFICES. In Amman, try the Ministry of Tourism and Antiquities (☎06 464 23 11 or 06 464 23 14) to collect a map, some glossy pamphlets, and fact sheets about the country. There's also a branch at Amman's Queen Alia Airport (☎06 445 12 56). In Jerash, the office is near South Gate (☎04 45 12 72); in Petra, it's at the entrance of the site (☎03 33 60 20).

CURRENCY AND EXCHANGE. The Jordanian dinar (JD) is a decimal currency, divided into 1000 fils. Notes come in denominations of JD20, 10, 5, and 1, and 500 fils. Coins are in denominations of 500, 250, 100, 50, 25, 20, 10, 5 and 1 fils. Prices are always labeled in fils, but the usual spoken practice is to call 10fils a piaster (pt, also called a *qirsh*). Prices are written in Arabic numerals, although the currency itself is marked with Western-friendly numbers.

Bank exchange hours are regularly 8:30am to 12:30pm, with some banks opening from 3:30pm to 5:30pm as well. Hours during Ramadan are 8:30am to 10am, although some banks open in the afternoon. All banks are closed on Friday. There are many branches of the national **Housing Bank** *(Bank al-Iskan)* outside Amman; there are also exchange offices in many of the *souqs*. Queen Alia International Airport has exchange facilities for incoming passengers. A passport is required to change traveler's checks. **Traveler's checks** may be exchanged for a hefty commission at most banks and exchange offices. **Credit cards** are only accepted in expensive hotels. **ATMs** work for local and international bank cards.

PRICES. Jordanian prices are generally very low; JD20 (US$28) should easily cover a day's budget travel.

TIPPING. A tip of 10% is expected in restaurants, unless "service included" appears on the menu; servers at fancier establishments expect a little something even if service is included. Taxi drivers do not expect tips but will round off fares to their advantage. Members of large sightseeing groups tip the bus driver about 500fils. A small tip (500fils) to room cleaners and porters in hotels is appropriate.

BUSINESS HOURS. All businesses close on Friday. Most stores and offices are open from 8 or 9am until 1pm, then reopen around 3 or 4pm. In the larger cities, the stores may remain open all afternoon. In Amman, retail stores close at 8 or 9pm. Banks and government offices retain only a skeleton crew in the afternoon.

HEALTH AND SAFETY

EMERGENCY	**Police:** ☎191 or 192. **Ambulance:** ☎193.

MEDICAL EMERGENCIES AND HEALTH. Health care is quite good in Jordan, and the World Health Organization's figures show that even in the mid-1980s, safe water and adequate sanitary facilities were accessible to 100% of the urban population and 95% of the rural population. Most doctors speak English, and pharmacies have a wide selection of medicines and other pharmaceutical products, including condoms. No vaccinations are necessary for entry into Jordan, except for those arriving from countries infected with yellow fever or cholera, but consider getting vaccinated for hepatitis, tetanus, and typhoid. Drink bottled water rather than tap water for the first few days until your system adjusts. Top-class hotels often have their own filtering systems, so their tap water is safe for drinking. Remember to wash all fruits and vegetables before eating them and be wary of food that has been sitting out, especially in the summer.

WOMEN TRAVELERS. Jordan is a modernized country, and women will generally feel quite comfortable, although harassment is not uncommon (just ignore it). Women should dress conservatively, as those dressed inappropriately will be punished with higher prices from offended merchants and possibly even pinches. For more tips, see **Women Travelers,** p. 39.

MINORITY TRAVELERS. No matter what color you are, if you're clearly not Jordanian, you can expect some staring. Jordanians tend to assume that all black people are Sudanese and therefore speak Arabic. Likewise, it is assumed that all Asians are Japanese tourists. Latinos usually blend in and will probably be left alone.

BGLT TRAVELERS. Jordan does not condone homosexual behavior. Be careful how you act in public.

ACCOMMODATIONS AND CAMPING

HOTELS. Regulated tourist hotels charge prices as high as Jordan's mid-summer temperatures. Bargaining is difficult, but hotel owners may be more flexible in the off-season winter months. Fall and spring are the busiest times, though sunny Aqaba sees the most activity during the winter and spring. Single women may feel uncomfortable at cheaper hotels and may not be admitted. Jordanian law bars unmarried couples from sharing a room; for foreign travelers, a "don't ask, don't tell" policy seems to be the norm. Most budget hotels do not abide by government

JORDAN

prices; "official" prices are listed in Arabic and cheaper ones in English. Most hotels add a 10% service charge; ask whether it's included in the price. Hotel owners may ask to hold your passport for the length of your stay, but they will return it after a night if you need to change money.

CAMPING. Camping is an option at government-approved sites, though facilities are virtually nonexistent. Approved areas include the beach north of Aqaba, Dibbin National Park, and the Dana Wildlands Campsite. Camping is allowed next to most government **Rest Houses** (free or JD1-2 per person per night, plus 10% tax). You'll need a sleeping bag or blanket for cool summer nights; winter evenings can bring freezing temperatures. You can also spend the night in a **Bedouin camp** on the outskirts of most towns and scattered around the desert. Tea, Arabic coffee, and meals are always included in an invitation, though showers and toilets are rare. While the Bedouin won't accept money, a pack of cigarettes is always appreciated.

KEEPING IN TOUCH

MAIL. Most post offices have **Poste Restante.** American Express offices (Amman and Aqaba) also hold mail. **Airmail letters** to North America cost 400fils, aerogrammes or postcards 300fils (to Europe 300fils/200fils). Airmail from Jordan gets to North America in five to seven days (quicker to Europe), if you're lucky. Make it clear that you want to send a letter airmail (and write "Airmail/*par avion*" on the envelope) or it may be sent via incredibly slow surface mail. Post office opening hours are Saturday to Thursday from 8am to 6pm. All are closed on Friday, except for the downtown post office on Prince Muhammad St. in Amman. International **Express Mail Service (EMS)** is available in major post offices and costs less than Western companies like DHL and FedEx.

TELEGRAMS. Telegrams may be sent from the Central Telegraph Office at the post office in 1st Circle, Jabal Amman or from major hotels and post offices.

TELEPHONE AND INTERNET ACCESS. Although the telephone system was recently revamped, international lines are often overloaded, especially around holidays. **Phone cards** have made a welcome appearance and are probably the easiest way to make both local and international calls; **no collect calls** can be made except from a private phone. **Calling card** calls can only be placed from private phones. You can make **international calls** from telephone offices (JD6.6 per 3min. to the US) or luxury hotels (fast but expensive). Use a private phone and reimburse the owner (to US, Europe, or Australia JD1.83-2.2 per min.; 30% less 10pm-8am). **International operator:** ☎0132. **Information:** ☎121. In most major cities, almost every place—from the hostel to the supermarket—is wired to the Internet, often at a cheaper rate (JD1-1.5) than cybercafes.

CUSTOMS AND ETIQUETTE

Jordan is socially conservative by Western standards, making modest dress a necessity for both sexes. Neither sex can wear shorts (except in hedonistic Aqaba), and women's skirts should be ankle-length. Shirts should cover the shoulders and upper arms. Sandals that expose feet are acceptable. Amman slackens its dress code at night and by the pool.

Jordanians have a very strong hospitality ethic. Bedouin invitations to coffee or tea should be strongly considered, as declining an invitation is often interpreted as a direct insult. If you choose to reject an offer, be calm and firm and repeat yourself until the point sinks in. Lone women should never accept an invitation from a single man. Most people who offer to help you, feed you, or take you somewhere are probably not con artists; they often represent the best of a culture that is serious about kindness to visitors.

AMMAN عمان ☎ 06

Noisy, crowded, and cosmopolitan, Amman thrives on its mix of modern business and traditional culture. The sidewalks in Amman are as packed with people as its streets are with cars, and the entire frenetic scene grooves to the beat of the popular Arabic music pouring out from downtown storefronts. When the sun goes down and the lights come up, the jasmine-scented streets provide the perfect setting for lazy summertime strolls through the city's seven hills. Hospitality is also a way of life in Amman; the greetings you hear are quite sincere, and chances are a "welcome" will lead to a cup of tea and a conversation. Seasoned globetrotters agree—travelers are welcome in Amman as in few places on earth.

Though it was the Ammonite capital in Biblical times, modern-day Amman was a mere village in the decades preceding 1948, when its population of 6000 could have easily fit inside the city's Roman Theater (see p. 452). Following the Arab-Israeli wars of 1948 and 1967, however, many Palestinians took refuge here, and Amman's population swelled exponentially. Descendants of these Palestinians now make up about 70% of Jordan's population. Some Palestinians are highly successful doctors, businessmen, bankers, and politicians, but many still live in Amman's huge refugee camps, much like their fathers and grandfathers did in Palestine. Egyptian and Southeast Asian workers also make up a large portion of the city's population, and after the Gulf War in 1991, they were joined by immigrants from Iraq and Kuwait. Today, Amman's more than 1.7 million inhabitants make up roughly one-third of Jordan's total population.

Amman's central location makes it the country's principal transportation hub and the base for exploring Jordan's other sights. The ruins at Jerash and Ajloun are just over 1hr. north, the Dead Sea is 1hr. west, Petra is 3hr. south, and the Desert Castles lie scattered to the east.

✈ INTERCITY TRANSPORTATION

FLIGHTS

Queen Alia International Airport (☎ 445 32 00, Royal Jordanian ☎ 445 33 33), 35km south of Amman. **24hr. buses** connect Abdali Bus Station and the airport (45min.; every 30min. 6am-10pm, every 2hr. 10pm-6am; JD1.5). Private **taxi** to the airport JD10, at night JD12; two pieces of luggage free, additional pieces 200fils. *Service* do not run to the airport. 24hr. banks and a tourist office (open daily 9am-2pm) in the airport. There is an **exit fee** of JD10 when leaving Jordan.

BUSES

Abdali Station, on King Hussein St. at Jabal al-Weibdeh. Minibuses to: **Ajloun** (500fils); **Irbid** (700fils); **Jerash** (350fils); **King Hussein/Allenby Bridge** (JD1.5); **Salt** (175fils).

Hashemi St. Station (also called **Raghadban Station** or **Interchange**), near the Roman Theater, launches northeast traffic to **Mafraq, Zarqa,** and points **east of Irbid.**

JETT Bus Station (☎ 566 41 46; fax 560 50 05) has two offices on King Hussein St., past Abdali Bus Station and opposite Army Headquarters. Both open daily 6am-9pm. Spacious, A/C buses to: **Aqaba** (4hr., 6 per day, JD4); **Beirut** (6hr., Su and Th 9am, JD15); **Cairo** (20-24hr.; Su, M, Tu, Th 6:30am; JD35); **Damascus** (4-5hr., 7am and 3pm, JD4.5, visa required); **King Hussein/Allenby Bridge** (1hr., 6:30am, JD6); **Petra** (3½hr.; Su, Tu, F 6:30am; JD5.5 round-trip JD11; admission to Petra paid at site JD20). Reserve one day in advance.

Wahdat Station, several kilometers from downtown Amman, just north of the Wahdat Refugee Camp, controls traffic to and from the south, sending slightly cheaper (read: non-A/C) buses to **Aqaba** (JD3). Buses also run to: **Karak, Ma'an, Madaba, Musa, Petra,** and **Wadi.**

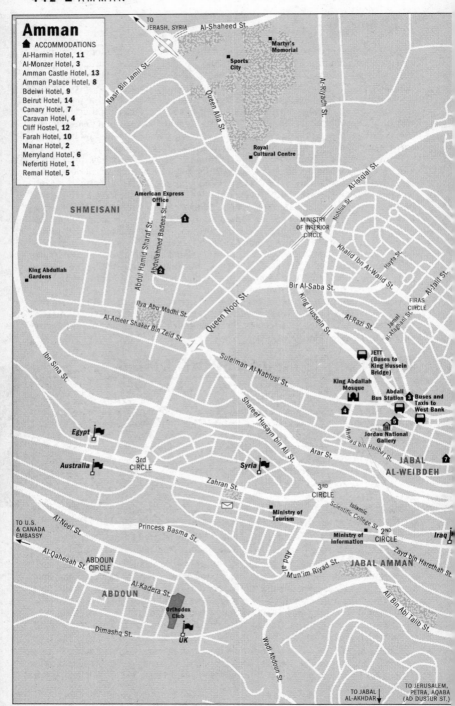

Amman

🏠 ACCOMMODATIONS

Al-Harmin Hotel, **11**
Al-Monzer Hotel, **3**
Amman Castle Hotel, **13**
Amman Palace Hotel, **8**
Bdeiwi Hotel, **9**
Beirut Hotel, **14**
Canary Hotel, **7**
Caravan Hotel, **4**
Cliff Hostel, **12**
Farah Hotel, **10**
Manar Hotel, **2**
Merryland Hotel, **6**
Nefertiti Hotel, **1**
Remal Hotel, **5**

TO
JERASH, SYRIA

Al-Shaheed St.

Martyr's
Memorial

Sports
City

Nasir Bin Jamil St.

Queen Alia St.

Ar-Riyadh St.

Royal
Cultural Centre

Al-Istqlal St.

American Express
Office

SHMEISANI

MINISTRY
OF INTERIOR
CIRCLE

Nablus St.

Abdul Hamid Sharaf St.

Abdulahmed Badees St.

King Abdullah
Gardens

Khalid Ibn Al-Walid St.

Hayfa St.

Al-Jalil St.

Ilya Abu Madhi St.

Bir Al-Saba St.

FIRAS
CIRCLE

Al-Ameer Shaker Bin Zeid St.

Queen Noor St.

King Hussein St.

Al-Razi St.

Jamal al-Afghani St.

Ibn Sina St.

Suleiman Al-Nablusi St.

JETT
(Buses to
King Hussein
Bridge)

Shareef Husayn bin Ali St.

King Abdallah
Mosque

Abdali
Bus Station

Buses and
Taxis to
West Bank

Egypt

Ahmad bin Hanbal St.

Jordan National
Gallery

JABAL
AL-WEIBDEH

Australia

3rd
CIRCLE

Syria

Arar St.

Zahran St.

3RD
CIRCLE

Al-Neel St.

Islamic
Scientific College St.

Ministry of
Tourism

Ministry of
Information

2ND
CIRCLE

Iraq

TO U.S.
& CANADA
EMBASSY

Princess Basma St.

Abu al-Mun'im Riyad St.

Zayd bin Harethah St.

JABAL AMMAN

Al-Qahesah St.

ABDOUN
CIRCLE

ABDOUN

Al-Kadera St.

Ali Bin Abi Talib St.

Orthodox
Club

Dimashq St.

UK

Wadi Abdoun St.

TO JABAL
AL-AKHDAR

TO JERUSALEM,
PETRA, AQABA
(AD DUSTUR ST.)

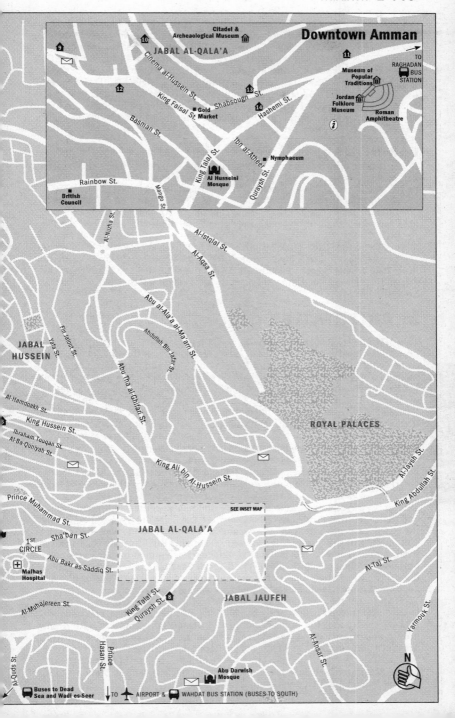

Downtown Amman

Citadel & Archaeological Museum

JABAL AL-QALA'A

Cinema al-Hussein St.

King Faisal St.

Shabsough St.

Hashemi St.

Gold Market

Basman St.

Ibn al-Atheer

King Talal St.

Quraysh St.

Nymphaeum

Al Husseini Mosque

Mango St.

Rainbow St.

British Council

Museum of Popular Traditions

TO RAGHADAN BUS STATION

Jordan Folklore Museum

Roman Amphitheatre

Al-Istqlal St.

Al-Nuzha St.

Al-Aqsa St.

Abu al-Ala a al-Ma'arri St.

Abdullah Bin Jafar St.

Abu Tha al-Ghifari St.

JABAL HUSSEIN

Yafa St.

Fin Jaraur St.

Al-Hamdoakh St.

King Hussein St.

Ibraham Touqan St.

Al-Ba-Quniyah St.

ROYAL PALACES

Al-Jaysh St.

King Ali bin Al-Hussein St.

King Abdullah St.

Prince Muhammad St.

SEE INSET MAP

JABAL AL-QALA'A

1ST CIRCLE

Sha'ban St.

Abu Bakr as-Saddiq St.

Malhas Hospital

Al-Taj St.

Al-Muhajereen St.

King Talal St.

Quraysh St.

JABAL JAUFEH

Al-Quds St.

Prince Hasan St.

Abu Darwish Mosque

Al-Ansar St.

Yarmouk St.

N

Buses to Dead Sea and Wadi es-Seer

TO AIRPORT & WAHDAT BUS STATION (BUSES TO SOUTH)

SERVICE

Intercity *service* leave from the same stations as buses and go to the same regions, but tend to be 40-50% more expensive. From **Abdali Bus Station,** *service* go to: **Ajloun** (775fils); **Irbid** (900fils); **Jerash** (500fils); **King Hussein/Allenby Bridge** (JD2); **Salt** (375fils). From **Wahdat Bus Station,** *service* go to: **Aqaba** (JD6); **Karak** via the King's Highway (JD1.5); **Ma'an** via the newer Desert Highway (JD3.5); **Madaba** (500fils); **Petra** (JD4). All prices, bus and *service* alike, are government-regulated, but regulations are not always observed and travelers will occasionally be approached by unaffiliated "tourist" drivers offering widely varying rates; ask around to find the lowest price.

CAR RENTAL

Prices depend on which cars are available, so the best deals come with flexibility and calling around a few days in advance. **Reliable Rent-a-Car** (☎ 592 96 76), **Avis** (☎ 569 94 20; fax 469 48 83), **Hertz** (☎ 553 89 58), and **Budget** (☎ 569 81 31; fax 567 33 12) all offer small sedans with automatic transmission, unlimited mileage, and air-conditioning for as low as JD25 per day, but only if you can find such a car available for your dates—otherwise, prices increase significantly. Check out **Firas** (☎ 467 29 27; fax 461 68 74), at 1st Circle and Shmeisani, which has small cars and a 200km limit for JD18. A CDW (Collision Damage Waiver) is available for around JD7 per day, and protects drivers from a JD300 deductible in the event of an accident. **Valid driver's license** and **passport** always required. Reserve in advance. Drivers under 21 may have more luck with local agencies than with corporate heavyweights.

✴ ORIENTATION

Take advantage of Amman's summits to get a perspective on this roller-coaster city. Rocky **Jabal al-Qala'a** ("Fortress Hill"), also known as the Citadel, where the Archaeological Museum sits amid Roman and Umayyad ruins, provides a panoramic view of tall buildings, mosques, and ruins, all of which serve as useful landmarks. The government has installed some street signs in downtown Amman, and most have English translations. Although most people know **King Faisal St.** and **Hashimi St.,** other inquiries are likely to produce blank stares. Successful navigation of Amman means knowing its landmarks. Try to find out which numbered circle your destination is near and you'll have an easier time finding your way.

Amman's downtown district, **al-Balad,** is neatly framed by the city's seven hills and is the best location from which to orient yourself. Al-Balad has three major landmarks: **al-Husseini Mosque (Masjid Malik Hussein),** the **Roman Theater,** and the **Central Post Office** *(maktab al-bareed).* Amman's eight **numbered traffic circles** follow a line leading westward out of town and through **Jabal Amman** on Zahran St. Beyond 3rd Circle (Amman's diplomatic center and home of most embassies), traffic circles have been replaced by busy intersections. Although the city is earnestly attempting to rename these intersections "squares," each is still fondly called a "circle," or *duwwar.* Following King Hussein St. northwest from the city center leads to **Jabal al-Weibdeh,** a tree-lined middle-class neighborhood perched on a hill. The **JETT** and **Abdali Bus Stations** are in this neighborhood. The blue dome and octagonal minaret of the Jabal's enormous **King Abdullah Mosque (Masjid Malik Abdullah)** are visible from all surrounding heights. To the north of the city lies **Jabal Hussein,** a largely residential district. This area is bordered to the northwest by the Ministry of Interior Circle *(Duwwar al-Dakhiliyyeh)* and the modern suburb of **Shmeisani,** complete with luxury hotels and American-style fast food restaurants. **Abdoun** and **Sweifiyyeh,** Amman's other hotbeds of Western-style decadence, lie west of al-Balad. To the southeast of the city, in the direction of the airport, rises **Jabal al-Ashrafiyyeh.** Its ornate **Abu Darwish Mosque** can be seen above the **Wahdat Bus Station** and the Wahdat Palestinian Refugee Camp.

▐ LOCAL TRANSPORTATION

To reach locations within the city or to find the departure point for **buses** and **service,** ask a downtown shopkeeper; be sure to know the name of your destination in Arabic, have someone write it down for you, or point to its Arabic name as printed in this book. You can flag buses and *service* anywhere along their routes, though *service* are often full (they take five passengers) from the beginning to the end of their pre-scribed courses. Public transportation stops at 8 or 9pm (a couple of hours earlier on Fridays). Walking is a safe alternative. Metered **taxis** prowl the streets and incessantly honk their horns at potential passengers. Make sure the driver is familiar with your destination before getting in, and then check that the meter is running. After 11pm, taxi drivers expect about double the daytime fare. It is an Arab custom for men to ride in the front seat of taxis. To avoid glares, women should always ride in the back seat.

BUSES

Buses traveling within Amman cost about 100fils, or a little more if heading for the suburbs. Flag any bus traveling in your direction and ask the driver if it stops where you want to go, or find out at any bus station. Pay the fare after the ride has begun. Drivers and their assistants don't like making change, and you don't want them trying to do so while maniacally driving 100km/hr anyway, so carry 100fils in change with you. Most buses have the name of their destination written in Arabic on the front, sides, or both. Some have numbers, but since buses going on different routes may display the same number, what worked one time may not the next. Asking around is the best way to find a bus.

SERVICE

Although it may cost a bit more, transportation by *service*, or white taxi, is much easier on the nerves than bus travel and offers frequent opportunities to meet Jordanians. *Service* routes are clear and comprehensive, with their numbers and the names of their routes listed on the doors in Arabic. All routes within the city originate downtown. Stopping a *service* en route is difficult—many drive at breakneck speed, so make yourself visible without stepping into the street, and then stick out your arm with the palm down. Popular routes include:

#1 (١): On Jabal Amman, from Center City through 1st–3rd Circles (100fils).

#2 (٢): From Basman St. (behind Cliff Hostel) along Jabal Amman to Malik 'Abd Ribiya St. and between 2nd and 3rd Circles (90fils).

#3 (٣): From Basman St. along Jabal Amman to 3rd and 4th Circles (100fils).

#4 (٤): From Omar al-Khayyam St. (the street running alongside and behind downtown post office) to al-Amaneh Circle and gardens, passing near all points of interest on Jabal al-Weibdeh (90fils).

#6 (٦): From Cinema al-Hussein St. (a.k.a. Malik Ghazi St.), along King Faisal and King Hussein St. to Ministry of Interior Circle, passing Abdali and JETT bus stations (100fils).

#6a (٠٦): From Cinema al-Hussein St. to Shmeisani near the Ambassador Hotel (110fils).

#7 (٧): From Cinema al-Hussein St. past Abdali to Shmeisani near Arab Bank (70fils).

Service and **minibuses** to Wahdat Bus Station start at Kureisha St. (or *Sakfi Seil*) near Petra Bank and pass near Abu Darwish Mosque on Jabal Ashrafiyyeh. *Service* directly to Wahdat Station from Abdali cost 120fils. Another route starts at Shabsough St. near the gold *souq* downtown, passing Abdali Bus Station and Jabal Hussein to Ministry of Interior Circle (90fils). Some prices are higher or lower than those listed, but drivers rarely cheat passengers, even tourists. Be wary of *service* drivers who "misinterpret" your directions to mean you want to hire the *service* as a private taxi. This usually only happens if you catch the *service* at the beginning of the route, but you can prevent it by insisting on waiting for other passengers, or by simply and firmly handing the correct fare (generally 100fils) to the driver.

🔢 PRACTICAL INFORMATION

TOURIST AND FINANCIAL SERVICES

Ministry of Tourism: P.O. Box 224 (☎464 23 11; fax 464 84 65). From 3rd Circle on Jabal Amman, walk down Abdul Muneim Riyad, then take the 1st right onto al-Mutanabbi St. to reach the imposing building on the right. Helpful office staff will do its best to answer questions (the more specific, the better) and has a small supply of excellent brochures and maps available. Open Su-Th 8am-3pm.

Tourist Office: (☎464 23 11), adjacent to the Roman Theater. The tourist office has many good brochures, some mediocre advice, and few bad maps.

Currency Exchange: Banks are open Su-Th, generally 8:30am-3pm. Many authorized **money changers** (found downtown between al-Husseini Mosque and the post office) are open daily, usually late into the evening. They offer roughly the same exchange rates as banks but will not charge a bank's commission. Passport sometimes required. **ATMs** are as common as stray cats in downtown Amman; most ATMs can give **cash advances** on MC and V and accept many bank cards on international networks (Cirrus, PLUS). This is rarely true of the stray cats.

American Express: P.O. Box 408 (☎560 70 14, emergency 79 58 44 64 or 79 52 05 76; fax 566 99 05; guest@traders.com.jo), on Abdul Hamid Sharaf St. opposite Shmeisani's Ambassador Hotel. Holds mail. Open daily 8am-6pm.

EMBASSIES AND CONSULATES

Australia (☎593 02 46, visa info 593 27 80), on Jabal Amman between 4th and 5th Circles, across from a large grassy knoll. Open Su-Th 7:30am-3pm, consular services M-W 9am-noon.

Canada (☎566 61 24; fax 568 92 27), in Shmeisani behind Jabri Restaurant, near Petra Bank. Open Su-W 8am-4:30pm, Th 8am-1:30pm; consular services 9-11am.

Egypt (☎560 51 75, visa info 560 52 03; fax 560 40 82), on Jabal Amman between 4th and 5th Circles, next to the Dove Hotel (Best Western). Take a right off Zahran St. after the grassy space; embassy is 50m down on the right. Bring photo and JD12 before noon; pick up visa same day. Open Sa-Th 9am-3pm; consular services 9am-noon.

Israel (☎552 54 07, visa info 552 61 57 or 552 61 58; fax 552 19 71, visa fax 552 51 76), in 4th Circle on Jabal Amman. Far from *service* routes, so take a yellow taxi. Visas issued Su-Th 9am-1pm (JD13). Open Su-Th 8am-4pm.

Lebanon (☎/fax 592 91 11), in Abdoun, behind UK Embassy. Bring photo and passport with no evidence of a trip to the West Bank or Israel, and get the visa in 24hr. UK and US citizens can also obtain visas upon arrival in Lebanon. One-month visa JD26; 3-month visa JD52. Open Su-Th 8am-2pm; consular services 8-11am.

Syria (☎464 19 35 or 464 19 45), on Jabal Amman up from 3rd Circle toward the reflecting building. Take a left at the intersection and head up the hill. Look for the Syrian flag (red, white, and black stripes with two green stars). Only issues work visas; apply for tourist visas before arriving in Jordan. In theory, a visa costs JD43.5, but they are difficult to obtain from the generally unhelpful staff—you must have a Jordanian entry stamp and no evidence of visits to the West Bank or Israel. Open Sa-Th 8:30am-2pm; consular services 9-10:30am.

UK (☎592 31 00; fax 592 37 59), in Abdoun on Damascus St. Instead of turning right to the US Embassy, continue on the road until reaching the Orthodox Club (the walled-in playground with the red jungle-gym). The embassy is behind, with a blue iron fence. Open daily 8:30am-3pm; consular services Su-Th 8:30am-noon.

US (☎592 01 01, visa info 592 32 93; fax 592 01 43), in Abdoun, head north on Zahran St., make a left at 5th Circle onto Muhammad Ali Jinnah St. and follow the street as it bends to the left after 1km. Take the 3rd right after the bend. The fortress-like complex is 500m down that road. Open Su-Th 8am-4:30pm; consular services 1:30-4pm.

LOCAL SERVICES

English-Language Bookstores: Al-'Ulama Bookshop (☎463 61 92; fax 465 60 17), uphill from the post office, has a friendly staff and a great selection of travel guides, dictionaries, and maps. Fax and photocopier (50fils per copy) available. Open Su-Th 8am-8pm, F 11am-8pm. **Gibraltar Bookshop** (☎462 37 99), next to Hashem Restaurant, sells up-to-date American, French, and British magazines, stationery, and postcards. Open daily 9:30am-8pm. **Istiqlal Library,** primarily a stationery and art supply store, has three locations in Amman: downtown, opposite the post office (☎462 24 75; open daily 7:30am-6pm); Shmeisani, downhill from Kentucky Fried Chicken (☎566 31 30; open Sa-Th 9am-1pm and 3-6:30pm); and Sweifiyyeh, around the corner from Turino Hotel (☎582 11 68). All have helpful English-speaking staffs.

Local and International Press: *Your Guide to Amman,* published monthly and available free, is a great resource but can be difficult to find. Some travel agencies and larger hotels may have copies, but the guide is most easily obtained by calling the publisher (☎ 465 65 93) and stopping by their office in 2nd Circle. The *Jordan Times* (200fils), a daily newspaper with good coverage of the Middle East and Africa, lists useful telephone numbers, 24hr. pharmacies, and cultural events in Amman. *Jordan Today,* published monthly and available at larger hotels, has valuable information on tourism, culture, and entertainment. The *International Herald Tribune* arrives at newsstands after 3pm one day late; *Time, Newsweek,* and *The Economist* are sporadically available. The weekly *Jerusalem Star* (350fils) lists cultural events. *The New York Times* is sometimes available one day late at the gift shop in the Marriott and Inter-Continental Hotels.

Cultural Centers: American Cultural Center (☎592 01 01, ext. 2052; fax 585 91 01), inside the American Embassy Complex; ask for the library. Free American films every Th at 5pm, lectures by scholars and visiting politicians. Library has American periodicals, comfy couches, a video library, and a good selection of (mostly non-fiction) books. Center and library open Su-Th 8am-5pm. **British Council** (☎463 61 47 or 463 61 48; fax 465 64 13) is on Rainbow St. Facing uphill at 1st Circle, go left; the British Council is past the Saudi Embassy on the right. Sponsors films and lectures and offers Arabic classes at reasonable rates. Language Center open Su-Th 11am-8:30pm; A/C library open Su-W 11am-6pm, Th 11am-3:30pm.

Laundromat: Laundromats are sparsely scattered throughout Amman, but many hotels and hostels provide laundry service (350fils per piece). **Al-Jami'a Laundry** (☎534 78 57), on the 1st right heading away from the city past the main gate of Jordan University, is a do-it-yourself joint. Wash and dry JD2. **Dry Clean** (☎464 19 55), 3rd Circle in Jabal Amman and 50m down the street from the Ministry of Tourism, charges 500fils for shirts and 750fils for pants.

EMERGENCY AND COMMUNICATIONS

Emergency: Ambulance: ☎193 **Police:** ☎192. **Fire:** ☎462 20 90 or 462 20 93.

Late-Night Pharmacies: The *Jordan Times* and *Your Guide to Amman* list 24hr. pharmacies and weekly rotating on-call doctors. The **Rawhi Pharmacy** (☎464 44 54), between 3rd and 4th Circles, has an English-speaking staff. For non-prescription medicine, try **Safeway,** on the edge of Nasser ibn Jamil St. near the northwestern edge of Shmeisani (☎568 53 11), or in 7th Circle (☎365 37 33); both are open 24hr.

Hospitals: The *Jordan Times, Jordan Star,* and *Your Guide to Amman* list doctors and hospitals. The **Shmeisani Hospital** (☎560 74 31) is most reputable; others include the **Jordan Hospital** (☎560 75 50) in 4th Circle, and the **Arab Heart Surgical Hospital** (☎592 11 99), an ultramodern research institute in 5th Circle.

Telephones: Overseas calls can be made from hotels, but it's cheapest to use payphones around Amman, which accept phone cards but not cash. **Alo** and **JPP** cards available at most newsstands and some restaurants in denominations of JD1, JD5, and JD15; good for both local and international calls. Private phone offices on Omar al-Khayyam St. To get there, take a left out of the post office and make the 1st left up the street across from the Cliff Hotel.

Directory Information: Amman: ☎121. **Jordan:** ☎131. **International:** ☎0132.

JORDAN

Internet Access: It is becoming easier and cheaper to access the Internet in Amman. A number of cafes can be found downtown and in other major commercial areas around the city. Many hotels also have their own computers for use by guests but tend to charge higher rates. 1hr. online should cost JD1, with a minimum charge of 500fils. The oddly named **Internet Yard** (☎ 461 31 23) is located just uphill from the post office and has a helpful staff managing 10 good computers running Win95.

Post Office: Generally open Sa-Th 7am-5pm in summer and 7am-3pm in winter, F 7am-1pm year round. The main post office is on Prince Muhammad St., uphill from where it joins King Faisal St. downtown. **Poste Restante** and stamps. **Faxes** (JD1.85 per page to US) can be sent from this office. Open Sa-Th 8:30am-7pm, F 8am-noon. **EMS** (☎568 81 90) is on Lifta St., a dead end behind Qawar Arthroscopy Center. From downtown, go up King Hussein St. past the Abdali and JETT Bus Stations. Take a right on Bir al-Sab'a St. and look left. Open daily 8am-8pm; holidays 8am-2pm.

ACCOMMODATIONS

Where you stay in Amman should depend on why you are in the city. **Downtown** draws backpackers in search of a cheap hotel, good food, and general chaos. The hotels vary greatly in quality and character, but you should be able to find something to fit your personality as well as your budget. Travelers using Amman as a transportation hub tend to congregate near the **Abdali Bus Station** in Jabal al-Weibdeh. Just beyond Jabal al-Weibdeh is the upscale **Shmeisani** district, a more relaxed setting with more expensive hotels and excellent restaurants. Prices come down during the ambiguously defined off season; basically, you pay more if the hotel is close to full, but it's always a good idea to ask for discounts and try to bargain.

DOWNTOWN

Farah Hotel (☎465 14 43 or 465 14 38; fax 465 14 37), on Cinema al-Hussein St. Follow red and yellow signs at the intersection of King Hussein and King Faisal St. through an alley and across a street to this 6-story behemoth. Each floor has four clean, smallish rooms with TVs, 2 bathrooms (free showers, no toilet paper), and a large fridge. International phone office with high rates downstairs. Laundry 350fils per piece. Breakfast JD1. Rooftop mattresses JD2.5; dorms JD4 per person; singles JD7; doubles JD9.

Bdeiwi Hotel, P.O. Box 182426 (☎464 33 94; fax 464 33 93), 50m from Prince Muhammad St., on the uphill side street across from the Cliff Hostel. Brightly painted, immaculate rooms and clean, shared bathrooms on a quiet sidestreet. Fans in all rooms and international telephone service at the front desk. A comfortable place for lone women travelers. Singles JD6; doubles JD8, with private bath JD10; shared room JD4.

Amman-Palace Hotel (☎464 61 72; fax 465 69 89; aplchoti@go.com.jo), on Quraysh St., 250m past the Nymphaeum, heading away from the Roman Theatre. A bit out of place in a downtown area teeming with budget hotels. Allows tired travelers to splurge on A/C and satellite TV without having to leave the appealing craziness of downtown. Big, relaxing rooms with private baths. Women welcome. Breakfast included. Singles JD18; doubles JD22; suites JD25.

Al-Harmin Hotel (☎465 58 90; fax 465 58 45), on al-Hashemi St. across from the Roman Theater. English-speaking manager welcomes visitors to the mirror-walled lobby and colorful rooms of this 2nd fl. hotel, accessible via an outdoor staircase. Singles JD5; doubles JD7; triples JD10.

Cliff Hostel, P.O. Box 184381 (☎462 42 73), heading away from al-Husseini Mosque, at the intersection of King Hussein and King Faisal St. bear left onto Prince Muhammad St. The entrance is off an alley on your left, beneath a Coca-Cola-postered terrace. Clean, high-ceilinged rooms with fans. Showers 500fils. Midnight lockout, but a knock will get you in later. Popular with backpackers, so reserve in advance during busy season. Terrace mattresses JD2; singles JD5; doubles JD8; triples JD3.5 per person; slightly lower prices in summer.

Amman Castle Hotel (☎/fax 464 68 09), on Shabsuq St. between al-Husseini Mosque and the Roman Theater, 75m up from where Shabsuq meets Quaraysh St. A sign marks the hotel entrance. The front desk is up a flight of stairs and through the door on the right. Few foreigners. Proprietors speak minimal English, but small rooms are comfortable and clean. 3rd fl. common kitchen. JD4.5 per person.

Beirut Hotel (☎463 69 86 or 463 80 99; fax 465 09 16), on al-Hashemi St. between al-Husseini Mosque and the Roman Theater. Walking from the mosque, look for the blue sign with white English letters on the left side of the street after about 90m. Carpeted rooms are small and the common bathroom is hygienically challenged. Predominantly male clientele. Singles JD5; doubles JD8.

NEAR ABDALI STATION

Canary Hotel, P.O. Box 9062 (☎463 83 53 or 463 83 62; fax 465 43 53; canary_h@hotmail.com), on Karmali St. in Jabal al-Weibdeh near Terra Sancta College. From Abdali Station, walk downhill along the right side of King Hussein St. When the main road forks downhill to the left, continue straight and uphill on al-Ba'oniyah St. Take the 1st right on al-Karmali St. and try to survive the final 1½-block climb. Pleasant, attractive facilities. Immaculate rooms have satellite TV, fans, and private bathrooms. Guests may even request a hardware and ring the on-call doctor—hopefully for unrelated reasons. Singles JD20; doubles JD24; triples JD30.

Caravan Hotel, P.O. Box 9062 (☎566 11 95 or 566 11 97; fax 566 11 96; caravan@go.com.jo), only 100m southwest of Abdali Bus Station, immediately south of King Abdullah Mosque. Entrance is on the right after a short walk down the street directly opposite the mosque. This hotel is owned by the same family as the Canary, and the spacious rooms, soft beds, and quality service reveal this connection. Request a balcony. Fans in every room and satellite TV in some. Free local calls. Internet available. Singles JD20; doubles JD24; triples JD30 (tax, service, and breakfast included). 15% *Let's Go* discount. Off-season and extended stay discounts. MC/V.

Merryland Hotel, P.O. Box 9122 (☎465 42 39; fax 463 03 70), on King Hussein St. Walk downhill on the right-hand side of King Hussein St.; Merryland is approximately 90m past Abdali Station, look for signs. The hotel-restaurant features glass chandeliers, a small bar, and a seedy disco downstairs (open daily 11pm-3am). Huge rooms have springy mattresses, color satellite TV, electric fans or A/C, and refrigerators. Check-out noon. Dry cleaning 250fils per shirt. Singles JD12; doubles JD15; triples JD18; quads JD21; quints JD25, A/C rooms may be more expensive in the summer. AmEx/MC/V.

Remal Hotel, P.O. Box 910477 (☎/fax 463 06 70; sufwat@go.com.jo), on Sa'id ibn al-Harith St. Look downhill from the Abdali Bus Station for the police station on the right; the hotel is 100m up the small street that runs up the right side of the station. Rooms have large and comfy beds with fluffy feather pillows. Some rooms have balconies. TVs, fans, and phones (free local calls). Singles JD14; doubles JD18; triples JD24; add 10% service charge. Student discounts. AmEx/V.

Al-Monzer Hotel, P.O. Box 926595 (☎463 94 69; fax 465 73 28; mfj@nol.com.jo), on the north side of King Hussein St. directly across from Abdali Station. The better of two hotels in the building. Rooms with fans and phones, some rooms come with in-room bath. Singles JD10; doubles JD14; triples JD19. Student discounts. MC/V.

SHMEISANI

Nefertiti Hotel, 26 al-Jahed St. (☎560 38 65 or 560 35 53), two streets downhill from the Ambassador Hotel. Less than 20m from al-Qasr Howard Johnson. All rooms are quite large. Some have gigantic glass-enclosed terraces, delightful places to enjoy the quiet neighborhood. Others have glass-enclosed bathrooms that afford spectacular toilet-seat views of Amman without compromising your privacy. Check out several rooms before committing; they differ enough that one may suit your taste more than another. Some rooms with private bath. Singles JD9; doubles JD13; triples JD15. Cash only.

Manar Hotel (☎566 21 86 or 568 48 11; fax 568 43 29), on Abdul Hamid Sharaf St., 200m south and on the opposite side of the street from the Ambassador Hotel. A/C rooms, outdoor pool, and in-room mini-bar with ice-cold beer help keep summer guests cool. Delightful staff and peaceful neighborhood provide a tranquil but more expensive alternative to downtown and Abdali. Breakfast included. Singles JD25; doubles JD35.

🖸 FOOD

RESTAURANTS

The better sit-down restaurants in Amman cluster near 3rd Circle, in Shmeisani, and in the area around Abdoun Circle. These places usually add a 10% service charge to the bill. Street vendor prices are drastically cheaper, and take-out food is usually excellent. The most common offerings, and sometimes the only ones, are shawarma (usually lamb and sometimes chicken, 300fils) or falafel, stuffed into a pita with french fries and fresh vegetables (150fils). If the listings are in Arabic only, ask the vendor to translate. The **souq** is near al-Husseini Mosque, across from the **Nymphaeum;** prices are stable and bargaining unnecessary. (Open Su-Th 8:30am-dusk.) When summer temperatures soar above 100 degrees, an ice cream cone can be priceless. Thankfully, the soft-serve vendors along Hashimi St. charge only 100fils for a fruity flavor in a colorful cone.

Westerners and wealthy Ammanites swear by the **Safeway** stores on the edge of Shmeisani and at 7th Circle, where you can find dry cleaning, shoe repair, a hardware store, Internet access, and a **Subway** sandwich joint—all open 24hr. American grease-to-go has also invaded Jordan: **McDonald's, Pizza Hut, Arby's,** and **KFC** draw locals and tourists to Abdoun Circle, Ilya Abu Madhi St. in Shmeisani, and the streets around the main gate of Jordan University in northern Amman.

🖾 **New Orient Restaurant (Abu Ahmad)** (☎ 464 18 79), 3rd Circle in Jabal Amman, behind the Amman Surgical Hospital. Walk down al-Amir Muhammad St. and turn right at the restaurant's sign. Splurge among vines, green tablecloths, and a hyper-attentive staff. Award-winning *nouvelle* Arabic cuisine. Appetizers 600fils-JD2. Entrees JD2-4.5. Open daily noon-4pm and 7pm-midnight. Traveler's checks/MC/V.

🖾 **Hashem Restaurant** (☎ 463 64 40), on Prince Muhammad St. in the alley directly opposite the Cliff Hostel. Middle Eastern fast food at its best. Almost on top of the intersection of King Faisal St., Prince Muhammad St., and King Hussein St., Hashem is a great place to see, hear, and taste Amman. *Fuul* served with an amazing pickled hot pepper concoction and fresh bread. Tea, hummus, and an evening's conversation with locals, all for well under 650fils. Take-out makes a good daytrip bag lunch. Open 24hr.

Al-Quds Restaurant (☎ 463 01 68), on King Hussein St. about 50m north of where King Faisal St. splits into Prince Muhammad St. and King Hussein St. Watch for the greenish awning on the right. Although it looks like an American pancake house, al-Quds serves authentic Middle Eastern food in a wonderfully clean setting. Try their variation on *mensaf*, made with chicken instead of lamb (JD2.4), or sample their kebab (JD1.9) and hummus (500fils). Check out the adjoining pastry shop's enticing array of desserts—the perfect way to end a meal, or start a meal, or both. Open daily 8am-10pm.

Salam Restaurant (☎ 462 26 26), on King Faisal St. ½ block up from al-Husseini Mosque on the left-hand side of the street, next to the Bata shoe store. Very small English sign; look for spitted chickens in the window. The manager has cleverly padded the perilously low ceiling beams in the upstairs dining room with pleasing blue foam. Tasty food and safe dining—what else could you possibly want? JD2.4 buys bread, bird, and fries at a table upstairs. Friendly service and English menu. Open daily 8am-10pm.

Cairo Restaurant (☎ 462 45 27). Facing away from al-Husseini mosque, head left past the clothing shops, turn left at the 2nd street, and look for the big red and white sign. Often crowded, the Cairo offers an extensive Arabic menu, including Jordanian *maglouba*, an "upside-down" dish of rice, chicken, and vegetables (JD1). Kebab JD1.3. Hummus 300fils. Open daily 6am-midnight.

Romero (☎ 464 42 27 or 464 42 28), 3rd Circle, Jabal Amman. Walking toward 2nd Circle from 3rd Circle, take the 2nd right. Romero is across from the Jordan Intercontinental Hotel. Take the hottie from the hostel to this romantic outdoor cafe for the best

Italian food in Amman. Pasta JD3-4.5. Meat and seafood JD5-9. Open daily 1-3:30pm and 8-11:30pm. Reservations recommended. AmEx/MC/V.

Abu Khamis and Abu Saleh Restaurant (☎462 27 82), on King Faisal St., 1 alley over from the Cliff Hostel in the direction of al-Husseini Mosque. A small facade masks a spacious, smoky interior. Half-chicken or kebab JD1.35. Open daily 7am-10pm.

L'Olivier Garden (☎592 95 64), in Abdoun, north of the circle. Serves tasty French cuisine in a clichéd cafe setting. The restaurant offers a bizarre "Car Park" buffet, in which take-out food is served from the backs of cars (JD8). Appetizers JD3-5. Entrees JD4-7. Open daily 10am-midnight. Reservations recommended.

Rasetelbab Restaurant (☎962 12 53). Walking from the Cliff Hostel toward al-Husseini mosque on the left side of King Faisal St., turn left up the alley next to the green Abu Sara Cousins store. Rasetelbab does not have an English sign, but it's the only restaurant in the alley. Look for the brightly colored straw stools and take a seat. Pleases patrons with omelets and meat with tomatoes (300-350fils). Open daily 7am-10pm.

CAFES

Find one of Amman's many traditional cafes, hidden in an alley or up an unmarked staircase, by following the trail of perfumed *argileh* smoke. Hosting card games and conversation over hot drinks and tobacco in its many forms, Jordanian cafes are great places to unwind in the cool evenings. Food is sometimes available, but cafes are primarily places for sipping and smoking. Tea, Turkish coffee, and Arabic coffee (a concentrated beverage made with cardamom and served in small portions—definitely an acquired taste) are staples, along with the ubiquitous *argileh* water pipe. Cafes **downtown** are mostly frequented by men, but women should feel comfortable at any of the cafes listed below.

Al-Sultan Coffee Shop (☎560 59 29), along Ilya Abu Madhi St., the main drag in Shmeisani. This popular outdoor cafe serves Turkish coffee (JD1) worthy of a sultan in a lively after-dinner family atmosphere. Live music nightly. Open 24hr.

Eco-Tourism Cafe (☎465 29 94), on King Faisal St. The facade of this absurdly named cafe is decorated with painted versions of flags from around the world, IHOP-style. Brings together a friendly mix of young and old Jordanian men for some backgammon, tea, and *argileh*. Open daily 9am-midnight.

Caffe Moka (☎592 62 85; fax 593 24 09; moka@go.com.jo), on al-Qahirah St. just off Abdoun Circle. Ritzy Abdoun elite enjoy tarts, sundaes, and various types of coffee (including relatively easy-to-drink Arabic), all for JD1-3. Open daily 7:30am-midnight.

Books@Cafe (☎465 04 57), on Omar bin al-Khattab St. (Mango St.) in Jabal Amman, about 500m from Abu Bakr al-Sideeq St. (Rainbow St.). The sprawling rooftop cafe serves tasty crepes (JD2) and pasta dishes (JD3), while the bookstore below offers speedy Internet access (JD2 per hr.) and sells English-language books and magazines.

Tourist Restaurant and Cafe (☎461 23 30), stretched along Hashimi St. in front of the Roman Theater in a chain of outdoor cafes. Despite its name, the cafe is popular with locals, who watch the world stroll by over a cup of coffee (650fils) or read the subtitles of the American action movies shown on the cafe's TV between puffs of an *argileh* (JD2). Open daily 8am-1am; closed in winter.

TCHE TCHE Cafe (☎593 20 20), on Abdoun Circle. Pronounced "Chi-Chi," this popular Abdoun hangout has mint *argileh* (a.k.a. the world's largest menthol cigarette; JD2.5). Fruit juice cocktails, milkshakes, and sandwiches all around JD2. Open 8am-midnight.

◉ SIGHTS

CITADEL HILL. From the Roman Theater or any other downtown locale, climb the steep steps and streets to the flat top of Citadel Hill (Jabal al-Qala'a). A trip to the top of Citadel Hill is a good idea for your first day in Amman, as the view gives the best perspective on the city's labyrinthine ups and downs. The trip is best taken with a companion (especially for women). The Citadel is the site of pre-modern Amman, formerly called Rabbath-Ammon or "The Great City of the Ammonites," (an ancient nation that makes several cameos in the Bible). Try wandering around the extensive ruins alone, since guides charge an outrageous JD5 to decipher the site's historical wealth, more of which Spanish and French archaeological teams are constantly uncovering. Tours lead visitors from the remaining columns of the Roman **Temple of Hercules** to the much younger and recently renovated **Umayyad Palace.** (Accessible by taxi from downtown for 500fils. Open daily 8am-5pm.)

ANCIENT ROMAN RUINS. Amman's best-preserved and most intriguing ruins lie behind the Archaeological Museum. Vaulted chambers tower 10m over a spacious courtyard where elaborate floral decorations can still be seen in the stonework. A 7th-century structure once supported a huge stone dome and was used as a mosque, auditorium, and residence. Below the Roman walls, directly to the north, an open pit leads into the underground passageway that connected the fortified city to a hidden water supply. Avoid the grassy area across from the Temple of Hercules: it's not part of the ruins, but rather a 40-year-old cemetery.

AL-HUSSEINI MOSQUE AND ENVIRONS. The Citadel was the heart of ancient Amman, but today Amman's pulse emanates from downtown, in and around this notable mosque ("Masjid al-Malik Hussein" in Arabic). The Ottoman-style mosque was built in 1924 on the site of a mosque built by Omar, the second caliph of Islam. On the corner of Quraysh St. and Ibn-al-Atheer St., behind the mosque, lies the **Nymphaeum,** a sacred fountain and bathing ground for the ancient city. In the alleys of King Faisal St. near its intersection with Shabsough St. is Amman's **gold souq,** featuring shop after shop of gold jewelry, as well as a few selling antique Bedouin silver jewelry. Although bargaining is a way of life in much of Amman, prices in the gold market are fixed at JD5.5 per gram. (Open M-Th and Sa 9am-9pm, Su 9am-1pm.)

KING ABDULLAH AND ABU DARWISH MOSQUES. Uphill—and barely out of a *muezzin*'s range—from al-Husseini Mosque stands Abdali's own place of worship, Masjid al-Malik Abdullah. Constructed over seven years in memory of modern Jordan's first king (the current Abdullah's great-grandfather), King Abdullah Mosque's blue mosaic dome can shelter 3000 Muslims kneeling together in prayer. Non-Muslims are permitted to enter the mosque and the connected **Museum of Islam** via a staircase to the right of the main gate. Tickets are available at a window across from the base of the stairs. Women are required to wear a head covering, which can usually be obtained at the entrance to the mosque. All visitors must remove their shoes before entering the buildings. The black-and-white checkered dome of nearby Abu Darwish Mosque *(Masjid Abu Darwish)* peeks over Jabal Ashrafiyyeh. In the 1940s, Circassians built this mosque—one of the most unusual religious structures in the Middle East—entirely from white rock and black basalt carted in from quarries in the northern part of the country. The two colors were also used for the mosque's ornamentation. (King Abdullah Mosque open Su-Th 8am-noon and 1:30pm-3pm; F 8am-11am. Museum of Islam entrance JD1.)

SWEIFIYYEH MOSAIC. Amman's finest Byzantine artifact was found during construction at the western edge of the city in 1970. The mosaic illustrates the passing of the seasons and once belonged to a 6th-century church. Ask the caretaker to hose down the floor for a better look at the bizarre creatures: leaf-bearded men, eagles with ears, and eel-men. Probably Jordan's finest mosaic north of Madaba. (Follow signs from the 1st left west of 6th Circle. Open Sa-Th 9am-4pm, F 9am-1:30pm. Free.)

ROMAN THEATER. The Roman Theater, on Jabal al-Qala'a downtown, is the most renowned of Amman's historical sights. Built by Roman Emperor Antonius Pius (138-161 CE), the Roman Theater was once able to accommodate all 6000 of Amman's inhabitants. Recently restored, the theater often hosts summer concerts

and theatrical productions; check for scheduled events at the nearby **tourist office.**
(Open daily 7am-7pm in summer; 7am-5pm in winter. Free.)

🏛 MUSEUMS

HERITAGE MUSEUMS. Two museums are built into the foundations of the Roman Theater on either side of the enclosed stage area. On the right, the **Folklore Museum** features dioramas on the diverse heritage of the Jordanian people—from Circassian military weaponry to Palestinian embroidery and Bedouin encampments. The **Museum of Popular Traditions** shows off attire and accessories from the country's past, including a sizable collection of traditional Bedouin jewelry. A well-documented display of semi-precious stones used by the Bedouin reveals a novel approach to natural medicine: rocks that cure jaundice, rocks that make you lactate, and so on. The gallery to the right of the entrance displays 6th-century mosaics from Madaba and Jerash. *(Folklore Museum ☎ 465 17 42. Open daily 8am-5pm. Museum of Popular Traditions ☎ 465 17 60. Open daily 9am-5pm. Both JD1.)*

ARCHAEOLOGICAL MUSEUM. This museum on Citadel Hill contains a chronologically organized series of finds from ancient sites throughout Jordan. Fragments of the **Dead Sea Scrolls** and 200,000-year-old rhinoceros teeth share the limelight with anthropomorphic Iron Age sarcophagi, minimalist Nabatean portraits, and sublime Roman marble statuary. In front of the museum are the foundations of a 2nd-century Roman temple that once housed a 10m statue of Hercules, to whom the temple was likely dedicated. Three of the statue's giant marble fingers hint at the shrine's former glory. *(☎ 463 87 95. Open daily 8am-5pm. JD2.)*

JORDAN NATIONAL GALLERY. The National Gallery's outstanding collection is comprised of contemporary works from artists throughout the Middle East and Africa. The image of Islamic culture that emerges is unlike anything you could glean from exploring ancient ruins. The gallery has a large permanent collection as well as a number of rotating exhibits. *(On Jabal al-Weibdeh, uphill from Abdali Bus Station. Heading down the street opposite the Remal Hotel, the gallery is on your right. Look for signs. ☎ 463 01 28. Open W-M 9am-5pm. JD1.)*

MUSEUM OF ISLAM. This museum lays out the chronology of Islam, with a focus on Jordan, among a collection of artifacts taken from successive periods. The English narrative helps to sort out all this talk of Umayyads and Ottomans within a religious context. *(Inside the King Abdullah Mosque complex. ☎ 567 21 55. Open Su-Th 8am-noon and 1:30pm-3pm, F 8am-11am. JD1.)*

🎵🎭 ENTERTAINMENT AND NIGHTLIFE

Most Jordanians prefer to spend their limited leisure time at home with their families, watching TV, or maybe going out to a movie. Strolling the lazy evening streets **downtown** and talking to friends or playing cards late into the night at a smoky cafe are also popular ways to mellow out after a week of work. However, the tranquil majority is steadily being won over by a variety of alcohol-oriented forms of nighttime debauchery. A western influence is obvious in the discos and pubs becoming popular with trendy locals, but **al-Vegas** (Jordanian "nightclubs") remain unique in *many* respects. The glitzy neighborhoods of **Shmeisani** and **Abdoun,** western suburbs of Amman, draw an energetic mix of young and wealthy locals every night of the week. The main streets are a flashy blur of European-style cafes, American franchise restaurants, and the occasional pricey bar or disco (most open until 2am). Women, gays, and lesbians will feel more comfortable going out in these two neighborhoods than anywhere else in Amman. *Service* run during the day to Shmeisani from downtown (150fils), but not yet to Abdoun, so take a taxi (JD1). If you seek a somewhat different scene, the region of Prince Muhammad St., downhill from 3rd Circle, is home to a cluster of Jordan's *Vegas,* and dozens of similar establishments are tucked into the cracks of reputable daytime businesses throughout the city. As the *Vegas* are almost exclusively frequented by men, a trip into Amman's underbelly will likely not appeal to everyone.

CINEMA AND THEATER

Four **cinemas** show English-language films: the **Philadelphia** (☎ 463 41 44), 100m down Prince Muhammad St. from 3rd Circle; **Concord** (☎ 567 74 20), in Abdali; **Plaza** (☎ 569 92 38), at the Forte Grande in Shmeisani; and the luxurious **Galleria 1 and 2** (☎ 594 47 93) in Abdoun. The daily **Jordan Times** lists movies and showtimes. A few scattered theaters show B-grade action movies from India and the US, as well as 1970s soft porn. The word on the street is that the censors have cut these cinematic masterpieces to ribbons by the time they hit the screens, so buyers beware. **Cinema al-Hussein,** downhill from the Farah Hotel, is a good spot for such titillating fare. **Nabil & Hisham's Theater** (☎ 462 51 55), on Rainbow St. in 1st Circle, occasionally produces plays in Arabic.

BARS AND DANCE CLUBS

Most Amman bars have dance floors, and it goes without saying that all dance clubs have bars, but whether the crowd chooses to emphasize sit-down-drinking or dancing-drinking is largely unpredictable. Thursday nights are consistently intense, and Sunday and Monday see their fair share of action. A few places have begun to capitalize on the potential Friday night scene, but the rest of the week can be rather mellow, especially in the winter.

Salute (☎ 465 14 58), between 1st and 2nd Circles, north of the Iraqi Embassy and across from the Fiker Adeen Restaurant. The place to be in Amman. Good-looking young Jordanians overflow the breezy outdoor patio and crowd the small dance floor, grooving to a mix of Arabic and western tunes. Drinks JD3-7. Cover JD2.5. Open daily until 2am.

The Big Fellow (☎ 593 47 66), part of the Sheraton Entertainment Center in Abdoun Circle. A favorite among Westerners for watching live soccer matches. Glitzy atmosphere and pool tables also draw sleek young locals. The daily drink specials are a great value (JD2). Cocktails JD3-5. Draft Guinness JD4. Amstel JD2.8. Open daily 1pm-2am.

Ciro's Pizza Pomodoro of Knightsbridge (☎ 492 85 15), on an alley off al-Kaldera St. heading away from Abdoun Circle, next to the Planet Hollywood. Transformed into a trendy bar and dance club at night, the DJ spins US Top 40 tunes for a swanky twenty-something crowd. Couples only Th. Drinks JD2-5. Cover JD5. Open M and W-F until 2am.

Irish Pub (☎ 569 76 01), in the basement of the Dove Hotel (Best Western), between 4th and 5th Circles, next door to the Egyptian Embassy. Less trendy elitism and more good ol'-fashioned drinking. If you ever wanted to get in on the diplomat scene, now is your chance. Beer JD3-4. Happy hour M 7-9pm. Open daily 6:30pm-2am.

Jordan Bar, buried in the left-most alleyway off Prince Muhammad St., facing away from Hashem Restaurant. The best of numerous downtown dives, this small bar serves tall beers at low prices (JD2). Almost exclusively male clientele. Open daily 5pm-1am.

AL-VEGAS

Jordanians refer to these well-known haunts simply as "nightclubs" and sometimes just as "bars." They are characterized by a female singer accompanied by a few male musicians (or sometimes just one guy banging obnoxiously on a synthesizer), waitresses in tight clothing using their feminine wiles in an entrepreneurial manner, and a horde of men (of all ages) seated at tables around the stage. The loud music and overpriced drinks lead many men to burst into mockingly sensual dances to the amusement of their friends and to throw five-dinar bills over the head of the female vocalist. This traditional Jordanian nightlife can be quite fun for the uninitiated who are open-minded, but it is rarely going to be cheap. Clubs usually charge for a table (up to JD15), split amongst the group, as well as an individual cover (JD5). Drinks range from expensive to absurd, and generous tips are expected. On the bright side, table prices usually include bar snacks (nuts, popcorn, and other salty delicacies), a surprisingly pleasant plate of fresh fruit, and the first round of drinks. Women will probably feel uncomfortable, but if accompanied by a group of (already-familiar) men, the seedy spectacle is likely to entertain.

La Fontaine (☎079 51 10 23), south of 2nd Circle on Zayd bin Harethah St., in the same building as Julfar Gardens. This smallish club is reputable and run by a friendly English-speaking manager. The attached restaurant has Middle Eastern food, but most people come for the cheap liquor and quality live music. No cover, no table charge, and bar snacks come with each drink order. *'Araq* (a potent anise liquor that turns cloudy white when mixed with water) and other shots JD2.5-3. Beer JD3. Open daily 6pm-1am.

Arizona, on the right as you head down Prince Muhammad St. about 200m south of 3rd Circle. Classic *Vegas:* live music, belly-dancers, and exorbitant prices. JD15 per table; be sure to bring a group of friends. Drinks about JD5. Cover JD5. Open daily 7pm-1am.

Al-Kinz, 100m south of Arizona. Enter this subterranean club through the above-ground shanty adorned with neon lights. Cheaper than Arizona with similar entertainment, but a little bit seedier. Table JD5. Beer JD3. Cover JD5. Open daily from 7pm-1am.

▶ DAYTRIPS FROM AMMAN

WADI AL-SEER AND ENVIRONS

*The easiest path begins from al-Husseini Mosque in Amman. Walk left past the screeching taxis to a fork in the road (10min.). Head left at the fork; the lines of **minibuses** off to the right will either go directly to Wadi al-Seer or to a nearby station where the driver can show you which bus will take you the rest of the way (150fils). From Wadi al-Seer, catch a minibus headed down the valley road (100fils). The whole trip takes 45min.-1½hr., depending on your driver's skill at avoiding stray chickens. Buses leave when full. Bring plenty of water and patience—you may have a bit of a wait for the return trip. Bus service stops in the evening, so try and plan your visit, which need not exceed 4-5hr., for the daytime.*

Burgeoning Amman has begun spreading westward into the quiet valley of Wadi al-Seer, a region first settled by the fair-skinned Circassians. Its high desert plateau suddenly gives way to the Jordan Valley, where a little stream *(wadi)* snakes through the countryside on its way to the Dead Sea. The narrow asphalt road that follows this valley out of town is ideal for daytripping motorists and tramping backpackers, even on scorching summer days. Groups of friendly children wander through the verdant pomegranate plants and olive trees lining the 12km road that runs southwest to the remains of Qasr Iraq al-Amir.

Soon after leaving Wadi al-Seer, you'll pass **al-Bassa Springs,** the source of the valley's fertility and site of a local swimming pool. Carved into the face of the cliff above the left bank of the *wadi* is **al-Deir,** the monastery. This extraordinary building merits the 20min. climb, even if you don't find any of the Roman gold that villagers claim is buried under the floor. Each of the thousands of triangular niches in the walls of the ossuary once cradled a monk's skull.

QASR IRAQ AL-AMIR قصرعراق الامير

This is the last stop at the end of the road from Amman through Wadi al-Seer. The guard or his son will let you in for free, though a donation of 100-200fils is appreciated.

The story behind the creation of this impressive rock palace is almost as fascinating as the carvings on its walls. Local legend holds that a love-smitten slave named Tobiah built Qasr Iraq al-Amir, also known as **Qasr al-'Abd** (Castle of the Slave), to win the hand of his master's daughter. Tobiah carved lions, panthers, and eagles into its walls while his master was away. Unfortunately, the boss returned before Tobiah could finish, and the slave's efforts went unrewarded, save his name carved in Aramaic near the entrance of one of the 11 hand-dug **caves,** 500m back up the valley road, high up on the side of the valley ridge. Killjoy historians, however, explain the inscription and castle remains with references to Tobiah the Ammonite Servant (of God), a rich priest in Jerusalem. Roman-era historian Josephus records yet another story about a wealthy Tobiah family and the exploits of their young son Hyrcanus, who built a strong fortress constructed entirely of white marble and enclosed by a wide, deep moat.

Regardless of who actually built the palace, it warrants a visit. Two red stone lions remain intact, though the roof does not. The lioness (without a mane) on the northwest corner is the more interesting of the two, but both lions have a unique twist: the male (with the flowing mane) is breast-feeding a baby, while the lioness, prowling the corner alone, has male genitals.

NORTH OF AMMAN

SALT السلط   ☎ 05

Salt (rhymes with "cult") thrived as an administrative center during Ottoman rule, making it a top candidate to become capital of the Emirate of Transjordan in 1921 (see **Modern History,** p. 432). But the more centrally located village of Amman won that honor, and Salt's main connection to government today is that the swanky prep school there can claim almost all of Jordan's high officials as alumni.

Nevertheless, Salt's position as a regional Ottoman stronghold is still very evident: whole sections of archways from a church destroyed during the reign of the Ottomans snuggle up beside older local homes. The Ottoman barracks (built over a 13th-century fortress destroyed to prevent its capture by Crusaders) also remain intact, and Salt's large Christian community has peppered the hillsides with church towers. In the second half of the 19th century, Salt again took center stage when industrious Saltis built Jordan's first hospital, modern church, and secondary school. A thriving craft industry, invigorated by the presence of the **Salt Handicraft Training Center** uphill from the bus station, still produces high-quality traditional Jordanian crafts to the delight of souvenir-seeking tourists. Downhill from the bus station in Salt lies **Wadi She'ib.** Natural streams bubble out of the ground and break through the pavement of the main road. Unexplored caves, abandoned stone houses, and numerous dirt paths wrap around the *wadis*, lush terraced farmlands, and eucalyptus groves—making a minibus ride up Wadi She'ib the best and most dramatic approach to the city.

▐ TRANSPORTATION. From Amman, corner an Abdali Station bus driver to find the **minibus** going to Salt (30min., 200fils). Minibuses depart when full, so be prepared to wait. Return minibuses run until 6pm (5pm in winter). To catch a minibus from Salt to **Jabal Yushah** (80fils), follow the only street heading uphill from the bus station, and veer right at the first intersection, onto Maydan St., which continues uphill. After you pass the Jordan Islamic Bank on your left, turn left down the next cross street; minibuses depart from a small bus terminal on this street.

▞▟ ORIENTATION AND PRACTICAL INFORMATION. To get downtown from the bus station, walk to the minibus terminal off Maydan St. There is a mosque on the left-hand side. **Amaneh St.** heads uphill opposite the mosque and leads directly into the heart of downtown Salt. Walk up Amaneh St., take a left at the first fork, and follow the street as it winds around to the right to reach the **post office,** which is on the left. (☎ 355 49 86. Open Sa-Th 7:30am-7pm, F 7:30am-1:30pm.)

▐▟ ACCOMMODATIONS AND FOOD. Although Salt has no hotels, Saltis are proud to uphold the Bedouin tradition of *khuttar*, whereby prominent (and not-so-prominent) local families take it upon themselves to host any visitors that cross their paths or knock on their doors.

For the best kebab north of Amman, head to **al-Amad's,** established in 1927 by Radi al-Amad and inherited by his son, who runs it today. From the bottom of Amaneh St., head uphill and bear left at the fork as if going to the post office. Amad's is at the top of the hill, just as the street begins to bend right. There are no signs, but a yellow facade and large ventilation pipe jutting out from above the entrance make it possible to find Salt's best-kept secret. (☎355 07 65. Kebab JD1.2. Chicken JD2.25. Open daily 7am-10pm.) Finish up with freshly baked pastries at the chain patisserie **al-Habiba** (☎355 33 75), across from the Archaeological Museum. The *warbaht*, a flaky pastry filled with cream cheese and rolled in copious amounts of honey, is especially good; you can get three for 500fils.

🔲 **SIGHTS.** To get to Salt's free museums, walk 300m uphill from the bus station, veering right. They're a stone building on the right with green wrought-iron balconies and a big black sign. The **Archaeological Museum** (☎355 56 51) consists of two rooms with piles of coins, pottery, and jewelry dating from the Chalcolithic period (4500 BCE) through the Islamic period (1516 CE). The reconstructed scenes of the **Folklore Museum** (☎355 36 53), one flight up from the Archaeological Museum, illustrate the integration of modern technology with traditional Bedouin lifestyles. (Both museums open Sa-Th 8am-7pm, F 9am-5:30pm.) The highest point in Salt is the 1000-year-old mosque on **Jabal Yushah,** which, according to Muslim legend, houses the tomb of **Joshua** (the biblical prophet who succeeded Moses and led the Israelites into Palestine). Minibuses leave irregularly for Jabal Yushah from the bus stop at the bottom of Amaneh St. (80fils). The bus driver will drop you at the turnoff about 1km from the mosque, and from there you can follow green English and Arabic signs about 1km to the tomb. A round-trip taxi from downtown Salt costs JD3. Since tradition holds that Yushah was 12m tall, his tomb is quite impressive. Moreover, the awe-inspiring view of the West Bank will make the trip up the hill worth your while. In the morning, it is possible to see all the way from the Dead Sea to Lake Tiberias in Israel.

JERASH جرش   ☎02

Abandoned and swallowed up by the surrounding deserts, the ancient city of Jerash lay buried and preserved in sand for centuries. Rediscovered when German traveler Ulrich Seetzen stumbled upon it in 1806, Jerash is one of the most extensive provincial Roman cities that you can visit today. Its main road, which still bears evidence of chariot traffic, extends several hundred meters through a magnificent series of columns, shops, temples, theaters, and arches. In ancient times it was called Gerasa and was an important member of the Decapolis League, a loose association of trading cities allied with Rome (see **Ancient History,** p. 430). Because of Jerash's isolation in a remote valley, it survived long after the other nine cities were destroyed.

    Jerash is typically Roman in design. The city's builders trampled over earlier settlements, so little evidence of pre-Roman days remains. Inscriptions calling the town **Antioch** reveal that the Seleucid king with that name had a prominent outpost here, but Jerash entered its golden age only after Roman general Pompey conquered it in 64 BCE. Over the following three centuries, Jerash experienced a period of prosperity rivaled only by the city's recent tourist boom. The city imported granite from as far away as Aswan, razing and rebuilding old temples according to the latest architectural trends. In 106 CE, the Emperor Trajan annexed the surrounding Nabatean lands and built a highway from Damascus to Aqaba that passed through Jerash. The impressive Triumphal Arch built for Emperor Hadrian's visit in 129 CE still stands. The town was later converted to Christianity and had its own bishop by the mid-4th century.

    Following the destruction of the Syrian trading center at Palmyra (see p. 590) and the decline of the Nabatean kingdom, trade routes shifted from the desert to the sea. Frantic construction continued through the 6th century, but without their former wealth, the citizens of Jerash could only replace the older monuments with inferior structures—which were subsequently plundered by invading Persians in 635. A great earthquake in 749 destroyed much of the area, and by the time the Muslim Arabs came to control the city, few remnants of the ancient Roman polis were left. The Crusaders described Jerash as uninhabited, and it remained aban-

JORDAN

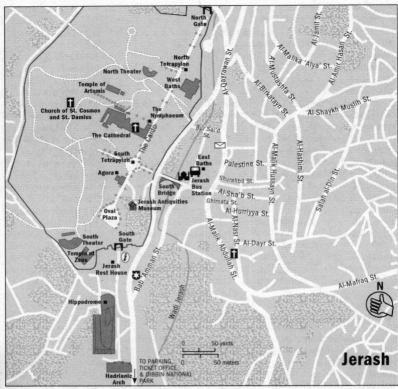

Jerash

doned until its rediscovery in the 19th century. After the invasion of the Ottomans, Circassians built the modern town in what was once the main residential area.

TRANSPORTATION

Getting to Jerash is painfully easy. **Minibuses** (300fils) and air-conditioned **buses** (350fils) leaving from Amman's Abdali Station make the 1hr. journey routinely throughout the day. **Service** are a bit pricier, somewhat faster, and also leave from Abdali. Ask the driver to stop at the Hadrianic Arch; otherwise he'll stop at the bus station across the river, next to the Eastern baths.

Buses and *service* leave town from the Jerash Bus Station. Buses go to: Amman (1hr.; 300fils, A/C 350fils); Ajloun (300fils); and Irbid (300fils). *Service* generally cost 50% more than buses. Public transportation shuts down around 6 pm. Hitchers to Amman, Dibbin, or Ajloun are known to walk south about 1km from the Visitors Center to the intersection with Hwy. 20. Turning right (west) leads to Ajloun and Dibbin National Park. Going straight leads to Amman. Buses pass frequently toward Amman and are easy to flag. Stand back from the road as you signal the bus—drivers seem to value time and speed more than they do toes.

ORIENTATION AND PRACTICAL INFORMATION

West of the Hadrianic Arch and adjacent to the parking area are the **ticket booths** where you must ante up to view Jerash's ruins (open 7am-7pm, JD5)—and the expected cluster of overpriced gift shops. Passing through the arch, walk 5min.

along the main road, past the Hippodrome, to reach the **Visitors Information Center,** which will appear on the right. (☎635 12 72. Open daily 8am-7pm; in winter 8am-5pm.) The **tourist police** station is opposite the Visitors Center, on the other side of the main road leading into town. The **Jerash Bus Station** is on the western edge of the new city, across the river from the Visitors Center. The **post office** is on King Abdullah St. behind the bus station. (Open daily 8am-5pm.)

Jerash dazzles along the 1km walk from the South Gate down the Street of Columns to the North Gate. The tiny Chrysoras (Golden) River separates the ancient ruins on the western bank from the new town on the eastern bank. Groups can hire **guides** (JD5; tip JD1 also expected). Booklets including maps and explanations of the sights invite leisurely exploration (JD1-6) and are easy to find at shops surrounding the ticket booths.

▐▜ ░ ACCOMMODATIONS AND FOOD

An easy daytrip from Amman, Jerash has few accommodations in town. The luxurious **Olive Branch Resort,** P.O. Box 2314, Amman 11181, is 5km uphill from the ancient ruins. A minibus runs about every 30min. from the Jerash Bus Station to a spot 800m below the resort (60fils) and taxis cost JD2 from downtown. The resort offers sparkling clean rooms and breakfast at high prices, but budget travelers can enjoy the mountaintop views, swimming pool, barbecue grills, billiard tables, and hot showers by camping on the grounds. (☎07 952 35 46 or 956 57 38; fax 06 582 60 34; olivekh@go.com.jo. Own tent JD5; resort's tent JD6; singles JD25; doubles JD38.) You might consider taking a taxi (JD3) or bus (500fils) to **camp** out at Dibbin National Park, about 8km away, or stay at the Dibbin Rest House (see p. 461). **Al-Khayyam Restaurant,** just past the Visitors Center on the right, serves bread, salad, and grilled meat (JD4). Escape the scorching sun on their open-air patio, complete with fountain and ceiling fans. (☎635 10 18. Open daily 8am-9pm.) The **Jerash Paradise Waterfall and Restaurant** (☎635 13 25), next door to al-Khayyam, offers similar fare, a similar setting, and slightly lower prices; mixed grill and kebab cost JD1.8 each. Street stands surrounding the bus station sell cheap falafel and *fuul* (100-200fils). Walking into town saves money and brings you to the lively streets of untouristed Jerash.

◉ SIGHTS

Jerash's ruins are its claim to fame. Nevertheless, over 75% of ancient Jerash still awaits excavation. (Unless otherwise stated, all sights open daily 7am-7pm. JD5.)

TRIUMPHAL (HADRIANIC) ARCH AND ENVIRONS. This arch, 400m south of the ancient walls, honors Emperor Hadrian's arrival in the winter of 129 CE. Spare parts strewn about the arch suggest how big the darn thing once was. Passing through it leads to the partially restored stables and bleachers of the **Hippodrome.** This arena hosted chariot races and other contests of skill for the amusement of up to 15,000 spectators, but shoddy construction brought an early end to the festivities, and the 245m-by-52m stadium was promptly turned into a tannery and pottery workshop. Continuing north, you'll see the Visitors Center and enter the site proper at the **South Gate,** leading into the **Forum** or Oval Plaza, the most photographed part of the city. The Ionic columns encircling the plaza have been reconstructed to first-century CE form. A statue once topped the central podium that is now home to the Jerash Festival flame.

SOUTH THEATER. A footpath to the left of the Forum leads to this theater, where Greek doodles reveal that 4000 of Jerash's wealthiest citizens reserved seats. The two-story backstage was once furnished with curtains and marble statues. Try to find "the spot," a groove in the floor of the lower stage where voices carry and amplify to several times their regular volume. The circular niches below the first row of seats are ancient telephones—speak into one and have a friend listen at any other "receiver." The top row of theater seats offers the best view of the ruined **Temple of Zeus,** which lies between the theater and the South Gate.

JERASH FESTIVAL The immensely popular Jerash Festival, instituted in 1981 by Queen Noor, takes place every summer in the second half of July. The South Theater and Artemis Steps provide a dramatic setting for musical, theatrical, and dance groups who come from all over the world to perform in celebration of past and present Jordanian and international culture. Performers have ranged from superstar Umm Kulthum to Spanish flamenco dancers, and from the Royal Jordanian Orchestra to the Royal Shakespeare Company. The festival has become very popular in recent years thanks to the presence of beloved Arab pop star Majdah al-Roumi (think Lebanese Celine Dion). The festival lasts two weeks, and spectators can buy one day passes (JD1) for most events but must buy separate tickets in advance for the top acts (JD5-10). Tickets are sold all over Amman (and usually sell out) in the weeks beforehand. Transport to and from Jerash is chaotic. Your best bet is to get a group together and share a private taxi. For details and line-up, check with the Jerash Festival Office, P.O. Box 910 582, Amman (☎06 567 51 99), look on the web at www.jerashfestival.com.jo, or read the *Jordan Times*. Also see **Jerash Festival,** p. 434.

CARDO. Otherwise known as the **Street of Columns,** the Cardo runs from the Forum to the **North Gate.** Its 260 pairs of columns are Corinthian replacements for earlier Ionic columns once capped by aqueducts carrying water throughout the city. The holes in the floor drained rainwater into a sophisticated sewer system. Enormous sidewalk coverings protected pedestrians from the sun, but only traces of these metropolitan parasols remain. The main avenue's first intersection is named the **South Tetrapylon** after its four huge slabs of stone, once accompanied by pillars and a large statue. Going west (left) at the cross street leads to the remains of a 7th-century Umayyad building. Back on the Cardo to the left, frescoes depicting lizards, cats, and turtles decorate the floor of the 4th-century **Cathedral,** built from and on top of the remains of a 2nd-century temple to Dionysus. Next along the avenue of arches is the **Nymphaeum,** built in 191 CE. Intricate stone carvings and the incorporation of marble and gypsum indicate that this two-story fountain was assembled at the height of Jerash's fortune; later it was used in an annual reenactment of the Miracle at Cana where Jesus changed water into wine (John 2:1-11). The gigantic bowl in front of the fountain was a pool that caught water as it cascaded over the Nymphaeum's facade.

JERASH ANTIQUITIES MUSEUM. Well hidden to the right, this museum lies a short way down the pillared promenade. Tall display cases mounted along the walls show neatly arranged artifacts from the Neolithic Age to the Ottoman period. Theater "tickets" made of stone, a three-dimensional model of the ruins, coins, and jewelry are highlights of the museum's small collection. Opposite the museum and across the Cardo is the city's **Agora,** a newly-restored meeting place with a central fountain. This small area served as the city's meat and fish market. *(Museum open daily 8am-6pm; in winter 8am-5pm. Free.)*

TEMPLE OF ARTEMIS. A short jaunt farther down the Cardo leads to the impressive Artemis Temple Stairway. Two flights up, the ominous columned structure at the top of the hill to the left of the Cardo is the Temple of Artemis. The patron goddess of Jerash, daughter of Zeus, and sister of Apollo, Artemis held special significance throughout the Decapolis, once the territory of similar goddesses Ishtar and Anat. Her temple consists of a Great Gate, a shrine-topped podium, and a courtyard surrounded by giant pillars. Descend the staircase and continue on the Cardo to the **West Baths,** including a 2nd-century cold bath *(frigidarium)*, warm bath *(tepidarium)*, hot bath *(caldarium)*, and changing rooms. The **East Baths,** across the *wadi* by the bus station, are even larger and more majestic. A left at the **North Tetrapylon** leads to the **North Theater.**

CHURCH OF ST. COSMOS AND ST. DAMIUS. Behind Artemis's monument, 200m to the left (facing the temple), lie a series of Byzantine churches built in the 6th century CE. Especially worth the walk is the Church of St. Cosmos and St. Damius, dedicated to a twin-brother team of doctors who treated their patients for free. Though barbed wire bars entrance to the church, peering over the edge from above affords a great view of its mosaic floor. Depicting the doctors surrounded by animals, the floor is one of the few pieces of art in the city to survive the 720 CE attempt of Umayyad Caliph Yazid II to destroy all images of God's creations. Walk like an archaeologist into the adjoining Church of St. John—hidden mosaics emerge with a gentle shuffle of the feet.

▓ DAYTRIP FROM JERASH: DIBBIN NATIONAL PARK

*An access road about 2km south of Jerash off the Amman-Jerash Highway leads to the park; look for signs. Take a **car** or hire a **taxi** (JD3), as neither buses nor service travel to the park. Alternatively, take a **bus** from Jerash to the nearby village of Dibbin and then **hike** 2km uphill from the village to the park.*

The pines and oaks of this fertile woodland are a sight for sore eyes in the middle of the desert wasteland. In the hills 10km southwest of Jerash and 65km north of Amman, Dibbin National Park (pronounced dib-EEN) encompasses some 20km of forest stretching south from a town of the same name. On weekends, hordes of locals flee nearby Irbid and Amman to picnic in Dibbin, somehow managing to bring a little of the urban frenzy along with them. So if you come seeking serenity, consider visiting Dibbin during the week, when you could easily be the only person in the park. The **Dibbin Rest House**, on the old road from Jerash past Dibbin village, offers private bungalows that come with refrigerators, TVs, and porches. (☎ 02 633 97 10; fax 635 11 46. Doubles JD25; camping JD3.)

AJLOUN عجلون ☎ 02

Atop the highest peak of the Ajloun region lies the ancient **Qal'at al-Rabad** (Ajloun Castle), an imposing fortress built in 1184 to thwart Crusader efforts. Its name loosely translates as "the castle that straddles a hill." Izz al-Din Usama, Salah al-Din's nephew, built the fortress in order to outdo the Castle of Belvoir on Lake Tiberias, but with its four corner towers and seven floors, Qal'at al-Rabadh more closely resembles Karak Castle, south of Amman (see **Karak**, p. 478). Filled with secret passages, dark corridors, and winding, crumbly staircases, the castle makes any gumshoe feel like Indiana Jones.

▐ GETTING THERE. Ajloun lies a mountainous 24km west of Jerash, an easy **bus** ride from Amman (1½hr., 450fils; last returns 5pm, in winter 3pm) or Irbid (45min., 250fils). The bus from Amman's Abdali Station stops a few streets down from the main circle. Follow the sound of honking cars and smell of shawarma a few blocks uphill until you reach the traffic circle at the center of town. From the circle, the castle is a strenuous, but not impossible, 4km hike up a mountain road (1hr.). Catch a **taxi** for 500fils-JD1 (be sure to negotiate before getting in) or take the poor **minibus** that struggles its way up the steep road to the castle (60fils). Especially on Fridays, public transportation can be slow—start walking uphill and flag the bus or a taxi on the way. Passersby may also offer you a lift if you're looking tired.

▐ PRACTICAL INFORMATION. Ajloun's **Directorate of Tourism**, about 200m downhill from the castle, gives out free maps and brochures and can arrange for a guided tour of the castle. (☎ 642 01 15. JD4, tip JD1.) Exchange money on the center circle at the **Housing Bank** (PLUS/V ATM) or at the **Bank of Jordan**. (Open Su-Th 8:30am-3pm.) The **post office** is about 1km from the center of town, back up the road toward Jerash. (Open Su-Th 8am-5pm.)

▐▊█ ACCOMMODATIONS AND FOOD. Both of Ajloun's hotels are within walking distance of the castle along the road to town, though it's hard to see why anyone would want to spend a night in town. At **al-Rabad Castle Hotel,** new rooms come with TV, phone, balcony with sunset view, and immaculate bathrooms. (☎642 02 02. Singles JD24; doubles JD32; with breakfast, add 10% service charge. Student discount.) The **Ajloun Hotel,** closer to the castle, offers clean, bright rooms, built-in closets, therapeutically hard mattresses, a swimming pool, and awesome views. (☎/fax 642 05 24; mobile 07 965 62 33; ajloun@firstnet.com.jo. Singles JD24; doubles JD32. Student discount if vacancy.) The restaurants of both hotels offer lunch with a view for a hefty JD4-6.

Those who prefer to fill their bellies rather than their eyes should stop in at the **Green Mountain Restaurant;** follow the signs from Ajloun's center circle. A half-chicken goes for JD1.25, a kebab sandwich is 300fils, and 850fils buys a complete meal. (☎642 09 05. Open daily 6:30am-9:30pm; in winter 6:30am-8pm.) The **Abu al-Izz Restaurant** (☎642 20 32), on the main circle in front of the Green Mountain, is a sprawling outdoor cafe that offers the usual Middle Eastern food for higher prices than the Green Mountain, but with leafy trellises and nicer ambiance. You can get half of a chicken for JD2 and add hummus for 500fils. The **Bonita Ajloun Restaurant,** adjacent to the Directorate of Tourism office, has a magnificent view of the castle with an expensive Middle Eastern buffet (JD6; salad JD4). The reasonably priced menu ranges from the benign (hummus 500fils) to the bizarre ("Brains in Brine" JD1.5). As always, **street vendors** provide economical and delicious alternatives.

◪ SIGHTS. The **Ajloun Castle** once controlled a long stretch of Jordan's northern valley and protected lines between Jordan and Syria. Crusaders spent decades trying to capture the castle and nearby village. After the Crusader threat dissipated, Salah al-Din used the castle as a base to control nearby iron mines, joining a chain of message posts stretched across the Middle East that were linked by beacon and pigeon. The network allowed messages to be sent from Baghdad to Cairo in only 12hr. During the Ottoman period, 50 soldiers were stationed in the castle at all times. After that, the castle was mostly uninhabited until 1812, when Swiss explorer J.L. Burkhardt (better known for discovering Petra the same year; see **Petra,** p. 481) found 40 members of the Barakat family living there. Two major earthquakes in 1837 and 1927 inflicted damage the Crusades never could. While the castle is in quite good condition today, parts of it are still under restoration by the Department of Antiquities. Hiring a guide is cheap, but it's more fun just to poke around with a flashlight. *(Open daily 8am-7pm; in winter 8am-5pm. JD1.)*

IRBID اربد ☎02

The streets that were once crowded with the residents of ancient Dion, a city in the Decapolis League, are now a fluorescent maze of Internet cafes and pool halls catering to the 18,000 students of **Yarmouk University.** Traces of Dion disappeared long ago from Irbid's environs, and unlike some of its more popular neighbors, Irbid has little to offer the ruin-hungry tourist. However, welcoming locals, great hotels and restaurants, and a rather unique nightlife combine to make Irbid the best location from which to explore the surrounding sites of Umm Qeis, Jerash, and Ajloun.

▐ TRANSPORTATION

Some Arab travelers may hitch to Irbid via Jerash, but the quickest and safest way to the city from Amman is with the **Hijazi Bus Co.,** which sends roomy, air-conditioned **buses** to Irbid from Amman's Abdali Station (1½hr., every 20min., 850fils). **Minibuses** to Irbid from Amman, Jerash, and Ajloun are slightly cheaper (600-700fils) but often slower and not nearly as convenient (especially for those with luggage). Both the Hijazi buses and the minibuses will drop you off at **New South Station,** also called **al-Janoubi Station** or "Mujma Amman Jadeed"—from which you can take a **service** downtown (80fils). **Taxis** from New South Station to downtown cost approximately 600fils, as do taxis from downtown to Yarmouk University. The latter may cost JD1 after midnight. *Service* from downtown to Yarmouk (120fils) leave from Othman bin Afan St., at its intersection with Jama St. (also known as University St., but "Shafeeq Rshaidat St." on street signs). From King Abdullah Sq., walk down Arar St. toward the obelisk monument. Continue in this direction after you pass the monument (you are now on Jama St.) for two blocks. The line of white *service* will be on the left. The walk between downtown and Yarmouk University is only 1km, and it follows Jama St. the entire way.

Leaving Irbid is insultingly simple. To travel north, go to **Shamali Station** (North Station). **Minibuses** to Umm Qeis and al-Himmeh leave every 30min. (250fils). To travel south (to Ajloun, Amman, or Jerash), head to New South Station. **Minibuses** run regularly to Ajloun (250fils) and to Amman's **Abdali Station** (825fils). The last **buses** depart for Amman at about 8pm (in winter 6pm). Between New South Station and Shamali Station, taxis cost 750fils.

Service also leave New South Station for **Damascus** (3-4hr. depending on border crossings, JD4). Bring your **visa** and JD5 exit fee; entering Syria should be painless as long as there is no evidence of a trip to Israel in your passport and you carefully follow your *service* driver's instructions (for details, see **Border Crossings**, p. 436). You'll first pass through Jordanian customs and then Syrian customs a mile later. Irbid also launches travelers to **Israel**. Take a *service* from East Station (Aghwar) to the bridge (bring passport and JD5 exit fee). **Al-Thinkah Company** buses (☎ 725 09 78) travel directly from East Station to Tel Aviv.

Irbid

⌂ ACCOMMODATIONS
Abu Bakr Hotel, **1**
Al-Amin al-Kabir Hotel, **2**
Omayed Hotel, **3**

◆ FOOD
Palestine Restaurant, **4**

② ORIENTATION AND PRACTICAL INFORMATION

Irbid has two town centers: the older **city center,** and the more modern one around Yarmouk University. The northern and southern boundaries of the old city center are Hashimi St. and King Hussein St. (often known as Baghdad St.), with **King Abdullah Sq.** (a traffic triangle with a fountain) at the focal point. The town **mosque** and **market** are about one block downhill from King Abdullah Sq., to the right. The **Housing Bank,** with PLUS/V **ATMs,** has branches at Hashimi St. and King Hussein St. To get to the **post office,** walk downhill past the fountain in King Abdullah Sq. and make a left onto King Hussein St. Walk about 150m, and the post office is on the right. (☎ 724 47 19. Open Sa-Th 7:30am-7pm, F and holidays 7:30am-12:30pm.)

Yarmouk University is across town to the south, just a short *service* ride or 15min. walk away. **University St.,** the main drag of the Yarmouk region, is packed with restaurants and **Internet providers** (500fils per hr.). Travelers should note that inhabitants of Irbid often call streets by names that are not written on street signs. A decent map of Irbid is published by the Ministry of Tourism (☎/fax 724 17 44 or 727 70 66). Some hotels will have copies at the front desk, but it is otherwise hard to find. Irbid is not a confusing city; knowing the location of a few landmarks (King Abdullah Sq. and Yarmouk University in particular) and which directions are north (*shimaal*) and south (*junub*) will be almost as useful as any available map.

▌ ACCOMMODATIONS

It is wise to stay around the older city center, as hotels in happening Yarmouk cost more. If you're up for the splurge, have about JD30 ready per night.

▨ Omayad Hotel (☎/fax 724 59 55), on Baghdad St., directly south of King Abdullah Sq. The entrance is through a corridor left of the Irbid Supermarket and up 3 flights of stairs. All rooms have phones, fans, private baths, and satellite TV that you can watch while you're on the can. Back rooms are quiet but street-side rooms afford spectacular views of the noise below. The English-speaking staff is helpful and hospitable. Singles JD14; doubles JD18. Add 10% tax. Student discount.

Al-Amin al-Kabir Hotel (☎ 724 23 84; al_ameen_hotel@hotmail.com.), on the southeast corner of King Abdullah Sq. Entrance is off Orouba St. Bright and breezy rooms, clean communal baths, courteous management, electric fans, and small kitchen for guest use. Street-side rooms have balconies. Hot shower 500fils. Singles JD5; doubles JD8.

Abu Bakr Hotel (☎ 724 26 95), around the corner from al-Amin on Wasfi al-Tal St., in same building as the Bank of Jordan. Rooms are clean but rather unexciting, all have ceiling fans, and some have private baths with tiny doors. Almost exclusively male clientele. Singles JD2; doubles JD4; triples JD6.

Al-Joude Hotel (☎ 727 55 15 or 727 55 16; fax 727 55 17; joud@go.com.jo), near Yarmouk University. Signs near the circle on University St. direct visitors down a quiet side street to the hotel entrance. The trying-to-be-trendy decor is surprisingly successful, and the spacious A/C rooms with satellite TV and private baths make al-Joude one of the best values in the overpriced Yarmouk area. Singles JD30; doubles JD42. Ask for discounts, particularly during the academic summer break (June-Aug.).

▐ FOOD

Streets around Yarmouk University are lined with sprawling restaurants, packed with families and procrastinating students, that serve filling regional dishes at low prices (JD1-4). Popeye's Fried Chicken, Subway, and Pizza Hut are on University St. near Yarmouk, but even if you've been unimpressed with falafel and shawarma so far, give the food stands around the university a chance. The cheapest food in Irbid is also some of Jordan's best (falafel 150fils; shawarma 250-300fils). The local market is downtown, near the mosque. The Irbid Supermarket, on King Hussein St. beneath the Omayad Hotel, is a good place to stock up on supplies for a daytrip.

Andalusia Restaurant (☎ 724 15 86), across from post office, on the 6th fl. of the building above Grindlay's Bank. Enter an interior corridor to the right of the bank entrance and take the rickety elevator up to the restaurant. The classy decor and friendly service complement Andalusia's extensive traditional menu. Hummus or *baba ghanoush* 400fils. Salad 600fils-JD1.1. Mixed grill JD2.5. Open daily 10am-10pm.

Palestine Restaurant, on King Hussein St., on the left as you head east past Andalusia. Full of famished Irbidians feeding on french fries, *fuul*, falafel, and Fanta for a few hundred fils. Open daily 6am-9pm.

Ish al-Hana Restaurant, on the right as you head south from the circle on University St., signs in Arabic. The best of many "open-air restaurant-cafes" that crowd the streets around the university. Mixed grill JD1.9. Hummus 450fils. Open daily 7:30am-midnight.

👁 SIGHTS

The university's **Museum of Jordanian Heritage,** 150m to the right as you pass through the campus' North Gate, offers Jordan's best and most comprehensive narrative of the nation's history from prehistoric times to the present. (☎724 56 13 or 750 00 71. Open W-M 10am-5pm. Free.)

🎵📺 ENTERTAINMENT AND NIGHTLIFE

Yarmouk University students have introduced two vices into Irbid's nightlife: the Internet and billiards. Nearly every business in the section of University St. near Yarmouk provides one or both of these services, and the local student-junkies still can't get enough. The scene can be pleasantly intense, but until someone figures out how to play pool over the Internet, there is a limited number of things to do. Those seeking a more mellow atmosphere can join swanky locals at the **News Cafe** in the basement of al-Joude Hotel for drinks (beer JD2.45), Jordan's version of MTV, and—of course—pool tables and Internet access. (☎727 55 15 or 727 55 16. Open daily 10am-midnight.) Or, for something completely different, step right up to thrills and spills (for a mere 200fils) at the **Yarmouk Amusement Park,** south of the circle on University St. (look for the Ferris wheel). Irbid residents scream and sing on the Pirate's Ship, while kids of all ages get belligerent on the bumper cars for 500fils. (Open daily until 11pm.)

UMM QEIS أم قيس ☎02

Umm Qeis was once the Biblical **Gadara,** where Jesus is said to have turned a sinner's demons into a herd of pigs that drowned in the Sea of Galilee. This thriving town was another of the 10 cities in the Decapolis League, founded by Pompey after his conquest of Syria and Palestine in 64 BCE. Its name comes from a Semitic word meaning "stronghold," reflecting the city's role as a fortified border town guarding the crucial land routes between southern Syria and northern Palestine. Once a satellite resort for Romans vacationing at al-Himmeh's therapeutic hot springs, Umm Qeis was renowned for its arts and orgiastic extravagances. Despite earthquakes and plagues in the 7th and 8th centuries CE, Umm Qeis survived through the subsequent Umayyad and Islamic periods and seems to have been continuously inhabited for over 5000 years. The last residents were run out of town as recently as 1972, when the Jordanian Department of Antiquities declared Umm Qeis to be an archaeological site not fit for habitation.

📧 TRANSPORTATION AND PRACTICAL INFORMATION. The **minibus** from Irbid's North (Shamali) Station will stop at the base of the ruins if you tell the driver where you are headed (250fils). Buy **water** at the stores in town or the two **gift shops** left of the road leading up to the ruins. (Shops open daily 7am-7pm.) To get to the **post office** in modern Umm Qeis, walk away from the ruins toward town, and turn right on the road across from the Umm Qeis Hotel. The post office is about 50m down the hill. (☎750 00 05. Open Su-Th 8am-2pm.)

🏠🍴 ACCOMMODATIONS AND FOOD. The value-packed **█Umm Qeis Hotel** is about 100m from the ruins. Walk away from the ruins on the main road toward town and look for signs on your left. The hotel is up a pink alley. Its brightly painted rooms have large windows, some overlooking the street. The best view is from the roof, where you can dine in sight of the ruins and, yes, the Golan Heights. Great for solo women travelers. (☎750 00 80. Breakfast JD2.5; dinner JD3-4. JD6 per person, with bath JD8.) The beautiful **Umm Qeis Rest House,** next to the museum, offers one of the best outdoor settings in Jordan. Reasonably priced refreshments (beer JD2), regional dishes (*mezze* JD1.5), and pastas (JD2-3) are welcome complements to the main dish (JD0)—a breathtaking view of the Sea of

Galilee. (☎750 05 55. Open 9am-10pm.) Typical Middle Eastern food is also available at a few relatively inexpensive establishments along the main road.

◪ **SIGHTS.** Visitors to the **Umm Qeis Ruins** wander among a mix of Greco-Roman, Byzantine, Ottoman, and Islamic architecture, strategically perched atop a mountain in northwest Jordan. (Open daily 7am-7pm. JD1.) The two-room **Umm Qeis Museum** (the white two-story building flying the Jordanian flag) has a small collection of artifacts for each period of the site's occupation. Don't miss **Tyche,** the patron goddess of Gadara. Though lacking a few key appendages, she still holds onto her fruit-filled cornucopia, a symbol of fertility. Journey back in time through the **Roman ruins.** The foundations of the **North Theater,** once able to accommodate audiences of 5000, is barely visible just outside the museum. The Ottomans used the actual stones of the structure to build the village on the hill. West of the North Theater is the **Basilica Terrace,** where black basalt Corinthian columns surround octagonally arranged white limestone ones (once belonging to a Byzantine church). Dug into a hillside southwest of the Basilica, the fully restored **West Theater** demonstrates the grandeur that characterized ancient Gadara. The Roman **Main Road** traverses the ancient village, running from the North Theater to the **Roman Bathhouse,** which lies at the northwest corner of the ruins. Alongside the road, you will see a series of barrel-vaulted rooms that once functioned as street-front **shops.** Near these rooms are the weed-entangled ruins of the **East Baths** and **Nymphaeum.** Looking downhill, you can see the **Roman Aqueduct** that brought water to Umm Qeis from present-day Syria.

▐ **DAYTRIP FROM UMM QEIS: AL-HIMMEH** الحمة

*A mere 10km from Umm Qeis, al-Himmeh is accessible by **bus** (150fils) or **taxi** (JD2); you can also take a bus from North Station in Irbid (300fils). To catch the bus from Umm Qeis, stand outside the Umm Qeis Hotel and flag down buses until you find one going to al-Himmeh. Get off the bus in front of al-Himmeh Hotel and Restaurant, just before the road forks; the driver will know the place. To return to Umm Qeis or Irbid from al-Himmeh, follow the same protocol outside al-Himmeh Hotel and Restaurant (last bus 5:30pm). Bring a **passport** along for the ride to al-Himmeh—there is a checkpoint along the way.*

The therapeutic hot springs and lush vegetation of al-Himmeh seduce visitors from all over the Arab world. The few Westerners who make it to al-Himmeh, which straddles Jordan's borders with Israel and Syria, find the village to be one of the most hospitable in Jordan. Covered with banana, guava, and lemon farms, al-Himmeh is an ideal place to swim, camp, and unwind in the shade.

The hotel and restaurant complexes are perfect if you're staying in town for more than a day. The **Sah al-Noun Hotel,** tucked among the banana farms at the base of the Golan Heights, boasts a hot springs canal in its garden restaurant. To get there, follow the road to the left as it forks after al-Himmeh Hotel and Restaurant. Sah al-Noun is about 100m down the road. The hospitable English-speaking manager, Samara Samara, will take guests for a swim in the Roman-style hot springs pool next door (JD1-3), arrange hunting tours, and tell you everything you ever wanted to know about his farm over tea. (☎750 05 10, 727 31 58, or 07 970 02 25. Breakfast included. JD6.5 per person. Foreign currency and traveler's checks accepted. Ask about camping options.) **Al-Himmeh Hotel and Restaurant** (☎ 750 05 05 or 750 05 11) is a resort-style establishment centered around a 40m pool of spring water. The adjacent hot, warm, and cool baths are popular with local residents and well worth the JD1 admission. They operate on a rotating segregated-sex schedule, so beware of the red sign outside the entrance to avoid offending anyone with your gendered presence. (Doubles JD10; triples JD11, chalet JD29; chalet quints JD40.)

EAST OF AMMAN

Originating as rain in the mountains of Syria, vast quantities of underground water flow undetected beneath the scorching black deserts of eastern Jordan. Until just a few years ago, this subterranean river bubbled through to the surface at a spot

75km east of Amman, forming the Azraq Oasis—an area of expansive wetlands teeming with lush vegetation and exotic wildlife. However, water is now being pumped into Amman at twice the rate that it is naturally replenished, and the water level at the oasis has now dropped below ground. The drying up of Azraq has not significantly altered the steady flow of trucks between Jordan, Iraq, and Saudi Arabia, but it has been a disaster for birds migrating between Europe and Africa. Fortunately, the Royal Society for the Conservation of Nature (RSCN) has established Azraq as a reserve and has begun to pump some of the exported water back into the former wetlands. With the return of water and a dramatic collection of bird life to the reserve, Azraq has become something of an environmental success story, though there is much work still to be done.

Water isn't the only thing that disappeared from Azraq. The most remarkable records of human habitation here are the scattered Umayyad castles (*qusur;* singular *qasr*), once part of a chain of fortresses from north of Damascus to near Jericho. Built in the 7th and 8th centuries CE, the castles were mysteriously abandoned a century later. The imposing stonework of Qasr Kharaneh and strategic location of Qasr Azraq support speculation that the castles sheltered caravans along the trade route between Syria, the Arabian peninsula, and the Far East. The baths near Qasr al-Hallabat and the magnificent frescoes at Qasr Amra provided respite from the vast, unforgiving desert. Still relatively tourist-free, these quietly majestic ruins will amaze you with the strength of their masonry and arches.

TRANSPORTATION

A trip to eastern Jordan is an exciting and unique experience for those who can afford to rent a car for two or three days; anyone bent on public transportation faces a substantial challenge. If you are only interested in the **Desert Castles,** you can attempt to bargain for a **taxi** from Amman, which should include a half-day's wheels and someone who knows the route (half-day JD25, full-day JD30). Another easy but constricting way to see the castles is to arrange a daytrip through the **Cliff Hostel** (JD15; see p. 448) or the **Farah Hotel.** These tours will usually skip the least spectacular castle, Qasr al-Hallabat. Individual trip prices are contingent on a full car, so arrange 2-3 days in advance or expect to pay more for empty seats. A trip to **Umm al-Jimal** can be included in a tour of the Desert Castles for an additional cost (about JD5), but you'll have to leave early if you expect to fit all this archaeology into one day. However, the easiest—though most expensive—way to enjoy the well-spaced-out splendors of eastern Jordan is to rent a car in Amman. Car rental agencies usually require a minimum rental of two days, so a drive out east will involve spending the night somewhere, most likely the hospitable **Azraq Oasis.** An air-conditioned, automatic transmission sedan with unlimited mileage should cost around JD30 per day, from either a big name like Avis or Budget or one of the local agencies (see **Car Rental,** p. 444). Renting and returning the car at the airport will save you the painful experience of "driving" in Amman.

As always, **hitchhiking** in the desert is potentially suicidal, and therefore discouraged. Hitchhikers should beware of the intense sun and vast, desolate spaces involved in the desert loop. Travelers report that ever-friendly Jordanians are quick to pick up hitchers, but vehicles can be few and far between in these parts. Those who decide to try their luck by thumb (or downward-turned palm, as tradition has it here) should bring a head covering and much more water than they think they will need. It is also wise to tell your hostel where you are going and when to expect your return. *Let's Go* does not recommend hitchhiking, though many travelers have and will continue to travel this way.

UMM AL-JIMAL ال ج ـ م ا ل

Lacking the monumental buildings of Jerash and Umm Qeis, the sprawling ruins of Umm al-Jimal exemplify the unadorned life of a rural Roman city. The builders of this black basalt town emphasized durability over grandeur, and up until a few decades ago, the 1400-year-old reservoir continued to fill up with run-off water—a level of sophistication in water management that modern Jordan is still struggling

JORDAN

NAVIGATING EASTERN JORDAN. The following description details a clockwise road trip to the major desert castles, Umm al-Jimal, and Azraq: (1) from Amman, head north on Hwy. 15 to Mafraq (70km); (2) go east on Hwy. 10 to Umm al-Jimal (15km); (3) backtrack to Mafraq, then go south on Hwy. 15 to Hwy. 30 near Zarqa (40km); (4) go east on Hwy. 30 and follow signs to Azraq (87km), passing Qasr al-Hallabat (30km from Zarqa); (5) leave Azraq to the west and continue west on Hwy. 40, passing Qasr Amra (25km from Azraq) and Qasr Kharaneh (40km from Azraq); (6) follow signs for the airport (90km from Azraq) and visit Qasr Mushatta (40km south of Amman). Public transportation is available between Amman, Zarqa, and Mafraq, but the return leg will be a struggle without your own car or hired taxi, and hitchhikers face a real danger of getting stranded. Accepting rides from the army is illegal, and they will take you only as far as whatever lonely desert depot they happen to be going to.

to attain. The site's history began in the 2nd or 3rd century, when Umm al-Jimal was a Nabatean farming village. In the 5th century, the installation of a Roman military station brought increased security to the city. Umm al-Jimal flourished a century later under Byzantine rule as a trade center, with a population of about 7000 ministered to by the 15 excavated churches you can see today. But an earthquake that struck in 747 CE marked the beginning of Umm al-Jimal's 1200-year period of decay. Today, the ruins rise up from mounds of black rock, giving the site the eerie feeling of a ghost town. Bedouin still make their homes here and shelter their camels amongst the standing buildings. (This practice is believed to have spawned the city's modern name: Umm al-Jimal means "Mother of Camels" in Arabic.) The adjacent farming village has several stores and food stands for those needing a snack before or after exploring this large site.

The main entrance is on the south side, opposite the **Visitors Center,** which offers much-needed drinks (water or soda 500fils) and less-needed guides. The **Barracks,** Umm al-Jimal's tallest structure, is just inside the main gate. Constructed by the Romans, the remaining three stories of the corner tower demonstrate the amazing durability of the stone arch. Heading north on the main road will take you past what is believed to have been a **Nabatean Temple** housing the characteristic sacrificial altar. Further to the north lie the ruins of a **Praetorium** (military headquarters) and the **West Church,** next to the **Gate of Commodus,** which has Byzantine crosses inscribed into its archways. Walking east from the Praetorium involves some delicate scrambling over piles of basalt and the standing walls of ruined houses, but eventually you'll reach the open-air pool of the **Main Reservoir.** The reservoir fed a network of canals that provided water to the underground reservoirs of the main houses and irrigation pools outside of town. The site stretches over almost ½ sq. km, with hundreds of buildings and homes clustered around larger, better-preserved structures, but the most impressive thing to note here is how different Umm al-Jimal is from the monumental Roman cities of western Jordan.

To get to Umm al-Jimal, drive east on Hwy. 10 from Mafraq and turn left down the marked access road. A minibus also travels sporadically between the site and Mafraq (30min., 200fils). The site is open daily during daylight hours; it is free.

QASR AL-HALLABAT قصر الحلابات

Qasr al-Hallabat's ruined arches appear in the desert approximately 30km east of Zarqa. From Hwy. 30 eastbound, turn left onto the paved road marked by a sign for the castle and follow this road for about 1km, until another sign directs you uphill to the gate. The gatekeeper's tent is to the right of the main gate, far from the crumbling castle. You're free to roam around whatever is there, but keep in mind that any gatekeeper who gives you information will expect a few hundred fils in return. Originally constructed as a Roman fort by the bath-obsessed emperor Caracalla (198-217 CE), Qasr al-Hallabat was later used by the Byzantines as a monastery. The Umayyads rebuilt it as a residential palace in the 8th century and added a mosque just meters away from the main fortress. Look for the Byzantine carvings on the remaining walls and fallen slabs of stone.

Back on the main highway, the sand and limestone desert to the south contrasts sharply with the gray volcanic desert to the north. Just off the road to the south is **Hammam al-Sarh,** a ruined bathhouse modeled after Qasr Amra. A 1000-year-old well covered by a rusty metal grating lurks to the left of the bathhouse. Though some daredevils have been known to climb onto the grating and peer into the abyss below, *Let's Go* does not recommend taking this risk.

AZRAQ الازرق   ☎06

On the long and grinding road east, you'll hear nothing but the entreaties of your overheating engine and the gentle rumble of tankers smuggling Iraqi crude oil into Jordan. The flat, rocky desert comes to a brief end at the former oasis of **Azraq Junction,** now a truck stop. Lined with colorful restaurants and gas stations, the stretch of road south of the junction offers a moment of relaxation to tourists on their way to desert castles and truckers on their way to Saudi Arabia. A couple of nice hotels and restaurants entice some visitors to spend the night. The nearby nature reserves are well worth an extended stay.

🛈 PRACTICAL INFORMATION. The Azraq **post office** is north of the castle, just off the main road. (☎383 40 02. Open Sa-Th 8am-2pm.) **Jordan Bank** and **Housing Bank** are on the main road as well, uphill from the castle, (Open for exchange Sa-W 9am-1pm and 4-5pm, Th 9am-1pm.) There are no ATMs in Azraq.

🛏🍴 ACCOMMODATIONS AND FOOD. The small markets and food stands surrounding Qasr Azraq are a good way for visitors to avoid the overpriced tourist traps nearby, but the best food and lodging is to be found south of the castle near Azraq Junction.

Five hundred meters north of Azraq Junction, down a tree-lined road, is the government-run **Azraq Resthouse.** Rooms include bath, air-conditioning, color TV, refrigerator, and a view of the pool, which non-guests may use (JD3). The expensive restaurant in the Resthouse serves meals for JD4.5. (☎383 40 06; fax 383 52 15. Singles JD20; doubles JD24.) The **Zoubi Hotel,** on the left as you head south through Azraq Junction, is a good value, even though all the beds have built-in radios that don't work. (☎383 50 12. Singles and doubles JD10.) If you insist on staying near Qasr Azraq, the slightly run-down **Sayad Hotel,** visible from the castle, is graced with an olive grove, a rose garden, and paintings of the owner. (☎383 40 94. Breakfast included. Singles JD24; doubles JD32.)

A slew of **24hr. restaurants** lines the main road south of Azraq Junction. Outfitted with flashy lights and kitschy fountains, they cater to truckers, and the Middle Eastern food is good and cheap. **Al-Arz,** on the main road 400m south of the gas station, will let you watch CNN as they fatten you up with generous kebab portions. (☎07 996 97 07. Hummus and kebab JD2. Open 24hr.) The **Azraq Palace Restaurant,** on the main road between the castle and Azraq Junction, offers a large buffet (JD6) and live music nightly (8-10pm), but the only real reason to suffer through this tourist buffet is to use the **■best bathrooms** in all of Jordan, in the rear of the restaurant. (☎/fax 439 71 44. Restaurant and bathrooms open daily 7am-11pm.)

◧ SIGHTS. About 13km north of Azraq Junction on the highway to Iraq stands **Qasr Azraq,** in excellent condition thanks to extensive restoration. The black basalt fort was built by the Romans in 300 CE and rebuilt by the Ayyubids in 1237. Of its three levels, only parts of the second level survived a 1927 earthquake, including a ceiling that exposes a web of basalt beams. The Druze gatekeeper will haul open the remarkable three-ton stone portal of the castle, and he might also show you his photocopied **Lawrence of Arabia** photograph collection (many of the photographs look suspiciously like the gatekeeper's grandfather). The most interesting attractions lie within a few meters of the entrance. Looking up from the main door,

JORDAN

you'll see the *machicoulis* (holes) through which boiling oil and molten lead were poured on the heads of invaders. Carved into the pavement behind the main gate is a Roman board game—ask the gatekeeper to show you how to play. In the center of the courtyard lies a small mosque, originally built as a Roman church. Just above the entrance was the living space of the aforementioned Larry, who used this fort as his headquarters during the Arab revolt against Ottoman rule in 1917.

Keep an eye out for the desert wildlife that has been making a comeback since Jordan began to protect its fragile habitat. In the **Shaumari Wildlife Reserve,** south of Azraq Junction and 5km down a well-marked turnoff, the RSCN is reintroducing ostriches, Persian onagers (wild asses), and gazelles. However, the star of the show is clearly the endangered Arabian oryx (antelope). Able to survive 22 days without drinking, these antelopes were sometimes followed by thirsty Bedouin aware of the animal's ability to smell water up to 150km away. Unfortunately, the oryx's survival powers were no match for hordes of ugly men. The oryx was hunted nearly to extinction for its horns, which were thought to be aphrodisiacs when ground up and burnt. The **Azraq Wetland Reserve** (☎ 383 54 25), 2km down a marked access road departing east from the center of Azraq Junction, offers visitors a glimpse of the former environment of Azraq Oasis. Wooden walkways lead visitors through the restored wetlands, over shallow pools, between corridors of reeds, and into a spectacular concentration of lizards, fish, and birds. The attached **Information Center** walks you through the fascinating history and precarious future of the oasis. (Both reserves open daily 8am-7pm; 8am-5pm in winter. Entry JD3 plus 10% tax. 50% student discount. Joint ticket for both reserves JD4.5.)

EAST OF AZRAQ AND THE IRAQI BORDER

A 150km chunk of desert extends to the northeast from Azraq to Iraq. The final junction is **Safawi,** the town where the roads from Mafraq (Hwy. 10) and Azraq (Hwy. 5) meet. From Safawi, Hwy. 10 leads to the border town of **al-Karama,** racing through the searing basalt desert (the undisturbed residue of prehistoric volcanic eruptions). The black horizon expands insistently in every direction, interrupted only by the occasional dust storm vortex and Bedouin encampment—as well as a blue sign every 10km listing the distance to Iraq. A steady stream of oil tankers make their way to and from the border, sharing the road with the occasional military truck or **minibus** on its way to Baghdad from Amman (13hr., JD8). There is little to see but a lot to experience in this region, which makes up one-quarter of Jordan's total land area. As your air-conditioned sedan chugs along—just hours from where mankind mastered nature, civilization was created, and religions were born—you find yourself in the middle of nowhere. It's unsettling.

QASR AMRA قصر عمرة

For a sneak preview of Qasr Amra, simply look at any half-dinar bill. Constructed under the auspices of Umayyad Caliph al-Walid ibn 'Abd al-Malik, the hunting lodge and bath complex of Qasr Amra impress visitors with the elegant simplicity of their design. The interior is also the best preserved of the desert palaces: its vaulted stucco ceilings are splashed with lively frescoes, and mosaics cover two of the floors. As you walk in, look to the right at the **mural** depicting the enemies of Islam—among them are the emperors of Byzantium, Persia, and China, as well as Spanish King Roderique. Their faces appear similar to traditional depictions of Jesus, leading many to believe that the artist was Roman rather than Muslim. Moreover, the frescoes throughout the castle ignore the Muslim tradition forbidding the pictorial representation of human beings. Especially surprising are the many portrayals of nude women, which somehow managed to escape the decree of Umayyad Caliph Yazid II (720-24 CE), a weekend visitor of the castle, who ordered all human images destroyed. An early portrayal of the zodiac covers the domed ceiling of the caldarium (hot room). The **Visitors Center,** next to the gatekeeper's office, pairs reproductions of the castle's artwork with historians' interpretations of each scene, and the detailed description of the bath construction presents an example of Umayyad ingenuity.

To reach Qasr Amra, take the road heading southwest of Azraq Junction (Hwy. 40). Qasr Amra is 28km from Qasr Azraq. The visitors center and castle are open daily 7am-7:30pm, 8am-4:30pm in winter. The very hospitable gatekeeper expects *bakhsheesh* of 250-500fils per person.

QASR KHARANEH قصرالخرانة

Qasr Kharaneh, about 15km west of Qasr Amra on Hwy. 40, is named for the small black stones (once more, basalt) that blanket the area. Some experts believe Kharaneh was a defensive castle; they point to the four corner towers, the square plan of a Roman fortress, and the arrow slits in the walls. Others think the slits were part of an elaborate ventilation system and argue that Kharaneh served as a retreat for Umayyad leaders to discuss state matters. Most historians, however, believe it was the first *khan* (inn) of the Islamic world, as the architectural style of the castle is similar to that which later typified Umayyad inns. A painted Arabic dedication in a second-story room dates the building's construction to 710 CE. Greek inscriptions on the doorjambs imply that the Umayyads built upon an earlier structure. Much of the second floor has been restored, setting up a maze of bedrooms, passageways and charming staircases. Two of the more precarious staircases lead up to the roof for a good view of the barren landscape stretching to Saudi Arabia and Iraq. The neighboring military base and the maneuverings of Jordanian troops are also visible. When you've finished exploring, the gatekeeper may let you ride his camel (500fils *bakhsheesh* should do). As he leads you around the castle, listen carefully: he insists that the ghosts of horses, camels, and people roam the ruins.

QASR MUSHATTA قصر مشتة

Getting to the expansive ruins of Mushatta can be a real challenge, but anyone with a sincere interest in Umayyad architecture or aviation (planes landing at Queen Alia International Airport fly within a few hundred feet of the road to the castle) should consider the effort. If driving to the castle, follow signs for the Airport and pass through the first military checkpoint about 2km from the terminals. At the next traffic circle, take the service road leading to the right, immediately after the entrance to the Alia Hotel. The service road winds around the airport, passing through three security checkpoints. (Tell the guards where you are headed and they'll probably just check your passport and point you in the right direction, but it is possible to be turned away). The castle will appear on your right after 4km. For those without a car, public transport to the airport is readily available from Amman or the village of **Muwaqaar** (southeast of Amman), and a taxi (JD5 roundtrip) or a 30min. walk can take you to the rest of the way. If walking, don't follow the service road, simply walk past the airport and then make a left past the Alia cargo terminal. Mushatta will appear on your left. There are a few security checkpoints along the way.

The entrance to the 8th-century castle once beckoned travelers with wonderfully carved floral designs, but most of these stones were delivered to Kaiser Wilhelm II as a gift from Ottoman Sultan Abdulhamid II, and only fragments remain. A piece of the wall now stands in the Berlin Museum. (Note to Jordanian museum curators: maybe you can finagle a slice of the Berlin Wall in return?) The castle rooms were cooled by a clever ventilation system, which on a windy day is still refreshingly effective. Although the size of the ruins attest to the builders' ambition, the castle was never completed. The upper levels of Mushatta were constructed with smaller, weaker bricks than the other castles, and the hastily erected portions still bear the graffiti and handprints of 8th-century masons.

SOUTH OF AMMAN

Three roads link Amman and Aqaba: the **King's Highway**, the **Wadi Araba Highway** (a.k.a. Jordan Valley), and the **Desert Highway.** Of these routes, the King's Highway (Wadi Mujib Rd.) is the best way to travel the length of Jordan. This ancient route winds through spectacular canyons, passing biblical sites, Crusader castles, and

Byzantine churches along the way. Allegedly traveled by the Israelites during the Exodus from Egypt, this road later became a popular spice trade route. Amman to Petra is 226km along the King's Highway, but the distances between sights along the way are more manageable: Amman to Madaba 32km, Madaba to Karak 86km, and Karak to Petra 108km. The only indoor accommodations are in Karak and Madaba (most people camp in the *wadis* north of Karak or between Karak and Petra). The easiest route is to see Madaba before heading to Karak for the night. If you leave early from Karak, the trip to Petra can be done comfortably in a day, stopping in Shobak along the way.

Service and **minibuses** run the route from Amman to Petra, but generally in the mornings only. **Hitchhiking** south of Amman is possible (hitchers stick their right arm out), though *Let's Go* does not recommend it, and it is risky and difficult along the deserted King's Highway. It is illegal to hitchhike on the Wadi Araba, which runs along the Israeli border. To get to the Desert Highway from downtown Amman, hitchhikers head south on Jerusalem St. (in Jabal Nadhif across Wadi Abdoun), which becomes Rte. 15 (the Desert Highway). To get to the King's Highway, prospective hitchers take a *service* or minibus to Madaba, then try out their thumbs on the road to Karak, which passes out of Madaba by the Apostles' Church. Small groups of hitchers stand by the mini-obelisk marking the intersection of the King's Highway and the Desert Highway, 18km south of Amman. To reach the intersection, take a Madaba-bound *service* from Wahdat Station.

DEAD SEA البحر الميت

The Dead Sea (*al-Bahr al-Mayit* to Jordanians) is the lowest point on earth, over 400m below sea level. Now a serenely quiet shore, the Dead Sea region is thought by many

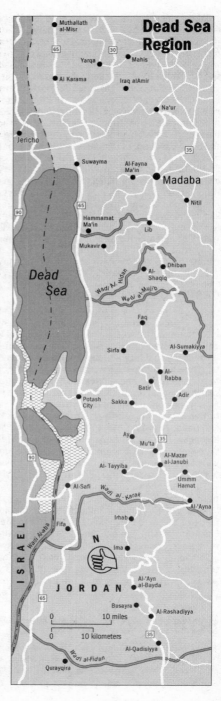

to be the site of five biblical cities: Sodom, Gomorrah, Admah, Zeboin, and Zowr. Indeed, a dried pillar of salt near the sea is believed to be the remains of Lot's wife, who, upon fleeing the damned city of Sodom, disobeyed God's command not to look back. Four times as salty as normal sea water, the peculiar buoyancy of this briny liquid forces even the densest swimmer into a back float, and the wealth of salts and minerals gives the sea its renowned curative powers, recognized for over 2000 years. Be warned that the awful-tasting salt water makes a tiny paper cut feel like a shark bite. Don't get any in your eyes, or you'll have to beg to use one of the eye-flushing water bottles that smart people tote along to the beach. The Dead Sea is easier and cheaper to reach by public transport if visited from Israel (see **Israel: Dead Sea,** p. 386). Its northeastern shore, about 1hr. from Amman or Deir Alla, hosts the only stretch of sand open to visitors on the Jordanian side.

▛ TRANSPORTATION. All **buses** to the Dead Sea leave from Amman's **Muhajereen Station,** on al-Quds (Jerusalem) St. Catch a minibus to Muhajereen from the circle at the western end of Quraysh St. (50fils) or a taxi from downtown (500fils). Don a Panama hat, bring plenty of water, and don't forget your passport—several military roadblocks along the way may demand identification. A few buses in the station marked in English as "The Dead Sea Express" go directly to the **Dead Sea Rest House;** they leave when full and fill up quickly (1¼hr., 500fils). Most salt-seekers take a bus to **Shouna al-Janubi** (1hr., every 30min. until 6pm, 400fils), where you can catch a second bus to the rest house (30min., 200fils). Another alternative is to arrange group daytrips with one of many Amman hotels (Farah Hotel charges JD15 per person). **Taxis** to the Dead Sea from Amman can be found for as little as JD8, but most will demand JD25; try bargaining. Temperatures rise rapidly along the descent from Amman—sometimes as much as 10 degrees Celsius—and the humidity is suffocating. Stay in the shade whenever possible and drink more water than you think necessary.

▛ ACCOMMODATIONS AND FOOD. The warm outdoor showers of the **Dead Sea Rest House** are open until sundown, but try as you might to get yourself clean, the salt will still be with you, somewhere, for at least a few days. (☎ 05 356 01 10. Access to the private beach, changing rooms, and showers JD3.) The rest house itself has bungalows with air-conditioning, bathroom, and TV. Singles JD25; doubles JD40; quads JD70. An overpriced restaurant completes the complex. (Hummus 650fils. Salad bar JD3. Soft drinks JD1. Water JD1. Open daily 6am-11pm.) You can save a few dinar by going to the **free beach** 200m to the right of the rest house. To get there from the bus stop at the rest house, backtrack along the road until you reach a junction, then take a left. The entrance to the free beach is off the parking lot at the end of this road. The beach includes a muddy shore, spartan changing rooms, very little privacy, and seaside **camping.** The showers are sometimes broken, and they are rather funky even when working. The rocky walk into the water can be tough, so consider foot protection. Shelters are available to ward off the sun. The last bus leaves the rest house at 6pm. If you get stranded, hike back to the main road (1km) and flag down any minibus headed north (a spectacular sunset will be taking place over the West Bank, on your left as you face north). The bus will stop at Shouna al-Janubi, from which the last bus to Amman leaves at 8pm in summer (1hr., 400fils). You could also hire a taxi, but don't look desperate, or the price is sure to go up. About 12km south of the resthouse, the natural spring of **Zara** is nestled between the Jordan Valley cliffs. Less than 30km south on the highway to Aqaba (Rte. 35) lies **Zarqa Ma'in,** a cascading hot spring.

▛ DAYTRIP FROM THE DEAD SEA

BETHANY (AL-MAGHTAS) المغتس

*Take any **minibus** to Shouna al-Janubi from Amman's Muhajereen Station (1hr., 400fils) or Madaba (45min., 500fils). From Shouna, a round-trip **taxi** to Bethany ("al-Maghtas") costs JD5, including ample time to look around while the driver waits. If **driving**, follow* *signs for the Dead Sea. When the road flattens out at the base of the valley, watch for the brown tourist signs reading "The Baptism Site" that will lead you right up to the site's main entrance. As Bethany is still being developed for tourism, there is no cost to see the site at this time. However, this is certain to change within the next year, and an admission price of a few JD is likely to be charged. **Open** daily 8am-7pm; closes at dusk in winter.*

The eccentric but endearing **John the Baptist** preferred to live and work (i.e. baptize) along the quiet eastern bank of the **Jordan River,** a stone's throw from Jericho and Jerusalem. The Bible refers to the area as "Bethany beyond the Jordan" (John 1:28). John chose Bethany for its historical connection to the prophet **Elijah,** who is believed to have ascended to heaven in a burning chariot from a nearby hill, and for its spring-fed stream (Wadi al-Kharrar), which allowed for much more pleasant baptisms than did the muddy, polluted waters of the Jordan.

Labeled on the mosaic Map of the Holy Land in Madaba (see p. 476) as "Ainon, where now is Saphsaphas" (Saphsaphas means "willow tree" in Arabic), the region was a major stop on the early pilgrimage trail until political turmoil limited access to this sensitive area at some point before the 2nd millennium CE. Unfortunately, turmoil has persisted in the area, and it wasn't until the 1994 Israeli-Jordanian peace accord—and three years of removing landmines—that archaeologists were finally granted access to the site. Following an extensive search, the ruins of churches, monasteries, mosaics, and an elaborate water routing system (used for filling the baptismal pools) have been uncovered. Excavations continue to unearth new finds, some dating to around 2000 years ago, supporting claims by archaeologists that they have at last rediscovered the site of **Jesus's baptism.** (According to Christian tradition, God commanded Jesus, on his way to Jerusalem from the Galilee, to stop off at John's House o' Baptisms and Pancakes.) Archaeologists landed a major endorsement in March 2000, when Pope John Paul II visited the site accompanied by 50,000 devotees, and after a 1000-year break, a steady stream of Christian pilgrims at last returned to the area. Even though most who visit *al-Maghtas* ("immersion" in Arabic; the Jordanian name for the site) are motivated by its religious significance, the site is interesting from a purely historical perspective as well, and is an easy detour from the Dead Sea.

MADABA مادبا ☎05

Perched atop a plateau of orange groves overlooking the Jordan Valley, Madaba lures visitors with its magnificent scenery, craft shops, and Byzantine mosaics. While the Roman columns scattered about town only hint at the flourishing trade center that Madaba once was, scientists at work in the downtown "Archaeological Park" have recently uncovered some of the city's past glories. A Roman road, a burnt palace, and several churches have been discovered only meters away from the Church

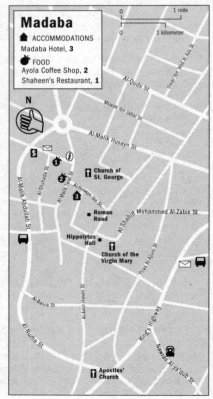

Madaba

⌂ ACCOMMODATIONS
Madaba Hotel, **3**

🍴 FOOD
Ayola Coffee Shop, **2**
Shaheen's Restaurant, **1**

0   1 mile
0   1 kilometer

Al-Quds St
Umar Ibn Abd Al Aziz St
Muadh Ibn Jabal St
Al-Malik Husayn St
Al-Shuhada St
Al-Malik Talal St
Al-Husayn Ibn Ali St
Church of St. George
Al-Malik Abdullah St
Muhammed Al-Zabin St
Al-Shahid St
Roman Road
Hippolytus Hall
Firas Al-Ajlun St
Church of the Virgin Mary
Al-Balua St
Al-Amir Hasan St
King's Highway
Al-Nuzha St
Nawras Al-Ya'qub St
Apostles' Church

of St. George (home of the famous **Map of the Holy Land,** see p. 476). The elaborate masterpieces scattered throughout this "City of Mosaics" attest to Madaba's importance as a Byzantine religious center. The town received its own bishop as early as the 5th century CE. Persians attacked Madaba in 614 CE, slaughtering the residents and damaging many Roman and Byzantine artifacts; an 8th-century earthquake finished off the job. Madaba remained a ghost town for the next 1100 years until Christian clans from Karak re-inhabited the city in the late 1800s. Madaba still hosts a sizable Christian population, most noticeable in the increased presence of bars and decreased presence of veils. Rural, quiet, and serene—the precise opposite of Amman—Madaba, and its quality accommodations, offer an appealing home base from which to take daytrips to **Mt. Nebo** (p. 477), **Jerash** (p. 457), or **Amman** (p. 441). However, women report that Madaba is particularly high on the nuisance list—expect to be talked to and stared at from the moment you arrive. Look out for tourist traps, but don't miss the carpet shops, where you can watch the fascinating process of loom weaving.

⌐ TRANSPORTATION

Minibuses: To Amman's **Wahdat** (200fils), **Raghadan** (250fils), and **Abdali Stations** (1hr.; last bus 7pm, in winter last bus 5pm; 300fils). **Service** don't run this route.

Hitchhiking: *Let's Go* does not recommend hitchhiking, but it doesn't get any easier than on the King's Highway.

◢◣? ORIENTATION AND PRACTICAL INFORMATION

To reach the city center from Madaba's bus station, take a **service** (70fils) or **taxi** (500fils) to the Church of St. George. Alternatively, walk 75m south from the bus station along the King's Highway and turn right onto al-Hashimi St. Follow al-Hashimi St. uphill as it becomes progressively more tourist-oriented: hardware stores, clothing, jewelry, and finally, postcards and Petra sand bottles. Turn right onto **King Talal St.** and walk one block to the center of old Madaba. Walking north on King Talal St. (which turns into **Yarmouk St.**) will take you past two traffic circles, the second of which is **al-Mouhafada circle,** where the better hotels cluster.

Tourist Office: (☎324 55 27), around the corner from the Church of St. George. Brochures with a semi-useful map of Madaba. Open Sa-Th 8am-3pm.

Banks: On Palestine St., which intersects King Talal St. opposite the entrance to the Church of St. George. **Housing Bank** open Su-Th 8:30am-5pm. **Arab Bank** (☎324 55 36) open Su-Th 8:30am-3pm. Both have international **ATMs.**

Emergency: ☎191. **Police:** ☎192. **Medical emergency:** ☎193.

Hospital: Nadim Hospital (☎324 17 00), 1km from town, is the nearest public hospital. **Mahabba Hospital,** near the entrance to town on the King's Highway. New and private.

Internet Access: TourDotNet (☎325 15 23), on King Talal St., north of the Church of St. George and opposite the **tourist police.** JD1 per hr. Open daily 9am-midnight.

Post Office: (☎324 40 05), across from the banks on Palestine St. Open Su-Th 7:30am-7pm, F-Sa 7:30am-1:30pm; in winter Su-Th 7:30am-5pm, F-Sa 7:30am-1:30pm.

▚ ACCOMMODATIONS

Blessed with high-quality budget hotels, Madaba soothes hostel-weary travelers.

▨ **Lulu's Pension** (☎324 36 78; fax 324 76 17; luluhotl@go.com.jo). Follow the signs north of al-Mouhafada circle to this hospitality haven. The gorgeous rooms upstairs come with clean bathrooms and breezy balconies. Guests are welcome to help themselves to fresh fruit from the garden, to use the common kitchen, and to receive discounted prices at a number of Madaba's finest restaurants. Ring the bell if door is locked. Breakfast included. Singles JD15, doubles JD25; triples JD35 with private bath; JD5 less for rooms with a shared bathroom.

Black Iris Hotel (☎/fax 324 19 59). The turnoff is 1 block south of al-Mouhafada Circle on Yarmouk St. Spacious rooms with attractive old furniture. Just wait until you see the size of their breakfast (included). Singles JD18; doubles JD25; triples JD35; cheaper with shared bath. Discounts available for guests staying longer than 1 night.

Queen Ayola Hotel (☎/fax 324 40 87; queenayola@yahoo.com), on King Talal St., 1 block south of the Church of St. George. This cozy hotel offers multilingual management and spotless rooms that come with fans, towels, and shampoo. Breakfast included. Doubles JD18-22. 10% student discount. V.

Madaba Hotel (☎324 06 43). Look for signs near the tourist office. The friendly staff maintains 14 clean rooms in a good location. Breakfast JD1. Shared bath. Singles JD10; doubles JD16. Student discount.

⚑ FOOD

🍴 **Haret Judoudna** (☎324 86 50), on King Talal St., across from the Queen Ayola Hotel. Easily the best restaurant in Madaba. Extensive menu includes Middle Eastern specialties like *siwani* (JD2.5-3.75), a stew of lamb or chicken, vegetables, and spices simmered to juicy perfection and served with pita so fresh that it comes to your table still inflated from the heat of the brick oven. The pizzeria-cafe downstairs lures a nightly crowd of wealthy locals with its excellent thin-crust pizza (JD2-4) and live music. Over 20 tourist shops toward the rear of the restaurant sell high-quality Jordanian handicrafts at inflated prices. Open daily 9am-1am.

Dana Restaurant (☎324 57 49), on al-Nuzha St., uphill from the Apostles' Church. Excellent, with prices slightly lower than most. Serves Middle Eastern, Indian, Chinese, and American food. Lamb-burger, fries, and coke JD1.75. Pasta JD2. Other entrees JD3-5. Open daily 8am-11pm.

Shaheen's Restaurant, off Palestine St., around the corner from the Ayola Cafe. Best falafel in town for 250fils and other generally cheap chow. Open daily 7am-midnight.

Al-Cardo (☎325 10 06; ☎/fax 325 10 07), across from the Archaeological Park. Entrees JD4-7. Western-style sandwiches JD1.5. Open daily 8am-midnight.

Ayola Coffee Shop, on Palestine St. Serves deli-style sandwiches (JD1) to a chatty crew of young locals. The western food is good for Jordan, but most patrons come to hang out rather than eat. Open daily 8am-11pm.

👁 SIGHTS

CHURCH OF ST. GEORGE. Built in 1896 atop the foundation of a Byzantine church, the prominent Greek Orthodox Church of St. George stands in the center of town, right off King Talal St. Parts of the 6th-century CE **Map of the Holy Land** (originally composed of 2.3 million tiles) are housed within the church's yellow brick walls. The map is the oldest preserved and most detailed of this region, once depicting the entire Middle East (as shown by the few remaining tiles of Turkey, Lebanon, and Egypt). Now only the cities of Byzantium, Nablus, Hebron, and Jericho remain, clustered around an intact representation of the Dead Sea that stretches from left to right across the peculiarly oriented map. The most well-known section of the mosaic is the inset map of Jerusalem at its center, with depictions of the buildings that existed in the 6th century (including the Church of the Holy Sepulchre, p. 301). According to some devout local Christians and Muslims, the Church of St. George received a visit by the Virgin Mary in 1978. A small shrine in the crypt contains an icon of Mary with a third arm and a blue "healing hand"—supposedly supernaturally imprinted on the icon during the Madonna's visit. (*Open M-Th and Sa 8am-6pm, F and Su 10:30am-6pm. Free.*)

■ARCHAEOLOGICAL PARK. The park's clever designers have used a maze of raised walkways to transform some recently excavated ruins into a veritable mosaic gallery. A well preserved **Roman road** runs alongside the **Church of the Virgin Mary** and notably non-virgin **Hippolytus Hall,** containing an amazing secular mosaic flaunting images of Aphrodite, scenes from Greek tragedies, and more nude women than all the maps of the holy land combined. *(From King Talal St., walk past the tourist office, make a right at the end of the road, and look for signs. Open W-M 8am-7pm; in winter W-M 8am-5pm. JD2; ticket also good for Madaba Museum.)*

MADABA MUSEUM. Madaba's museum is divided into three sections: the Old House of Madaba, the Folklore Museum, and the Archaeological Museum. The complex features a collection of mosaics (including a depiction of the Garden of Eden), traditional Jordanian dresses, and pottery dating back to 4500 BCE. *(Turn left where al-Hashimi St. meets the southern tip of King Talal St. and follow signs to the museum's alleyway entrance. Open W-M 9am-5pm. JD2; ticket also good for Archaeological Park.)*

APOSTLES' CHURCH. This reconstructed church was built to house Madaba's largest mosaic, which was completed in the 6th century CE. Distorted flora and fauna border the intriguing image of a woman's face at the mosaic's center. *(At the intersection of the King's Highway and al-Nuzha St., about 500m past the bus station.)*

■ DAYTRIP FROM MADABA: MT. NEBO

No buses go to Mt. Nebo. Take a *taxi* (round-trip JD4, including 30min. wait at the site; add JD2 for a short trip to Khirbet al-Mukheiyat and 'Ain Musa) or a **service** from Madaba to Feisaliyyeh (150fils). At Feisaliyyeh, walk to Mt. Nebo or bargain with the driver to take you there once other passengers get off (JD2.5 for the extra 3km up, 30min. wait, and trip back to Madaba). Without a prearranged ride, the only way off Mt. Nebo is to **walk** back to Feisaliyyeh. **Buildings** and **Siyagha Peak** open daily 7am-7pm; in winter 7am-5pm. 500fils; pay the guard an extra 500fils to see the sunset.

The view from Mt. Nebo is so spectacular that Moses's last request to God was for a view of the Promised Land from its heights. Although the Bible says that "no man knows the place of [Moses's] burial to this day" (Deuteronomy 34:6), his grave is rumored to be in a cave somewhere along 'Ain Musa. On Nebo's **Siyagha Peak,** the Christians of Madaba built a three-nave **Memorial Church,** next to which looms an imposing serpentine cross. Archaeological work has revealed a complete mosaic floor in the church dating from 531 CE, as well as foundations of monasteries from the 3rd century CE. In the 7th century, the **Chapel of the Theotokos** (or Mary, Mother of God) was added, with lavish decorations adorning the walls.

Just beyond Feisaliyyeh, a marked turnoff leads to **Khirbet al-Mukheiyat,** once known as the ancient village of **Nebo,** on the southern base of the mountain. A hike (1hr. round-trip) will allow you to see the fishing, hunting, and wine-making scenes that decorate another finely preserved Byzantine church floor. Despite repeated warnings by the Surgeon General, cigarettes are the preferred *bakhsheesh* for the Bedouin gatekeeper who lives on the hill at the end of the paved road. If you're out of smokes, 500fils is plenty. (Church open until dusk, or whenever the gatekeeper leaves.) Further up the road to Nebo's peak lies **'Ain Musa** (Spring of Moses), alleged to be the spot where two strikes of Moses' staff caused water to spew forth—much to the delight of the hordes of parched Israelites fleeing from Egypt. Moses and his staff have been replaced by a pipe stuck into a rock, and the role of the thirsty Jews is now filled by a steady stream of thirsty goats, donkeys, and cab drivers. To get there, take a right before the Mt. Nebo sign and follow the road down into the valley; walk around the old pump buildings and follow the path down to the right.

The trip out to Mt. Nebo is worth the schlep: the mosaics are astounding and the views are—well, good enough to make it onto a dying prophet's wish list. Those with their own transportation or willing to splurge for the JD10 round-trip cab ride should consider taking the breathtaking drive from Nebo to the Dead Sea. The main road passes to the left of the peak and is well marked and well maintained along its dramatic plunge between rocky cliffs and windswept ridges, down 1000m to the lowest point on Earth.

KARAK الكرك ☎ 03

Once the capital of ancient Moab, Karak now humbles itself in the shadow of **Karak Castle,** the largest of the mountaintop Crusader castles that stretch from Turkey to the Sinai. A colorful cluster of restaurants and hotels have sprung up around the castle to greet the steady stream of air-conditioned tour buses making a brief pit stop in Karak on their way to Petra. However, the modern city, sloping to the north and east away from the castle, is wonderfully removed from the goings-on of "Castle Plaza" (as the newly developed tourist area has been unfortunately named). This breezy mountain town settles down each evening to enjoy a spectacular sunset over the Dead Sea, and as dusk turns to dark, the streets grow quiet and mellow, filled with the murmurs of carefree conversation and the aroma of livestock.

▐ TRANSPORTATION. Travel to Karak from Amman's **Wahdat Station** by **minibus** (2hr., 750fils) or **service** (JD1.2) along the Desert Highway. A **taxi** along the King's Highway from Madaba costs around JD10. The most reliable way to reach Petra from Karak is to first take a **minibus** from the **Karak Bus Station** to Ma'an (2hr., 1050fils) and then take another **bus** from Ma'an to Petra (45min., 500fils). To get to the Karak station, **walk** east of the castle for about 20min., turning right at the bottom of the hill, or take a **taxi** (JD1). A slightly less direct route involves taking a **bus** from the Karak station to Tafilah (30min., 500fils), from there to Shobak (1hr., JD1), and finally from Shobak to Petra (30min., 250fils). *Service* rarely run along these routes. During the high season, **buses** may travel directly from Karak to Petra, depending on tourist traffic (2hr., 9am); **private taxis** charge a hefty JD40. Those who hitch the route along the King's Highway say it's easy, though *Let's Go* does not recommend hitchhiking. If you're traveling in the late afternoon, don't expect to see cars or sleep anywhere besides the homes of hospitable locals or grounds of Shobak Castle. The desert mountains can get cold and lonely at night—it is best to stay in warm Karak and leave on a morning bus.

▐▌▐ ORIENTATION AND PRACTICAL INFORMATION. The two main landmarks in town are the **castle** and the **center circle,** which has a statue of Salah al-Din looking passionately off-balance atop his horse. The former is at the top of the hill, while the latter is at the bottom. The area along **al-Hadar St.,** running in front of the castle and **al-Qala'a St.,** is a self-sustaining tourist ecosystem. Visitors could easily spend their entire time in Karak within 50m of the castle, and judging from what's available elsewhere in the city, most do. Karak's renovated **tourist office** (☎235 11 50) is next to the Peace-Ram Restaurant on al-Hadar St. (Open Sa-Th 8am-2pm.) **Banks** and **ATMs** cluster downhill from the castle, on the side street across from the Jordan National Bank on al-Qala'a St. Karak's **Italian Hospital** (☎235 11 45 or 235 10 45) is downhill from the road leading to the castle, in the direction of Mr. al-Din's dagger. The **police station** (☎235 10 69) is across from the tourist office and next to the huge radio tower. Karak's **post and telephone office** is right next door. (Open Sa-Th 8am-2pm.) You can't access the **Internet** in Karak, but there are a few cyber cafes in Marij, about 3km east of the castle, along the road to Amman. (Taxi JD1. Minibus 50fils. Internet access 750fils per hr.)

▐▐ ACCOMMODATIONS AND FOOD. The **Karak Rest House,** next to the entrance to Karak Castle, offers the nicest rooms and the best views in town. (☎235 11 48; fax 235 31 48. Breakfast included. Singles JD25; doubles JD35; triples JD45. Slow business brings discounts of JD10-15. AmEx/MC/V.) The Rest House restaurant offers full meals including salad, main dish, dessert, and coffee for JD6. (Open daily 7:30-10am, noon-4pm, and 7:30pm-10pm.) The management of the Rest House also runs the **Karak Guest House,** downhill from the castle on al-Qala'a St. It offers similar services and facilities at consistently lower prices than its neighbor. (☎235 55 64. Breakfast included. Singles JD15; doubles JD25; triples JD35.) The **Ram Cottage Hotel,** on al-Hadar St. is spotless, and prices are negotiable, especially in the off season. (☎/fax 235 13 51; fax 235 11 05. Singles JD10; doubles JD15, in the off-season JD10.) The **Towers Castle Hotel,** between the Rest and the Guest, has rooms that are not as nice as those at the Ram Cottage. (☎235 24 89; ☎/fax 235 42 93. Singles JD10; doubles JD15; triples JD20.) Despite its noisy, stuffy atmosphere, the **New Karak Hotel,** on Italy St. west of Salah's circle, has hot showers and low prices. (☎235 19 42. JD3 per bed; JD6 for private room.)

AN ENGLISHWOMAN IN ARABIA Wrapped in a heavy sun hood, with her skirts and petticoats whipping up the dry sands, **Gertrude Bell** traveled throughout the Arabian desert advising *sheikhs,* documenting archaeological sites, and hosting proper teas with her Wedgwood china. In the 1880s, Bell was one of the first women to study at Oxford University, where she gained high honors but shocked professors with her brazenness. Her family sent her to Bucharest, Romania, to be schooled in the ways of Victorian femininity, but Bell's insatiable wanderlust would have none of it. Soon Bell was traveling farther East and in 1909, with a bevy of male servants in caravan, she set out for "Mesopotamia." Dubbed an "honorary man" by the Arabs she met, Bell befriended graduate student T.E. Lawrence (later to be known as Lawrence of Arabia) and became the only woman to be drafted into Cairo's Arab Bureau as an intelligence agent at the break of World War I, igniting controversy with her support of Arab self-determination. After the war, she published an official report on the administration of Mesopotamia. When Iraq rebelled in 1920, she served as one of King Faisal's closest aides. Bell took her own life in 1926. The next day, crowds filled the streets of Baghdad to pay respects to this "uncrowned queen of Iraq."

The restaurants near Karak Castle cater to tourists. The meals at **Kir Heres Restaurant,** adjacent to the Towers Castle Hotel, are good, and the setting is colorful and charming. (☎235 55 95. Kebab JD4.5. *Mezza* JD1-2. Open daily 9am-10pm.) The **Peace Ram Restaurant,** across the street from the police station and the radio tower, offers oven-warmed frozen pizza or *mensaf* with salad starting at JD1.5. (☎235 37 89. Open daily 8am-10pm.) Popular with tourist groups, the **Fida Restaurant,** down the street from the Ram Cottage Hotel, serves an open buffet luncheon for JD5. (☎235 26 77. Open daily 8am-10pm.) A handful of restaurants around Salah al-Din's circle serve cheaper, more traditional Jordanian food to a crowd of locals. Despite the smoky smell of roasting chicken wafting throughout the **Turkey Restaurant** on the eastern side of the circle, the kebab—served beneath two slices of tasty seasoned pita—makes the best meal downhill from the castle. Kebab, hummus, and drink JD3. (☎07 973 04 31. Open daily 7am-10pm.)

◘ SIGHTS. Built into and on top of the hill overlooking its sleepy hamlet, **Karak Castle** is full of secret passageways and hidden rooms. Bring a flashlight for easier exploration, and allow at least 2hr. In 1142 CE, Baldwin I of Jerusalem built the castle midway between his capital and Shobak, on the site of an Iron Age citadel mentioned in the Mesha Stele of 850 BCE. The fortress was soon inherited by the charming Renauld de Chatillon, who delighted in tossing prisoners over the western wall (with wooden boxes fastened around their heads so they wouldn't lose consciousness before hitting the ground some 400m below). Renauld's stronghold was so heavily fortified—protected by a **glacis** (a steep smooth slope of stone blocks) and dizzying natural cliffs—that it is a wonder that anyone even considered attacking it. However, the 1187 Battle of Hittim saw the castle fall to the Ayyubids and their courageous leader Salah al-Din, who personally saw to it that Chatillon's head was removed. Although the fortress's walls have mostly collapsed since the castle's renovation in 1188, its presence still looms over the city. The few surviving above-ground towers and fortifications provide a nice backdrop for group photos, but the real adventure is to be had below ground, where tunnels, hallways, and narrow stairwells stretch deep into the blackness beneath the mountain. Bring a flashlight (or a couple of cigarette lighters), a lack of lizard-phobia, and a healthy amount of caution—the ruins are dotted with ventilation shafts which are poorly marked and only sometimes covered with a pathetic excuse for metal grating. To the right of the castle entrance is a stone staircase that descends to the **Archaeological Museum.** A copy of the **Mesha Stele** rests alongside original Nabatean, Roman, and Mamluk artifacts. (Castle open daily 8am-6pm. Museum open daily 10am-4pm. Castle and museum JD1.)

▶ DAYTRIP FROM KARAK: MAZRA'A

A round-trip taxi to the Mazra'a area with an hour or so wait costs JD10. Bring your passport along for the military checkpoint, and remember that the Dead Sea basin is substantially warmer and far more humid than the breezy heights of Karak (bring a hat and some water). In the towns surrounding Karak, tourist services are nonexistent. If you are lost or need a ride or a place to stay, approach a store owner or businessperson and ask for help (offer 500fils-JD1 in return). Solo women should refuse hospitality from single men.

West of Karak, Hwy. 49/80 (some call it Hwy. 50) drops over 1500m from the King's Highway to the Dead Sea "port" of **Mazra'a** and al-Lisan ("Tongue") Peninsula. Five kilometers before reaching Mazra'a and the Wadi Araba Highway to Aqaba, Hwy. 49/80 passes a group of large mounds that rise suspiciously from the flat rocky desert with a strange reddish hue. The mounds are the remains of **Bab al-Dhira,** a Bronze Age village with a cemetery containing 20,000 shaft tombs containing 500,000 bodies (an unfortunate ratio). The reddish color comes the shattered fragments of what was once more than three million pottery vessels. The length of the bones indicates that the average height in Bab al-Dhira was a sturdy 2m (over 6½ ft.), which explains why the Bible describes its inhabitants as giants. The main site is surrounded by a barbed wire fence and accessed through a gate along the main road. The gate is usually open, but there is no one around to let you in if it happens to be locked. However, a portion of the site is on the other side of the road where there is no fence to impede your morbid meanderings.

The mosques at **Mu'tah** and at the nearby village of **Mazar** (bus 150fils) commemorate the Muslim generals who died in the first great battles between the forces of Islam and Byzantium in 632 CE. The green-domed mosque in Mazar houses a small **Islamic museum** on the first floor. (Usually open daily 9am-4pm.)

SOUTH OF KARAK

SHOBAK شوبك

The first castle of King Baldwin I of Jerusalem pales in comparison to his later creation at Karak. **Shobak Castle,** originally known as "Mons Realis" or "Montréal," is 4km from the marked turnoff at the northern edge of Shobak Village. The castle first fell to Salah al-Din in 1189, just 74 years after it was built. In 1260, the Mamluks gained possession of the castle, restored it, and inscribed records of their work on its main walls and towers. Present day excavation and restoration projects promise to develop the castle in a manner similar to Karak, with a museum, descriptive plaques, and an admission fee—but as of now Shobak remains in a raw, earthquake-ravished form. The few tourists that make it out here will find the remains of rectangular enclosing walls and a few towers perched atop a lonely slab of white rock. Villagers who lived inside the castle walls depended upon the water from the rock-hewn well, 375 steps deep. Entry to the well has been prohibited for safety reasons, but a network of equally precarious and still-accessible tunnels lead deep into the castle's rocky foundation.

From Karak, **minibuses** regularly head to Tafilah (30min., 250fils), where you can catch a connection to Shobak (JD1, 1hr.). Amman-bound minibuses (500fils) reach Shobak Village from Wadi Musa (the modern town next to Petra), leaving from the traffic circle in front of al-Wadi Restaurant in the early morning. Ask your hotel manager about getting to Shobak from Petra, as bus departure times and frequencies change throughout the year. If you hire a taxi (at most JD10 from Karak, JD5 from Wadi Musa), make sure the driver waits while you explore. Entrance is free.

DANA NATURE RESERVE

Stretching from the mountains south of Karak to the Wadi Araba basin, the **Dana Nature Reserve** is Jordan's largest protected ecosystem. The bulky mountains, some topping 1600m, shelter a substantial (nocturnal) population of jackals, wolves, and hyenas. The reserve's misty valleys host one of the most beautiful sunsets in the country. The reserve affords many opportunities for guided and unguided hiking, camping, and treks to remote archaeological sites. The Dana Visitors Center (☎227 04 97; fax 227 04 99), located next to the Dana Guesthouse, has ample information about all reserve-related activities.

Perched on a rocky ledge 1200m above sea-level, the 500-year-old ◼**Dana village** maintains the traditional lifestyle that once existed throughout the area. An asymmetric maze of stone buildings and thatched roofs, the village barely survived the wave of modernization, but its wonderfully authentic setting is now protected as part of the reserve. The village's 84 families still farm the fruit-bearing hills, though a few have decided to till the fertile soils of Jordanian tourism. Fortunately, the two hotels in Dana are sensitively run and have adapted to (rather than corrupted) the traditional setting. The **Dana Tower Hotel,** located on the edge of town (and the edge of a cliff) at the end of the road leading into the village, has clean rooms built shrewdly into an old stone building. Dinner is served on the roof, along with the best views in town. The friendly manager can arrange treks and camping in the reserve. (☎227 02 37. Breakfast and dinner included. Shared baths. Singles or doubles JD7.5 per person.) The **Dana Hotel,** near the entrance to town and well marked, has clean rooms with stylish beds, shared baths, and no view. (☎/fax 227 05 37. Breakfast included. Other meals JD5. Rooms JD10 per person.) The **Dana Guesthouse** is just outside of town, down a turnoff marked along the main road. Overhanging a cliff, the hotel's marble floors and beige interior serve as an upscale attempt to maintain a traditional look. (☎227 04 97; fax 227 04 99. Breakfast included. Lunch and dinner JD6. Singles JD20, with balcony JD25; doubles JD25, with balcony JD35. Add 10% service charge. 20% student discount.) **Camping** is available in the reserve at designated sites only, and is surprisingly expensive. (Single tent JD18; double tent JD30. Entrance to the reserve included.)

Buses between Tafilah and Shobak (JD1) can drop you off along the King's Highway in Qadessiya near Dana village, or near the entrance to the reserve. In either case you'll have to **hitch** or **hike** the last few kilometers. *Let's Go* does not recommend hitchhiking. A **taxi** from Karak or Petra should cost around JD7, and the latter may include short stops at al-Barid and Shobak Castle for an extra JD3. Entrance to the reserve is JD5.

PETRA (WADI MUSA) البترا ☎03

Match me such marvel save in Eastern clime,
a rose-red city 'half as old as Time'!
——Dean Burgon, *Petra*

Follow the ancient path of Nabatean priests hauling the rectangular stone vessels of their gods through a deep and narrow fissure eroded from solid rock. Ghostly images of wind-worn carvings hide in the darkness until—suddenly—the shadows yield to a brilliant pink flash, the first light of the lost city of Petra seeping between the canyon walls. Discovered in 1812, Petra is a city hewn from raw mountain, blood-red cliffs manipulated by a skillful chisel into impossibly delicate structures that were somehow lost for over 1000 years. Petra ("stone" in ancient Greek) is perhaps the most astounding ancient city left to the modern world, and certainly a must-see for visitors to the Middle East.

For decades after Petra's rediscovery, the Bedouin adapted to the influx of tourists by providing them with food and accommodations in the ancient city itself, a practice outlawed from 1984-85 out of concern for Petra's monuments. While many Bedouin have been relocated to a housing project in the hills outside of **Wadi Musa** (the modern town near the ancient site), a large portion still make their homes in the more remote caves and hills of the city (which spans 50km, most of which tourists never see). Some Bedouin sell souvenirs and drinks amidst the ruins, and others herd goats—don't be surprised to smell a barnyard stench emanating from an ancient tomb. If you venture on paths that go beyond the standard one-day itinerary, you will notice stones piled into neat columns; as long as these cairns are in sight, you're near a trail, and Bedouin will pass by.

HISTORY

For 700 years, Petra was lost to all but the few hundred members of a Bedouin tribe who guarded their treasure from outsiders. In the 19th century, Swiss explorer Johann Burkhardt heard Bedouin speaking of a "lost city" and vowed to find it. Though initially unable to find a guide willing to disclose the city's location, he guessed that the city he sought was the biblical Sela, which should have been near Mt. Hor, the site of Aaron's tomb. Impersonating a Christian pilgrim, Burkhardt hired a guide, and on August 22, 1812, he became the first non-Bedouin in centuries to walk between the cliffs of Petra's *siq* (the mile-long rift that was the only entrance to the city). In the nearly two centuries since Burkhardt's discovery, Petra has become a featured tourist attraction, admired by visitors from all over the world, including the crew of *Indiana Jones and the Last Crusade.*

Humans first set foot in the area in the 8th millennium BCE, but the region's occupants didn't enter the written record until Edomite King Rekem unwisely denied Moses and his followers passage through his territory on their way to the Promised Land. The Judean kings held a grudge, and they ultimately enslaved and exterminated the Edomites. The fall of the Edomites (which was literal as well as figurative, as many were thrown off cliffs within Petra), made room for the Nabateans, who arrived in the 6th century BCE. Originally nomads attracted by Petra's abundant sources of water, the Nabateans settled down upon realizing they could control the trade routes between the Mediterranean Sea and Fertile Crescent. Over the next three centuries, the Nabateans carved their temples out of the mountains, looking to Assyrian, Egyptian, Greek, and Roman styles for inspiration. Their most distinctive symbol is an evolution of the Assyrian crow-step pattern. The crow-steps so closely resemble inverted staircases that the people of Meda'in Salih in Saudi Arabia claimed that God had thrown Petra upside down and turned it to stone to punish its people for their wickedness.

More historically verifiable evidence suggests that the Nabatean King Aretes defeated Pompey's Roman legions in 63 BCE. The Romans controlled the entire area around Nabatea, however, prompting the later King Rabel III to strike a cowardly deal: as long as the Romans did not attack during his lifetime, they would be permitted to move in after he died. In 106 CE, the Romans claimed the Nabatean Kingdom and inhabited this city of rosy Nubian sandstone. In its heyday, Petra housed as many as 30,000 people, but after an earthquake in 363 CE, a shift in trade routes to Palmyra (see p. 590), expansion of the sea trade around Arabia, and another earthquake in 747, much of Petra deteriorated to rubble.

▐ TRANSPORTATION

Petra lies in the rocky wilderness near the southern extreme of the King's Highway, 282km from Amman (262km via the Desert Highway). **JETT buses** leave Amman daily and drop off passengers at the Petra Visitors Center (3½hr.; 6:30am; JD5.5, same-day roundtrip JD11). Make reservations in person well in advance (especially in fall and spring) at JETT stations; questions can be handled by phone (☎566 41 46). More than one day is needed to really explore the site, but the "day-trip from Amman" JETT bus service allows travelers with limited time to get a decent taste of Petra. **Service** also run to Petra from Wahdat Station in Amman, but there is a wait in Ma'an (5hr., JD2). *Service* drivers will stop at **al-Anbat** or **Musa Spring Hotel** and at the center circle of Wadi Musa in front of al-Wadi Restaurant;

Petra

1 Visitor's Center/
   Ticket Booths
2 Djinn Blocks
   (Ghost Tombs)
3 Obelisk Tomb
4 The Kazneh
   (Treasury)
5 High Place
6 Lion Fountain
7 Garden Tomb
8 Triclinium
9 Tomb of the Roman
   Soldier
10 Roman Theater
11 Um Tomb
12 Corinthian Tomb
13 Palace Tomb
14 Tomb of Sextius
   Florentinus
15 Mughar al-Nasara
   (Caves of the
   Christians)
16 Nymphaeum
17 Byzantine Church
18 Temple of the
   Winged Lions
19 Fara'aun
   (Pharaoh's Pilar)
20 Great Temple
   Complex
21 Temenos Gate
22 Qasr Bint Far'aun
23 Nabatean Baths
24 Qasr Habis
   (Crusader Castle)
25 Archaeological
   Museum
26 Basin Restaurant
   and Nabatean
   Museum
27 Turkmaniyyeh Tomb
28 Lion's Tomb
29 al-Deir (The
   Monastery)
30 Snake Monument

JORDAN

from Wadi Musa, walk 2km or take a **private taxi** to Petra (JD1). From Aqaba, take a **minibus** (2hr., JD3). Start early in the morning to make any of these connections.

To reach Petra from the King's Highway, take the well-marked turnoff and head west into the colorful, steep-sided town of **Wadi Musa**. The main road makes a few twists and turns as it descends into the valley, passing Wadi Musa's tourist district—a mess of hotels and restaurants clustered around the central traffic circle, about halfway down. After a final loop along the side of a ridge, the road reaches the entrance to Petra, 2km downhill from the circle. The cluster of buildings here includes the Visitors Center, a group of five-star hotels, and the gatehouse to the valley that leads to the *siq* and Petra proper.

To leave Petra, catch a **minibus** or **service** to Aqaba (JD3), Amman (JD3), or Wadi Rum (JD3) at the center circle of Wadi Musa or at the Musa Spring Hotel. Buses leave early in the morning (6-8am); ask your hotel to reserve you a spot on the morning bus, and the bus will pick you up from the hotel (even budget hotels offer this service). A local **bus** to Ma'an also leaves early in the morning (500fils). Ask at your hotel for exact information.

✴ 🔋 ORIENTATION AND PRACTICAL INFORMATION

The town of Wadi Musa stretches along the switchback road starting at **'Ain Musa** ("Spring of Moses," a bountiful spring and the main reason that ancient Petra became a raucously wealthy trade center), passing **Shaheed circle** at the center of Wadi Musa village, and bottoming out near the **Petra Visitors Center.** Next to the Visitors Center are the **rest house** and the swinging gate that mark the beginning of the trail down to the *siq*.

> 👁 **TOURING PETRA.** For a "low-tour" of the city center, hire an official guide (2½hr., JD8). More comprehensive tours include the city center and one "high" site: options are al-Madbah (JD22), al-Deir (JD22), and Jabal Harun (JD35-60, half-day city-center tour and 5-6hr. hiking). For more remote areas, arrange trips directly with a guide (full-day tour JD35). You can rent a horse (JD7) for a short trip to the entrance of the *siq*, or a two-person carriage (JD20) for a longer ride all the way to the Treasury. Horses, donkeys, and camels are available inside the site for more negotiable prices, sometimes useful as a means of transportation, but most often hired for the ability to say, "I have ridden a <your mammal here> in Petra." If you have a guide tagging along, you are responsible for renting his ride as well. Without much effort, you can hook up with another guided group or form your own. However, groups of 10 or more are required to hire a guide, so split up before buying tickets if you want to avoid the extra cost. Various guidebooks are available at the Visitors Center, but there's no substitute for the expertise of an official guide on the remoter hikes to al-Barid or al-Madras.

Tourist Office: The **Vistors Center** (☎215 60 20) houses an excellent (and expensive) gift store, stocks the best selection of books about the site, and arranges all the (official) guide services. Open daily 7am-10pm.

Banks: Not surprisingly, banks are conveniently located near the hotels in Wadi Musa, with a few near the entrance to the site. The 2 largest, the **Arab Bank** (☎215 68 02) and the **Housing Bank** (☎215 70 75), are uphill from Shaheed circle and have international **ATMs**. Both open Sa-Th 8:30am-3pm. **Cairo Amman Bank** is in the Mövenpick Hotel, just outside the entrance to Petra. Open daily 8:30am-3pm. All banks extract exorbitant commissions for exchanges and **cash advances**.

Tourist Police (☎215 64 41), opposite the Visitors Center, munching on cigar ends.

Pharmacy: Wadi Musa Pharmacy (☎215 64 44), 10m downhill from Shaheed circle. Open 8am-10pm.

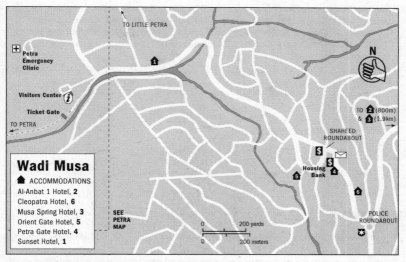

Wadi Musa

🏠 ACCOMMODATIONS

Al-Anbat 1 Hotel, **2**
Cleopatra Hotel, **6**
Musa Spring Hotel, **3**
Orient Gate Hotel, **5**
Petra Gate Hotel, **4**
Sunset Hotel, **1**

Medical Assistance: The **government health center** (☎215 60 25) is a 15min. walk uphill from the circle. Open 24hr.

Internet Access: Rum Internet Cafe (☎215 79 08), just downhill from Shaheed circle. JD2 per hr. with a 1hr. minimum. **Petra Internet Cafe** (☎215 72 64), off the circle and well marked by signs. Sells computer equipment. Fast connections. JD2 per hr. with a 30min. minimum.

Post Offices: (☎215 62 24), next to the Musa Spring Hotel. **Poste Restante.** Open Sa-Th 7:30am-7pm, F 7:30am-12:30pm. A 2nd branch (☎215 66 94) is behind the Visitors Center, by the entrance to the *siq.* Open Sa-Th 8am-7pm.

🏠 ACCOMMODATIONS

When Jordan and Israel signed a peace treaty in 1994, visitors from all over the world invaded Petra, and the once quiet town of Wadi Musa erupted in a hotel construction frenzy, building some 40 new hotels in the past seven years alone. Unfortunately, the recent resurgence of violence in the region has taken its toll on tourism in Wadi Musa, and the city routinely finds itself with more beds than paying guests. This makes for a favorable situation for budget travelers, making some nice rooms available for JD2-3 per night. However, economic woes have also contributed to some less desirable practices, such as taxi drivers (particularly from Amman) recommending a hotel to passengers and then taking a hefty commission. Also, women travelers should be wary of super-cheap rooms (JD1 or less) offered by men advertising hotels around the streets of Wadi Musa. There have been a few instances where accepting an amazing bargain has been taken as an implicit invitation to unwelcome advances. **Camping** inside Petra is illegal, but lingering explorers (especially women) may receive invitations for overnight stays from Bedouin; use your judgment and be sure you'll be staying with a family. Others pick off-the-beaten-path caves for the night. Camping is available in Wadi Musa at some hotels.

🏠 **Al-Anbat 1 Hotel** (☎215 62 65; fax 215 68 88; alanbath@joinnet.com.jo), downhill from the spring, about 1km uphill from the center of Wadi Musa. The staff, the view, and the meals are wonderful, making al-Anbat the most popular hotel in Petra. Single and double rooms upstairs have private baths and big TVs; some have balconies. Breakfast and transport to Petra included. Nightly dinner buffet draws as many non-guests as guests (6-9pm, JD4). Mattresses in the breezy "greenhouse" and campsites with pink-walled bathroom facilities JD2 per person. Student dorms JD4; singles JD14; doubles JD16.

Al-Anbat 2 Hotel (☎215 72 00; fax 215 68 88; alanbath@joinnet.com.jo). From the center of Wadi Musa, follow the sign downhill from Shaheed circle. Same great service as its older brother, but no dorm/budget rooms, and the view is of the "cityscape" variety. Super-clean rooms have private baths, fans, and TVs. Breakfast and transport to Petra included. Dinner buffet JD4. Singles JD14; doubles JD16.

Petra Gate Hotel, P.O. Box 120, Wadi Musa (☎215 69 08), 40m up the hill from Shaheed circle in Wadi Musa, on the right, overlooking the valley. A homey atmosphere with smallish rooms and home-cooked dinners. Helpful employees live up to the "funky and friendly staff" slogan. Free billiards plus free laundry equal backpacker heaven. Breakfast JD1.5. Dinner buffet JD3, veg. JD2. Rooftop mattresses JD1.5; dorms JD2; singles JD7; doubles JD8; triples JD10.5.

Orient Gate Hotel and Restaurant, P.O. Box 185, Wadi Musa (☎/fax 215 70 20), left of the traffic circle, facing downhill. Cozy rooms, some with downhill view and balcony, house backpacker clientele. 2 nearby mosques and their competing *muezzins* create an interesting aural experience. Breakfast JD1-2. Dinner buffet JD2.5-3. Rooftop mattresses 500fils; singles JD3, with bath JD8; doubles JD8-10; triples JD15.

Sunset Hotel, P.O. Box 59 (☎215 65 79; fax 215 69 50), 200m uphill from the Visitors Center. A good value, especially considering what you would pay elsewhere to stay this close to the entrance to Petra. Clean rooms and a helpful staff. Breakfast JD2. Singles JD8, with bath JD15; doubles JD10, with bath JD20. V.

Cleopetra Hotel, P.O. Box 125 (☎/fax 215 70 90), 50m uphill from the main traffic circle, on the left. Colorful, small rooms offer backpackers a more mellow atmosphere than Petra or Orient Gate. Friendly manager gives maps and info. Breakfast included. Rooftop mattresses JD2.5; singles JD8; doubles JD12; triples JD16.

Musa Spring Hotel and Restaurant (☎215 63 10; fax 215 69 10), downhill from 'Ain Musa, the first hotel as you arrive from Amman. Big, clean rooms with satellite TV and decent views of the valley. Free shuttle to Petra and free use of the kitchen. Breakfast JD1.5. Dinner buffet JD3. Rooftop mattresses with hot showers JD2; dorm beds JD4; doubles JD8, with bath JD10.

🌀 FOOD

The farther you go from the ruins, the less you'll pay for falafel. Wadi Musa boasts the best bargains, especially in the streets off Shaheed circle. Many hotels have all-you-can-eat buffets at reasonable prices, and after an exhausting day of hiking, the ability to stumble from the dining room table to your bed is sometimes worth a few extra dinar. **Star Supermarket,** on the left and uphill from Shaheed circle, has cheap water (300fils) and reasonably priced basics for bag lunches. Even if you can't afford to eat dinner there (buffet JD14), the **Mövenpick** offers affordable ice cream (JD1.5 per scoop), an excellent salad lunch buffet (JD4.5), and a deliciously air-conditioned interior. The Mövenpick and its rival, the **Petra Forum Hotel,** also house the most pleasant bars in town. The former is in a tea garden on the roof of the hotel, while the latter sits on a lobby-level terrace at the base of the Petra hills, offering the best (and closest) view of the sunset over Petra (drinks JD3-5).

Al-Wadi Restaurant (☎07 979 56 26), in the city center on Shaheed circle. The popular breakfast omelets (JD1.5) have energized many a ruin-hungry tourist. Minibuses to and from Wadi Musa stop in front of the restaurant, and the English-speaking manager is helpful in transportation matters. Soups and salads 500fils. Meals (including dessert) JD1-3. 10% student discount. Open daily 6am-midnight.

Red Cave Restaurant (☎215 77 99; fax 215 69 31), up the street from Petra. A long hallway (or "cave," if you like) leads to this beautiful, breezy, bamboo-covered restaurant. Delicious food matches elegant setting. Daily specials and *mensaf* (JD4-5). Grills JD4. Appetizers JD1. Open daily 9am-midnight.

Al-Arabia Restaurant (☎215 76 61), next door to al-Wadi Restaurant. A little more stylish than al-Wadi, with a fountain spewing colored water and retro-modern furniture. The restaurant draws a good crowd of locals, quite an accomplishment for tourist-infested Wadi Musa. Kebab JD2. Appetizers JD1. Drinks 500fils. Open 6am-midnight.

Cleopatra Restaurant (☎079 68 39 47), to the left of the main circle when facing downhill. Friendly cooks serve rice, salad, bird, and bread (JD2.5). Arabic breakfast JD1.5. Kebab or mixed grill JD2.5. Buffet JD4. Soda 75fils. Free Middle Eastern sweets with any meal or sandwich purchase. Open daily 6am-midnight.

Rose City Restaurant (☎215 73 40), just uphill from the site. Pick up a sandwich lunch for the park at this diner and souvenir shop. Hummus 600fils. Sandwiches 400fils-JD1. Grills JD3. Soda 400fils. Open daily 6:30am-11pm.

Petra Pearl (☎079 81 01 85), across the street and 10m uphill from Cleopatra. Serves up a chicken buffet (JD3) and *ad hoc* Arabic lessons. Falafel 150fils. Shawarma 500fils. Open daily 6am-midnight.

👁 SIGHTS

It is possible to see Petra's top monuments in 1 very full day, usually via a tour of the city center and a hike up to al-Deir, but there are enough longer hikes and remote ruins to occupy 3-4 days of exploration. Guides are expensive but recommended for distant sites. Bring water bottles from outside; Bedouin sell water throughout the park, but at JD1-1.5 per bottle, you'll need to empty the Treasury to stay hydrated. Open daily 6am-6:30pm, in winter 6am-5:30pm; but hours loosely enforced. If you stay to see the sunset, you should have no problem getting out. 1 day JD20, 2 days JD25, 4 days JD30; under 15 free.

Officially, the Nabateans had only two deities—Dushara, the god of strength, and al-Uzza (Atargatis), the goddess of water and fertility—but worship of money was by far the most common practice. If the size of a man's tomb truly does reflect his wealth, Petra was once home to a lot of very wealthy people. Tombs and temples clog the brightly colored sandstone cliffs, stretching deep into the diverging valleys away from Petra's main attractions. Climbing into these hills will quickly remove you from the waves of tourists, but it is nearly impossible to find even one breathtaking vista that escaped the skillful manipulations of a Nabatean chisel.

OBELISK TOMB. If you head toward the canyon-like *siq*, large *djinn* monuments (ghost tombs) and caves will stare down at you from the encroaching rocky hills. The Obelisk Tomb is built high into the cliff on the left, a testament to the architectural influence of Ptolemaic Egypt. Closer to the entrance of the *siq*, rock-cut channels once cradled the ceramic pipes that brought 'Ain Musa's waters to the city and the surrounding country. A nearby dam burst in 1963, and the resulting flood killed 28 tourists in the *siq*. While engineers designed the new dam, the Nabateans' ancient dam was uncovered and used as a model.

▨ KHAZNEH. As you enter the *siq*, 150m walls on either side begin to block out the sunlight, casting enormous shadows on the niches that once held icons meant to hex unwelcome visitors (you should be safe if you've paid the admission fee). The *siq* winds around for 1.5km, then slowly emits a faint pink glow at the first peek of the Khazneh (Treasury). At 28m wide and 39m tall, the Khazneh is the best preserved of Petra's monuments, though bullet holes are clearly visible on the upper urn. Believing the urn to be hollow and filled with ancient pharaonic treasures—hence its modern name, Khazneh—Bedouin periodically fired at it, hoping to burst this petrified *piñata*. Actually, the Treasury is a royal tomb of distinctly Hellenistic style, leading some to believe that monument was actually designed by foreign architects. The Khazneh's rock face changes color as the day progresses: in the morning, the sun's rays give the monument a rich peach hue; in late afternoon it glistens rose; and by sunset it drips blood red.

ROMAN THEATER. Along the road to the right as you face the Khazneh, rows of tombs line hillside, sporting the traditional crow-step facade. The older tombs have one row of steps, while the younger tombs have more. At the end of this **Street of Facades,** Wadi Musa opens up to the 7000-seat Roman Theater. The (once) three-story, fully enclosed theater is carved into the red stone beneath a Nabatean necropolis, and the ancient cave tombs still yawn above it. The theater has been restored to its 2nd-century appearance, and audiences are returning after a 1500-year intermission. A marble Hercules (now in the museum) was discovered just a few years ago in the curtained chambers beneath the stage.

ROYAL TOMBS. Farther down the *wadi,* high up on the face of Jabal Khutba, are the Royal Tombs. The **Urn Tomb,** with its unmistakable recessed facade, commands a panoramic view of the valley. The two-tiered vault beneath the pillared facade is known as the **prison,** or *sijin.* A Greek inscription on an inner wall describes how the tomb, originally dedicated to the Nabatean King Malichus II in the first century CE, was converted to a church 400 years later. Nearby are the **Corinthian Tomb** (allegedly a replica of Nero's Golden Palace in Rome) and the **Palace Tomb** (Tomb in Two Stories), which juts out from the mountainside. Workers completed the tomb by attaching preassembled stones to its top left-hand corner. Around the corner to the right is the **Tomb of Sextus Florentinus,** who was so enamored of the hewn heights that he asked to be buried in this ultimate outpost of the Roman Empire.

CARDO MAXIMUS. Around the bend to the left, a few restored columns are all that remain of the paved Roman main street. Two thousand years ago, columns lined the full length of the street, shielding markets and residences. At the beginning of the street on the right, the **Nymphaeum** ruins outline the ancient public fountain near its base, where the waters imported all the way from 'Ain Musa finally resurfaced. On a rise to the right, before the triple-arched gate, recent excavations have uncovered the Temple of al-Uzza (Atargatis), also called the **Temple of the Winged Lions.** In the spring you can watch the progress of US-sponsored excavations that have already uncovered several workshops and some cracked crocks.

BYZANTINE CHURCH. A team of Jordanian and American archaeologists has excavated an immense Byzantine church, home to a wealth of mosaics. The site lies several hundred meters to the right of the Roman street, near the Temple of the Winged Lions (from which some of the church's column bases and capitals were probably lifted). Each of the church's side aisles is paved with 70 sq. m of remarkably preserved mosaic, depicting people of various professions, representations of the four seasons, and indigenous, exotic, and mythological animals. Recent studies attest that the church was the seat of an important Byzantine bishopric in the 5th and 6th centuries.

GREAT TEMPLE COMPLEX AND ENVIRONS. A team from Brown University in the US has recently unearthed the remarkable remains of a 7000 sq. m **Great Temple.** The Nabatean temple's short, wide columns were constructed of many cylindrical sections (unlike the slender Roman columns along the Colonaded Street). White hexagonal paving stones cover an extensive tunnel system. Farther along, the triple-arched **Temenos Gate** was once the front gate of the **Qasr Bint Fara'un** (Palace of the Pharaoh's Daughter), a later Nabatean temple built to honor the god Dushara. Like many of Petra's monuments, the walls of Qasr Bint Fara'un were once decorated with colored plaster, the bleached remains of which can still be seen today. On the left before the gate are the **Nabatean Baths.** On a trail leading behind the temple to the left, a single standing column, **Amud Fara'un** (Pharaoh's Pillar), gloats beside its two fallen comrades.

MUSEUMS. To the right of the Nabatean temple, a rock-hewn staircase leads to a small **archaeological museum** holding the spoils of the Winged Lions dig as well as carved stone figures from elsewhere in Petra. On the way to the monastery, next to the Basin Restaurant, the **Nabatean Museum** has well-documented exhibits and air-conditioned restrooms with what is probably the ◪**world's best toilet seat view.** *(Both museums open daily 9am-4pm. Free.)*

◙ HIKING AROUND PETRA

HIKE	DURATION
Wadi Turkmaniyyeh	30min.
Al-Habis	1hr.
◙ Jabal Harun (Mt. Hor)	4-6hr.
Jabal Umm al-Biyara	10-12hr.
High Place of Sacrifice	1½ hr.
Al-Madras	4-8hr.
Al-Barid	6hr.

Many people rave about Petra's most accessible 10 percent, content with what they can see in one day. The Bedouin say, however, that in order to appreciate Petra, you must spend enough time there to watch your nails grow long. The following seven treks fill two strenuous days, but you can easily spend a week wandering, especially if you venture beyond the ancient city limits. Four of these seven hikes require a guide (officially JD35, but good luck finding one who charges less than JD50): **Jabal Harun,** the **Snake Monument, al-Madras,** and **al-Barid.** It's unwise to hike the remote hills alone. If you feel lost, keep a sharp eye out for remnants of donkey visits, which can serve as a trail of crumbs.

WADI TURKMANIYYEH وادى تركمانية

The shortest and easiest of the hikes leads down the *wadi* to the left of and behind the Temple of the Winged Lions. Fifteen minutes of strolling down the road running through the rich green gardens of Wadi Turkmaniyyeh leads to the only tomb at Petra with a Nabatean inscription. The lengthy invocation above the entrance beseeches the god Dushara to protect the tomb from violation. Unfortunately, Dushara took a permanent sabbatical, and the chamber has been stripped bare.

AL-HABIS الحابس

A second, more interesting climb begins at the end of the road that descends from the Pharaoh's Pillar to the cliff face, a few hundred meters left of the museum. The trail winds up to al-Habis, the prison. While the steps have been restored recently, they do not lead up to much. A path winds all the way around the mountain, however, revealing gorgeous canyons and (you guessed it) more tombs, on the western side. The climb to the top and back takes less than 1hr.

◙ JABAL HARUN (MT. HOR) جبل هارون

This climb begins just to the right of Jabal Habis, just north of the Nabatean Museum. Winding staircases lead panting tourists up the narrow ravine of Wadi Deir, passing shrewd Bedouin selling water (JD1). A sign marks a trail diverging off to the left that leads to the **Lion's Tomb.** The anthropomorphic hole in the tomb's facade is the skilled work of Mother Nature's persistently eroding breeze.

Back on the path, keep climbing to reach the most rewarding summit in all of Jordan, which the Nabateans have sculpted into **al-Deir** (the Monastery), Petra's largest monument. Larger (50m wide and 45m tall) but less ornate than the Khazneh, al-Deir has a single inner chamber that dates back to the first century CE. Most scholars believe that al-Deir was originally either a Nabatean temple or an unfinished tomb dedicated to one of the later Nabatean kings. It picked up its orthodox appellation in the Byzantine period. Straight across the *wadi* looms the highest peak in the area, **Jabal Harun** (Aaron's Mountain or Mt. Hor). On top of the mountain, a white church reportedly houses the **Tomb of Aaron.** The hike straight up to al-Deir (no side trips) takes 30min., but the whole trip takes a few hours. Expect to spend a few more hours if you detour into **Wadi Siyah** and visit its seasonal waterfall on the way back.

JABAL UMM AL-BIYARA جبل أم البيارة

It takes a grueling 3hr. hike to ascend **Jabal Umm al-Biyara** (Mother of Cisterns Mountain), which towers over the Crusader castle on Jabal Habis. Follow the trail from the left of the Nabatean temple past the Pharaoh's Pillar and down into the *wadi* to the right. A 50m scramble up the rock chute to the left of the blue sign leads to the beginning of a stone ramp, which leads to the top. Exercise caution on the ramp, as the footing is fickle. It was here, at the site of Petra's original acropo-

JORDAN

lis and the biblical city of Sela, that a Judean king supposedly hurled thousands of Edomites over the cliff's edge. The gigantic piles of shards, over 8000 years old, are the only remnants of the mountain's first inhabitants.

If you continue south along Wadi Tughra (which runs by its base) instead of climbing Umm al-Biyara, you'll eventually reach the **Snake Monument,** one of the earliest Nabatean religious shrines. From here, it's about 2hr. to the **Tomb of Aaron** on Jabal Harun. The path meanders around Jabal Harun before ascending it from the south. When it disappears on the rocks, follow the donkey droppings. As you start to climb Jabal Harun you'll see a lone tent. Inside, a Bedouin (the official holder of the keys) will escort you the rest of the way and open the building for you to explore. The entire trek takes 5-6hr.

HIGH PLACE OF SACRIFICE المكان العالى

One of the most popular hikes is the circular route to the **High Place of Sacrifice** on **Jabal al-Madhbah,** a site of sacrifice with a full view of Petra—even the tourist police come here to watch the sunset. A staircase sliced into the rock leads to the left just as the Roman Theater comes into view. Follow the right prong when the trail levels and forks at the top of the stairs. On the left, **Obelisk Ridge** presents obelisks dedicated to Dushara and al-Uzza. On the peak to the right, the High Place supports a string of grisly sights: two altars, an ablution cistern, gutters for draining away sacrificial blood, and bleachers for an unobstructed view of the whole thing. Head downhill past the Pepsi stand, leaving the obelisks behind you, and backtrack under the western face of the High Place. A hard-to-find staircase leads down to a sculptured **Lion Fountain.** The first grotto complex beyond it is the **Garden Tomb.** Below it is the **Tomb of the Roman Soldier** (named for the tough guy carved in the facade) and across from it a rock **triclinium** (feast hall), which has the only decorated interior left in Petra. The trail then leads into Wadi Farasa and ends near the Pillar. The circle, followed either way, takes about 1½hr.

AL-MADRAS المدرس

Tourism beyond Petra disappears rapidly. The isolated antiquities can only be reached by donkey or foot. All roads lead back to the King's Highway.

A trail branching to the left just past the Obelisk Tomb and before the entrance to the *siq* leads to **al-Madras,** an ancient Petran suburb with almost as many monuments as Petra. On the way, watch for the short-eared desert hare and a full spectrum of small lizards in dazzling purple, fuchsia, and iridescent blue—one camouflage for each color of Petra's sandstone. Come with water, a snack, and a guide. The round-trip takes 4-8hr.

AL-BARID البارد

Past the Tomb of Sextus Florentinus and the **Mughar al-Nasara** (Caves of the Christians), a trail chisels into the rock that leads to the northern suburb of **al-Barid,** affectionately known as "Little Petra." A road passing the new hotel in Wadi Musa also approaches this archaeological site. Al-Barid is a fascinating miniature of Petra, complete with a short *siq* and several carved tombs, but almost no tourists. If you don't feel like hoofing it, a Wadi Musa **taxi** will take you there and wait at the entrance for 1hr. (JD7). Also off the new road past the hotel is **al-Beidha.** Excitement runs high among the members of the excavating expedition here—they've uncovered traces of a pre-pottery Neolithic village, a sedentary society dating from the 8th millennium BCE. Conclusive evidence of this site's age would make al-Beidha, along with Jericho, one of the oldest known farming communities in the world. A Bedouin guide can lead you here via a painless trail, about 3hr. each way. Bring an extra JD2-3 or some trinkets (such as cigarettes) to trade.

AQABA العقبة ☎ 03

Set in a natural theater beneath a crescent of rugged hills on the Egyptian and Israeli border, Aqaba is Jordan's sole link to the sea. Beneath the water, legions of brilliantly colored fish flit through a universe of coral. Aqaba's reefs are in better condition than the damaged reefs of Eilat, but they aren't quite on par with the spectacular snorkeling spots that circle the southern Sinai. Above the water,

Aqaba serves as an important trade and military center and has become the darling of Arab elites in need of periodic respite from dry cityscapes. At the tip of the gulf of the same name, Aqaba's strategic setting has been its greatest asset since biblical times, when King Solomon's copper-laden ships made Aqaba their home base. The Romans stationed their famous Tenth Legion here, and the Crusaders fortified the port and Pharaoh's Island, 7km off the coast (now in Egyptian territory). During the 1917 Arab Revolt, Faisal Ibn Hussein and T.E. Lawrence staged a desert raid on the Ottoman fortifications and captured the port. In 1965, King Hussein not-so-shrewdly traded the Saudis 6000 sq. km of southeastern desert (before he knew there was oil beneath the sand) for 13km of coastline, and started developing the city. The reopening of the Suez Canal in 1957 and the Iran-Iraq War in the '80s boosted Aqaba's importance as a regional port. During the 1991 Gulf War, Aqaba was Iraq's chief outlet for illicit exports, but a blockade slowed traffic considerably. Recently, Aqaba has bounced back, as trade has resumed and the open border with Israel has exposed the city to tourism.

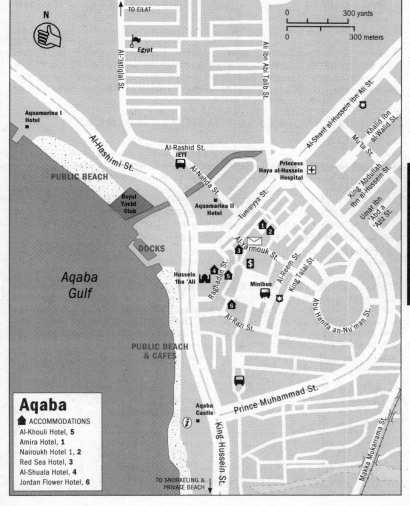

Aqaba

ACCOMMODATIONS

Al-Khouli Hotel, 5
Amira Hotel, 1
Nairoukh Hotel 1, 2
Red Sea Hotel, 3
Al-Shuala Hotel, 4
Jordan Flower Hotel, 6

JORDAN

▐ TRANSPORTATION

Flights: Royal Jordanian (☎201 24 03), a 10min. walk northeast of town on al-Sharif al-Hussein Ibn 'Ali St., just past the rotary. 1 flight daily to and from **Amman** (40min.; 8am; JD30). More flights during high season. Some hotels run buses from Aqaba International Airport to the center of city. Taxis to airport JD2-3 per person. **Caution:** It is recommended to wait at least 24hr. before flying after scuba diving.

Buses and Minibuses: The **minibus station** (☎201 63 78) is uphill past the post office; turn right onto King Talal St. and walk 2 blocks. Daily minibuses to **Petra** leave when full (2hr.; 8:30, 10:30am, noon; JD3); sometimes another bus departs in early afternoon. Another way to Petra is to take a minibus to **Ma'an** (1½hr., JD1) and catch a Petra bus from there (1½hr., JD1). There is normally only 1 minibus to **Wadi Rum** (1½hr., 7am, JD1.50), but during busy season others sometimes leave in the afternoon. Check times in advance. **JETT buses** (☎201 52 22), just north of the Miramar Hotel, go to **Amman** (4hr.; 7, 9, 10:30am, noon, 2, 3:30, 4:30, 5:30pm; JD4.2).

Taxis: Talal (☎201 24 77) offers groups of up to 4 people quick transport to: **Aqaba ferry terminal** (10km, JD3); **Petra** (3hr., JD30); **Wadi Rum** (1¼hr., JD20).

Car Rental: Prices have come down in Aqaba and are now similar to those in Amman. Rentals longer than 3 days include unlimited mileage; otherwise, the 1st 100km is free and each additional 100km is JD10. Daily rates for compact cars hover around JD25, mid-size cars around JD35; prices on 4WDs vary greatly. **Avis** (☎202 28 83), on King Hussein St. next to Nairoukh 2 Hotel, has the best deals on 4WDs (JD60-90 per day). **Hertz** (☎201 62 06), in front of the Aquamarina II Hotel, may have better rates on other cars, depending on what is available.

✳ ▐ ORIENTATION AND PRACTICAL INFORMATION

Aqaba is essentially one elongated beach, extending from the royal villa on the Israeli border to the huge, fenced-in port facilities 4km southeast down the arching corniche. Luxury hotels and military complexes have gobbled up a good part of the beach near town. Four countries come together in the small northern tip of the Gulf of Aqaba: Egypt meets Israel near the conspicuous resort hotels at Taba, Israel's Eilat faces Jordan's Aqaba across the border, and Saudi Arabia looms to the southeast. (For information on **border crossings,** see p. 436.)

Colorful shops, markets, and restaurants fill the streets between the **minibus station** and **Hussein ibn 'Ali Mosque.** Most of Aqaba's budget hotels and better restaurants are hidden in alleys surrounding the mosque, and its conspicuous metallic dome and howling minaret are useful landmarks for navigating the city. The mosque sits along King Hussein St. opposite the beach and downhill from the minibus station. Raghadan St., behind the mosque, is the heart of Aqaba; it is crowded and safe well past midnight every night of the week. South of the port and 10km from central Aqaba, the **ferry dock** handles the thousands of Egyptian workers and occasional foreign travelers who cross the Gulf of Aqaba to Nuweiba in Egypt. The **Marine Research Center** is about 1km past the ferry port. Past the center lie Aqaba's finest coral reefs and a sandy beach that stretches south to the Saudi border.

Visitors Center: (☎201 33 63 or 201 37 31), on the grounds of the Aqaba Museum, about halfway to the port from the town center. Short walk or 500fils taxi ride. Free maps, brochures, and info on travel to nearby cities. Open Su-Th 7:30am-2:30pm.

Egyptian Consulate: (☎201 61 71), on al-Istiqlal St. Turn right along the curve 800m northwest of the Aquamarina II Hotel; look for the guard booth. Same-day **Egyptian visas.** Bring passport, photo, and JD12 (JD15 for a multiple-entry visa). Apply for visa 9am-noon, pick-up 2pm. Open Su-Th 9am-2pm.

Currency Exchange: Arab Bank (☎201 35 45), just north of the park in the main square, is open for exchanges Su-Th 8:30am-3pm. **Jordan National Bank** (☎202 23 51), 10m downhill from the post office on the 1st street to the right, allows MC withdrawal. Hefty JD3 commission on traveler's checks. Open Su-Th 8:30am-3:30pm.

ATM: Arab Bank (see above). Also, **Housing Bank** has an ATM pagoda in front of the post office. Both accept MC/V and international debit cards.

American Express: International Traders Travel Agency Office (☎201 37 57). Walk downhill from the post office, take the 1st left, and continue for 30m. The office is just before the 'Ali Baba. Holds mail for anyone. Open daily 8:30am-1pm and 4-7pm.

English-Language Bookstores: Redwan Library (☎201 37 04), across from the Arab Bank along the street opposite the post office, has loads of quality novels, magazines, and newspapers in English, French, and German, as well as books about Aqaba and Islam, and a thick selection of used guidebooks discounted 50%. Open daily 8am-10pm. If you can't find what you want at Redwan, try the smaller selection at the **Yamani Bookshop** (☎201 22 21) next door, which also sells film, snorkeling gear, sunscreen, and other odds and ends. Open daily 8:30am-2pm and 6pm-10pm. MC/V.

Laundromat: Most hotels provide expensive laundry service. **Al-Abbi Dry Cleaning** (☎201 57 22), 1 block down from the minibus and *service* station on King Talal St., is cheaper. Shirts 500fils. Pants JD1. They'll also wet wash your sack of filth for negotiable prices (JD5-10). Open Sa-Th 8am-9pm.

Police: (☎192 or 201 35 03), uphill past the post office. Turn right onto King Talal St. and walk 2 blocks; it's across from the minibus station. **Tourist police** (☎201 97 17), at the Israeli border. **Ambulance** (☎199).

Pharmacies: Aqaba Pharmacy (☎201 22 37), next to Jordan Flower Hotel. Open Sa-Th 8am-1am, F 8pm-1am. MC/V. **Jerusalem Pharmacy** (☎201 47 47), on Tunisiyya St. next to al-Zeitouna Hotel. Open Sa-Th 7:30am-midnight.

Hospital: Princess Haya al-Hussein (☎201 41 11), a 10min. walk northeast of town on al-Sharif al-Hussein Ibn 'Ali St., just past the rotary near Royal Jordanian Office. One of the best, with decompression chambers and staff who deal with diving accidents.

Telephones: JPP and ALO phone cards are available throughout the city, but the smaller denominations (JD1-3) cannot be used for international calls. Cheaper F or after 8pm.

Post Office: (☎201 39 39). Turn left out of bus station and take the next left. Next to the large radio tower. **Poste Restante** and **EMS.** Open Sa-Th 7am-6pm, F 7am-2pm.

▚ ACCOMMODATIONS

Aqaba is where Jordanians go to be tourists. The balmy weather in winter and cool waters in summer draw crowds throughout the year, which makes it difficult to bargain for "low-season" rates. Prices at the beach resorts are exorbitant (JD100-200), but the one luxury you'll want to pay for in summer is air-conditioning, available at all the hotels listed below. **Camping** is free, common, and legal south of the port; the only legal camping north of the port is on the lots beside some of the larger hotels. The Aqaba Hotel, along the beach north of the city, also has a small campsite; the JD6 fee includes access to the private beach and showers.

▨ **Nairoukh Hotel 1,** P.O. Box 1138 (☎201 92 84; fax 201 92 85). With your back to the Hussein Ibn 'Ali Mosque, head to the left down Raghadan St., round the corner, and turn down the alley between the Han 'Ali and 'Ali Baba restaurants to reach the hotel entrance. There are 2 different Nairoukhs (**Nairoukh 2** is along King Hussein St. and charges JD20 for a single room with a beach view). The friendly staff cleans incessantly, and the place sparkles. Spacious rooms have A/C, TV, fridge, towels, and phone. Breakfast JD1.5. Singles JD10; doubles JD15; triples JD20.

Red Sea Hotel, P.O Box 65 (☎201 21 56; fax 201 57 89; redseahotel@firstnet.com.jo), next door to Nairoukh 1. Simple rooms come in 2 flavors (and prices). 1st class: Western toilet, TV, and fridge. 2nd class: Turkish toilet and "fun" hose. All rooms have A/C. Singles JD12/7; doubles JD18/12; triples JD21/18. Helpful manager 'Amer can arrange snorkeling with lunch for JD18.

Al-Shuala Hotel, P.O. Box 211 (☎201 51 53 or 201 51 54; fax 201 51 60), on Raghadan St., behind Hussein Ibn 'Ali Mosque. Luxury hotel with low prices. Some rooms have bidets, balconies, and a charming view of Eilat. Singles JD15, with breakfast JD18; doubles JD24, with breakfast JD28.

Al-Khouli Hotel (☎/fax 203 01 52), 1 street over from Raghadan St., almost directly behind al-Shuala Hotel. Small entrance with bigger rooms. A/C, fan, TV, fridge, and phone. Singles JD10; doubles JD14. Add 7% tax.

Amira Hotel, P.O. Box 383 (☎201 88 40; fax 201 25 59), next to Nairoukh 1. Bright, clean rooms come with TV, towels, fridge, private bath, and A/C. Some rooms have seaside balconies. Breakfast included. Singles JD14; doubles JD18; triples JD24.

Jordan Flower Hotel, P.O. Box 681 (☎201 43 77; fax 201 43 78), 10m down a side-street to the left as you head downhill from the bus station. Dreary entrance but comfortable rooms. Some have balcony seaview and A/C (add JD2). Breakfast JD1. Singles with shared bath JD5-6; doubles JD8, with private bath JD10; triples JD12.

🗚 FOOD

Fresh fish is surprisingly hard to find in Aqaba, despite its seaside location. A low plankton count in the northern waters of the Gulf of Aqaba forces hungry sea creatures to forage elsewhere, Jordanians are not permitted to fish the richer Saudi waters, and the Egyptian export tax is outlandish. Whatever the local fishermen do manage to haul in either ends up as a JD10 entree in one of the city's luxury restaurants or packed on ice next to crate upon crate of Fanta at the crowded **market** south of al-Khouli Hotel. (Open daily 7am-11pm.) Shops around Raghadan St. sell everything from ice cream and **fried sloth** to a dazzling array of imported cigarettes. A few upscale and Western fast food restaurants (Pizza Hut et al.) can be found along al-Nahda St. in front of the Aquamarina II Hotel, but the eateries around Hussein ibn 'Ali Mosque are much more interesting and generally a better value. **Gelato Uno,** a popular chain serving frozen treats throughout Aqaba, has one franchise on al-Nahda St. (500fils per scoop of ice cream. Open 10am-midnight.)

◪ 'Ali Baba Restaurant (☎201 39 01). Heading north on Raghadan St. with the mosque on your left, the restaurant is on the right after you go around the bend. A diverse menu of excellent food served in a quintessential beach town atmosphere. Top-notch french onion soup JD1. Hamburgers JD1.75. Pasta JD3. Lobster JD9.9. Huge variety of steaks JD7. Open daily 8am-midnight. AmEx/MC/V.

Al-Shami Restaurant (☎201 61 07), on Raghadan St., next to al-Shuala Hotel. A good value, popular with locals for its A/C and cheap chicken. Salads 500fils. Mixed grill JD2.5. Large chicken dishes JD2-3. Fish JD5-6. Open daily 10am-midnight.

Hani 'Ali Restaurant (☎201 52 00), next to 'Ali Baba Restaurant. Not as good-lookin' as its neighbor, but the wonderful pastries (600fils) and ice cream (450fils per scoop) are the perfect way to ruin any nutritionally balanced meal. Open daily 8am-11pm.

Shamea, down an alley to the left of al-Khouli Hotel. Not marked in English, but the sign above the glass display case contains the word 'pizza' several times. Syrian pizzeria warms pizza and other Middle Eastern snacks in a brick oven while you wait. Za'tar pizzas (mana'eesh) 100fils. Small Western-style pizzas 500fils. Open daily 8am-11pm.

Captain's Restaurant (☎201 69 05), on al-Nahda St., by Aquamarina II Hotel. Look for the blue-and-white boat-shaped veranda. One of Aqaba's best, even if it goes overboard on the naval decor. Fresh fish from Egypt and Yemen. Spaghetti with fresh cheese JD2. Meat dishes JD3-6.25. Seafood JD5. Simple omelets 700fils. Open daily 9am-11pm.

China Restaurant (☎201 44 15), on the 3rd fl. of a building behind the lot stretching uphill from the post office. Gaudy red interior and varied menu of quality food (entrees JD2-4.8). Hits the spot if you have a hankering for Chinese; even the king eats here. Open daily 11:30am-3pm and 6:30-11pm.

Tikka Chicken (☎201 36 33), on al-Nahda St., west of the Aquamarina II Hotel, on the right. Seven different chicken entrees with various side dishes JD2-3.25. Herbivores will enjoy the veg. salad (600fils) and hummus (500fils). Open daily noon-midnight.

👁 SIGHTS

Aqaba should thank its lucky starfish for its aquatic splendors, because the sights above sea level are all washed up.

RUINS OF AILA. The recently discovered ruins of Aila ("god" in Aramaic) are one of the few above-ground sights worth seeing. In a plain beachside lot across from the Miramar Hotel, archaeologists have uncovered a 120m-by-160m city established in the first century CE as a Nabatean port. Recent excavations have focused on the Islamic period of the 7th to 10th centuries, when Aila was part of a trade network stretching from Morocco to China. Visitors are free to wander amid signs explaining the paltry ruins. Items recovered in the excavations, including Greek and Arabic inscriptions and pottery shards, are displayed in the recently completed **Aqaba Museum,** in the same building as the Visitors Center, which also houses artifacts from excavations in Wadi Rum. The semi-dilapidated **Aqaba Castle,** next to the Visitors Center, was a beach resort during the Mamluk and Ottoman periods for Muslim pilgrims on their way to Mecca. *(Open daily 7am-7pm; in winter 7am-5pm. Aila and Castle ruins free. Museum JD1.)*

PHARAOH'S ISLAND. An accord between Jordan and Egypt has recently opened the Egyptian **Pharaoh's Island** (known as **Gezirat Fara'un;** see p. 193), 7km offshore, to tourists from Jordan. The scenic setting is host to some excellent snorkeling and the scattered remains of ancient ports. Pharaoh's Island (rather than Eilat) is increasingly believed to be the location of Ezion-Geber, the prosperous trade center of King Solomon. The **Aquamarina II Hotel** (☎201 62 50), on al-Nahda St., runs full-day trips to the island, including meals. (JD4. Reserve 24hr. ahead.) The Aquamarina also runs day-long snorkeling jaunts (JD10) and trips to **Wadi Rum** (JD40).

AQUARIUM. The Marine Science Station Aquarium, 1km south of the ferry terminal (taxi JD2), holds a colorful selection of the Red Sea's marine life. It also makes for a good stop before a dive or snorkeling trip if you want to sound smart by identifying the creatures you see in the water. *(☎201 51 44. Open daily 8am-5pm. JD1.)*

🤿 UNDERWATER ADVENTURES

Whether you're hiding from the relentless sun or exploring an ethereal undersea wonderland, Aqaba's blue waters will reward everyone who decides to dive in.

BEACHES. The majority of Aqaba's cleaner, emptier, and more scenic public beaches are quite far away, but a free and relatively clean **public beach** awaits near the Miramar Hotel. Southeast of downtown, a free **pebble beach** hides behind a "Restricted Area—No Camping" sign. Both public beaches are mostly male scenes, and women may become the focus of unwanted attention. The **Aquamarina Hotel** has a gorgeous white sand beach, but will gouge you JD2.5 for the privilege of burning your feet (shade and lounge chairs are reserved for guests). The beaches south of the port, off the road leading to Saudi Arabia (taxi JD3-5), are more remote, but they have beautiful views and great snorkeling.

SNORKELING. Yemeniyyeh Reef, starting just south of the Marine Research Center beyond the port, ranks among the world's best snorkeling spots for scoping fish. The **Royal Diving Center** (☎201 70 35; fax 201 70 97), in the Yemeniyyeh area, can help you get into the water. They rent snorkeling gear (JD3) and conduct beach dives (JD10, for 2 JD17). Novices can enroll in a four-day dive course (JD220). Entrance to the center costs JD2, which includes use of the private beach and saltwater swimming pool. A bus runs to and from major hotels in Aqaba. (To diving center 9am, back to Aqaba 4-5pm. 500fils.) Otherwise, it's a 15min. taxi ride south of the city (JD3). Most luxury hotels also rent out equipment and organize outings. Armed with a mask, snorkel, and pair of fins, aquatic adventurers can wander off alone to more isolated spots near the Saudi border, where the fish run on high octane. Wherever you snorkel, apply sunscreen frequently (it washes off!) or consider wearing a wetsuit or T-shirt: the cool water surface acts as a magnifying glass for the sun's rays, and floating on your stomach for a few hours can lead to the worst sunburn you've ever had. For important information on snorkeling and scuba diving, see **Scu-better Watch Out,** p. 184.

OTHER WATERSPORTS. The **Seastar Watersports Center,** in al-Cazar Hotel on al-Nahda St., conducts dives daily at 9am and 2pm; arrive 30min. early. Snorkeling gear costs JD7 per day. Beginners can take a test dive for JD34; a full PADI course course costs JD280. All prices include transportation. (☎201 41 31; fax 201 41 33; alcsea@alcazar.com.jo; www.seastar-watersports.com. 1 dive JD24; 2 JD38; discounts for multiple dives.) The **Yamani Bookshop,** oddly enough, has a good selection of masks and fins (see p. 493). The **Aquamarina Club** at the Aquamarina Hotel, offers a number of **watersports.** (☎201 62 50. Waterskiing JD4.3. Wind surfing JD5 per hr. Jet skiing JD1 per min. Kayaking JD5 per hr. Tubing JD2.)

⚡ DAYTRIP FROM PETRA OR AQABA: WADI RUM وادي رام

Taxis constantly run to Wadi Rum from Aqaba (1hr., JD15) and Petra (2hr., JD20). A **minibus** to Wadi Rum leaves every morning (around 7am) from Aqaba (JD1.5) and from Petra (JD3.5); ask your hotel manager to find out the exact departure time. **Buses** and **service** along the Desert Highway can drop off passengers 25km north of Aqaba at the turnoff marked "Rum 30km." From there it is possible to hitch a ride to the government rest house at Wadi Rum, though Let's Go does not recommend hitchhiking. Another option is to rent a **car** in Aqaba (see **Amman: Transportation,** p. 492). 4WDs are unnecessary unless you plan on exploring the desert alone. Arranging a trip to Wadi Rum from a travel agency or hotel in Petra or Aqaba eliminates the uncertainty of transportation and finding a guide, and can even save you money. **Wadi Rum Desert Service** (☎ 201 38 82), based in Aqaba near al-Khouli Hotel, offers very reasonable prices. (Daytrip from Aqaba JD25; overnight trip JD35. Prices include all transportation, guides, and meals. Discounts for longer treks. Open daily 9am-1:30pm and 4-9pm.) **Buses** leave Wadi Rum in the morning for Petra (2hr., 8:30am, JD3) and Aqaba (1½hr., 7am, JD1.5)–inquire about exact times. Entrance fee JD1, includes a cup of tea or coffee; JD5 extra if you bring your own car.

Two tectonic plates split to create the sublime desert valley of Rum. At the northern end of the *wadi* lies the village of Rum, home to hundreds of Bedouin, the Desert Police, and a government rest house. At the southern end of the valley stands the fort of the **Desert Camel Corps,** the descendants of the British-trained Arab Legion. The members of the Desert Patrol proudly pose for photographs in their green robes and red *kefyehs.* When not posing for visitors, they chase smugglers and renegade Bedouin or offer desert jaunts to beautiful star-gazing areas.

Just beyond the village of Rum, a vast wilderness of sand and rock begins. Massive rust-colored cliffs tower over the desert floor, sculpted into surreal structures by the gentle but persistent breeze. Although there is little escape from the sun during the day, evenings bring fantastic shadows, transforming the desert into a vast jigsaw puzzle of light and dark. The whopping slabs of granite and sandstone erupted from beneath the desert floor millions of years ago, and it's easy to imagine that Wadi Rum has not changed a bit since then. In *Seven Pillars of Wisdom,* **T.E. Lawrence** (a.k.a. Lawrence of Arabia) wrote that when he passed between these rusty crags, his "little caravan fell quiet, ashamed to flaunt itself in the presence of such stupendous hills." The hills and dunes provide a magnificent setting for a few days of desert exploration and camping.

With its otherworldly lavender mountains set against an empty sky, Wadi Rum deserves the name **Valley of the Moon.** For a set price, posted on the signs in front of the rest house, a Bedouin guide will lead you by camel or jeep to the valley's most impressive sights. South of Rum village, **Lawrence's Well,** a small spring next to which Mr. Of Arabia once napped, is the usual first stop on more extensive desert excursions. (30min. by jeep, 2hr. by camel. JD7.) The narrow *siq* through **Jabal Khaz'ali** is covered by shade during the day, making it a great place to explore a classic Rum landscape before climbing atop one of the nearby peaks to drink tea and watch the sunset. (3hr. by jeep; JD32. 6hr. by camel; JD40.) Other popular sights include the **Rock Bridge,** a huge rock with an arch through the middle, and the elusive **moving sand dune.** (Rock Bridge JD40 by jeep. Sand dune JD25 by jeep, JD40 by camel. Trips to the Rock Bridge and Sand Dune will stop at the Well and Khaz'ali canyon along the way.) For multi-day treks, a guide and transportation for each day (about 6hr.) will cost JD30 for a camel and JD45 for a jeep.

The only place to stay in the village is the **government rest house,** which has a nice restaurant but no indoor accommodations. (☎201 88 67. Breakfast JD3, other meals JD6. Rooftop JD2; tents JD3 per person.) A few small shops along the main road south of the rest house sell drinks and food for reasonable prices. A large tent beside the rest house is often the site of **traditional Bedouin music and singing** in the evenings. The **tourist police** hang around their office beside the rest house, providing advice and answering questions about trips into the desert. (☎201 82 15. Open 24hr.) A **Visitors Center,** located in the converted train car beside the rest house, has some free maps and some not-free maps (JD1.5) of equivalent utility.

A ROCKIN' GOOD TIME Rock climbing is a fabulous but little-known way to enjoy Wadi Rum. Many Europeans (especially the French) arrive each year and suit up for sheer-face scaling in this spectacular region. Experienced climbers will take thrill-seekers of all levels on trips all over the valley. The widely-available pocket-sized *Walks and Scrambles in Rum,* by Tony Howard and Di Taylor (JD3), contains descriptions of a number of different climbing routes and visitors' accounts of their adventures. One day of climbing, including equipment rental and a guide, will cost JD50-100 and can be split among your group.

Stunning as the desert landscape might be, it cannot compare to the wondrous night sky. Sleeping under the stars in Wadi Rum is easily some of the ▨**best night-life in Jordan.** A night in the desert can be arranged by the rest house at one of the valley's official campsites for JD25-50 (including meals and shelter but not transportation). However, the Bedouin guides sitting around the tables in front of the tourist police office will only charge JD15 (JD30 including transportation). If you bring your own food or buy some in town, it should be easy to bargain for a jeep ride to a beautiful remote location, a sleeping bag and mattress, and a ride home in the morning for JD20. However, don't count on getting much sleep—the desert evenings are cool, ridiculously quiet, and safe, but the frequent meteors lighting up the sky are bound to keep you awake well into morning.

LEBANON لبنان

LEBANESE POUND (L£)

US$1 = L£1510	L£1000 = US$0.66
CDN$1 = L£979	L£1000 = CDN$1.02
UK£1 = L£2160	L£1000 = UK£0.46
IR£1 = L£1750	L£1000 = IR£0.57
AUS$1 = L£805	L£1000 = AUS$1.24
NZ$1 = L£665	L£1000 = NZ$1.50
ZAR1 = L£181	L£1000 = ZAR5.53
EUR€1 = L£1380	L£1000 = EUR€0.72
E£1 (EGYPTIAN POUND) = L£356	L£1000 = E£2.81
JD1 (JORDANIAN DINAR) = L£2140	L£1000 = JD0.47
NIS1 (NEW ISRAELI SHEKEL) = L£357	L£1000 = NIS2.80
S£100 (SYRIAN POUNDS) = L£2840	L£1000 = S£35.3
TL10,000 (TURKISH LIRA) = L£11.5	L£1000 = TL866,000

PHONE CODES   **Country Code: 961. International dialing prefix:** 00.

Lebanon has long enjoyed its privileged position at the crossroads of three continents, proving its resilience from millennia of foreign invasions and natural disasters. Before the Lebanese Civil War of 1975-1990, Lebanon was the multifaceted "jewel of the Middle East," with *souqs*, ritzy hotels, and cutting-edge fashions. The self-proclaimed Lebanese sophistication is a blend of Mediterranean and Arab elements with a healthy dose of panache from the French, whose 1918-1943 occupation of the area left a lasting impression on the cuisine, language, and culture of the country. Four major religious groups—Sunni and Shi'ite Muslims, Druze, and Christians of different denominations—vie for political power and influence. In times of peace, this diversity adds flavor to the famed sights and natural splendor of the country. Tension between them, however, can make things explosive.

The country has emerged from the civil war with its spirit—if not its buildings—intact. A wave of reconstruction has allowed Lebanon to reclaim its cosmopolitan air, and welcome back a growing number of tourists. Beirut in particular is more alive than ever, rising from the ashes of its internal strife. Ba'albeck's international festival, world famous in the 1960s, is once again a hot ticket. Ancient cities, pristine mountains, hot springs, and other historical and natural monuments make Lebanon a worthwhile destination, while the ambitious and worldly spirit of its people distinguish it within the Middle East.

⊠ HIGHLIGHTS OF LEBANON

SAMPLE the international flavor of **Beirut** (p. 510), known for its chichi shopping, party-till-dawn nightclubs, and world class jazz.

FROLIC AND BRONZE on the sandy **Tam-Tam Beach** (p. 533), off the coast of Byblos.

HIKE AND SKI in the **Qadisha Valley** (p. 542), where thousand-year-old cedar trees rub shoulders with regal mountains and secluded monasteries.

LONG for the good old days of pagan abandon, as you admire the stellar Roman ruins and take in the famous arts festival at **Ba'albeck** (p. 545).

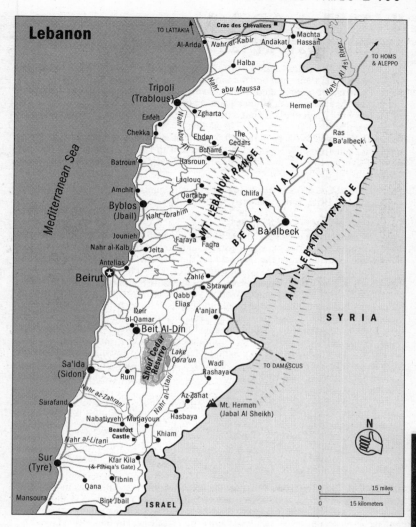

LIFE AND TIMES

Lebanon is a study in contrasts: it is home to numerous factions of Christians and Muslims. Its geography, complete with coastal beaches and interior mountain ranges, permits hiking, skiing, and swimming, in the same day. Its cultural rhythms combine Islamic culture with a distinctly Western beat, as old-school street vendors share commercial space with upscale bars and lively discotheques. But combination sometimes brings conflict, and Lebanon has had more than its fair share. Civil war, Israeli occupation, and Syrian paternalism have disrupted Lebanese life over the past twenty years. Still, Lebanon's drive to modernization remains steady, and Beirut's status as the most cosmopolitan city in the Middle East irrefutable.

HISTORY

ANCIENT HISTORY (3500 BCE-1516 CE)

THE ABC'S. The earliest settlers of Lebanon were the **Phoenicians,** who hailed from the Arabian Peninsula and spread their 22-letter alphabet everywhere they went. Phoenicians established Beirut, Ba'albeck, and the port cities of Byblos, Sidon, and Tyre as cultural, political, and especially commercial centers. The people of **Tyre** were particularly resourceful, building one of the first business empires in history nearly 3000 years ago. The sailing-savvy Phoenicians from Tyre also founded the city of **Carthage** in the 9th century BCE, and the remaining Tyrian settlers cut their own swathe through the heart of the Mediterranean, colonizing parts of Cyprus, Rhodes, and the Aegean Islands before sailing around Africa and settling the Straits of Gibraltar.

FOREIGN RULE AND INSURRECTION. Egyptian domination of Phoenician cities began in 1500 BCE, and was nearly as ineffective as any modern-day Egyptian bureaucracy. Toward the end of the 14th century BCE, the Egyptian Empire began to weaken, allowing Lebanon to slowly regain its independence. Freed from foreign rule and enriched by Phoenician literacy, navigation, and shipbuilding know-how, Lebanon enjoyed a 300-year period of unmatched prosperity. But the joyride soon came to an end when the rising tide of the **Assyrian Empire** washed over Lebanon's harbors in 875 BCE. Assyrian rule deprived the Phoenician cities of their independence and was peppered with repeated unsuccessful rebellions which were always ruthlessly crushed. When Tyre and Byblos revolted, the Assyrian ruler Tiglath-Pileser subdued the rebels and imposed heavy tributes. When oppression continued unabated, Tyre resisted again, this time against Sargon II (722-705 BCE), who besieged the city and punished the rabble-rousers. About 100 years later, Sidon followed suit and was completely razed by Esarhaddon (681-668 BCE), who proceeded to sell its inhabitants into bondage and build a new city on its ruins. But by the end of the 7th century BCE, Assyria was sufficiently weakened by the successive revolts to succumb to Babylonia, a new regional power led by the legendary king Nebuchadnezzar.

The Achaemenids ended Babylonian rule when King Cyrus, founder of the Persian Empire, captured Babylon in 538 BCE, and Phoenicia and its neighbors passed into Persian hands. Cyrus's son continued his father's policy of conquest and became ruler of Syria, Lebanon, and Egypt. The Phoenician navy supported Persia during the Greco-Persian War (490-449 BCE). But when the Phoenicians were overburdened with heavy tributes imposed by the successors of King Darius I, rebellion resumed in the Lebanese coastal cities.

CLASSICAL CIVILIZATION. Alexander the Great overthrew the Persians in 332 BCE, marking the beginning of the Greco-Macedonian cultural domination of the Middle East during the following 800 years. After Alexander's death, his empire was divided among his Macedonian generals, who were in turn succeeded by the Seleucid Dynasty. Phoenicia was thoroughly Greek when the Roman general **Pompey** added Syria and Lebanon to the Roman Empire. Economic and intellectual activities flourished in Lebanon during the *Pax Romana*. The inhabitants of the principal Phoenician trading cities of Byblos, Sidon, and Tyre were granted Roman citizenship. Economic prosperity led to a revival in construction and urban development; temples and palaces were built throughout the country, as were paved roads that linked the cities.

RELIGIOUS REFUGE. Phoenicia's geographical inaccessibility made it a safe asylum for minorities fleeing persecution. In the 6th century CE, the Christian sect that later became the **Maronite Church** (named after founder St. Maron) settled in the northern districts of the Lebanese mountains to avoid persecution from other Christian sects and conversion to Islam by Arabs who controlled the surrounding area. Seeking a similar spirit of religious tolecrance, Shi'ite Muslims sought refuge there during the 9th century, and the Druze followed suit two centuries later.

THE ARAB CONQUEST. Under the banner of *jihad*, the Prophet Mohammed's successor Abu Bakr brought Islam to Lebanon in 634 CE, soon after which the Umayyad (660-750) and Abbasid (750-1258) dynasties took root in the region. Under the Abbasids, philosophy, literature, and the sciences received great attention, and Lebanon made a notable contribution to this intellectual renaissance. Physician Rashid al-Din, jurist al-Awazi, and philosopher Qusta ibn Luqa were leaders in their respective disciplines. The country also enjoyed an economic boom, shipping textiles, ceramics, and glass. Lebanese products were widely sought after throughout the Mediterranean Basin.

CRUSADERS AND MAMLUKS. The first Crusade was proclaimed by Pope Urban II in 1095 CE at the Council of Clermont-Ferrand in France. After taking Jerusalem, the Crusaders turned their attention to the Lebanese coast. Tripoli capitulated in 1109; Beirut and Sidon, a year later while Tyre stubbornly resisted until 1124. Although they failed to establish a permanent presence, the Crusaders left conspicuous impressions on Lebanon's landscape, including the remains of towers, castle ruins, and numerous churches. The Crusaders were driven out by the Mamluks, intially a band of Turkish slaves brought in by the Muslim Ayyubid sultans of Egypt to serve as their bodyguards. One of these slaves, Muez Aibak, assassinated the Ayyubid sultan al-Ashraf Musa in 1252 CE and founded the Mamluk sultanate, which would rule Egypt and Syria for more than two centuries.

MODERN HISTORY (1516 CE-PRESENT)

THE OTTOMANS AND EMIR FAKHR AL-DIN. During the late Middle Ages, Lebanon was divided into fiefdoms, each governed by **Ottoman-sponsored emirs,** or hereditary sheiks. In the early 17th century, nationalist hero Emir Fakhr al-Din succeeded in uniting the small fiefdoms that compose most of modern Lebanon. A gentleman of great taste and remarkable administrative power, Fakhr al-Din was loved for his commitment not simply to the development of land, but to the well being of the people within. His vision to stimulate the economy began with the modernization of the ports in Sidon and Beirut. He then set about improving olive oil production under the expertise of Italian engineers and developed an extensive silk industry. Fakhr al-Din continued to gain momentum among the people as his domain grew. Fearful of his rise to power, the Ottoman leadership dispatched Syrian and Egyptian troops in 1633 to bring the territory back under Istanbul's control. Fakhr al-Din fled to a nearby cave (that can now be visited in the **Shouf Cedar Reserve,** p. 552), but could not escape. He was executed two years later. Today, Fakhr al-Din's memory as a national hero survives in the hearts of the Lebanese, in the lyrics of Fairouz, and as a miniature wax statue in **Deir al-Qamar** (see p. 552). The Ottomans ruled Lebanon until the middle of the nineteenth century, and it was during their rule that the term Greater Syria was coined to designate the approximate area included in present-day Lebanon, Syria, Jordan, and Israel.

THE FRENCH MANDATE. Muslim Druze and Christian Maronites coexisted peacefully under Ottoman rule, but once Turkish power began to decline, the two sects began fighting ruthlessly until **World War I.** When the Ottoman Empire was dismantled in the wake of the war, the League of Nations authorized France to administer Lebanon. French educational reforms formalized the study of the Arabic language, which ironically fueled the rising tide of Pan-Arabism while instilling a French cultural and political affiliation in Lebanon's consciousness.

INDEPENDENCE AND CONFLICT. In 1926, Lebanon became a republic in name only, becoming official only once the French granted **independence** on November 22, 1943. The infant government that came to power was militantly nationalistic, and tried to cut itself off from France immediately and completely. Riots erupted when the French refused to comply and muscled their way back into Lebanese

LEBANON

political matters. But the country reeked so much of anti-French sentiment that French administrators finally left after **World War II.** The US has been the most important Western influence on Lebanese society since.

Postwar Western leanings concentrated governmental power in the hands of Lebanon's Christian population, to the exclusion of the Muslim citizenry. But when Yasser Arafat moved the headquarters of the **Palestinian Liberation Organization (PLO)** from Amman to Beirut in 1970, the already stormy political climate worsened. Predominantly Muslim **Palestinian refugees** added their numbers to the growing Lebanese Muslim population, making Christians the demographic minority. The Christian-led government reacted violently against Palestinians, in a "defense" measure that was considered an act of outright aggression in the eyes of many Lebanese Muslims. Many Muslim soldiers defected and joined anti-Christian factions, leaving the Lebanese National Army significantly weakened by 1980.

Citing security concerns along its northern border, in the 1970s, Israel began attacking the southern half of Lebanon, where the anti-Israel PLO forces were stationed. Much of the predominantly Shi'ite Muslim population in the area migrated to **West Beirut** to escape the attacks, essentially dividing the capital between an impoverished "Belt of Misery" in the west and an overflowing gut of Maronite wealth in **East Beirut.** On June 6, 1982, Israel initiated **Operation Peace for Galilee,** a plan that ultimately involved surrounding and shelling Beirut at an immense civilian cost. This attack led to public outcry against ruthless Israeli military tactics, which in turn led to the formation of the fundamentalist Muslim guerrilla fighters party, the **Hezbollah** ("Party of God"), which was determined to act against Israel with more immediacy and violent extremity than the PLO had done.

CIVIL WAR. The **Lebanese Civil War** came to the global forefront in 1982—although it had been ravaging the country since 1975—after Islamic fundamentalists started taking **hostages.** The target for kidnappings were Westerners who lived and worked in Beirut, particularly those who resided in the expat Hamra district. In July, David Dodge, president of the American University of Beirut, became the first foreign hostage; such tactics persisted until the last hostage was released in June 1992, two years after the war's end. By then, 50 foreigners had been taken, some kept chained and blindfolded for years. The US government instituted a ban on American travel to Lebanon that lasted until 1997, though Europeans visited the country for several years before the US ban was lifted. The US government still advises that travelers exercise extreme caution when traveling in Lebanon.

POLITICAL AND ECONOMIC RESHUFFLING. Rebuilding the country after the civil war has required restructuring of the government's composition. Until 1990, an unwritten agreement called the **National Pact** required that the President be a Maronite Christian, the Prime Minister a Sunni Muslim, the speaker of Parliament a Shi'ite Muslim, and the Chief of the Armed Forces a Maronite, and this arrangement had heightened tensions between the communities. Because of high Muslim birth rates and Christian emigration, Muslims began to outnumber Christians and became discontent with Christian minority rule. Under the reforms of the **peace accord** that ended the civil war in 1990, many of the powers of the Christian president were shifted to a half-Christian, half-Muslim cabinet, and the Muslim Prime Minister was required to countersign presidential decrees.

Syrian intervention in Lebanese affairs has been a significant political factor since 1976, when Syria deployed 40,000 troops in Lebanon, fearing the potential partition of the country and Israeli occupation in the event of a Christian victory. Although parliamentary elections were held in 1992, with Hezbollah winning the largest number of seats, it is hardly a secret that Syria continues to control most aspects of Lebanese foreign and internal affairs. Although a significant number evacuated in July 2001, Syrian troops continue to occupy much of Lebanon, and Syria is the sugardaddy of Hezbollah, the most prominent political force in the country. Current Lebanese President **Emile Lahoud** was elected in October 1998.

Lebanon has few natural resources, so the economy is dependent on banking, commerce, and tourism. Before the war, the country was the "gateway to the Mediterranean," where backpackers and jet-setters frolicked side by side. It was also the banking capital of the Middle East, holding half the wealth of the Arab world in Swiss-style bank accounts. Wartime inflation forced the economy to adopt a more stable currency than the Lebanese pound. The invisible hand chose the US dollar.

IN THE NEWS

The summer of 1999 marked a tit-for-tat bombing struggle between the Israeli Army occupying South Lebanon and **Hezbollah** guerrillas. In September 1999, Israeli Prime Minister Ehud Barak announced plans for a historic Israeli pullout scheduled for July 2000. Barak hoped the pullout would indicate Israeli goodwill and encourage peace talks with neighboring Syria. Escalating skirmishes through the winter, however, prompted Barak to advance the pullout to June 1, 2000. When Hezbollah attacks intensified, Barak realized that holding out a few extra days would lead to unnecessary conflict. On May 24, Israeli forces withdrew from South Lebanon, and with them fled 2000 refugees from the Christian, Israeli-backed South Lebanese Army. Israel's 20-year occupation of South Lebanon ended.

As Hezbollah's flag waves over South Lebanon, many questions remain regarding the Lebanese government's future. South Lebanese, finally returning to their homes, see Hezbollah as their leaders and Hezbollah has since acquired additional seats in the Lebanese Parliament. The death of iron-fisted Syrian president Hafez al-Assad, Syria's partial military evacuation from Lebanon, and its suspension of peace talks with Israel have all added an additional layer of uncertainty regarding Lebanon's role in the future of the Middle East. This future depends on how the hot-blooded Hezbollah, old-school politicians such as President Lahoud, and the self-interested Syrian government reconcile their political differences.

RELIGION AND ETHNICITY

Lebanon's religious composition differs greatly from that of the rest of the Arab world. The country has more **Shi'ite** than **Sunni** Muslims (who makes up a majority of the Muslim population everywhere else in the world except Iran) and also has a sizeable **Druze** population of about 300,000. **Maronite Christians** are the most prevalent Christian denomination. The beginnings of Maronite Christianity are unclear. The sect is named after St. Maron, a 5th-century hermit from Syria, and St. John Maron, a monk who later preached St. Maron's theology. For the most part, religious groups have remained geographically separate. Before the start of the war, Shi'ite Muslim communities dominated southern Lebanon (including Sur) and the northeast region along the Syrian border. The Maronite Christian population held the majority in Central Lebanon, including East Beirut, and the northwestern coastline. Tripoli, North Lebanon, and West Beirut were populated primarily by Sunni Muslims.

LANGUAGE

The official language of Lebanon is **Arabic,** but it is unique among its neighbors in the degree of **French** that is spoken, especially in densely Christian areas. Today, **English** is the most widely spoken second language in Beirut and most of Lebanon. Street signs are written in Arabic and French. Radio programming airs in French, English, and Arabic. French is taught in predominantly Christian areas, while English is the more common second language of Muslims. There is also a minority of Armenian speakers. There is no local English daily newspaper, but newsstands carry an assortment of British and American dailies and weekly magazines. Two English-language weeklies, *Monday Morning* and the *Daily Star,* review local news and social events. The local French newspaper is *L'Orient le Jour.*

LEBANON

THE ARTS

LITERATURE. Largely because of its liberal political history, Lebanon has one of the richest and most diverse literary traditions in the Arabic-speaking world. In the 19th century, Beirut led a broad Arab cultural renaissance. Mystic, romantic poet, novelist, and painter **Khalil Gibran** (1883-1931) is most famous for his work *The Prophet*. A museum in his hometown, Bcharré (p. 542), is devoted to his life and works (for more on Gibran's life, see **The Wanderer,** p. 543). **Amin Ma'alouf** has published four historical novels in French, including the brilliant *Léon L'Africain*, that have established his presence as an expatriate Lebanese writer. He made history when his novel *The Rock of Tanios*, about a 19th-century Lebanese village, won the distinguished French *Prix de Goncourt* in 1993. **Amin Rihani** (1876-1940) is a 20th-century poet whose work is classified as *Adab al-Mahjar*, or "Literature of the Migration." Influenced by American poet Walt Whitman, Rihani introduced free verse into Arabic poetry. These writers and many modern Lebanese authors often wrote from abroad. What makes their work "Lebanese" is its enduring fascination with and love of Beirut, its interest in the problems of war and strife, and its form. Especially noteworthy female writers dealing with these questions include Hanan al-Sheikh, in her groundbreaking *Story of Zahra*, a fictional first-person narrative of a mentally ill woman trying to live out the war in safety. Hoda Barakat's masterful *Stone of Laughter* deals with a gay man's experience as a journalist who refuses to leave Beirut even during the worst waves of sniper and rocket attacks. Lebanese **poetry** has developed the *zajal* form, in which verses are sung rather than recited. World literature has also contemplated the civil war. Kamal Salibi's *A House of Many Mansions* recounts events of the war. Robert Fisk's *Pity the Nation: Lebanon at War* gives a first-hand account of the conflict and its major players. Italian journalist Oriana Fallaci's *Insh'allah* also tackles the topic of the civil war through a personal account of her time in the capital city; her book has been translated into many languages.

VISUAL AND PERFORMING ARTS. Lebanon's cities and villages come alive with annual festivals that feature traditional folk dancing and music. The largest of these is in Ba'albeck (see p. 545). **Belly dancing** is a popular form of entertainment at nightclubs and even at private parties. A type of provincial dance is the **dakle,** in which dancers wearing traditional mountain garb enact themes from village life. The national dance is the ▨**dabke,** a line dance performed to the rhythmic beat of feet pounding on the floor.

Modern **theater** in Lebanon took off in the 1950s and '60s, and was featured in many of the annual festivals around the country. The luxurious Hotel al-Bustan in Beit Meri, a suburb of Beirut, hosts Lebanon's main dramatic and musical festival, the **International Festival of the Performing Arts,** for five weeks in February and March. The war has colored theatrical themes—most contemporary theater ponders the effects of conflict. **Cinema** has undergone a similar evolution. The Lebanese film industry now revolves around documentaries somehow incorporating the civil war. An especially good example is *West Beirut*, directed by Ziad Doueiri (known also for his work as first camera on *Pulp Fiction* and HBO's *Tales from the Crypt*). Popular movie theaters play mainly American and European films.

MUSIC. Lebanese consumers really appreciate a good diva, and with the exception of **Amr Diab** (the best-selling musical artist ever in the Arab world), female artists dominate the music scene. In the summer of 2001, Najwah Karem's album "Nadmana" topped the charts. **Laure Daccache** is a master of introducing melodies of classical repertoire into her music. She has composed over 120 songs and invented a new Arabic rhythm, accomplishments that have secured her the respect of her male counterparts. Nouhad Haddad, more popularly known as **Fairouz,** is more than just a singer's name—she is the voice of Lebanon, a woman whose songs touch on ethnic and nationalistic as well as musical and poetic themes. During most of her singing career, Fairouz was part of a three-member team including the two **Rahbani brothers,** whose poetic and musical genius aided in the success of her songs. Fairouz performed at the Beit al-Din Festival in July 2001. **Nour al-Houdda**, whose name means "light of guidance," sang more than 100 songs during a career that spanned more than 60 years. She earned the respect of conservative Arabs and was given medals by the Russian and Eastern Orthodox churches not only because she was thought to be the "girl with the golden voice," but also because she refused to kiss or wear revealing clothing on screen or in performance. Live performances are rare, except during summer festivals. Most albums are available from outdoor cassette stands for US$1-3.

FOOD AND DRINK

Lebanese food is known all over the Middle East for its variety, flavor, and quality. Vegetarian dishes are common, especially in the form of very good and very cheap sandwiches from outdoor stands. **Tabouleh** is the national dish, made with parsley, *burghul* (cracked wheat), onions, tomatoes, lemon juice, and spices. **Fattoush** is a salad of lettuce, tomato, and cucumber with small pieces of toasted pita mixed in to soak up the dressing. Lebanese *mezze* (appetizers) include any combination of green peppers, cucumbers, radishes, scallions, olives, pickles, hummus, *baba ghanoush*, eggplant, and fuzzy raw almonds. *Mujeddra* is a lentil stew cooked with sauteed onions and spices. *Kibbeh naye* is raw beef and spices, whipped into a dip and eaten with pita. There are different varieties of **pita** as well: *marqooq* is a paper-thin bread cooked on a metal dome in a wood fire, common both in the mountains and at stands in Beirut; *ka'ak* is a sesame bread, molded either into little round balls or breadsticks. These are customarily dipped into Turkish coffee.

Lebanese meals often finish with cornucopias of fresh fruit, but sweets are also popular. The best are made with secret recipes closely guarded by those who possess them (mostly Sunni Muslims). Tripoli is especially famous for sweets like *halawat al-jibn* (unsalted cheese kept in a warm place for a few days and then rolled out with semolina into long sheets with sugar, syrup, and sweet cream. See **SweetNothings,** p. 539, for more treats). Lebanon is most famous for its **'araq,** an aniseed liquor similar to Greek *ouzo*, produced in small villages by families that have passed on techniques for years. The non-alcoholic specialty is *jellab*, a raisin syrup served with pine nuts.

FACTS AND FIGURES

OFFICIAL NAME: Republic of Lebanon

GOVERNMENT: Republic

CAPITAL: Beirut

LAND AREA: 10,452 sq. km.

GEOGRAPHY: Narrow coastal plane bounded by mountain ranges on the north and south; bordered by the Mediterranean Sea on the west.

CLIMATE: Rain and cool season with snow in the mountains from Dec.-Mar.; hot season with little rain from Apr.-Dec.

MAJOR CITIES: Beirut, Tripoli, Byblos (Jbail), Sa'ida (Tripoli), Sur (Tyre), Ba'albeck.

POPULATION: 1,504,900; urban 88%, rural 12%.

LANGUAGES: Arabic, French, English.

RELIGIONS: Muslim (70%), Christian (30%).

INCOME PER CAPITA: US$2700

MAJOR EXPORTS: Food and tobacco (20%), textiles (12%), chemicals (11%).

LEBANON

FESTIVALS AND HOLIDAYS

Although the practice is officially discouraged, Shi'ite Muslims beat themselves with a variety of instruments as a sign of devotion on **Ashura,** a religious holiday recalling the martyrdom of **Imam Hussein.** This grandson of **Prophet Muhammad** was slain in a doomed battle against a rival Muslim force more than 1300 years ago.

On a livelier note, the **Tyre Festival** boasts performances of Lebanese heritage, culture, and artistic activities through national music and folk dances in the ancient **Roman Hippodrome** every summer. An even bigger and more international show, the **Beit al-Din Festival** entertains thousands with books, music, photo exhibits, and ballet by artists from around the world.

In addition to the perpetual rustle and bustle inherent to Lebanon, the world-renowned **Ba'albeck Festival** further enlivens the country each summer. The festival began in 1955 and continued until 1974, drawing performers like Ella Fitzgerald, Rudolf Nureyev, and Margot Fonteyn. Over the last couple of years, the festival has been revived, and has been wildly successful, with recent appearances by Elton John, Sting and Fairouz. For a calendar of holidays and festivals celebrated in Lebanon, see **Life and Times,** p. 61.

ESSENTIALS

DOCUMENTS AND FORMALITIES

CONSULAR SERVICES ABROAD

Lebanese embassies and consulates abroad include:

Australia: Embassy: 27 Endeavour St., Red Hill ACT 2603, Canberra (☎02 62 95 73 78; fax 62 39 70 24). **Consulate:** Level 5, 70 William St., Sydney NSW 2000 (☎02 93 61 54 49 or 93 61 08 43; fax 93 60 76 57). **Consulate:** 117 Wellington St., Windsor, Victoria 3181 (☎03 95 29 45 88 or 95 29 44 98; fax 95 29 31 60).

Canada: Embassy: 640 Lyon St., Ottawa, Ontario, K1S 3Z5 (☎613-236-5825; fax 232-1609; www.synapse.net/~emblebanon). **Consulate:** 40 Chemin Cote Ste. Catherine, Outremont, Quebec H2V 2A2 (☎514-276-2638; fax 276-0090).

South Africa: Embassy: 7 16th Ave., Lower Houghton, Johannesburg 2198 (☎11 483 11 07; fax 483 18 10).

UK: Embassy: 21 Kensington Palace Gardens, London W8 4QN (☎020 7229 7265; fax 7243 1699; emb.leb@btinternet.com). **Consulate:** 15 Kensington Palace Gardens, London W8 4RA (☎020 7727 6696).

US: Embassy. 2560 28th St. NW, Washington, D.C. 20008 (☎202-939-6300; fax 939-6324; embLebanon@aol.com; www.lebanonembassy.org). **Consulate:** 9 E. 76th St., New York, NY 10021 (☎212-744-7905; fax 794-1510; lebconsny@aol.com).

CONSULAR SERVICES IN LEBANON

Embassies and consulates of other countries in Jordan include:

Australian Embassy: Farra Building, Rue Bliss, Beirut (☎01 37 47 01; fax 37 47 09, 37 47 14, or 37 47 16; austemle@cyberia.net.lb; www.austemb.org.lb).

Canadian Embassy: 434 Autostrade Jal al-Dib, Coolrite Building, Jal al-Dib (☎04 71 39 00; fax 71 01 95; berut@dfait-maeci.gc.ca).

Irish Honorary Consulate: Rue de Chilie, Kollelat Building, P.O. Box 11-746, Beirut (☎01 86 30 40 or 86 32 39; fax 01 86 00 76). The **embassy** with jurisdiction over Lebanon is located in Egypt: 3 Abu al-Fada St., Zamalek, Cairo (☎02 340 82 64; fax 341 28 63; irishembassy@rite.com).

UK Embassy: 8th St., Rabieh, P.O. Box 60180, Beirut (☎04 41 70 07; fax 40 20 32; britishemb@britishembassy.org.lb; www.britishembassy.org.lb). **Consulate:** 434 Coolrite Building, Jar al-Dib (☎04 71 59 04).

US Embassy and Consulate: P.O. Box 70-840, Awkar, Lebanon (☎04 54 26 00; fax 54 41 36; usvisas@inco.com.lb; www.usembassy.com.lb).

ENTRY REQUIREMENTS

PASSPORT. Passports are required of all visitors to Lebanon. If you visit **Israel** before a trip to Lebanon, insist that Israeli customs place **no stamp** in your passport. Instead, have them stamp a piece of paper inserted in your passport that can be removed. Be warned that Lebanese border officials may still refuse entry into the country if they see that you have no Jordanian stamp or have an Egyptian exit stamp from Taba.

VISAS AND PERMITS. All nationalities require a visa to enter Lebanon, and most need to arrange for one in advance. Citizens of **Canada, Ireland, New Zealand,** the **UK,** the **US,** and most of the **EU** can obtain a visa upon arrival at Beirut International Airport or at any official surface-entry border post with a valid passport. Single entry visas cost US$15 for two weeks and US$34 for three months; multiple entry visas cost US$70. If you need to obtain a visa in advance, print out an application online at http://www.lebanonembassy.org/consular_affairs/visas.html. You can also send a letter of request to the nearest embassy or consulate, specifying length of stay and the reason for your trip. Applications require a completed form, passport (*sans* evidence of a trip to Israel), one passport-sized photograph, a contact address in Lebanon (any Beirut hotel is fine), a money order for the type of visa you are requesting, and a self-addressed stamped envelope.

INOCULATIONS AND MEDICATIONS. There are no inoculation requirements for entry into Lebanon. Recommended vaccinations include hepatitis B, typhoid, immunoglobulin, polio and tetanus. Malaria pills, while not necessary, may foil those nasty mosquitoes.

BORDER CROSSINGS

TO SYRIA. Syria will only provide visas at the border for those who do not have a Syrian embassy in their home country (see **Syrian Consular Services Abroad,** p. 570). This excludes citizens of Canada, South Africa, the UK and the US, and most European countries. If at all possible, get a visa before leaving home, as there is no Syrian consular representation in Lebanon and it is difficult to get a visa at the Syrian embassy in Jordan. The crossing may take a long time due to hyper-security at the border. You will be denied entry into Syria if your passport contains evidence of having visited Israel, including stamps from Egyptian and Jordanian crossing points. Daily buses run from Tripoli or Beirut to Damascus, and from Beirut to Aleppo and Lattakia. Though costly, it is possible to hire a *service* to Damascus.

TO ISRAEL. Though Lebanon borders Israel, direct travel between the two countries is impossible at this time. Most travelers go to Syria, then into Jordan, where the Israeli border is open (see **Border Crossings: To Israel,** p. 436).

GETTING AROUND

BY BUS. Most **buses** are privately owned and efficient. Some are luxury Pullmans, while others are older vehicles with vinyl seats, no air-conditioning, and tacky interiors. The only way to find out schedules is to ask locals.

BY CAR. Renting a **car** is easy in Beirut, but not advisable. There are few universally understood or respected traffic signals in Lebanon, and most drivers graduated from the bat-out-of-hell school of driving. Whenever you ride in a car, **buckle-up.** A new, strictly enforced law mandates seatbelt safety throughout Lebanon.

BY THUMB. While **hitchhiking** is common in some rural areas, it is dangerous and not recommended by *Let's Go*, especially due to the tense political situation in the mountains of southern Lebanon. Most places are accessible by *service* or bus.

TOURIST SERVICES AND MONEY

TOURIST OFFICES. The National Council of Tourism in Lebanon is on 550 Central Bank St. in Beirut. (Mail to P.O. Box 11-5344.) Other tourist offices are in major cities throughout Lebanon. While local staff is often unhelpful or simply not knowledgable, the maps and brochures they hand out are a good tool. The Embassy of Lebanon website offers some useful advice for tourists and a nifty interactive map of Lebanon www.lebanonembassy.org. See **Useful Information,** p. 508, for other resources. Private tour offices in Beirut are an excellent, and often more knowledgable, alternative to government-run tourist infrastructure (see **Tours,** p. 515).

LEBANON

CURRENCY AND EXCHANGE. The basic unit of currency is the **Lebanese pound** (L£), sometimes known locally as the **lira**. Bills are in denominations of L£100, 250, 500, 1000, 5000, 10,000, 50,000, and 100,000, while coins of L£100, 250, and 500 are now in circulation. US dollars are widely accepted, especially at restaurants and hotels. **ATMs** give cash advances on **MC** and **V**; and most are plugged into the **Cirrus** and **PLUS** network. Only major banks accept or exchange **traveler's checks.** Except at upscale establishments, credit cards are not widely accepted in Lebanon.

PRICES. Because of Lebanon's westernization, prices are significantly higher than in neighboring Jordan, Syria, Egypt, and Turkey, but still lower than in Israel. There ae few hostels or camping facilities, while pensions range US$5-10 per night and midsize hotels US$20-35. US$30 should cover an average day's budget travel. For information on camping in Lebanon, see **Accommodations and Camping,** p. 509.

BAKHSHEESH, TIPPING, AND BARGAINING. *Bakhsheesh* (see p. 14) may be necessary in far-out places, but is not as widespread as in Egypt, Jordan, and Syria. However, since prices are higher and travelers tend to be wealthier than those in other countries, spoiled guards and officials may expect more palm-greasing than their counterparts in other countries. 15% is usually automatically added at nicer restaurants and another 5% is expected on top of that; budget establishments don't expect a tip but welcome it. *Service* drivers do not expect tips, but taxi drivers should get a little something extra (especially for long rides or ones that include many military checkpoints). **Always bargain** with *service* and taxi drivers, and do not be afraid to turn down the first cab. Bargaining at cheaper hotels that seem empty will often land a discount of up to 50%.

BUSINESS HOURS. Government offices are open M-F 8am-2pm and Sa 8am-noon. Banks are open M-F 8am-12:30pm and Sa 8am-noon. Other businesses are open M-Sa 8am-5pm. Muslim-owned shops close Fridays. The Lebanese week ends on Sunday.

USEFUL INFORMATION. For a comprehensive links page dealing with Lebanese politics, culture, and tourism, as well as hard facts about visas, customs, and international embassies, visit www.lebanonlinks.com or www.lebanon-online.com. Find additional hard facts at the **World Travel Guide's** Lebanon site at www.wtgonline.com/data/leb. You may also contact one of the **Lebanon Tourist Offices** abroad: **Egypt,** 1 Talaat Harb St., Maidan al-Tahrir, Cairo (☎/fax 20 2 393 75 29); **France,** Office du Tourisme Libanais, 124, Rue du Faubourg, St. Honoré, 75008 Paris (☎33 143 59 10 36, 143 59 12 13; fax 143 59 11 99); and the **UK,** Lebanon Tourist and Information Office, 90 Piccadilly St., London W1V 9HB (☎44 20 7409 2031; fax 7493 4929; abdallah@lebanon.demon.co.uk).

HEALTH AND SAFETY

EMERGENCY	Police: ☎ 112. Ambulance: ☎ 140. Fire: ☎ 175.

MEDICAL EMERGENCIES. In a medical emergency, dial ☎ 140 for an **ambulance** or ☎ 86 55 61 for the **Red Cross.** In Beirut, head to the **American University of Beirut Hospital** in Hamra (see p. 517), the best in the country. **Pharmacies** generally have someone on hand who can prescribe medication for those who know what they need. Payment is usually in cash.

WOMEN TRAVELERS. Women traveling alone should encounter fewer problems here than in most Middle Eastern destinations, due to the French influence that still lingers after decades of French colonial presence. Women travelers have nevertheless frequently reported unwanted attention, ranging from innocent leers and catcalls to being followed around town for a day. Marriage proposals are a common conversation ice breaker. While there is little violent crime, women should stay on their guard, referring constantly to a muscular husband or brother who is meeting them back at the hotel. For more tips, see **Women Travelers,** p. 38.

MINORITY TRAVELERS. Lebanese are often noted as hospitable people, and this is reflected in their good treatment of visitors from ethnic backgrounds other than their own. Discrimination against people who do not appear to be native is mostly limited to price-gouging in taxis and sandwich shops. An easy solution to this problem is to know how much items should cost and negotiate. In less expensive hotels and pensions, Arabs may feel uncomfortable, because some proprietors think that the presence of Arabs drives off Western visitors. Asian travelers will find that they are assumed to be Japanese, while black visitors will be treated as a novelty by locals. Though annoying, this treatment is generally free of animosity.

BGLT TRAVELERS. Homosexuality is illegal in Lebanon, but attitudes toward gays are more relaxed than in other parts of the Middle East, especially along the urbanized coast. Visible gay populations live in Beirut and Tripoli. Travelers, however, should take note: many Lebanese see no problem in mocking or making offensive comments about gays, and fundamentalist groups may severely harass them.

ACCOMMODATIONS AND CAMPING

HOTELS AND HOSTELS. Wartime inflation caused prices to skyrocket, and lodging prices are particularly astronomical. Availability varies based on location. Accommodations fall under four unofficial categories: uninhabitable but very cheap, cheap but surprisingly nice, "middle range" establishments that start at around US$20 per night, and luxury resort havens patronized mostly by vacationing Arabs from the Gulf States. Along the coast and in Beirut, accommodations are plentiful and expensive. Places to stay in all but the ski villages tend to be more reasonably priced (and negotiable when less crowded), but many medium-sized towns (especially in formerly-occupied South Lebanon) lack lodging of any kind.

CAMPING. It is hard to learn about camping sites, as they are not well publicized. There are four commercially-run campgrounds in the country: in Amchit, al-Jord, the Shouf Cedar Reserve, and the Afqa Reserve.

KEEPING IN TOUCH

MAIL. Poste Restante is not perfectly reliable—though service is improving, mail sent to the main post office in Beirut has been known to disappear. **Liban Post** is the new national mail service, with branches sprouting around the country. Sending a letter or postcard costs L£1000 within Lebanon or to Syria and L£1500 abroad. Mail from Lebanon takes four to seven days to reach the US, and two to four days to reach Europe. Lebanon also sports **DHL** offices, but no Federal Express service. Packages take up to four days for international express delivery.

TELEPHONES. Telephone communication is very difficult in Beirut without a **cellular phone**—there are no phone cards available and connections are spotty, at best. International calls must be placed from public telephone offices; there is one in every Beirut district, though not in every Lebanese city. To try and access **MCI World Phone,** dial (01) 42 76 27. You can also (theoretically) access **AT&T USADirect** operators from any phone by dialing ☎(01) 42 68 01. Do not try to make a collect call from telephone offices. The attendant will likely figure out what you're doing and scream at you to hang up. Cellular phones are available for rental. Telex and fax services are also available, though mostly in Beirut. For more advice on staying in touch by phone, see **E.T. Can't Phone Home,** p. 517.

INTERNET ACCESS. It's easy to find Internet access in all urban centers. In major cities like Beirut and Tripoli, Internet access might be easier to find than a phone with a reliable long-distance connection. Rural villages lag behind in this respect, but almost everything in Lebanon is only a daytrip from Beirut.

CUSTOMS AND ETIQUETTE

Lebanon's Westernization is reflected in its liberal attitudes toward dress and demeanor. In the big cities and along the coast, tank tops and shorts are perfectly acceptable for men and women. Beirutis are chic—travelers who are dressed down will stand out in many areas. Nevertheless, both sexes should dress modestly when touring the country's rural areas and when visiting monasteries and other religious sites. Men should wear loose-fitting pants and shirts. Women should wear long skirts and loose-fitting shirts with sleeves below the elbow, and cover their hair with a hat or scarf. People in Lebanon smoke everywhere. If you are smoking in a *service* or microbus, it is considered good manners to offer cigarettes to your neighbors.

BEIRUT بيروت

 PHONE CODES. The phone code in Beirut is **01** for land lines, **03** cellular.

Fourteen centuries ago, the Roman gods shook the city of Berytus with a powerful tidal wave that erased everything. Archaeological evidence confirms that since then, Beirut has actually been destroyed seven times—by earthquakes, fires, tidal waves, and war. After each disaster, Beirut emerged with a new and stronger face. In the golden years of the 1960s, Europeans could sample the flavors of the Orient while lounging in western comfort, and wealthy Arabs could sneak away to a hedonistic haven of pleasures condemned by their more conservative home nations. A tightly knit group of international jet-setters, journalists, and socialites unwound at seaside cafes, casinos, and resorts. Beirut appeared to be a happy home to a rare spectrum of religious, cultural, and political lifestyles. But it is this very diversity that shook the ostensibly content melting pot and carved deep scars during the war. The reality was that a growing underclass of disaffected refugees had been living in squalor on the edges of the city; exiled Palestinians and Shi'ites were silently witnessing the extravagant lifestyle of the expats and chic crowds, as Muslims, Druze and Maronite Catholics competed for a coherent definition of Lebanese religious and national identity.

While the civil war blew away the illusion of Beirut as a multicultural melting pot, in the 12 years since the war's end a renaissance has swept the city. Walking its streets today is a surreal voyage into the heart of Beirut's numerous rebirths. At opposite ends of the spectrum lie glittering high-rises and the remains of shell-shocked neighborhoods, battered into an eerie silence by years of sniper attacks. From the dust left behind by the war, a multi-billion-dollar reconstruction project has restored buildings of such immense beauty that their soft perfection appears almost painted on the fading canvas of rubble and pock-marked walls. But the truth is that the reconstruction is merely cosmetic. Most of the buildings downtown are still only superficially healed; the insides remain empty. Beirut's true resilience thrives in neighborhoods where bakers preside patiently over the suffocating heat of stone ovens and grocers sit and tell jokes; it is in the colorful tales of *service* drivers; it is in the hopeful ideals of Beirut's intellectuals, young and old, who ponder issues of identity as they sip Turkish coffee in European-style cafes.

For those who can afford the Western-style prices, Beirut is as hedonistic and forward-thinking as any European metropolis. The city's dedication to luxury and fun is in full effect in its many jazz clubs, Internet cafes, and opulent shopping districts. Arab tourists are returning in force, and even Europeans (and to a lesser extent, Americans) are once again exploring this erstwhile Paris of the East.

✈ INTERCITY TRANSPORTATION

FLIGHTS

Beirut International Airport (☎629 065 or 629 066), 5km south of downtown, is serviced by over 40 international airlines, including Air France, British Airways, Alitalia, KLM, Royal Jordanian, Turkish Airlines, and Gulf Air. **Middle East Airlines (MEA)** is the official national carrier, offering direct flights between Europe, Australia, and the Middle East. Buses and *service* do not go directly to the airport terminals. **Taxis** from the airport should cost about L£10,000 for the 20min. ride into town; beware of prices inflated to as much as US$25-30. If you are feeling adventurous, it is possible to **hike** 1km out to the airport traffic circle and flag down a bus or *service* heading north into the city for L£500-L£2000.

BUSES AND SERVICE

Currently, the only land border open for crossing without an advance **visa** is from Lebanon to **Syria**. Those wishing to visit Syria from Lebanon should plan to obtain a Syrian visa from the embassy at home (for more information, see **Border Crossings**, p. 507). Bus traffic is heavy between Beirut, Tripoli, and most destinations in Syria. There are three main transportation hubs for **buses** and **service** in Beirut.

CHARLES HELOU STATION

Located near the port in western Beirut, this station can be reached by bus or service from the anywhere in the city. Buses, minibuses, taxis, and *service* to Tripoli and most destinations in Syria originate here. Bus tickets must be bought in person. It is highly recommended to reserve at least 24hr. in advance.

Tripoli Express sends buses to **Tripoli** (1¼hr., every 15min. 5am-6pm, L£2000).

Pullman Buses (☎587 466) run to: **Aleppo** (6hr., every 30min. 7:30am-12:30am; L£11,000); **Damascus** (3½hr., every hr. 5:30am-8pm, L£7000); **Hama** (6hr., every hr. 7:30am-9:30pm, L£9000); **Homs** (4hr., every hr. 7:30am- 9:30pm, L£9000); **Tripoli** (1½ hr., every 20min. 5am-6pm, L£1500). Daily buses to **Amman** (9hr., 9am, L£25,000) via **Damascus** (3½hr.), and **Istanbul** (30hr., 10pm, US$40). From Amman. connections can be made to **Israel, Egypt,** and the **Gulf States.** Istanbul provides ready access to the rest of Turkey and most of **Europe.** Numerous other land connections possible via Damascus.

Beirut Taxi (☎ 587 460 or 03 296 846), a faster and more comfortable alternative to buses. To: **Aleppo** (6hr.; US$15 per person, US$75 per car); **Amman** (4½hr.; US$27 per person, US$110 per car); **Damascus** (3½hr.; US$10 per person, US$50 per car); **Homs, Hama, Lattakia, Tarsus** (about 6hr.; US$10 per person, US$50 per car). Taxis run 24hr., but those wishing to travel on the per-person fares should travel 5am-1pm.

COLA BRIDGE

This bridge in southern Beirut can be reached by any city bus or *service* headed to the National Museum. Cola Bridge is a congregation point for buses and *service* leaving to all points **south of Beirut**, including Shtawra in the Beqa'a Valley (p. 545) and southern Lebanon (p. 551). Buses or *service* to: **Ba'albeck** (3hr., L£7000); **Beit al-Din** (1½hr., L£5000); and **Sur** (Tyre) (3½hr., L£5000) via **Sa'ida** (Sidon) (2hr., L£1000). Bus schedules vary greatly. *Service* depart when full.

DAWRA

Many city buses and *service* terminate at this traffic circle in western Beirut. Transportation congregates here for local routes and shorter jaunts to the north. Buses to **Byblos** (1½hr., L£500) via **Jounieh** (45min.) and **Tripoli** (1hr. or longer, depending on frequency of stops).

LEBANON

N

CORNICHE

Avenue de Paris

American Univerty
of Beirut

Bains Francais
R. Ibn Sina

Hard Rock Cafe

Rue Ahm

MINAT
AL-HISN

Rue Fakhr ad-Din

Rue Omar Daouk

**Military
Camp**

MANARA

Australia

Lighthouse

Rue Bliss

Rue John Kennedy

Rue Clémenceau

AIN AL-
MREISSE

R. Sidani

Rue Sourati

Rue Magmari

Ave. du General de Gaulle

Rue Naguib Aradati

Rue du Koweit

Rue Sourati

HAMRA

Rue Makdissi

Rue de Rome

Rue d'Amerique

Rue l'Armée

Wadi Ab

Rue de S

Rue Labbane

Rue Hamra

Rue de Ba'albeck

Rue Emile Edde

Rue Banque du Liban

Rue Spears

SEE HAMRA INSET

Sanayeh
Public
Garden

Parl

**Lebanese
American
University**

Henry J. Bean's

Rue Madame Curie

SANAYEH

RAOUCHE

Rue Chatila

*Pigeon
Rock*

Rue Yakey Edoline Solh

Rue de Tenir

Rue Rafic Aran

Rue d'Australie

R. Andaboue

Rue Itani

Rue Dunant

Rue d'Alger

Ave. de l'Independance

R. Osman
Bin Affan

Rue Ahmed Bey

Rue Al-Rachidine

MUSSAITBEH

Rue Vienna

BASHM

Rue Abdallah Sabbah

Rue Verdun

Rue Unesco

Rue Mazra'a

Rue Mar Elias

Rue Selim Ali al-Salaam

MEDITERRANEAN
SEA

Egypt

**Lebanese
University**

Boulevard Sa'ed Salam

Rue Al-Mussaitbeh

Rue Bor Abi-Haidar

Boulevard Sa'ed

Rue Maz

*Ramlet
al-Baida
Public Beach*

Ave. Rafiq Hariri

Rue Habib Abu Shala

Cola Bridge

**Arab Univer
of Beirut**

Rue Suleiman al-Bustani

Rue
al-

Rue de la République

Rue Akhtal Al-Saghir

Ave. Camille Chamoun

*Côte d'Azur
Beach*

St. Simon Beach

St. Michel Beach

**Sports
City**

Beirut

⌂ ACCOMMODATIONS
Cederland Hotel, **11**
Embassy Hotel, **14**
Hotel Al-Nazih, **4**
Lord's Hotel, **1**
Mayflower Hotel, **12**
Pension Valery, **3**
Talal's New Hotel, **5**
University Hotel, **10**
West House Residence, **15**
YWCA, **2**

🍴 FOOD
Hamadeh Snack, **17**
Le Chef, **9**

♪ NIGHTLIFE
B018, **18**
Barbar, **16**
Taj Al Moulouk, **7**
Tribers, **8**
Walimah, **13**

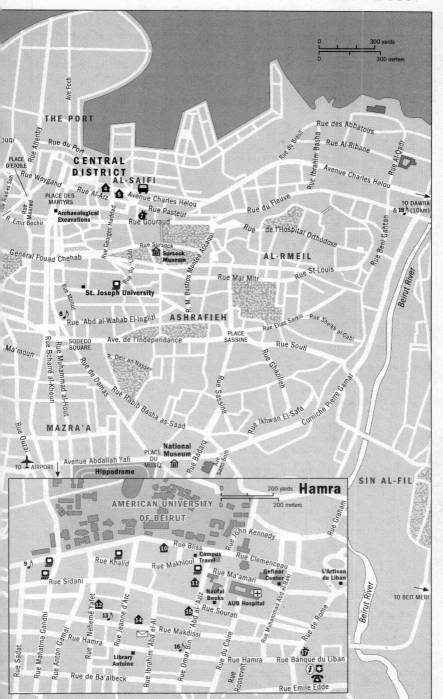

CAR RENTAL

Rental is no hassle in Beirut, but it takes nerves of steel to actually drive it through Lebanon's chaotic roadways.

Budget Car Rental (☎ 740 741). Offices all around the country offer rentals starting at US$35 per day. Taxi and shuttle services available, as well as chauffeurs for hire (8am-8pm, US$25 per day).

Europcar (☎ 480 480 or 502 200), in the Sa'arti Building on Hayek Ave. in Sin al-Fil. Another office in 'Ain Mreisse (☎ 602 223). Prices and options similar to Budget's.

■ ORIENTATION

Located at the foothills of the Mt. Lebanon range, Beirut elegantly dips her toes into the blue waters of the Mediterranean. The city is located on a promontory that juts out into the sea, bounded by waves on the north and west. **Ave. Général de Gaulle** borders the sea on the west shore, turning into **Ave. de Paris** on the north coast. Parallel to the sea is a popular walking, jogging, and lounging path known as the **corniche.** The corniche begins at the **Pigeon Rocks** in **Raouche** and continues to the **Hard Rock Cafe** in **'Ain Mreisse.**

Each of Beirut's districts has a slightly different feel. The **Hamra** district in western Beirut is centered around Rue Hamra, a major commercial street flanked by cafes, restaurants, accommodations, shops, banks, and many of the administrative buildings that were displaced from downtown during the war. Just north of **Rue Bliss** in Hamra is the **American University of Beirut (AUB),** whose beautiful hilltop campus cascades down towards the sea and inspires the intellectual air in Hamra and much of Beirut. Heading east along the corniche leads to the quieter streets of the **'Ain Mreisse** district, a residential area that is home to several hotels running the gamut from glamorous intercontinental to dirt cheap. Continuing east leads to the port and downtown, also known as **Beirut Central District,** or BCD. Downtown was heavily damaged in the war but is rapidly taking shape around reconstruction in its main squares: **Place de l'Etoile** and **Place des Martyrs.** It is expected that downtown will regain its status as a center of city life within the next few years.

Continuing east of downtown on Ave. Charles Helou leads first to the **Charles Helou Bus Station,** then (several kilometers later), to the transport hub of **Dawra.** Heading south from downtown on **Rue de Damas** leads to the **Ashrafiye** district, with its two centers at **Place Sassine** and **Sodeco Sq.** Continuing south finds the **National Museum** and **Hippodrome** racetrack. From here, **Blvd. Sa'ed Salam** heads back to the sea in the direction of **Cola Bridge** and, farther south, **Beirut International Airport.**

⊏ LOCAL TRANSPORTATION

Beirut traffic is a nightmare, which makes walking the most pleasant way to travel. The districts are small, and almost all listings are centrally located in **Hamra, 'Ain Mreisse,** and **Ashrafiye** districts. Although walking between neighborhoods is reasonable (30min. from Raouche's Pigeon Rocks to 'Ain Mreisse), an alternative is to take a *service* or bus and get off on a main road in the vicinity of your destination.

BUSES

Local buses in Beirut cost L£500 and are surprisingly easy to use. There are two companies in Lebanon, both running nearly identical routes. **Government** buses are blue and white, while the red-and-white buses are those of the **Lebanese Commuting Company (LCC).** Over 20 lines criss-cross the city, making buses ideal for getting to well-traveled destinations such as Cola Bridge, Hamra, the National Museum, Dawra, or the Pigeon Rocks in Raouche. Schedules are posted, but most locals find it worthless to memorize the ever-mutating routes. The easiest way to use buses is to treat them like *service:* stand on the proper side of a busy street and shout your destination as the bus slows down. Buses leave when full but generally run every 5-15min. beginning as early as 5:30am and shutting down around 8pm.

OFF THE BEATEN TRACK Eager to introduce foreigners and nationals to Lebanon's amazing natural diversity, the Ministry of Tourism has dubbed 2002 the year of **"Eco Tourism."** Unfortunately, because there are few organized trails in the country and fewer reliable detailed maps of the mountains, much of the country's beauty remains difficult to access. Signs are rare in remote areas and directions survive most vividly in the minds of shepherds and villagers. Although such secrets recall a romantic era of oral traditions and unexploited land, it makes travel very difficult for those who do not speak some Arabic. Trekking and adventure organizations are rapidly breaking ground, planning group trips to various regions around the country. Many are also eager to offer route suggestions and advice for those who would rather travel alone. It is advised that one start any off-the-beaten-track exploration with advice from knowledgeable guides. Although companies have sprung up around Lebanon in the past few years (e.g. **al-Jord,** p. 549), most offices are still concentrated in Beirut.

SERVICE

Service are found everywhere in the city. Rides within central Beirut cost about L£1000, while rides to suburbs or off central routes will run around L£2000. Look for the red license plates and be sure the driver knows you are looking for *service* and **not** a private taxi. *Service* thin around 9pm and stop running by midnight.

TAXIS

Fares for private taxis within greater Beirut will rarely be more than L£5000-10,000. Be sure to agree on the fare **before** getting in and don't feel pressured to take the first offer. If you think it's too expensive, send the driver off and another will shortly slow down. Taxis can be called 24hr.; **Allo Taxi** (☎366 661), **Radio Taxi** (☎352 250) and **Lebanon Taxi** (☎340 717 or 353 153) are reputable companies.

🛈 PRACTICAL INFORMATION

TOURIST SERVICES

Tourist Office: Ministry of Tourism (☎34 30 73; www.lebanon-tourism.gov.lb), at the intersection of Rue de Rome and Rue Banque du Liban in Hamra. Enter the covered enclave from the corner; the information office is the 1st door on your left opposite the tourist police. Fluent English speakers distribute sleek, up-to-date maps and brochures for every region of the country. The **GeoProjects** maps are the best available (also found at most bookstores, L£12,000). Open M-F 8am-2pm, Sa 8am-1pm.

TOURS

Nakhal Tour Company (☎389 389; fax 389 282; www.nakhal.com.lb), in the Ghorayeb Building on Rue Sami al-Solh. Offers 8 different day-long tours of Lebanon leaving from Beirut (US$35-55, lunch included). If you feel the need for a tour bus-style orientation, Nakhal is one of the cheapest and most reliable options around. Historical tours of Beirut (half-day US$20) and weeklong tours to Syria, Jordan, Cyprus, Egypt, Turkey, and Greece. Check online to save US$5-10 on select "Eco" days.

Liban Trek (☎390 790; www.libantrek.com, info@libantrek.com). Guided hiking, trekking, and cultural expeditions for all levels and interests. Founder Michel Moufarege is knowledgeable and inspiring, offering superb wisdom and advice. Check online for set weekend trips (L£20,000-30,000). Tailor-made excursions available.

Club Thermique (☎03 288 193; www.clubthermique.com.lb), based in Ajaltoun near Faraya. This offshoot of a French paragliding school offers well-organized adventures in the Mt. Lebanon Range. Tandem discovery flights US$35-50. Paragliding school US$350, including 7 flights. Mountain biking US$15 for 5hr. 4WD treks to multiple destinations including Qoronet al-Sawda, Lebanon's tallest peak.

Lebanese Adventure (☎/fax 01 398 982; www.lebanese-adventure.com). Organizes reasonably priced hiking, rafting, rock climbing, mountain biking, snowshoeing, and star gazing trips on weekends. Among the most popular excursions are hikes for all levels in the Shouf Cedar Reserve (US$15 for 1 day, including Reserve entrance fee), whitewater rafting on Nahr al-Asi near Hermel (US$30 for rafting and overnight camping accommodations), mountain biking (US$30 for 1 day including bike and transportation), and rock climbing near Faraya and Faqra. Web site posts monthly and weekly schedules.

Wild Expeditions (☎615 381, or 03 293 210; www.wild-expeditions.com). Biking, hiking, rock climbing, rafting, and other weekend excursions US$20-35. Includes transportation. Full-day private guides US$75-125. Call or check online for weekly schedules.

EMBASSIES AND CONSULATES

Australia: (☎374 701; fax 374 709), in the Farra Building on Rue Bliss in Ras Beirut.

Canada: 434 Autostrade (☎04 710 576; fax 710 595), Coolrite Building, in Jal al-Dib.

Egypt: (☎867 917, 868 295; fax 863 751), on Rue Thomas Edison, in Ramlet al-Baida.

Jordan: (☎05 922 500, or 922 501; fax 922 502), Rue Elias Helou in Ba'abda.

UK: (☎41 70 07, 40 36 40, or 40 50 70; fax 402 032), on Rue No. 8 in Rabieh.

US: (☎04 542 600 or 543 600; ☎544 037 for visa documents; fax 544 136), in Aoucar. Take a *service* headed anywhere north of Beirut (Byblos or Tripoli), and ask to be dropped off at Dbayye. From Dbayye, take a taxi (L£5000) to the embassy.

LOCAL AND FINANCIAL SERVICES

Currency Exchange: Exchange foreign currency at any bank or currency exchange booth. US dollars are universally accepted at shops and hotels, and on buses. Like banks, **ATMs** can be found on all main roads. Most are plugged into the Cirrus and Plus networks and can give cash advances on MC/V. Don't wait until you are in a crunch to get cash, as network connections can be unreliable. **Fransabank** (☎340 180) is across from the tourist office in Hamra. Open M-F 8:15am-2:30pm, Sa 8:15am-noon.

American Express: (☎34 18 25 or 34 18 56), in the Gefinor Center on Rue Clemenceau in western Hamra. Will hold mail for card members and frequently for non-members who ask nicely. Open M-F 9am-4pm, Sa 8:30am-1:30pm.

English-Language Bookstores: Naufal Booksellers (☎354 898), on Rue Sourati near the intersection with Rue 'Abd al-'Aziz, across from the Idriss Market. Extensive selection of English-language fiction, magazines, newspapers, journals, and travel guides. Open M-F 9:30am-6pm, Sa 9:30am-2pm. MC/V. **Librairie Antoine** (☎341 470 or 341 471), Rue Hamra near Rue Jeanne d'Arc. Mostly French, with a smaller selection of English books and dailies. Open M-F 8:30am-7pm, Sa 8:30am-6pm.

Laundry: Although there are no laundromats in Beirut, many dry cleaners and hotels will do your laundry. Balconies draped with colorful laundry remind visitors that clothes can still be washed the good old fashioned way. Try Five Star Cleaners (☎74 28 56), on Rue Nehme Yafet just off Rue Sidani. Laundry and dry cleaning services. Shirts L£3000. Pants L£4000. Socks L£1000. Open M-F 8am-6pm, Sa 8am-4pm.

EMERGENCY AND COMMUNICATIONS

Emergency: Ambulance: ☎140. **Police:** ☎112. **Fire:** ☎125. **Information:** ☎120.

Tourist Police: (☎350 901 or 343 286), within the Ministry of Tourism enclave, opposite the tourist office. Start here with complaints of scams, overpricing, petty crime, and theft. More serious issues should be directed to the city police. There is not always an English speaker on duty, though someone can translate for you while the tourist office is open. If you find the language barrier insurmountable, and can't wait for the tourist office to open, call city police. Open 24hr.

Pharmacy: Pharmacie Rishani (☎34 28 31), on Rue Sourati opposite Naufal Booksellers in Hamra. English and French spoken. Open daily 8am-8pm. **Mazen Pharmacy** (☎313 362), in Mazra'a. English speakers not always on duty. Open 24hr. **Wardieh Pharmacy** (☎343 678) offers free home delivery 24hr.

Hospital: American University of Beirut Hospital (☎34 04 60 or 35 00 00), at the inter-section of Rue Ma'amari and Rue Claire in Hamra.

Telephones: Telephone service in Lebanon is hard to come by and completely unreliable. There is a **telephone office** (☎348 930) in Hamra in the Ministry of Tourism complex. Write the number you are calling on a piece of paper and the operator at the table will dial for you and direct you to a booth. Long lines, so come armed with patience. L£1,500 per min. to the US (L£1,100 during non-peak hours) and L£1,500 per 3min. within Lebanon. Open daily 8am-11pm.

E.T. (CAN'T) PHONE HOME. Almost everyone in Beirut carries a **cell phone,** in large part because regular phone service is hard to come by and unre-liable. If you anticipate having to make a lot of calls, it may be worthwhile to rent or purchase a used cell phone. Cell phone service is paid for in units known as "clicks" following a scheme similar to phone cards. A click phone line costs US$70 for the chip and first 125 units, and US$20 for every subsequent 40 units. (1 click per min. for local calls; up to 8 clicks per min. for international calls. Received calls do not use up units). There are some **public phones** scat-tered around Beirut (L£500), but they often do not accept international phone cards. As of August 2001, local phone cards were not available. To make calls from the public phones, insert a L£500 coin in the slot, push the slot, and dial the number. Push the button to release your coin only after you've heard a voice on the receiving end. When the red light starts flashing, quickly open the slot, insert a new coin, and push the button. **Collect calls** cannot be dialed directly in Lebanon. To make call the US collect, call AT&T at ☎426 801. Lebanon's telephonic primitivism is partly made up for by easy **internet** accessibility.

INTERNET ACCESS

The majority of Internet cafes in Beirut are located in Hamra near AUB.

Virus: The Cyber Infection (☎374 794), on 2nd fl. of the Blue Building (not named for its color) at the corner of Rue 'Abd al-'Aziz and Rue Bliss in Hamra. One of the best rates in town (L£3,000 per hr.) and great hours (9am-3am or later). Dark, well-decorated operation with TVs playing music videos and one of the only nonsmoking sections in the country. Snacks and sandwiches L£500-3000.

PC Club (☎74 53 38), on Rue Mahatma Gandhi. Walk along Rue Bliss keeping AUB to your right, and take a left at Popeye's Chicken. Network games L£3000 per hr. Internet L£5000 per hr. Billiards L£1000. Open 24hr.

The Net (☎740 157), next door to PC Club. Less of a hangout than its neighbor, but faster connections. L£3000 per hr. Open 24hr.

Web Cafe (☎348 880), on Rue Khaldi near the intersection with Rue Jeanne d'Arc in Hamra. L£5000 per hr. Slightly more expensive than other places, perhaps because it takes itself more seriously. Open daily noon-midnight.

Images Computer Services (☎338 933), on Rue Lebanon near St. Joseph University in Ashrafiye. L£5000 per hr., but expected to drop to L£3500 early in 2002. Open M-F 8:30am-9pm, Sa 8:30am-8pm.

New Age Cafe (☎797 101), in the Dunes Shopping Center, Verdun. High-class setting begets high-class prices. L£6000 per hr. Open 10am-10pm.

Post Office: Liban Post, 2nd fl. of the Matta Building, on Rue Makdissi, between Rue Ibrahim Abdel Ali and Rue Cheikh Elias Gaspard. Services include regular, express, and registered mail, **Poste Restante, Western Union,** and **UPS.** Bring packages to the post office ready to send, as boxes and envelopes are not available, though they may be pur-chased at **Star Stationery** next door (☎354 848). Open M-F 8am-5pm, Sa 8am-1pm. (The main headquarters for Liban Post will be moved to the **Riad al-Solh** branch down-town as soon as restoration is complete—anticipated in 2002.) **DHL** (☎98 33 97) in the Lazaristes building, on the corner of Rue Emir Barchir and Rue Bechara al-Khoury, facing Place des Martyrs. Open M-F 8am-5pm, Sa 8am-3pm.

LEBANON

⌐ ACCOMMODATIONS

Most budget lodgings in Beirut were destroyed during the war, but new options are slowly emerging. The **Lebanese Youth Hostel Federation** (☎366 099) is working to reestablish facilities in Beirut and the rest of Lebanon. As of August 2001, fliers advertised bed and breakfast for US$10-15, but facilities in Beirut had not yet opened. For updates call the Federation or Mr. Anis 'Abd al-Malik (☎03 338 442).

▨ **Destination Liban** (☎293 066 or 03 497 762; lucien@intracom.net.lb). Lucien arrived in Lebanon from France 4 years ago, and has dedicated himself to helping backpackers, temporary workers, and new immigrants find their way. He has a few rooms in Achrafiye with communal kitchen, bathroom, and washing machine. Lucien also helps organize budget lodgings and homestays in remote areas of the country. Airport pickup, guided daytrips, and car rental available. It is best to email him with your needs about 1 week before of your arrival. Singles US$17; doubles US$25; triples US$30; quads US$32 per night. Private apartments available for rent at US$150 per week for one person, US$250-450 for 2-4 people).

▨ **Pension Home Valéry** (☎362 169), on Rue Phoenicia in 'Ain Mreisse. Keeping the Hard Rock Cafe on your left, walk 100m down the street and take a right; enter just after the Wash Me Carwash. There is no sign at the front entrance; continue to the stairs at the end of the hallway. Although the 1st, 2nd, and 3rd fl. (French floor system) are all home to establishments calling themselves the Pension Valéry, make no mistake: you are looking for the **2nd** fl. One of Beirut's top backpacker stops. Clean, boxy rooms with super fans. Internet L£4000. Laundry service L£1000 for large pieces, smaller pieces free. Dorms US$5; singles US$8; doubles US$12.

▨ **Talal's New Hotel** (☎562 567), on Ave. Charles Helou. From the Helou Bus Station, go up the stairs behind the Beirut Taxi office near the station's south end. Facing the sea on Ave. Charles Helou, turn left and the hotel will be on your left. Renovations in the last few years make this a welcoming backpacker niche. Dorms are small, but come with satellite TV, use of kitchen and hot shower, and (usually) friendly company. Laundry L£3000 per load. Dorms US$4. One double available US$10.

University Hotel (☎36 53 91), just off Rue Bliss in Hamra across from AUB. Private bathrooms, A/C, and excellent location in the heart of budget Beirut compensate for smallish rooms. Singles L£30,000; doubles L£45,000; triples L£52,500. Student monthly rate L£225,000. Reserve in advance, as hotel is often fully booked.

YWCA (☎367 750 or 367 751), in 'Ain Mreisse. Keeping the Hard Rock Cafe on your left, walk 100m and take a right at the Wash Me Carwash. Turn right just after the Holiday Inn and it will be on your right. This international center is usually populated by students and is **open to women only.** Comfortable rooms with private bath and fridge. Many rooms have large balconies with laundry wires. 1am curfew is actually enforced; do not be late. Dorms US$15; singles US$25; doubles and triples US$30.

Al-Nazih Hotel (☎564 868), on Ave. Charles Helou just past Talal's New Hotel. Renovations expected for 2002; name may change to Pension Nazih. Laundry $3 per load. Dorms US$4; comfy rooms with satellite TV and private toilet US$12.

Al-Shahbaa Hotel (☎564 287), on Ave. Charles Helou. From Helou Bus Station, go up the stairs behind the Beirut Taxi office. The hotel will be immediately behind you. Communal shower and kitchen. Dorms L£5000; private rooms US$10 per person.

Cedarland Hotel (☎340 233), on Rue 'Abd al-'Aziz near the intersection with Rue Sourati. Popular with folks studying at AUB. Comfortable rooms with A/C, desk, and private bath. Singles US$30; doubles US$35. US$400-600 per month.

Lord's Hotel (☎74 03 85; fax 74 03 85), on Rue du Koweit, near the intersection with Ave. Général de Gaulle, opposite the Luna Park on the corniche. The best value for seaside rooms. If you crave that touch of luxury, A/C, private bath, maid service, satellite TV, and mini fridge are a nice change of pace. July-Aug. singles L£60,000; doubles L£75,000. Sept.-June singles L£52,500. Budget rooms L£45,000.

Mayflower Hotel (☎34 06 80 or 34 70 80), on Rue Nehme Yafet, 2 blocks off Rue Hamra. A splurge, but truly excellent. TV, A/C, private bath, maid service, and proper colonial rooms. Budget rooms L£52,500; singles L£97,500. Add 5% service charge.

Embassy Hotel (☎34 08 14; fax 34 08 15), on Rue Makdissi opposite the post office. Pleasant lobby and clean rooms with A/C, TV, mini fridge, private bath, and springy mattress. Plant-filled indoor and outdoor restaurant and Beirut's only hotel garden present a bucolic escape from the urban jungle outside. Breakfast L£5250. Laundry service. Singles L£50,000; doubles L£70,000; triples L£82,000; 14% service charge. Student discount often lowers price to about US$25.

West House Residence (☎35 04 50), near the corner of Rue Sourati and Rue 'Abd al-'Aziz. Ultra-funky '70s apartments out of *A Clockwork Orange* fully equipped with A/C, private bath, TV, and kitchenette. Streetside rooms are noisy, but worth the pretty polly you'll save. Don't go by the board—the "official" rate means nothing. Singles and doubles L£48,000 per night; L£300,000 per week; L£975,000 per month. Add 5% tax. V.

▗ FOOD

Beirut's reputation as the meeting ground of East and West is well reflected in its food options. Traditional Lebanese mezze, grills, exotic international cuisine, European pub grub, Western fast food, and cafe fare are all widely available. "Snacks" are sandwich shops with little ambiance but good value. The **Hamra** district, especially Rue Bliss across from AUB, is packed with small, affordable eateries. The **Raouche** district is home to many of Lebanon's most renowned restaurants, with fantastic open-air seating and sunset views of the Pigeon Rocks. New restaurants and cafes are opening at a staggering pace in the reconstructed downtown area, especially around **Place de l'Etoile**.

▧ **Restaurant Le Chef** (☎445 373), on Rue Gouraud near the post office in the Gemayze District. From the Sursock Museum, take a left onto the main road. A large path of stairs on the right descend to Rue Gouraud. Le Chef is immediately on the left at the bottom of the stairs. Choice of 6 home-cooked *plats du jour* L£3000-5000. A daily stop for international students and Lebanese families alike. Sharbi, the brilliant waiter, specializes in finding company for all at the family-sized tables. Open 8am-6pm.

▧ **Zaatar wa Zeit** (☎614 302), on Rue Seifeddine al-Khatib near the intersection with Ave. de l'Independence in Sodeco Sq. in Ashrafieh. Just around the corner from Rue Monot, Zaatar is a favorite post-clubbing hangout. Sandwiches and *saj* wraps (L£1000-3000) satisfy late-night cravings. Open 24hr. Free delivery.

Restaurant Mashawi Assaf (☎372 364), on Rue Phoenecia in 'Ain Mreisse. From Wash Me Carwash, walk past Holiday Inn and the restaurant will be on your left. Favorite stop for Pension Home Valéry guests seeking cheap, filling, and appetizing Lebanese sandwiches. Craving steak? Try their *Brochettes Grillées* sandwich (L£3000). Take it to go or make it a plate (L£7000). Open daily 7am-3am.

Walimah (☎745 933), on Rue Makdissi in Hamra next to the White Marble Hotel just before Rue Nehme Yafet. 2 Lebanese women have transformed a white house with blue shutters into a comfortable restaurant serving 3 daily home-cooked *plats du jour* (L£7000-15,000). Fortune-telling from your coffee cup Friday at lunch. Weekly menu available. Open M-Sa 8am-midnight.

Flying Pizza (☎35 19 04 or 35 39 75), in Hamra, on Rue Makhloul at Rue Jeanne d'Arc, next door to Web Cafe. Create your own Lebanese pizza off the checklist-menu: small L£5500, toppings L£1000 each. Open daily 11am-midnight. Free delivery in Hamra.

Al-Amadouli (☎340 552), on the corner of Rue Makdissi and Rue Nehme Yafet, diagonal from the White Tower Hotel. Downstairs is a takeout bar, upstairs is a sit-down restaurant whose interior design somehow combines gold, pastel, fake greenery, oversized chandeliers, and Christmas decorations. Tasty dishes L£6000-8000. Live lute player W-Su evenings (cover L£1000). Beer L£2000. Open daily noon-midnight.

Hamadeh Snack (☎34 26 70), at the corner of Rue de Rome and Central Bank St. in Hamra, across the street from the Ministry of Tourism. Popular morning stop for commuters. Nothing beats a *beeza* with olives (L£3500). Delicious *mana'eesh* with *za'tar*, lamb, and cheese L£1000-2500. Open daily 6am-5pm.

Barbar (☎ 753 330), on Rue 'Abd al-'Aziz just south of Hamra across from the old Piccadilly Theater. Outdoor stands take up an entire corner, serving nearly every fast food imaginable. Falafel L£1500. Grills L£3000. *Plat du jour* L£7500. Subs L£3000. Fruit, and ice cream. A frightening monopoly, Barbar is a fast food cultural experience, with convenient location and 24hr. service. Free delivery.

'Abd al-Wahab Restaurant (☎200 552), on Rue 'Abd al Wahab al-Inglizi around the corner from Rue Monot. *Mezze* L£2800-4000. Grills L£9000-12,000. *Plat du jour* L£12,000. Unique fusion of traditional and modern Middle Eastern fare. Amazing oven-fresh bread arrives hot at your table. Skyroom or rooftop terrace overlooking the neighborhood is ideal for a late evening *argileh* (L£10,000). Open noon-11pm.

Cafe Met (☎984 444), on Rue Maarad in the Place de l'Etoile downtown. Overlooking the Roman ruins, this European-style restaurant has a lively, sophisticated feel. Salads, sandwiches, and entrees exemplify Beirut's metropolitan air. A great deal for downtown, at US$10-20 per person.

Tiger Restaurant (☎04 870 564), in Beit Marie, about a 1km walk uphill from the main traffic circle (just ask a local), or take bus #7 (L£500) from the National Museum. This cat's been roaring for about a century. A good deal with a mountain view of Beirut to boot. Entree and selection of *mezze* L£15,000. Open daily 10am-midnight.

▓ COFFEE AND SWEETS

Cafes are everywhere in the city, but three popular locations are near the intersection of Rue Hamra and Rue 'Abd al-'Aziz, downtown, and along the corniche.

▓ The Terrace (☎999 777), on the roof of the **Virgin Megastore,** located downtown in the old opera center on Rue Weygand near Place de l'Etoile. One of the best rooftop views of the city. A great spot to watch the restoration progress over coffee (L£3000) or drinks (L£4000-5000). Open daily 12:30pm-1:30am. Due to immense popularity, reservations are required for all times except 3:30-8:30pm.

Modca Cafe (☎345 501), Rue Hamra at the intersection with Rue 'Abd al-'Aziz. A chic place to sip coffee (L£2500), read a newspaper, or people-watch. Open 6:30am-1am.

Cafe de Paris (☎341 115), on Rue Hamra across the street from Modca. Full of history, the atmosphere here has been attracting morning commuters, backgammon masters, and intellectuals for decades. Excellent coffee L£3000. Open 8am-10pm.

Tribeca (☎339 123), on Rue 'Abd al-Wahab al-Inglizi, around the corner from Rue Monot. The bagel (L£1250) and bagel sandwich (L£4500-8500) find their way to Lebanon in this trendy NY-style hangout. Excellent freezers L£5,500. Open daily 8am–1am.

Taj al-Moulouk, 2 locations: 1 on Rue Bliss just before Rue Sadat in Hamra (☎365 797), and another on the corniche in 'Ain Mreisse (☎370 096). Perhaps the best sweets in Lebanon, the desserts are shipped regularly around the world. Although most sales are by the kilo (L£10,000-18,000), their sample plate with 5 pieces (L£3600) makes for a luscious initiation (see **Sweet Nothings**, p. 539). Open 7am-midnight.

◉ SIGHTS

For a city with a 5000-year heritage, Beirut is somewhat slim on sights of archaeological importance. Since the war ended in 1990, the reconstruction effort and urban digging initiatives have peeled back otherwise inaccessible layers of destroyed cityscape. Though archaeologists have uncovered ancient ruins, most are not yet available for public viewing, as they are still in the process of being excavated and catalogued.

LEBANON

PIGEON ROCKS. Created by an earthquake eons ago, these two rocks just off the coast are captivating formations. One has an open arch through which small boats and swimmers pass. Today home to daredevil divers, the shores near the Pigeon Rocks have yielded the oldest evidence of human presence in Beirut. Flints and tools found here are now displayed in the AUB Archaeological Museum. Ministry of Tourism pamphlets proclaiming these rocks to be Beirut's major natural landmark neglect to mention the neon signs and fast food-riddled landscape that clutter the scene. Scramble down the path to the base for a pure cliffside view. *(Off the coast of Raouche. Take a minibus or #15 bus along the corniche from 'Ain Mreisse or Hamra (L£500) or walk away from the port and central Beirut along the corniche.)*

AMERICAN UNIVERSITY OF BEIRUT (AUB). In 1866, the Rev. Daniel Bliss spent weeks searching the cacti and sands of undeveloped Ras Beirut for a site on which to found his college. When he arrived at the site where AUB now stands, Bliss wrote "immediately we decided that we had found the finest site in all of Beirut, if not all Syria." He exaggerated only a little. The campus rolls down a lush cliff full of flowers and broad green leaves overlooking the sparkling waves of the Mediterranean. Benches scattered across the campus allow visitors to sit, think, discuss, cuddle, and take in the view. Long the intellectual heart of Beirut and much of the Middle East, the university provides a dynamic fusion of Western and Middle Eastern thought. Athletes will love the track, soccer-field, tennis, volleyball, and basketball courts on the lower campus.

SANAYEH PUBLIC GARDEN. Before the Solidere projects, this was Beirut's only public garden. With quiet benches and a playground, it's a favorite spot to relax.

LE GRAND SERAIL. Built in 1853 as Ottoman military barracks on a hill in the Beirut Central District, the Serail became the headquarters of the French governor during the French Mandate. Following extensive renovation in 1998, the magnificent Serail is once again a Government Palace. *(Open to the public Su 10am-2pm.)*

PLACE DES MARTYRS. Named in honor of martyrs executed by the Ottomans in 1915, this open space in the heart of the Central District was completely razed during the war. The only feature that remained in the dust and ruins was the Martyrs' Statue. Today, the statue stands amidst new developments and garden flowers—at once a powerful symbol of what was destroyed and the spirit of survival.

MOSQUES AND CHURCHES. Al-Omari Mosque (Grand Mosque) on the corner of Rue Maarad and Rue Weygand was originally the Crusader Church of St. John the Baptist. In 1291 CE, Salah al-Din recaptured Beirut and transformed the building into the present mosque. Nearby is the 18th-century **St. Louis Capuchin Church.** Both the **Emir Assaf Mosque,** opposite the municipal building, and the **Emir Munzir Mosque,** housing 8 Roman columns in its courtyard, are still functional. The **Greek Orthodox Cathedral of St. George,** built in 1767, was the oldest functioning church in Beirut until the war. By the 5 Roman columns of the Cardo Maximus, the **Maronite Cathedral of St. George** is one of several sites competing for recognition as the location where St. George is said to have slain the dragon and rescued the princess.

ANCIENT AND MODERN RUINS. The Beirut Central District holds the largest concentration of ancient ruins. Anticipating completion by 2003, the Heritage Trail and Garden of Forgiveness will take visitors through all of the major religious and historical sites centered around the remains of the **Roman Cardus Maximus.** After visiting the ancient ruins, walk along Rue Damascus (Tari' al-Sham, or Rue Damas) to see the modern ruins. Rue Damascus traces the **Green Line** of the civil war, demarcating Muslim West Beirut and Christian East Beirut. Although many of the buildings have been restored, the line follows some of the most dramatic visual contrasts left in the city, with glittering high-rises emerging from rubble.

ARS LONGA, BELLUM BREVE When officials at Beirut's National Museum realized that civil war was about to break out, they moved quickly to save the precious artwork in their care. The Roman sarcophagi and statuary (arguably the most impressive works) could not be moved due to their weight, so they were encased in nearly 3 ft. of concrete. Many of the smaller pieces were sent to Germany or stored in National Bank vaults. Space and time were limited, however, and much of the pottery could only be unceremoniously dumped in cardboard and stored in the basement to wait out the hostilities. Unfortunately, the intense humidity in the flooded basement caused the cardboard to disintegrate, damaging many of the ceramics and other pieces. The war itself caused inevitable damage: snipers poked holes through priceless mosaics, the museum's majestic columns were so badly bullet-riddled that they were left barely standing, and giant exhibit halls brimmed with debris. Nevertheless, a high proportion of the art was preserved. Since the war ended, the museum's facade has been given a facelift, the bank vaults have been emptied, the oil and grime staining the pottery have been removed, and—most gloriously—the cement cases have been opened. Today's National Museum is as much a monument to the resilience and ingenuity of the modern Lebanese people as it is to their fascinating and varied history.

🏛 MUSEUMS

▣ NATIONAL MUSEUM. An excellent introduction to the ancient people's and civilizations that have defined Lebanon over the millennia, the museum is a crucial stop on any archaeological journey through the country. The collection of stone pieces and mosaics on the first floor is highlighted by 4 intricately carved Roman sarcophagi, a mosaic of the Seven Wise Men from Ba'albeck, and the Colossus of Byblos. Although the civil war forced the National Museum to close its doors (see **Ars Longa, Bellum Breve,** p. 522), extensive restoration was completed in 1999 and the collection continues to grow today. Don't miss the second-floor display of articles damaged during the war, or the 27 eerily lit anthropomorphic coffins in the basement. (*On Ave. Abdullah Yafi behind the Hippodrome, the museum is near the race track and can be reached by service from nearly anywhere in the city. Open Tu-Su 9am-5pm. L£5000, students and those under 18 L£1000.*)

SURSOCK MUSEUM. Donated in 1952 by Lebanese philanthropist Nicholas Ibrahim Sursock, the museum is housed in a mansion whose *fin de siècle* Lebanese-Italian architectural style is a spectacle in itself. The museum rotates photography and art exhibits focusing on Lebanese heritage and cultural themes. Shows culminate in the annual Salon d'Automne, which showcases the best of modern Lebanese art. A visit to the museum should include a walk through the neighborhood to see the parade of beautiful homes lining the streets, most of which escaped the war unscathed. (*On Rue Sursock in Ashrafieh. ☎ 334 133. Open daily 10am-1pm and 4pm-7pm. Free. Closes when exhibits are being changed; call in advance to avoid disappointment.*)

AUB ARCHEOLOGICAL MUSEUM. This museum maybe small, but it's full of local history, excellent glazed work, and sublime ivory carvings. The front of the museum displays the prehistoric Stone and Bronze Age findings from the Pigeon Rocks, as well as glass, pottery, and coin collections from ancient Lebanon, Egypt, and Palestine. (*On the AUB campus on Rue Bliss, in Hamra. ☎ 340 549. Open M-F 10am-2:30pm; in winter M-F 10 am-4pm. Free.*)

PLANET DISCOVERY. Recently opened Children's Science Museum has interactive displays for children aged 3-15 years. (*☎ 980 650. In Central District, on Rue Omar al-Daouk near the Starco Building. Open M-F 9am-6pm, Sa-Su 10 am-8pm. L£5000.*)

▲🖪 ACTIVITIES AND ENTERTAINMENT

SPORTS

HORSERACING. Behind the National Museum, pure-bred Arabian steeds race every Sunday at the **Hippodrome Beirut Racetrack**. Be warned that there are a limited number of horses, and it is not uncommon for races to be canceled because a few have become ill. (☎ 632 520. Entrance US$3-10.)

FUTBOL. Beirut futbol (soccer) is dominated by two teams, **Beirut Nejmeh** and **Beirut Ansar**. Matches are held on the pitch at the City Sports Complex south of the city. During the summer of 2001, the league was suspended for months while officials sorted through a shady inter-league plot of match-fixing and other scandals. (Check www.cyberia.net.lb or newspapers for match schedules.)

SWIMMING. The Mediterranean is quite polluted around Beirut, but most locals don't seem to mind. While many hit the beaches just north or south of the city (see **Beaches**, p. 533), those who stick around usually visit one of several **beach clubs** with concrete platforms along the sea that are open to visitors. To enjoy the sea free of charge, either jump the wall over the corniche or go to the public beach at **Ramlet al-Baida**. The sand here is littered with small bits of trash, but great beach futbol and volleyball courts make up for it. During the summer, nearby sand courts host professional matches. (L£10,000-20,000 per day for use of pool and facilities.)

GOLF. Beirut Golf Club in Bir Hassan is a posh club open to visitors, who may use the nine-hole course, squash and tennis courts, and swimming pool. The club has survived some difficult times: in 1982 the Israeli army bulldozed the gold club pavilion, and later during the civil war, hundreds of shells landed on the course. Re-landscaping efforts have restored the course's face, where new flora blossoms. (☎ 822 470. Use of facilities L£20,000.)

CINEMA AND THEATER

Movie listings appear in newspapers and in a publication called *The Guide*. Beirut's three main theaters host plays in French, Arabic, and sometimes English. Listings usually appear in the newspaper. The *Agenda Culturelle* has all theater listings, but is normally only available by subscription. Walimah Restaurant has copies at the desk; you can also try some of the more expensive hotels. For information, it might be easiest to simply call the theaters themselves.

Empire Cinema, in the Dunes Center in Verdun (☎ 792 123), and in Sodeco Sq. (☎ 616 707) shows movies daily at 4:30, 7:30, and 10:15pm. L£10,000. M L£5000.

Theatre Monot (☎ 320 782 or 202 422), on Rue de L'Universite Saint-Joseph not far from the intersection with Rue Monot. Frequent drama performances.

Beirut Theater (☎ 343 988), on Rue Idriss in 'Ain Mreisse not far from Hard Rock Cafe.

Al Madina Theater (☎ 371 962), on Rue Justin Niel just off of Rue Clemenceau. Look for the red buttresses.

⬘ SHOPPING

Beirut's world-renowned *souqs* were destroyed during the war. Currently, construction of a new market is in progress, anticipated to open by 2003 at the corner of Rue Weygand and Rue Patriarche Hoayek downtown. In high fashion, Beirut is best known for the **boutiques** concentrated around **Rue Verdun** and **Rue Hamra**. Prices for name brands on the racks are reasonable. For traditional **crafts** try:

L'Artisan du Liban (☎ 364 880), on Rue Clemenceau just past the Gefinor Center. A non-profit organization, working with the Mouvement Social to encourage local artisans to continue their trade while also supporting the poor. Profits donated to needy Leba-

LEBANON

> # THE GARDEN OF FORGIVENESS
> Despite the often restless drive to erase all marks of war from the city center, the restoration project is currently focusing on developing a public space where citizens can congregate to remember, contemplate, resolve, and ultimately forgive. Following an international landscape competition for the proposed Hadiqat al-Samah (Garden of Forgiveness), a design was chosen by an eight-member jury in March 2000. The garden will lie between Nejmeh Sq. and Place des Martyrs on the 2.3 hectare Roman Cardo Maximus archaeological site, possibly the location of Fakhr al-Din's 17th-century gardens. To be symbolically placed on the garden's skyline are two pillars of spiritual life in Beirut: the minaret of al-Omari Mosque and the bell tower of St. Louis Capuchin church. At prayer times, it is not uncommon for the *muezzin* and church bells to sound in unison. Both sites of worship were heavily damaged during the war and have undergone extensive restoration. Targeted for opening in spring 2002, the garden will be one of the key public spaces along the Heritage Trail, a path that will circuit the district's historic core, linking its ancient ruins, historic restorations, and religious buildings.

nese families. Levantine furniture, blown glass, pottery, linens, Jezzine cutlery, Rachaya silver jewelry, and other traditional items. Open M-F 9am-7pm, Sa 10am-3pm.

Maison de l'Artisanat (☎ 368 461), on Ave. de Paris across from the Hard Rock Cafe. Another branch of L'Artisan du Liban, selling traditional items and classy gifts. Prices are reasonable, but definitely not cheap. Open M-Sa 9:30am-7:30pm.

Souq al-Barghout, every July in the streets of the Place de l'Etoile. A bargain flea market that doubles as a center for high-end art collections, the event attracts flocks of Beirutis. Check *The Guide* for specific dates and times.

♬ NIGHTLIFE

Beirut's nightlife is bursting with energy. Hotspots tend to shift on a whim, and many clubs open and close overnight due to competition. First centered in **Ras Beirut,** the scene has expanded to include **Rue Monot, Sodeco,** and **Ashrafiye.** Crowds are rapidly growing in the **downtown area** as empty buildings in the Central District near completion and begin to fill with cafes, pubs, restaurants, and clubs. Luckily, it's not too hard to figure out where everyone is going. *The Guide*, a monthly publication sold at most newsstands, offers updates surveying the scene and posts listings for all venues.

>
> **LET'S NOT GO THERE.** A word to the wise: so-called super night clubs are common in Lebanon. Many visitors wrongly assume that "super" means "very good." Those in the know simply call these clubs "brothels." So unless your planet is lonely, avoid this scene.

Nighthawking in Beirut doesn't start until late. Most Beirutis begin with dinner around 9 or 10pm, and clubs are nearly empty before midnight or 1am. Although the wild beats of the beach and night clubs in the suburbs attract large crowds on the weekends, they are reachable only by private taxi. An incentive to stick to the city is that *service* are available until midnight, and taxis roam the streets into the wee hours of the morning, going almost anywhere in the city for L£5000-10,000.

BARHOPPING

🎵 **The Smugglers** (☎ 03 619 382), on Rue Makhloul in Hamra, on the left as you walk from Rue 'Abd al-'Aziz. Begins the evening as a bar with some tables, but by midnight customers dance in the lava lamp-lit aisles. Unlike many places in Beirut, the music—though loud—does not stifle conversation. Almaza beer L£3000 (L£2000 during happy hour, 7pm-9:30pm). House tea blends L£2000. Open daily 6pm-3am.

Bongos (☎03 407 439), on Rue Monot. Casual hangout where spunky waiters drum to jazz, funk, and Latin beats. Diverse crowd bridges the fashion gap between alterna-chic and eurotrash. Cocktails L£9500. Draft beer (L£3500-5000). Open 8:30pm-4 or 5am.

Pacifico, on Rue Monot in Ashrafieh. "The goddess made me a cup of tea with a spot of rum, but she herself drank only rum." Heine's words on the menu may inspire you to imitate the goddess with the L£6500-10,500 shooters. Alternately, worship her with cigars (L£9500-33,500), fancy meals (L£14,500-24,500), Almazas (L£4000) or Coronas with lime (L£6000). Happy hour 7-8pm.

Zinc (☎612 612), on Rue Seifeddine al-Khatib in Sodeco. Funky portraits of Dizzy Gillespie and geckos in various colors line the walls. Variety gives this jazz and blues restaurant-pub creative energy. Drinks L£5000-15,000. Wild virgin blends L£5000. Open daily noon-late.

Blue Note (☎743 857), on Rue Makhloul in Hamra. The original home of jazz in Beirut. Pasta lunch L£22,500-30,000. Dinner L£30,000-37,500. A budget-friendlier option is to fill up on the *mezze*. Beer L£3900-5200. Live bands on F and Sa nights with cover charges from L£6000-12,000 (more when NY bands are featured). Open M-Th noon-1am, F-Sa noon-2am. AmEx/MC/V.

Hole in the Wall (☎03 803 202), on Rue Monot. A typical English pub typically full of foreigners. Sing-a-long crowds get riled up to tunes of the "American Pie" variety. Happy hour 6-8pm and 12:30am till closing.

L'Escroc (Cheap Shots) (☎03 965 198), on Rue al-Inglisi near Banque Audi in Ashrafieh. Although this local favorite's name means "crook" in French, you won't be swindled, but wasted (◪cheap shots L£2500). Very crowded on weekend nights. Many people seem to just stop in for a cheap drink before heading out to graze in more glamorous pastures. Those who like to inhale with their alcohol can join the *argileh* crowd. Open daily noon-1am.

Janneh (☎04 87 31 20), in Beit Marie. A pain to reach—take the #7 bus from the National Museum to Beit Marie. Patrons heading home after 7:30pm will have to grab a private taxi to get home. This tropical food-and-drink complex nearly lives up to its name ("heaven"). Waterfall, pond, and crossbridge flow through 2 restaurants serving Middle Eastern (all you can eat, L£37,500) and French (prix-fixe L£33,000) cuisine. Pub serves drinks for L£4000-10,000. Open daily 9am-5am..

CLUBBING

◪**Rai** (☎338 822), on Rue Monot. Proof that despite being dominated by Western-style clubs, Beirut nightlife is not totally severed from Middle Eastern ties. Arcaded walls, mosaic designs, seat cushions, and a Moroccan flavor color the air while DJs spin mixes of traditional Arabic music with modern beats. Only here can Cafe del Mar and Umm Kulthum commune. No cover. Cocktails US$10. Beer US$5. Open Tu-Su 10:30pm-late.

◪**B018** (☎03 800 018), next door to the Forum de Beyrouth in Karantina. The Forum is easily visible from the coastal highway en route to Charles Helou Station and the north. One of the few clubs in the area to prove its staying power, B018 has been heating up every weekend for 3 years running. Music starts out light, building into techno, house, and "trip hop" mixes as crowds pick up. When dancing gets too hot, the roof retracts to let off steam and reveal a starry night sky. A bit spooky: each area of the club is dedicated to the memory of a different artist and coffins double as platforms for dancing and seating. No cover. Beer L£10,000. Mixed drinks L£15,000. Open daily 10 pm-dawn; the superstars don't really come out until after 1am. AmEx/MC/V.

Fubar (☎612 100), in Sodeco Sq. All the rage during the summer of 2001: the only hope to get in was to make reservations several days or weeks in advance. "Buddha bar" music fades into trance and rave. Fubar has a reputation for crazy dancing (beyond all recognition) on tables, bar, and stage. The club's name sparked controversy for months. No cover. Drinks $US10.

Babylone (☎219 539), on Rue 'Abd al Wahab al-Inglizi around the corner from Rue Monot. Stylish international restaurant by evening, Babylone gradually escalates into a

LEBANON

BEIRUT, ANYONE? To many Westerners, Beirut conjures up images of Islamic fundamentalists taking hostages and of a glittering cosmopolitan city ravaged by a protracted civil war. To those who actually pay Beirut a visit, the city is often remembered for its vibrant nightlife, unparalleled elsewhere in the Middle East. The "Beirut" of thousands of American college students, however, is something profoundly different. Sometime during the Lebanese Civil War, innovative American fraternity brothers (some say it was Lehigh University's chapter of Theta Delta Chi, in around 1990) coined the term "Beirut" to describe a variant of **beer pong**—a drinking game that dates at least as far back as the 1950s. While beer pong involved table tennis paddles, Beirut was less equipment-intensive, requiring players only to throw ping-pong balls into plastic cups filled with beer or some other liquid. The simpler game spread like wildfire across American college campuses—and though the last Beiruti hostage was released in 1992, the game of Beirut continues. Cup size, number, and placement on the table vary from place to place, as do rules regarding defense tactics (blowing or slapping a ball away from a cup). Whether your Beiruti nightlife includes Rue Monot barhopping or ping-pong ball lobbing, *Let's Go* recommends that you drink responsibly.

nightclub centered around the bar and grand piano. Plays international mixes, attracting a crowd where the artsy and the fartsy can mingle effortlessly. Drinks US$10-15.

Acid (☎ 03 714 678), in Sin al-Fil by the Futurscope. The selling point: an open bar where ladies get in free F and Sa before midnight. Men pay only US$20 for endless drinks until 4am. The music is a pretty standard mix of club and Arabic favorites, but boy does the crowd know how to enjoy them. Open late daily.

Club 70 (☎ 366 686), on Rue Phoenicia in 'Ain Mreisse across from the Wash Me Car Wash. The night starts in elegance with dinner, wine, and gentle dancing and gradually picks up as the moon rises. Live violin or *oud* Th-Sa nights starting at midnight. No cover. Red label L£8000. Black label L£15,000. Cocktails L£10,000. Open late daily.

◪ DAYTRIPS FROM BEIRUT

JOUNIEH جونية

*Take a **bus** or **service** to Dawra from Ave. de Paris (bus L£500; service L£1000; if you take service from anywhere other than Ave. de Paris it will cost double or more). "Dawra" in Arabic refers to the landmark roundabout where taxis, service, and buses congregate. Buses or service going past Jounieh to Byblos and Tripoli can drop you off on their way. The trip takes 25min. by service (L£2000) and up to 1hr. by bus (L£500). Service and taxis try to accommodate the Jounieh night-owls, but be sure to ask about return trips while the night is young if you don't wish to spend the night. Budget accommodations exist in Jounieh but tend to be less than desirable.*

High-stakes risk-takers gamble and bikini-clad women gambol at the casinos, clubs, and luxurious beach resorts of Jounieh, the capital of Lebanese hedonism. Wealthy Beirutis and well-heeled visitors make the 21km jaunt north of Beirut to frolic at the three coastal towns—Kaslik, Jounieh, and Ma'ameltein—that compose the area collectively referred to as Jounieh. Despite its history as a quiet fishing bay, Jounieh today betrays no hint of antiquity to compromise its many disco floors, Western-style steakhouses, pizza factories, and falafel stands. During the war, Jounieh's sleepy ports took on a sleeker, louder persona as night clubs, beaches, resorts, and casinos sprang up to which wealthy Beirutis could flee from the chaos transpiring at home. Jounieh continues to attract large crowds of visitors looking to let loose, blow lots of cash, and catch some sun.

KASLIK

On the south end of the bay. Coined the "Rodeo Drive of Lebanon," **Kaslik Ave.** is best known for high-class stores and night clubs, a favorite place to window-shop and people-watch. In June 2001, Kaslik attracted a new wave of attention with the opening of ⬛**Hektic,** which at six levels and space for 2500 people, is now the largest dance club in the Middle East. Professional dancers perform underwater inside huge transparent balloons in a giant aquarium while foam cannons shoot torrents of bubbles. Look for alcohol-free afternoon clubbing on Saturday and Sunday for under-18 crowds. International guest DJs perform every two weeks, while resident jockeys spin every night. Cover US$20. Beer US$10. Other popular clubs include **Ozone** and **Amor Y Liberdad.** After swallowing the inflated prices of Kaslik's nightlife, regulars flock to the only real budget restaurant in town, **Zaatar wa Zeit** (☎09 831 601), open 24hr. to satisfy post-clubbing cravings. Their trademark *za'atar* wraps are tasty, filling, and super cheap (L£1000).

JOUNIEH

Heading north along the bay, the Beirut-Tripoli freeway leads to Jounieh proper where beaches and "super" **night clubs** litter the shore. Be weary of the modifier: although super night clubs may sound better, locals will tell you their title usually just means "sketchier," often implying strip shows and other associated activities. Jounieh's primary attraction during hot summer days is its **swimming.** Most of the coast has been consumed by beach clubs with private pools and cover charges from L£2000 to as much as L£15,000 (often cheaper if you arrive early in the day). Walking along **Rue Mina,** the main road that hugs the sea, you can check out all of the beach fronts in less than half an hour before settling into a spot. Do not come expecting Caribbean-style dunes; the coast here is rocky, concrete slabs are plentiful, and sand is a rarity. Most beaches are open until 3-4am, some until dawn. Meals in Jounieh are relatively expensive in most restaurants and clubs, but budget snack stands abound. **Sailor's Snack** (☎09 635 700, open 24hr.) serves up munchies ranging from cheeseburgers and *shish tawouq* to tuna and chicken liver (L£2500-4000). **Snack Crepe Marie** (☎03 449 570) has a tropical seaside seating area and serves crepes and yummy fruit juices (L£3000).

HARISSA MOUNTAIN

Overlooking crashing waves on an overdeveloped shore, the peaks of Harissa Mountain offer a stunning perspective of the coastline. The best mode of ascension is via ⬛**Téléférique** (☎914 324), a nine-minute gondola skyride that leaves from the municipal building at the center of Jounieh proper. When it gets too steep for the cable cars, a funicular takes over the ascent to the pinnacle, a 500m climb. (Open daily July-Sept. 10am-10:30pm; Oct.-June 10am-midnight. L£7500, ages 4-10 L£3500.) Absorb the views while puffing an *argileh* (L£10,000) at the **Téléférique Restaurant.** The menu runs the gamut from budget to bank-breaking; grab a *saj* or sandwich for L£3500. (Open daily 10am-midnight.) Just above the restaurant, a statue of **Notre Dame de Liban** embraces the nation with forgiving arms. The white glow of the **Church of the Virgin of Lebanon** sharply contrasts with the nearby **Maronite Cathedral,** a modernist cascade of glass and concrete. Locals joke that gamblers come here to pray for big bucks. (Open daily 10am-9pm. Services M-Sa 7:30am, 5, 6pm; Su and holidays every hr. 7am-noon and 4-7pm.)

MA'AMELTEIN

The two major attractions here are the world-famous **Casino du Liban** (☎853 222) and fishing port restaurant **al-Jazira Chez Louis** (☎854 040). In its heyday, the casino dueled with Monte Carlo for Mediterranean gaming supremacy and was filled with celebrities, international jet-setters, and suave British spies sipping martinis. War shut down the fun-house, but it recently reopened with several new facilities to accommodate more musical and artistic performances. The opulent excess of the three gaming rooms, five restaurants, two auditoriums, and eight bars will shake, if not stir you. The doorman may sneer at dirty backpackers, and those in sandals will be turned away. Signs say no shorts, but shorts-clad gamblers abound. (21+. Game rooms open daily 8pm-4am, slots noon-4am.)

Al-Jazira is reputed to serve up the best fish and the best views in all of Lebanon. Though pricey at US$18-30 per meal, if you are going to splurge, this is the place to do it. For those who would rather enjoy the same view for free, scramble down the shore just south of Chez Louis and meet Abu Ray'yd Al-Sa'id (Happy Abu Ray'yd). After loosing both legs in the war, Abu Ray'yd moved his family to the beach where they now live out of a pop-up Volkswagen camper and invite visitors to share the sun and the view. A trailer nearby serves cold drinks and coffee for as much as you would like to pay. Abu Ray'yd presence is proof that the charm of Arabic coffee rests not in the taste of the beans, but in the company it keeps. This is also a great spot to observe local fishermen trying out new trapping techniques.

JEITA GROTTO مغارة جيتا

Getting to Jeita (20km north of Beirut) is going to involve a lot of walking, a lot of cash, or a lot of smooth talking. Start by catching a **bus** *from Dawra to Jounieh or Byblos (L£500) and asking to be let off at "Mafra' Jeita" just after Nahr al-Kalb. From here, a private* **taxi** *can take you to "Maghaarat Jeita" (Jeita Grotto) for about L£10,000. Otherwise, you can take service to the center of town by the sign indicating the turnoff to the caverns and* **hike** *the last 2km downhill. The parking attendant specializes in hooking carless visitors up with rides, but some must brave the uphill climb on the return journey. ☎09 220 840. Open Tu-Su 9am-5pm, May-Sept. Tu-Su 9am-6pm; lower grotto closed for 20 days or so in Jan. and Feb. when water level is too high for tour boats to pass through the cave. L£16,500; under 12 L£9250; under 4 free. No photography.*

One of the largest and most intricate caverns in the world, the Jeita Grotto formed where the waters of the Nahr al-Kalb gradually hollowed out the insides of the wooded mountains that stand in its path. Drop by drop, massive calcite formations accumulated, secretly fighting entropy underground for millions of years. Today, the caverns house the turbulent waters of the river's source within a magical, soaring cathedral of latticed stalactites and stalagmites. Credit for modern discovery of the grotto goes to Reverend William Thomson, an American missionary who ventured 50m into the cave in 1836. Once he reached the underground river, he fired his gun, and the echo revealed the subterranean immensity. In his honor, the still water in the cavern's lower gallery is named **Thomson's Pool.**

Efforts to make the make the grotto more tourist-friendly have been underway for years. Visitors are whizzed to the entrance of the **upper grotto** in one of four "Austrian" cable cars. An unnecessary amenity, the ride at least serves to justify the steep entrance fees. But have patience and don't let the tourist traps turn you off; the caverns are amazing and should not be missed. The **lower grotto** is accessible via a short boat ride into the cavern. In winter, water levels are sometimes too high and unnavigable. A theater near the upper cave plays a short film detailing the caves' history (20 min., once per hr. in English, French, and Arabic). Two restaurants and multiple ice cream and snack shops keep visitors grotting.

NAHR AL-KALB

On the way to Jeita Grotto, most *service* will drop you off just past the mouth of the Nahr al-Kalb (Dog River), which gets its name from the legend of a dog statue that once guarded the river, howling at the approach of invaders. No one knows exactly how this worked, but it is believed to have been some type of acoustic wind trap. The dog appears to have disappeared, but 17 stelae inscribed by Assyrian, Egyptian, Greek, Roman, Arab, British, and French armies over several centuries commemorate the river's long history. Before the modern multi-lane highway was constructed, crossing Nahr al-Kalb was exceptionally dangerous; armies were forced to move single file through the gorge. After successful passage, generals would leave some type of inscription or memorial as thanks for their safety. For history buffs, or those who enjoy scrambling around busy roads, the stelae begin at the intersection with the highway and follow a railed stair climb over the double-arched tunnel. The climb is fairly steep and not in great condition, but near the top, the seal of Ramses II offers a mystical reward.

NEAR BEIRUT

FARAYA AND FAQRA فـرايـة وفـقـرة ☎ 09

Venture just east of Beirut into the Mt. Lebanon area, and suddenly the diversity of Lebanon's terrain becomes apparent—and the nickname "Little Switzerland" comes to life. A ½hr. and 1hr. drive from the coast, respectively, Faraya (elevation 2465m) and Faqra (elevation 2001m) are frequented by die-hards eager to be beach and ski bums on the same day. The two mountain towns offer some of the best skiing in Lebanon and one of the most unique winter landscapes in the world. Visitors come both for the snow and to revel in the art of Lebanese *après-ski*. The **ski season** begins in December and lasts through April. In the off season, Faraya and Faqra enter a period of hibernation. Although somewhat eerie during this lapse, the ghost town emptiness translates into drastic discounts on accommodations, making the area a good base for mountain day trips and exploration.

▐ TRANSPORTATION. Faraya (45km from Beirut) and Faqra (55km from Beirut) are challenging, but not impossible to reach via public transportation. From Dawra, take a *service* or bus north to Jounieh and ask to be let off at Mafra' Jeita. Here, *service* can usually be found waiting to trek passengers up the mountain. *Service* make the ½hr. trip to Faraya year-round (LS3000), but Faqra—about 30min. farther—is rarely visited in the off season. In the summer, your best bet is to take a *service* to Faraya and then a private taxi to Faqra (LS10,000). For the return trip, make arrangements in advance with whoever drops you off.

▐ ACCOMMODATIONS. Because Faqra is a private club, the only option, aside from being invited to stay in a private chalet, is to book a spot in the glamorously expensive **L'Auberge de Faqra** (starting around US$230 a night). Fortunately, Faraya offers more reasonable lodging, especially in the off season. The family-run **Coin Vert Hotel and Restaurant** (☎ 321 260), on the left side of the main road just before the center traffic circle, offers 24 laundry-fresh rooms (some with balconies and TVs), private baths, free breakfast, and entrance to **Le Kayak** disco during the ski season. (Singles US$30; doubles US$40; triplesUS$50; off season at least US$5 less). Bear left at the center traffic circle to find **The Grand Hotel** (☎ 321 534), one of Faraya's oldest and most accommodating facilities. Although not large, rooms with private baths have up to four beds and are well suited for piling in big groups (US$25-40 per night, US$300 per month). Visitors have access to a communal kitchen and a restaurant with home cooked meals (LS2000-3000 per plate).

▐ FOOD. Designed to feed hungry skiers, Faraya has plenty of snack shops along the main road with options ranging from pizza to *saj* wraps. For a longer, more scenic meal, try **Al-Nahr al-Hawi Restaurant** (☎ 720 260), just past the main traffic circle in Faqra (Arabic sign only, النهر الهوى.) *Mezze* LS3500 per dish, entrees LS4000-17,000. MC/V. In Faraya, **Restaurant Jisr al-Kamer** (☎ 03 877 993) sits alongside a babbling brook and is well-equipped with large outdoor patios and a range of *argileh* flavors (LS7000). *Mezze* LS18,000, grill entrees LS4000-12,000. MC/V.

▲ SKIING. With 16 lifts and 17 slopes, **Faraya Mzaar** (☎ 341 034) is the largest ski facility in Lebanon. Although often overcrowded, it boasts challenging slopes and a reputation for thrills (lifts Sa-Su US$15-4; M-F US$13-26). Rentals are available from Coin Vert and several other stores, starting at US$10 per day. **Faqra** is the only resort in Lebanon to offer night skiing, but unfortunately the slopes are often open by invitation only. See **www.skileb.com** for updates on conditions and prices.

◉ SIGHTS. On the road between Faqra and Faraya, be sure to notice the unassuming **natural bridge**. It is easily spotted on the right, but often overlooked as just another man-made bridge. For centuries, debate circled as to whether the bridge was a natural or human construction. The final verdict is that it is a natural formation. *Service* usually don't mind pulling over for a few minutes, and if you have time, the climb down to the base is an adventure. Along with its ski slopes and natural wonder of the bridge, the mountain region also bears the ruins of over 3000 years of continuous settlement, including ancient Greek and Romans buildings. The **main temple,** about 50m northwest of the tower, is believed to be dedicated to Adonis. Its Corinthian columns were restored during the 20th century and are tourist postcard favorites, especially when covered in snow. Near the temple stand a small temple and several free-standing altars. (Open W-M 8:30am-dusk, L£3000.)

The nearby town of **Hrajel** is home to two grottoes, al-Karkouf and Nabeh al-Maghara. As of August 2001, these caves were closed to the public, but avid spelunkers should inquire with locals or a Beirut trekking company (see **Tours,** p. 515) for further details.

NORTH OF BEIRUT

BYBLOS (JBAIL) جبيل ☎09

The charm of Byblos is born from the sea and thrives in its port. For seven thousand years, it has drawn sailors and civilizations to its shores, placing the city among Jericho, Damascus, and Aleppo in the rankings of "oldest continually inhabited city in the world." Though each civilization—Neolithic, Phoenician, Egyptian, Greek, Roman, Persian, and Ottoman—has left its distinct mark, the city somehow remains remarkably unified. Despite a small wave of modern expansion, life here is still simple, thankful, and content in the arms of its Mediterranean port. Located within the Maronite Catholic heartland of Lebanon, small shrines and chapels dedicated to the Virgin Mary and other saints line the streets, beckoning those passing by on foot or by car. Deep sunset colors, beautiful cedar doors, inviting window-scapes, and a unique layering of time have made Byblos a favorite spot for Lebanese artists and poets.

▐ TRANSPORTATION

Buses: Buses run between Dawra in **Beirut** and Rue Jbail in Byblos, stopping at a taxi hub near the Mobil gas station (L£500). Buses return from Byblos until about 9pm. Late at night, a private **taxi** may be the only option.

Minibuses: To **Tripoli** and the **north** (every 15min., L£2000). Walk up to the Beirut-Tripoli *autostrade* (highway) and flag down a minibus en route.

Service: To **Amchit** (L£2000), from in front of the Mobil station on Rue Jbail.

✳ ▐ ORIENTATION AND PRACTICAL INFORMATION

Byblos is easy to negotiate on foot. The modern city is centered around **Rue Jbail,** where buses and *service* congregate. Walking up Rue Jbail away from the highway takes you to **Rue al-Mina,** which follows the medieval wall to the sea. Here, the road curves left to the old port (*al-mina* in Arabic), where most of the city's restaurants sit admiring the view to the waterside. Rounding the port leads to the ancient **ruins** and **souq.** Climbing a side street here completes the circuit back to Rue Jbail.

Ministry of Tourism: (☎540 325), just outside the entrance to the archaeological site. Pamphlets and advice, but no comprehensive map of the city. Open M-Sa 9am-4:30pm, Su 10am-1pm; in winter M-Sa 9am-4:30pm, Su 10am-2pm.

Byblos Bank: (☎540 035), on Rue Jbail. Open M-F 8am-5:30pm, Sa 8am-1pm.

Emergency: Medical: ☎140. **Police:** ☎112. Police station located across the street from Ministry of Tourism (sign reads "Gendarmie").

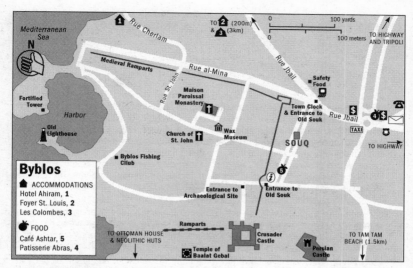

Byblos

🏠 ACCOMMODATIONS
Hotel Ahiram, **1**
Foyer St. Louis, **2**
Les Colombes, **3**

🍴 FOOD
Café Ashtar, **5**
Patisserie Abras, **4**

Internet: CD Master and **S@m Internet,** next door to each other at the intersection of Rue Jbail and Rue al-Mina. Both charge L£2000 per hr. Both open 24hr.

Post Office: (☎540 003), off Rue Jbail on a side street, at the corner with the Coral gas station. Open M-F 7:30am-5pm, Sa 8am-2pm.

Telephone: Central Telephone Office, on the north end of Rue Jbail. A privately owned **Telephone Office,** 50m past the post office on the left, across from DHL, offers unbeatable international rates. L£750-1100 per min. to the US. Open daily 8am-midnight.

🏠🏠 ACCOMMODATIONS & CAMPING

Many travelers to Byblos tend to stay outside the city, as there are only limited budget accommodations options.

Foyer St. Louis (☎03 301 523), follow Rue Jbail from the center of town past Safety Food, keeping the Wadih Restaurant on your right; it will be on your right about 5min. down the road. This newly purchased apartment complex is a newcomer to the budget accommodation scene in Byblos. Each room US$15 per night, US$25 per month. Subject to availability, so call in advance.

Hotel Ahiram (☎540 440; fax 944 726), on Rue al-Mina, the last right before the sea. The cheapest downtown hotel option. Rooms have A/C, TV, private bath, and windswept balconies with priceless seaside views. You will fall asleep to the sound of crashing waves. Before leaving, ask to see Karim's marine archaeological collection. Breakfast included. Singles US$45; doubles US$65; triples US$75; add 5% tax. Bargain if staying longer than 2 nights, or if business seems quiet. AmEx/MC/V.

Lebanese Youth Hostel Federation (☎09 750 370 or 03 649 235). Will put you up at a priest's home in Meaad, 15km from Byblos (US$10-15). Call for availability.

Les Colombes (Camping Amchit) (☎54 03 22), in Amchit, a short *service* ride (L£1000) or 3km walk north on Rue Jbail. On a lush cliffside overlooking the sea, where a small path beckons swimmers down to the waves. Must bring your own **tent** for camping. Alternatively, small **bungalows** with 2 beds and a bathroom also available. Be warned that bungalows often come with noisy neighbors and can get stuffy fast. In summer, the site attracts long-term visitors who set up tents and extensive lounge areas. Comfier **chalets** are equipped with dining rooms and kitchenettes, but no cookware. Bring insect repellent. Tents US$3; bungalows US$20; chalets US$30.

FOOD

Snack stands and fast food shawarma joints are scattered throughout Byblos, but the beauty of the city rests in its portside restaurants. If camping at Les Colombes, you will find a variety of small groceries and fresh fruit stands in Amchit to assemble sandwiches and meals. Most stay open until 11pm, but hours vary. Ask locals or the camp office for details.

■ **Byblos Fishing Club** (☎540 213), in the old port. Once the most glamorous restaurant in the Middle East, the Club's 90-year-old owner, ■ Pepe "the Pirate" Abed, has entertained guests including Marlon Brando, Charles de Gaulle, Brigitte Bardot, and JFK. Visitors marvel at glamor shots of Pepe with famous friends. Despite his fame, the charismatic and unconventional Pepe remains humbly grounded and an active humanitarian. A one-time cock fighter, sea turtle racer, marine archaeologist, and world traveler, Pepe has a special place in his heart for free spirits and students. The prix-fixe menu with meat (L£26,000) or fish (L£30,000) may be pricey, but this is the place for a sunset drink or dessert. Open daily 10am-1am; in winter 10am-11pm. AmEx/MC/V.

Cafe Ashtar (☎03 746 044), on the 1st street to the left after entering the old *souq* from the gate by the archaeological site. Outdoor seating captures all the atmosphere of the *souq* without any of the haggling. Attracts lounging munchers, *argileh* puffers and peaceful conversation seekers. Sandwiches and *mezze* L£2000-5000.

Safety Food, at the intersection of Rue Jabail and Rue al-Mina. Seating available, but sandwiches are better enjoyed on the rocks by the sea. Rotisserie and whole grilled chickens L£7000. Open daily until midnight.

Patisserie Abras, on Rue Jbail at the corner of the intersection leading to the highway. Delicious and affordable way to satisfy sweet cravings. Pistachio, vanilla, and almond ice cream is the best and cheapest around (L£1000-2000). Open daily 5am-midnight.

◎ SIGHTS

ANCIENT BYBLOS. Once brilliant and impressive landmarks announcing the city to distant sea travelers, the ruins of ancient Byblos now sit weathered on the coast, whispering the strength of their survival. Remnants span Byblos's 7000 years, beginning with early Neolithic and Chalcolithic huts. Enter the site through the **Crusader Castle,** the largest and best preserved of the ruins. Although the highest tower may be closed for restoration, panoramic views from lower towers serve as a useful orientation to the rest of the site. Built by the French in the 12th century, the castle is built with some of the largest stones in the Middle East, many of which are believed to have been pillaged from Roman buildings. Towards the sea, six prominent Roman columns dating to 300 CE line the route to the **Temple of Baalat Gebal.** Originally built in the 4th century BCE, the temple foundation is the oldest in Byblos, while the temple itself was rebuilt during the Amorite period following a major fire. A small **Roman Theater,** reconstructed in the 20th century to less than half its original size, sits right on the sea cliff. Between the pillars and the theater, the **Royal Necropolis** (2nd millennium BCE) houses nine tombs of Byblos kings, including that of King Ahiram. Further down the shore sits an **Ottoman house** with a red-tiled roof framed by a lone palm tree. En route to the house is the **King's Well,** a depression of impressive depth that remained in use until Hellenistic times. Nearby lie the crushed limestone floors of Byblos's earliest settlements. Dating from the Neolithic (5th millennium BCE) and Chalcolithic (4th millennium BCE) eras, these settlements are among the earliest human remains in the world. Walking east away from the sea, finds the **Obelisk Temple.** Originally built on the site of the 5000-year old **Temple of Resheph,** the obelisks were moved to this site to facilitate further excavation. The eastern-most ruins are the scattered remains of a Persian castle. Keep your eyes peeled for camouflaged newts and the beautiful collection of wild flowers. Sturdy shoes are recommended, as the marked path may not take you everywhere you want to go. (☎546 333. Open daily 8am-sunset. L£6000, students L£1500; guides available for L£15,000 or more depending on group size).

OLD SOUQ. The *souq* is famous for its collection of prehistoric fish fossils, ancient antiques, and other excavated treasures. Be especially careful to scope out the market before making any purchases. A stroll through the alleyways after shops have closed uncovers their hidden face—a beautiful array of cedar doors, some of which are among the oldest in Lebanon.

CHURCH OF ST. JOHN THE BAPTIST. This famous Romanesque Maronite cathedral was built in 1115 CE as the Crusader church of St. John the Baptist. It was later destroyed, rebuilt, and eventually expanded. *(From Rue al-Mina, head straight down Rue St. John, bearing left at the end of the road. The church will be on your right.)*

WAX MUSEUM. The display travels through time, depicting scenes from ancient and modern Lebanese history. The wax sculptures are far from artistic masterpieces, so unless this is really your thing, the 15min. excursion is hardly worth the admission price. *(Turn left at the end of Rue St. John, pass the church, and the museum will be on your left. Open daily 9am-6pm. L£5000.)*

BYBLOS FISHING CLUB. This famous restaurant is a sight unto itself (see **Food**, p. 532). Check out Pepe the Pirate's free museum, featuring antiquities he recovered during diving expeditions. The museum structure dates back 800 years and UNESCO has declared it a World Heritage Site.

 BEACHES

TAM-TAM BEACH. One of the few public sand beaches in Lebanon, making it a popular spot on the weekends, buzzing with youth listening to Bob Marley and drinking too much beer. Breaking the waves on surfboards with double-headed oars is a tough Mediterranean adventure, though locals make it look easy. Consult with lifeguards before swimming or surfboarding as undercurrents, known locally as "twisters," are notorious for pulling swimmers out to sea. At its northern end, Tam-Tam turns into a gay hangout known as **Paradise Beach.** Two snack stands provide food, drinks, and a variety of loud music. *(Tam-Tam is a 15min. walk south of Byblos or a short L£1000 service ride along the coastal highway. Entrance is L£1000, and includes use of shower facilities. Surf board rental L£7000 per hr.)*

PEBBLE BEACH. Byblos's other public beach, with free entrance and free use of surfboards. Swimming here is more private than at Tam-Tam, but (duh) the beach is covered with pebbles. *(Located in front of the Ahiram Hotel.)*

 DAYTRIPS FROM BYBLOS

AFQA GROTTO AND ADONIS VALLEY

*The Afqa Grotto and Adonis Valley are a 1hr. drive from Byblos, but no service run the route. Haggling with local **taxi** drivers can get you a chauffeur for a whole day for around US$30. Rides available to Afqa Nature Reserve from Beirut or Byblos, call in advance.)*

The Afqa Grotto marks the source of Nahr Ibrahim (River of Abraham), which flows through a deep gorge known as the Adonis Valley, one of the most beautiful regions in the country. According to an ancient semitic myth (later adopted by the Greeks), the handsome Adonis was slain by a wild boar at the river's source, turning the waters red. Every spring, melting snow brings an iron-rich, red mineral deposit to the river, symbolizing the period when Adonis is temporarily reunited with his lover Astarte. Ruins of a Roman temple dedicated to Astarte (a.k.a. Aphrodite a.k.a. Venus) are nearby. The valley is a great spot for picnics, swims, and hikes along the river. Although water pipes serving most of the region detract from the natural feel of the Grotto, it remains quite majestic. To explore the cave, bring flashlights and be prepared for extremely cold water (and temperatures) at the source. Young locals will eagerly guide you through the cave's many windows.

LEBANON

AFQA NATURE RESERVE (LA RESERVE)

5min. from the Afqa Grotto. From the Beirut-Tripoli highway, take the main road just past Nahr Ibrahim that leads to Qartaba; after the town of al-Majdel, follow signs to La Reserve Afqa. ☎03 727 484; 286 670; www.lareserve.com.lb. Tents US$10 per person, with 4 beds, pillows and one solar energy outlet; bring your own sheets or sleeping bag. Tent sites US$5. Bathroom, shower, and health food restaurant. Space is limited; call for reservations.

An ideal hub for **hiking** and **climbing** daytrips, the Afqa reserve overlooks the Adonis Valley and Nahr Ibrahim, comprising probably the most beautiful area of the Mt. Lebanon region. While there are no detailed maps of the area available, the wise staff provides guides and regional advice to send you safely on your way. Ask about the "road of the peaks" hike from **Qoronet al-Sawda** (the highest peak in Lebanon) to **Sanine**, via Faraya and the Cedars of Lebanon. Mountain biking, climbing, rappelling, and caving by request.

BATROUN بترون ☎06

A quiet fishing town with unsuspecting ingenuity, Batroun has adopted a modern reputation as the "City of Lemonade." The technique is simple, but surprisingly delicious: Lemons are quartered, doused in sugar, and pressed by hand until the juice has been full extracted and flavored by the rind. The mixture is then diluted with water, filtered, and chilled. Inhabited by Phoenicians, Greeks, and Romans, Batroun has long taken advantage of its natural resources in interesting ways, including acting as a hub for the ancient world's sponge diving trade. Today, archaeological sites are fluidly integrated into modern life, making them an adventure and unconventional pleasure to discover. In the old *souq*, fresh fish, fresh fruit, and—of course—fresh lemonade flavor the coastal air.

TRANSPORTATION. Service depart for Batroun from Byblos and Tripoli (L£2000-4000). Alternatively, **buses** serving the north-south coastal route between Byblos and Tripoli will drop you off on the highway (L£1500); it's a short walk along the exit ramp into town.

ORIENTATION AND PRACTICAL INFORMATION. The two-lane coastal highway is the main street in Batroun. All major shops flank this highway, while historical sites tend to lie just off it. An English tourist map, free at most shops, simplifies navigation. If the map is unavailable, walk to the large **statue of a diver** on the north side of town (a reminder of the town's past as a sponge diving center), and follow the site-specific arrows. West of the main street lies the **Old City** with its surviving **souq** and **port.**

ACCOMMODATIONS. Because Batroun is just a short ride from both Byblos and Tripoli, it is probably not worth spending the night. The cheapest accommodation, a seaside resort called **Aqualand** (☎742 741), is on the main road at the south end of town. Weary travelers with enough money can enjoy their sauna, whirlpool, and Turkish baths. (All rooms US$50. MC/V.)

FOOD AND ENTERTAINMENT. On the east side of the main street near the center of town, **Chez Hilmi** has been owned by the Rahim family for over 85 years. Their home-brewed, tangy **lemonade** comes in three sizes (large L£2000) and is responsible for initiating Batroun's lemonade craze. Hilmi also serves ice cream and homemade sweets so good that they are regularly ordered over the Internet and shipped around the world. (☎740 068. www.chezhilmi.com. Open daily 7am-11pm. AmEx/MC/V.) **Hannouch Restaurant,** on the main street a few blocks south of the diver statue, is a cheaper option, serving sandwiches (L£3000), *mana'eesh* (L£1000) and a slightly tangier lemonade. (☎740 438. Open daily 8am-midnight.) For a droopy good time at **Droopy Rest Snack,** follow the main road south past the intersection that leads to the highway; it is at the corner just as the main road begins to bend towards the sea. TV plays music videos,

Discovery Channel, and sports matches while crowds down fruit cocktails (L£2500), beer (L£3000 with *mezze*), and a variety of snacks. (☎743 464. Open daily 10am-2am.) **Le Marin,** across from Droopy, is the place for fresh fish and seaside views. Although a full meal with *mezze* and grill will cost L£30,000, you can order just a fish plate for L£6000. (☎744 016. Open daily noon-midnight.) **Taiga Pub,** Batroun's lone nightclub, sits on the east side of the main street near the center of town. During the week, sparse crowds sip brewskies (L£2000), but come Friday and Saturday nights, young clubbers from Tripoli and Jounieh pack the place, jamming to Arabic and Euro techno. (☎03 499 408. L£5000 cover F and Sa. Open Tu-Th and Su 6pm-midnight, F-Sa 6pm-5am.)

◨ SIGHTS. Towering on the east side of the coastal highway 2.5km north of Batroun is **◨Musheilla Castle.** Buses en route can easily drop you off. Built in the 16th century, the castle stands on a majestic 25m stone outcrop. Although the rubbish-strewn field and highway noise detract from the area's charm, you'll forget these blemishes after ascending the stone stairway to explore the castle's interior. Wear sturdy shoes and be careful: the castle is full of uneven steps and unmarked ledges, and the fall is a long, long way.

In the **Old City** of Batroun, blue signs through laundry-draped alleyways lead to a **Phoenician wall and castle,** an ancient **port,** and several old churches. The most notable are **St. George's Church** (1867), **St. Estephan Cathedral** (1900), and the **Church of Mary Our Lady of the Sea,** originally the site of a Roman temple. Most shops in the old *souq* have closed due to slow business, but fresh fruit stands and the atmosphere have managed to survive. To get to the **Roman Amphitheater,** follow the main road north of Chez Hilmi and turn left at the corner of the Pharmacie Traboulsi. Heading uphill, you will see the Agfa Studio Jammal. The amphitheater has been incorporated into the garden of the photo studio and is often the backdrop to photo displays of natural wonders in Lebanon.

TRIPOLI (TRABLOS) طرابلس   ☎06

Conservatism and religion—predominantly Islam—are much more important in Tripoli, Lebanon's second-largest city, than in Beirut. Blessed and cursed with natural ports, offshore islands, and a once-strategic position along the trade route of the Abu Ali River, Tripoli's coast has seen waves of natural destruction and conquest alternating with periods of rapid growth. In 551 CE, an earthquake and tidal wave erased nearly all signs of Phoenician, Roman, and Byzantine civilization. By 635 CE, Tripoli reemerged as a commercial and shipbuilding center under the Umayyads—only to be sieged, pillaged, and burned by Crusaders in 1109 CE. Crusader Tripoli soon fell in 1289 to the Mamluk Sultan Qalaoun, who ordered the old port city (present-day al-Mina) destroyed and a new inland city built near what is today the Citadel of St. Gilles. This early distinction between *al-madina* (the city) and *al-mina* (the port) is evident in the present division of the city. Most of the surviving architecture in the city is the original product of Mamluk rule, later built over by the Ottomans during their reign of 1516-1918.

Tripoli's history is matched in variety only by the city's cultural diversity. Tripolitans shuffling along the seaside corniche dress in fashions ranging from miniskirts to Islamic head coverings. In the Old City, colorful *souqs*, bathhouses, and mosques with their adjoining *madrasas* (theological schools) recall a declining past that is nonetheless unwilling to change. Old men gather in *ahwas* (coffeehouses), nostalgically puffing *argileh* and throwing dice against elaborate backgammon boards. As the lazy Mediterranean sun lingers on the horizon, cars zip past each other in a chaotic race home, and Tripoli's fishermen call it a day and begin their coffeehouse lounging. Along the corniche in al-Mina, an endless train of families and couples walk for hours, stopping only for three pleasures—ice cream, coffee, and a glimpse of the sun laying to rest in the sea.

▐ TRANSPORTATION

Tripoli is easily reached from anywhere along the Beirut-Tripoli highway. Just flag
down a *service* or bus heading your way.

Buses: Ahdab Station, on Rue Tell just west of the clocktower, adjacent to al-Soufi
snack stretch. Smoking and non-smoking buses go to Helou Station in **Beirut** (2hr.;
every 15min. 5am-7pm; L£2500).

International Buses: Kotob Bus Travel, on Rue Fouad Chehab. Turn right from Ahdab
Station and look for the sign across the street, next to the Big Bite Restaurant. To:
Aleppo (5hr., every hr., L£7500); **Hama** (3hr., every hr., L£6000); **Homs** (2½hr., every
hr.; L£6000); **Lattakia** (3½hr., 3pm, L£7500) via **Tartus** (2hr., 3pm, L£4500). Buses
to **Turkey** and destinations in **Europe** (most leave at midnight; US$20-60).

Service: There are 2 primary depots in town. *Service* from Tell Sq. go to **Beirut**
(L£4000), **al-Mina** (L£500), and numerous destinations in Syria and Lebanon. Al-
Koura Sq. serves **Bcharré** (L£3500) and the mountains.

Taxis: The occasional private taxi will take you to **Ba'albeck** for about US$30.

✷ ORIENTATION

The major north-south road in Tripoli is **Rue Fouad Chehab.** Approaching from
Beirut on this road, you arrive at **al-Karami** traffic circle with its distinctive "Allah"
(الله) sign in the middle. The next major intersection, marked by **Big Bite Restaurant,**
separates **Rue Jemayzat** to the left and **Rue Tell** (officially Rue 'Abd al-Hamid
Karami) to the right. Turning right on Rue Tell leads to **Tell Sq.** ("Sahet al-Tell")
with its landmark **Tell Clocktower.** Behind the clocktower is a public garden, and
across the street is the dusty **Jamal 'Abd al-Nasser Sq.** This area forms the heart of
modern Tripoli and is filled with *service* drivers boisterously hawking rides in a
chorus of horns and shouts. Taking the first right after al-Nasser Sq. leads to **Koura
Sq.,** and a left at Koura Sq. leads to **al-Nejmeh Sq.** From here the towering citadel is
visible, and almost all of the historical sights are a short walk away. **Al-Mina** (the
port) is 2km from the city center. *Service* to al-Mina (L£500) will drop you off on
Rue Ibn Sina, the main seaside road, also referred to as the **corniche.**

▟ PRACTICAL INFORMATION

Tourist Office: (☎433 590), in al-Karami Sq. near the "Allah" sign. Provides a great historical map of Tripoli and pamphlets on all major tourist destinations in Lebanon. Be
insistent if they cannot find the historical map. Open M-Sa 8am-5pm. **Ali Khawaja**
(☎433 838) is a respected local resident who will answer questions and show you
around town for free (for more information, see **Sights,** p. 539).

Banks: Banque Libano-Française (☎430 180), in al-Karami Sq. **ATM.** Multilingual staff.
Open M-F 8:15am-2:30pm, Sa 8:15am-noon. **Bank of Beirut and the Arab Countries
(BBAC)**(☎430 460), on Rue Tell next to Ahdab Station. **ATM.** Multilingual staff. Open
M-F 7:30am-2:30pm, Sa 7:30am-1:30pm. Exchange traveler's checks at **Walid Masri**
(☎430 115), across the street from Tell Clocktower.

Laundromat: Express Laundry (☎625 825), from the tourist office in Karami Sq., walk
counterclockwise around the rotary taking the 1st right; it's on your left as you approach
the tree in the middle of the road. Shirts L£2500. Pants L£4000. Open M-Th and Sa
7:30am-6pm, F 7:30am-3pm; in winter M-Th and Sa 7:30am-4:30pm, F 7:30am-3pm.

Emergency: Police: ☎112. **Ambulance:** ☎140.

Pharmacy: Ayoub Pharmacy (☎624 295), in Tell Sq., directly opposite the clocktower.
Multilingual staff. Open M-F 8am-5pm, Sa 8am-2pm. **Assaray Pharmacy** (☎444 56
74), opposite the post office. Open M-F 8am-9pm, Sa 8am-8pm.

Hospital: Mazloum Hospital (☎430 325 or 628 303). Emergency room. X-rays. Will air-
lift seriously ill or injured patients to Beirut.

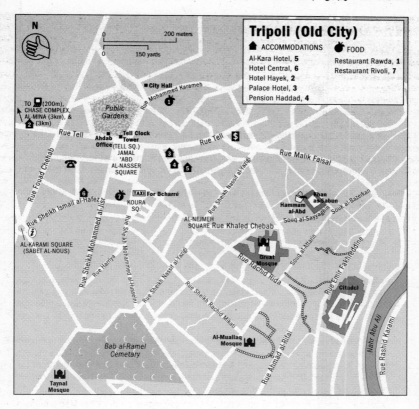

Tripoli (Old City)

🏠 ACCOMMODATIONS
Al-Kara Hotel, **5**
Hotel Central, **6**
Hotel Hayek, **2**
Palace Hotel, **3**
Pension Haddad, **4**

🍅 FOOD
Restaurant Rawda, **1**
Restaurant Rivoli, **7**

Telephones: EasyNet (☎447 041 or 03 917 362). From Tell Sq., bear right at al-Koura Sq., then bear left where the road forks at the City Land toy store; EasyNet is on the right. Friendly English-speaking staff will place international calls to the US, Western Europe, Australia, and Canada (L£1000 per min). Open daily 9am-midnight. **Central Telephone Office** is on the 1st side street parallel to Rue Tell near the clocktower. Facing Ayoub Pharmacy with the clocktower on your right, the street is on your left. Clerks speak little English and rates are posted only in Arabic. International L£4500 per 3min.; Local L£1000 per 5min. Open 7am-midnight.

Internet Access: Most Internet facilities are located in or near the City Complex on Rue Riad al-Solh (popularly referred to as Rue Mina). From Tell Sq., head past Rue Fouad Chehab, bearing right at the square with the wire sculpture, until you reach Rue Mina. City Complex is on your left. **In-Side**, on the 1st fl. of the City Complex, has the fastest connections in Lebanon (L£3000 per hr.; 10am-noon L£2000). Open 10am-midnight. Also in the City Complex are **WLan** and **Drop Zone**. Both L£3000. Open 10am-1am. Turning left at the 2nd intersection past City Complex, **Net & Chat** will be on your right. L£3000 per hr.; L£2000 on Tu. Open M-Sa 9am-midnight, Su 3pm-midnight.

Post Office: (☎432 101), on Rue Dr. Hashem al-Housseini. From the "Allah" sign, take Rue Fouad Chehab towards the municipal building. The 1st right will be Rue Dr. Hashem al-Housseini (sign also to Mazloum Hospital); the post office is on the right. **Western Union** and **UPS** available. Open M-F 7am-5pm and Sa 7am-noon. **DHL** (☎433 205) is off Rue Fouad Chehab in Helou Plaza, about 500m north of Big Bite Restaurant. Open M-F 8am-5pm, Sa 8am-3pm. AmEx/MC/V.

ACCOMMODATIONS

Tripoli's accommodations are generally much cheaper and less crowded than those in Beirut. Many tourists visit Tripoli as a daytrip from Beirut, but a few nights' stay makes Tripoli a good hub for exploring the mountains and northern half of the country. Most budget hotels in Tripoli accept both Lebanese pounds and US dollars, but usually not credit cards.

Pension Haddad (☎06 624 392 or 03 507 709; haddadpension@hotmail.com), on Haddad Alley just off of Tell Sq. Facing Fahim Coffee (Arabic sign with blue Pepsi logo and a fence separating *argileh* smokers from the rest of the street) it is in the 1st alley on the left. A haven for weary backpackers, staying here is like staying at your Lebanese grandmother's house. Immaculate, well-furnished bedrooms and shared bathroom with a brilliant three-nozzled shower. Anti (Grandma) Haddad and the rest of the family eagerly provide maps, travel advice and TLC. Full breakfast L£3000. Meals L£5000. Tea, coffee, and morning croissant included. Fans, satellite TV, and laundry. Mixed dorm US$7. Singles US$10; doubles US$16; triples US$21.

Al-Koura Hotel (☎03 326 803) in Tell Sq., 1 alley to the left of Haddad. A variety of private and dorm-style rooms in a comfortable family-run flat. Though somewhat pricey, al-Koura's 3 renovated rooms with private baths, cedar-rafter ceilings, and original Ottoman-era brickwork are worth it. A/C. Breakfast included. Laundry US$5 per load. Singles US$10-15; doubles US$30; triples US$45. Less well-maintained dorms US$5.

Palace Hotel (☎432 257), on Rue Tell, just past Haddad Alley. The regal reception area with lovely ceiling and stained glass earns the hotel its name. Manager will call the English-speaking owner to communicate with you. A/C units do not work, but a pleasant breeze blows into rooms facing Rue Tell. Laundry service. Private rooms US$10 per person; with bath US$15 per person.

Hotel Central (☎441 544). From tourist office, walk counterclockwise around the rotary and take the 1st right. Look up as you approach the large tree; the hotel is on the 6th fl. with flags and blue railings. Shared balcony has a great view of downtown, from the castle to the sea. All rooms have sinks and fans. Shared baths. US$10 per person.

Hotel Hayek (☎601 311), on Rue ibn Sina, 1 street behind the corniche, just south of al-Mina Mosque. Not right on the water, but seaside rooms overlook the Mediterranean and its refreshing breezes. Game room on the 1st fl. with billiards and ping pong for L£4000 per hr. 3 meals US$12. Singles US$17; doubles US$20; triples US$30.

FOOD

Tripoli is bursting with *hallabs* (sweet shops) that continue to expand and improve, as they compete for the most refined taste buds. Prices are very reasonable (L£2000-3000) and nearly identical at most *hallabs*, so "sweet-hopping" from one place to the next is a good way to find your favorite. **Hallab Brothers** (☎444 433), on Rue Tell, is one of the oldest in town and still one of the best. With the clocktower on your left, walk past the square and it will be on your right. A new location is scheduled to open in 2002 just past the City Complex. Open daily 5am-10pm, although hours often extend until midnight. For the pre-game, Middle Eastern eateries and shawarma stands line **al-Soufi** stretch, along Rue Tell just past the clocktower. As with the *hallabs*, competition here has refined the best fly-by sandwiches in town (L£1000-3000). Shawarma, falafel, rotisserie chicken, and a daring potato and coleslaw pocket are the favorites. Extreme budget travelers can live on sesame and cheese sandwiches (L£500) and freshly squeezed orange, carrot, or lemon juice (L£500) sold from pushcarts around Tell Sq.

Restaurant Rivoli (☎624 227), approaching al-Koura Sq. from the clocktower, bear to the far right and make the 1st right; the restaurant is on your right. Sit-down establishment with a relaxed atmosphere. Offers a different Middle Eastern special each day with salad and watermelon (L£5000). Open daily 6am-9pm.

> ## SWEET NOTHINGS
> Tripoli is famous for its sweets, most notably those containing a special kind of cream called *ashta*, collected from the curdling top of boiling milk. All sweets are doused in a sugar and rosewater syrup known as *atir*. The following primer on Lebanese desserts should start your tongue watering:
>
> **Zinoud al-sit:** Plump cream pastries, so named because they are said to resemble the upper portion of a curvaceous woman's arm.
>
> **Halawat al-jibn:** Soft pastry stuffed with blended cheese and cream. The local specialty.
>
> **Mafroukeh:** A caramelized blend of sugar, butter, and farina.
>
> **Karboosh hallab:** A layered mix of pistachios, marshmallow fluff, and farina crust.

Restaurant Rawda (☎ 433 339), opposite City Hall, just outside of the public garden in Tell Sq. With the clocktower on your left, turn left around the public gardens and City Hall will be in front of you. Sign only in Arabic, but look for the Lebanese flag. A popular casino before the war, Rawda reopened its doors in 2001 to serve affordable traditional Lebanese meals. Spacious and quiet with great views of the public gardens. Daily plate L£5000. Open 6am-midnight.

Captain Fish Restaurant (☎ 613 031), off Rue Ibn Sina south of the mosque in al-Mina, on the 3rd fl. of al-Balha Ice Cream. Fresh fish cooked however you like it. Pick-your-fish pay-by-the-kilo meals; 1kg of fish is enough for 4 or 5 (L£45,000 per kg). Elaborate mirrored ceiling, balanced by a simple open window on the sea. Open daily noon-midnight.

Tasty (☎ 612 909), on the corniche south of al-Mina Mosque, near the end of the boat launches to the islands. Western and Middle Eastern fast food draws young crowds from their seaside strolls. Food (L£2000-6000) lives up to the restaurant's name. Beer L£1500. Open daily 10am-midnight.

Big Bite (☎ 43 01 56 or 44 09 65), landmark restaurant on the corner of Rue Tell and Rue Fouad Chehab. Falafel and french fries—together at last! Garnish your burger (L£3000) with a side of hummus (L£1000), or go with a respectable veg. pizza (L£4500). Open daily 4am-10pm.

CAFES

Al-Badi'a Cafe, at the end of the corniche walk. With the sea to your left, stroll to the end of the main path, where a small dirt road continues to the cafe (but look for the blue Pepsi awning). The only place on the corniche that is directly on the water. A bit pricey (*argileh* and Turkish coffee L£6000), but the view of fishing boats silhouetted against the sky is worth it. Open daily 9am-1am.

Tal al-'Ali (High Hill), opposite City Hall in Tell Sq. Stairs leading up to the garden are to the right of Restaurant Rawda (see **Food,** p. 538). Once an open-air theater, this beautiful canopy of trees and grapevines has been converted to a garden for lounging Coffee and *argileh* L£2000. Perhaps the greenest and most peaceful spot in the city. Open daily afternoon-midnight.

Ahwa Musa, outside the east corner of Bab al-Ramel Cemetery, down a street off al-Koura Sq. A small garden amidst the concrete and stone of the city, Musa's fountainside cafe has attracted the backgammon and card sharks of Tripoli for over 100 years. The crowd is typically all male, but women perceived as foreigners usually aren't bothered. Turkish coffee L£750. Soft drinks L£1000. *Argileh* L£1500. Open daily 5pm-2am.

SIGHTS

A maze-like array of narrow alleys, vibrant *souqs*, picturesque mosques, and steamy *hammams*, the Old City is the heart of Tripoli's charm and a testament to its Mamluk history. Because the *souq* is hard to navigate and mocks all presumption of linear planning, it is best to begin with the **historical map** provided by the tourist office. Don't be afraid simply ask locals for specific locations. Keys to many sights rest in the hands of nearby street vendors, who often don't speak much English or French; if you speak no Arabic or are simply feeling overwhelmed by the *souq*, it may be worthwhile to hire a guide. ◪**Ali Khawaja**, son of a late community leader, will show you every nook and cranny of the Old City for free (most visitors offer him L$4000-7000, which he donates to poor families). Look for Ali in front of Taynal Mosque; he can also be reached at home before 10am or after 8pm (☎ 433 838). If Ali is not around, the tourist office can recommend someone else; expect to pay around US$25 for a half-day tour.

An ideal sightseeing strategy is to begin your tour at **al-Nejmeh Sq.** From here, take **Rue Khaled Chehab** (the street to the left of the "Dr. Ezzat Moukadem" sign) to an entrance of the Old City known as *souq al-sayaghin* (Jewelers Market) or *souq al-dahab* (Gold Market). Just before the entrance to the souq is the Great Mosque and its attached theological school, followed by a concentration of sights. The numbers in brackets in the descriptions below correspond to the numbers on the historical map provided by the tourist office.

THE GREAT MOSQUE (AL-MANSOURI AL-KABIR) [#2]. Built from 1294 to 1315 on the remains of a 12th-century Crusader cathedral, al-Mansouri is the oldest and largest of Tripoli's mosques. Architects adapted several features of the old church to fit a traditional mosque layout; most notably, the church's Lombard-style bell tower was transformed into the present minaret. Attached to the mosque are two *madrasas* (theological schools) from the same period; **Madrasa al-Shamsiya** and **Madrasa al-Mashad.** Across the street are two more schools, **al-Khairiah Hassan** and **al-Nouriyat.** Ask nearby shopkeepers for the keys. *(Modest dress required. Women must wear a cloak available at the entrance. Do not enter during prayer hour. No shoes.)*

BAB AL-HADEED. Tripoli was one of the first cities to have discovered and produced soap *(sabun)*. The 400-year old **Khan al-Sabun [#10]** is the most prominent factory, located near the beginning of Souq al-Dahab. *Khan* means inn; rooms on the upper floor were used as sleeping quarters for factory workers. Their trademark soap is made purely of olive oil and honey, scented with natural oils and colored with henna, saffron, keratin, or chlorophyll. Vendors sell 800-year old fragrant blends now referred to as "aromatherapy" (try the Jasmine soap). Around the corner from Khan al-Sabun is **Hammam al-'Abd** (Bath of the Slave), Tripoli's only functional *hammam.* Here, men come to rejuvenate mind and body with a traditional routine of sauna, massage, Turkish bath, and *argileh* smoking. *(☎ 03 724 556. Open daily 7am-midnight. L£15,000. For a look around, the doorman may expect L£1000-2000. The facilities can be reserved for use by groups of up to 10 women for US$100.)*

THE CITADEL (QAL'AT SINJIL) [#1]. This old castle has been destroyed, altered, and renovated by myriad conquerors over hundreds of years, which has resulted in a unique layering of architectural styles. The castle is now named Qal'at Sinjil (Citadel of St. Gilles), after Raymond of St. Gilles, a Crusader leader who occupied the hill in 1099 CE. Towering over the Old City and Abu 'Ali River, the Citadel has an amazing view of Tripoli. *Hammams* can be identified in the distance by their domes inlaid with colored glass. *(Open daily 8am-6:30pm; in winter 8am-5pm. L£5000.)*

HAMMAM AL-JADEED [#35]. This bathhouse is the largest in Tripoli, built in 1740 but non-functional since the Lebanese militia used it as a base in the 1970s. Still, the faded grandeur of the interior is worth a peek. The fountain in the main entrance was designed as an optical illusion. Walk around it in circles, moving closer and farther away—watch the water and marvel at the mystery. The colored glass in the domed ceiling of each room lets sunlight pass while keeping peeping Toms away. If you have a pair of sunglasses, hold them so that the glass lights are visible on their surface and observe the patterns. One room reveals a magnificent Maltese cross. *(The keymaster hangs out in a local shop and will ask for a L£2000 donation.)*

TAYNAL MOSQUE [#39]. Built in 1336 by Saif al-Din Taynal on the site of a ruined Carmelite church, Taynal is the most beautiful mosque in Tripoli. Following a familiar theme in Tripoli's architecture, the mosque was adapted from the Carmelite structure. Visitors are sometimes allowed to climb the minaret, but entry depends on the presence of the guard. *(Women must wear a cloak, available at the entrance. Visitors should not enter at prayer time, normally between 11:30am and 1pm. Free.)*

🔊 🎵 NIGHTLIFE AND ENTERTAINMENT

With the exception of one club and one movie theater, Tripoli's nightlife consists of three activities, often performed simultaneously: walking, smoking, and eating sweets (see **Sweet Nothings**, p. 539). Perhaps one more option is sitting, smoking and drinking coffee at one of the city's *argileh* joints (see **Cafes**, p. 539). Teenagers and young families flock to the **corniche** for evening strolls and ice cream. The rocks are a favorite spot to set up camp for swimming and lounging as the sun quietly sinks into the sea.

Clou Club (☎ 03 254 622), in the City Complex. Tripoli's club scene is limited, but local hipsters swear by this young, tropical-style pub. Beers and liquors L£3000-6000; add L£2000 on Sa. Open Tu-Th 7:30pm-1:30am, F-Sa 7:30pm-3am.

Ciné Planete (☎ 442 471), in the City Complex. 4 theaters play a new rotation of American movies every week, usually about 6 months behind initial release. Daily showings at 3, 5:30, 8, 10:30pm. L£5000. Night shows on T and Th-Su L£10,000.

🛥 🏖 BOATING AND BEACHING

There are several **islands** just off Tripoli's coast that can be reached by boats docked along the waterfront (L£2000-5000). These rocky but pleasant isles are popular launch sites for hard-core Mediterranean fishers and swimmers. The **Palm Islands,** 5km from Tripoli, are a protected area aiming to preserve the marine ecosystem from coastal development. In winter and spring, the islands serve as a breeding ground for a wide variety of birds and turtles. They are open to the public July-September only, and your visit will require a (free) permit from the tourist office in Tripoli (see **Practical Information**, p. 536). A private boat to make the trip costs L£50,000, but can be split between up to 20 passengers.

The sandy **beaches** of the largest island attract heavy swimming crowds during these months, making wildlife difficult to spot. Aside from the Palm Islands and rocky pseudo-beaches along the corniche, Tripoli proper has little to offer when it comes to sand and sun. Most locals head about 20min. south along the coastal highway to **Chekka,** where sandy beaches line a scenic bay (minus a nearby concrete factory). The beaches are excellent and charge a tolerable L£5000, shower included. Surfboards, known locally as "huskies," go for L£5000 per hr. Any bus heading south of town can let you off at the turnoff to Chekka's "Florida Beach."

MT. LEBANON RANGE   ☎ 06

Heading through the olive groves southeast of Tripoli, the roadside is packed with increasing numbers of crosses, a harbinger of the predominantly Christian Mt. Lebanon Range ahead. After passing through **Zgharta**, the road enters **Ehden**, a small town rumored by locals to have been visited by Jesus on a donkey. If traveling by private taxi, ask the driver to take you to the **Sayyid David Maoda** memorial for a beautiful view of the coast. Adjacent to the memorial is the **Chapel of Our Lady of the Castle**, which originally served as a Roman lookout post. Near Ehden is the **Horsh Ehden Nature Reserve**, a great place for day hikes. For information on wildlife or for a tour of the area, check in with the ranger, Sarkis Khawaja (☎ 03 389 973).

> **TRANSPORTATION TO THE MOUNTAINS.** Because bus and *service* schedules to the mountains tend to thin out around 3-4pm, travel can be difficult. One option is to hire a **private taxi** from Tripoli for the day (about L£50,000), which provides greater flexibility and allows you to make stops along the way. It is usually possible to share the fare with fellow budget-minded travelers (groups up to 5), making a fully-loaded taxi more affordable than any other option. If you are traveling alone, the Pension Haddad (see **Accommodations**, p. 538) is a good place to round up groups to split the fare for private taxis. Make sure the driver understands where you want to go before you depart. To avoid any miscommunication, it is a good idea to familiarize yourself with the names of mountain towns in Arabic, or to have a local write down your itinerary.

BCHARRÉ بشرى   ☎06

A small Christian village, Bcharré sits about 1400m above the ▮Qadisha Valley, arguably one of the most beautiful natural regions in Lebanon. Most travelers come to Bcharré to explore the Qadisha Valley and Mt. Lebanon Range. The mountains write poetry, while waterfalls blur the ink in a tranquil mess of green and blue. Apart from its lush natural beauty, the Qadisha Valley houses a number of churches, monasteries, and hermitages, recalling its role over the millennia in protecting persecuted religious minorities (mostly Maronite Christians). Bcharré is also the birthplace and inspiration of Khalil Gibran, Lebanon's greatest poet and artist, who dealt with the universal question of humanity's relation to nature.

▮ TRANSPORTATION. Buses are supposed to depart for Bcharré from near the tourist office in Tripoli (every hr., 10am-3pm, L£2500), but schedules vary enough to make buses hard to catch. The best way to reach Bcharré is by **service** from Tripoli's al-Koura Sq. (1hr., L£3000). *Service* back to Tripoli leave from St. Saba Church on the main road in the center of town. Start your trip early; traffic thins later in the day. Alternatively, private **taxis** are sensible if you have travel buddies.

▮▮ ORIENTATION AND PRACTICAL INFORMATION. Bcharré is located near the eastern head of Qadisha Valley, making it an ideal place to start hikes along the **Qadisha Floor** and **Abu Ali River** (see **Hiking**, p. 543). On the main road in the center of Bcharré, the monumental **St. Saba Church** is the largest of the churches in Bcharré and a prominent landmark. Taxis and *service* depart from the **square** in front of the church. Clustered just east of this square are a **pharmacy, bank, and supermarket.** A **post office, police station** and small **hospital** are located northwest of the church, between the main street and Rue Gibran. **Lentine Internet** is across from the Palace Hotel. (L£4000 per hr. Open daily 9am-1am.)

▮▮ ACCOMMODATIONS AND FOOD. The **Palace Hotel,** located just off the main road 100m past St. Saba Church, is the cheaper of Bcharré's two hotels. Rooms are comfortable, with private baths and peaceful views of the town and mountains. (☎03 671 005; fax 671 460. Singles US$30; doubles US$40; triples US$48. Some US$20 singles available. Negotiate prices if business seems slow.)

Shallal Restaurant is next to the waterfall, on the main road en route from Bcharré to the Gibran Museum. Be one with the rhythm of falling water in the mountains and enjoy a variety of sandwiches (L£3000) or grill plates (L£7000.) (☎03 698 471. Open daily 9am-9pm.) Just west of the Palace Hotel is **Maklouf Elie Restaurant.** Plates of grilled meat with *mezze*, dessert, and coffee (L£10,000), come with a view of the mountains. (☎672 585. Open 10am-5pm and 6pm-midnight.)

▮ SIGHTS. The ▮Khalil Gibran Museum, located on a marked turnoff below the sculpture of Gibran's head, is in itself worth a trip to Bcharré. The museum houses a large collection of Gibran's paintings as well as the author's personal library, along with his manuscripts and letters. A useful guidebook is available for L£7500; copies may be borrowed for free. (L£3000; students L£2000. Open daily 9am-5pm; in winter Tu-Su 9am-5pm.)

THE WANDERER

Khalil Gibran was a romantic, fascinated by nature and the tides of change and contrast. A journal entry in the museum reads, "There are no miracles beyond the seasons...." Gibran's paintings have a mystic quality inspired by visions of man's intermediary place between nature and God. Born in Bcharré in 1883, he immigrated to Boston at a young age. After returning to Beirut to study Arabic and French, Gibran went to Paris to work under the sculptor Auguste Rodin. (Rodin would later refer to Gibran as the William Blake of the 20th century.) Among Gibran's favorite places as a child was the Mar Sarkis hermitage, a cave settled by Carmelite monks in the 17th century. Gibran asked to buy Mar Sarkis from the monks and spend his final days living there. To Gibran, the hermitage reflected man's ability to resign to his surroundings—it is often difficult to tell which stone was placed by the hand of man and which by the hand of nature. When he died in 1931, Gibran had written 17 books in Arabic and English; his masterpiece, The Prophet, has been translated into numerous languages. In the last room of the museum built at his tomb an Arabic epigram reads, "I am alive like you and I am standing beside you. Close your eyes, turn around, and you will see me."

■ **HIKING.** Declared a UNESCO World Heritage Sight, the Qadisha Valley is one of the most gorgeous spots in Lebanon. From Bcharré, the best way to descend is on foot, along an old goat path that begins behind **St. Saba Church,** shortly after a series of stairs used by nearby homes. The path is not well defined and at times difficult to follow. Be prepared to keep your eye on the dirt path and small restaurant below and to traverse apple and pear orchards. The hike to the restaurant takes about 30-45min. From here, a road follows the valley with a turnoff to **Deir Mar Elisha,** a monastery built into the cliffside by the Lebanese Maronite Order in 1695. Returning to the road along the valley floor, it is possible to continue hiking for several kilometers, passing a series of chapels, monasteries, and hermitages magnificently nestled into cliffside grottoes.

Another option for exploring the valley is to descend from the town of **Hadchit,** 3km west of Bcharré. Behind the Church of St. Raymond, there is a more accessible path that leads to **Deir al-Salib,** a 12th-century stone monastery housing two of the area's few surviving frescoes. Continuing west along the valley finds the following major sites (in order): **Deir Qannoubin** (40min.-1hr.), the **Cave Chapel of Marina** (30-40min.), **Hawka Monastery** and the **Chapel of Saydet Hawka** (30-45min.). From here, a stair path ascends to the **Church of Saydet Hawka** in the town of Hawka. From Deir al-Salib, expect this route to take a minimum of 4hr.

As of August 2001, Hawka Monastery was home to an elderly Colombian monk who came to the mountains of Lebanon to spend his last days. He speaks Spanish, French, and English and is very pleasant, but asks that you respect his privacy and often unconventional sleeping hours.

NEAR BCHARRÉ

THE CEDARS OF LEBANON أرز الرب

It is impossible to understand Lebanon without knowing the Cedars. A small patch of trees perched in the mountains, Arz al-Rab (Cedars of God), are the few survivors on a mountain range once covered with cedar trees. Strong, flexible, and remarkably old, the cedars are a revered symbol of the modern Lebanese nation (one appears on the flag). The Cedars are cited throughout the Book of Psalms for their grandeur and uprightness, symbolizing the ideal of righteousness. For centuries, the fragrant and durable cedar wood was a lucrative cash crop. The rise of Phoenician civilization is often attributed to its shipbuilding, temple construction, and timber exports. However, after thousands of years of exploitation, very little remains of these slow-growing trees. Today, just over 350 cedars remain in Arz al-Rab, and they are under strict protection. The path through the cedars has been fenced off to avoid too much traffic, but the seeing the trees is still a moving experience. Near the top of the grove, one of the oldest cedars was transformed into a biblical sculpture by artist Rudy Rahmé in honor of an 1825 visit to the grove by the French poet, Alphonse Lamartine.

TRANSPORTATION AND PRACTICAL INFORMATION. From Bcharré, private **taxis** leave to the Cedars from the St. Saba Church—you should be able to bargain the fare down to about L£10,000. **Walking** to the Cedars involves a long (1-1½ hr.) uphill climb. There are two roads, but only the old road accesses the Qadisha Grotto. Traffic is heaviest in the morning and evening as workers travel to and from their jobs at the Cedars. A donation of L£2000 is encouraged at the entrance to the cedar grove. Gates are open Tu-Su 9am-5pm.

ACCOMMODATIONS. Hotels in the cedar grove area are generally expensive resorts that rely on the high season (December-March) for survival. Look for deals in the off-season. **Hotel Mon Refuge** (☎03 617 212), offers singles (L£30,000, L£45,000 with breakfast during ski season) and doubles (L£45,000-60,000). The best deal for those traveling in a group is Mon Refuge's **chalet,** which comfortably sleeps 8-10 people (L£150,700, L£226,000 during ski season). **Hotel Cortina** (☎678 061), on the main road, has private rooms with double or single beds and nice balconies (US$15 per person, US$30 during the ski season). **Hotel Rancho Grande** (☎678 071), offers a few moderately well-maintained rooms with private bath (US$10 per person, US$30 per person during the ski season). Unfortunately, the cheaper prices here sacrifice mountain views. From the main road, follow the sign to the Auberge des Cèdres; it will be on your left. **Centre Tony Arida** (☎671 195) has chalet-style suits—multiple rooms with private bath, sitting area, kitchen, and fireplace. Arida operates a full-service complex for skiers, including ski area, restaurant, and nightclub. (Doubles US$50; singles US$25 in low season only. Suites sleeping 8-10 depend on season and time of week, starting at US$100 for low-season weekdays and peaking around US$200. Ski rental US$20 per day, including a ride to the resort. Skiing lessons US$15 per hr.).

FOOD. There are a few snack shops across from the cedar grove, near al-Arze Restaurant. **Al-Arze Restaurant** (☎671 130), across from the cedar grove, serves *mezze* and sandwiches (L£3000). **Centre Tony Arida** boasts a sports-bar restaurant (open 24hr.) and a retro-'70s nightclub. (Open Sa 10:30pm till late.) **Le Pichet** (☎678 189) is a high-end piano bar offering a *plat du jour* for L£12,000, and fondue for L£23,000 per person. (Open 8:30am-1am.)

SIGHTS. The **Qadisha Grotto** offers amazing views and features intricate rock formations. To get to the grotto, turn off from the old road to the Cedars at L'Agilon Hotel. If you have already seen the Jeita Grotto it might not be worth the $4000 admission fee; the cavern is less expansive and the formations not nearly as beautiful. However, if you have time, the 15min. walk to the entrance loops around the head of the Qadisha Valley with amazing views. The path is lined with broom, a delicate yellow wildflower that blooms atop thin bamboo-like stalks. (Grotto open 9am-7pm, closed in winter.)

HIKING. The main ski lift in the Cedars is just under a 1hr. walk north of the grove. From here, the lift ascends through a pass known as **Fam al-Mizab** (left peak 2820m, right peak 2970m). The lift is controlled by the Lebanese army and can be opened on request from 8am-2pm for L£3000. The ride takes 20min. by lift and about 2hr. on foot. Continuing over the pass from the top of the lift, you will find a dirt path that leads to Lebanon's highest peak, **Qoronet al-Sawda** (3090m). While the hike itself is straightforward, because Qoronet al-Sawda is rounded at the top and a mere 10m taller than surrounding mountaintops, its peak can be difficult to find. There are no signs in the area, and the tripod once marking the peak has tumbled into a pile of stones. Fog often rolls in off the valley, severely limiting visibility, and snow grottoes remain throughout the summer months. Bring plenty of water, wear layered clothing, and start early. From the bottom of the chair lift, the hike takes about 8hr. round-trip. Hikers should seek guidance from the tourist office in Beirut or consider hiring a guide from one of the several reputable trek companies there (see **Tourist Services,** p. 515).

SKIING. The cedar grove is especially elegant when cloaked with snow, and nearby peaks offer some of the best skiing in Lebanon. Talk to the tourist office in Beirut or check **www.skileb.com** for updates and details.

BEQA'A VALLEY البقعة

A checkerboard of green, red, and golden plains, the Beqa'a Valley is situated between the snow-capped Mt. Lebanon Range and its arid counterpart, the Anti-Lebanon Range. Although its location between these two ranges minimizes rainfall, the central and southern Beqa'a are blessed with fertile soils and fresh springs bursting out of mountain slopes. One of the first regions within the fertile crescent to be settled, the Beqa'a today remains the breadbasket of Lebanon.

GETTING AROUND THE VALLEY. Whatever your destination in the Beqa'a Valley, you may have to change cars in **Shtawra,** the transportation hub of the region. Located in the northern valley 44km from Beirut, Shtawra's mini-buses or *service* go to most major destinations in Lebanon and Syria, including **Beirut, Sidon,** and **Homs.** To get to Shtawra, catch a *service* from Beirut's Cola Bridge (L£6000). Alternatively, take a minivan from Beirut bound for Zahlé and ask to be dropped off at Shtawra (1½hr., L£2000).

BA'ALBECK بعلبك ☎ 08

Known to the Greeks and Romans as **Heliopolis** ("City of the Sun"), Ba'albeck houses a magnificent temple complex that is unofficially considered among the wonders of the ancient world. Constructed over several hundred years beginning in the first century BCE, the temples represent the single largest surviving corpus of Roman architecture in the world. Standing at 22.9m, the columns of the **Temple of Jupiter** are the tallest ever erected. Three stones in the west corner of the Temple known as the Trilithon are among the largest ever hewn, each weighing in at over 800 tons. The **Temple of Bacchus,** referred to as the "small temple" of the complex, is larger than the Parthenon in Athens. Yet, from a distance and in postcards, the harmony of the temples' proportions disguises their huge dimensions. On the horizon, Ba'albeck seems as contained as a toy model.

Every year in July and August, the Great Court of the temple complex is transformed into a magnificent concert venue for the world-famous **Ba'albeck Festival.** Modern lights, risers, and sound systems bring fresh life to the ancient days of music, dance, and revelry once familiar to the temple walls. Performances run the gamut from traditional Lebanese music to French operas and Western pop artists. Mansour Rahbani and Sting performed back-to-back in 2001.

Today, Ba'albeck is also known as the headquarters of **Hezbollah,** an Islamist fundamentalist organization that has claimed responsibility for numerous acts of terrorism in the West and in Israel. Although ever-present pictures of Ayatollah Khomeini, Seyyed Hassan Nassrallah, and Hezbollah martyrs may give tourists pause, there is no cause for concern. As of August 2001, Hezbollah and the local population openly welcome Western tourists; many have been known to go out of their way to explain that their quarrels are with the US government and not its citizens, though it is best to keep abreast of the political situation in the area. Out of respect for local customs, it is recommended that visitors dress modestly.

LEBANON

TRANSPORTATION

Buses and minibuses: Run to Ba'albeck from Cola Bridge in beirut (L£3000). From Ba'albeck, some minibuses go directly to **Beirut** (L£3000), while others run via **Shtawra** (L£1000). Minibuses depart to Shtawra from near the Temple of Venus.

Service: The most common way to travel between Ba'albeck and **Beirut** (L£8000). *Service* regularly shuttle between Beirut's Cola Bridge and Ba'albeck's Temple of Venus.

ORIENTATION AND PRACTICAL INFORMATION

There are two main roads in Ba'albeck that intersect just before the Temple of Venus. **Rue 'Abd al-Halim Hajar,** leading to Ba'albeck from Beirut, is home to most hotels. The other main street is **Ras al-'Ain Boulevard,** which crosses Rue Hajar just past al-Shams Hotel. A left at the intersection leads to the temples; a right takes you along the river to a park area known as **Ras al-'Ain,** which is full of football games and outdoor restaurants with lush gardens and tasty grills. On the other side of the park are the **Hezbollah Headquarters.**

Bank: BBAC Bank (☎374 015), on Rue Hajar just before the Palmyra Hotel as you approach from Beirut. **ATM.** Open M-Sa 8am-3pm. No traveler's check exchange; use one of the many exchange booths on Rue Hajar.

Police: ☎112. **Tourist Police:** ☎371 177. Open 24hr.

Pharmacy: Pharmacy Ghassan (☎370 320), on Rue Hajar, across the street from al-Shams Hotel. English and French. Open M-Sa 8am-10pm.

Telephones: Centrale Telephone Office: located 1 street parallel to Ras al-'Ain Blvd., on the left about 150m before the large building with Sarah's Sweets. If you cannot find it, ask locals for directions to *maktab al-bareed* In the same building as the post office. L£4500 per min. to US, Australia, and Europe. Open 24hr.

Internet Access: Network Center (☎370 192), around the corner from the Palmyra Hotel on Rue Hajar L£3000 per hr. Open 9am-1am.

Post Office: Same building as the phone office. Open M-F 8am-5pm, Sa 8am-2pm.

ACCOMMODATIONS

Most budget accommodations in Ba'albeck cluster around the ancient temples. **Jawhari Cafe** offers some pension-style rooms (see **Food,** below).

Pension Shuman (☎370 160), in front of the Temple of Venus on Ras al-'Ain Blvd. Spectacular view of the ruins. Dorms with sink and communal shower L£10,000.

Al-Shams Hotel (☎373 284), on Rue Hajar just before the intersection with Ras al-'Ain Blvd. Clean bedrooms and bathrooms accompanied by slightly obstructed views. Owner is a friendly dentist who provides tooth-talk free of charge and might let you camp out on his balcony. Dorms L£9000; doubles L£22,500.

Jupiter Hotel (☎376 715), near the ruins. Rents furnished apartments, plus a few rooms. Some are incredibly large. Rooms with private bath US$10-20 per person; less if space is available.

Palmyra Hotel (☎370 230). Familiar to all in Ba'albeck. A great place to powder your nose and travel back to the heyday of Victorian tourism in the Middle East. Built in 1874, its guestbook includes Kaiser Wilhelm II, Kemal Atatürk, and Charles de Gaulle. Vine-lined **Palmyra Cafe** serves dinner on temple fragments, preserving a bygone era of European decadence. Many rooms have views of the temple (some with balconies) and are cooled by valley breezes. Singles L£57,000; doubles L£79,500; triples L£94,500.

FOOD

Cheap Middle Eastern sandwich shops line **Rue Hajar.** Quality outdoor restaurants serving large portions of traditional Lebanese *mezze* and grills line **Ras al-'Ain Blvd.** Peruse the bill carefully, as some restaurants specialize in ripping off tourists.

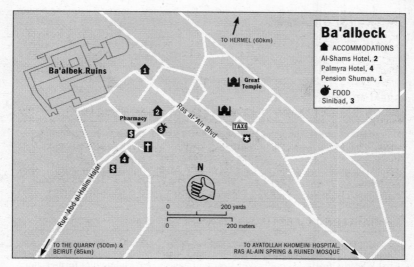

Sindibad (☎ 37 02 71), next to Ghassan Pharmacy on Rue Hajar. Best eatery on the street. No English sign, but you can't miss the shawarma spit. Friendly owner wraps up a variety of meat and vegetable sandwiches for L£1500-2500. Open daily 8am-11pm.

Asyla Cafe (☎ 371 356), on Rue Hajar across the street from the Palmyra Hotel. Garden-side view of the temples that can also be enjoyed by night. Colorful Lebanese decor. A full meal is a bit pricey (L£18,000 per person), but *mezze* (L£2500) and coffee let you enjoy the atmosphere. Open in summer only, noon-11:30 pm; later on festival nights.

Ananas Restaurant, also on Rue Hajar. Unique sandwich combinations and fresh juices at reasonable prices.

Jawhari Cafe (☎ 373 943), across the park from Ras al-'Ain Blvd. Outdoor seating serving ice cream (L£500), *argileh* and coffee. A few pension-style **rooms** (US$10 per person) available. Open daily 9am-11pm.

👁 SIGHTS

■ **TEMPLE COMPLEX.** The tourism office just outside the gate has a free brochure with a simple map of the site and brief historical background. To gain a more thorough appreciation of the magnitude of the temples and their construction, it is a good idea to visit the free **museum** before entering the ruins. Check out the displays featuring site reconstructions and information on how the great stones were cut, moved, and erected.

Visitors enter the Temple Complex through the **Propylaea** and **Hexagonal Court,** two structures added in the 3rd century to introduce the **Great Court** and sacrificial **altar** that follow after them. The entrance, like the majority of the complex, was once covered with a cedar roof and tiled with mosaics. Six 22.9m Corinthian columns are all that remain of the 54 columns that once supported the famous **Temple of Jupiter.** Each column is made up of three stone pieces joined by small bronze pegs, whose sockets are carved only 30cm deep into the stone. No mortar was used in the temples, so each stone had to be perfectly hewn to fit its neighbors.

The **Temple of Bacchus,** parallel to the much larger Temple of Jupiter, is the best-preserved building in the complex; its size and the intricate detail of its adornments make it one of the world's greatest surviving Roman temples. Completed in the 2nd century CE, the temple was dedicated to Venus, but exquisite reliefs of grapes and poppies on the main door indicate that it probably belonged to a cult of

LEBANON

Bacchus, whose members were infamous for drinking wine and smoking opium during rituals. (*Let's Go* does not recommend opium.) Several meters above eye level in the temple interior, 19th-century graffiti marks the level where earth buried the temple before excavation began in 1898. The circular **Temple of Venus,** facing the present-day entrance, is much smaller than the site's other temples and a fence prevents visitors from entering. *(Temples open daily 8:30am until 30min. before sunset. L£10,000; students L£2500. Museum open 9am-5pm. Free.)*

GREAT MOSQUE. An ancient house of worship in its own right, the Great Mosque seems positively youthful compared with the Roman temples it faces. Originally built as a Byzantine church dedicated to St. John, the edifice was adapted by the Umayyads around 700 CE using material borrowed from ancient monuments.

ROMAN QUARRY. The stones used to construct the behemoth temples at Ba'albeck were hewn from this quarry, opposite a large new mosque off Rue Hajar in the direction of Beirut. Most of the stones were cut from **Hajar al-Hubla,** or "Pregnant Woman's Stone." Weighing 2000 tons and measuring 22x5x4m, the stone is rumored to (noticeably) influence the fertility of any woman who touches it.

🎵 BA'ALBECK FESTIVAL

Inaugurated in 1956, the Ba'albeck Festival has hosted celebrity artists including Duke Ellington, Ella Fitzgerald, Rudolf Nureyev, and Joan Baez. Silenced by the Lebanese Civil War, the festival reopened in 1997 and has since reclaimed its former glory. Blockbuster performances begin early in July and continue through late August. Buy tickets well in advance as only 5000 seats are available in the Great Court. Showtime is usually 8pm. Tickets (L£30,000-200,000) are available online at **www.trading-places.com.lb** or by phone from several outlets in Beirut, Tripoli, and Ba'albeck. In Beirut, call Sodeco Square's **Bloc C** (☎01 611 600). Tickets prices will double if you wait to buy from scalpers at the gate. **Tania Travel** provides transportation from Beirut, departing between 4-5pm from three locations (☎01 616 555; L£10,000). Buses and *service* are also available from Beirut's Cola Bridge for about the same price.

🏛 DAYTRIPS FROM BA'ALBECK

RAS BA'ALBECK رأس بعلبك

*To get to Ras Ba'albeck, take a **minibus** north from Ba'albeck (L£1000) or south from Hermel or Nahr al-Assi (L£500). Drivers drop you off at a turnoff 1km from the town's center.*

Ras Ba'albeck ("head of Ba'albeck") acquired its name because it provides a vantage point on all of northern Beqa'a, scrunched against the base of the Anti-Lebanon Range. Romans used it as an outpost to identify attacking armies. Today, it is one of the few Christian pockets in the heavily Muslim region of northern Beqa'a.

The **Melkite (Greek Catholic) Monastery,** along the main street on the east side of town, is Ras Ba'albeck's main attraction. Ancient stonework on the bottom of the southern wall betrays its Roman builders. In 1759 CE, an earthquake destroyed most of the original structure, leaving only the small chapel built in 1111. The monastery was rebuilt soon after the earthquake, and was reconstructed for the last time in 1943. A **museum** features various Roman, early Christian, Byzantine, and Melkite artifacts. A small garden behind the monastery shelters remains of various Roman structures. (☎21 04 84. No official hours; call ahead or arrive 10am-4pm.)

The ruins of a **Roman temple** rest on the left side of the road into town. Little preservation work has been done, but the altar area is in decent shape and the rest of the site is worth a walk-through. Don't miss the few old houses still standing proudly amidst the drab concrete of the main street.

Ras Ba'albeck has few accommodations, but several small sandwich shops dot the main drag near the center of town. On the northwest corner of the intersection of the highway and the main road, **Restaurant Abou-Khalaf's** multilingual staff assembles delicious sandwiches for L£2000-3000. (☎21 00 62. Open 24hr.)

HERMEL حرمل

*To get to Hermel, take a **minibus** north from Ba'albeck (L£3000). Deir Mar al-Maroun is located on a turnoff about 10km south of Hermel. Heading north on the main road to Hermel, the turnoff will be on the left, 1.5km south of Hermel Pyramid, which is visible for miles around. It is a 3km walk to the monastery from the intersection with the main road. Continuing north on the main road, the pyramid will be on your right about 600m off the road. If walking doesn't appeal to you, private **taxis** can be hired from Hermel to take you to the pyramid and back (US$15-20).*

The northernmost city in the Beqa'a, Hermel is a green haven amidst the dry plains of the north. Once a Hezbollah stronghold, the city grew rapidly during the Lebanese Civil War, functioning as a safe haven for Shi'ites fleeing the fighting. After the war, Hermel became a hub for drug and counterfeit currency trade. Since 1998, the town has been under the firm control of Syrian and Lebanese authorities pledging funds to provide economic support. Though Hermel itself is nothing special, its ruins are quite captivating.

Deir Mar Maroun, on a cliff overlooking Nahr al-Assi (Assi River) several kilometers south of Hermel, is intimately linked to the early days of Maronite Catholicism (see **Religion and Ethnicity,** p. 503). St. Maron, founder of the Maronite order, established the monastery in the 5th century CE as a haven for his persecuted followers. In later centuries, Muslims used the monastery as a fortress. The grotto has a high and low chamber; the lower chamber is easily reached, but the higher requires a tricky climb up a short, creviced rock face. Ambitious explorers can ascend still farther to the upper chamber's second (but not third) level, via a spiral staircase. Be very **careful** entering the upper chamber; there is a 100m well to the left of the doorway. Also, bats tend to nest on the second floor, so before entering you may have to duck low for a while as they evacuate. No worries—the bats feast only on insects and fruit. It is not a good idea to go alone; the area is a bit challenging and rarely frequented. Be sure to bring a **flashlight.**

A gravel road at the monastery's base leads to the shady banks of the river; either direction will take you to the fresh spring water.

Just north of the turnoff to the monastery and visible for miles around is a large box-like stone structure capped by a pyramid. The structure, estimated to be over 2000 years old, is known as the **Hermel Pyramid,** or "Haram Hermel." Although its origin remains a mystery, obscure hunting scenes on all four faces have led many to speculate that it is a tomb marker for an unknown Syrian prince.

AL-JORD الجرد

Nestled in the mountains 86km east of Tripoli between Hermel and Akkar, al-Jord is an "ecolodge" that covers 500km sq. of forest at altitudes of several thousand meters. From this beautiful spot, you can see the summit of Qornet al-Sawda above, and peek down at the Mediterranean Sea below. Run by a new community-based tourism company, al-Jord offers a range of outdoor activities in the Beqa'a Valley region, aiming at the same time to preserve its ecological and cultural resources. The company organizes 1-3 day treks throughout the valley, and can arrange horseback riding, mountain-biking, rock-climbing and spelunking adventures. Options for (eco)lodging include basic huts, stone houses (up to 6 people), Bedouin-style tents, and cheap camping (US$6-20 per person). Visitors are picked up free from Hermel, Sir al-Dinniye (L£1500 *service* ride from Tripoli), and occasionally Beirut. For more information, contact Imm Henri Qassir, 8 Rue Choucri Assali, Acharafieh, Beirut (☎/fax 01 336 820; mobile 03 235 303 or 03 764 048; info@aljord.com; www.aljord.com).

ZAHLÉ زحلة ☎ 08

Known locally as the "Bride of the Beqa'a," Zahlé is an enchanting red-roofed city renowned for its food and wine, and for the work of its food-consuming, wine-imbibing poets. The primarily Greek Orthodox Christian town has several interesting Ottoman-era houses and religious buildings that survived the civil war.

TRANSPORTATION. From Beirut, Zahlé is accessible by **service** from Cola Bridge (L₤7000). Alternatively, **minivans** from Cola Bridge will take you to Shtawra (L₤1000); from there, *service* continue north to Zahlé (L₤1000). From Ba'albeck, **minivans** traveling to Shtawra or Beirut can drop you off along the way (L₤1000).

ORIENTATION AND PRACTICAL INFORMATION. The city spreads along both banks of the **Bardaouni River,** with the older section of town on the higher ground of the west bank and the shopping district on the east bank. **Rue Brazil** is the main street in town, with **Rue Ste. Barbara** running parallel. At the northern end of Zahlé (a 20-30min. walk from the city's traffic circle), is a famed area of the Bardouni River known as **Wadi al-Aarayesh** ("Grapevine Valley"). Accessible only by foot, the valley is home to legendary outdoor restaurants serving traditional Lebanese grills and *mezze.*

Local services in Zahlé, including **banks** and the **post office,** are all clustered around the city center on Rue Brazil alongside the river. **Dataland Internet Cafe** is next door to the Banque du Liban, also on Rue Brazil. In an emergency, call the police (☎803 521) or an ambulance (☎824 892).

ACCOMMODATIONS. Along with its fine wine and poetry, Zahlé is known for its old houses, several of which have been turned into budget hotels. Situated on Rue Brazil directly across from the Khoury Hospital (a 20min. walk from the main traffic circle), **Hotel Akl** is an inviting 100-year-old home with high ceilings, fans, and sunlit salons. The rooms are kept spotless by friendly, trilingual mother-and-daughter management team. (☎820 701. L₤25,000 per person, with private bath L₤30,000. Tea or coffee L₤1500.) Next door, the similarly bedecked **Hotel Traboulsi,** is run by Umm George (George's mom), and has tidy rooms, baths, big beds, and patio sitting areas. (☎812 661. L₤20,000.)

FOOD. Fine waterside dining is perhaps the best reason to come to Zahlé. Similar restaurants flank both sides of the valley, but the first two you will encounter are among the oldest grandes dames of Lebanese dining. **Casino Arabi** and **Casino Mhanna,** 80 and 100 years old, respectively, are similar in character and share the same fountainside view. Both serve meals for L₤30,000-60,000 per person. Arabi is on the left as you walk upstream. (☎820 144. Open May-Oct. 6:30am-1:30am. AmEx/MC/V.) Mhanna is across the stream from the Arabi on the right side of the main walkway—you can't miss the *saj* baker baking fresh bread. (Open 12:30pm-2:30am. AmEx/MC/V.) For a super-budget meal, grab a sandwich (L₤2500) with freshly squeezed juice or fruit cocktail at **Adonis Cocktails and Sandwiches,** on the left side of the main street facing uphill after the taxi stand. (☎820 329. Open M-Sa 6:30am-10:30pm, Su 6:30am-noon and 5-10:30pm.)

DAYTRIPS FROM ZAHLÉ

KSARA WINERY

*Take a **service** from Zahlé or Shtawra (L₤1000-2000). Get out when you see the large "Caves de Ksara" sign and a beautiful vineyard. To get a service back to Zahlé or Shtawra, ask to be pointed to Ksara Village.*

The prized home of *Le vin du Liban,* Ksara Village lies just south of Zahlé. Although there are several wineries in the village, the most famous is the world renowned Ksara Winery (Caves de Ksara). The wine of Ksara was first produced by an order of Jesuit monks who discovered the caves in 1856. By 1973, Ksara had built a reputation for *the* wine of Lebanon. Soaked in prosperity, the Jesuits were forced to sell the winery when the Second Vatican Council ordered that the church no longer participate in commercial activities. Ksara offers free three-part guided **tours** in English, French, or Arabic. The visit begins in the caves winding through an extensive labyrinth of tunnels totalling nearly 2km. First discovered and enlarged by the Romans, the tunnels naturally remain at a constant 11 to 13 degrees Celsius—the ideal natural conditions that are believed to be the secret to the delicately aged wine. Bottles of wine dating back to 1918 and cognac dating back to 1910 are preserved in the tunnels by a natural mold that protects the cork from decay. The tour ends with a video and wine tasting. (☎ 813 495. Open daily 9am-7pm; in winter M-Sa 9am-4pm.)

ANJAR عنجر

Service from Shtawra run to Mafra' Anjar (L£1000-2000); signs direct you down a 500m road to the site. Site open daily 7am-7pm; L£6000.

While most archaeological sites in Lebanon reveal a rich layering of civilizations over time, Anjar is unique in that it was built exclusively by the Umayyads. The Umayyads were the first hereditary dynasty to rule after the Prophet Muhammad's death and are generally credited with earliest conquests that established the Islamic Empire (see **From Hellenism to Islam**, p. 49). Founded by Caliph Walid ibn 'Abd al-Malik between 705 and 715 CE, Anjar flourished for only a few decades before fading back into the fertile land from whence it emerged. Although short-lived, Anjar's sprawl was extensive, covering a staggering 114,000m sq. Following a Roman layout, the site is almost a perfect square with two perpendicular roads crossing in the center. The **Cardo Maximus** runs north-south, and the **Decumanus Maximus** runs east-west. Four **tetrapylons** mark the intersection, one of which has been reconstructed with its trademark four columns. Both main roads are lined with a partially reconstructed columned arcade, flanked by about 600 shops. Past the tetrapylon on the left is the **mosque** and monumental **Great Palace.**

Besides with its ruins, Anjar is famous for its trout ponds and fresh fish **restaurants,** many located on the ponds themselves. To get there, follow the fish signs visible from the entrance to the ruins. It is about 3km to the heart of the ponds.

SOUTH OF BEIRUT

▨ BEIT AL-DIN بيت الدين

Beit al-Din is 17km down the coastal highway south of Beirut and 26km inland. Accessible from Cola Bridge in Beirut by **service** (1hr., L£4000) or A/C **bus** (1 hr., L£3000). Slightly cheaper **microbuses** (L£500) run to "Mafra' Damour," also called "Mafra' Beit al-Din," at the intersection with the coastal highway. From there take a service to Beit al-Din (L£2000). Service that travel this route can drop you off at **Deir al-Qamar, Musa's Castle,** or any other point along the way. The Beirut tourist office has a brochure and map of the palace. Palace and museums open Tu-Su 9am-6pm. L£7500, students studying in Lebanon L£2000.

The palace at **Beit al-Din** (House of Faith) is a breathtaking example of 19th-century Italian-influenced Baroque architecture. Built over a 30-year period by Emir Bechir al-Shehab II, ruler of Mt. Lebanon for over half a century, it bears triumphant testimony to his long reign. Near the entrance on the ground floor is the **Jumblatt Museum,** dedicated to the life of Druze leader Kamal Jumblatt. A Parliament member and cabinet minister, Jumblatt founded the Progressive Socialist Party in 1949. The collection contains photographs, correspondence with world leaders, and personal mementos. To the right of the entrance to the outer courtyard (Dar al-Baraniyya, where courtiers once mingled) is the two-story **al-Madafa,** originally used for receiving guests and now home to two museums. It is said that visitors to the palace were luxuriously hosted for at least three days in these quarters before being asked their identity or the reason for their visit. On the ground level is an exhibit of photographs by well-known Lebanese and European shutterbugs. Upstairs, the long corridors of the **Rashid Karami Archaeological and Ethnographic Museum** culminate in a model of the palace complex.

The middle section of the palace (directly ahead, with al-Madafa on the right) leads to a large courtyard complete with a fountain and countryside view. Surrounding the courtyard are the richly furnished reception rooms used by the Emir Bechir's secretaries. Notice the soldiers guarding the building in front of you.

Handpicked to guard the president's summer house, they are better dressed and taller than most Lebanese soldiers. Named **Dar al-Harim,** this building once housed the private apartments of the emir. To the right of the presidential pad is the palace's **hammam,** and beyond the baths lies the tomb of **Sitt Chams,** the emir's first wife. (The emir's ashes were added in 1947.) The lower portion of the palace overlooks a beautiful terrace and houses an extensive collection of Byzantine mosaics, most of which were excavated from a church in Jiyyeh.

In addition to his own palace, Emir Bechir built a palace for each of his three sons—Qassim, Khalil, and Amine. Qassim's palace is now in ruins, and Khalil's is used as Beit al-Din's seat of local government. **Emir Amine Palace** is perched on the hill above Beit al-Din a 15min. climb from the ruins, and is now a fully restored luxury hotel with 24 magnificent rooms. The facade of the central courtyard is among the palace's most beautiful features. The courtyard has an elegant pool and lounging space. It may be hard to justify spending L£185,000 for a single or L£220,000 for a double during high season, but the prices are slashed by 50% October-early June. (☎05 501 315. AmEx/V.) The hotel has three restaurants serving Middle Eastern and international cuisine. **Al-Diwan Terrace** has a great view of the valley, but it unfortunately comes at a steep price (sandwiches L£8100-11,600; soft drinks L£3500). **Al-Hatemia Restaurant,** near the main square, is more affordable. (☎500 526. Grilled sandwiches L£2500. Beer L£3000 at table, L£2000 to go. Open daily 7:30am-4am.) There are also a number of snack stands around the palace.

Beit al-Din Festival, held every July and August in the palace's outdoor courtyard, draws thousands of visitors and features internationally renowned musicians. Performances in 2001 included Elton John and the legendary Lebanese diva Fairuz (see p. 504). Tickets (L£30,000-200,000) available from the Starco Center in the Beirut central district or online at www.beiteddine.org.

DEIR AL-QAMAR

*Reached by **service** en route to Beit al-Din ☎05 512 777. Open daily 9am-8pm. L£6000.*

This peaceful, red-roofed mountain village, whose name means "monastery of the moon," is home to the **Palace of Fakhr al-Din** and **Marie Baz Wax Museum.** The palace was built in 1620 in Fakhr al-Din's chosen capital (on the Emir's historical legacy, see **p. 501**). Four years ago, its present owners, the Baz family, decided to transform the lower rooms into a wax museum. The collection is growing rapidly, with new figures of Charles de Gaulle, Yasser Arafat, and Hezbollah general secretary Hassan Nassrallah expected to join the ranks of Pope John Paul II and former US president George Bush. At the museum's entrance stands a wax life-sized figure of Fakhr al-Din. Just outside of the museum is Fakhr al-Din's prized **Silk Khan,** while across the road stand the **Serail of Youssef Chehab** and **Mosque of Fakhr al-Din.** For a post-palace snack, Malkat al-Saj (loosely, "the Burrito Queen"), has a stand in the Silk Khan near the road, where she transforms simple cheese and za'atar *saj* wraps into decorative art. (Stand open daily 7:30am-3pm, often later.)

MUSA'S CASTLE

1km past Deir al-Qamar on the main road to Beit al-Din. Open daily 8am-7pm. L£6000.

As a child, Musa dreamed of living in a castle. His dream never died, and after years of doing hard labor and saving money, he began building the castle by hand. Thirty-five years later, the 70-year old Musa can still be spotted chiseling intricate engravings upon each stone of the fairy-tale castle of his dreams. A drawbridge crosses the moat to the entrance, where amusing mechanical displays depict traditional Lebanese activities and moments from Musa's life. At the end of the tour, a man serves Turkish coffee brewed in a charcoal pit.

▨ SHOUF CEDAR RESERVE

*There are 3 points of entry to the Shouf Cedar Reserve: 1 in Barouk, 1 in 'Ain Zhalta, and 1 in Masser al-Shouf. Barouk is the easiest to access by public transportation. From Mafra' Damour, several **service** will continue past Beit al-Din to Barouk (L£3000). Trek* *agencies in Beirut can arrange transportation and tours (see p. 515). To enter on your own, you must first visit the information office located next to the Barouk Palace Hotel near the center of town. The Reserve provides transportation from the hotel. All* **hikes** *are led by guides along a developing trail network. L£5000 on foot for a 30min. loop; L£10,000 for longer hikes and 4WD tours. www.shoufcedar.org. Open daily 9am-6pm.*

Under government protection since 1996, the Shouf Cedar Reserve is home to the world's southernmost cedar trees. The reserve covers 5% of Lebanon's land, and contains the majority of the country's species diversity. There are three separate forests in the reserve (corresponding to the three points of entry), each with a different mix of flora. The **Barouk forest** is the oldest and has the highest concentration of cedars. It is home to a famous cedar known as al-Khityara (the Old One), said to be the model for the tree on the Lebanese flag. Near the town of Niha in the **Masser al-Shouf forest** is the cave to which Fakhr al-Din fled from the Ottomans (see p. 501). **'Ain Zhalta** is the youngest forest with a great number of trees planted during re-forestation efforts.

Camping in the reserve will be available beginning in the summer of 2002 at the **Cedar Camp.** All-season tents come equipped with beds, sheets, and solar power. Toilets and showers are free; telescopes, tennis, basketball, and volleyball are available for a small fee. Call for transport information and arrangements. (☎ 03 806 026 or 05 240 730. Breakfast included. US$10 per night.)

In September 2001, the Shouf Cedar Reserve was host to its first **Cairn to Cairn Mountain Marathon.** The marathon may become an annual event; call for details.

SA'IDA (SIDON) صيدا ☎ 07

The largest city in South Lebanon, Sa'ida is an expansive port and commercial center. Although much of modern Sa'ida is concrete construction, the land surrounding the city is flanked by banana and citrus plantations. The town's foundations recall its days as Sidon, one of the three great Phoenician city-states (along with Byblos and Tyre). Unfortunately, the majority of Sidon's ancient artifacts were plundered by treasure hunters in the 19th century and sold on the black market. The port flourished in the Phoenician era (12th-10th centuries BCE) and peaked during the occupation of the Achaemenid Persians (550-330 BCE). Although glass was its biggest industry, Sidon also achieved fame alongside Tyre for textiles dyed with the purple extract of Murex snail shells (see **To Dye For,** p. 555). Like other Phoenician city-states, Sidon suffered under a succession of conquerors, including Alexander the Great, the Romans, the Crusaders, and Salah al-Din. Sa'ida fell into obscurity during the French Mandate, but has been revived as an urban center over the past century.

Modern Sidon is not as fun-filled as its ancient incarnation, but its neighborhoods maintain a pleasant small town air. Mediocre places to stay and a nonexistent nightlife conspire to make Sa'ida's ruins ideally visited as a day trip from Beirut or Sur. The *souq* is one of the liveliest in Lebanon and, for those with patience and a careful eye, full of treasures.

▐ TRANSPORTATION

Buses and Service: Depart from Sahet al-Nejmeh on Rue Riad al-Solh for **Sur** (Tyre) (buses L£500, *service* L£2500). Buses go to Sa'ida from Cola Bridge in **Beirut** (L£1000). *Service* also run to **Shtawra** (L£7500) in the Beqa'a Valley.

▟ ORIENTATION AND PRACTICAL INFORMATION

Though Sa'ida is large, almost all sights (and the only hotel) fall within a small area. Lined with banks, shops, and pastry stands, **Rue Riad al-Solh** is the main north-south road through town. Buses and *service* arrive and depart from **Sahet al-Nejmeh,** the main traffic circle at the north end of Rue Riad al-Solh. The street continues south past Sahet al-Nejmeh and becomes **Rue Fakhr al-Din** near the **Castle of**

St. Louis. Heading toward the castle, a right turn off Riad al-Solh leads to **Rue Shakrieh,** home to the only hotel in Sa'ida. Follow Rue Shakrieh south to reach the Castle of St. Louis and north (toward the sea) to reach the **Sea Castle.**

Currency Exchange: Kotob Exchange (☎ 720 322), just south of Sahet al-Nejmeh. One of the few places that exchanges traveler's checks. L£3000 charge per check. Open M-Sa 8:30am-2pm, F 8:30am-noon.

Emergency: Police (☎ 112); **Ambulance** (☎ 140).

Pharmacy: Atef Bissat (☎ 721 821), across the street from the Kotob Exchange. Longest hours in town. Staff speaks English and French. Open daily 8am-10:30pm.

Hospital: Hamoud Hospital (☎ 723 111 or 721 021) is the best in Sidon.

Internet Access: PC Net (☎ 721 218), 150m north of the post office on the left. L£3000. Open daily 9:30am-2am.

Post Office: 200m north of Sahet al-Nejmeh (toward Beirut) on the left of Rue Riad al-Solh. Open M-Th 8am-2pm, F 8am-1pm.

■ ACCOMMODATIONS

Hotel d'Orient (☎ 720 364), on Rue Shakrieh 200m south of the Sea Castle. Arabic sign: نازل الشرق, (Nazel al-Sharq). The only hotel in Sa'ida. Dorm-style rooms have grimy floors and mattresses, and unpleasant communal bathroom. Private rooms are cleaner with TVs and fans. Dorms L£15,000; singles L£20,000; doubles L£30,000.

Mounes Hotel (☎ 03 666 657; fax 07 390 607; fakihco@cyberia.net.lb), halfway between Sa'ida and Sur in Sarafand. Hop a bus or *service* bound for Sur and ask to get out at the Mounes. The 4-star hotel is a splurge, but comes with a saltwater pool, dock for ocean swimming, outdoor restaurant, private baths, refrigerators, and A/C. Call in advance as rooms are usually booked on summer weekends. Singles L£45,000; doubles L£60,000; triples L£75,000. Pool L£5000 for non-guests; children L£3000.

■ FOOD

Food options in Sa'ida are unspectacular, with few exceptions. Pastries are easy to find in stands across town. The city is especially famous for a sugar cookie-like treat known as *señora*. Local legend has it that a beautiful Spanish immigrant introduced the recipe to the town; since she was known as "the mysterious *señora*," the cookie assumed her name.

Rest House (☎ 722 469). This government-owned eatery is the best in town. Outdoor patio seating amid palm trees, with views of the Sea Castle. Salads L£3000-7500. Meat or fish entrees L£5500-17,000. Tourist menu L£18,000 (tax included, for groups of 6 or more). Add 20% tax. Open daily 11am-midnight. MC/V.

Al-'Arabi (☎ 720 342), the 1st restaurant when coming from Beirut, about 2km north of central Sa'ida on the right side of Rue Riad al-Solh. *Mezze* and entree L£15,000 per person. Beer L£3000. Cocktails L£7500. Open daily noon-midnight. AmEx/MC/V.

'Aroosat Kheyzaran (☎ 03 249 231), in Sarafand, 350m up the main road toward Sa'ida on the left side. No English sign. Specializes in weddings. Free pool and deck. Fish and *mezze* for 2 L£15,000-20,000. Open daily noon-midnight.

Patisserie Kanaan (☎ 720 271), on the right just south of Sahet al-Nejmeh. Famous for *señoras* and a secret ice cream recipe (large L£3000). Open daily 5am-midnight.

◎ SIGHTS

Developed at the end of the Crusader period, the **Old City** contains numerous *souqs, khans,* and other medieval remnants. The main attraction in Sa'ida proper is the **Sea Castle,** a Crusader fortress built in 1228 on a small island connected to the shore by a stone walkway. The southwestern tower combines Crusader and Mamluk influences. A small Ottoman-era mosque sits atop the northeastern Crusader tower. Fishermen mend their nets on the beach by the entrance.

TO DYE FOR Since antiquity, the royal wardrobes of the world have been made from fabrics of the deepest purple hue. The color's regal associations originated off the coast of Lebanon near Sidon and Tyre, where two species of **mollusk**, *Murex* and *Buccinum*, live in great numbers. Legend has it that the intense purple ink within their shells was discovered when the lovesick god **Melkart** was wooing the nymph **Tyrus.** One day, Melkart's dog playfully bit into a shell and his muzzle turned purple. Tyrus then demanded that Melkart make her a purple garment from the shell in exchange for some bootay. Melkart quickly pulled some strings, establishing a precedent for the dye's importance in trade and romance. Phoenician production of purple dye was considerably more complex and messy, and probably less rewarding. Narrow-necked baskets baited with frog or mussel meat were placed in the sea; when mollusks gathered, they were brought to the factories. The yellowish sacs, which turn purple when exposed to light, were removed and boiled in lead pots. The Phoenicians did not like to clean up after themselves—shell refuse now forms the 50m high Murex Hill.

Khan al-Franj (Inn of the French), across the road from the Sea Castle near the entrance to the *souqs*, is a beautifully restored *khan* representative of Fakhr al-Din's work to encourage economic exchange with France. Today, the *khan* serves as Sa'ida's cultural center. Next door to the Hotel d'Orient is the **Sidon Soap Museum,** a landmark in the city. The museum is one of a kind in Lebanon, displaying historical artifacts and soaps from Sa'ida, Tripoli, and Aleppo. The soap museum also gives out two very useful maps of the city. (☎ 733 353. Open daily 9am-6pm.) A cafe adjoined to the museum serves coffee and *señora* (L₤2000).

The *souqs* lie between the Sea Castle and the **Castle of St. Louis,** a ruined 13th-century castle erected on top of a Fatimid fortress during a crusade led by French King Louis IX. Locals call it al-Muizz Citadel, as it was restored by Muizz al-Din, a Fatimid caliph. The castle is at the end of Rue Shekrieh heading away from the sea. Unfortunately, the interior of the castle has been locked for several years with little hope of reopening soon. **Murex Hill** (see To Dye For, p. 555), is just south of the Castle of St. Louis and is partially covered by a cemetery. The **Great Mosque** (Al-Omari Mosque), is south of the *souq*. Ask locals in the *souq* for directions. Originally built during the Crusades, the building was converted into a mosque by the Mamluks. Most of the current structure is new, rebuilt after suffering damage during the Israeli invasion of 1982.

🔲 DAYTRIP FROM SA'IDA: TEMPLE OF ECHMOUN

*On **foot** from Sa'ida, follow Rue Riad al-Solh north, with the beach on the left. After the fairgrounds, take a right and then bear left following the bank of the river. The temple is on the left. **Taxis** cost about L₤4000 from Sa'ida; ask for Bustan al-Sheikh. If you are planning to visit both the Temple of Echmoun and Sa'ida in the same day from Beirut, you will save time and distance by getting dropped off at the intersection that leads to the Temple of Echmoun first, and then continue into town. Open daily 8am-6pm. Free.*

Known locally as Bustan al-Sheikh, the ◼Temple of Echmoun is about 2.5km out of town along the rushing Nahr al-Awali. Dedicated to Echmoun, the god of healing and rejuvenation, the temple complex is the only Phoenician site in Lebanon that has retained more than just its foundations. At the far end of the site is the **healing basin** where most of Echmoun's miracles took place. Families would often present small marble statues of their cured children at the temple, several of which are on display at the National Museum in Beirut (see p. 522). The Greeks associated Echmoun's healing powers with Asklepios, their god of medical arts, and he was often depicted holding a staff with coiled snake. The modern medical symbol, or *caduceus* (a staff intertwined with two serpents), is thought to derive from this symbolic representation of Echmoun. The large, pyramidal temple is the oldest part of the complex, while the colonnade, surrounded on both sides by mosaics, is a later Roman addition. Climb to the top of the temple for a view of the surrounding land. Perhaps the most intriguing piece in the complex is the **Throne of Astarte,** carved out of granite and flanked by two sphinxes. Ancient myth tells how Astarte (the Phoenician equivalent of Aphrodite and Venus) fell madly in love with the dashing Echmoun. Interested in nothing but hunting, the young Echmoun mutilated himself to escape her love. Refusing to give up, Astarte brought him back to life as a god. The throne is on the right near the stairs of the temple.

SUR (TYRE) صور ☎ 07

The modern city of Sur sits alongside and atop the remains of the ancient Phoenician city-state of Tyre, 80km south of Beirut. When Herodotus, "Father of History," visited Tyre's Temple of Hercules in the 5th century BCE, the port city had already been in existence for nearly 3000 years. Tyre originally sprawled over two islands and the mainland. In the 10th century BCE, King Hiram joined the two islets with a landfill. Later, in a protracted siege to take the city, Alexander the Great used the ruins accumulated in his destruction of the mainland to build a causeway to the island. Over the years, the debris sedimented, and the ancient island became the modern-day peninsula. The city was as powerful as it was old; during the golden era of Phoenician civilization, the Mediterranean Sea became known as the Tyrian Sea. Worn by royalty throughout the ancient world (including Shakespeare's fictional Pericles), Tyre's purple-dyed textiles became a powerful mark of wealth. One gram of dye extracted from Murex mollusks was worth 10-20 grams of gold. Sur's long history would not be complete without the requisite list of invaders and conquerors: Tyreans resisted Babylonian Nebuchadnezzar for 13 years in the 6th century BCE, but they didn't do so well against Alexander in the 4th century BCE, the Romans in 64 BCE, the Umayyads in 634 CE, the Crusaders in 1124, the Mamluks in 1291, or the Ottomans in the 16th century.

Today, the old port remains relatively unspoiled. At sunset, fishermen set out with elaborate basket traps to await the bounty of the sea. Rolling with the waves through the dark hours of the night, they return at dawn with just enough time to prepare the fish for market. Towering over the Mediterranean, Sur claims an some of the impressive ruins in Lebanon, including one of the largest Roman hippodromes ever found, an extensive necropolis, and parts of the ancient agora.

▐ TRANSPORTATION

Buses: A/C Pullman (L£1500) and minibuses (L£500) run between Sur and Sa'ida. From Beirut, Pullman buses (L£2500-3000) and minibuses (L£2000) go to Sa'ida; from there, you can pick up a ride to Sur.

Service: Direct *service* run between Beirut's Cola Bridge and Sur (L£5000-6000).

✴ ▐ ORIENTATION AND PRACTICAL INFORMATION

Modern Sur rests on a promontory that was once an island but has long since been silted over. The two harbors are named for the directions they face—the **Sidonian harbor** to the north and the **Egyptian harbor** to the south. The **taxi stand** and **bus station** are in the center of town, a few meters from the Sidonian port. Walking south from the taxi stand toward the Egyptian harbor, take the first left to reach **Rue Abu Dib,** Sur's main shopping thoroughfare. The first right off this street leads to the unfortunately named **Area I** ruins, also called Assar Ja'afariyya. A 25min. walk farther along Abu Dib leads to Sur's highlight, the **Roman Ruins (Area III),** known as Assar Romaniyya. When entering the ruins, the **Rest House** is 150m toward the sea.

Currency Exchange: Bank Audi, between the post office and pharmacy, has an **ATM.**

Emergency: Police: ☎ 740 009. **Ambulance:** ☎ 140.

Pharmacy: Saed Pharmacy (☎ 344 227), the 2nd pharmacy down the street with the post office on the right. Helpful staff speak English and French. Open M-Sa 8:30am-9pm; Su pharmacies in town open by rotation.

Telephones: In the same building as the post office. Open 24hr. L£1500 per min. to US; L£500 per 3min. locally.

Internet Access: Cafe Net (☎03 846 097), next to Hotel Elyssia on the sea, along the Egyptian harbor. Open daily 9am-1am. **Alpha Net** is north of the main traffic circle on Rue Abu Dib. With Restaurant Abu Dib on your left, head straight across the traffic circle. Open 10:30am-1am. Both charge L£2000 per hr.

Post Office: (☎740 018), 200m east of the taxi stand across from the UN building on Rue Bawaba. **Poste Restante** available. Open M-F 8am-5pm, Sa 8-1:30 pm.

ACCOMMODATIONS

Hotel Fanar (☎741 111), on the water next to the lighthouse. Follow signs from the port. Clean, homey rooms overlooking the sea come with breakfast, private bath, and A/C. Restaurant serves fresh fish (about US$15 for a full meal with *mezze*). Recently extended its services to the beachfront; look for #100 at the far end.

Rest House (☎740 677; fax 345 163; www.resthouse-tyr.com.lb), luxurious A/C rooms with porches opening onto the beach. Singles and doubles US$98; F-Su US$256. Non-guests can use pool, whirlpool, and sauna for L£10,000; F-Su L£15,000. AmEx/MC/V.

Murex Hotel (☎34 71 11), about 200m north of Area I. Directly across the street from the beach. Singles L£105,000, in winter L£67,500; doubles L£127,500, in winter L£82,500. 10% student discount. AmEx/MC/V.

FOOD AND ENTERTAINMENT

Cheap eateries cluster around the taxi stand and throughout the *souq*. Nightlife in Sur tends to revolve around smoking *argileh*, sipping coffee, and licking ice cream by the sea. Facing the water from the lighthouse at the tip of the peninsula turn left towards the Egyptian port to find the city's main park. The **public beach** in Sur, located south of the Egyptian port, past the Rest House, is one of the best in Lebanon. Part of the beach has been divided up into 100 small restaurants, each owned by a local family. Farther down, there remain untouched tracts of clean sand.

Crab Restaurant (☎03 483 126), on the water in the Sidonian port. Serves *mezze* (L£2000) and fresh fish from a converted boat. Depending on your picks, fish will cost L£15,000-100,000 per kg; 1 kg serves about 4.

Le Phénicien (☎740 564), among the last buildings along the harbor toward the sea. Once owned by Pepe the Pirate (see **Byblos: Food**, p. 532), it was frequented by some of the same jet-setters who chilled at his famous Fishing Club. A Lebanese feast costs L£20,000, and you can cap it off with Almaza for L£2000. Note the inscription by Brigitte Bardot above the bar. Open daily 8am-5pm.

Ali Restaurant (☎741 305), along the seacoast about 250m southeast of Area I. Sandwiches L£2000-3000. Full meals L£10,000. Open daily 7am-11pm.

Pizzeria Italia (☎74 25 62), on Rue Abu Dib, across from Restaurant Abu Dib. Pizzas L£1500-L£9000. Open daily 9am-11pm.

SIGHTS

There are three archaeological sites in Sur, dryly designated as Areas I, II, and III by the Tourism Ministry. Only Areas I and III are open to visitors. Located behind Area I, the Crusader Castle foundations of Area II can be seen from the road.

AREA III (ROMAN RUINS). From the entrance to the site, bear right to reach the main colonnaded east-west road. This path winds through an extensive **necropolis** with Roman and Byzantine marble sarcophagi. Continuing along the road leads to the three-bay **Triumphal Arch,** a postcard favorite marking the entrance to the Roman town. Near the arch are the remains of an **aqueduct** that carried water from Ras al-'Ain, 6km south of the city. Behind the arch is the 480m long **hippodrome**

(once buried under 6m of sand). Check out the stonework underneath the bleachers before climbing the stairs for stellar views on both ends. Imagine yourself lost in a crowd of 20,000 crazy Roman spectators cheering daredevil chariot racers as they dodge and burn seven times around the ever-standing turnstiles. The hippodrome is the world's largest and best preserved of its kind. *(Locally called al-Bas, the site is a 30min. walk from Areas I and II, west of the promontory. Service will take you there for L£1000.* ☎ *740 530. Open daily 8am-7pm, 8am-sunset in winter. L£6000, students L£3500.)*

AREA I. The smaller minor ruins of Area I are filled with swirled colonnades and intricate mosaic floors. Across from the main colonnaded road are the remains of a large, heated Roman bathhouse. Notice the piles of stone discs on the ground: these were used to support a raised floor, or **hypocaust,** that was heated by air flowing underneath. Across the way are remarkably well-preserved living quarters, and the remains of a Roman temple and sarcophagi. This site is famous for its columns dramatically overlooking the sea. Offshore, you will notice what appear to be a series of small islands; they are actually the remains of Phoenician breakwaters. *(Locally called al-Mina.* ☎ *740 115. Open daily 8am-7pm. L£6000, students L£2500.)*

■ DAYTRIPS FROM SUR

TOMB OF HIRAM

On the right hand side of the road from Sur to Qana, a few kilometers before Qana. **Service** *(L£1500-3000) will stop here between the two towns, as will private* **taxis** *(L£5000 to the tomb, L£7000-8000 to Qana).*

The **Tomb of Hiram** is commonly believed to be that of the famous king of Tyre, dating back to 1200-800 BCE. The area around the tomb is littered with rubbish and the tomb itself has been defaced with graffiti. Still, its age, sheer immensity, and accompanying **sarcophagus** make it worth a look. The sarcophagus for Penymer, architect of many (now lost) Phoenician monuments, is in the same style as that of King Ahiram of Jbail, but is now on display at the National Museum in Beirut (p. 522).

QANA قانا

Take a **service** *from Sur (30min., L£2000-3000). Do not stay late, as service are virtually nonexistent at night. On weekends, you may need to hire a private* **taxi** *(L£7000-8000).*

Qana is disputedly the Biblical city of **Cana,** where Jesus is said to have performed his first miracle, transforming water into wine. Many biblical scholars have identified Qana's two adjacent caves as the actual site of this miracle. Recently, the site was transformed into a park, with benches and a path that leads down the valley wall and caves. The first cave contains a carving of a woman believed to be the bride of Qana and is brilliantly named **Woman's Cave.** Carvings of 13 figures on a stone bed nearby are believed to be Jesus and his 12 apostles. Continue down the steps to reach the cave where the miracle itself is said to have occurred, a conclusion first reached in 1976 by Lebanon University archaeologist Yusef Hourani.

A bit over 1km from the grottoes, the heart of Qana captured tragic international attention in 1996, when 102 civilians and UN soldiers were killed and more than 120 injured durning an Israeli shelling of the UN base. By 1996, Israel's decade-long occupation of southern Lebanon began to face increased opposition from Hezbollah guerrillas launching sporadic attacks into northern Israel. In April of 1996, Israel launched "Operation Grapes of Wrath," an air and naval attack aimed to destroy Hezbollah bases in Lebanon. On April 18, the UN peacekeeping base in Qana was sheltering hundreds of civilians from the fighting when Israeli shells struck. Israel maintains that it had not known the base was sheltering civilians and had directed the attack in a defensive strike against Hezbollah guerrillas who had entered the site. However, a UN investigation acquired evidence suggesting that Israel had deliberately targeted the base. The **Qana Memorial** and **Art Museum** were built to commemorate the tragedy. The gatekeeper sleeps in the museum and will open the doors at any time. There is also a moving and graphic photographic collection in a room behind the memorial.

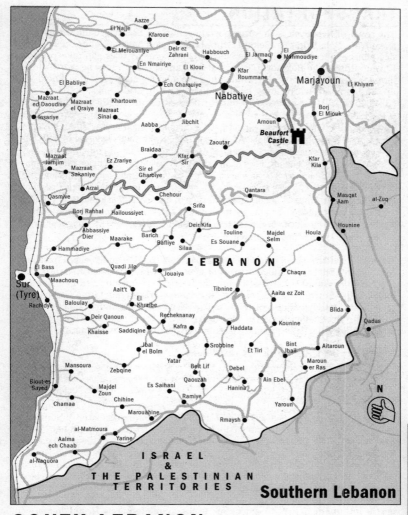

Southern Lebanon

SOUTH LEBANON

South Lebanon witnessed much of the worst fighting during the Lebanese Civil War, and a 60km strip of land along the Israeli border remained under Israeli occupation after the war's end. When the Lebanese army collapsed in 1976, Israel backed the Lebanese Christian forces under Major Sa'ad Haddad. By May 1980, Haddad's troops became known as the South Lebanon Army (SLA), which grew from 2000 soldiers to nearly 10,000 and took control of the region. During the late '90s, the Israeli-SLA alliance met increased resistance from South Lebanon's Shi'ite Muslim majority, in the form of Hezbollah guerrilla attacks on northern Israel. In January 2000, Hezbollah activity intensified, eventually gaining the withdrawal of Israeli troops and the collapse of the SLA. Today, the region—less developed than the rest of Lebanon—is beginning a psychological and economic recovery after years of neglect. With vast stretches of lush, unspoiled land, South Lebanon attracts the majority of its visitors (still mostly Lebanese) on weekends.

TRANSPORTATION

The town of **Nabatiyeh** is the transportation hub for South Lebanon. **Microbuses** leave from Cola Bridge in **Beirut** (1½hr., L£3000) and **Sa'ida** (45min., L£2000); **service** charge twice as much. From Nabatiyeh, *service* or **taxis** can take you to al-Khiyam Prison, the Beaufort Castle, and the Fatima Gate. It may be worthwhile to hire a private taxi for the day—individual fares between destinations quickly add up, and *service* traffic may be infrequent during odd hours. Expect to pay L£35,000-50,000 for a 4hr. taxi around the sites. Fares are highly negotiable.

> **CAUTION!** Since Israel pulled out of South Lebanon in May 2000, the area has been open to visitors. As of August 2001, the south was safe to visit, but travelers should exercise caution by keeping abreast of current events and avoiding travel during times of unrest. A good way to see the region is by daytripping from Beirut or Sur, as tourism is new to the area and accommodations are scarce. Stick to well-traveled roads—there are still **landmines** littering parts of the area. When in doubt, err on the side of caution and **ask locals.** If you feel uncomfortable visiting the south alone, the safest and most hassle-free alternative is to go with an **organized tour** (see **Beirut: Tours,** p. 515). Bring your **passport;** you may need to present it at checkpoints.

If you decide to take a guided tour, **Nakhal Tours** (p. 515) and **Concord Travel** both run one-day English-language trips that leave from Beirut. Concord's office is in the Saroulla Building on Rue Hamra in Beirut. The air-conditioned bus tour includes the Beaufort Castle, al-Khiyam Prison, Marjayoun, and the Fatima Gate. Reserve three days ahead of time. (☎01 340 644. Lunch included. Tours F-Su. L£25,000.) **Destination Liban** (p. 518) and other ecotourism companies can also arrange guided daytrips and hikes to southern destinations, including Mt. Hermon.

BEAUFORT CASTLE قلعة الشقيف

*Aside from organized **tours**, Beaufort Castle can only be reached by private **taxi** (L£10,000-15,000 round-trip from Nabatiyeh). There are no guides at the castle.*

Poised at the top of an cliff 900m above the Litani River valley in Arnoun, the imposing Beaufort Castle (Qal'at al-Shaqif) is a symbol of shifting power in South Lebanon. Built by French Crusaders in 1179 CE, Beaufort was later reinforced by Muslims, who used it as a strategic lookout over the road between Damascus and the Beqa'a Valley. T.E. Lawrence once described it as the finest medieval castle in the Arab world. Unfortunately, recent history has taken its toll on the once-magnificent site. Palestinian guerrillas occupied the castle during the 1970s, and in 1982 it suffered further damage when seized by Israel (it was one of the last sites to be de-occupied by Israeli forces in May 2000). Damage is visible on the exterior and on the two towers now marked by Lebanese and Hezbollah flags. Be careful exploring the interior chambers (the structure is not completely sound), and do not wander from the main castle grounds—the surrounding area may still have **landmines.**

MARJAYOUN مرجعيون ☎ 07

*Catch a **microbus** from Nabatiyeh (L£2000). **Service** are harder to find (L£5000).*

Founded in 1139 CE, Marjayoun ("Spring Meadow") was known for its prosperity before the Israeli conflict. Today, this small town near the Israeli border is a good starting point from which to visit the Fatima Gate or al-Khiyam prison. Uphill from the main square is **St. Georges,** a beautiful Greek Orthodox church. The paintings and chandeliers inside are stunning, but electric candle mania has unfortunately hit this church, lessening the aura of the place. There are no set hours; to be let in, ask a local to take you to Father John Dib.

The **post office** is just off the main square. (Open M-Sa 8am-2pm.) Currently, the only quasi-budget accommodation lies outside of town. The **Racha Hotel,** several kilometers before Marjayoun on the left side of the road from Nabatiyeh, has clean, recently renovated doubles with fridge, private bath, and air-conditioning. (☎ 03 752 426. Breakfast L£7500. Lunch L£15,000. Doubles L£53,000.) Ask your driver to let you off at the hotel before arriving in Marjayoun. For a quick bite to eat, try **Falafel Imad,** 300m from the main square, on the right when walking toward Nabatiyeh. Look for the red-on-white Arabic sign. A falafel sandwich costs L£1500. Several hundred meters south is the **Rajed Restaurant,** which features delicious steak sandwiches for L£2000. (☎ 03 705 653. Open daily 8am-9pm.)

FATIMA GATE باب فاطمة

*Take a **service** from Marjayoun or Nabatiyeh (L£3000-4000). Private **taxis** cost L£12,000-15,000 round-trip. Visitors occasionally encounter trouble getting through the checkpoints on the way to the gate; be sure to have your **passport** on hand.*

Located along the Israeli border in the town of Kfar Kila, Fatima Gate was a border crossing for Lebanese working in Israel during the occupation. It became a prime tourist attraction and darling of international television news during and after the Israeli withdrawal, as thousands of Lebanese, Palestinian, and other Arabs (including Arab-American intellectual Edward Said) gathered to throw stones in the direction of the Israeli border, in controversial symbolic expression of frustration. Today, the site is significantly calmer, attracting mostly Lebanese families on weekend trips. Buy roast corn or a Hezbollah keychain before walking the length of the fortified military post, from which you can look out on Israel.

AL-KHIYAM PRISON سجن الخيم

*Take a **service** (L£3000) or private **taxi** (L£5000) from Marjayoun. Bring a flashlight, as some rooms are dark. Tours in English. Open daily 9am-5pm. Free.*

Originally constructed in 1932 as a camp for French forces, al-Khiyam prison became a detainment camp during the civil war where the SLA held their political enemies. Notorious for torture, the prison is one of the more depressing sights in Lebanon. Soon after the SLA disbanded, al-Khiyam was opened to tourists and has been turned into a memorial museum. All rooms have signs in Arabic and English. Some tours are led by former prisoners, who describe their experiences with solitary confinement, electrical shock torture, and 40-day waits between showers.

HASBAYA حسبايا ☎ 03

Service run to Hasbaya from Marjayoun (L£1500), Nabatiyeh (L£5000), and Beirut (L£12,000). Microbuses run from Marjayoun (L£1000) and Nabatiyeh (L£3000). Citadel open daily 8am-1pm and 3-8pm. Bring a flashlight. In the mosque, women must dress modestly and cover their hair with a scarf. Mosque closed to public during prayer times.

Hasbaya's **Citadel,** dating from the Crusader era, was turned into a palace by the Shehab princes in the 12th century. There is an extensive system of cellars to your right as you enter; you'll need a flashlight to explore them. As you walk farther into the main courtyard, you'll notice the residences still occupied by the Shehab family, descendants of the princes. In fact, there remains one prince, Talal Irslan, who serves in the Lebanese Parliament. Beyond the courtyard are the upper levels of the compound. Though old furniture lies about in disarray, spiral staircases, stunning arches, and impressive stonework make this a worthwhile stop. Ask the family's permission to enter. Across the street is the Hasbaya **mosque,** built in the 13th century, with thick walls similar to those of the Citadel. It has been well preserved—its intricate stonework was not, as in many other mosques, plastered over and painted puke green during the 1930s.

In the *souqs,* you will notice Hasbaya's large Druze population dressed in traditional black-and-white garments. The men wear pants with a pleated, skirt-like center called a *shilwaal.* Elderly men wearing *shilwaals* in the mountain regions often fill the pleats with stones to achieve an elegant swaying motion in the folds as they walk. A dramatic sway was once perceived as irresistibly handsome. If all the swaying makes you hungry, try **al-Amana Restaurant.** (☎ 267 011, ext. 2054. Sandwiches L£1500. Open daily 6:30am-11pm.)

JEZZINE جزين ☎ 07

Accessible by service from Sa'ida (L£3000).

The area now called Jezzine has been inhabited since Roman times, but the modern town was founded in the 18th century. Today, this picturesque Maronite Christian town is home to craftsmen and moderately priced restaurants and hotels. Dropping 40m from the edge of town into the valley below, the Jezzine waterfall is the highest in Lebanon. In 1635, Prince Fakhr al-Din hid from the Ottomans in a cave in this valley. He was eventually captured and taken to Istanbul after Ottoman soldiers smoked him out. Israel controlled the hills surrounding Jezzine from 1982 to 1999 and frequently entered the town, which was administered by the SLA. Now that the Israelis have left, Jezzine is a favorite spot among Lebanese city dwellers seeking a mountain escape. Visitors should arrive early on weekend evenings if they hope to find a seat at one of the town's many cafes.

Among Jezzine's sights are the restored **municipal buildings** (originally built in 1898), on the right as you enter town from Sa'ida. Next to the Jezzine Pharmacy is the **Bsharn Rhuyyen Factory,** where locals craft the cutlery for which Jezzine is famed. The workers don't mind visitors watching them work. (Usually open for viewing M-Sa 8am-1pm.) Nearby shops sell these wares, often at half the price they fetch in Beirut. Single utensils and letter openers can be had for less than L£7600, but you'll have to fork out nearly L£3,000,000 for a flashy sword. Jezzine also has a few **churches** dating from the 18th century.

There are no hostels or pensions in Jezzine, but the **Wehbe Hotel** provides a lot of bang for your buck, with large, well-appointed rooms and private baths. Although there is neither air-conditioning nor fans, large windows let in a nice breeze that keeps the temperature pleasant even in summer. (☎ 780 217. Singles L£37,800; doubles L£53,000; triples L£68,000.) The best restaurant in town, the **Rock of the Waterfall** (Mat'am al-Sakra), is just off the main drag and next to the waterfall, overlooking the valley. Lebanese fare will set you back about L£23,000, but the view is priceless. (☎ 03 425 525. Almaza beer L£3000. Pepsi L£1500. Open daily 9am-midnight.)

The **police** can be reached at ☎ 780 089. The well-stocked **Jezzine Pharmacy** lies on the main commercial street, one street over from the road to Sa'ida, on the right when facing the town from Sa'ida and the valley. The staff speaks English and French. (☎ 780 305. Open M-Sa 8am-1pm and 3-9pm, Su 8am-noon.) The **Jezzine Hospital** (☎ 780 106) is on the main road on the way in from Sa'ida.

RASHAYA رشاية ☎ 03

Minibuses run from Chtura and Zahlé (45min.-1hr., L£1500). Rashaya is the closest you can get to Mt. Hermon without hiring a taxi or renting a car, so it is frequently used as a starting point for treks up the mountain. Citadel open daily 8am-8pm. Free.

Rashaya is located at the south end of the Beqa'a Valley in the shadow of Mt. Hermon, the highest peak in the Anti-Lebanon range (2814m). Most of the town was destroyed by Druze rebels in the 1920s and has since been rebuilt.

The **Citadel** is currently used as an army base. Soldiers tend to be very friendly to visitors, and it is likely that there will be an English (or at least French) speaker handy to serve as a guide. As always, ask before photographing anything that might be military-related. Originally built in 1800 for use by the Shehab princes, the Citadel was reconstructed by the French in 1923 to serve alongside the Suweida and Hasbaya Citadels as a bulwark against rebellious Druze. On October 23, 1925, British-backed Druze rebels besieged the Citadel. A plaque inside commemorates the November 22, 1943 release of the prime minister, foreign minister, and other officials of the nascent Lebanese republic, who were imprisoned here by the French. The reconstructed **souq** lies just off the town square. Stores sell crafts and jewelry at generally reasonable prices. One shops features a workshop where visitors can watch the production of gold and silver jewelry; ask for Wisam al-Laham. (Most shops open daily 8:30am-7:30pm.)

The staff at **al-Kalaa Pharmacy** in the *souq* speaks French and some English. (Open M-Sa 8am-9pm, Su 9am-7pm.) The **Castle Restaurant,** at the entrance to the castle, has sandwiches (L£1000-2000) and a great view of the Citadel and countryside below. (☎ 872 142. Open daily 8am-11:30pm.)

MT. HERMON جبل الشيخ   ☎ 03

Mt. Hermon (Jabal al-Sheikh) has carried religious significance since antiquity and is often refered to as the Holy Mountain. Phoenician and Roman temples were usually built to face it, and it is considered sacred by Druze, Muslims, and Christians. It is believed that the slopes of Hermon witnessed the transfiguration of Jesus and later became the site where Jesus advised his followers to "turn the other cheek" (Matthew 5:39). The mountain has no tree cover or water sources, making the 6-8hr. rocky ascent from the lower peak rather treacherous in summer heat. The tallest of the three peaks that cluster to form Mt. Hermon is also the highest point in the Anti-Lebanon range at 2814m, and is covered with snow year-round (except during years of low precipitation). Locals advise against relying on snow for drinking water. Hermon's zenith affords an amazing view of Lebanon, Syria, Israel, and Jordan. The summit is technically in **Syrian territory.** *Let's Go* does not recommend illegal border crossings (especially for those who do not hold a valid Syrian visa), but the Syrian side of the mountain and the surrounding areas are currently a UN-occupied security zone, and locals report that friendly Austrian peacekeepers permit trekkers from the Lebanese side of the border to reach the summit. It is difficult and potentially dangerous to climb Mt. Hermon without a guide. There are no signs or clearly delineated paths, and much of the surrounding area is disputed territory (including the Chebaa Farms) riddled with **landmines**. Ecotourism offices in Beirut, including Wild Expeditions and Lebanese Adventure, can provide updates for potential climbers as well as guide contacts. Rashaya resident **Michel Malik** (☎ 03 639 776) is also well informed. **Mehdi Fayek** (☎ 963 378), a local guide, provides donkeys and leads treks up the mountain. For one person, an overnight trek will cost L£45,400. For groups of four or more, the price drops to L£15,150-22,700 per person. The journey takes you past a monastery on the mountainside and to the summit, where travelers often spend a cold night huddled between rocky enclaves, awaiting the glorious sunrise.

SYRIA سوريا

US$1 = S£53.5	S£100 = US$1.87
CDN$1 = S£34.6	S£100 = CDN$2.89
UK£1 = S£77.7	S£100 = UK£1.29
IR£1 = S£62.3	S£100 = IR£1.61
AUS$1 = S£28.6	S£100 = AUS$3.50
NZ$1 = S£23.5	S£100 = NZ$4.25
ZAR1 = S£6.37	S£100 = ZAR15.7
EUR€1 = S£49.1	S£100 = EUR€2.04
E£1 (EGYPTIAN POUND) = S£12.6	S£100 = E£7.96
JD1 (JORDANIAN DINAR) = S£75.5	S£100 = JD1.33
L£100 (LEBANESE POUNDS) = S£3.53	S£100 = L£2830
NIS1 (NEW ISRAELI SHEKEL) = S£12.6	S£100 = NIS7.94
TL100,000 (TURKISH LIRA) = L£3.73	S£100 = TL2,680,000

SYRIAN POUND (S£)

PHONE CODES | **Country Code: 963. International dialing prefix: 00.**

Surrounded by the Caspian Sea, the Indian Ocean, the Black Sea, and the Nile River—and criss-crossed by the trade routes connecting them—Syria has been one of civilization's first proverbial cradles, and home to at least seven great empires. The silk road, linking China with the Mediterranean, made Doura Europos an ancient center of trade. The kingdom of Ugarit (Ras Shamra) on the Mediterranean coast developed the first alphabet in history, and a royal palace at Ebla (see p. 615) contains one of the largest documentary archives of the ancient world. Copper was discovered at the ancient site of Tel Halaf, and bronze was also invented in Syria.

After a recent history of closed regimes and enmity with Israel, Syria is now open to travelers. From the sparsely populated Syrian Desert in the east to the west's balmy seashore, the country's natural beauty remains unmolested by masses of tourists, as backpackers and tourist groups are only beginning to discover Syria's treasures. Get there before they do, and discover magnificent Roman ruins, medieval castles, and prices that haven't changed since the dawn of time. Syria is one of the last frontiers of budget adventure in the Eastern Mediterranean.

HIGHLIGHTS OF SYRIA

DEFY the tug of time at the amazing ruins of **Palmyra** (p. 590), much like the legendary queen that once inhabited its castles.

IT'S a castle on Crac! See **Crac des Chevaliers** (p. 596), the Crusader fortress that even Salah al-Din couldn't conquer.

AMBLE through the Arcadian city of **Tartus** (p. 606), home to sunsets, sea breezes, and the best Crusader ruins this side of Jerusalem.

LIFE AND TIMES

For years, Egypt and Israel garnered the glitz and glamour of the Middle East while Syria played the ugly second cousin. But in the last decade, travelers have begun to discover what Syrians knew all along—that Syria is the hidden jewel of the Middle East. Syria's ancient ruins rival Semitic sites anywhere, and the developing economy keeps prices low enough to soothe budget travelers' pockets. Syria has been cushioned from the assault of Western culture, thanks partially to former President Hafez al-Assad's efforts. Despite their unabashed marvel at foreigners, Syrians are helpful and accommodating to tourists. Just walk to the nearest *souq* to catch a glimpse of the vibrant Middle Eastern culture that Syria has to offer.

SYRIA

Adana
Gaziantep
Karatas
Iskenderun
TURKEY
Tall Ahmar
NUR DAGLARI
Manbij
Euphrates River
40 miles
Afrin
Al-Bab
40 kilometers
Saint Simeon
HALAB
N
Antakya (Antioch)
Darret 'Azzay
Aleppo
Samandag
Idlib
Jabal al Hass
Buhayrat al-Asad
Saraqib
Ugarit
Ebla
Salma
IDLIB
Al-Haffeh
Maaret Al-Noman
Lattakia
Qal'a Salah Al-Din
Suqaylabiyah
Khirbat
AL-LADHIQIYAH
Apamea
HAMA
Baniyas
Qal'at Al-Marqab
Masyaf
Hama
Salamiyah
JABAL RASHRID
JABAL ABU RUJMAYN
TARTUS
Jabal al-Bil'as
Huwaysi
Tartus
Safita
Jabal al Shawariyah
Jabal al-Abyad
Jabal as-Safra
Arwad
Crac Des Chevaliers
Homs
Jabal as-Satih
Mediterranean Sea
Lake Qattine
HOMS
Al-Qasr
Tripoli
Palmyra (Tadmor)
Batroun
Bcharre
Hermel
Hisyah
Qasr al-Hayr
Byblos (Jbail)
Al'Aqurah
LEBANON
LEBANON MTS.
Al-Nabk
Jounieh
Ba'albeck
JABAL LUBNAN
Beirut
Ma'alula
Zahleh
ANTI-LEBANON
Sab'Abar
Syria
Beit al-Din
Al-Zabadani
Seydnaya
Khan Abu Shamat
Tanf
Saida (Sidon)
Damascus
Marjayoun
Al Kiswah
Damascus International Airport
Mt. Hermon
Banyas
AL QUNAYTIRAH
Buraq
GOLAN HEIGHTS
Quneitra
Katzan (Qasnien)
AL-SUWEIDA'
Sea of Galilee
Fiq
DAR'A
Shahba
Beit She'an
Shaykh Miskin
Izra
Al-Suweida'
Irbid
Dar'a
Safah
Salkhad
Bosra
Imtan
Mafraq
Jabal Ajlun

SEE MAIN MAP
TURKEY
Aleppo
Euphrates R.
Mediterranean Sea
SYRIA
Deir ez-Zur
Palmyra (Tadmor)
Homs
LEBANON
Damascus
IRAQ
ISRAEL
JORDAN

HISTORY

ANCIENT HISTORY (8000 BCE-1516 CE)

EARLY HISTORY. Andrea Pavrot, a former director of the Louvre Museum in Paris, once said, "Each person has two homelands: his own and Syria." Her words are not far from the truth. Most modern civilizations owe a huge debt to the ancient civilizations of Syria. The oldest alphabet in the world—and the precursor to most ancient and modern alphabets—was discovered at **Ugarit**, a site near Lattakia (p. 602). Excavations at **Mureybet** have revealed a settlement where inhabitants were among the first potters and farmers, cultivating *einkorn*, a single-grained wheat, as early as the 9th millennium BCE. Bronze, an alloy of copper and tin, was first produced in Syria in the middle of the 4th millennium BCE. Last but not least, the city of Damascus is the world's oldest continually inhabited city.

Greater Syria, a land area incorporating present-day Lebanon, Israel, Jordan, and Syria, has been the locus of countless land squabbles since ancient times and continues to be fought over today. The list of conquerors and rulers of the region is a who's-who of ancient history. After the rise and fall of Ebla around 2500 BCE, the Assyrian king **Shamshi-A'adad I** established his capital at Shubat Enlil (known today as Tel Leilan, in northeast Syria) around 1800 BCE. The **Hittites** moved in 200 years later and ruled until the **Egyptians**, took control of the area another two centuries later. The **Aramaeans** migrated into Syria around 1200 BCE and established several minor kingdoms. An endless array of conquerors had their way with Syria in the following years: the Assyrians returned, quickly succeeded by the Babylonians, the Persians, and finally the Seleucids, who gave Syria the its modern name.

ROMAN AND ARAB RULE. **Alexander the Great** added Syria to his empire during in 333 BCE, establishing the city of **Antioch** as its capital. Next up were the Romans under Pompey, who, in 64 BCE, reduced the entire region to one of a long list of Roman provinces. The region remained a Roman province for several centuries.

The Arabs wrested Syria from the Romans in 636 CE and established Damascus as the capital of the powerful **Umayyad** caliphate. The Abbasid caliphs, who took over in 750 CE, were puzzlingly immune to Damascus's many charms; they moved the capital to Baghdad. Muslim rule ended in the 11th century, when the Crusaders arrived and made Syria part of the Christian Kingdom of Jerusalem. Syria, along with the rest of the Arab world, was freed from Christian control when **Salah al-Din** overthrew the Kingdom of Jerusalem at the end of the 12th century. The **Mamluk sultans** of Egypt moved in soon after and ruled until the coming of the Ottomans.

MODERN HISTORY (1516 CE-PRESENT)

THE OTTOMAN PERIOD. Most of the coastal region of modern-day Syria officially became part of the **Ottoman Empire** in 1516 CE, beginning an era in Syrian history that lasted until the onset of World War I. While Syria's economy and population did not exactly thrive overall during the four centuries of Ottoman rule, the market towns of **Damascus** and **Aleppo** reaped the benefits of their location along the trade routes between Persia (modern-day Iran) and Europe.

WORLD WAR I AND ARAB NATIONALISM. During World War I, **Emir Faisal** and his Arab nationalist army defied the Ottoman Empire (which sided with Germany), backing the British, who promised Arab independence. After emerging victorious, however, the British betrayed Faisal, carving up the Levant and placing Syria under French control. In response, Faisal and British colonel T.E. Lawrence (**Lawrence of Arabia**) conquered Damascus in October 1918.

WORLD WAR II AND INDEPENDENCE. A bit peeved, the French strong-armed their way back into control with the help of the 1920 mandate from the League of Nations. They governed militarily, Frenchifying every aspect of Syrian culture and battling nationalist rebels in and around Damascus until the outbreak of World War II. After a brief stint under German control, Syria was "liberated" by the French. However, it took United Nations involvement and British threats before Syria was truly liberated, gaining independence when the last of the French troops withdrew on April 17, 1946 (now celebrated as **Evacuation Day,** a national holiday).

SYRIA AFTER INDEPENDENCE. The first few decades of independence were anything but peaceful. In March 1949, the country came under the first of a series of military dictatorships. **Pan-Arabism** became a major political force in Syria (and the rest of the Middle East) during the 1950s, heralded mainly by the rise of the **Ba'ath Party** (the Arab Socialist Resurrection Party). In 1958, Syria officially merged with Egypt, forming the so-called **United Arab Republic.** The union was far from a match made in heaven, as Syria backed out of the partnership in 1961, ending Egyptian President **Gamal 'abd al-Nasser's** dreams of ruling the entire Arab world. The Syrian Ba'ath Party has been the strongest political force in Syria since rising to power in the 1963 **March Revolution.** The party was dealt a major blow by the **Six Day War** against Israel in June 1967, which cost Syria the **Golan Heights.** Syria suffered further casualties, both in terms of lives and morale, when Jordanian forces defeated Syrian-backed Palestinian guerrillas in the **Black September** hostilities of 1970 (see **Jordan: Modern History,** p. 432). After much frantic finger-pointing among government officials, **Hafez al-Assad,** the Ba'ath's fair-haired boy and commander of the Syrian Air Force, seized control of the country and was sworn in as president on March 14, 1971.

BACK THAT ASSAD UP. From 1971 through June 10, 2000, Assad ran Syria as a tight-fisted dictatorship, though two events in the early years of his rule challenged his supremacy. First, in 1973, Assad and Egypt's President Anwar al-Sadat launched a surprise attack on Israel known as the **October War** or **Yom Kippur War** (see **Egypt: Modern History,** p. 66). After early Arab gains, the Israelis surged forward and came within 35km of Damascus, forcing Assad to sign an armistice. Second, in February 1982, the militant **Muslim Brotherhood** launched a rebellion from Hama. Assad's forces retaliated successfully, but by most estimates they took between 5000 and 25,000 lives in the process. When Israel invaded Lebanon in 1982, Assad responded by backing the main Lebanese Muslim militias, Amal and **Hezbollah.** Over the next few years, Israel and Syria clashed; by 1985, Israel withdrew from Lebanon but Syria did not. Though formally independent, Lebanon continues to take its political cues from Damascus.

The money gained from **oil sales** in the 1970s allowed Assad to pursue a program of capital formation, but industries were haphazardly chosen and poorly run, leaving Syria with inefficient factories. The Syrian economy today suffers from rapid population growth and the legacy of hyperinflation (which reached 300% in late 1991). Unemployment stalled at 35% in the '70s and '80s, and the colossal government bureaucracy is also enormously inefficient. Western economic aid has been scarce, due to Syria's connections with terrorist groups, support of Iran, and skirmishes with Jordan. However, in exchange for its support of the US-led coalition against Iraq in the **Gulf War,** Western powers granted Syria a free hand in Lebanon. In more recent times, Assad sought Western aid to revitalize Syria's plodding economy, loosening travel restrictions for Syrian Jews and negotiating with Israel to curry favor with Western governments and investors.

In 1999, Assad was "elected" to his fifth presidential term with 99% of the vote. Overall, Assad's policies stabilized Syrian politics, as he diluted the Ba'ath's centralized power by mandating the election of local councils (of which at least 51% were required to be workers or peasants). His political longevity, however, could also be attributed to the aggressive repression of his enemies. The omnipresent internal security forces, known as the **Mukhabarat,** quelled all anti-Assad sentiment. The government also had an abysmal human rights record, and has repeatedly been accused of harboring terrorists.

On June 10, 2000, Assad died, leaving the country in the hands of his son, **Bashar al-Assad.** The new president is Syria's first Western-educated leader, having spent most of his adult life practising ophthalmology in Britain. World leaders now look to Bashar to take new strides in Syria's quest for peace, and Syrians are hopeful that he will develop and modernize Syria's economy.

Today, as in the former President Assad's time, all political parties are associated with the **National Progressive Front (NPF),** a coalition dominated by the Ba'ath Party. The **People's Council** is a 250-member legislative body, but since it is controlled by the NPF, Ba'ath policies pass with minimal opposition.

IN THE NEWS

Animosity continues between Syria and Israel over the **Golan Heights,** which have been under Israeli control since 1967 though Syria claims historic and cultural ownership of them. In June 2001 Syrian troops pulled out of key government sectors in Beirut, making a first move towards easing out of Lebanese affairs. This is a process that was supposed to have begun in 1992.

RELIGION AND ETHNICITY

Islam is the dominant religion of Syria, the faith of 88% of the country's 17 million inhabitants. About 74% of Syrians are **Sunni** and 14% are **Shi'ite.** The Shi'ite branch is split into several sects, two of the most popular being the Alawis (12%) and the Isma'ilis (2%). The former group counts President Bashar al-Assad as one of its adherents. About 10% of Syrians belong to the Catholic or Eastern Orthodox churches. Two percent are Druze, and a very small minority are Jewish.

About 85% of Syria's population are ethnic Arabs. The rest is a mix of Kurds, Turks, Armenians, and Circassians. Part of the Kurdish minority has long since vowed to create an independent state, which would also include Kurds in Turkey, Iran, and Iraq. Their grievances have not yet been accompanied by constructive action; pamphlets distributed in 1992 brought about the arrest of 200 Kurdish activists. For more on the struggle for Kurdish independence, see **Turkey: Religion and Ethnicity,** p. 628.

LANGUAGE

The official state language of Syria is **Arabic. French** has been the unofficial second language since the days of colonialism, but in the past few years **English** has surged forward, catching up with and threatening to overtake French. Minority groups, such as the Kurds in the east and the Armenians in Aleppo, continue to use their native languages. In some villages, you may encounter Turkish or even Aramaic (the language spoken 2000 years ago by Jesus Christ). For some handy Arabic phrases, consult the **Phrasebook,** p. 701.

THE ARTS

LITERATURE. Although the earliest known alphabet has its origins in Syria, it is only recently that the rest of the world has started paying attention to Syrian letters. One of the greatest poets in contemporary Arabic literature is the iconoclast **Adonis** (Ali Ahmad Sa'id). Adonis, born in Syria in 1930 and educated in Syria and Lebanon, is one of the founding fathers of modernism in Arabic literature. Some claim he transformed Islamic culture as radically as Dante influenced Christianity. Adonis was the central figure of the **New Poets,** a group of Arabs who used poetry to challenge language, religion, and authority in the 1960s and '70s. The first of Adonis's seven poetry collections, *Aghani Mihyar al-Dimashqi* (*Songs of Mihyar the Damascene,* 1961), is readily available in English translation.

Possibly the most popular contemporary Syrian poet, **Nizar Qabbani** was born in Damascus in 1923 and worked as a diplomat for many years before turning his full attention to his two loves: poetry and women. His poetry has a two-sided appeal: on the one hand it is extremely sensual, with women ever the focus of the poems, and on the other hand it gives a voice to Arab nationalism and anti-authoritarianism, using the oppression of women as a metaphor for Arab political problems. Widely hailed as a national hero in Syria, Qabbani saw his poems turned into pop songs and political battle cries. He died of a heart attack in 1998.

VISUAL AND PERFORMING ARTS. Glassblowing was invented in Syria over 2000 years ago, and it continues to be a popular art form today. Vessels for everyday and luxury use were produced commercially in Syria and exported to all parts of the Roman Empire. In Syria, as in the rest of the Middle East, calligraphy is one of the most respected and popular of the visual arts. Syrian **Muhammad Ghanoum,** born in Damascus in 1949, is considered one of the greatest calligraphers in the Arab world.

Esteemed Syrian playwright **Sa'adullah Wannous** was born in Hussein al-Bahr, where there is a theater festival in his honor each June. Other theater festivals include the **Syrian Theater Festival** in June, the **Bosra Folklore Festival** in September, and the **Damascus Film Festival** and the **Theater Arts Festival** in October. Do not count on watching much television, though, as Syria has only three channels: one in Arabic, one in English and French, and one by satellite only.

MUSIC. The jewel of Syrian music is **Farid al-Atrash,** the artist known as the "sad singer." As a child, he was unable to express his feelings while singing, so his instructor advised him to cry as he sang, and this advice worked and remained a theme that lasted throughout his career. Farid is also known to Arab musicians as the best *oud* player of his time. In an effort to create a niche for himself beside established giants like Muhammad 'Abd al-Wahab and Umm Kulthum, Atrash adopted European musical elements such as flamenco and tango, mixing Arabic and European styles. Atrash is so well respected that he is often unabashedly imitated by other Syrian singers.

FOOD AND DRINK

Syrian meals feature the typical Levantine staples: hummus, falafel, shawarma, shish kebab, and *shish tawouq*, among others. A particularly common dish is *farooj*, roasted chicken served with chilis and onions. Syrian desserts are delicious: *ba'laweh* is pistachio- or almond-filled filo-dough; *burma* is shredded, fried dough with pistachios; and *basbouseh* is wheat pastry with syrup. Don't leave without trying the desert banana *bybil* for desert; its short growing season (culminating in a harvest around October 1) makes it one of the most prized

MARY ATE A LITTLE LAMB Anyone with knowledge of Middle Eastern cooking knows that Syrian cuisine is one of the region's best. Such a claim should not be put forth sheepishly; it is supported by the large numbers of high-quality patisseries and Arab eateries that dot the streets of most major cities. The uninitiated should note, however, that some dishes require an acquired taste. Notorious "sheep eggs," which are actually **testicles,** are the most famous example. Sheep also get special treatment in a Damascene favorite, *ma'adim,* which consists of sheep hooves drenched in a hummus-like dressing and served over bread. Moving up the sheep anatomy, we arrive at *mukh,* sheep brains: these are normally mixed with lettuce and lemon to create the intriguing "brain salad." If such a mix proves to be a gastrointestinal disaster, consider washing it down with a soothing cup of *zghourat,* a tea made from "useful plants in the ground" that tastes curiously close to its rough English translation.

fruits in the world. Other fruits are available in abundance and *aseer* (fruit juice), available at stands everywhere, is a sweet way to rehydrate. Arabic coffee is a potent and bittersweet brew known as *ahwa*. Be careful when adding milk, though—Syrian milk is not always pasteurized. *Mandarin* is a Syrian-brewed soft drink. Liquor ranges from locally brewed beers such as Sharq and Barada (as well as Amstel smuggled from Lebanon) to *'araq*, an anise-flavored liqueur mixed with water and consumed from shot glasses. Ask for *booza*, though, and you'll get ice cream—not alcohol.

FACTS AND FIGURES

OFFICIAL NAME: Syrian Arab Republic

GOVERNMENT: Republic under military regime

CAPITAL: Damascus

LAND AREA: 184,050 sq. km.

GEOGRAPHY: Narrow coastal plane with semi-arid desert conditions and mountains in the east

CLIMATE: Hot, dry summers from June-Aug. and mild, wet winters from Dec.-Feb.; desert-like in the east

MAJOR CITIES: Damascus, Aleppo, Lattakia, Palmyra

POPULATION: 17,213,871; urban 53%, rural 47%

LANGUAGE: Arabic, some French

RELIGIONS: Muslim (90%), Christian (10%)

AVERAGE INCOME PER CAPITA: US$2500

MAJOR EXPORTS: Petroleum (65%), textiles (16%), food and livestock (13%), other (6%)

ESSENTIALS

DOCUMENTS AND FORMALITIES

SYRIAN CONSULAR SERVICES ABROAD

Syria's embassies and consulates abroad include:

Canada Embassy: 151 Slater St., Ste. 1000, Ottawa, Ontario, K1P5H3 (☎613-569-5556; fax 569-3800).

South Africa Embassy: 772 Government Ave., East Clyff/Arcadia, Pretoria, South Africa (☎12 342 47 01; fax 342 47 02).

UK Embassy: 8 Belgrave Sq., London SW1X 8PH (☎171 245 90 12; fax 235 46 21 or 235 89 76).

US Embassy: 2215 Wyoming Ave. NW, Washington, D.C. 20008 (☎202-232-6313; fax 265-4585)

CONSULAR SERVICES IN SYRIA

Embassies and consulates of other countries in Syria include:

Australian Embassy: 128/A al-Farabi St., E. Villas, Damascus (☎11 613 23 23; fax 613 24 78; austdmas@go.com.jo).

Canadian Embassy: Block 12 al-Mezzah, Damascus (☎11 611 68 51; fax 611 40 00).

UK Embassy: 11 Muhammad Kurd Ali St., Kotob Building, Malki, Damascus (☎11 371 25 61 or 371 25 62; fax 37135 92). **Consulate:** Aleppo (☎21 268 05 02 or 268 05 03; fax 268 05 01).

US Embassy: 2 al-Mansour St., Abu Roumaneh, Damascus (☎333 13 42, emergency ☎333 13 42; fax 224 79 38).

ENTRY REQUIREMENTS

PASSPORT. Passports are required of all visitors, except for citizens of Lebanon—who hold national ID cards.

 TRAVEL TO ISRAEL. If you visit **Israel** before a trip to Syria, insist that Israeli customs place **no stamp** in your passport, or more practically, have them stamp a piece of paper inserted in your passport that can be removed. Be warned that Syrian border officials may still refuse entry if they see that you have no Jordanian entry stamp or have an Egyptian exit stamp from Taba.

VISA AND PERMIT INFO. Visas are required by all but Arab nationals to enter Syria. Australian citizens may obtain visas at the border. All other applicants must apply for a visa before entering Syria. Applications are available from any Syrian embassy. Send two completed applications (no photocopies), passport (without evidence of a trip to Israel), two passport photographs, a self-addressed stamped envelope (US$5), and money order (US$61) to a Syrian embassy. All visitors staying in Syria for more than two weeks (even those with six-month visas) must apply for a **visa extension** on the 13th day of their stay. It makes sense to do this in a smaller city where the lines will be shorter.

BORDER CROSSINGS

Hard currency is needed to cross the Jordanian and Lebanese borders to Syria. Fees vary according to nationality and duration of stay, but ideally you should carry US$100 in cash (you will not need the full amount). This is the best way to avoid extremely poor exchange rates at the borders. There is a S£200 departure tax if you fly out of Syria.

TO LEBANON. Crossing into Lebanon may take a long time due to security at the border, but the path is well-trodden and simple. Daily buses run from Damascus to Tripoli or Beirut, Aleppo and Lattakia to Beirut, and Homs to Tripoli. Though costly, it's possible to hire a *service* to drive across the border from Damascus. Citizens of Canada, Ireland, the UK, the US, and most European countries can obtain a Lebanese visa at the border (L£20,000 for US citizens), though prices depend on your nationality and are subject to change. Syrian visas, however, are not available if crossing from Lebanon to Syria. If you have a single-entry visa, you may reenter Syria within 48hr. after departure for US$10. After this time, the price and difficulty to return will increase. The word on the street is that a Syrian single-entry visa is good for two entries from Lebanon before the visa expires. It is also possible to return to Syria with a **multiple-entry Syrian visa,** though it is more expensive and hard to obtain (there is no Syrian representation in Lebanon and it is difficult to get a visa of any kind at the Syrian embassy in Amman).

TO JORDAN. The official road crossing into Jordan runs through the town of Dera. Daily buses run from Damascus or Aleppo to Amman. *Service* from Damascus are faster, but also more expensive. Jordanian visas are available at the border. Bring US dollars or use the bank next door. They charge according to nationality; US citizens must pay about US$50. For true penny-pinchers, the painfully slow Hijaz railway chugs (and chugs, and chugs) between Damascus and Amman. The train departs Amman at 8am every Monday, arriving at Damascus at 5pm, and leaves Damascus every Sunday at 7:30am to arrive in Amman at 5pm.

TO TURKEY. Of the four official land crossings between Syria and Turkey, the Bab al-Hawa post on the Aleppo-Antakya road is the most popular, and often gets so congested that it takes a few hours to cross. Buses run from Damascus, Aleppo, and Lattakia to a number of Turkish destinations, most commonly Istanbul and the travel hubs of Antakya and Iskenderun near the border. Buy a Turkish visa at the border for US$20.

TO ISRAEL AND IRAQ. Syria's borders with Israel and Iraq are closed; neither situation is likely to change soon. The most common route between Syria and Israel is via Jordan and the West Bank. In the past few years, a few trade delegations have been permitted to travel by road between Baghdad and Damascus, but it remains to be seen whether a loosening of border restrictions will follow.

GETTING AROUND

BY PLANE. Syrian Arab Airlines fly from Damascus to Aleppo, Palmyra, Deir al-Zur, and Lattakia. Fares tend to be very inexpensive.

BY TRAIN. Strictly speaking, trains connect some cities in Syria; frankly speaking, roller skates would serve you better. Trains are slow, crowded, and dirty, and in most places they drop you off about 30km out of town. Use the buses.

BY BUS. Karnak, the government-run bus company, has extensive routes and low fares on orange-and-white, air-conditioned buses. Buses occasionally depart on schedule, and reservations are required. **Pullman** buses are a step below Karnak. Over 50 **private bus companies** now operate in Syria; they have ship-shape coaches and competitive prices. Reservations are a good idea for these buses too. Karnak, Pullman, and private buses usually leave from different stops—make sure you're at the right one. All tickets must be bought at the stations, as drivers do not handle money. **Microbuses** (MEEK-ro-bus) are easy, cheap, and relatively hassle-free. They are white minivans that drive on set routes within Damascus and to outlying areas. Like most *service*, they usually depart only when full. Untangling their confusing schedules may be difficult at first (destinations are often written in Arabic on the side of the vehicle), but they are cheaper than taxis for long rides. Fees in Damascus are set, but vary everywhere else depending on where you get off; ask the person next to you (not the driver) how much to pay or wait to see what other people are paying. Microbuses differ from clattery old **minibuses,** which are becoming less frequent on the roads.

BY TAXI. Yellow private taxis, also known as *service* (ser-VEES), are 50-70% more expensive than buses. But *service* are more user-friendly and still relatively cheap. To hail one, hold out your hand with the palm down. Taxis have meters, but drivers rarely use them; negotiate a price before getting in. If a driver refuses to bargain, just point to the meter to get a fair rate. Beware and be firm—many drivers specialize in cheating newly arrived travelers.

BY CAR. Very few people in Syria own private cars, which is why public transportation is good. If you want to risk your life driving one, cars can be rented at a few places in Damascus (see **Damascus: Car Rental,** p. 578). Cars are generally not worth the expense, as all the sights you could possibly want to see are easily accessible via cheap public transportation. For negotiable prices, some *service* drivers will be your private chauffeur for the day—a cheaper option than renting a car if you want the freedom to visit out-of-the-way places and don't want to risk your life on the way.

BY THUMB. There is no need to hitchhike in Syria. If you stand by the side of a road, an ultra-cheap microbus will eventually stop. It is not unusual, however, for truck drivers to pick up passengers in order to subsidize their trips (they usually expect S£1-2 per km). Hitchers caught by the police may be hauled in for questioning or given a stern warning. *Let's Go* does not recommend hitchhiking.

TOURIST SERVICES AND MONEY

TOURIST OFFICES. The **Ministry of Tourism** runs an office in Damascus on Abu Firas al-Hamandi St. (☎11 223 74 90 or 224 28 52; fax 224 26 36; min-tourism@syri-atel.net; www.syriatourism.org), as well as a **Tourist Information Center** on 29 May Street (☎11 232 39 53).

CURRENCY AND EXCHANGE. The basic unit of currency is the **Syrian pound** (S£). Each pound is divided into 100 **piasters** (pt), or *qirsh*. Bills are in denominations of S£5, 10, 25, 50, 100, 500, 1000, while coins are in denominations of S£1, 2, 5, 10, 25. You may bring as much foreign currency into the country as you like, but may not leave with more than you brought in. Amounts up to US$5000 do not need to be declared. The Commercial Bank of Syria has exchange desks at its many branches, as well as in major hotels. US dollars are the preferred currency for exchange.

Credit cards cannot be used to obtain cash advances, though major credit cards are increasingly accepted at large hotels and stores for purchases (V, MC, AmEx are the most widely accepted). It is illegal to cash traveler's checks anywhere besides the bank, but the AmEx office will do it in an emergency. If you are in a bind, some shopkeepers in the Damascus *souq* will disguise a cash advance as a purchase, although the exchange rate will be lower than the official bank rate. **Black market** exchange is not the flourishing industry it once was, as secret service agents have begun to clamp down upon illicit dealings. Still, it is common in *souqs* or near al-Marjeh Sq. in Damascus, where some trading takes place beneath the thumb of secret service agents on the lookout for offenders. Some hotels will unofficially change money for you at the black market rate, but these days that rate isn't much better than the official one. Transactions using US dollars are illegal (except to pay hotel bills); in 1986, a law was passed making illegal exchange or possession of hard currency punishable by up to three years in prison.

It used to be the case that nothing would get done in Syria without a bit of **palm-greasing.** Now, increased contact with the world market is changing the general attitude toward *bakhsheesh*. While bribes are no longer necessary to accomplish the smallest task (and are inappropriate when dealing with high government officials and police officers), **tipping** makes everything run a little smoother. Taxi drivers, waiters, and movie theater employees should be given at least a 10% tip. If you stay multiple nights at a hotel that cleans its rooms daily, a small thank you (S£20-40 per day) to the person responsible is appropriate.

PRICES. Due to its struggling economy, Syria's prices are among the lowest in the Middle East. S£900 (US$20) should easily cover a day's budget travel.

 SIGHT SAVVY. Admission to sights in Syria is literally 20 times more expensive (usually S£300 instead of S£15) without an ISIC card. At all costs, get an ISIC card in your home country before departure.

BUSINESS HOURS. The work week begins on Saturday and ends on Thursday. Friday is the official day off. Stores are generally open 8:30am-2pm, then again from 4:30-8pm. Some stores stay open all day in the winter. Government offices are open 9am-2pm; banks 8:30am-1pm. Museums always close on Tuesdays, and are generally open November to March from 9am-6pm and April to October from 9am-5pm. Restaurant hours vary. Most establishments serve food from 11am until the last few patrons leave (often after midnight).

USEFUL ADDRESSES. For a comprehensive bibliography of Syrian politics, culture, and tourism, as well as hard facts about visas, customs, and embassies, visit www.cafe-syria.com. Find additional hard facts at the **World Travel Guide's** Syria site (www.wtgonline.com/data/syr/syr.asp).

HEALTH AND SAFETY

EMERGENCY   Police: ☎112. Ambulance: ☎110. Fire: ☎113.

MEDICAL EMERGENCIES. The Syrian government runs several hospitals and clinics, and there are also many private practices. Syrian facilities, however, are not state-of-the-art, and in cases of serious emergency, travelers should consider traveling to Lebanon or Jordan (or, ideally, Israel), or returning to their home countries. In case of **medical emergency,** dial ☎110.

HEALTH. While no **vaccinations** are necessary for entry, those for hepatitis B, typhoid, immunoglobulin, and malaria are recommended. Syria is a clean and healthy country, and water in cities is normally chlorinated and safe to drink. Outside of the main cities, however, most tap water is likely to be unsterilized. Bottled water is readily available and advised in small towns. Make sure milk is pasteurized. Eat only well-cooked meat, fish, and peeled vegetables and fruits. There are numerous pharmacies in Syria and no shortage of Western medicine. Quality and prices are regulated by the Ministry of Health.

WOMEN TRAVELERS. Common sense is the best companion for women traveling in Syria. Men may make comments, but remember that ignorance is bliss; the best way to deal with harassers is simply to ignore them. If they prove persistent, raise your voice and threaten to call the police. If things get out of hand, alert the tourist police. Many female travelers have found that wearing a wedding band wards off many unwanted advances. Females traveling alone should know their destination ahead of time so that they do not appear bewildered on the street. Women should not venture out alone at night. For more tips, see **Women Travelers,** p. 38.

MINORITY TRAVELERS. Unlike other Middle Eastern countries, Syria surprises Western travelers with its lack of outward hostility toward those who are obviously not Syrian. Blacks and whites exist in Syrian society; those from East Asia will stand out, but not to a dangerous degree. All travelers should avoid discussing Israeli politics, unless they are equally informed about the countering Arab side.

BGLT TRAVELERS. Homosexuality can land you in jail, which doesn't mean that it doesn't exist. The *souq* in Aleppo is known for its gay pick-up scene. You may want to read Robert Tewdwr Moss's *Cleopatra's Wedding Present*, an account of a gay journalist's travels in Syria (Duckworth, UK). As in other Middle Eastern countries, it is best to be discreet.

ACCOMMODATIONS AND CAMPING

HOTELS. Two hotel options span opposite ends of price and quality: expensive international chain resorts or basic hole-in-the-wall, bed-and-a-roof crash sites. The higher the room quality, the more likely owners will require payment in US dollars; all hotels two-star or higher carry this requirement. In most places, there is an even split between hotels that charge Syrian pounds and those that demand US dollars, but in heavily touristed towns like Palmyra, prepare to part with dollars. Different employees from the same establishment often quote contradictory rates; bargaining can save some money. Damascus and Aleppo hotels are less likely to respond to haggling, but if they look empty, give it a shot. Even posted rates can sometimes be brought down, if only by a few pounds. Unmarried couples may have a difficult time getting a room together; this is less of a problem in more expensive hotels. There are no hostels in Syria.

OTHER LOCAL ACCOMMODATIONS. Guest houses are available in Damascus, Aleppo, Zabadani, Idlib, and Bosra. *Cités Universitaires* also offer summer accommodations.

CAMPING. You can find official campsites in Aleppo, Lattakia, Palmyra, and Tartus. Camping is also permitted near resorts.

KEEPING IN TOUCH

MAIL. Poste Restante service is available in Damascus's main post office; bring your passport and enough money to cover customs charges on parcels (letters carry no charge). The **American Express** office in Damascus (see **Practical Information,** p. 580) also holds mail. A one-pound package to Syria costs US$8.48 from the US and AU$21 from Australia. Mail from Syria is inexpensive but slow. Parcels to

Europe take one week to arrive, while parcels to the US can take up to three weeks. Overseas letters cost about S£18; postcards cost S£11. Take packages to a post office for inspection before wrapping them up.

TELEPHONES. Damascus has a 24hr. telephone office where you can place international calls, but you'll need your passport, lots of money, and patience (at least an hour's worth). Some other cities have offices as well. Most hotels have direct-dial international capabilities, but rates from Syria are exorbitant (US$12 per 3min. to the US), and hotels charge at least double the phone office rates. It's much cheaper to have your party call you back or to call collect. The access code for **MCI's World Phone** program is 0800, **AT&T's USADirect** 0801, and **Sprint** 0888 (only to the US). You can now use phone cards to make local calls; they are available at most post offices. Inside Syria, you need to dial 0 before the city code.

INTERNET ACCESS. In the last year, Internet cafes have sprung up in Damascus like worms after the rain. Although Internet access is not allowed for the public sectors, these cafes get their connections through doctors or other professionals. You can usually access anything thanks to the brilliant site www.safeweb.com.

CUSTOMS AND ETIQUETTE

Conservative dress is the norm for both sexes. Shorts, tank tops, and short skirts will invite stares, comments, and possibly sexual advances. Pants and skirts should fall to at least mid-calf and shirts should cover the shoulders and upper arms. It is considered impolite to point directly at someone or to point the sole of your shoe at someone (as when sitting down and placing an ankle on one knee). When Syrians tip their heads up and make a clucking noise, this means "no"—Westerners have been known to mistake it for a sign of acknowledgment or a "get in the back seat" gesture by a taxi driver.

DAMASCUS دمشق ☎ 11

When pre-Islamic Arabs saw the site of present-day Damascus, they named it *Balad al-Shaam:* a phrase denoting luscious green hills, rich brown soil, and an otherwise blessed Heaven on Earth, as it is sometimes referred to by its denizens. During the intervening centuries other colors have infiltrated Damascus: the red battle flag of the Roman legions, the green banner of Islam, the French tricolor, and today the yellow of omnipresent *service* taxis. The product is a city as unique as the Syrian presidency is long.

Though Aleppo likes to claim this distinction for itself, Damascus is the oldest continuously inhabited city in the world. Early historical references to Damascus include the 3000 BCE Ebla tablets, 15th-century BCE pharaonic inscriptions, and records of the city as the capital of the Aramaic Kingdom. Centuries later, Roman invaders left their mark in the form of the Temple of Jupiter, built by Apolodor the Damascene (see p. 583). During the Byzantine era, Christians converted this temple into a church and built other monuments that you can see still standing today. In 636 CE, Khalid ibn al-Walid, known as the "Sword of God," conquered Damascus in the name of Islam. The city served as the capital of the Umayyad Empire for almost a century, wielding enormous influence during Islam's formative years. The city's situation took a turn for the worse when the Abbasids replaced the Umayyads and moved their capital to Baghdad. In the ensuing centuries, Damascus fell under the thumb of various Muslim dynasties and empires, including the Ottoman Turks, whose influence remains quite visible in existing Damascene architecture. During World War I, German and Turkish armies used Damascus as a base. When the United Nations placed Syria under French control, Damascus became the seat of Syrian resistance. In 1925, the French crushed a popular revolt in the unruly city. With Syrian independence in 1946, Damascus won its long-awaited status as the capital of a modern nation-state.

SYRIA

Damascus Old City

♪ NIGHTLIFE
Casablanca, **2**
Marmar, **1**
Piano Bar, **3**

Aththawra St.

Al-Naser St.

Baroudi St.

Zaghloul Souk

Hamidiyya Souk

Ibn Khaldoun St.

A Al-Albeit St.

Al-Badawi St.

Jarrah St.

Al-Mamoun St.

Sinan Pasha
Bab al-Gabla

Al-Shaghour St.

Bab al-Saghir

Madhat Basha St.

Moawiyah St.

Al-Hamidiyya St.

Dar al-Hadith

Medicine and Sciences

Arabic Epigraphy

Al-Jumrok Khan

Nureddin al-Shahid

Al-Kilyateen Mosque

Aladliya School

Alzahiriya Library

Aljaqmaqa School

Alzahiriya

Umayyad

Museum of Popular Arts and Traditions

Damascus Citadel

Bab al-Faraj

Bab al-Faradis

Bab al-Salaam

Al-Malek Faysal St.

Rougayya Mosque

Hassan al Kharat St.

Souk Bzouriyeh

Hammam Nureddin

Hassad Pasha Khan

Al-Azem Palace

Beit Jabri

Badreddin
Al-Hassan St.
Al-Nawfara

Temple of Jupiter

Nizam

Al-Sha'l House

Al-Amin St.

Al-Qaimariyh Ln.

Al-Bakri St.

Hammam Bakri

Protestant

Roman Arch

St. Mary's

Al-Jourah St.

Al-Bayanya

Bab Kissan

Ibn 'Asaker St.

Bab Sharqi St.

Bab Tuma St.

Marijjos Cathedral

Al-Azarya

Hananla

Ananias St.

Franciscan

Bab Tuma

Qassa St.

Bab Sharqi

SYRIA

AL-ITTIHAD SQUARE

Al-Zablatani St.

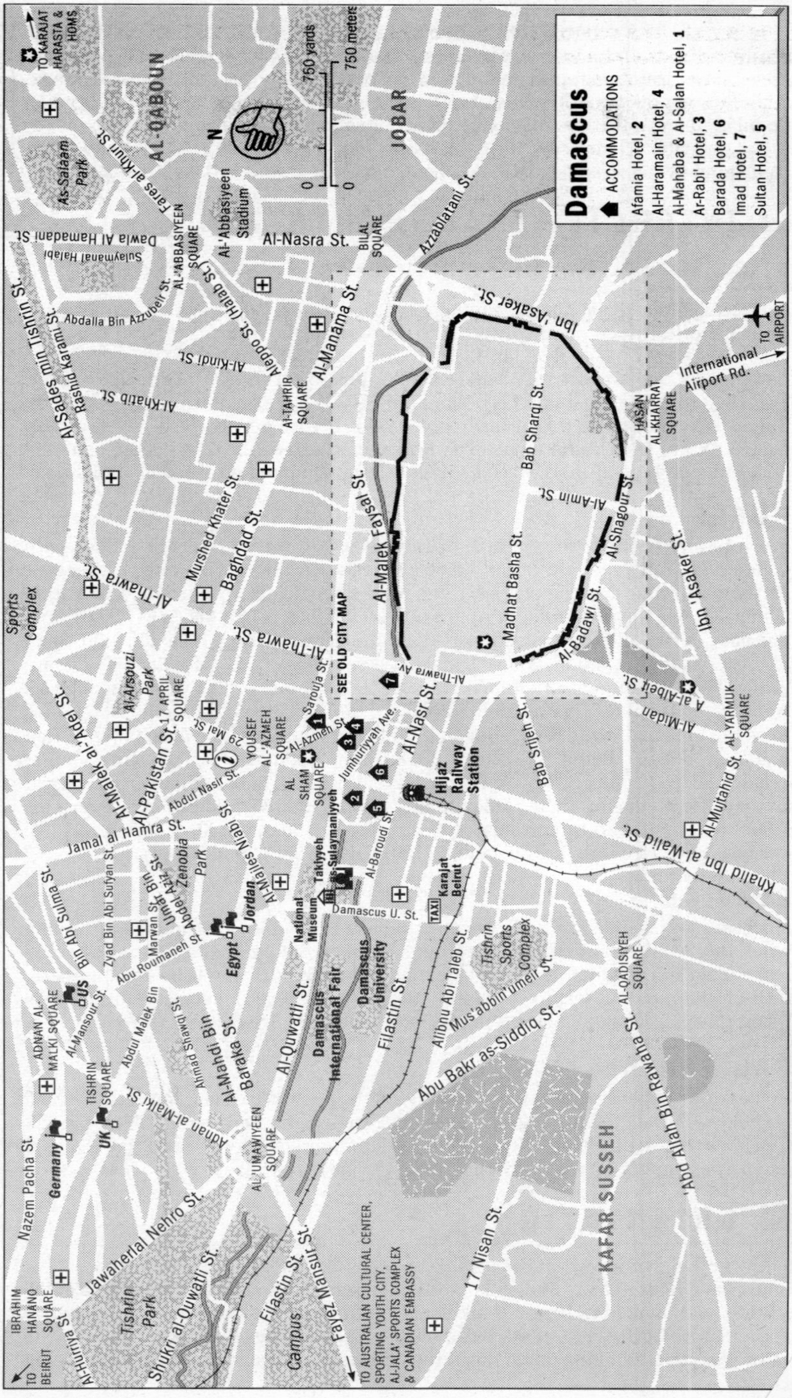

Damascus
ACCOMMODATIONS
Afamia Hotel, 2
Al-Haramain Hotel, 4
Al-Mahaba & Al-Salan Hotel, 1
Ar-Rabi' Hotel, 3
Barada Hotel, 6
Imad Hotel, 7
Sultan Hotel, 5
750 yards
750 meters
N
AL-QABOUN
As-Salaam Park
TO KARAJAT HARASTA & HOMS
Fares al-Khuri St.
Al-'Abbasiyeen Stadium
AL-'ABBASIYEEN SQUARE
Dawla Al Hamadani St.
Sulaymanal Halabi
Al-Nasra St.
BILAL SQUARE
JOBAR
Azzablatani St.
Ibn 'Asaker St.
TO AIRPORT
International Airport Rd.
HASAN AL-KHARRAT SQUARE
Bab Sharqi St.
Al-Amin St.
Al-Shagour St.
Madhat Basha St.
Al-Badawi St.
Ibn 'Asaker St.
Al-Midan
A al-Albeit St.
AL-YARMUK SQUARE
Al-Mujtahid St.
Khalid Ibn al-Walid St.
Bab Srijeh St.
Al-Sades min Tishrin St.
Rashid Karami St.
Abdalla Bin Azzubeir St.
Al-Kindi St.
Aleppo St. (Halab St.)
Al-Manama St.
Al-Khatib St.
AL-TAHRIR SQUARE
Al-Malek Faysal St.
SEE OLD CITY MAP
Murshed Khater St.
Baghdad St.
Al-Thawra St.
Al-Thawra St.
Al-Thawra Av.
Sports Complex
Al-Arsouzi Park
17 APRIL SQUARE
Al-Malek al-'Adel St.
Al-Pakistan St.
29 Mai St.
YOUSEF AL-'AZMEH SQUARE
Sarouja St.
Al-Azmeh St.
AL SHAM SQUARE
Jumhuriyyah Ave.
Al-Nasr St.
Hijaz Railway Station
Abdul Nasir St.
Jamal al Hamra St.
Al-Majles Nabi St.
Takiyyeh as-Sulaymaniyyeh
Al-Baroudi St.
Karajat Beirut
National Museum
Damascus U. St.
Zenobia Park
Jordan
Egypt
Bin Abi Sulma St.
Zyad Bin Abi Sufyan St.
Marwan St.
Bin Umar Aziz St.
Abdel
Abu Roumaneh St.
US
ADNAN AL-MALKI SQUARE
Al-Mansour St.
Abdul Malek Bin
Ahmad Shawqi St.
Al-Mahdi Bin Baraka St.
Al-Quwatli St.
Damascus International Fair
Damascus University
Filastin St.
Alibnu Abi Taleb St.
Tishrin Sports Complex
Mus'abbin'umeir St.
AL-QADISIYEH SQUARE
Abu Bakr as-Siddiq St.
Abd Allah Bin Rawaha St.
KAFAR SUSSEH
17 Nisan St.
TISHRIN SQUARE
UK
Adnan al-Malki St.
Germany
Nazem Pacha St.
AL-'UMAWIYEEN SQUARE
Jawaherlal Nehro St.
Fayez Mansur St.
Filastin St.
Campus
TO AUSTRALIAN CULTURAL CENTER, SPORTING YOUTH CITY, AJ-JALA' SPORTS COMPLEX & CANADIAN EMBASSY
IBRAHIM HANANO SQUARE
Tishrin Park
Shukri al-Quwatli St.
Al-Hurriya St.
TO BEIRUT

Today, the city reflects both contemporary reality and historical splendor, as satellite dishes and minarets tower over its streets. Damascus is a city of many faces: large fountains, parks, and wide avenues grace the newer part of town, while the winding cobblestone streets of the Old City house a sizable Christian population and a plethora of small, old-fashioned craft shops and bakeries. Downtown, pedestrians and cars thrust and parry in perennial street-level duel while fruit stand owners and pastry makers pull chairs up to the curbs and look on.

✈ INTERCITY TRANSPORTATION

FLIGHTS

Damascus International Airport, southeast of Damascus. Buses to the airport leave from Victoria Bridge on al-Quwatli St. (S£10 per piece of luggage, free if no luggage). Taxis S£300-500. Regular flights to European and Arab capitals and domestic one-way flights daily to: **Aleppo** (S£900); **Deir al-Zur** (S£900); **Lattakia** (S£500). Travelers to **Beirut** must pay US dollars (US$60, 21-day round-trip ticket US$100). Flights may be canceled arbitrarily up to 24hr. before departure. There is an **exit fee** (S£100) to leave Syria by air. The **SyrianAir** office (☎222 07 00) is opposite the post office n Sa'ad al-Jabri St. Open daily 8:30am-7pm; tickets issued 8:30-11am.

BUSES

For intercity transportation north of Damascus, 30 private bus companies with competitive rates operate out of **Karajat Harasta,** on the eastern edge of the city. Arrive at any time and chances are a bus will be leaving for your destination within 30min. Among the most reliable operators are the **Damas Tour Co.** (☎511 90 67) and **Qadmoos** (☎512 22 60). Buses depart daily to: **Aleppo** (4½hr.; 11:30am, 1:30, 3pm; S£150); **Hama** (3hr., noon, S£85); **Lattakia** (4hr., every hr., S£150); **Suweida** (1½hr., S£50). The government-run **Karnak Bus Co.** (☎231 14 93 or 231 61 36) is a 5-min. walk from Jisr al-Ra'is (President's Bridge), on Damascus University St., across from big blue and white SANA building. Run-down buses serve: **Amman** (4hr., 7am and 3pm, S£270); **Beirut** (3-3½hr.; 7:30, 8:30am, 3:30pm; S£175); **Bosra** (30min.; 11am, 2:30, 5, 7:30pm; S£50). Similarly decrepit Karnak buses depart from Karajat Harasta to: **Aleppo** (4-4½hr., 7:30am and 4:30pm, S£130); **Homs** (2hr., every hr. 7:30am-6:30pm, S£60); **Lattakia** (4-4½hr.; 7:30, 8:30am, 1:30, 2:30pm; S£125); **Palmyra** (3hr.; 10, 11am, 1, 2:30, 6pm; S£100); **Tartus** (5hr., 2pm, S£100).

SERVICE

Minibuses and **service** are fairly cheap and have the dubious advantage of leaving when full. Domestic *service* leave from Abbaseen Stadium; international *service* leave from Barumkeh. Shout your destination to the driver—if he's going there, he'll motion you in. *Service* travel to: **Aleppo** (3hr., S£300); **Amman** (4hr., S£400); **Beirut** (3hr., S£400-500); **Sidon** (4hr., S£500); **Tripoli** (5hr., S£500).

CAR RENTAL

Remarkably expensive. A few places around the post office rent, but little English is spoken. For helpful driving information in English, try **Hertz** (☎221 66 15; fax 222 61 81) at the Cham Palace Hotel. Rent with unlimited mileage for a day (S£3000 and up per day) or on a weekly basis (S£2700 and up per day).

✵ ORIENTATION

With the help of a few landmarks, Damascus is easy to navigate on foot. The impressive **Hijaz Railway Station** is at the intersection of **al-Nasser St.** and **Sa'ad al-Jabri St.,** with an old railway car on display in front of its stone steps and an extra-large picture of the late Assad. Sa'ad al-Jabri St. stretches directly away from the railway station. Walking down this street, the **post office** and **exchange bank** are on your left. Across the well-traveled footbridge crossing **al-Quwatli St.,** Sa'ad al-Jabri St. becomes **Port Said St.** Continuing on Port Said St. leads to **Yusef al-'Azmeh Sq.** Radiating from the right of this landmark are **29 Mai Ave.** (called **29 Ayyar Ave.** in Arabic) and the **Tourist Information Center.** To the left are **Maysaloun St.** and the five-star **Cham Palace Hotel** (pronounced "sham"). Continuing past Cham Palace brings you to **Abu Roumaneh St.** (officially named **al-Jala'a Ave.**), a nicer residential area that is home to several embassies and cultural centers.

Those seeking cheap eats and hotels, pistachio desserts, or money changing should head over to **al-Marjeh Sq.**—officially named al-Shuhada (Martyr's) Sq.— two blocks off al-Nasser St. in line with the post office. Al-Marjeh Sq. has developed something of an ill reputation, as Russian prostitutes frequent many of its cheaper hotels. In the center of the square, the **Barada River** surfaces from its underground lair in the form of a big fountain. Just up from al-Marjeh Sq., across al-Quwatli St., and to the right of al-'Azmeh Sq. is the **Bahsa** district, home to some of the nicest budget hotels in the Middle East. Continue right on al-Nasser St. from the Hijaz Station to enter the **Souq al-Hamidiyyeh** and the **Old City.** A walk through the covered *souq* brings you to the **Umayyad Mosque.**

A left turn from the Hijaz Station onto **al-Baroudi St.** eventually leads to the site of the annual international exposition, **Foire Internationale de Damas,** where the now defunct Barada River bed lies and fountains shoot high in the air. The **Taqiyyeh al-Suleimaniyyeh Mosque** and the **Military Museum** are on the right as you walk away from the station. The **National Museum** borders the dried-up river. The local **bus** and **service station** can be found under **Jisr al-Ra'is** (President's Bridge) on al-Quwatli St.

▣ LOCAL TRANSPORTATION

MICROBUSES

These white minivans (also called *service*) have predetermined routes and pick up passengers along the way. If one is going your way, flag it down. Tell the driver your destination when you get in to avoid confusion later. *Service* run to Mezzeh from the beginning of al-Thawra St. and to Muhajereen and Abu Roumaneh from under Jisr al-Ra'is (President's Bridge). A *service* also connects Baramkeh Station with Karaj Halab. As rides only cost S£3-10, even a short ride is usually worth it.

TAXIS

Private or **service taxis** (yellow cars) have meters, and drivers are required by law to use them. If the meter isn't turned on (starting fare S£3), either demand that the driver use it or negotiate a fair price before getting in. Longer trips, like the one from Hijaz Station to Karajat Harasta, shouldn't cost more than S£80. If you think that the driver is cheating you, point to the side of the road and indicate that you are getting out; if this doesn't work, try opening the door. Although drivers are likely to act annoyed, they will usually concede if you remain firm. Most drivers, however, will give you an honest rate and appreciate a small tip (S£5-10).

▣ PRACTICAL INFORMATION

TOURIST AND FINANCIAL SERVICES

Tourist Office: 29 Mai Ave. (☎232 39 53). From Yusef al-'Azmeh Sq., walk to the right of the modern white building; the clearly marked office will be on the left. Free maps and information in English. Open 24hr.

Tours: Allied Tours Kiwan (☎223 02 71 or 222 18 88, fax 224 52 41, kiwan@net.sy, www.alliedtour.com), in al-Marjeh Sq., 2nd fl. of al-Faiha building. More helpful than the disorganized official office. Whether you are an adventurer or a religious pilgrim, this well-situated office will get you where you want to go at the most reasonable prices around. Airport pickup can be arranged for S£1250. Open daily 9am-9pm.

Embassies:

Canadian, Block 12, al-Mezzeh (☎611 68 51; fax 611 40 00). Open Su-Th 8am-noon.

Egyptian (☎333 35 61), on al-Jala'a Ave. in Abu Roumaneh. Open Sa-Th 9am-3pm.

Jordanian (☎333 93 13), on al-Jala'a Ave. in Abu Roumaneh. Open Sa-Th 8am-2pm.

Turkish, 48 Ziad ibn Abi Sufyan St. (☎333 14 11). Open M-W 8am-3:15pm, Th 8am-2pm.

UK (☎373 92 41 or 373 52 28; fax 373 16 00), on Malki Kurd Ali St. Open M-Th 8:30-10:30am.

US, 2 al-Mansour St. (☎333 13 42, emergencies 333 32 32; fax 224 79 38). Take al-Jala'a Ave. (in Abu Roumaneh) away from al-Quwatli to Rawdat Abu al-'Ala'a Sq. The embassy is on the left. Consular section open Su-Th 7:30am-3:30pm; observes US and most Syrian holidays.

Visa Extension Office: Head to the Baramkeh station and cross the street. Turn right before the SANA news agency, and the brown **Immigration Office** will be to your left. Travelers staying in Syria for longer than 2 weeks must register with the police and apply for a visa extension. This will take all morning, so plan for lunch in the area. Bring 4 photographs and a copy of your passport. Start at the 3rd fl. and follow instructions. Open 8am-2pm. Go early!

Currency Exchange: Less of a chore than it used to be. Even though it's illegal, some shop owners and travel agents in Damascus discreetly offer to change foreign currency at slightly better rates than banks. This practice has greatly declined in the past year, as the cost of getting caught outweighs the meager rewards of the black market. Talk to locals and other travelers for advice on the current climate. Banking hours are Sa-Th 8am-2pm; many banks are also open 4-8pm. The **Commercial Bank of Syria,** at Yusef al-'Azmeh Sq., has a busy foreign cash exchange window and changes traveler's checks at no charge. Open M-Th 8:30am-12:30pm, Su 9:30am-12:30pm.

American Express (☎221 78 13; fax 221 79 38), to the right of the Sudan Airways office on al-Mutanabbi St. Heading away from Hijaz Station toward Yusef al-'Azmeh Sq., take a left on Fardous St., and al-Mutanabbi is the 1st left; go up the stairs. Holds mail for AmEx cardholders. Staff are among the most well-informed in Damascus. Open Sa-Th 8:30am-1:30pm and 5-8pm.

LOCAL SERVICES

English-Language Bookstores: The **Librairie Universelle** (☎223 23 00, ask to be transferred), in the Cham Palace Hotel near Yusef al-'Azmeh Sq., has 2 big shelves full of paperbacks in various languages. Yesterday's *International Herald Tribune* and last week's *Time* and *Newsweek* available. Open daily 9am-10pm. The **Sheraton** and **Meridien Hotels** have smaller selections.

Cultural Centers: American Cultural Center, 87 Ata Ayoubi St. (☎333 18 78). Frequent film screenings and concerts. Open Su-Th 8am-4pm. **British Council** (☎331 06 31), at Rawdah Sq. on the left side of al-Jala'a Ave. in Abu Roumaneh. A/C reading room. Open Sa-Th 8am-9pm.

Laundromat: Al-Ahram, next to al-Haramein Hotel in Bahsa, off al-Marjeh Sq. Pants and shirts S£20. Open Sa-Th 9am-9pm.

EMERGENCY AND COMMUNICATIONS

Emergency: Police: ☎112. **Ambulance:** ☎110. US citizens may call the embassy (☎333 32 32). For medical problems call the **Red Crescent** (☎442 16 00) or **al-Assad al-Jami'i Hospital** (☎212 65 00).

Tourist Police (☎222 00 00, ask to be transferred to Tourist Police). Take al-Quwatli St. past the National Museum; the office will be directly under Jisr al-Ra'is Hafez (President's Bridge), on the left side of the street. English-speaking. Open 24hr.

Late-night Pharmacies: Pharmacies are generally open Sa-Th 9am-1:30pm and 5-9:30pm. Try **Kassar** (☎222 73 47), across from the post office on Sa'ad al-Jabri St. Pharmacies rotate late hours; if you can't read the posted Arabic lists, inquire at a larger hotel. The all-night **Central Pharmacy,** on Saba 'Abhar Sq., is closed 1-5pm.

Telephones: The telephone office is on al-Nasser Ave., 1 block to the right of the Hijaz Station toward the Old City. Open daily 8am-10pm. For international calls, bring your passport, lots of cash, and a good supply of patience—placing calls can take up to 1hr. A far easier way to place both domestic and international calls is to buy an **Easycomm phone card** from the post office. Cards come in various denominations and can be used at any of the many Easycomm phone booths that dot the city. You cannot, however, dial toll-free Syrian numbers with these cards. Your only hope of using a foreign phone card is at a hotel.

Internet Access: ⬛Zoni Internet Service (☎232 46 70), behind Al-Haramein Hotel toward the big parking lot. No hotmail or telnet. Open a USNet or Yahoo! account before you go. S£750 per 5hr., S£5 per min. Open Sa-Th 9am-midnight, F 10am-midnight.

Post Office (☎223 82 00, then dial 2725), on the left side of Sa'ad al-Jabri St. as you head down the street directly in front of the Hijaz Railway Station. Open Sa-Th 8am-7pm, F 9am-noon. **Poste Restante** charges for parcels. Rates depend on Syrian customs. The **EMS Office** (☎223 69 00) is directly behind the post office, in a little building in the parking lot. Delivery to North America or Europe normally takes 3 days and is more expensive than at the post office, but probably worth it. Open Sa-Th 8am-6pm.

◤ ACCOMMODATIONS

In two-star or better hotels, prices for foreigners are listed in US dollars, though other Western currencies are often accepted. In all but one-star hotels, the Syrian government, eager to grab greenbacks, charges all foreigners (with the exception of Lebanese) two to three times what Syrians and those with residence permits pay. Most hotels accept traveler's checks and will give change in US dollars, but it's a good idea to have small bills on hand to simplify exchange and avoid horrible exchange rates. Most two-star hotels are near Hijaz Station and the post office, but al-Marjeh Sq. has cheaper, equally comfortable options. Many "hotels" in this area moonlight as brothels and may turn you away if you're not paying extra for a bedmate, but don't let the sleazy places keep you from finding jewels—inexpensive hotels with high ceilings, tidy bathrooms, and bug-free beds. If you're willing to give up satellite TV and a minifridge, many one-star hotels are both cheaper and cleaner than the two-star joints. Try the safe and lively Bahsa district first. Never forget to bargain, especially in the off season or if a place looks empty.

BAHSA

⬛**Al-Haramein Hotel** (☎231 94 89 or 231 42 99), on Bahsa St. With your back to the Cham Palace in Yusef al-'Azmeh Sq., walk down the winding road next to a big parking lot until you come to a sharp right. The hotel is on the right, on a shady, ivy-laced street. This charming old house, complete with an courtyard, has a super-friendly staff you'll want to take home with you. Breakfast S£75. Hot showers (S£35 for non-guests); shared bathrooms. Reserve 20 days in advance; during busy season even the roof is full. 4-bed dorms S£185; singles S£235; doubles S£400; triples S£555. MC/V.

⬛**Al-Rabi' Hotel** (☎231 83 74; fax 231 18 75), on Bahsa St. next door to al-Haramein Hotel. Similar in style to al-Haramein with a larger and greener courtyard, though less homey. International phone service, airport transport, help with hotel reservations. Breakfast S£75. Staff recommends reservations up to 10 days in advance during summer. 3-bed dorms S£185; singles S£250; doubles S£395; triples S£555. About S£150 more for private bathroom with miniscule shower. MC/V.

Al-Mahabba & al-Salaam Hotel (☎231 65 84), on Bahsa St., toward Yusef al-'Azmeh Sq. This "love and peace" hotel offers just that to weary travelers. Known to fill up when al-Haramein is full. Tidy and comfortable rooms, with spotless bathrooms. Bargain away—they take pity on students. Doubles S£900; triples S£1100.

AL-MARJEH SQ.

Imad Hotel (☎231 42 25), next to al-Tal Hotel. Walk toward Bahsa on the bridge in al-Marjeh Sq; al-Shuhada St. is the 2nd right near the live animal *souq*. A nice option in al-Marjeh, with refrigerators, fans, A/C, satellite TV, and the most comfortable beds around. Some rooms have breezy balconies with great views. Single woman-friendly. Breakfast US$2. Singles US$23; doubles US$24; triples US$30.

NEAR HIJAZ STATION

Barada Hotel (☎221 25 46 or 224 14 45), directly across from post office on Sa'ad al-Jabri. Sparkling, sunny rooms, nice common spaces, friendly staff, and a homey atmosphere make this family-owned hotel ideal for single women. Singles US$15; doubles US$18; triples US$23; television and private bath US$3 extra.

Sultan Hotel (☎222 57 68 or 221 69 10; fax 224 03 72), on al-Baroudi St. With your back to the station, turn left. The student-filled, tourist-friendly Sultan is a block down across the street. Colorful rooms with red and green carpets, and a small multi-language library in the lobby. Recommended for single women. In summer reserve at least 10 days in advance. Breakfast US$2.5. Singles US$19; doubles US$24; triples US$29.

Afamia Hotel (☎222 91 52 or 222 89 63; fax 221 46 83), off Jomhoriyyah St. directly behind the post office; take the 1st left after the big building. For a few more dollars, you can get one of the rooms on the top floor, which are brand-new and equipped with Art Deco furniture and such rare commodities as hair dryers. Single women might want to scope it out before booking a room. Singles US$20; doubles US$24; triples US$39.

◘ FOOD

There are as many food stands around al-Marjeh Sq. as portraits of Assad—hummus, falafel, and shawarma are Damascene staples. Fresh fruit stands serve juices that can be meals in themselves. Prices are fairly low (hummus S£30, falafel S£15, shawarma S£25, large juice S£40-50). The best pastry shops are around al-Marjeh Sq.—don't miss *ba'laweh*, sinfully honey-glazed pistachio treats.

Maysaloun St., just off Yusef al-'Azmeh Sq. past the Cham Palace Hotel, is home to numerous sit-down restaurants and ice cream parlors. In the evenings, the street fills with cologne-scented sweet-lovers strolling with a sundae or large juice in hand. ▨**Damer Patisserie** is the best ice cream parlor in Damascus. (Open Sa-Th 9am-12:30am.) If you've had enough of hummus, pizzerias line Abu Roumaneh St., one block down from Damer Patisserie. The **Christian Quarter** in the Old City (Bab Touma Sq.) has a great atmosphere and boasts falafel as well as pizza joints. Christian Syrians are known to flaunt their freedom from alcohol restrictions here.

▨ **Al-Shamiat** (☎222 72 70), off Abu Roumaneh St. in al-Nijma Sq. Beaded lamps, tables with hand-sewn embroidery, fresh flowers, and hanging baskets create a kitsch conspiracy. This local favorite caters to an eclectic crowd of expats and intellectuals. Appetizers S£10-30; entrees S£60-100; drinks S£15-25. Open daily 7am-3am.

▨ **Scheherazade Palace Restaurant** (☎544 59 00). Walk down Souq al-Hamidiyyeh to the Umayyad Mosque; Scheherazade is directly behind the mosque on the right. This gorgeous restaurant is relatively inexpensive, and its delectable dishes take Syrian cuisine to a new level. Outdoor seating available. Appetizers S£20; main courses S£100. Open daily 10am-1am. Reservations recommended Thursday nights.

Beit Jabri Restaurant (☎541 62 54 or 544 32 00). All roads lead to Beit Jabri. Follow the yellow signs from Al-Azem Palace or from the Umayyad Mosque. Built in the 18th century, this newly converted Damascene house is now known as an "intellectual restaurant." The bougainvillea and grapevine shades make for a laid-back ambiance late into the night. Fast service and great food. Try the "Fool with yogurt" (*fu'ul* is the arabic word for beans), a meal in itself for just S£40. Appetizers S£30-40; main courses S£100. Also offers Internet facilities (S£200 per hr.) and a TV room. Open daily 9:30am-1:30am. Reservations recommended after 6pm.

Nadi al-'Ummal (☎231 87 69). Turn right off 29 Ayyar Ave. at Cinema al-Sufara (across from the tourist office) and follow the lamp-lined path to the end of the street. You won't find many proletarians at this "Workers' Club," but you will find excellent appetizers (S£50-70) and grills (S£85-100) while relaxing in the *argileh*-scented breezes of an old Damascene courtyard. Barada beer S£60. *Argileh* S£80. Open Sa-Th 5pm-12:30am.

Abu al-Ezz (☎221 81 74 or 224 60 05). With your back to the Umayyad Mosque, walk through the arch of the Temple of Jupiter and take the 1st right; it's on the left. One of the best places around to soak up Syrian atmosphere and food. Try the *bas bashkat* (S£85). Lunch and dinner S£350-400. Live music and whirling dervishes in the Bedouin tent after 9:30pm. Open daily 8am-2am. Reservations required for dinner.

Pizza Roma (☎331 64 34), off Maysaloun St., on the right just past the Cham Palace. A modern and authentic pizza joint with a rare (but feeble) salad bar. Create your own pizza with a variety of swineless toppings. Pizza S£50-150. Open daily 11am-1am.

Abu Kamal (☎222 42 65), in Yusef al-'Azmeh Sq, upstairs in the Ministry of Labor building on the corner of Fardous St. Bow-tied waiters bring succulent entrees (S£125-225) while you gaze through large windows onto the square. Delicious *kebbeh* (breaded lamb fried with onions). Appetizers S£35-100; desserts S£50. Open daily 7am-1am; reservations recommended on weekends. MC/V.

'Ali Baba (☎222 54 34), in Yusef al-'Azmeh Sq. under Abu Kamal. A monumental achievement in Arab aesthetics, the basement is a womb of Arab decor and decorum. Shares kitchen and prices with Abu Kamal. Whirling dervishes entertain happy eaters during the summer Th and Sa 8:30-11pm. Open daily 7am-1am. AmEx/MC/V.

👁 SIGHTS

CITADEL. Built by the Seljuks in 1078 CE, the Citadel once housed elaborate baths, mosques, and schools. During the Crusader invasions, it functioned as headquarters for Egyptian and Syrian sultans, including Salah al-Din. Ayyubid Sultan Malik al-'Adil demolished and rebuilt the Citadel in 1202 CE because he felt it was no longer suitable for contemporary warfare. The new fortress has 300 arrow slits and was once surrounded by a deep moat, now filled in to serve as the *souq* floor. As of August 2001 the Citadel was closed for renovations, but you can still peek through the wrought iron gate. *(Next to the entrance of Souq al-Hamidiyyeh in the Old City.)*

SOUQ AL-HAMIDIYYEH. A rich and colorful trail of desserts, spices, nuts, tawdry dancing garb, glitzy cloth, and carved wooden artifacts, Souq al-Hamidiyyeh assails your senses as you whisk through seemingly endless tunnels that buzz with the sounds of the marketplace. *(Beginning next to the Citadel and stretching to the Temple of Jupiter and the Umayyad Mosque.)*

UMAYYAD MOSQUE. Caliph Walid ibn 'Abd al-Malik supervised the building of the Umayyad Mosque, one of the oldest and grandest mosques in the world. Originally the site of an ancient temple dedicated to Hadad (an Aramaean god revered around 1000 BCE), it was later the temple of Jupiter the Damascene. In the 4th century, a Byzantine church dedicated to St. John the Baptist was erected on this site. When the church was destroyed to make room for the grand mosque, the only relic that survived was the head of St. John (known to Muslims as the Prophet Yahya) which now rests in its own shrine in the mosque's prayer hall. The shrine is a site of worship for both Christians and Muslims. Today, the mosque is a crowded, center of socialization, business, gossip, and worship. The mosque's three minarets were built in different styles, reflecting the changes under different empires. Intricate mosaics decorate the walls and ceilings of the mosque, and on the central dome are the names of some of the most significant figures in early Muslim history. *(Follow Souq al-Hamidiyyeh to the end. Open daily 9:30am-9pm, closed for prayer F 12:30-2pm. Use the visitors' entrance to the left of the main entrance. S£50 includes entrance and elegant brown gowns for women who are not appropriately dressed.)*

SALAH AL-DIN'S TOMB. The famed fighter's body lies under a red dome in a peaceful garden mausoleum. Built in 1193 CE and later restored by Kaiser Wilhelm II of Germany in the 19th century, the building contains both a wooden and a marble tomb in the place of honor. The marble was a gift from the Kaiser, but Salah al-Din chose to stay in the wooden one. Before the Umayyad Mosque at the end of Souq al-Hamidiyyeh stand the remains of the 3rd-century CE **Temple of Jupiter**, now a source of shade for magazine and Qur'an vendors. *(Follow Souq al-Hamidiyyeh down to the end. The tomb is to the left of the Umayyad Mosque, on the way to its visitors' entrance. Open daily 9am-5pm; in winter 10am-4pm. Free.)*

IRANIAN MOSQUE (SAYYIDA RAQAI'YA'S MOSQUE). Financed by Iranians, this stunning mausoleum and mosque was built for Lady Raqai'ya, the daughter of Imam Hussein. Beautiful blues and yellows of mosaics surround her golden, chandelier-lit shrine, reflected in the mirrors and crystals of the mosque ceiling. *(Near the Umayyad Mosque, but farther north toward the Barada River. Open daily 4am-2am. Conservative dress and headscarf required; provided free. All faiths welcome.)*

AL-AZEM PALACE. First built under the Ottomans in 1749 for As'ad Basha al-Azem, the governor of Damascus, this palace also briefly housed King Faisal after the Ottomans' fall in World War I. Surrounding the courtyard are various rooms with reenacted Ottomanesque scenes, including a multi-room Turkish bath (note the pained expression on the man who is being scrubbed) and a bridal room complete with mother-in-law, unwed daughters, and maids. Inside, the **Museum of Popular Traditions** has the usual stone-faced mannequins in anatomically impossible poses, with French-only labels. *(On the right side of the Umayyad Mosque when approaching from Souq al-Hamidiyyeh. Palace and museum open W-M 9am-5:30pm; in winter 9am-3:30pm. S£300, students S£15.)*

CHRISTIAN QUARTER. The **Chapel of Ananias,** dedicated to the Christian disciple who restored sight to St. Paul, is here. *(Follow Souq al-Hamidiyyeh to the Umayyad Mosque. Circle to the right around the mosque and continue farther down any road. You're in the Christian Quarter when mosques turn to churches. Cross Bab Touma St. and the chapel is ahead. Open daily 9am-1pm and 4-7pm., in winter 9am-1pm and 3-5pm. Free.)* Across Midhat Basha St. stands **St. Paul's Chapel,** the Armenian Orthodox church from which the saint was lowered out of a window to escape arrest by his enemies. You may have to knock at the gate to enter; the friendly multilingual staff will be happy to let you in and give you a religious history lesson. *(Open daily 8am-1:30pm. Free.)*

TAQIYYEH AL-SULEIMANIYYEH MOSQUE. Though this downtown mosque is open only to Muslims, its simple yet striking exterior is a compelling expression of Ottoman architecture. Built in 1554 CE by the famed architect Sinan, its two lofty minarets frame an imposing dome reflected in a courtyard fountain. The surrounding *madrasa* was converted into the **Artisanat,** an Ottoman market offering silver jewelry, oil paintings, and mother-of-pearl inlaid backgammon boards. *(From Yusef al-'Azmeh Sq., walk down Port Said St. to Salam al-Baroudi St. Take a right; the mosque and market are down on the right. Most shops open daily 9am-9pm. MC/V.)*

🏛 MUSEUMS

📖NATIONAL MUSEUM. Admire the collection of writings in Ugarit (the first alphabet, dating from the 14th century BCE), Aramaic (the language that Jesus spoke), and Arabic amidst the shady green courtyard littered with ruins. The permanent collection contains Syrian sculpture, a Qur'an collection, Palmyran textiles from the first three centuries CE, original scientific writings of Ibn Sina, and a reconstructed underground tomb from Palmyra. Beyond the door at the end of the last hall stand the frescoed walls of a synagogue excavated from the 3rd-century CE town of Doura Europos. *(One street over from the Taqiyyeh al-Suleimaniyyeh mosque. Open M-W 9am-6pm; in winter 9am-4pm. S£300, students S£15. Ask the guard to let you in.)*

MILITARY MUSEUM. Stacked with swords and guns, this museum testifies to the military past of Syria. On display are ancient and modern weapons and photographs paying homage to those who have served their country. *(Across the street from the cafe of the National Museum, next door to the Taqiyyeh al-Suleimaniyyeh mosque. Open W-M 8am-2pm. S£5, students S£3.)*

> **WHY YOU GOTTA (FORE)PLAY ME LIKE THAT?** No self-respecting Damascus movie theater lacks eye-catching advertisements. Go to any of these movie houses and you will likely encounter posters depicting couples in titillating positions, captured *in flagrante delicto,* adding a bit of erotic flair to the already frenzied Damascene streets. Anyone hoping that the promises made outside the theater will come to fruition inside will be disappointed: Syrian censorship laws require that sexually explicit material be deleted from films. Laws say nothing about ads, however, and movie house managers accordingly exploit the loophole.

⚑ NIGHTLIFE

When it comes to nightlife, Damascus knows how to sit back and relax. Soak in a *hammam* before heading off to a cafe or bar for the night. If you'd rather catch a movie, the high-quality **Cham Palace Theater** has regular showings of American films (every 3hr. 12:30-9:30pm, S£100).

CAFES

As the evenings cool, Damascenes of all stripes take to the streets. Outdoor cafes pepper the area behind the Umayyad Mosque. By the end of the evening this area grows into a big street party as people pull up chairs to drink or smoke *argileh.* Try one of the best Old City cafes, **al-Nawafara,** which features nightly Arabic storytelling (7-8pm; in winter 6-7pm). Take Souq al-Hamidiyyeh to the Umayyad Mosque. Turn right at the mosque and proceed around the wall. Take the first right; the cafe is on the immediate right. Unlike most cafes, this one welcomes single women. (☎543 68 13. *Argileh* S£50; Turkish coffee S£25. Open daily 7:30am-midnight.) Younger people line **Maysaloun St.** in downtown Damascus, at the crossroads of Yusef al-'Azmeh St. and Port Said St. If you scream for ice cream, check out **Damer** and **Shimi,** opposite one another on Maysaloun St.

BARS

Much late-night and early-morning activity in Damascus takes place in the bars of larger hotels and in the Christian quarter around Bab Touma, where alcohol restrictions are thrown by the wayside. Women will not be received warmly at most local bars, though hotels and nicer bars in Bab Touma are exceptions. It is wise for women to find trustworthy male companions. Many embassies rotate hosting parties on Thursday nights; call the American embassy for details.

Mar Mar (☎541 00 41), in Bab Touma near Hammam Bakree, across from the Elissar Restaurant. The closest approximation to a mellow Western bar. Its lovely decor and setting in an old mansion explain its popularity. Local stars and wealthy young jet-setters drink beer (S£100) and eat steak (S£275) while listening to fresh Arab-American-Latin tunes. Open Th-Su until 2am. Reservations recommended Th and Sa nights.

Casablanca, on the last left off of Hanamia St. before Bab Sharqi in the Old City, down the street from Le Piano. A very classy joint with super-friendly staff, beautiful roofed courtyard, and fountained terrace. Serves luxurious drinks and expensive dinners, but ask for the group rate and you might get a fixed menu 5-course dinner for S£250. Live oldies music. Beer S£100-150; wine S£450-900. Open daily noon-12:30am.

Le Piano (☎543 03 75), on the last left off of Hanamia St. before Bab Sharqi in the Old City. This cramped, music-themed bar serves cold beer (S£140) and features karaoke. No cover. Reservations necessary. Only singles admitted.

POOLS AND BATHS

You can take a dip for S£200 in the numerous **swimming pools** in Damascus (many at larger hotels). True decadence, however, is most closely approximated at the *hammams* (Turkish baths) that gurgle around the *souq.*

Hammam Nour al-Din (☎222 95 13), in the covered street between the Umayyad Mosque and Midhat Basha St. The most luxurious *hammam* in the city caters to men only. Full massage, bath, soap, and sauna S£300. Open daily 8am-midnight.

Hammam al-Ward (☎231 43 07), near the black and white al-Ward Mosque in Bahsa, 2 streets behind al-Haramein Hotel. Great for women who want to experience a Damascene *hammam*. Have the whole Turkish bath to yourself for S£1500. The works S£200. Open noon-5pm; Tu-W for women, Th-M for men.

▣ DAYTRIPS FROM DAMASCUS

BOSRA بصرى

*Microbuses from Karaj Dar'a on the southern edge of Damascus go to Dar'a (2hr., S£45); it's another 30min. and S£15 to Bosra. A **private taxi** will take you directly to Bosra for S£700. **The Citadel** is open daily 8am-7pm. S£300, students S£15.*

For an under-touristed part of Syria and solitude amid Roman ruins, make your way to Bosra, 20km from the Jordanian border. Nineteen centuries ago, Bosra was the northern capital of the Nabateans, who are best known for building and abandoning the castles at Petra, Jordan (see p. 481). The Romans annexed the city in 106 CE, renamed it *Neatrajana Bustra*, and made it the capital of the Province of Arabia. Muslim control began in 634 CE, and the 6000-seat theater (with standing room for 3000 more) was converted into a Citadel over the next six centuries: fortifications were added, a second outer wall was constructed, and more rooms were built to accommodate increasing numbers of horses and soldiers.

Enter Bosra through the stark **City Gate,** constructed around 200 BCE and known to former inhabitants as *Bab al-Hawa* (Gate of the Wind). Several Roman columns greet you at the entrance. Straight ahead is the **Cryptoportic,** a great market constructed in the first half of the 2nd century. The well-preserved 3rd-century **Central Arch,** known to locals as *Bab al-Qandil* (Gate of the Candle), stands to the right. Continue to the right to reach the splendid **Roman Baths.** The guard will show you around the baths; a tip of S£100 is appropriate. To see the most impressive structure in Bosra, the **Roman Theater-Arab Citadel** complex, retrace your steps to the Central Arch and turn left. The Roman Theater is one of the best-preserved in the world, with secret stairways and an original stage.

Bosra boasts historically significant Muslim sights as well. The 7th-century **Mosque of Omar** is purportedly the world's third-oldest mosque, still maintaining some of its original form as a pagan temple. The **Mabrak Mosque** is where, according to legend, a camel delivered the first Qur'an in Syria. The 3rd-century **basilica** is where Prophet Muhammad allegedly met Nestorian monk Bahira, who was the first to predict the Prophet's future greatness. South of the City Gate is *Birkat al-Hajj* (Pool of Pilgrimage), a huge reservoir dug by the Romans. A branch of Wadi Zeid fed by a conduit system flowed down from the hills and emptied itself into this reservoir. For a moment of peace, walk east toward Suweida to the **Cistern.**

If sightseeing makes your tummy grumble, face away from the reservoir gate and look for the biggest restaurant in the right-hand corner of the tourist courtyard. The four-star **Bosra Cham Palace Hotel** provides fast food favorites (salad, hummus, french fries), as well as freshly prepared dinners. Food is prepared at a different location, so call ahead to avoid a long wait. (Appetizers S£22-45. Entrees S£110-125. ☎015 79 08 81. Open daily 7am-11pm.)

MA'ALULA معلولا

*Ma'alula is an easy daytrip from Damascus, with frequent **minibuses** from Karaj Ma'alula on the east side of town (1hr., S£20). To get to Karaj, take a **service** to Abbaseyeen Sq.; it's down al-Nasra St. on the left. Alternatively, take a **taxi** (S£30).*

The small town of Ma'alula (56km northeast of Damascus) is tucked into al-Qalamoun Mountains. Ancient churches and weathered mosques drowse among blue houses, precipitously clinging to steep slopes beneath staggering cliffs. The urban culture of nearby Damascus is gradually infiltrating Ma'alula (in the form of graffiti on the walls of the mountain paths, for example), but it has not yet gained a secure foothold. This is one of the few places in the world where townspeople still speak **Aramaic,** the language in which Jesus preached and the Lord's Prayer was authored. Aramaic remained the vernacular of Syria until replaced by Arabic after the Islamic conquests of the 7th century. The language only survives among the few Christians who live in isolated villages in the mountains.

The **Monastery of St. Taqla** was carved into the face of a nearby barren cliff in the 4th century to hold the remains of the young saint. The daughter of a Seleucid prince, Taqla was a disciple of St. John and a Christian convert before such behavior became popular. She ran away from home when a servant revealed that her father had plans to kill her. As the legend goes, Taqla was being pursued on the night she was sentenced to be burned. She was led by an angel toward safety: a mountain opened up for her and then quickly closed, crushing her father's soldiers. Ask for the "information nun" to learn more about the monastery and its history. Spending one night at the monastery is free; each subsequent night is S£200.

The road around to the left of the town and the cliffs leads to the mountaintop chapel of **Mar Sarkis,** named after a Syrian horseman who lived during the reign of King Maximus (3rd century CE). If you continue along the road past the Safir Hotel, you'll see the entrance to the mountain path at the bridge on the left. This takes you to St. Taqla's Monastery; take a right for cliffs and spectacular views.

DEIR MAR MUSA

*To get to Deir Mar Musa, take a **microbus** or **bus** from Karajat Harasta in Damascus to Nebek (1hr., every 30min. or when full, S£35). Deir Mar Musa is a 30min. drive from the town of Nebek (80km from Damascus). Anything on wheels will take you from Nebek to the monastery for S£300 (you may find other travelers to split the fare with). To return to Nebek, arrange for a driver to pick you up or get a free ride with the monastery bus (M-Sa, 2:30pm). From Nebek, take a bus back to Damascus from the main bus station (1hr., 5am-8pm, S£35). For more information contact the monastery at ☎ 723 1301; deirmarmusa@mail.sy; www.deirmarmusa.org.*

Nestled in the deserted mountains of the Qalamoun, Deir Mar Musa offers a Heidiesque setting without the Swiss greenery. The newly restored monastery is home to a tight-knit community that welcomes all faiths and species. The residents' daily life is centered around meals, meditation, prayer, and caring for the monastery's 40 goats and other assorted livestock. All of the priests are musically inclined, and the daily musical interlude follows meditation hour. Hospitality is one of the monastery's priorities and the heterogeneous group of monks and nuns will be happy to put you up for as long as you like (donations accepted, of course).

After the short hike up to the Monastery, you will be welcomed into the main building with a quick cup of tea and a tour of the frescoed walls of the 11th-century church, the small museum, and the underground library. The numerous caves around the monastery are ideal for spiritual retreat, but are occasionally used to house campers who have been known to leave their marks on the walls. The view from the summit is worth the hike, and the beautiful starlit sky is reason enough to put your bags down for the night.

SAYIDNAYA صيدنايا

*To get to Sayidnaya, take a **bus** from Karaj Ma'alula on the east side of town (40min., S£13). To get to Karaj, take a taxi or service to Abbaseyeen Sq.; it's down al-Nasra St. on the left. **Microbuses** connect Sayidnaya and Ma'alula (5:30am-8:30pm, S£250-300).*

Sayidnaya (Arabic for "Our Lady"), a sandstone town of small shops, beautiful views, and a glowing hilltop chapel, rests 29km between Damascus and Ma'alula. The Byzantine **Chapel of the Virgin** in the center of town was built in 547 CE to honor the spot where the Virgin Mary appeared, in the form of a gazelle, before Emperor Justinian I. The gazelle ordered Justinian to build a church on that very spot, and later returned in a dream with the blueprints. Today, the church serves as both a small orphanage and school, demonstrating the communal interplay between religion and education. Within a maze of stone stairways, a shrine to the Virgin contains an **icon** (said to have been painted by St. Luke), to which miracles throughout the ages have been attributed. To the right of the church is the entrance to a small underground **sanctuary** where Mary supposedly stood. It may be necessary to get the security guard to ask one of the nuns to open the mirrored doors protecting the icon and sanctuary. The inscription outside the entrance echoes the commandment given to Moses before the Burning Bush (Exodus 3:5): "Take off your shoes, for the ground you are treading upon is sacred." Sayidnaya was second only to Jerusalem as a place of pilgrimage during the Crusades, and was called (redundantly) Notre Dame de Sayidnaya. Pilgrims and respectful visitors may be allowed to spend one night in the convent for free.

QUNEITRA قنيطرة

*Visitors must obtain permission from the Syrian Ministry of the Interior before going to Quneitra. The free permit can be obtained at the Fir' al-Muhajireen office behind Palace Adnan al-Malki. Go up the stairs from the white monument and look for men with rifles out front. Bring your **passport** (which will often be checked on the way to Quneitra). Permit office open Su-Th 8am-2pm; permit valid for the same day or the next. **Buses** leave every 10min. (or when full) from Baramkeh Station for Khan Arnabeh (1½hr., S£20), then from Khan Arnabeh to Quneitra (15min., S£5). Pick up your mandatory guide/security officer between Khan Arnabeh and Quneitra. Don't take pictures of anything vaguely official-looking: your roll of film could be confiscated.*

The war-ravaged town of Quneitra (a diminutive form of *qantara*, "bridge") owes its misfortune to its location beside the Golan Heights, at an intersection of roads leading to four often militant countries. Quneitra was destroyed during the Syrian-Israeli conflict in 1967 (see **Modern History**, p. 566) and was recently opened by the Syrian government as a "museum." The incident on the Golan was a major factor in the political destabilization that allowed the still-governing Ba'ath Party to seize control in November 1970. Quneitra is a fair distance from Damascus, but a visit to the town is worthwhile—although the museum itself is unimpressive as a memorial to those who perished during the bombings, the town does offer a firsthand look at the aftermath of military conflicts that have long plagued the Middle East. Visitors are left to explore the modern ruins and walk through the crumbled streets under the close supervision of their security officer. The partially destroyed mosque, church, and hospital have been stripped bare and are riddled with bullet holes. Sometimes, especially Fridays, you can see families yelling at each other by megaphone between the Golan and the Syrian UN border (only 2km long). Binoculars are provided at the Quneitra Restaurant to gaze out over the UN Military Security Zone at Israel, just 500m away.

SUWEIDA سويدة

*Buses from Damascus to Suweida (130km southeast) leave from Karaj Suweida, which is, confusingly, actually the same place as Karaj Dar'a (1½hr., S£40). **Service** from Damascus to Suweida leave Karaj Suweida frequently (1½hr., S£40). Damas Tours also offers regular **buses** to Suweida (1½hr., S£50). To get to Suweida from Bosra, take a **service** from the town to Karaj Suweida in Damascus (30min., S£10).*

In the 3rd century, the Romans considered Suweida (then known as Dionysis) one of the most important towns in the Province of Arabia. Late in the Nabatean period, the area was called Suwada ("little black town") because it was constructed with black volcanic rock. In recent decades, however, this provincial town has been bulldozed to make way for new houses to accommodate the growing population. Suweida has little to offer travelers as a daytrip from Damascus, and is best visited on the way to Qanawat. Don't leave, without checking out the well-organized and informative **Suweida Museum**, 1km up the hill from the bus station. Many of Suweida's ruins have been preserved in this museum, built and organized in 1991 with French aid. It contains artifacts ranging from the Stone Age to the Roman Empire, including many well-preserved basalt statues. The first floor is populated by plaster figures engaged in traditional Druze activities. The highlights are the mosaics from Shaba in the main room, especially the beautiful "Artemis Surprised while Bathing" from the mid-3rd century CE. (Open daily 9am-6pm; in winter 9am-4pm. S£300, students S£15.)

If you're hungry, you will several restaurants in the city center *(wust al-balad).* For a unique East-meets-West experience, turn your back to the bus station and admire the gaudy, mirrored **Lotus Restaurant** in Basil Hafez al-Azem Sq. (Appetizers S£25-50; entrees S£100-150. ☎23 01 59. Open daily 9am-midnight. Western style toilets, but bring your own paper.)

▧ QANAWAT قنوات

Buses to Qanawat (S£2-5) leave in the morning from the main bus station in Suweida. After noon, take a taxi to Suweida's other bus station, or walk up to the Suweida Museum and hop on the 1st bus that comes by. Buses from Damascus to Suweida leave from Karaj Suweida (same location as Karaj Dar'a. 1½hr., S£40). Service from Damascus to Suweida leave Karaj Suweida frequently (1½hr., S£40).

Once a member of the mercantile Decapolis League, ancient Qanawat flourished under Ghassanid rule in the first century BCE. After the monuments at Bosra, those at Qanawat are the most impressive and richly decorated in the region. Ancient carved stones litter the ground, hide in present-day dwellings, and soar up as haughty columns. Qanawat today prides itself on being a quasi-exclusive residence and a pilgrimage site for the **Druze,** a secretive sect derived from the Ismai'ili branch of Shi'ite Islam (see **Religions,** p. 60). They have been living in the region known as Jabal al-'Arab since the 11th century CE.

A cluster of columns from a 2nd-century temple marks the entrance to present-day Qanawat. The village square is on the site of the ancient forum, and old paving-stones still cover parts of the ground. Take a left from the village square to see the gorge of Wadi al-Ghar, lined with the shady roofs of Druze homes built from the Roman ruins. Within the gorge, a pillared structure encloses a green pool, where local children take a dip during the warm summer afternoons.

Christian buildings sprinkled among the Roman ruins testify to Qanawat's role as a bishopric under Byzantine Christianity. Columns of an ancient temple, contained in a basilica in the 4th and 5th centuries CE, still stand. A characteristic floral pattern marks the walls of this building as well as the many fragments lying on the ground. The right slope of the valley is home to a few steps of a small theatre, the remains of a nymphaeum and an aqueduct, and the foundations of two towers. The street up the hillside also leads to the **Temple of Zeus,** which boasts a view over the entire valley, and the *Serai,* a group of monuments on the highest point in Qanawat. The monuments are surrounded by a little wall, but the gatekeeper will let you in (S£150, students S£15).

IZRA'

Microbuses to Izra' (S£15) leave from the Dar'a Post Office, 1km from the main bus station in Dar'a, 7am-4pm. A taxi will make the trip for S£400. Microbuses leave from Izra' to Damascus from the Izra' bus station (S£25)—the driver will take you up to the churches at no extra fee. Service is irregular; ask when the last bus leaves when you get there (no buses leave after sunset).

After a long stretch of countryside tapestried with grazing sheep, olive trees, and endless strips of golden wheat, Izra' itself appears lacking in color. Its two historic churches, however, are well worth the trip.

Superstitious locals are very attached to their churches, and proud to see that they attract visitors from afar. They will be happy to help you in your search for the key keepers and kindly show you to the donation box. Founded in 515 CE, the Greek Orthodox **Church of St. George,** known by locals as *Mar Georgis,* is believed to contain the tomb of St. George. Walking down from the church of St. George, remainders of a mosque prayer hall lie on the left. Amid the rubble, two pillars stand side by side, and legend has it that only those who can pass between the pillars are *wlad halal,* or legitimate children.

Take a left after the pillars and walk up the street to reach the more utilized Greek Catholic **Church of St. Elias.** Founded in 542, this church has only recently begun to arouse archaeological interest; scholars are currently deciphering the Greek inscriptions on the church doors that recount the history of the building.

CENTRAL SYRIA

PALMYRA تدمـر   ☎ 31

The desert oasis of Palmyra ("City of Palms," also known locally as **Tadmor,** "City of Dates") first offered travelers shade in the first century BCE, when it was a stopover for caravans passing from the Persian Gulf to the Mediterranean. Palmyrenes prospered from tax revenues collected from tired, thirsty traders and grew even wealthier when their city became a Roman colony in 129 CE. Palmyra became the keystone of a thriving trade between Rome, the Middle East, and India, and most of the city's surviving ruins date from this period of prosperity.

During the middle of the 2nd century CE, reduced trade and increased distaste for Persian rule inspired Palmyran resident **Odenathus** to overthrow the city's senate and declare himself king. Odenathus and his son were assassinated in 267 CE, after defeating the encroaching Persians. Odenathus's multilingual and strikingly beautiful second wife **Zenobia** took control of the city. Possessing "manly understanding" (according to 18th-century historian Edward Gibbon), this woman not only secured Palmyra's full independence from Rome, but also attacked the Roman territories and took possession of lower Egypt and much of Asia Minor. The minting of coins emblazoned with her image was the last straw: infuriated Roman emperor Aurelian captured Palmyra and carted Zenobia off to Rome.

In succeeding years, Palmyra served as a Roman border fortress until Muslims conquered it in the 7th century CE. Local emir Fakhr al-Din built the castle overlooking the site in the early 1600s, but the ruined city was only sporadically inhabited. By mid-century, no one knew the once-proud metropolis had ever existed. In 1678, two English merchants rediscovered the city, but excavations did not begin until 1924. First centered in the courtyard of the Temple of Bel, the modern town was relocated northeast of the ruins between 1929 and 1932. Today, Palmyra's column-lined avenues stand proudly in a lush oasis surrounded by miles of uninhabited desert. The city's ruins, though weathered by centuries of war and sandstorms, rank among the most spectacular in the Middle East. As a result, large tourist buses are perpetually stationed at its gates. Near the ruins, the city's main street is lined with colorful souvenir shops while the little back alleys are bland, distinguished only by tourist-enthralled children. Nevertheless, as the sun sets over majestic ruins, Palmyra's beauty astounds.

⌐ TRANSPORTATION

Luxury Buses:

Karnak Station (☎91 02 88), near the circle by the tourist office, sends buses to: **Damascus** (3hr.; 10:15am, 12:30, 1:45, 5:15pm; S£100); **Deir al-Zur** (2hr.; 11:30am, 1:45, 3:15, 5:30, 7:30, 9:15pm; S£75); **Homs** (2hr., 7:30am and 2:30pm, S£65).

Qadmous (☎91 00 89), nicer buses but not very punctual, is on the main highway about 3km from the town center. Sends buses to: **Damascus** (3hr., every hr. 7:30am-9pm, S£110); **Deir al-Zur** (2½hr., every 30min. 8:30am-5am, S£85); **Tartus** and **Lattakia** via **Homs** (2hr.; 2:15pm; S£65).

Damas Tours has luxurious private buses to **Damascus, Homs,** and several smaller towns. Schedules are unpredictable; ask your hotel manager for updated info.

Service and public buses: A 5min. walk down the street to the left of the tourist office; the station is to the left, right before the cemetery wall. To **Homs** (2hr.; every hr. or when full; S£35-60).

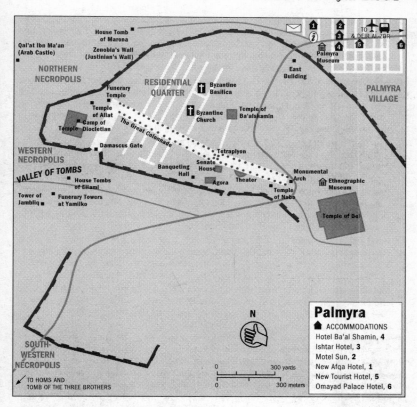

Palmyra

🏠 ACCOMMODATIONS

Hotel Ba'al Shamin, **4**
Ishtar Hotel, **3**
Motel Sun, **2**
New Afqa Hotel, **1**
New Tourist Hotel, **5**
Omayad Palace Hotel, **6**

🛈 PRACTICAL INFORMATION

Tourist Office: (☎91 05 74), on the main street, next to the post office. New, bilingual office provides maps, brochures, and tea. Open Sa-Th 8am-2pm. More helpful books and guides at the entrance to the Museum of the Temple of Bel.

Currency exchange: Commercial Bank of Syria has a booth right next to the museum. Open daily 9am-2pm and 6-9pm.

Police: An English-speaking representative of the **tourist police** can be reached at the Temple of Bel (☎91 05 17), while the **police station** (☎91 01 58) is on the main street off the highway as you reach the 1st hotels in the new town.

Pharmacy: (☎91 04 55), just down from the Spring Restaurant on the right side of the main street. Open Sa-Th 9am-2pm and 6-9:30pm.

Hospital: (☎91 05 51). East of the city, call 91 29 02 for an ambulance.

Telephones: Outside the post office, inside the Temple of Bel, and outside the museum. Purchase a phone card in the post office.

Post Office: Near the circle on the highway. Friendly staff. Open Sa-Th 8am-2pm.

🏠 ACCOMMODATIONS

Despite steadily rising prices, a number of friendly inexpensive options remain. Most hotels and restaurants are on the main street, starting at the highway. Hotels that charge in US dollars are more comfortable, but six times more expensive.

■ **New Afqa Hotel** (☎ 91 03 86), near the post office and the new tourist office, before the Karnak station. This family-run hotel is the best budget deal in town. A/C reception area is a great place to while away the afternoons, sipping tea or suffering backgammon defeat at the hands of local youngsters. Pleasant, well-kept rooms and clean sheets. Breakfast included. Singles S£250; doubles S£500; triples S£750.

■ **Ishtar Hotel** (☎ 91 30 73; fax 91 32 60), on the left at the beginning of the main street; one of the 1st hotels you'll see upon entering the city. Warren Beatty never had service this good. An occasional dancing troupe spices up the pleasant cave-like bar downstairs. Doubles with A/C, bath, and breakfast US$24. In high season price rises to US$30 and reservations are needed up to 2 months in advance. AmEx/MC/V.

New Tourist Hotel (☎ 91 03 33), down the main street on the right, is actually the oldest in Palmyra. The effusive comments in the guestbook confirm that this is a backpackers' haven. The owners sell and trade from their used book collection. Rooftop mattresses S£100; 3-bed dorms S£125, with bath S£150; singles S£200; doubles S£325.

Omayad Palace Hotel (☎ 91 07 55), 250m down the main street to the right of the fountain. Rest like a caliph in the pastel-hued lobby and spacious, shaded courtyard of this old Palmyrene house. Spartan but pleasant rooms. Breakfast S£50. Singles S£200; doubles S£400; triples S£600; quads S£800.

Hotel Ba'al Shamin (☎ 91 04 53, fax 91 29 70), 1 block south of the main street and a block down from the museum. Spacious rooms and the cheapest inhabitable singles in Palmyra. Check out the oblong, private baths bent L-shaped around the bedrooms. Singles S£150; doubles S£300; triples S£450. Group discounts available.

Motel Sun (☎ 91 11 33). Walk away from the ruins and take the 1st left after the Ishtar Hotel. More like a homey bed-and-breakfast than a motel, but prices are fair for small but well-maintained rooms. Singles S£200; doubles S£300; triples S£400.

🍴 FOOD

Palmyra's main street abounds with restaurants catering to tourists' every desire. Meals are universally decent, but prices vary with tourist traffic. Some hotels serve local beer (S£75) until 11pm. Local diners are also ready and eager to feed you, but don't let them rip you off. The best option is to get invited for some down-home Syrian cooking. Be sure to sample the traditional Levantine dish *mensaf* (see **Jordan: Food and Drink**, p. 435).

Palmyra Tourist Restaurant (☎ 91 03 46). Dazzles with fountains, canopies, an in-house boutique, and reasonably priced meals. *Mezze* chicken, mineral water, and salad S£200. Hummus with meat S£75. Soup S£30. Beer, wine, and *'araq* also served. Open daily 7:30am-11:30pm.

Spring Restaurant (☎ 91 03 07), on the right of the main street. Offers tasty *mensaf*, served with a choice of chicken or lamb and yogurt on the side (S£200-250). Get meat entrees (S£125) in the relaxing upstairs Bedouin tent. A breakfast of omelets and cheese goes for S£50. Open daily 7am until the shawarma runs out.

Villa Palmyra Restaurant (☎ 91 01 56), right before Spring Restaurant. This 3-star hotel offers a full buffet dinner in tourist season (S£400; you may be able to bargain it down). The 4th fl. dining room overlooks the ruins.

👁 SIGHTS

It takes a full day to explore Palmyra. The best way to see the ruins is to wake up at dawn, catch the spectacular sunrise, and begin exploring before the sun is directly overhead. In summer bring about 2L of water and finish sightseeing no later than noon—it is **hot**.

TEMPLE OF BEL. This mammoth building, enclosed in a high, largely reconstructed wall, is a good place to begin exploring Palmyra. The **gatehouse** has books on Syria and Palmyra, and the guides who gather here are useful for a more in-

SYRIA

depth appreciation of the ruins (around S£1000 per day, but in low season bargaining can bring prices down). The existing Temple of Bel was constructed in 32 CE over an older Hellenistic site. Bel is a Babylonian pronunciation of the Semitic word *Ba'al* ("master"), the name for the supreme deity who was identified with the Greek god Zeus. The **altar** in the middle of the temple was used for animal sacrifices; blood ran into the drain in the floor and was emptied into a sophisticated plumbing system (only a large stone pipe sitting beside the drainage hole remains). The impressive **cella** ("shrine")—the free-standing building in the center of the temple—was built from 17 to 32 CE. Small shrines to the right and left reflect the multitude of deities that were associated with the mighty god Bel. Several intricate carvings of grapes and pineapples, hinting at Palmyra's rich agricultural past, can be found outside the entrance and at the bottom of the stone slab. *(Gatehouse open daily 8am-1pm and 4-6pm; in winter 8am-4pm. S£300, students S£15.)*

MONUMENTAL ARCH. The Great Colonnade once led from the Temple of Bel to the Monumental Arch and the rest of the city. Constructed in 200 CE, the oft-photographed structure is richly decorated with rows of pears, acorns, and palm trunks, as well as acanthus, oak, and grape leaves. On the left, just past the arch, stands the **Temple of Nabo,** raised 2m off the ground. Dedicated to the Babylonian god of writing (later identified with Apollo), this first-century CE construction (along with **Zenobia's Baths** to the right) is largely in ruins. Up the colonnade and to the left is a newly renovated **theater.** The stage, chorus pit, and foundations of the dressing rooms remain visible.

AGORA AND ENVIRONS. Farther down the street to the left are the not-so-distinct remains of the agora (public market) and the **Senate House.** Social position determined one's placement in the agora: Palmyran and Roman officials sat in the northern portico, senators in the eastern portico, soldiers in the western portico, and merchants and caravan leaders in the southern portico. Next door is the **Banqueting Hall,** where religious fraternities congregated to celebrate holidays. The prominent Tetrapylon consists of four groups of poorly rebuilt columns. The pedestals in the center of each group once supported statues, including likenesses of the fabulous Zenobia and her husband, Odenathus. To the right of the Tetrapylon, near the Zenobia Hotel, is the **Temple of Ba'alshamin,** dedicated to Zeus Ba'alshamin, the god of storms and fertilizing rains, whose name means "Master of the Heavens." The locked vestibule of the temple has six columns with platforms as bases for statues. To the right, the ruins partially covered by the Zenobia Hotel used to be a colonnaded courtyard surrounded by rooms and a chapel. This complex's role within the temple remains unknown.

QAL'AT IBN MA'AN. The imposing Qal'at Ibn Ma'an, also called **Arab Castle,** is attributed to Fakhr al-Din, who once ruled the area between Mt. Lebanon and the Syrian desert. This fortress, built in the 12th or 13th century to protect Palmyra from Crusader attacks, is *the* place to be at sunset, though bus loads of photo-snapping tourists can mar the experience during high season (Mar.-May). Climb the 150m slope for free (30-45min.) or bargain for a ride from town; S£200 including 2hr. wait is reasonable. *(Open daily until just after sunset. S£150, students S£15.)*

FUNERARY TOWERS. To the left of Qal'at Ibn Ma'an are funerary towers, known as "eternal houses" in Palmyra. Each of the most important families had its own mausoleum, though there are also individual sepulchres. The locked tombs are a 30min. walk from the main city. As always, there's a catch—the keymaster won't move a muscle until you've arranged transportation. If you haven't rented a car, this means getting a taxi (S£200 after bargaining), many of which prowl outside the museum around tour time. You can hire a guide to the tombs for around S£300, but once at the towers most guides will let you latch on to their group for a small fee. *(Tombs unlocked W-Th and Sa-M 8:30, 10, 11:30am, 4:30pm; Tu 9, 11am; F 8:30am, 10am, 4:30pm; Oct.-Mar. last opening 2pm. Cars leave from the Palmyra Museum, where tickets are sold. S£150, students S£10.)*

VALLEY OF THE TOMBS. The 4-story **Tomb of Elahbel,** which belonged to a rich Palmyran family, has stairs to its roof for a good view of the Valley of the Tombs. The underground **Tomb of the Three Brothers** is southwest of the city. The center panel of the tomb's colorful wall frescoes depicts Achilles hiding in drag among the daughters of Lycomedes. He did this upon hearing the Delphic oracle foretell his death, which would come only after the cross-dressing hero was suited up for war and shot in his now-famous left heel. More underground tombs will cost you—for S£300 more to your driver and a generous S£150 to the keymaster, you may gain access to the **Tomb of Borfa Borha,** with a carving of Medusa at its entrance to prevent evil spirits from entering, and the 2nd-century CE **Tomb of Art-aban** with an actual mummy in one of the crypts.

MUSEUMS. The **Palmyra Museum,** at the entrance to the new town, is larger and more interesting than most Syrian museums. Statues from family tombs, coins with godly depictions, and a tacky model of an ancient Palmyran cave and its semi-naked inhabitants highlight the collection. The **Ethnographic Museum,** where mildly interesting displays attempt to catalogue different aspects of Bedouin life with wax statues, won't leave Madame Tussaud melting with envy. (*Palmyra Museum open Apr.-Sept. daily 8am-1pm and 4-6pm; Nov.-Mar. W-M 8am-1pm and 2-4pm. S£300, students S£15. Ethnographic Museum open W-M 8:30am-2:30pm. S£150, students S£20.*)

▶ DAYTRIP FROM PALMYRA

QASR AL-HEIR AL-SHARQI
Decrepit cars parked in front of the Palmyra Museum charge S£1200 for the trip to Qasr al Heir, but your hotel might provide a better (and safer) alternative. For S£2000, the tourist office will hook you up with a top-of-the-line vehicle. To get the keys to the eastern castle, take the road to the left before reaching the castle. S£150; students S£10.

The Umayyad caliph chose this site for Qasr al-Heir al-Sharqi, built in the in the 8th century CE, because it coupled excellent hunting with prime location for maintaining control of the trade route between the Euphrates and Damascus. The *qasr* is actually two castles were built side by side, separated by a square minaret. The exterior walls are the most exciting remains; inside you'll find only an occasional column or arch. The eastern castle, with its richly decorated towers, is thought to have served as an inn to accommodate passing caravans, while the larger western castle was a mini-city in itself, with residential quarters, a cistern, and a mosque.

HOMS حمص ☎ 31
Any Syrian will tell you that oil is the most refined thing in Homs. All over the Levant, "Homsies" are the butt of jokes ridiculing their supposed stupidity, but they thrive despite this abuse and are some of the most genuine people in Syria. Now an industrial wasteland strewn with bent telephone poles, hanging electrical wires, half-finished buildings, and rank streets, Homs has seen better days. In ancient Roman times (when it was known as Emesa), Homs was an important metropolis along the Palmyra trade route. Most buildings of historical interest, however, have been destroyed by wars and earthquakes, and now Homs is a destitute sister to fair Palmyra. As much as travelers try to avoid the smoke-belching city, Homs often serves as a default transportation hub; roads from Hama, Palmyra, Damascus, and Tartus converge here, and Crac des Chevaliers is only a short bus ride away. Be it ever so humble, there's no place like Homs.

▐ TRANSPORTATION

Buses from **Karnak Station,** next to the public bus station, run daily to: **Damascus** (2hr., 10 per day 6:15-3:30am, S£60); **Hama** (45min.; 1:30am, 1:30, 2:30, 7:30pm; S£25); and **Tartus** (1hr., 4pm, S£40). From **Pullman Station** Kadmous buses leave to: **Damascus** (2hr., 12 per day 6:30-4:05am, S£70); **Tartus** (1¼hr., 9 per day 5am-

11:15pm, S£40); **Lattakia** (2¼hr.; 5, 6:15am, 7pm; S£80). **Minibuses** to **Crac des Chevaliers** (1hr., every hr. 8am-5pm, S£25). **Microbuses** run frequently to: **Aleppo** (2½hr., S£55); **Damascus** (2hr., S£45); **Hama** (45min., S£15); **Tartus** (1hr., S£25). Take S£10 off the price if you want to brave a microbus *sans* A/C.

⚡🔢 ORIENTATION AND PRACTICAL INFORMATION

The **bus station** sits at the intersection of **al-Corniche St.** and **Hama St.** A right turn out of the station leads to the Hama St. intersection, where you'll find food vendors and small, cheap restaurants. Hama St. intersects **Quwatli St.,** past the Khalid ibn al-Walid Mosque, at a bus stop and fountain. A right onto Quwatli St. brings you to a clocktower and most of Homs's accommodations. The public **bus station** is past the small clocktower circle on Hama St., near Khalid ibn al-Walid Mosque.

Tourist Booth: (☎47 38 98). On Quwatli St. in the middle of a small park past the hotels. Don't expect much more than a smile. Open Sa-Th 8am-2pm and 4-9pm. The best source of information for tourists is Ahmed at the Nasser al-Jadid Hotel, who speaks near-flawless English.

Passport Office: On the right side of Ibn Khaldoun St. at the Quwatli St. intersection, 3rd fl. Take a right before the Homs Museum. For visas and renewals you'll need 4 passport-sized photographs, available from the photo office to the left of the passport office. Open for visa extensions Sa-Th 8am-2pm.

Currency Exchange: Facing away from the entrance of Hotel Nasser al-Jadid, 50m up the street, on the left. **Commercial Bank of Syria** cashes traveler's checks and changes money at the usual rates. Open Sa-Th 8:30am-12:30pm.

Police: (☎112) Headquartered in the government building on Hashem al-Atasi St., a sharp left from the clocktower on Quwatli St.

24-Hour Pharmacy: Umaliyya Pharmacy (☎46 62 49). Across from the mosque on Hama St.

Hospital: (☎110 for an ambulance) On al-Corniche St. at the intersection with al-Salamiyeh St.

Telephone Office: At the end of Quwatli St. to the right of the new clocktower; phone cards available. Open daily 8am-10pm.

Internet Access: Compu Serv (☎49 99 90). Take a left at the clocktower and a right onto Tarablos St.; it is tucked away in a building on the right before the intersection with Midan St. S£100 per hr., students S£75. Open daily 10am-2am.

Post Office: On Riad St.; head away from the clocktower circle and the Army Club on the right. The post office immediately follows on the left. **Poste Restante** available.

🏠 ACCOMMODATIONS

Hotel options in Homs border on awful, especially for women and single travelers. Most rooms are in large, old buildings in various states of disrepair on Quwatli St.

Hotel Nasser al-Jadid (☎22 74 23), on Quwatli St. about 50m past the park. Amiable, English-speaking manager Ahmed will show you to the well-worn but tidy rooms. Shared baths with hole-in-the-ground toilets. Cold showers S£25. Hot showers S£50; give manager 2hr. notice in winter and 30-40min. in summer. Singles S£200; doubles S£300; triples S£400; quads S£500.

Ghazi Hotel (☎22 21 60), on Quwatli St. one block from the Nasser al-Jadid toward the park. Marked by a sign that says "HOTEL." The pretty tile floors and the curtains' leafy print fail to compensate for the overall gloominess and rock-hard mattresses. Hot showers S£35. Singles S£17; doubles S£275; triples S£375.

New Basman Hotel (☎43 10 81), on Damascus St., across from the small park in front of Qala'at Usama. If the sketchy downtown accommodations are getting you down, the trek out to this hotel is worth it, despite the not-so-helpful staff. Revamped rooms with A/C, fridge, phone, and two-channel TV are more expensive but oh, so nice. Singles S£600; doubles S£750; triples S£900. Add S£300 for renovated rooms.

SYRIA

◧ FOOD

Falafel, shawarma, and pastry shops line Hama St. between the bus station and Quwatli St. Most stay open until midnight. Roving merchants hawk fresh-boiled corn on the cob, fruits, vegetables, and nuts. Myriad juice and snack shops squeeze onto the street parallel to Quwatli, behind Hotel Nasser al-Jadid. Most are open until midnight and offer affordable sandwiches (S£15) and cocktails (S£25-50).

City Cafe (☎ 22 40 85), the yellow-and-blue building at the end of Quwatli St., to the left of the new clocktower. The chefs of this hip joint cook up steak, filet, pizza, kebab, and *shish tawouq* (S£100-200). Open 24hr in summer; 8am-2am in winter.

Nile Restaurant, near City Cafe. Specializes in what locals call *sha'abi,* or "of the people." The people eat *fatteh*—a huge bowl of chickpeas with pita, lemon juice, and olive oil—real Homstyle cooking (S£22).

Rawda Cafe, across Quwatli St. from the Nile Restaurant, provides welcome relief from the industrial decay. Homsboys calmly smoke *argileh* (S£35), sip tea (S£15), and play backgammon around a tree-lined fountain. Foreigners might feel more welcome in the family section to the right.

Dick al-Jinn (☎ 51 76 46 or 51 27 83), on Mimas St. (taxi S£30). A limited bar serves up beer (S£36), *'araq* (S£54), and local wine (S£152). Outdoor seating overlooks the Orontes River. Open 8am-2am.

Ward Club, adjacent to Dick al-Jinn, serves as a nightclub for 30+ Homsies on alternate Thursdays (10pm-2am).

◉ SIGHTS

KHALID IBN AL-WALID MOSQUE. This silver-domed mosque-turned-community center should be your first (and perhaps last) sightseeing stop in Homs. It is dedicated to the Arab commander known as the "Sword of God," who brought Islam to Syria in 636 CE. His alms-laden tomb lies inside. The mosque mixes Byzantine, Ottoman, and Arab styles. Ask the attendant in the office for a guided tour. The **Museum of Islamic Ruins** is nestled inside the mosque, but you are lucky indeed if you find it open. *(On Hama St. between the city center and bus station. Robes provided. Museum open Th 10am-12pm. Free.)*

GREAT AL-NOURI MOSQUE AND ENVIRONS. Built in 1162 CE by Ayyubid commander Nour al-Din Zanki (Nuraddin), this simple mosque is famous for its square minaret and wooden pulpit. The nearby *souqs* date from the Ayyubid, Mamluk, and Ottoman periods. *(On the left when walking toward the souq from Khalid Ibn al-Walid Mosque, behind the black and white striped building.)*

UMM AL-ZUNNAR CHURCH. Built in 59 CE, Umm al-Zunnar served as the holy house for Homs's earliest Christians. They worshiped here secretly, fearing persecution by their pagan rulers. The church was expanded during the Christian era and now holds the so-called Belt of the Virgin Mary, a 74cm silk and linen rope found under the altar in 1953. *(In the Old City, take a left at the souq and make a right at the 1st major street. Then follow the street to the left. The church is on the right.)*

◈ DAYTRIPS FROM HOMS

▧ QAL'AT AL-HISN (CRAC DES CHEVALIERS) قلعة الحصن

Buses and service leave Homs station for Qal'at al-Hisn daily (1hr., every hr. 7am-5pm, S£25). Officially, the last bus returns to Homs around 5pm. In low season, however, shark-like service drivers may claim to be private taxis after 3pm and charge an outrageous S£300 for the return trip. Microbuses leave when full from the entrance of the castle. Start the trip in early morning to avoid the heat and allow ample time to explore. Open June-Nov. W-M 9am-6pm; Oct.-Apr. W-M 9am-4pm, Tu 9am-3pm. S£300, students S£15. Guided tours S£100, groups S£300.

This must-see mountaintop Crusader castle, known as both Qal'at al-Hisn and Crac des Chevaliers, ranks among the best sights in Syria. Those who proclaim it the Greatest Castle in the World are not far off the mark. The Crac is really a castle within a castle, separated by a moat, with a larger moat surrounding the entire structure. The governor of Homs built the original structure in 1031 CE, leaving a Kurdish garrison to defend the castle against enemy attacks on the Tripoli-Homs-Hama road. In 1110, Crusaders more or less destroyed the fortress in the process of capturing it. They built a new castle on the ruins of the old and used it to control the "Homs Gap," a narrow pass linking the coast to the Orontes Valley. Possession of this pass, the only gap in a 250km stretch of mountainous terrain, guaranteed control over inland Syria. The Crusaders held the medieval fortress for 161 years; Salah al-Din supposedly withdrew his troops upon viewing the imposing castle. The stronghold finally fell to the Mamluk army under the command of Sultan Baybars in 1271, after a month of intense fighting. Perched on a hill 750m above sea level and spreading over 30,000 sq. m, the castle's high towers afford panoramic views of the Mediterranean, the Port of Tripoli, and Homs Lake. Only from afar can the size of the building be fully appreciated, and the best views of the castle come as you approach it.

Upon entering through the main door, continue up the ramp past the **guard rooms** and **stables.** Straight ahead, through the door of the first tower, are the moat and outer wall. To get to the **main courtyard,** take a sharp right. In front of the courtyard, the **seven-arched facade** is the castle's most aesthetically impressive feature. Behind it is the **main assembly room,** where Crusader kings were received by the knights of the castle under a vaulted Gothic roof. The long room against the castle's back wall contains a huge **oven,** 5m in diameter. To the right is a **cathedral** that was converted into a mosque in 1271; a simple stone *minbar* adorns the arch. The intriguing nooks in the rest of the castle lend themselves to impromptu exploration—a map might cramp your style, but a **flashlight** makes a great companion. Be sure to trek up to the southern towers for an inspiring view of the Syrian countryside, with Lebanon visible in the distance. Those accustomed to warmer climates should bring a sweater.

At the **Roundtable Restaurant and Hotel,** 150m to the left and up the hill from the castle entrance, passable beds and baths await for S£500. Full meal S£200, buffet S£250, beer S£50. The **Restaurant des Chevaliers,** in front of the main entrance, has similar food but a better view of the mountain. (☎74 04 11. Buffet S£150, beer S£100, hummus S£25, coffee or tea S£25.) If you get hungry or thirsty exploring the site, visit the **Castle Restaurant** in the **Princess Tower,** Rapunzel-style on the top level of the castle toward the northern end. *Mezze* (S£100) accompanied by lovely, if foggy, views and a helpful English-speaking manager. (☎74 00 07. Open daily, same hours as the castle.) **Camping** (☎74 02 80. S£125 per person), shower included, is also an option at the Roundtable Hotel.

DEIR MAR GEORGIS

Service from the Qal'at Al Hisn intersection frequently connect the castle with this monastery (S£5). Alternatively, take a *bus* or *service* from the Homs station to Marmarita and ask to be dropped off at Deir Mar Georgis (S£15). Once you reach the monastery, you can ask for a tour at the information office. Donations recommended if you don't want to be treated like the anti-Christ.

Balanced atop one of the lush hills surrounding Crac de Chevaliers, the Monastery of St. George is an easy trip from the Crac. A short visit is enough to become acquainted with this high-walled working monastery. Three churches have been built on this site, one on top of the other. While the oldest building is now completely buried under its younger siblings, the second, 800-year-old church is still healthy and active. It contains icons of St. George—one of which was stolen, sold in England, and later returned to its spot in the intricate wooden frame.

HAMA حماه ☎ 33

Although the city of Hama was once an important trade center, the only remaining monuments to its former glory are the *norias* (Aramaic for "waterwheels") scattered throughout the city. The low-pitched groaning of wood rubbing wood has echoed through Hama since the *norias'* construction in the Middle Ages. The Orontes river is no longer what it used to be, but the wheels continue to turn in the summer months, as they are still indispensable for the city's morale if not for its agriculture. Parks and cafes line the shores, conglomerating at the critical *noria* locations. The graceful turning of these irrigation devices has long set the pace for this town. Hama's serenity makes it difficult to remember that the city was ground zero for the government's bloody quelling of the Muslim Brotherhood uprising of 1982. Nevertheless, Hama's high-quality budget accommodations make it an ideal locale to lose track of time and spend a relaxing couple of days. The best way to see Hama's sights is to make like a *noria* and roll along the banks of the river.

▐ TRANSPORTATION

Buses:

Al-Ahliah Bus Station: (☎52 25 51) has luxury service to all major Syrian cities. Walking toward the post office, go past the Basman Grand Hotel, and take a left after the large white government building. The station is around the corner on the left. Frequent service to: **Aleppo** (2hr., every hr., S£65); **Damascus** (3hr., every hr., S£90); **Homs** (40min.; 5:30, 6, 7am, 12:15, 2, 6:15pm; S£20); **Lattakia** (3hr.; 6am, 12:15, 6:15pm; S£100); **Raqqa** (4hr.; 6:45am, 3:30, 4:30, 5:30, 6:30, 8:45pm; S£145); **Tartus** (2hr.; 6am, 12:15, 5, 6:15pm; S£70).

Qadmous Bus Station: On the corniche in the middle of town (right before the Afamia restaurant). Regular service to: **Aleppo** (1:30, 8:15, 11:15am, 1:15, 3:15, 6:15, 11:15pm; S£65); **Damascus** (7:30am, 3:15pm; S£85), **Homs** (7:00, 8:15am, 3, 4:15, 6:45pm; S£20); and **Lattakia** (6:30, 9:30am, 12:30, 3:30, 6:30pm; S£60), as well as less frequent trips to **Tartus** and **Qamishli.**

Al-Rayyan Bus Company: (☎22 79 77 or 52 37 16), behind the Riad Hotel. Runs to: **Aleppo** (S£65); **Damascus** (S£90); and **Homs** (S£20).

Minibuses: The station is a left turn away from the river at the intersection of Murabet and Quwatli. Conquer the hill on foot (20min.) or take a city bus (S£2). Minibuses depart when full to: **Aleppo** (2hr., S£25); **Damascus** (3hr., S£35); **Homs** (45min., S£11); and **Suqelbia** (1hr., S£20).

Service: Opposite the minibus station. Impractical and hugely expensive *service* run to: **Aleppo** (S£150); **Damascus** (S£200); and **Homs** (S£40).

✳ ▐ ORIENTATION AND PRACTICAL INFORMATION

Navigating the small city of Hama is easy and can be done almost entirely on foot. The intersection of **Quwatli St.** and **Sadiq Ave.** is the city center. Most budget hotels and restaurants are on Quwatli St., facing the bank and the post office across the intersection. Continuing in this direction leads to **Murabet St.** and the city's second major intersection. Walking toward the grinding sound will bring you to the river.

As holds true for most of Syria, your best bet for advice and tourist information is to find a knowledgeable, English-speaking hotel manager to introduce you to the city. In Hama, the best person to contact is Anas, manager of the **Cairo Hotel.** He can provide information on everything from the transportation to visa requirements for almost any nationality.

Tourist Office: (☎51 10 33), on Sadiq Ave. across the river from the central intersection. Provide more maps than advice. (Open daily 8am-6pm.)

Passport Office: Walk past the tourist office and take a right at Ziqar St.; it's about 15min. away, on the left. Alternatively, hop on a microbus across the street from the tourist office and ask to be dropped off (S£3). Bring 4 passport-sized photographs and S£50 to renew visas. Open Sa-Th 8:30am-1pm.

Bank: Commercial Bank of Syria: Next to the post office. Exchanges cash and traveler's checks. Open daily 9am-2pm and 5-8pm.

Emergency: Police: ☎ 112. **Ambulance:** ☎ 110.

Hospital: (☎ 51 58 01, 51 58 02, or 51 58 03), uphill from al-Ahliah Bus Station.

Pharmacy: Ummalia Pharmacy, 8 Ayyar St. (☎ 225 097). Follow al-Mutanabbi St. away from the river, turn right at the large crossing, and continue to the end of 8 Ayyar St.; the pharmacy is on the left, marked by a large red sign in Arabic. Open 24hr. Contact your hotel manager first about getting medicine; he will probably know where to procure necessary items at the best prices.

Internet Access: The **ELIWI** shop behind the post the post office doubles as a cyber cafe complete with printer and scanner (☎ 23 60 10; 10am-2:30pm and 6-10:30pm, S£150 per hr.), and most hotels have Internet facilities.

Post Office: On Quwatli St. just past the Sadiq Ave. intersection. Minimal services, but very efficient. **EMS** and **phone cards.** Open daily 8am-2pm.

ACCOMMODATIONS

Hama's hotels outshine those in almost any other Syrian city. Amenities abound, floors sparkle, and managers practically tap dance to keep visitors happy. Still, you should not believe opportunistic managers who try to convince you that there are no other decent lodgings in Syria. Prices vary drastically between high season (summer) and low season (winter). It never hurts to ask for a discount, especially if the hotel looks deserted.

■ **Cairo Hotel** (☎ 22 22 80; fax 23 72 06; cairohot@scs-net.org.), on Quwatli St. near the intersection with Gamal 'Abd al-Nasser St. A 2-star hotel with 1-star prices. Some travelers have dubbed Anas, the helpful manager, a Syrian national treasure. Well-maintained rooms have fridges, beautiful bathrooms, and color TVs. Breakfast S£75, dinner S£150. Rooftop mattresses S£100; dorm beds S£150; singles S£250; doubles S£375; triples S£525; June-Aug. S£50-150 more; A/C and fridge S£75. AmEx/MC/V.

■ **Riad Hotel** (☎ 23 95 12 or 23 55 40, fax 51 77 76), next door to the Cairo Hotel. With its young, hip, and super-friendly manager, Abdullah, Riad is a worthy match for its neighbor. Clean rooms have fridges and speakers connected to a central sound system. Beer sold out of a lobby cooler in the lobby. Breakfast S£75. Full bath or shower S£50. Rooftop mattresses and facilities S£75-100; singles S£280; doubles S£405; triples S£505; quads S£605. AmEx/MC/V.

Noria Hotel (☎ 51 24 14; fax 51 17 15), across the street from the Riad Hotel. Under the same impeccable management as the Cairo. All rooms come with central A/C, continental breakfast, and a bevy of 4-star services. Magnificent suites (for 2-5 people) have a kitchen, a tastefully decorated living room, and views of the *norias*. Singles US$20; doubles US$28; triples US$36; suites US$30-50. AmEx/MC/V.

🍴 FOOD

Most of Hama's restaurants are of the standard chicken, meat, and falafel variety. A full meal shouldn't cost more than S£100. Along Quwatli St. the diners have plumper chickens and larger portions and pastry shops abound. The local specialty, not to be missed, is a deliciously gooey cheese pastry called *halawiyyat al-jibn*. More expensive restaurants line the waterfront.

Sultan Restaurant (☎ 23 51 04), behind the Hama Museum. Provides a memorable riverside meal in an Ottoman insane asylum. If the grinding noise from the neighboring *noria* doesn't drive you mad, Hama's fit-inducing specialty, *batursh* (layered eggplant, mincemeat, and tahini eaten with bread; S£55), surely will. Entrees S£15-20.

Dream House (☎ 41 16 87), off Medina Sq. near the Grand Mosque. An unorthodox spread of spring rolls (S£45), excellent pizzas (S£90-110), and genuine banana splits (S£70). Barada beer (S£60) and a variety of liquors and local and imported wines (S£300-600) ensure happy dreams. Open daily 10am-1am.

Four Norias (☎ 22 10 13). Walk 15min. from the center of town with the river to your left. This upscale riverfront restaurant has a splendid view of its namesakes and the fountains. Check out yet another regional specialty, *sajaia* (your choice of lamb or chicken cooked with pistachios and almonds in yogurt; S£85). *'Araq*, Sharq beer (S£36), and whiskey (S£95) also available. Yes, those creatures flying along the water are bats. Full meal S£200-250. Open daily 8am-2:30am.

👁 SIGHTS

OLD CITY AND OTTOMAN BATH. When facing the Orontes from the center of town, walk left along the bank and enter the cobblestone-paved Old City. The narrow, winding streets were built to provide protection from the sun at all hours. A small sign above an old door on the left that reads "Automan Public Bath" marks the Hammam Othmania, a Turkish bath from the Ottoman era. *(Open for men 7am-noon and 7-11pm; women noon-5pm. Bath with soap and massage S£100.)*

MUSEUM OF POPULAR TRADITIONS. This museum, was built as a residence for As'ad Pasha al-Azem, governor of Hama from 1700 to 1742. After al-Azem was promoted to a Damascus post, he built an even grander structure of the same name. The palace's men's section *(Salamlek)* and women's section *(Haramlek)* conveniently join at the baths. The museum has lost some of its most important pieces to the new Hama Museum across the river. *(Directly across from the Ottoman Bath in the Old al-Azem Palace. Open W-M 8am-2:30pm. S£150, students S£20.)*

HAMA MUSEUM. Inaugurated in the year 2000, the pompous Hama museum is all marble, gazebos, and water fountains. Try to wrench your eyes away from the sumptuous architecture to turn your attention to the museum's impressive collection, which includes a wooden *minbar* yanked from al-Nouri Mosque, a 5th-century CE *noria* mosaic from Apamea, and the remarkable 3rd-century CE Maryameen Mosaic. *(Cross the Jisr al-Ra'is bridge right after the Citadel, and the museum will be to your right.)*

AL-NOURI MOSQUE AND CITADEL. After passing al-Jabariyya waterwheel (home to daredevil child divers in the late afternoon), the road opens up at al-Nouri Mosque. Built in 1162 by Ayyubid commander Nour al-Din Zanki (Nuraddin), the mosque thrusts a square minaret into the Syrian sky, mirroring its cousin in Homs. A left turn at the mosque leads to the Citadel, the center of the old city and a popular spot for evening strolls. Relics from the 6th millennium BCE were unearthed beneath this hill. Today, the only digging is done by kids playing in the huge park planted on top. *(Open only during prayer times, and visitors should be discreet so as not to disturb the worship. You may be asked to pay a S£10 entrance fee.)*

GRAND MOSQUE. The Citadel once hid Hama's Grand Mosque, which contains the tombs of two 13th century Ayyubid kings, Muhammad II and al-Muzaffar III. The mosque and tomb were roughed up during the 1982 uprising, and they have yet to be fully reconstructed. Greek writing from a previous edifice marks some of the fallen stones. *(Free.)*

▶ DAYTRIPS FROM HAMA

APAMEA افاميا

*To reach Apamea, take a **microbus** from Hama to Suqelbia (S£20), then a **service** to Qasr al-Mudiq (S£10). The colonnade is 2km farther up. Leave early in the day, when transportation is more frequent. Open W-M 8am-2:30pm. Ruins S£300, students S£15; combination ruins and museum S£350, students S£30.*

Apamea lies on a hill overlooking the lush Ghab Valley and the Orontes River *(Nahr al-Assi)*, 55km north of Hama. The Macedonians knew the city as Barnakeh, but a smitten King Sahicos renamed the military stronghold after his beloved wife Afamia in 310 BCE. After Apamea fell in 64 BCE, the victorious Romans supplied the city with a rock-hewn water canal and ornate stone **colonnades** (the longest of which is 1850m)—still the city's most awesome features. They also built an **amphitheater** and a **public bath** (about 500m downhill and to the left of the colonnade), which have weathered the years far less gracefully. While in Apamea, you will likely encounter several moped-riding sharks offering rides up to the ruins and selling antiques supposedly found in nearby graves. Beware—chances are these "antiques" were manufactured in nearby shops just hours before your arrival.

The **cathedral,** to the left when facing the Afamia cafeteria, is floored with centuries old mosaics, in surprisingly good shape considering the centuries of erosion from weather and warfare that they have endured. It still houses a cross and set of jewels given to the King of Persia in 540 CE. The Persians nonetheless invaded and razed the city 33 years later, enslaving almost 300,000 Apameans. Muslim Arabs entered the city on peaceful terms under the leadership of Abu Obeida ibn Jarrah. Between 1137 and 1170, inhabitants likely abandoned Hama after a series of earthquakes. One of the more noteworthy buildings is the circular **al-Mudiq Castle,** about 2km from the colonnade, near modern Apamea. The Ottoman Stan Pasha built a great *khan* (courtyard inn) inside the castle that contained an inn, a stable, and a market. Now a museum, the *khan* is worth checking out. The museum **cafeteria** has standard Syrian fare at slightly inflated prices.

QAL'AT AL-SHMAYMIS

Buses from Hama to the nearby town of Salamiyeh leave frequently from in front of the White House restaurant, to the right of the post office (1hr., every 30min., S£5). From Salamiyeh, get a taxi to take you to the Citadel, or your bus driver may be willing to take you to the sight and back to the town for S£200.

The sight of Qal'at Al-Shmaymis from the foot of the hill on which it stands is reason enough to visit the place. Though the hike up to the Citadel may look daunting, the windy view from the summit—bedouin tents peppering the golden green hillside—more than compensates for the effort. There is not much left of this 13th century Ayyubid fort. Scattered bits of masonry and a lackluster cave can be found at the summit. There is also a dizzying well-like hole in the ground, which, according to local legend, was dug by a Ayyubid king at the behest of his beloved, who wanted a passage between the Citadel and the town of Salamiyeh.

MEDITERRANEAN COAST

LATTAKIA اللاذقية ☎ 41

With its aesthetically pleasing buildings, crowded streets, and fashionable student population, Lattakia has a decidedly cosmopolitan feel. A nice beach, plenty of cheap eats, and budget accommodations make Lattakia a good base for relaxing or exploring the ruins at Ugarit and the castle of Salah al-Din. Founded in the 2nd century BCE by the Seleucids, Lattakia once welcomed St. Peter and Mark Antony to its shores, but the only remaining witnesses to its glorious past are a few columns, a Roman arch, and some Ugaritic artifacts—all housed in the overpriced museum inside the Ottoman Khan al-Dukhan. As Syria's largest seaport and the country's major international trade center, Lattakia dedicates much of its coastline to industry, but there are still plenty of beaches. Still, as in most Syrian cities, life remains centered around the shopping district; unlike other Syrian cities the shopping district here is dominated by man-hunting, scandalously clad women.

▐ TRANSPORTATION

Intercity Buses: Three different carriers service Lattakia. All luxury buses depart from **Pullman Bus Station**, near al-Yaman Pl. traffic circle. Take the 1st right as you walk away from the train station.

Kadmous Transport Co. makes regular trips to **Damascus** (4hr., every hr., S£150) and **Deir al-Zur** (7hr.; 12:30, 2:30, 11pm; S£230) via **Palmyra** (4½hr., S£150) and **Homs** (2½hr., S£80). Kadmous also sends **minibuses** to **Baniyas** (45min., every 15min., S£15), not accessible by microbus.

Jallouf runs buses to **Aleppo** (3hr.; 1:30, 6,7, 8am, 2:30, 4, 5, 6pm; S£100).

Al-Hasan Transport Co. (☎23 90 08) sends buses to **Turkey**. Bring your passport and US$45 to get a **Turkish visa** at the border. Buses to: **Istanbul** (17hr.; 8, 9am; S£1500) via **Antakya** (2½hr., S£500).

Within the city, travel by **taxi** (refuse to pay more than S£25) or **service.** To get to the **microbus station,** with regular departures to neighboring areas, walk down Ramadan St. toward the tourist office, turn left on al-Maghreb al-Arabi St. at the big traffic circle, take the first right, and walk 500m.

▐ ORIENTATION AND PRACTICAL INFORMATION

The main thoroughfare, **14 Ramadan St.,** runs northeast from the harbor and ends at the clueless **tourist office.** (☎41 69 26. Open daily 8am-8pm.) Farther inland, running north-south from the beginning of 14 Ramadan St., is **8 Azar St.,** which turns into **Baghdad Ave.** at **al-Quds St.** intersection. Heading east on al-Quds St. (which soon morphs into **al-Ghafiqi St.**) leads to the large **al-Yaman Pl.** traffic circle.

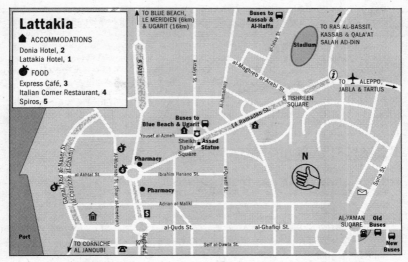

Lattakia

🏠 ACCOMMODATIONS
Donia Hotel, **2**
Lattakia Hotel, **1**

🍴 FOOD
Express Café, **3**
Italian Corner Restaurant, **4**
Spiros, **5**

Commercial Bank of Syria faces the sea on 8 Azar St. before the traffic circle. (Open daily 8am-2pm and 5-8pm; changes traveler's checks before 2pm only.) At the intersection of 14 Ramadan St. and Ibrahim Hanano St., Hanano Pl. (also known as **Sheikh Daher**) is home to the **Assad statue**, the **police station** (☎112), and many budget hotels. **Sani Daker Pharmacy,** on 8 Azar St. before the Karnak office, has excellent multilingual service. (☎47 69 79. Open Sa-W 9am-1:30pm and 5-8:30pm.) In a medical emergency, call the **Assad Hospital** (☎48 77 82), on 8 Azar St. To reach the overcrowded **telephone office,** turn right onto Haria St. from Baghdad Ave. (Open daily 8am-11pm.) **Internet access** is also available at the telephone office but come armed with patience. (Open daily 8am-8pm, S£120 per hr.) To get to the surprisingly efficient **post office,** face away from the train station and take the second right off the circle; it's 50m down on the left. **Poste Rapide** and **Poste Restante** available. (Open daily 8am-7pm.)

🏠🛏 ACCOMMODATIONS AND FOOD

To get to **Hotel Lattakia,** walk a direct line from Assad's much admired backside until you reach a sprawling outdoor coffee shop; look for the flashing yellow sign in the alley to the right. The knowledgeable management provides spacious rooms with comfy beds and balconies. The vast majority of guests are men. (☎47 95 27. Rooftop mattresses S£75; singles S£100, with bath S£175; doubles S£200-250; triples S£300-375.) To reach the **Dounia Hotel,** face away from the Assad statue and adjacent outdoor cafe and take the second right after the gas station; the small hotel is on the left. The Dounia is a good deal, though its lack of private baths and the dubious quality of the shared baths make it a runner-up. (☎42 12 96. Singles S£100; doubles S£200; triples £300; quads £400.) The more expensive **Safwan Hotel** is a homier option for lone travelers. Situated near the sea on al-Corniche al-Gharbi St., Safwan's clean rooms and airy balconies provide repose from the hustle of the city. Washing machine and fridge available. (☎46 15 64 or 47 86 02. Singles S£300; doubles S£500; suites S£1000.)

Dining is more central to the Lattakian experience than that of the average Syrian town. Budget food stops line the area around the Assad statue, while more upscale restaurants sit on and around America St. For mouth-watering kebab, visit **Spiro,** on Gamal 'Abd al-Nasser St. in front of the harbor. Fish is pricey at S£1000, but savory Syrian delicacies are more reasonable at S£75-300. (Open 11am-1am.) To reach the

Italian Corner Restaurant and Bar, near America St., follow Ramadan St. toward the sea and take a right at the end. The staff serves up several noble attempts at Western meat dishes (filet mignon S£160), a wide array of pizzas (S£85-120), cocktails (S£90-115), and beer (S£75). (☎47 72 07. Open daily 1pm-12:30am.) The brand-spanking new **Express Cafe** is at the heart of America St.; living up to its street name, the joint flaunts its shiny frontage at the passersby. Take a seat for ice cream (S£50-65) or a crepe (S£50-100) on the teeming first floor, or treat yourself to a piña colada (S£200-250) in the basement at the **Express Bar** (☎45 62 00. Restaurant open 9am-midnight, bar open 6pm-2am). Take a cab to Corniche al-Janoubi (S£25) for restaurants with great views of the sea and the best people-watching in town. **Somar** doles out cocktails for S£50. (☎23 25 64. Open daily 8am-1am, go early for a good spot near the sea.)

📷 DAYTRIPS FROM LATTAKIA

UGARIT (RAS SHAMRA) راس شمرة

*To get to Ugarit, take the last left before the rear of the Assad statue and walk to the 1st intersection on the right. Hop on a **service** (S£5) heading to Ras Shamra and ask to be dropped off at the ruins. To get back, hail a service on the main road; they come more frequently earlier in the day. Open daily 9am-6pm; in winter 9am-4pm. S£300, students S£15. Trilingual guidebooks S£50-100.*

The historic Kingdom of Ugarit once stood upon the site of this tiny town, 16km north of Lattakia. Ugarit's greatest gift to civilization is its 28-letter **alphabet,** preserved in a stone tablet from the 14th century BCE now sitting in the National Museum in Damascus (see p. 584). The oldest phonetic alphabet in the world, it is the probable ancestor of Phoenician, Hebrew, Latin, and Greek alphabets. In 1928, a peasant farmer discovered this site when he unearthed a few slabs of stone marking a spot originally settled in the 7th millennium BCE. Since the Kingdom of Ugarit was built with stone, its architectural legacy has been better preserved than that of almost all other Bronze Age cities, which typically consisted of mud-brick houses. Nevertheless, snail-covered weeds are winning the war against the ruins. English signs help decipher the fascinating remains and explain the elaborate system of waterworks. As you enter, the **royal palace** stretches out to the right, and farther down are the **residential quarters** and **acropolis.**

QAL'AT SALAH AL-DIN قلعة صلاح الدين

*Take a **microbus** from the main station to al-Haffeh (45min., S£10). For easy thrills, hire the services of one of the Honda **motorcycles** across the street, though women should be extra careful about jumping on a bike with a stranger (possible 1hr. wait, round-trip S£75). Your microbus driver may agree to wait for you for S£150, provided you make your visit brief. **Taxis** ask for S£100 one-way—they know how few cars drive along the winding 7km road to the castle (hitchers, think twice). Open W-M 9am-6pm; in winter 9am-4pm. S£300, students S£15.*

This fortress, 35km east of Lattakia, is named for the exalted warrior who took the "impregnable" castle from the Crusaders in 1188 CE. Perched on a plateau flanked by two deep gorges, the site's most impressive feature is the 156km long, 18m wide, and 28m deep **trench** that laborers cut by hand to completely isolate the fortress from the adjacent land. This is arguably the pinnacle of the Crusaders' architectural achievement. The lone column of rock that stands in the gorge once supported a drawbridge. Inside the walls, you'll find the arched entry to a stable on your right and a **dungeon** in the drawbridge tower. Holes in the dungeon walls mark where prisoners' chains were drilled into the stone. Up the path and inside the next tower, a hollow column conceals a **secret staircase** that soldiers on the roof would descend in order to attack the enemy from behind. Across from the entrance sits a huge **cistern** that collected rain water for 4000 soldiers' tea. To the left are remains of Byzantine and Crusader **churches,** and directly in front is a **mosque.** Views from the tops of many of the buildings take in the surrounding valley. Though no warriors remain to guard it, the castle's highest point is virtually impenetrable due to the thick tangle of prickly briars.

SYRIA

JABLEH جبلة

Buses leave for Jableh every 30min. from Lattakia (S£10). *Taxis* are a costlier option, but you should refuse to pay more than S£200.

A small coastal town near Lattakia, Jableh has a slow pace and sparsely-touristed streets that make it a nice place to spend the afternoon. Stroll from the main bus station toward the sea, taking notice of Jableh's past. The quaint local **mosque** sits right behind the *karaj*. Built on the site of an old Byzantine church, it is home to the shrine of Muslim saint Ibrahim ibn Adham as well as a house for daily worship. The **Roman amphitheater,** to the left of the mosque, seems to hold little interest for locals but its austere hallways deserve at least a quick look. (Open W-M 8am-6pm. S£150, students S£10.) Behind the gates and to the left, a small passageway leads through the scenic medina straight to the port.

If sightseeing gives you an animal appetite, stop off by the sea at the ■**Zoo-zoo Restaurant and Cafe** (☎83 38 15). Famed locally for its breakfasts, Zoo-zoo's proprietors also sell kebab for an affordable S£200. Take a break before returning to the bustle of the city by snoozing on the rocks while your stomach does the work.

KASSAB كساب

Buses leave Lattakia for Kassab frequently until around 8pm (S£25). In the off season, be prepared to pay S£50 or wait endless hours until the microbus fills up. *Microbuses* travel between Kassab and Aleppo at noon and 3pm (S£125).

Crisp air, lush spruce forests, stone settlements, and stunning vistas surround the traveler all the way to Kassab, and the town itself is equally beautiful. Sharing a dense, forested border with Turkey, Kassab has been home to Armenians for over 1000 years and was a shelter for those who fled 1915 Armenian Genocide. Kassab's shops and churches bear signs in Armenian as well as Arabic. Locals will tell you about their Armenian dialect, which is spoken only in Kassab. Brave bathers should catch the bus to Ras al-Bassit to take advantage of its black-sandy beaches (30min.; 9:45am, return 4:15pm; S£25). When you get there, use a luxury hotel's private beach—locals frown on public skin-bearing.

Al-Sakhra Restaurant (☎71 07 50), up the hill (microbuses make the trip for S£50), has the best views of the mountains and even better food. (Open 24hr., live music summer evenings.) If you want to stay more than a day, try **Mokhtar Hotel,** past the Kassab Karaj. It's a cozy place with snug rooms, new furniture, kitchens and common rooms. (☎71 00 49. Doubles S£500, triples S£700, quads S£1000.)

SLUNFEH

Microbuses to Slunfeh leave when full from the main station in Lattakia (1hr.; 6am-9pm in summer, S£20). Alternatively, reach Slunfeh from al-Haffeh (20min; S£10). To reach the Slunfeh Karaj, take the 1st left from the town square and walk up to the right.

The area's fresh summer temperatures and temperate flora induced the French to establish the town of Slunfeh during their mandate in Syria. Some of the buildings testify to French control, including the Slunfeh Grand Hotel in the teeming town square. Slunfeh's numerous restaurants make it a popular destination for well-off Lattakians out for some fresh air. Take a right from the town square to reach some of the nicer restaurants. Another right at the next roundabout leads past the **phone office** to **al-Khawabi Restaurant**. Positioned next to a natural park scattered with benches, the restaurant serves typical Syrian dishes at Slunfeh prices. Warm bread makes up for the inflated cost.

QAL'AT MARQAB

*To get to Qal'at Marqab, take a Qadmous **microbus** from Tartus (40min., S£12) or from Lattakia (45min., S£15) to the seaside Baniyas. From the Baniyas Qadmous station, walk 200m to the left and take the 1st left to reach the Karnak station, where microbuses leave to Zobeh (S£10). Hop into one of these buses and ask for Qal'at Marqab. Microbuses back to Baniyas are sporadic but usually keep running until 5pm. Open W-M 8:30am-6pm, winter 8:30am-4pm. S£300, students S£15. Free maps.*

The thick-walled Qal'at Marqab, built by Mamluks in 1062 CE, overlooks the sea and is within sight range of Crac des Chevaliers, with which the Crusaders exchanged messages during their brief occupation of the castle. Despite its sad state of disrepair, the remains are evidence of the castle's illustrious past. The fortress was passed from hand to conquering hand for centuries: the Byzantines, the Crusaders, the Ottomans, the Ayyubids under Salah al-Din, and the French each had their turn controlling Qal'at Marqab, which remained inhabited until 1950. The main courtyard, to the right as you enter, opens to an impressive Gothic chapel. A little room to the left is decked with a painting of the Last Supper of Jesus and his disciples, along with more recent works of decorative wall art left by castle visitors. Off the main courtyard, you can reach bakeries and other buildings dating from the Ottoman occupation of the castle. For panoramic views, climb up the dim stairs of the Central Tower, past the Church and the water-tank hall. The watchtower near the sea was built along with the castle to assure its security.

TARTUS طرطوس ☎ 43

Syria's second major seaport is Tartus, the charming older sister to buck-toothed Lattakia 90km to the south. The Phoenicians called this Mediterranean town Antardus, reflecting its secondary importance to the more secure island of Arwad ("Anti-Arwadus" means "the town opposite Arwad"). The Crusaders called it Tortosa, and they not only fortified the town's seaport, but also built its **Cathedral Church of Our Lady of Tortosa.** Many consider the cathedral to be the premier piece of Crusader religious architecture standing outside Jerusalem. Salah al-Din made short work of the fortifications in 1188 CE, while the Templar garrison cowered in the dungeon. Nonetheless, Tartus served as the last Crusader stronghold on the mainland, remaining secure until 1291, when the Crusaders retreated to Arwad for a decade of ineffectual revolt.

Modern-day Tartus is a veritable Shangri-la of sunsets, sea breezes, delectable food, and welcoming accommodations. Cafes spread their tables across the corniche, where bare-armed beauties parade from designer store to gourmet ice cream parlor with their tan and tattooed partners. Tourists attract no more attention than the tame pelicans that roam the fish market each evening. Don't let the showy face of Tartus trick you—Tartusians still inhabit the narrow lanes and arched buildings of the old town, and their calls to prayer still echo off the water every day.

⬛ TRANSPORTATION. Kadmous Transportation Co. (☎ 31 67 30 or 31 28 29), near the intersection of Ibn al-Walid St. and al-Thawra Ave., sends **buses** to: Aleppo (4hr.; 6:30, 9, 11:30am, 1:30, 4:30, 6:30, 9, 11:30pm; S£65) via Hama (1½hr., S£65); Baniyas (30min., every 15min., S£12); Damascus (3½hr., every 2hr. 2am-10:30pm, S£110); Homs (1hr.; 9am, 12:30, 1:45, 3:45, 6:30, 9, 11:30pm; S£40); Lattakia (1hr., every 15min., S£30). To get to **Lebanon,** hop on a bus bound for Homs and transfer to another bus there, or hire a **service** from either the clocktower or the side street about 50m before the microbus station (Tripoli S£200, Beirut S£400). Remember to have a **Lebanese visa** and a **multiple-entry Syrian visa** for reentry into the country (or exit visa), and carry some hard currency just in case.

For local transportation, the **microbus** station, a 15min. walk from the town center, services nearby destinations. Take either Wahda St. or Ibn al-Walid St. away from the sea, pass al-Thawra Ave., and turn right on Tichrin Ave.

⬛ ORIENTATION AND PRACTICAL INFORMATION. Three main streets and the corniche bind the downtown area of Tartus into a rectangle. **Wahda St.** and **Ibn al-Walid St.** run from the sea to **al-Thawra Ave.** Walking down the hill toward the sea on Ibn al-Walid St. takes you past the **post office,** at the intersection with 6 Tishrin Ave. (Open Sa-Th 8am-2:30pm, EMS available 8am-12:30pm, **Poste Restante** pickups 9-10am). A left off of Ibn al-Walid St. two blocks before **Basil Park**

leads to the **Immigration and Passport Office** (open Sa-Th 8am-2pm). Resume your descent to the sea and you will come across the **police station** at the intersection of Ibn al-Walid St. and al-Thawra Ave. Take a left at the next street to reach the **Commercial Bank of Syria,** which changes traveler's checks for those wary of the black market (open Sa-Th 8am-2pm.) The **telephone office** is a block down from the police station and to the right of al-Thawra Ave. (Calls to the US S₤75 per min. Open daily 7am-11pm.) A left onto al-Thawra Ave. leads to the clocktower circle and Wahda St., running east from the corniche at the **Arwad dock.** Most of Tartus's reasonably priced hotels and restaurants line Wahda St. Across from the Daniel Hotel is the friendly and efficient **al-Iman Pharmacy.** (Open Sa-W 8:30am-1:30pm and 5-8pm, Th 8:30am-1:30pm.) **Razi Hospital** is on Baghdad St., off al-Thawra Ave., right before the intersection with Iskandaroun St. (☎22 39 03, open 24hr.) Backtracking to the clocktower circle and hanging a left on Ibn al-Walid St. leads straight to the corniche in front of the **Old City.** The newly relocated **tourist office** is miles away (at the intersection of al-Talaei and 6 Tishrin Ave.) and probably not worth the trek. Speak to the amiable and informative manager of the Daniel Hotel, Elie, instead.

▟▊ ACCOMMODATIONS AND FOOD. Tartus houses enough budget hotels and restaurants to make a brief stay pleasant. **◼Daniel Hotel,** one of Syria's best budget hotels, sits a block and a half up from the beach on Wahda St. Large, sunny rooms boast fans and tidy bathrooms, and some even come with balconies. Manager Elie is an opinionated, generous conversationalist who will enlighten you on everything from the best places to visit in Tartus to the political situation in the Middle East. The friendly hotel rents mountain bikes and runs trips to beaches along the Syrian coast. (☎22 05 81; fax 31 65 55. Breakfast S₤75. Singles S₤350, doubles S₤600, triples S₤800.) Two and a half blocks up the beach on Wahda St., to the right of the next intersection, is the **Republic Hotel.** Reasonably clean rooms come with sink and phone. There is a communal refrigerator. (☎22 25 80. Hot showers ₤35. Singles S₤200, doubles S₤275, triples S₤375.) A step down in quality, the **Hotel Seyaha ("Tourism")** farther up Wahda St. on the left, offers habitable rooms for the lowest prices in town, but lacks private bathrooms. (☎22 17 63. Hot showers S₤25. Singles S₤200; doubles S₤250; triples S₤350; quads S₤450.) For the best quality (and highest prices) in town, go to the **Blue Beach Hotel,** on the corner of Wahda St. and the corniche. Sunny rooms come with balconies overlooking the big blue sea. Fans, heat, and phones included. (☎22 06 50 or 32 63 75. Singles US$13; doubles US$17; triples US$21. Discount for groups of six or more.)

For luxurious dining, explore **The Cave,** 300m from the dock on the waterfront by the Old City. Chef Ahmed spent 18 years as a cook on a Greek ship and occasionally brews his own *'araq* (S₤15). The calamari is a tasty, hefty treat for about S₤350. (☎22 10 16. Open daily 10am-10pm.) For a cheaper fish experience, try **al-Nabil Restaurant.** On the right of Wahda St. as you approach the sea, al-Nabil offers choose-your-own seafood, with quality fish (S₤200) and shrimp (S₤250). *Mezze* (S₤25) and beer (S₤50) round off the menu. (☎31 95 64. Open daily 7am-12:30am, winter 7am-10pm) At the **Venicia Restaurant,** near the corner of the corniche and Wahda St., the fresh fish is a catch at S₤1500 per kilo. Tables for two on the balcony overlook the sea. For Western-style dining, check out the hip **Tic Tac Restaurant,** across from Port Arwad. Chow down on cheeseburgers for S₤120 and shrimp pizzas for S₤135. (Open daily 9am-midnight.)

◙ SIGHTS. Almost entirely unrenovated, the sturdy walls of the medieval **Old City** enclose a hive of activity and chronologically jumbled architecture. With your back to The Cave restaurant on the waterfront, walk left until you reach a large, white mosque. Walk up the hill to the right of the mosque to reach the fortified 12th-century **cathedral,** which claims to house the world's oldest altar dedicated to the Virgin Mary. Now a museum, it displays an eclectic collection of artifacts from all over coastal Syria. (Open W-M 8am-6pm; winter 8am-4pm. S₤300, students

S£15.) Take a break at **Basil (al-Assad) Park,** on the corner of al-Thawra Ave. and Ibn al-Walid St. With its low bushes and meandering aged Tartusians, this fountained eden is perfect for a picnic or quiet read.

🎒 DAYTRIPS FROM TARTUS

ARWAD ارواد

*Ferries run about every 15min. from Port Arwad in Tartus. (20min.; round-trip S£20, pay before returning; last boat leaves 8:30pm.) The choppy ride can be nauseating for the weak of stomach. There are no formal lodgings available on the island, so don't let yourself get stranded. **Crusader fort** open W-M 9am-6pm. S£150, students S£10.*

Arwad, Syria's sole island, floats just 3km from the coast of Tartus. In ancient times, Arwad served as a sanctuary for those seeking protection from foreign invaders. As such, it was the last Crusader stronghold to return to Muslim hands. More recently, the French used it as a prison for Syrian nationalists. The Phoenician kingdom of Aradus was centered on the island, and though little remains of its defensive walls, two grand medieval forts stand their ground. One of them now calls itself a museum. Suntanned children and wary cats roam the narrow lanes of the island while Arwad's men take a break from fishing or building boats to enjoy a seaside cup of tea. The scenic port is followed by a picturesque market. Stop for Turkish beer (S£50) and a great view of the traffic flow at the second floor of **al-Samak** restaurant, to the left of the port. Take a 30min. walk around the island for a more realistic view. The environmental police would have a heart attack over the litter scattered liberally over Arwad's beautiful backside.

CASTLE LE BLANC

To get to Castle le Blanc, take a microbus from Tartus to Safita (40min., S£10). From Safita center, hop on a service to the base of a cobblestone side street (ask for al-Burj). On foot from Safita center, walk up the steepest street and look for the cobblestone side street on the right leading up to the tower. It may seem like a good idea to continue from Castle le Blanc to Crac des Chevaliers, but be warned that the return trip to Tartus is quite complicated. Site open daily 9am-7pm. Free, donations are appreciated.

Only one remaining tower of the once majestic Castle le Blanc stands guard over the tile-roofed houses and olive trees of the small mountain town of Safita. A beautiful chapel graces the tower's entrance level. Never deconsecrated, it continues to serve as a place of worship today. Upstairs are spacious living quarters, which represent one of the finest examples of Romanesque architecture in Syria. Another steep flight of stairs leads to the roof, which offers panoramic views of Lebanon and, on a clear day, Crac des Chevaliers (see p. 596).

Al-Burj restaurant, flanking the tower, has the same great views plus meals made with love. Middle Eastern staples are available at reasonable prices, but for a treat try the succulent vegetarian dish *kama* (S£150), made with rare desert mushrooms, accompanied by a glass of mountain wine. (☎52 17 73. Open 24hr.)

HOSN SULEIMAN

Microbuses to Hosn Suleiman leave from Safita at irregular intervals, more frequently earlier in the day (45min., 6am-3pm, S£10); service on Fridays is rare. Ask about the last returning microbus before leaving. To get to Safita, take a microbus from Tartus (40min., S£10).

Giant stones up to 14m long form the outer walls of this ruined Roman temple, dating from the first century CE. The remarkable rectangular temple with a gate in each wall, nestled in a valley in the middle of the mountains, serves today as a playground for little village children, but its history is not so innocent. It was built upon a site that used to be the home base for the cult of Zeus, and before that housed yet another cult dedicated to the Phoenician god Baotececian Baal. The interior of the temple is cluttered with fallen columns, and stairs and thorns lead up to what used to be the altar. The northern gate is the most elaborate, while the southern gate leads to a shady backyard. All four have eagles with spread wings carved onto their ceilings. To the right of the temple, another eagle watches over a structure with three mossy walls, and an engraved stone (yet to be deciphered) lies abandoned on the ground. Parts of the temple have been know to disappear, so make your visit while supplies last!

AMRIT

 WARNING. Women should absolutely not walk from the bus stop to the ruins alone. Amrit is a remote, wild area, and there have been numerous claims of harassment and assault along the road to the ruins.

To get to nearby Amrit (7km from Tartus), take a microbus to Hamidiyeh from the Karaj and ask to be dropped off at Mafra' Amrit (S£10). Walk about 15min. down the the road to the right of the blue sign at Mafra' Amrit to get to the 1st of the ruins.

Set back into the wilderness just off the coast, the ruins at Amrit, dating from the fifth century BCE, are an impressive mixture of Phoenician styles, drawing influence alternately from Egyptian and Mesopotamian traditions. A gate to the right of the road from the bus stop leads to the necropolis, where two tall towers mark the entrance to dark passages leading into the graves (ask the guards for a flashlight if you are inclined to venture in). Wandering too far behind these two towers leads into a military zone and is not advisable.

To reach the **Temple of Melqart,** head back to the main road and continue past the rusty "Amrit Touristic Project" sign until you reach a crossing of two dirt roads. While the path to the left heads toward the ocean, turning right leads to the temple and a rectangular stadium (of which little remains). The awesome temple sits in a lush green area home to frogs and all things that crawl. In ancient times it was flooded by an underground spring believed to possess healing powers. In the center of the temple is the altar from which an idol of the god Melqart presided.

NORTHERN SYRIA

ALEPPO (HALAB) حلب ☎ 21

Aleppo, 350km north of Damascus, has flourished since the 3rd millennium BCE. Abraham is said to have milked his gray cow on the acropolis here—hence its Arabic name Halab, "to milk." Situated at the crossroads of several vital trade routes, ancient Aleppo controlled the Great Syrian Passage connecting Mesopotamia and Persia with the Mediterranean Sea. Though previously occupied by the Romans, Persians, and Byzantines (whose Christian influence is still felt), Aleppo reached its cultural peak in the days of the Arab Hamadanis. Sayf al-Dawla, who established the Hamadani state in 944 CE, built the city's towering Citadel, hosted the great poets al-Mutanabbi and Abu al-Firas, and filled the city with splendid mosques, schools, and tombs. The city's *khans* were built later to accommodate the many traders passing through; several still stand. Construction continued during Ottoman rule, when the majority of the ancient city's covered *souqs* were built.

Along with the city's Arab Muslim population, today's Aleppans include Armenians, Kurds, Russians, Greek Orthodox Christians, and the occasional Sephardic Jew. The cafes and outdoor restaurants that crowd its wide, tree-lined streets make Syria's second-largest city a sophisticated metropolis, with some of the best shopping available along the eastern Mediterranean. The downside of Aleppo's modernity is that it lacks some of the ethical uprightness of which Syrians are so proud, and can be a challenge for women traveling alone. Some tourists may also be disappointed by Aleppo's pollution and hunkering socialist architecture. Nevertheless, cosmopolitan Aleppo retains many of its erstwhile charms and constitutes a must-see stop on any Syrian itinerary.

SYRIA

▐ TRANSPORTATION

Flights: Aleppo International Airport (☎478 69 00), 30km east of the city center. Buses leave for the airport across from the tourist office (about 1 per hr. 6am-7:30pm; S£5 per person and piece of luggage). *Service* are more flexible (S£150).

International Buses: Afamia for Travel and Tourism (☎221 23 74), opposite the tourist office on al-Ma'ari St., organizes transportation to **Turkey.** Open 9am-10pm and 2am-5am. Buses run to: **Antakya** (3hr., 5am and 1pm, S£250); **Iskenderun** (11hr., S£1200); and **Istanbul** (22hr., S£1200). US$20 buys a **visa** at the border. **Karnak Station** (☎221 02 48), facing the Baron Hotel, sends buses to **Amman** (8½hr., 10pm, S£450) and **Beirut** (7hr., 1pm and midnight, S£250);

Intercity Buses: Most intercity luxury buses depart from **Karnak Hanano** on Ibrahim Hanano St., a short walk to the right facing the Amir Palace.

Kadmous (☎224 88 37 or 221 33 27) makes trips to: **Damascus** (4¼hr., every hr., S£150); **Deir al-Zur** (4½hr.; 12 per day; S£135); **Hama** (1¾hr., 6:30am, S£65); **Homs** (2¼hr., 6:30am, S£80); **Raqqa** (2½hr.; 10:30am, 5, 11pm; S£85); **Tartus** (3½hr.; 9 per day; S£115).

Al-Wafa Co. (☎ 223 16 39), near Kadmous. Buses to **Hama** (S£65) and **Homs** (S£85) every hr.

Jallouf Co. is the best bet to **Lattakia** (3hr.; 14 per day; S£100).

Karnak Station, facing the Baron Hotel, sends buses to: Homs (2½hr., 10am and 1pm, S£75) via Hama (1½hr., S£60); Lattakia (3½hr., 7am, S£65).

Local Buses: To ride **local** buses, purchase a card valid for 4 rides (S£10).

Service and Taxi: *Service* stop next to the **Pullman Station** behind Amir Palace Hotel (S£3-5). Private taxi rides should not cost more than S£25; drivers don't use meters.

✳ ▐ ORIENTATION AND PRACTICAL INFORMATION

Mastering Aleppo's layout is simple. Almost all budget accommodations and some restaurants are in the area bounded by **al-Ma'ari St.** and **Quwatli St.** (running east-west) and **Baron St.** and **Bab al-Faraj St.** (running north-south). Be careful when walking in the vicinity of Bab al-Faraj St. at night, especially when the kung fu and porn movies let out. The National Museum, tourist office, private bus services, travel agents, and a few fancy restaurants lie on al-Ma'ari St. A sharp right onto **al-Walid St.,** which turns into **Sa'adullah al-Jabri St.,** leads to the **Christian Quarter,** where the wealthy strut around restaurants and cafes. It is pleasant to stroll through the enormous **Public Garden** opposite the Christian Quarter, but it is not recommended at night or if alone. South of Bab al-Faraj St. is the congested **al-Mutanabbi St.,** which eventually leads to the **Citadel.** Any right turn will lead to the bustling **souqs.** The easiest way to gain perspective on Syria's second-largest city is to hike up the Citadel's bridge and climb the western wall.

Tourist Office: (☎222 12 00), on al-Ma'ari St. at the intersection with Baron St., across from the National Museum. Pick up helpful Historic Trails pamphlets along with the usual map. Open Sa-Th 8:30am-2pm.

Currency Exchange: Changing anything but cash is a hassle. **Commercial Bank of Syria,** on Baron St. just past the Ugaritic theater, changes traveler's checks for a small commission; bring your passport. Other branches on al-Mutanabbi St. only change cash. All branches open daily 8:30am-12:30pm. An **exchange booth** at the intersection of Quwatli and Bab al-Faraj St. changes cash only. Open daily 9am-7pm.

English-Language Bookstore: Kussa Library (☎223 26 48), on Homsi St. Walk down Baron St. away from the tourist office, passing the kung fu theaters. Take a right after Ma'had al-Mahabba School (a bombed-out building on the right); the small bookstore is on the immediate left. Carries the previous week's copy of the *Sunday Times,* new copies of *Times* and *Newsweek,* and English editions of Lebanon's *Daily Star,* Egypt's *al-Ahram,* and Saudi Arabia's *Arab News.* Open daily 9am-2pm and 5-9pm.

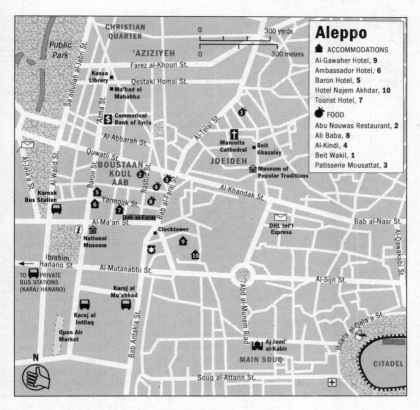

Aleppo

🏠 ACCOMMODATIONS
Al-Gawaher Hotel, **9**
Ambassador Hotel, **6**
Baron Hotel, **5**
Hotel Najem Akhdar, **10**
Tourist Hotel, **7**

🍴 FOOD
Abu Nouwas Restaurant, **2**
Ali Baba, **8**
Al-Kindi, **4**
Beit Wakil, **1**
Patisserie Mousattat, **3**

Emergency: Police and Medical: ☎ 112. **Hospital:** ☎ 110.

Tourist Police: (☎ 222 12 00), on Bab Antakia St., just past the clocktower to the left. Same telephone number as the tourist office; ask to be transferred.

Late-Night Pharmacy: Pharmacies rotate late-night duties. **Ummal al-Najl Pharmacy** (☎ 225 14 78), next to the entrance of Baghdad Station, is open 24hr. Other pharmacies open 9:30am–2pm and 5–9:30pm.

Medical Assistance: Dr. Faher (☎ 225 52 52) offers medical assistance in English.

Telephones: Phone booths are scattered all over the city. They take S£1 coins only, so your best bet is to buy a Syrian Telecom card. Ask at a nearby bookstore or juice-stand where these can be purchased. Cards of S£500 or more can be used for international calls and offer good rates. S£75 per min. to the US, Canada, or Australia, S£50 to Europe. Half price after midnight.

Internet Access: A few cyber cafes dot the Aziziye area, but the most reliable is **Grand Internet** in Souq al-Intaj on Razi St., near the Razi hospital. (☎ 228 24 78. S£100 per hr. Open 10am–1am.) The pricey **Dream Park** fast food joint in the public park (walk around the park to enter), has a lone computer with intermittent Internet access. (☎ 226 66 23. Open 9am–1am. S£200 per hr.)

Post Office: (☎ 147), on al-Jala'a St., just before the park, under a giant radio tower. Open daily 8am–8pm. **EMS** open Sa-Th 8am–1pm; bring your passport. For **DHL** (☎ 224 09 88), walk down Quwatli St. and take the 2nd right after Bab al-Faraj St.; it's in a small alley to the right. Open Sa-Th 9am–2pm and 4–8pm.

ACCOMMODATIONS

Hotels in Aleppo range from the lap of luxury to the seat of sleaze. Higher-priced options cluster on Baron St. in the center of town; more affordable places are scattered among the car parts and hole-in-the-wall eateries near the Bab al-Faraj clocktower. Those searching for the very cheapest should be warned that some are frequented by Russian prostitutes. Look carefully before parting with your cash.

Tourist Hotel (☎ 221 65 83), off Yarmouk St. across from the museum. Walking away from the clocktower on al-Ma'ari St., take a right just before the Syria Hotel sign; it is 75m down on the left past an intersection. Spotless rooms with comfy beds and some with huge, beautiful balconies. Common areas with antique furniture and multi-colored flowerpots. Distinguished owner Madame Olga gives good deals and sends up cookies with customer tea. Breakfast S£100. Singles S£350, with bath S£400; doubles with bath S£700; triples with bath S£1050.

Baron Hotel (☎ 221 08 80; fax 221 81 64), on Baron St. When Aleppo was the end of the line on the Orient Express, the Baron was a stopover for illustrious guests like T.E. Lawrence, Agatha Christie, and Kemal Atatürk, all of whom have been outlived by the hotel's palatial grandeur. The bar is a great retreat, serving local beer and rare stiff cocktails (gin and tonic S£150). Breakfast included. Reserve in advance. Singles US$30; doubles US$40; add US$5 for renovated rooms. Stunning 3-4 person suites US$80.

Al-Gawaher Hotel (☎/fax 223 95 54), on Bab al-Faraj St. With your back to the clocktower, walk toward the library (keeping it on your left), and take the 1st left. Small, clean rooms open up to a fountained, high-ceilinged common room. Communal dining room, rooftop views, and quiet neighborhood are a bonus. Reservations advised in high season. Breakfast S£75. Laundry service available: shirt S£20, pants S£30. Singles S£300-375; doubles S£650-750; triples S£900-1050; quads S£1350.

Hotel Najem Akhdar (☎ 223 91 57). Facing the library from the clocktower, take a left and then a right around the mosque; the hotel is on the right. Full of life, with birds, a cat, and ultra-friendly management. Ice cream awaits in the lobby. Rooftop restaurant has excellent views. There is a catch: rooms have seen better days and "showers" resemble meat lockers. Breakfast S£75. Rooftop mattresses S£150; dorms S£200; singles S£250-350; doubles S£350-500; triples S£450-700; quads S£600-700.

Ambassador Hotel (☎ 221 02 31), on Baron St. next to the Baron Hotel. Rooms cheerfully decorated with blue curtains, bedspreads, tablecloths, and Impressionist-style paintings. Less pricey than its neighbor, but ambiance is lacking and little English is spoken. All rooms have nice bathrooms. Some have balconies. Breakfast US$2. Singles US$15; doubles US$21; triples US$25. Add US$2.50 for A/C, TV, and fridge. V.

FOOD

For great inexpensive restaurants and cafes, turn around the corner from the exchange booth on Quwatli St. onto Bab al-Faraj St. Take a right at the **fruit shake stands** and you'll see six or seven places on the right, their waiters trying to lure passing tourists with calls of "Kebab!" and "Welcome!" Baron St. is lined with rooftop restaurants. The Christian Quarter, near the park off Sa'adullah al-Jabri St., is home to true Middle Eastern opulence.

Beit Wakil (☎ 221 71 69 or 224 70 83), in the Christian Quarter. Head down Khayali St. toward al-Hatab Sq., take a left at the end of the street and an immediate right onto Sissi St. The sweetest splurge in Syria is on the left, not far from the Maronite church. Ottoman architecture and design provide an authentic backdrop, and the congenial manager caters to all budgets. Huge entrees S£300-500. Quiet but well-stocked bar is a great place for a cocktail (S£170). Discounts for groups. Restaurant open 12-4pm and 6pm-1am; bar 10am-2am. 10% charge for DC/MC/V.

Abu Nouwas (☎221 03 88). From Bab al-Faraj clocktower, walk up al-Ma'ari St. and take the 1st right; it's 2 blocks uphill on the left. A/C diner with distinctive orange sign. No menu: the manager gives tours of the kitchen where you choose from lip-smacking veg. and meat dishes. Outstanding lentil soup S£50. Tasty kebab with pita, soup, salad, and drink S£200. Syrian-style breakfast S£75. Open daily 8am-midnight.

Al-Kindi (☎223 11 54 or 221 08 89). Walking uphill on Bab al-Faraj St. from the clock-tower, take the 2nd left; al-Kindi is on the right. Synchronize your mastication with the whacking of a distant meat mallet in this cheap, local favorite. Lightning-quick service. Extensive English (but not veg.-friendly) menu featuring well-prepared kebab (S£80), *shish tawouq* (S£70), and lamb eggs (S£70). Open daily 7am-2am.

Ali Baba Restaurant (☎221 50 24). From the clocktower, head up Bab al-Faraj St. and take the 1st left at the fruit shake stands. The rooftop eatery specializes in *kebab halabi* (S£80). All-male crowd sips beer (S£36) and *'araq* (S£24). Open daily 9am-2am.

Patisserie Mousattat (☎21 27 47), 3rd left up from the clocktower, off Bab al-Faraj St., next to the exchange booth. Classic *ba'laweh* bakery. Bring your morning munchies here and ask for *mamouniya:* a farina-like starch drenched in warm syrup, doused with cin-namon, and eaten with pita bread (S£25). Open daily 5am-midnight.

👁 SIGHTS

CITADEL. Begin your sightseeing tour with an outstanding view of Aleppo from the Citadel. Built in the 10th century CE by Sayf al-Dawla, the Citadel stands 50m above the city on a hill (or *tel*), created by the accumulated remains of prior civilizations. In times of war, Aleppans equipped themselves with provisions and took refuge in this fortress. Its enormous gate is fortified with three sets of steel doors, and the 12th-century **moat** (20m deep and 30m wide) is lined with smooth stones to make climbing difficult (some of the tiles are still in place today). The watery defense is now full of refuse, and not for the first time. Historical accounts describe in gruesome detail how in 1400 CE, invaders from central Asia forces couldn't penetrate the Citadel until the moat brimmed with fallen soldiers' bodies.

Inside and to the immediate left of the main path lies a **bath** that was once used as a metal working studio, probably part of an Ayyubid palace. Beyond the bath is the **small mosque** (with a well in the middle of its courtyard), the **Great Mosque** (bigger, but with a fountain rather than a well), and a cafeteria serving overpriced food and drinks (soda S£35; no fountain or well). Connected to the cafeteria are the **barracks,** now a museum displaying sundry objects found during the Citadel's excavation. Below the barracks is a modern **amphitheater** that stages occasional performances (including the annual **Euro-Syrian Jazz Festival**). To the right of the main path are **storage rooms,** followed by stairs leading to the **Royal Palace.** One of the most interesting sections of the Citadel, this area has its own baths and a courtyard paved with black and white marble. From the palace, a passage leads to the opulent **Throne Room,** which sits directly above the main entrance. *(Open W-M 9am-6pm; in winter 9am-4pm. S£300, students S£15. Museum S£150, students S£15.)*

HAMMAM YALBOAGHA AL-NASIRI. Outside the Citadel, **Hammam Yalboagha al-Nasiri** awaits to steam, and massage the grime off sore bodies. This beautiful 14th-century bath is heavily marketed by the Ministry of Tourism. *(☎362 31 54. Take a left with your back to the Citadel entrance. Open for women Sa, M, Th 9am-5pm; in winter, Sa, M, W 9am-5pm. Open for men daily 9am-1:30am. Soaping, massage, and cup of coffee or tea S£415; unassisted bath with own soap S£200. Outside regular hours by appointment, S£450.)*

▨ MAIN SOUQ. Between the *Hammam*-Citadel area and the hotel district is the best souq in Syria. Nine kilometers of ancient, winding passageways burst with leather, silk, backgammon boards, carpets, Qur'ans, *argilehs*, brass, gold and silver jewelry, and even lingerie. Several **khans** (courtyard inns) in the *souq* housed international traders during the Mamluk and Ottoman periods. On Friday evenings, the dark and deserted *souq* invites leisurely exploration on foot. For those short on time or too faint-hearted to venture into the endless passageways, the renovated Khan al-Shouneh, behind the coffee shops facing the Citadel entrance, offers a good array of the *souq*'s produce—at tourist prices. *(Walking around the* souq *is generally safe even during less-busy hours, but women travelers should not walk alone in the evenings. Open Sa-Th early morning until 7-8pm.)*

AL-JAAMI' AL-KABIR. Appropriately situated just behind the gold market, **al-Jaami' al-Kabir,** the Great Mosque of the Umayyads (also called **Zacharias's Mosque,** after the father of John the Baptist), is a real gem. Built on top of a Byzantine cathedral in the 8th century, its square minaret with five levels of arches is a remarkable architectural feat. To the left of the main entrance stands an empty 600-year-old **insane asylum** in good condition. A fragrant smell emanates from two **soap factories** around the corner. Aleppo's high-quality soap (made from olive or laurel oil) is known throughout the Middle East. Both factories have been in the same unsullied families for generations. *(Expected to be under renovation until 2004, but still open to the public. Requisite robes S£10; don't be tricked into paying more.)*

NATIONAL MUSEUM. Aleppo's National Museum is second in quality only to the one in Damascus. On display are several 100,000-year-old Ugaritic flint axes, a 3rd-millennium BCE basalt altar from Ebla, and a stone lion from an 18th-century BCE temple. An excellent modern art wing on the third floor offers a rare look into the experience and psyche of Syrian artists. *(Opposite the tourist office on Baron St. Open W-M 9am-5:30pm; winter 9am-3:30pm; Ramadan 9am-3pm. S£300; students S£15.)*

CHRISTIAN QUARTER. Fabulous 17th- and 18th-century homes line the narrow streets of the Christian Quarter. Within a few blocks, there are churches representing four different denominations. Walk down Quwatli St. past Bab al-Faraj St. and take the second left across from the parking lot onto an airy, tiled street. Past the **museum** and the **Ghazale House** (under renovation; knock for a peek) take the first left to get to the 19th-century **Maronite Cathedral** in Farhat Sq. To the right of the cathedral is a gorgeous **Greek Catholic Church.** Take a left around the Greek Catholic church and a right at the end of the street to reach the **Greek Orthodox Church** and the **Armenian Church of the Forty Martyrs.** These buildings feature 3rd-century artwork, engraved marble altars, and antique chandeliers.

▓ DAYTRIPS FROM ALEPPO

BASILICA OF ST. SIMEON قلعة سمعان

*To reach St. Simeon from Aleppo, take a **microbus** from Karaj al-Mu'ahad to Darrat 'Azzeh (1hr., S£10). From this small town, negotiate with locals for the 8km ride to the cathedral. **Service** minivans S£100 1-way, S£300 round-trip. English-speaking guides hanging out at the entrance will show you around for S£200. Guidebooks S£200. Open daily 9am-6pm; in winter 9am-4pm. S£300, students S£15.*

Born in 392 CE, **St. Simeon of Stylites** acquired his name by spending almost 40 years preaching from atop a stylite, or pillar. Simeon's popularity with locals and his ability to starve himself made his superiors jealous, so they banished him to a nearby hillside. Peasants hounded the local legend for advice, and the game of "Simon Says" was born. While he would gladly address the questions of men, Simple Simeon refused to talk to women. As his disenchantment with humanity grew so did the pillar—at the time of his death in 459 CE he was sitting 11m in the air.

Simeon's death did not stop pilgrims from visiting his pillar, and the emperor Zenon had a **cathedral** built around his home, which is considered a masterpiece of pre-Islamic architecture. A large dome covered the octagonal courtyard where the pillar stood, surrounded by four basilicas that formed a giant cross. One basilica was a chapel; the other three housed pilgrims. The rear wall of the chapel was decorated with delicate acanthus leaves and Byzantine crosses. An earthquake destroyed the structure less than 50 years after its completion, causing pilgrims to question the site's holiness and deterring pious investors from rebuilding the cathedral. The 5th-century remains are beautiful, but years of souvenir-seekers chipping away at the pillar have reduced it almost to a large boulder. In the 10th century, the site was converted to a Byzantine fort with 12 towers, one for each apostle, along the wall. The fortifications are easily distinguishable from the cathedral ruins and afford panoramic views of the rocky terrain leading up to Turkey.

If you have time, make a side trip to **Qatura**. This Roman tomb, the resting place of the warrior Titus Flavius Julianus, is carved into rock about 1km off the road to St. Simeon. Above the entrance to the tomb, an eagle—identical to one in Palmyra's Temple of Bel (p. 592)—poses with spread wings, a symbol of the soul.

EBLA أبلا

*From the Aleppo Karaj al-Intilaq, take a **minibus** headed to Ma'arat al-Nu'man (S£20) and ask to get off at the road to Ebla. It's a 30min. **walk** to the site. If you bring food and water, able will you be ere you see Ebla. Back on the highway it's easy to catch a **bus** back to Aleppo; they come frequently from both Ma'arat al-Nu'man and Hama. To include a visit to the **Idlib museum**, take a **microbus** from Aleppo to Idlib (S£20); **minibuses** from Idlib to Ma'arat al-Nu'man pass in front of the museum, and will stop at the road to Ebla (S£5). Museum open 9am-6pm; in winter 9am-4pm. S£300, students S£15. Ebla open daily 6am-6pm. S£200, students S£15 (if the guard isn't off tending to his sheep).*

This *tel*, 60km south of Aleppo, was discovered in 1964, and excavations are still in progress. Ebla is thought to have been the oldest city in Syria, dating back to the 3rd millennium BCE. Over 17,000 **cuneiform tablets** have been recovered in an ancient **palace library**, revealing much about Syria's early history. Apparently, Ebla was the center of an important North Syrian empire during the 3rd millennium BCE, but as fate would have it, the city was to prove itself a rather irritating obstacle to the expansion of empires. Both Sargon of Akkad (around 2300 BCE) and the Hittites (around 1600 BCE) razed Ebla almost completely. Today, signs insist that you remain on the edges of the site. This shouldn't be too disappointing, as little more than clusters of stones surrounded by stubby walls remain of the once-prominent city. Colorful plaques, however, remind the visitor of Ebla's pre-pillage glory.

The **Idlib Museum** gives a more complete picture of the Ebla's heyday. The second floor houses a reconstruction of the palace library and the cuneiform tablets found there. The actual tablets, with writings ranging from magical incantations to political treaties, are displayed behind glass. The modern art wing is also decent.

MA'ARAT AL-NU'MAN معارة النعمن

*To get to Ma'arat al-Nu'man, take a **service** or **minibus** from Karaj al-Intilaq in Aleppo or Hama (S£17, buy your tickets from a booth to the left of the karaj). From town, hire a local or private **taxi** to take you around the Dead Cities (S£600, lower if you bargain).*

The road to Ma'arat al-Nu'man betrays few hints of the splendor of its main attraction, the neighboring **Dead Cities**. Despite its bustling populace and *souq*, this dusty peripheral town has only one minor point of interest. Two hundred meters left of the bus terminal and directly next to the *souq* stands an old Ottoman *khan* that has been converted into a **museum**. The fourth exposition room, to the left of the entrance, houses a remarkable collection of Roman mosaics from the 3rd century CE, boasting of Hercules's exploits. The extensive collection of Byzantine mosaics, restored from surrounding churches and old houses, gives you a good idea of the past majesty of the Dead Cities. (Open W-M. S£300, students S£15.)

AL-BARA. Ten kilometers west of town and 5km to the north lies the least inspiring of the Dead Cities. This 5th-century city was one of Syria's major wine producers, as well as an important religious site. Al-Bara's main attractions are two well-preserved **pyramid tombs** that house Christian carvings. Today, al-Bara is home to wandering sheep, green orchards, and a modern Bedouin village.

SERJILLA. Seven kilometers east of al-Bara on a lonely road is Serjilla, perhaps the grandest of the Dead Cities. Built on a plateau, the town once housed 11,000 people. Its baths, olive oil mills, Roman and Byzantine churches, and tavern have remarkably withstood the test of time. Townspeople spoke Syriac and Greek until the 1148 Muslim conquest, led by Nour al-Din. A **guide** *(Sa-M and W-Th 9am-4pm; S£200, students S£10, tips appreciated)* can teach you about Serjilla's complex water-heating system and its hidden **underground caverns** and **cisterns.**

RUWEIHA. Twelve kilometers north of Ma'arat al-Nu'man, Ruweiha sports standard Dead City sights (churches, baths, mills, and villas). Bedouins have settled into many of the ruins. The highlight of the town is a grandiose columned 5th-century **basilica,** which serves as a storage area for inhabitants of modern Ruweiha.

QALB LOZEH AND HARIM

*Take a **microbus** from Karaj al-Mu'ahad (1½hr., S£30) to Harim. From there negotiate with a driver for the remaining distance to Qalb Lozeh (30min., round-trip around S£300).*

 WARNING: Women should absolutely not make this trip alone. There have been numerous claims of harassment and assault by both drivers and locals.

The journey to Qalb Lozeh is long and strenuous, and the finale, though rewarding, may not be worth the trouble to if you're not keen on 6th century CE churches. The renowned **Church of Qalb Lozeh** stands solidly in the little Druze village, its arches fenced up to keep children and horses from straying inside. Intricately decorated pillars and intact corinthian arches make this remote church one of the most beautiful and historically significant in Syria.

On the road to Harim, you'll get a brief glimpse of a paved Roman road that disappears under the asphalt to the left and stretches into the fields. The **Ayyubid castle,** a short hike up from the Harim bus station, might be worth a stop. Views from the top are splendid, but little remains of the original structure. To the right, the ruins of a *hammam* greet the visitor, and farther along is a bottomless well.

'AIN DARA

*To get to 'Ain Dara, take a **minibus** from Karaj al-Intilaq in Aleppo to 'Afrin (1hr., S£13). From there, hop on a **microbus** headed to Jandarah (S£10) and ask to be dropped off at the 'Ain Dara intersection. A pleasant 20min. **walk** (taking a left at the fork) leads to the 'Ain Dara hill. Guards in the mission house at the foot of the hill collect the entrance fee (S£150, students S£10). To return to 'Afrin, hail any microbus going in your direction. Take a minibus back to Aleppo; as microbuses (S£25), though faster and more comfortable, will only drop you on the outskirts of the city.*

The *tel* housing the 'Ain Dara ruins appears from a distance, marked by red tape and a hedge of cement. Work on the site is still unfinished, and Tokyo University experts return yearly to carry on their mighty task. Overlooking cultivated hills, the top of the *tel* boasts a magnificent Hittite-era temple. Winged sphinxes and 3000-year-old lions guard the temple's southern facade, with the well-preserved features of the feminine creatures providing a model of the Hittite ideal of beauty. The small museum in the mission house contains other noteworthy sculptures, as well as pottery and miscellaneous findings from the site (ask the guard to let you have a peek). Beside the lions and sphinxes, three decorated basalt steps lead up to the temple entrance, where the limestone blocks of the threshold bear the marks of huge footprints, purportedly of divine origin.

EASTERN SYRIA

DEIR AL-ZUR دير الزور ☎ 51

Tourists may consider Deir al-Zur out of the way, but its remote location has always been its greatest asset. The city first flourished due to its strategic position next to the Euphrates River, at the crossroads of two major trade routes. In the 1980s, oil was discovered beneath the city's sands, fueling a huge growth

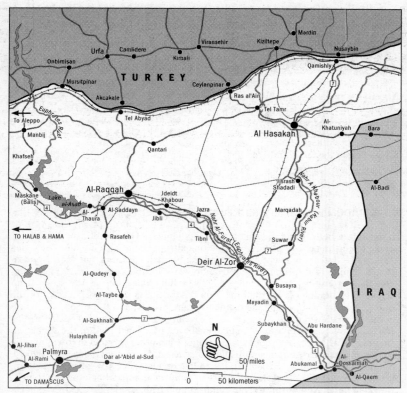

spurt. Fortunately, the Turkish dams harnessing the river's hydraulic force have not stripped Deir al-Zur of its splendor. Enjoy its troubled waters from a safe distance on the **suspension bridge** built by the French, or from one of the many restaurants that line the riverbanks. Aside from a first-class museum and magnificent views of the river, dry and distant Deir al-Zur offers travelers little more than a base for visiting the nearby ruins at Rasafeh, Halabiyyeh, and Zalabiyyeh, and the chance to experience the hospitality of the desert people of eastern Syria.

▐ TRANSPORTATION. The **bus/microbus station,** Karaj al-Intilaq, is about 1km out of town on 8 Azar St. Hourly microbuses go to: **Homs** (4½hr., S£95); **Mari** (2hr., S£50); **Raqqa** (2hr., S£50-60); and other southern destinations. Buses leave less frequently to **Aleppo** (5hr., S£85) and **Damascus** (6hr., S£110) via **Palmyra** (2¼hr., S£75). The **luxury bus station** is about 2km out of town: pass Karaj al-Intilaq and take a right at the mosque. Karnak Bus Co. (☎22 18 85) runs to **Damascus** (5hr.; 12:45, 8, 10, 11:15am, 3pm; S£150) via **Palmyra** (2hr.; S£75). Qadmous (☎21 29 21) has buses every 30-45min. to **Aleppo** (5hr., S£135) and **Damascus** (5½hr., S£175) via **Palmyra** (2½hr., S£85). Also to **Hama** (5hr.; noon and midnight; S£170) via **Homs** (4½hr., S£150), and **Lattakia** (7hr.; 1:15am, 2pm, midnight; S£230) via **Tartus** (6hr., S£190).

▐▐ ORIENTATION AND PRACTICAL INFORMATION. Deir al-Zur is easy to navigate. Hotels, restaurants, and shopping areas are centered around the main intersection of **8 Azar** and **al-Imam St.** (also called **Shari' al-'Amm**). The **statue** of late

President Hafez al-Assad's late son Basil on a horse is a handy landmark—nearly everything is a 5min. walk. Most signs are in Arabic; rely on maps and landmarks.

The **tourist office** is east of the square, 1 block south of Khalid ibn al-Walid St. English skills are tenuous and maps rarely available. (☎22 61 50. Open Sa-Th 8am-2pm.) The office also has a booth at the luxury bus station that keeps the same hours. Most hotels will **exchange cash** but the best way to change money is at the **Commercial Bank of Syria,** a 10min. walk along al-Imam Ali St. Changing **traveler's checks** is a 15min. procedure. Bring your passport. (Open Sa-Th 8:30am-12:30pm.) The **police** (☎112) are around the corner from the old museum on 6 Ayyar St., across from the river. For an **ambulance** call ☎110. **Al-Shifa'a Pharmacy** (☎22 12 41) is next to al-Jamia'a Hotel, east of the main square. There are two **post offices:** a new one is near the bus station on 8 Azar St. and offers **Poste Restante** and **EMS** services (open Sa-Th 8am-2pm); the old office sells expensive **phone cards** and is a 5min. walk west of the square on al-Imam Ali St. (Open 8:30am-1:30pm). The only **public phones** are around the corner from the old post office.

⌂ ACCOMMODATIONS AND FOOD. Cheap lodgings in Deir al-Zur are limited to dingy-looking buildings in disrepair. Don't count on private showers or immaculate beds. **Hotel al-Jamia'a al-'Arabia** jams on Grande St., the third right away from the central square. A spacious sitting room with TV and balconies makes this hotel somewhat cheery, and the English-speaking manager, Noureddin, is a mine of information and friendly even to non-guests. (☎22 13 71. Singles S£200; doubles S£325; triples S£425.) **Hotel Damas,** across the street from the smaller branch of the Euphrates on 8 Azar St., is the most peaceful of the bunch. Rooms overlooking the main street are breezy, and some come with balconies with views of the river. (☎22 14 81. Singles S£200; doubles S£325; triples S£425; quads S£525.) **Hotel al-'Arabi al-Kabir,** about a block east of the square on Khalid ibn-Walid St., is brighter and cleaner than other options in town, but the rock-hard mattresses and earsplitting noise are definite drawbacks. (☎22 20 70. Singles S£250; doubles S£300; triples S£450; quads S£600.) West of the square, on the second right off of the main street, material comfort beckons you to pristine **Ziad Hotel.** New furniture, air-conditioning, fridge, satellite TV, fresh sheets and spic-and-span showers make it well worth the extra cash. (☎ 21 45 96; fax 21 19 23. Breakfast included. Singles US$17; doubles US$26. Discount for groups of 12 and more.)

Don't expect fine dining, either—most culinary options come from the small falafel, shawarma, and pastry shops and the fresh-produce **souq** around 8 Azar Sq. If the stand-up routine grows tiresome, there are a few sit-down places around the square and on the river. **Nadi al-Muhandisin Restaurant** is opposite the suspension bridge, to the right, in a cool setting with nice views. Slow service gives you ample time to enjoy fish from the river (S£350 per kg) or just sit back with a beer. (☎ 22 04 69. Open noon-5pm and 8pm-3am). **Sahara Restaurant,** a short walk west of the square, tucked within a building to the right, provides cheap, filling meals for S£60. (☎22 23 73. Open 6am-11:30pm.)

◉ SIGHTS. Deir al-Zur's **National Museum,** considered one of the best in Syria, was opened in response to a growing number of archaeological discoveries in the area. It was established in 1996 as a joint venture of the Syrian Antiquities Department and the Frei Universität of Berlin, Germany. The museum presents the region's history starting with the biblical era, moving through Arab-Islamic culture, and ending in the present day. Especially fascinating is the Roman-era "Twin Pot Grave" containing the remains of a 14-year-old girl bedecked with a ring and bracelet. The museum pays particular attention to the region's delicate environmental situation. *(South of the central square, a short walk past the central bank. Open W-M 9am-6pm; in winter 9am-4pm. S£300, students S£15.)*

🔃 DAYTRIPS FROM DEIR AL-ZUR

MARI

To get to Mari, take a microbus from Karaj al-Intilaq headed to Boukmal and ask to be dropped off at the sight (2hr., S£50). To return, hail a microbus in the opposite direction and ask if it's going to Deir al-Zur. Open daily. S£300, student S£15.

The ancient city of Mari was established around 2900 BCE. Today its ruins comprise the most important Mesopotamian site in Syria that is still open to visitors. The most visible and well preserved monument here is the **Royal Palace,** covered by a protective white tent. It was built by 8th century BCE Mesopotamian ruler Zimrilim and contained over 300 rooms. Like most of the remainders of the city, the palace is partially buried, its narrow hallways made of delicate mud bricks.

Beyond the palace, little remains of ancient Mari. Hopping into the numerous holes where buildings once stood, you can see shattered pieces of pottery and what looks like water canals dug within the walls. The remains of five different temples and a ziggurat are hard to spot.

The faithful guard, Abu 'Ali, offers visitors water and tea in the Bedouin shelter at the entrance to the site. Across from the ticket office (doubling as 'Ali's home), the mission house shelters artifacts awaiting shipment to various museums.

DOURA EUROPUS

Microbuses to Boukmal (1¼hr., S£50) will drop you off within walking distance of the ruins. Ask for 'Athar al-Salihiyay. Don't be fooled if the Palmyra Gate looks close; it's is a 20min. walk on the main road (walk with the electricity towers to your back). Bring plenty of water since, apart from the occasional grazing sheep and goats, the arid region is completely deserted. Open 6am-7:30pm. S£150, students S£10.

Doura Europus, founded in the 3rd century BCE, occupied a defensive position on the road linking two important Seleucid military encampments. Romans occupied the city from 164 to 256 CE, when it fell to the Persians, whose ransacking rendered the site uninhabitable forevermore.

The magnificent **Palmyra Gate** and sandy ramparts are the most impressive remains of the ancient city and the most accurate indicators of the past grandeur of Doura Europus. The gate had fortified towers on either side, connected by a passage over the arch. The path from the main gate leads past the scant remainders of the **Temple of Adonis** and the **Agora** to the more impressive ruins. The imposing front of the **Palace of the Strategion** emerges to the right, with little cave-like rooms at its feet. Farther on, beyond the stretching remainders of 2nd century BCE houses, the Euphrates river forges on, bringing with it unexpected greenery.

RAQQA رقة ☎22

Looking around modern Raqqa, one would hardly guess at the glorious past of this bustling market town. On the left bank of the Euphrates, between Aleppo and Deir al-Zur, Raqqa was founded in the 4th century BCE by Alexander the Great and rebuilt many times throughout the ages, though few ruins remain to attest to its former splendor. In 662 CE, Abbasid Caliph Mansour built a new city atop Raqqa's ruins, with a semi-circular plan inspired by Baghdad. The southern, straight side of this horseshoe-shaped city was aligned with the Euphrates. Raqqa reached its apex in the beginning of the 9th century under notorious Abbasid Caliph Harun al-Rashid, but virtually ceased to exist after Mongol invasions in 1260. It was not until the end of World War II that Syrians revitalized the city as a commercial hub, once again rebuilt on top of its own ruins. Wide, dusty, homely streets run across the city today, and rows of trees struggle hopelessly against the scorching sun. During the hottest hours, sleepy bodies find refuge under the shade of their carts, drowsily waking up in the evening to crowd the streets.

TRANSPORTATION. The **microbus station** is about 200m south of the clock-tower past the statue of Assad. Microbuses leave regularly to **al-Mansoura** (30min., S£15) and **Aleppo** (3hr., S£75). The main **bus station** is across the street. The cheapest of the luxury bus lines is **Karnak** (☎22 28 16), with one daily bus to **Damascus** (5½hr., noon, S£150) via **Homs** (3¼hr., S£100). The nicer **Qadmous** (☎22 16 28, last ticket office in the line) runs to: **Aleppo** (2½hr.; 7:15am, 2:15, 8pm; S£85); **Damascus** (6hr.; 1:15, 8, 9:45am, noon, 2:30, 4:30pm; S£190) via **Homs** (3½hr., S£125); and **Deir al-Zur** (2hr.; 9am, 3, 9:30pm; S£60). Luxury bus line **al-'Aliah** (☎22 23 06) services **Aleppo** (2½hr.; 12:30, 7, 8, 9, 11:30am, 1, 3:30, 6:30, 9pm; S£85).

ORIENTATION AND PRACTICAL INFORMATION. Finding your way around Raqqa is easy from the **clocktower** in the central square and **Assad Sq.** (marked by a statue of Assad) downhill to the south. Don't expect much help from the distant **tourist office,** a 20min. walk down the second street off the right side of Assad Sq., coming from the clocktower. (☎23 03 41. Open Sa-Th 8am-2pm.) In contrast, the **hospital** (☎22 23 40), just west of the clocktower on al-Shahid Basil al-Assad St., is clean, economical, and friendly. The **telephone office,** east of the clock-tower, is often the only place to make international phone calls, but the staff's poor English and unhealthy suspicion of foreigners make it hard to get any assistance. (Open Sa-Th 8am-9pm. S£75 to call US, Canada and Europe; S£90 to Australia). There are orange phone booths south of the central square, but they are usually out of order. **Phone cards** for use in the booths are available outside the phone office (S£100, 500, or 1000). The **post office,** on the southeast corner of the central square, has **EMS** (Sa-Th 8am-2pm).

ACCOMMODATIONS AND FOOD. Hotel Karnak, also known as **Tourist Hotel,** is a 10min. hike west of the Assad statue along winding al-Shahid Basil al-Assad St. The **Karnak Hotel** is a gem compared to other options in Raqqa. The English-speaking receptionist is helpful even to non-guests, and big rooms come with clean baths, air-conditioning, and fridge. Ask for one of the top-floor rooms complete with balconies and tremendous views. (☎23 22 66. Breakfast included. Singles $24; doubles $30; triples $35. Traveler's checks accepted.) The well-situated **'Ammar Hotel** is a short walk north of the clocktower, on the first street to the left. The hotel is male-dominated and has nondescript but relatively clean dorm-style rooms with sinks but no showers, as well as a communal kitchen. (☎22 26 12. Singles S£200; doubles S£400; student rooms S£150.) **Hotel Tourism,** just east of the clocktower on the main street, might make you think twice before leaving home again. Perks like showers, fridges, air-conditioning, and TV fail to compensate for crumbling furniture and sheets in dire need of sterilization. Ask the manager to turn on the hot water or you'll be in for a frigid shock. (☎22 07 25. Singles S£300; doubles S£400; triples S£500. S£100 extra for private bathroom, A/C, and TV.)

Many falafel and shawarma stands cluster around the main square, and delight-ful pastry shops beckon the hungry north of the clocktower. Finding a sit-down restaurant is often as rewarding as it is difficult. **Al-Rashid Restaurant** (☎24 19 19) is about a block west of the clocktower through a small park. Sit back and enjoy a splendid Syrian meal (S£200) with beer (S£100) in the comfort of al-Rashid's air-conditioned dining room with artsy decor and views of the garden. The **Hotel Karnak Restaurant** serves cheap eats (S£200) that can be enjoyed on the patio over-looking the main street and lawn.

SIGHTS. Most of Raqqa's former splendor has been lost over time, but there are a few exceptions. To the east and northeast of the clocktower, parts of the Abbasid wall remain. Raqqa's 12th-century city gate, **Bab Baghdad,** is a 10min. walk east of the clocktower. The area around Bab Baghdad is by far the most pleasant part of town. A left at the gate leads to the Abbasid palace known as the **Palace of the Maidens,** uncovered by Syrian and French archaeologists and surrounded by a metal fence (ask the guard to let you in). To the northwest lie the remains of the old

Grand Mosque, built during the 8th-century reign of the Abbasid Caliph al-Mansour. Only parts of the wall and the arcade of the sanctuary wall still stand. To the east of the clocktower, the third left takes you right to the **Raqqa Museum.** The first floor of this small building details the archaeological finds from the province of Raqqa, and the second floor contains items found in the city proper. Scattered explanations in English and German. On the first floor, at the heart of the museum, you can see the grandiose plan for a new museum to be constructed in the near future on the banks of the Euphrates. *(Museum open W-M 8am-2pm. S£200, students S£30.)*

■ DAYTRIPS FROM RAQQA

RASAFEH رسا فة

*Service depart from Raqqa to al-Mansoura (30min., S£15), where drivers of little Suzukis offer to take you to Rasafeh and back for S£150. **Microbuses** from Raqqa will do the same for S£500 and are a better alternative for larger groups. **Hitchhiking** is a popular option, though Let's Go does not recommend it. Hitchers first walk the short distance to al-Mansoura's main road to look for a lift. It may take about 1hr. and could require a few different rides, so bring water, small bills to offer your driver(s), and plenty of patience. Women should not travel to Rasafeh without a male companion. Open site. S£150, student S£10.*

Thirty kilometers south of Raqqa and the Euphrates, the towering walls of Rasafeh—one of the most extraordinary desert cities in the Middle East—appear suddenly from the flat desert expanse. Around 300 CE, **Sergius,** a Christian officer in the Roman army, was tortured to death for refusing to worship the Roman god Jupiter, sending shockwaves though Syria's Christian community. Sergius became the patron saint of Rasafeh, where his shrine became a major pilgrimage site. The city was renamed Sergiopolis in the 5th century, then fell to Persian Muslims in the 7th century. The Umayyads eventually depopulated and then deserted the area. Today, Rasafeh's relative inaccessibility means that few tourists crowd the town.

Enter Rasafeh through the Byzantine **North Gate,** often called one of the loveliest city entrances in Syria. Three corinthian columns support the richly decorated triple entrance and serve as a graceful frame for the city beyond. Climb the ramparts for a better view of the whole fortress. The bulk of the site has yet to be excavated, so the interior looks somewhat like a lunar landscape, with high ground where walls once stood and depressions where roofs collapsed. In front of the gate is a run-of-the-mill Roman **basilica** and about 100m farther lies the **khan.** To the west, the arched openings of the enormous **cisterns** lead to vast underground caverns, supplied by aqueducts connected to a huge open reservoir. These caverns were capable of holding enough water to supply the entire city for two to three years. To the east stands the early 6th-century **Basilica of St. Sergius,** the best-preserved building in Rasafeh and one of the most ornate cathedrals in the region. The Rasafeh **cafeteria** does not serve food, but its fairly priced drinks are a life-saver after exploration of the colossal site.

HALABIYYEH AND ZALABIYYEH

*Getting to these towns is an arduous process. From Deir al-Zur, take a **microbus** to Tibne (30min., every hr., S£15). From this turnoff, you'll have to hitch or suffer the 2hr. walk to Halabiyyeh. Getting to Zalabiyyeh is much harder and probably not worth it. From Halabiyyeh, cross the bridge just beyond town, walk for 3hr. along the main road, pass through the tunnel under the railway (just after the station), and proceed up the hill.*

Previously called Zenobia (after the Palmyrene queen under whose auspices it was built), the 3rd-century CE town of Halabiyyeh once guarded trade routes along the Euphrates and the desert. The Romans took Halabiyyeh after destroying Palmyra. In the following years, the town was a stronghold against the encroaching Sassanian Persians. Its Citadel was once heralded as the greatest Byzantine fortification outside Constantinople. The city was destroyed and eventually abandoned after sieges in 540 and 610. Nevertheless, Halabiyyeh's outer walls and upper fortifications remain relatively intact, and it is still possible to make out the foundations of some churches and baths. What isn't difficult at all to discern is the incredible view of the Euphrates. The twin fortress town of Zalabiyyeh, 3km downstream on the opposite bank, once defended the approaches to Halabiyyeh. With the exception of the main gateway, the site has been almost completely destroyed.

TURKEY (TÜRKİYE)

TURKISH LIRA (TL)		
US$1 = TL1,480,000		TL1,000,000 = US$0.68
CDN$1 = TL970,000		TL1,000,000 = CDN$1.04
UK£1 = TL2,130,000		TL1,000,000 = UK£0.47
IR£1 = TL1,716,000		TL1,000,000 = IR£0.59
AUS$1 = TL783,000		TL1,000,000 = AUS$1.29
NZ$1 = TL642,000		TL1,000,000 = NZ$1.57
ZAR1 = TL180,000		TL1,000,000 = ZAR5.60
EUR€1 = TL1,351,000		TL1,000,000 = EUR€.75
E£1 (EGYPTIAN POUND) = TL308,000		TL1,000,000 = E£3.24
JD1 (JORDANIAN DINAR) = TL1,860,000		TL1,000,000 = JD0.538
L£100 (LEBANESE POUNDS) = TL86,600		TL1,000,000 = L£1,154
NIS1 (NEW ISRAELI SHEKEL) = TL309,000		TL1,000,000 = NIS3.23
S£100 (SYRIAN POUNDS) = TL2,460,000		TL1,000,000 = S£40.7

The modern Republic of Turkey is one of the world's great paradoxes: it is neither Europe, Asia, nor the Middle East, but rather a kaleidoscope of the three. The empires that shaped Asia Minor over the past 10,000 years—the Hittites, Assyrians, Romans, Byzantines, and Ottomans—each left their mark, layering history upon history: Urartian fortresses tower over Armenian churches converted into Selçuk mosques. Though resolutely secular by government decree, every facet of Turkish life is graced by the religious traditions of a 99% Muslim population. The terrain ranges from the ribboned, white sand beaches of the Aegean Coast resort towns, across the great Anatolian plains to the harsh, forbidding peaks of Mt. Ararat in the East. Millionaire playboys dock at the exclusive clubs of İstanbul in private yachts, while shepherds and farmers eke out an often desperate living in the southeast. Every year, tourists cram the Sultanahmet district of İstanbul, the glittering western coasts, and the ever-popular moonscapes of Cappadocia, while the rest of Anatolia remains a purist backpacker's paradise: pristine alpine meadows, cliffside monasteries, medieval churches, tiny fishing villages, and countless cups of *çay* offered by people who take pride in their tradition of hospitality.

▓ HIGHLIGHTS OF TURKEY

BE DAZZLED by İstanbul's **Blue Mosque** (p. 643), a six-minaret wonder whose creation once threatened the singularity of the mosque at Mecca.

ENVY Süleyman the Magnificent's house and harem at the **Topkapı Palace** (p. 644) in Istanbul, and pore over the visual treasures of the Islamic World.

HACK your way through an Amazonian forest to find ruins of an ancient city overrun by crabs, turtles, birds, and lizards in **Olimpos (p. 673)**.

SLEEP in a cave pension and spend the afternoon at the **Göreme Open-Air Museum** (p. 691), where you can tour six frescoed Byzantine cave churches.

LIFE AND TIMES

Human beings have been living in what is now Central Turkey (known as "Anatolia" or "Asia Minor") since the 8th millennium BCE, making it one of the world's oldest continuously inhabited areas. Since the first human settlements appeared, Turkey has hosted the greatest of civilizations, each waxing with exuberance and then fading with despair.

HISTORY

HITTITES TO OTTOMANS (2000 BCE-1922 CE)

FOREIGN RULERS. By the start of the 2nd millennium BCE, the iron-forging **Hittites** had migrated from the Caucasus into central Anatolia to establish a millennium-long feudal empire headquartered at Hattuşaş (modern **Boğazkale,** p. 686). Despite Hittite dominance in central Anatolia (and beyond—the Hittites even controlled Syria), other groups established themselves in the area of present-day Turkey, most notably the Phrygians (a.k.a. the Trojans). **Troy** sprung up at the mouth of the Dardanelles, and archaeological excavations suggest that the Trojans unsheathed their swords for the Trojan War around 1250 BCE. After the collapse of the Hittites came the Persians, who used Turkey as a base for forays into Greece. Next in line was **Alexander the Great,** who invaded the region and took it from the Persians in less than a year. The Mediterranean coast's importance in the Roman province of Asia Minor paved the way for the creation of the East Roman Empire, centered in the city of **Constantinople** (now İstanbul). Founded by Emperor Constantine in 324 CE over the Greek city of Byzantium, Constantinople became the center of Greek Orthodox culture and the capital of a renewed empire stretching from the Balkans through Greece to the Levant and Egypt.

By the 9th century, the ancestors of the Turks had begun to migrate from Central Asia and resettle everywhere from Iran to India. In the 11th century, **Seljuk Turks** from inner Mongolia established states in Persia (modern-day Iran) and Anatolia. Great Seljuk Sultans from this latter state—namely Tughril-Beg and Alp Arslan—led raids into the Byzantine realm they bordered, and the Seljuks in Anatolia became increasingly independent of the Great Seljuk Sultanate, centered in Persia. The Turks gained a foothold in Anatolia in 1075, when **Süleyman** (the son of Alp Arslan) captured Nicaea from the Byzantines, renamed it İznik, and set it up as the capital of the newly reorganized **Sultanate of Rum,** which declared its independence from the Great Seljuks in Persia a decade later. By its heyday in the 13th century, the Sultanate of Rum had developed into one of the most important Islamic states of its time, with thriving trade, agriculture, and arts.

THE OTTOMAN EMPIRE. When Seljuk rule broke down in the 14th century, separate Turkish principalities picked up the pieces. A general named **Osman** claimed the northwest corner of Anatolia and united several fiefdoms against the Byzantines, laying the religious and cultural foundations for one of the largest and most enduring empires in the history of the world: the *Osmanlı,* or **Ottoman,** Empire. From the mid-14th to the mid-15th century, Ottoman rulers slowly gnawed away at the Byzantine Empire. In 1453, after a 54-day siege, Constantinople fell to **Mehmet the Conqueror,** who went directly to the great Byzantine basilica Aya Sofia and prayed to Allah (thus converting it into a mosque). The city, renamed **İstanbul,** became the capital of Mehmet's new empire, which included Greece, Cyprus, and the Balkans as far as Belgrade. **Selim I** (1512-20) added Syria, Palestine, Egypt, and the Arabian Peninsula to the Empire, making the Ottoman Sultan the guardian of the three holy places of Islam—Mecca, Medina, and Jerusalem.

Such a vast and heterogeneous empire was necessarily politically decentralized. The hinterland regions developed almost entirely independently; this eventually led to the Ottomans' downfall. Non-Muslims were left to practice their religions freely, but had to pay the **cizye,** a special head tax. Many of the empire's minorities, including Greeks and Jews, were peacefully incorporated into Ottoman society, and many fared better under Muslim authority than they had under the Crusaders and Spanish monarchs.

Süleyman (1520-66) doubled the empire's size, securing borders that stretched from the Balkans and Greece north to the Black Sea (and even knocked on the gates of Vienna), west to Iraq, and south into the Arabian Peninsula and Africa. Süleyman's military conquests and lavish lifestyle earned him the sobriquet of "Magnificent" among Europeans. Süleyman's administrative, artistic, literary, and

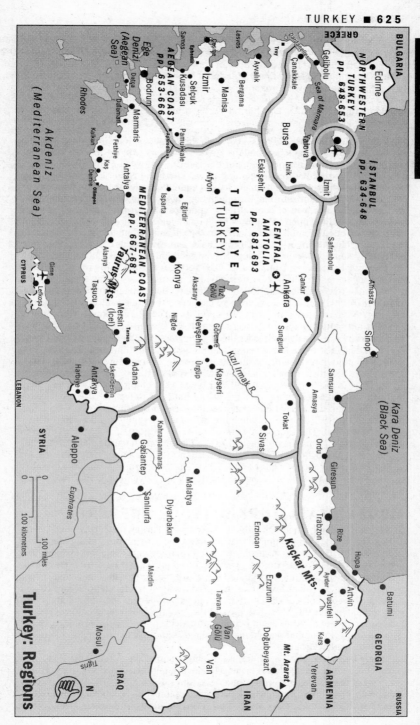

Turkey: Regions

architectural legacies were equally dramatic. His commitment to legislation earned him the title of **Kanuni** (the Lawgiver), and his patronage of Mimar Sinan, the great Ottoman architect, resulted in some of the greatest of Ottoman monuments. Süleyman the Magnificent appointed his son Selim the not-so-magnificent (a.k.a. **Selim the Sot**), who transferred all his political power to the Grand Vizier and presided over an era of palace infighting (before he drowned in his tub in a drunken stupor in 1574). This period is sometimes referred to as the **rule of the women,** as mothers of potential sultans had rivals' sons knocked off.

FALL OF THE OTTOMAN EMPIRE. By 1812, the Ottomans had lost all of their territories north of the Black Sea, and the government was growing weaker as it went deeper into debt. A series of administrative reforms known as the **Tanzimat** ("Reorganization") were instituted, beginning in 1839 with the Noble Edict of the Rose Chamber that declared all Ottoman citizens equal regardless of ethnicity, race, or religion. Despite major reforms, European and Russian diplomats feared that time was up for the **sick man of Europe** (as the empire was known), and feared even more what would happen to the European balance of power as a result. The 19th century saw one rebellion after another in the Ottoman domains (including uprisings among the Albanians, Serbs, Bulgarians, and Armenians). In response to an impending sense of doom, a group of bourgeois intellectuals that included the poet Namık Kemal (see **Literature,** p. 628) formed a group known as the **Young Turks.** They sought to draft a Western-style constitution providing for an elected parliament—a wish that was fulfilled in 1876 upon the ascension of **Sultan Abdülhamid II** (1876-1909), though he suddenly suspended the constitution and all democratic reforms two years later. In 1908, the **Young Turk Revolution** ended Abdülhamid's stranglehold on power and restored the 1876 constitution. The new leaders, known as the **Committee for Union of Progress (CUP),** embarked on a reform program designed to increase centralization and promote industrialization. CUP leaders continued with reforms, but these were far overshadowed by such bloodbaths as the Albanian uprisings and the **Balkan Wars** (1912-13). Bloody disaster was all the Ottoman Empire saw in World War I, when the empire sided with Germany and was completely humiliated save at the **Battle of Gallipoli** (1916), when the Turks defended the Dardanelles against the Allies. Festering domestic tensions erupted in the 1915 Armenian genocide, when approximately 1.5 million Armenians were killed. The Unionists were not gone or forgotten, and under Ottoman general **Mustafa Kemal** they plunged into the **Turkish War of Independence** (1920-22) against the Allies, who were looking to partition Anatolia amongst themselves. An armistice was signed on October 11, 1922. The new Grand National Assembly (under President Kemal) abolished the sultanate on November 1, 1922 and set up the **Turkish Republic** by 1923.

MODERN (ATA)TURKEY (1922-PRESENT)

As part of his determined campaign to westernize Turkey (and forge a distinctly Turkish identity), Kemal required that all Turks adopt surnames, taking **Atatürk,** or "father of the Turks," for himself. Many city names also changed; Angora, for instance, became **Ankara.** Atatürk oversaw the adoption of a Western-style constitution, abolished polygamy, prohibited the use of the *fez* (traditional Islamic headwear), instituted secular law codes, adopted the Gregorian calendar, and closed religious schools and courts. By 1928, Islam was no longer the official state religion. As Alexander the Great had purged the country of Persians before, Atatürk purged Turkish of all Arabic and Persian influences, replacing the Arabic alphabet with a Latin version, and mandating that the *adhan* (call to prayer) be recited in Turkish instead of Arabic.

Shortly before World War II, the increasingly autocratic Atatürk died and was replaced by his associate **İsmet İnönü.** The government remained neutral until the very end of the war, when Turkey joined the Allies. During the Cold War, the country's position within firing range of the Soviet Union and its control over the Bosphorus made it strategically vital to both Soviet and US interests. Even today,

Turkey remains one of the largest recipients of US economic and military aid. Politics became increasingly polarized during the turbulent 1970s, reaching a fever pitch when **Abdüllah Öcalan** formed the **Workers' Party of Kurdistan (PKK),** advocating Kurdish sovereignty. Turkey's foreign relations were no calmer than its domestic affairs. Fearing that Cyprus would be annexed by Greece, Turkey invaded the island in 1974; economic and arms embargoes soon followed, and Turkey responded by closing foreign military installations. The **Turkish Republic of Northern Cyprus** is still only officially recognized by the Republic of Turkey itself.

In September 1980, General **Kenan Evren** led a bloodless coup against the government and instituted brutally-enforced martial law throughout the country until 1983. Elections that year brought the **Motherland Party** (ANAP) of **Turgut Özal** to power. Özal encouraged free-market principles and foreign trade, but worldwide recession brought massive inflation, budget deficits, and unemployment to Turkey. Disaffected youth in the PKK, based in Syria and Iraq, waged guerrilla warfare against the government, catching civilians in the crossfire. In response, the government banned the use of the Kurdish language and outlawed expressions of sympathy for the Kurds.

While discussion of the Kurdish issue has been forcibly silenced, the secularist tenets of the Turkish state have been the subject of increasing debate. In May 1993, the True Path Party elected **Tansu Çiller** the first female prime minister. Controversy arose around Turkey's secular **dress code,** which attempted to curb religious attire such as head scarves in schools and universities. Religious female students have protested and circumvented this rule by holding street demonstrations and wearing showy blond wigs over their head scarves (since the code dictates that the women's hair must be showing).

In early 1995, Turkey was accepted into the **European Customs Union** (after being rejected in 1989) on the condition that the Turkish Parliament make hundreds of new laws and changes to the constitution. The European Union again denied Turkey candidacy for membership in December 1997. The EU's simultaneous selection of Cyprus as a candidate greatly incensed Turkey, which threatened in March 1998 to begin a new war with Cyprus.

IN THE NEWS

Nature has not been kind to Turkey in recent years. On August 17, 1999, an **earthquake** hit İzmit, killing 18,000 people, injuring tens of thousands more, destroying 60,000 buildings, and leaving 200,000 homeless. While neighboring countries and international relief groups aided the rescue, the Turkish government was criticized for slowness and disorganization. In December 1999, the Helsinki European Council nominated Turkey as a full candidate for membership to the EU, contingent on peace with Greece and the relinquishment of Northern Cyprus. Tensions in the southeast have decreased since the spring 1999 capture, arrest, and death sentence of PKK leader **Abdüllah Öcalan.** In June 2000, Parliament voted to end the state of emergency that had been in place for more than a decade for certain predominantly Kurdish southeastern provinces. In early May 2000, the Turkish Grand National Assembly elected **Ahmet Necdet Sezer** the 10th president of the Turkish Republic. A career judge, Sezer stated in his May 16 inaugural speech that he would focus on higher standards for democracy, secularism, and rule of law. In the summer of 2001, Turkey was in the midst of the worst **economic crisis** of its history. Spurred by politicians' reckless campaign promises, the crisis broke in February 2001, when the lira devalued by almost 50% essentially overnight. Over 600,000 people lost their jobs over the next six months. Two hopes linger on the horizon: the first in the person of **Kemal Dervis,** the economy minister, who many believe will help bring an end to the endemic corruption of Turkey's government. The second is the tourist industry, which pulls in US$10 billion per year and has begun to attract Germans, Russians, and Americans in greater and greater droves.

RELIGION AND ETHNICITY

Though Atatürk set modern Turkey on a secular course, Islam has played a key role in the country's evolution. About 99% of Turks are **Muslim,** while about 26,000 are **Jews,** concentrated mainly in İstanbul with large communities in İzmir and Ankara. **Orthodox Christians** of Greek, Armenian, and Syrian backgrounds compose the other religious minority. The **Alevi** are Shi'ites who follow simple moral norms rather than the *sharia* (Islamic law) and the traditional pillars of Islam. "Alevi" has also come to refer to the numerous heterodox communities that make up 15-25% of the population. Roughly 12 to 15 million **Kurds** make up a quarter of Turkey's population, making them the largest ethnic group in the world without its own nation. Kurdish nationalist movements have existed since before the fall of the Ottoman Empire, but the most famous and extreme of these, the **Workers' Party of Kurdistan** (or **PKK**) was founded by Abdüllah Öcalan in 1978 (see **Modern History** and **In The News,** above). Until the early 20th century, ethnic **Armenians** comprised approximately 10% of the Anatolian population, but after the deportation and slaughter of about 1.5 million Armenians in 1915, almost none are left in Eastern Anatolia today. In the past few decades, Armenians and their supporters have demanded that Turkey officially recognize the genocide and provide some form of apology or compensation. The **Laz, Hemşin,** and **Circassian** people are Caucasian minorities that live in Eastern Turkey and the northern Caucasus region.

LANGUAGE

Turkish, the official language of Turkey, is spoken by approximately 55 million people domestically, and about one million more abroad. It is the most prominent member of the Turkic language family, which also includes Azerbaijani, Kazakh, Khirgiz, Uyghur, and Uzbek. Turkish is also related to other languages spoken in central Asia such as Mongolian and Manchu. Korean is sometimes included in this group as well. Originally written in Arabic script with strong Arabic and Persian influences, Atatürk reformed the language in 1928 using a romanized alphabet and attempted to purge any foreign borrowings so as to minimize Islam's influence on secular life. This linguistic cleansing was not absolute; common Arabic and Persian words such as *merhaba* (hello) remain.

English is widely spoken wherever tourism is big (mostly in the major coastal resorts). In the rest of Anatolia, only university students know English. French and German are also widely spoken in cities. For Turkish pronunciation tips and handy phrases, see the **Phrasebook,** p. 705.

THE ARTS

LITERATURE. The Sufi poetry of **Celaleddin-i-Rumi** and **Yunuş Emre** survived the Ottoman centuries, as did *The Book of Dede Korkut,* a collection of 12 legends of the noble Oğuz Turks, the ancestors of modern Turks. Among these folk tales, those of **Nasrettin Hoca**—a friendly, anti-authoritarian, religious man—are particularly popular, plastered on *ayran* cups and well known by children.

Satire has always been important in Turkish literature. Poet **Namık Kemal** is particularly famous for his satire of the Ottoman Empire during its final years. A fervent republican and free-speech advocate, **Aziz Nesin** was a provocative Alevi writer. **Yaşar Kemal,** author of *Memed, My Hawk,* has been nominated several times for the Nobel Prize for Literature. He has been charged with anti-Turkish activities by the government for criticizing Turkish society and government in his work. The magical realism of **Orhan Pamuk** has made him the best-selling author in Turkish history. He is internationally known for his three major novels, *The White Castle, The New Life,* and *The Black Book.*

VISUAL ARTS. Long before Atatürk's revolution, Ottoman painting had gradually begun to adopt Western forms. In 1883, the **Academy of Fine Arts** was founded by the Ottoman artist, museum curator, and archaeologist **Osman Hamdi Bey.** In 1914, the Ottoman government opened an Academy of Fine Arts for Women headed by the painter **Mihri Müşfil Hanım,** whose work blended the world of veiled ladies in İstanbul with the Parisian flair for Levantine fashions. The two eventually merged, and the Academy (as the combined institution is known) has had an unparalleled influence on the artistic movements of modern Turkey: the **Çallı group** of the 1920s, the **'D' Group** of the '30s, and the **New Group** of the '40s, '50s, and '60s.

FOOD AND DRINK

Turkish cuisine reflects its Ottoman heritage. The ubiquitous **kebap** (kebab) and **pilav** (rice) are flavored by the cuisine of the nomadic Central Asian tribes of Asia Minor. Fans of Greek, Armenian, and Levantine food will recognize their favorites on Turkish menus. Lunch and dinner often begin with **meze**, which ranges from simple *beyaz peynir* (feta cheese) to more complicated vegetable dishes. Meals often involve meat (usually lamb), and especially **köfte** (small spiced meatballs) or **mantı** (tiny meat-filled ravioli). Dessert highlights include **baklava** (a flaky nut pastry with pistachio), *kadayif* (shredded pastry dough filled with nuts, in syrup), *tavukgöğsu* (creamy, made of chicken fibers), and *helva* (sesame paste).

Turkey's national drink must be the strong, black tea known as **çay,** served everywhere in small, hourglass-shaped glasses. *Elma çayı* (apple tea), which tastes like warmed cider, is a good alternative to conventional Turkish tea's strong brew. A demitasse-jolt of pure caffeine, **kahve (Turkish coffee)** can be ordered *sade* (black), *orta* (medium sweet), or *şekerli* (very sweet). When you finish your *kahve,* read your fortune in the goop remaining in the bottom of your cup.

Alcohol is widely available but frowned upon in the more conservative parts of the country. Restaurants that post *içkili* serve alcohol, while *içkisiz* do not. **Bira** (beer) is ever-popular: *Efes Pilsen* and *Tüborg* are the leading brands. The best domestic white wines are *Çankaya, Villa Doluca,* and *Kavaklıdere*, made in Cappadocia. The best red wines are *Yakut* and *Kavaklıdere.* Ice-cold **rakı,** a clear-anise-seed liquor with the taste of licorice, is Turkey's national alcohol. Customarily mixed in equal parts with water, *rakı* is similar to Greek *ouzo* or Levantine *'araq,* but even stronger. İstanbul's local specialty is *balyoz* ("sledge hammer" or "wrecking ball"). It's easy to get wrecked with this combination of *rakı,* whiskey, vodka, and gin mixed with orange juice.

ESSENTIALS

DOCUMENTS AND FORMALITIES

CONSULAR SERVICES ABROAD

Turkish embassies abroad include:

Australia Embassy: 60 Mugga Way, Red Hill, Canberra ACT 2603 (☎02 6295 0227; fax 6239 6592; turkembs@ozemail.com.au; http://members.ozemail.com.au/İturkembs.).

Canada Embassy: 3 Crescent Rd. Rockcliffe, Ontario KIM ON1 (☎613-748-3737, 789-3720, or 749-0739; fax 789-3442; turkish@magma.ca).

Ireland Embassy: 11 Clyde Rd., Ballsbridge, Dublin 4 (☎01 668 5240 or 660 1623; fax 668 5014; turkemb@iol.ie).

New Zealand Embassy, 15-17 Murphy St., Level 8, Wellington (☎04 472 1290 or 472 1292; fax 472 1277; turkem@xtra.co.nz).

South Africa Embassy: 1067 Church St., Hatfield, Pretoria 0028 (☎012 342 6053, 342 6054, or 342 6055; fax 342 6052; pretbe@global.co.za; www.turkishembassy.co.za).

UK Embassy: 43 Belgrave Sq., London, SWIX 8PA (☎020 7393 0202; fax 7393 0066; info@turkishembassy-london.com; www.turkishembassy-london.com).

US Embassy: 2525 Massachusetts Ave. NW, Washington, D.C. 20008 (☎202-612-6700 or 612-6701; fax 612-6744; info@turkey.org; www.turkey.org).

CONSULAR SERVICES IN TURKEY

Embassies and consulates of other countries in Turkey include.

Australian Embassy: 83 Nenehatun Cad., Gaziosmanpaşa, Ankara (☎312 446 11 80 or 446 11 87; fax 446 11 88).

Canadian Embassy: 75 Nenehatun Cad., Gaziosmanpaşa, Ankara (☎312 436 12 75, 436 12 76; fax 447 21 73; ankara@dfait-maeci.gc.ca.)

Irish Embassy: Ugur Mumcu Cad. MNG Binasi, B Bloc, Kat 3, Gaziomanpaşa, Ankara (☎312 446 61 72; fax 446 80 61).

New Zealand Embassy: 13/4 İran Cad., Kavaklıdere, Ankara (☎312 467 90 56; fax 467 90 13; newzealand@superonline.com.)

South African Embassy: 27 Filistin Sok., Gaziosmanpaşa, Ankara (☎312 446 40 56; fax 446 64 34; saemb@ada.net.tr; www.southafrica.org.tr).

UK Embassy: 46/A Şehit Ersan Cad., Çankaya, Ankara (☎312 455 33 44; fax 455 33 56; britembank@ankara.mail.fco.gov.uk; www.britishembassy.org.tr.)

US Embassy: 110 Atatürk Bul., Kavaklıdere, **Ankara** (☎312 455 55 55; fax 468 61 31).

ENTRY REQUIREMENTS

As of August 2001, citizens of Australia, Canada, Ireland, the UK, and the US require a visa (US$45) in addition to a valid passport to enter Turkey. Citizens of New Zealand and South Africa do not need visas to enter Turkey. New Zealanders may stay for up to three months with a valid passport, South Africans for up to one month. Though visas can be obtained from a Turkish embassy or consulate in your home country, it is most convenient (and cheapest) to get them at the airport upon arrival in Turkey. Visitors on a tourist visa need a **work permit** to hold a job in Turkey. Exchange students must obtain a **student visa.**

BORDER CROSSINGS

TO SYRIA. Daily buses connect **Antakya** (p. 679) to **Aleppo** (see p. 609; 4-5hr., including formalities). The border crossing is hassle-free, but you must get a visa beforehand in **Ankara** (p. 681), **İstanbul** (p. 634), or another Syrian embassy or consulate. Try to obtain the visa in your home country; it is not always easy, or even possible, to get one from a Syrian embassy or consulate in Turkey.

TO GREECE AND EUROPE. Buses leave from İstanbul's **Esenler Otobüs Terminal** and trains from İstanbul's **Sirkeci Gar** station (p. 635) to various European cities, including Athens, Sofia, Vienna, Munich, Bucharest, and Moscow. **Ferries** also leave from many cities on the Aegean close to the Greek islands, which are in turn connected by boat to Athens. Citizens of the US, Canada, Australia, New Zealand, and EU countries do not need a visa to enter Greece. South Africans must obtain a visa beforehand from any Greek embassy or consulate.

TO NORTHERN CYPRUS. Daily **Seabuses** (2½hr.) and **ferries** (5hr.) run from Taşucu in mainland Turkey to **Girne** in Northern Cyprus. Less frequent ferries also travel to Girne from Alanya and Anamur, and three night ferries per week embark from Mersin to Mağusa. Turkish air carriers are the only ones that fly into Northern Cyprus; flights run between Lefkoşa's Ercan airport (☎231 46 39) and most major airports in Turkey.

GETTING AROUND

BY PLANE. Turkish Airlines (*Türk Hava Yolları*, THY) flies to over 30 cities in Turkey, including Ankara, Antalya, Bodrum, İstanbul, and İzmir. **İstanbul** and **Ankara** are the hubs for domestic flights. See individual city listings for schedules and prices. Domestic flights average about US$90 one way, but passengers from ages 12 to 24 may receive a discount. It is often cheaper to purchase tickets for domestic flights in Turkey. In some cities, an airport shuttle bus leaves from the downtown ticket office 30-90min. before flights (for an extra fee). There are reduced fares for passengers who book international flights with THY.

BY BUS. Frequent, modern, and cheap **buses** run between all sizeable cities. In large cities, the *otogar* (bus station) is often a distance from the city center, but many bus companies have branch offices downtown. Buy tickets in advance (10% ISIC discount on some lines). Fares go up during summer and religious holidays.

Because road safety is a serious concern in Turkey, *Let's Go* strongly recommends that you only travel on reputable bus lines (such as **Varan, Ulusoy,** and **Kamıl Koç**), particularly for long trips. Although these are the most expensive tickets, the extra money allows companies to take additional safety precautions.

Fez Travel, 15 Akbıyık Cad., Sultanahmet, İstanbul (☎ (212) 516 90 24; fax 638 87 64; feztravel@escortnet.com; www.feztravel.com), Turkey's flexible "backpacker bus" service, runs around a long loop encompassing İstanbul, Çanakkale, Gallipoli, the Aegean and Mediterranean coasts (including Ephesus, Troy, Kuşadası, Bodrum, Marmaris, Pamukkale, Antalya, and Side), Konya, Cappadocia, Ankara, and Bursa. A season pass (June-Oct. US$175, under 26 US$168) allows you to get on and off along the route at your own whim. There are also various scheduling alternatives, including cheaper passes that cover smaller portions of the route. Buses have English-speaking staff full of information on accommodations and activities. Tickets can also be purchased through **STA Travel** (p. 30).

BY DOLMUŞ. Extensive *dolmuş* (shared taxi) service follows fixed routes within larger cities and between small towns. *Dolmuş* post their final destinations in their front windows, but if you're headed to an intermediate destination, you'll probably need to ask locals which is the right one for you: *"Bu dolmuş X gidiyor mu?"* (Does this *dolmuş* go to X?). To ask your neighbor or the driver how much it costs to go to your destination: *"X kadar ne kadar?"* (How much is it to X?). The driver may remember your stated destination and stop there without any reminder. Otherwise, clearly say *"inecek var"* (getting off).

BY TRAIN. Despite low fares, trains within Turkey are no bargain, as they are slow and follow circuitous routes. First class gets you a slightly more padded seat, but most Turks travel 2nd class. Since couchettes are available, overnight train trips are preferable to overnight bus trips. Lock your compartment door and keep your valuables on your person. Reserve at least a few hours ahead at the station.

BY BOAT. Ferries do not serve the west coast, but a **Turkish Maritime Lines** (TML) cruise ship sails between İstanbul and İzmir (21hr., 1 per week). A weekly boat connects İstanbul with destinations on the Black Sea Coast. İstanbul has frequent service to Bandırma and Yalova. Larger ports have ship offices; otherwise, just get on the boat and find the purser. Most Turkish ferries are comfortable and well-equipped, though ferry food is outrageously pricey; bring your own provisions. Fares jump sharply in July and August. Student discounts are often available.

BY MOPED AND MOTORCYCLE. Motorized bikes are a good way to tour coastal areas and countryside. Exercise extreme caution—they're uncomfortable for long distances, dangerous in the rain, and unpredictable on rough roads and gravel. Always wear a helmet and never ride with a backpack. Expect to pay about US$20-35 per day; remember to bargain. Motorcycles normally require a license. Ask if the quoted price includes tax and insurance, or you may be hit with an additional fee. Avoid handing your passport over as a deposit; if you have an accident or mechanical failure, you may not get it back until you cover all repairs.

MONEY MATTERS

If you stay in hostels and prepare your own food, expect to spend anywhere from US$15-30 per day. Carrying cash with you, even in a money belt, is risky but necessary; though banks will exchange traveler's checks, most establishments in Turkey do not accept them. The **Turkish lira (TL)** is the main unit of currency in Turkey. Western currency, particularly US dollars and German marks, will sometimes be accepted. Credit cards are generally accepted by larger businesses. Because of constantly fluctuating exchange rates and Turkey's high inflation, prices are quoted in US dollars to minimize increases.

The high inflation rate means that it's best to convert small amounts of money on a regular basis despite the commission charges. Using an ATM or a credit card will often get you the best rates. **ATMs** are widespread throughout the country; larger banks usually accept Cirrus and PLUS, and major credit cards—particularly Mastercard and Visa—can also be used for cash advances. Most stores and offices are open Monday to Friday 8:30am-12:30pm and 1:30-5:30pm. Unlike in the rest of the Islamic world, the official weekend is on Saturday and Sunday.

Tipping is widely accepted and expected, and leaving a bit of change at your table after a meal or with a taxi driver or hotel porter is appreciated. Only luxury restaurants require a 15-20% service charge *(servis dahil)*, usually included in the bill; an additional small tip is customary. Turkey has a 10-20% **value-added tax,** known as the *katma değer vergisi* or **KDV,** which is included in the prices of most goods and services (including meals, lodging, and car rentals). Before you pay, check whether the KDV is included in the price to avoid paying it twice. Theoretically, it can be reclaimed at most points of departure, but this requires much persistence.

TOURIST AND TRAVEL SERVICES

MEDICAL EMERGENCIES AND HEALTH. Serious medical problems should be taken to the *klinik* or **hospital** *(hastane).* Private hospitals, located in urban areas, provide much better care than state-run institutions *(devlet hastanesi)* and are not much more expensive for foreigners. Most doctors speak some English, and cash payments are expected. **Pharmacies** *(eczane)* in each town stay open all night on a rotating basis; signs in their windows and local newspapers tell which is on duty *(nöbetçi).* For **medical emergencies,** dial 112 (ambulance) or call your consulate; they can provide a list of English-speaking doctors.

USEFUL ADDRESSES. Turkish cities and popular tourist towns have tourist offices with maps and lists of accommodations in the area. Turkish tourist offices abroad include: **UK,** 1st fl., 170-173 Piccadilly, London W1V 9DD (☎0171 629 777; fax 0171 491 0773; tto@turkishtourism.demon.co.uk) and **US,** 821 UN Plaza, 4th fl., New York, NY, 10017 (☎212-687-2194; fax 599-7658; tourny@idt.net; www.turkey.org/turkey). Surf on over to **Türkiye on the Web** (www.columbia.edu/Isss31/Turkiye) or **All About Turkey** (web.syr.edu/~obalsoy/Turkiye).

ACCOMMODATIONS

There are very few accredited International Youth Hostels in Turkey, and if you ask for a hostel *(yurt)*, you'll probably be directed to **university dormitories.** Many colleges and universities open their residence halls to travelers when school is not in session—some do so even during term-time. **Pensions** that call themselves **aile** (family-style) try to maintain a wholesome atmosphere, and may be preferable for women traveling alone in remote parts of Turkey, particularly the East and the

Black Sea coast. In the more touristed areas along the Aegean and Mediterranean coasts, Turks are accustomed to **unmarried couples** staying together, but such relations are often culturally unacceptable in rural and conservative regions, including the Black Sea coast and southeastern Turkey. It is generally a good idea to wear rings to help gain admittance. Men may be turned away from pensions if there are no other men staying in the house.

KEEPING IN TOUCH

Airmail from Turkey averages one to two weeks to reach its destination. If regular airmail is too slow, there are faster, more expensive, options such as *Acele Posta Servisi* (APS). **Poste Restante** is available at the **PTT** (post, telegraph, and telephone office) in most towns.

For phone calls, a **calling card** is your best bet. Deposit a **prepaid card (telekart)** or a token-like **jeton** (buy both at the PTT) to activate the phone. To call home with a calling card, dial the appropriate access numbers for Turkey: **AT&T** (☎888-288-4685); **Sprint** (☎800-877-4646); **MCI** (☎800-444-4141); **Australia Direct** (☎13 22 00); **Canada Direct** (☎800-565-4708); Telecom Éireann **Ireland Direct** (☎800 250 250); **Telecom New Zealand** (☎0800 00 00 00); **Telkom South Africa** (☎09 03); British Telecom **BT Direct** (☎800 34 51 44). To place a **collect call,** dial 115 for an international Türk Telekom operator. You can reach an English-speaking operator through the appropriate service provider listed above, and they should place a collect call even if you don't have a phone card.

Internet access is available in most regions of the country for US$1-2 per hr. Access is widespread in areas of İstanbul, Cappadocia, and the Aegean and Mediterranean coasts, but thins out a bit along the Black Sea and in Eastern Turkey.

SPECIAL CONCERNS

WOMEN TRAVELERS

Foreign women, especially those traveling alone, attract significant attention in Turkey. Because Western movies and TV often depict women as seductive sex symbols, female travelers are frequently perceived as likely sexual partners; however, although verbal harassment is common, physical harassment is rare. If harassed, women can attract attention by making a scene and using the expression *"ayıp!"* ("shame!") or *"haydi git"* ("go away"). If a situation becomes threatening, holler *"imdat"* (eem-DAHT, "help") or *"polis"* (PO-lees, "police"). More touristed cities like İstanbul, the Northwest, the Aegean and Mediterranean coasts, Cappadocia, and Ankara are more comfortable for women. Only experienced female travelers should venture into Central and Eastern Anatolia and along the Black Sea coast. For more tips, see **Essentials: Women Travelers,** (p. 39).

DRESS AND ETIQUETTE

Shorts scream "I am a tourist." Women will find a headscarf handy, and even essential in more conservative areas. Long skirts and loose pants are most acceptable (and practical), but T-shirts are fine, though it's a good idea to cover your arms in more religious parts of the country. While topless bathing is common around the resorts, it is a bad idea elsewhere. Nude sunbathing is officially illegal.

Turks value hospitality and will go out of their way to offer travelers a meal or a cup of çay (tea). If you are invited as a guest, it is customary to bring a small gift such as flowers or chocolates and to remove your shoes before entering. When making conversation, do not speak with disrespect or skepticism about Atatürk, the founder of modern Turkey, and avoid other sensitive subjects such as the Kurdish issue, Northern Cyprus, Armenia, and Turkey's human rights record.

İSTANBUL

Straddling two continents and almost three millennia of history, İstanbul unfolds

  PHONE CODES: The code is **212** on the Europe side, **216** on the Asia side.

against a dense historic landscape of Ottoman mosques, Byzantine mosaics, and Roman masonry. In its current incarnation, İstanbul is the most crowded and cosmopolitan city in the Turkish Republic. This urban supernova explodes out into the surrounding countryside behind an ever-expanding front of new construction sites, but no cement truck could hope to keep up with the pace of İstanbulian life.

Legend has it that in the 7th century BCE, **Byzas**, a Greek speculator looking for prime real estate, consulted the infallible Oracle at Delphi, who told him to settle "opposite the Land of the Blind." Byzas and his crew settled here in 667 BCE, and the city was named **Byzantium** in his honor. Roman infighting at the beginning of the 4th century CE determined the city's fate for the next millennium. The victorious Constantine declared Byzantium **"New Rome"** and renamed it **Constantinople,** the capital of what became the Byzantine Empire. **Justinian,** the most famous Byzantine emperor, doubled the city's glory with the Aya Sofia and other architectural monuments—many of which were destroyed centuries later by marauding Crusaders. Constantinople fell to the Ottomans on May 29, 1453, and the new sultan, **Mehmet II,** transformed the city into the administrative, cultural, and commercial center of his empire. Under Ottoman rule, the city, which came to be called İstanbul (a Turkish corruption of the Greek phrase *"steen poli,"* or "to the city"), remained one of the world's major cosmopolitan centers and an architectural treasure trove, best known for its collection of Imperial mosques.

Ankara is now the governmental capital of the Republic of Turkey, but İstanbul remains its cultural heart. Since 1960, the city's population has increased tenfold—to over 13 million inhabitants. Even as İstanbul's centuries-long expansion has engulfed entire towns, each neighborhood of the city retains a distinct character: the poverty of İstanbul's *gecekondus* (shanty towns) coexists with a commercialism as audacious and ostentatious as any in New York or London. The challenge is to see beyond the Ottoman palaces, carpet salesmen, and backpacker bars, and venture out into neighborhood produce markets, back-alley tea shops, and Byzantine fortifications.

✈ INTERCITY TRANSPORTATION

FLIGHTS

İstanbul's airport, **Atatürk Havaalanı,** is 30km from the city. **Buses** (every 20min. 6am-11pm) connect domestic and international terminals. To get to **Sultanahmet,** take a Havaş shuttle bus from either terminal to Aksaray (every 30min. 6am-9pm, US$7). From there, take an Eminönü-bound **tram** to Sultanahmet (walk uphill along the overpass to the Lâleli tram stop). You can also take a **taxi** (US$4) to the Yeşilköy train station and take the commuter rail **(tren)** to the end of the line in Sirkeci. A direct taxi to Sultanahmet costs US$9. To **Taksim,** take the Havaş shuttle to the end of the line (every 30min. 6am-9pm, US$6). To get to the airport, have a service such as **Karasu** (☎638 66 01) or **Zorlu** (☎638 04 35) pick you up from your hostel (US$5.50), or take the Havaş shuttle from the Taksim McDonald's (45min., every 30min., US$6.75).

TRAINS

It's quicker and cheaper to take the bus. **Haydarpaşa Garı** (☎(216) 336 04 75 or 336 20 63), on the Asian side, sends trains to Anatolia. Take the ferry from Karaköy pier #7 (every 20min. 6am-midnight, US$0.65), halfway between Galata Bridge and the Karaköy tourist office, where rail tickets for Anatolia can be bought in advance at the **TCDD** office upstairs. To: **Ankara** (6½-9½hr., 6 per day, US$6-22) and **Kars** (11-13½hr.; daily 8:35am; US$10). **Sirkeci Garı** (☎212 527 00 50 or 527 00 51), in Eminönü sends trains to Europe via: **Athens** (24hr., 1 per day, US$60); **Bucharest** (17½hr., 1 per day, US$30); **Budapest** (40hr., 1 per day, US$90).

BUSES

Esenler Otobüs Terminal (☎658 00 36). Take the tram to Yusufpaşa (US$0.50), walk to the Aksaray Metro, and take it to the *otogar* (15min., US$0.50). Most companies have courtesy buses, called *servis*, that run to the *otogar* from Eminönü, Taksim, and other city points (free with bus ticket purchase). From İstanbul, buses travel to every city in Turkey. **Aydin** (☎658 09 09) runs to: **Ankara** (6hr., 7 per day 8:15am-1am, US$11); **Bodrum** (14hr.; 8:30 and 9:30pm; US$15); **İzmir** (9hr.; 9am, 1:30, 10:30, 11pm; US$12); **Pamukkale** (10hr.; 7 per day 8:30am-11:30pm; US$16). For service to **Tehran,** try **İgdir** (No. 165-6), next door to Mar-Soy and Van (36hr., daily 1pm, US$30). **Nur** (☎58 05 43 or 658 05 44) has buses to: **Amman** (26hr.; 1:30, 4:30, 7:30pm; US$45, students US$40) and **Damascus** (23hr.; 1:30, 4:30, 7:30pm; US$40, students US$30). Unlicensed companies have been known to offer discounts on trips to Western European destinations and then ditch passengers in Eastern Europe.

FERRIES

Turkish Maritime Lines (☎249 92 22), near pier #7 at Karaköy, to the left of the **Haydarpaşa** ferry terminal (blue awning marked *Denizcilik İşletmeleri*), ferries travelers to **İzmir** (combo ticket US$10-25) via **Bandırma.** Buy the schedule *(feribot tarifesi)* for US$0.60 at any pier, or call **Seabus Information** (☎(216) 362 04 44).

✈ ORIENTATION

Waterways divide İstanbul into three sections. The **Bosphorus Strait** (Boğaz) separates Asia **(Asya)** from Europe **(Avrupa).** The **Golden Horn,** a sizeable river originating just outside the city, splits Avrupa into northern and southern parts. Directions in İstanbul are usually further specified by neighborhood. **Sultanahmet, Taksim** (both on the European side), and **Kadıköy** (on the Asian side) are the most relevant for sightseers. The other half of Avrupa is centered on commercial **Taksim Sq.** Asya is primarily residential.

▣ LOCAL TRANSPORTATION

PUBLIC TRANSPORTATION. AKBİL is an electronic ticket system that saves you 15-50% on fares for municipal ferries, buses, trams, seabuses, and subway (but not *dolmuş*). After an initial deposit of US$5, add money in 1,000,000TL increments at the white IETT public bus booths, **AKBİL satılır.**

BUSES

These run 5am-midnight, less frequently after 10:30pm, arriving every 10min. to most stops. Hubs are **Eminönü, Aksaray** (Yusuf Paşa tram stop), **Beyazıt, Taksim, Beşiktaş,** and **Üsküdar.** Signs on the front indicate destination, and signs on the right-hand side list major stops. **Dolmuş** are more comfortable but less frequent than buses. Most *dolmuş* gather on the side streets north of Taksim Sq.

TRAMS

The **tramvay** runs from Eminönü to Zeytinburnu (US$0.50 per ride). A ramshackle **commuter rail** (known locally as *tren*) runs between Sirkeci Gar and the far western suburbs. A two-stop **metro** runs from the Karaköy side of Galata Bridge to Tünel, where an old-fashioned trolley car continues along İstiklâl Cad. to Taksim.

İstanbul

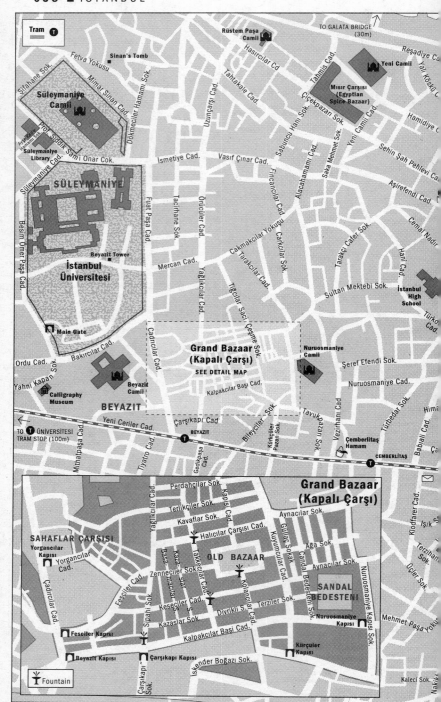

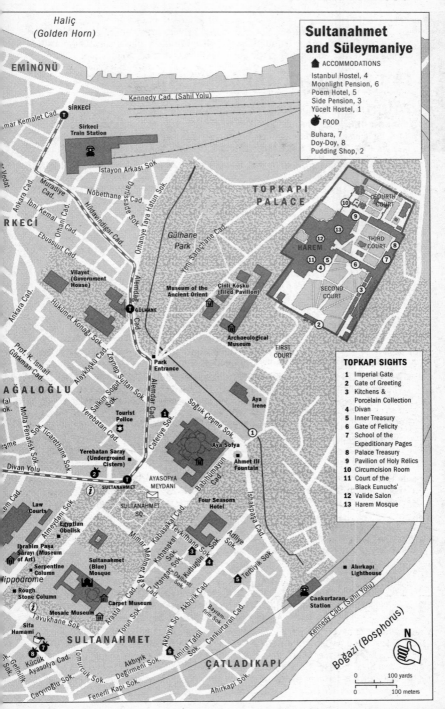

Haliç (Golden Horn)

EMİNÖNÜ

Sultanahmet and Süleymaniye

🏠 ACCOMMODATIONS

Istanbul Hostel, 4
Moonlight Pension, 6
Poem Hotel, 5
Side Pension, 3
Yücelt Hostel, 1

🍎 FOOD

Buhara, 7
Doy-Doy, 8
Pudding Shop, 2

Kennedy Cad. (Sahil Yolu)

SİRKECİ

mar Kemalet Cad.

Sirkeci Train Station

Istayon Arkası Sok.

Muradiye Cad.
İbni Kemal Cad.
Ankara Cad.
Orhani Cad.
Nöbethane Cad.
Darüssade Cad.
Hüdavindigar Cad.
Orhaniye Tava Hatun Sok.

RKECİ

Ebussuut Cad.

Gülhane Park

TOPKAPI PALACE

Vilayet (Government House)

Ankara Cad.
Hükümet Konağı Sok.

Alemdağ Cad.

GÜLHANE

Museum of the Ancient Orient

Yeni Saraçhane Cad.

Çinli Köşkü (Tiled Pavilion)

HAREM

FOURTH COURT
THIRD COURT
SECOND COURT

10
9
13
12
11 5
4
6
7
8
3
2

Prof. K. İsmail
Gürkman Cad.

AĞALOĞLU

fal ok.

Molla Fenarisi Sok.
Ticarethane Sok.

Salkım Söğüt Sok.
Zeynep Sultan Sok.
Alayköşkü Cad.

Archaeological Museum

FIRST COURT

Aya Irene

Divan Yolu

Tourist Police

Yerebatan Cad.

Cağeriye Sok.

Soğuk Çeşme Sok.

Park Entrance

TOPKAPI SIGHTS

1 Imperial Gate
2 Gate of Greeting
3 Kitchens & Porcelain Collection
4 Divan
5 Inner Treasury
6 Gate of Felicity
7 School of the Expeditionary Pages
8 Palace Treasury
9 Pavilion of Holy Relics
10 Circumcision Room
11 Court of the Black Eunuchs'
12 Valide Salon
13 Harem Mosque

Yerebatan Saray (Underground Cistern)

SULTANAHMET

Aya Sofya

Babıhumayun Cad.

Ahmet III Fountain

AYASOFYA MEYDANI

Law Courts

Atmeydanı Sok.

Egyptian Obelisk

İbrahim Paşa Sarayı (Museum of Art)

Serpentine Column

Hippodrome

Rough Stone Column

Mosaic Museum

Sifa Hamamı

Tavukhane Sok.

Küçük Ayasofya Cad.

SULTANAHMET

SULTANAHMET SQ.

Mimar Mehmet Ağa Cad.

Sultanahmet (Blue) Mosque

Carpet Museum

Arasta Sok.

Torun Sok.

Kabasakal Cad.

Tevkifhane Sok.

Four Seasons Hotel

Adliye Sok.

İshakpaşa Cad.

Dalbastı Sok.

Utangaç Sok.

Akbıyık Cad.

Bayram fırın Sok.

Cankurtaran Cad.

Terbıyık Sok.

Ahırkapı Lighthouse

Cankurtaran Station

Kennedy Cad. (Sahil Yolu)

Boğazı (Bosphorus)

Akbıyık Degirmeni Sok.

Amiral Tafdil Sok.

ÇATLADIKAPI

Caryıroğlu Sok.

Fenerli Kapı Sok.

Ahırkapı Sok.

N

0 —— 100 yards
0 —— 100 meters

TAXIS

Little. Yellow. Fiats. Better? Not really; taxi drivers are even more reckless and speed-crazed than other İstanbul drivers. 1 light on the meter means day rate; 2 means night rate. Rides within the city shouldn't cost more than US$5.

⓰ PRACTICAL INFORMATION

TOURIST AND FINANCIAL SERVICES

Tourist Office: 3 Divan Yolu (☎/fax 518 87 54), at the north end of the Hippodrome in Sultanahmet. Open daily 9am-5pm. Branches in Taksim's **Hilton Hotel Arcade** on Cumhuriyet Cad., **Sirkeci train station, Atatürk Airport,** and **Karaköy Maritime Station.**

Budget Travel: Indigo Tourism and Travel Agency, 24 Akbıyık Cad. (☎517 72 66; fax 518 53 33; www.indigo-tour.com), in Sultanahmet's hotel cluster. Sells bus, plane, and ferry tickets, arranges airport shuttle service and tours, and holds mail. Internet US$1.50 per hr. GO25 cards US$10. Open daily 8:30am-7:30pm; in winter M-Sa 9:30am-6pm.

Consulates: Australian, 58 Tepecik Yolu, Etiler (☎257 70 50; fax 257 70 54). Visas 10am-noon. **Canadian,** 107/3 Büyükdere Cad., Gayrettepe (☎272 51 74; fax 272 34 27). **Irish** (honorary), 25/A Cumhuriyet Cad., Mobil Altı, Elmadağ (☎246 60 25); visas 9:30-11:30am. **New Zealand,** 100-102 Maya Akar Center, Büyükdere Cad., Esentepe (☎275 28 89; fax 275 50 08). **South African,** 106/15 Büyükdere Cad., Esentepe (☎288 04 28; fax 275 76 42). Visas M-F 9am-noon. **UK,** 34 Meşrutiyet Cad., Beyoğlu/Tepebaşı (☎293 75 40; fax 245 49 89). Visas M-F 8:30am-noon. **US,** 104-108 Meşrutiyet Cad., Tepebaşı (☎251 36 02; fax 251 32 18). Visas M-F 8:30-11am.

Currency Exchange: *Bureaux de change* around the city open M-F 8:30am-noon and 1:30-5pm. Most don't charge commission. **ATMs** generally accept all international cards. Most banks exchange **traveler's checks.** Exchanges in Sultanahmet have poor rates and a 2% commission, but are open late and on the weekends.

American Express: Türk Express, 47/1 Cumhuriyet Cad., 3rd fl. (☎235 95 00), uphill from Taksim Sq. Open M-F 9am-6pm. Branch in Hilton Hotel, Cumhuriyet Cad. (☎241 02 48). Open daily 8:30am-8:30pm. No cash advances or wired money.

LOCAL SERVICES

English-Language Bookstores: In Sultanahmet, *köşk* (kiosks) at the Blue Mosque, on Aya Sofia Meydanı, and on Divan Yolu, sell international papers. **Galeri Kayseri,** 58 Divan Yolu (☎512 04 56), caters to thinking tourists with books on Turkish, Islamic, and Byzantine history, as well as a host of guidebooks in multiple languages.

Laundromat: Star Laundry, 18 Akbıyık Cad. (☎638 23 02), below Star Pension in Sultanahmet. Wash and dry US$1.50 per kg; 2kg min. Open daily 8am-8pm.

EMERGENCY AND COMMUNICATIONS

Tourist Police: In Sultanahmet, at the beginning of Yerebatan Cad. (24hr. hotline ☎527 45 03 or 528 53 69). Speak excellent English, and their mere presence causes hawkers and postcard-selling kids to scatter. In an **emergency,** dial from any phone.

Hospitals: American Hospital, Admiral Bristol Hastanesi, 20 Güzelbahçe Sok., Nişantaşı (☎231 40 50), applauded by İstanbul natives and tourists. Has many English-speaking doctors. **German Hospital,** 119 Sıraselviler Cad., Taksim (☎251 71 00), also has a multilingual staff and is conveniently located for Sultanahmet hostelers.

Internet Access: In low-rent corners and ambitious hostels all over Sultanahmet and Taksim. **The Antique Internet Cafe,** 51 Kutlugün Sok., offers a fast connection and serves tasty meals. US$1.50 per hr. Open 24hr. **Sinem Internet Cafe,** 16 Dr. Emin Paşa Sok. (☎513 62 77), in an alley off Divan Yolu by the Metro stop. Waits are rare at this cafe with full drink service. US$1.25 per hr. Open daily 9am-midnight.

PTT: All PTTs accept packages. **Main branch** in Sirkeci, 25 Büyük Postane Sok. Stamp and currency exchange services open daily 8:30am-midnight. 24hr. phones. The **branch** off Taksim Sq. at the mouth of Cumhuriyet Cad. is convenient for mailing packages or making calls. 24hr. international phone office. No collect calls. Open M-F 8am-8pm, Sa 8am-6pm. Phone cards available in increments of 30, 60, or 100 *kontür* (credits). **Sirkeci postal code:** 5270050 and 5270051

■ ACCOMMODATIONS

Budget accommodations are concentrated in **Sultanahmet** (a.k.a. Türist Şeğntral), bounded by Aya Sofia, the Blue Mosque, and the walls of the Topkapı Palace. The side streets around **Sirkeci** railway station and **Aksaray** have dozens of dirt-cheap (and pretty-dirty) hotels. Hotels in **Lâleli** are the center of prostitution in İstanbul and should be avoided. Rates sometimes rise by 20% in July and August. All accommodations below are in Sultanahmet.

■ **İstanbul Hostel,** 35 Kutlugün Sok. (☎516 93 80; fax 516 93 84; info@valide.com or istanbulhostel@hotmail.com; www.istanbul-hostel.com). Downhill from the Four Seasons Hotel. All major amenities, and the cleanest bathrooms in town. Breakfast US$1. Lunch and dinner US$2. Happy hour 6:30-9:30pm. Internet US$2.20 per hr. Dorms US$6; quads US$7; doubles US$16; deluxe with TV and bath US$30.

■ **Moonlight Pension,** 87 Akbıyık Cad. (☎517 54 29 or 518 85 36; fax 516 24 80; moonlight@superonline.com; http://abone.superonline.com/~moonlight). A few blocks away from the hustle and bustle of the backpacker scene. Clean rooms. Fax available. Internet US$1.50 per hr. Laundry US$4 per load. Snacks US$3. Breakfast US$2. 15 rooms; ask for one with a shower (same price). Dorms US$5; doubles US$16; triples US$21. MC/V.

■ **Side Pension/Hotel Side,** 20 Utangaç Sok. (☎517 65 90; fax 517 65 90; info@sidehotel.com; www.sidehotel.com). Near the entrance of the Four Seasons Hotel. This hotel/pension combination occupies the 2 buildings by the corner of Tevkifhane Sok. and Utangaç Sok. Pension singles US$20; doubles US$25; triples US$35. Add US$10 for clean, modern bathroom. Hotel singles US$40; doubles US$50; triples US$60. Basement apartment with kitchen, bath, TV also available. Subtract 20% in winter. MC/V.

■ **Poem Hotel,** Akbıyık Cad., 12 Terbıyık Sok. (☎/fax 517 68 36; hotelpoem@superonline.com). Quiet, luxurious rooms are marked with titles of Turkish poems instead of room numbers; all have Bosphorus views. Breakfast included. Free Internet. Lunch, dinner US$10. 12 rooms with safe-deposit, TV, A/C, and superb full bath. Singles US$45; doubles US$65; triples from US$80. Prices 25% lower in winter. MC/V.

Seagull Pension, Küçük Ayasofya Cad., Aksakal Sok. 22 (☎517 11 42; fax 516 09 72; seagullpension@hotmail.com; www.seagullpension.cjb.net). Blissfully removed from the rest of touristy Sultanahmet. A great bargain and unbeatable access to the sea and the train. Breakfast included. Internet US$1.75 per hr. Airport transportation US$3.50 per person. 24hr. hot water. Dorms US$5; private rooms US$8-10.

Yücelt Hostel/Interyouth Hostel (HI), 6/1 Caferiye Cad. (☎522 95 01; fax 512 76 28; info@yucelthostel.com; www.yucelthostel.com). On the left side of Aya Sofia. Tons of amenities and a friendly staff make this a backpacker favorite. Dinner US$3. Breakfast US$3. Dorms US$7-9; singles US$18; doubles US$18; triples US$27. MC/V.

◘ FOOD

İstanbul's restaurants, like its clubs and bars, often stick by the golden rule that if it's well advertised or easy to find, it's not worth a visit. Sultanahmet's heavily advertised "Turkish" restaurants aren't difficult to find, but much better meals can be found on İstiklâl Cad. and around Taksim. Small Bosphorus suburbs such as **Arnavutköy** and **Sarıyer** (on the European side) and **Çengelköy** (on the Asian side) are the best places for fresh fish. *Vişne suyu* (sour cherry juice) is sold by vendors in Ottoman costume wearing big steel teapots on their backs (US$0.20-0.30). The best open-air market is the daily one in **Beşiktaş,** near Barbaros Cad.

TURKEY

■ **Doy-Doy,** 13 Şifa Hammamı Sok. (☎517 15 88). From the south end of the Hippodrome, walk down the hill around the edge of the Blue Mosque and look for the blue and yellow sign high in the trees. The best and cheapest of Sultanahmet's cheap eats, 3-story Doy-Doy keeps locals and backpackers coming back for more. Tasty *kebap* and refreshing salads US$3.50 and under. Open daily 8:30am-late.

■ **Haci Abdullah,** 17 Sakizağacı Cad. (☎293 85 61 or 293 08 51), down the street from Ağa Camii is your best bet to find what comes out of a real Turkish kitchen (hint: it's not *kebap*). This family-style restaurant has been going strong since 1888. Entrees US$3-6. Delicious soups US$1. Open daily noon-11pm (kitchen closes at 10:30pm).

■ **Naregatsi Cafe,** upstairs at the mouth of Sakizağacı Cad., across from the Ağa Camii. Gourmet cafe fare in the midst of a galactic, high-speed collision of kitsch and concept art. Warhol would feel right at home. Open noon-11:30pm.

Buhara, just across from Doy-Doy on Şifa Hammamı Sok. Hefty portions and a good veg. selection. Munch on fresh bread as you ponder a wide range of mouth-watering choices. Buhara special US$3.50. Turkish special *kebap* US$3. Open daily 9am-late.

Haci Baba, 49 İstiklâl Cad. (☎ 244 18 86 or 245 43 77), has perfected a wide range of Turkish standards. The unassuming entrance hides a large dining room with a terrace overlooking the courtyard of Aya Triada in back. Extensive menu. Entrees about US$3.50-6.50. 10% service charge. Open daily 10am-10pm. AmEx/MC/V.

Pudding Shop, 6 Divan Yolu Cad. (☎522 29 70; fax 512 44 58). A major pitstop on the Hippie Trail to the Far and Middle East during the '70s. The setting for the drug deal scene in *Midnight Express* is now clean and tasty. A/C upstairs. Meat dishes US$2-2.50. Veg. dishes US$1.50.

◎ SIGHTS

İstanbul's incomparable array of churches, mosques, palaces, and museums can keep an ardent tourist busy for weeks. Most budget travelers spend a lot of time in **Sultanahmet,** the area around the **Aya Sofia,** south of and uphill from **Sirkeci.** Merchants crowd the district between the **Grand Bazaar,** east of the university, and the less touristy **Egyptian Spice Bazaar,** just southeast of Eminönü.

AYA SOFİA (HAGIA SOPHIA)
Museum open Tu-Su 9:30am-4:30pm. Gallery open Tu-Su 9:30am-4pm. US$6.50, students US$2.50.

Aya Sofia was built by Justinian in 537 CE, and at that time its area (7570 sq. m) and height (55.6m) made it the biggest building in the world. Upon entering the church, which was even larger than King Solomon's temple in Jerusalem, Emperor Justinian exclaimed, "Solomon, I have outdone you!" Twenty years later, an earthquake brought the dome crashing to the ground, and in 1453 the entire building fell to the Ottomans and was converted into a mosque (as it remained until 1932, when Atatürk declared it a museum).

Aya Sofia's austere interior amplifies its awesome size. The nave is overshadowed by the gold-leaf mosaic dome lined with hundreds of circular windows that make it seem as though the dome is floating on a bed of luminescent pearls. The *mihrab*, a calligraphy-adorned portal pointing toward Mecca, stands in the apse, the space that housed the altar during the mosque's Orthodox incarnation. The marble square on the floor marks the spot where Byzantine emperors were once crowned. The *minbar*, a platform used to address the crowd at prayer time, is the stairway right of the *mihrab*. The gallery contains Byzantine mosaics uncovered from beneath a thick layer of Ottoman plaster as well as the famed sweating pillar, sheathed in bronze. The pillar has a hole where you can insert your finger to collect the odd drop of water, believed to possess healing powers.

▧ BLUE MOSQUE (SULTANAHMET CAMİİ)

Open Tu-Sa 8:30am-12:30pm, 1:45-3:45pm, and 5:30-6:30pm. The Blue Mosque is a working religious facility, so don't attempt to visit during prayer times, which are marked by the call to prayer issued five times daily. Dress modestly and remove your shoes. Women should cover their heads. On your way out, expect to make a small donation of US$1. Tomb open Tu-Su 9:30am-4:30pm. Tomb US$1, students free.

The mosque between the Hippodrome and Aya Sofia is the Blue Mosque (Sultanahmet Camii), so named for the beautiful blue İznik tiles that decorate the interior. Completed in 1617, it was Sultan Ahmet's "size doesn't matter" response to Justinian's Aya Sofia. The mosque has several modern constructions: the internal framework of iron bars across its domes allows the entire structure to bend in earthquakes (it's withstood 20 so far), and an underground pool moderates the mosque's interior temperature. Numerology is the name of the game at the Blue Mosque: Sultan Ahmet was the 16th sultan of the Ottoman state and the sixth since the Turkish conquest of Constantinople; consequently, the mosque has 16 balconies and six **minarets**—the primary source of the mosque's fame. Only the mosque at Mecca had that many minarets at the time of the Blue Mosque's construction, and the thought of equalling that sacred edifice was considered heretical. Sultan Ahmet circumvented this difficulty by financing the construction of a seventh minaret at Mecca. The interior was originally lit with candles, the chandelier structure intended to create the illusion that tiny starlights floated freely in the air. A small stone from the Ka'aba at Mecca is almost invisible from the tourists' area. The small, square, single-domed structure in front of the Blue Mosque is **Sultanahmet'in Türbesi,** or Sultan Ahmet's Tomb, which contains the sultan's remains and his family's; it also has İznik tiles. The reliquary in the back contains strands of the Prophet Muhammad's beard.

HIPPODROME (AT MEYDANI)

Though all of the major Sultanahmet sites provide insight into pre-Ottoman and Ottoman history, few conjure images of the glory of Byzantine Constantinople like the **Hippodrome**, behind the Blue Mosque. Built by the Roman Emperor Septimus Severus in 200 CE, it served as the stage for chariot races and public executions. The politically opposed **Hippodrome Factions** arose out of the Hippodrome's seating plan, which was determined by social standing. The "blues" were wealthy citizens seated in the front rows and the "greens" urban plebeians in cheap seats. In 532 CE, a tax protest turned into the full-out Nika Revolt. The city was ravaged in the ensuing melee, and Justinian's post-revolt reconstruction efforts culminated in the building of the Aya Sofia. The tall, northernmost column with hieroglyphics is the **Dikili Taş,** an Egyptian obelisk erected by the Pharaoh Thutmose III in 1500 BCE and brought to Constantinople in the 4th century by Emperor Theodosius I. Farther south, the subterranean bronze stump is all that remains of the **Serpentine Column,** originally placed at the Oracle of Delphi. The southernmost column is the **Column of Constantine,** whose original gold-plated bronze tiling was looted by Crusaders during the sack of Constantinople.

MUSEUM OF TURKISH AND ISLAMIC ART

Museum and cafe open Tu-Su 9:30am-4:30pm. US$2, students US$1.20.

This superb museum (also known as İbrahim Paşa Sarayı) features a large Islamic art collection organized by period. The museum's main wing consists of a long hall with carpet and silver displays, off of which the rooms contain works from specific periods. The Selçuk displays and the Ottoman calligraphy with *tuğras* (seals) of sultans are particularly impressive.

UNDERGROUND CISTERN (YEREBATAN SARAYI)

As you stand with your back to Aya Sofia, the entrance lies 175m from the mosque in the small stone kiosk on the left hand side of Yerebatan Cad. Open daily 9:30am-5:30pm. US$4, students US$3.25.

This underground "palace" is actually a vast cavern whose shallow water eerily reflects the images of its 336 supporting columns, all illuminated by colored ambient lighting. The echoing sounds of dripping water and the muted strains of classical tunes will accompany your stroll across the elevated wooden walkways. Underground walkways originally linked the cistern to Topkapı Palace, but were blocked to curb rampant trafficking in stolen goods and abducted women.

TOPKAPI PALACE (TOPKAPI SARAYI)

Open W-M 9am-4:30pm. Each day's open galleries are posted next to the ticket window. Palace US$6.50. Harem closes at 4pm. The only way to visit is on one of the tours that leave every 30min. 9:30am-3:30pm. Harem US$4.

Towering from the high ground at the tip of the old city and hidden behind walls up to 12m high, Topkapı Palace (Topkapı Sarayı) was the nerve center of the Ottoman Empire. Topkapı offers unparalleled insights into the wealth, excess, cruelty, and artistic vitality that characterized the Ottoman Empire at its peak. Built by Mehmet the Conqueror between 1458 and 1465, the palace became an imperial residence during the reign of Süleyman the Magnificent. The palace is divided into a series of courts, all surrounded by the palace walls.

FIRST AND SECOND COURTYARD. The **first courtyard,** through the **Imperial Gate,** was the popular center of the Palace. The general public was permitted entrance to watch executions, trade, and view the nexus of the Empire's glory. At the end of the first courtyard, the capped conical towers of the **Gate of Greeting** (Bab üs-Selam) mark the entrance to the **second court.** To the right, beyond the colonnade, the **Imperial Kitchens,** with their distinctive conical and vaulted chimneys, house porcelain and silver collections. The last set of doors on the left of the narrow alley open into the palace's deservedly world-famous Chinese and Japanese **porcelain collections.** Across the courtyard, where ostriches and eunuchs once roamed, lies the divine **Divan** (also known as Kubbealtı), with its window grilles, awnings, walls, and ceilings slathered in gold leaf. The **Council Chamber,** the room closest to the Harem, retains its original classical Ottoman *faience* decor. The plush Rococo-style room abutting the Council Chamber was where the Grand Vizier would receive foreign dignitaries. Next door and to the right is the **Inner Treasury,** where various instruments of cutting, bludgeoning, and hacking are kept.

THIRD COURTYARD. The **third court,** officially known as **Enderun** (inside), is accessible through the **Gate of Felicity.** In the **Expeditionary Force Dormitory** is a costume collection that traces the evolution of imperial dress. Moving along the colonnade brings you to the awesome **Palace Treasury.** One of the highlights is the legendary **Topkapı dagger** (essentially three giant emeralds with a knife sprouting out of them), a gift Sultan Mahmut I intended to present to Shah Nadir of Iran in return for the solid-gold throne displayed elsewhere in the treasury. Wrestle your way to the front of the line leading up to all 86 karats of the Pigot Diamond, better known as the **Spoonmaker's Diamond** because it was traded to a spoonmaker in exchange for three spoons. A nearby glass compartment reportedly contains some of John the Baptist's bones. This display is excellent preparation for the **Pavilion of Holy Relics,** just on the other side of the courtyard and leagues ahead in beauty and elegance. Even the most İzniked-out traveler will be amazed by the calligraphied tiles of this holy site. The pavilion holds the booty taken from Egypt by Selim the Grim as well as relics from Mecca, including the **staff of Moses,** hairs from **Muhammad's beard,** and some of the Prophet's personal effects (including his bow and mantle, a handwritten letter, and two swords).

FOURTH COURTYARD. Three passages lead into the **fourth courtyard.** If Topkapı was the nerve center of the Ottoman Empire, then the fourth courtyard certainly qualifies as its pleasure center—it was amongst these pavilions, gardens, and fountains that the Ottomans really got their mojo working. Uninterrupted vistas of the Sea of Marmara and the Bosphorus extend from the broad marble terrace at the west end. At one end of the portico is the **Circumcision Room,** a chamber hanging over the edge of the pavilion, built by Ibrahim the Mad.

HAREM. The harem's 400-plus rooms housed the sultan, his immediate family, and an entourage of servants, eunuchs, and general assistants. The mandatory tour begins at the **Black Eunuchs' Dormitory,** which is just what its name says it is. Next up is the women's section of the harem, the center of which are the lavish chambers of the **Valide Sultan,** the sultan's mother and the most powerful woman in the Harem. Surrounding the room of the queen mum are the chambers of the **concubines,** the women who put the slut back in sultanate. If a particular woman attracted the sultan's affections or if the sultan spent a night with her, she would be promoted to coveted "odalisque" status (immortalized in Ingres' nudes), which meant she had to stay in İstanbul (concubines were allowed to leave after nine years) but got nicer quarters in exchange for her undying ministrations.

ARCHAEOLOGICAL MUSEUM COMPLEX

150m downhill from the Topkapı Palace's 1st courtyard. When the palace is closed, enter the museums through Gülhane Park, where a separate road next to the park ticket booths leads to the museum complex. A single ticket theoretically gets you into all 3 museums, although one or another is often closed. Museum complex open Tu-Su 9:30am-5pm. US$5.

TILED PAVILION AND ANCIENT ORIENT MUSEUM. The **Tiled Pavilion** (*Çinli Köşk*) exposes more than you ever wanted to know about the omnipresent İznik tiles. The once fully tiled pavilion was built in 1472 by Mehmet to view the athletic competitions below, but fires and earthquakes have destroyed much of the original *faience*. The displays cover the full spectrum of Ottoman tilemaking, including some rare early İznik tiles. The smaller cement building adjacent to the Tiled Pavilion is the **Ancient Orient Museum,** which houses treasures so rare that the curator seems reluctant to let anyone see them. If you catch this place when it's open, don't miss the excellent collection of 2nd-millennium BCE stone artifacts from the ancient Middle East (including Anatolia, Mesopotamia, and Egypt). The pride of this museum is the **Treaty of Kadesh,** the world's oldest-known written treaty, drafted after a battle between Ramses II of Egypt and the Hittite King Muvatellish (a copy graces the entrance to the United Nations).

ARCHAEOLOGY MUSEUM. The 19th-century Archaeology Museum has one of the world's great collections of Classical and Hellenistic art. The first portion of the building is a walking tour through Classical sculpture. The highlight is the misnamed **Alexander Sarcophagus,** modeled on a Greek temple and covered with intricate carvings; it actually holding the remains of the Sidonese king Abdalonymous. Other exhibits include "İstanbul Through the Ages" and "Ancient Turkey."

GRAND BAZAAR

From Sultanahmet, follow the tram tracks toward Aksaray for 5min. until you see the Nuruosmanıye Camii on the right. Walk down Vezirhanı Cad. for one block, keeping the mosque on your left. Follow the crowds left into the bazaar. www.grand-bazaar.com. Open M-Sa 9am-7pm. A small number of stores close 1-2hr. before the rest of the store

Consisting of over 4000 shops, several banks, mosques, police stations, and restaurants, the enormous **Grand Bazaar** (*Kapalı Çarşısı*, "covered bazaar") could be a city in itself. Now the largest covered bazaar in the world, the Grand Bazaar began in 1461 as a modest affair during the reign of Mehmet the Conqueror. Today, the enormous Kapalı Çarşısı forms the entrance to the massive mercantile sprawl that starts at Çemberlitaş and covers the hill down to Eminönü, ending at the **Egyptian Spice Bazaar** (*Mısır Çarşısı*) and the Golden Horn waterfront. This colorful, chaotic, labyrinthine world combines the best and worst of shopping in Turkey. Though the bazaar is loosely organized according to specific themes, much of it is a jumble of shops selling hookah pipes (*argilehs*), bright baubles, copper filigree shovels, Byzantine-style icons on red velvet, Turkish daggers, rugs, embroidered pillows, amber jewelry, silver flintlock guns with mother-of-pearl handles, musical instruments, chess sets, ornaments, and the ubiquitous evil-eye bedecked keychains. Through banter, barter, and hassle, a day spent at the Kapalı Çarşısı is bound to tempt and tantalize on a scale unmatched by even the most frenetic of *souqs* elsewhere in the Middle East. You'll surely get lost, so enjoy the ride.

SÜLEYMANİYE COMPLEX

From the university, follow the line of stalls to the left of the mosque down the hill of Fuatpaşa Cad. Keep the stone wall on your left; follow it around to the left and the mosque will come into view. From Sultanahmet, either walk along the tramvay (15min.) or take the tramvay to the "Üniversite" stop, walk across the square, and take Besim Ömer Paşa Cad. past the walls of the university to Süleymaniye Cad. Open Tu-Su 9:30am-4:30pm, except during prayer.

To the north of İstanbul University stands the elegant **Süleymaniye Camii**, one of Ottoman architect Sinan's great masterpieces. This mosque is part of a larger *külliye* (complex), which includes **tombs**, an **imaret** (soup kitchen), and several **madrasas** (Islamic schools). Prof. Sıddık Sami Onar Sok. is the major street running between the university and the mosque. Passing through the graveyard brings you to the **royal tombs** of Süleyman I and his wife, Haseki Hürrem. Walk along the Süleymaniye Camii's southwest side to the large arch just below the dome and enter the mosque's central courtyard through the smaller tourist entrance to the left of the main door. After removing your shoes and covering your head, proceed inside the vast and perfectly proportioned mosque—the height of the dome (53m) is exactly twice the measurement of each side of the square base. The **stained-glass windows** are the sobering work of the master Sarhoş İbrahim (İbrahim the Drunkard). The İznik tile İnzanity all started here: the area around the *mihrab* showcases Sinan's first experiment in blue tiles.

⬛ HAMMAMS (TURKISH BATHS)

Most baths have separate women's sections or women's hours, but not all have designated female attendants.

◼ Çemberlitaş Hammamı, 8 Verzirhan Cad. (☎522 79 74). Just a soap-slide away from the Çemberlitaş tram stop. Built by Sinan in 1584. Marble interiors. Vigorous "towel service" after the bath requires a tip of US$1.50-3. Bath with own towel and soap US$9; with a sudsy rubdown, massage and wash US$15 (tip included, but after you've changed, the washers wait around, expecting another US$1-3). Open daily 6am-midnight.

Çinli Hammamı. In Fatih, near the butcher shops at the end of Itfaiye Cad. Built for the pirate Barbarossa, this bath is excellent, even retaining a few of its original İznik and Kütahya tiles. Large facilities mean ample space on the hot stone. Bath US$2.30; *kese* US$1.50 massage US$3. Both men's and women's sections open daily 8am-8pm.

Mihrimah Hammamı (☎523 04 87). Right next to Mihrimah Mosque on Fevzi Paşa Cad., about 50m from Edirnekapı. Definitely one of the better local baths: it's large, quiet, clean, cheap, and hot. Women's facilities are good, though smaller. Bath US$3; massage US$2.50. Men's section open 7am-midnight; women's section 8am-7pm.

▣ NIGHTLIFE

Turkish nightlife divides into three categories. The first includes male-only *çay* houses, backgammon parlors, and dancing shows. Women are not prohibited but are unwelcome and should avoid these places; they are often unsafe for men as well. *Let's Go* does not endorse patronage of these establishments. The second

HAMMAM-O-RAMA *Hammams* can be intimidating for first-timers, but they're well worth the effort. Pay the entrance fee plus massage and *kese* (abrasive mitt). Bring your own shampoo, soap, and towel, or pay to use the bath's. Some *hammams* have cubicles *(camekan)* for personal storage. You will be given a large towel *(peştemal)*. Men generally strip and wrap the *peştemal* around their waists, but don't drop that sucker! Turkish women frequently strip naked (in the *hammam*).

Some *hammams* have a hot, sauna-like room. After you've worked up a sweat, proceed to the warm main room with its large, heated stone *(göbek taşı)*. Mix hot and cold water and pour it over yourself with the bowl provided.

A wash and **massage** on the large, heated marble stone costs a little more. Usually, the masseur is your gender; female visitors may request a female masseuse. The massage is often very vigorous; try the phrase *"lütfen daha yumuşak"* (gentler please) if need be. The *kese* used can also be purchased at pharmacies. Following the massage and *kese*, you will usually be sponged gently and shampooed. When you're clean as a whistle, rehydrate with water and a have a nap.

category includes **cafe-bars, rock bars,** and **backpacker bars.** Cafe-bars are smaller and more relaxed than the sometimes cavernous rock bars. Backpacker bars are concentrated in the Sultanahmet area. **Clubs** and **discos** comprise the third nightlife category. The hippest İstanbul clubs often move from unlisted locations in Taksim during the winter to unlisted open-air summer locations throughout the city. Even taxi drivers can't keep up with the scene. Nightlife is centered around **Taksim** and **İstiklâl Cad.** In **Sultanahmet,** all pubs are within 100m of each other and have standardized beer prices (US$1-1.25). The Beşiktaş end of **Ortaköy** is a maze of upscale hangouts; along the coastal road toward Arnavutköy are a string of open-air clubs. Cover charges are high (US$18-45), and bouncers highly selective, but wander between **Ortaköy** and **Bebek** and try your luck.

■ **Jazz Stop,** at the end of Büyük Parmakkapı Sok. in Taksim. A mixed group of music lovers mostly sit while live bands lay the funk, blues, and jazz on thick. The owner, a talented drummer from one of Turkey's oldest and most respected rock groups, occasionally takes part in the jams. Live music nightly 11pm. Beer US$3; liquor US$6 and up. June-Aug. no cover; Sept.-May F-Sa cover US$10. Open daily 11am-4am.

■ **Riddim,** 6 Büyük Parmakkapı Sok. in Taksim. If you are looking for Jah, he is here, in the only bar in Taksim dedicated to spinning reggae all night long. Crowd is a mixed group that likes to dance, and the DJs are generally great, spinning the Jamaican export as well as other African and island music. Unaccompanied men will be turned away on weekends. Beer US$2.50. Open F-Sa 8pm-4am, Su-Th 9pm-1:30am.

■ **Madrid Bar,** İpek Sok. Off Küçük Parmakkapı Sok., which is itself off İstiklâl Cad. An understated bar with a fascination for surrealist Spanish paintings. This small, mellow spot is popular with Turkish students and young foreigners looking for one of the cheapest pints in Taksim (US$1.25). Open daily 2pm-2am.

Cheers, on Akbıyık Cad. in Sultanahmet. The best music on backpacker alley, Cheers attracts locals (except in Jul. and Aug.) as well as the normal tourist crowd to its comfortable, outdoor benches. Delicious fresh fruit soaking in bottled water and a very friendly scene make this one of the best places to grab a beer in the area.

Buzz Bar, 35 Kutlugün Sok. in Sultanahmet, at the Istanbul Hostel. By far the homiest and cleanest of the backpacker bars, Buzz Bar plays nightly movies on their huge satellite TV. Has a very pleasant outdoor seating area for more relaxed conversation. The *Efes* flows just as much upstairs on their sea-view terrace, but it's less of a party than the basement. A brick interior and fireplace make this the place to be in the winter months.

China White, 120 Muallim Naci Cad. in Ortaköy (☎259 54 80). Just under the bridge. By far the best spot in Ortaköy. As classy as its sister location in London. Outdoor funfest of Asian decor on several tiers of cushy teak terraces. While there is no cover, the drinks are pricey. *Efes* US$5. Imported liquor US$9-11. Open daily 7pm-4am.

NORTHWESTERN TURKEY

The only part of the country actually on the European continent, Northwestern Turkey wraps around the Sea of Marmara with a dazzling array of cities and towns—fantastic quick escapes from İstanbul's urban sprawl. As the dusty streets of the big city filter into winding highways, pavement gives way to terra cotta soil, silvery olive groves, and fields of peach trees. This is the area that nourished the young Ottoman Empire, and it has two Ottoman capitals, **Bursa** and **Edirne,** to show for it. The regions's artistic achievements, including Edirne's masterful architecture, İznik's ceramic tilework, and Bursa's silk, are world-famous. The Gallipoli Battlefields remain a major pilgrimage site for those commemorating the bloody World War I battle for control of the Dardanelles.

EDİRNE
☎ 284

Edirne has worn many masks throughout its almost 2000 years of historical prominence: founded as the Roman outpost Hadrianopolis by the humble Emperor Hadrian, Edirne has been an Ottoman capital (and is still home to the Turkey's greatest Ottoman mosque, *Selimiye Camii*) and a modern Greek military possession. In the 19th century, Edirne was still the seventh-largest city in Europe; now, though, it has a frontier town feel, removed from the rest of Turkey. Trakya University, which serves European Turkey, keeps Edirne young. Not coincidentally, the finest brand of *rakı* is produced nearby.

⌐ TRANSPORTATION. Buses depart from the **otogar,** 2km from the city center, to: Ankara (Edirne Ece Turizm; 9hr., 9:30pm, US$20); Antakya (21hr., 5:30 and 7:30pm, US$28.25); Antalya (17hr., 7:45pm, US$23); Bursa/Mt. Uludağ (7hr., 5pm, US$16.50); Çanakkale (Edirne Ece Turizm; 4hr., 7:45pm, US$8.25); İstanbul (3½hr.; 5:30, 7am, then every 30min. until 6:30pm; US$5) or (2hr., every 30min. 7am-7pm, US$8.25); İzmir (9hr., 7:45pm, US$15.50). *Dolmuş* leave from the dusty gravel lot behind the Rüstem Paşa Kervansaray Hotel (US$0.25-0.45).

▄▐ ORIENTATION AND PRACTICAL INFORMATION. Two of Edirne's major roads, **Mimar Sinan Cad.** and **Talat Paşa Cad.,** converge at the fountain at the center of city. To the south sits **Eski Camii,** the **Bedesten,** and one of the city's central cafe squares. **Talat Paşa Cad.,** the city's main east-west thoroughfare, starts at the fountain and runs through town to the Tunca River. The other half of **Talat Paşa Cad.** begins behind Eski Cami, runs southeast out of the city, and continues on to İstanbul. **Mimar Sinan Cad.** runs up toward the main mosque and Edirne's major **museums.** The city's shops are on **Saraçlar Cad.,** reached by walking on Talat Paşa Cad., away from Selimiye Camii, and making the first left. Farther down Talat Paşa Cad., at the intersection with **Maarif Cad.,** you'll find the tourist office and a variety of cheap accommodations. The magnificent **Selimiye Camii** towers above the city, visible from several kilometers away. Though few of the streets are marked, the large map in the square is a good reference. The **tourist office,** 17 Talat Paşa Cad., 300m down the road from the center of town, hands out free maps. (☎213 92 08. Open M-F 8:30am-5:30pm.) **Türkiye İş Bankası** and **Vakıfbank,** both on Saraçlar Cad., exchange **traveler's checks** and have **ATMs.** (Both open M-F 9am-12:30pm and 1:30-5:30pm.) Take *dolmuş* #1 to the Mega Park stop (10min., US$0.25) to reach the **police** (☎213 92 40). For pharmaceutical fancies, go to **Şifa Eczanesi,** on Talat Paşa Cad. (☎225 46 36. Open M-F 8:30am-7:30pm.) There are two **hospitals** in town: the private **Özel Trakya Hastanesi** (☎213 92 00) and the public **Edirne Devlet Hastanesi** (☎225 46 03). The **PTT** is at 17 Saraçlar Cad. (Open daily 8:30am-5pm; phones until 10pm.) **Postal Code:** 22100.

▛▟ ACCOMMODATIONS AND FOOD. Plenty of hotels are scattered along Maarif Cad., the first left after passing over Saraçlar Cad. on Talat Paşa Cad. Travelers to Edirne during the Kırkpınar Grease Wrestling Festival should call ahead, since the town is filled with spectators for the event during the first week of July. When the flow of travelers through the city falls off, bargaining can be productive. ▨**Efe Hotel,** 13

Maarif Cad., offers luxurious rooms with modern bathrooms, phones, and TV, and features an "English Pub" with live music. The friendly staff is the only one in town that speaks English. (☎213 61 66; fax 213 60 80; www.efehotel.com. Breakfast included. Singles US$16.50; doubles US$23; triples US$27; suites US$35.) **Hotel Kervansaray,** a.k.a. **Rüstempaşa,** 57 Iki Kapılı Han Cad., was built in the 1550s as a resting place for camel caravans trudging between Europe and the East. Its courtyard and stone hallways complement modern facilities (bath, TV, phone) and a billiards/Internet parlor. (☎225 71 95; fax 212 04 62. Singles US$30; doubles US$60; triples US$90. MC/V.)

Saray Restaurant (☎212 13 92), directly behind the PTT and identifiable by its red awning, stands out as a local favorite, serving daily lunch specials for US$0.50-1 per serving. **Lalezar** (☎212 24 89 or 213 06 00), to the right of the Meriç River bridge, is high-class by Edirne standards. There's no menu, but the language barrier shouldn't be a problem as waiters bring mouth-watering *mezes* directly to your wooden pavilion, before moving on to the standard *şiş* and *döner* fare, with the added selection of fresh fish. Be warned, there is more being devoured here than the food, as the river's standing water brings tons of mosquitoes.

◙ SIGHTS. Every July, competitors from all over Turkey travel to Edirne, don giant leather breeches, slather themselves in oil, and hit the mats. The champions of the **Kırkpınar Grease Wrestling Festival** are assured lasting fame and a portrait in the wrestling room of the Islamic Art Museum (see below).

Edirne is *really* famed for its magnificent mosque architecture. **Selimiye Camii** is considered the finest mosque in all of Turkey, surpassing İstanbul's Aya Sofia (Hagia Sophia) in size, structural stability, and aesthetic unity. Construction of the famous Ottoman architect Sinan's self-proclaimed masterpiece did not actually begin until 1567, the year after Sinan died. The interior fills with light from 999 windows, illuminating the colorful lace patterns and calligraphic inscriptions on the 32m interior dome (as well as the *minbar* and *mihrab*). The former *madrasa* of the mosque houses the **Turkish and Islamic Art Museum,** which has a special room recounting the history of the Kırkpınar Wrestling Festival.

Edirne's two other mosques (both on Hürriyet Meydanı) trace the architectural transition from the Selçuk style of Konya and Bursa to the distinctly Ottoman style of Selimye Camii. The nine-domed **Eski Camii** ("Old Mosque") and its marble *mihrab* are an excellent example of pre-conquest Ottoman architecture. The limestone **Üç Şerefeli Camii** ("Three Balconies Mosque") replaced Eski Camii as the main mosque for Friday prayers upon its completion in 1447. The mosque is known for its 23m dome, the largest Ottoman dome of its time.

BURSA   ☎224

Surrounded by fertile plains and blessed with vast gardens and parks, the city has earned the moniker "Green Bursa"—a name with double significance, as Bursa is one of Turkey's holiest cities (green is the symbolic color of Islam). While the city's 14th-century mosques and tombs still receive visitors, Bursa's rapid economic growth has spawned a wealthy resort area, including one of Turkey's most popular skiing spots. Silk trade remains a major industry here, as attested by the silkworm cocoon harvests held every June and September. The town also claims a number of culinary triumphs: the *İskender kebap* and *İnegöl Köfte* (a type of meatball) were both invented in Bursa's kitchens. Anticipating the gastric distress such tasty victuals would conjure, Sultan Süleyman's Grand Vizier had cure-all several mineral baths constructed here.

▐ TRANSPORTATION

Bursa's **bus terminal,** 20km outside the city center, is reached by local bus #90/A (every 30min. 6:20am-midnight, US$0.45). **Buses** go to: **Ankara** (5½hr., every hr. 6am-3am, US$6); **İstanbul** (3½hr., US$5); and **İzmir** (5hr., every hr., US$5), among other cities. Small **dolmuş** (US$0.40-0.60 per person) leave from Atatürk Cad., behind the *Adliye*, and from the Atatürk statue in Heykel.

TURKEY

✦? ORIENTATION AND PRACTICAL INFORMATION

Except for the Ulu Cami, which is right on the main road, all of Bursa's sights lie about 1½km east and west of either end of **Atatürk Cad.**, while all of the hotels and restaurants, except those in the Arap Şükrü district, are within a block of Atatürk Cad. in the area called **Heykel.** The **tourist office,** is on Atatürk Cad. near the Atatürk statue, down the stairs and to the left. (☎220 18 48. Open May-Sept. daily 8:30am-6pm; Oct.-Apr. daily 8am-5pm.) **Police** can be reached at ☎221 66 11. Hospitals come in private (**Vatan Hastanesi;** ☎220 10 40; on İnönü Cad.) and public (**Devlet Hastanesi;** ☎220 00 20) varieties. Get yourself connected at **Elite Internet Cafe,** 37 Yeşil Cad., before the overpass leading to Emir Sultan Camii. (☎327 03 34. US$0.30 per hr. Open daily 10am-1am). The **PTT** is opposite Ulu Camii. (Open daily 8am-11pm; airmail and currency exchange until 5:30pm.)

⌂☾ ACCOMMODATIONS AND FOOD

A number of Bursa's budget hotels lie off Atatürk Cad., to the south of the PTT. Hotels closer to the main street tend to be noisy. Bursa's budget hotels are off Atatürk Cad., south of the PTT. Clean, quiet **Otel Güneş,** 75 İnebey Cad. also has shared baths. (☎222 14 04. Singles US$5; doubles US$7.50; triples US$14.50; quads US$20.) **Otel Deniz,** 19 Tahtakale Veziri Cad., is left off Atatürk Cad. after the Sümerbank. (☎222 92 38. Singles US$4; doubles US$8.) The birthplace of *İskender kebap* has many restaurants claiming maternity, of which 🔲**Kebapçı İskender** is the tastiest. It has two locations (7 Ünlü Cad. and on Atatürk Bul. by the cultural center) serving the same *İskender kebap* since 1867. (☎221 46 15. Open daily 11am-9pm.) **Çiçek Izgara,** 15 Belediye Cad., behind the town hall on Atatürk Cad., serves delicious *köfte* and *kasarlı köfte* (meatballs and cheese) for US$2. (☎221 65 26. Open daily 11am-4pm and 6-9:30pm.)

◉ SIGHTS

ULU CAMI. The unique layout and domed splendor of the immense Ulu Cami Mosque, in the heart of town on Atatürk Cad., was a compromise between Sultan Beyazıt I and Allah. Beyazıt promised he would build 20 mosques in exchange for victory, but when he squashed his enemy, he built one with 20 domes. The interior columns and walls are bedecked with Selçuk calligraphic excerpts from the Qur'an. The *mihrab* contains an astronomical guide with pictures of the planets.

YEŞİL TÜRBE AND YEŞİL CAMII. The gorgeous **Yeşil Türbe** (Green Tomb) stands atop a hill, its blue-green, tile-sheathed octagonal form rising out of the surrounding foliage (right off Atatürk Cad., along Yeşil Cad.). Inside, everything is covered with beautiful İznik tiles, even the sarcophagus of Ottoman hero Sultan Mehmet I (who is best known as the patron of the Harem of the Topkapı Palace in İstanbul; see p. 634). Across the street stands the 15th-century **Yeşil Camii** mosque, whose Selçuk influence is apparent in its brick-and-stone construction and its almost onion-shaped minarets. The mosque's real beauty lies within, where intricately stenciled İznik tiles adorn the walls. The balcony that hangs low above the entrance was built so that the sultan could enter and pray unobserved, while keeping his eyes peeled for potential assassins. The large, central dome is one of the first used in Ottoman architecture. *(Tomb open daily 8:30am-noon and 1-5:30pm.)*

MURADIYE. *Şehade* (royal sons) are buried in the tombs around the Muradiye Camii, a testament to the early Ottoman practice of fratricide. In order to ensure a smooth succession, the eldest son would execute his younger or weaker brothers. The complex includes 12 tombs, but at the time of publication, only four were open to the public. Cem Sultan's tomb, covered in İznik tiles, is particularly spectacular. Adjacent to the tomb is the Muradiye or **Murat II Camii,** built in the same style as the Yeşil Camii. *(Catch one of the frequent "Muradiye" dolmuş or buses from the Atatürk Cad./Heykel area. Open daily 8:30am-noon and 1-5:30pm. US$0.60.)*

ENTERTAINMENT

Entertainment in Bursa means winding down at a mineral bath. The bars and clubs of **Arap Şükrü** district, near Altıparmak Cad., are as close to nightlife as Bursa gets.

MINERAL BATHS. Bursa's fabled mineral baths are in the Çekirge ("Grasshopper") area west of the city. One of the finest in the country, ■**Eski Kaplıca** ("Old Bath") features a hot pool, a hotter pool, and a great massage room. (Open daily 7am-10:30pm. Men US$4, women US$3.30.) The three-bath complex **Yeni Kaplıca** ("New Baths") was constructed by Süleyman the Magnificent's Grand Vizier atop the remains of another built by Justinian. (Men only; bath US$2-4.25, massage US$2.50, *kese* US$2; open daily 5am-11pm.) The **Kaynarca** is a women's bath. (US$2.50, massage US$2.50, *kese* US$1; open daily 7am-11pm). Soak in a tub of smooth, pasty mud at **Karamustafa.** (US$4. Open for men 7am-5pm, for women 8am-4pm.) *(Take bus #40 from Heykel or any dolmuş with a "Çekirge" sign. Get off on Çekirge Cad. by the Atatürk Museum. For Eski Kaplıca, walk west and bear right at the fork onto Yeni Kaplıca Cad. Signs point down the stairs.)*

MARKETS. The **Koza and Emir Hans** have been the centers of the city's silk *(ipek)* trade for the past 500 years. Restored by the Ağa Khan, the **Koza Han** draws silk cocoon dealers every July and September. The rest of the year, the *han* is home to a slew of silk fabric shops. The **Emir Han** is concerned only with the sale of the finished product. Both *hans* open into the 14th-century **bedesten** (covered market), similar to İstanbul's Grand Bazaar. *(On Atatürk Cad. behind the Ulu Camii.)*

ÇANAKKALE ☎286

Modern Çanakkale presides over the mythic and eternally strategic Dardanelles, straits that have seen poets and soldiers come and go for centuries. With inexpensive accommodations and frequent bus connections to nearby sights and cities, Çanakkale is an easy base from which to explore Gallipoli and Troy. Though not the most scenic locale, it is improving as the central Cumhuriyet Meydanı is refurbished and local tourist establishments are expanded. Around ANZAC Day (Apr. 25), Çanakkale hosts thousands of Australians and New Zealanders who come to commemorate the soldiers that died at Gallipoli in World War I; expect every hotel in town to be booked solid at this time of year.

☐ TRANSPORTATION. Buses run to: **Ankara** (11hr., 10 per day 7am-1pm, US$11); **Bursa** (4½hr., 9 per day 7am-1am, US$6.50); **İstanbul** (5hr.; 7 per day 7am-1am; US$9); and **İzmir** (5hr., 16 per day 6:45-2:30am, US$8); and **Selçuk** (6hr.; 8am, 7:30, 11:15pm, 1:45am; US$7.50). *Dolmuş* (US$0.75) leave from near the small bridge over the Sarı Çay inlet to **Troy** (25min., leaves when full).

▉☐ ORIENTATION AND PRACTICAL INFORMATION. Most things related to the mechanics of budget travel are within one block of the ferry dock and the clocktower. From the *otogar*, turn left along **Atatürk Cad.,** make a quick right onto **Demircioğlu Cad.,** and follow the signs marked "Feribot."

The English-speaking staff at the **tourist office,** 67 İskele Meydanı, distributes free maps and helps find rooms. (☎/fax 217 11 87.) For several **banks** with Cirrus/ PLUS **ATMs,** walk up Demircioğlou Cad. and take the fourth right from Anzac House; follow this street to a 4-way intersection. (Banks open M-F 9am-12:30pm and 1:30-5:30pm.) The **police** (☎257 52 60 are off İnönü Cad., next to the PTT. Pharmacy **Pelini Eczanesi** (☎217 12 60) is on Demircioğlou Cad. just down from Anzac House. Hospitals include **Devlet Hastanesi** (public; ☎217 10 98), off İnönü Cad. across from the PTT, and **Özel Hastanesi** (private; ☎217 74 62), 1km from the tourist office. The **PTT** is on İnönü Cad. (Open daily 8am-midnight.) **Postal Code:** 17100.

⌐ ACCOMMODATIONS. Budget accommodations cluster around the clock-tower, with good restaurants and bars only a few steps away. Many feature a nightly screening of *Gallipoli*, starring Mel Gibson, and can arrange Gallipoli and Troy tours. To reach **Efes Hotel**, 5 Aralık Sok., walk to the left of the clocktower, then turn left onto Aralık Sok. Completely tiled, this spotless hotel has spacious rooms with baths. (☎217 3256. Breakfast US$2.50. Singles US$7.50; doubles US$9; triples US$13.50.) Another backpacker hangout, **Yellow Rose Pension,** 5 Yeni Sok., is around the corner, 50m from the clocktower. It has a garden, moderately clean single-sex dorms, laundry facilities, Internet access (US$2 per hr.), and interna-tional phone and fax services. (☎/fax 217 33 43. yellowrose1@mailexcite.com; www.yellowrose.4mg.com. Breakfast US$1. Dorms US$3; singles US$6; doubles US$9.) **Anzac House,** 61 Cumhuriyet Meydanı, across from the taxi stand, is a popu-lar spot for Aussies and Kiwis, with refurbished rooms and clean communal baths with hot showers. Perks include laundry service, Internet access, and a barbecue every evening. (☎217 01 56; fax 217 29 06; hasslefree@anzachouse.com; www.anzachouse.com. Laundry US$3; Internet access US$1.50 per hr. Breakfast US$0.75-1.50. Dorms US$3; singles US$7; doubles US$11. AmEx/MC/V.)

⌂ FOOD AND ENTERTAINMENT. Çanakkale's restaurants serve the catch of the day along the waterfront, and its bars and clubs are close by on the streets just inland. **Boğaz 2000,** 4 Saat Kulesi Meydanı, is on your left when facing the clocktower. Step inside, choose small portions, and the waiter will bring you your meal. Specialties include *döner kebap* for US$1.50, and *Kemal Paşa Tatlısı,* a dessert with cheese inside, for US$0.50. (☎214 08 88. Open daily for lunch and dinner.) Excellent *İskender kebap* (US$2.50) and *lahmacun* (US$0.45), has made **Doyum Pide ve Kebap Salonu,** on the right side of Demircioğlu Cad., up from Anzac House, a local favorite. (☎217 46 87). The best of the bars is the explosive **TNT Bar/Garden,** on Saat Kulesı Meydanı, which draws in hostelers to play pool (US$2.50 per hr.). The garden serves drinks and quality meals (US$3-5). (☎217 07 74. Open daily 4pm-3am; in winter 2pm-1am. MC/V.)

NEAR ÇANAKKALE

Several agencies provide group tours of Troy and the Gallipoli Battlefields, which generally include round-trip transportation, breakfast or lunch, an English-speak-ing guide, and admission. ▧ **TJ's Tours** (☎814 31 21; fax 814 31 21; TJs_TOURS@excite.com) offer daily Gallipoli tours (noon, US$19) and Troy tours (8:45am, US$14) when there is sufficient demand. Call ahead to reserve a space. **The Hassle Free Travel Agency,** (☎213 59 69; hasslefree@anzachouse.com; www.anzachouse.com), 61 Cumhuriyet Meydanı, has daily Gallipoli tours (Apr.-Nov. 11:45am, Dec.-Mar. 10:45am; US$19) and almost-daily Troy tours (Apr.-Nov. 8:45am, Dec.-Mar. 7:45am; US$14) that depart from Anzac House.

BATTLEFIELDS OF GALLIPOLI (GELIBOLU)

Gallipoli's battle sights and memorials are spread out, so your best bet is to take an ***orga-****nized tour (see above). Bring along your swimsuit, since tours often make a short stop for a swim. If you want to visit the area on your own, take a* ***dolmuş*** *to the Kabatepe Müzesi (☎814 12 97) from Eceabat. The museum has a good collection of memorabilia, including 2 bullets that collided in midair. Museum open daily 8:30am-noon and 1-5:30pm. US$1.20.*

The strategic position of the Gallipoli Peninsula on the Dardanelles made it the site of one of the most catastrophic Allied offensives in World War I. According to a plan proposed by Britain's young First Lord of the Admiralty, **Winston Churchill,** the Allies could conquer Constantinople, drive Turkey out of the war, and open communications with Russia by attacking at this spot. Eighty thousand Turks and more than 200,000 soldiers of the British Empire—including a disproportionate sacrifice by the Australian-New Zealand Army Corps (ANZAC)—lost their lives in the entrenched stalemate in December 1915. This battle launched its hero, **Atatürk,** on a rapid rise toward his status as Turkey's founding father. Each year, thousands of Aussies and Kiwis make pilgrimages to Gallipoli's war cemeteries, and April 25, the date of the Allied landing, is an important day of remembrance Down Under.

TRUVA (TROY)

*32km south of Çanakkale. Troy-bound **dolmuş** leave from the Çanakkale lot every 30min. until dark (US$0.75). Site and Excavation House open daily in summer 8am-7pm; otherwise 8am-5pm. Admission to both US$3, students US$1.50.*

For the casual visitor with no romantic attachment to Homer, Troy's jumbled, partially excavated ruins may well prove a disappointment. People raised on stories of the Trojan War should not get their expectations up—the city Homer wrote about came tumbling down 3000 years ago. When Heinrich Schliemann rediscovered Troy in the 1880s, it had been a ghost town for at least 13 centuries. The site is confusing and not immediately striking to the imagination, a situation hardly improved by the hokey wooden horse and academic dryness of the displays in the excavation house. The site's presentation focuses more on what people ate or how they made pottery than on the quasi-historical legacy of Homer, who was quite a storyteller but not exactly a stickler for details. Troy offers extensive ruins of unmatched significance; nine distinct strata contain the remains of different cities that stood here, dubbed Troy I (from 3200 BCE) through Troy IX. The city of Homer's *Iliad* is now believed to be Troy VI, not Troy II, the city Schliemann excavated. An illustrated explanation of each stratum is available in the **Excavation House** (on your right after passing the horse). Look out for house foundations, city walls, a temple, and a theater.

BOZCAADA (TENEDOS)

*Ferries run from Geyikli (Yükyeri dock) to Bozcaada (daily in summer 10am, 2, 7, 9pm. midnight) and back to Geyikli (daily in summer 7:30am, noon, 5:30, 8, 11pm). **Minibuses** run from the Çanakkale otogar (1hr., every hr., US$1) and arrive in Geyikli near, but not at, the ferry dock. To get to the dock, take a **dolmuş** from the bus stop to the Yükyeri dock (5min., US$0.35). Dolmuş wait for ferries coming back from the island before heading to Çanakkale (20min., US$0.60) and other local destinations. Castle open daily 10am-1pm, 2-7pm. US$1, students US$0.50.*

Sandy coves, rolling hills, a perpetual cool breeze, and plentiful wine make Bozcaada a natural paradise. The charm of the white-washed, pastel-trimmed houses of the island's only town provides a distinctively Greek feel. The island is short on residents (pop. 2500), and even the summer arrivals aren't enough to crowd the place. Beaches abound, and there's enough wine to go around; this tiny island supplies more than 10% of Turkey's wine. In antiquity, Bozcaada's wine was considered some of the finest in the world. Today's product standard has dropped a bit, but it's cheap and available everywhere except (maybe) the post office.

The well-preserved **castle** dominates the area around the harbor. The edifice was constructed in the Byzantine period and later remodeled by the Venetians, Genoese, and Ottomans. The island's main attractions, however, are its beaches and cliffs, from which you can gaze out over the cobalt sea. The best way to check it all out is by bike. **Ada Cafe**, in the main square, rents bikes and provides maps. (☎697 87 95. www.geocities.com/adaturzim. Bikes US$1 per hr., US$5 per day. Open daily 8:30-2am, off-season 8:30am-midnight.) The beautiful beaches of **Ayana, Ayazma, Solubahçe,** and **Habbele** are the best on the island and also the most popular, though they are rarely crowded.

AEGEAN COAST

Fabulous classical ruins and a sinuous coastline concealing sublime beaches have helped transform Turkey's once-tranquil Aegean coast into an increasingly popular destination. Framed by 5000 years of mythology and history, the region's rich culture is an eyeful for photographers, archaeologists, nature-lovers, and pleasure-seeking travelers alike. Hellenistic ruins stand as weathered testaments to the coast's glorious heritage.

İZMİR ☎232

İzmir, formerly ancient **Smyrna** (reputed to be the birthplace of Homer), has risen from the rubble of the 1922 Turkish War of Independence to become Turkey's third-largest city. Due to İzmir's sheer size, many travelers find themselves here for a bus transfer or even an overnight stay en route to the Aegean coast's more impressive sights. The city is only worth a more extended visit between June and August, when it hosts the **International İzmir Festival,** attracting world-renowned musical, dance, and theater performers.

⊏ TRANSPORTATION

Airport Adnan Menderes, 20km south of İzmir, connects Turkey to major European cities and other Turkish cities. Take the Havaş bus from the tourist office (30min., 12 per day 4:15am-8:30pm, US$2). **Turkish Airlines,** 1/F Gazi Osman Paşa (airport office ☎274 24 24 or 274 28 00, ticket office 484 12 20, reservations 455 53 63), just up from the tourist office, runs flights to **Ankara** (1hr., US$75, students US$60) and **İstanbul** (45min., US$75, students US$60). **Intercity bus** destinations include: **Ankara** (8hr., 12 per day 9am-1am, US$9); **Antalya** (8hr., 17 per day 4am-1am, US$9); **Bodrum** (via **Selçuk;** 4hr., every hr., US$5); **Bursa** (5hr., 10 per day 9am-1am, US$6); **İstanbul** (9hr., every hr., US$11); **Kuşadası** (1hr., 7 per day 8:30am-7:30pm, US$2); and **Marmaris** (5hr., every hr. 8am-9pm, US$7). For **Selçuk,** take a Bodrum or Kuşadası bus and tell the driver where you're going (1hr., US$2). To get to the city center and to Basmane from the **Yeni Garaj,** İzmir's new intercity bus station, take **local bus** #601, 605, 50, 51, 53, 54, or 60.

✺🔁 ORIENTATION AND PRACTICAL INFORMATION

Cumhuriyet Meydanı, on the waterfront, is the city's financial center. Many budget hotels and inexpensive restaurants, along with several bus company offices and the **Basmane train station,** are located around **9 Eylül Meydanı,** the center of the Basmane district. Many banks have offices along the waterfront.

🔏🔁 ACCOMMODATIONS AND FOOD

Head for 9 Eylül Meydanı and don't look back. To reach the **Lâleli Otel,** 1368 Sok. No. 5-6, walk 1 block from 9 Eylül Meydanı on 1369 Sok. and turn left. All rooms have showers and ceiling fans. (☎484 09 01 or 484 09 02. Breakfast US$1. US$5 per person. AmEx/MC/V.) **Hotel Oba,** 1369 Sok. No. 27, four blocks west of 9 Eylül Meydanı (away from the train station), is more expensive, but has great amenities, including a lobby bar. Each room has a private bath, TV, and air-conditioning. (☎441 96 05 or 441 96 06; fax 483 81 98. Breakfast included. US$11 per person.) **Güzel İzmir Lokantaları,** No. 8/B at the Basmane end of the 1369 Sok., is the best *lokanta* in the vicinity, serving up traditional dishes in a clean setting. Meat dishes US$1, vegetable dishes US$0.75. Open daily 7am-11pm. A display case at the front of **Basmane Kebap Salonu,** 157/A Fevzipaşa Bul., on the dead-end leading to the train station, holds the meats from which you create a fantasy *şiş* mix (US$2-2.50). Ask for the *içli köfte* (meatballs with deep-fried batter, US$1.50 each. ☎425 50 19. Open daily 11am-11:30pm. V.)

🔁 DAYTRIP FROM IZMIR: PERGAMON (BERGAMA)

*Pergamon gazes across the river at the modern town of Bergama. Buses run to: **Ankara** (10hr., 9pm, US$11); **İstanbul** (10hr., 10am and 9:15pm, US$13); and **İzmir** (2hr., every 45min. 6am-7:30pm, US$2.25). Acropolis open daily 8:30am-6pm. US$2.25, students with ISIC card free. Asclepion open daily 8am-6:30pm. US$2.25, students free.*

Once a dazzling center of cultural activity, Pergamon did a stint as the capital of the Roman province of Asia and had one of the two largest libraries in the ancient

BLACK, WHITE, AND READ WITH ENVY In ancient times, only the **Great Library of Alexandria** (see p. 152) surpassed Pergamon's, which contained over 200,000 volumes in repositories all over the city. So great was Alexandria's jealousy of the Pergamenes' literary hoard that they made what they thought was a brilliant strategic move: they limited the flow of Egyptian papyrus to Pergamon. The Pergamenes countered by writing all subsequent volumes on parchment pages made from goat hide, an exponentially more durable, manageable medium. The scheming Alexandrians were foiled only temporarily. After the Alexandrian library burned down, **Marc Antony** and his boys plundered Pergamon's shelves and presented the pilfered publications to Cleopatra, as a token of his love to replace the charred editions. In 640 CE, the ill-fated collection was put to the torch by the **Caliph Omar.** If the books agreed with the Qur'an, Omar argued, they were superfluous, and if they disagreed with the Qur'an, they were heretical and fit for combustion.

world, second only to the one at Alexandria (see p. 152). The ruins of this great Hellenistic and Roman city dominate the top of the hill, while buildings from later eras, when the city's stature and importance declined, cling lower down at the hill's feet. Pergamon traces its roots back to the Aeolian Greeks, who built a settlement here in the 9th century BCE. The city was beautified by Philataeros, a successor of Alexander the Great, but all his work was undone by an earthquake in the 2nd century CE and subsequent kicks to the proverbial stomach from various ancient conquerors.

From the river (near the Pension Athena), cross the bridge and head up the hill through the old town. Follow the paved road until you come upon a gate, and take the path to the right of the gate (which eventually turns into a stone-paved road) up to the temples and marble ruins of the **Acropolis** looming over the city. On your way up, take in the breathtaking view of the Hellenistic **theater** that once seated 10,000. Farther up, try to land three coins on top of the column inside the **wishing well** for good luck. Follow the yellow signs from Atatürk Meydanı on the west side of town to reach the famed **Asclepion,** an ancient healing center where the foremost doctor of the ancient world, Galen (born in Pergamon), once worked. A marble colonnade, theater, and healing rooms remain visible today. Near the river and the old part of Bergama stand the remnants of **Kızıl Avlu,** a pagan temple that became one of the Seven Churches of the Apocalypse mentioned in the Book of Revelations—"this is where Satan has his altar" (Rev. 2:3).

SELÇUK   ☎ 232

Selçuk serves as the most convenient base from which to explore nearby Ephesus, and offers several notable archaeological sites of its own. The Selçuk castle dominates the city's skyline, and the Basilica of St. John (where the apostle John is buried), the İsa Bay Camii, and the ruins of the Temple of Artemis lie just below. The House of the Virgin Mary *(Meryemana)* can also be reached from Selçuk. Selçuk is home to the famous Camel Wrestling Festival, held annually during the third weekend of January near Pamucak Beach, a short *dolmuş* ride away (contact the tourist office for more information).

▐ TRANSPORTATION

Buses: The **otogar** is at the intersection of Şahabettin Dede Cad. and Atatürk Cad. To: **Ankara** (9hr.; 6:30, 11am, 11pm; US$10); **Bodrum** (3hr., every hr. 8:15am-1:15am, US$4.50); **Fethiye** (6hr., every 2hr. 8:15-1:15am, US$7); **İstanbul** (10hr.; 5 per day 9:45am-12:30pm US$10); **İzmir** (1hr., every 30min. 6:20am-8:30pm, US$1.25); **Marmaris** (4hr.; every hr. 8:45am-7:45pm, midnight, US$5). From May-Sept., you can take a bus directly to **Pamukkale** (3hr.; 8:45, 9:15, 9:45am, 4, 5pm; US$5). In off-season, you must go first to **Denizli** (3hr.; 10:30am, 1, 4, 5:30pm; US$3.75) and then catch a *dolmuş* to **Pamukkale** (20min.).

Minibuses: Run to **Kuşadası** (20min.; every 15min. May-Sept. 6:30am-11:30pm, Oct.-Apr. 6:30am-8:30pm; US$0.80).

✴️🛈 ORIENTATION AND PRACTICAL INFORMATION

The İzmir-Aydın road, **Atatürk Cad,** is one of Selçuk's main drags. **Dr. Sabri Yayla Bul.,** also called **Kuşadası Cad.,** meets Atatürk Cad. from the west, and **Şahabettin Dede Cad.** meets Atatürk Cad. from the east to form the town's main crossroads.

Tourist Office: 35 Agora Çarşısı, Atatürk Mah. (☎892 63 28; fax 892 69 45; info@selcukephesus.gen.tr; www.selcuk.gov.tr), at the intersection of Kuşadası Cad. and Atatürk Cad. Free maps. Open M-F 8am-noon and 1-5pm; Apr.-Dec. also open Sa-Su 9am-5pm.

Banks: Türkiye İş Bankası, 17 Namık Kemal Cad., İsabey Mah. (☎892 61 09 or 892 65 14), under the aqueduct. Exit the PTT, turn left, and walk 1 block. **Currency** and **traveler's check exchange** and a Cirrus/MC/Plus/V **ATM.** Open M-F 8:30am-5:30pm.

Police: (☎892 60 16). Office beside Türkiye İş Bankası, and a booth at the corner of the *otogar* on Atatürk Cad.

Hospital: (☎892 70 36), across Kuşadası Cad. from the tourist office.

Internet Access: Net House Cafe, 7/A Siegburg Cad. (☎892 23 70). To the right, off Atatürk Cad. when walking away from the *otogar.*

PTT: 1006 Sok., No. 9 (☎892 90 65 or 892 64 25), 1 block west of All Blacks Pension (away from train tracks) on Cengiz Topel Cad. Full service M-F 8:30am-12:30pm and 1:30-5pm. **Currency, traveler's check exchange,** and **phone** open daily 8am-11pm. **Postal Code:** 35920.

📭 ACCOMMODATIONS

🏠**Artemis Guest House ("Jimmy's Place"),** Atatürk Mah., 1012 Sok., No. 2 (☎892 61 91; jimmy@egenet.com.tr; www.artemisguesthouse.com). Guests are greeted with a refreshing drink; shown to a carpeted room complete with bath, towels, and fans; and invited to dinner in the garden (US$2.50) or to watch one of owner Jimmy's 100 movies. Excellent organized travel information. One of the few gay-friendly establishments in Turkey. Arranges group excursions to the *hammam* for women. Free transportation to Ephesus, and to Pamucak and Tusan beaches in the morning and from Kuşadası harbor. Internet US$0.80 per hr. Laundry US$2.50. Breakfast US$1.60. US$5 per person. 2 hotel-style rooms with A/C US$30 per night.

🏠**All Blacks Hotel and Pension,** Atatürk Mah., 1011 Sok., No. 1 (☎892 36 57; abnomads@egenet.com.tr; www.allblacks.8m.com). Named after the famous Kiwi rugby squad. Some of the nicest rooms in the budget circuit, with ultra-clean tile floors and bathrooms. Rooftop terrace with views of the fortress. Great company; wonderful staff. Free transportation to and from Ephesus, Pamucak Beach, and Kuşadası harbor. Ring the bell to enter. Guest kitchen. Laundry US$3.75 per load. Internet US$1.50 per hr. Breakfast US$1.75. Singles US$6; doubles US$9.

Australian New Zealand Guest House, 7 Prof. Miltner Sok. (☎892 60 50; www.anzturkishguesthouse.com), behind the museum. A backpacker's haven. Terrace on roof with nightly BBQs and Turkish dinners (veg. options available). Free service to Ephesus, Kuşadası harbor, and the beach. Trips to Şirince for groups of 3 or more. Boat tickets to Samos (Apr.-Nov., US$30) and winter trekking packages available. 20% discounts for trekking groups larger than 7. Laundry US$3.75 per load. Internet US$1.50 per hr. Breakfast and dinner included. Dorms US$7; double with bath US$15.

Diana Pension, Zafer Mah., 3004 Sok., No. 30 (☎892 12 65; jesseakin@hotmail.com), beyond the railroad tracks. After crossing the bridge, walk 50m with the track on your left, turn right onto 3008 Sok., walk 3 blocks, and turn left onto 3004 Sok.—or just follow the signs. Immaculate rooms, cozy garden, and terrace with views of the castle. Free transport to Ephesus and Şirince. Guest kitchen. 24hr. hot water. Laundry US$3.75. Breakfast US$1.50. US$3.75 per person with bath. Double with A/C US$19.

⬛ FOOD

Karameşe Restaurant (☎892 04 66), Tarihi İsabey Camii Önü, beside İsa Bey Camii. A maze of stone paths wind through miniature waterfalls, fountains, and gazebos. Bench seating or low tables surrounded by cushions. In the rear, a miniature zoo is home to swans, ostriches, and monkeys. All *ayran* and yogurt made with the milk from on-site cows. *Gözleme* US$1.75. *Kebap* US$1.50. *Ayran* US$0.40. Open daily 9am-3am.

Özdamar Restaurant, 33 Cengiz Topel Cad., Atatürk Mah. (☎892 00 97). Outdoor seating with a view of the castle. Dine on just about any Turkish dish imaginable. (US$0.75-2.75). Open daily 8am-midnight.

Eski Ev (Old House) Restaurant and Cafe, Atatürk Mah., 1005 Sok., No. 1/A (☎892 93 57), around the block from the PTT. Quiet dining in the garden of a century-old home. *Meze* US$1.25; bottle of Pamukkale wine US$5.25. Open daily 8:30am-1am.

◉ SIGHTS

Selçuk's archaeological sights have always been overshadowed by the towering majesty of neighboring Ephesus. However, they should not be overlooked.

BASILICA OF ST. JOHN. The colossal and unadvertised Basilica of St. John lies on the site of St. John's grave. The Byzantine church's entrance is inaccurately called the **Gate of Persecution;** believed to depict a Christian being thrown to a lion, it in fact shows Achilles slaying a lion. If it were complete, it would be the seventh-largest cathedral in the world today. *(Open daily 8am-7pm. US$1.50, students US$0.75.)*

İSA BEY CAMİİ. This stunning Selçuk mosque, built in 1375 on the order of Aydınoğlu İsa Bey, features columns taken from Ephesus, which the Ephesians had in turn pilfered from Aswan, Egypt. Inside the courtyard is an enormous collection of well-preserved Ottoman and Selçuk tombstones and inscriptions. The façade features Persian-influenced geometric black and white stone inlay. *(Open daily 10min. before and 10min. after times of prayer.)*

EFES MÜSEZİ. Back in town, directly across from the town's tourist office, Selçuk's **Efes Müzesi (Ephesus Museum)** houses a world-class collection of recent Hellenistic and Roman finds from Ephesus. Most of the earlier finds are in Vienna. The collection includes the infamous statue of **Beş** (Priapus) that graces postcards throughout Turkey, rather tastelessly displayed in peep-show setting: push the button for a 10s glimpse. While this particular piece was found in the vicinity of the Ephesian brothels, the image of the erect, and generously endowed, demi-god was actually a fairly common piece of iconographic currency in the ancient world. The museum also houses an excellent collection of statuary. *(Open daily 8:30am-noon and 1-7pm; in winter 8:30am-noon and 1-5:30pm. US$3.)*

TEMPLE OF ARTEMIS. A few hundred meters down Dr. Sabri Yayla Bul., as you walk away from town with the tourist office on your right, are the sad remains of the **Temple of Artemis.** Once the largest temple in the ancient world, it's now a reconstructed column twisting upward from a bog that approximates the area of the temple's foundation. *(Open daily 8:30am-5:30pm. Free.)*

HOUSE OF THE VIRGIN MARY. Nearer to Selçuk than to any other town, but still a US$15 round-trip cab ride away, the tranquil House of the Virgin Mary lies 100m off the road from Ephesus to Bülbüldağı (Nightingale Mountain). About five years after the death of Christ, St. John is said to have accompanied the Virgin Mary to Ephesus, where they lived in a small house on the slopes of Bülbüldağı. It is a popular pilgrimage destination for both Christians and Muslims, who leave wishes and prayers in the form of tissue tied to chain-link screens.

✈ DAYTRIP FROM SELÇUK: EPHESUS (EFES)

*Ephesus lies 2-3km outside of Selçuk along the main Kuşadası-Selçuk road called **Dr. Sabri Yayla Bul.** The easiest way to get to Ephesus from Kuşadası or Selçuk is to take advantage of the free **shuttle** service offered by practically every hotel and pansiyon. Otherwise, to get to Ephesus from the Selçuk otogar, take a Pamucak-bound **dolmuş** toward Kuşadası (5min.; May-Oct. every 15min., Nov.-Apr. every 30min.; US$0.60). **Taxis** also run from Selçuk to Ephesus (US$4) and to the House of the Virgin Mary (9km, US$15 roundtrip including 45min. to visit the house). The site is also an easy walk (25min.) from Selçuk along a fig tree-shaded path (beside Dr. Sabri Yayla Bul.) that passes by the spectacular Ephesus Museum (see **Selçuk: Sights,** p. 657) and the Temple of Artemis. The lower entrance, which you reach by dolmuş or on foot, has **toilets** (US$0.20) and a **PTT**. Bring water and sunscreen. ☎ 892 64 02. Open daily 8am-7pm. US$5.60, students US$2.50.*

Fiery and intense, Ephesus's history has all the makings of an ancient tragedy. Out of devotion to its patron goddess Artemis, it stayed close to her colossal temple near modern Selçuk. When the harbor silted up, deteriorating into a mosquito-infested wasteland and resulting in a massive malaria epidemic, this decision proved disastrous, sealing the city's fate by the 6th century.

Ephesus' origins are equally romantic. The Delphic Oracle had prophesied that a fish and a wild boar would determine the ideal site for the city. Soon after, Androclus was passing through a seaside village where fish were being roasted along the shore. One fish, covered in burning wood, fell from the fire, igniting a nearby bush and upsetting a wild boar, who tore out from the foliage. Androclus slew the boar, and, heeding the oracle, he founded the city on the site, now 10km inland.

The ancient traveler Pausanias deemed Ephesus the "most wondrous of the Seven Ancient Wonders" and "the most beautiful work ever created by mankind." The first major structure built entirely of marble and the largest edifice in the ancient Greek world, the **Temple of Artemis** was four times as big as the Parthenon. Remarkably, the Temple of Artemis was actually built twice. It was set afire during the reign of Mad King Hesostratos in 356 BCE on the night of Alexander the Great's birth. According to legend, the pyro-king succeeded only because Artemis—watching over Alexander's birth at the time—was absent. Fittingly, Alexander himself offered to restore the temple when he passed through the city. The Ephesians, however, declined his offer and rebuilt the temple even more splendidly with their own resources and the offerings made by hundreds of thousands of pilgrims. Today, little remains of the magnificent structure. Goths sacked the sanctuary in the 3rd century, and the Byzantines followed suit.

Ephesus reached its zenith after 129 BCE, when the Romans established the province of Asia with Ephesus as the capital. After Rome, it was second only to Alexandria in population, with more than 250,000 inhabitants. St. Paul, recognizing the significance of the metropolis, arrived in 50 CE and converted a small group of Ephesians to Christianity. Not surprisingly, many perceived the development of the new religion as a threat to Artemis and Cybele (mother goddess of Anatolia) and forced St. Paul and his followers to depart. Eventually, however, Ephesus became a center of Christianity in the Roman Empire, so much so that the Ecumenical Council met here in 431. Pope Paul VI visited the site in 1967 and prayed in the ruins of Ephesus's 4th-century church to the Virgin Mary.

Stretching from early archaic times to the 6th century CE, Ephesus's glorious prosperity has not gone the way of other notable ancient cities. To this day, Ephesus boasts a concentration of Classical art and architecture surpassed only by Rome and Athens. As both the capital of Roman Asia and the site of a large, wealthy port, Ephesus accumulated almost unparalleled wealth and splendor, the marble specter of which still leaves visitors in awe. The ruins, with their extensive marble roadways and columned avenues, rank first among Turkey's ancient sites in terms of sheer size and state of preservation.

VEDIUS GYMNASIUM AND STADIUM. On the left as you walk down the road from Dr. Sabri Yayla Bul. to the lower entrance, the Vedius Gymnasium was built in 150 CE in honor of Artemis and then-emperor Antonius Pius. Beyond the vegetation lie the horseshoe-shaped remains of the city's stadium, originally constructed by the Greek architect Lysimachus and then expanded during the reign of Nero. The dual construction highlights the fundamental differences between Hellenic and Roman public entertainment. The original Greek structure would have been a semi-circular theater whose shape followed the contours of the land to add a natural emphasis to the staged dramas. The Roman stadium was built atop the old theater for the viewing of such martial spectacles as bloody gladiator games, wild beast hunts, and public executions.

ON THE WAY TO THE ARCADIANE. Of the three holy Christian sites in the Efes vicinity, only the very long, skinny building of the **Church of the Seven Councils** is in Ephesus itself. Just inside the lower entrance, a dirt path leads to the right; follow this path and turn right where it splits to the ruins of the Church. Here, the Ecumenical Council met in 431 CE to iron out the **Nestorian Heresy,** in which the bishop Nestor called into question the humanity of Christ. This was also the site of Pope Paul VI's visit in 1967. Beside the Church of the Seven Councils is the **Archbishop's Place,** which was destroyed by Arabs in the 6th century CE.

ALONG THE ARCADIANE. Back at the main entrance gate, a tree-lined path leads straight ahead to the Arcadiane, Ephesus' main drag. Running from the Grand Theater to what was once the harbor, the magnificent, colonnaded marble avenue would have been thronging with stevedores (men who unload ships' cargoes) and carts bringing wares to sell in the *agora*. The street eventually liquefied into a small marsh, and only a few marble stumps remain of the covered arcade which ran along the sides of the main road. The large expanse of column stones laid out in tidy rows to the left as you face the theater are the remnants of the **Theater Baths and Gymnasium.** This area, used in the Roman Period for training actors, is currently a focus of excavation. The **Grand Theater,** at the end of the Arcadiane, is a stunning 30m by 145m heavily restored beast. Its *cavea* (seating area), carved into the side of Mt. Pion, had a capacity of 25,000 people. (Archaeologists have used this number to estimate the population of this and other Hellenistic cities.) The hard marble and the sound-catching colonnade across the top gave the theater excellent acoustics. The *skene* (where the scenery and props stand in a modern theater) is a forest of columns, stelae, and statues dating mostly from the reigns of Claudius and Trajan. Denizens of Ephesus placed 89 golden idols of Artemis here to celebrate the goddess's annual festival each April. St. Paul railed against these same false gods. Today, the **International Efes Festival** is held here in September.

THE MARBLE ROAD. From the Grand Theater, approach the Street of Curetes by walking along the Marble Road. To your right as you walk along the Marble Road is the **agora,** which is currently off-limits, but was once a large commercial area built during the reign of Nero. A square stone in the center marks all that remains of the city's **horologium,** a sundial and water clock that kept accurate time. At the southern end of the *agora* is the **Gate of Maxeus and Mithridates,** two wealthy men who had the gate built and dedicated to the first Roman emperor, Augustus. About halfway to the Street of Curetes, on the right-hand edge of the Marble Road, stands a small metal barrier surrounding and protecting a rough-hewn inscription thought to be the **world's first advertisement.** The inscription consists of a picture of a foot, a cross, a woman, and a heart-shaped blob. The ad-wizards of the day intended this to designate the **brothel** down the road. The foot indicated the viewer's position as well as the need to walk to the crossroads ahead, represented by the cross. The heart above and to the left of the cross showed the house's position at the intersection, and the woman depicted is just that, a woman.

THE STREET OF CURETES. A slight incline signals the beginning of the Street of Curetes, which connected the city to the Temple of Artemis, now in Selçuk. Ruts in the road are evidence of the enormous concentration of traffic between the temple and the city, and gaps between the slabs reveal glimpses of the city's **sewer system.** At the very bottom of the Street of Curetes is the **Library of Celsus,** which was restored by Austrian archaeologists. A memorial to Gaius Julius Celsus and a general fount of knowledge, the library was covered with inscriptions recording important events and once contained 12,000 scrolls. The facade's frontal curvature and the slight thinning of the peripheral columns serve to create an impression of greater width. Scholars suspect that the large building behind the library is the **Temple of Sarapis,** an Egyptian god associated with grain.

Walking up the Street of Curetes from the library, the **brothel** is on your left. Romantic commerce took place by oil light in the windowless side rooms, where archaeologists unearthed the infamous statue of **Priapus,** the god of fertility, now in Selçuk's Efes Müzesi (see p. 657). Adjacent to the brothel are the **Baths of Scholastica,** built in the 5th century at the behest of a wealthy woman. You will find a **public restroom** just beyond the brothel.

Farther up the Street of Curetes on the left are the imposing ruins of the **Temple of Hadrian.** It is marked by its double-layered column construction, several friezes depicting the creation of Ephesus, and a bust of the goddess Cybele that adorns the keystone. The temple was built in 118 CE—during Hadrian's rule. This is atypical for Romans, who usually preferred to deify their emperors only after death. Covering the hillside on the right are the famous stephouses, home to the local bourgeoisie. Since they are currently under excavation, most are off limits. Farther up the hill on the left are the ruins of the exquisite **Fountain of Trajan.** A statue of the **Emperor Trajan** once stood before the fountain; today only its base remains.

Two pillars in the middle of the road mark the location of the **Gate of Hercules.** Farther uphill and to the left is the **Prytaneion.** Dedicated to the worship of **Vesta** (Hestia to the Greeks), goddess of the hearth and home, the Prytaneion contained an eternal flame that was tended by the **Vestal Virgins,** a small group of priestesses who served Vesta. Worship of Vesta was of such great significance to Romans that the Vestal Virgins were afforded social standing close to that of men.

Adjacent and in fine repair is the **odeon** (bouleterion), a small theater and meeting place that seated approximately 1500 people. The **state agora** on the right was the heart of political activity from the first century BCE until the city's final demise. On the left after the odeon lie the upper **baths.**

OTHER SIGHTS. The road that runs by the top entrance of Efes leads to the **House of the Virgin Mary** (8km, 1-1½hr. walking), where, according to a legend supported by some archaeological and literary evidence, she lived with the Apostle John and later by herself after leaving Jerusalem (see **Selçuk: Sights,** p. 657). Much closer to the Ephesus site are the **Caves of the Seven Sleepers,** easily reached by leaving Ephesus through the bottom gate, turning right at the "Seven Sleepers" sign, and walking for 10-15min. Legend has it that seven youths fleeing religious persecution under Emperor Decius slept in the cave for what they thought to be a night. Upon waking up, they discovered that they had slept for 112 years, during which time Christianity had become the official religion of the Empire. Amazed by their story, Emperor Theodosius II built a church atop the caves and decreed that the sleepers' remains be buried there. All that remains of the church is a fence in front of the cave. It is covered with tiny napkins representing wishes. The youths' tombs are at the top of the hill, abutting the fence. *(Always open. Free.)*

PAMUKKALE (HIERAPOLIS) ☎ 258

Whether as modern Pamukkale ("Cotton Castle") or ancient Hierapolis ("Holy City"), this village has been drawing the weary and the curious to its thermal springs for more than 23 centuries. The Turkish name refers to the extraordinary surface of the shimmering, snow-white limestone, shaped over millennia by calcium-rich springs. Legend has it that the formations are actually solidified cotton (the area's principal crop) that giants left out to dry. Most of the ancient terraces are currently under restoration. In any case, the site remains impressive, even its springs are not open for bathing. Overshadowed by natural wonders, Pamukkale's Roman ruins and museum have gone unadvertised by travel agencies.

⌐ TRANSPORTATION

Buses to Pamukkale stop in Cumhuriyet Meydanı in the center of **Pamukkale Köyü (village)**. Most direct buses come from Kuşadası and pass through Selçuk (3½hr.; daily May-Aug. 9am, return 5pm; US$6.50), but the more common route is through Denizli. **Dolmuş** run between Denizli and the beginning of the Pamukkale walking path, where Atatürk Cad. meets Mehmet Akif Ersoy Bul. (25min., every 15min. in summer 7am-11pm, US$0.40). Alternatively, a Pamukkale pension can arrange free pick-up from the Denizli *otogar*, with the added benefit of bypassing the barrage of pension hawkers at the *dolmuş* stop.

⚹🛈 ORIENTATION AND PRACTICAL INFORMATION

Pamukkale is roughly divided into two areas: **Pamukkale Köyü**, or village, is home to hotels and restaurants; the **Pamukkale site** contains the pools and the ruins of Hierapolis. The road to the tourist complex begins from the central square, curves around to the left (past bus company offices), and heads uphill to the site. It's also possible to ascend to the top of the deposits by climbing up the calcium mountain face starting from the main square. At the top of the hill within the site gates are: the **tourist office** (☎272 20 77; fax 272 28 82; open May-Sept. 8am-noon and 1:30-6:30pm; in winter M-F 8:30am-noon and 1-5:30pm); **tourist police** (☎272 29 09; open 24hr.); and the **PTT** (☎ 272 21 21; open M-F 8:30am-12:30pm and 1:30-5:30pm. 8:30am-7pm). **Pharmacies** can be found in the village.

🛏🍴 ACCOMMODATIONS AND FOOD

Both hotels listed have swimming pools filled with Pamukkale thermal water and offer free pickup from the Denizli bus station. With a warm welcome to backpackers, ▨ **Meltem Guest House**, Atatürk Cad., 14 Şirin Sok., just outside Cumhuriyet Meydanı, offers satellite TV with stereo sound for nightly movie showings. Owner Ali Baba runs daily trips to the red springs, his "secret waterfall," and a nearby mud bath for a "magic massage" (US$12). The tidy rooms all have baths. Enjoy the view of Pamukkale mountain from the top-floor restaurant/lounge. (☎272 24 13; fax 272 24 14; meltemmotel@superonline.com.tr. Internet US$1.20 per hr. Laundry US$4. Breakfast US$1.60. US$4 per person; dorm US$3.20; rooms with A/C and bath US$8 per person; roof US$1.60.) ▨ **Koray Hotel**, 27 Fevzi Çakmak Cad., has carpeted rooms around an inner courtyard, where guests can relax and eat their meals by the pool. It also offers TV, a bar, daily trips to Aphrodisias, Internet access, laundry, and a restaurant. (☎272 23 00; fax 272 20 95. Breakfast buffet included. Unlimited dinner buffet US$5. Singles US$16; doubles US$24.)

Most of the pensions serve better dinners than those available in town. The large buffet at the **Koray Hotel** is the best option. **Konak Sade**, on Atatürk Cad., has a traditional Turkish salon and pool-side terrace seating with a view of cornfields and the Pamukkale mountain. (☎272 20 02. Chicken US$3.40. *Kebap* US$3.80. Ice cream US$1.20. Free swimming for diners. Open daily 9am-2am.) **Gürsoy Aile Restaurant**, 3 Atatürk Cad., in Cumhuriyet Meydanı, offers simple outdoor dining. The house special is *gürsoy kebap* (US$2), but salads, omelets and pasta dishes (US$1.20) will satisfy vegetarians. (☎272 22 67. Fish US$1.60. Unlimited lunch buffet US$4. 10% student discount. Open daily 9am-midnight.)

👁 SIGHTS

BATHS. A favorite getaway for vacationing Romans almost two millennia ago, the warm baths at Pamukkale still bubble away. Elegant, shallow pools at the top of the hill gradually deepen farther down the slope, while the center of the formation is graced with intricately shaped terraces. Pools are off-limits to public bathing due to overuse, but small walkways leading down the slope still allow barefoot visitors to touch the thermal waters. Don't leave Pamukkale without a dip in the **Sacred Spring** at the Pamukkale Motel, the only place where you can still swim in the fizzy waters. On the pool's floor rest remains of Roman columns, toppled by the earthquake that created the spring. *(Open 24hr. US$3.20, students US$0.80.)*

RUINS OF HIERAPOLIS. Just past the PTT is a wire fence, with an opening 50m up. From here you can walk to the right to explore the **nymphaeum**, a fountain temple dedicated to the frisky nymphs, and remains of the 3rd-century **Temple of Apollo**. Carved into the side of the mountain, the enormous **Grand Theater** is one of the best-preserved in Turkey; many carved stage decorations and much of the 25,000-person seating area remain intact. Ancient priests performed rituals at the nearby **Plutonium** (a.k.a. *Cin Deliği* or "Devil's Hole"), a pit emitting toxic carbonic acid gas. After demonstrating the hole's potency by killing off a couple birds, the priests would duck inside while holding their breath, then reemerge having supposedly made a trip to the underworld. Down the road to Karahayıt are the north **city gate,** the ruins of a 5th-century Christian **basilica** dedicated to St. Philip (martyred here 1000 years ago), and a **necropolis,** holding some 1200 tombs and sarcophagi. These plots were prime real estate; it was believed that proximity to the hot springs and vapor-emitting cracks would ease one's trip to the underworld.

◪ DAYTRIP FROM PAMUKKALE: GEYRE (APHRODISIAS)

Buses leave daily from Pamukkale (2hr., round-trip US$10). Site open daily in summer 8am-8pm; in winter 8am-5pm. Museum open daily 9am-6:30pm; in winter 9am-5pm. Site and museum US$3.20, students US$1.20.

The ruins of Aphrodisias are still very much under excavation, but some archaeologists predict that they will eclipse Ephesus in grandeur after another 50 to 60 years of work. Ancient Greeks came here to pay respects to the goddess of love, **Aphrodite,** and ask for her blessing. Aphrodisias was well-known as a center for astronomy, medicine, and mathematics, but above all as a showcase for sculpture chiseled from the famed white and bluish-gray marble quarried in the nearby foothills. The highlights of a visit to Aphrodisias are the three magnificent structures at the back of the site. The soaring Ionic columns of the **Temple of Aphrodite** mark the original home of a famous statue of the goddess. Sculpted nearly 2000 years ago, the statue was similar in appearance to the many-breasted Artemis of Ephesus. So far, only copies of the original have been unearthed. The grand **tetrapylon,** the gateway into the ancient city, has elegant spiral-fluted Corinthian columns and floral reliefs on its pediment. Its name, which means "four gateways" in Greek, refers to the four rows of four columns that comprise the structure. The ancient 30,000-seat **stadium** is one of the most intact ever excavated. Even the marble blocks that once marked the starting line for foot races remain in the central arena. The new **museum,** near the site entrance, displays an impressive collection of Roman-era sculpture. Among the highlights are the large statues of Aphrodite, her priests, and a satyr carrying the child Dionysus.

BODRUM

☎252

Before it became the "Bedroom of the Mediterranean," the ancient city of Halicarnassus was known for Herodotus, the "father of history," and the 4th-century BCE Mausoleum of Halicarnassus, so magnificent that it was declared one of the Seven Wonders of the Ancient World. While Bodrum's night scene is the most notorious in Turkey, the surrounding Acadian Peninsula is famous for its silica beaches, lush forests, secluded swimming coves, and ancient ruins. As multitudes of Turkish jetsetters, international yachtsmen, backpackers, and package tourists attest, it's easy to get sucked into Bodrum's daily rhythm of sun, shopping, sight-seeing, and watersports—but all of these relatively innocent activities are a mere prelude to the bacchanalian delights that begin once night falls.

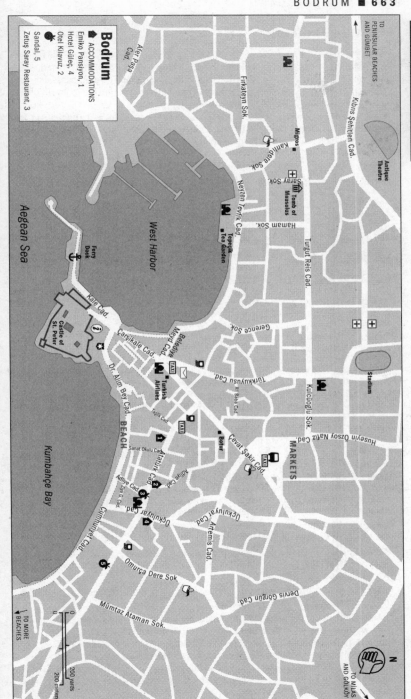

TURKEY

TO
PENINSULAR BEACHES
AND GÜMBET

Antique
Theatre

Kıbrıs Şehitleri Cad.

Fırkateyn Sok.

Migros

Kamlarie Sok.

Neyzen Tevfik Cad.

Saray Sok.

Tomb of
Mausolus

Hamam Sok.

Turgut Reis Cad.

Tepecik
tea garden

West Harbor

Aegean Sea

Ferry
Dock

Kale Cad.

Çarşıkale Cad.

Castle of
St. Peter

Gerence Sok.

Belediye
Meyd. Cad.

Türkkuyusu Cad.

Baba Cad.

Stadium

Dr. Alim Bey Cad.

Turkish
Airlines

TAXI

Taşlık Cad.

Kulcuoğlu Sok.

BEACH

TAXI

Botur

Çevat Şakir Cad.

Huseyin Özsoy Nafiz Cad.

Sanat Okulu Cad.

Atatürk Cad.

Adliye Cad.

TAXI

MARKETS

Adliye Cad.

Üçkuyular Cad.

Kumbahçe Bay

Cumhuriyet Cad.

Üçkuyular Cad.

Artemis Cad.

Omurça Dere Sok.

Derviş Görgün Cad.

TO MORE
BEACHES

Mümtaz Ataman Sok.

0   200 yards
0   200 meters

N

TO MILAS
AND GÖLKÖY

Bodrum

⚓ ACCOMMODATIONS

Emiko Pansiyon, 1
Hotel Güleç, 4
Otel Kılavuz, 2
Sandal, 5
Zetuş Saray Restaurant, 3

◰ TRANSPORTATION

Flights: The Bodrum Airport is about 45min. out of town. Buses to the airport depart from the *otogar* (US$5). The **Turkish Airlines Office** (☎317 12 03/04), has moved outside of the town's center to the Oasis shopping center in Gümbet, accessible by *dolmuş*. Open daily 8:30am-7:30pm. To **Ankara** and **İstanbul** (1hr.; 5 per day 6:00am-10:15 pm; İstanbul US$106, Ankara US$98).

Buses: The *otogar* is on Cevat Şakir Cad. To: **Antalya** (8hr., 9:30am and 10pm, US$12); **İstanbul** (12hr., 6 per day, US$19-26); **İzmir** (4hr.; 8:45am, noon; US$7); **Kuşadası** (2½hr.; 9:45am, noon; US$6); **Pamukkale** (5hr.; 8:30, 10:30am, 3:30pm; US$7.50); **Selçuk** (3hr.; 8:45am, noon; US$8).

Dolmuş: Depart from the *otogar* to **Marmaris** (3hr., every hr. 7am-8pm, US$6).

Ferries and Hydrofoils: Tickets sold through travel agents. **Bodrum Express Lines**, 18 Kale Cad. (☎316 40 67 or 316 10 87; fax 313 00 77), has offices in the *otogar* and near the castle. To: **Kos** (1½hr.; daily 9am, return 4:30pm; arrive at the jetty 30min. early for passport check); **Datça** (M, W, F 9am, return 4:30pm). Children under 11 free. Call for off-season schedule changes.

Car and Moped Rentals: Botur Agency (☎313 90 52), on Cevat Şakir Cad. Cars US$36-96 per day. Mopeds US$14-72 per day.

✳❼ ORIENTATION AND PRACTICAL INFORMATION

Streets in Bodrum are marked by small blue signs, though it is often easier to navigate using landmarks. The main streets in town radiate from the Castle of St. Peter *(Kale)*. **Cumhuriyet Cad.**, the main commercial drag, runs along the water, twisting slightly inland to allow room for a small beach before returning to the sea. Ferries, hydrofoils, and yacht cruises depart from the breakwater and **Kale Cad.**, which runs between the castle and the marina, ending at a mosque. **Belediye Meyd Cad.**, the street that hugs the port's coast between the ships and cafés, turns into **Neyzen Teyfik Cad.**, the western harbor coastal road. Through the canopy of **Carşikale Cad.**, a commercial pedestrian road, **Türkkuyusu Cad.** curves slightly to the left and **Çevat Şakir Cad.** branches to the right. **Atatürk Cad.** stems to the right off of Çevat Şakir Cad. as it moves away from the harbor.

Tourist Office: 48 Barış Meydanı (☎316 10 91; fax 316 76 94), at the foot of the castle. Pension information, room listings, and free brochures with maps. Open Apr.-Oct. daily 8:30am-5pm; Nov.-Mar. M-F 8am-noon and 1-5pm.

Travel Agencies: Botur, 24/A Çevat Şakir Cad. (☎316 90 52). Open 9am-10:30pm. Organizes bus trips to: **Pamukkale** and **Ephesus** (48hr.; W, Th 7:30am; return Su 8pm; US$54 includes overnight stay in a 4-star hotel); **Dalyan and Kaunos** (12½hr.; Th, Su 6:30am, return 8pm; US$26). **Village tour** (daily 11:30am, return flexible; US$8).

Consulate: UK, Kıbrıs Şehitleri Ca. no. 421 1B (☎317 00 93/4), in Konacik. A 15min. bus ride from Bodrum. Open M-Th 9am-12:30pm and 2:30-4:30pm.

ATMs: Cirrus/Plus/MC/V ATMs located throughout the shopping areas. **Türkiye İş Bankası** (☎316 10 12), on Çevat Şakır Cad., is about halfway between the bus station and the castle. Open M-F 9am-12:30pm and 1:30-5:30pm.

Police: 50 Barış Meydanı (☎316 10 04). At the foot of the castle, next to the tourist office. Open 24hr. **Emergency Police:** (☎316 12 15).

Pharmacies: Especially prevalent on Cumhuriyet Cad., Çevat Şakir Cad., and Atatürk Cad. All open daily 8:30am-8pm. All post the nighttime on-duty pharmacy.

Hospital: Bodrum Devlet Hastanesi (☎313 14 20 or 313 21 27), Kıbrıs Şehitleri Cad., uphill from the amphitheater. Public and open 24hr; English spoken.

Internet Access: Reklam Bigisayar Internet, 49 Atatürk Cad. (☎313 38 79), past Uçuluyar Cad. Open April-Sept. 24hr., Oct.-Mar. 9am-9pm. US$1.50 per hr. **Cyber Internet,**

30 Çevat Şakir Cad. (☎313 85 47) is a block toward the sea from the *otogar* in an alleyway to your left. Open 9am-1am. US$1 per hr. **Nese-Immuhabbet Internet Café** 85 Türkkusuyu Cad. (☎313 76 08/03) has a lounge and TV as well as Internet access. Open 10am-2am, US$1 per hr.

PTT: (☎316 12 12), on Çevat Şakir Cad., 4 blocks from the *otogar* (when heading toward the castle). **Poste Restante,** international phone, stamps, and faxes. Open daily 8:30am-midnight. **Postal Code:** 48400.

⌇ ACCOMMODATIONS

Pensions are plentiful in Bodrum. Rates rise and reservations are recommended during the high season (July and August). Cheap pensions cluster behind the PTT and to the left of the castle facing inland.

⌇ **Emiko Pansiyon,** Atatürk Cad., 11 Üslü Sok. (☎/fax 316 55 60). From the *otogar*, follow Çevat Şakir Cad. toward the water, turning left onto Atatürk Cad. After 50m, turn right down the alley marked with a blue sign for the Emiko Pansiyon, not Uslu Sok (which is the next street). Run by Emiko, a gently attentive Japanese woman, this white-washed pension offers 8 simple rooms with baths and hardwood and tile floors. Guests enjoy breakfast under the shade of grape leaves on the stone patio. Guest kitchen. Sept.-Mar. singles US$7, doubles US$12; Aug. singles US$10, doubles US$16.

⌇ **Otel Kilavuz,** No. 25 Atatürk Cad. (☎316 38 92; fax 316 2852). From the *otogar* follow Çevat Şakir Cad. toward the castle, turning left onto Atatürk Cad. After 50m, turn left onto Adliye Sok; the hotel is directly before the mosque on your right. Modern hotel with a garden, pool, and bar. Each of the 12 rooms has a large bathroom, phone, and art on the walls. Laundry free with *Let's Go*. Breakfast included. Sept.-Mar. singles US$10, doubles US$16; June-Aug. singles US$13, doubles US$20. Discounts with *Let's Go*.

Hotel Güleç, 18 Üçkuyular Cad. (☎316 52 22 or 313 73 91). From the *otogar*, take Çevat Şakir Cad. toward the sea and make a left onto Atatürk Cad. Take a left onto Üçkuyular Cad.; the hotel is on the right. Trimmed by a pleasant garden, this white-washed hotel has fresh, clean rooms replete with oak furnishings and bath. Breakfast and laundry included; discounts for large parties. Apr.-June singles US$8, doubles US$15; July-Sept. singles US$10, doubles US$22.

⌁ FOOD

Cheap eats in Bodrum consist of the usual *kebap* stands (*kebap* and chips US$3) and the small cafeteria-style joints on Çevat Şakir Cad. (meals US$2). Steaming corn on the cob (US$0.50) and baked potatoes (US$1.50) are sold from small carts on the streets.

⌇ **Sandal,** 76 Atatürk Cad. (☎ 316 91 17 or 316 35 59). Turn onto Atatürk Cad. from Çevat Şakir Cad. and walk 200m past the mosque on your right. The restaurant is on the block after Omurça Dere Sok on the right. For those craving the taste of the east, Sandal provides an extensive offering of Chinese and Thai food *al fresco*. Munch on *pad thai* under the thatched roof while listening to the rush of the outdoor waterfall. Open daily noon-midnight. Dinner around US$10. AmEx/MC/V.

⌇ **Zetaş Saray Restaurant** 12 Atatürk Cad. (☎316 68 48/47). Turn onto Atatürk Cad. from Çevat Şakir Cad. and follow it until just before the mosque on your right. Well regarded by Bodrum citizens for the high quality of its Turkish dishes, Zetaş Saray has *kebaps* (US$3) and a filling set menu (US$7-8). Veg. option available. Reservations for parties of 10+. Wheelchair-accessible. Open 9am-3am. AmEx/MC/V.

Tepeçik Tea Garden, 1 Neyze Teyfik Cad. (☎313 86 66). Follow the road along the coast away from the castle; the tea house will be on your left past a small shopping center. Gaze at the Bodrum coast under the blanket of dried *harıp* leaves or curl up like a sultan on the pillows of an Ottoman corner (*şark*) with apple tea (US$0.50) and a sandwich (US$2-5) in this government-owned tea garden. Open daily 7am-4am.

SIGHTS

RUINS OF HALICARNASSUS. Despite what everyone says about the nightlife, the ruins of ancient Halicarnassus are Bodrum's most noteworthy attraction. Unfortunately, most of the remains were either destroyed, buried beneath the modern town, or shipped to London's British Museum. The old city walls and the large but uninspiring remains of the theater are still partly visible. The **Mausoleum**, one of the seven wonders of the ancient world, once rose to a height of 50m, but Crusaders demolished the structure to fortify the Castle of St. Peter (see below). The memory of King Mausolus, here interred, lives on in the word *mausoleum*. Covered with a pyramidal roof, the mausoleum was crowned by a statue of Mausolus driving a chariot drawn by four horses. Today the mausoleum site houses a small porch with reconstructions of the mausoleum's friezes and an open-air museum with columnar fragments. *(To reach the Theater, take a* dolmus *toward Gümbet on Kibris Sehitler Cad. Ask to get off when you see the ruins to your right. To reach the mausoleum, take Kulucüoglu Sok. from behind the otogar; it will be on your right. Theater and Mausoleum open Tu-Su 8am-noon and 1-5pm. US$2.50, students US$1.)*

CASTLE OF ST. PETER. Crusaders from the Knights of St. John decimated the nearby Mausoleum of Halicarnassus to construct Bodrum's formidable castle over the ruins of an ancient acropolis during the 15th and 16th centuries. Decorated with 249 coats-of-arms, the castle towers have been dubbed the English, French, German, and Italian Towers after the nations responsible for their construction. Despite their extensive fortifications, the Crusaders' towers were no match for Süleyman the Magnificent's forces, who overpowered the knights in 1523. Under Ottoman rule, the castle's importance waned, and in 1895 it was converted into a prison; it now houses a museum with maritime and cultural exhibits. *(The Castle is the central landmark in Bodrum. Facing the sea on the harbor, walk left for 300 ft. toward the ferries.* ☎ *316 25 16. Open Tu-Su 8:30am-noon and 12:30-5pm. US$5, students with ISIC free.)*

🎵 **ENTERTAINMENT**

Bodrum, a.k.a. the "Bedroom," can be a wild flesh-pot whose excesses seem to bring out everyone's extremes. Loud, exciting discos and calm, sophisticated bars are merely the foreplay to what goes on when the music dies down. Most clubs also open daily as restaurants. Prices rise in July and August. For a wild taste of England in Turkey, hop over the western ridge of Bodrum to Gümbet, where more discos and bars can be found glittering in the night (30min. walk or 10min. *dolmuş* ride; *dolmuş* leave the *otogar* every 5min.; US$0.60).

■ **Halikarnas Disco,** Z. Müren Cad. On the hill at the end of Cumhuriyet Cad., 1km from the center of town. The 2nd-largest open-air disco in the world, this famed colosseum of rhythm juts out into the ocean, where its strobe lights reflect off the sails of nearby yachts. The club's dressed-to-be-seen clientele makes serious moves on the dance floor, while spectators gaze from above. Daily shows featuring 25 performers, great music, and a celebrity-style entrance tunnel make this club the definitive Bodrum experience. US$12 cover charge includes 1 drink. **Foam parties** on Sa in Jul. and Aug. Beer US$3.

■ **Temple** (☎316 17 21). A popular club where excitable dancing coincides with sly socializing, as the spasmic dance floor lights dart above the flicker of candlelight from the dark wooden bar. Beer US$2. *Rakı* US$2. Cocktails US$3-6. Open daily 7pm-5am.

■ **Hadi Gari** (☎313 80 97). Next to the luminous castle, the oldest disco in Bodrum fuses elegance and funkiness. Stylish customers get down under twinkling white lights on the large outdoor dance floor. Others recline on plush rose and silver cushions in the softly lit interior. An unbeatable view of Bodrum's colorful nightlife. Beer US$3; *rakı* US$4; cocktails US$7-9. Open daily 6pm-4am.

Ora Bar, 17 Cumhuriyet Cad. (☎316 39 03). A swanky candle-lit interior with the feel of a castle, where a lively, polished crowd bustles from table to table to the sounds of rock and pop. Popular with a vivacious Turkish crowd. Beer US$2.40; *rakı* US$3; cocktails US$4-6; prices strangely higher on Muslim holidays. Open 7pm-4am.

MEDITERRANEAN COAST

Alternately chic, garish, and remote, Turkey's Mediterranean coast stretches along lush national parks, sun-soaked beaches, and expansive pine forests. Natural beauty and ancient ruins have made the western Mediterranean one of the most touristed regions in Turkey. While increasingly over-run with pushy touts, Armani sportswear and mega-hotels, the western coast also caters to the backpacker circuit. By day, travelers take tranquil boat trips, hike among waterfalls, and explore submerged ruins; by night, they exchange stories over *Efes*, dance under the stars, and fall asleep in seaside pensions and treehouses.

MARMARİS ☎252

Marmaris's popularity with tourists has engendered a peculiar blend of tradition and transaction. The town bazaar sells both finely crafted traditional wares and forged signature accessories, and local fishermen are increasingly doubling as tour guides ready to ferry tourists to and from uninhabited coastal crannies. Native charm packaged for tourists can be found in this tacky pleasure-haven's namesake, Marmaris Castle. The town owes its name to Süleyman the Magnificent's order to "hang the architect" *(mimarı as)*; exactly what was so distasteful about this understated castle is hard to say, as throngs of appreciative international tourists swarm to the landmark each summer.

◤ TRANSPORTATION

Buses: To reach the *otogar* (☎412 30 37), walk down Ulusal Egemenlik Bul. from the statue and make a sharp right onto Mustafa Münir Elgin Bul. after the Türk gas station. The bus station is on the left, around the corner from the shopping center. Buses run to: **Ankara** (10hr.; 10am, 9pm; US$14); **Antalya** (7hr., 10am and 11pm, US$12); **Bodrum** (3¾hr., 8:30am-5:30pm, US$6); **Eskişehir** (10hr., 7pm, US$16); **Göreme** (14hr., 3pm, US$18); **İstanbul** (12½hr., 7 per day 9am-1pm, US$18); **İzmir** (4½hr., 5:15am-3am; US$10); **Konya** (10hr.; 4:40, 6:40, 10pm; US$14); **Kuşadası** (5hr., 10:45am, US$9); **Pamukkale** (4½hr., 8:15am-5:15pm, US$7).

Dolmuş: Inter-city dolmuş: From the hub at the Tansaş Shopping Center to: **Dalaman** (2hr., every 30min., US$4); **Fethiye** (3hr., 7:30am-11pm, US$5); **İçmeler** (10min., every 5min. 7am-1am, US$0.50); **Köyceğiz** (1hr., every 30min. 7:30am-10pm, US$2); **Milas** (2½hr., 8:30am-9:30pm, US$6); **Muğla** (1hr., every 30min. 9am-midnight,

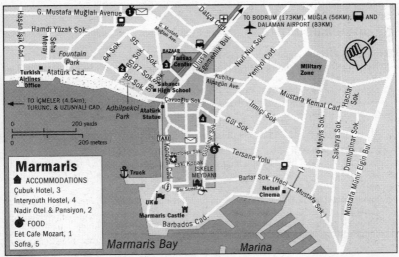

Marmaris

▲ ACCOMMODATIONS
Çubuk Hotel, 3
Interyouth Hostel, 4
Nadir Otel & Pansiyon, 2

✉ FOOD
Eet Cafe Mozart, 1
Sofra, 5

US$1.50); **Ortaca** (1½hr., 7:30am-10pm, US$3.50). **Kalkan** and **Kaş** can be reached from Fethiye, and **Dalyan** can be reached from Ortaca. **Local Dolmuş:** Two main inner-city *dolmuş* routes both start at Tansaş Shopping Center.

✳🛈 ORIENTATION AND PRACTICAL INFORMATION

From the bus station, outside of town on Mustafa Münir Elgin Bul., take a dolmuş (US$0.40) or taxi (US$3) to the town center. There, on **Ulusal Egemenlik Bul.**, are the **Tansaş Shopping Center,** bus offices, and the *dolmuş* hub. Across from a large school at the intersection of Ulusal Egemenlik Bul. and the sea, the **Atatürk Statue** is a good reference point. Facing the water at the monument, turn left down **Kordon Cad.** to reach the tourist office and harbor. **Barlar Sok.** (Bar Street), the bazaar, and the **castle** are also to the left. **Atatürk Cad.** and **Uzunyalı Cad.** run from the right of the statue. Atatürk Cad. leads to the popular waterfront walkway and public beach before veering right and becoming **Kemal Seyfettin Elgin Bul.** Most smaller streets are numbered Soks. labeled with small blue signs.

Tourist Office: (☎412 10 35; fax 412 72 77), 250m down Kordon Cad. English-speaking and very helpful. Open May-Sept. daily 8:30am-7:30pm; Oct.-Apr. M-F 8am-5pm.

Budget Travel: Interyouth Hostel, Tepe Mah., 42 Sok No. 45 (☎412 36 87; fax 412 78 25; interyouth@turk.net), can help find cheap airline, bus, and boat tickets. Jeep and moped rentals. There's also an extraordinary Backpacker's Cruise on the hostel's beautiful yachts (US$200 for 5 days).

Consulates: UK (☎412 64 86 or 412 64 87; fax 412 50 77), in the Yeşil Marmaris office building on the harbor, around the corner from the tourist office. Open M-F 7:30am-noon and 2:30-5pm.

Police: (☎412 14 94), on 49 Sok., by Kordon Cad., past the PTT. Little English spoken.

Hospital: Public Devlet Hastanesi (☎412 45 49 or 412 10 29), on Datça Yolu Üzeri. From the Atatürk statue, walk 500m up Ulusal Egemenlik Bul., turn left on Datça Cad., and continue 900m uphill.

Internet Access: There are many cyber cafes in the bazaar, especially at the entrance. Most have A/C, charge US$1.50 per hr., and are open daily 9am-midnight. **The Blue Internet Cafe** (☎413 63 28) is on Mustafa Muğlalı Cad., past Tansaş Cad.

PTT: The main PTT (☎412 12 12), on Mustafa Muğlalı Cad., is on the right side heading inland from the Atatürk statue. Open daily 8:30am-midnight. A smaller branch is in the bazaar, to the left off Kordon Cad.

Postal Code: 48700.

🏠 ACCOMMODATIONS

▓**Interyouth Hostel,** Tepe Mah., 42 Sok. No. 45 (☎412 36 87; fax 412 78 23; interyouth@turk.net). Not to be confused with the imposter Interyouth Hostel at Kemeraltı Mah., the real deal is deep within the bazaar. From the Tansaş Shopping Center, enter the bazaar and make your 1st right. The hostel features a book exchange, Internet access (US$4 per hr.), international phone, free videos, and laundry (US$5). Can arrange cheap travel. Breakfast in the terrace bar and nightly spaghetti dinners (7:30pm, free for guests). 4-night cruises US$200 per person. Dorms US$5; July-Aug.: US$6; private room US$12. US$1 discount for ISIC, HI, and IYTC holders.

Sezin Apart-Otel (☎413 61 43; fax 413 14 55). From Mustafa Muğlatı Cad., take a right onto 98 Sok. past the PTT, and then a left onto 91 Sok. The lap of luxury, with a pool, bar, and enormous rooms, each with bath, private kitchen, and balcony. A/C available US$15 per room; July-Aug. US$25. Discount with *Let's Go.*

Çubuk Hotel (☎412 67 74; fax 412 67 76). Head down Atatürk Cad. from the statue and turn right on the 1st street after the park; the hotel is on the left corner. 27 carpeted, pastel-hued rooms with bath, phones, balconies, and A/C. Included breakfast served in a room with parakeets. US$10 per person; July-Aug. singles US$13, doubles US$25.

Nadir Otel and Pansiyon, Kemeraltı Mah., 56 Sok. (☎412 11 67 or 412 18 06), the 1st left off Mustafa Muğlalı Cad. All rooms have TV and balcony. Ask for the side away from the shopping center. The hotel has 24 doubles with bath. Breakfast included. Singles US$12; doubles US$17; July-Aug. singles US$12, doubles US$20. The pension has 20 rooms, some with bath, no breakfast. US$5 per person; July-Aug. US$8.

TURKEY

🍴 FOOD

■ **Kervansaray Restaurant** (☎412 64 84). From the statue, head straight on Ulusal Ege-menlik Bul., turn left on Datça Yolu, and take another left on Yunus Nadi Cad.; the res-taurant is on the 1st corner on the right. For US$12, feast on a large meal with Turkish wine or beer, and enjoy live Turkish music, wrestling, and traditional folk dances. The finale features the most famous male belly dancer in Marmaris. Ask at the Interyouth Hostel for more information, as groups often go from there. Open daily Apr.-Oct.

Sofra (☎413 26 31), 3 blocks into the bazaar from the PTT, on the right. Well-recom-mended by the tourist office, Sofra serves *kebap* (US$1-3.50), lamb and mushroom dishes (US$4), and European fare (US$6) to locals and tourists alike. Enjoy the wine bottle on every table and the music from the record store across the street. Open 24hr.

Eet Cafe Mozart, Mustafa Muğlalı Cad. #1-2-4 (☎413 87 64). Head straight down Ulusal Egemenlik Bul. and turn left on the street after Tansaş Shopping Center; look for the large french-fry man by the PTT. This charming Dutch cafe/patisserie/restaurant serves European fare (fish and chips wrapped in newspaper; US$8.50). The chef is open to creating new dishes. Turkish breakfast US$2.50; English breakfast US$3; apple tart US$3; falafel US$4.40. Open daily 8:30am-12:30am.

🎭 ENTERTAINMENT

It's hard to tell which is hotter in Marmaris: the burning sun or the blazing night-life. Eleven o'clock is showtime for Barlar Sok., Uzunyalı Cad., and Barbados Cad. (the harbor), when bars and clubs kick into high gear. Loud, bright, and conta-gious music and neon lights spill onto the street.

To reach **Barlar Sok.** (Bar St.), face the tourist office and take road to the left of the office. Turn left into the bazaar at the next corner and walk straight. **Uzunyalı** is on the opposite side of Marmaris, right on the waterfront past the Atatürk Statue, with larger bars, clubs, and karaoke. **Barbados Cad.** is the pavement along the har-bor. Most bars and clubs have no cover, and all clubs feature dancing. At bars with both indoor and outdoor seating, drinks are usually cheaper outside.

Backstreet (☎412 40 48). On Bar St. An open-air tropical oasis, where ultra-hip danc-ers groove to international rock and pop while onlookers chill and pool sharks hunt under palm trees along a tiny, fish-filled creek. Beer US$2.50; *rakı* US$3.50; cocktails US$4-8. Open May-Sept. daily 9am-4am.

Greenhouse (☎412 50 71). Halfway down Bar St. Known for its cutting-edge music and comfortable setting, this electric-green, A/C dance club and bar is a Marmaris favorite. Beer US$2. *Rakı* US$3.50. Cocktails US$5-10. Open daily 9pm-5am.

Beach Club (☎412 11 88). On the beach at the far end of Uzunlyalı. Famous for its cabana-like exterior decorated with fluorescent surfboards and zebra-print bar stools, plus an outdoor bar painted with tropical fish. Inside, the sophisticated surroundings reverber-ate with the top-notch electronic sounds of hip-hop, house, and Top 40. Beer US$1.20-2; *rakı* US$2; cocktails US$5. Open daily 8am-4am in winter Sa-Su 8am-4am. 18+; single men usually not admitted.

Magic Garden Bar (☎413 12 96), on the right at the beginning of Bar Street. This col-orful refuge is a great place to talk and people-watch. Sit at jungle-green terrace tables under a canopy of grapes. Cider US$3. Special mixed drinks US$7. Open daily 2pm-4am.

TURKEY

SAND AND SURF

BEACHES. Only 1500m away, Günlücek National Park offers a small, quiet beach and picnic tables set against a forest of fragrant frankincense trees. Follow the harbor road past the marina and across the wooden footbridge, or catch a *dolmuş* from in front of the Tansaş Shopping Center (US$0.40). While the crowded beach in Marmaris proper is lively, quieter and prettier beaches in the area are accessible only by boat. Pleasant İçmeler beach is an easily reached exception. *Dolmuş* from the front of Tansaş Shopping Center or anywhere along Atatürk Cad go to İçmeler (10min., every 5min. 8am-1am, US$0.50), or take the water *dolmuş* to İçmeler from the waterfront next to the tourist office (20min., in summer 7am-7pm, US$4).

BOAT TRIPS. Water *dolmuş* going to **Turunç Beach** depart from the waterfront behind the Atatürk statue (45min., in summer every hr. 7am-7pm, US$1). Full-day boat tours stop at **Paradise Island Beach**, the **Akvaryum** (aquarium), and some phosphorous caves. Others go to **Dalyan and Kaunos,** including **Turtle Beach** and the mud baths (US$18). Most continue to the **Gölenye Springs,** whose waters reputedly cure intestinal ills; the less crowded **Kumlu Buk Beach,** near the remains of a fortress; and the tiny village of **Keçi,** in the heavily-wooded Nimara Peninsula (US$10-15 per person; lunch included). Legends say that Marc Antony imported the white sand from the Red Sea some 2100 years ago in an attempt to get Cleopatra into the sack. Those less romantically-inclined suspect that fossilized plankton make the sand so white. Take a boat to **Kleopatra's Island** through an organized tour (45min., in summer 17 per day from 10:30am, return 7pm.) Book through a travel agency.

FETHİYE
☎252

A big city with a small-town feel, Fethiye rests peacefully on a harbor surrounded by pine forests and mountains. Its inexpensive pensions and nearby islands make it a popular stop on the Mediterranean backpacker circuit. Still, Fethiye has managed to maintain its calm, leaving the carousing to its southerly neighbor Ölüdeniz.

■ TRANSPORTATION. Ulusoy (☎612 37 37), **Kamil Koç** (☎612 06 36 or 614 19 73), and **Pamukkale** (☎614 14 51 or 614 19 99) bus companies serve Fethiye and have offices on Atatürk Cad. The *otogar* is on Ölüdeniz Cad. Buses running along the coastal road can drop off passengers anywhere, so there's no need to wait for a bus to a specific destination. Ulusoy, Kamil Koç, and Pamukkale send buses to: **Alanya** (5hr., 2:15pm and 2:15am, US$9); **Ankara** (9hr., 10 and 11pm, US$15); **Antalya** (4hr., 2:15pm and 2:15am, US$7); **Bodrum** (4½hr., 3:30am and 4pm, US$8); **Bursa** (10hr., 5 and 10:30pm, US$15.50); **Cappadocia** (13hr., 6pm, US$14.50); **Eskişehir** (7hr., 5 and 10:30pm, US$13.50); **İstanbul** (13hr.; 5, 9, 10:30pm; US$18.50); **İzmir** (6½hr., US$9.50); **Kaş** (2hr.; 3, 7, 9, 10am; US$3); **Marmaris** (3hr., 2pm, US$5); **Pamukkale** (4½hr, 7 per day 7am-6:30pm, US$6.50). To reach **Selçuk,** take the İzmir bus and change in Aydın. *Dolmuş* run from the stop near the intersection of Hastane and Atatürk Cad. to: **Çalış Beach** (15min., every 3min. 6am-12:30am, US$0.35); **Ölüdeniz** (20-25min., every 5min. 7am-12:30am, US$1.15); **Kayaköy** (40min., every hr. 7am-10pm, US$1.50); **Saklıkent** (1hr., every 20min. 7:30am-5pm, US$2). On Atatürk Cad., across from the Atatürk head, there is a **24hr. taxi service** (☎614 44 77).

■■ ORIENTATION AND PRACTICAL INFORMATION. The *otogar* is 2km from the center of town, on the way to Ölüdeniz. If there are no *servis* shuttles to the town center, leave the terminal, cross the street, and wait for a *dolmuş* heading to Fethiye (about 10min., frequent, US$0.40). The *dolmuş* runs on the main street, **Atatürk Cad.,** past a mosque, PTT, and the Atatürk head on a pedestal. As the harbor ends, Atatürk Cad. becomes **Fevzi Çakmak Cad.** Facing the PTT, the harbor, tourist information office, and old town are on the left. The ritzy **Çalış Beach** is to the right along **Sedir Sok.,** which becomes **Akdeniz Cad.** Near the PTT and the edge of the bazaar, **Çarşı Cad.** branches off Atatürk Cad. The **Tourist Office** is at 1/A İskele Meydanı, at the end of the harbor, past the Atatürk head and antique theater, toward the *jandarma*. (☎/fax 612 19 75. Open daily 8:30am-5pm; in winter M-F 8:30am-5pm.) **Fetur,** past the tourist office on Fevzi Çakmak Cad., arranges flights and tours. (☎614 20 34; fax 614 38 45; www.fethiye-net.com. Open daily 8:30am-5pm; in winter M-F 8:30am-5pm.) The **European Diving Center** (☎614 97 71; fax 614 97 72), on Atatürk Cad. in the bazaar, offers beginning and advanced scuba dives for US$64. Several banks with 24hr. **ATMs** line Atatürk Cad. **Money exchange** open daily 8:30am-5:30pm. The **Police** (☎614 10 40) are around the corner from the tourist office, near the ancient theater. A larger branch (☎614 13 09) is on Atatürk Cad., across from the PTT. **Kestepli Eczanesi Pharmacy** is across from the mosque. The **Letöon Hospital,** on Patlanak Mahaller Cad., has English-speaking doctors. (☎612 54 84. Open 24hr.) Public hospital **Devlet Hastanesi** (☎614 40 17 or 614 40 18) is near the PTT at the intersection of Atatürk and Hastane Cad. **Internet Cafe,** on Atatürk Cad. next to Imagine Bookstore, has Internet access. (US$1.80 per hr. Open daily 9am-midnight.) The **PTT,** on Atatürk Cad., offers **Poste Restante,** international phone calls, money exchange, and fax. **Postal Code:** 48300.

▐▐ ACCOMMODATIONS AND FOOD. Cheap pensions cluster around Hastane Cad. and Fevzi Çakmak Cad. To reach **Ideal Pension** take a left up the large hill as the harbor ends. The peach-colored exterior gives way to helpful, friendly service and 34 clean and orderly rooms. (☎614 19 8; idealpension@hotmail.com; www.idealpension.net. US$7 per person.) **Ferah Pansiyon,** 2 Karagözler Ordu Cad. No. 21, is one of the best hostels in Turkey, with spacious rooms (most with bath) and a free pool. (☎/fax 614 28 16; call for free pickup from the *otogar*. Breakfast included. Laundry US$3. Dinner US$5. Dorms US$3.60; rooms US$10-12.) **Meğri Lokantası,** Cumhuriyet Mah. 13/A Çarşı Cad., off Atatürk Cad. by the harbor, features an enormous selection of sumptuous Turkish fare. (☎614 40 74. *Mezze* US$1.40, *şiş* US$3.60. Open 24hr.) **Yörükoğlu,** on Çarşı Cad., serves huge "Turkish burritos" for US$2. (☎612 20 64. Open daily 8am-1am.) The large, outdoor **Meğri Restaurant,** in the main square of the bazaar, specializes in fresh fish. (☎614 40 47. Fish US$4-7. *Mezze* US$2. Open daily 9am-1am.)

▐ ENTERTAINMENT. Ottoman Bar, on the right, before Maman Sok. runs into Çarşı Cad., is fit for a *pasha:* fragrant smoke drifts from the large selection of water pipes as the crowd lounges outdoors or dances. (☎612 11 48. Water pipe US$3.60; beer US$1.80; *rakı* US$2. Open daily noon-3am.) **Car Cemetery Bar,** 33 Hammam Sok., across from the old *hammam* in the old city, offers beer amidst deceased car parts. Cocktail names like "sperm of the barman" will be sure to spice up your evening. (☎612 78 72. Beer US$1.80; *rakı* US$2; cocktails US$4-6. Open daily 10am-4am.) Everybody dance now at tourist favorite **The Music Factory,** on Hammam Sok., a pumping metallic cage with two levels of flashing dance floors. (☎617 51 72. Beer US$1.80; *rakı* US$2. Open daily 5pm-5am.)

NEAR FETHİYE

ÖLÜDENİZ AND THE BUTTERFLY VALLEY

*Small wooden **dolmuş boats** heading to Butterfly Valley leave from the beach to the right of Ölüdeniz (45min.; 11am, 2, 4pm; return 1, 5pm; US$3 each way). Fancier **yacht tours** will also take you on a daytrip that includes Butterfly Valley for a much higher price.*

The town of Ölüdeniz's main attraction is the **Blue Lagoon,** an idyllic peninsula cradled in wooded hills and lapped by shining clear water. Enter from Tabiat Park, on the right of the road from Fethiye, where potable water, bathrooms, and showers are available. The next best thing to swimming in the Blue Lagoon is seeing it from above while tandem **paragliding,** available through **Sky Sports Paragliding** (☎617 05 11; fax 617 03 24; info@skysports-turkey.com). Passengers are driven to the top of Baba Dağı and given take-off and landing instructions (2hr., US$130; book in advance). The tiny turquoise bay known as ▧**Butterfly Valley** near Ölüdeniz is home to waterfalls and several species of butterfly, including the nocturnal orange and black Jersey Tiger. From the entrance to the valley, follow the blue dots up the rocky path to the two **waterfalls**. Spending the night means camping on the beach (US$1.60 per tent), renting a mattress in the treehouse (US$3 per person), or bedding down in **The Greek Home** (US$3 per person). All accommodations have toilets and showers. Food is readily available at the local eatery (US$4 per plate). It isn't hard to find **The Rock Cafe,** built into the sides of the cliffs.

KAŞ   ☎242

Sandwiched between the deep sea and stunning mountains, cosmopolitan Kaş is refreshingly hassle-free. Its streets are lined with inexpensive, hospitable places to stay, excellent restaurants, and laid-back bars. Kaş is a great base for exploring the sunken city of **Kevova** and the beautiful beaches of the Blue Caves nearby.

📻 **TRANSPORTATION.** Buses run to: **Ankara** (12hr., 8:30pm, US$19); **Antalya** (3hr., every 30min. 7am-7:45pm, US$5.40); **Bodrum** (7hr., 9:30am, US$10); **Bursa** (12hr., 8pm, US$17); **Fethiye** (2hr.; 9, 9:30am, 6:30, 8:30, 9pm; US$2.50); **İstanbul** (15hr., 6:30pm, US$21); **İzmir** (9hr., 9am and 9pm, US$12.50); and **Selçuk** via **Aydin.** To get to **Olimpos,** take any Antalya-bound bus.

🖼🛈 **ORIENTATION AND PRACTICAL INFORMATION.** Most of the activity centers around the small harbor along the main street, **Cumhuriyet Cad.** At its west end near the mosque, Cumhuriyet Cad. intersects **Hastane Cad.** before becoming **Atatürk Cad.** At its east end near the Atatürk statue, Cumhuriyet Cad. intersects **Çukurbağlı Cad.** (also known as **Şübe Sok.**), which leads to the **PTT.** From the Atatürk statue, **Hükümet Cad.** passes above the harbor to the two beaches. The street that runs uphill behind the tourist office—the one with most of the souvenir shops—is **Uzun Çarşı Cad.** The **tourist office**, 5 Cumhuriyet Meydanı, is to the left of the Atatürk statue. (☎836 12 38. English spoken. Open daily 8am-noon and 1-7pm; in winter M-F 8am-5pm.) Nearly all **travel agencies** have tours to **Kevova. Bougainville Travel,** 10 Çukurbağlı Cad., offers diving courses, **kayaking** trips to Kekova (US$35), and **Jeep Safaris.** (☎836 37 37; fax 836 16 05. Open daily 8:30am-10pm.) **Simena Tours,** 1 Elmalı Cad. (☎836 14 16), near the *otogar*, books airline tickets and popular daytrips to **Kevova.** For emergencies, the **police** (☎836 10 24) are opposite the entrance to Küçük Çalık Plaj (Little Pebble Beach). The **hospital** (☎836 11 85) is on Hastane Cad., 500m past the mosque by the tourist office. **Munise Ozan** (☎836 41 42), offers free services and has a certified tourism doctor. The **PTT,** on Çukurbağlı Cad., does **currency exchange** until 5pm. (☎836 14 50. Open daily 8:30am-midnight.)

🛏🍴 **ACCOMMODATIONS AND FOOD.** There are many pensions on the side streets to the right of Atatürk Bul. The best is **Ateş Pension,** Yeni Cami Cad. No. 3., on the right side of Hastane Cad., uphill from the mosque. A popular backpacker hangout with simple rooms, some with bath and balcony, and an adjoining pension with stenciled flowers on the walls and mosquito nets. (Singles US$7; doubles US$14.) **Hermes Pension,** 2 İmdi Cad., 1 block from Atatürk Cad., has clean, airy rooms with bath and balcony. (☎836 32 22. Singles US$9; doubles US$14; triples US$16.) The best dining is at **Bahçe,** uphill from the monument tomb. Known for the best *mezes* this side of İstanbul, this garden restaurant does it all. Try the fish wrapped in paper (US$6.50) or the *saç kavurma* (meat cooked on the table, US$5) for a taste of house specialty. (☎836 23 70. Open daily noon-midnight.

🏖 **BEACHES.** Kaş's two main beaches are both are tucked in rocky coves surrounded by rocky cliffs. The entrance to **Küçük Çalık Plajı** (Little Pebble Beach) is at the top of the hill on Hükümet Cad., while the less crowded **Büyük Çalık Plajı** (Big Pebble Beach) is 15min. down the road to the left of the tourist office. Most travelers who pass through Kaş take a dip in the **Blue Caves,** 15km from Kaş and home to the Mediterranean's only **seal colony.**

NEAR KAŞ

KEKOVA

Trips from Kaş, often on glass-bottom boats, cost around US$30. Kayaking (US$35) allows for the best views of the ruins and some hearty exercise. Inquire at Bougainville Travel in Kaş for more details (see p. 672). In the morning it is less crowded, and the sea is calmer and clearer. You can also get to Kekova from Demre.

The Lycian city of Kekova lies submerged beneath the clear Mediterranean waters as a result of an earthquake that struck in 25 CE. During the Hellenistic and Arab eras, the city served as a lookout post and refuge from marauding pirates. From craggy Kekova Island, it is possible to see through calm water to the underwater walls and staircases (calm seas afford views sharp enough to discern details on amphoras). Above sea level, a motley assortment of doors and walls still bear evidence of long-gone floors and ceilings. The highlight of the trip is the partially submerged Lycian sarcophagus near the village of Kale. **Swimming or snorkeling among the ruins is forbidden.**

DEMRE AND MYRA

*From the otogar, **buses** run to: **Antalya** (3hr., every 30min. 7am-8:45pm, US$4); **Fethiye** (3¼hr., every hr. 9am-4:45pm, US$4); **Kaş** (1hr., every hr. 8:15am-11:15pm, US$1.50). Myra Otogar Taksi (☎871 43 43) has **taxis** at the otogar. Other services include: **banks** and an **ATM** on Noel Baba Cad., including a **Türkiye İş Bankaşı** on the way to St. Nicholas Church from the otogar (open 11am-5:30pm); a **police station** (☎871 42 21), near the otogar; and a **PTT**, 200m to the right of the T-junction. (☎871 55 19. Open 8:30am-6pm.)*

The ancient ruins of Myra, a mixture of Lycian rock tombs, sculptures, and a Roman theater, are truly awe-inspiring. St. Paul is said to have stopped here in Demre in 61 CE on his way to Rome. Demre was the diocese of St. Nicholas, better known as **Santa Claus.** The kind-hearted saint, born in Patara (60km west of Demre), became the Bishop of Myra in the early 4th century. The town has a nearby beach and cold springs accessible by car.

Myra was one of the most important cities in the Lycian League, a federation that included 70 cities, including Xanthos, Patara, Olimpos, and Tlos. Myra is divided into three areas: the **sea necropolis** in the southwest part of the site, the **acropolis** area and its surrounding walls, and the **river necropolis.** The **rock tombs** built into the sea and the river necropolis are of particularly high quality. The site also has a **theater** with 35 consecutive rows of seats and a still-intact stage. (Open daily in summer 8am-7:30pm; in winter 8am-5:30pm. US$1.15, students US$0.70.)

Demre's other major attraction is the **Church of St. Nicholas,** thought to be built on the site of the saint's tomb. An Orthodox service takes place in the theater on December 6, the anniversary of St. Nicholas's death. The 8th-century structure, which suffered centuries of neglect, was repaired by the Russian Tsar in the 19th century, only to be covered with sand and mud years later. Excavations since 1989 have uncovered new rooms and treasures, and scholars generally agree that the tomb of St. Nicholas is in the southern nave of the church. His remains were stolen in 1087 by Italian merchants and taken to Bari, Italy, leaving behind only those that appear in the **Antalya Museum** (see p. 677; open daily 9am-7:30pm; in winter 8am-5:30pm. US$5, students US$2.).

OLİMPOS ☎242

Enchanting Olimpos is a true backpacker's town, one of the few budget spots along the Turkish Riviera. Olimpos brings travelers closer to the heavens by giving them the chance to sleep in a treehouse and make a nighttime ascent of the Chimaera, where a naturally occurring flame has burned since ancient times.

▐ TRANSPORTATION

To get to Olimpos from Antalya, take a Kaş- or Demre-bound bus and ask to be let off at Olimpos. From Kaş, take an Antalya-bound bus. **Buses** stop at a rest station

"YES, PLEASE" The Turkish language is replete with multipurpose expressions. One particular favorite is *"çok güzel,"* literally "very beautiful," which can be used in reference to pretty much anything one finds agreeable. Another is *"buyurun,"* from the verb *buyurmak* meaning "to order" or "to command." *"Buyurun"* is a prompting word used in a number of different contexts. A waiter bringing food might use it to express "here you are," or a shopkeeper might use it to express "what can I do for you?" The possibilities are endless. Sadly, the linguistic wizard charged with teaching English to generations of Turks decided that there was a direct English translation of *"buyurun:"* specifically, "yes, please." Not only does "yes, please" make no sense in the contexts in which it is so often used by Turkish restaurateurs and hawkers, but the equivalent Turkish *"evet, lütfen"* is equally nonsensical. When you think you'll turn murderous the next time you hear "yes, please," keep in mind that the speaker is trying to find the equivalent of a friendly and welcoming—and untranslatable—expression.

on the main road. From there, **dolmuş** run down the 10km dirt road that leads to the treehouses (15min., every hr. 8:30am-10pm, US$1.25), dropping passengers off at the pensions of their choice. From Olimpos, *dolmuş* return to the main road (15min., every hr. 8am-6pm, US$1.25).

ⓘ PRACTICAL INFORMATION

Olimpos has no PTT, pharmacy, bank, or police station. Many pension owners accept US dollars, offer international phone calls, and arrange tours that include trekking or rafting. **Postal Code:** 07350.

ⓘ ACCOMMODATIONS

All prices for treehouses include breakfast and dinner. **Bayram's Treehouse Pension,** on the beach, has colorful bungalows and a friendly staff. (892 12 43; fax 892 13 99. US$7 per person.) **Şaban Pansiyon** is a welcoming family-run pension with tasty dinners and 24hr. service to Antalya airport for US$42. (☎892 12 65. US$7 per person; doubles US$20; camping US$6.) More like a sprawling Ewok village than a pension, **Kadir's Yörük Treehouses** is a post-adolescent summer camp: volleyball and ping-pong included. (☎892 12 50; fax 892 11 10. Dorm beds US$6; doubles US$14; bungalows US$13 per person.) Kadir's hits puberty after dark, though, when it becomes the focus of Olimpos nightlife (beer US$1.15; cocktails US$2.35).

ⓖ SIGHTS

■ **CHIMAERA.** Olimpos's proximity to this perpetual natural flame in the mountainside (once so bright that ships navigated by it) inspired the residents of the city to worship Hephaestos, god of fire and the forge. Today's Olimpians are less reverent: most bring marshmallows to toast. The ancients believed the flame was the breath of the Chimaera, a mythical beast that was part lion, part goat, part serpent—and pure evil. Geologists have not produced a better explanation, but they suspect natural gas plays a role. *(Best seen at night. Ask pension owners about bus tours (2½hr., 9:30pm, US$2.80). Bring a flashlight for the tricky 20min. uphill trek to the flame.)*

RUINS. The ruins at Olimpos are a jumbled pastiche of everything from ancient temples to crumbling walls of medieval castles. Follow the road from the pensions to the beach. The ruins tend to be overgrown with vines and dry bushes, and inhabited by **snakes** and **scorpions,** so be very cautious when exploring the site. About 10m beyond the entrance booth, you can cross the dry river bed to reach a row of tombs and one of the crumbling arches. If you continue on the main path about 40m farther, a small path leads off to the left, climbing uphill past the overgrown **necropolis** to a rather large but unimpressive **archway.** Beyond the archway it is easy to get lost in overgrown orange groves and reeds. The sign at the beginning of the pathway reads simply "temple."

On the other side of the road across the stream are the decrepit **theater** and **medieval walls.** Though it is not unusual to see locals at the stream swimming and drinking, tourists should avoid doing so. Continuing along the main path leads to the **Harbonu memorial tombs** just before the beach, where the best of the ruins loom over the water on a rocky cliff to the right. *(Open 8am-7pm. US$5, students US$2. Hold on to your ticket stub, as it will be good for multiple entry to the beach and site.)*

ANTALYA   ☎242

Capital of the so-called Turquoise Riviera and linked by air with Munich, Moscow, and Amsterdam, Antalya is a city of many faces. This busy metropolis encircles Kaleiçi ("inside the fortress"), the crescent-shaped old city that brims with cobblestone streets, Ottoman houses, tourist businesses, and carpet dealers. At Kaleiçi's heart, pricey eateries and cutting-edge nightclubs line the ancient walled harbor that once sheltered Roman ships and now welcomes luxury yachts.

▐ TRANSPORTATION

Flights: Antalya International Airport, 15km from town (domestic flight info ☎330 30 30, international flight info 330 36 00). **THY** (reservations ☎444 08 49) has an office on Cumhuriyet Cad., next to the tourist office. Open M-F 10am-7pm, Sa-Su 9am-5:30pm. Buses run between THY and the airport (10 per day 4:45am-2:30am, US$3). Flights to **İstanbul** (US$61, students US$51; round-trip US$79, students US$61).

Buses: To: **Ankara** (10hr., 10am-midnight, US$12); **Fethiye** (5hr., 10:30am, 12:30, 11pm, US$6); **Cappadocia** (9hr.; 8:30, 9:30, 10pm; US$15); **İstanbul** (12hr., 9:30am-11pm, US$16); **İzmir** (8hr., 6:30am-midnight, US$12); **Kaş** (3hr., every 30min. 5:45am-8pm, US$5).

Dolmuş: Antalya has 2 *dolmuş* hubs. **Doğu Garaj** sends *dolmuş* to **Lale** and **Lara Beaches.** To get there from Atatürk Cad., turn right on Ali Çetinkaya Cad., walk 1 block, and turn right at the Start Hotel. The **Meydan Garajı,** at the intersection of Mevlâna Cad., Aspendos Bul., and Ali Çetinkaya Cad., 1.5km from the city center, has *dolmuş* to **Perge** and **Aspendos.** *Dolmuş* to and from the *otogar* are white with a blue stripe.

Trams: A new tram system runs from the Antalya Museum along Cumhuriyet Cad., then down Atatürk Cad. to the stadium (every 20min., US$0.25). Blue signs mark stops.

✸ ▐ ORIENTATION AND PRACTICAL INFORMATION

In 1997, Antalya gave birth to a gargantuan orange **otogar,** replete with fountains, several **ATMs,** cafes, air-conditioning, and labyrinthine bathrooms with seat toilets. Unfortunately, this wonderland is 4km out of town at **Anadolu Kavşağı,** the intersection of Namık Kemal Cad. and Dumlupınar Bul. Gray buses (US$0.40) run from outside the *otogar* to the city center, near **Kaleiçi,** the old city. **İşıklar Cad.,** at the intersection of **Kazım Özalp Cad.** and **Cumhuriyet Cad.,** is marked by a brick-red fluted minaret and a stone clocktower. Hostels, restaurants, and historically important ruins and buildings, are in this area. The two beaches are on the outskirts of town.

Tourist Office: (☎241 17 47), on Atatürk Cad., toward the Antalya Museum. Helpful, English-speaking staff distributes free maps. Open M-F 8am-7pm, Sa 9am-5:30pm.

Consulates: UK, Dolaplıdere Cad. Pırıltı Sitesi, 1st fl. (☎244 53 13; fax 824 67 03). **The Turkish Republic of Northern Cyprus (TRNC),** Kışla Mah. 35th Sok. Dörteldemir Apt. 11 PK 633 (☎323 43 64).

Banks: For cash transfers, go to **Koç Bank,** opposite Hadrian's Gate on Atatürk Cad. Banks, many with **ATMs,** are clustered about the main streets outside Kaleiçi.

Hospital: The closest hospital to Kaleiçi is the private **Akdeniz Sağlık Vakfı Hastanesi,** 17 Ali Çetinkaya Cad. (☎247 90 01 or 247 90 02; fax 247 90 03), on the left side of Cumhuriyet Cad., 400m past the intersection with Atatürk Cad.

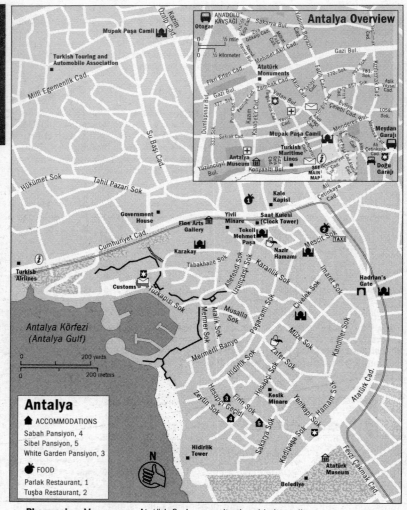

Antalya Overview

Antalya

⌂ ACCOMMODATIONS

Sabah Pansiyon, 4
Sibel Pansiyon, 5
White Garden Pansiyon, 3

🍎 FOOD

Parlak Restaurant, 1
Tuşba Restaurant, 2

Pharmacies: Many are on Atatürk Cad., opposite the old city walls.

Internet Access: Sörk Cafe, across from Hadrian's Gate, on an alley off Atatürk Cad. US$1 per hr. Open daily 8am-midnight. In Kaleiçi, try **Cool Exhibitions** (☎244 56 71), next to Sabah Pansiyon on Hapaçi Sok. US$1 per hr. Open daily 8am-midnight.

PTT: To get to the **main branch** (☎243 45 79), head down Cumhuriyet Cad. toward Atatürk Cad. and take the 1st major left onto Anafartalar Cad. Open daily 8:30am-5:30pm for stamps, **Poste Restante,** and **currency exchange.**

Postal Code: 07100 (Kaleiçi). Mail sent Poste Restante should be addressed 07000.

🏠🍴 ACCOMMODATIONS AND FOOD

The best place to stay is within the ancient walls of **Kaleiçi,** which contain over 200 pensions and hotels. Unless otherwise stated, all include private shower and breakfast. Through Hadrian's Gate and down Hepaçı Sok. in Kaleiçi, **White Garden**

Pansiyon has 15 beautiful rooms, proving that less is more, with a nice garden patio and helpful, English-speaking management. (☎241 91 15; fax 241 20 62; gardenşmail.koc.net. Singles US$10; doubles US$15.) To reach **Sibel Pansiyon**, 30 Firin Sok., take the second right after the Kesik Monument on Hespaçı Sok., past Hadrian's Gate. Sibel sports large, clean rooms with air-conditioning, and a sunny, overgrown garden. (☎241 13 16; fax 241 36 56. Singles US$12; doubles US$20.) **Sabah Pansiyon**, Kaleiçi, 60 Hesapçı Sok., is a popular backpackers' hangout with a pleasant courtyard area. (☎247 53 45; fax 247 53 47. Veg. and regular dinners US$3.50. Beer US$0.80. Laundry US$4 per load. Bike/scooter rental US$15 per day; car rental US$24 per day. Singles US$7; doubles US$8, with bath US$13, with A/C US$18; roof, couch, or floor US$3; camping US$2.50-3.) Facing the street, turn left off Atatürk Cad. to find **Tuşba Restaurant** (☎244 43 81) for the best *kebap* in Antalya, served sizzling with fresh, warm flatbread (US$2.50). Lightning-fast service with a finale of free watermelon. **Parlak Restaurant** is in the shopping center by the clocktower, with a classy, air-conditioned interior and a rotisserie. (☎241 65 53. Open daily 11am-midnight.)

🎴 SIGHTS

🏛**ANTALYA MUSEUM.** This museum is one of Turkey's best and a winner of the 1988 European Museum of the Year Award. The exhibits chronicle the history of Turkey from prehistoric times to the founding of the Turkish Republic. One of the museum's highlights is the **Salon of the Gods,** with large 2nd-century BCE statues of Nemesis, Zeus, Aphrodite, Tyche, Athena, Artemis, Hermes, and Dionysus, and their Egyptian sidekicks Serapis, Isis, and Horus. The **Salon of Small Objects and Underwater Remains,** to the right, houses several gorgeous silver and ivory Phrygian statuettes; the gem of the collection is a magnificently painted Grecian urn, mysteriously labeled "Tibet Crater." The adjoining **Icon Hall** is home to a small collection of Orthodox Christian icons, among them a portrait and bones of St. Nicholas. The **Hall of Money and Jewelry** contains a few of the world's first coins, minted between 640 and 630 BCE by the Lydians from white gold or electrium. *(2 Konyaatı Bul., about 2½km from town along Cumhuriyet Bul., which changes its name to Konyaaltı Bul. as it heads out of town. Dolmuş labeled "Konyaaltı/Liman" head along this street, (US$0.30). Get off when you see the yellow museum signs before the dolmuş heads downhill to the beach. ☎238 56 97. Open Tu-Su 9am-7:30pm; in winter 8am-5pm. US$5, students US$2.)*

OTHER SIGHTS. Near the entrance to Kaleiçi, at the intersection of Cumhuriyet Cad., stands the symbol of Antalya, the unique red-tinted **Yivli Minare** (fluted minaret). Dating from the 13th century, this minaret was constructed by the Selçuk Sultan Alaeddin Keykubad. Down Atatürk Cad., on the right, stands the three-arched **Hadrian's Gate,** built in 130 CE to commemorate the visit of the emperor Hadrian. Through this gate to the old city, about halfway down Hesapçı Sok., is the **Kesik Minare** (Broken Minaret). The ruined mosque traces Antalya's history: it was once a Roman temple, then a three-nave basilica, and finally a Selçuk mosque. At the far end of Hesapçı Sok. is the **Hıdırlık Tower,** which resembles a Roman-era mausoleum but is believed to have been built as a lighthouse in the 2nd century.

🎵 ENTERTAINMENT

From elegant dance clubs to rowdy bars, there's no shortage of nightlife in Antalya. **Cinemas** generally show English-language films with Turkish subtitles. **Oscar,** Zafer Sok., along Atatürk Cad., shows Hollywood blockbusters and other foreign films (US$3.50). **Club Alley,** above the harbor, is the be all and end all of nightlife for Antalya's young and affluent. Eight independently-owned bars encircle a central bar in this spacious outdoor establishment. The evening begins with mellow hip-hop, while bass-heavy dance beats pick up the pace as the night wears on. (Beer and *rakı* US$6; cocktails US$10. Cover Su-Th US$7.50, F-Sa US$10; includes 1 drink. Open daily 10pm-4am.) **Club 29** is uphill along the harbor. Megabass Euro,

Turkish, and American pop blasts from all directions on the open dance floor and chic white seats. On weekends, young Turks pack the floor until daybreak. (☎241 62 60. Beer US$3.50; *rakı* US$5. Cover M-Th US$5, F-Sa US$7.50. 18 and up. Open daily 11pm-4am.) Disgruntled grungesters still mourning Kurt pack the **Rock Bar**, downhill from the clocktower. Loud, angry, live music plays 10:30pm-1:30am. (☎248 89 41. Open daily 2pm-3:30am.) Antalya's two beaches, **Lara** and **Konyaaltı**, are both accessible by *dolmuş* (from the Doğu Garaj to Lara, from Konyaaltı Bul. to Konyaaltı; US$0.30). On the way to Lara, you might want to stop at the **Lower Düden Waterfall**, a cascade that tumbles 20m into the sea. Spectacular **Upper Düden Falls**, 10km from Antalya, are included in most tours of Termessos.

İSKENDERUN ☎326

Formerly known as **Alexandretta**, İskenderun was founded by Alexander the Great to commemorate his decisive victory over the Persians at Issus. As the principal port city of Antioch, Alexandretta became a powerful and cosmopolitan burg in its own right. Modern-day İskenderun has retained very little of historical interest, but its waterfront promenades and wide boulevards are pleasant to walk, and its position on the Mediterranean trade routes has protected the diversity of the towns' Christian, Muslim, and Jewish populations. To the south, some pleasant **beaches** make İskenderun a popular destination for Turkish and Arab tourists.

⊏ TRANSPORTATION. İskenderun is a major waystation for all buses connecting Antakya to points north and east.

⑦⚡ ORIENTATION AND PRACTICAL INFORMATION. Travelers arrive at the **otogar**, 1km north of the town center. **Atatürk Cad.** runs along the waterfront park, and intersects the town's two main boulevards, **Sehit Pamir Cad.** and **Ulu Camii Cad.**, at the Atatürk statue. All travelers' needs can be met on these three streets. South on Atatürk Cad., the **tourist office**, 49B Atatürk Cad., has mimeographed maps and brochures. (☎614 16 20. Open M-Sa 8am-noon and 1-5pm.) Next door, the **tourist police** (☎613 61 76) is open daily 24hr. **Banks** and **pharmacies** line Sehit Pamir Cad.; exchange is best at the **Türkiye İş Bankası**, by the Atatürk statue. Hospital **Devlet Hastahnesi** (☎613 35 70) offers 24hr. medical care. **Ambulance** ☎122; **pharmacy** information ☎118. The **PTT** is up Sehit Pamir Cad. on the right. Open 8:30am-5:30pm. **Postal Code:** 31200.

🏠🍴 ACCOMMODATIONS AND FOOD. Hotel Açıkalin, 13 Sehit Pamir Cad. (☎617 37 32) is the best deal in town, with clean air-conditioned rooms and shared bath for US$5 per person. Next door, the **Turistik Hotel Imrenay**, 5 Sehit Pamir Cad., is a step up with air-conditioning, bath, fridge, and TV for only a little more. (☎613 21 17. Singles US$8.50, doubles US$17.) One block over on Ulucamii Cad. No. 16, the **Hotel Cabir** (☎612 33 91) offers suites with powerful climate control and spotless bathrooms for US$15 per person. For those seeking a beachside locale, the **Arsuz Otel**, 30min. south on in the resort town of **Uluçınar,** provides 3-star luxury with private beach, restaurant, and waterfront bar. (US$20 per person.)

İskenderun has several nondescript *lokantas;* the exception is the atmospheric **Hasan Baba Restaurant**, 35 Ulu Camii Cad. (☎613 27 25), famous for its tasty *iskender kebap* (US$3), served in a well-lit garden with fountains and terraces.

🔲 SIGHTS. Plenty of Turkish and Syrian tourists come to İskenderun for the nice stretches of **beach** south of the city, which somehow avoid the pollution that fouls the beaches in southern Hatay. The most popular destination is **Uluçınar,** a pretty resort town with beachside cafes and sandy beaches over clear water. The coastal highway ends at Uluçınar, but the town has the southernmost outpost of the Kharamanmaraş ice cream chain **46 Edem,** with glorious US$0.40 cones.

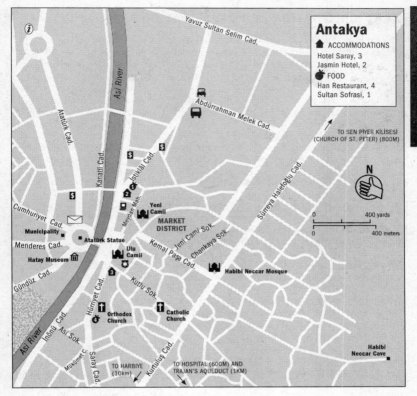

Antakya

🏠 ACCOMMODATIONS
Hotel Saray, 3
Jasmin Hotel, 2
🍴 FOOD
Han Restaurant, 4
Sultan Sofrasi, 1

TO SEN PİYER KİLİSESİ
(CHURCH OF ST. PETER) (800M)

ANTAKYA (HATAY)   ☎326

In Antakya, site of the ancient city of **Antioch**, the throngs of tourists diminish, as does the Mediterranean resort atmosphere. Antakya offers sprawling markets in the old sections of town, manicured tea gardens, and the renowned Hatay Museum, housing the world's finest collection of Roman mosaics. It was in Antioch that Christianity received its name; the side of Mt. Stauros is riddled with caves and tunnels where the underground religion was kindled, including the legendary Grotto of St. Peter—the oldest church in the world. The crumbling walls along the surrounding mountain ridge are evidence of the city's former glory. Modern-day Antakya thrives in the bustle of its market streets, the buzz of border traffic to Aleppo and Damascus, and the mouth-watering concoctions of Antakya's kitchens, the fusion of Turkish and Syrian palates.

▟ TRANSPORTATION

The *otogar* runs **buses** to: **Ankara** (10hr., 6 per day 10am-10pm, US$13); **Antalya** (14hr., 10 per day 9am-6:15pm, US$13); **İstanbul** (16hr., 8 per day 2:30-6pm, US$19); and **İzmir** (16hr., 4 per day 12:30-7pm, US$19). **Buses** also run to **Aleppo** (3-4hr., 4 per day 9am-6pm, US$8) and **Damascus** (9hr., 9:30am and noon, US$15) in Syria. For more information on border crossings to Syria see p. 630 and p. 681. *Dolmuş* leave opposite the station to **İskenderun** (30min., every 15min., US$1).

TURKEY

✦ ? ORIENTATION AND PRACTICAL INFORMATION

The **Asi River** divides Antakya into two parts. At the center of town in the western half of the city, a theater, the PTT, a government office, and the museum snuggle up to the Atatürk statue rotunda. The eastern half has the budget hotels, restaurants, markets, *otogar*, and old neighborhoods. To reach the center of town, turn left at the exit of the *otogar*, make another left onto **İstiklâl Cad.**, and continue 700m to the river. Cross the second bridge into the square with the Atatürk statue.

The **Tourist Office** (☎216 06 10) is in the Valiliki building, at the end of İstiklâl Cad., just past the Antik Beyazıt Hotel. (☎216 06 10. Open M-F 8am-noon and 1:30-5:30pm.) **Türkiye İş Bankası** has branches on İstiklâl Cad. and on Hürriyet Cad. down from the Saray Hotel, both with **currency exchange** and 24hr. **ATMs.** The *otogar* and the exchange office on İstiklâl Cad. change Syrian pounds at better rates. **Devlet Hastanesi** (☎214 54 30), 4km from town, is the best **hospital** (taxi US$3-4). The **PTT**, in the center of town, has 24hr. phone service (mail service 8:30am-6pm.)

☗ ☖ ACCOMMODATIONS AND FOOD

Most accommodations are not well suited to the budget traveler. ▨ **Jasmin Hotel,** 14 İstiklâl Cad., has shared bathrooms, a rooftop patio, and lawn furniture. Rooms open into a central atrium. (☎212 71 71. Singles US$5; doubles US$8; triples US$10.) **Hotel Saray,** 3 Hürriyet Cad., the best of the mid-range choices, offers a pleasant breakfast salon and new rooms with bath. (☎/fax 214 90 01. Breakfast included. Singles US$10; doubles US$16; triples US$25.) Culinary enthusiasts will swoon over Antakya's specialty, *içli köfte* (a.k.a. *oruk*), spicy bulgur wheat and red pepper served with seasoned lamb and pine nuts. *Ekşi aşı*, a variation on *oruk*, is covered in tomato sauce. For dessert, *künefe* (or *peynirli kadayıf*) is a baklava-style pastry stuffed with white cheese. Much of this Syrian-influenced Turkish cuisine is unavailable in the rest of Turkey. **Han Restaurant** is on Hürriyet Cad. Despite the external appearance, Han has a smashing upper level with a grove of fruit trees. The *mezes* are simply extraordinary. (☎214 17 16. Full meal US$4-5. Open 10am-midnight.) ▨ **Sultan Sofrasi,** 18 İstiklâl Cad., is unrivaled. Sample *mumbar*, *aşur*, and *sultan sarma* in air-conditioned comfort. (☎213 87 59. Open daily 7am-10pm.) ▨ **Anadolu Restaurant,** 50/C Hürriyet Cad., down the street from the Saray Hotel, serves vegetarian *mezze* and excellent hummus, with the option of outdoor seating. (☎215 15 41. Full meal US$5-6; open daily 10am-midnight.) **46 Edem Dondurma** (☎214 53 36), on Atatürk Cad., 100m from the center of town, scoops up fruit flavors and three varieties of *dövme* (thick ice cream; US$1).

◉ SIGHTS

HATAY MUSEUM. Except for the ruins of the ancient walls, earthquakes and marauders have destroyed much of Antioch's ancient splendor. Only the breathtaking and world-renowned Hatay Museum hints at the magnificence of the ancient city. The museum houses one of the world's best collections of **Roman mosaics,** assembled by an archaeological team from Princeton University, the British Museum, and the Chicago Oriental Institute. Painstakingly pieced together from thousands of tiny tiles, these huge mosaics depict images with near-photographic precision. Highlights are a 2nd-century wild boar hunt ("A Pig Hunt in Calydonia"); the striking "Personification of Soteria"; the small, priapic hunchback mosaic ("The Happy Hunchback"); and a scantily clad man running in horror from an enormous levitating eye radiating farm implements ("Evil Eye"). The most imposing mosaic is the giant 5th-century hunting scene on the floor; climb the spiral staircase for a complete view. An air-conditioned salon houses coins, jewelry, and mounted heads. Sarcophagi and additional mosaics fill the garden outside. *(Open Tu-Su 8:30am-noon and 1:30-6pm. US$3.50, students US$1.50.)*

ST. PETER'S CHURCH (SEN PİYER KİLİSESİ). Founded by the Apostle Peter, who preached here with Paul and Barnabas, this church (a.k.a. St. Peter's Grotto) was built into a cave so that services could be conducted in secret. The original congregation here coined the term "Christianity" to describe their new religion, making this the oldest Christian church in the world. The hillside above the church, riddled with the remains of tunnels, natural caves, and bits of Antioch's city walls, has been a holy place since pagan times. Inside the cave are an escape tunnel, an ancient baptismal font, and a stone altar that is still regularly used for services. The external facade was built by 11th-century Crusaders. The terraced garden in affords a great view of the city below. A path zigzags 200m to a high relief of a veiled figure, alternately described as a windblown Mary or as the Syrian goddess of Hierapolis flanked by Charon, boatman of Hades. *(To reach the church, walk 2km north on Kurunus Cad. (20min.) and take the erratic city bus #6 or taxi (US$2). Open Tu-Su 8am-noon and 1:30-4:30pm. US$3, students US$1. There is no regular mass; check with the Antakya Catholic Church (☎ 215 67 03). Relief open Tu-Su 8am-noon and 1:30-5:30pm. Free.)*

✈ BORDER CROSSING: SYRIA

The overland crossing at Bab al-Hawa on the Aleppo-Antakya road takes less than 30min. each way. Obtain your Syrian visa in advance from your home country or at the Syrian embassy in Ankara. In theory, only travelers from countries without Syrian embassies can purchase border visas; otherwise they can cost up to US$100 at the border. Three-month double-entry visas cost US$61. Any passport with evidence of a trip to Israel will be refused a visa or entry.

Several Antakya bus companies, including **Has**, offer service to **Aleppo** (3-4 per day, US$8). Avoid Öztur, which uses substandard buses without air-conditioning. Allow 4-5hr. for the journey and border formalities. The border has two stops on each side. At one stop on the Turkish side, you will have to leave the bus and go through passport control. Passport control and luggage searches are slower on the Syrian side, sometimes as long as 1½hr. You'll get a better-than-official rate changing money Antakya, so it's best to do your exchange before crossing.

CENTRAL ANATOLIA

Central Anatolia fosters the traditional spirit of Turkish culture. The astonishing landscapes and improbable natural formations of Cappadocia are some of the most fascinating in the world. The proximity of Cappadocia, an ancient Christian stronghold, to Konya, Turkey's most conservative Islamic city, hints at the area's diversity. A vibrant culture, welcoming atmosphere, and inspiring landscape characterize these windswept plains of Turkey's heartland.

ANKARA ☎ 312

Ankara's history and character sometimes lead would-be visitors to dismiss the city as a functional, soulless capital city. Such an attitude ignores 3200 years of history and Ankara's place as Turkey's premier college town. Its old houses and twisting streets lie in a confusing tangle beneath imposing Byzantine walls, concealing dozens of cafes with breathtaking views, while nearby Kızılay, the main student area, has bars and an active nightlife to suit all tastes. The Museum of Anatolian Civilizations may well be Turkey's best museum, and one can begin to understand Atatürk's pivotal place in the national consciousness after visiting his mausoleum. In Ankara you can secure visas to the rest of the Middle East.

◤ TRANSPORTATION

Flights: *Havaş* buses (every 30min. 4am-11:30pm, US$5) to **Esenboğa Airport** (☎ 398 00 00) leave from Hipodrom Cad. (next to the train station). Major carriers serving

Ankara include: Aeroflot, Air France, Alitalia, Austrian Airlines, British Airways, Canadian Airlines, Delta, Iberia, JAL, KLM, Lufthansa, and Swissair. **Turkish Airlines (THY),** 154 Atatürk Bul., Kavaklıdere (info and reservations ☎419 28 00, sales 468 73 40 or 468 73 41), has direct flights to: **Antalya** (1hr., 3 per day, US$70); **Bodrum** (1¼hr., 5 per day, US$82); **Diyarbakır** (1½hr., 2 per day, US$68); **İstanbul** (1hr, 15 per day, US$82); **İzmir** (1¼hr., 12 per day, US$82). THY open M-F 8:30am-8pm, Sa-Su 8:30am-5:30pm. Travel agencies between Kızılay and Kavaklıdere sell tickets.

Buses: The **otogar** is the westernmost stop on the Ankaray subway line (take any train to Kızılay). To get to Ulus, take a *dolmuş* (US$0.60), city bus (US$0.50), or taxi (US$6.25), or ride the metro 2 stops north to Cumhuriyet Cad. Buses to **Boğazkale** via **Sungurlu** (3hr., 20 per day 6am-1am, US$5). **Varan,** 34/1 İzmir Cad., Kızılay (☎418 27 06 or 224 00 43), and **Ulusoy,** 18/A İnkılâp Sok., Kızılay (☎419 40 80 or 224 01 72 or 286 53 30) offer safer, more comfortable, faster service to major cities.

Local Dolmuş: Hubs near Hacı Bayram Camii and at the intersection of Denizciler-Adnan Saygun Cad. US$0.35-0.60, depending on distance. Student fare available.

Subway: Ankara's new, clean subway system provides possibly the fastest and easiest way to get around the city. The east-west Ankaray line (stations marked by a white "A" on a green background) connects the bus station to Dikimevi, with stops in Tandoğan, Maltepe, Kızılay, and the Colleges (Kolej). The north-south Metro line (white "M" on red background) also stops in Kızılay, running north to Sıhhiye, Ulus, and the northwestern suburbs. 5-ride passes US$2.50, students US$1.50. Open 6:15am-midnight.

✦🄙 ORIENTATION AND PRACTICAL INFORMATION

The city's main street, **Atatürk Bulvarı,** runs north-south. At its north end is the **Ulus** precinct, centered around an Atatürk statue. The traditional village of **Hisar** (Citadel) is east of Ulus and crowned by the 9th-century **Ankara Fortress** *(Ankara kale)*. Ulus and Hisar comprise **Eskişehir** (Old City). Farther south along Atatürk Bul. is **Kızılay,** the center of **Yenişehir** (New City). West of Kızılay is **Maltepe,** a district full of grim nightclubs and cheap student dorms. **Kavaklıdere, Çankaya,** and **Gaziosmanpaşa,** south of Kızılay, have lush residential areas, embassies, and nightclubs. Bus #413 runs the length of Atatürk Bul., from the Atakule tower to the equestrian statue in Ulus. The **Ankaray suburban railway line** is the subway system in Ankara, running east-west from its center in Kızılay.

Tourist Offices: 121 Gazi Mustafa Kemal Bul. (☎231 55 72). Directly outside the Maltepe stop on Ankaray (from Kızılay, take the train headed toward AŞTİ). The friendly, English-speaking staff provides free city and country maps and can interpret your needs to the **tourist police** (☎303 63 53). Open daily 9am-5pm.

Embassies: Egypt, 126 Atatürk Bul., Kavaklıdere (☎426 10 26; fax 427 00 99). **Greece,** 9-11 Ziaürrahman Cad., Gaziosmanpaşa (☎436 88 60; fax 446 31 91). Visa applications M-F 9:30am-noon. **Israel,** 85 Mahatma Gandhi Cad., Gaziosmanpaşa (☎446 29 20; fax 426 15 33). **Jordan,** 18A Mesnevi Dede Korkut Sok., Aşağı Ayrancı (☎440 20 54; fax 440 43 27). **Lebanon,** 44 Kızkulesi Sok., Gaziosmanpaşa (☎446 74 85; fax 446 10 23). **Northern Cyprus,** 20 Rabat Sok., Gaziosmanpaşa (☎437 60 31; fax 446 52 38). **Syria,** 40 Sedat Simavi Sok., Çankaya (☎440 96 57, visa department 440 17 21; fax 438 56 09) Visa applications M-F 8:30-9:30am.

Banks: All large banks offer **currency exchange,** but only major banks such as **Akbank** (no commission) and **Garanti** will cash **traveler's checks. Türkiye İş Bankası, Yapı ve Kredi, Pamukbank,** and **Garanti Bankası** are open 24hr. and accept Cirrus/MC/Plus/ V; Vakıfbank and Akbank also accept AmEx. AmEx cardholders can send and receive moneygrams at Koçbank by the statue in Ulus Meydanı. **ATMs** lurk on most corners.

Hospital: Bayındır Tıp Merkezi, Kızılırmak Mah. #3-3A, 28th Sok., Söğütözü (☎287 90 00), is Ankara's best private hospital. Centrally located, brand-new **Bayındar Kilnik,** 201 Atatürk Bul. (☎428 08 08), Kavaklıdere, is smaller but offers all services.

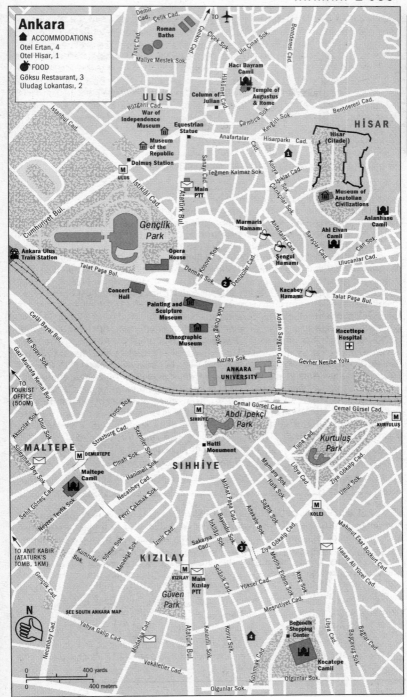

Ankara

🏠 ACCOMMODATIONS
Otel Ertan, 4
Otel Hisar, 1

🍎 FOOD
Göksu Restaurant, 3
Uludag Lokantası, 2

Internet Access: Most of Ankara's Internet cafes are in Kızılay. Many are fairly smoky. Several post connection speeds in their windows. ■**Internet Center Cafe,** 107 Atatürk Bul. (☎419 27 54; fax 425 79 27), on the 3rd fl. of the Engürü İş Hanı, is one of the best. Fast connection, color printing, photocopying, and scanning. US$1.25 per hr. Open daily 9am-11pm.

PTT: In **Ulus,** on Atatürk Bul., just south of the equestrian statue. Open 24hr., although services are limited at night. **Poste Restante.** In **Kızılay,** on Atatürk Bul. just off Kızılay Square, opposite the metro. Open M-Sa 8am-8pm; Su 8:30am-12:30pm, 1:30-7:30pm. In **Kavaklıdere,** on Cinnah Cad. just off the Kavaklıdere roundabout. Open daily 8:30am-12:30pm and 1:30-5pm. In the **train station** on Talat Paşa Cad. Open daily 7am-11pm. All offer full services.

✴🛏 ACCOMMODATIONS AND FOOD

The lively, student-oriented Kızılay neighborhood is more expensive but more pleasant than the dustier, noisier Ulus (which is nearer the sights). Going south along Atatürk Bul., take the fourth left after McDonald's onto Meşrutiyet Cad., then the third right onto Selanik Cad. to reach **Otel Ertan,** 70 Selânik Cad. Great value on a peaceful street, yet close to the Kızılay nightlife. 20 rooms, all with shower, toilet, and TV. (☎418 40 84. Singles US$15.50; doubles US$24.50.) Across from Ertan, 3-star **Otel Büyük Erşan,** 74 Selânik Cad., has 85 rooms, each with toilet, shower, TV, and refrigerator, with prices to match. The hotel feels like something out of a '60s movie. (☎417 60 45; fax 417 49 43. Singles US$26; doubles US$38; triples US$57.) In Ulus, try **Otel Hisar,** 6 Hisarparkı Cad., east of the equestrian statue, for comfortable rooms and Hisar views. (☎311 98 89 or 310 81 28. Singles US$6.50; doubles US$11.)

The main food hotspots are Gençlik Park (cheap), Kızılay (mid-range), and Hisar and Kavaklıdere (upscale). **Hoşdere Cad.,** southeast of Atakule Tower, lays claim to many good restaurants. The supermarket **Gima** has branches on Atatürk Bul. in Kızılay and on Anafartalar Cad. in Ulus. ■**Göksu Restaurant,** 22/A Bayındır Sok., one of the classier places in Kızılay, offers excellent Turkish and European food. (☎431 22 19. Filet mignon US$4.50. Open daily noon-midnight.) ■**Daily News Cafe,** 1 Arjantin Cad., Kavaklıdere, lets patrons peruse a free copy of the English-language *Turkish Daily News* or just pore over the newspaper decor. (☎468 45 13. Fusilli with porcini mushrooms US$6. Open daily 9am-midnight.) **Uludağ Lokantası,** 54 Denizciler Cad., Ulus (☎309 04 00; fax 312 18 19; www.uludagkebap.com.tr), is possibly the best restaurant in Ankara, serving wonderful, reasonably priced food (*ozel Uludağ kebap* US$3.50).

👁 SIGHTS

■**MUSEUM OF ANATOLIAN CIVILIZATIONS.** This restored 15th-century Ottoman building won Europe's Museum of the Year Award in 1997. It houses a collection of astoundingly old artifacts tracing the history of Anatolia from the 6th millennium BCE onward. The museum boasts artifacts from every age of Turkey's ancient history, from Çatalhöyük, the blockbuster of all Neolithic sites, through the early Bronze Age, Assyrian trade colonies, the Phrygian kingdom of Midas, and the Urartians. Highlights include perfectly preserved Hittite bull vessels, original gate figures from Boğazkale, and a life-size reproduction of King Midas's tomb at Gordion. Equally impressive is the room of 3300-year-old hieroglyphic tablets, ranging from one written by the wife of Ramses II to a tablet of the Hittite Queen Puduhepa. An underground section features ancient coins. (*2 Gözcü Sok. Walk to the top of Hisarpark Cad., turn right at the base of the Citadel steps, and follow the Citadel boundaries to a set of steps leading up to the entrance. ☎324 31 60; fax 311 28 39. Museum open Tu-Su 8:30am-5:30pm. US$3, students US$2.*)

ATATÜRK'S MAUSOLEUM (ANIT KABİR). Upon Atatürk's death, Turkey held an international contest to select a plan for his mausoleum. The winner, Emin Onat, designed the Hittite-influenced Anıt Kabir. Now covering 750,000 sq. m near Tandoğan Sq., the building took nine years to complete and is simple in execution but monumental in scope (like Atatürk himself). Six unhappy statues at the mausoleum's entrance represent Turkey's grief for its father's death. Across the courtyard is the tomb of **İsmet İnönü**, first prime minister of the Republic. The mausoleum complex has such Atatürkana as his 1936 Lincoln sedan and even photographs taken after his death showing cloud formations shaped like his profile. *(Anıt Cad. Take the Ankaray line to Tandoğan and follow the Anıt Kabir signs along Anıt Cad. The unmarked entrance is guarded by two soldiers. It's a 10min. uphill walk from the gate to the mausoleum entrance. ☎ 231 79 75. Open M 1:30-5pm, Tu-Su 9am-5pm; winter 9am-4pm. Free.)*

HİSAR (CITIADEL). On a high hill overlooking the city, the original, pre-republican hill-town of Ankara remains more or less unchanged, and has managed to preserve a village feel despite being mere meters away from the urban hub. Protected by its imposing Byzantine walls, still in excellent condition, the Hisar provides a vantage point over the new city and the contrasts between the old and the new, and the remarkable range of civilizations to have dominated the city and plains beyond. The network of narrow, twisting streets is full of merchants and craftsmen of every variety, and it's probably the best place in town to go looking for carpets or *kilim*. At the very top of the hill, the eastern tower *(Şark Kulesi)* and the northern tower *(Ak Kale)* offer excellent views. Buy shoes, sheets, and Superman outfits on Çıkrıkçılar Sok., which runs just southwest of the Citadel, downhill from the entrance to the Museum of Anatolian Civilizations. From the restaurant area, follow the road uphill and then climb the steps. Descend the Hisar from the other side, toward the **Hacı Bayram Mosque,** for a view of beautiful gardens and a picnic area amid the steps leading down. *(Fortress open 11am-5pm. Free.)*

MOSQUES. Completed in 1987, **Kocatepe Mosque** is a 20th-century take on 16th-century piety, complete with electric chandeliers, digital clocks blipping away prayer times, and an underground shopping strip. Inside is a model of the mosque at Medina (the second-holiest Muslim site in the world), a gift from Saudi Arabia's King Fahd. Amid the nearby Roman ruins is one of Ankara's most important mosques, the **Haci Bayram Camii,** built alongside the tomb of dervish saint Haci Bayram Veli. The mosque first did time as the Roman Temple of Augustus. *(Kocatepe: east of Kızılay on Mithat Paşa Cad. Haci Bayram: east of Ulus' equestrian statue on Anafartalar Cad.; take a left at Gima supermarket.)*

🖼 🎵 NIGHTLIFE AND ENTERTAINMENT

Ankara's chat-over-a-beer, listen-to-live-music nightlife is centered around Kızılay. Pub life thrives on **İnkilâp Sok.** and **Bayındır Sok.,** east of Kızılay Sq. Bar prices are fairly uniform: a pint of *Efes*, the local favorite, goes for US$1.10-1.50; mixed drinks are US$3-4. In Kızılay, enjoy acoustic renditions of Turkish tunes at **Brothers Bar,** 61 Selânik Cad., just past the Ertan Hotel. (☎419 41 26. Open daily 11am-midnight.) **Zx Bar Disco,** 14/A Bayındır Sok., Kızılay, packs a three-floor Turkish pop punch: disco downstairs, live music upstairs, and a bar in the middle of it all. (☎431 35 35. Beer US$1.50. Open daily noon-12:30am.) At Kavaklıdere's **Süleyman Nazif Club,** 97 Güvenlik Cad., a young, mostly Turkish crowd lets loose. (☎468 57 83. Open W-Sa 10pm-2am.) Also in Kavaklıdere, **Marilyn Monroe,** 54/A Büklüm Sok., serves the Anglo-American expat crowd. (☎467 12 12. Open daily 10am-midnight.) **Metropol Sanat Merkezi Movie House,** 76 Selanik Cad., Kızılay, offers six screens of artsy and pop films, mostly American. (☎425 74 78. US$3.75, students US$2.50.)

NEAR ANKARA: SUNGURLU AND BOĞAZKALE

☎364

Nowhere is the former glory of the 4000-year-old Hittite civilization more evident than at its ruined capital, Hattuşaş, on the outskirts of present-day Boğazkale (just over 200km east of Ankara and 30km off the Samsun highway). Beginning in 1600 BCE, the great Hittite kings occupied Hattuşaş for four centuries, competing with the Egyptians for control of the fertile lands and trade routes of Mesopotamia. The 8km loop passing through the site makes for a beautiful hike through a wild landscape of cliffs and valleys. Two kilometers northeast of the site is Yazılıkaya, an open air temple with bas-reliefs of 100 of the 1000 or so Hittite gods. On the main road, Boğazkale's museum maintains a collection of the site's artifacts.

▐ TRANSPORTATION

The only way to get to Boğazkale is via the town of **Sungurlu**. From there, **dolmuş** run to Boğazkale. **Buses** to Sungurlu stop on the main highway or at the *otogar*, just off the highway across from a Petrol Ofisi gas station. Buses leave the *otogar* for: **Ankara** (3hr.; 13 per day 7:15am-8pm; US$4.80, students US$3.50); **Antalya** (10hr.; 6, 7, 8pm; US$13, students US$11.50); **Bodrum** (10hr.; 6:30pm; US$13.50, students US$12); **Fethiye** (10hr.; 7pm; US$13.50, students US$13); **İstanbul** (9hr.; 8:30pm; US$13, students US$12); **İzmir** (10hr.; 8pm; US$13, students US$12).

▐ PRACTICAL INFORMATION

Sungurlu is nothing more than a jumping off point for Boğazkale. **Türkiye İş Bankası**, within sight of the Hotel Fatih, cashes **traveler's checks** and has an **ATM**. The local hospital is **Devlet Hastanesi** (☎311 80 07).

▐▐ ACCOMMODATIONS AND FOOD

If you're stuck in Sungurlu, crash at **Hotel Fatih**, 24 Cengiztopel Cad., which offers 15 sunny rooms, most with a view and bath; a Turkish toilet is on each floor. (☎311 34 88. Singles US$8, with shower US$12; doubles US$16, with shower US$22; triples US$24.) In the center of town, across from the Türkiye İş Bankası, is the simple but functional **Otel Ferhat**, 3 Baykal Sok., with 17 basic rooms and one lucky Turkish toilet per floor. (☎311 80 67. Singles US$4.50, with bath US$5.50; doubles US$9.50, with bath US$11.) You can find a decent meal at **Birand Restaurant**, inside Özel İdare İşhanı. Follow Lise Cad. past the intersection with Cengiztopel Cad. and take the next right onto Çorum Cad. The comprehensive menu includes *dolma* for US$1.50 and cold *mezes* for US$1.25. (☎311 99 16. Open daily 6am-11pm.) Crunchy *leblebi* (roasted chickpeas), a regional specialty, are available at dozens of shops throughout town.

◉ SIGHTS

HATTUŞAŞ

Hattuşaş is where many of the Hittite artifacts housed at the Museum of Anatolian Civilizations in Ankara were unearthed. The Hattuşaş road runs from the ticket kiosk in a 8km loop following the city walls. Walking the loop in a counter-clockwise direction, you'll first pass the **Büyük Mabet**, a temple dedicated to the weather god Hatti and the sun goddess Arinna. Farther in are the quarters of the priests, musicians, scribes, and soothsayers, as well as the temple's warehouses, where thousands of cuneiform tablets documenting commerce were found in 1907. Downhill from the temple were the offices of Assyrian merchants. Here, archaeologists found a parallel text in Akkadian and Hittite hieroglyphics that allowed scholars to translate Hittite. The smooth round holes bored into many of the stones originally held bronze rods that kept the stones together.

Up the hill, the right fork of the road passes the Hittite kings' ruined summer castle, **Yenicekale,** and then winds steeply up to meet the city walls. On the right is the **Aslanlı Kapı,** or Lion's Gate, consisting of two crumbling doorways framed by lion statues. Only one statue survives. The grooves about a foot above the ground were for the hubs of entering chariot wheels. A photographic computer reproduction posted nearby shows what the gate might have looked like in the 13th century BC. Follow the restored city walls running atop the embankment up the hill to the **Yer Kapı,** or Ground Gate. Popularly known as the **Sfenksli Kapı,** or Sphinx Gate, it was guarded by four sphinxes until one was taken to Berlin and another to İstanbul. Only one remains, as the fourth one has been missing since the city's discovery. Climb up the stairs to see the site's most intriguing feature: a 71m-long tunnel leading from inside the city walls to the outside. It was once suggested that the tunnel served a military function, allowing for surprise exits in times of siege. However, scholars now agree that it had a ceremonial function. To get a sense of the wall's overwhelming size, walk though the tunnel, take a left, and walk about 100m along the wall to the corner staircase. Once on top, you can walk back toward the gate, the city's highest point. From here, you can observe several razed *mabet* (temples) and a Byzantine church, now little more than blueprints marked out by limestone blocks. The plum tree to your left as you pass through *Sfenksli Kapısı* marks where the cuneiform and hieroglyphic-inscribed Boğazkale tablets, now in Ankara, were found (see **Museum of Anatolian Civilizations,** p. 684).

Moving eastward and downhill along the wall, the next place of interest is the **Kral Kapı,** or King's Gate. The giant figure is a reproduction; the original is in the Museum of Anatolian Civilizations. Originally believed to be the gate's namesake king, this fellow is actually a war god carrying a battle axe to symbolically defend the gate. Follow the road down a few hundred meters; on your right side are two stone chambers, each containing cuneiform characters. Unremarkable **Chamber 1** is less striking than **Chamber 2,** 50m farther down. Enter the opening opposite Nişantaş and follow the path up to a large stone arch-shaped chamber. These were commissioned in 1200 BCE by **King Shuppiluliuma II,** the last king of Hattuşaş. The enclosed cult chamber contains a relief of the king holding a symbol with an inscription mentioning a "divine earth road," the symbolic entrance to the underworld. Just across the road is **Nişantaş,** a rocky mound whose eastern side bears a badly weathered 10-line hieroglyphic inscription, believed to be a narration of the deeds of Shuppiluliuma II. Last on the tour, and worth skipping if you're short on time, is the **Büyük Kale,** a ruined complex of archives, offices, and royal apartments linked by courtyards. This was the main fortress of the Hittite kings, and it contained most of their documents. Archaeologists found 8000 cuneiform tablets here, including a treaty between Hattuziliz II and the Egyptian Pharaoh Ramses II. Though the ruins are scattered and difficult to make out, it's easy to appreciate the size and scope of everyday city life. From here it's 1km back to the ticket office.

YAZILIKAYA

The nearby holy shrine of Yazılıkaya was originally a series of narrow ravines in the rock (Yazılıkaya means "inscribed rock" in Turkish) with reliefs of gods and goddesses on parade. Goddesses appear in profile, wearing long, trailing robes; gods face forward, and their rank can be inferred by the number of horns on their hats. Archaeologists believe that **Chamber A** was used to celebrate the Hittite New Year every spring. Here, reliefs of 42 gods face 21 goddesses. On the far wall, the sculpture culminates in the marriage of the Hittite's most powerful deities, **Teshub,** the storm god, and **Hepatu,** the sun goddess. Facing the procession of deities is the famous 2.6m high relief representing **King Tudhaliya IV** (c. 1250-1220 BCE), who stands astride two mountains under a winged sun disk. **Chamber B,** accessible via a passage to the right of the entrance, was the site of animal sacrifice and contains a relief of 12 sword-carrying gods that are believed to represent the months of the year. *(Both sites open daily 8am-7pm; in winter 8am-6:30pm. US$2. Ticket is valid for both Hattuşaş and Yazılıkaya. Since Hattuşaş isn't near any restaurants, you may want to pack a lunch.)*

CAPPADOCIA

No other place on earth looks quite like Cappadocia. The unique landscape began to take shape 10 million years ago, when volcanic lava and ash hardened into a layer of soft rock called *tufa*. Rain, wind, and flooding from the Kızılırmak River shaped the *tufa* into a striking landscape of cone-shaped monoliths called *peribaca* ("fairy chimneys"), which are grouped in cave-riddled valleys and along gorge ridges. Throughout Cappadocia's other-worldly moonscapes, stairs, windows, and sentry holes have been carved into the rock.

TRANSPORTATION

From June to September, **dolmuş** follow the Ürgüp-Göreme-Çavuşin-Zelve-Avanos circuit (leaving Ürgüp M-F every 2hr. 10am-6pm and returning from Avanos M-F every 2hr. 9am-5pm). In winter, most connections within Cappadocia must be made via Nevşehir, from which **buses** depart every 30min. for all major Cappadocian towns. Transportation within this region costs between US$0.60 and US$2.50. Most visits to southern Cappadocia must be made through Aksaray. **Buses** from Nevşehir to Ankara stop in Aksaray (every hr., US$2.50).

If you have the funds, **car and motorbike rentals** can be a great way to stray from the beaten path and explore the captivating landscape and mysterious caves. Cars start at about US$30 per day, though prices skyrocket to about US$50 for automatic transmission. **Europcar** (☎341 34 88 or 341 43 15) in Ürgüp rents automatics with air-conditioning for US$90 per day. Agencies in Göreme and Ürgüp rent **bicycles** (US$3 per hr. or US$14 per day), **mopeds** (US$8 per hr. or US$20 per day), and **motorcycles** (US$50 per day). **Chimney Tours** next to the Goreme Otogar has a beautiful 5-seater 1970 custom Ford convertible in its rental fleet (US$45 per day).

Guided tours of Cappadocia's major sites are organized by agencies in Göreme and Ürgüp. Packages typically include a day-long tour of the region, as well as bus, lunch, and admission to all sites (US$30).

GÖREME ☎ 384

The village of Göreme is indisputably the capital of Cappadocia's backpacker scene. Surrounded by picturesque fairy chimneys, Göreme offers tourists no fewer than 50 pensions, mostly cave dwellings carved into the soft *tufa*. Its central location makes it the best base for exploring Cappadocia, and the glorious Open-Air Museum is only a short walk away. A local adage says, "once you've tasted Göreme's water, you're bound to come back." The staggering number of foreign brides (locals say there are 200) who've settled here suggests a different allure...

▐ TRANSPORTATION

From the *otogar*, buses travel via **Nevşehir** to: **Ankara** (4hr., 9 per day 8:15am-midnight, US$8); **Bodrum** (14hr.; 7:30, 9pm, midnight; US$20); **Bursa** (10hr.; 5:30, 7:30pm; US$16); **İstanbul** (11hr., 7 per day 8:30am-9pm, US$16); **İzmir** (12hr.; 6 per day 6:45-10pm; US$16); **Marmaris** (14hr., 5 per day 8pm-midnight, US$20); **Olimpos** (12hr., 8 per day 6-10:30pm, US$19); **Pamukkale** (10hr., 4 per day 7:30pm-midnight, US$14); and **Selçuk** (13hr., 6 per day 6:45pm-midnight, US$19).

✴▐ ORIENTATION AND PRACTICAL INFORMATION

Göreme main road heads out west toward Nevşehir and northeast toward Çavuşin. The *otogar*, just off the main road, is at the eastern end of the town center. At the eastern end of town, a road to the Open-Air Museum breaks off from the main road, uphill. Restaurants are mostly near the main road, and *pansiyons* are everywhere.

Tourist Office: (☎271 25 58). In the *otogar,* this cooperative provides info on almost all of Göreme's lodgings. Doing your own research here will acquaint you with Göreme's myriad pensions. Additionally, **Backpacker Information** (on your left as you exit the *otogar;* ☎271 27 36) can help "the independent traveler" organize an itinerary and offers hostel-based connections through Cappadocia and Turkey's western coast (US$10 per day covers lodging and transportation).

Tours: There are many tour companies in Göreme that offer various walking and driving tours (usually US$30-US$150). In order to find the company best-suited for your needs, as well as to get your money's worth, check that a particular company has insurance, good vehicles, and licensed guides (a licensed guide should have an actual license that he can show you). **Alpino Tours** (☎271 27 27; fax 271 27 28; alpino@alpino.com; www.alpino.com.tr) has a very good reputation in town and offers jeep tours (you drive) in addition to the traditional routes. **Zemi Tours** (☎271 25 76; fax 271 25 77), on the left side of the road leading from the *otogar* to the Open-Air Museum, offers a unique 2-day Ihlara Gorge Camping Trip (US$50 per person) with tents, beds, and meals. **Kapadokya Balloons** (☎271 24 42; fax 271 25 86; www.kapadokyaballoons.com), with an office next door to Cafe Doci@, offers breathtaking 90min. balloon tours, a.k.a. "aerial nature walks," through the Cappadocian landscape. Multilingual, professional pilots fly as high as 700m and low enough to pick flowers. Balloons fly for 1½hr. with 8 or 12 passengers Apr.-Nov. daily at dawn, weather permitting. They are fully insured and licensed, unlike some other balloon companies in the region. US$210 per person, US$230 if you pay by credit card; book at least two days in advance.

Banks: Next to the Open-Air Museum. Open daily 9am-5:30pm. There is an **ATM** in the center of Göreme, across from the *otogar* and to the left.

Laundromat: (☎271 25 79), behind the *otogar*, across from the Göreme Belediye Handicrafts Market. Wash and dry US$7, with ironing US$6. Open daily 9am-8pm.

Pharmacy: Kapadokya Pharmacy (☎271 21 37), on the main road near the hospital. Open daily 8am-8pm.

Medical Assistance: The **Göreme Sağlık Ocağı Hospital** (☎271 21 26), near the PTT, is actually a Community Health Clinic, but it also serves medical emergencies.

Internet Access: Cafe Doci@ (see **Food and Entertainment**); **Flintstone's Internet,** next door to Fat Boy's Bar; and **Neşe C@fe.** All open from around 8am until around 11pm and offer cold drinks and a few American-style keyboards to preserve your sanity.

PTT: Though many street-side stores offer PTT services (money exchange, stamps, phone cards), the official post office is on the main road just after the turn-off for the Open-Air Museum. Offers the best exchange rate in town. Open daily 8:30am-12:30pm and 1:30-5:30pm.

Postal Code: 50180.

ACCOMMODATIONS

Under Göreme's government, all pensions have fixed minimum prices for non-dormitory rooms: US$5 per person, with bath US$7, and up to US$10 for a single. Establishments designated as starred hotels may charge higher rates. Hit the tourist office (see above) for more complete comparative information on all of Göreme's accommodations, most of which will provide transportation to their establishments if you call ahead. A few pensions accept credit cards, but all of them, like every business in Göreme, strongly prefer that you pay in cash or traveler's checks.

■ **Kelebek Pension** (☎271 25 31; fax: 271 27 63; ali@kelebekhotel.com; www.kelebekhotel.com). A clean, comfortable, and very well-run pension. Just uphill from Kookabura and Tuna Caves, Kelebek offers cave, "fairy chimney," and regular rooms. Each of the several levels of terrace has spectacular views of Göreme and the surrounding valleys. Lounge with satellite TV and English news. Late-arrivals room, complete with shower, open 24hr. for guests wishing to check in the next morning. Dorms US$4; fairy chimney rooms US$12, with shower US$18; super-deluxe US$50.

■ **Tuna Caves Pension** (☎271 26 81; tunacaves@hotmail.com). Heading from the *otogar*, take the 1st right after the ATM and follow the signs. New owners totally refurbished Tuna Caves in 2001 with 17 rooms in an old Greek house. The stone courtyard offers a fireplace and a shady *kilim*-ed lounge area with a stereo. The terrace has a great view. (Cave and non-cave rooms US$6, some with shower; dorms US$4; deluxe US$23).

Special Cave Pension (☎271 23 47; cheilker@yahoo.com). The coziest cave pension in town. Clean, private showers in every room. The friendly staff, *kilim*-ed terrace, and plush cave bar make this a fun stay. US$7 per person.

Köse Pansiyon (☎271 22 94; fax 271 25 77), just behind the PTT. Makeshift Ottoman divans, vine-covered ceilings, swimming pool, yin-yang murals, and helpful Scottish-Turkish owners make Köse quite backpacker friendly. Breakfast US$2. Veg. and 4- course dinners US$4. 2 dorm rooms with mattresses on the floor (US$4 per person; bring your own sleeping bag, if possible) and 13 rooms, some with private bath.

Göreme Dilek Camping (☎271 23 96), across from Peri Pansiyon. Vast, floral campsite and pool. US$4.50 per site, US$3 per person, US$8 per tent, US$10 per caravan.

FOOD AND ENTERTAINMENT

Local Restaurant On the right as you turn onto the road heading to the Open-Air Museum. A recent addition to Göreme's dinning choices, the Turkish crafts and wooden furniture give Local a touch of tradition, and the house specialties are Turkish dishes unique among Göreme's restaurants. Like most tourist establishments in town, Local stays open as long as it has guests.

Fat Boys Bar. The newest bar in town. Its good music, central location in the town's promenade, and cheap happy hour (2 big local beers for US$1) have made it an instant success. Backpackers (especially Aussies) often keep Fat Boys fun into the wee hours.

Pacha Bar (☎271 23 40). Well-situated in the middle of Göreme's central promenade and marked by celestial murals, Pacha is often the busiest bar in town. Back to back *Simpsons, South Park* and *Friends* episodes play every day from 6-8pm and English language films also play in the earlier afternoons. Enjoy beer (US$1) or mixed drinks (US$3) at the bar or on cushioned benches. Open until business ends.

🔍 SIGHTS

GÖREME OPEN-AIR MUSEUM. With seven Byzantine churches, a convent, and a kitchen/refectory, the Open-Air Museum is a delight to history, art, and religion buffs. In the 4th century, St. Basil founded one of the first Christian monasteries here, setting down religious tenets that influenced the entire Western monastic tradition, which was put to a halt in the 15th century under Turkish rule. From then until the 1923 Population Exchange, the Greeks and Turks used the old churches to store goods. Today, the remains offer tourists some of Cappadocia's most spectacular frescoes. A close look at the 10th-century frescoes in the **St. Basil Church,** an early Christian monastery, reveal the artist's fingerprints. The **Çanklı Kilise (Sandal Church)** earns its name from the footprints, supposed molds of Jesus' feet, inside. The church itself dates back to the 11th century, rendering the holy footprints but a popular myth.

Yilinlik Kilise (Dragon Church), marked by frescoes of St. George slaying the dragon and of a hermaphroditic figure, is also known as St. Onuphrius church. One popular legend claims that the Egyptian girl Onophirios was so beautiful that she could not drive away all the men seeking to ravish her. She prayed for assistance and was granted a long white beard and moustache, which solved all her problems. Another tale tells of St. Onuphrius, who belonged to a 4th-century commune of Egyptian hermits. **Karanlik Kilise (Dark Church)** houses the most impressive artwork in the museum. The dome also houses a rare fresco of a teenage Jesus. *(From Göreme village, follow Open-Air Museum Way about 2km east, walking uphill. Open year-round 8am-5pm. US$5.25. Dark Church US$10.)*

A ticket to the Open-Air Museum will also admit you to a number of nearby churches. The first, the **Tokalı Church,** is right outside the museum's entrance and contains three smaller churches and a chapel. About 250m from the entrance are the **Church of Mother Mary** and the 10th-century **Church of St. Eustathios.**

🥾 HIKING

When good Christians die, they go to heaven; when good hikers die, they go to Cappadocia. Mountain ranges with spectacular views and eerie rock formations are all within throwing distance of Göreme. Follow the road leading to the Open-Air Museum 1km past the museum, take a left on the dirt road by Kaya Camping, turn left again at the next paved road, and walk 3km to reach **Sunset Point** (US$0.60). From there, you can descend into the **Rose Valley,** where bizarre, multi-colored rock formations make for one of the area's better hikes. After getting lost a few times, you'll eventually end up in Çavuşin; take the Avanos-Nevşehir **bus** or the Avanos-Zelve-Göreme-Ürgüp minibus back to Göreme (every 30min. until 6pm, weekends every hr.), or take a **taxi** (US$5). Follow the canal west of the bus terminal to reach **Pigeon Valley,** whose namesakes have unfortunately been hunted almost to extinction. This hike is somewhat confusing, but ultimately you'll end up in Uçhisar. To the north of Göreme is **Love Valley,** affectionately known as "Penis Valley" because of the 🔲 phallic rock formations that would give even Dirk Diggler a complex. If you're short on time, consider a **guided tour** of the nearby terrain.

⚡ DAYTRIP FROM GÖREME

UNDERGROUND CITIES: KAYMAKLI AND DERİNKUYU

By **dolmuş,** *Kaymaklı and Derinkuyu are about 30min. and 45min. from Göreme, respectively, with a connection in Nevşehir. From Göreme, dolmuş run to Nevşehir (every 30min. 6:30am-7pm, US$0.50) and then go to Kaymaklı (US$0.60) and Derinkuyu (US$0.80). Both sites open daily 8am-5pm. Each site US$3.75.*

Although Cappadocia encompasses almost 30 **underground cities** carved from *tufa*, Kaymaklı and Derinkuyu are the largest. Some think the cities began as cave dwellings that were later used by the Hittites for storage and ambushes. Between the 5th and 10th centuries, the Byzantines expanded them into full-fledged cities that shielded people from Iconoclast and Sassanid raids.

Low and narrow passages, easily blocked off by massive millstones, hindered prospective invaders. It was forbidden for anyone to leave while the cities were occupied, lest their departure give away the hideouts. Strangely enough, no evidence of a permanent settlement has been conclusively found in either Derinkuyu or Kaymaklı.

Derinkuyu, 45m deep with a 55m well, is slightly more impressive than Kaymaklı. With eight levels open to the public, Derinkuyu has sizeable rooms and halls, good lighting, and relatively easy access. Kaymaklı, smaller than Derinkuyu, boasts a more complex structure. The village has been built around the underground city, so residents could enter storage areas through tunnels in their courtyards.

At both sites, red arrows lead down, blue arrows up. Although all explorable areas are lit, a flashlight may come in handy. Stick to the marked and lighted areas. Just remember that these cities were designed to foil potential trespassers, who would fall to their deaths from sudden drops hidden behind corners.

ÜRGÜP ☎ 384

Ürgüp emerges from a pastiche of rock formations, early Christian dwellings, and old Greek mansions. With fewer *pansiyons* and neo-hippies than Göreme, Ürgüp appeals to independent travelers fleeing the commotion of tourism.

▤ TRANSPORTATION. English-speaking Aydın Altan of **Nevtur** (☎341 43 02) answers bus-related questions. **Buses** run to: **Ankara** (5hr., 5 per day 7am-5:30pm, US$8); **Bodrum** (14hr., 7pm, US$19); **Fethiye** (15hr., 3 per day 6-8pm, US$19); **İstanbul** (12hr., 4 per day 6-8pm, US$16); **İzmir** (12hr., 6:30pm, US$16); **Konya** (4hr., 6 per day 8am-7pm, US$6); **Kuşadası** (13hr.; 6:30 and 7:30pm; US$18); **Marmaris** (15hr., 7pm, US$19); **Pamukkale** (10hr., 7pm, US$15); and **Selçuk** (13hr., 6:30pm, US$18). Several **vehicle rental agencies** are near the *otogar*. You can rent: bikes for US$5-10 per day; mopeds for US$15-20 per day; cars from US$30 per day. Roads are reasonably organized in this area, though only the skilled will conquer the hills.

▤▨ ORIENTATION AND PRACTICAL INFORMATION. The main square, marked by a *hammam* and an Atatürk statue, is 20m down **Güllüce Cad.** from the *otogar*. This road forks uphill into two smaller roads, both near accommodations. Intersecting Güllüce Cad. in the main square is **Kayseri Cad.** The **Tourist Office** is inside the garden on Kayseri Cad. English- and German-speaking Zeki Güzel offers maps and brochures. (☎341 40 59. Open Apr.-Oct. daily 8am-7pm; Nov.-Mar. 8am-5pm.) Alternatively, fork left at the *hammam* and walk up to the **Turkish Airlines Office,** which doubles as a classier tourist office. Arrange plane tickets, get info, or simply cool off in the stone building that was once Ürgüp's prison. (Open daily 8am-5pm.) The reliable and affordable **Erko Tours** (☎341 32 52; fax 341 37 85; www.erkotours.com.tr) in the *otogar*, organizes tours of Cappadocia. Upscale and professional **Argeus Tours** operates out of the Turkish Airlines Office. (☎341 46 88; www.argeus.com.tr. US$70 for all-inclusive day tours.) The **Tarihi Şehir Hammamı,**

in the main square, is co-ed, with only a male masseur. (Open daily 7am-11pm.) The **hospital,** off Kayseri Cad. just behind Tourist Information, can be reached at ☎341 40 31. The **Cappadocia Health Center,** 28 Dumlupınar Cad. (☎341 54 27 or 341 54 28; fax 341 34 92), offers private out-patient clinical care. For **Internet Access,** go to **Asia Teras** (see **Food,** below). To reach the **PTT,** turn right out of the tourist office and take the first right uphill. It offers telephone services, stamps, fax, and currency exchange. (☎341 80 12. Open daily 8:30am-7pm; in winter 8am-5pm. Currency exchange closed noon-1:30pm.) **Postal Code:** 50400.

▐▐ ACCOMMODATIONS AND FOOD. Hotel Kemer, on İstiklâl Cad., is the closest pension to the center of town and offers clean, basic rooms with shower and towels. (☎341 21 68; fax 341 85 16. US$9 per person.) Its *kilim*-ed lounge and bar, parking space, cave restaurant, and ping-pong table make **Hotel Surban** ideal for groups, and lots of fun. Rooms have private bath and towels. (☎341 47 61 or 341 46 03; fax 341 32 23. Singles US$15; doubles US$25; triples US$30.) At the **Hotel Elvan,** İstiklâl Cad., 11 Barbaros Hayrettin Sok., downhill from Hotel Akuzun, to the left off the *hammam,* Maternal Fatma Hanım will boil medicinal teas for guests' weak stomachs. Rooms are tidy and have private bath. (☎341 41 91; fax 341 34 55. Singles US$14; doubles US$25; triples US$30. MC/V.) Fork right at the mosque, climb up the hill and steer left at the next fork to reach the **Türkerler Otel, Camping and Swimming Pool** (☎341 33 54). Pitch a tent for a couple of bucks on the environs of this tiny pension. Call ahead to check if the swimming pool is in fact filled, and cut a price with the laid-back owners (Turkish business at its best). If camping's lost its novelty, patrons can check into the on-grounds hotel or pension.

Heavy with Turkish spirit, ▉**Han Çırağan** (☎341 25 66) is in a 300-year-old *caravanserai* whose rooms are still used by traveling merchants. Try the filling *döner* special (US$4). The **Şömine Cafe** (☎341 84 42; fax 341 84 43), across from the Atatürk statue, caters largely to the tourist scene with a multilingual menu and professional service. Entrees US$2-4. **Asia Teras,** 20m to the left when exiting the tourist office offers billiards (US$2 per hr.) and Internet access (US$2.50 per hr.), along with mediocre American food like burgers for US$1-1.50. (☎341 38 39; asiateras@hotmail.com. Beer US$1; *rakı* US$2. Open daily 10am-midnight.)

▐▐ WINE AND NIGHTLIFE. Cappadocia is one of Turkey's major viticultural regions, with its center in Ürgüp. Uphill to the right behind the Atatürk statue, the renowned **Turasan Winery,** supplier of 60% of Cappadocia's wines, offers free tours and tastings in its rock-carved wine cellar. (Open daily 8am-8pm. Tours available until 5pm.) Several wine shops around the main square also offer free tastings. In late September, the Ürgüp **wine festival** brings eager competitors from France, Italy, Argentina, and the US, among others.

If you find yourself still energized after a day of boozing and trooping through Ürgüp's narrow cobblestone streets, put on your dancing shoes. ▉**Kaya Bar,** Ürgüp's most relaxed bar, overlooks the town square from the second floor of the large Sukurogullari pastry shop. Featuring live music, Kaya is big with backpackers and younger locals. (☎235 13 57. Beer US$1.50. *Rakı* US$2.) The ▉**Prokopi Pub Bar,** right in the town square, is popular with tourists. This hip bar plays an excellent selection of electronica, dance beats, and American and Brit pop. For the inspired or intoxicated there is a dance floor. (☎341 64 98. Beer US$2.50; *rakı* US$3; mixed drinks US$4-6. Open until the party dies, usually around 3am.) **Bar Barium** features funky mirrored walls and a solid mélange of Turkish and American pop. (Beer and *rakı* US$2.50. Open until 4am.)

EASTERN ANATOLIA

Welcome to Eastern Turkey, a secret kept even from its own people. Racial and political faultlines traverse this part of the world. Fortunately, tensions have subsided somewhat and once again, one of the world's richest anthropological and historical regions welcomes visitors. Snowy peaks and thundering cascades, the Silk Road and shimmering Van Gölü, hauntingly beautiful Ani and Paşa Palace will, more often than not, be enjoyed without another traveler in sight. After checking passports, once-twitchy police now share apricots and *çay* with travelers. Hotel keepers remember your name, and Eastern Anatolians will consider you their *misafir* (guest) and offer you the utmost hospitality.

> **! TRAVEL WARNING.** Though tensions have decreased significantly in recent years, travel in Eastern Turkey should be approached with caution. Travelers should be aware of all consular advisories and travel warnings, and should be careful to adhere to local rules and laws. That said, Eastern Turkey has begun to develop a tourist infrastructure, and no traveler should avoid Eastern Turkey because of safety concerns.
>
> *Let's Go* does not recommend that **women** travel alone to Eastern Turkey. Even with a headscarf and long, concealing clothes, women may be considered fair game for wandering eyes and forward flirtations, though the constant accompaniment is almost always benign. To avoid unwanted advances, dress conservatively, memorize some key phrases, particularly about a soon-to-return husband or boyfriend, and stay in more expensive hotels (see **Women Travelers,** p. 633).
>
> The unpredictable nature of travel in Eastern Anatolia requires that travel schedules be flexible. Aside from large luxury buses, arrival and departure times for transportation should be considered tentative.

GAZİANTEP   ☎342

The largest city in southeast Turkey has a rich heritage dating back to the Stone Age. Yet with the exception of fortress, floodlit at night upon a man-made hill, this heritage is giving way to a veneer of modernity. Today, Gaziantep competes with its neighbors for pre-eminence in trade and industry. At night, locals flock to Centenary Park, complete with water gardens, bike tracks, shopping, and a cinema. Beyond the city, a fertile plain of pistachios, olive trees, and vineyards extends in all directions. Gaziantep is a crossroads town for travelers heading west to the Mediterranean coast, south to Antakya and Syria, or east to Van. The Turkish Grand National Assembly granted the town its epithet *Gazi* (war hero/veteran) in 1921 for its resistance to foreign occupation during the War of Independence.

 TRANSPORTATION

Flights: THY (☎230 15 65) serves 60 European and Middle Eastern cities worldwide.

Trains: There are 3 rail routes out of Gaziantep. The service to the west runs to tiny Narli to meet the **Adana-Elazig Express** to **Adana, Konya,** and **İstanbul.** One train leaves daily for Narli to meet the **Diyarbakır Express,** via Malatya and Elazig. Another runs east along the Syrian border to a dead end at **Nusaybin,** 50km beyond Mardin. The station (☎323 30 15) lies conveniently enough at the northern end of İstasyon Cad.

Buses: The *otogar* is a palatial structure 3km north of town. Regular minibuses (US$0.40) run from İstasyon Cad. at the waterway. **Hidayet Turizm** (☎328 96 96) is one of many companies with offices here, running to: **Adana** (3hr., 5 per day, US$5); **Ankara** (10hr., 5 per day 7:30am-midnight, US$14.50); **Antakya** (3½hr., 9 per day, US$5); **Antalya** (14hr.,10 per day, US$16); **Diyarbakır** (5½hr., 8 per day, US$7); **Erzurum** (6½hr., 4 per day, US$15); **İstanbul** (16hr., 6:30am-9pm, US$17); **İzmir** (16hr., 2 per day 4-7pm, US$17); **Kahramanmaraş** (1hr, plenty, US$2.50); **Kars** (19hr., US$18); **Kayseri** (8hr., US$10); **Sivas** (18hr., 5 and 8pm, US$11); **Trabzon** (18hr., 6 per day, US$18); **Van** (10hr., 9pm and midnight, US$14).

ORIENTATION AND PRACTICAL INFORMATION

Gaziantep has a disorderly street plan, centered upon its **Antep Kalesi fortress** and divided by a park-lined waterway, **Allenben Deresi**. **İstasyon Cad.** crosses the waterway before intersecting with **Atatürk Bul.** to the right and **Eski Saray Cad.** To the left at the town's commercial center.

Tourist Office: A large information office (☎230 99 60) in Centenary Park. Regional info, maps, brochures. Open M-F 8am-noon and 1:30-5:00pm.

Banks: All major banks have **ATMs** and line Atatürk and Eski Saray Cad. Open 9am-noon, 1:30-4pm.

Hammam: 2 of the city's better *hammams* are in the shadows of the fortress. **Naip** and **Paşa** both admit women by day, but switch to male-only clientele after dusk.

Police: (☎230 18 30). The headquarters are across the Parki on Aksöy Bul. and 4 Cad.

Hospital: Public **Devlet Hastanesi** (☎220 93 37). **Sani Konukoğlu Tip Merkezi** (☎220 95 00) provides care at international standards. Most convenient is the private clinic **Özel Hayat Hastenesi** (☎230 60 60) at 17 İstasyon Cad. US$10 per patient. 24hr.

Internet Access: The **Eksen Internet Cafe**, 14 Atatürk Bul., 1st fl. (☎231 41 48), 100m from İstasyon Cad. US$0.75 per hr. Open 8am-midnight.

PTT: On İstasyon Cad., just past Atatürk Cad., on the right. Open 24hr.

Postal Code: 27000

ACCOMMODATIONS AND FOOD

Gaziantep carries the full range of price and quality. Prices are generally negotiable. **Bulvar Palas Oteli**, at 11 İstasyon Cad., has simple rooms and an uneven foyer reminiscent of the Addams Family. (☎231 34 10; singles US$7; doubles US$10). For slightly nicer accommodations, the **Hotel Büyük Murat**, 15 Suburcu Cad. (☎231 84 49) and the **Hotel Güllüoğlu**, 18 Suburcu Cad. (☎232 43 63) offer nearly equivalent amenities next door to each other just off Eski Savey Cad. Both feature large, clean rooms with full bath; singles US$10, doubles US$15. The **Hotel Katan**, on İstasyon Cad. by the waterway, is a step up, with a terrace restaurant, balcony, and fridge. (☎220 69 69. Singles US$15, doubles US$20.)

Wander 500m along Eski Saray Cad. from İstasyon Cad. to ▨ **Cavusoğlu** (☎231 30 69) or the less pretty ▨ **Cagdas** (☎234 40 00), one block off to the left on Uzun Carsi 14. Both offer quality *kebap* and *baklava* for US$3 per person. (Both open 9am-11pm.) Tucked off İstasyon Cad., on Sayi Ahmet Sok., is quiet **Sadirvan** (☎231 81 88). Visitors to the Anthropological Museum can relax at the nearby **Fuar Restaurant** (☎323 69 69) and sample *alinazik*, a combination of local yogurt dip and *kebap*. Beware the rapidly mounting bill. The uncontested *baklava* master is ▨ **Güllüoğlu** on Suburcu Cad. 20. (☎231 22 82. Open 7am-8:30pm.)

SIGHTS AND ENTERTAINMENT

Daytrippers should target Gaziantep's **Archeological Museum** (☎231 11 71), just beyond the stadium on İstasyon Cad., and if possible, the **Ethnographic Museum** (☎230 47 21), on Hamfioğlu Cad. in the Bey district. (Both open Tu-Su 8am-noon, 1-5pm.) **Duluk** village, one of Anatolia's earliest habitations lies 10km north. It contains an archaeological site where Hittite and Roman influences blend in underground stone churches and mausoleums. Take a minibus from İstasyon Cad. (US$1) and sit in the village *çay* house until a bus returns. Taxis cost US$7 but may not wait for you to explore the site.

Three key sites lie outside Gaziantep. **Belkis** (Zeugma) is just off the Şanlıurfa road, 10km from Nizip village. Hellenistic, Roman, and Byzantine influences are combined in a series of villa remnants, many of which will flood with the construction of the Birecik Dam. Check with locals to establish what remains visible after water levels stabilize. **Yesemet** is a field of Hittite statues, progressively excavated over the last 100 years. It is a 2hr. detour from the town of Ishlahiye, accesible by taxi. **Rum Kale**, 25km from Yazuveli and 62km from Gaziantep, requires an additional day to visit. This late-Hittite castle is said to have held St. John's biblical manuscripts. Rising water levels from a nearby dam are likely to flood the approaches to Rum Kale, so inquire at tourist information first.

Gaziantep's nightlife includes a good deal of prostitution and pornography; check your surroundings carefully before ordering a drink. Close to Güllüoğlu is **Dedikodu,** Gaziantep's favorite **disco,** though ravers would prefer **Taj Mahal,** 3km out of town. Walking from town along the Parki offers outdoor drinking, light dining, and live music, ideal for evenings.

ŞANLIURFA ☎414

Though officially known as Şanlıurfa (Glorious Urfa), for its contribution to the struggle for Turkey's independence, this city is known as *Peygamberler Şehri* to Muslims: City of Prophets. Şanlıurfa is a place of pilgrimage, being the putative birthplace of Abraham and the home of the prophet Job, as well as ten other Biblical figures including Jethro, Joseph, and Moses. Şanlıurfa is mind-bogglingly old, with newly-excavated temples at Göbeklitepe dating back to 9000 B.C. The city has changed hands many times along the millennia: from Hittite to Assyrian to Alexandrine to Commagene, Aramaean, Roman, Persian, Byzantine, Arab, Latin, and Selçuk, before finally joining the Ottoman Empire in 1637. These diverse influences have simmered gently in the city to form a distinctive style of architecture, still visible today. It's also the best base from which to visit the spectacular 2000-year-old funerary ruins at Nemrut Dağı (see p. 698).

▐ TRANSPORTATION

Buses: The *otogar* is 1.5km from the town center. Take a taxi for US$4-5, or stop any *dolmuş* and mention your preferred hotel (US$0.20), as all listed are on the main route. Some bus companies have free shuttle service to the *otogar*. **Buses** run to: **Ankara** (12hr., 8 per day, US$16); **Antakya** (6hr., 3 per day, US$8); **Diyarbakır** (3hr., 20 per day, US$5); **Doğubeyazıt** (16hr., 4 per day, US$22); **Gaziantep** (2hr., 20 per day, US$3); **İstanbul** (17hr., 9 per day, US$23); **İzmir** (17hr., 2 per day, US$23); **Konya** (12hr., 3 per day, US$14); and **Van** (12hr., 1 per night, US$13).

Dolmuş and **minibuses** leave from the same parking lot.

▐ PRACTICAL INFORMATION

Tourist Office: 20m from the doors of the Hotel Edessa (opposite Hasan Pasa Camii), the state tourist office (☎215 24 67) is heralded by marble steps and a small sign. Locals are oblivious to its existence. The office organizes a US$17 taxi tour. Open M-F 8am-noon and 1:30-5:30pm.

Banks: Those with **ATMs** are concentrated around Fuar and Sarayönü Cad.

Hospital: The **Özel Şan-Med Hastanesi** is a good private hospital at the center of town (☎216 27 72, 216 36 16, or 215 43 48). Open 24hr. MC/V.

Internet: Maviatnet, off Atatürk Cad. by the main circle, is open late. US$0.50 per hr.

Post Office: The main **PTT** is located between the Şan-Med Hospital and the bazaar. Services include **Poste Restante** and 24hr. card telephones. Open daily 8am-noon, 1:30-5:30pm. **Internet** services are also available here.

Postal Code: 63100 or 63200.

▚ ACCOMMODATIONS

Şanlıurfa's heat persists through the night, so consider splurging on rooms with air-conditioning. Because Şanlıurfa's visitor flow varies, try negotiating prices.

- **▨ Hotel Ugur Palas** (☎313 13 40), near Hotel Harran, off Atatürk Cad. on Koprubasi Cad. Clean and breezy: a budget dream. Tidy rooms with shared baths. US$3 per person.
- **▨ Valiligi Konuk Evi** (☎215 93 77), on Vali Fuat Bey Cad. Not as budget-oriented as other options, but hey, how often do you get the chance to stay in an 800-year old mansion? With only 6 rooms, this exquisitely restored mansion books out in advance. Staff wear traditional dress. Singles US$22; doubles US$40; suite US$50.
- **Hotel Bakey** (☎215 19 79), on Asfalt Cad., off Sarayönü Cad. Popular with groups, this fading giant offers A/C and showers for a decent price. Singles US$10; doubles US$18.

▣ FOOD

Şanlıurfa is renowned for its culinary wonders, but beware: many foods (especially meats) become infested with bacteria in the sweltering heat, and visitors often leave with stomach problems. Specialties include *patlıcanlı kebap* (eggplant and meatball on a skewer) and *domatesli kebap* (meatball and tomato on a skewer). Restaurants often give you a complementary dish of *lebeni* (fresh yogurt and bulgur wheat) before your meal, and end with a ritual cup of *mirra* coffee.

- **▨ Gulizar Konuk Evi** (☎215 05 05), by the Ulu Camii. Walk 20m up Irfaniye Sok. from Sarayonu Cad. Housed in a newly-restored Urfan mansion, with *kilim*-carpeted terraces, pigeon houses, and intricate stone latticework. Full meal US$3-4. Open until 10pm.
- **Cardakli Kösk Restaurant** (☎217 10 80), next to the Edessa. Offers terraces with traffic-free views of the floodlit fortress. Urfa specialties US$3-5.
- **Güney Lokantası**, 17 Köprübaşı (☎313 22 37), across from Hotel İpek Palas., is one of the few welcoming places for vegetarians in the city. They offer about 4 dishes with absolutely no meat, including *fasulye* (beans with red sauce) and *bamya* (okra in tomato-oil sauce). Full meal US$2. Open 6am-midnight.

◉ SIGHTS

A walking tour of Şanlıurfa starts on Atatürk Cad., past the post office. Cross the road and visit Şanlıurfa's oldest **hammam**, the **Vezir,** then continue around the corner for a cold glass of *biyanbali* from **Serbetci Abdullah** (☎216 77 99), the best source in town. Make sure you visit the **Ulu Camii,** built between 1170 and 1175. It is on the right toward the fortress. The mosque has a beautiful courtyard and a Byzantine bell tower that now serves as a minaret. The engaging *imam* Muhammed Guhadaroğlu enjoys guiding visitors (US$1 donation). The first mosque on Göl Cad. is the late Ottoman **Haşon Paşa Camii.** Behind it lies the large **Mevlid Halil Camii,** which houses the supposed **birth cave** of the prophet Abraham. There are separate entrances for men and women; women can go all the way into the sacred cave, while men may only look through a barred fence, praying in the proper direction. (Dress respectably.)

The fantastic **bazaar** begins at the far south end of Atatürk/Sarayönü/Divan Cad, and simply has no peer in Eastern Turkey. Enter any portal for a surreal adventure in the tiny alleys that stretch for kilometers. Each is disorienting, filled with the sounds of machinery and the smell of spices. A few notable spaces are the dark alleys of the coppersmiths market, the sumptuous displays of silk scarves and *hişvali* embroidery near the Kazzazpazarı bedestan, rows of sheepskins (US$3-7), wool, and pigeon-sellers. Most impressive is the local craft of *keçe*, a wool felt pressed and dyed by the sweat of burly, half-naked men in steam rooms. The market's culinary peak is the *tavulc döner* of **Kadiz Usta,** available near the Gümrük

Han. If you want to leave, ask for **Gölbaşı,** the park near the pools of sacred carp. On the southwestern side, the **Halil-ür Rahman** mosque stands in a Byzantine church dating to 504 CE. Across the pool is an elegant Ottoman *madrasa*.

The entrance to the **Citadel** is marked by **Corinthian columns,** constructed in 242 BCE, from which, according to legend, Nemrut shot firebrands at Abraham. (Open daily 8am-6pm. US$2, students US$1.) There are two entrances: the stairway on the front wall in the blazing sun and a cave walkway lit by lamps, 50m east. On top, the view is spectacular. Three kilometers south is **Eyyüp Peygamber,** which contains the cave where Job endured seven years of torture. (Take an "Eyyübe" *dolmuş* from Atatürk Cad., by the tourist office (US$0.20). Open daylight hours. US$1.)

NEAR ŞANLIURFA

NEMRUT DAĞI

Accessible from Malatya, Kahta, Adiyaman, and Şanlıurfa. The site is at the base of a cone-shaped pile of rocks, at the bottom of which are three terraces on the north, west, and east. The Malatya road ends 100m below the eastern terrace, while the road from Kahta ends in a parking lot 1km from the summit. Beside the parking lot is Nemrut Kafeteria, offering 24hr. food, drinks, and a bathroom. Allow at least 2hr. to explore the site, including the walk up. Rough winds can cause chills and dehydration: bring layers and water. Open during daylight hours. US$3.50, students US$2.

Upon the highest peak in the region (2150m), King **Antiochus I** ordered the construction of this 75m pyramid of rubble, flanked by massive statues (which have long since been decapitated by earthquakes—most recently in 1938—and time). At dawn and dusk, solitude and silence prevails on this impressive funerary monument, the calm broken only by the whipping of a constant wind. The site holds relics dating back to the Commagene kingdom, a border kingdom which managed to fend off the Romans and Persians encroaching from either side between 162 BCE and 72 CE. The kingdom flourished under Antiochus, son of Mithradates, who claimed direct ancestry to **Alexander the Great** on his father's side and to the Persian **Darius the Great** on his mother's, thus embodying the unification of east and west in one royal line. Antiochus is best remembered for installing a brand new pantheon of syncretic gods like Apollo-Mithras and Zeus-Oromasdes. He commissioned 10m high statues of these gods in their honor; they are seen bestowing the divine mandate upon a 10m statue of himself. The Herculean labor of constructing this shrine from six-ton stone blocks, as well as the 75m tall peak (now eroded to 50m) of crushed rock thought to hide the tomb itself, leads archaeologists to think the tomb may rival Tutankhamun's for wealth and majesty. Meanwhile, the collection of 3m tall stone heads continues to attract visitors to the site.

DİYARBAKIR (AMED)
☎ 412

Diyarbakır is one of the world's oldest cities, a fact immediately apparent to any traveler who arrives in this ancient maze of cobbled streets, perched on the shores of the Tigris River in the crook of the Fertile Crescent. The black basalt walls which encircle the city—5km long and reportedly visible from space—are of Roman and Byzantine construction, a relatively recent addition in a place whose archaeological record shows evidence of continuous occupation spanning 7500 years and 26 distinct civilizations. Nowadays the crescent isn't so fertile, but the Tigris floodplain still yields bushels of Diyarbakır's famous 50kg watermelons—a welcome treat in a town whose summer heat is regularly above 43°C.

⊏ TRANSPORTATION

Bus: The *otogar* is 4km from town, accessible by *dolmuş* in front of the hotels on Kilbris Cad. **Mardin minibuses** (1 hr., US$3) leave from the intersection of Melek Ahmet and Gazi Cad to: **Ankara** (13hr., 9 per day 11:30am-8pm, US$18); **Antakya** (8hr.; 9am, 8,

9:30pm; US$12); **Doğubeyazıt** (8hr., 9pm, US$12); **Gaziantep** (5hr., 8 per day 7:30am-5:30pm, US$7); **Şanlıurfa** (2½hr., 11 per day 9:30am-11:30pm, US$4).

Taxis: Avoid taxis in Diyarbakır, where the meters spin like roulette wheels.

⚡ PRACTICAL INFORMATION

Tourist Office: In the basement of the **Dağ Kapisi** (☎221 21 73). The director, **Zeki Genes**, speaks some English. Also contact the well-traveled **Ubeydullah Calisir**, nick-named "Japonali" (☎229 22 71; mobile (535) 259 34 66), who enjoys helping tourists find their way without obligation.

Banks: Every major bank lines Gazi Cad. from the İnönü Cad. intersection toward the center of town. Open 9am-5:30pm. **ATMs** available 24hr.

Police: On Gazi Cad., next to Hasan Paşa Hani. Emergency ☎155. Open 24hr.

Pharmacy: Akdeniz Eczane, 11/A Kibris Cad. (☎222 56 68). Open 8am-6:30pm. Part of a group of pharmacies that rotate 24hr. duty.

Hospital: Devlet Hastanesi (☎228 5430), outside the city walls. Turn left 200m on Yusef Azizoğlu Cad.

Internet Access: The city's 20 cafes are wonderfully concealed, and the joy of discovery almost compensates for slow connections and daily power outages. For **Number 1 Computer Internet House,** cross from the hotels on Kibris Cad, traverse the *dolmuş* lot, then walk 200m left down Selim Amca Sofra Sal. US$0.75 per hr.

PTT: The main branch is on the corner of İnönü and Vilayet Cad. Postal services open 8:30am-noon and 1:30-5:30pm.

▟ ACCOMMODATIONS

Diyarbakır has an excellent range of accommodations, concentrated on İnönü, Kibris and Izzet Paşa Cads. Travelers in summer months may find air-conditioning to be more necessity than luxury. Room rates are negotiable, and giving up breakfast can often be a crucial bargaining point.

▨**Aslan Palas,** Kibris Cad. 21 (☎221 12 27). With TV, private bath, and A/C in rooms above the parrot-filled lobby, this is the top choice in town. Singles US$5, doubles US$10.

Hotel Kristal (☎224 25 50; fax 224 01 87), in a small alley of Kibris Cad., has large, clean rooms. A bit pricier, but with the added luxuries of a refrigerator, new carpeting, and a tiled bath. Singles US$10, doubles US$15.

Hotel Kenan, (☎221 66 14), on Izzet Paşa Cad., past İnönü Cad. Similar accommodations to Aslan Palas, with A/C, private bath, and laundry facilities. US$5 per person.

◐ FOOD

Traditional food reigns in Diyarbakır, with a forlorn Burger King exiled beyond the city walls. Speak to locals about the type of dishes that are best avoided (e.g. dairy, pre-cooked, undercooked, reheated). It is a crime to leave Diyarbakır without sampling the local watermelon.

Sarmasik Ocakbasi, 31 Kibris Cad. (☎224 25 97). The best for cheap, reliable food. Try *guvec,* a delicious crock pot of lamb and vegetable. Full meal US$3. Open 24hr.

Tuccarlar, Ticaret Merkezi Kat 1, 5th fl. (☎228 90 21). City views, breezes, great alternatives to *kebap* (*semiz otu* yogurt, pepper, and juicy *bostane* salad each US$1), and live traditional music until 1am.

Guneydoğa Gazeteciler Cemiyeti (☎229 21 17), or "Journalists Club," opposite Tuccarlar and disguised as a *çay* garden, happily serves tourists *içli köfte* (crumbed meat and vegetable ball) and *kie-mumbar* (intestine stuffed with minced meat and vegetable), as well as a full range of drinks. Full meal US$5-7.

TURKEY

 SIGHTS

A circuit of Diyarbakır's **walls** can be made in a few hours, but the secrets hidden within its labyrinthine center can take days to discover. The walls are among the city's chief draws: 12m high and 5m thick, covered in inscriptions from 12 distinct historical periods. The southern and western walls can be climbed easily, and one can stroll for a good distance atop the fortifications. Within the walls of the old city, several major sites can be seen in just a few hours. Start at the Selçuk **Ulu Camii,** then have a cup of *çay* in the restored **camel market** across the road. The **bazaar,** like the camel market, winds down after 6pm. Finding the **Meryamana Kilisesi,** a 3rd-century Aramaic church and convent, requires a plunge into the tangled knot of ancient alleys. Any number of old men or young boys will be happy to guide you; the church is nearly impossible to find without help. This magnificent structure, flanked by carved lions and Aramaic inscriptions, continues to hold services in the original language of Jesus. To the south on Gazi Cad., the restored Ottoman *kervanseray* that has become the **Grand Kervansaray Hotel** is a good place for a drink and a dip in the beautiful pool (US$8). Next is the restored home of **Cahit Sitki Taranci, Atatürk's house,** south of town, and the **Ducle bridge,** built in 1065.

APPENDIX

MEASUREMENTS

The metric system is used throughout the Middle East.

MEASUREMENT CONVERSIONS

1 inch (in.) = 25.4 millimeters (mm)	1 millimeter (mm) = 0.039 in.
1 foot (ft.) = 0.30m	1 meter (m) = 3.28 ft.
1 yard (yd.) = 0.914m	1 meter (m) = 1.09 yd.
1 mile = 1.61km	1 kilometer (km) = 0.62 mi.
1 ounce (oz.) = 28.35g	1 gram (g) = 0.035 oz.
1 pound (lb.) = 0.454kg	1 kilogram (kg) = 2.202 lb.
1 fluid ounce (fl. oz.) = 29.57ml	1 milliliter (ml) = 0.034 fl. oz.
1 gallon (gal.) = 3.785L	1 liter (L) = 0.264 gal.
1 acre (ac.) = 0.405ha	1 hectare (ha) = 2.47 ac.
1 square mile (sq. mi.) = 2.59km^2	1 square kilometer (km^2) = 0.386 sq. mi.

ARABIC (AL-'ARABIYA) العربية

Dialects of Arabic vary from country to country—it is not uncommon to see a
Moroccan and a Palestinian speaking French because their dialects are so different. There may even be dialectal differences within countries. In Upper (south)
Egypt, the Nubians (also called Sa'idis) replace the Classical Arabic *q* with a hard
g. In Lower Egypt and in most other dialects, *q* is dropped completely and
replaced with a glottal stop (a sound similar to that of the middle syllable of the
word "butter" pronounced with a Cockney accent), indicated with a ' in transliteration. The main phonetic difference between the Egyptian and Levantine (includes
the dialects of Jordan, Syria, Lebanon, the West Bank and Gaza) tongues is that the
Levantine *j* sound (as in fu**dge**) becomes a hard *g* (as in **g**ulf) in Lower Egypt. Egyptian is the most widely understood dialect because of Egypt's prolific film and television industry. It's also considered to be the best dialect in which to tell jokes.

Arabic is read from right to left, but numerals are read from left to right. Arabic
uses eight sounds not heard in English. *Kh* (خ) is like the German *ch*; *gh* (غ) is like
the French *r*. There are two *h* sounds; one (ه) sounds like the English "h" and the
other (ح, in Muhammad) is somewhere between *kh* and plain *h*. The letter *'ayn*
(ع) comes from the throat; it is indicated by ' in transliteration. *R* is pronounced as
a trill, just as it is in Spanish. The sounds *dh* (as in this), *d*, *t*, *k*, and *s* all have
emphatic equivalents. Vowels and consonants can be either long or short (it
means the difference between a *hammam*, bathroom, and a *hamam*, pigeon).
The definite article is the prefix *al*. When *al* comes before the sounds *t*, *th*, *j*, *d*,
dh, *r*, *z*, *s*, *sh*, or *n*, the *l* is not pronounced, and the *l* elides to become the letter
which follows it (e.g., *al-noor* is properly pronounced *an-noor*).

EMERGENCY

ENGLISH	ARABIC	
Help!	Saa'idoonee	
Stop!	Waqif/Waqfoo (pl)	
I'm ill.	Ana marid (m)/Ana marida (f)	
It hurts me here. (Levant/Egypt)	Bituja'ani hun/Bituga'ani hina	
I'm tired.	Ana ta'aban (m), Ana ta'abana (f)	
Water	Mayya	
Hospital	Mustashfa	

ENGLISH	ARABIC
Doctor	Duktoor
(Tourist) police	Bolees (al-seeyaaha)
I'm calling the police. (Levant/Egypt)	Hakhabar al-bolees/Hagiblak al-bolees.
Go away!	Imshee
Passport	Basbor/Jawaz (Levant), Gawaz (Egypt)
(American) Embassy	Safaarah (al-Amrikiya)

GREETINGS

ENGLISH	ARABIC
Informal hello; Formal hello (Response); Goodbye	Marhaba; As-Salaamu aleikum(Wa Aleikum as–salaam); Ma' as-salaama
Good morning (response).	Sabah al-kheir (Sabah an-noor/Sabah al-ishta)
Good evening (response).	Masa' al-kheir (Masaa' an-noor)
How are you? (Levant/Egypt)	Keefak?/Izzayyak?
I'm fine. (Levant/Egypt)	Mabsuut/Kwayyis (m), Mabsuuta/Kwayyisa (f)
Yes; Yes (formal); No; Maybe	Eeh (Levant)/Aywa (Egypt); Na'am; La; Mumkin
Never mind, no big deal.	Ma'alesh
Thank you.	Shukran
Please. (Levant/Egypt)	Min fadlak (f)/Law samaht (m), Law samahti (f)
I'm sorry.	Ana aasif (m), Ana aasfa (f)
Enough	Hajeh or kaafi
Excuse me (to get attention).	'An iznak (m), 'An iznik (f)
Excuse me (to apologize).	'Afwan
God willing; Praise God	Inshallah; Al-hamdu lillah
I don't know.	Mish 'aarif (m), Mish 'aarifa (f)
What is your name?	Shoo ismak (m), Shoo ismik (f)
My name is...	Ismee...
Student	Talib (m)/Taliba (f)
Tourist	Sayah (m), Sayaha (f), Suwwaah (pl)
I don't understand.	Mish faahim (m), Mish faahma (f)
I don't speak Arabic. (Levant/Egypt)	Ma bahki 'arabi/Mabatkallimish 'arabi
Do you speak English?	Tatakalim inglizi? (m), Tatakalimee inglizi? (f)
Please speak slowly.	Kalimnee biraaha min fadlak
What is that? (Levant/Egypt)	Shoo hey/Eh da?
Where? What? Why? Who? When?	Feyn? Shoo? Leysh? Meen? Imta?

DIRECTIONS

ENGLISH	ARABIC
Let's Go!	Yallah!
Can you tell me how to get to [the main] Street?	Shaari'a [al-markazi] fein?
Straight (Levant/Egypt)	Dughree/'Ala tool
Right/Left	Yameen/Shimal
North/South/East/West	Al-shamal/Al-ganoub/Ash-sharq/Al-gharb
I'm lost. (Levant/Egypt)	Ana daayi'a/Ana tuht.
Station	Mahatta (Mahattat when followed by name)
Public Square	Midan
I would like a ticket for... (Levant/Egypt)	Bidi bitaa'a ila/'Aayiz (f: 'Aayza) tazkara rayhah...
One way/Round-trip	Bass/Rayih gayeh
What time does the (bus) leave?	Biyitla' imta (al-Autubis)?
Bus	Al-Baas (Levant), Al-Autubees (Egypt)
Train	Al-Atr
Automobile	As-Sayyaara (Levant), Al-'Arabiyya (Egypt)
Airport	Mataar

DATE AND TIME

ENGLISH	ARABIC
What time is it? (Levant/Egypt)	Addeish al-saa'a?/El-saa'a kaam?
Hour, Time	Saa'a
Day/Week/Month/Year	Yom/Usbuu'/Shahr/Sana
Yesterday/Today/Tomorrow	Imbaarih/Al-yom (Egypt: Al-nahar da)/Bukra
What time do you open/close?	Ayyeh saa'a bitiftah/bitsakker? (Levant); Bitiftah/ Biti'fil al-saa'a kam? (Egypt)
Sunday/Monday/Tuesday	Yom al-ahad/Yom al-itnein/Yom at-talaat
Wednesday/Thursday/Friday/Saturday	Yom al-arba'/Yom al-khamees/Yom aj-juma'a (Egypt: Yom ig-guma'a/Yom as-sabt

MONEY

ENGLISH	ARABIC
How much is this? (Levant/Egypt)	Addaysh?/Bikam?
Will you take half?	Taakhud nuss? (m) Taakhdee nuss? (f)
I want... (Levant/Egypt)	Biddee/'Aayiz (m), 'Aayza (f)...
Is there a student discount?	Fi takhfid lit-talaba?
Cheap/Expensive	Rikhees/ghaalee
No way! Impossible!	Mish mumkin
Money	Masaari (Levant), Fuloos (Egypt)
Change	Fraata (Levant), Fakka (Egypt)

HEBREW (IVRIT) עברית

The Hebrew language contains 22 characters, written from right to left. Although Hebrew is read from right to left, **numerals** are read from left to right. Vowels are generally left unwritten, but may appear underneath regular characters as smaller markings. Modern spoken Hebrew contains a large number of Hebraicized versions of English words that may be understandable to perky-eared English-speaking listeners. The transliterations ḥ (ח) and kh (כ and ך) are both guttural, as in the German word *ach*. The Hebrew *r* is close to the French *r*, although an Arabic (or even English) *r* is also understood. The definite article is the prefix *ha*. Feminine adjectives add an "-ah" at the end; feminine verbs usually add an "-at" or an "-et."

EMERGENCY

ENGLISH	HEBREW
Help!	Hatzeeloo!
Stop!	Tafseek! (m)/Tafseekee! (f)
Don't touch me!	Al teegah bee
I'm ill.	Anee ḥoleh (m)/Anee ḥolah (f)
I'm hurt.	Anee patzoo'ah (m)/Anee ptzoo'ah (f)
Water	Mayim
Hospital	Beit-ḥolim
Doctor	Rofeh
I need a doctor.	Anee tzariḥ rofeh (m)/Ani tzriḥa rofeh
I'm calling the police.	Anee kore (m) (f: koret) lamishtara
Leave me alone!	Azov otee!
Go away/Go to hell!	Tistalek/Lekh l'azazel
Police/Fire fighters/Ambulance	Mishtara/Meḥabei esh/Ahmboolance

GREETINGS

ENGLISH	HEBREW
Hello/Goodbye.	Shalom
Good morning/Good evening.	Boker tov/Erev tov
Could you help me?	Atah yaḥol la'azor lee(m)/At yeḥola la'azor lee (f)?

ENGLISH	HEBREW
How are you?	Ma nishma?
Excellent/Fine/Not good	Metzuyan/Be-seder/Lo tov
Yes/No/Maybe	Ken/Lo/Oolai
Thank you.	Todah
Please/You're welcome.	Bevakasha
Excuse me/I'm sorry.	Sliha
I don't know.	Anee lo yodeah (m)/Anee lo yoda'at (f)
What is your name?	Eikh korim lekhah? (m) Eikh korim lakh? (f)
My name is...	Shmee...
I'm a student.	Anee student (m)/studentit (f)
How do you say...?	Eikh omrim...
I don't understand.	Anee lo mevin (m)/Anee lo mevinah (f)
I don't speak Hebrew.	Anee lo medaber (f: medaberet) ivrit
Do you speak English?	Ata medaber ivrit? (m)/At medaberet ivrit? (f)
Please repeat yourself.	Tagid (f: tagidi) od pa'am, bevakasha
Please speak slowly.	Tedaber (f: tedabri) le'at bevakasha

DIRECTIONS

ENGLISH	HEBREW
Where is...?	Eyfoh...?
Straight	Yashar
Right/Left	Yameen/Smol
North/South/East/West	Tzafon/Darom/Mizrah/Ma'arav
I'm lost.	Ne'ebadetee
Do you know where... is?	Ata yodeah (f: At yoda'at) eifoh nimtzah... ?
Do you stop at...?	Ata otzer b'...?
From where does the bus leave?	Mi'eifo ha-otoboos ozev?
Center of town	Merkaz ha'ir
Central bus station	Tahana merkazit
Bus stop	Tahanat otoboos
I would like a ticket for...	Ani rotzeh (f: rotzah) kartees le...
One-way/Round-trip	Keevoon ehad/Haloh ve'hazor
Please stop!	Atzor, bevakasha
What time does the (bus) leave?	Matai ha (otoboos) ozev?
Bus	Otoboos
Taxi	Monit/Taxi
Automobile	Mekhonit
Train	Rakevet

SERVICES

ENGLISH	HEBREW
Do you know of a cheap hotel?	Ata makeer (m) (f: makeera) malon zol?
Do you have a single/double room?	Yesh lahem heder le'yaheed/kafool?
How much is the room?	Kama oleh haheder?
Hotel/Hostel	Malon/Ahsania
Breakfast/Lunch/Dinner	Aruhat boker/Aruhat tzohora'im/Aruhat erev
Do you have vegetarian food?	Yesh lahem ohel tzimhonee?
I am vegetarian.	Ani tzimhonee/tzimhoneet
Coffee/Tea	Kafeh/Teh
Bathroom	Sherutim
Room	Heder

ENGLISH	HEBREW
Restaurant	Mees'ada
Telephone	Telephon
I'd like to make a call to [the US].	Anee rotzeh (m) (f: rotzah) letalfen leh [amerika]
Passport	Darkon
Pharmacy	Beit Markaḥat
Post office	Do'ar
Street	Reḥov
Market	Shuk
Museum	Muzaion
Synagogue	Beit knesset
Church	Knessia
Mosque	Misgad
Beach	Ḥof
Grocery store	Makolet

DATE AND TIME

ENGLISH	HEBREW
What time is it?	Ma hasha'ah?
Hour, Time	Sha'ah
Day/Week/Month/Year	Yom/Shavuah/Ḥodesh/Shanah
Early/Late	Mookdam/Me'ooḥar
Today/Yesterday/Tomorrow	Ha-yom/Etmol/Maḥar
Morning/Afternoon/Evening/Night	Boker/Tzohora'im/Erev/Lyla
What time do you open/close?	Matai atem potḥim/sogrim?
Open/Closed	Patoo'aḥ/Sagoor
Sunday /Monday/Tuesday/Wednesday	Yom rishon/Yom shaini/Yom shlishi/Yom revi'i
Thursday /Friday/Saturday (Sabbath)	Yom ḥamishi/Yom shishi/Yom Shabbat

MONEY

ENGLISH	HEBREW
Do you have...?	Yesh lekha...? (m) Yesh lakh...? (f)
How much is this?	Kama zeh oleh?
I want...	Anee rotzeh... (m)/Anee rotzah... (f)
I don't want... (male/female)	Lo rotzeh (male) Lo rotzah (female)
Is there a student discount?	Yesh hanaḥa le'studentim?
Cheap/Expensive	Zol/Yakar
Do you accept credit cards/traveler's checks?	Atem mekablim kartisei ashrai/hamḥaot nos'im?
Money	Kesef
Change	Odef

TURKISH (TÜRKÇE)

Turkish is phonetic: each letter has only one sound that is always pronounced distinctly (except ğ, which lengthens the vowels adjacent to it). Special vowel and consonant pronunciations include: c (jacket); ç (check); ı (i without a dot, cousin); i (peace); j (zh, pleasure); ö (deux); ş (short); u (boot); ü (cue). Special letter combinations include: ay (pronounced eye); ey (play); oy (toy); uy (phooey).

EMERGENCY

ENGLISH	TURKISH
Help!	İmdat (Eem-daht)
Stop!	Ayıp (Ah-yup)
I'm ill.	Hastayım (has-TA-yuhm)

ENGLISH	TURKISH
Water	Su (soo)
Hospital	Hastane (has-ta-NE)
I need a doctor.	Doktora ihtiyacım var (dohk-TOR-ah eeh-tee-YA-cum vahr)
Go away!	Haydı git (Hah-dee git)
Police	Polis (polees)

GREETINGS

ENGLISH	TURKISH
Hello /Goodbye (morning)/Goodbye (evening)	Merhaba (Mehrhaba)/İyi günler (eee-YEE goon-lehr)/ İyi akşamlar (eee-YEE ak-SHAM-lar)
How are you?	Nasılsın?(nah-sil-sihn)
Fine	İyiyim
Yes/No/Maybe	Evet (eh-veht)/Hayır (hyer)/Belki (behl-kee)
Thank you.	Teşekkur ederim (tesh-ekur edeh-rim)
You're welcome.	Bir şey değil. (beer shey dee-eel)
Please.	Lütfen (loot-fahn)
Excuse me/I'm sorry.	Pardon (pahr-don)/Özür dilerim (oz-oor deel-er-rim)
My name is...	İsmim (Ees-meem)
What is...?	...ne? (neh)
I'm a student.	Oğrenciyim (OH-ren-jee-yeem)
I don't understand.	Anlamadım (ahn-luh-mah-dim)
I don't speak Turkish.	Turkçe bilmiyorum. (Toork-che BEEL-mee-YOR-uhm)
Do you speak English?	İnglizce biliyor musun? (een-gul-EEZ-je beel-ee-YOR muh-SUN?)
Please speak slowly.	Yavaş lütfen (yah-vash loot-fahn)
Are you a pimp?	Pesevenk misin? (pehs-seh-vehnk mih-sihn?)

DIRECTIONS

ENGLISH	TURKISH
Where is... ?	...nerede? (...nehr-eh-deh?)
How far is...?	...a ne kadar uzakta (a neh kahdahr oozakta?)
Straight	düz (dooz; to a taxi driver); doğru (doh-oo; said in all other instances)
Right/Left	Sağ (saa)/Sol (sohl)
North/South/East/West	Hangisi (han-gee-see)/Güneye (goo-ne-YE)/Doğuya (do-ghoo-YA)/Batıya (ba-tuh-YA)
I'm lost.	Yolumu kaybettim (yol-oo-moo kay-bet-teem)
I'm going to...	...'a gidiyorum (ah geed-EE-yohr-uhm)
Central bus station	otogar (oh-tow-gar)
Bus stop	otobüs durağı (oto-boos doo-raa)
I would like a ticket.	Bir bilet alabilir miyim? (beer bee-let ala-bee-LEER mee-yeem?)
One-way/Round-trip	Gidiş (gee-deesh)/Gidiş-dönüş biletin (gee-deesh doo-noosh bee-le-teen)
What time does the ___ leave?	Saat kaçta kalkiyor? (sah-at kach-tah kahlk-ee-yor?)
Bus	otobüs (oto-boos)
Taxi	Taksi
Automobile	Bir araba (beer ah-ra-bah)

SERVICES

ENGLISH	TURKISH
Is there an available room?	Boş odanız var mı? (bosh odaniz vahr mih?)
Single/double/triple	Tek (tehk)/Çift (cheeft)/Üç kişilik (ooch keesheeleek)

ENGLISH	TURKISH
How much is the room?	Bir günlük fiyat ne kadar?
Hotel/Pension	Otel (oh-tell)/Pansiyon (pan-see-yown)
Breakfast/Lunch/Dinner	Kahvaltı (kah-val-tuh)/öğle yemeği (oo-le yeme-ee)/ akşam yemeği (aksham yeme-ee)
Do you have food without meat?	Etsiz yemek var mı? (eht seez yemek vahr mi?)
I am vegetarian.	Vejetariyanım (vej-e-tar-iyan-im)
Coffee/Tea	Kahve (Turkish coffee, kah-veh)/Çay (chai)
Bathroom	Tuvalet (too-wallet) or Banyo
Restaurant	lokanta
Telephone	Telefon
Can I make a call to (the US)?	(Amerika'ya) nasıl telefon edebilirim (ame-REE-kaya nasul telefon ede-bee-lee-reem?)
Passport	Pasaport
Pharmacy	Eczane (ej-ZAH-ne)
Post office	Postane
Market	Çarşı (charshi), Bedesten (be-de-STEN)
Museum	Müze (moo-zeh)
Mosque	Camii (jamee-ee)

DATE AND TIME

ENGLISH	TURKISH
What time is it?	Saat kaç? (Sa-at ka-ch?)
Hour	saat (sa-AT)
Day/Week/Month/Year	Gün (goon)/Hafta (hahfta)/Ay (ay)/Yıl(yil)
Yesterday/Today/Tomorrow	Dün (doon)/Bugün (boo-goon)/Yarıin (yah-rin)
Are you open/closed?	Açık/kapalı mısın? (a-chik/kah-pah-li misin)
Sunday /Monday/Tuesday/Wednesday	Pazar (pa-ZAR)/Pazartesi (pa-ZAR-te-see)/ Salı (saluh)/Çarşamba (char-sham-ba)
Thursday /Friday/Saturday	Perşembe (per-shem-be)/Cuma (joo-ma)/ Cumartesi (joo-mar-tee-see)

MONEY

ENGLISH	TURKISH
How much is...?	...ne kadar? (NE ka-dar?)
I want...	Biraz .... istiyorum
I don't want...	...istemedim (eestemedim)
Is there a student discount?	Öğrenci var mı? (Oo-ren-jee var muh?)
Do you accept credit cards?	Kredi kartı alıyor musunuz? (kredee kartuh aluh-YOR moo-soo-nooz?)
Money	Para (pahrah)

TELEPHONE CODES

CYPRUS	357
Limassol, Paphos	05, 06
EGYPT	**20**
Alexandria	03
Aswan	097
Bahariyya	010
Cairo	02
Dakhla	092
Hurghada	065
Kharga	092

LEBANON	961
Ba'albeck	08
Bcharré	06
Beirut	01
Sa'ida (Sidon), Sur (Tyre)	07
Tripoli	06
SYRIA	**963**
Aleppo	21
Damascus	11
Hama	33

Luxor	095
Port Said	066
Sinai Peninsula (incl. Suez)	062
ISRAEL	**972**
Be'er Sheva	07
Eilat	07
Golan	06
Haifa	04
Jerusalem	02
Tel Aviv	03
Tzfat	06
JORDAN	**962**
Amman	06
Aqaba	03
Azraq (Desert)	06
Dead Sea	05
Irbid	02
Madaba	08

Homs	31
Lattakia	41
Palmyra	34
WEST BANK	**972**
All locations	02
GAZA	**972**
Gaza City	07
TURKEY	**90**
Ankara	312
Antalya	242
Bodrum	252
Göreme	384
İstanbul (Asia/Europe)	216/212
İzmir	232
Marmaris	252
Trabzon	462

GLOSSARY

'ain: spring
ankh: Egyptian symbol for life, Coptic cross
bab: door, gate
bakhsheesh: tip, bribe
bir: well
booza: ice cream
caretta: donkey-drawn taxicart
corniche: from the Fr., long avenue along the water
dabke: Lebanese line dance
dakle: Lebanese dance in which themes from village life are enacted
deir: monastery
djinn: ghost
emir: prince
felucca: Egyptian sailboat
galabiyya: long gown worn by men
hammam: hot baths; bathroom
hantour: horse carriage
hibis: plow
hijab: traditional women's head-covering
hurriyya: liberty; freedom
iconostasis: icon-covered screen in a mosque that separates the nave from the sanctuary
imam: Muslim leader
irwan: arcaded porch in a mosque surrounding the central open courtyard
jabal: hill, mountain
kalish: from the Fr. calèche, a horse-drawn carriage
kefyeh: traditional black-and-white checkered headscarf
khan: caravanserai, courtyard inn
khanqah: home for sufi mystics
khedive: Turkish for viceroy

khuttar: tradition in which prominent Bedouin families host any visitors that cross their path
kuttab: Qur'anic school
lakaban: marble basin
madrasa: school or college of Islamic law
margunah: large, decorated woven basket
mashrabiyya: interlaced wooden screen
mawlid: festival celebrating events from the Qur'an or birthdays of Coptic or Muslim saints
mayda'a: ablution fountain
midan: square
mihrab: richly decorated prayer niche in a mosque pointing in the direction of Mecca
minbar: pulpit in a mosque next to the mihrab where sermons are delivered
muezzin: person who does the call to prayer
papyrus: ancient Egyptian paper made from reeds
pronaos: vestibule
qala'a: fortress, citadel
qasr: castle
Ramadan: Muslim holy month of fasting
rue: Fr. for street
sabil: water dispensary
saha: central open courtyard in a mosque
service: group taxi
siq: narrow passageway in rock
souq: market
tarfudit: veils
umm: mother
wadi: small river or riverbed

FOOD & DRINK
ahwa: Arabic coffee
'araq: strong anise liquor
argeleh, sheesha: water pipe, hookah

'asab: sugar cane juice

aseer: fruit juice

baba ghanoush: pureed eggplant with lemon juice, mayonnaise, and spices

ba'laweh: pistachio- or almond-filled filo dough (baklava)

basbouseh: wheat pastry with syrup

burma: shredded, fried dough with pistachios

farooj: roasted chicken served with chilis and onions

fattoush: salad of lettuce, tomato, and cucumber with small pieces of toasted pita mixed in.

falafel: fried chickpeas, shaped into balls

fuul: cooked, mashed fava beans with garlic, lemon, olive oil, and salt on bread and vegetables

halawat al-jibn: unsalted cheese with semolina, sugar, syrup, and sweet cream

hummus: ground chickpeas with oil and spices

jamid: tangy yogurt-based sauce

jellab: raisin syrup with pine nuts

kibbeh naye: raw beef and spices

kofta: spiced ground beef grilled on skewers

kushari: starch-laden Egyptian dish of pasta, rice, lentils, and dried onions in tomato sauce

lagbi: sweet, palm tree juice

mahshi: stuffed grape leaves (stuffed with mincemeat, rice, and onions)

mana'eesh: pizza with za'tar

marqooq: paper thin baked bread

mensaf: rice on a large tray of flat bread, topped with pine nuts, lamb or goat, and a tangy yogurt-based sauce

mezze: appetizers

musakhan: chicken baked with olive oil, onions, and spices, served on bread

mujeddra: lentil stew with sautéed onions and spices

mulukhiyya: green Egyptian vegetable

na'na': mint

shawarma: fatty lamb rolled onto pita

shay: tea

shish kebab: skewered lamb

shish tawouq: skewered chicken

ta'amiyya: Egyptian version of falafel, discuslike in both shape and hardness

tahina: sesame-based sauce

tabbouleh: parsley, cracked wheat, onions, tomatoes, lemon juice, and spices mixed together

tawila: backgammon

zaghlouta: ululation

za'tar: thyme mixed with sesame seeds and spices

INDEX

MAPS

ABOUT LET'S GO

FORTY-TWO YEARS OF WISDOM

For over four decades, travelers crisscrossing the continents have relied on *Let's Go* for inside information on the hippest backstreet cafes, the most pristine secluded beaches, and the best routes from border to border. *Let's Go: Europe*, now in its 42nd edition and translated into seven languages, reigns as the world's bestselling international travel guide. In the last 20 years, our rugged researchers have stretched the frontiers of backpacking and expanded our coverage into the Americas, Australia, Asia, and Africa (including the new *Let's Go: Egypt* and the more comprehensive, multi-country jaunt through *Let's Go: South Africa & Southern Africa*). Our new-and-improved City Guide series continues to grow with new guides to perennial European favorites Amsterdam and Barcelona. This year we are also unveiling *Let's Go: Southwest USA*, the flagship of our new outdoor Adventure Guide series, which is complete with special roadtripping tips and itineraries, more coverage of adventure activities like hiking and mountain biking, and first-person accounts of life on the road.

It all started in 1960 when a handful of well-traveled students at Harvard University handed out a 20-page mimeographed pamphlet offering a collection of their tips on budget travel to passengers on student charter flights to Europe. The following year, in response to the instant popularity of the first volume, students traveling to Europe researched the first full-fledged edition of *Let's Go: Europe*. Throughout the 60s and 70s, our guides reflected the times—in 1969, for example, we taught you how to get from Paris to Prague on "no dollars a day" by singing in the street. In the 90s we focused in on the world's most exciting urban areas to produce in-depth, fold-out map guides, now with 20 titles (from Hong Kong to Chicago) and counting. Our new guides bring the total number of titles to 57, each infused with the spirit of adventure and voice of opinion that travelers around the world have come to count on. But some things never change: our guides are still researched, written, and produced entirely by students who know first-hand how to see the world on the cheap.

HOW WE DO IT

Each guide is completely revised and thoroughly updated every year by a well-traveled set of nearly 300 students. Every spring, we recruit over 200 researchers and 90 editors to overhaul every book. After several months of training, researcher-writers hit the road for seven weeks of exploration, from Anchorage to Adelaide, Estonia to El Salvador, Iceland to Indonesia. Hired for their rare combination of budget travel sense, writing ability, stamina, and courage, these adventurous travelers know that train strikes, stolen luggage, food poisoning, and marriage proposals are all part of a day's work. Back at our offices, editors work from spring to fall, massaging copy written on Himalayan bus rides into witty, informative prose. A student staff of typesetters, cartographers, publicists, and managers keeps our lively team together. In September, the collected efforts of the summer are delivered to our printer, who turns them into books in record time, so that you have the most up-to-date information available for your vacation. Even as you read this, work on next year's editions is well underway.

WHY WE DO IT

We don't think of budget travel as the last recourse of the destitute; we believe that it's the only way to travel. Our books will ease your anxieties and answer your questions about the basics—so you can get off the beaten track and explore. Once you learn the ropes, we encourage you to put *Let's Go* down and strike out on your own. You know as well as we that the best discoveries are often those you make yourself. When you find something worth sharing, please drop us a line. We're Let's Go Publications, 67 Mount Auburn St., Cambridge, MA 02138, USA (feedback@letsgo.com). For more info, visit our website, www.letsgo.com.

Will you have enough stories to tell your grandchildren?

Yahoo! Travel

Do You Yahoo!?

CHOOSE YOUR DESTINATION SWEEPSTAKES

No Purchase Necessary.

**Explore the world with Let's Go® and StudentUniverse!
Enter for a chance to win a trip for two to a Let's Go destination!**

Separate Drawings! May & October 2002.

GRAND PRIZES:
Roundtrip StudentUniverse Tickets

✓ Select one destination and mail your entry to:

☐ Costa Rica
☐ London
☐ Hong Kong
☐ San Francisco
☐ New York
☐ Amsterdam
☐ Prague
☐ Sydney

* Plus Additional Prizes!!

Choose Your Destination Sweepstakes
St. Martin's Press
Suite 1600, Department MF
175 Fifth Avenue
New York, NY 10010-7848

Restrictions apply; see offical rules for
details by visiting Let'sGo.com or sending SASE
(VT residents may omit return postage) to the address above.

Name: _____

Address: _____

City/State/Zip: _____

Phone: _____

Email: _____

Grand prizes provided by:

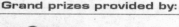 **StudentUniverse.com**   Real Travel Deals